Planning Permission

Planning Permission

Richard Harwood QC

39 Essex Chambers

Bloomsbury Professional

BLOOMSBURY PROFESSIONAL LTD, MAXWELTON HOUSE, 41–43 BOLTRO ROAD, HAYWARDS HEATH, WEST SUSSEX, RH16 1BJ

© Bloomsbury Professional Ltd 2016

Bloomsbury Professional, an imprint of Bloomsbury Publishing plc

All rights reserved. No part of this publication may be reproduced in any material form (including photocopying or storing it in any medium by electronic means and whether or not transiently or incidentally to some other use of this publication) without the written permission of the copyright owner except in accordance with the provisions of the Copyright, Designs and Patents Act 1988 or under the terms of a licence issued by the Copyright Licensing Agency Ltd, Saffron House, 6–10 Kirby Street, London EC1N 8TS. Applications for the copyright owner's written permission to reproduce any part of this publication should be addressed to the publisher.

Whilst every care has been taken to ensure the accuracy of the content of this work, no responsibility for loss occasioned to any person acting or refraining from action as a result of the material in this publication can be accepted by the authors or by the publisher.

Warning: The doing of an unauthorised act in relation to a copyright work may result in both a civil claim for damages and criminal prosecution.

Crown copyright material is reproduced with the permission of the Controller of HMSO and the Queen's Printer for Scotland. Any European material in this work which has been reproduced from EUR-lex, the official European Communities legislation website, is European Communities copyright.

A CIP Catalogue record for this book is available from the British Library.

ISBN: 978 1 78043 491 9

Typeset by Phoenix Photosetting, Chatham, Kent
Printed in the United Kingdom by CPI Group (UK) Ltd, Croydon, CR0 4YY

For Cathan

Preface

The outcome of the planning process is the carrying out or the restriction of construction and the use of land. Policy planning and design are extremely important, and crucial to achieving a positively planned environment, but without work and uses being authorised, nothing will happen.

Deciding what can happen in the public interest is the function of planning permission. It is the essential mechanism which operates the planning system. The purpose of this book is to explain how it works in law, policy and practice.

Primary legislation on planning permission is contained in the Town and Country Planning Act 1990, principally Part III which runs from sections 55 to 106C. For the practitioner, that both overstates and understates the amount of law which has to be dealt with. In everyday practice, fewer than 10 of these sections are likely to be referred to with any regularity.

These are, though, just the basic structural elements of a decision-making process the majority of which is laid out in secondary legislation, Ministerial directions and policy. Even then, the legislation is, as Sir Malcolm Grant has long pointed out, simply a framework. It says what requires consent and how that consent may be given or withheld, but gives few pointers as to whether planning permission should be granted. The outcome of a planning application is a combination of political determination, the public interest and professional judgment, guided by and reflected in policy. Both the operation of the process and determination of outcomes has been the subject of case law. There are, though, fewer planning judicial review and similar proceedings than might be imagined. Fewer than 0.1% of planning applications ultimately end up in the Planning Court. The courts, however, perform the vital role of ensuring that decisions are taken in accordance with the rule of law. That protects everyone interested in planning, from the developer who wants its scheme considered on its merits, to the local residents and interest groups concerned that only suitable development proceeds.

Planning has become extremely complex. In part this is because of the number of issues which it is expected to address, including whether the proximity of a proposed hot food takeaway to a school would encourage childhood obesity. Unlike other regulatory systems, planning is able to address a proposal holistically and so ends up looking at every issue unless there is a good reason why it should not. There are, though, two other reasons why planning encompasses so much, and good reasons they are too. Planning is the epitome of public consultation. Whatever problems may arise in practice, many of which are chronicled in this book, there is a determination to include the public in the process in a way which is unmatched in other regulatory systems. Finally, and most importantly, it is the democratic regulatory system. Decisions are either taken by politicians or, if that is not the case, then those officials making decisions, whether council officers or planning inspectors, are subject to closer political scrutiny than in any other area of regulation.

Preface

Beyond the fair reasons for complexity, there are some well-intentioned but less good ones. Concern at perceived slowness or misuse of the planning system has prompted a variety of adjustments, tweaks and alternatives. Some have been useful. Some have produced a legislative dead-end, unused even by the governments that devised them, such as section 76A major infrastructure inquiries or planning inquiry commissions. Others have added exceptions, loopholes and detail, which is the enemy of efficiency and public understanding, for little if any benefit.

Since 2010 Ministers in England have had great success in cutting down the volume of planning policy with the publication of the *National Planning Policy Framework* and the *Planning Practice Guidance*. There has also been a programme of reform of secondary legislation, much of it low-key, which has operated as a brake on the legislative juggernaut if not yet a reverse gear. Primary legislative reform has further to go. Through the maze of redundant provisions and unhelpful bits of assistance, a relatively simple process still exists. It is time to put it on display.

The book deals with the law and policy in England and Wales. There are important differences, as separate administrations find their own solutions to problems which are not always identical. However, it often remains a case of the same thing being done by different legislation or policy. The text therefore picks up the similarities and differences between the two nations.

Planning practice involves a great number of people and potential stages, from the developer's decision as to what scheme to promote, through public consultation, consideration by officers and councillors, appeals to Ministers and inspectors and High Court proceedings. Throughout the book I seek to give some advice as to how the various participants can play their part.

The coincidence of working through the first proofs over the Christmas holidays means that I have sought to state the law as at 1 January 2016. I have also covered legislation which has been enacted but not yet brought into force, in particular mayoral development orders and the development management changes in the Planning (Wales) Act 2015. When finally introduced, these provisions will have to be considered with their secondary legislation and any guidance. The book also addresses the relevant provisions of the Housing and Planning Bill, working from the text as amended in Public Bill Committee in November and December 2015. Some potential amendments are picked up in the course of the analysis.

All of this explains, and if necessary, excuses, the length of this book. The task of writing it has been made incomparably easier by the work of judges and counsel in the court analysing, explaining and pulling together the legislation, policy and case law. At the forefront of these decisions has been Sir Jeremy Sullivan, whose judgments explained planning law with utter clarity for the last two decades. He was fearless in striking down bad decisions and correctly interpreting the law even if that had dramatic consequences. For nearly 20 years he dominated the planning case law in the High Court and then the Court of Appeal before his retirement in September 2015.

My understanding of planning law has, as always, benefited from discussion and debate with colleagues, clients, opponents and judges. When faced with an issue to advise on or argue in court or inquiry I have turned to the draft book. If it has not covered the point sufficiently I have added a short paragraph or footnote to the chapter. Sometimes I have revised the text after receiving the judgment.

Preface

Thanks are also due to the team at Bloomsbury Professional. Leanne Barrett was encouraging from the start and did not bat an eyelid when the manuscript came in at twice the length I had originally promised. Jenny Lank, Hannah Johnson and Harriet Espin-Bradley have been immensely helpful in marketing and design. Maria Skrzypiec did a fantastic job of editing the text, picking up on references to statutory instruments which were not quite right.

Much of the book has been written on trains, so I would like to thank my fellow commuters on the 0648 and 1735 for the elbow room and the South West Trains crews for the coffee. The remainder has been written in evenings, weekends and holidays. I owe therefore the greatest of thanks to Gráinne and to Cathan, James and Sophie for their love and tolerance.

Richard Harwood OBE QC
39 Essex Chambers
81 Chancery Lane
London
WC2A 1DD
January 2016

Contents

Preface	vii
Table of Statutes	xxvii
Table of Statutory Instruments	xxxix
Table of Cases	lxiii

Chapter 1	**Outline of the planning system**	
	The purpose of the planning system	1
	Planning authorities	4
	Planning legislation	5
	The need for planning permission	5
	Planning policy	6
	Permitted development rights	9
	The planning application process	10
	Notification and consultation on planning applications	11
	Statements of Community Involvement	12
	Environmental Impact Assessment	13
	The determination of applications by local planning authorities	14
	The planning permission or refusal	16
	Planning conditions	16
	Planning obligations	17
	Referral of planning applications to the Secretary of State or Welsh Ministers	18
	Referrals to the Mayor of London	19
	Appeals	20
	Development consent orders	22
	The grant of planning permission by orders and other means	23
	Other planning controls	23
	Breaches of planning control	24
	Section 215 notices on the condition of land	26
	High Court challenges	26

Chapter 2	**The meaning of development**	
	The meaning of development	28
	Operational development	29
	Building operations	29
	Engineering operations	30
	Mining operations	30
	Other operations	31
	Exclusions from operational development	31
	Demolition	34
	Fish farming	35

Contents

	Material change of use of land	35
	Primary and ancillary uses	37
	The planning unit	38
	The carrying on of a use	38
	Exceptions to material changes of use	39
	Changes of use which are material	42
	Short-term lettings in London	43
Chapter 3	**Use classes**	
	The basis of use classes	45
	The Use Classes Order	46
	Uses outside the use classes	46
	Subdivision of land or buildings in the same use class	48
	Removal of the use class by planning condition	48
	Categorisation	50
	Part A: shopping area uses	51
	Part B: business and industrial uses	53
	Part C: residential uses	56
	Class D: community uses	61
	Town and Country Planning (Use Classes) Order 1972	62
Chapter 4	**The need for planning permission**	
	The need for planning permission	65
	Exceptions to the need for planning permission	66
	Abandonment of a lawful use	68
	Interventions which end lawful uses	69
	Statutory powers to remove the right to develop or to retain development	70
	Completion notices	71
	Revocation or modification	72
	Discontinuance orders	74
Chapter 5	**Permitted development rights**	
	Permitted development rights: general principles	79
	Article 3 restrictions on the grant of permission	79
	Permitted development restricted by Sch 2	80
	Conditions on other planning permissions which withdraw permitted development rights	80
	Only lawful development benefits from permitted development rights	82
	Environmental Impact Assessment and permitted development rights	82
	Habitats	84
	Particular acts limited to particular permitted development rights	85
	Prior approval of details	86
	Failure to give notice of a decision	88
	The effect of a prior approval determination	89
	Attaching conditions to prior approvals under permitted development rights	89
	Planning obligations and prior approval	90

	The effect of changes to permitted development rights or their application	90
	Changes to the GPDO	91
	The effect of an Article 4 direction	91
	Changes to the designation of the land	92
	Changes of the underlying circumstances on the ground	93
	The making of Article 4 directions	93
	England	93
	English procedures for making Article 4 directions	95
	Welsh procedures for making art 4 directions	98
	Article 5 directions restricting certain mineral permitted development	99
	Types of permitted development rights	100
	Interpretation of the permitted development rights	102
	Particular issues which arise across the classes	103
	The permitted development rights	105
	Part 1 Household permitted development rights	105
	Part 2 Minor operations	107
	Part 3 Changes of use	108
	Part 4 Temporary buildings and uses	113
	Part 5 Caravan sites and recreational campsites	115
	Part 6 Agricultural and forestry	117
	Part 7 Non-domestic extensions, alterations etc	119
	Part 8 Transport related development	121
	Part 9 Development relating to roads	121
	Part 10 Repairs to services	122
	Part 11 Heritage and demolition	122
	Part 12 Development by local authorities	123
	Part 13 Water and sewerage	123
	Part 14 Renewable energy	124
	Part 15 Power related development	125
	Part 16 Communications	126
	Part 17 Mining and mineral exploration	128
	Part 18 Miscellaneous development	130
	Part 19 Development by the Crown or for national security purposes	130
Chapter 6	**Planning applications**	
	Types of planning applications	133
	Local planning authorities	136
	Stages in the application process	139
	Working up the scheme	140
	Pre-application advice	142
	Planning Performance Agreements	144
	Pre-application consultation	144
	Local authority policies and pre-application consultation	145
	Statutory pre-application consultation	145
	Non-statutory pre-application consultation	146
	The application process	146
	Notice of the application to landowners and agricultural tenants	146
	The offence of giving an inaccurate certificate of notice	148

Contents

The planning application	149
Drawings	149
Crown land	150
Fees for planning applications	151
Changes to fees for different applicants	154
Design and access statements in England	156
Design and access statements in Wales	157
Environmental statement	158
Local lists	159
Acknowledgment of a valid application	160
The effect of a failure to give notice or submit the required documents	160
Determining the validity of a planning application	162
The planning register	163
Declining to determine applications	164
Statements of community involvement and legitimate expectations	167
Examples of breaches of legitimate expectation	169
Consultation and publicity	170
Publicity	170
Planning applications affecting the setting of listed buildings or conservation areas in England	171
Statutory consultees	172
Consultation with county planning authorities	189
Consultation by county councils with districts	189
Consultation by National Park Authorities	190
Consultation on s 73 applications and certain renewals	190
Consultation period with statutory bodies	190
Making consultation responses	191
Taking into account consultation responses	193
Amendments to schemes	193

Chapter 7 Environmental Impact Assessment

EIA in outline	194
The need for EIA	195
Screening	207
Screening on receipt of a planning application	209
Below threshold screening decisions	210
The screening decision	211
Reasons in screening decisions	215
Screening decisions kept on or with the planning register	217
Changes to the scheme post-screening	217
Scoping of proposed environmental statements	217
Environmental statements	219
Publicity and consultation on the environmental statement and other material	221
The submission of additional information	223
Consideration of the environmental information	224
Subsequent applications	224
Publicity of EIA decisions	225

Chapter 8	**Determining planning applications**	
	The decision-making process	226
	Decision-making	226
	Common delegation arrangements	228
	Area planning committees	229
	Compliance with the scheme of delegation	230
	Committee reports	232
	Access to documents on the planning application	234
	General rights of access: Environmental Information Regulations 2004, the Freedom of Information Act 2000 and the Data Protection Act 1998	234
	Access to committee reports and background documents under the Local Government Act 1972	238
	Legitimate expectation of publication	239
	Access to viability reports and sensitive material	240
	Making representations to the committee	241
	Oral representations to the committee	243
	Committee meetings	244
	Resolutions	245
	Bias	246
	Principles	246
	Predetermination	248
	Bias	248
	The Localism Act 2011	251
	Can one person taint the committee?	252
	Summary of predetermination/bias	252
	Which persons are subject to the rules on predetermination and bias?	252
	The role of non-committee members	253
	Role of a disqualified member	254
	Reasons for planning decisions	255
	Former English duty to give reasons for the grant of planning permission	256
	Why a planning decision was taken by a committee	258
	Recording of meetings	260
	Reasons for officer decisions	261
	Reasons for refusal	262
	Reasons for rejecting advice from Natural England	262
Chapter 9	**Material considerations and policy**	
	Material considerations and the structure of policy	263
	What are material considerations?	263
	The time when material considerations are addressed	265
	The weight to be given to material considerations	266
	Statutory duties to have regard to various matters	266
	Policy	267
	National planning policy – England	270
	National planning policy – Wales	272
	Other national bodies' guidance as material considerations	273
	The interpretation of policy	273
	Substantive material considerations	275
	Sustainable development	275

Contents

Effects on neighbouring land and amenity	277
Amenity effects on the occupants of the proposed development	279
Extremely sensitive neighbours and users	280
Coal mining operations	280
Safety and control of major accident hazards	280
Economy	281
External costs – impacts on services	283
Green Belt	283
Appropriate and inappropriate development	284
Health	287
Historic environment	288
Housing policy	291
Affordable housing	292
Starter homes, self-build and custom housebuilding	293
Landscape and visual impact	294
Minerals	297
Nature conservation	297
Personal circumstances and impacts	304
Waste	308
Welsh language	310
Structural material considerations	310
Alternatives	310
Financial considerations	312
Local finance considerations	314
Interference with other legal rights	315
Precedent	316
Prematurity and the weight to be attached to emerging policy	317
Planning uses and planning decisions	320
The fallback position	320
Previous planning decisions	320
The unlawfulness of a previous decision	322
The protection of existing or proposed uses and users of land	322
Existing unlawful development	323
The effect of a planning application on an existing planning permission	324
The effect of other regulatory regimes on a planning decision	324
Housing technical standards	325
The risks on appeal	325

Chapter 10 London

The Mayor of London's powers over applications	327
Applications of potential strategic importance	327
Time for exercising the powers	330
Pre-application consultation	331
Initial consultation on a planning application	331
Consultation prior to the decision being issued	331
Directions to refuse planning permission	332
The power to become the local planning authority for an application	334

	Determination of reserved matters	336
	Appeals involving mayoral decisions	336
	Directions to consult the Mayor on planning applications	337
	The Mayor's involvement in planning generally	337
	Mayoral Development Orders	337
Chapter 11	**Planning conditions**	
	The power to impose conditions	338
	The legal tests for planning conditions	339
	Planning purpose	340
	Fairly and reasonably relate	340
	Unreasonable	340
	The geographical extent of planning conditions	341
	The application site	341
	Other land under the applicant's control	341
	Land outside the application site or the applicant's control	342
	Davenport – the scope of planning conditions	342
	Positive and negative conditions	343
	Conditions restricting or controlling matters which are not otherwise subject to planning control	344
	Conditions removing permitted development and use class order rights	345
	Conditions affecting existing lawful uses	345
	Limits as to whether conditions can affect the substance of a planning permission	346
	Conditions providing for later approval of details	346
	Conditions providing for later variations to approved details	346
	Conditions requiring the transfer of land or the making of payments	347
	Planning conditions requiring agreements	348
	Conditions and highways agreements	349
	The time for implementing planning permission	349
	Full planning permissions	350
	Outline planning permissions	350
	Extensions of time if the consent is challenged	351
	Minerals planning conditions	351
	Condition delaying the start of operations likely to damage a site of special scientific interest	353
	Permissions in part	353
	Determining conditions	353
Chapter 12	**Planning obligations**	
	Section 106 planning obligations	355
	Planning obligations contained in a deed	356
	The limits of planning obligations	356
	Unilateral imposition of land or obligations	357
	Interests in land	358
	Formal requirements	360
	Deed	360
	Identification of the nature of the obligation	360
	Publicity and consultation on planning obligations	362

Contents

Legality and the relationship with planning permission	363
Regulation 122	364
Regulation 123	365
Submission of planning obligations and heads of terms in planning applications	367
Submission of planning obligations and heads of terms in planning appeals	367
The interpretation of planning obligations	369
Enforcement of planning obligations	371
Modification or discharge of planning obligations	371
Modification or discharge by agreement	372
Applications for the modification or discharge of a planning obligation	372
Section 106A modification or discharge applications	373
Section 106BA affordable housing modification or discharge applications	376
Section 106BA applications	377
Section 106BC appeals	379
Avoiding a need for early modification of any planning obligation	381
A planning obligation is not discharged by a breach	381
Pre-1991 Act planning agreements	381
Other forms of agreements and powers	383
The use of planning conditions to require payments	383
The general power in the Localism Act 2011, s 1	384
Contractual agreements under the Local Government Act 1972 and other provisions	384

Chapter 13 Planning permission for variations, retrospective and replacement consents

Section 73 variations	386
The breadth of the s 73 consideration	387
The need for an extant planning permission	389
Extension of time for implementation and reserved matters applications	390
Reserved matters	391
Retrospective planning applications under s 73A	392
'Minor material amendments'	393
Interpretation issues	394
Section 73 or 73A application?	394
Replacement planning permissions in England	394
Renewal applications in Wales	395
Procedures for s 73 and replacement planning applications	395
Procedures for retrospective planning applications	396
Fees payable	397

Chapter 14 The issuing of planning permission

The issue of a planning permission	398
Events between a resolution and decision notice	399
Content of the decision notice	399
Generally	399

	Date of the decision	400
	Conditions and notes	400
	Refusals	401
	Drawings	401
	The positive working statement in England	402
	Duty to give notice of the commencement of development in Wales	402
	EIA planning permission	402
	The appeal notification	402
	Publicity of planning decisions	403
	Inability to issue a second decision notice	404
	Potential remedies for erroneous decision notices	405
Chapter 15	**Non-material amendments to planning permissions**	
	The implicit ability to make immaterial changes	406
	Town and Country Planning Act 1990, s 96A	408
	Procedure for non-material amendments under s 96A	409
	The decision	411
	Challenges to local planning authority decisions	411
	Use of non-material amendments	412
Chapter 16	**Reserved matters and the approval of details under conditions**	
	Scope of details under reserved matters or conditions	413
	Omission of approved elements	416
	Conditions on reserved matters approvals	417
	Applications for reserved matters approval	418
	Fees for reserved matters applications	419
	Publicity and consultation on reserved matters and approvals of details	419
	EIA and subsequent applications	420
	Multiple applications and approvals	421
	Applications for the approval of details under conditions	421
	Deemed discharge of details under conditions	423
	Appeals on reserved matters applications or applications for the approval of details	425
	Revision of planning permission decision notices in Wales	425
Chapter 17	**Call-ins and the role of Ministers**	
	Ministerial powers of intervention	427
	Directions preventing the determination of applications (Article 31 directions)	428
	Persuading a Minister to make a direction	429
	Persuading a Minister to lift a direction	429
	Duties to refer applications to the Minister	429
	Town and Country Planning (Consultation) (England) Direction 2009	429
	WGC: 07/2012: The Town and Country Planning (Notification) (Wales) Direction 2012	432
	Town and Country Planning (Safeguarded aerodromes, technical sites and military explosives storage areas) Direction 2002	434

Town and Country Planning (Safeguarding
    Meteorological Sites) (England) Direction 2014   434
Safeguarding directions   434
Health and safety   434
Other referral provisions   435
Call-ins   435
Section 77   435
Call-in policy   436
Challenges to decisions whether or not to call-in
    applications   437
Section 76A and major infrastructure projects in
    England   439
Revocation of a decision to call-in an application   441
The call-in process   441
Planning applications made directly to the Secretary of
    State or the Welsh Ministers   442
Recovery of appeals   442
Recovery procedure   444
Ministerial conduct of planning matters   444
Planning Inquiry Commission   445

Chapter 18   Planning applications made directly to the Minister
The right to apply to the Secretary of State in England
    under the Town and Country Planning Act 1990,
    s 62A   447
The s 62A application process   450
The right to apply to the Welsh Ministers under s 62M   452
Applications for nationally significant development in
    Wales under s 62D   453
Section 62D application procedure   454
Urgent Crown development   455

Chapter 19   Planning appeals: preliminaries and tactics
The entitlement to appeal   457
The role of the appeal   459
Time limits for appealing   460
Inability to appeal for non-determination for
    timing reasons   462
The notice of appeal and accompanying documents
    in England   462
The notice of appeal and accompanying documents
    in Wales   464
Notice of the appeal for owners and agricultural tenants   465
Dual jurisdiction: determining applications after they have
    been appealed in Wales   465
The decision to appeal   466
Refusals   466
Grant of permission subject to conditions   467
Non-determination   467
Other avenues and further applications   468
Amendment of schemes on appeal   468
Withdrawal of an appeal   469

	Deciding upon the mode of determination	469
	Mode of determination in England	470
	Mode of determination in Wales	472
Chapter 20	**Householder and minor commercial appeals**	
	Householder, advertisement and minor commercial appeals	474
	Scope of the English simplified written representations	475
	Scope of the Welsh simplified written representations	477
	The simplified procedure	478
	Site visits	480
	Further representations and issues	481
Chapter 21	**Written representations**	
	The procedure in England under the 2013 amendments	485
	The starting date	485
	Notice to third parties	485
	Questionnaire	486
	Five-week representations by the local planning authority	487
	Third party representations	487
	Responses to the five-week representations	488
	Written representations in Wales and those in England prior to the 2013 amendments	489
	Fairness	490
	Site visits	493
Chapter 22	**Hearings**	
	Procedure	496
	Submission of the appeal	496
	Decision on mode of determination	496
	'Starting date' notice of hearing and preliminaries	496
	Statements of case and third-party representations	496
	Further information and representations	498
	Statement of common ground	498
	Potential to change the mode of determination	499
	The hearing	499
	Appearances at the hearing	499
	The hearing date	499
	Notice of the hearing date	500
	Hearing venue	500
	The rigour of a hearing	500
	Procedure at a hearing	501
	Late evidence at the hearing	502
	Tactics and preparation	503
	Adjournment of the hearing to site or a site visit	503
Chapter 23	**Inquiries**	
	The start of the process	511
	Timetabling	512
	Initial publicity of the appeal or call in inquiry	512
	Ministerial cases – pre-inquiry meetings and outline statements of case	513

Contents

Statements of case in inquiries	514
Appellant's statement of case	514
Local planning authority's statement of case	515
Mayor of London	515
Third parties and r 6 status	515
Copies of statements of case and referenced documents	516
Further information	516
Pre-inquiry meetings called by inspectors	516
Statement of matters	518
Timetable	518
Persons entitled to appear at the inquiry or hearing	518
Representatives of government departments at the inquiry	519
Date of the inquiry	520
Notification of the inquiry or hearing date	521
Advocates and witnesses	522
The inquiry	523
Assessors	523
Proofs and statements of evidence	524
Statement of common ground in inquiries	526
Requiring the production of documents or the attendance of witnesses	527
The inquiry proceedings	528
Inquiry venues	528
Procedure at the inquiry	529
Inquiry conduct	534
Communication with the inspector outside the formal hearing	535
Interests of inspectors	536
Inspector conduct generally	536
Recording inquiries and hearings	538
Site visits	538
The fairness of inquiry proceedings	539
The inspector's role during the giving of evidence	541
Reference to material not produced by the parties	542
National security cases	544
Urgent Crown development	546

Chapter 24 Decisions and costs in appeals and call-ins

Ministerial decision-making	547
'Minded to' letters	550
Inspector's decision-making	550
New matters following the close of an inquiry or hearing	550
Split decisions	551
Reasons	551
Reasons for ministerial and inspector decisions	552
Decisions subject to Environmental Impact Assessment	553
Costs in planning appeals and call-ins	554
Unreasonable conduct	555
Unnecessary or wasted expenditure	558
Making a costs application in time	558
Making a costs application	559
Costs and interested parties	560

	Assessing costs	560
	Correction of errors in decisions	561
	Inability of Ministers to withdraw issued decisions	563
Chapter 25	**High Court challenges**	
	Public law grounds of review	566
	Illegality	567
	Unreasonableness	567
	Natural justice	568
	High Court challenges to planning decisions	569
	Alternative remedies	574
	Challenges to costs decisions in planning appeals	575
	Procedures for High Court challenges	576
	Application to the High Court under s 288	576
	Grounds of challenge	576
	Standing to bring s 288 applications	577
	The commencement of s 287 and 288 proceedings	580
	Time for commencing proceedings	581
	Pre-action processes	583
	Section 288 and judicial review proceedings from commencement	584
	Documentation filed with the proceedings	584
	The commencement of the proceedings	585
	Service of proceedings	585
	Acknowledgments of service and summary grounds	586
	Consideration of permission	586
	Post-permission	587
	The former s 288 procedure	588
	Evidence in statutory applications and judicial review	588
	Evidence about the inspector or Minister's reasoning	589
	Disclosure	590
	Cross-examination in statutory applications and judicial review	591
	Interim orders	592
	The hearing of the case	592
	Remedies	593
	Severance of unlawful parts of decisions	595
	Costs of High Court appeals and applications	596
	Costs protection for parties	597
	Appealing to the Court of Appeal in judicial review and s 288 cases	599
	The effect of quashing	600
	The redetermination of an appeal or call-in following a quashing	600
	Redetermination of a planning application which was before the local planning authority	601
	Declarations as to the planning status of land	602
	The Planning Court: structure and organisation	602
	The Planning Court	602
	Jurisdiction	603
	Significant cases and timetabling	604
	Judges	606

Contents

Chapter 26	The grant of planning permission by orders and other means	
	Special development orders	608
	Local development orders	608
	The LDO-making process	609
	Register of LDOs	612
	Neighbourhood planning	613
	Neighbourhood Areas	613
	Parish councils and neighbourhood forums	613
	Neighbourhood development plans	614
	Neighbourhood development orders and community right to build orders	614
	Policy on neighbourhood development orders and community right to build orders	619
	Register of neighbourhood development orders and community right to build orders	619
	Mayoral development orders	620
	The content of a Mayoral development order	621
	Revocation and revision	621
	Simplified planning zones	622
	Enterprise zones	624
	Deemed planning permission	625
	Planning permission in principle under the Housing and Planning Bill 2015	626
	Grant of planning permission in principle by development order	627
	Grant of planning permission in principle on application	628
	Technical details consent	629
Chapter 27	Community Infrastructure Levy	
	The purpose of CIL	631
	Liability to pay CIL	632
	The nature of the development	633
	Development categories subject to CIL	633
	Exemptions and reliefs	633
	Exclusion of retained and replacement floorspace	638
	Development not subject to CIL for timing reasons	639
	The CIL rates applied	639
	CIL rates for development under planning permission granted on an application	639
	CIL rates for development under a general consent	640
	The calculation of the chargeable amount	640
	Apportionment and assumption of liability	641
	Appeals	641
	Payment	642
Chapter 28	The effect and interpretation of planning permission	
	The effect of planning permission	644
	Planning permission benefits the land unless specified otherwise	645
	Interpretation of a planning permission	646
	Interpretation of conditions	650

Chapter 29	**Implementation of planning permission**	
	Initiated, begun and commenced	653
	Implementation of prospective planning permissions	654
	Material operations	654
	Works which are not in exact accord with the permission	655
	Conditions on the planning permission	658
	No need for an intention to implement	665
	Duty to give and display notice of the commencement of development in Wales	667
	Planning obligations	667
	Retrospective permissions	667
	Carrying out conflicting planning permissions	667

APPENDIX: STATUTORY MATERIALS

Town and Country Planning Act 1990, ss 55–106C, 284, 288, 319–323	671
Town and Country Planning (Use Classes) Order 1987, SI 1987/764	772
Town and Country Planning (Inquiries Procedure) (England) Rules 2000, SI 2000/1624	779
Town and Country Planning Appeals (Determination by Inspectors) (Inquiries Procedure) (England) Rules 2000, SI 2000/1625	815
Town and Country Planning (Hearings Procedure) (England) Rules 2000, SI 2000/1626	839
Town and Country Planning (Appeals) (Written Representations Procedure) (England) Regulations 2009, SI 2009/452	858
Town and Country Planning (Development Management Procedure) (England) Order 2015, SI 2015/595	869
Town and Country Planning (General Permitted Development) (England) Order 2015, SI 2015/596	939
Index	1115

Table of Statutes

[All references are to paragraph number]

Airports Act 1986	
Pt V (ss 57–62)	2.21
s 57A	5.142
82(1)	5.184
Alkali etc Works Regulation Act 1906	3.27, 3.30
Ancient Monuments and Archaeological Areas Act 1979	
s 1	7.13
2	1.76
Banking and Financial Dealings Act 1971	5.43
Building Act 1984	9.209
s 2B	9.209
Caravan Sites and Control of Development Act 1960	5.131; 6.127
s 5	5.131
Sch 1	
para 2–10	5.130
12, 13	5.130
Coal Industry Act 1994	
s 53(2)	9.62
Companies Act 2006	
s 44(7)	12.26
46(1), (2)	12.26
Countryside and Rights of Way Act 2000	9.118
s 82	9.118
(1)	7.13
85(1)	9.119
Criminal Justice and Courts Act 2015	25.3, 25.17, 25.45
s 91	25.30, 25.45
92	25.45
Sch 16	25.17, 25.45
Data Protection Act 1998	6.33; 8.25, 8.29, 8.31
s 1(1)	8.31
2, 4, 7	8.32
Deregulation Act 2015	2.51
s 25	2.49
42	9.209
Deregulation Act 2015 – *contd*	
s 43	9.209
44(3)	2.51
(4)	2.52
Electricity Act 1989	26.65
s 36	1.17; 26.63, 26.64
37	26.63, 26.64
(1)	5.154
Sch 9	
para 1(1), (2)	26.65
Energy Act 2004	
s 82(6), (8)	5.151
Equality Act 2010	26.11, 26.12
s 19	17.62
149	9.149, 9.154
Flood and Water Management Act 2010	
s 6(7)	6.128
Freedom of Information Act 2000	6.33; 8.24, 8.25, 8.29, 8.40; 24.10; 25.78
s 1, 8, 10, 21–24, 30, 31, 35, 36, 39, 41–43	8.30
Gas Act 1965	5.153
s 7	5.153
Greater London Authority Act 1999	1.13, 1.18; 10.4
s 41(5)(a)	10.19
344(9)	10.6
Greater London Authority Act 2007	10.4
s 31	10.7
Greater London Council (General Powers) Act 1974	
s 16	12.108
25	2.49
25A	2.51, 2.52
25B	2.52
(3), (5)	2.52
Greater London Council General Powers Act 1981	
s 18	3.37

Table of Statutes

Growth and Infrastructure Act
    2013 .... 12.79; 18.3
  s 4(1) 5.6, 5.36
  5(2) 26.18
  6 .... 6.84
  7(1), (4), (5) 12.79
Highways Act 1980 .... 2.20;
                                5.143; 14.19
  Pt V (ss 62–105) 2.20
  s 278 .... 11.35; 12.32,
                          12.43; 14.19; 16.39
  329(1) 2.20
Historic Buildings and Ancient
    Monuments Act 1953
  s 8C 6.127
Hotel Proprietors Act 1956
  s 1(3) 3.35
Housing Act 1974
  s 129 .... 3.36
Housing Act 1985
  s 622 .... 3.36
  Sch 1
    para 4ZA 27.16
    12 .... 27.16
      (1)(h) 27.16
    12ZA 27.16
Housing Act 2004 .... 3.48
  s 254 .... 3.44, 3.48
    (2)(e) 3.48
    (3)(b) 3.48
    (4)(f) 3.48
    (5) 3.48
  255, 256 .... 3.48
  257 .... 3.44, 3.48
  258 .... 3.43, 3.48
    (2)–(4) 3.48
  Sch 14
    para 4, 9 .... 3.48
Housing and Planning Act 1986: 26.54
  s 90 .... 26.3
Housing and Planning Bill 2015: 26.3,
                      26.40, 26.42, 26.68,
                      26.69, 26.72, 26.77,
                           26.82; 27.21
  cl 8(1) 27.21, 27.22
  102(2) 26.70, 26.78
  103 .... 26.70
  105 .... 26.78
  Sch 6
    para 11(2) 26.77
Human Rights Act 1998
  s 6(1) 9.149

Infrastructure Act 2015 .... 5.143;
                                        26.46
  s 1, 2 .... 2.20
  Sch 4
    para 12 .... 26.50
Land Charges Act 1972 ....
  s 2(4) 15.12
Land Commission Act 1967 .... 29.38
Land Compensation Act 1961
  s 5 r 4 .... 4.36
Land Drainage Act 1991
  s 72(1) 5.149
Landlord and Tenant Act 1954
  Pt II (ss 23–46) 9.202
  s 30(1)(g) 9.202
Law of Property Act 1925
  s 84 .... 12.59, 12.100,
                                        12.102
    (1)(a) 12.102
Law of Property (Miscellaneous
    Provisions) Act 1989
  s 1(2) 12.24
    (3) 12.27
  2 .... 12.27
Lee Valley Regional Park Act
    1966
  s 14(8) 17.28
Local Democracy, Economic
    Development and Con-
    struction Act 2009 ....
    1.18, 1.25
Local Government Act 1972 ...... 8.13,
                          8.24, 8.33, 8.40
  s 100A 8.4
    (3) 8.35
    (7A)–(7F), (9) 8.114
  100B 8.4, 8.23
    (1) 8.34
    (3) 1.44; 8.18, 8.33
  100C 6.21; 8.4; 18.12
  100D 6.21; 8.4; 18.12
    (1) 8.33, 8.34
    (4) 8.34
    (5) 8.33, 8.34
  100E 1.44; 6.21;
                           8.4, 8.18; 18.12
  101 .... 8.4, 8.9, 8.10
    (1), (2) 8.5
    (4) 8.7
    (5) 8.6
  111 .... 6.34; 12.7
    (1) 12.105

Table of Statutes

Local Government Act 1972 – *contd*
s 250 .... 23.95
   (2)................................ 23.80
   (3)................................ 23.81
   (4)................................ 10.35
   (5).............. 10.35; 24.29, 24.51
270 .... 8.3
Sch 12 .... 8.4
  para 39(1) 8.13
    (2) 8.109
  44 .... 8.109
    (1) 8.13
Sch 12A 8.117
  Pt I
    para 1–3, 5–7 .... 8.36
  Pt II
    para 9 .... 8.37
Local Government Act 2000 ...... 8.3
s 9D, 13 .... 5.71
  48(4)................................. 8.3
Local Government Act 2003
s 93 .... 6.34; 12.104
  (1)–(4) 6.34
Local Government (Miscellaneous
  Provisions) Act 1982
s 33 .... 12.107
Local Government Finance Act
  1992
s 6 .... 2.51
Local Government, Planning and
  Land Act 1980
s 148(1), (2) 26.4
Sch 32 .... 1.73; 26.2, 26.60
Localism Act 2011 .... 1.18, 1.25,
        1.26; 6.40, 6.42;
        8.75, 8.84; 9.5,
        9.172; 18.2; 26.24
s 1 .... 12.104
  3(2).................................... 12.104
  25(2).................................. 8.75, 8.77
    (4)................................. 8.76
  29, 30 .... 8.84
  31 .... 8.84
    (2)–(4).......................... 8.84
Magistrates' Courts Act 1980
s 127 .... 6.56
Mobile Homes (Wales) Act 2013: 6.127
National Parks and Access to the
  Countryside Act 1949 .... 7.13;
        9.118
s 5(1), (2), (2A) 5.109
  11A(1), (2)......................... 9.114

Natural Environment and Rural
  Communities Act 2006
s 2 .... 8.120
  4(1).................................... 8.120
    (2), (3)...............................
  8.120; 14.19
  40(1).................................. 9.146
    (3)................................. 9.146
New Roads and Street Works Act 1991
s 1(4)..................................... 9.170
New Towns Act 1946 .... 1.8
Norfolk and Suffolk Broads Act
  1988 .... 9.115
s 2(1), (3)............................... 9.115
  (4)...................................... 9.116
  17A 9.117
    (1)................................. 9.117
  Sch 2.................................. 9.115
Party Wall etc Act 1996............. 9.208
Planning Act 2008............. 1.13, 1.16,
        1.18, 1.71; 6.39;
        9.34; 12.59; 17.71;
        18.1, 18.26; 19.50;
        25.18; 26.28; 27.3, 27.10
s 52 .... 12.47
  57(6).................................. 4.8
  118 .... 25.18, 25.46
  190(2)................................ 15.7
  196 .... 19.51
  203 .... 19.53
  205(2)................................ 27.19
  206(1), (2)......................... 27.4
    (3)(a)............................ 27.4
  209(1)................................ 27.9
    (2).................................. 27.9
    (a)................................. 27.9
  211(1), (2)......................... 27.4
  212, 213 .... 27.6
  214(1)................................ 27.6
  216(1)............................ 12.45; 27.4
  221 .... 12.35
Planning and Compensation Act
  1991 .... 4.9; 9.19;
        12.59, 12.101; 29.10
Planning and Compulsory Purchase Act 2004........... 1.13, 1.18,
    1.19, 1.23, 1.24, 1.28, 1.38;
    2.19; 3.41; 4.30; 5.56;
    6.63, 6.140; 9.16, 9.23,
    9.26, 9.28, 9.38; 11.44;
    13.15; 17.41, 17.45, 17.71;
    18.29; 19.36; 24.53; 27.2

Table of Statutes

Planning and Compulsory Purchase Act 2004 – *contd*
Pt 2 (ss 13–37)...................... 1.21
s 14A 26.70, 26.71
   (1), (4), (7) 26.71
17 .... 1.38
   (5)...................................... 9.26
18 .... 6.112
   (2).................... 1.38; 6.41, 6.112
19 .... 6.112
20 .... 26.39
26, 28 .... 6.112
38 .... 10.3
   (2)...................................... 26.27
   (3).......................... 1.26; 26.27
   (5)...................................... 9.26
   (6).................... 1.46; 4.26; 5.116;
             9.18, 9.19, 9.21,
             9.22, 9.50; 10.18,
             10.30; 12.61; 13.32;
             16.11, 16.35; 17.18;
             19.13; 26.67, 26.77
38A 1.26; 26.27
38B, 38C 26.27
39 .... 9.47
   (2), (2A)......................... 1.6
40 .... 26.7
42 .... 6.70
45 .... 26.54
54 .... 6.140
   (3)...................................... 6.36
56 .... 24.54, 24.63
   (3)(b).............................. 24.55
     (c).............................. 24.58
   (4).................................. 24.55
   (6).................................. 24.58
57(1).................................. 24.59
58 .... 24.60
59 .... 24.63
   (4)........................ 24.53, 24.54
   (5).................................. 24.55
Pt 6 (ss 60–78)...................... 1.21
s 60I.................................. 9.16
113.................................. 1.81
Sch 8.................................. 9.23
Planning and Energy Act 2008
  s 1(1)(c) 9.209
   (1A).............................. 9.209
Planning (Consequential Provisions) Act 1990........ 1.13; 25.49
Planning–gain Supplement (Preparations) Act 2007 .... 27.2

Planning (Hazardous Substances) Act 1990 .... 1.13; 17.47; 25.49
Planning (Listed Buildings and Conservation Areas) Act 1990 .... 1.13; 6.140; 17.47; 25.49
s 1, 7 .... 1.75
14 .... 23.39
18 .... 28.19
22(2)................................. 19.51
63, 65 .... 1.81
66 .... 9.99
   (1)...................... 9.12, 9.88, 9.93
69 .... 9.96
72 .... 9.95, 9.96, 9.97, 9.99
   (1)...................... 9.12, 9.94, 9.96
   (2)...................................... 9.94
75 .... 5.145
88D 19.51
Planning (Wales) Act 2015 ... 1.19, 1.28, 1.32; 6.43, 6.84, 6.102; 9.16, 9.38, 9.48, 9.160; 13.15, 13.18; 14.16; 18.17, 18.21; 29.43
s 2(5)................................. 9.48
6 .... 9.16
17, 18 .... 6.43
19 .... 18.22
23 .... 18.17
28 .... 6.84
31(2)................................. 9.160
32 .... 6.102; 19.8
33 .... 14.13; 16.43
34 .... 14.16; 29.43
35(4)................................. 13.15
36(4)................................. 13.15
Postal Services Act 2011
  s 30, 31 .... 5.163
Public Health Act 1936
  s 269 .... 5.132
Radioactive Substances Act 1993.................................. 7.21
Regional Development Agencies Act 1998.......................... 17.46
Sch 1.................................. 17.46
Road Traffic (Driver Licensing and Information Systems) Act 1989
  s 8, 10 .... 5.162

Self-build and Custom Housebuilding Act 2015 .... 9.111; 27.21
  s 1(A1) 27.21
    (A2) 27.22
    (1) 9.111
  2 .... 9.111
Senior Courts Act 1981
  s 31(2A), (2B), (3D), (3E) 25.40,
                                    25.89
    (6) 25.88
Town and Country Planning Act
  1932 .... 4.10
  s 34 .... 12.98
Town and Country Planning Act
  1947 .... 6.61; 12.98
  s 77(1) 4.10
Town and Country Planning Act
  1968 .... 17.67; 29.38
Town and Country Planning Act
  1971 .... 9.95; 12.98
  s 29, 30 .... 11.5
  43 .... 29.37
  52 .... 12.8, 12.99, 12.100
  Sch 24
    para 88 .... 12.98
Town and Country Planning Act
  1990 .... 1.13, 1.81; 2.4,
                    2.7; 4.19; 5.6, 5.13,
                    5.90, 5.91; 6.39, 6.62,
                    6.100, 6.101; 9.94;
                    10.4, 10.35; 12.2;
                    17.29; 18.2; 21.7,
                    21.26; 25.23, 25.45,
                    25.46, 25.49; 26.49
  Pt I (ss 1–9) 20.5
  s 1 .... 1.11; 6.17
    2A 1.12, 1.65; 10.7
      (1), (1A), (1B) 10.7
    2B 1.65; 10.7
      (2), (3) 10.28
      (4)–(7) 10.25
    2C 1.65; 10.7
      (1) 10.33; 16.19
      (3) 10.33
    2D 1.65; 10.7
    2F 10.7
    2E 1.56
      (2) 10.30; 12.30
      (4) 10.31; 12.30
      (5) 10.31; 12.58
    2F(2)–(5) 10.32
    4A 1.12; 6.16

Town and Country Planning Act
  1990 – *contd*
  s 5 .... 1.12; 6.16; 15.8
  6, 7, 7A, 8, 8A 1.12; 6.16
  38(6) 4.30
  52 .... 12.15
  54A 1.46; 9.19; 16.11
  Pt III (ss 55–106C) 6.112; 7.8
  s 55 .... 2.19, 2.32; 27.10
    (1) 1.3, 1.14; 2.2,
                          2.22, 2.49; 3.1;
                          5.123, 5.134
    (1A) 2.6
    (2) 2.15, 2.37; 3.2
      (a) 1.15; 5.152; 11.24
      (e) 5.133
      (f) 3.4, 3.5
    (2A) 1.15; 2.19; 27.8
    (3) 2.45
      (a) 3.9
    (4) 2.11
    (4A) 2.23
    (5) 2.48
  56 .... 29.9, 29.37
    (1) 29.4
    (2) 29.4, 29.7, 29.9
    (4) 29.7, 29.8, 29.11
  57 .... 1.16; 27.10
    (1) 4.2
    (1A), (2) 4.8
    (3) 4.6, 4.8, 4.9
    (4) 4.9
    (5), (6) 4.8
    (7) 4.10
  58(1) 4.3
  59 .... 1.73; 26.2
    (1), (2) 5.2
    (3) 26.4
    (b) 4.3
  59A(1)(a) 26.70
    (b) 26.77
    (2) 26.70, 26.73
    (7) 26.78
  60(1) 5.6; 26.4
    (2), (2A)–(2C) 5.6, 5.36
    (4) 5.125
  61 .... 17.67
  61A 1.73; 26.2, 26.7
    (2), (4) 26.7
    (6) 26.20
  61B(1) 26.17, 26.18
    (3), (4) 26.18

Table of Statutes

Town and Country Planning Act
1990 – *contd*

s 61B(5)–(7)	26.17, 26.18
(7A)	26.18
(9)	26.20
61C(1), (2)	26.8
61D	5.56, 5.57; 26.21
(1)	5.56, 5.57
(2), (3)	5.57
61DA	1.73; 26.2, 26.46
(1), (2)	26.47
61DB(1)–(5)	26.50
(6), (7)	26.51
(8)	26.50
61DC(1)–(5)	26.48
(6)	26.49
61DD(1)	26.52
(2)–(4)	26.49, 26.52
(5)	26.49
(6)(a), (b)	26.52
(7)	26.52
61DE	1.73; 26.2 26.46
(3)–(7)	26.53
61E	1.73; 26.2, 26.28
(2)	26.37
(4)	26.42
(b)	26.42
(5)	26.42
(6)	26.30
(8)	26.42
61F	26.27
(1), (4)–(7)	26.26
61G	26.25
61H	26.41
61I	26.27
61J	26.37
(1), (2), (4), (5)	26.28
61K	26.28
61L	26.37
(1), (2), (5)	26.29
61M	26.27
61N	26.27
(1)–(3)	25.46
61O, 61P	26.17
61Q	1.73; 4.9; 19.6; 26.2
61W	6.21, 6.42
(1)	6.43, 6.45
(2)–(4), (7)	6.43
61Z	6.43
61Z1, 61Z2	6.43
62	17.67; 28.9

Town and Country Planning Act
1990 – *contd*

s 62(3)	6.82, 6.93
(4)	6.82
(4A)	6.84
(5)	6.70
(8)	6.45
62A	1.32; 6.103, 6.104; 10.7; 17.5, 17.56; 18.2, 18.3, 18.6, 18.7, 18.11, 18.12, 18.13, 18.15, 18.16, 18.17, 18.21, 18.24; 19.51; 24.54; 25.13
(2)	18.8
(b)	18.7
(3), (4)	18.13
62B	18.6
(1)	18.9, 18.10
(2)–(4)	18.9
(5)	18.10
(6)	18.10
62C	18.6, 18.12, 18.15
62D	1.32; 18.2, 18.22, 18.23, 18.25, 18.26, 18.27, 18.28
(1), (3), (4)	18.22
(5)–(7)	18.23
62E	18.26
62F(1)	18.24
(3)	18.25
(6)	18.24
62G	18.25
62H(1), (2)	18.24
62I	18.26
62J(2), (3)	18.27
62K	18.26
62L	18.28
62M	18.2, 18.17, 18.20, 18.21, 18.23
(5), (6)	18.17
62N	18.17, 18.18
(7), (8)	18.18
62O	18.17
62Q	18.20, 18.26
62R	18.20, 18.26
63	17.67
64	27.35
64A(3)	27.35
65	1.35; 6.2, 6.21, 6.56, 6.89, 6.90; 18.12
(1), (3)	6.48

Town and Country Planning Act
1990 – *contd*

s 65(5)	6.89
(6)	6.56, 6.88
(7), (9)	6.56
66–68	6.2
69	6.2
(1)(aza)	26.78
(8)	6.96
70	1.51, 1.52; 5.50; 6.2, 6.21; 9.185; 11.3, 11.6, 11.16; 13.14, 13.29; 17.48; 18.12; 25.6
(1)	1.51; 11.4, 11.13; 26.77, 26.82
(1A)	26.77
(2)	1.45; 8.64; 9.4, 9.9, 9.12, 9.17, 9.22, 9.48, 9.160, 9.172; 10.30; 13.32; 19.13; 26.67, 26.77
(aa)	9.160
(b)	9.172
(2A)	1.46; 9.5
(2ZA)	26.80
(2ZB)	26.79
(2ZC)	26.80
(4)	8.22; 9.173
70A	6.101, 6.102, 6.103, 6.105, 6.106, 6.109, 6.110; 18.14; 19.5, 19.8, 19.39
(1)–(4), (4A), (4B)	6.103
(8)	6.105
70B	6.101, 6.102, 6.104, 6.105, 6.106, 6.109; 18.14; 19.5, 19.8, 19.39
70B(1)(a)	6.104
(2)	6.104
(3)	6.104; 1942
(4)	6.104
(5)	6.105
70C	6.101, 6.102, 6.107, 6.109; 18.14; 19.5, 19.8, 19.9
(1)	6.107, 6.108
71	6.2
(3), (4)	6.127
71ZA(4), (5)	16.43
71ZB	14.16; 29.43

Town and Country Planning Act
1990 – *contd*

s 71ZB(3)	29.43
(4)–(6)	14.16
72	1.51, 1.52; 5.50; 6.2, 6.21 9.95; 11.3, 11.5, 11.15; 18.12; 26.82
(1)	11.4; 17.48
(a)	11.5, 11.16
(b)	11.5
(2)	11.4
(3), (4)	29.4
(5)	17.48
73	6.2, 6.3, 6.59, 6.60, 6.72, 6.135, 6.136; 10.7; 11.29; 13.1, 13.3, 13.4, 13.5, 13.6, 13.7, 13.8, 13.9, 13.10, 13.11, 13.12, 13.13, 13.14, 13.15, 13.16, 13.17, 13.18, 13.19, 13.24, 13.27, 13.28, 13.29, 13.32, 13.33, 13.34, 13.35, 13.36, 13.37, 13.38; 14.7; 15.7, 15.20, 15.22, 15.23; 18.7, 18.23; 19.13, 19.41; 26.51; 27.32; 29.47
(2)	13.6, 13.7, 13.12
(4)	13.9, 13.10, 13.14
(5)	13.15
(b)	13.16, 13.18
73A	6.2, 6.3, 6.59; 13.1, 13.13, 13.20, 13.23, 13.24, 13.25, 13.28, 13.29, 13.32, 13.33, 13.34, 13.36, 13.37, 13.38; 14.8; 15.20, 15.22; 17.48; 19.13
(1)	13.20
(2)	13.21
(3)	13.22
74	1.75; 6.21; 18.12
(1)(a)	17.8
(b)	9.22
(1B)	10.6
(1C)	10.18
74A	16.38

Table of Statutes

Town and Country Planning Act
1990 – *contd*

s 74A(9)	16.39
75	28.5
(1)	28.6
(2)	28.3
(3)	28.3, 28.4
76A	6.103; 17.29, 17.45, 17.47, 17.48, 17.49, 17.50; 24.54; 25.13
(1)	17.46
(2), (3)	17.47
(4), (5)	17.48
(7)	17.50
(9)	17.46
(10)	17.48
(12)	17.45
76B(2)–(4)	17.48
76C(1)	18.14
76D(1), (2)	18.16
(6)	25.13
76E	18.16
77	1.60; 6.100, 6.103; 17.29, 17.47, 17.50; 18.12, 18.33; 19.5, 19.51, 19.53; 23.3; 24.54; 25.13, 25.27, 25.31; 26.67
(1)	10.32; 17.30
(2)	17.32, 17.52
(5), (6A)	17.55
78	6.104; 23.6, 23.7; 24.54; 25.13, 25.27, 25.31; 26.50
(1)	5.47; 19.4, 19.38; 20.5
(b)	16.42
(c)	5.50; 15.21; 26.50
(2)	16.42; 19.5, 19.48; 20.5; 24.19
(3)	1.68; 19.16; 24.19
(4)	19.16
78A	19.36, 19.38
(1)	19.37
(3), (4)	19.38
79(1)	11.50; 19.12, 19.13; 24.18
(4)	19.13
82	1.73; 26.2; 26.54
(2), (3)	26.55

Town and Country Planning Act
1990 – *contd*

s 83–87	26.54
85(1), (2)	26.58
86(2)–(5)	26.58
87(1)	26.59
88	1.73; 26.2
(1)–(6), (8)	26.60
90	1.17, 1.73; 4.3; 5.8; 16.39; 17.7; 25.18; 26.3, 26.67; 27.29
(1)	26.61
(2)	26.63
(2A)	26.66
(2ZA)	26.64
(3)	25.18; 26.67
(4)	26.61
(5)	26.63
91	11.3, 11.41; 29.3, 29.4, 29.5, 29.9, 29.46
(1)–(3)	11.41
(3A), (3B)	11.43; 13.15; 29.3
(3C), (3D)	13.15
(3ZA)–(3ZD)	13.15
(4)(b)	11.40
(c)	11.40; 29.5
(d)	29.8
92	11.3, 11.42; 15.4; 29.3, 29.4, 29.5, 29.9, 29.15
(1)	11.42
(2)	11.42
(b)(i)	11.42
(3), (5)	11.42
93(4)	13.7
94	4.20; 29.9
(1)	4.22
(2)–(4)	4.23
(5), (6)	4.24
95	25.13
(1)	4.23
(2), (3), (5)	4.24
96A	15.2, 15.7, 15.8, 15.9, 15.12, 15.13, 15.14, 15.17, 15.18, 15.21, 15.23, 15.24; 16.29
(1)	15.8
(2)	15.10

Table of Statutes

Town and Country Planning Act 1990 – *contd*

s 96A(3)	15.9
(4)	15.12
(5)	15.14
(6), (7)	15.12
97	4.25, 4.26, 4.30; 9.170; 14.20, 14.21; 19.11; 24.63
(1), (2)	4.26
(3), (4)	4.27
98	4.30; 14.21; 19.11; 24.53
(1)–(6)	4.28
99	4.29; 14.21; 19.11; 24.53
(1), (8)	4.29
100	14.21; 19.11; 24.53
(1)	4.30
(3)–(5)	4.30; 26.20
(6)	26.20
101	17.67; 19.11
(2)	17.67
(3)	17.68
102(1)	4.34
(2), (4), (5), (8)	4.35
103	4.37
(4)	4.37
104	4.38
106	1.56, 1.57 1.58; 6.21; 10.30; 11.38; 12.3, 12.4, 12.7, 12.14, 12.21, 12.98, 12.104; 27.16
(1)	1.56; 12.3, 12.4, 12.5, 12.6, 12.36
(a)	12.7
(5), (6)	1.57; 12.55
(9)	12.20, 12.23
(a)	12.21
(aa)	12.22
(c)	12.17
106A	12.63, 12.64, 12.65, 12.66, 12.67, 12.68, 12.79, 12.80, 12.87; 25.18
(1)	12.60
(2)	12.60
(3)	12.65, 12.66
(4)	12.66
(5)	12.65, 12.87
(6)	12.71, 12.75

Town and Country Planning Act 1990 – *contd*

s 106A(7)	12.76
(10)	12.59
(11)	12.59, 12.63
106B	1.57; 12.64, 12.78; 19.51; 24.56; 25.18
(4)	12.78; 19.51
(7)	12.78
106BA	1.57; 12.79, 12.80, 12.82, 12.85, 12.91, 12.92; 25.18
(2)	12.80
(3)	12.82, 12.88
(4)	12.88
(6)	12.87
(a)	12.87
(b)	12.88
(7)	12.88
(8)	12.83
(11)	12.84
(12), (13)	12.80
(16)	12.85
106BB	12.79, 12.85
(2)–(4)	12.85
106BC	1.57; 12.79, 12.80, 12.90, 12.91; 19.51; 24.56
(1)	12.90
(3)	12.91
(4), (5)	12.90
(6)	12.91
(9)	12.90, 12.91
(11)	12.92
(13)	12.92
107	4.31; 5.60, 5.69; 14.21
108	5.60, 5.69
(2A)	5.69
(3B)(a)	5.69
(3C)	5.69
109(b)	12.16
115	4.36
171A	1.77
171B	5.21
(1)	1.79; 15.4
(2), (2A), (3), (4)	1.79
171BA, 171BC	1.79
172, 172E, 174	1.78
177(1)	25.13
183	1.78
187A	1.78
187B	1.78; 25.120

Table of Statutes

Town and Country Planning Act
1990 – *contd*

s 189(1)	4.38
190	4.39
191	4.9; 5.21
192	5.21
195(1)	25.13
196D	5.145; 6.18
(3), (9)	13.23
197	9.147
198	9.147
(1)	9.147
202	1.75
206	9.147
215	1.80
220, 221	1.75; 24.13
222	1.75; 2.48
223, 224	1.75
235(1)	27.9
262	5.96
(1), (3)	2.21
264	16.39
265, 266	24.2
278	6.99, 6.100; 11.38; 12.32
Pt XII (ss 284–292)	25.13
s 284	24.66; 25.13
(1)	25.14
(f)	18.33; 25.13
(g)	25.17
(2)	4.37
(3)	25.13
(i)	18.33
(3A)	25.17
(4)	25.18
286(1)	6.18
287	1.81; 25.12, 25.14, 25.41, 25.46, 25.58
(4)	25.46
(5)(b)	25.46
288	1.81; 4.37; 6.98; 18.33; 24.66; 25.3, 25.7, 25.12, 25.13, 25.14, 25.15, 25.16, 25.17, 25.19, 25.21, 25.27, 25.28, 25.30, 25.31, 25.32, 25.35, 25.41, 25.43, 25.44, 25.46, 25.49, 25.54, 25.58, 25.59, 25.60, 25.68, 25.69, 25.79, 25.80, 25.81, 25.85, 25.87, 25.91, 25.100, 25.102, 25.104, 25.105, 25.106; 26.67

Town and Country Planning Act
1990 – *contd*

s 288(1)	25.32, 25.35
(1A)	25.17
(3)	25.15, 25.46
(4)	25.15
(5)	25.34
(b)	25.87
(9)	25.32
289	1.81; 25.12, 25.120
292A	5.177
(1)	6.62
293(1)	6.63; 18.30
(2)	18.30
293A	6.63; 16.39; 18.2, 18.29, 18.30, 18.33; 24.54
(1)	18.30
(2)	6.100
(3)	18.30
(4)(a)	18.30
(b)	18.31
(7)	18.32
(9)(a)	18.32
(10)	18.32
(11)	18.33
316	6.18; 28.7
319A	1.68; 12.78; 19.38, 19.51; 24.19
(3)	19.51; 21.3; 23.3
(4)	19.51
(6)	19.52
319B	1.68; 19.38, 19.53
(3)	21.3
(4), (6)	19.53
320	23.83
(2)	23.80, 23.95; 24.29
(3)	24.29
321	10.35
(2)	23.143
(3)	23.82, 23.115, 23.143
(4)	23.143
(5), (6), (9)	23.144
321A	23.144
321B(2)	23.144
322	10.35
(1AA)	24.29

Table of Statutes

Town and Country Planning Act
1990 – contd
s 322A, 322B.......................... 10.35
327A 6.87, 6.89, 6.90
336 .... 2.3; 5.10, 5.89
(1)..................... 1.13; 2.7, 2.12,
2.20, 2.39; 3.5;
5.90, 5.153, 5.163;
26.9; 29.8
Sch 1.................................. 1.11; 6.17
para 1 .... 6.17
(a)–(h).................... 26.28
3................................. 5.17
4...................... 6.134; 16.22
6................................ 6.133
(2) 14.19
7...................... 6.25, 6.131
(4), (5)..................... 6.131
(10) 6.131
8......................6.21, 6.128;
18.12, 18.15
9............................... 26.55
10............................. 4.21
11............................. 4.26
14............................. 6.96
Sch 1A.................................. 19.18
para 2 .... 18.26
Sch 2...................................... 5.14
Sch 4...................................... 4.10
Sch 4A
para 2(1)–(3)..................... 26.22
3............................... 26.16
Sch 4B................................... 26.27
para 5 .... 26.34
6.............................. 26.34
7(4)–(6)..................... 26.36
8(1) 26.37
(2) 26.38
(6) 26.39
9(1) 26.39
(2)(a)....................... 26.39
(3), (6)..................... 26.39
10, 12 .... 26.40
14, 15 .... 26.41
Sch 4C
para 2 .... 26.29, 26.37
3............................... 26.30
4............................... 26.30
(2) 26.30
(5) 26.34
6(1)(a), (b) 26.33
8............................... 26.37

Town and Country Planning Act
1990 – contd
Sch 5..................................... 19.13
para 1(1)–(3)..................... 11.46
(6) 11.46
2(1) 11.47
(2)(a), (b) 11.47
(3)–(7)..................... 11.47
3............................... 11.48
4...................... 11.48; 16.36
5, 6........................... 16.37
Sch 6.............................. 12.78; 17.67
para 1 .... 17.57
2(7) 25.13
(8) 25.15
3(1) 17.57
(2) 17.63; 24.64
(5A), (5B) 17.64
8............................... 24.19
Sch 7
para 1(1), (2)..................... 26.55
2(1) 26.56
3(1)–(4).................... 25.56
4............................... 26.56
5, 6........................... 26.57
8(1) 26.58
9(1)–(3).................... 26.58
Sch 8..................................... 17.67
para 1(1) 17.69
2............................... 17.69
3(1) 17.69
(2), (4)..................... 17.70
4(2), (3).................... 17.68
5............................... 17.70
Sch 9..................................... 4.35
Town and Country Planning Bill
1947................................. 1.8
Town and Country Planning
(Consultation) (England)
Direction 2009................... 1.60
Town and Country Planning
(Interim Development) Act
1943................................. 4.10
s 1, 2 .... 4.10
Town and Country Planning (Noti-
fication) (Wales) Direction
2012................................. 1.62
Transport Act 2000
Pt I Ch I (ss 1–40) 2.21
Transport and Works Act 1992... 1.73;
25.119; 26.3
s 1, 3 .... 26.66

Table of Statutes

Tribunals and Inquiries Act 1992:	25.32, 25.87
s 10	24.19
Well-being of Future Generations (Wales) Act 2015	9.48
s 2, 4	9.48
5(1), (2)	9.48
Wildlife and Countryside Act 1981	
s 28(1)	7.13

Wildlife and Countryside Act 1981 – *contd*	
s 28G	9.145
(1)–(3)	9.145
28I(2), (3)	6.128
(4)	6.138
(6)	11.49
41(3)	5.97, 5.98
Pt III (ss 53–66)	6.119

Table of Statutory Instruments

[*All references are to paragraph number*]

Air Navigation Order 2009, SI
  2009/3015
  art 255................................ 5.182
Building Regulations 2010, SI
  2010/2214........................ 9.209
  reg 4(1B)............................ 9.209
  Sch 1
    Pt M 9.209
Civil Procedure (Amendment No
  3) Rules 2014, SI 2014/610
  r 3 .... 25.117
Civil Procedure Rules 1998, SI
  1998/3132............. 25.101, 25.120
  Pt 8 (rr 8.1–8.9)............ 25.41, 25.43,
                            25.61, 25.68
  r 8.2 .... 25.43
    8.3, 8.4 .... 25.68
    8.5(3), (4)........................ 25.61
    8.6(2), (3) 25.79
  PD 8 .... 25.68
  PD 8A.................................. 25.70
  PD 8C.................... 25.41, 25.55,
              25.56, 25.59, 25.60,
              25.61, 25.62, 25.63,
              25.64, 25.67, 25.82
  r 44.3(2)(a) 25.94
    45.41 .... 25.100
  PD 45 .... 25.100
  r 46.5 .... 24.51
  PD 46 .... 24.51
  r 52.3(6) 25.107
    52.15(2)............................ 25.64
    52.15B.............................. 25.106
      (1), (2).......................... 25.106
      (3) 25.64,
                                        25.106
  Pt 54 (rr 54.1–54.36)............ 25.55
  r 54.1 .... 25.79
    54.5(A1) 25.49
      (1), (4).......................... 25.48
      (5).................................. 25.46,
                              25.48, 25.54
    (6)................................ 25.54

Civil Procedure Rules 1998, SI
  1998/3132 – *contd*
  r 54.7 .... 25.59
    54.8(1).............................. 25.60
      (2)................................ 25.62,
                                        25.63
      (4).................................. 25.60
    54.13(4)............................ 25.64
    54.14(1)............................ 25.67
    54.21(2)............................ 25.119
      (b) 25.124
    54.22(1)............................ 25.117
      (2) 25.118,
                                        25.119
      (3)................................ 25.130
  PD 54A........................ 25.5, 25.56,
                              25.63, 25.82
  PD 54E........................ 25.41, 25.57,
              25.63, 25.69, 25.117,
              25.125, 25.127
  PD 66 .... 25.59
Community Infrastructure Levy
  Regulations 2010, SI 2010/
  948 .... 12.103; 27.3
  reg 2(1) 27.13, 27.20, 27.34
    4(1).................................. 27.15
    (2).................................. 27.13
    5(3) 27.29, 27.35
    6(1)(a), (b), (d) 27.9
    (2).................................. 27.9
    8...................................... 27.34
    (7) 27.29, 27.35
    9(1) 27.10
    13(1) 27.5
    14...................................... 27.4
    25...................................... 27.6
    31–34, 36........................ 27.37
    40(4) 27.33
    (5).................................. 27.36
    (7) 27.30, 27.36
    (8).................................. 27.36
    (11) 27.27, 27.28
    41...................................... 27.26

Table of Statutory Instruments

Community Infrastructure Levy Regulations 2010, SI 2010/948 – *contd*	
reg 42	27.12
42A	27.13
(2)	27.41
42B(1)	27.14
(2)	27.14
(a)	27.14
(3), (6)	27.14
42C	27.13
43(1)–(3)	27.15
44(1)–(4)	27.15
45, 46	27.15
49	27.16
(1)	27.17
49(3)–(7), (7A), (11)	27.16
49A, 49B	27.16
49C(2)–(5)	27.17
50–52	27.18
53	27.20
(3)	27.20
54	27.18
54A(1), (2)	27.21
(3)–(6), (8)	27.23
54B(2)	27.24
(a)	27.24
(3)	27.24
54C	27.24
54D(2)	27.24
(b)	27.24
(5), (6)	27.24
55(1)	27.25
(3)	27.25
(a), (b)	27.25
56	27.25
57(4)(d)(ii)–(iv)	27.26
(5)	27.26
59E, 59F	12.42
64	27.29, 27.35
(2)	27.35
64A(3)	27.35
65(1), (3), (12)	27.44
67	27.45
(1)	27.45
(1A)	27.45
(aa)	27.14
68	27.45
69	27.37
70	27.45
112(1)	27.42
(2)(c)	27.41

Community Infrastructure Levy Regulations 2010, SI 2010/948 – *contd*	
reg 112(3)	27.43
113(1)–(3), (7)	27.39
114	27.39
(4)	27.38
115	27.38, 27.40
116	27.40
(3)	27.38
116A	27.41
(3)	27.38
116B	27.42
(3)	27.38
117–119	27.42
120(1), (4), (5), (7), (9)	27.43
121	27.43
122	12.9, 12.36, 12.39, 12.40, 12.43, 12.47, 12.53
(2)	1.59; 12.35
123	12.9, 12.41, 12.43, 12.45, 12.53
(1)	12.41, 12.44
(2)	12.41, 12.43; 27.19
(2A)	11.39
(2B)	12.43
(3)	11.39; 12.44, 12.46
(4)	12.41, 12.42, 12.44, 12.45, 12.46
128(1)–(3)	27.31
128A, 128B	27.32
Conservation (Natural Habitats etc) Regulations 1994, SI 1994/2716	5.26; 9.141, 9.144
reg 60–63	5.8
Conservation of Habitats and Species Regulations 2010, SI 2010/490	1.76; 4.26; 5.7, 5.12; 9.130; 26.6, 26.9, 26.59, 26.60
reg 3(3)	5.30
5	5.27
9(5)	9.140
41, 53–58	9.131
60	5.30; 9.131
61	9.131
(1)	5.30; 9.132

Table of Statutory Instruments

Conservation of Habitats and Species Regulations 2010, SI 2010/490 – *contd*
- reg 61(2)–(4) 9.137
- (6) 5.30; 9.133
- 62 .... 9.131
- (1) 9.134
- (2) 9.135
- 63 .... 4.26
- 66 .... 9.135
- 68 .... 9.132
- 69 .... 4.26
- (6) 4.26
- 70–72 .... 4.26
- 73 .... 5.7, 5.8, 5.26
- (1) 5.31
- 74 .... 5.7, 5.8, 5.26
- (6) 5.28
- 75 .... 5.7, 5.8, 5.26, 5.27, 5.28, 5.29, 5.30, 5.31; 12.104
- (2) 5.28
- (4), (5) 5.27
- (6), (7) 5.29
- 76 .... 5.7, 5.8, 5.26
- 77 .... 26.6
- 78A 26.33
- 79 .... 26.59
- 80 .... 26.60

Criminal Justice and Courts Act 2015 (Commencement No 1, Saving and Transitional Provisions) Order 2015, SI 2015/778
- art 3 .... 25.89
- Sch 2
  - para 6 .... 25.89

Criminal Justice and Courts Act 2015 (Commencement No 3 and Transitional Provisions) Order 2015, SI 2015/1778
- art 3, 4 .... 25.30

Electricity (Applications for Consent) Regulations 1990, SI 1990/455 .... 26.63
- reg 5–9 .... 26.65

Electricity Generating Stations and Overhead Lines (Inquiries Procedure) (England and Wales) Rules 2007, SI 2007/841 .... 26.63

Electricity Works (Environmental Impact Assessment) (England and Wales) Regulations 2000, SI 2000/1927 .... 26.63

Environmental Impact Assessment (Land Drainage Improvement Works) Regulations 1999, SI 1999/1783 .... 5.25

Environmental Information Regulations 2004, SI 2004/3391: 6.33; 7.61; 8.24, 8.25, 8.26, 8.30, 8.34, 8.40, 8.41; 24.10
- reg 2(1) 8.26
- 5 .... 8.29
- (1), (2) 8.29
- 9 .... 8.29
- 12 .... 8.29
- (1), (2) 8.29
- (5)(e) 8.42
- 13 .... 8.29

Environmental Permitting (England and Wales) Regulations 2010, SI 2010/675 .... 1.76; 6.27
- reg 2 .... 3.26

Hazardous Waste (England and Wales) Regulations 2005, SI 2005/894
- reg 6 .... 2.47; 3.6

Hazardous Waste (Wales) Regulations 2005, SI 2005/1806
- reg 6 .... 3.6

Highways (Environmental Impact Assessment) Regulations 2007, SI 2007/1062 .... 5.25

Legal Aid, Sentencing and Punishment of Offenders Act 2012 (Fines on Summary Conviction) Regulations 2015, SI 2015/664 ... 6.56

Licensing and Management of Houses in Multiple Occupation and Other Houses (Miscellaneous Provisions) (England) Regulations 2006, SI 2006/373 .... 3.48

Licensing and Management of Houses in Multiple Occupation and Other Houses (Miscellaneous Provisions) (Wales) Regulations 2006, SI 2006/1715 .... 3.48

Table of Statutory Instruments

Local Authorities (Executive Arrangements) (Functions and Responsibilities) (Wales) Regulations 2007, SI 2007/399	
Sch 1......................................	8.3
Local Authorities (Executive Arrangements) (Meetings and Access to Information) (England) Regulations 2012, SI 2012/2089	8.33
Local Authorities (Functions and Responsibilities) (England) Regulations 2000, SI 2000/2853	
Sch 1......................................	8.3
Local Government (Access to Information) (Variation) Order 2006, SI 2006/88.....	8.36
Neighbourhood Planning (General) Regulations 2012, SI 2012/637	1.26
reg 3.......................................	26.30
5–7......................................	26.25
8–12....................................	26.26
13..	26.30
14–20..................................	26.27
21..	26.30
(a)	26.30
(b)(i), (ii)	26.31
(c)	26.31
22..	26.30
(1)	26.32
23..	26.30
(1)	26.35
(a)(v)........................	26.35
(2).................................	26.35
24............................ 26.30, 26.36	
25............................ 26.30, 26.40	
26............................ 26.30, 26.42	
27..	26.30
Neighbourhood Planning (Prescribed Dates) Regulations 2012, SI 2012/2030 .... 26.27, 26.41	
Neighbourhood Planning (Referendums) Regulations 2012, SI 2012/2031 .... 26.27, 26.41	
Openness of Local Government Bodies Regulations 2014, SI 2014/2095	8.24, 8.100, 8.115
Openness of Local Government Bodies Regulations 2014, SI 2014/2095 – *contd*	
reg 4.......................................	8.114
7(1).................................	8.115
(2).................................	8.115, 8.116
(3).................................	8.116
8..	8.117
9..	8.117
Planning Act 2008 (Commencement No 1 and Savings) Order 2009, SI 2009/400	
art 3(j).....................................	19.51
Planning (Listed Buildings and Conservation Areas) Regulations 1990, SI 1990/1519:................................	6.141
reg 3(1A)	6.74
3A..	6.74
5A........................... 6.124; 13.35	
(1), (2)...........................	6.124
(2A)–(2C)....................	18.12
(3) 6.128; 21.7	
(4)	6.124
Planning (National Security Directions and Appointed Representatives) (England) Rules 2006, SI 2006/1284	
r 4	23.144
(1)...................................	23.145
5, 6, 8–11, 14	23.145
Planning (National Security Directions and Appointed Representatives) (Wales) Rules 2006, SI 2006/1387	
r 4	23.144
(1)...................................	23.145
5, 6, 8–11, 14	23.145
Planning (Wales) Act 2015 (Commencement No 2 and Transitional and Saving Provisions) Order 2015, SI/2015/1987	9.48
Public Gas Transporter Pipe-line Works (Environmental Impact Assessment) Regulations 1999, SI 1999/1672.................. 5.25, 5.153	
Rules of the Supreme Court 1965, SI 1965/1776	25.2

Town and Country Planning Appeals (Determination by Inspectors) (Inquiries Procedure) (England) Rules 2000, SI 2000/1625 .... 1.68; 23.130
r 2(1).................................. 23.7, 23.26, 23.39
3A....................................... 23.7
4(1)–(3)............................... 23.11
(4)................................. 23.12
5 .... 23.57
6(1)..................................... 23.22, 23.26
(3)................................. 23.26
(6).......................... 23.25, 23.26
(8).......................... 23.25, 23.27
(10)............................... 23.25
7(1)..................................... 23.36
(2), (3)........................... 23.29
(4)................................. 23.30
8 .... 23.10
(1)–(3)............................ 23.37
9 .... 23.57, 23.62
10(2), (2A), (3)................... 23.51
(4).................... 23.48, 23.51
(5)................................. 23.52
(6)................................. 23.53
(7)................................. 23.54
11(1)........................... 23.39, 23.40
(2)................................. 23.43
12(1).......................... 23.45, 23.46
(2)................................. 23.46
(3)................................. 23.46
14(1), (2).............................. 23.68
(3)......................... 23.37; 24.15
(4)................................. 24.15
(5)................................. 23.94
15(1)................................... 23.77
16(2)................................... 23.89
(4)................................ 23.89, 23.92, 23.104
(5)................................. 23.96
(6)....................... 23.98, 23.100
(9)................................. 23.112
(12)............................... 23.100
(14)............................... 23.91
17(2), (3) 23.106, 23.125
19(1)................................... 24.19
20 .... 24.20; 25.110
21 .... 23.10
24 .... 10.34; 23.23
(3)................................. 23.41

Town and Country Planning Appeals (Determination by Inspectors) (Inquiries Procedure) (Wales) Rules 2003, SI 2003/1267 .... 1.68
r 2(1).............................. 23.9, 23.76
3A....................................... 23.9
r 4(1)–(3)............................ 23.11
(4)................................. 23.12
4A....................................... 23.9
5 .... 23.57
6(1)..................................... 23.22, 23.26
(3).......................... 23.20, 23.21, 23.26
(5)................................. 23.26
(6).......................... 23.25, 23.26
(8).......................... 23.25, 23.27
(10)............................... 23.25
7(1)..................................... 23.36
(2), (3)........................... 23.29
(4)................................. 23.30
8 .... 23.10
(1)–(3)............................ 23.37
9 .... 23.57, 23.62
10(2), (2A), (3)................... 23.51
(4).................... 23.48, 23.51
(5)................................. 23.52
(6)................................. 23.53
(7)................................. 23.54
11(2)................................... 23.43
12 .... 23.46
(1).......................... 23.45, 23.46
(3)................................. 23.46
14(1).......................... 23.68, 23.72
(2)................................. 23.68
(3)......................... 23.37, 23.72; 24.15
(4)................................. 24.15
(5)................................. 23.94
15(1)................................... 23.77
16(2)................................... 23.89
(4)................................ 23.89, 23.92, 23.104
(5)................................. 23.96
(6)....................... 23.98, 23.100
(9)................................. 23.112
(12)............................... 23.100
(14)............................... 23.91
17(2), (3) 23.106, 23.125
19(1)................................... 24.19
20 .... 24.20; 25.110
21 .... 23.10

Table of Statutory Instruments

Town and Country Planning (Appeals) (Written Representations Procedure) (England) Regulations 2009, SI 2009/452
reg 2(1) 20.3, 20.5, 20.6, 20.8, 20.22; 21.12
3(2), (3) 20.4
Pt 1 (regs 4–10) 1.67; 20.2
reg 4 .... 20.22
5 .... 20.23
6(1), (2) 20.24
7(1) 20.18
(2) 20.23
8(1) 20.25
9(1) 20.4
Pt 2 (regs 11–16) 1.67; 20.4; 21.2, 21.3
reg 11 .... 21.6
12 .... 21.9
13(1) 21.7, 21.14
(2) 21.8
14 .... 21.20
(1) 21.4
(2) 21.9
(3) 21.12
(5), (6) 21.16
(7), (7A) 21.17, 21.18
15(1) 21.14
(2)(a), (b) 21.16
(7) 21.20
16(1) 21.18
(2) 21.18, 21.20
(b) 21.20
(3), (4) 21.20
18 .... 10.34; 20.3; 21.6

Town and Country Planning (Applications) Regulations 1988, SI 1988/1812 .... 1.33
reg 3(1) 1.34; 6.57
(3) 13.33

Town and Country Planning (Assessment of Environmental Effects) Regulations 1988, SI 1988/1199 .. 1.41; 7.4

Town and Country Planning (Compensation) (England) Regulations 2015, SI 2015/598
reg 2 .... 5.69

Town and Country Planning (Control of Advertisements) (England) Regulations 2007, SI 2007/783: 20.12
Sch 3
Class 8 .... 5.121

Town and Country Planning (Control of Advertisements) Regulations 1992, SI 1992/666 .... 2.48; 20.12
Sch 3
Class 8 .... 5.121

Town and Country Planning (Determination of Appeal Procedure) (Prescribed Period) (England) Regulations 2009, SI 2009/454: 1.68
reg 2(1) 19.51

Town and Country Planning (Determination of Appeals by Appointed Persons) (Prescribed Classes) Regulations 1997, SI 1997/420
reg 3(1) 17.57
4 .... 17.57

Town and Country Planning (Determination of Procedure) (Prescribed Period) (England) Regulations 2009, SI 2009/454
reg 2 .... 21.3; 23.3
12 .... 21.3
13(1) 21.3
14(3), (5), (7) 21.3
15(1) 21.3
(2)(a), (b) 21.3
16 .... 21.3

Town and Country Planning (Determination of Procedure) (Prescribed Period) (Wales) Regulations 2014, SI 2014/2775
reg 2 .... 19.53; 21.3; 23.3
12 .... 21.3
13(1) 21.3
14(1) 21.3
15(3)–(5), (7) 21.3
16(2)(a), (b) 21.3
(3) 21.3
17, 18 .... 21.3

Town and Country Planning (Determination of Procedure) (Wales) Order 2014, SI 2014/2773 .... 1.68; 24.29
art 2................................. 19.53
Sch 1
   para 2 .... 17.55
Town and Country Planning (Development Management Procedure) (England) (Amendment) Order 2013, SI 2013/2932
art 7(a)............................... 8.93
Town and Country Planning (Development Management Procedure) (England) Order 2010, SI 2010/2184: 1.33; 1.36, 1.66; 6.2, 6.94; 9.121; 10.12; 17.11; 18.11; 26.57
art 2(1)......................... 6.5, 6.6; 19.17
   3................................... 2.19
     (1)............................... 6.44
   3A................................. 6.21
     (1)............................... 6.44
   3B................................. 6.21
   4......................... 6.21, 6.45; 28.10
     (2)......................... 6.21; 18.12
   5................................... 6.21
   6............................ 1.34; 6.21
     (1)(a), (b)....................... 6.57
     (c) 6.59
     (2)............................... 6.60
     (4), (4A)......................... 6.57
   7......................... 6.21, 6.63
   8................................... 6.21
   9(2)............................... 15.14
     (3)............................... 15.15
     (4)............................... 15.16
     (5)............................... 15.18
   10.................................. 6.21
     (3)(a), (b)....................... 6.82
     (c) 6.85
   11.............................. 1.35; 6.21
     (1)............................... 6.49
     (2)............................... 6.52
     (2A)............................. 6.53
   12............................ 6.21, 6.51
   13................. 1.36; 6.118; 16.22
     (2)............................... 6.119
     (5)............................... 6.122

Town and Country Planning (Development Management Procedure) (England) Order 2010, SI 2010/2184 – contd
     (7)............................... 6.122
   14.................................. 17.53
   15.................................. 17.48
     (7), (10) 6.123
   16(1)(a), (b), (d), (e).......... 6.126
     (2), (3)........................... 6.126
     (5), (6)........................... 6.137
     (7)............................... 6.148
   18........................... 6.3, 6.59
   19.................................. 6.137
   22.................................. 6.36
     (3)(a) 14.19
   23............................ 6.21; 18.12
     (1)............................... 6.137
     (3)............................... 17.54
     (a) 14.19
   25............................ 1.61; 6.21
   31.................................. 6.21
     (1)(a)(iii) 8.94
   27.................................. 9.22
   28............................ 6.21; 18.12
     (2)............................... 14.19
   29(1)............................... 14.4
     (3)............................... 6.93
   31(1)(a) 14.10
     (b)............................... 14.11
     (c) 14.12
     (cc).............................. 14.14
     (d)............................... 14.18
     (2)............................... 7.75
   33............................ 1.66; 20.3
     (2)......................... 14.4, 14.18
     (b), (c).......................... 19.16
     (7)............................... 19.16
   Sch 2................................ 6.50
   Sch 3................................ 6.123
   Sch 5......................... 6.118, 6.127
     para (zc)......................... 6.126
     1 .... 6.127
Town and Country Planning (Development Management Procedure) (England) Order 2015, SI 2015/595 .. 1.33; 5.2; 6.94; 13.31; 14.10, 14.18; 17.48; 18.31; 19.17; 21.2; 23.11

Table of Statutory Instruments

Town and Country Planning (Development Management Procedure) (England) Order 2015, SI 2015/595 – *contd*

art 2(1)	1.36, 1.66; 6.5, 6.6, 6.73; 19.16; 20.20
3	6.21
(1)	6.44
(2)	13.35
4	6.21, 6.45; 18.12
(2)	19.16
5	6.21; 28.10
6	16.18
(c)	16.19
7	6.21; 18.12
(1)	1.34
(a)	13.35
(b)	6.57; 13.35
(c)	6.59; 13.35, 13.36
(2)	6.60; 16.19
(4), (5)	6.57
8	6.21, 6.63; 18.12
9	6.21, 6.71
(1)	6.71
(3)	6.74
(4)	6.71; 13.35
10	18.12
(2)	15.14
(3)	15.15
(4)	15.16
(5)	15.18
11	6.21
(1)	16.19
(2)	6.86; 16.20
(3)(a), (b)	6.82
(d)	6.85
(4)	6.133; 16.22
(5)	16.20
12(1)–(4)	6.94
13	1.35; 6.21, 6.55, 6.89; 13.35; 18.12; 19.35
(1)	6.49, 6.52; 23.39
(2)	6.52
(a)	6.53
(3)	6.53
(4)–(6)	6.54
(9)	6.50

Town and Country Planning (Development Management Procedure) (England) Order 2015, SI 2015/595 – *contd*

art 14	6.21, 6.89; 13.35; 18.12; 19.35
(1)	6.51, 6.56
(2)	6.56
15	1.36; 6.21, 6.118; 16.22
(2)	6.119; 7.69
(c)	6.119
(3)	6.120
(4)	6.121
(5)	6.122
(7)	6.54, 6.120, 6.121, 6.122; 20.11
16	6.21; 7.77; 16.26; 18.12
17	6.21; 17.53; 18.12; 23.3
18	1.37; 6.21, 6.125, 6.136, 6.137; 7.69; 18.12
(1)(a)–(d)	6.126
(e)	6.126; 13.35
(2), (3)	6.126
(5), (6)	6.137
19	6.21; 18.12, 18.32
20	6.3, 6.21, 6.59, 6.64, 6.126, 6.135, 6.136, 6.137; 13.1, 13.38
(1)(b)	6.72, 6.74; 13.30
(c)	6.72, 6.74
(2)	13.35
21	6.21, 6.137
22(1)–(3)	6.36, 6.141
23	6.142
24	18.12
(1)	6.133, 6.148
(2)	6.133
(3)	17.54
(b)	14.19
25	6.21; 18.12; 23.3
(1)	6.137
(2)	6.148
(3)	17.54
(a)	14.19
26	6.21

Town and Country Planning
(Development Management Procedure) (England)
Order 2015, SI 2015/595 –
contd

art 26(1)(a)–(c)	6.128
27	16.22
(1)	16.30
(b)	16.30
28(2)	16.41
29(2), (4)	16.40
31	1.61; 6.21; 17.11, 17.12, 17.14; 18.12
(1), (3)	17.9
33	6.21; 20.3
34	16.42
(1)	6.95; 14.4
(2)	6.95; 16.42
(a), (b)	19.16
(3)	6.95
(4)	6.51, 6.90; 7.75
(6)(c)	6.94
35	6.21; 9.22
(1)	8.91
(a)(i)	14.10
(ii)	11.23; 14.10
(b)	14.11
(c)	8.92; 14.12
(2)	8.92; 14.14
(3)	14.18
(4)	14.17
(5)	14.10
36	19.35; 23.3
(1)(a), (b)	19.30
(3)	19.24
37	1.66; 19.24; 21.3, 21.4; 22.4; 23.3
(1)	19.24; 20.17
(b)	19.30
(bb)	20.19
(2)	14.18; 19.16
(2)(a)	14.4; 20.17
(b)–(d)	19.16
(3)(a)	20.18
(ii)	19.21; 20.19
(b)(viii)	23.20
(x)	23.77
(4)	23.77, 23.147
(8)	19.16, 19.28; 20.20; 23.26
38(1), (2)	26.10
(3)	26.11

Town and Country Planning
(Development Management Procedure) (England)
Order 2015, SI 2015/595 –
contd

art 38(4), (5)	26.13
(6)	26.9, 26.14
(a), (b)	26.14
(7), (8)	26.15
(9), (10)	26.16
(12)(a), (b)	26.9
(13)	26.20
40(2)	6.97
(3)	6.99
(a)	16.22
(b)	12.32
(4)	6.100; 14.19
(e)	16.22, 16.33
(f)	12.32
(5)	15.17
(13)	6.98
(14)	15.17
41	26.23
(2)(a), (b)	26.23
(3)–(5)	26.23
42	26.45
(2)	26.45
(d)	26.45
(4)	26.45
44	1.15; 2.19; 27.9
47(2), (3)	6.2
(5)	16.39
Sch 2	6.50; 23.39
Sch 3	6.118, 6.123
Sch 4	6.36, 6.125, 6.127, 6.136
Sch 5	26.31
para 1(j)	17.16
Sch 6	16.39

Town and Country Planning
(Development Management Procedure) (Wales)
(Amendment) Order 2015,
SI 2015/1330 .... 2.19

art 2(1)	6.5, 6.11
3	6.21
(2)	6.21
(3)–(5)	6.11
4	6.21
5	6.21
(1)(c)	6.59
6	6.137

Table of Statutory Instruments

Town and Country Planning (Development Management Procedure) (Wales) (Amendment) Order 2015, SI 2015/1330 – *contd*
art 6, 7	6.21
8	1.66; 6.21
(2)(b)	19.20
9	6.21
10	6.49
(2)	6.52
(3)–(5)	6.54
11	6.51
12–18, 21, 24	6.21

Town and Country Planning (Development Management Procedure) (Wales) Order 2012, SI 2012/801 .. 1.33, 1.36; 2.19; 5.2, 5.3; 6.2, 6.137; 18.17; 20.3; 21.2
art 2(1)	19.21
(c)	14.18
2A	1.15; 2.19; 27.9
3	28.10
4	20.3
(1), (2)	16.19
5	1.34; 13.33; 20.3
(1)(a)	1.34; 13.35
(b)	13.35
(c)	13.35, 13.36
(2)	6.60
6	6.63
(1)	20.3
7	6.75
(1)	6.75
(c)	6.78
(2)	6.78
(3), (4)	6.76
(5)	6.77
(6)	6.76
8(1)	16.20
(2)(a)	6.85
(b), (c)	6.82
(3)	16.20
10	1.35
11	20.3
(1), (2)	6.56
12	1.36; 6.118; 16.26
(2)	7.69
(c)	6.119
(3)	6.120

Town and Country Planning (Development Management Procedure) (Wales) Order 2012, SI 2012/801 – *contd*
art 12(4)	6.121
(5)	6.122
(7)	6.120, 6.121, 6.122, 6.123
(10)	6.123
13	17.53
14	6.125, 6.142; 7.69; 15.17
(1)(a), (b)	6.126
(2)	6.126
(4)	6.137
(5)	6.148
15	18.32
15A	6.142
(1), (2)	6.36, 6.142
15B	6.142
16(3)	14.19
17(1)(a)–(c)	6.128
18	1.51; 17.10
20	9.22
22(1)	14.4
(2)	16.42
23	16.30, 16.31, 16.42
24(1)	8.93
(a)	14.10, 14.11
(b)	14.12
(2)	7.75; 14.17
25	19.35; 20.17; 23.3
26	1.66; 14.19; 19.32; 20.17; 23.3
(1)	19.32, 19.34
(b)	20.19
(2)	1.66; 6.98; 19.19, 19.21; 20.17
(a)	20.17
(b)	14.4
(3)(a)	19.32; 20.18
(ii)	20.19
(b)	19.33
(7)	20.20
26A	19.37
27(1), (2)	26.10
(3)	26.12
(h)–(j)	26.12
(4), (5)	26.13

Town and Country Planning (Development Management Procedure) (Wales) Order 2012, SI 2012/801 – *contd*

art 27(6)	26.14
(a), (b)	26.14
(7), (8)	26.15
(9)	26.16
(10)	26.17
(13)	26.9, 26.20
(a)	26.9
28A(2)	15.14
(3), (5), (6)	15.17
(7)	15.18
29(1)	6.96
(2)	6.97, 6.99
(a)	16.22
(3)	6.97, 6.100; 14.19
(e)	16.22, 16.33
(3A)	15.17
(5)	26.23
(a), (b)	26.23
(6)–(8)	26.23
(15)	6.98
(16)	15.17
Sch 3	6.118, 6.123; 7.69
Sch 4	6.125
para (x)	6.126
Sch 5	14.18

Town and Country Planning (Environmental Impact Assessment) (Amendment) Regulations 2015, SI 2015/660 .... 1.41
reg 4, 5 .... 7.21

Town and Country Planning (Environmental Impact Assessment and Permitted Development) Regulations 1995, SI 1995/417 .... 5.25

Town and Country Planning (Environmental Impact Assessment) (England and Wales) Regulations 1999, SI 1999/293 .... 1.41; 5.24; 6.2, 6.118; 7.4, 7.7, 7.9, 7.22, 7.50, 7.75; 13.35; 16.25; 18.31
reg 2(1) 7.9, 7.12, 7.13, 7.23, 7.57, 7.61, 7.62, 7.69, 7.70; 16.23; 24.25

Town and Country Planning (Environmental Impact Assessment) (England and Wales) Regulations 1999, SI 1999/293 – *contd*

reg 3(2)	7.75; 14.17; 16.24; 24.25
4	6.21
(2)(a)	7.33
(5)	7.36
(7)	7.27, 7.49
(8)	7.34
5	6.21, 7.24
(2)	7.24
(3), (4)	7.26
(5)	7.52
(6)	7.27
(7)	7.27, 7.28
6	6.21
(1), (3)	7.28
(4)	7.27
(5)	7.53
7(1)	16.25
10(1), (2)	7.56
(4)	7.57, 7.58
(5)	7.58
(6)	7.57
(7)	7.59
(9)	7.60
11(1)–(4)	7.59
(6)	7.60
12(1)–(4)	7.61
13	7.69
(1)	7.69
(3A)	16.26
(4)	7.69
14	7.69
(4)(b)	7.69
(5)	7.69
(6)	7.72
(7)	7.69
(8)	7.69
15	19.31
17, 18	7.69
19	16.24
(1)	7.70
(2)–(6)	7.71
(7)	7.72
(8)	7.71
20	7.53
(1), (2)	7.52
21	14.19

Table of Statutory Instruments

Town and Country Planning (Environmental Impact Assessment) (England and Wales) Regulations 1999, SI 1999/293 – *contd*
reg 21(1) 7.78
    (c) 24.26, 24.27
    (2) 24.26, 24.27
    (3) 24.27
  34 .... 2.47
Sch 1 .... 7.11
  para 21 .... 7.18
Sch 2
  para 13 .... 7.18
Sch 4 .... 7.55
Town and Country Planning (Environmental Impact Assessment) Regulations 2011, SI 2011/1824 ..... 1.41; 2.47; 4.26; 5.24; 6.2; 7.4, 7.21, 7.49, 7.51, 7.75; 18.31; 26.9
reg 2(1) 7.9, 7.12, 7.13, 7.57, 7.61, 7.62, 7.69, 7.70; 16.23; 24.25
    (5) 7.35
  3 .... 6.21; 18.12
    (4) 7.73, 7.75; 14.17; 16.24; 24.25
  4 .... 6.21; 18.12
    (2) 7.33
    (6) 7.36
    (8) 7.25
    (9) 7.19, 7.34
  5 .... 6.21; 18.12
    (1) 7.25
    (4) 7.26
    (5) 7.26, 7.52
  6 .... 6.21; 18.12
    (3) 7.28
    (4) 7.27, 7.28
    (5) 7.53
  7(1) 7.29
  8(2), (3) 16.24
  9 .... 16.25
  10A 18.12
  13(1), (2) 7.56
    (4) 7.57, 7.58
    (6) 7.57
    (7) 7.59
    (9) 7.60

Town and Country Planning (Environmental Impact Assessment) Regulations 2011, SI 2011/1824 – *contd*
reg 14(1)–(4) 7.59
    (6) 7.60
  15(1), (3)–(5) 7.61
  16 .... 7.69
    (1) 7.69
    (2)(d) 7.69
    (4) 7.77; 16.26
    (5) 7.69
  17 .... 7.69
    (5)(b) 7.69
    (6) 7.69
    (7) 7.69, 7.72
    (8) 7.69
  18 .... 19.31
  20 .... 7.69
  21 .... 6.21; 7.6
  22 .... 16.24
    (2) 7.70, 7.71
    (3)–(6) 7.71
    (7) 7.72
    (8), (9) 7.71
  23(1), (2) 7.52
  24 .... 6.21; 18.12
    (1) 7.78; 14.19
    (c) 24.26, 24.27
    (2) 24.26, 24.27
    (3) 24.27
  27 .... 26.59
  28 .... 26.59, 26.60
  29A 26.33
  60 .... 2.47
  61 .... 19.16
Sch 1 .... 2.47; 7.11, 7.30, 7.31; 26.9, 26.59
  para 21 .... 7.18
Sch 2 .... 1.41; 7.12, 7.30, 7.31, 7.34; 26.33, 26.59
  col 1 .... 7.33
Sch 4 .... 7.55
Town and Country Planning (Fees for Applications and Deemed Applications) Regulations 1989, SI 1989/193 .... 1.34; 6.64

Table of Statutory Instruments

Town and Country Planning (Fees for Applications, Deemed Applications and Site Visits) (Wales) Regulations 2015, SI 2015/1522............... 1.34; 6.64
reg 3...................................... 15.14
    4.. 6.66
    5, 6..................................... 6.67
    9.. 6.68
    13(1).................................. 5.40
    15(1)................................ 16.31
      (2)................................ 16.32
Sch 1..................................... 6.64
  Pt 1
    para 1 .... 6.69; 16.21
        2 .... 6.68
        3 .... 6.64
        4 .... 6.69; 16.21
        5–7 .... 6.64; 13.38
        9–13 .... 6.65
  Pt 2..................................... 16.21
Town and Country Planning (Fees for Applications, Deemed Applications, Requests and Site Visits) (England) Regulations 2012, SI 2012/2920: 1.34; 6.64, 6.67
reg 2A 18.12, 18.14
    4.. 6.66
    5, 5A, 6 .... 6.67
    7.. 6.68
    9A..................................... 16.21
    11A(1)–(7)....................... 18.14
    12...................................... 18.31
    14.. 5.40
    16(1)................................ 16.31
      (2)................................ 16.32
    17...................................... 15.14
Sch 1
  Pt 1
    para 1 .... 6.69; 16.21
        2 .... 6.68
        3 .... 6.64
        4 .... 6.69; 13.38; 16.21
        5, 6 .... 6.64; 13.38
        7 .... 6.64
        10 .... 6.65
        11 .... 6.65
          (1A).................. 6.65
        12–14 .... 6.65

Town and Country Planning (Fees for Applications, Deemed Applications, Requests and Site Visits) (England) Regulations 2012, SI 2012/2920 – *contd*
  Sch 1 – *contd*
    Pt 2................................... 16.21
Town and Country Planning (General Development Procedure) (Amendment) (England) Order 2010, SI 2010/567
  art 18(1)(b), (c)...................... 27.32
Town and Country Planning (General Development Procedure) (Amendment) (Wales) Order 2006, SI 2006/3390......................... 6.70
Town and Country Planning (General Development Procedure) (England) (Amendment) Order 2003, SI 2003/2047 .... 8.94, 8.95
Town and Country Planning (General Development Procedure) Order 1995, SI 1995/419...................... 5.3; 6.15; 17.11
  art 19..................................... 22.8
    22(1)(a) 8.95
      (b)(i) 8.95
Town and Country Planning (General Permitted Development) (England) Order 2015, SI 2015/596.. 1.17, 1.29; 4.3, 4.8; 5.4, 5.7, 5.35, 5.41, 5.52, 5.54, 5.57, 5.61, 5.87, 5.91, 5.92, 5.99, 5.115, 5.125, 5.134, 5.157, 5.158, 5.177, 5.190; 11.38; 16.38
  art 1(10)................................. 5.45
    2.. 5.10
      (1)................................. 5.91, 5.92, 5.93, 5.94, 5.96, 5.101, 5.103, 5.163, 5.185
      (3).............................. 5.42, 5.97, 5.103, 5.158, 5.159

Table of Statutory Instruments

Town and Country Planning (General Permitted Development) (England) Order 2015, SI 2015/596 – *contd*
- art 2(4) 5.97, 5.136
- (5) 5.97
- (9) 5.45
- 3 .... 5.66
  - (1) 5.12, 5.26
  - (2) 5.13
  - (4) 5.15
  - (5) 5.20, 5.21, 5.22, 5.101
  - (6) 5.33
  - (8) 5.34
  - (9) 5.34
  - (10), (11) 2.22; 5.24
  - (12) 2.22; 5.25
    - (c) 5.25
- 4 .... 5.19, 5.54, 5.60, 5.61, 5.65, 5.67, 5.68, 5.69, 5.71, 5.72, 5.75, 5.80, 5.81
  - (1) 5.66, 5.73, 5.81, 5.82, 5.83
  - (2) 5.81, 5.84
    - (a) 5.62
  - (3) 5.68
  - (5) 5.62
- 5 .... 5.81
  - (3)–(5) 5.86
- 6 .... 5.81
- 7 .... 5.43
- Sch 1 .... 5.25, 5.97
- Sch 2 .... 1.30; 4.8; 5.13, 5.14, 5.20, 5.25, 5.33, 5.43, 5.62, 5.66, 5.87
  - Pt 1 .... 5.100, 5.105
    - para A 5.100, 5.103, 5.110
      - condition A1(e) . 5.103
        - (f) . 5.42
        - (g) 5.42, 5.103
      - 4 ..... 5.42
        - (3) 5.13, 5.49
        - (7) 5.42

Town and Country Planning (General Permitted Development) (England) Order 2015, SI 2015/596 – *contd*
- Sch 2 – *contd*
  - Pt 1 – *contd*
    - Class A para A2(c) 5.106
    - Class B 5.100, 5.110
      - para B1(d) 5.64
        - 2(b)(i) (bb) 5.103
    - C 5.100, 5.110
    - D 5.108, 5.100, 5.110
    - E 5.108, 5.100, 5.102, 5.107, 5.110
    - F 5.100
    - G 5.100, 5.1025.110
    - H 5.100, 5.104, 5.110
    - I–W 5.110
  - Pt 2 .... 5.108, 5.109
    - Class A 5.108
      - para A1 .... 5.108
      - B–F 5.108
      - C 2.9
  - Pt 3 .... 5.110, 5.115
    - Class A para A1,A2 ...... 5.111
    - B 3.23
      - para B1, B2 ..... 5.111, 5.119
      - B8 .... 5.119
    - C 5.36, 5.113, 5.114
    - J 5.36, 5.113
    - M, N 5.113, 5.114
    - O 5.97, 5.113
    - P–T 5.114
    - V 5.119
    - W 5.114
      - para W(2) 5.114

Table of Statutory Instruments

Town and Country Planning (General Permitted Development) (England) Order 2015, SI 2015/596 – *contd*
  Sch 2 – *contd*
    Pt 3 – *contd*
      Class W para W(3) 5.14, 5.49, 5.115
        (4) 5.115
        (5), (6), (8) 5.116
        (10)(b) 5.116
        (11) 5.117
        (13) 5.53, 5.117
    Pt 4 .... 5.120
      Class A 5.120, 5.121, 5.123
        para A2 .... 5.130
      B 5.120, 5.124
        para B1(b)–(e). 5.124
      C 5.126
      D 5.127
      E 5.128
      F para F 5.124
    Pt 5 .... 5.129
      Class A 5.130
      B 5.131
      C 5.132
        para C1(e) 5.127
        C2 .... 5.132
        (f) 5.127
      D para D1(f) 5.127
        D2(a), (c), (e), (f) 5.127
    Pt 6 .... 5.133, 5.137
      Class A 5.134, 5.135, 5.136, 5.139
        condition A2(1)(a) 5.135
        (2) 5.136
        (iv) 5.41
        (3) 5.136
        para A1(k) 5.135
      Class B 5.134, 5.135, 5.136
        condition B5(1) 5.135
        B5(2) 5.136

Town and Country Planning (General Permitted Development) (England) Order 2015, SI 2015/596 – *contd*
  Sch 2 – *contd*
    Pt 6 – *contd*
      Class B para B1(d) 5.135
      C 5.134
      D para D 5.134
        (1) 5.134, 5.135
        (6)–(8) .. 5.139
      E 5.134, 5.136
        condition E2(1) 5.136
    Pt 7 .... 5.140, 5.142
      Class A 5.140, 5.142
        para A1(a) 5.64
      B–N 5.140, 5.142
      O 5.140
        para O 5.140, 5.142
    Pt 8 .... 5.141, 5.142
      Class A 5.185
    Pt 9 .... 2.20; 5.143
      Class A–E 5.143
    Pt 10 .... 5.144
      Class A 5.144
    Pt 11 .... 2.22; 5.145
      Class A 5.145
      B 5.145, 5.146
        para B1(a)–(c). 5.145
        B3 .... 5.145, 5.146
      Class C 5.145, 5.146
    Pt 12 .... 2.20; 5.147, 5.148
      Class A 5.148
        para A1 .... 5.148
      B 5.148
    Pt 13 .... 5.149
      Class A, B 5.149

Table of Statutory Instruments

Town and Country Planning (General Permitted Development) (England) Order 2015, SI 2015/596 – *contd*
  Sch 2 – *contd*
    Pt 13 – *contd*
      Class C 5.149, 5.150
        para C1 .... 5.149
      D 5.150
    Pt 14 .... 5.151
      Class A–O 5.152
        para P 5.151, 5.152
    Pt 15 .... 5.153
      Class A 5.153
      B 5.154
        para B1(a) 5.154
    Pt 16 .... 5.47, 5.155
      Class A 5.156
        condition
        A.3(7) 5.46
        B, C 5.161
        D 5.162
        E 5.163
    Pt 17 .... 5.165
      Class A 5.166
      B 5.39, 5.52, 5.167
        para B2 .... 5.167
      C 5.168, 5.169
      D–G 5.169
      H 5.170
        para H3 .... 5.167
      I 5.170
      J 5.171
        para J1(a) 5.171
      K 5.66, 5.171
        para K1(a) 5.171
      L 5.172
      M 5.66, 5.173
        para M2(b)–(d) 5.173
        (3) 5.173
      N para N1 .... 5.167, 5.172
    Pt 18 .... 5.174
      Class A 5.175

Town and Country Planning (General Permitted Development) (England) Order 2015, SI 2015/596 – *contd*
  Sch 2 – *contd*
    Pt 18 – *contd*
      Class B 5.176
    Pt 19 .... 5.177
      Class A 5.178
      B 5.179
      C 5.181
      D 5.181
      E 5.182
        para E2, E4 ...... 5.182
      F–J 5.183
      K, L 5.184
      M 5.185
      N 5.186
      O, P 5.187
      Q 5.188
      Q para Q1, Q2 ..... 5.188
      R–T 5.189
        para U 5.182
    Pt 24
      Class A 5.63
        para A2(4), (5) 5.159
        3(1), (2) 5.160
        (5)–(7) 5.160
    Pt 27
      Class A 5.132
  Sch 3
    para 1(1) 5.72
      (c) 5.72
    (2) 5.72, 5.78
    (3) 5.72
    (4) 5.70, 5.73
    (5), (6) 5.72
    (7) 5.70
    (8) 5.72
    (9) 5.74
    (10) 5.79
    (11), (12) 5.74
    (13) 5.75, 5.79
    (15) 5.75, 5.79
    (16)–(18) 5.75
    2(1) 5.76
    (2) 5.77
    (3) 5.75, 5.77
    (4) 5.75
    (5) 5.77
    (6) 5.78, 5.79

Town and Country Planning (General Permitted Development) (England) Order 2015, SI 2015/596 – *contd*
  Sch 3 – *contd*
    para 2(7)–(9)...................... 5.79
  Sch 16
    Class A para A1(5) 5.158
Town and Country Planning (General Permitted Development) Order 1995, SI 1995/418 .... 1.17, 1.29; 4.3, 4.8; 5.3, 5.4, 5.16, 5.26, 5.34, 5.41, 5.43, 5.57, 5.60, 5.87, 5.99, 5.115, 5.157, 5.158, 5.177; 17.31; 19.6
  art 1(2)............................. 5.91, 5.93, 5.94, 5.96, 5.101, 5.103, 5.166
    (5)............................... 5.98, 5.140, 5.158
    (6).................................... 5.98
  2(3).................................... 5.42
  3(1)............................... 5.8, 5.12
    (2)............................. 4.8; 5.13
    (4).................................... 5.15
    (5)............... 5.20, 5.21, 5.22
    (8).................................... 5.34
    (9).................................... 5.34
    (10)............................. 2.22; 5.24
    (11)............................. 2.22; 5.24
    (12)............................. 2.22; 5.25
      (c) 5.25
  4................................. 5.19, 5.54, 5.60, 5.61
  5................................. 5.85, 5.86
    (3)–(6), (8)..................... 5.82
    (10).................................. 5.83
    (11).................................. 5.82
    (12)–(17) 5.83
  6(1)–(10) 5.84
  7... 5.85
    (3)–(5)............................ 5.86
  Sch 1................................... 5.25
  Sch 2.................. 1.30; 5.9, 5.13, 5.14, 5.20, 5.25
    Pt 1........................... 5.9, 5.100
      Class 12, 13 .... 2.20

Town and Country Planning (General Permitted Development) Order 1995, SI 1995/418 – *contd*
  Sch 2 – *contd*
    Pt 2
      Class C 2.9
    Pt 3..................................... 5.110
      Class A,AA,B, C, CA, D–I, IA, J–M, MA, MB, N 5.110
      J 5.97
      MA, MB 5.36
      N para N(11)......... 5.52
    Pt 4..................................... 5.120
      Class A........................ 5.121
      B para B1(b)–(e). 5.124
    Pt 5..................................... 5.129
      Class A........................ 5.130
      B 5.131
      C 5.131
    Pt 6..................................... 5.133
      Class A condition A.2(2)(iv) 5.41
    Pt 7..................................... 5.133
    Pt 8
      Class A–E.................... 5.140
    Pt 9..................................... 5.143
    Pt 10................................... 5.144
    Pt 11................................... 5.145
      Class A........................ 5.175
    Pt 12................................... 5.147
    Pt 13
      Class A, B 5.143
    Pt 14
      Class A........................ 5.149
    Pt 15
      Class A........................ 5.150
    Pt 16
      Class A........................ 5.149
    Pt 17
      Class A–D 5.142
      E 5.149
      F 5.153
      G 5.154
      H 5.143
      I 5.142
      J 5.163
    Pt 18
      Class A–I..................... 5.142
    Pt 19
      Class A........................ 5.166

Table of Statutory Instruments

Town and Country Planning (General Permitted Development) Order 1995, SI 1995/418 – *contd*
  Sch 2 – *contd*
    Pt 19 – *contd*
      Class B 5.167
      C 5.168
    Pt 20
      Class A–E 5.169
    Pt 21
      Class A, B 5.170
    Pt 22
      Class A 5.171
      B 5.66, 5.171
    Pt 23
      Class A 5.172
      B 5.66, 5.173
    Pt 24 .... 5.47
      Class A 5.46, 5.156, 5.158
    Pt 25
      Class A, B 5.161
    Pt 28
      Class A 5.176
    Pt 29
      Class A 5.162
    Pt 30
      Class A 5.143
    Pt 31 .... 2.22
      Class A, B 5.146
    Pt 32
      Class A, B 5.140
    Pt 34
      Class A–D 5.181
    Pt 35
      Class A–F 5.183
      G 5.184
      H 5.184
    Pt 36
      Class A 5.185
      B–D 5.187
    Pt 37
      Class A 5.188
    Pt 38
      Class A–C 5.189
    Pt 39
      Class A 5.190
    Pt 40 .... 5.150, 5.151
      Class A–I 5.152
      J para J 5.151, 5.152

Town and Country Planning (General Permitted Development) Order 1995, SI 1995/418 – *contd*
  Sch 2 – *contd*
    Pt 41
      Class A, B 5.140
    Pt 42
      Class A–C 5.140
    Pt 43 .... 5.150, 5.151
      Class A–F 5.152
Town and Country Planning General Regulations 1992, SI 1992/1492 .... 28.7
  reg 3 .... 6.18; 8.8, 8.37
  4 .... 6.18
  4A 6.18
    (1) 6.128
  9 .... 6.18; 28.7
  9A, 9AA 6.18
  10 .... 8.8
Town and Country Planning (Hearings and Inquiries Procedures) (England) (Amendment) Rules 2009, SI 2009/455
  r 4 .... 23.15
Town and Country Planning (Hearings Procedure) (England) Rules 2000, SI 2000/1626 ... 22.3; 24.4
  r 2(1) 22.4, 22.7, 22.8, 22.10
    (4), (8) 22.11
  3A 22.4
  4(1) 22.4, 22.8
  (2) 22.4, 22.9
  6(1) 22.4, 22.8
  (1A) 22.4, 22.11
  (2) 22.14
  (3) 22.4
  (5) 22.4, 22.13
  (6), (6A) 22.13
  (7) 22.4, 22.13
  6A(1) 22.4, 22.18
  7(1) 22.4, 22.23
  (2) 22.4, 22.24
  (2A), (3), (4) 22.24
  (5), (7) 22.25
  8(3) 22.19
  (4) 22.20
  9(1), (2) 22.22

Table of Statutory Instruments

Town and Country Planning (Hearings Procedure) (England) Rules 2000, SI 2000/1626 – *contd*
r 9(3)	22.32
11(2)	22.28, 22.30
(3)	22.19
(4), (5)	22.28
(6)	22.31
12(1)	22.36
(2)	22.38; 23.127
(4)(a), (b)	22.38
13	24.11
15	24.20
(2)	24.19
16	24.20
(2)	24.19
17	25.110

Town and Country Planning (Hearings Procedure) (Wales) Rules 2003, SI 2003/1271 .... 1.67; 22.3; 24.4
r 2(1)	22.4, 22.7, 22.8
(4), (8)	22.11
3A	22.4
4(1)	22.4, 22.8
(2)	22.9
4A	22.4
6(1)	22.4, 22.12
(2)	22.13
(3)	22.4, 22.12
(4)	22.4, 22.15
(5)	22.4, 22.13
(6), (6A)	22.13
(7)	22.4, 22.13
7(1)	22.4, 22.23
(2)	22.4, 22.24
(2A), (3), (4)	22.24
8(1)	22.19, 22.21
(2)	22.21
9(1), (2)	22.22
(3)	22.32
11(2)	22.28, 22.30
(3)	22.19
(4), (5)	22.28
(6)	22.31
12(1)	22.36
(2)	22.38; 23.127
(4)(a), (b)	22.38
13	24.11
15	24.20

Town and Country Planning (Hearings Procedure) (Wales) Rules 2003, SI 2003/1271 – *contd*
r 15(2)	24.19
16	24.20
(2)	24.19
17	25.110

Town and Country Planning (Inquiries Procedure) (England) Rules 2000, SI 2000/1624 .... 1.68; 17.49; 23.2, 23.15
r 2(1)	23.6, 23.17, 23.19, 23.39, 23.76
3	17.49
3A	23.3, 23.6
4(1)–(3)	23.3, 23.11
(4), (5)	23.3, 23.12
5	23.57
(1)	23.13
(2)	23.3
(a)	23.30
(ii)	23.15, 23.36
(c)	23.15
(d)	23.15, 23.30
(3)	23.15
(5)	23.3, 23.30
(6)	23.3
(7)	23.18, 23.30
(8)	23.31
(10)	23.3
6(1)	23.3
(3)	23.3, 23.21, 23.29
(4)	23.3
(5)	23.26
(6)	23.3, 23.25, 23.26
(8)	23.3, 23.25, 23.27
(10)	23.25
(12)	23.36
7(1)	23.3, 23.29
(2)	23.3, 23.30
(3)	23.31
8	23.10
(1)	23.3, 23.37
(2), (3)	23.37
9	23.57, 23.62
10(1)	23.3, 23.48
(2)	23.48

lvii

Table of Statutory Instruments

Town and Country Planning (Inquiries Procedure) (England) Rules 2000, SI 2000/1624 – *contd*
  r 10(3).................................. 23.3, 23.51
    (3A) 23.51
    (4), (5) 23.48, 23.51
    (6) 23.3, 23.52
    (7) 23.3, 23.53
    (8) 23.54
  11(1) 23.18, 23.39
    (2) 23.43
  12(1) 23.45, 23.46
    (2) 23.46
    (3) 23.36
  13 .... 24.11
    (1) 23.68, 23.72
    (2) 23.68
    (3) 23.3, 23.37, 23.72
    (5) 23.94
  14 .... 23.3
    (1) 23.77
  15 .... 23.3
    (2) 23.89
    (4) 23.89, 23.92, 23.104
    (5) 23.96
    (6) 23.98, 23.100
    (9) 23.112
    (12) 23.100
    (14) 23.91
  16 .... 23.3
    (2) 23.106, 23.125
    (2A) 23.148
    (3) 23.106, 23.125
  17 .... 23.3; 24.4
    (1) 24.5
    (2), (3) 23.62; 24.7
    (4) 24.16
    (5)–(7) 24.11
  18 .... 1.69; 23.3; 24.4
    (1) 23.62; 24.19
    (2) 24.13
  19 .... 25.110
    (1) 23.62
  20 .... 10.34; 23.10; 24.40
  21 .... 24.20, 24.40
  23 .... 10.34; 23.23
    (3) 23.41

Town and Country Planning (Inquiries Procedure) (England) Rules 2000, SI 2000/1624 – *contd*
  r 23A 23.147
    (2) 23.150
  Sch 1
    Pt 1 .... 23.147
      para 7 .... 23.148
    Pt 2 .... 23.150
Town and Country Planning (Inquiries Procedure) (Wales) Rules 2003, SI 2003/1266 .... 1.68; 23.2, 23.3; 24.4
  r 2(1) 23.7, 23.15, 23.17, 23.19, 23.76
  3A 23.3, 23.7
  4(1)–(3) 23.3, 23.11
  (4), (5) 23.3, 23.12
  4A(1) 23.3
  5 .... 23.57
    (1) 23.13
    (2) 23.3, 23.15
      (a) 23.30
      (ii) 23.15, 23.36
      (c) 23.15
      (d) 23.15, 23.30
    (3) 23.15
    (5) 23.30
    (6) 23.3
    (7) 23.18, 23.30
    (8) 23.31
    (10) 23.3
  6(1) 23.3, 23.26
    (3) 23.3, 23.22, 23.26, 23.29
    (4) 23.3
    (5) 23.26
    (6) 23.3, 23.25, 23.26
    (8) 23.3, 23.25, 23.27
    (10) 23.25
    (12) 23.36
    (14), (15) 23.3
  7(1) 23.3, 23.29
    (2) 23.3, 23.30
    (3) 23.31
  8 .... 23.10
    (1) 23.3, 23.37
    (2), (3) 23.37

Town and Country Planning (Inquiries Procedure) (Wales) Rules 2003, SI 2003/1266 – *contd*
r 9 .... 23.57, 23.62
  10(1) 23.3, 23.48
    (2) 23.48
    (3) 23.3, 23.51
    (3A) 23.51
    (4), (5) 23.48, 23.51
    (6) 23.3, 23.52
    (7) 23.3, 23.53
    (8) 23.54
  11(1) 23.18, 23.40
    (2) 23.43
  12 .... 23.46
    (1) 23.45, 23.46
    (3) 23.46
  13 .... 24.11
    (1) 23.68, 23.72
    (2) 23.68
    (3) 23.3,
                      23.37, 23.72
    (5) 23.94
  14(1) 23.3, 23.77
  15 .... 23.3
    (2) 23.89
    (4) 23.89,
                  23.92, 23.104
    (5) 23.96
    (6) 23.98, 23.100
    (9) 23.112
    (12) 23.100
    (14) 23.91
  16 .... 23.3
    (2) 23.106, 23.125
    (2A) 23.148
    (3) 23.106, 23.125
  17 .... 23.3
    (1) 24.5
    (2), (3) 23.62; 24.7
    (4) 24.16
    (5)–(7) 24.11
  18 .... 23.3
    (1) 23.62; 24.19
    (2) 24.13
  19 .... 25.110
    (1) 23.62
  20 .... 23.10
  21 .... 24.20
  22B 23.147
    (2) 23.150

Town and Country Planning (Inquiries Procedure) (Wales) Rules 2003, SI 2003/1266 – *contd*
Sch 1
  Pt 1 .... 23.147
    para 7 .... 23.148
  Pt 2 .... 23.150
Town and Country Planning (Local Development) (England) Regulations 2004, SI 2004/2204 .... 9.28
Town and Country Planning (Local Planning) (England) Regulations 2012, SI 2012/767 .... 1.27
  reg 6 .... 1.27
  Pt 5 (regs 11–16) 9.28
Town and Country Planning (London Borough of Camden) Special Development (Amendment and Revocation) Order 2010, SI 2010/569 .... 26.5
Town and Country Planning (London Borough of Camden) Special Development (Amendment) Order 2004, SI 2004/2355 .... 26.5
Town and Country Planning (London Docklands Urban Development Area) Special Development Order 1981, SI 1981/1082 .... 26.4
Town and Country Planning (Major Infrastructure Project Inquiries Procedure) (England) Rules 2005, SI 2005/2115 .... 17.49
r 3, 5, 7, 8 .... 17.49
  9(5) 17.50
Town and Country Planning (Mayor of London) Order 2008, SI 2008/580 .... 1.65; 10.4, 10.11; 18.12; 23.41
  art 1(2) 10.8
    (3) 10.7
  4 .... 10.15
    (1), (2) 10.14
  5 .... 10.15
    (2) 10.14
  6(1) 10.18

Table of Statutory Instruments

Town and Country Planning (Mayor of London) Order 2008, SI 2008/580 – *contd*	
art 6(2)	10.19
(4)	10.22
(5)	10.23
(6)	10.22
(7), (8)	10.23
7(1)	10.26
(2)	10.28
(3), (4)	10.27
(5), (6)	10.12
(7), (8)	10.28
8	10.29
9	10.32
Sch 1	
para 1	10.10
(2)	10.8
2	10.10, 10.25
3	10.10, 10.11
4	10.9, 10.10
Town and Country Planning (Minerals) Regulations 1995, SI 1995/2863	
Sch 1	
para 1	29.9
Town and Country Planning (Modification and Discharge of Planning Obligations) (Amendment) (England) Regulations 2013, SI 2013/147	12.67
Town and Country Planning (Modification and Discharge of Planning Obligations) Regulations 1992, SI 1992/2832	12.64, 12.67
reg 3	12.67
(1), (2)	12.68
4(1), (3)–(5)	12.69
5(1)–(4)	12.70
6(1)–(3)	12.76
7(1)	12.77
(2)(a), (c)	12.77
8	12.78
Schedule	
Pt 1	12.69
Pt 2	12.69

Town and Country Planning (Non-Material Changes and Correction of Errors) (Wales) Order 2014, SI 2014/1770	
art 2(2)	15.7
Town and Country Planning (Operation Stack) Special Development Order 2015, SI 2015/1635	26.5
Town and Country Planning (Prescription of County Matters) (England) Regulations 2003, SI 2003/1033	6.17
reg 2	6.17; 26.28
Town and Country Planning (Referrals and Appeals) (Written Representations Procedure) (Wales) Regulations 2003, SI 2003/390	1.67; 21.3, 21.22, 21.22
Town and Country Planning (Referrals and Appeals) (Written Representations Procedure) (Wales) Regulations 2015, SI 2015/1331:	21.22
reg 2(1)	20.3, 20.13, 20.15, 20.22
3	21.22
(2), (3)	20.4
Pt 1 (regs 4–11)	1.67; 20.2
reg 4	20.22; 21.22
5	20.23; 21.22
6	21.22
(1), (2)	20.24
7	21.22
(1)	20.18
(2)	20.23
(7)	21.22
8	21.22
(1)	20.25
(2)(b)	21.22
9(1)	20.4
11	24.19
Pt 2 (regs 12–18)	1.67; 21.2, 21.3, 21.22
reg 15(7)	21.20
16(2)	21.20
(b)	21.20
(3), (4)	21.20
18	21.21

Town and Country Planning (Referrals and Appeals) (Written Representations Procedure) (Wales) Regulations 2015, SI 2015/1331 – *contd*
  reg 22 .... 21.3
    (2) 20.2
  Schedule
    para 1–3 .... 20.16
Town and Country Planning (Section 62A Applications) (Hearings) Rules 2013, SI 2013/2141 .... 18.6, 18.11
  r 6(2) 18.6
Town and Country Planning (Section 62A Applications) (Procedure and Consequential Amendments) Order 2013, SI 2013/2140 .... 18.6, 18.11
  art 3, 3A, 3B 18.12
    4–14A, 17–21 .... 18.12
    23 .... 18.3
    24, 25 .... 18.12
    28–49 .... 18.13
Town and Country Planning (Section 62A Applications) (Written Representations and Miscellaneous Provisions) Regulations 2013, SI 2013/2142 .... 18.6
  reg 3 .... 18.8
Town and Country Planning (Simplified Planning Zones) Regulations 1992, SI 1992/2414 .... 26.54
  reg 3–5 .... 26.57
    7 .... 26.58
    8, 9, 11–13 .... 26.59
Town and Country Planning (Tree Preservation) (England) Regulations 2012, SI 2012/605
  reg 4(2) 9.147

Town and Country Planning (Use Classes) (Amendment) (England) Order 2015, SI 2015/597 .... 3.7, 3.20
  art 3 .... 3.7
Town and Country Planning (Use Classes) Order 1972, SI 1972/1385 .... 3.52
  art 2(2) 3.52
Town and Country Planning (Use Classes) Order 1987, SI 1987/764 .... 1.15; 2.43, 2.45; 3.3, 3.4, 3.9, 3.10, 3.36, 3.40, 3.52; 4.6; 5.18; 11.25; 20.9
  art 2 .... 3.40
    3(1) 2.43; 3.3, 3.5
    (2) 3.5
    (3) 2.44; 3.5
    (6) 2.43; 3.6, 3.19; 20.9
      (h) 3.30
      (i) 3.36
    (6A) 3.7
    (7), (8) 3.24
    4 .... 3.9
Valuation for Rating (Plant and Machinery) (England) Regulations 2000, SI 2000/540
  Schedule
    Class 4
      Table 4 .... 5.93
Waste (England and Wales) Regulations 2011, SI 2011/988
  reg 18, 19 .... 9.158
    20(1), (2) 9.159

Table of Cases

[All references are to paragraph number]

A

A-G v Wilts United Dairies Ltd (1921) 37 TLR 884; *upheld* (1922) 38 TLR 781 .... 11.32; 12.103
A-G ex rel Co-operative Retail Services v Taff-Ely Borough Council (1979) 38 P & CR 156; *revs'd* (1979) 39 P & CR 223, (1979) 250 EG 757, [1979] JPL 466; *aff'd* (1981) 42 P & CR 1 .... 28.8
A-G ex rel Scotland v Barratt Manchester Ltd (1992) 63 P & CR 179, [1992] JPL 148, [1991] EG 73 .... 12.98
Aannemersbedrijf PK Kraaijeveld BV v Gedeputeerde Staten Van Zuid-Holland (Case C-72/95) [1996] ECR I-5403, [1997] 3 CMLR 1, [1997] All ER (EC) 134 .... 7.17, 7.21
Abraham v Région Wallonne (Case C-2/07) [2008] ECR I-1197, [2008] Env LR 32 .... 7.17
Aerlink Leisure Ltd (in liquidation) v First Secretary of State [2004] EWHC 3198 (Admin), [2005] 2 P & CR 15 .... 29.8
Agecrest Ltd v Gwynedd County Council [1998] JPL 325, [1996] NPC 106 .... 29.20, 29.21, 29.23, 29.38
Airwave MM02 Ltd v First Secretary of State [2005] EWHC 1701 (Admin), [2006] JPL 362, (2005) 102 (28) LSG 33 .... 5.42
Alliance Against the Birmingham Northern Relief Road v Secretary of State for the Environment, Transport and the Regions *see* R v Secretary of State for the Environment, Transport & the Regions, ex p Alliance against the Birmingham Northern Relief Road (No 2)
Allied London Property Investment Ltd v Secretary of State for the Environment (1996) 72 P & CR 327, [1997] JPL 199, [1996] EG 52 ... 13.7
Alnwick District Council v Secretary of State for the Environment, Transport & the Regions (2000) 79 P & CR 130, [1999] 4 PLR 43, [2000] JPL 474 .... 4.31; 9.170
Anderson v Secretary of State for Communities & Local Government [2015] EWHC 3005 (Admin) 23.100; 25.82
Antaios Compania Naviera SA v Salen Rederierna AB (The Antaios) [1985] AC 191, [1984] 3 WLR 592, [1984] 3 All ER 229 .... 12.54
Archid Architecture & Interior Design v Dundee City Council [2013] CSOH 137, 2014 SLT 81, [2014] JPL 336 .... 14.21; 24.62
Argyll & Bute District Council v Secretary of State for Scotland 1976 SC 248, 1977 SLT 33 .... 2.3
Arnold v Britton [2015] UKSC 36, [2015] AC 1619, [2015] 2 WLR 1593 .... 12.55; 28.14
Arnold v Secretary of State for Communities & Local Government [2015] EWHC 1197 (Admin), [2015] JPL 1053 .... 5.64
Arun District Council v Secretary of State [2006] EWCA Civ 1172, [2007] 1 WLR 523, [2007] 1 P & CR 10 .... 20.6

Table of Cases

Ashbridge Investments Ltd v Minister of Housing & Local Government
 [1965] 1 WLR 1320, [1965] 3 All ER 371, (1965) 129 JP 580 .... 25.33
Ashton v Secretary of State for Communities & Local Government *see*
 Historic Buildings & Monuments Commission for England (English
 Heritage) v Secretary of State for Communities & Local Government
Associated Provincial Picture Houses Ltd v Wednesbury Corpn [1948] 1 KB
 223, [1947] 2 All ER 680, (1947) 63 TLR 623 .... 1.47, 1.54, 1.58;
 7.16, 7.37; 8.64; 9.11; 11.6,
 11.12, 11.26, 11.27, 11.30; 12.8,
 12.12, 12.33, 12.103; 25.7; 29.31
Aston v Secretary of State for Communities & Local Government [2013]
 EWHC 1936 (Admin), [2014] 2 P & CR 10 .... 7.48; 9.121; 23.97
Avon County Council v Millard (1985) 50 P & CR 275, 83 LGR 597, [1985]
 1 EGLR 171 .... 12.101

B

BAA plc v Secretary of State for Transport, Local Government & the Regions
 [2002] EWHC 1920 (Admin), [2003] JPL 610..................................... 7.42
BDW Trading Ltd (t/a Barratt Homes) v Cheshire West & Chester Borough
 Council [2014] EWHC 1470 (Admin)... 26.39
Ball v Secretary of State for Communities & Local Government [2014]
 EWCA Civ 372, [2014] JPL 1016... 17.65; 24.12
Ball v Secretary of State for the Environment, Transport & the Regions
 [2000] 1 PLR 64, [2000] PLCR 299, (2000) 97 (4) LSG 34 .... 21.27;
 23.138
Barchester Healthcare Ltd v Secretary of State for Communities & Local
 Government [2010] EWHC 2784 (Admin), [2011] JPL 544 .... 3.40
Barclays Bank Ltd v Quistclose Investments Ltd [1970] AC 567, [1968] 3
 WLR 1097, [1968] 3 All ER 651 .... 12.14
Barclays Mercantile Business Finance Ltd v Mawson (Inspector of Taxes)
 [2004] UKHL 51, [2005] 1 AC 684, [2004] 3 WLR 1383..................... 5.92
Barker v Hambleton District Council [2011] EWHC 1707 (Admin); aff'd
 [2012] EWCA Civ 610, [2013] PTSR 41, [2013] 1 P & CR 1 .... 25.45,
 25.46, 25.50
Barnes v Sheffield City Council (1995) 27 HLR 719, [1995] NPC 87 .... 3.47
Barnett v Secretary of State for Communities & Local Government [2008]
 EWHC 1601 (Admin), [2009] 1 P & CR 24, [2009] JPL 243; aff'd
 [2009] EWCA Civ 476, [2010] 1 P & CR 8, [2009] JPL 1597............. 28.9
Barvis Ltd v Secretary of State for the Environment (1971) 22 P & CR 710 .... 2.8;
 5.90
Bayliss v Secretary of State for Communities and Local Government [2013]
 EWHC 1612 (Admin) 9.41
Bedford Borough Council v Secretary of State for Communities & Local
 Government [2008] EWHC 2304 (Admin), [2009] JPL 604 .... 29.19,
 29.29, 29.32
Belize Alliance of Conservation Non-Governmental Organisations v
 Department of the Environment [2004] UKPC 6, [2004] Env LR 38.... 25.76
Belmont Farm Ltd v Minister of Housing & Local Government (1962) 13 P
 & CR 417, 60 LGR 319, [1963] JPL 256.. 2.40
Belmont Riding Centre v First Secretary of State [2003] EWHC 1895
 (Admin), [2004] 2 PLR 8, [2004] JPL 593 .... 2.44; 3.4

Table of Cases

Berkeley v Secretary of State for the Environment, Transport & the Regions
(No 1) [2001] 2 AC 603, [2000] 3 WLR 420, [2000] 3 All ER 897 ...... 25.86
Berkeley v Secretary of State for the Environment, Transport & the Regions
(No 2) [2001] EWCA Civ 1012, [2001] 3 CMLR 11, [2002] Env LR
14 .... 7.16, 7.22, 7.35
Bernard Wheatcroft Ltd v Secretary of State for the Environment (1980) 43 P
& CR 233, (1981) 257 EG 934, [1982] JPL 37 .... 6.148; 13.5; 19.44
Beronstone Ltd v First Secretary of State [2006] EWHC 2391 (Admin)........ 2.14
Blackpool Borough Council v Secretary of State for the Environment (1980)
40 P & CR 104, [1980] JPL 527 .... 3.46
Bloor Homes East Midlands Ltd v Secretary of State for Communities and
Local Government [2014] EWHC 754 (Admin)................................... 9.21
Bluebell Cemetery Ltd v Secretary of State for Communities & Local
Government [2015] EWHC 2339 (Admin).................................. 19.52; 25.15
Bolton Metropolitan District Council v Secretary of State for the Environment
(Costs) [1995] 1 WLR 1176, [1996] 1 All ER 184, [1995] 3 PLR 37 ... 25.96,
25.97
Botton v Secretary of State for the Environment [1992] 1 PLR 1 .... 25.17
Bovale Ltd v Secretary of State for Communities & Local Government
[2009] EWCA Civ 171, [2009] 1 WLR 2274, [2009] 3 All ER 340...... 25.69
Bovis Homes Ltd v New Forest District Council [2002] EWHC 483
(Admin) 8.66, 8.69,
8.74, 8.78, 8.106
Bovis Homes (Scotland) Ltd v Inverclyde District Council [1982] SLT 473,
[1983] JPL 171 .... 6.98; 19.22
Bowen-West v Secretary of State for Communities & Local Government
[2012] EWCA Civ 321, [2012] Env LR 22, [2012] JPL 1128........... 7.37, 7.42
Bradford City Council v Secretary of State for the Environment (1987) 53 P
& CR 55, [1986] 1 EGLR 199, [1986] JPL 598 .... 11.33
Braintree District Council v Secretary of State for the Environment (1995) 71
P & CR 323, [1997] JPL 217, [1995] NPC 152.................................... 16.5
Bramall v Secretary of State for Communities & Local Government [2011]
EWHC 1531 (Admin), [2011] NPC 63.. 4.14
Brazil (Concrete) Ltd v Amersham Rural District Council (1967) 18 P & CR
396, 65 LGR 365, 202 EG 413... 2.29
Breckland District Council v Secretary of State for the Environment (1992)
65 P & CR 34, [1992] 3 PLR 89 .... 19.46
Brentwood Borough Council v Secretary of State for the Environment (1996)
72 P & CR 61, [1996] JPL 939 .... 9.192
Brewer v Secretary of State for the Environment [1988] 2 PLR 13, [1988]
JPL 480... 9.176
British Airports Authority v Secretary of State for Scotland 1979 SC 200,
1979 SLT 197 .... 11.9, 11.19
British Railways Board v Secretary of State for the Environment [1993] 3
PLR 125, [1994] 02 EG 107, [1994] JPL 32.. 11.22
Broadview Energy Developments Ltd v Secretary of State for Communities
& Local Government [2015] EWHC 1743 (Admin), [2015] JPL 1355,
[2015] ACD 122 .... 17.66
Brown v Hayes & Harlington Urban District Council (1963) 15 P & CR 284,
62 LGR 66, 188 EG 785... 5.123
Bubb v Wandsworth London Borough Council [2011] EWCA Civ 1285,
[2012] PTSR 1011, [2012] HLR 13 .... 25.80

Table of Cases

Burdle v Secretary of State for the Environment [1972] 1 WLR 1207, [1972] 3 All ER 240, 70 LGR 511 .... 2.33
Burroughs Day v Bristol City Council [1996] 1 PLR 78, [1996] 1 EGLR 167, [1996] 19 EG 126 .... 2.18
Bushell v Secretary of State for the Environment [1981] AC 75, [1980] 3 WLR 22, [1980] 2 All ER 608 .... 23.133
Butler v Derby City Council [2005] EWHC 2835 (Admin), [2006] 1 WLR 1346, (2006) 170 JP 285 .... 9.149

C

CF v Ministry of Defence [2014] EWHC 3171 (QB) 23.149
Cadogan v Secretary of State for the Environment (1993) 65 P & CR 410, [1993] JPL 664, [1992] EG 123 .... 11.27
Cala Homes (South) Ltd v Chichester District Council (Time Limits) [2000] CP Rep 28, (2000) 79 P & CR 430, [1999] 4 PLR 77 .... 25.57
Calcaria Construction Co (York) Ltd v Secretary of State for the Environment (1974) 27 P & CR 435, 72 LGR 398, (1974) 118 SJ 421 .... 16.5
Camden London Borough Council v Secretary of State for the Environment [1993] JPL 466 .... 16.4, 16.9
Campaign for the Protection of Rural Wales v Secretary of State for Wales (unreported, 7 April 2000) 24.12
Campbell v Argyll & Bute District Council 1997 SCLR 197 .... 29.40
Carpet Décor (Guildford) Ltd v Secretary of State for the Environment (1982) 261 EG 56, [1981] JPL 806 .... 3.10
Carroll v Secretary of State for Communities & Local Government [2015] EWHC 316 (Admin) 19.46; 21.17, 21.28, 21.30, 21.31
Carter Commercial Developments Ltd (In Administration) v Secretary of State for Transport, Local Government & the Regions [2002] EWHC 1200 (Admin), [2003] JPL 35; *aff'd* [2002] EWCA Civ 1994, [2003] JPL 1048 .... 28.11, 28.20
Castell-Y-Mynach Estate, Trustees of v Secretary of State for Wales & Taff Ely Borough Council [1985] JPL 40 .... 4.14
Castleford Homes Ltd v Secretary of State for the Environment, Transport & the Regions [2001] EWHC Admin 77, [2001] PLCR 29, [2001] JPL 1217 (Note) 23.134
Chartbrook Ltd v Persimmon Homes Ltd [2009] UKHL 38, [2009] 1 AC 1101, [2009] 3 WLR 267 .... 12.55; 28.18
Chelmsford Corpn v Secretary of State for the Environment & Homes East Anglia Ltd (1971) 22 P & CR 880, 70 LGR 89 .... 16.16
Chichester District Council v First Secretary of State [2006] EWHC 1876 (Admin), [2007] JPL 389 .... 23.129
City of London Corpn v Secretary of State for the Environment (1971) 23 P & CR 169, 71 LGR 28 .... 3.10; 11.25
Clyde & Co v Secretary of State for the Environment [1977] 1 WLR 926, [1977] 3 All ER 1123, 75 LGR 660 .... 9.203
Coal Contractors Limited v Secretary of State for the Environment [1995] JPL 421 .... 9.98
Cocks v Thanet District Council [1983] 2 AC 286, [1982] 3 WLR 1121, [1982] 3 All ER 1135 .... 25.76
Cocktails Ltd v Secretary of State for Communities & Local Government [2008] EWCA Civ 1523, [2009] LLR 170, [2009] JPL 953 .... 3.4

Table of Cases

Coghurst Wood Leisure Ltd v Secretary of State for Transport, Local Government & the Regions [2002] EWHC 1091 (Admin), [2003] JPL 206, [2002] 24 EG 145 (CS) 29.22
Coleshill & District Investment Co Ltd v Minister of Housing & Local Government [1969] 1 WLR 746, [1969] 2 All ER 525, (1969) 133 JP 385 .... 2.14
Collis Radio Ltd v Secretary of State for the Environment (1975) 29 P & CR 390, 73 LGR 211, (1975) 119 SJ 302 .... 9.178
Commercial & Residential Property Development Co Ltd v Secretary of State for the Environment [1982] JPL 513, 80 LGR 443 .... 3.37
Commercial Land Ltd v Secretary of State for Transport, Local Government & the Regions [2002] EWHC 1264 (Admin), [2003] JPL 358 .... 29.14, 29.16
Commission of the European Communities v Italy (Case C-486/04) [2006] ECR I-11025, [2007] Env LR D10 .... 7.17
Commission of the European Communities v Spain (Case C-227/01) [2004] ECR I-8253, [2005] Env LR 20 .... 7.17
Commission the European Communities v United Kingdom (C-508/03) [2006] QB 764, [2006] 3 WLR 492, [2006] ECR I-3969 .... 7.6
Connors v Secretary of State for Communities & Local Government [2014] EWHC 2358 (Admin), [2015] JPL 196 .... 25.15
Cooper v Wilson [1937] 2 KB 309, [1937] 2 All ER 726 .... 8.82
Copas v Secretary of State for Communities and Local Government [2014] EWHC 2634 (Admin), [2015] JPL 83 .... 9.85
Corus UK Ltd v Erewash Borough Council [2006] EWCA Civ 1175, [2006] CP Rep 41, [2007] 1 P & CR 22 .... 25.58
Council for National Parks Ltd v Pembrokeshire Coast National Park Authority [2004] EWHC 2907 (Admin), [2005] JPL 1362 .... 8.74
Crane v Secretary of State for Communities and Local Government [2015] EWHC 425 (Admin) 9.51
Crawford-Brunt v Secretary of State for Communities and Local Government [2015] EWHC 3580 (Admin) 25.38
Creighton Estates Ltd v London County Council (The Times, 20 March 1958) 28.8
Cynon Valley Borough Council v Secretary of State for Wales (1987) 53 P & CR 68, 85 LGR 36, [1986] 2 EGLR 191 .... 4.6, 4.8

D

DPP v Hutchinson [1990] 2 AC 783, [1990] 3 WLR 196, (1991) 155 JP 71 .. 12.13
Davenport v London Borough of Hammersmith & Fulham (1999) 78 P & CR 421, [1999] 2 PLR 96, [1999] JPL 1122 .... 1.52; 11.5, 11.16, 11.17, 11.19
Davill v Pull [2009] EWCA Civ 1309, [2010] 1 P & CR 23, [2009] NPC 142 .... 12.55
Dear v Secretary of State for Communities and Local Government [2015] EWHC 29 (Admin) 9.200
Deitsch v Secretary of State for the Environment [1993] JPL 579 .... 3.49
Delta Design & Engineering Ltd v Secretary of State for the Environment, Transport & the Regions (2000) 80 P & CR 76, [2000] 4 PLR 1, [2000] JPL 726 .... 11.10
De Mulder v First Secretary of State [2005] EWHC 2640 (Admin), [2005] NPC 138 .... 24.12

Table of Cases

Dimes v Grand Junction Canal Proprietors (1852) 3 HL Cas 759, 10 ER 301: 8.69
Dimsdale Developments (South East) Ltd v Secretary of State for the Environment & Hounslow London Borough Council [1985] 2 EGLR 183, (1985) 275 EG 58, [1986] JPL 276.. 9.37
Doncaster Metropolitan Borough Council v Secretary of State for the Environment, Transport and the Regions [2002] EWHC 808 (Admin), [2002] JPL 1509, [2002] 16 EG 181 (CS)... 9.180
Drexfine Holdings Ltd v Cherwell District Council [1998] JPL 361............. 8.102
Dunoon Development Ltd v Secretary of State for the Environment & Poole Borough Council (1993) 65 P & CR 101, [1992] 2 PLR 128, [1992] JPL 936... 3.11, 3.12; 5.18; 11.25
Dunsford Park Ltd v Secretary of State for Communities & Local Government [2013] EWHC 1878 (Admin), [2013] BLGR 861, [2013] JPL 1568..... 29.34
Durham County Council v Secretary of State for the Environment (1989) 60 P & CR 507, [1990] 1 PLR 103, [1990] JPL 280 .... 29.49
Dyason v Secretary of State for the Environment, Transport & the Regions (No 1) (1998) 75 P & CR 506, [1998] 2 PLR 54, [1998] JPL 778 .... 1.67; 22.27
Dyer v Dorset County Council [1989] QB 346, [1988] 3 WLR 213, (1988) 20 HLR 490.. 2.37

E

E v Secretary of State for the Home Department [2004] EWCA Civ 49, [2004] QB 1044, [2004] 2 WLR 1351 .... 25.5
Earthline Ltd v Secretary of State for the Environment, Transport and the Regions [2002] EWCA Civ 1599, [2003] 1 P & CR 24, [2002] 4 PLR 94... 9.200
East v Pantiles (Plant Hire) [1982] 2 EGLR 111, (1982) 263 EG 61............. 28.17
East Barnet Urban District Council v British Transport Commission [1962] 2 QB 484, [1962] 2 WLR 134, [1961] 3 All ER 878 .... 2.26; 9.148
East Dunbartonshire Council v Secretary of State for Scotland 1999 SLT 1088, 1999 SCLR 396, [1999] 1 PLR 53...29.40, 29.42
East Lindsay District Council v Thompson [2001] EWHC Admin 81, (2001) 82 P & CR 33, [2001] 2 PLR 26 .... 6.50
East Northamptonshire District Council v Secretary of State for Communities and Local Government; *sub nom* Barnwell Manor Wind Energy Ltd v East Northamptonshire District Council [2014] EWCA Civ 137, [2015] 1 WLR 45 [2014] JPL 731 .... 9.12, 9.93, 9.97
Eco-Energy (GB) Ltd v First Secretary of State [2004] EWCA Civ 1566, [2005] 2 P & CR 5, [2005] 2 PLR 33... 25.39
Ecologistas en Acción-CODA v Ayuntamiento de Madrid (Case Case C-142/07) [2009] PTSR 458, [2008] ECR I-6097, [2009] Env LR D4 .. 7.20
Ecotricity Ltd v Secretary of State for Communities & Local Government [2015] EWHC 801 (Admin)... 23.130
Ecotricity (Next Generation) Ltd v Secretary of State for Communities & Local Government [2014] EWHC 2699 (Admin), [2014] JPL 1338; *aff'd* [2015] EWCA Civ 657 .... 24.12
Edinburgh City Council v Secretary of State for Scotland [1997] 1 WLR 1447, [1998] 1 All ER 174, 1998 SC (HL) 33 .... 9.19, 9.20, 9.21
Ellis v Worcestershire County Council (1961) 12 P & CR 178....................... 29.50
English Clays Lovering Pochin & Co Ltd v Plymouth Corpn [1973] 1 WLR 1346, [1973] 2 All ER 730, 71 LGR 412 .... 5.88; 29.9

Table of Cases

Enoch & Zaretzky, Bock & Co's Arbitration, Re [1910] 1 KB 327 .... 23.136
Etheridge v Secretary of State for the Environment (1983) 48 P & CR 35,
  [1984] JPL 340 .... 16.20; 29.40
Europa Oil and Gas Ltd v Secretary of State for Communities and Local
  Government [2013] EWHC 2643 (Admin), [2014] 1 P & CR 3, [2014]
  JPL 21; aff'd [2014] EWCA Civ 825, [2014] PTSR 1471, [2014] JPL
  1259 .... 9.78
Evans v Secretary of State for Communities & Local Government [2014]
  EWHC 4111 (Admin), [2015] JPL 589 .... 5.22, 5.106

F

F Hoffmann-Le Roche & Co AG v Secretary of State for Trade & Industry
  [1975] AC 295, [1974] 3 WLR 104, [1974] 2 All ER 1128 .... 25.108
F Lucas & Sons Ltd v Dorking & Horley Rural District Council (1964) 17 P
  & CR 111, 62 LGR 491 .... 29.53, 29.54
FG Whitley & Sons Co Ltd v Secretary of State for Wales (1992) 64 P & CR
  296, [1992] 3 PLR 72, [1992] JPL 856 .... 29.18, 29.19,
                                                                   29.20, 29.23, 29.26,
                                                                   29.28, 29.29, 29.31, 29.33
Fairmount Ltd v Secretary of State for the Environment [1976] 1 WLR 1255,
  [1976] 2 All ER 865, 75 LGR 33 .... 21.27; 23.131
Fairstate Ltd v First Secretary of State [2005] EWCA Civ 283, [2005] JPL
  1333, [2005] JPL 369 .... 2.50; 4.9
Farleyer Estate v Secretary of State for Scotland 1992 SC 202, 1992 SLT 476,
  1992 SCLR 364 .... 2.31
Fawcett Properties Ltd v Buckingham County Council [1961] AC 636, [1990]
  3 WLR 831, [1960] 3 All ER 503 .... 28.11, 28.20
Federal Steam Navigation Co Ltd v Department of Trade & Industry (The
  Huntingdon) [1974] 1 WLR 505, [1974] 2 All ER 97, [1974] 1 Lloyd's
  Rep 520 .... 28.17
Fidler v First Secretary of State [2004] EWCA Civ 1295, [2005] 1 P & CR
  12, [2005] JPL 510 .... 2.25, 2.42,
                                                                                      2.44; 3.4
Field v First Secretary of State [2004] EWHC 147 (Admin), [2004] JPL
  1286, [2004] 6 EG 145 (CS) 29.10
Finlay (M) v Secretary of State for the Environment & Islington London
  Borough Council [1983] JPL 802 .... 9.53
Finn-Kelcey v Milton Keynes Borough Council [2008] EWCA Civ 1067,
  [2009] Env LR 17, [2009] JPL 493 .... 25.47
Fitzpatrick Developments Ltd v Minister of Housing and Local Government
  (1965) 194 EG 911 .... 9.177
Fordent Holdings Ltd v Secretary of State for Communities and Local
  Government [2013] EWHC 2844 (Admin), [2014] 2 P & CR 12, [2014]
  JPL 226 .... 9.73, 9.74
Fox Strategic Land and Property Ltd v Secretary of State for Communities
  and Local Government [2012] EWCA Civ 1198, [2013] 1 P & CR 6 ... 9.199

G

G Percy Trentham Ltd v Gloucestershire County Council [1966] 1 WLR 506,
  [1966] 1 All ER 701, (1966) 130 JP 179 .... 2.29, 2.33
Gambone v Secretary of State for Communities and Local Government
  [2014] EWHC 952 (Admin) 9.192

Table of Cases

Gateshead Metropolitan Borough Council v Secretary of State for the Environment [1995] Env LR 37, (1996) 71 P & CR 350, [1994] 1 PLR 85 .... 9.207
George Wimpey UK Ltd v Tewkesbury Borough Council *see* MA Holdings Ltd v George Wimpey UK Ltd
Gillespie v First Secretary of State [2003] EWCA Civ 400, [2003] Env LR 30, [2003] JPL 1287 .... 7.41
Golding v Secretary of State for Communities & Local Government [2012] EWHC 1656 (Admin) 25.27
Good v Epping Forest District Council [1994] 1 WLR 376, [1994] 2 All ER 156, 92 LGR 306 .... 12.8, 12.47
Grampian Regional Council v Secretary of State for Scotland 1984 SC (HL) 58, 1984 SLT 197, (1984) 47 P & CR 633 .... 1.53; 11.22
Granada Hospitality Ltd v Secretary of State for the Environment, Transport & the Regions (2001) 81 P & CR 36, [2001] PLCR 5, [2001] JPL 222 (Note) 6.148; 11.27; 19.45
Gransden & Co Ltd v Secretary of State for the Environment (1987) 54 P & CR 86 .... 24.23
Grant v Secretary of State for the Environment [1990] JPL 110 .... 21.32
Grantchester Retail Parks plc v Secretary of State for Transport, Local Government & the Regions [2003] EWHC 92 (Admin) 9.200
Gravesham Borough Council v Secretary of State for the Environment (1984) 47 P & CR 142, [1983] JPL 307 .... 3.44
Greater London Council v Secretary of State for the Environment [1985] JPL 868 .... 25.21
Green v Secretary of State for Communities & Local Government [2010] EWCA Civ 64, [2010] JPL 1022, [2010] NPC 16 .... 28.15
Green v Secretary of State for Communities & Local Government [2013] EWHC 3980 (Admin) 29.14, 29.16, 29.34
Greyfort Properties Ltd v Secretary of State for Communities & Local Government [2011] EWCA Civ 908, [2011] 3 EGLR 93, [2012] JPL 40 .... 29.19, 29.29, 29.31, 29.32, 29.33, 29.34
Guerra v Italy (1998) 26 EHRR 357, 4 BHRC 63, [1998] HRCD 277 .... 9.151

H

Halifax Building Society v Secretary of State for the Environment (1983) 267 EG 679, [1983] JPL 816 .... 23.137
Hall v Secretary of State for the Environment, Transport & the Regions [1998] JPL 1055 .... 4.4
Hall & Co Ltd v Shoreham-by-Sea Urban District Council [1964] 1 WLR 240, [1964] 1 All ER 1, (1964) 128 JP 120 .... 11.33; 25.92
Handoll v Warner Goodman & Streat (1994) 70 P & CR 627, 93 LGR 293, [1995] 1 EGLR 173 .... 29.13
Harris v Harris (The Times, 9 April 1952) 23.136
Harrison v Secretary of State for Communities and Local Government [2009] EWHC 3382 (Admin), [2010] Env LR 17, [2010] JPL 885 .... 9.208
Harrods Ltd v Secretary of State for the Environment, Transport & the Regions [2001] EWHC Admin 600, [2002] JPL 437, [2001] 31 EG 101 .... 2.30
Harrogate Borough Council v Crossland [2012] EWHC 3260 (QB) 5.48, 5.139

Table of Cases

Hart District Council v Benford [2006] EWHC 240 (QB), [2006] JPL 1318,
 [2006] 9 EG 183 .... 5.124
Hartley v Minister of Housing & Local Government [1970] 1 QB 413, [1970]
 2 WLR 1, [1969] 3 All ER 1658 .... 2.35; 4.12
Hatton v United Kingdom (Application 36022/97) (2003) 37 EHRR 28, 15
 BHRC 259 .... 9.150
Hawes v Thornton Cleveleys Urban District Council (1965) 17 P & CR 22,
 63 LGR 213 .... 5.125
Henry Boot Homes Ltd v Bassetlaw District Council [2002] EWCA Civ 983,
 [2003] 1 P & CR 23, [2003] JPL 1030 .... 16.20; 29.24
Heron Corpn Ltd v Manchester City Council (1977) 33 P & CR 268, 5 LGR
 298, (1976) 247 EG 209 .... 14.20; 16.12,
 16.14, 16.27; 24.62
Hertfordshire County Council v Secretary of State for Communities & Local
 Government [2012] EWHC 277 (Admin), [2012] JPL 836 *aff'd* [2008]
 EWHC 198 (Admin), [2008] JPL 1486 .... 4.9
Historic Buildings & Monuments Commission for England (English
 Heritage) v Secretary of State for Communities & Local Government
 [2010] EWCA Civ 600, [2010] JPL 1645 .... 25.37, 25.40
Hopkins Development Ltd v Secretary of State for Communities & Local
 Government [2014] EWCA Civ 470, [2014] PTSR 1145, [2014] JPL
 1000 .... 9.208; 21.25,
 21.27; 23.130, 23.132
Hopkins Homes Ltd v Secretary of State for Communities and Local
 Government [2015] EWHC 132 (Admin) 9.103
Hounslow London Borough Council v Secretary of State for Communities
 and Local Government (Planning Inspectorate) [2009] EWHC 1055
 (Admin) 9.198
Hoveringham Gravels Ltd v Chiltern District Council (1978) 35 P & CR 295,
 76 LGR 533, 243 EG 911 .... 29.49
Hoveringham Gravels Ltd v Secretary of State for the Environment [1975]
 QB 754, [1975] 2 WLR 897, [1975] 2 All ER 931 .... 9.98
Howell v Secretary of State for Communities and Local Government [2014]
 EWHC 3627 (Admin) 9.117
Howell v Sunbury-on-Thames Urban District Council (1964) 15 P & CR 26,
 61 LGR 477, 187 EG 393 .... 2.24
Hughes v Doncaster Metropolitan Borough Council [1991] 1 AC 382 [1991]
 2 WLR 16, [1991] 1 All ER 295 .... 4.36
Hughes v Secretary of State for the Environment, Transport & the Regions
 (2000) 80 P & CR 397, [2000] 1 PLR 76, [2000] JPL 826 .... 2.35; 4.13
Hulme v Secretary of State for Communities & Local Government [2011]
 EWCA Civ 638, [2011] NPC 55 .... 28.20
Hunston Properties Ltd v Secretary of State for Communities and Local
 Government [2013] EWCA Civ 1610, [2014] 1 EGLR 79, [2014] JPL
 599 .... 9.44, 9.101
Hunter v Canary Wharf [1997] AC 655, [1997] 2 WLR 684, [1997] 2 All
 ER 426 .... 9.6, 9.58
Hussain v Secretary of State for the Environment (1972) 23 P & CR 330,
 (1971) 221 EG 627 .... 2.30
Hyde Park Residence Ltd v Secretary of State for the Environment, Transport
 & the Regions (2000) 80 P & CR 419, [2000] 1 PLR 85, [2000] JPL
 936 .... 2.50

Table of Cases

I

IRC v Barclay, Curle & Co Ltd [1969] 1 WLR 675, [1969] 1 All ER 732, [1969] 1 Lloyd's Rep 169	5.92
Iddenden v Secretary of State for the Environment [1972] 1 WLR 1433, [1972] 3 All ER 883, 71 LGR 20	4.15
Impey v Secretary of State for the Environment (1984) 47 P & CR 157	2.24, 2.36
I'm Your Man Ltd v Secretary of State for the Environment (1999) 77 P & CR 251, [1998] 4 PLR 107, [1999] PLCR 109	5.13
Infocus Public Networks Ltd v Secretary of State for Communities & Local Government [2010] EWHC 3309 (Admin), [2011] JPL 1048, [2011] NPC 2	5.45
International Sociey for Krishna Consciousness v Secretary of State for the Environment & Hertsmere Borough Council (1992) 64 P & CR 85, [1992] JPL 962, [1992] COD 251	2.30
Inverclyde District Council v Lord Advocate; Inverclyde District Council v Secretary of State for Scotland 1982 SC (HL) 64, 1982 SLT 200, (1982) 43 P & CR 375	16.28
Investors Compensation Scheme Ltd v West Bromwich Building Society (No 1) [1998] 1 WLR 896, [1998] 1 All ER 98, [1998] 1 BCLC 531	12.54
Ioannou v Secretary of State for Communities & Local Government [2013] EWHC 3945 (Admin), [2014] 1 EGLR 83, [2014] JPL 608	25.74
Iskcon v United Kingdom (Application 20490/92) (1994) 18 EHRR CD 133:	9.149
Islam v Secretary of State for Communities & Local Government [2012] EWHC 1314 (Admin), [2012] JPL 1378	2.8

J

JB Trustees Ltd v Secretary of State for Communities & Local Government [2013] EWHC 3555 (Admin), [2014] JPL 656, [2013] 48 EG 124 (CS)	25.39
JJ Gallagher Ltd v Secretary of State for Transport, Local Government and the Regions [2002] EWHC 1812 (Admin), [2002] 4 PLR 32, (2002) 99 (36) LSG 42	9.199
James Hay Pension Trustees Ltd v First Secretary of State [2006] EWCA Civ 1387, [2007] 1 P & CR 23, [2007] JPL 643	14.22
Jeffrey v First Secretary of State [2006] EWHC 2920 (Admin), [2007] JPL 907; aff'd [2007] EWCA Civ 584	4.40
Jelson Ltd v Derby City Council [1999] 4 PLR 11, [1999] 3 EGLR 91, [1999] 39 EG 149	12.27
Jennings Motors Ltd v Secretary of State for the Environment [1982] QB 541, [1982] 2 WLR 131, [1982] 1 All ER 471	4.18
Johnson v Secretary of State for Communities & Local Government [2007] EWHC 1839 (Admin)	24.18
Jones v National Coal Board [1957] 2 QB 55, [1957] 2 WLR 760, [1957] 2 All ER 155	23.136
Jones v Secretary of State for Wales (1995) 70 P & CR 211, [1995] 2 PLR 26, (1995) 159 LG Rev 689	25.79
Jory v Secretary of State for Transport, Local Government & the Regions [2002] EWHC 2724 (Admin), [2003] 1 PLR 54, [2003] JPL 549	23.140

K

Kalra v Secretary of State for the Environment (1996) 72 P & CR 423, [1996] 1 PLR 37, [1996] JPL 850	3.21

Table of Cases

Kaur (Pritam) v S Russell & Sons Ltd [1973] QB 336, [1973] 2 WLR 147,
  [1973] 1 All ER 617 .... 5.46; 25.50
Kendall v Rochford District Council [2014] EWHC 3866 (Admin), [2015]
  Env LR 21 .... 7.78; 24.27
Kensington & Chelsea Royal London Borough Council v Secretary of State
  & Mia Carla Ltd [1981] JPL 50 .... 2.25
Kent County Council v Secretary of State for the Environment & Burmah-
  Total Refineries Trust (1976) 33 P & CR 70, 75 LGR 452, [1976] 241
  EG 83 .... 11.50; 13.5
King's Lynn and West Norfolk Borough Council v Secretary of State for
  Communities and Local Government [2015] EWHC 2464 (Admin) 22.27
Kingston-Upon-Thames Royal London Borough Council v Secretary of State
  for the Environment [1973] 1 WLR 1549, [1974] 1 All ER 193, 71
  LGR 206 .... 11.26
Kingsway Investments (Kent) Ltd v Kent County Council [1971] AC 72,
  [1970] 2 WLR 397, [1970] 1 All ER 70 .... 16.4, 16.8,
                                                                16.16, 16.34, 16.42
Kingswood District Council v Secretary of State for the Environment (1989)
  57 P & CR 153, [1988] JPL 248 .... 9.10; 25.108
Knott v Secretary of State for the Environment (1998) 75 P & CR 65, [1997]
  JPL 713, [1996] EG 175 (CS) 28.23
Koumis v Secretary of State for Communities and Local Government [2014]
  EWCA Civ 1723, [2015] JPL 682 .... 28.14

L

LOUP v Secretary of State for the Environment; Trustees of the Viscount
  Folkestone Settlement (LOUP) v Secretary of State for the Environment
  (1995) 71 P & CR 175, [1996] JPL 22, [1995] EG 93 .... 9.21
LTSS Print & Supply Services Ltd v Hackney London Borough Council
  [1976] QB 663, [1976] 2 WLR 253, [1976] 1 All ER 311 .... 4.8, 4.9
Lafarge Redland Aggregates Ltd v Scottish Ministers 2001 SC 298, 2000
  SLT 1361, [2001] Env LR 27 .... 17.62
Laing Homes Ltd v Secretary of State for Transport, Local Government and
  the Regions [2002] EWHC 1967 (Admin), [2003] 1 P & CR 18, [2003]
  JPL 559 .... 9.165
Lakin Ltd v Secretary of State for Scotland 1988 SLT 780 .... 17.42
Landelijke Vereniging tot Behoud van de Waddenzee v Staatssecretaris van
  Landbouw Natuurbeheer en Visserij (Case C-127/02) [2004] ECR
  -7405 [2005] 2 CMLR 31, [2005] All ER (EC) 353 .... 9.134,
                                                                  9.136, 9.138
Lardner v Renfrewshire District Council 1997 SC 104, 1997 SLT 1027, 1997
  SCLR 454 .... 25.38
Larkfleet Ltd v Secretary of State for Communities and Local Government
  and South Kesteven District Council [2012] EWHC 3592 (Admin) 9.186
Lawson Builders Ltd v Secretary of State for Communities & Local
  Government [2015] EWCA Civ 122, [2015] PTSR 1324, [2015] JPL
  896 .... 13.8, 13.13,
                                                                  13.25, 13.29
Leelamb Homes Ltd v Secretary of State for Communities & Local
  Government [2009] EWHC 1926 (Admin) 3.40
Leisure Great Britain plc v Isle of Wight Council (2000) 80 P & CR 370,
  [2000] PLCR 88, [1999] NPC 80 .... 29.20, 29.23

Table of Cases

Lenlyn v Secretary of State for the Environment (1984) 50 P & CR 129, [1985] JPL 482, (1985) 82 LSG 358 .... 25.18
Lever (Finance) Ltd v Westminster Corpn [1971] 1 QB 222, [1970] 3 WLR 732, [1970] 3 All ER 496 .... 5.47; 15.3, 15.5, 15.6, 15.9; 16.29
Lilo Blum v Secretary of State for the Environment [1987] JPL 278 .... 2.25; 9.53
Lloyd, ex p (1822) Mont 70 .... 23.136
Lloyd v Secretary of State for Communities and Local Government [2014] EWCA Civ 839, [2014] JPL 1247 .... 9.79
Lobb v Secretary of State for the Environment [1984] JPL 336 .... 29.52
London & Henley (Middle Brook Street) Ltd v Secretary of State for Communities & Local Government [2013] EWHC 4207 (Admin) 25.128
London Borough of Croydon v Gladden *see* Runnymede Borough Council v Harwood
London Borough of Southwark v Secretary of State for the Environment [1987] JPL 36 .... 21.26
London County Council v Allen [1914] 3 KB 642 .... 12.2
London Residuary Board v London Borough of Lambeth (1989) 58 P & CR 256, [1988] 2 PLR 79; *revs'd* (1989) 58 P & CR 370, [1990] JPL 200, [1990] COD 72 *revs'd* [1990] 1 WLR 744, [1990] 2 All ER 309, (1991) 61 P & CR 65 .... 3.25, 3.26; 9.204
Lopez Ostra v Spain (A/303-C) (1994) 20 EHRR 277 .... 9.151
Lord Advocate v Dumbarton District Council [1990] 2 AC 580, [1989] 3 WLR 1346, [1990] 1 All ER 1 .... 6.61
Lord Baker of Dorking v Information Commissioner EA/2006/0043 .... 24.10
Lough v First Secretary of State [2004] EWCA Civ 905, [2004] 1 WLR 2557, [2005] 1 P & CR 5 .... 9.152
Lydcare Ltd v Secretary of State for the Environment (1984) 49 P & CR 186 .... 2.30

M

MA Holdings Ltd v George Wimpey UK Ltd [2012] EWCA Civ 12, [2008] 1 WLR 1649, [2008] 3 All ER 859 .... 25.107
MWH Associates Ltd v Wrexham County Borough Council [2012] EWCA Civ 1884, [2013] Env LR 27, [2013] RVR 112 .... 4.31
McAlpine (David) v Secretary of State for the Environment [1995] 1 PLR 16, (1995) 159 LG Rev 429, [1994] EG 189 (CS) 2.37; 5.101
Macarthur v Secretary of State for Communities & Local Government [2013] EWHC 3 (Admin) 24.24
McCarthy & Stone (Developments) Ltd v Richmond-upon-Thames London Borough Council [1992] 2 AC 48, [1991] 3 WLR 941, [1991] 4 All ER 897 .... 6.34; 12.103
Mackman v Secretary of State for Communities & Local Government [2015] EWCA Civ 716, [2016] Env LR 6, [2015] JPL 1370 .... 7.21
Main v Secretary of State for the Environment (1999) 77 P & CR 300, [1999] JPL 195, (1998) 95 (22) LSG 30 .... 2.29
Main v Swansea City Council (1985) 49 P & CR 26, [1985] JPL 558 .... 6.90, 6.129
Malvern Hills District Council v Secretary of State for the Environment (1983) 46 P & CR 58, 81 LGR 13, (1982) 262 EG 1190 .... 29.8, 29.37

Manchester City Council v Secretary of State for the Environment & Mercury
    Communications [1988] JPL 774.. 24.28
Mannai Investments Co Ltd v Eagle Star Life Assurance Co Ltd [1997] AC
    749, [1997] 2 WLR 945, [1997] 3 All ER 352...................................... 12.54
Martin v Secretary of State for Communities and Local Government [2015]
    EWHC 3435 (Admin) 9.91; 25.87
Martins' Application, Re (1988) 57 P & CR 119, [1988] 3 PLR 45, [1989] 05
    EG 85... 12.102
Matthews v Secretary of State for the Environment, Transport & the Regions
    [2001] EWHC Admin 815, [2002] 2 P & CR 34, [2002] JPL 716 .... 25.50
Mayflower Cambridge Ltd v Secretary of State for the Environment (1975)
    30 P & CR 28, 73 LGR 517, (1975) 119 SJ 590.................................... 3.35
Medina Borough Council v Proberun (1991) 61 P & CR 77, [1990] 3 PLR 79,
    [1991] JPL 159... 16.8
Methuen-Campbell v Walters [1979] QB 525, [1979] 2 WLR 113, [1979] 1
    All ER 606 .... 2.37; 5.101
Middle Level Comrs v Atkins Ltd [2012] EWHC 2884 (TC), [2012] CILL
    3257, [2013] JPL 355... 5.150
Mid Suffolk District Council v Clarke (Preliminary Issue) [2005] EWHC
    3099 (QB), [2005] 4 PLR 27.. 28.4, 28.12
Milebush Properties Ltd v Tameside Metropolitan Borough Council [2010]
    EWHC 1022 (Ch), [2010] 2 EGLR 93, [2010] JPL 1303.............. 12.27, 12.55
Miles v National Assembly for Wales [2007] EWHC 10 (Admin), [2007] JPL
    1235... 5.124
Miller-Mead v Minister of Housing & Local Government [1963] 2 QB 196,
    [1963] 2 WLR 225, [1963] 1 All ER 459... 28.8
Millington v Secretary of State for the Environment, Transport & the Regions
    [1999] 3 PLR 118, [2000] JPL 297, [1999] EG 95 (CS)................... 2.40; 3.51
Minister for Immigration v Bhardwaj (2002) 187 ALR 117 .... 24.65
Ministry of Agriculture, Fisheries & Food v Jenkins [1963] 2 QB 317, [1963]
    2 WLR 906, [1963] 2 All ER 147... 6.61
Moore v Secretary of State for Communities & Local Government & Suffolk
    Coastal District Council [2012] EWCA Civ 1202, [2012] 3 EGLR 91,
    [2013] JPL 192 ....3.46; 17.62
Moore v Secretary of State for the Environment & New Forest District
    Council (1999) 77 P & CR 114, [1998] 2 PLR 65, [1998] JPL 877 ...... 3.46
Morbaine Ltd v First Secretary of State [2004] EHWC 1708 (Admin), [2005]
    JPL 377... 25.39
Mordue v Secretary of State for Communities and Local Government [2015]
    EWCA Civ 1243 .... 24.21, 24.23
Mossell (Jamaica) Ltd (t/a Digicel) v Office of Utilities Regulations [2010]
    UKPC 1 ....9.200; 25.108
Mouchel Superannuation Fund Trustees v Oxfordshire County Council
    [1992] 1 PLR 97.. 25.92
Mulvenna v Secretary of State for Communities and Local Government
    [2015] EWHC 3494 (Admin).. 24.67
Murrell v Secretary of State for Communities & Local Government [2010]
    EWCA Civ 1367, [2012] 1 P & CR 6, [2011] JPL 739 .... 5.38

N
Newark & Sherwood District Council v Secretary of State for Communities
    & Local Government [2013] EWHC 2162 (Admin)............................. 28.17

Table of Cases

Newbury District Council v Secretary of State for the Environment [1981]
AC 578, [1980] 2 WLR 379, [1980] 1 All ER 731 .... 1.54; 3.52;
4.11, 4.17; 11.6, 11.7,
11.10, 11.24, 11.30; 12.8
Newcastle-upon-Tyne City Council v Secretary of State for Communities &
Local Government [2009] EWHC 3469 (Admin), [2010] 2 P & CR 5,
[2010] JPL 904 .... 6.90, 6.93, 6.94
Newlyn Dean v Secretary of State for Communities and Local Government
[2014] EWCA Civ 193... 9.75
Nicholson v First Secretary of State [2005] EWHC 378 (Admin).................. 5.109
Nicholson v Secretary of State for Energy (1977) 245 EG 139, 76 LGR 693,
[1978] JPL 39 .... 23.97
Norris v First Secretary of State [2006] EWCA Civ 12, [2007] P & CR 3,
[2006] JPL 1574 .... 29.27
North v Brown (1974) 231 EG 737 .... 5.130
Northampton Borough Council v Secretary of State [2005] EWHC 168
(Admin), [2005] JPL 1213, [2005] 7 EG 142 (CS)...........................3.12; 28.23
North Cornwall District Council v Secretary of State for the Environment,
Transport & the Regions [2002] EWHC 2318 (Admin), [2003] 1 P &
CR 25, [2003] JPL 600.. 5.123
North Kesteven District Council v Secretary of State for the Environment
[1989] JPL 445 ....25.17, 25.27
Northumberland County Council v Secretary of State for the Environment
(1989) 59 P & CR 468, [1979] JPL 700... 9.170
North Wiltshire District Council v Secretary of State for the Environment
(1993) 65 P & CR 137, [1992] 3 PLR 113, [1992] JPL 955.......... 9.194; 24.19
Nottingham City Council v Calverton Parish Council [2015] EWHC 503
(Admin), [2015] PTSR 1130, [2015] ACD 97 .... 25.50
Novalong Ltd v Secretary of State for Communities & Local Government
[2008] EWHC 2136 (Admin).. 24.12

O

Oakimber v Elmbridge Borough Council *see* R v Elmbridge Borough
Council, ex p Oakimber Ltd
Oxford Diocesan Board of Finance v Secretary of State for Communities and
Local Government [2013] EWCA Civ 1718, [2014] JPL 530................ 9.36
Oxfordshire County Council v Secretary of State for Communities & Local
Government [2015] EWHC 186 (Admin), [2015] JPL 846, [2015]
PTSR D24 .... 6.17; 12.3, 12.39
Oxton Farms v Selby District Council (unreported, 18 April 1997)................ 8.18

P

PF Ahern (London) Ltd v Secretary of State for the Environment *see* R v
Secretary of State for the Environment, ex p PF Ahern (London) Ltd
PG Vallance Ltd v Secretary of State for the Environment [1993] 1 PLR 74,
[1994] JPL 50 .... 23.91
Palisade Investments Ltd v Secretary of State for the Environment &
Kensington & Chelsea Royal London Borough Council (1995) 69 P &
CR 638, [1994] 3 PLR 49, [1994] EG 188 (CS).................................. 3.21
Panayi v Secretary of State for the Environment (1980) 50 P & CR 109,
[1985] JPL 783 .... 2.27; 3.36, 3.37

Table of Cases

Parker v Secretary of State for Communities & Local Government [2009] EWHC 2330 (Admin) 6.90
Parkes v Secretary of State for the Environment [1978] 1 WLR 1308, [1979] 1 All ER 211, 77 LGR 39 .... 2.3
Patel v Brent London Borough Council (No 3) [2005] EWCA Civ 644, [2006] 1 P & CR 7, [2005] 3 PLR 114 .... 12.97
Payne v Secretary of State for Communities & Local Government [2010] EWHC 3528 (Admin), [2011] JPL 767 .... 22.38, 22.39; 23.128
Peche D'Or Investments v Secretary of State for the Environment [1996] JPL 311 .... 5.107
Pedgrift v Oxfordshire County Council (1991) 63 P & CR 246, [1992] JPL 731, [1991] EG 89 (CS) 25.92
Pennine Raceway Ltd v Kirklees Metropolitan Borough Council [1983] QB 382, [1982] 3 WLR 987, [1982] 3 All ER 628 .... 12.15
Pertemps Investments Ltd v Secretary of State for Communities and Local Government [2015] EWHC 2308 (Admin) 9.196
Petticoat Lane Rentals Ltd v Secretary of State for the Environment [1971] 1 WLR 1112, [1971] 2 All ER 793, 69 LGR 504 .... 4.17
Philgrow Ltd v Secretary of State for the Environment (1986) 51 P & CR 1, (1984) 270 EG 1192, [1985] JPL 318 .... 2.28
Phillips v First Secretary of State [2004] EWHC 2415 (Admin), [2003] 4 PLR 75, [2004] JPL 613 .... 5.37, 5.159; 9.164; 21.28, 21.29
Pilkington v Secretary of State [1973] 1 WLR 1527, [1974] 1 All ER 283, 72 LGR 303 .... 4.16; 29.48, 29.49, 29.50, 29.52, 29.53
Pioneer Aggregates (UK) Ltd v Secretary of State for the Environment [1985] AC 132, [1984] 3 WLR 32, [1984] 2 All ER 358 .... 2.4, 2.35; 4.16, 4.17, 4.20
Porter v Magill [2001] UKHL 67, [2002] 2 AC 257, [2002] 2 WLR 37 .... 8.68, 8.69, 8.74
Poundstretcher Ltd v Secretary of State for the Environment [1988] 3 PLR 69, [1989] JPL 90, [1988] EG 89 (CS) 9.178
Proberun Ltd v Secretary of State for the Environment (1991) 61 P & CR 77, [1990] 3 PLR 79, [1991] JPL 159 .... 16.16, 16.34
Prossor v Minister of Housing & Local Government (1968) 207 EG 139, 67 LGR 109, 118 NLJ 516 .... 4.17
Pugh v Secretary of State for Communities and Local Government [2015] EWHC 3 (Admin) 9.98
Pye v Secretary of State for the Environment, Transport & the Regions & North Cornwall District Council [1998] 3 PLR 72, [1999] PLCR 28, [1998] EG 80 (CS) 13.6, 13.7, 13.8; 29.47
Pyx Granite Co Ltd v Ministry of Housing & Local Government [1958] 1 QB 554, [1958] 2 WLR 371, [1958] 1 All ER 625 .... 11.6

Q
Qureshi v Barnet London Borough Council [2014] PAD 52 .... 5.108

R
R v Alnwick District Council, ex p Robson [1997] EWHC Admin 993 .... 6.114

Table of Cases

R v Amber Valley District Council, ex p Jackson [1985] 1 WLR 298, [1984] 3 All ER 501, (1985) 50 P & CR 136.................. 8.74
R v Arfon Borough Council, ex p Walton Commercial Group Ltd [1997] JPL 237................ 29.39, 29.50
R v Ashfield Borough Council, ex p Shepway District Council [1999] PLCR 12, [1998] JPL 1073 .... 6.13; 28.11
R v Ashfield District Council, ex p Bolsover District Council *see* R v Bolsover District Council, ex p Ashfield District Council & Nottinghamshire District Council
R v Ashford Borough Council, ex p Shepway District Council [1999] PLCR 12, [1998] JPL 1073 .... 16.5; 28.8, 28.9, 28.12, 28.13, 28.18
R v Aylesbury Vale District Council, ex p Chaplin (1998) 76 P & CR 207, [1997] 3 PLR 55, [1998] JPL 49 .... 9.210
R v Basildon District Council, ex p Martin Grant Homes Ltd (1987) 53 P & CR 397, [1987] JPL 863.................. 28.2
R v Bateman (Henry William) (1946) 31 Cr App R 106 .... 23.136
R v Berkshire County Council, ex p Wokingham District Council [1997] Env LR 545, (1997) 73 P & CR 430, [1997] 1 PLR 87 .... 6.17, 6.20
R v Bolsover District Council, ex p Ashfield District Council & Nottinghamshire District Council (1995) 70 P & CR 507, [195] 2 PLR 57, [1995] EG 73 .... 3.4; 6.13; 16.5
R v Bolsover District Council, ex p Paterson [2001] JPL 211, [2000] EG 83 (CS), (2000) 97 (27) LSG 40.................. 25.90
R v Bow Street Metropolitan Stipendiary Magistrate, ex p Pinochet Ugarte [2000] 1 AC 119 .... 8.78
R v Bradford City Council, ex p Corris [1990] 2 QB 363, [1990] 2 WLR 247, [1989] 3 All ER 156 .... 8.109
R v Braintree District Council, ex p Halls (2000) 80 P & CR 266.................. 12.106
R v Caradon District Council, ex p Lovejoy (1999) 78 P & CR 243, [2000] JPL 186.................. 5.45
R v Castle Point District Council, ex p Brooks [1985] JPL 473.................. 16.7
R v Chief Constable of the Merseyside Police, ex p Calveley [1986] QB 424, [1986] 2 WLR 144, [1986] 1 All ER 257.................. 25.11
R v Clewer (Brian Edward) (1953) 37 Cr App R 37 .... 23.136
R v Cotswold District Council, ex p Barrington Parish Council (1998) 75 P & CR 515.................. 25.52
R v Coventry City Council, ex p Arrowcroft Group plc [2001] PLCR 7 .... 11.27; 13.4, 13.5
R v Derbyshire County Council, ex p Poole [2001] PLCR 3, [2001] JPL 221 (Note).................. 8.61
R v East Hertfordshire District Council, ex p Beckman (1998) 76 P & CR 333, [1998] JPL 55, [1997] EG 104 (CS).................. 8.102
R v East Sussex County Council, ex p Reprotech (Pebsham) Ltd *see* R (on the application of Reprotech (Pebsham) Ltd) v East Sussex County Council
R v Elmbridge Borough Council, ex p Health Care Corpn & Prime Commercial Properties (1992) 4 Admin LR 242, (1991) 63 P & CR 260, [1991] 3 PLR 63.................. 29.18
R v Elmbridge Borough Council, ex p Oakimber Ltd (1991) 62 P & CR 594, [1991] 3 PLR 35, [1992] JPL 48 .... 29.18
R v Flintshire County Council, ex p Somerfield Stores [1998] PLCR 336, [1998] EG 53 (CS) 16.30; 29.20, 29.23

Table of Cases

R v Gillingham Borough Council, ex p Parham Ltd (1987) 58 P & CR 73, [1988] 1 PLR 7, [1988] JPL 336 .... 12.8
R v Hammersmith & Fulham London Borough Council, ex p Greater London Council (1985) 51 P & CR 120, [1986] JPL 528, (1985) 82 LSG 3532: 16.13
R v Hendon Rural District Council, ex p Chorley [1933] 2 KB 696 .... 8.87
R v Hereford & Worcester County Council, ex p Wellington Parish Council [1996] JPL 573, 94 LGR 159, (1996) 160 LG Rev 161 .... 8.61
R v Hillingdon London Borough Council, ex p Royco Homes Ltd [1974] QB 720, [1974] 2 WLR 805, [1974] 2 All ER 643 .... 11.6, 11.27; 25.25
R v Kensington & Chelsea Royal London Borough Council [1999] 1 WLR 1415, [1999] 3 All ER 929, (2000) 79 P & CR 467 .... 2.50
R v Lambeth London Borough Council, ex p Sharp (1986) 55 P & CR 232, [1987] JPL 440 .... 23.56
R v Lambeth London Borough Council, ex p Sharp (1988) 55 P & CR 232, [1987] JPL 440 .... 6.129
R v Lancashire County Council, ex p Huddleston [1986] 2 All ER 941, (1986) 136 NLJ 562 .... 25.76
R v Leeds City Council, ex p Hendry (unreported, 14 December 1993) 25.24
R v Leicester City Council, ex p Powergen UK plc (2001) 81 P & CR 5, [2000] JPL 1037, [2000] EG 64 .... 13.7, 13.8, 13.18; 29.22, 29.35, 29.47
R v London Borough of Bromley, ex p Barker *see* R (on the application of Barker) v Bromley London Borough Council
R v London Borough of Bromley, ex p Barker (C-290/03) *see* R (on the application of Barker) v Bromley London Borough Council (Case C-290/03)
R v London Borough of Hammersmith & Fulham, ex p CPRE London Branch (Leave to Appeal) (No 1) [2000] Env LR 549, (2001) 81 P & CR 7 ..... 7.6
R v London County Council, ex p Akkersdyk [1892] 1 QB 190 .... 8.88
R v London Docklands Development Corpn, ex p Sister Christine Frost (1997) 73 P & CR 199 .... 13.7
R v Mendip District Council, ex p Fabre (2000) 80 P & CR 500, [2000] JPL 810, [2000] COD 372 .... 8.20, 8.23, 8.103
R v Monopolies and Mergers Commission ex p Argyll Group [1986] 1 WLR 763 .... 25.40
R v Newbury District Council, ex p Chieveley Parish Council (1998) 10 Admin LR 676, [1999] PLCR 51, [1998] EG 131 (CS) 16.5, 16.6, 16.7
R v Newbury District Council, ex p Stevens & Partridge (1993) 65 P & CR 438, [1992] 3 PLR 34, [1992] JPL 1057 .... 16.16
R v North Yorkshire County Council, ex p Brown [2000] 1 AC 397, [1999] 2 WLR 452, [1999] 1 All ER 969 .... 7.6
R v Richmond-upon-Thames London Borough Council, ex p McCarthy & Stone (Developments) Ltd *see* McCarthy & Stone (Developments) Ltd v Richmond upon Thames London Borough Council [1992] 2 AC 48, [1991] 3 WLR 941, [1991] 4 All ER 897 .... 12.103
R v Rochdale Metropolitan Borough Council, ex p Milne (No 1) [2000] Env LR 1, [1999] 3 PLR 74, [2000] JPL 54 .... 6.14; 7.6
R v Rochdale Metropolitan Borough Council, ex p Milne (No 2) [2001] Env LR 22, (2001) 81 P & CR 27, [2001] JPL 470 .... 6.14

Table of Cases

R v Rochdale Metropolitan Borough Council, ex p Tew *see* R v Rochdale Metropolitan Borough Council, ex p Milne (No 1)
R v Royal Borough of Kensington and Chelsea, ex p Stoop [1992] 1 PLR 58, [1991] JPL 1129, [1992] COD 87 .... 9.210
R v St Edmundsbury Borough Council, ex p Walton [1999] Env LR 879, (1999) 11 Admin LR 648, [1999] JPL 805 .... 7.44
R v Salford Assessment Committee, ex p Ogden [1937] 2 KB 1, [1937] 2 All ER 98 .... 8.81
R v Secretary of State for the Environment & SJ Investments, ex p Allied London Property Investments Ltd [1991] JPL 637 .... 25.15
R v Secretary of State for the Environment, ex p Baber [1996] JPL 1034 ...... 9.195
R v Secretary of State for the Environment, ex p Corby Borough Council (1994) 68 P & CR 544, [1994] 1 PLR 38 .... 13.10
R v Secretary of State for the Environment, ex p Ealing London Borough Council (unreported, 22 April 1999) 25.29
R v Secretary of State for the Environment ex p Gosport Borough Council [1992] JPL 476 .... 24.12
R v Secretary of State for the Environment, ex p Kent (1989) 57 P & CR 431, [1988] 3 PLR 17, [1988] JPL 706 .... 23.56
R v Secretary of State for the Environment, ex p Kirkstall Valley Campaign Ltd [1996] 3 All ER 304, [1997] 1 PLR 8, [1996] JPL 1042 .... 8.66, 8.78
R v Secretary of State for the Environment, ex p Leeds City Council [1995] JPL B61 .... 23.49
R v Secretary for the Environment, ex p Middlesbrough Borough Council [1988] 3 PLR 52 .... 17.43
R v Secretary of State for the Environment, ex p PF Ahern (London) Ltd [1998] Env LR 189, [1998 JPL 351, [1997] EG 94 (CS) 9.192
R v Secretary of State for the Environment, ex p Percy Bilton Industrial Properties Ltd (1975) 31 P & CR 154, 74 LGR 244, (1975) 237 EG 491 .... 29.21, 29.40
R v Secretary of State for the Environment, ex p Slough Borough Council (1995) 70 P & CR 560, 94 LGR 376, (1995) JPL 1128 .... 28.8
R v Secretary of State for the Environment, Transport & the Regions, ex p Alliance against the Birmingham Northern Relief Road (No 2) [1999] JPL 426, [1998] EG 146 (CS), [1998] NPC 143 .... 9.170
R v Secretary of State for the Environment, Transport & the Regions, ex p Bath & North East Somerset Council [1999] 1 WLR 1759, [1999] 4 All ER 418, (1999) 11 Admin LR 997 .... 6.92
R v Secretary of State for the Environment, Transport & the Regions & the National Assembly for Wales (CO/3109/99, 24 November 1999) 25.41
R v Solihull Borough Council, ex p Berkswell Parish Council (1998) 77 P & CR 312 .... 9.176
R v Somerset County Council, ex p Dixon [1998] Env LR 111, (1998) 75 P & CR 175, [1997] JPL 1030 .... 12.13; 25.40
R v South Northamptonshire District Council, ex p Crest Homes plc [1994] 3 PLR 47, 93 LGR 205, [1994] EG 158 (CS) 12.7
R v Surrey County Council, ex p Bridge Court Holdings Ltd [2000] 4 PLR 30, [2000] PLCR 344, (2000) 97 (8) LSG 38 .... 6.50
R v Sussex Justices, ex p McCarthy [1924] 1 KB 256 .... 8.81
R v Swale Borough Council, ex p Royal Society for the Protection of Birds (1990) 2 Admin LR 790, [1991] 1 PLR 6, [1991] JPL 39 .... 7.32

Table of Cases

R v Swansea City Council, ex p Elitestone Ltd (1993) 66 P & CR 422, [1993]
2 PLR 65, [1993] 46 EG 181... 2.8; 8.33
R v Teeside Development Corpn, ex p William Morrison Supermarket plc
[1998] JPL 23, [1997] NPC 78.. 8.62
R v Thanet District Council, ex p Tapp *see* R (on the application of Tapp) v
Thanet District Council
R v Waltham Forest London Borough Council, ex p Baxter [1988] QB 419,
[1988] 2 WLR 257, [1987] 3 All ER 671.. 8.77
R v Wealden District Council, ex p Charles Church South East Ltd (1990) 59
P & CR 150, [19889] JPL 837, [1989] COD 565 .... 12.8
R v West Dorset District Council, ex p Searle [1999] JPL 331 .... 9.98
R v Westminster Council, ex p Monahan [1990] 1 QB 87, [1989] 3 WLR 408,
[1989] 2 All ER 74 .... 9.169; 12.37
R v West Oxfordshire District Council, ex p C H Pearce Homes Ltd (1986)
RVR 156, [1986] JPL 523 .... 14.3
R v Yeovil Borough Council, ex p Trustees of Elim Pentecostal Church,
Yeovil (1972) 23 P & CR 39, 70 LGR 142, (1972) 116 SJ 78....... 14.20; 24.62
RG Kensington Management Co Ltd v Hutchinson IDH Ltd [2002] EWHC
1180 (Ch), [2003] 2 P & CR 13 .... 12.27
RJ Williams Le Roi v Secretary of State for the Environment [1993] JPL
1033, [1993] EG 23 (CS), [1993] NPC 17.. 5.56
RWE Npower Renewables Ltd v Welsh Ministers [2012] EWCA Civ 311,
[2012] Env LR 39.. 23.135; 24.24
R (on the application of Adlard) v Secretary of State for Transport, Local
Government & the Regions [2002] EWCA Civ 735, [2002] 1 WLR
2515, [2002] HRLR 37... 17.37, 17.41
R (on the application of Akester) v Department for the Environment, Food &
Rural Affairs [2010] EWHC 232 (Admin), [2010] Env LR 33, [2010]
ACD 44... 24.23
R (on the application of Alconbury Developments) v Secretary of State for
the Environment, Transport & the Regions *see* R (on the application
of Holding & Barnes plc) v Secretary of State for the Environment,
Transport & the Regions
R (on the application of Ashley) v Secretary of State for Communities &
Local Government [2012] EWCA Civ 559, [2012] JPL 1235 .... 20.31;
21.28, 21.30
R (on the application of BT) v Gloucester City Council [2001] EWHC Admin
1001, [2002] 2 P & CR 33, [2002] JPL 993... 7.44
R (on the application of Baker) v Bath and North East Somerset District
Council [2009] EWHC 595 (Admin), [2009] JPL 1498 .... 7.18
R (on the application of Barker) v Bromley London Borough Council [2001]
EWCA Civ 1766, [2002] Env LR 25, [2002] 2 P & CR 8 .... 7.6
R (on the application of Barker) v Bromley London Borough Council (Case
C-290/03) [2006] QB 764, [2006] 3 WLR 492, [2006] ECR I-3949..... 7.6
R (on the application of Barker) v Bromley London Borough Council [2006]
UKHL 52, [2007] 1 AC 470, [2006] 3 WLR 1209................................ 7.6
R (on the application of Barr) v North Somerset Council [2015] EWHC 1735
(Admin) 15.24
R (on the application of Basildon) v First Secretary of State [2004] EWHC
2759 (Admin), [2005] JPL 942 .... 9.81
R (on the application of Batchelor Enterprises Ltd) v North Dorset District
Council [2003] EWHC 3006 (Admin), [2004] JPL 1222 .... 12.61, 12.72

Table of Cases

R (on the application of Bateman) v South Cambridgeshire District Council [2011] EWCA Civ 157, [2011] NPC 22 .... 7.37, 7.47
R (on the application of Bedford) v Islington London Borough Council [2002] EWHC 2044 (Admin), [2003] Env LR 22............................ 8.37, 8.40, 8.41; 9.185
R (on the application of Belgrave Land) v Bedford Borough Council [2001] EWHC Admin 1127 .... 16.5, 16.15; 25.19; 28.15
R (on the application of Berky) v Newport City Council [2012] EWCA Civ 378, [2012] 2 CMLR 44, [2012] Env LR 35...................................... 5.46; 7.47; 8.78; 25.50
R (on the application of Bibb) v Bristol City Council [2011] EWHC 3057 (Admin), [2012] JPL 565 .... 9.206
R (on the application of Billings) v First Secretary of State [2005] EWHC 2274 (Admin), [2006] JPL 693 .... 19.22
R (on the application of Bishop's Stortford Civic Federation) v East Hertfordshire District Council [2014] EWHC 348 (Admin), [2014] PTSR 1035, [2014] BLGR 161 .... 8.85
R (on the application of Bleaklow Industries Ltd) v Secretary of State for Communities & Local Government [2009] EWCA Civ 206, [2009] 2 P & CR 21, [2009] JPL 1477... 29.9
R (on the application of Blewett) v Derbyshire County Council [2004] EWCA Civ 1508, [2005] Env LR 15, [2005] JPL 620 .... 9.158
R (on the application of Blue Green London Plan) v Secretary of State for the Environment, Food & Rural Affairs [2015] EWHC 495 (Admin)......... 25.46, 25.50
R (on the application of Brown) v Carlisle City Council [2010] EWCA Civ 523, [2011] Env LR 5, [2010] JPL 1571.. 7.42
R (on the application of Buglife: The Invertebrate Conservation Trust) v Thurrock Thames Gateway Development Corpon [2008] EWHC 475, [2008] Env LR 31, [2008] 2 P & CR 7.. 9.146
R (on the application of Burkett) v London Borough of Hammersmith & Fulham (No 1) [2001] Env LR 39, [2001] 3 PLR 1, [2001] JPL 775*revs'd* [2002] UKHL 23, [2002] 1 WLR 1593, [2002] 3 All ER 97: 1.50; 14.3; 25.19, 25.20, 25.47, 25.50, 25.88
R (on the application of Burridge) v Breckland District Council [2013] EWCA 228, [2013] JPL 1308, [2013] 18 EG 102 (CS)......................... 7.32
R (on the application of CBRE Lionbrook (General Partners) Ltd) v Rugby Borough Council [2014] EWHC 646 (Admin), [2014] Env LR D3 ...... 7.54
R (on the application of Cala Homes (South) Ltd) v Secretary of State for Communities & Local Government [2010] EWHC 2866 (Admin), [2011] BLGR 204, [2010] JPL 553.. 1.25
R (on the application of Cala Homes (South) Ltd v Secretary of State for Communities & Local Government (No 3) [2011] EWCA Civ 639, [2011] 2 EGLR 75, [2011] JPL 1458.. 1.25; 9.181, 9.189
R (on the application of Campaign for Real Ale) v Bradford Metropolitan Borough Council 25.117
R (on the application of Campbell Court Property) v Secretary of State for the Environment, Transport & the Regions [2001] EWHC Admin 102, [2002] PLCR 4, [2001] JPL 1322 (Note)... 28.14

Table of Cases

R (on the application of Candlish) v Hastings Borough Council [2005]
 EWHC 1539 (Admin), [2006] Env LR 13, [2006] JPL 22 .... 7.32
R (on the application of Carlton-Conway) v Harrow London Borough Council
 [2002] EWCA Civ 927, [2002] 3 PLR 77, [2002] JPL 1216................ 8.17
R (on the application of Carroll) v South Somerset District Council [2008]
 EWHC 104 (Admin), [2008] JPL 991, [2008] ACD 40................ 11.37; 12.29
R (on the application of Catt) v Brighton & Hove City Council [2007] EWCA
 Civ 298, [2007] Env LR 32, [2007] JPL 1517 .... 7.41;
 25.19, 25.20
R (on the application of Champion) v North Norfolk District Council [2013]
 EWHC 1065 (Admin), [2013] Env LR 38; rev'sd [2013] EWCA Civ
 1657, [2014] Env LR 23; aff'd [2015] UKSC 52, [2015] 1 WLR 3710,
 [2015] 4 All ER 169 .... 7.40, 7.41;
 8.3; 9.136;
 25.19, 25.86
R (on the application of Chelmsford Car & Commercial Ltd) v Chelmsford
 Borough Council [2005] EWHC 1705 (Admin), [2006] 2 P & CR 12,
 [2006] JPL 375 .... 9.165
R (on the application of Cherkley Campaign Ltd) v Mole Valley District
 Council [2013] EWHC 2582 (Admin), [2014] 1 P & CR 12, [2014]
 ACD 42... 9.23, 9.24, 9.122
R (on the application of Cherwell District Council) v First Secretary of State
 [2004] EWCA Civ 1420, [2005] 1 WLR 1128, [2005] 1 P & CR 22 .... 6.61
R (on the application of Commercial Estates Group) v Secretary of State
 for Communities & Local Government [2014] EWHC 3089 (Admin),
 [2015] JPL 350 .... 25.19
R (on the application of Condron) v National Assembly for Wales [2006]
 EWCA Civ 1573, [2007] BLGR 87, [2007] JPL 938 .... 8.61
R (on the application of Copeland) v London Borough of Tower Hamlets
 [2010] EWHC 1845 (Admin), [2010] LLR 654, [2011] JPL 40............ 9.86
R (on the application of Corbett) v Cornwall Council [2013] EWHC 3958
 (Admin), [2014] PTSR 727... 7.70
R (on the application of Corbett) v First Secretary of State [2005] EWHC
 2433 (Admin), [2006] 1 P & CR 32, [2006] JPL 505 .... 19.47
R (on the application of Corner House Research) v Secretary of State for
 Trade & Industry [2005] EWCA Civ 192, [2005] 1 WLR 2600, [2005]
 4 All ER 1 .... 25.102, 25.103
R (on the application of Corrie) v Suffolk County Council [2014] EWHC
 2490 (Admin), [2015] Env LR 5.. 15.13
R (on the application of Corus UK Ltd (t/a Orb Electrical Steels) v Newport
 City Council [2010] EWCA Civ 1626 .... 25.86
R (on the application of Costas Georgiou) v London Borough of Enfield
 [2004] EWHC 779 (Admin), [2004] BLGR 497, [2004] 2 P & CR 21 .. 8.70,
 8.71, 8.74
R (on the application of Crownhall Estates Ltd) v Chichester District Council
 CO/3299/2014 .... 26.43
R (on the application of Crownhall Estates Ltd) v Chichester District Council
 CO/2669/2015 .... 26.43
R (on the application of Cummins) v London Borough of Camden [2001]
 EWHC Admin 1116 .... 8.69
R (on the application of Daniel) v East Devon District Council [2013] EWHC
 4114 (Admin) 15.23

Table of Cases

R (on the application of Davey) v Aylesbury Vale District Council [2007] EWCA Civ 1166, [2008] 1 WLR 878, [2008] 2 All ER 178 .... 25.61
R (on the application of Davies) v Carmarthenshire County Council [2015] EWHC 230 (Admin), [2015] Env LR 29, [2015] JPL 908 .... 7.37
R (on the application of Davies) v Secretary of State for Communities & Local Government [2008] EWHC 2223 (Admin), [2009] ACD 12 .... 7.42
R (on the application of Daws Hill Neighbourhood Forum) v Wycombe District Council [2014] EWCA Civ 228, [2014] 1 WLR 1362, [2014] PTSR 570 .... 26.25
R (on the application of Derwent Holdings Ltd) v Trafford Borough Council [2011] EWCA Civ 832, [2011] NPC 78 .... 12.36
R (on the application of Dry) v West Oxfordshire District Council [2010] EWCA Civ 1143, [2011] 1 P & CR 16, [2011] JPL 579 .... 9.10
R (on the application of Eastleigh Borough Council) v First Secretary of State [2004] EWHC 1408 (Admin), [2004] 24 EG (CS), (2005) 101 (24) LSG 33 .... 3.3
R (on the application of Edwards) v Environment Agency (C-260/11) [2013] UKSC 78, [2014] 1 WLR 55, [2014] 1 All ER 760 .... 25.103
R (on the application of Ellaway) v Cardiff County Council [2014] EWHC 836 (Admin), [2015] Env LR 19, [2014] PTSR D12 .... 29.21
R (on the application of Elvington Park Ltd) v York Crown Court [2011] EWHC 2213 (Admin), [2012] Env LR 10, [2011] LLR 833 .... 23.95
R (on the application of Embleton Parish Council) v Northumberland County Council [2013] EWHC 3631 (Admin), [2014] Env LR 16 .... 6.114, 6.117, 6.124; 7.50; 9.56; 25.80
R (on the application of English) v East Staffordshire Borough Council [2010] EWHC 2744 (Admin), [2011] JPL 586, [2011] ACD 34 .... 8.41
R (on the application of Evans) v Attorney General [2015] UKSC 21, [2015] AC 1787, [2015] 2 WLR 813 .... 8.28
R (on the application of Ewing) v Office of the Deputy Prime Minister [2005] EWCA Civ 1583, [2006] 1 WLR 1260, [2006] LLR 18 .... 25.61
R (on the application of Freud) v Oxford City Council [2013] EWHC 4613 (Admin) 8.84
R (on the application of Friends of Basildon Golf Course) v Basildon District Council [2010] EWCA Civ 1432, [2011] Env LR 16, (2010) 154 (48) SJLB 35 .... 7.47
R (on the application of Friends of Hethel) v South Norfolk Council [2010] EWCA Civ 894, [2011] 1 WLR 1216, [2011] PTSR 630 .... 6.124, 6.129; 7.78; 8.13, 8.14, 8.110; 11.19
R (on the application of Friends of the Earth England, Wales and Northern Ireland) v Welsh Ministers [2015] EWHC 776 (Admin), [2016] Env LR 1, [2015] PTSR D28 .... 9.145
R (on the application of Garden and Leisure Group Ltd) v North Somerset Council [2003] EWHC 1605 (Admin), [2004] JPL 232 .... 12.75
R (on the application of Garner) v Elmbridge Borough Council [2010] EWCA Civ 1006, [2011] 3 All ER 418, [2012] PTSR 250 .... 25.103
R (on the application of Garner) v Elmbridge Borough Council [2011] EWHC 86 (Admin); aff'd [2011] EWCA Civ 891, [2012] JPL 119 ..... 9.92
R (on the application of Gavin) v London Borough of Haringey [2003] EWHC 2591 (Admin), [2004] 2 P & CR 13, [2004] 1 PLR 61 .... 25.51

Table of Cases

R (on the application of Gerber) v Wiltshire Councl [2015] EWHC 524 (Admin), [2015] Env LR 33, [2015] JPL 1021 .... 6.117, 6.129; 25.51
R (on the application of Ghadami) v Harlow Borough Council [2004] EWHC 1883 (Admin), [2005] BLGR 24, [2005] 1 P & CR 19 .... 8.71
R (on the application of Gibson) v Waverley Borough Council [2012] EWHC 1472 (Admin) 6.130
R (on the application of Gilbert) v Secretary of State for Communities & Local Government [2014] EWHC 1952 (Admin); aff'd [2015] EWCA Civ 314 .... 7.51; 25.19
R (on the application of Gill) v Central Bedfordshire Council [2015] EWHC 3458 (Admin) 6.104, 6.108
R (on the application of Gleeson Developments Ltd) v Secretary of State for Communities & Local Government [2014] EWCA Civ 1118, [2014] PTSR 1226, [2014] JPL 1386 .... 14.21; 17.63, 17.64; 24.53, 24.63
R (on the application of Goodman) v London Borough of Lewisham [2003] EWCA Civ 140, [2003] Env LR 28, [2003] JPL 1309.................... 7.16, 7.21, 7.31, 7.37, 7.45
R (on the application of Gopie) v Mayor of London [2002] EWHC 656 (Admin) 10.20, 10.22
R (on the application of Gopie) v Mayor of London [2002] EWCA Civ 1186... 25.23
R (on the application of Gregan) v Hartlepool Borough Council [2003] EWHC 3278 (Admin), [2004] JPL 1088... 28.16
R (on the application of Grove Park Community Group) v London Borough of Lewisham (CO/7847/2011).. 8.14
R (on the application of Groves) v Boston Borough Council [2014] EWHC 3950 (Admin) 25.80, 28.22
R (on the application of H) v Ashworth Special Hospital Authority [2002] EWCA Civ 923, [2003] 1 WLR 127, (2002) 5 CCL Rep 390 .... 25.108
R (on the application of HS2 Action Alliance) v Secretary of State for Transport [2014] EWHC 2759 (Admin), [2014] PTSR 1334, [2015] JPL 309; aff'd [2015] EWCA Civ 203, [2015] PTSR 1025, [2015] 2 Costs LR 411 .... 17.26; 25.101
R (on the application of Halebank Parish Council) v Halton Borough Council; Avich & Kilchrenan Community Council (Aarhus Convention Compliance Committee: ACCC/2012/68).. 25.101
R (on the application of Hall Hunter Partnership) v First Secretary of State [2006] EWHC 3482, [2007] 2 P & CR 5, [2007] JPL 1023 .... 2.8; 5.130
R (on the application of Hammerton) v London Underground Ltd [2002] EWHC 2307 (Admin), [2003] JPL 984, [2002] 47 EG 148 (CS) 25.115; 29.19, 29.23, 29.26, 29.27
R (on the application of Hampton Bishop Parish Council) v Herefordshire Council [2014] EWCA Civ 878, [2015] 1 WLR 2367 .... 9.20, 9.21; 12.36, 12.38
R (on the application of Harbige) v Secretary of State for Communities & Local Government [2012] EWHC 1128 (Admin), [2012] JPL 1245..... 3.4
R (on the application of Harris) v Secretary of State for Communities & Local Government [2014] EWHC 3740 (Admin)............................... 20.29
R (on the application of Harrison) v Richmond upon Thames London Borough Council [2013] EWHC 1677 (Admin).................................... 6.104

Table of Cases

R (on the application of Hart Aggregates Ltd) v Hartlepool Borough Council [2005] EWHC 840 (Admin), [2005] 2 P & CR 31, [2005] JPL 1602.... 29.19, 29.27, 29.29, 29.30, 29.32, 29.33

R (on the application of Hart DC) v Secretary of State for Communities & Local Government [2008] EWHC 1204 (Admin), [2008] 2 P & CR 16, [2009] JPL 365 .... 9.136, 9.138; 24.23

R (on the application of Hasan) v Secretary of State for Trade and Industry [2008] EWCA Civ 1312.. 24.19

R (on the application of Hautot) v London Borough of Wandsworth [2003] EWHC 900 Admin 13.35

R (on the application of Health & Safety Executive) v Wolverhampton City Council [2012] UKSC 34, [2012] 1 WLR 2264, [2012] 4 All ER 429.. 4.26; 9.8, 9.63, 9.170

R (on the application of Henry Boot Homes Ltd) v Bassetlaw District Council 2002] EWHC 546 (Admin), [2002] JPL 1224, [2002] 13 EG 100 (CS): 29.21

R (on the application of Hewitson) v Guildford Borough Council [2011] EWHC 3440 (Admin), [2012] BLGR 637, [2012] JPL 951 .... 8.109, 8.110

R (on the application of Holder) v Gedling Borough Council [2013] EWHC 1611 (Admin), [2013] JPL 1426 .... 7.48; 14.20; 24.62

R (on the application of Holder) v Gedling Borough Council [2014] EWCA Civ 599, [2014] JPL 1087 .... 9.82, 9.83, 9.168, 9.180; 25.86, 25.88

R (on the application of Horner) v Lancashire County Council [2007] EWCA Civ 784, [2008] Env LR 10, [2008] JPL 209 .... 7.21

R (on the application of Holding & Barnes plc) v Secretary of State for the Environment, Transport & the Regions [2001] UKHL 23, [2003] 2 AC 295, [2001] 2 WLR 1389... 9.3; 17.1

R (on the application of Hossack) v Kettering Borough Council [2002] EWCA Civ 886, [2003] 2 P & CR 34, [2002] 2 PLR 114 .... 3.36, 3.47

R (on the application of Hourhope Ltd) v Shropshire Council [2015] EWHC 518 (Admin), [2015] PTSR 933 .... 27.28

R (on the application of Hunt) v North Somerset Council [2015] UKSC 51, [2015] 1 WLR 3575, [2016] 1 All ER 95... 25.94

R (on the application of IM Properties Development Ltd) v Lichfield District Council [2014] EWHC 2440 (Admin), [2014] PTSR 1484.................. 8.77

R (on the application of I'm Your Man Ltd) v North Somerset Council [2004] EWHC 342, [2004] 4 PLR 1, [2004] JPL 1563 .... 2.30

R (on the application of Island Farm Development Ltd) v Bridgend County Borough Council [2006] EWHC 2189 (Admin), [2007] BLGR 60, [2007] LLR 230... 8.61

R (on the application of Islington London Borough Council) v Secretary of State for Communities & Local Government [2013] EWHC 4009 (Admin) 5.97

R (on the application of J (a child) v North Warwickshire Borough Council [2001] EWCA Civ 315, [2001] 2 PLR 59[2001] PLCR 31 .... 9.165

R (on the application of JM & NT) v Isle of Wight Council [2011] EWHC 2911 (Admin), [2012] Eq LR 34, (2012) 15 CCL Rep 167 .... 9.155

R (on the application of Jedwell) v Denbighshire County Council [2015] EWCA 1232 .... 7.49; 25.80

R (on the application of Joicey) v Northumberland County Council [2014] EWHC 3657 (Admin), [2015] PTSR 622, [2015] BLGR 1 .... 6.114, 6.117; 8.24, 8.34, 8.38

Table of Cases

R (on the application of Jones) v English Heritage CO/1932/2013................. 25.121
R (on the application of Jones) v Mansfield District Council [2003] EWCA
    Civ 1408, [2004] Env LR 21, [2004] Env LR 391 .... 7.37, 7.41
R (on the application of Kelly) v London Borough of Hounslow [2010]
    EWHC 1256 (Admin) 1.44; 6.114, 6.117
R (on the application of Kelton) v Wiltshire Council [2015] EWHC 2853
    (Admin).. 8.69, 8.84
R (on the application of Kides) v South Cambridgeshire District Council
    [2002] EWCA Civ 1370, [2003] 1 P & CR 19, [2002] 4 PLR 66 .... 1.47;
                                                                                9.9; 24.17; 25.40
R (on the application of Koumis) v Secretary of State for Communities &
    Local Government [2012] EWHC 2686 (Admin), [2013] JPL 215 .... 25.113
R (on the application of Kverndal) v London Borough of Hounslow [2015]
    EWHC 3084 (Admin) 9.192
R (on the application of Lady Hart of Chilton) v Babergh District Council
    [2014] EWHC 3261 (Admin), [2015] JPL 491............................... 9.98; 17.16
R (on the application of Lebus) v South Cambridgeshire District Council
    [2002] EWHC 2009 (Admin), [2003] Env LR 17, [2003] JPL 466....... 7.23,
                                                                                7.38, 7.39, 7.41, 7.43
R (on the application of Lee Valley Regional Park Authority) v Broxbourne
    Borough Council [2015] EWHC 185 (Admin)....................................... 9.85
R (on the application of Lewis) v Redcar & Cleveland Borough Council
    [2008] EWCA Civ 746, [2009] 1 WLR 83, [2008] BLGR 781 .... 8.70,
                                                                                8.72, 8.73, 8.74
R (on the application of Lichfield Securities Ltd) v Lichfield District Council
    [2001] EWCA Civ 304, [2001] PLCR 32.. 12.31
R (on the application of Ling (Bridlington) Ltd) v East Riding of Yorkshire
    Council [2006] EWHC 1604 (Admin), [2007] JPL 396 .... 8.98, 8.99
R (on the application of Littman) v London Borough of Barnet [2007] EWHC
    3411 (Admin).. 5.95
R (on the application of Loader) v Secretary of State for Communities &
    Local Government [2012] EWCA Civ 869, [2013] PTSR 406, [2012] 3
    CMLR 29... 7.37
R (on the application of Lowther) v Durham County Council [2001] EWCA
    Civ 781, [2002] Env LR 13, [2002] JPL 197 .... 8.19
R (on the application of Lucchetti) v South Norfolk District Council [2012]
    EWHC 3557 (Admin) 5.51
R (on the application of Lyons) v Secretary of State for Communities & Local
    Government [2010] EWHC 3652 (Admin).. 5.138
R (on the application of McClellan) v London Borough of Lambeth [2014]
    EWHC 1964 (Admin) 8.21
R (on the application of Majed) v London Borough of Camden [2009] EWCA
    Civ 1029, [2010] JPL 621 .... 1.38; 6.113,
                                                                                6.114, 6.117;
                                                                                23.56; 25.88
R (on the application of Malster) v Ipswich Borough Council [2001] EWHC
    Admin 711, [2002] PLCR 14, [2002] Env LR D7 .... 7.37
R (on the application of Marson) v Secretary of State for the Environment,
    Transport & the Regions [1999] 1 CMLR 268, [1998] Env LR 761,
    (1999) 77 P & CR 202.. 7.45
R (on the application of Mayor of London) v First Secretary of State [2008]
    EWHC 631 (Admin), [2008] NPC 41... 10.35

Table of Cases

R (on the application of Mellor) v Secretary of State for Communities & Local Government C-75/08 [2010] PTSR 880, [2009] ECR I-3799, [2010] Env LR 2 .... 7.46, 7.47, 7.50
R (on the application of Midcounties Co-operative Ltd) v Wyre Forest District Council [2009] EWHC 964 (Admin) 5.47; 11.29; 12.32; 15.5; 25.93
R (on the application of Mid-Counties Co-operative Ltd) v Wyre Forest District Council [2010] EWCA Civ 841, [2011] JPL 173, [2010] 32 EG 60 (CS) 28.11
R (on the application of Mid-Suffolk District Council) v Secretary of State for Communities & Local Government [2009] EWHC 3649 (Admin) 24.60; 25.28; 28.4
R (on the application of Miller) v North Yorkshire County Council [2009] EWHC 2172 (Admin) 9.91
R (on the application of Millgate Developments Ltd) v Wokingham Borough Council [2011] EWCA Civ 1062, [2012] 3 EGLR 87, [2012] 39 EG 120 .... 12.7, 12.58, 12.61
R (on the application of Milton Keynes Council) v Secretary of State for Communities & Local Government [2011] EWCA Civ 1575, [2012] JPL 728, [2012] ACD 40 .... 3.48
R (on the application of Morge) v Hampshire County Council [2010] EWCA Civ 608, [2010] PTSR 1882, [2011] Env LR 8; aff'd [2011] UKSC 2, [2011] 1 WLR 268, [2011] 1 All ER 744 .... 7.37; 9.142
R (on the application of Morland) v Secretary of State for Communities & Local Government [2009] EWHC 310 (Admin), [2010] JPL 176 .... 29.17
R (on the application of Mount Cook) v Westminster City Council [2003] EWCA Civ 1346, [2004] CP Rep 12, [2004] JPL 470 .... 9.162; 25.66
R (on the application of National Association of Health Stores) v Secretary of State for Health [2005] EWCA Civ 154 .... 24.10
R (on the application of Newsmith Stainless Ltd) v Secretary of State for the Environment, Transport & the Regions [2001] EWHC Admin 74 .... 25.7
R (on the application of Noble Organisation Ltd) v Thanet District Council [2005] EWCA Civ 782, [2006] Env LR 8, [2006] 1 P & CR 13 .... 7.43
R (on the application of O'Brien) v West Lancashire District Council [2012] EWHC 2376 (Admin) 6.51
R (on the application of Obar Camden Limited) v London Borough of Camden [2015] EWHC 2475 .... 6.86
R (on the application of Orange Personal Communications Services Ltd) v Islington London Borough Council [2005] EWHC 963 (Admin), [2006] 1 P & CR 12, [2006] JPL 396 aff'd [2006] EWCA Civ 157, [2006] JPL 1309, (2006) 103 (6) LSG 30 .... 5.60, 5.63
R (on the application of Ortona) v Secretary of State for Communities & Local Government [2009] EWCA Civ 863, [2010] 1 P & CR 15, [2010] JPL 361 .... 23.120
R (on the application of Park Pharmacy Trust) v Plymouth City Council [2008] EWHC 445 (Admin), [2008] 2 P & CR 11 .... 6.57, 6.90; 8.100
R (on the application of Payne) v Secretary of State for Communities & Local Government CO/8053/2011 .... 25.113
R (on the application of Peel Land & Property Investments plc) v Hyndburn Borough Council [2013] EWCA Civ 1680 .... 28.5
R (on the application of Perry) v Hackney London Borough Council [2014] EWHC 1721 (Admin), [2014] JPL 1329 .... 8.41

Table of Cases

R (on the application of Persimmon Homes Ltd) v Secretary of State for Communities & Local Government [2007] EWHC 1985 (Admin), [2008] JPL 323 .... 17.43, 17.44
R (on the application of Plant) v Pembrokeshire County Council [2014] EWHC 1040 (Admin), [2015] Env LR D4 .... 7.49
R (on the application of Plunkett) v Sefton Borough Council [2011] EWHC 368 (Admin) 25.86
R (on the application of Prideaux) v Buckinghamshire County Council [2013] EWHC 1054 (Admin), [2013] Env LR 32 .... 9.142
R (on the application of Pridmore) v Salisbury District Council [2004] EWHC 2511 (Admin), [2005] 1 P & CR 32, [2005] JPL 655 .... 6.51, 6.90
R (on the application of Prokopp) v London Underground Ltd [2003] EWCA Civ 961, [2004] Env LR 8, [2004] JPL 44 .... 13.35; 25.81; 28.19; 29.26, 29.27
R (on the application of Prudential Assurance Ltd) v Sunderland City Council [2010] EWHC 1771 (Admin), [2011] JPL 322 .... 2.17; 28.5
R (on the application of RB) v Devon County Council [2012] EWHC 3597 (Admin), [2013] Eq LR 113 .... 9.154
R (on the application of RWE Npower Renewables) v Milton Keynes Council [2013] EWHC 751 (Admin) 9.28
R (on the application of Raissi) v Secretary of State for the Home Department [2008] EWCA Civ 72, [2008] QB 836, [2008] 3 WLR 375 .... 9.43
R (on the application of Redditch Borough Council) v First Secretary of State [2003] EWHC 650 (Admin), [2003] 2 P & CR 25, [2004] JPL 21 .... 25.21
R (on the application of Renaissance Habitat Ltd) v West Berkshire Council [2011] EWHC 242 (Admin), [2011] 2 EGLR 80, [2011] JPL 1209 ...... 12.58, 12.61, 12.72, 12.73, 12.74
R (on the application of Reprotech (Pebsham) Ltd) v East Sussex County Council [2002] UKHL 8, [2002] JPL 821 .... 25.115; 29.21, 29.22, 29.25
R (on the application of Robert Hitchins Ltd) v Worcestershire County Council [2014] EWHC 3809 (Admin), [2015] PTSR D5 .... 29.47
R (on the application of Roudham & Larling Parish Council) v Breckland Council & Paul Rackham Ltd [2008] EWCA Civ 714, [2009] 2 Costs LR 282, [2009] LLR 545 .... 7.21
R (on the application of Sainsbury's Supermarkets Ltd) v Wolverhampton City Council [2010] UKSC 20, [2011] 1 AC 437, [2010] 2 WLR 1173: 1.47; 9.11, 9.171; 12.37
R (on the application of Samuel Smith Old Brewery (Tadcaster)) v Secretary of State for Energy & Climate Change [2012] EWHC 46 (Admin), [2012] 2 All ER 849 .... 25.18; 26.65, 26.67
R (on the application of Saunders) v Tendring District Council [2003] EWHC 2977 (Admin) 8.59; 9.63; 16.7, 16.10
R (on the application of Save Britain's Heritage) v Secretary of State for Communities & Local Government [2011] EWCA Civ 334, [2011] PTSR 1140, [2011] LGR 493 .... 2.4, 2.22; 5.146; 6.129; 7.21, 7.28, 7.42; 29.23
R (on the application of Save Britain's Heritage) v Gateshead Metropolitan Borough Council [2014] EWHC 896 (Admin) 14.5

Table of Cases

R (on the application of Save Britain's Heritage) v Gateshead Metropolitan Borough Council [2010] EWHC 2919 (Admin), [2011] JPL 339 .... 25.81
R (on the application of Save Wooley Valley Action Group Ltd) v Bath & North East Somerset Council [2012] EWHC 2161 (Admin), [2013] Env LR 8, [2012] ACD 124.. 2.4, 2.8, 2.14; 7.21
R (on the application of Sellars) v Basingstoke & Deane Borough Council [2013] EWHC 3673 (Admin), [2014] JPL 643, [2013] 49 EG 76 (CS): 2.33
R (on the application of Silus Investments SA) v London Borough of Hounslow [2015] EWHC 358 (Admin), [2015] BLGR 391 .... 6.117
R (on the application of Siraj) v Kirklees Metropolitan Borough Council [2010] EWCA Civ 1286; [2011] JPL 571 .... 8.99; 9.167
R (on the application of Skillcrown Homes Ltd) v Dartford Borough Council [2014] EWHC 365 (Admin), [2014] JPL 988.. 6.109
R (on the application of Smith) v Cotswold District Council [2007] EWCA Civ 1341 .... 8.100
R (on the application of Springhall) v Richmond-upon-Thames London Borough Council [2006] EWCA Civ 19, [2006] BLGR 419, [2006] JPL 970... 8.17
R (on the application of Sumption) v London Borough of Greenwich [2007] EWHC 2776 (Admin), [2008] 1 P & CR 20, [2008] JPL 783 .... 2.37; 5.101
R (on the application of Symphony Limited) v Reigate and Banstead Borough Council (17 December 2015, unreported)... 12.60
R (on the application of Tait) v Secretary of State for Communities & Local Government [2012] EWHC 643 (Admin).................................. 21.35; 23.127
R (on the application of Tapp) v Thanet District Council (2001) 81 P & CR 37, [2001] PLCR 2, [2001] JPL 225 .... 2.25, 2.28
R (on the application of Tata Steel UK Ltd) v Newport City Council *see* R (on the application of Corus UK Ltd (t/a Orb Electrical Steels) v Newport City Counci
R (on the application of Taylor) v Maidstone Borough Council [2004] EWHC 257 (Admin) 25.24
R (on the application of Telford Trustee No 1 Ltd) v Telford & Wrekin Council [2011] EWCA Civ 896, [2012] PTSR 935, [2011] JPL 1596.. 8.97, 8.99
R (on the application of Threadneedle Property Investments Ltd) v London Borough of Southwark [2012] EWHC 855, [2013] Env LR 1 .... 7.35
R (on the application of Timmins) v Gedling Borough Council [2014] EWHC 654 (Admin); aff'd [2015] EWCA Civ 10, [2015] PTSR 837, [2015] 2 P & CR 12 .... 9.73, 9.76
R (on the application of Trashorfield Ltd) v Bristol City Council [2014] EWHC 757 (Admin) 8.21
R (on the application of Treagus) v Suffolk County Council [2013] EWHC 950 (Admin), [2013] Env LR 36 .... 11.29; 25.93
R (on the application of Trillium (Prime) Property GP Ltd) v London Borough of Tower Hamlets [2011] EWHC 146 (Admin) 6.38, 6.113
R (on the application of Tromans) v Cannock Chase District Council [2004] EWCA Civ 1036, [2004] BLGR 735, [2005] JPL 338 .... 8.110
R (on the application of Trustees of the Friends of the Lake District) v Secretary of State for the Environment [2001] EWHC Admin 281, [2002] 1 P & CR 23, [2002] JPL 72... 17.50

R (on the application of Viera) v London Borough of Camden [2012] EWHC
287 (Admin) 6.115, 6.117;
8.15; 23.56
R (on the application of Wainwright) v London Borough of Richmond-upon-
Thames [2001] EWCA Civ 2062, (2002) 99 (9) LSG 29 .... 25.88
R (on the application of Wall) v Brighton & Hove City Council [2004] EWHC
2582 (Admin), [2005] 1 P & CR 33, [2004] 4 PLR 115......................... 8.96
R (on the application of Warley) v Wealden District Council [2011] EWHC
2083 (Admin), [2012] Env LR 4 .... 7.21; 9.56
R (on the application of Warners Retail (Moreton) Ltd) v Cotswold District
Council [2014] EWHC 2504 (Admin)... 9.66
R (on the application of Watts) v Secretary of State for the Environment,
Transport & the Regions [2002] EWHC 993 (Admin), [2002] JPL 173:   5.64
R (on the application of Welcome Break Group Ltd) v Stroud District Council
[2012] EWHC 140 (Admin)... 12.36
R (on the application of Wells) v Secretary of State for Transport, Local
Government & the Regions (C-210/02) [2004] ECR I-723, [2004] 1
CMLR 31, [2005] All ER (EC) 323 .... 7.6
R (on the application of West Berkshire District Council and Reading Borough
Council) v Secretary of State for Communities and Local Government
[2015] EWHC 2222 (Admin), [2015] BLGR 884, [2016] JPL 35.........   9.32,
9.106
R (on the application of Westminster City Council) v Secretary of State for
Communities & Local Government [2015] EWCA Civ 482, [2015]
JPL 1276 .... 2.24, 2.33; 3.36
R (on the application of Wilkinson) v Rossendale Borough Council [2002]
EWHC 1204 (Admin), [2003] JPL 82... 3.15;
11.25; 13.24
R (on the application of Williams) v Secretary of State for Energy & Climate
Change [2015] EWHC 1202 (Admin), [2015] JPL 1257....................... 25.46
R (on the application of Williams) v Powys County Council (2016) 6.126
R (on the application of Wilsdon) v First Secretary of State [2006] EWHC
2980 (Admin) 5.121
R (on the application of Wingrove) v Stratford-on-Avon District Council
[2015] EWHC 287 (Admin)... 6.108
R (on the application of Woolley) v Cheshire East Borough Council [2009]
EWHC 1227 (Admin), [2010] Env LR 5, [2009] 3 EGLR 89 .... 9.141
R (on the application of Wrenn) v Wiltshire Council [2011] EWHC 2198
(Admin)... 28.10
R (on the application of Wye Valley Action Association Ltd) v Herefordshire
Council [2011] EWCA Civ 20, [2011] PTSR 1011, [2011] Env LR 20: 7.21
R (on the application of Young) v Oxford City Council [2002] EWCA Civ
990, [2003] JPL 232, [2003] JPL 232 .... 8.104; 9.40
R (on the application of Zurich Assurance Ltd (t/a Threadneedle Property
Investments)) v North Lincolnshire Council [2012] EWHC 3708
(Admin)... 9.66
Rael-Brook Ltd v Minister of Housing & Local Government [1967] 2 QB 65,
[1967] 2 WLR 604, [1967] 1 All ER 262... 3.26
Rambridge v Secretary of State for the Environment (1997) 74 P & CR 126 .. 5.107
Ramsey v Secretary of State for the Environment, Transport & the Regions
[2002] EWCA Civ 118, [2002] JPL 1123, [2002] 7 EG 120................. 5.125
Rasbridge's Application, Re [2012] UKUT 246 (LC), [2012] JPL 1521 .... 12.102

Table of Cases

Reading Borough Council v Secretary of State for the Environment & Commercial Union Properties (Investments) Ltd (1986) 52 P & CR 385, [1986] JPL 115 .... 24.16

Redhill Aerodrome Ltd v Secretary of State for Communities and Local Government [2014] EWCA Civ 1386, [2015] PTSR 274, [2015] JPL 416 .... 9.52, 9.79

Redrow Homes Ltd v First Secretary of State [2003] EWHC 3094 (Admin), [2004] 2 PLR 51, [2004] JPL 1273 .... 6.12; 16.16; 28.8

Reed v Secretary of State for Communities & Local Government [2014] EWCA Civ 241, [2014] JPL 725 .... 2.25

Reid v Secretary of State for Transport, Local Government & the Regions [2002] EWHC 2174 (Admin), [2002] 42 EG 158 (CS), (2002) 99 (40) LSG 35 .... 13.28

Revival Properties Ltd v Secretary of State for the Environment [1996] JPL B86 .... 9.91

Richmond-upon-Thames London Borough Council v Secretary of State for the Environment, Transport & the Regions [2000] 2 PLR 115, [2001] JPL 84, [2000] EG 47 (CS) 2.27, 2.45

Richmond-upon-Thames Royal London Borough Council v Secretary of State for the Environment [1973] 1 WLR 1549, [1974] 1 All ER 193. [1974] QB 720 .... 11.27; 13.4

Riordan Communications Ltd v South Buckinghamshire District Council (2001) 81 P & CR 8, [2000] 1 PLR 45, [2000] JPL 594 .... 29.42

River Wear Commissioners v Adamson [1877] 2 App Cas 743 .... 28.15

Riza v Secretary of State for Communities & Local Government [2014] EWHC 909 (Admin) 19.52

Robert Hitchins Ltd v Secretary of State for the Environment (1995) 72 P & CR 579, [1995] EG 101 (CS) 9.98; 21.27; 23.141

Royal Aquarium & Summer & Winter Garden Society v Parkinson [1892] 1 QB 431 .... 23.113

Royal Borough of Greenwich v Information Commissioner (EA/2014/0122): 8.42

Royal Borough of Kensington & Chelsea v CG Hotels (1981) 41 P & CR 40, [1981] JPL 190 .... 2.18

Royal London Mutual Insurance Society Ltd v Secretary of State for Communities & Local Government [2013] EWHC 3597 (Admin), [2014] JPL 458 .... 3.14, 3.16

Rugby Football Union v Secretary of State for Local Government, Transport & the Regions [2001] EWHC Admin 927, [2002] JPL 740 .... 2.27; 3.11; 3.51; 11.25

Rumsey v Secretary of State for the Environment, Transport & the Regions (2000) 81 P & CR 32, [2001] JPL 1056 .... 9.179; 25.74

Runnymede Borough Council v Harwood (1994) 6 Admin LR 697, 92 LGR 561, (1994) 68 P & CR 300 .... 2.37

Rydon Homes v Secretary of State for the Environment (1995) 70 P & CR 657, [1997] JPL 145 .... 22.29

S

St Albans City & District Council Secretary of State for Communities and Local Government [2015] EWHC 655 (Admin) 9.194

Table of Cases

St George Developments Ltd & Kew Riverside Developments v Secretary of State for the Environment [1996] JPL 35, [1994] 3 PLR 33, [1994] EG 153 (CS), [1994] NPC 121 .... 16.11
Sage v Secretary of State for the Environment, Transport & the Regions [2003] UKHL 22, [2003] 1 WLR 983, [2003] 2 All ER 689 .... 2.16; 15.4, 15.5, 15.7; 29.15
Sampson's Executors v Nottinghamshire County Council [1949] 2 KB 439, [1949] 1 All ER 1051, 65 TLR 376 .... 2.38
Samuel Smith Old Brewery (Tadcaster) v Secretary of State for Communities and Local Government [2009] EWCA Civ 333, [2009] JPL 1326 .... 9.192
San Vicente v Secretary of State for Communities & Local Government [2013] EWCA Civ 817, [2014] 1 WLR 966, [2014] 1 P & CR 7 .... 25.57
Save Britain's Heritage v Secretary of State for the Environment; Save Britain's Heritage v Number 1 Poultry Ltd [1991] 1 WLR 153, [1991] 2 All ER 10, 89 LGR 809 .... 25.38
Schofield v Hall (R & H)[1975] STC 353, 49 TC 538 .... 5.92
Scrivens v Secretary of State for Communities & Local Government [2013] EWHC 3549 (Admin), [2014] JPL 521 .... 24.52
Scurlock v Secretary of State for Wales (1977) 33 P & CR 202, (1976) 238 EG 47 .... 3.49
Sea Estates Ltd v Secretary of State for Communities & Local Government [2012] EWHC 2252 (Admin) 19.52
Searle v Secretary of State for Communities & Local Government [2012] EWHC 2269 (Admin), [2013] PTSR D4 .... 24.12
Secretary of State for the Environment, Transport & the Regions v Hughes *see* Hughes v Secretary of State for the Environment, Transport & the Regions
Seddon Properties Ltd v Secretary of State for the Environment (1981) 42 P & CR 26, (1978) 248 EG 951, [1978] JPL 835 .... 25.33
Shadwell Estates Ltd v Breckland District Council [2013] EWHC 12 (Admin), [2013] Env LR D2 .... 24.23
Shemara Ltd v Luton Corpn (1967) 18 P & CR 520 .... 16.5
Silver v Secretary of State for Communities & Local Government [2014] EWHC 2729 (Admin), [2015] JPL 154 .... 29.14, 29.16, 29.34
Simplex GE (Holdings) v Secretary of State for the Environment (1989) 57 P & CR 306, [1988] 3 PLR 25, [1988] JPL 809 .... 25.88
Singh v Secretary of State for Communities & Local Government [2010] EWHC 1621 (Admin) 29.54
Skerrits of Nottingham v Secretary of State for the Environment, Transport & the Regions (No 1) [2001] QB 59, [2000] 3 WLR 511, (2000) 80 P & CR 516 .... 2.37; 5.101
Skerritts of Nottingham v Secretary of State for the Environment, Transport & the Regions (No 2) [2000] 2 PLR 102, [2000] JPL 1025, [2000] EG 43 (CS) 2.7, 2.8
Slough Borough Council v Secretary of State for the Environment *see* R v Secretary of State for the Environment, ex p Slough Borough Council
Slough Estates Ltd v Slough Borough Council (No 1) [1971] AC 958, [1970] 2 WLR 1187, [1970] 2 All ER 216 .... 28.8
Smith v Secretary of State [2003] EWCA Civ 262, [2003] Env LR 32, [2003] JPL 1316 .... 11.29; 12.10
Smith v Secretary of State for the Environment (1984) 4 P & CR 194 .... 4.8

Table of Cases

Smout v Welsh Ministers [2011] EWCA Civ 1750, [2010] EWHC 3307 (Admin), [2011] Env LR 17, [2011] PTSR D19 .... 4.26
Solvay v Region Wallonne (Case C-182/10) [2012] 2 CMLR 19, [2012] Env LR 27 .... 9.139
Sosmo Trust Ltd v Secretary of State for the Environment [1983] JPL 806 ... 9.169
Southampton City Council v Hallyard Ltd [2008] EWHC 916 (Ch), [2009] 1 P & CR 5, [2008] JPL 1440 .... 12.14
South Buckinghamshire District Council v Porter (No 2) [2004] UKHL 33, [2004] 1 WLR 1953, [2004] 4 All ER 775 .... 8.99; 24.21
South Gloucestershire Council v Secretary of State for the Environment [1999] JPL B99 .... 29.39
South Lakeland District Council v Secretary of State for the Environment [1992] 2 AC 141, [1992] 2 WLR 204, [1992] 1 All ER 573 .... 9.95, 9.97
South Northamptonshire Council v Secretary of State for Communities and Local Government [2014] EWHC 573 (Admin) 9.103
South Oxfordshire District Council v Secretary of State for the Environment (1994) 68 P & CR 551, [1994] 1 PLR 72, [1994] EG 80 (CS) 23.81
South Oxfordshire District Council v Secretary of State for the Environment, Transport & the Regions [2000] 2 All ER 667, [2000] PLCR 315, (2000) 97 (2) LSG 32 .... 2.30
Spackman v Wiltshire County Council [1977] 1 All ER 257, (1977) 33 P & CR 430, [1977] JPL 173 .... 29.12, 29.14, 29.37
Sporrong and Lönroth v Sweden (A/52) (1983) 5 EHRR 35 .... 9.150
Staffordshire County Council v NGR Land Developments Ltd [2002] EWCA Civ 856, [2003] JPL 56 .... 29.50
Staffordshire County Council v Riley [2001] EWCA Civ 257, [2002] PLCR 5, [2001] JPL 1325 (Note) 29.13, 29.14, 29.51
Staffordshire Moorlands District Council v Cartwright (1992) 63 P & CR 285, [1992] JPL 138 .... 28.8
Steinberg v Secretary of State for the Environment (1989) 58 P & CR 453, [1989] 2 PLR 9, [1989] JPL 258 .... 9.96
Stevenage Borough Council v Secretary of State for Communities & Local Government [2010] EWHC 1289 (Admin) 11.24
Stockton-on-Tees Borough Council v Secretary of State for Communities & Local Government [2010] EWHC 1766 (Admin), [2011] JPL 183 .... 2.35
Stringer v Minister of Housing & Local Government [1970] 1 WLR 1281, [1971] 1 All ER 65, 68 LGR 788 .... 1.48; 9.6, 9.45, 9.60
Sunbury-on-Thames Urban District Council v Mann (1958) 9 P & CR 309, 56 LGR 235 .... 5.123
Sustainable Shetland v Scottish Ministers [2015] UKSC 4, [2015] 2 All ER 545, [2015] Env LR 23 .... 26.65
Sweetman v An Bord Pleanala (Case C-258/11) [2014] PTSR 1092, [2013] 3 CMLR 16, [2015] Env LR 18 .... 9.138
Sykes v Secretary of State for the Environment (1981) 42 P & CR 19, (1981) 257 EG 821, [1981] JPL 285 .... 2.41

T

TA Miller Ltd v Minister of Housing & Local Government [1968] 1 WLR 992, [1968] 2 All ER 633, [1969] RPC 91 .... 4.12
Tapecrown v First Secretary of State [2006] EWCA Civ 1744, [2007] 2 P & CR 7, (2007) 151 SJLB 64 .... 5.48

Table of Cases

Tariq v Home Office [2011] UKSC 35, [2012] 1 AC 452, [2011] 3 WLR
322 .... 23.149
Taylor & Sons (Farms) v Secretary of State for the Environment, Transport
& the Regions [2001] EWCA Civ 1254, [2002] 1 PLR 16, [2002]
PLCR 11 .... 5.139
Taylor Wimpey (South West Thames) Ltd v Secretary of State for Communities
& Local Government [2011] EWHC 2090 (Admin), [2011] 44 EG 106
(CS), [2011] NPC 110 .... 13.25
Tegni Cymru Cyf v Welsh Ministers [2010] EWCA Civ 1635, [2011] JPL
1342 .... 24.24
Telford & Wrekin Council v Secretary of State for Communities & Local
Government & Growing Enterprises Ltd [2013] EWHC 79 (Admin),
[2013] 1 EGLR 87, [2013] 17 EG 100 .... 3.16; 28.8
Tesco Stores Ltd v Dundee City Council [2012] UKSC 13, [2012] PTSR 983,
2012 SC (UKSC) 278 .... 9.43, 9.66
Tesco Stores Ltd v North Norfolk District Council [1998] PLCR 183; aff'd
(1999) 78 P & CR 359, [1999] JPL 920, [1999] EG 39 (CS) 16.17, 16.30;
29.28, 29.29, 29.39
Tesco Stores Ltd v Secretary of State for the Environment [1995] 1 WLR 759,
[1995] 2 All ER 636, 93 LGR 403 .... 1.47, 1.59; 9.11,
9.12, 9.43, 9.44, 9.67,
9.169; 11.33; 12.7, 12.9, 12.34
Tessier v Secretary of State for the Environment (1976) 31 P & CR 161, 74
LGR 279, (175) 120 SJ 8 .... 3.6
Tewkesbury Borough Council v Keeley [2004] EWHC 2954 (QB), [2005]
JPL 831 .... 2.14
Thames Heliport v London Borough of Tower Hamlets [1995] JPL 526........ 2.3
Thames Heliport v London Borough of Tower Hamlets (1997) 74 P & CR
164, [1997] 2 PLR 72, [1997] JPL 448 .... 2.26; 5.125
Thayer v Secretary of State for the Environment [1991] 3 PLR 104, [1992]
JPL 264, [1992] COD 89 .... 29.13, 29.38
Thomas David (Porthcawl) Ltd v Penybont Rural District Council [1972] 1
WLR 1526, [1972] 3 All ER 1092, 71 LGR 89 .... 2.13
Thomas Newall Ltd v Lancaster City Council [2013] EWCA Civ 802, [2013]
RVR 309, [2013] JPL 1531 .... 24.22
Thurrock Borough Council v Secretary of State for the Environment [2002]
EWCA Civ 226, [2002] 2 PLR 43, [2002] JPL 1278 .... 2.34
Thurrock Borough Council v Secretary of State for the Environment,
Transport & the Regions & Holding [2001] CP Rep 55, [2001] 1 PLR
94, [2001] 3 EG 132 .... 25.41
Times Investment Ltd v Secretary of State for the Environment (The Times,
21 June 1990) 25.35, 25.37
Trapp v Mackie [1979] 1 WLR 377, [1979] 1 All ER 489, 1979 SC (HL) 38: 23.113
Trinder v Sevenoaks Rural District Council (1967) 204 EG 803 .... 28.4
Truman, Hanbury, Buxton & Co's Application, Re [1956] 1 QB 261, [1955]
3 WLR 704, [1955] 3 All ER 559 .... 12.101
Truro City Council v Cornwall City Council [2013] EWHC 2525 (Admin) .. 9.186,
9.187
Trustees of Walton on Thames Charities v Walton & Weighbridge District
Council [1970] 21 P & CR 411, 68 LGR 488 .... 28.20
Trusthouse Forte Hotels Ltd v Secretary of State for the Environment (1986)
53 P & CR 293, [1986] 2 EGLR 185, (1986) 279 EG 680 .... 9.166

Table of Cases

Turner v Secretary of State for Communities & Local Government [2015]
EWHC 375 (Admin), [2015] JPL 936.. 23.35,
23.81, 23.137
Turner v Secretary of State for the Environment (1973) 28 P & CR 123, 72
LGR 380, (1973) 228 EG 335 .... 25.37

V

Valentino Plus Ltd v Secretary of State for Communities & Local Government
[2015] EWHC 19 (Admin), [2015] JPL 707...................................... 5.118
Venn v Secretary of State for Communities & Local Government [2014]
EWCA Civ 1539, [2015] 1 WLR 2328, [2015] CP Rep 12 .... 25.100
Vergos v Greece (Application 65501/01) (2005) 41 EHRR 41 .... 9.149

W

Wallington v Secretary of State for the Environment (1991) 62 P & CR 150,
[1991] 1 PLR 87, [1991] JPL 942 .... 2.37
Walsall Metropolitan Borough Council v Secretary of State for Communities
& Local Government [2012] EWHC 1756 (Admin), [2012] JPL 1502.. 5.47
Waltham Forest London Borough Council v Secretary of State for
Communities & Local Government [2013] EWHC 2816 (Admin) 5.103
Walton v Scottish Ministers [2012] UKSC 44, [2013] PTSR 51, 2013 SC
(UKSC) 67 .... 25.35, 25.38, 25.86
Wealden District Council v Secretary of State for the Environment (1988) 56
P & CR 286, [1988] 1 PLR 87, [1988] JPL 268 .... 2.40
Wealden District Council v Taylor [1992] 1 PLR 42, [1992] JPL 1036 .... 29.52
Weber v Minister of Housing & Local Government [1968] 1 WLR 29, [1967]
3 All ER 981, (1967) 132 JP 86 .... 4.12
Welwyn Hatfield Council v Secretary of State for Communities & Local
Government [2011] UKSC 15, [2011] 2 AC 304, [2011] 2 WLR 905 .. 2.24;
4.17
Wenman v Secretary of State for Communities and Local Government [2015]
EWHC 925 (Admin) 9.51, 9.103
Westerleigh Group Ltd v Secretary of State for Communities & Local
Government [2014] EWHC 4313 (Admin).. 25.15
West Midlands Probation Committee v Secretary of State for the Environment,
Transport & the Regions 1998) 10 Admin LR 297, (1998) 76 P & CR
589, [1998] JPL 388 .... 9.53
Westminster City Council v British Waterways Board [1985] AC 676, [1984]
3 WLR 1047, [1984] 3 All ER 737.. 2.31; 9.202
Westminster City Council v Davenport [2011] EWCA Civ 458, [2011] JPL
1325, [2011] NPC 45 .... 4.8
Westminster City Council v Great Portland Estates [1985] AC 661, [1984] 3
WLR 1035, [1984] 3 All ER 744 .... 1.49; 9.7, 9.148
Westminster City Council v Secretary of State for Communities & Local
Government [2013] EWHC 23 (Admin), [2013] JPL 842.................... 2.34
Westminster City Council v Secretary of State for Communities & Local
Government [2013] EWHC 690 (Admin) 12.6, 12.49
Westminster City Council v Secretary of State for Communities & Local
Government *see* R (on the application of Westminster City Council) v
Secretary of State for Communities & Local Government
Westminster City Council v Secretary of State for Communities & Local
Government [2014] EWHC 708 (Admin)... 17.44

Table of Cases

Westminster City Council v Secretary of State for the Environment & City Commercial Real Estates Investments [1984] JPL 27.................. 21.26, 21.27
Whitsbury Farm & Stud Ltd v Hemens (Valuation Officer) [1988] AC 601, [1988] 2 WLR 72, [1988] 1 All ER 72... 2.40
Williams v Minister of Housing & Local Government (1967) 18 P & CR 514, 65 LGR 495, (1967) 111 SJ 559 .... 2.40
Wilson v Secretary of State for the Environment [1973] 1 WLR 1083, [1974] 1 All ER 428, 71 LGR 442... 25.38
Wilson v West Sussex County Council [1963] 2 QB 764, [1963] 2 WLR 669, [1963] 1 All ER 751 .... 28.4, 28.8
Wiltshire Council v Secretary of State for Communities and Local Government [2015] EWHC 1459 (Admin)... 25.85
Wimpey Homes Holdings Ltd v Secretary of State for the Environment & Winchester City Council [1993] 2 PLR 54, [1993] JPL 919 .... 12.10, 12.11
Winchester City Council v Secretary of State for Communities & Local Government [2007] EWHC 2303 (Admin), [2008] 1 P & CR 15, [2008] JPL 315... 2.42; 3.26
Wind Prospect Developments Ltd v Secretary of State for Communities & Local Government [2014] EWHC 4041 (Admin).................................... 24.12
Wipperman v Barking London Borough Council (1966) 130 JP 102, 64 LGR 97, (1966) 17 P & CR 225.. 2.33
Wood v Secretary of State for Communities & Local Government [2015] EWHC 2368 (Admin) 28.4

Y

Yarmouth v France (1887) 19 QBD 647... 5.92
Young v Secretary of State for the Environment [1983] 2 AC 662, [1983] 3 WLR 382, [1983] 2 All ER 1105 .... 4.8, 4.9
Younger Homes (Northern) Ltd v First Secretary of State [2003] EWHC 3058 (Admin), [2004] JPL 950 .... 7.43; 25.20, 25.88
Younger Homes (Northern) Ltd v First Secretary of State & Calderdale Metropolitan Borough Council [2004] EWCA Civ 1060, [2005] Env LR 12, [2005] JPL 354 .... 7.53
Yuill v Yuill [1945] P 15, [1945] 1 All ER 183... 23.136

Chapter 1

Outline of the planning system

1.1 This chapter briefly outlines the working of the planning system in England and Wales, both to place planning permission within its context and to summarise how planning permission is obtained.

THE PURPOSE OF THE PLANNING SYSTEM

1.2 Works which affect land and the use of land are controlled by the planning system by requiring planning permission for the carrying out of development. A very wide range of matters are considered when deciding whether to grant planning permission.

1.3 There is no statutory definition of 'planning', nor any legislative purpose for the planning system as a whole. However, some principles can be drawn out of the legislation.

At its most straightforward, planning permission is required for the carrying out of development. 'Development' is defined by the Town and Country Planning Act 1990, s 55(1):

> 'Subject to the following provisions of this section, in this Act, except where the context otherwise requires, "development" means the carrying out of building, engineering, mining or other operations in, on, over or under land, or the making of any material change in the use of any buildings or other land'.

1.4 There are various inclusions and exclusions to the meaning of development and the need for planning permission, discussed further below and in Chapters 2 and 3, but the general propositions that development is 'operational development' and the making of a 'material change of use' of land and that such development requires planning permission are the starting point. Planning legislation does encompass various other consent requirements – for buildings of special architectural or historic interest, tree works, advertisements and hazardous substances – but those are separate to the need for planning permission.

1.5 The bald statement that planning permission is required for development does not explain what is to be taken into account in deciding whether permission should be granted. What is the planning system about?

On its face the legislative code provides some answers, but these are only partial. Statute does require the planning system to deal with various matters, but this legislation is of comparatively recent origin. Rather than changing or defining the role of planning, it emphasises certain elements or uses planning to deal with other

1.6 *Outline of the planning system*

regimes which fall within its ambit. These legislative references therefore provide illumination rather than a statutory purpose.

1.6 There is a statutory duty to exercise local planning policy making functions 'with the objective of contributing to the achievement of sustainable development'[1]. Sustainable development is, however, not defined in the legislation, although in England regard must be had to the desirability of achieving good design for these purposes[2].

1.7 Planning authorities are specifically required to take certain matters into account when making decisions: the effect of development on listed buildings and conservation areas. Several EU environmental measures are principally implemented in the UK by the planning process: Environmental Impact Assessment, Strategic Environmental Assessment and the protection of sites under the Birds and Habitats Directives. Various general duties on public authorities have been accepted as applying to planning decisions, ranging from effects on areas of outstanding natural beauty, to the public sector equality duty in respect of protected characteristics such as a person's age, sex, race and disability. Whilst showing the weight of obligations upon the planning system, they complicate rather than set out its purpose.

1.8 An explanation can more profitably start with the Second Reading speech of the Minister of Town and Country Planning, Mr Sam Silkin MP, on the Town and Country Planning Bill 1947, which set the framework of the present system[3]:

'The objects of town and country planning are becoming increasingly understood and accepted. Primarily, they are to secure a proper balance between the competing demands for land, so that all the land of the country is used in the best interests of the whole people. This is especially necessary in these small, densely populated islands. More than ever, there is today heavy pressure on our limited supply of land. And many of the demands on the use of our land are conflicting. Some must result in more land being brought into development; for example, the housing programme, including the clearance of slums and the rebuilding of blitzed areas, the redevelopment of obsolete and badly laid out areas; the dispersal of population and industry from our large, overcrowded cities to new towns under the New Towns Act. Then there are the re-equipment of industry, the expansion of the social services, particularly the new schools, on present day standards, the construction of new and wider roads and airfields. Again, the House is very familiar with the postwar needs of the Service Departments for land for training and experimental purposes. All these involve the use of additional land. On the other hand, town and country planning must preserve land from development. A high level of agricultural production is vital. More land must be kept for forestry. We have to see that our mineral resources—both surface and underground—are properly developed and are not unnecessarily sterilised by erecting buildings on the surface. And it is important to safeguard the beauty of the countryside and coast-line, especially now that holidays with pay will enable more people to enjoy them, and because we must develop the tourist industry as a source of foreign exchange.

All this involves sterilisation of land, and these conflicting demands for land must be dovetailed together. If each is considered in isolation, the common interest is bound to suffer. Housing must be so located in relation to industry that workers are not compelled to make long, tiring and expensive journeys to and from work. Nor must our already

---

[1] Planning and Compulsory Purchase Act 2004, s 39(2).
[2] Planning and Compulsory Purchase Act 2004, s 39(2A).
[3] 432 HC Official Report (5th series) cols 947–948, 29 January 1947.

large towns be permitted to sprawl, and expand, so as to eat up the adjacent rural areas and make access to the countryside and to the amenities in the centre of the town more difficult. Green belts must be left round towns, and the most fertile land must be kept for food production. The continued drift from the countryside must be arrested. Today, four-fifths of our people live in towns, and the rural population is declining. We have, in the past, neglected the planning of our villages and allowed some of the most beautiful of them to be spoiled by wholly inappropriate development. Life in the countryside must be made more convenient, and its attractiveness maintained'.

Mr Silkin concluded:

'I believe that the vast majority of people in this country are prepared to face up to the implications of planning. We as a nation have led the world in our industrial revolution, but at what a price in human lives, misery and squalor. Now we have a great opportunity of leading the world once more in a better cause, of showing that we in these islands are in no sense decadent, but intend to assume the proud position which we have, in many respects, held in the past. Already the world is looking eagerly to this country to see how we intend to solve the problem of the rebuilding of our blitzed towns and cities and the redevelopment of our dreary, ugly, squalid industrial towns; how we are to decongest the overcrowded large towns, and how we intend to build our new towns; how we are going to reconcile the growth of great new industrial activity with desirable, convenient and attractive conditions of living. I am convinced that we can and that we shall do all these things. When this Bill becomes law, we shall have created an instrument of which we can be justly proud; we shall have begun a new era in the life of this country, an era in which human happiness, beauty, and culture will play a greater part in its social and economic life than they have ever done before'.

1.9 Those extracts indicate a dizzying array of issues, some of which would often be in tension. They emphasise the economic and social roles of planning, to create a prosperous and well-fed nation but also desirable, convenient and attractive conditions of living. Since 1947 the principal change in the purpose of planning has been its increased environmental role. Mr Silkin mentioned environmental matters in terms of public enjoyment of the countryside and the decongestion of the cities. The protection of the environment for its own sake—flora and fauna, geology, air and water and the historic environment—was not mentioned. Those have become more important issues in their own right, and as concerns of the planning system rather than being left to other legal regimes.

1.10 A more current political explanation was given by the Minister for Planning, Greg Clark MP, in the foreword to the 2012 National Planning Policy Framework:

'The purpose of planning is to help achieve sustainable development.

Sustainable means ensuring that better lives for ourselves don't mean worse lives for future generations.

Development means growth. We must accommodate the new ways by which we will earn our living in a competitive world. We must house a rising population, which is living longer and wants to make new choices. We must respond to the changes that new technologies offer us. Our lives, and the places in which we live them, can be better, but they will certainly be worse if things stagnate.

Sustainable development is about change for the better, and not only in our built environment.

Our natural environment is essential to our wellbeing, and it can be better looked after than it has been. Habitats that have been degraded can be restored. Species that have been

1.11 *Outline of the planning system*

isolated can be reconnected. Green Belt land that has been depleted of diversity can be refilled by nature – and opened to people to experience it, to the benefit of body and soul.

Our historic environment – buildings, landscapes, towns and villages – can better be cherished if their spirit of place thrives, rather than withers.

Our standards of design can be so much higher. We are a nation renowned worldwide for creative excellence, yet, at home, confidence in development itself has been eroded by the too frequent experience of mediocrity.

So sustainable development is about positive growth – making economic, environmental and social progress for this and future generations'.

What both politicians emphasised – 65 years apart – was a positive role for planning. It is making things happen, in an encouraging rather than purely defensive way.

PLANNING AUTHORITIES

1.11 Planning is a locally administered system, which is subject to a degree of national direction and influence. At the local level most planning matters are dealt with by local planning authorities which are usually district, borough and unitary authorities. In England, minerals and waste matters are dealt with by county councils within their areas, as are applications for development by those authorities[4]. Some parish councils and neighbourhood fora are able to establish more local policy and secure certain approvals ('neighbourhood planning'). The Secretary of State for Communities and Local Government is able to influence decisions by national policy, has powers to direct that policy documents and applications are approved by him and determines appeals against local planning authority decisions. In practice, most appeals are determined by an Inspector from the Planning Inspectorate. The Mayor of London has power to decide or to direct the refusal of defined planning applications of potential strategic importance.

In Wales the local planning authorities are usually the unitary councils (whether county, county borough or city councils). The Welsh Ministers perform the functions of the Secretary of State. The Planning Inspectorate also operates in Wales, so is answerable to the administrations in London and Cardiff.

1.12 There may be other bodies who are local planning authorities in both England and Wales. National park authorities are the local planning authorities for their areas for all purposes, as is the Broads Authority for the Norfolk and Suffolk Broads[5]. The Mayor of London may take over certain major planning applications and become the local planning authority for those[6]. Other bodies who may be designated as the local planning authority for particular areas, but might not be, are enterprise zone authorities[7], urban development corporations[8], Mayoral development corporations in London[9], housing action trusts[10] and the Homes and Communities Agency[11].

---

[4] See Town and Country Planning Act 1990, s 1 and Sch 1.
[5] Town and Country Planning Act 1990, ss 4A, 5 respectively.
[6] Town and Country Planning Act 1990, s 2A.
[7] Town and Country Planning Act 1990, s 6.
[8] Town and Country Planning Act 1990, s 7.
[9] Town and Country Planning Act 1990, s 7A.
[10] Town and Country Planning Act 1990, s 8.
[11] Town and Country Planning Act 1990, s 8A.

PLANNING LEGISLATION

1.13 Primary legislation on planning is principally contained in the following Acts:

- Town and Country Planning Act 1990: planning authorities, planning permission, enforcement, trees, advertisements, powers of acquisition, neighbourhood planning in England;
- Planning (Listed Buildings and Conservation Areas) Act 1990: as the name says, the listed building and conservation area aspects of the historic environment;
- Planning (Hazardous Substances) Act 1990: controls over the quantity of certain substances on land;
- Planning (Consequential Provisions) Act 1990: transitional provisions made in 1990[12];
- Greater London Authority Act 1999: the Mayor of London's powers over strategic planning policy and planning applications;
- Planning and Compulsory Purchase Act 2004: planning policies adopted by local planning authorities in England and Wales, correction of Ministerial decisions;
- Planning Act 2008: national policy statements, development consent orders for nationally significant infrastructure projects and community infrastructure levy.

The 1990 Acts were consolidating legislation so did not substantively alter the law. Subsequent changes have been made by amending the existing legislation (including by the insertion of large numbers of new sections) and only retaining legislation in standalone Acts if a substantial new element is being created, such as the major infrastructure regime in the Planning Act 2008. This does mean that legislation on a particular topic is kept together and where the reader would expect to find it.

THE NEED FOR PLANNING PERMISSION

1.14 As mentioned above, the Town and Country Planning Act 1990, s 55(1) sets out the definition of development:

> 'the carrying out of building, engineering, mining or other operations in, on, over, or under land, or the making of any material change in the use of any buildings or other land'.

By s 55(1A)(a) 'building operations' includes:

> '(a) demolition of buildings;
> (b) rebuilding;
> (c) structural alterations of or additions to buildings; and
> (d) other operations normally undertaken by a person carrying on business as a builder'.

---

[12] The four 1990 Acts are identified as 'the planning Acts' in legislation: Town and Country Planning Act 1990, s 336(1).

1.15 *Outline of the planning system*

1.15 There are a number of exceptions, for example internal alterations to buildings and works to a building which do not materially affect its external appearance are not development[13]. The Town and Country Planning (Use Classes) Order 1987[14] defines various categories of uses, such as shops, restaurants and cafes, and assembly and leisure within which any change of use is not development.

1.16 Subject to limited exceptions, development may only be carried out following the grant of planning permission or deemed planning permission (or, for nationally significant infrastructure projects, the making of an order for development consent)[15].

1.17 Planning permission may be granted:

(i) by the local planning authority on an express application;

(ii) by Ministers on express application in particular circumstances;

(iii) by permitted development rights contained in the Town and Country Planning (General Permitted Development) (England) Order 2015 or in Wales the Town and Country Planning (General Permitted Development) Order 1995[16]; or

(iv) by various specific orders, such as Local Development Orders. Deemed planning permission may be granted by the Secretary of State with certain other applications, for example, Transport and Works Act applications for infrastructure or Electricity Act 1989, s 36 consents for large power stations[17].

PLANNING POLICY

1.18 Planning policy is a combination of documents adopted under statutory powers and policies which are non-statutory.

In England planning policy may be:

(i) non-statutory national policy adopted by a Secretary of State usually on planning matters. This is now contained in the National Planning Policy Framework but until 2012 was in Planning Policy Statements (PPSs), Planning Policy Guidance Notes (PPGs), Mineral Planning Statements (MPSs) and Mineral Policy Statements (MPGs). Further detail is contained in the Planning Practice Guidance, first published in March 2014 and revised on an ad hoc basis. Confusingly, this is also abbreviated to PPG;

(ii) National Policy Statements, which are statutory policies on particular types of development[18];

---

[13] Town and Country Planning Act 1990, s 55(2)(a). As an exception to the general exemption of internal works, the installation of mezzanine floors in retail premises may be development: s 55(2A) and Town and Country Planning (Development Management Procedure) (England) Order 2015, SI 2015/595, art 44; Town and Country Planning (Development Management Procedure) (Wales) Order 2012, SI 2012/801, art 2A. See Chapter 2.

[14] SI 1987/764. For the use classes, see Chapter 3.

[15] Town and Country Planning Act 1990, s 57: see Chapter 4. An order for development consent may be made by the Secretary of State for nationally significant infrastructure projects under the Planning Act 2008.

[16] SI 2015/596 and SI 1995/418 respectively.

[17] Town and Country Planning Act 1990, s 90. See Chapter 26.

[18] Adopted under the Planning Act 2008.

(iii) other national policy. This may be specific to planning, often in the form of a Written Ministerial Statement to Parliament, or other national policy which explicitly or implicitly guides planning decisions;

(iv) remaining elements of regional strategies adopted by the Secretary of State under the Local Democracy, Economic Development and Construction Act 2009. These were mostly abolished under the Localism Act 2011;

(v) the London Plan adopted by the Mayor of London[19];

(vi) Local Plans or Development Plan Documents adopted by local planning authorities;

(vii) Supplementary Planning Documents adopted by local planning authorities[20];

(viii) Local Development Documents adopted by local planning authorities and which are not Local Plans, Development Plan Documents or Supplementary Planning Documents;

(ix) neighbourhood development plans prepared by town and parish councils or neighbourhood fora and adopted by local planning authorities following a referendum[21].

1.19 In Wales planning policy may be:

(i) non-statutory national policy adopted by the Welsh Ministers in the form of Planning Policy (Wales)[22] and Technical Advice Notes (TANs) with older circulars;

(ii) the Wales Spatial Plan adopted under the Planning and Compulsory Purchase Act 2004[23];

(iii) a National Development Framework for Wales to be introduced by the Planning (Wales) Act 2015 replacing the Wales Spatial Plan;

(iv) a strategic development plan to be introduced by the Planning (Wales) Act 2015;

(v) local development plans adopted by local planning authorities (which are due to replace unitary development plans);

(vi) non-statutory supplementary planning guidance adopted by local planning authorities.

1.20 In addition in both countries there has been a mass of supporting material which may be relevant to decision making, such as 'Companion Guides' or 'Good Practice Guides' to national policy guidance and letters to local authorities from the Chief Planner. Since 2010 there has been a concerted effort in England to cut down this further documentation. Guidance documents from specialist government agencies might also be material.

---

[19] Adopted under the Greater London Authority Act 1999. See Chapter 10. It is proposed that similar strategic plans may be adopted under devolution powers in other local authority areas.
[20] Development Plan Documents and Supplementary Planning Documents are adopted under the Planning and Compulsory Purchase Act 2004.
[21] Adopted under the Localism Act 2011.
[22] Currently the 7th edition (2014).
[23] Adopted in 2004 and updated in 2008.

1.21 *Outline of the planning system*

1.21 Traditionally, development plans have been prepared by local planning authorities and set out their policies and proposals for the development and use of land[24]. Although they have more recently been prepared by a wider range of bodies, development plans contain area-wide policies, site-specific designations and sites allocated for particular forms of development.

1.22 It is worth tracing the more recent history of the development plan system, since some older documents are still in force. Prior to the Planning and Compulsory Purchase Act 2004, county councils published structure plans containing strategic policies, and district councils within counties prepared more detailed local plans. Most unitary authorities, including all metropolitan councils and London boroughs, were required to prepare unitary development plans (UDPs) which combined the functions of structure and local plans. Part I of a UDP contained strategic policies equivalent to a structure plan, whilst detailed local plan-style policies were contained in Part II. Some unitary authorities prepared joint structure plans with the neighbouring county council and their own local plan.

1.23 The Planning and Compulsory Purchase Act 2004 replaced this development plan system with a range of documents. The Regional Spatial Strategy (RSS), adopted by the Secretary of State, replaced the non-statutory Regional Planning Guidance. The Mayor of London has had responsibility since 2000 for the adoption of London's Spatial Development Strategy (SDS, known as 'The London Plan'). The 2004 Act made the Regional Spatial Strategy and the London Plan part of the development plan for their respective areas. District and borough councils are required to prepare a portfolio of documents as a local development framework. Some of these documents will be development plan documents and the remainder will have a lower, but still statutory, basis. The development plan documents will include a core strategy and a proposals map as well as more detailed plans for particular areas.

1.24 Since the Planning and Compulsory Purchase Act 2004 county councils in two-tier areas have no longer prepared their own structure plans, but were able to contribute to sub-regional elements of the Regional Strategies. Counties continue to prepare minerals and waste development frameworks for their areas and consequently adopt minerals and waste development plan documents.

1.25 The Local Democracy, Economic Development and Construction Act 2009 turned the Regional Spatial Strategies into Regional Strategies with effect from April 2010. In May 2010 the Coalition government announced its intention to abolish the Regional Strategies and the Secretary of State advised that the intention to get rid of these strategies was material to the determination of planning matters. In short, less weight should be attached to them. In July 2010 the Regional Strategies were revoked by order, but this decision was quashed by the High Court in November 2010[25]. The Secretary of State immediately reaffirmed his intention to abolish Regional Strategies in the Localism Bill and said that this intention should be taken into account in decision making[26]. The Localism Act 2011 provided for the revocation

---

[24] The current local planning authority powers are in the Planning and Compulsory Purchase Act 2004, Part 2 (for England) and Part 6 (for Wales).

[25] *R (on the application of Cala Homes (South) Ltd) v Secretary of State for Communities and Local Government (No 1)* [2010] EWHC 2866 (Admin), [2010] JPL 553.

[26] A challenge to the materiality of this intention was rejected: *R (on the application of Cala Homes (South) Ltd) v Secretary of State for Communities and Local Government (No 3)* [2011] EWHC 97 (Admin), [2011] JPL 887; [2011] EWCA Civ 639, [2011] JPL 1458.

of these strategies by order. The Regional Strategies have now all been revoked, either in their entirety or with the retention of limited, location specific policies on matters which are not covered by local plans.

1.26 Whilst regional strategies were to be abolished, the Localism Act 2011 allowed neighbourhood development plans to be initiated by parish councils and neighbourhood fora in England. The local planning authority would adopt a neighbourhood development plan following an independent examination and a local referendum[27]. An adopted neighbourhood development plan is part of the development plan[28].

1.27 Development plan documents are now known as 'local plans' in the Town and Country Planning (Local Planning) (England) Regulations 2012[29] and the National Planning Policy Framework, although they remain referred to as development plan documents in primary legislation.

1.28 Consequently, the development plan for an area in England is:

(i) for unitary authorities outside Greater London, any remaining parts of the Regional Strategy for the area, the development plan documents adopted by the local planning authority for the area (including any adopted jointly), any old development plans which have not yet expired and any neighbourhood development plan for the relevant part of the area;

(ii) for areas outside Greater London with two-tier authorities, again any remaining parts of the Regional Strategy, the development plan documents adopted by the district authority (including any adopted jointly), the minerals and waste development plan documents adopted by the county council as minerals and waste planning authority, any old development plans which have not yet expired and any neighbourhood development plan for the relevant part of the area;

(iii) for areas within Greater London, the London Plan and the development plan documents adopted by the local planning authority (including any adopted jointly), any old development plans which have not yet expired and any neighbourhood development plan for the relevant part of the area.

In Wales the development plan system is simpler. Local planning authorities had each adopted a unitary development plan. Under the Planning and Compulsory Purchase Act 2004 these were to be replaced in each authority with local development plans. Strategic development plans are introduced by the Planning (Wales) Act 2015.

PERMITTED DEVELOPMENT RIGHTS

1.29 The concept of development is very wide. The consequence is that planning permission is required for many activities that will have limited impact. The Town and Country Planning (General Permitted Development) (England) Order 2015

---

[27] Planning and Compulsory Purchase Act 2004, s 38A. Procedures for designating neighbourhood areas and 'neighbourhood forums' are contained in the Neighbourhood Planning (General) Regulations 2012, SI 2012/637.
[28] Planning and Compulsory Purchase Act 2004, s 38(3).
[29] Town and Country Planning (Local Planning) (England) Regulations 2012, SI 2012/767, reg 6.

1.30 *Outline of the planning system*

(GPDO 2015) and, for Wales, the Town and Country Planning (General Permitted Development) Order 1995 (GPDO 1995)[30] therefore grant planning permission for certain operations and material changes of use[31]. The rationale is that the benefits of avoiding the need to submit a planning application outweigh any environmental harm which might arise from the development permitted; alternatively that the planning merits of the scheme have been considered under another consent process.

1.30 Permitted development rights are contained in Sch 2 to each GPDO. These are organised into 19 Parts in England and 42 Parts in Wales. Each Part contains one or more Classes of development. In each Class there is a description of the development permitted, a description of development which would otherwise fall into the Class but is not permitted, and then conditions and limitations which apply to the development permitted. Usually a person may carry out permitted development without notifying the local planning authority. However certain permitted development can only be carried out if the developer has applied to the local planning authority for a determination as to whether prior approval of particular details of the development is required. The developer can them only proceed if: (a) there has been a determination that prior approval is not required; (b) there has been a determination that prior approval is required and that approval has been granted; or (c) the local planning authority has failed to say whether prior approval is required within a particular period of the application.

1.31 Various restrictions are placed on permitted development rights for environmental reasons. If Environmental Impact Assessment is required then permitted development rights are lost and in some circumstances permitted development rights are subject to a screening decision that Environmental Impact Assessment is not required. Permitted development rights may be removed by an Article 4 Direction made by the local planning authority or the Secretary of State or Welsh Ministers. Some permitted development rights are restricted in their own terms on land subject to natural or historic environmental designations. Additionally, consent is needed for the exercise of any permitted development rights which are likely to have a significant effect on a European nature conservation site.

Permitted development rights only grant planning permission. They do not affect any need for other consents, such as scheduled monument, listed building or advertisement consent.

THE PLANNING APPLICATION PROCESS

1.32 Planning applications are normally made to the local planning authority[32]. Where local planning authorities have been designated as underperforming, a planning application may be made directly to the Secretary of State[33]. In Wales, nationally significant development applications will in future have to be made directly to the Welsh Ministers[34].

---

[30] SI 2015/596 and SI 1995/418 respectively.
[31] See Chapter 5.
[32] For the planning application process, see Chapter 6.
[33] Under Town and Country Planning Act 1990 s 62A: see Chapter 18.
[34] Town and Country Planning Act 1990, s 62D, prospectively inserted by the Planning (Wales) Act 2015.

The planning application process **1.36**

1.33 Planning applications to local planning authorities are made formally. The planning application procedure in England is governed by the Town and Country Planning (Development Management Procedure) (England) Order 2015 (DMPO 2015) and for applications pre-dating 15 April 2015, the Town and Country Planning (Development Management Procedure) (England) Order 2010[35] (DMPO 2010). In Wales applications are governed by the Town and Country Planning (Applications) Regulations 1988 and the Town and Country Planning (Development Management Procedure) Order 2012[36] (DMPO Wales).

1.34 In England, applications must be made on a prescribed form, known as 1APP, or a form to substantially like effect. This can be obtained from the relevant local planning authority or via the Planning Portal website[37]. The application must include the particulars specified in the form and, with limited exceptions, be accompanied by a location plan and any other plans, drawings and information necessary to describe the development which is the subject of the application. Unless the form is submitted electronically, three copies of all this material must be provided[38].

In Wales, standard forms are also produced by the Welsh Ministers[39]. The application must include the particulars specified in the form and be accompanied by a plan which identifies the land to which it relates and any other plans and drawings and information necessary to describe the development which is the subject of the application. Three copies of the form and plan must be provided if it is submitted by hard copy[40].

The application may have to be accompanied by a design and access statement.

The planning application must usually be accompanied by a fee[41].

Notification and consultation on planning applications

1.35 The applicant has to give notice of the application to the freehold owner, leaseholders with more than seven years remaining on the lease and agricultural tenants prior to submitting the application[42]. Certificates on the application form have to be completed to show that has been done.

1.36 Statutory publicity may take the form of displaying a site notice, notifying neighbours by letter, placing a notice in a local newspaper and notice on the local

---

[35] SI 2015/595 and SI 2010/2184 respectively.
[36] SI 1988/1812 and SI 2012/801 respectively.
[37] www.planningportal.gov.uk.
[38] DMPO 2015, art 7(1); DMPO 2010, art 6.
[39] These are required to be used by DMPO Wales, art 5(1)(a). However the Town and Country Planning (Applications) Regulations 1988, reg 3(1) provides for a paper submission on a form provided by the local planning authority or an electronic submission on a form provided by the Minister. This is inconsistent with the newer DMPO Wales, but appears not to have been revoked.
[40] DMPO Wales, art 5.
[41] The fees are set out in the Town and Country Planning (Fees for Applications, Deemed Applications, Requests and Site Visits) (England) Regulations 2012, SI 2012/2920 and the Town and Country Planning (Fees for Applications, Deemed Applications and Site Visits) (Wales) Regulations 2015, SI 2015/1522. Both sets of regulations have been subject to regular amendment.
[42] Town and Country Planning Act 1990, s 65; DMPO 2015, art 13; DMPO 2010, art 11, and DMPO Wales, art 10.

1.37 *Outline of the planning system*

planning authority's website[43]. Additionally local authorities may issue press releases for major applications and hold public meetings. Applications fall into three categories:

(i) applications for projects requiring Environmental Impact Assessment, or which do not accord with the development plan or which would affect a public right of way[44], which require a site notice and local newspaper advertisement;

(ii) other applications for major development[45], which require a site notice or notice to any adjoining owner or occupier and local newspaper advertisement;

(iii) any other applications require a site notice or notice to any adjoining owner or occupier.

Notice of all applications has to be given on local planning authority websites in England[46].

There are some additional publicity requirements in other legislation.

1.37 Local planning authorities may be required to consult particular organisations (usually government agencies or other local authorities) on particular applications. These duties will be contained either in legislation (principally the DMPO 2015, art 18 and the DMPO Wales, art 14) or in directions made by the Secretary of State or Welsh Ministers. Occasionally government policy will recommend consultation in particular circumstances.

Statements of Community Involvement

1.38 The Planning and Compulsory Purchase Act 2004 introduced a requirement that local planning authorities in England adopt a Statement of Community Involvement (SCI) as part of their suite of Local Development Framework documents[47]. A Statement of Community Involvement is a statement of the authority's policy as to the involvement of the public and persons interested in development in the formulation of planning policy and the consideration of planning applications[48]. There is a legitimate expectation that the local planning authority will act in accordance with promises made in its SCI[49].

---

[43] DMPO 2015, art 15; DMPO 2010, art 13, and DMPO Wales, art 12.
[44] Footpath, bridleway, restricted byway or byway open to all traffic.
[45] Major development means one or more of (art 2(1) of DMPO 2015, DMPO 2010 and DMPO Wales):
 '(a) the winning and working of minerals or the use of land for mineral-working deposits;
 (b) waste development;
 (c) the provision of dwellinghouses where—
   (i) the number of dwellinghouses to be provided is 10 or more; or
   (ii) the development is to be carried out on a site having an area of 0.5 hectares or more and it is not known whether the development falls within sub-paragraph (c)(i);
 (d) the provision of a building or buildings where the floor space to be created by the development is 1,000 square metres or more; or
 (e) development carried out on a site having an area of 1 hectare or more'.
[46] DMPO 2015, art 15, DMPO 2010, art 13. There is no duty to give notice on an authority website in Wales, although in practice this is done.
[47] Planning and Compulsory Purchase Act 2004, s 17. These documents are usually found under the planning policy section of the relevant authority's website.
[48] Planning and Compulsory Purchase Act 2004, s 18(2).
[49] *R (on the application of Majed) v London Borough of Camden* [2009] EWCA Civ 1029, [2010] JPL 621 at para 14.

The planning application process **1.42**

Additional consultation and publicity requirements arise in Environmental Impact Assessment cases.

Environmental Impact Assessment

1.39 The process of Environmental Impact Assessment (EIA) has become an integral part of the planning process for large-scale development projects[50].

EIA is prescribed by European Directive 2011/92/EU, which codifies the original EIA Directive 85/337/EEC which had been amended by Directives 97/11/EC, 2003/35/EC and 2009/31/EC[51]. The critical obligation in the EIA Directive is contained in art 2(1):

> 'Member States shall adopt all measures necessary to ensure that, before consent is given, projects likely to have significant effects on the environment by virtue, *inter alia*, of their nature, size or location are made subject to a requirement for development consent and an assessment with regard to their effects. These projects are defined in Article 4'.

1.40 Article 4 identifies two categories of projects. Projects listed in Annex I of the Directive will automatically require EIA: these include developments such as an oil refinery, a motorway or a large power station (described in the UK as Schedule 1 development). Where projects fall within Annex II, member states are required to determine through a case-by-case examination or thresholds or criteria whether EIA is required. Annex II covers a wide range of projects from intensive agriculture, to mineral extraction, urban development, the food industry and flood defence works (described in the UK as Schedule 2 development). The essential question is whether these projects are likely to have significant effects on the environment.

1.41 In the UK EIA has either been integrated into existing consent regimes or new regimes have been devised, and in either case separate regulations have been produced. The English regulations applying to planning applications are the Town and Country Planning (Environmental Impact Assessment) Regulations 2011[52]. Planning applications in Wales (and those made in England prior to 24 August 2011) are subject to the Town and Country Planning (Environmental Impact Assessment) (England and Wales) Regulations 1999[53]. Consents under other regimes such as highways, pipelines, harbours and electricity projects are governed by separate EIA regulations. Where it takes place, EIA is usually part of the process of granting planning permission or another domestic law consent rather than a separate consent.

1.42 EIA processes involve the following stages:

(i) deciding whether EIA is required using selection criteria (screening);

(ii) if EIA is required, considering what impacts should be subject to assessment (scoping);

---

[50] Environmental Impact Assessment is considered in Chapter 7, and addressed in more detail in Tromans *Environmental Impact Assessment: Law and Practice* (2nd edn, 2012) Bloomsbury Professional.
[51] The 2011 Directive is to be amended again by Directive 2014/52/EU, with implementation of these changes required by 16 May 2017.
[52] SI 2011/1824. Amended with respect to Sch 2 by the Town and Country Planning (Environmental Impact Assessment) (Amendment) Regulations 2015, SI 2015/660.
[53] Planning applications made before 14 March 1999 were subject to the Town and Country Planning (Assessment of Environmental Effects) Regulations 1988, SI 1988/1199.

1.43 *Outline of the planning system*

(iii) the preparation of an environmental statement by the developer. The statement will explain the scheme, the environmental baseline which is capable of being affected by the scheme, the likely significant effects of the scheme, the mitigation proposed in respect of those effects and the alternatives considered by the developer. As part of the statement, there will be a non-technical summary produced;

(iv) consultation of public bodies and the public on the environmental statement and any further information produced by the developer;

(v) consideration of the environmental statement, the developer's further information and the responses to the consultation by the decision-maker;

(vi) the production of a reasoned decision on the application and its subsequent publication.

The determination of applications by local planning authorities

1.43 Planning applications are decided by planning committees of councillors or by officers under delegated powers, or by similar arrangements in non-council local planning authorities[54]. The council's constitution will set out the arrangements delegating power to committees or officers to determine particular applications. The majority of applications are decided by officers, but larger or more controversial schemes will tend to be decided by committee.

1.44 The agenda and reports for a committee meeting have to be published in advance of the meeting. Subject to exceptions in urgent cases, this must be five clear working days before the meeting in England or three clear working days before in Wales[55]. The local authority may allow applicants or members of the public to speak at planning committee meetings. The procedures will be set out in the statement of community involvement or separate notes for meetings[56].

1.45 In determining a planning application in England, the local planning authority shall have regard to (Town and Country Planning Act 1990, s 70(2))[57]:

'(a) the provisions of the development plan, so far as material to the application,

(b) any local finance considerations, so far as material to the application, and

(c) any other material considerations'.

Local finance considerations means government grants and Community Infrastructure Levy contributions.

1.46 A similar duty arises in Wales with the omission of reference to local finance considerations[58]. In both countries there is a presumption in favour of the development plan (Planning and Compulsory Purchase Act 2004, s 38(6))[59]:

---

[54] See Chapter 8.
[55] Local Government Act 1972, s 100B(3), applied by s 100E.
[56] There may be limits on speaking time or numbers of speakers, or requirements to notify an intention to speak in advance, so these need to be considered carefully. The authority might also promise to give notice of the meeting: see *R (on the application of Kelly) v London Borough of Hounslow* [2010] EWHC 1256 (Admin).
[57] For material considerations, see Chapter 9.
[58] Town and Country Planning Act 1990, s 70(2A) omits para (b) in Wales.
[59] This duty was previously in the Town and Country Planning Act 1990, s 54A.

'If regard is to be had to the development plan for the purpose of any determination to be made under the planning Acts the determination must be made in accordance with the plan unless material considerations indicate otherwise'.

Other material considerations are matters relevant to land use planning, including national policy contained in the National Planning Policy Framework or Planning Policy Wales[60].

1.47 In *R (on the application of Kides) v South Cambridgeshire District Council*[61], the Court of Appeal addressed what was a material consideration in the planning context. Jonathan Parker LJ said:

'In my judgment a consideration is "material", in this context, if it is relevant to the question whether the application should be granted or refused; that is to say if it is a factor which, when placed in the decision-maker's scales, would tip the balance to some extent, one way or the other. In other words, it must be a factor which has some weight in the decision-making process, although plainly it may not be determinative. The test must, of course, be an objective one in the sense that the choice of material considerations must be a rational one, and the considerations chosen must be rationally related to land use issues'.

The weight to be attached to any material consideration is a matter for the decision maker, subject to *Wednesbury* unreasonableness[62].

1.48 In *Stringer v Ministry of Housing and Local Government*[63] the potential of proposed development to interfere with radio astronomy at Jodrell Bank was capable of being a material consideration in determining a planning application. Cooke J said:

'It may be conceded at once that the material considerations to which the Minister is entitled and bound to have regard in deciding the appeal must be considerations of a planning nature. I find it impossible, however, to accept the view that such considerations are limited to matters relating to amenity. So far as I am aware, there is no authority for such a proposition and it seems to me wrong in principle. In principle, it seems to me that any consideration which relates to the use and development of land is capable of being a planning consideration'.

1.49 In *Westminster City Council v Great Portland Estates*[64] the House of Lords held that the test of what is a material consideration in the planning context was whether it served a planning purpose relating to the character of the use of land. However Lord Scarman, with whom the other law lords agreed, said[65]:

'It would be inhuman pedantry to exclude from the control of our environment the human factor. The human factor is always present, of course, indirectly as to the background to the consideration of character of land use. It can, however, and sometimes should be given direct effect as an exception under a special circumstance. But such circumstances when they arise will be considered not as a general rule but as exceptions to a general rule to be met in special cases'.

---

[60] 7th edn, 2014.
[61] [2002] EWCA Civ 1370, [2003] JPL 431 at para 121.
[62] *Tesco Stores Ltd v Secretary of State for the Environment* [1995] 1 WLR 759; *R (on the application of Sainsbury's Supermarkets Ltd) v Wolverhampton City Council* [2010] UKSC 20, [2011] 1 AC 437 at para 70.
[63] [1971] 1 WLR 1281.
[64] [1985] AC 661.
[65] At 670E–F.

1.50 *Outline of the planning system*

The planning permission or refusal

1.50 A planning application is finally determined when the decision notice is sent out by the local planning authority[66]. A resolution by the committee to grant planning permission does not create a planning permission. The issue of a permission may be delayed by a number of matters, including referral to the Secretary of State or Welsh Ministers, referral to the Mayor of London, and the drafting of planning obligations.

Planning conditions

1.51 Conditions can be attached to a grant of permission under the Town and Country Planning Act 1990, ss 70 and 72[67]. Section 70(1) simply permits authorities to grant planning permission 'either unconditionally or subject to such conditions as they think fit'. Section 72(1) is more detailed:

> 'Without prejudice to the generality of section 70(1), conditions may be imposed on the grant of planning permission under that section—
>
> (a) for regulating the development or use of any land under the control of the applicant (whether or not it is land in respect of which the application was made) or requiring the carrying out of works on any such land, so far as appears to the local planning authority to be expedient for the purposes of or in connection with the development authorised by the permission;
>
> (b) for requiring the removal of any buildings or works authorised by the permission, or the discontinuance of any use of land so authorised, at the end of a specified period, and the carrying out of any works required for the reinstatement of land at the end of that period'.

1.52 Section 72 deals explicitly with two situations: applying conditions to land outside the application site but under the control of the applicant (this is usually marked on application drawings by blue lines); and temporary planning permissions. The s 70 power is wider than the more specific provision in s 72. Conditions may be imposed to require works to be carried out or to restrict or control activities on the planning application site (whether or not owned or controlled by the applicant) or on land under the ownership or control of the applicant (whether or not it is within the application site). A condition might require actions or limit activities of the developer or person occupying the application site if that person would be able to comply with the condition. For example, a condition could prohibit the operators of a car repair garage from parking cars under their control in a particular street[68], but could not prohibit their visitors from parking where they wish.

1.53 Conditions are often described as positive or negative. A positive condition would require the developer to do a certain act: for example, 'The windows shall be constructed in accordance with drawing 545/02A'. A negative condition prevents something from being done until something else has occurred: for example, 'The development shall not be brought into use before the completion of the junction improvements shown on drawing 545/08'. This negative form allows activities on the site to be restricted until an off-site event has occurred, even if it would not be

---

[66] *R (on the application of Burkett) v London Borough of Hammersmith and Fulham* [2002] 1 WLR 1593, HL. For the issue of a planning permission, see Chapter 15.
[67] See Chapter 11.
[68] *Davenport v London Borough of Hammersmith and Fulham* [1999] 2 PLR 96.

The planning application process **1.56**

lawful to require the developer to carry out the works for the off-site event. Negative conditions are often known as Grampian conditions[69]. A condition may have positive and negative elements. For example, it is common to require details to be submitted and approved before development commences and for the development to be carried out in accordance with those approved details.

1.54 To be lawful a condition must:

(i) apply to the application site, land under the control of the applicant or (subject to the restrictions discussed above) other land;

(ii) be for a planning purpose;

(iii) fairly and reasonably relate to the development permitted;

(iv) not be *Wednesbury* unreasonable.

The last three criteria were set out by the House of Lords in *Newbury District Council v Secretary of State for the Environment*[70]. In that case it was held to be *Wednesbury* unreasonable for a condition on a planning permission for a temporary use of an existing building to require the demolition of the building at the end of the temporary use period.

1.55 In the NPPF the Secretary of State says[71]:

'Planning conditions should only be imposed where they are necessary, relevant to planning and to the development to be permitted, enforceable, precise and reasonable in all other respects'.

The requirement of necessity is the main policy addition to the legal tests.

Planning obligations

1.56 The developer may also enter into a planning obligation under the Town and Country Planning Act 1990, s 106 requiring him to do or refrain from doing various acts on site or to make payments for off-site activity, in connection with the planning application[72]. A planning obligation is a deed made by a person interested in land in the area of a local planning authority[73]:

'(a) restricting the development or use of the land in any specified way;

(b) requiring specified operations or activities to be carried out in, on, under or over the land;

(c) requiring the land to be used in any specified way; or

(d) requiring a sum or sums to be paid to the authority (or, in a case where section 2E applies, to the Greater London Authority) on a specified date or dates or periodically'.

---

[69] Following the House of Lords decision in *Grampian Regional Council v Secretary of State for Scotland* 1984 SC (HL) 58.
[70] [1981] AC 578.
[71] NPPF, para 206. This continues longstanding guidance, most recently in Circular 11/95, Part 1, para 14 and similar guidance in Wales.
[72] See Chapter 12.
[73] Town and Country Planning Act 1990, s 106(1). See Chapter 11.

1.57 *Outline of the planning system*

1.57 The obligation may either be signed by those involved in the land alone (a unilateral obligation) or also signed by the local planning authority (a planning agreement)[74]. The obligation is enforceable by the local planning authority in contract and also by statutory injunction or by going onto the land to carry out works[75]. A planning obligation may be modified or discharged either by an agreement by all parties to it and the local planning authority, or on an application made to the local planning authority five years or more after the obligation was made, or (in England) on an application made at any time on the basis that affordable housing requirements make the scheme unviable[76].

1.58 A planning obligation will be lawful if it complies with the formalities in s 106 and those of deeds, is for a planning purpose and is not *Wednesbury* unreasonable.

1.59 Planning obligations are usually made in connection with the grant of planning permission. The content of a planning obligation (or proposed obligation) must satisfy the tests in the Community Infrastructure Levy Regulations 2010, reg 122(2)[77]:

'A planning obligation may only constitute a reason for granting planning permission for the development if the obligation is:

(a) necessary to make the development acceptable in planning terms;

(b) directly related to the development; and

(c) fairly and reasonably related in scale and kind to the development.'

The necessity test had previously just been contained in policy[78]. Being directly related and fairly and reasonably related in scale and kind were in substance existing legal tests[79].

Referral of planning applications to the Secretary of State or Welsh Ministers

1.60 An application may have to be referred to the Secretary of State for Communities and Local Government or Welsh Ministers for a decision whether to 'call in' the application for their own determination under s 77 of the Town and Country Planning Act 1990, prior to the local planning authority issuing a decision notice[80]. In England any requirement to refer would usually arise under the Town and Country Planning (Consultation) (England) Direction 2009.

1.61 If the local planning authority does 'not propose to refuse the application' falling within the Direction (ie they propose to approve it), they must send a copy of the application, the notice given of it, the representations made and their report to the Secretary of State. The Secretary of State then decides whether to call in the

---

[74] In two-tier local government areas district and county councils can sign as local planning authorities regardless of which authority determines any related planning application.
[75] Town and Country Planning Act 1990, s 106(5), (6).
[76] Town and Country Planning Act 1990, ss 106A, 106BA. There are rights of appeal against the refusal or non-determination of section 106A and BA applications: ss 106B, 106BC.
[77] SI 2010/948.
[78] Circular 05/05 *Planning Obligations*, para B5. This circular is revoked by the National Planning Policy Framework, Annex 3.
[79] *Tesco Stores Ltd v Secretary of State for the Environment* [1995] 1 WLR 759, HL.
[80] See Chapter 17.

application within the 21-day period in the Direction. If more time is needed to make a decision then the Secretary of State can make a direction under DMPO 2015, art 31[81] to prevent the authority approving the application until that direction is lifted.

1.62 These directions will not permanently prevent a permission being issued. A delay may be imposed until, for example, a planning inspector has reported on a development plan document, but ultimately ministers have to call in the application or allow the local authority to determine it.

Duties to refer applications to the Welsh Ministers are contained in the Town and Country Planning (Notification) (Wales) Direction 2012.

1.63 The Secretary of State and Welsh Ministers may make directions preventing determination of an application or calling it in whether or not the application has to be referred to ministers under a direction. It is not uncommon, therefore, for requests to be made for directions to be made preventing local authorities from issuing permissions as applications are being considered at committee.

1.64 The Secretary of State's policy on calling in planning applications is[82]:

'The policy is to continue to be very selective about calling in planning applications. We consider it only right that as Parliament has entrusted local planning authorities with the responsibility for day-to-day planning control in their areas, they should, in general, be free to carry out their duties responsibly, with the minimum of interference. …

The Secretary of State will, in general, only consider the use of his call-in powers if planning issues of more than local importance are involved. Such cases may include, for example, those which in his opinion:

- may conflict with national policies on important matters;
- may have significant long-term impact on economic growth and meeting housing needs across a wider area than a single local authority;
- could have significant effects beyond their immediate locality;
- give rise to substantial cross-boundary or national controversy;
- raise significant architectural and urban design issues; or
- may involve the interests of national security or of foreign Governments.

However, each case will continue to be considered on its individual merits'.

Referrals to the Mayor of London

1.65 The Mayor of London is able to direct local planning authorities within Greater London to refuse certain planning applications falling within defined categories (known as applications of potential strategic importance). These are a limited number of very major applications. The Mayor has a 14-day period to direct refusal following notification of the local authority's proposed decision. He is also able to take over some of those applications and grant planning permission[83].

---

[81] SI 2015/595, formerly DMPO 2010, art 25. In Wales these directions are made by the Welsh Assembly Government under DMPO Wales, art 18.
[82] 551 HC Official Report (6th series), cols 71-72WS, 26 October 2012.
[83] Town and Country Planning Act 1990, ss 2A–2D, 74; Town and Country Planning (Mayor of London) Order 2008, SI 2008/580. See Chapter 10.

1.66 *Outline of the planning system*

Appeals

1.66 The applicant for planning permission has a right of appeal to the Secretary of State for Communities and Local Government (in England) or the Welsh Ministers (in Wales) against the refusal of an application, its grant subject to conditions or non-determination of the application. In England an appeal must be brought[84]:

(i) within six months of the refusal or grant, unless the application is a householder or minor commercial application[85] (when the period for appealing against refusal is 12 weeks) or an enforcement notice has been recently served[86]; or

(ii) within six months of the expiry of the period for determining the application, including the expiry of any extended period which had been agreed in writing by the applicant and local planning authority.

In Wales the general time limit for appealing is six months from refusal or grant of the application subject to conditions[87]. Householder or minor commercial applications made from 22 June 2015 are subject to a 12-week period for appeal from a decision[88]. There is no time limit for appealing for non-determination in Wales[89].

The appeal must be brought on the relevant form and include certificates that notice of the appeal has been given to landowners.

1.67 Appeals may be determined by four main procedures:

(i) As householder and minor commercial appeals, a system introduced in England in 2009 and Wales in 2015. Householder appeals are appeals against the refusal or non-determination of householder applications for the development of an existing dwellinghouse or land within its curtilage for incidental purposes. Minor commercial appeals concern small-scale works to existing retail and food and drink uses. Where these appeals proceed by written representations a planning inspector will simply consider the application documents, the representations submitted on the planning application by third parties and statutory consultees, the decision notice, any report by the local planning authority on the application, and the appellant's comments made with the appeal form and carry out a site visit[90]. Further information may be requested by the inspector or Secretary of State (ie the Planning Inspectorate) prior to determination.

---

[84] DMPO 2015, art 37, DMPO 2010, art 33. For appeals, see Chapters 19–24.
[85] Article 2(1) of the DMPO 2015 and DMPO 2010 define 'householder application' and 'minor commercial application', discussed under appeal procedures.
[86] DMPO 2015, art 37, DMPO 2010, art 33 set out shorter, 28-day time limits where such enforcement action has been taken.
[87] DMPO Wales, art 26.
[88] DMPO Wales, art 26(2), amended by the Town and Country Planning (Development Management Procedure) (Wales) (Amendment) Order 2015, SI 2015/1330, art 8.
[89] DMPO Wales, art 26(2), amended by the Town and Country Planning (Development Management Procedure) (Wales) (Amendment) Order 2015, art 8.
[90] The procedure is in the Town and Country Planning (Appeals) (Written Representations Procedure) (England) Regulations 2009, SI 2009/452, Part 1 and the Town and Country Planning (Referrals and Appeals) (Written Representations Procedure) (Wales) Regulations 2015, SI 2015/1331, Part 1. See Chapter 20.

The planning application process **1.67**

(ii) Written representations. In England, the appellant will set out its full case with the notice of appeal and the local planning authority will then send copies of the material considered with the application (attached to a questionnaire). The local planning authority and third parties will have an opportunity to make further representations in a five-week period after the 'starting date' set by the Planning Inspectorate. The appellant and local planning authority have a further opportunity to comment on those 'five week' representations within a further period of two weeks. An inspector will then carry out a site visit[91]. In Wales, the appellant's initial case is submitted with the appeal and they may then send further representations six weeks after the starting date, as may the local planning authority and third parties. The appellant and local planning authority may comment on those representations within a further three weeks[92].

(iii) Following a hearing. The Planning Inspectorate will receive the appeal form and any submissions with it and, from the local planning authority, the documents considered with the application. The appellant, local planning authority and third parties are required to provide their hearing statements (which include all their evidence not put in during the application process) within five weeks of the starting date (six weeks in Wales). A hearing will then be held, which is a structured discussion (with an agenda) led by the inspector[93]. A hearing is an inquisitorial process, with cross-examination not being allowed, but must be sufficiently rigorous to ensure a thorough and fair investigation[94]. The hearing may then be adjourned to the site for discussion to continue or the hearing may be closed and a site visit will then be carried out.

(iv) Following a public inquiry. Again the Planning Inspectorate will receive the appeal form from the appeal and the questionnaire documents from the local planning authority. The appellant and local planning authority will have to produce a statement of case within five weeks of the starting date (six weeks in Wales). A statement of case is not evidence, but sets out the case which the party will advance (like a pleading in court proceedings) and lists the documents which will be referred to. These parties have to file proofs of evidence four weeks before the inquiry starts (unless a different timetable is set at a pre-inquiry meeting)[95]. Any other person who wishes to play a major role at the inquiry should ask to become a 'rule 6 party'. They will then be required to produce a statement of case and proofs of evidence, but will have the same rights to participate at the inquiry as the main parties. Other persons may make written representations within six weeks of the start date, speak at the inquiry (but only cross-examine with the permission of the inspector) and have written submissions handed in to the inspector.

---

[91] The procedure is in the Town and Country Planning (Appeals) (Written Representations Procedure) (England) Regulations 2009, Part 2. See Chapter 21.
[92] Town and Country Planning (Referrals and Appeals) (Written Representations Procedure) (Wales) Regulations 2015, SI 2015/1331, Part 2.
[93] The procedure is in the Town and Country Planning (Hearings Procedure) (England) Rules 2000, SI 2000/1626 and the Town and Country Planning (Hearings Procedure) (Wales) Rules 2003, SI 2003/1271. See Chapter 22.
[94] *Dyason v Secretary of State for the Environment* [1998] 2 PLR 54.
[95] Statements of evidence are required to be produced in Wales, which are the same as proofs.

1.68 *Outline of the planning system*

In England the Secretary of State (in reality the Planning Inspectorate) will decide whether a planning appeal is dealt with by written representations, a hearing or inquiry[96]. From November 2014 similar provisions were introduced in Wales[97].

1.68 Most appeals are decided by planning inspectors. However Ministers may 'recover jurisdiction' over any particular appeal and decide it themselves.[98] In those cases an inspector will write a report to the Minister, usually following an inquiry or hearing, and the Minister will then determine the appeal[99].

1.69 The inspector or Minister will then issue a written decision which will also set out the reasons for the decision[100]. The usual principle is that the parties to a planning appeal bear their own costs but costs may be awarded against a party if: (a) an application is made at the appropriate time; (b) the party has acted unreasonably; and (c) that unreasonableness has caused the applying party to suffer wasted costs. Unreasonableness in this context has its ordinary meaning and is usually considered in terms of substantive conduct (for example, bringing an appeal which was bound to fail or refusing planning permission when an appeal was bound to succeed) or procedural conduct (such as forcing an adjournment by producing evidence late without justification)[101].

1.70 Procedural guidance on the appeals process in England is issued by the Planning Inspectorate. The principal documents are *Procedural Guide Planning appeals – England*[102] and *Procedural Guidance Enforcement appeals – England*[103].

Guidance on the appeals process in Wales is contained in National Assembly of Wales Circulars NAW 07/03 Planning (and analogous) Appeals and Call-in Procedures and NAW 08/03 Enforcement Appeal Procedures.

DEVELOPMENT CONSENT ORDERS

1.71 Certain major infrastructure projects are considered under the development consent procedure in the Planning Act 2008[104]. An order for development consent replaces any requirement for planning permission, listed building, conservation area

---

[96] Town and Country Planning Act 1990, ss 78(3), 319A; Town and Country Planning (Determination of Appeal Procedure) (Prescribed Period) (England) Regulations 2009, SI 2009/454.
[97] Town and Country Planning Act 1990, s 319B, inserted by the Town and Country Planning (Determination of Procedure) (Wales) Order 2014, SI 2014/2773.
[98] The criteria for recovering jurisdiction are set out in the Planning Practice Guidance. See Chapter 17.
[99] The procedural rules vary (although not significantly) between Inspector-determined appeals and recovered jurisdiction appeals. The relevant rules for ministerial decisions are the Town and Country Planning (Inquiries Procedure) England Rules 2000, SI 2000/1624 and the Town and Country Planning (Inquiries Procedure) Wales Rules 2003, SI 2003/1266, and for inspectors' decisions the Town and Country Planning Appeals (Determination by Inspectors) (Inquiries Procedure) (England) Rules 2000, SI 2000/1625 and the Town and Country Planning Appeals (Determination by Inspectors) (Inquiries Procedure) (Wales) Rules 2003, SI 2003/1267. See Chapter 23.
[100] For example, Town and Country Planning (Inquiries Procedure) England Rules 2000, r 18.
[101] Guidance on costs in planning appeals is given in the Planning Practice Guidance and Welsh Office Circular 23/93 *Awards of Costs incurred in Planning and Other (Including Compulsory Purchase Order) Proceedings*.
[102] The latest edition is 31 July 2015 and subject to frequent online revisions.
[103] Dated 10 July 2015.
[104] See Humphries *National Infrastructure Planning Handbook 2015* (Bloomsbury Professional).

or scheduled monument consent. Policy for certain types of major infrastructure is contained in statutory National Policy Statements.

THE GRANT OF PLANNING PERMISSION BY ORDERS AND OTHER MEANS

1.72 Planning permission may be granted by several other mechanisms[105]. The UK planning system has essentially operated by a case-by-case consideration of proposals or nationally set permitted development rights. Plan-making has been to establish policies which can be applied when case-by-case applications are determined. This is distinct from a zoning approach, where an area-wide document will grant permission for development of certain classes in certain locations. Proposals which do not accord with the zone may be permitted on an individual application. Whilst the zone might establish the principle of the use up to certain dimensions, the detail of the scheme is likely to require individual approval. Zoning in these terms is adopted widely in Europe, the United States and some former British colonies, including Hong Kong.

1.73 Zoning has periodically appealed to ministers as a concept, with the result that there are now seven mechanisms for granting planning permission by zones or local orders of some kind:

- the making of a special development order by the Secretary of State[106];
- local development orders made by the local planning authority[107];
- neighbourhood development orders initiated by a parish council or designated neighbourhood forum[108];
- community right to build orders initiated by community organisations[109];
- mayoral development orders in London[110];
- simplified planning zones made by the local planning authority[111];
- designation of an enterprise zone[112].

Additionally the Secretary of State or Welsh Ministers may grant deemed planning permission under s 90 where authorisation for the development is given under other mechanisms, such as the Transport and Works Act 1992[113].

OTHER PLANNING CONTROLS

1.74 There are several other consent regimes in the planning system. These consents are not considered in detail in this book, although the matters which they

---

[105] Considered in more detail in Chapter 26.
[106] Town and Country Planning Act 1990, s 59.
[107] Town and Country Planning Act 1990, s 61A.
[108] Town and Country Planning Act 1990, s 61E.
[109] Town and Country Planning Act 1990, s 61Q.
[110] Town and Country Planning Act 1990, ss 61DA–61DE.
[111] Town and Country Planning Act 1990, s 82.
[112] Local Government, Planning and Land Act 1980, Sch 32 and Town and Country Planning Act 1990, s 88.
[113] Town and Country Planning Act 1990, s 90.

1.75 *Outline of the planning system*

address may be relevant to the determination of a planning application. Additionally the content of a planning permission, in particular its conditions, may be affected by the existence of the other consent regime if duplication is to be avoided.

1.75 The planning consent regimes are:

- tree preservation order consent to cut down, top, lop, uproot or wilfully damage or destroy a tree which is subject to a tree preservation order[114];
- advertising consent for the display of advertisements[115];
- listed building consent for works for the demolition of a listed building or for its alteration or extension in any manner which would affect its character as a building of special architectural or historic interest[116]. A listed building is one listed by the Secretary of State for Culture, Media and Sport or by the Welsh Ministers as being of special architectural or historic interest[117];
- conservation area consent for the demolition of unlisted buildings in conservation areas in Wales[118].

1.76 Other consent regimes which have an impact on the planning system include:

- scheduled monument consent for works affecting scheduled ancient monuments[119];
- environmental permits for the carrying out of particular activities[120];
- species licences for the killing, disturbance, capture of European protected species and the destruction of their breeding grounds and resting places[121].

With the exception of advertisement consent, none of these various regimes obviate any need for planning permission.

BREACHES OF PLANNING CONTROL

1.77 The carrying out of development without planning permission or contravening a condition on a planning permission is a breach of planning control[122].

---

[114] Town and Country Planning Act 1990, s 202. This is considered from an enforcement perspective in Chapter 17 of Harwood *Planning Enforcement* (2nd edn, 2013) Bloomsbury Professional.
[115] Town and Country Planning Act 1990, ss 220–224, again discussed in *Planning Enforcement* at Chapter 18.
[116] Planning (Listed Buildings and Conservation Areas) Act 1990, s 7. Listing is considered in Chapters 6 and 7 of Harwood *Historic Environment Law* (Institute of art and Law, 2012) and the *Historic Environment Law Supplement 2014*.
[117] Planning (Listed Buildings and Conservation Areas) Act 1990, s 1.
[118] Town and Country Planning Act 1990, s 74. Conservation area consent was abolished in England in October 2013 and demolition previously subject to that consent is now dealt with entirely by planning permission. For conservation areas see Chapter 8 of *Historic Environment Law* and for the 2013 changes, the *Historic Environment Law Supplement 2014* by Richard Harwood QC.
[119] Ancient Monuments and Archaeological Areas Act 1979, s 2 (see Chapter 4 of *Historic Environment Law*).
[120] Under the Environmental Permitting (England and Wales) Regulations 2010, SI 2010/675.
[121] Conservation of Habitats and Species Regulations 2010, SI 2010/490.
[122] Town and Country Planning Act 1990, s 171A. See Harwood *Planning Enforcement* (2nd edn, 2013) Bloomsbury Professional.

Breaches of planning control **1.79**

Except for the demolition of an unlisted building in a conservation area, failure to comply with planning control is not an immediate criminal offence.

1.78 The local planning authority can take the following measures:

(i) issue an enforcement notice requiring the ending of the contravention and any steps required to remedy the consequences of the breach[123]. An enforcement notice may be appealed to the Secretary of State or Welsh Ministers on grounds including that no breach of planning control has taken place or can any longer be enforced against, or that planning permission should be granted[124]. An enforcement notice does not take effect until the period for appealing has expired and any appeal has been finally determined. Once it has taken effect and the period for compliance has expired, then the failure of the site owner or occupier to comply is a criminal offence. The local planning authority may also at that point go onto the land and carry out any works in the notice;

(ii) serve a breach of condition notice where the contravention is a failure to comply with a condition[125]. It is an offence to fail to comply with the notice once the period for compliance has expired. There is no ability to appeal against a breach of condition notice and so its validity can only be challenged by judicial review or as a defence to a prosecution under the notice;

(iii) serve a stop notice[126]. As an enforcement notice only takes effect once any appeal has been disposed of it cannot require an immediate halt to unlawful activities. A stop notice may be served to prohibit activities in breach of planning control provided that an enforcement notice has already been issued. Failure to comply with such a notice is a criminal offence. No appeal may be brought against a stop notice so its validity can only be challenged by judicial review or as a defence to a prosecution under the notice. A stop notice will cease to have effect once its related enforcement notice has taken effect. If the stop notice is served against activities that are in fact lawful then compensation for any loss caused is payable by the local planning authority.

(iv) serve a temporary stop notice[127]. Stop notices were seen to have the disadvantage that an enforcement notice had to be issued before or at the same time. A temporary stop notice can be served before any enforcement notice is issued and has effect for up to 28 days. A similar approach to criminal offences, validity and compensation arises as for stop notices;

(v) apply to the High Court or county court for an injunction under the Town and Country Planning Act 1990, s 187B to restrain an actual or apprehended breach of planning control. An injunction is the only measure that can be taken before a breach has occurred so could be used if there is good reason to consider that an irrevocable act, such as demolition of a building or ground works in an important archaeological site, is about to take place.

1.79 Where the breach of planning control consists of operational development or a change of use of a building to a dwellinghouse then any enforcement notice must

---

[123] Town and Country Planning Act 1990, s 172.
[124] Town and Country Planning Act 1990, s 174.
[125] Town and Country Planning Act 1990, s 187A.
[126] Town and Country Planning Act 1990, s 183.
[127] Town and Country Planning Act 1990, s 172E. This power does not apply in Wales.

1.80 *Outline of the planning system*

be issued or breach of condition notice served within four years of the breach[128]. For other breaches of planning control the time limit is ten years[129], except that there is no time limit for unauthorised demolition within conservation areas in England[130].

Section 215 notices on the condition of land

1.80 A local planning authority may serve a notice requiring land to be properly maintained if its condition is adversely affecting the amenity of part of the authority's area or the area of an adjoining authority. These notices under the Town and Country Planning Act 1990, s 215 will specify the steps required to be taken to remedy the position.

HIGH COURT CHALLENGES

1.81 As with challenges to listed building decisions there are a variety of means of challenging planning decisions in the Administrative Court of the High Court. Different procedures apply to different decisions and care needs to be taken to identify the correct type of proceedings. Each proceeding has different procedural rules and time limits. There are five main types:

(i) application to the High Court under the Town and Country Planning Act 1990, s 288 against the Secretary of State or inspector's decision on a planning appeal and local authority tree preservation order decisions. A similar application arises under the Planning (Listed Buildings and Conservation Areas) Act 1990, s 63 against a listed building consent appeal decision. The application must be made within a six-week period;

(ii) application to the High Court under the Town and Country Planning Act 1990, s 287 against a simplified planning zone scheme or its alteration within six weeks of publication of its making;

(iii) appeal to the High Court under the Town and Country Planning Act 1990, s 289 against the Secretary of State or Inspector's decision on an enforcement notice appeal. Appeals to the High Court against listed building enforcement notice appeal decisions are made under the equivalent Planning (Listed Buildings and Conservation Areas) Act 1990, s 65. The appeal should be brought within four weeks of notice of the decision, although an extension of time might be granted;

(iv) application to the High Court under the Planning and Compulsory Purchase Act 2004, s 113 against the adoption of a development plan document. Proceedings must be brought in the six-week period from the adoption of the document;

(v) judicial review. Judicial review is the mechanism for challenging any public authority decision which is not subject to a right to make a statutory application

---

[128] Town and Country Planning Act 1990, s 171B(1), (2).
[129] Town and Country Planning Act 1990, s 171B(3). There are limited circumstances in which enforcement action may be taken within four years of any previous attempted enforcement or breach of condition notice (s 171B(4)). Where a breach of planning control has been deliberately concealed then a local planning authority may apply to the magistrates' court for 'planning enforcement order' allowing it to take enforcement action out of time: Town and Country Planning Act 1990, ss 171BA–171BC.
[130] Town and Country Planning Act 1990, s 171B(2A).

High Court challenges **1.81**

or appeal to the High Court or an alternative remedy (such as appealing to the Secretary of State). In the planning context it is most commonly used to challenge the grant of planning permission by a local planning authority but arises in other circumstances, such as challenges to decisions whether to enforce planning control and the adoption of non-local plan documents. Judicial review proceedings of decisions under the Town and Country Planning Act 1990 should be brought within six weeks of the decision.

Applications under Town and Country Planning Act 1990, ss 287 or 288 or the Planning and Compulsory Purchase Act 2004, s 113 against decisions made on or after 26 October 2015 require an application for permission from the court to bring the proceedings. These processes are now closely modelled on those used in judicial review. Section 287 and 288 applications and judicial review proceedings are discussed in more detail in Chapter 25.

Chapter 2

The meaning of development

2.1 The key concept in planning is 'development'. Subject to limited exceptions, matters which amount to development require planning permission. This chapter considers what development is.

THE MEANING OF DEVELOPMENT

2.2 'Development' is defined by the Town and Country Planning Act 1990, s 55(1):

> 'Subject to the following provisions of this section, in this Act, except where the context otherwise requires, "development" means the carrying out of building, engineering, mining or other operations in, on, over or under land, or the making of any material change in the use of any buildings or other land'.

2.3 This definition divides into two categories: operational development, 'building, engineering, mining or other operations'; and the making of a material change of use. Lord Denning MR observed in *Parkes v Secretary of State for the Environment*[1]:

> 'in the first half "operations" comprises activities which result in some physical alteration to the land, which has some degree of permanence to the land itself: whereas in the second half "use" comprises activities which are done in, alongside or on the land but do not interfere with the actual physical characteristics of the land'.

Land means any corporeal hereditament[2] and this includes water (tidal or otherwise) in a river[3].

2.4 Several general principles apply to interpreting the meaning of development:

(i) planning is concerned with works which physically alter the land or change its use;

(ii) planning is concerned with protecting the public interest, and 'development' will therefore tend to be interpreted in a way which includes activities and works which should be regulated in the public interest;

---

[1] [1978] 1 WLR 1308 at 1311.
[2] Town and Country Planning Act 1990, s 336.
[3] *Thames Heliport v London Borough of Tower Hamlets* [1995] JPL 526. The seaward limit of the requirement for planning permission has generally been taken to be to the low-water mark: see *Argyll and Bute District Council v Secretary of State for Scotland* 1976 SC 248, although the position has historically been complicated by the Crown's ownership of the seabed and most of the foreshore and the immunity of the Crown from planning control.

(iii) the Town and Country Planning Act 1990 and the secondary legislation made under it provide a 'comprehensive code of planning control'. The courts must give effect to the intention of Parliament as evinced by that comprehensive statutory code[4];

(iv) to give effect to European law, 'development' should be construed as far as possible as including all projects which fall within the Environmental Impact Assessment Directive unless they are subject to other English legislation requiring EIA[5].

OPERATIONAL DEVELOPMENT

2.5 Operational development involves making a physical change to land. It must, though, fall within one of the four categories of operational development.

Building operations

2.6 By the Town and Country Planning Act 1990, s 55(1A) 'building operations' includes:

'(a) demolition of buildings;

(b) rebuilding;

(c) structural alterations of or additions to buildings; and

(d) other operations normally undertaken by a person carrying on business as a builder.'

Consequently building operations is defined in an inclusive but not exclusive fashion in sub-s (1A).

2.7 Whether building operations have been carried out can often be answered by asking whether they have resulted in a building. 'Building' must be considered, in its wide definition in the Town and Country Planning Act 1990, as including any structure or erection or part of a building[6]. Whether an object is a building is often judged by reference to three factors: size; the nature and degree of attachment; and the degree of permanence. Permanence is concerned with 'a sufficient length of time to be of significance in the planning context'[7] and this may be something erected on a seasonal basis.

2.8 Examples of structures which the courts have said could be buildings include a seven-bay marquee erected in the grounds of a hotel for eight months in a year[8], a tower crane resting on a steel track[9] and polytunnels over large areas

---

[4] *Pioneer Aggregates (UK) Ltd v Secretary of State for the Environment* [1985] AC 132 at 140–141 per Lord Scarman.
[5] *R (SAVE Britain's Heritage) v Secretary of State for Communities and Local Government* [2011] EWCA Civ 334, [2011] LGR 493; *R (Save Woolley Valley Action Group Ltd) v Bath and North East Somerset Council* [2012] EWHC 2161 (Admin), [2013] Env LR 8 at paras 112–114 per Lang J.
[6] Town and Country Planning Act 1990, s 336(1).
[7] *Skerritts of Nottingham v Secretary of State for the Environment, Transport and the Regions* [2000] JPL 1025 at 1034 per Schiemann LJ.
[8] *Skerritts of Nottingham.*
[9] *Barvis Ltd v Secretary of State for the Environment* (1971) 22 P &CR 710.

2.9 *The meaning of development*

of farmland for nine months a year[10]. The setting up of umbrellas and side panels to create a marquee-type structure in the rear garden of a shisha lounge was also a building operation[11]. 'Poultry units', each housing up to 1,000 birds and said to be moved periodically around their paddocks, could also be buildings (or the product of building operations)[12]. An object may be a building in planning law without being incorporated into the land, as part of the realty[13].

2.9 Some building operations do not result in buildings. For example, laying a tarmac drive is normally undertaken by a builder. Similarly the categories include structural alterations to buildings. Painting the exterior of a building has permitted development rights[14] so legislators must have assumed that painting could be development, even though it would not be a structural alteration.

Engineering operations

2.10 It is perhaps too simplistic to suggest that engineering operations are operations carried out by engineers. Operations in planning are concerned with effects on land, so engineering operations tend to fall within the civil engineering disciplines. Those operations include the construction of roads, earthworks, lakes and ponds, being physical works to land which do not result in buildings, structures or erections. Many of these operations will not be carried out by engineers at all.

Mining operations

2.11 Mining operations include[15]:

'(a) the removal of material of any description:

(i) from a mineral-working deposit;

(ii) from a deposit of pulverised fuel ash or other furnace ash or clinker; or

(iii) from a deposit of iron, steel or other metallic slags; and

(b) the extraction of minerals from a disused railway embankment'.

2.12 Mineral working deposit and minerals are further defined[16]:

'"mineral-working deposit" means any deposit of material remaining after minerals have been extracted from land or otherwise deriving from the carrying out of operations for the winning and working of minerals in, on or under land;

"minerals" includes all substances of a kind ordinarily worked for removal by underground or surface working, except that it does not include peat cut for purposes other than sale'.

---

[10] *Hall Hunter Partnership v First Secretary of State* [2006] EWHC 3482, [2007] 2 P & CR 5.
[11] *Islam v Secretary of State for Communities and Local Government* [2012] EWHC 1314 (Admin), [2012] JPL 1378.
[12] *R (Save Woolley Valley Action Group Ltd) v Bath and North East Somerset Council* [2012] EWHC 2161 (Admin), [2013] Env LR 8.
[13] *R v Swansea City Council, ex p Elitestone* (1993) 66 P & CR 422.
[14] Town and Country Planning (General Permitted Development) Order 2015, SI 2015/596, Sch 2, Part 2, Class C (in England); Town and Country Planning (General Permitted Development) Order 1995, SI 1995/418, Sch 2, Part 2, Class C (in Wales).
[15] Town and Country Planning Act 1990, s 55(4).
[16] Town and Country Planning Act 1990, s 336(1).

Operational development **2.16**

Minerals therefore include sand, gravel, stone and coal but also oil and gas.

2.13 The extraction of further minerals from an existing quarry or the digging of the ground to gain access to it, is a mining operation. Even where mining has taken place on land, it is still a mining operation to carry out further extraction on that land, such as by digging deeper. Lord Denning MR said in *Thomas David (Porthcawl) Ltd v Penybont Rural District Council*[17] 'Every shovelful is a mining operation'.

Other operations

2.14 Such is the breadth of building, engineering or mining operations that the final category of 'other operations' has rarely been relied upon. This residual category is not limited to operations of the same class as building, engineering or mining operations[18]. *Beronstone*[19] concerned the erection of hundreds of wooden stakes to mark out plots of land and accessways, which amounted to other operations[20]. In *Save Woolley Valley* the construction or installation of the poultry units could have been other operations had it not fallen within building operations.

Exclusions from operational development

2.15 The Town and Country Planning Act 1990, s 55(2) sets out various operations or uses of land which do not involve development. With respect to operational development these are:

'(a) the carrying out for the maintenance, improvement or other alteration of any building of works which:

(i) affect only the interior of the building, or

(ii) do not materially affect the external appearance of the building,

and are not works for making good war damage or works begun after 5th December 1968 for the alteration of a building by providing additional space in it underground'.

2.16 This exception is of considerable practical importance, as it excludes from control a very large number of building operations, although its meaning and application have been open to some debate. In *Sage v Secretary of State for the Environment, Transport and the Regions*[21] the House of Lords held that the sub-paragraph only applied to an existing building. This was described in *Sage* as a 'fully detailed structure of a certain character'[22]. Consequently it would not be possible to partly construct a building and then use sub-para (a) to alter the internal layout from

---

[17] [1972] 1 WLR 1526 at 1531.
[18] *Coleshill and District Investment Co Ltd v Minister of Housing and Local Government* [1969] 1 WLR 746 and *Beronstone Ltd v First Secretary of State* [2006] EWHC 2391 (Admin), *R (Save Woolley Valley Action Group Ltd) v Bath and North East Somerset Council* [2012] EWHC 2161 (Admin), [2013] Env LR 8 at para 74 per Lang J (the latter decision disagreeing with *Tewkesbury Borough Council v Keeley* [2004] EWHC 2954 (QB), [2005] JPL 831 at para 37, which appears to decide to the contrary).
[19] *Beronstone v First Secretary of State* [2006] EWHC 2391 (Admin).
[20] Small plots had been sold on the dubious potential of development in the Green Belt and stakes were used to mark the plots to avoid restrictions on permitted development rights for fences.
[21] [2003] UKHL 22, [2003] 2 All ER 689.
[22] *Sage* at para 18, 23 per Lord Hobhouse of Woodborough.

2.17 *The meaning of development*

the approved plans, although internal changes could be done as soon as the building was complete.

2.17 There has been some debate as to whether internal works are classed as development if they are part of a project which includes external alterations which are themselves development. The issue has arisen in unusual circumstances, as where planning permission is granted for the external works it rarely matters whether it is actually required for the internal works. However the view was taken in *R (on the application of Prudential Assurance Ltd) v Sunderland City Council*[23] that planning permission was required for the insertion of internal walls in a retail unit as part of a sub-division which involved material alterations to the exterior of the building.

2.18 Under the second proviso to the exception, materially affecting the external appearance of a building involves an impact capable of having some effect in planning terms. Whether an alteration is material does depend upon the building, its character, the change and the available viewpoints. For example an alteration which is only visible from an aircraft would not be material[24]. In *Royal Borough of Kensington and Chelsea v CG Hotels*[25] 11 floodlights had been fixed to the walls of a hotel or placed on balconies, but as these were unnoticeable and virtually invisible from the street during the day an inspector held that they were not development because of the paragraph (a) exception. This was upheld by the Divisional Court, who considered that the effect of floodlighting at night did not alter the external appearance of the building. Historically it has been considered that conventional television aerials and their poles or mountings have not affected the external appearance of buildings so have not been development and a similar view can be taken of burglar alarms and microcell telecommunications antennae[26].

2.19 The exception for internal works allowed the installation of mezzanine floors in retail warehouses (unless restrained by planning condition) which could significantly increase sales floorspace and so retail and traffic impact. Section 55 was consequently amended by the Planning and Compulsory Purchase Act 2004 to allow specified floorspace additions to be removed by order from the exception from development[27]. Subsequently in England operations which have the effect of increasing the gross floor space of a building by more than 200 square metres are capable of being operational development if the building is used for the retail sale of goods other than hot food[28]. From 22 June 2015 the same extension to what is development applies in Wales[29].

---

[23] [2010] EWHC 1771 (Admin), [2011] JPL 322.
[24] *Burroughs Day v Bristol City Council* [1996] 1 PLR 78 at 88 per Richard Southwell QC, suggesting that 'all roof alterations which can be seen from any vantage point on the ground or in or on any neighbouring building or buildings would be capable of affecting the "external appearance" of the building in question'.
[25] (1981) 41 P & CR 40.
[26] See the former Planning Policy Guidance 8: *Telecommunications* at Appendix, para 43.
[27] Inserting Town and Country Planning Act 1990, s 55(2A).
[28] Town and Country Planning (Development Management Procedure) (England) Order 2015, SI 2015/595, art 44 and the former Town and Country Planning (Development Management Procedure) (England) Order 2010, SI 2010/2184, art 3.
[29] Town and Country Planning (Development Management Procedure) (Wales) Order 2012, SI 2012/801, art 2A, inserted by the Town and Country Planning (Development Management Procedure) (Wales) (Amendment) Order 2015, SI 2015/1330, art 4.

2.20

'(b) the carrying out on land within the boundaries of a road by a highway authority of any works required for the maintenance or improvement of the road but, in the case of any such works which are not exclusively for the maintenance of the road, not including any works which may have significant adverse effects on the environment'.

Sub-paragraph (b) provides a general exception for maintenance or improvement works carried out by the highways authority[30] within the existing boundaries of a road. 'Improvement', in relation to a highway, has the same meaning as in the Highways Act 1980[31]. The Highways Act definition of 'improvement' is 'the doing of any act under powers conferred by Part V of this Act'[32]. Part V contains a series of powers including dualling, building roundabouts, cycle tracks, footways, guard rails, pedestrian refuges, subways, the widening and levelling of highways, fencing, installing cattle-grids, road humps, other traffic calming works, bridge repairs, installation of speed cameras, lighting, metalling and drainage of highways, filling roadside ditches and protecting against natural hazards. It would have to be checked that the works are within these powers but the primary constraints are that the works are within the existing boundaries of the road and any improvement works are not likely to have 'significant adverse effects on the environment'.

Permitted development rights apply to other works which may have significant adverse effects, maintenance or improvement works adjoining the road and street furniture[33].

2.21

'(c) the carrying out by a local authority or statutory undertakers of any works for the purpose of inspecting, repairing or renewing any sewers, mains, pipes, cables or other apparatus, including the breaking open of any street or other land for that purpose'.

This exception relates to works to and for existing apparatus. There are extensive permitted development rights for new apparatus. Statutory undertakers are defined as[34]:

'persons authorised by any enactment to carry on any railway, light railway, tramway, road transport, water transport, canal, inland navigation, dock, harbour, pier or lighthouse undertaking or any undertaking for the supply of hydraulic power and a relevant airport operator (within the meaning of Part V of the Airports Act 1986)' and

'any gas transporter, water or sewerage undertaker, the Environment Agency, the Natural Resources Body for Wales, ... the Civil Aviation Authority and a person who holds a licence under Chapter I of Part I of the Transport Act 2000 (air traffic services)'.

---

[30] Highways England is the highways authority for motorways and trunk roads in England (being a strategic highways company and taking over the functions of the Secretary of State, as the Highways Agency: Infrastructure Act 2015, ss 1, 2), Transport for London (as part of the Greater London Authority) is the highways authority for certain important roads in Great London, whilst the county or unitary council is the highways authority for the remainder.
[31] Town and Country Planning Act 1990, s 336(1).
[32] Highways Act 1980, s 329(1).
[33] Town and Country Planning (General Permitted Development) Order 2015, Sch 2, Parts 9 and 12; Town and Country Planning (General Permitted Development) Order 1995, Sch 2, Parts 12 and 13.
[34] Town and Country Planning Act 1990, s 262(1), (3).

2.22 *The meaning of development*

Demolition

2.22

> '(g) the demolition of any description of building specified in a direction given by the Secretary of State to local planning authorities generally or to a particular local planning authority'.

Demolition is dealt with in planning in this way[35]:

(i) considering s 55(1) on its own, demolition will tend to fall within the categories of operational development. The demolition of buildings is a building operation under s 55(1A), and the demolition of other works (such as a road or bund) may be an engineering operation or other operation;

(ii) the demolition of the whole of a building with a cubic content (measured externally) which does not exceed 50 cubic metres, or the demolition in whole or part of any gate, fence, wall or other means of enclosure, is excluded from the definition of development in England by the Town and Country Planning (Demolition – Description of Buildings) Direction 2014 and in Wales by the Town and Country Planning (Demolition – Description of Buildings) Direction 1995[36];

(iii) where demolition is development, it will need planning permission, even if scheduled monument, listed building or (in Wales) conservation area consent is also required;

(iv) planning permission may be granted on application to the local planning authority, by the Secretary of State, by permitted development rights or by order. Permitted development rights in the Town and Country Planning (General Permitted Development) (England) Order 2015 (GPDO 2015), Sch 2, Part 11 and, for Wales, the Town and Country Planning (General Permitted Development) Order 1995 (GPDO 1995), Sch 2, Part 31, exist to authorise demolition (except that the demolition of buildings in conservation areas does not have permitted development rights in England and conservation area consent is required for such demolition in Wales). However these permitted development rights may be withdrawn by an article 4 Direction or may need to be subject to a determination that EIA is not required[37];

(v) unless planning permission, scheduled monument, listed building or conservation area consent has already been granted for the demolition, or demolition is required by a planning obligation, the local planning authority must be asked

---

[35] This issue is discussed in more detail in Harwood *Historic Environment Law* (Institute of Art and Law) at pp 160–170 and in its 2014 Supplement.

[36] The 1995 Demolition Direction (which operated in England and Wales) had excluded from the definition of development demolition which was authorised by scheduled monument, listed building or conservation area consent or the demolition of any building which was not a dwellinghouse or adjoining a dwellinghouse. The effect was that most commercial, infrastructure and public buildings could be demolished without being subject to planning control. The Court of Appeal in *R (SAVE Britain's Heritage) v Secretary of State for Communities and Local Government* [2011] EWCA Civ 334, [2011] JPL 1016 held that these exclusions were contrary to the EIA Directive as those projects could avoid a need for EIA. Those parts of the Demolition Direction were declared unlawful, bringing almost all demolition within the need for planning permission. The 2014 Demolition Direction is essentially the 1995 Direction without the parts which were ruled unlawful in *SAVE*.

[37] EIA requirements for permitted development are in the GPDO 2015, art 3(10)–(12), and GPDO 1995, art 3(10)–(12).

whether prior approval of the method of demolition and any proposed restoration of the site is required for permitted development rights for demolition (except of means of enclosure) to be carried out.

Fish farming

2.23 One inclusion within operational development is fish farming (including shellfish) in non-tidal waters. 'The placing or assembly of any tank in any part of any inland waters for the purpose of fish farming' is treated as an 'engineering operation' if it would not otherwise be development[38]. In this context 'tank' includes any cage and any other structure for use in fish farming.

MATERIAL CHANGE OF USE OF LAND

2.24 Material change of use requires a 'material change in the definable character of the use of the land'[39]. The character of a use is broad and does not allow the planning authorities to exercise detailed control over the use of land in the way that conditions on a planning permission may do. A change of use may occur when the activity on the site changes and sometimes when works are carried out to alter the use of land, such as physical conversion of a building for residential purposes without actual occupation having taken place[40]. In deciding whether a change of use has occurred, relevant elements include any change in the physical state of the land[41] and off-site effects[42].

2.25 Usually a material change of use will involve a change in the description of the use, for example from office to residential, or shop to café. In some cases the character of the use may change because the purpose of the activity may affect its extent. For example, a home occupier using his garage for repairing his cars would usually be acting within the residential use, but if he repairs other people's cars, particularly for payment, then this is likely to be a material change of use[43]. It is possible that a mere intensification of a use of land can be a material change of use – doing more of the same thing – but such cases will be very rare. Usually the new use is capable of being described differently by the activity or its purpose. There may be occasions when a material change of use resulting from changes in intensity can affect the overall character of the use, even though the descriptions of the uses do not change[44]. However it is important to remember that any intensification must change

---

[38] Town and Country Planning Act 1990, s 55(4A).
[39] *Hertfordshire County Council v Secretary of State for Communities and Local Government* [2012] EWHC 277 (Admin), [2012] JPL 836 at para 46 per Ouseley J, approved by the Court of Appeal [2012] EWCA Civ 1473 at para 11 per Pill LJ.
[40] *Impey v Secretary of State for the Environment* (1984) 47 P & CR 157 approved in *Welwyn Hatfield Council v Secretary of State for Communities and Local Government* [2011] UKSC 15. *Impey* suggested that the test may be whether the premises are usable for the new purpose.
[41] *Howell v Sunbury-on-Thames Urban District Council* (1964) 15 P & CR 26 per Upjohn LJ.
[42] *Westminster City Council v Secretary of State for Communities and Local Government* [2015] EWCA Civ 482 at para 41 per Richards LJ.
[43] See the comments of Sullivan J in *R v Thanet District Council, ex p Tapp* (2001) 81 P & CR 37 at para 54.
[44] See *Fidler v First Secretary of State* [2004] EWCA Civ 1295, [2005] 1 P & CR 12 at para 29 per Carnwath LJ doubting the relevance of Donaldson LJ's comment in *Kensington and Chelsea RBC v Secretary of State and Mia Carla Ltd* [1981] JPL 50 that 'If the planners were incapable of formulating what was use after intensification and what was use before intensification then there had been no material change of use' to the post-1991 legislation.

2.26 *The meaning of development*

the character of the use[45]. In assessing whether there has been a change of character in the use, the impact of the use on other premises is relevant, but cannot be considered in isolation from what is happening on the land[46]. In *Reed v Secretary of State for Communities and Local Government*[47] the inspector had found that doubling the number of residential caravans from one to two amounted to a material change of use of the land. The decision was remitted in the absence of any explanation as to why that should be the case, beyond simple mathematics, and the failure of the inspector to say that there had been a change in the character of the use of the land, let alone why he thought that was the case.

2.26 The identity of the user of the land will usually be immaterial to whether a material change of use takes place. The question will be the nature of the activities which are carried out on the site and this may have implications for the characterisation of the use of the land. For example, in *East Barnet Urban District Council v British Transport Commission*[48] the handling of a different commodity at a rail transit depot was not a material change of use. What the character is and what is taken into account in a change has been the subject of inconclusive judicial comment. In *Thames Heliport plc v Tower Hamlets London Borough Council*[49] Schiemann LJ said:

> 'Planning law was concerned ... with the effects of the making of material changes in the use of land ... focusing the eye on what mattered from an environmental point of view'.

2.27 In *Richmond-upon-Thames London Borough Council v Secretary of State for the Environment, Transport and the Regions*[50] Christopher Lockhart-Mummery QC, sitting as a Deputy High Court Judge, followed *Panayi v Secretary of State for the Environment*[51], holding that a change of use that gave rise to planning considerations could be material. In that case the implications of losing seven units of small accommodation was relevant when considering a building's conversion back to a single dwellinghouse. However, Ouseley J took a relatively narrower approach to change of use in *Rugby Football Union v Secretary of State for Local Government, Transport and the Regions*[52]:

> 'I have some reservations about the extent to which an assessment of likely impact from the way in which a particular use may be carried out at a particular place is really the key to whether there is a change in the character of the use of land. A change in the character of the use of land can of course occur even where on the facts of a particular case there is little impact and may not occur even where there is a substantial impact'.

2.28 Where land is being used for more than one activity, the cessation of one of the uses is not by itself a material change of use[53]. The issue is whether the remaining

---

[45] *Lilo Blum v Secretary of State for the Environment* [1987] JPL 278 at 280 per Simon Brown J.
[46] *Hertfordshire County Council v Secretary of State for Communities and Local Government* [2012] EWCA Civ 1473 at para 26 per Pill LJ.
[47] [2014] EWCA Civ 241, [2014] JPL 725.
[48] [1962] 2 QB 484.
[49] [1997] JPL 448 at 450.
[50] [2001] JPL 84.
[51] (1980) 50 P & CR 109 at 117.
[52] [2001] EWHC Admin 927, [2002] JPL 740 at para 52.
[53] *Philgrow Ltd v Secretary of State for the Environment* [1985] JPL 318, CA.

use has changed to such a degree as to amount to a material change of use. In *R v Thanet District Council, ex p Tapp*[54] it was accepted that a change from military use of an airfield to civilian use was not a material change of use.

Primary and ancillary uses

2.29 A use of land includes uses which are ordinarily incidental or ancillary to the primary use. This is a judge-made concept[55] designed to cater for the common situation that different and smaller uses will be part of a main use (for example, a shop may have an office for its management[56]; a sports centre might have a store for equipment). There must be a relationship between the potential ancillary use and the main use[57], otherwise there would be two separate uses or a mixed use.

2.30 'Ordinarily' excludes particularly unusual uses, but is wider than 'commonly'. In *Harrods Ltd v Secretary of State for the Environment*[58] the courts held that whilst a car park was an incidental part of the retail use of a department store, a helicopter landing pad on the roof for the Harrods chairman was not. Sullivan J focused his judgment on the ordinarily incidental issue. In the Court of Appeal, Schiemann LJ agreed in broad terms with the High Court analysis, but said the proper approach was to consider whether, ignoring the Use Classes Order, what is involved amounts to a material change of use[59]. Examples of activities found not to be ancillary to the main use are: the keeping and slaughtering of chickens for sale (some 300 per week) was not incidental to the shop use of the premises[60]; providing coin-operated booths for viewing films in a shop[61]; and holding major festivals at a residential theological college[62].

2.31 Whilst there is Scottish authority that an ancillary use may be offsite[63], the ancillary use must be within the same planning unit (a concept discussed below): see *Westminster Council v British Waterways Board* per Lord Bridge[64]:

> 'The concept of a single planning unit used for one main purpose to which other uses carried on within the unit are ancillary is a familiar one in planning law. But it is a misapplication of this concept to treat the use or uses of a single planning unit as ancillary to activities carried on outside the unit altogether'.

---

[54] (2001) 81 P & CR 37.
[55] First appearing in *Percy Trentham Ltd v Gloucestershire County Council* [1966] 1 WLR 506 at 512 per Lord Denning MR and 514 per Diplock LJ.
[56] An example used in *Brazil Concrete Ltd v. Amersham RDC* (1967) 18 P & CR 396 at 399 per Lord Denning MR.
[57] *Main v Secretary of State for the Environment* (1999) 77 P & CR 300.
[58] [2001] EWHC Admin 600, [2002] JPL 437, affirmed [2002] EWCA Civ 412, [2002] JPL 1258.
[59] Court of Appeal at paras 20, 21. For some reason helicopter movements tend to prompt disputes about ancillary uses: *South Oxfordshire District Council v Secretary of State for the Environment, Transport and the Regions* [2000] 2 All ER 667 (dwellinghouse); *R (on the application of I'm Your Man Ltd) v North Somerset Council* [2004] EWHC 342, [2004] JPL 1563 (aviation museum).
[60] *Hussain v Secretary of State for the Environment* (1971) 23 P & CR 330.
[61] *Lydcare Ltd v Secretary of State for the Environment* (1984) 49 P & CR 186.
[62] *International Society for Krishna Consciousness v Secretary of State* [1992] JPL 962.
[63] *Farleyer Estate v Secretary of State for Scotland* 1992 SC 202.
[64] [1985] AC 676 at 684–685. The need to be in the same planning unit appears to have been overlooked in *Farleyer*.

2.32 *The meaning of development*

The planning unit

2.32 In considering whether a material change of use has taken place, it is necessary to identify the appropriate planning unit. This is the most appropriate physical area against which to determine whether a material change has taken place. As with primary and ancillary uses, the planning unit is a judge-made concept – it is not in the legislation – but one which enables the identification of the relevant land in s 55.

2.33 Three broad categories for determining the planning unit were identified by Bridge J in *Burdle v Secretary of State for the Environment*[65]:

> 'First, whenever it is possible to recognise a single main purpose of the occupier's use of his land to which secondary activities are incidental or ancillary, the whole unit of occupation should be considered. That proposition emerges clearly from *G Percy Trentham Ltd v Gloucestershire County Council* [1966] 1 WLR 506 , where Diplock LJ said, at p 513:
>
>> "What is the unit which the local authority are entitled to look at and deal with in an enforcement notice for the purpose of determining whether or not there has been a 'material change in the use of any buildings or other land'? As I suggested in the course of the argument, I think for that purpose what the local authority are entitled to look at is the whole of the area which was used for a particular purpose, including any part of that area whose use was incidental to or ancillary to the achievement of that purpose."
>
> But, secondly, it may equally be apt to consider the entire unit of occupation even though the occupier carries on a variety of activities and it is not possible to say that one is incidental or ancillary to another. This is well settled in the case of a composite use where the component activities fluctuate in their intensity from time to time, but the different activities are not confined within separate and physically distinct areas of land.
>
> Thirdly, however, it may frequently occur that within a single unit of occupation two or more physically separate and distinct areas are occupied for substantially different and unrelated purposes. In such a case each area used for a different main purpose (together with its incidental and ancillary activities) ought to be considered as a separate planning unit'.

Applying the categories is not always simple. The evidence needs to be considered with care and may be incomplete or inconsistent, particularly where the use is not derived from a planning permission. The planning unit might also be larger than the area which is the subject of the particular application[66]. In a composite or mixed use it is possible that different elements are not associated with particular parts of the premises[67].

The carrying on of a use

2.34 A use may be carried on even if at that moment there is no activity on site. For example, a building and land would still be in a factory use if the factory was

---
[65] [1972] 1 WLR 1207.
[66] For example, model aircraft flying on a farm: *R (on the application of Sellars) v Basingstoke and Deane Borough Council* [2013] EWHC 3673 (Admin), [2014] JPL 643.
[67] *Wipperman v Barking London Borough Council* (1966) 17 P&CR 225 at 229 per Widgery J, followed in *Westminster City Council v Secretary of State for Communities and Local Government* [2015] EWCA Civ 482 at paras 8, 27 per Richards LJ.

closed for the weekend or for a summer holiday[68]. Similarly an area of pavement was used for seating ancillary to a restaurant even though the tables and chairs were put away at night and during cold weather[69].

2.35 A lawful use will survive a lengthy period of inactivity on the land. Abandonment is possible in relation to prior use[70] though not in relation to rights acquired under a planning permission still capable of being implemented according to its terms[71]. There is some debate as to whether a use instituted under a planning permission can be abandoned by lack of use[72].

Conversely if a use is not lawful then it will need to be actively carried out for the limitation period to become lawful.

2.36 Identifying in legal terms the start of a use is not straightforward. It could not be later than the actual commencement of a use (for example, when the shop started trading). However the physical conversion of a building might give rise to a change of use before the use by the occupiers commences, for example, carrying out works to convert a building to residential use. The point in the process at which the change takes place has not been firmly resolved by the courts. Donaldson LJ suggested in *Impey v Secretary of State for the Environment*[73] that the test may be whether the premises are usable for the new use.

Exceptions to material changes of use

2.37 By s 55(2) various matters are not material changes of use:

'(d) the use of any buildings or other land within the curtilage of a dwellinghouse for any purpose incidental to the enjoyment of the dwellinghouse as such'.

Such uses include gardens, swimming pools for the use of occupants, the keeping of family pets, car parking and storage. The use must be incidental to the enjoyment of the dwellinghouse as such, rather than the particular interests of the owner. It is legitimate to consider what people normally do in dwellinghouses, and so the keeping of 40 dogs or having a replica Spitfire aircraft in the back garden were not incidental[74]. The term 'curtilage' covers land and buildings which are 'part and parcel' of the land comprised with a building[75]. Curtilage is not necessarily confined to a small area around a building. In the context of a mansion house the curtilage could cover a significant area and is likely to include stables and outbuildings[76]. That said,

---

[68] *Thurrock Borough Council v Secretary of State for the Environment* [2002] JPL 1278 at para 28 per Schiemann LJ.
[69] *Westminster City Council v Secretary of State for Communities and Local Government* [2013] EWHC 23 (Admin) at paras 57–61.
[70] *Hartley v Minister of Housing and Local Government* [1970] 1 WLR 413; *Secretary of State for the Environment, Transport and the Regions v Hughes* (2000) 80 P & CR 397.
[71] *Pioneer Aggregates (UK) Ltd v Secretary of State for the Environment* [1985] AC 132 at 143 per Lord Scarman.
[72] See *Stockton-on-Tees Borough Council v Secretary of State for Communities and Local Government* [2010] EWHC 1766 (Admin), [2011] JPL 183.
[73] (1980) 47 P & CR 157.
[74] *Wallington v Secretary of State for the Environment* [1991] JPL 942 and *London Borough of Croydon v Gladden* (1994) 68 P & CR 300 respectively.
[75] See *Methuen-Campbell v Walters* [1979] 1 QB 525 at 543 per Buckley LJ.
[76] *Skerritts of Nottingham Ltd v Secretary of State for the Environment, Transport and the Regions* [2001] QB 59.

2.38 *The meaning of development*

a large estate may well have the main house with a curtilage defined by the extent of formal gardens or a ha-ha, and parkland or grazing outside the curtilage[77]. Collins J observed in *R (on the application of Sumption) v London Borough of Greenwich*[78]:

> 'In an urban environment, land attached to a dwelling house which is able and intended to be used in conjunction with the house (whether or not formally described as its garden) is likely to be within its curtilage'.

2.38 A change to the curtilage of a building will usually be a consequence of operational development or the making of a material change in the use of land (for example from agricultural to residential), so a landowner cannot simply take advantage of the exception by extending the curtilage without planning permission[79].

2.39

> '(e) the use of any land for the purposes of agriculture or forestry (including afforestation) and the use for any of those purposes of any building occupied together with land so used'.

Agriculture has a special, and relaxed, status in planning law. A material change of use from any use to agriculture or forestry is not development and agricultural and forestry operational development has substantial permitted development rights. Agriculture is defined as including[80]:

> 'horticulture, fruit growing, seed growing, dairy farming, the breeding and keeping of livestock (including any creature kept for the production of food, wool, skins or fur, or for the purpose of its use in the farming of land), the use of land as grazing land, meadow land, osier land, market gardens and nursery grounds, and the use of land for woodlands where that use is ancillary to the farming of land for other agricultural purposes, and "agricultural" shall be construed accordingly'.

2.40 The sale of produce grown on a site is part of the agricultural use, but the sale of products grown elsewhere is not[81]. The stationing of a caravan for mixing cattle food and for the farmer to shelter in during the day (but not to live) was also an agricultural use[82]. In *Millington v Secretary of State for the Environment, Transport and the Regions*[83] the growing of grapes for winemaking and the making of wine at the farm from those grapes was an agricultural use, the latter being ancillary to the farming activities. The keeping of horses is not agricultural unless they are used in farming: *Belmont Farm Ltd v Minister of Housing and Local Government*[84]. This approach has been consistently followed, not least by the House of Lords in the rating case of *Whitsbury Farm and Stud Ltd v Hemens (Valuation Officer)* where Lord Goff said[85]:

---

[77] For example, in *Dyer v Dorset County Council* [1989] QB 346 not all of a 100-acre park was within the curtilage and in *McAlpine v Secretary of State for the Environment* [1995] 1 PLR 16 a grassed area used for recreation beyond the formal garden of a large house was held to be outside the curtilage.
[78] [2007] EWHC 2776 (Admin), [2008] 1 P & CR 336 at para 24.
[79] *Sampson's Executors v Nottinghamshire County Council* [1949] 2 KB 439.
[80] Town and Country Planning Act 1990, s 336(1).
[81] *Williams v Minister of Housing and Local Government* (1967) 18 P & CR 514.
[82] *Wealden District Council v Secretary of State for the Environment* [1988] JPL 268, CA.
[83] [2000] JPL 297. The case contains a useful examination of the agricultural use authorities.
[84] (1962) 13 P & CR. 417.
[85] [1988] AC 601 at 616.

'those operations were the grazing of thoroughbred horses in the course of breeding and rearing. ... I do not regard the operation of breeding and rearing of thoroughbred horses for the purposes of what can broadly be called recreation as an agricultural operation'.

2.41 Consequently the use of land for keeping or breeding horses (unless those horses are used in farming) is not agricultural. Whilst the use of land for the grazing of any kind of horse is agricultural, keeping is not. The distinction was discussed by Donaldson LJ in *Sykes v Secretary of State for the Environment*[86]:

'If horses are simply turned out on to the land with a view to feeding them from the land, clearly the land is being used for grazing. If, however, horses are being kept on the land and are being fed wholly or primarily by other means so that such grazing as they do is completely incidental and perhaps achieved merely because there are no convenient ways of stopping them doing it, then plainly the land is not being used for grazing but merely being used for keeping the animals. On the other hand, of course, if animals are put on to a field with a view to their grazing and are kept there for 24 hours a day, seven days a week over a period, it would not, I would have thought, be possible to say that, as they were being kept there, they were not being grazed. It is quite possible for horses to be both grazed and kept in the same place.'

2.42 There may be exceptions to agricultural uses. For example, in *Winchester City Council v Secretary of State for Communities and Local Government*[87] the production of pathogen-free eggs was an industrial rather than an agricultural process. Agricultural contracting might be ancillary to agricultural activities if it is the use of equipment which is also used to a significant degree on the farmer's own land. Otherwise agricultural contracting is a separate use of land to agriculture[88].

2.43

'(f) in the case of buildings or other land which are used for a purpose of any class specified in an order made by the Secretary of State under this section, the use of the buildings or other land or, subject to the provisions of the order, of any part of the buildings or the other land, for any other purpose of the same class'.

The use classes are set out in the Town and Country Planning (Use Classes) Order 1987 and are considered in more detail in Chapter 3. Where a building or other land is within one use class a change of use to another use within the same use class is not development[89].

The use classes are not comprehensive. There will be uses of land or buildings which fall outside the wording of all of the classes, described informally as *sui generis*. Certain uses are expressly excluded by the Order even if they would otherwise be within a class[90].

2.44 The concept of primary and ancillary uses remains, so land may be within a use class because of its primary use and still have ordinarily incidental uses[91]. A

---

[86] (1981) 42 P & CR 19 at 23.
[87] [2007] EWHC 2303 (Admin), [2008] JPL 315.
[88] See *Fidler v First Secretary of State* [2004] EWCA (Civ) 1295, [2005] JPL 510 at para 20 per Carnwath LJ.
[89] Town and Country Planning (Use Classes) Order 1987, SI 1987/764, art 3(1).
[90] Town and Country Planning (Use Classes) Order 1987, art 3(6).
[91] Town and Country Planning (Use Classes) Order 1987, art 3(3).

2.45 *The meaning of development*

mixed use comprising one or more use classes, or a use class and a *sui generis* use does not have the benefit of the use classes order[92]. For example, if a sandwich shop was in mixed A1/A3 use, the use classes order could not be relied upon to change to an A1 or A3 use.

Changes of use which are material

2.45 Section 55(3) provides that the following are material changes of use (whether they would be otherwise):

> '(a) the use as two or more separate dwellinghouses of any building previously used as a single dwellinghouse involves a material change in the use of the building and of each part of it which is so used'.

The conversion of a dwellinghouse into flats is therefore development (and also does not benefit from the Use Classes Order), as would be the subdivision of an existing flat within a building. A change of use to another form of residential use, such as a house in multiple occupation or lodgings, is not covered by this subsection although such changes will often be material in any event. Changing from two or more dwellinghouses into a single dwellinghouse is not within the subsection. Whether such a change is material has to be considered on its own facts. In *Richmond-upon-Thames London Borough Council v Secretary of State for the Environment, Transport and the Regions*[93] an inspector's decision that the conversion of a house back from seven flats to a single dwelling was not development was quashed as the inspector did not consider that small flats may fulfil a planning purpose. However the general approach of inspectors and local planning authorities is that a change of a building from two dwellings to a single dwelling is not a material change of use.

2.46

> '(b) the deposit of refuse or waste materials on land involves a material change in its use, notwithstanding that the land is comprised in a site already used for that purpose, if—
>
> (i) the superficial area of the deposit is extended, or
>
> (ii) the height of the deposit is extended and exceeds the level of the land adjoining the site'.

The deposit of waste on a temporary or permanent basis tends to be seen as a use of land. To provide a degree of planning control over long-established sites, the area and height of waste deposits is restricted.

2.47 The landfilling of hazardous waste, as defined by the Hazardous Waste (England and Wales) Regulations 2005, reg 6, is within the Town and Country Planning (Environmental Impact Assessment) Regulations 2011[94], Sch 1 and so requires EIA. Hazardous waste is defined by the Hazardous Waste Directive 91/689/EEC as amended (which include the European Council decisions providing that

---

[92] *Fidler v First Secretary of State* [2004] EWCA Civ 1295, [2005] JPL 510 at para 28 per Carnwath LJ, endorsing *Belmont Riding Centre v First Secretary of State* [2003] EWHC 1895 (Admin), [2004] JPL 593.
[93] [2001] JPL 84.
[94] SI 2011/1824.

asbestos in various contexts (including in construction waste) is hazardous waste). By reg 60 of the EIA Regulations 2011 the change in the use of land or buildings for the incineration, chemical treatment or landfilling of hazardous waste is a material change of use[95].

2.48 Additionally, by the Town and Country Planning Act 1990, s 55(5):

> 'the use for the display of advertisements of any external part of a building which is not normally used for that purpose shall be treated for the purposes of this section as involving a material change in the use of that part of the building'.

This enables the planning enforcement powers to be used against unlawful advertisements in addition to the advertising controls in the Town and Country Planning Act 1990, Part VIII. If the advertisements are displayed in accordance with the relevant Advertisements Regulations, then they have deemed planning permission[96].

Short-term lettings in London

2.49 A local variation to the meaning of development is provided by the Greater London (General Powers) Act 1973, s 25, which makes the use of residential premises in Greater London for short-term lets a material change of use. However, this was revised by the Deregulation Act 2015. Section 25 provides:

> '(1) For the purposes of section 55(1) of the Town and Country Planning Act 1990, the use as temporary sleeping accommodation of any residential premises in Greater London involves a material change of use of the premises and of each part thereof which is so used.
>
> (2) In this section:
>
> (a) "use as temporary sleeping accommodation" means use of sleeping accommodation which is occupied by the same person for less than 90 consecutive nights and which is provided (with or without other services) for a consideration arising either:
>
>   (i) by way of trade for money or money's worth; or
>
>   (ii) by reason of the employment of the occupant; whether or not the relationship of landlord and tenant is thereby created;
>
> (b) "residential premises" means a building, or any part of a building, which was previously used, or designed or constructed for use, as one or more permanent residences'.

2.50 In *R v Kensington and Chelsea Royal London Borough Council*[97] Lord Clyde explained the objective of this section:

> 'The purpose of the provision was plainly to control the extent to which residential property could be put to use for certain forms of short-term transitory occupation.

---

[95] Town and Country Planning (Environmental Impact Assessment) (England and Wales) Regulations 1999, SI 1999/293, reg 34, which is still in force in Wales, is to the same effect.

[96] Town and Country Planning Act 1990, s 222. The regulations are the Town and Country Planning (Control of Advertisements) (England) Regulations 2007, SI 2007/783, and in Wales the Town and Country Planning (Control of Advertisements) Regulations 1992, SI 1992/666.

[97] [1999] 1 WLR 1415. Section 25 is not overcome by the Use Class C3 dwellinghouse: *Hyde Park Residence Ltd v Secretary of State for the Environment, Transport and the Regions* [2000] JPL 936.

2.51 *The meaning of development*

That was achieved by requiring the obtaining of planning permission where residential property was going to be used for such purposes. The point is stressed in the explanation which I have already quoted in the grant of planning permission in the present case for the imposition of the condition in question. What the planning authority was seeking to do was to preserve a sufficiency of permanent accommodation in their area, no doubt on social, economic and environmental grounds, and to control the extent to which the character of the area and the amenity of particular residential premises might be affected by a constantly changing population of transitory residents'.

Even if a change from temporary sleeping accommodation to longer term residential accommodation is not a material change of use, a reversion to temporary sleeping accommodation would be a material change of use[98]. The section only applies to buildings previously used, designed or constructed for use as permanent residences, so does not apply to those designed as hotels or hostels.

2.51 The Deregulation Act 2015 introduces a limited exception by inserting s 25A, which provides that no material change of use occurs if the total number of nights use as temporary sleeping accommodation in that calendar year is no more than 90 and one or more of the persons providing the sleeping accommodation was liable to pay council tax for the premises[99]. Council tax liability falls on residents (whose sole or main residence is in the dwelling) and only in the absence of any residents on the owner[100].

2.52 The Secretary of State or the local planning authority may direct that the s 25A exception does not apply to particular residential premises or areas if 'it is necessary to protect the amenity of the locality'[101]. Unless the Minister directs or determines otherwise, the making of a direction by a local planning authority requires the Secretary of State's consent[102]. Directions may be revoked by the Minister.

---

[98] *Fairstate Ltd v First Secretary of State* [2005] EWCA Civ 238, [2005] JPL 1333, affirming [2005] JPL 369. In *Fairstate*, the occupation of temporary sleeping accommodation for 155 days by one person meant that the next short period of occupation was a material change of use.
[99] Greater London (General Powers) Act 1973, s 25A, inserted by the Deregulation Act 2015, s 44(3).
[100] Local Government Finance Act 1992, s 6.
[101] Greater London (General Powers) Act 1973, s 25B, inserted by the Deregulation Act 2015, s 44(4).
[102] Greater London (General Powers) Act 1973, s 25B(3), (5).

Chapter 3

Use classes

3.1 The definition of development in the Town and Country Planning Act 1990, s 55(1) is very wide, so the planning system has always sought to limit its operation when changes are small or presumed to be desirable. One such mechanism is the creation of use classes.

Use classes are defined categories of use. If land is in use within a particular use class then a change to any other use within that use class will not be development unless the ability to make that change has already been excluded by a planning permission. Use classes are quite separate to permitted development rights: permitted development rights automatically grant planning permission, but that may be removed; a change within a use class does not require planning permission at all. There is, though, a complex web of interrelationships between use classes and permitted development rights.

THE BASIS OF USE CLASSES

3.2 Amongst the actions excluded from the definition of development by the Town and Country Planning Act 1990, s 55(2) are those in para (f):

'(f) in the case of buildings or other land which are used for a purpose of any class specified in an order made by the Secretary of State under this section, the use of the buildings or other land or, subject to the provisions of the order, of any part of the buildings or the other land, for any other purpose of the same class'.

3.3 Where a building or other land is within one use class a change of use to another use within the same use class is not development[1]. The current order is the Town and Country Planning (Use Classes) Order 1987 (generally referred to as the Use Classes Order)[2]. Since use classes are a potent symbol of whether activities are seen as politically desirable in principle differences have arisen between the English and Welsh versions.

3.4 Several preliminary points are worth setting out:

(i) not all uses are in use classes;

---

[1] Town and Country Planning (Use Classes) Order 1987, art 3(1). Even if it would involve a material change of use, such as intensification, for example, *Eastleigh Borough Council v First Secretary of State* [2004] EWHC 1408 (Admin).
[2] SI 1987/764.

3.5 *Use classes*

(ii) to have the benefit of the use classes, the use must already be taking place within the use class[3];

(iii) a use which is a mix of uses in two or more use classes does not have the benefit of the Use Classes Order[4];

(iv) a change from a use within one use class to a use in a different use class or outside the use classes altogether will not necessarily be a material change of use, similarly for a change to a use class;

(v) the use class only excludes the need for planning permission for what would otherwise be a material change of use. Planning permission may still be required for operational development associated with that change, although permitted development rights for operational development are provided for particular use classes.

The Use Classes Order

3.5 The effect of the Use Classes Order is set out in its art 3(1):

> 'Subject to the provisions of this Order, where a building or other land is used for a purpose of any class specified in the Schedule, the use of that building or that other land for any other purpose of the same class shall not be taken to involve development of the land'.

References to 'a building' include 'references to land occupied with the building and used for the same purposes'[5]. The Use Classes Order is concerned with the primary use of land or buildings. Ancillary uses ('included in and ordinarily incidental to any' use class) would still fall within the use class of the primary use even if their description is within a different use class[6]. For example, a light industrial factory (use class B1) may have areas or buildings used for storage of materials to be processed or the finished product but the whole use remain as B1.

USES OUTSIDE THE USE CLASSES

3.6 Not all uses of buildings or land are within the classes in the Use Classes Order. There is no presumption that the use classes should be interpreted to seek to

---

[3] See 'are used' in Town and Country Planning Act 1990, s 55(2)(f). In *R v Ashfield District Council, ex p Bolsover District Council* (1995) 70 P & CR 507 it had been left open whether a use needed to have commenced by activity (in that case by shops starting to trade) before the Use Classes Order could be relied upon, but such use is required. The original use need not be lawful for a further use not to be development: if a material change of use takes place to a use within a use class without planning permission then a change to a different use within the same use class will not be a fresh act of development: *R (on the application of Harbige) v Secretary of State for Communities and Local Government* [2012] EWHC 1128 (Admin), [2012] JPL 1245.

[4] *Belmont Riding Centre v First Secretary of State* [2004] JPL 593 at para 31 per Richards J, approved in *Fidler v First Secretary of State* [2004] EWCA Civ 1295, [2005] JPL 510 at para 28 per Carnwath LJ and *Cocktails Ltd v Secretary of State for Communities and Local Government* [2008] EWCA Civ 1523, [2009] JPL 853 at para 8 per Pill LJ.

[5] Town and Country Planning (Use Classes) Order 1987, art 3(2), giving effect to the Town and Country Planning Act 1990, s 55(2)(f). A building includes part of a building: see Town and Country Planning Act 1990, s 336(1).

[6] See Town and Country Planning (Use Classes) Order 1987, art 3(3).

Uses outside the use classes **3.7**

include uses. Uses may simply fall outside the use classes[7]. Additionally some uses are specifically excluded by the Order, whether or not they would fall within the terms of the classes. Article 3(6) lists the excluded *sui generis* uses in England as follows:

'(a) as a theatre,

(b) as an amusement arcade or centre, or a funfair,

(c) as a launderette,

(d) for the sale of fuel for motor vehicles,

(e) for the sale or display for sale of motor vehicles,

(f) for a taxi business or business for the hire of motor vehicles,

(g) as a scrapyard, or a yard for the storage or distribution of minerals or the breaking of motor vehicles,

(h) for any work registrable under the Alkali, etc Works Regulation Act 1906,

(i) as a hostel,

(j) as a waste disposal installation for the incineration, chemical treatment (as defined in Annex I to Directive 2008/98/EC under heading D9) or landfill of hazardous waste as defined (in relation to England) in regulation 6 of the Hazardous Waste (England and Wales) Regulations 2005 or (in relation to Wales) in regulation 6 of the Hazardous Waste (Wales) Regulations 2005,

(k) as a retail warehouse club being a retail club where goods are sold, or displayed for sale, only to persons who are members of that club,

(l) as a night-club,

(m) as a casino,

(n) as a betting office,

(o) as a pay day loan shop'.

The *sui generis* categories in Wales, again set out in art 3(6), exclude sub-paras (l)–(o).

3.7 A 'pay day loan shop' means premises[8]:

'(a) from which high-cost short-term credit is provided principally to visiting members of the public and includes premises from which such credit is provided in addition to other financial or professional services, and

(b) which, but for provision made in this article, would fall within Class A2 (financial and professional services) of the Schedule to this Order.'

---

[7] *Tessier v Secretary of State for the Environment* (1976) 31 P & CR 161. Lord Widgery CJ indicated at 166 'the desirability of not stretching the Use Classes Order to embrace activities which do not clearly fall within it, because it is no bad thing that unusual activities should be treated as *sui generis* for this purpose'.
[8] Town and Country Planning (Use Classes) Order 1987, art 3(6A). The same paragraph defines '*high-cost short-term credit*' as having the meaning given in the edition of the Financial Conduct Authority's Handbook which came into effect on 1 April 2014 (following an amendment by the Authority in the Consumer Credit (Consequential and Supplementary Amendments) Instrument 2014).

3.8 *Use classes*

The betting shop and pay day loan shop exclusions came into force in England on 15 April 2015[9].

3.8 The reasons for *sui generis* uses are three-fold: they may be uses which government does not want to allow an automatic right to change *to* because of concerns about their proliferation (such as night clubs); uses which there is a reluctance to lose without control, such as laundrettes; and uses which might be a springboard to an undesirably located use (car showrooms are often at out of town centre business estates where conventional retailing would be discouraged).

Subdivision of land or buildings in the same use class

3.9 The Use Classes Order applies to part of a building as well as the whole, so sub-division of a building is not a material change of use. However the sub-division of a dwellinghouse is specifically excluded from this permissive approach[10]. Since internal works would not be operational development, the only element giving rise to the need for planning permission may be external alterations.

Removal of the use class by planning condition

3.10 The benefits of the Use Classes Order can be removed by planning condition, see *City of London Corpn v Secretary of State for the Environment*[11] where the use class could not be relied upon with a condition which said 'premises shall be used as an employment agency and for no other purpose'. In *Carpet Decor (Guildford) Ltd v Secretary of State for the Environment* Sir Douglas Frank said[12]:

> 'As a general principle, where a local planning authority intend to exclude the operation of the Use Classes Order or the General Development Order, they shall say so by an imposition of a condition in unequivocal terms, for in the absence of such a condition it must be assumed that those orders will have effect by operation of law'.

3.11 However this may be an unnecessary gloss and it is well established that removal may be by implication (such as providing that use be for a certain purpose and 'for no other use'): *Rugby Football Union v Secretary of State for Transport, Local Government and the Regions*[13] where the court considered a condition relating to stands at Twickenham Rugby Football Ground, which was worded that the stands, 'shall only be used ancillary to the main use of the premises as a sports stadium and for no other use' excluded the order. Mr Justice Ouseley held:

---

[9] By the Town and Country Planning (Use Classes) (Amendment) (England) Order 2015, SI 2015/597. Transitional provisions allow changes from A2, A3, A4 and A5 uses to a betting shop provided a betting premises licence had been issued or a change from an agricultural building provided that prior approval had been secured or determined not to be required, or a Class D(a) health centre provided that notice had been given to the local planning authority in all cases before that date: Town and Country Planning (Use Classes) (Amendment) (England) Order 2015, art 3.

[10] Town and Country Planning (Use Classes) Order 1987, art 4, reflecting the requirement of Town and Country Planning Act 1990, s 55(3)(a) that the subdivision of a dwellinghouse is development.

[11] (1971) 23 P & CR 169.

[12] (1982) 261 EG 56, [1981] JPL 806.

[13] [2001] EWHC Admin 927, [2002] JPL 740.

'56 ... The words "for no other use" are clear. They have no sensibly discernible purpose than to prevent some other use which might otherwise be permissible without planning permission. The Use Classes Order is an obvious source of such a permission.

57 I am satisfied that those words meet the test of being sufficiently clear for the exclusion of the Use Classes Order in relation to the three stands in question. The test is set out in *Dunoon Developments*'.

3.12 The test for excluding permitted development rights in *Dunoon Development Ltd v Secretary of State for the Environment and Poole Borough Council*[14] was that if the exclusion was not explicit, 'The question, therefore, is whether it is to be implied from the words themselves, in the context in which they are used, to so exclude them'. For example, in *Northampton Borough Council v Secretary of State*[15] a condition that 'the total non-food retail space ... shall not exceed 150,000 sq ft ...' prevented future increases.

3.13 Conditions may limit uses to particular activities which fall within a use class and so implicitly exclude the operation of the Use Classes Order to allow other activities within that class. Carrying on the prohibited activities would be a breach of condition. Government guidance accepts that implicit exclusion is possible. Circular 11/95 provides a model condition for non-food retailing in the following terms[16]:

> 'The premises shall not be used for the sale of food for consumption off the premises other than confectionery'.

This is effective to prevent Class A1 sales of food (other than what in practice are bars of chocolate stacked by the checkouts).

3.14 The effectiveness of a similar condition was considered in *Royal London Mutual Insurance Society Ltd v Secretary of State for Communities and Local Government*[17]. A condition on planning permission for a retail warehouse park provided:

> 'The retail consent shall be for non-food sales only in bulky trades normally found on retail parks which are furniture, carpets, DIY, electrical goods, car accessories, garden items and such other trades as the council may permit in writing'.

Mrs Justice Patterson held[18]:

> 'the words of the condition ... have no other sensibly discernible purpose than to prevent some other use that might otherwise be permissible without planning permission'.

She also took the view, necessarily, that the restriction had continuing effect.

3.15 In *R (on the application of Wilkinson) v Rossendale Borough Council*[19] a condition that 'The premises shall be used solely for the sewing, making up and

---

[14] (1993) 65 P & CR 101.
[15] [2005] EWHC 168 (Admin), [2005] JPL 1213.
[16] Appendix A, Model Condition 49.
[17] [2013] EWHC 3597 (Admin), [2014] JPL 458.
[18] At para 36.
[19] [2002] EWHC 1204 (Admin) at paras 75–78 per Sullivan J.

3.16 *Use classes*

repairing of tarpaulins and for no other purpose' excluded other industrial activities permissible under the then Use Classes Order.

3.16 Whilst the language of 'unequivocal terms' has been adopted in subsequent cases[20] it is more of a warning than a rule. There are many conditions which fail to express their stance in unequivocal terms and may indeed be hard to construe, but which have a meaning and significant consequences. Since removing the use classes is an important, and usually non-routine, step, it would normally be done clearly, even if implicitly.

CATEGORISATION

3.17 The use classes are as follows:

Part A: shopping area uses

    A1: Shops[21]

    A2: Financial and professional services

    A3: Restaurants and cafes: use for the sale of food and drink for consumption on the premises

    A4: Drinking establishments: use as a public house, wine-bar or other drinking establishment

    A5: Hot food takeaways: use for the sale of hot food for consumption off the premises

Part B: business and industrial uses

    B1: Business (offices, light industrial and research)

    B2: General industrial (now includes previous classes B3–B7)

    B3–B7: repealed

    B8: Storage or distribution

Part C: residential uses

    C1: Hotels

    C2: Residential institutions

    C2A: Secure residential institutions

    C3: Dwelling houses

    C4: Houses in multiple occupation

Part D: community uses

    D1: Non-residential institutions

    D2: Assembly and leisure.

---

[20] *Telford and Wrekin Council v Secretary of State for Communities and Local Government and Growing Enterprises Ltd [2013] EWHC 79 (Admin)* at para 33; *Royal London Mutual Insurance Society Ltd v Secretary of State for Communities and Local Government* at para 14.

[21] After 21 April 2005, class A1 uses include internet cafés.

Categorisation **3.20**

Part A: shopping area uses

3.18   The essence of Part A is that these are walk-in, commercial-type services which are offered to members of the public, although profit making is not required. Planning has always favoured A1 shops over other A class uses; for example, permitted development rights allow changes from those uses to A1 but not usually from A1 and policies have tended to protect the proportion of A1 uses in the best shopping streets.

Class A1: shops

3.19   There is a lengthy list of activities which are defined as shops:

'Use for all or any of the following purposes:

(a)   for the retail sale of goods other than hot food,

(b)   as a post office,

(c)   for the sale of tickets or as a travel agency,

(d)   for the sale of sandwiches or other cold food for consumption off the premises,

(e)   for hairdressing,

(f)   for the direction of funerals,

(g)   for the display of goods for sale,

(h)   for the hiring out of domestic or personal goods or articles,

(i)   for the washing or cleaning of clothes or fabrics on the premises,

(j)   for the reception of goods to be washed, cleaned or repaired,

(k)   as an internet café; where the primary purpose of the premises is to provide facilities for enabling members of the public to access the internet;

where the sale, display or service is to visiting members of the public'.

The sale of cold food for consumption off the premises is within class A1, as is the sale of hot or cold drinks[22]. The sale of food and drink for consumption on the premises or of hot food for consumption off the premises is covered by a later A class. Several of the art 3(6) exceptions also impinge on the A1 class: petrol filling stations, car showrooms and retail warehouse clubs are *sui generis*, as are launderettes[23].

The internet café category only applies in England.

Class A2: financial and professional services

3.20   Class A2 comprises:

'Use for the provision of:

(a)   financial services, or

---

[22]   Food and drink are separately identified in class A3.
[23]   Launderette is of the self-service type; dry cleaners are A1. The exclusion of launderettes is primarily to protect them from being turned into shops. The *sui generis* nature of car showrooms restricts the conversion of those uses, often on business estates, into unrestricted retail.

3.21 *Use classes*

(b) professional services (other than health or medical services), or

(c) any other services which it is appropriate to provide in a shopping area,

where the services are provided principally to visiting members of the public.'

In Wales, after 'other services' the class says '(including use as a betting office)'. This was removed in England from 15 April 2015, when betting offices were made *sui generis*[24].

3.21 The A2 uses are classically banks and estate agents, and include bureaux de change[25]. The professional services category is constrained by the exclusion of health or medical services (which tend to be D1 community uses), but also by the need for the services to be provided 'principally to visiting members of the public'. In *Kalra v Secretary of State for the Environment*[26] the Court of Appeal held that solicitors' offices who base themselves in or close to shopping areas in the hope of attracting clients who walk in off the street could be A2 uses[27]. That the public might need appointments did not alter the position: hairdressers have them but are still A1[28].

Food and drink (classes A3–A5)

3.22 The sale of food and drink for consumption on the premises, or of hot food for takeaway was traditionally a single use class. That remains the case in Wales where use class A3 is:

'**Food and drink**

Use for the sale of food or drink for consumption on the premises or of hot food for consumption off the premises'.

3.23 The use class was split into three in England in 2005:

'**A3 Restaurants and cafes**

Use for the sale of food and drink for consumption on the premises.

A4 Drinking establishments

Use as a public house, wine-bar or other drinking establishment

A5 Hot food takeaways

Use for the sale of hot food for consumption off the premises'.

This change was to control what was seen as a proliferation of pubs and takeaway uses arising out of previously innocuous restaurants[29].

---

[24] By the Town and Country Planning (Use Classes) (Amendment) (England) Order 2015, SI 2015/597.
[25] *Palisade Investments Ltd v Secretary of State for the Environment* (1995) 69 P & CR 638.
[26] (1996) 72 P & CR 423.
[27] These would include private law firms as well as Citizens Advice Bureaux and law centres.
[28] *Kalra* at 429 per Henry LJ.
[29] The preference is reflected in the permitted development rights to change from A4 or A5 to A3 but neither from A3 to A4 or A5, or from A4 to A5: Town and Country Planning (General Permitted Development) (England) Order 2015, Sch 2, Part 3, Class B.

Part B: business and industrial uses

3.24

'**B1 Business**

Use for all or any of the following purposes:

(a) as an office other than a use within class A2 (financial and professional services),

(b) for research and development of products or processes, or

(c) for any industrial process,

being a use which can be carried out in any residential area without detriment to the amenity of that area by reason of noise, vibration, smell, fumes, smoke, soot, ash, dust or grit.

Class B2. General industrial

Use for the carrying on of an industrial process other than one falling within Class B1 above.

Class B8. Storage or distribution

Use for storage or as a distribution centre.'

In Wales, class B8 (storage or distribution) does not include use of that building or land for the storage of, or as a distribution centre for, radioactive material or radioactive waste[30].

3.25 The three sub-paragraphs in class B1 are all within the same use class, so whilst there may be reference to B1 office or B1 light industrial there may be any change or mix between those sub-paragraphs. 'Office' is not defined in planning legislation. In *London Residuary Board v London Borough of Lambeth*[31] an Inspector was entitled to regard the former Greater London Council headquarters, County Hall, as not being a B1 office because of the characteristics of public debate and decision making associated with it, including debating chamber, committee rooms and use for public meetings, although the Secretary of State's agreement with this was quashed because of erroneous reliance on the use not being commercial.

3.26 An 'industrial process' is defined as[32]:

'a process for or incidental to any of the following purposes:

(a) the making of any article or part of any article (including a ship or vessel, or a film, video or sound recording);

(b) the altering, repairing, maintaining, ornamenting, finishing, cleaning, washing, packing, canning, adapting for sale, breaking up or demolition of any article; or

(c) the getting, dressing or treatment of minerals;

in the course of any trade or business other than agriculture, and other than a use carried out in or adjacent to a mine or quarry'.

---

[30] Town and Country Planning (Use Classes) Order 1987, art 3(7). The radioactive definitions are as contained in the Environmental Permitting (England and Wales) Regulations 2010, SI 2010/675: Use Classes Order, art 3(8).
[31] (1989) 58 P & CR 370 at 382–383 per Slade LJ.
[32] Town and Country Planning (Use Classes) Order 1987, art 2.

3.27 *Use classes*

It therefore extends beyond 'metal-bashing' to include tailoring and food preparation along with many digital and creative businesses. The primary use and ancillary uses may need to be carefully identified[33]. For example, if bread is baked to be sold from the premises then the use would be an A1 shop. However if most of the bread is taken offsite and sold from other premises then the site would be in a B1 or (possibly) B2 use. The trade or business need not be profit-making or commercial and may include a public authority or charity's activities[34].

3.27 Several of the *sui generis* categories are pertinent to industrial processes: a scrapyard, or a yard for the storage or distribution of minerals or the breaking of motor vehicles, works registrable under the Alkali Works Regulation Act 2006 or waste disposal installations involving hazardous substances.

Various particular obnoxious industrial processes had been listed in classes B3 to B7 but these were revoked in 1995. Those activities are now within B2.

3.28 Flexibility between B1 and B2 uses on a mixed use site is provided by art 3(4):

> 'Where land on a single site or on adjacent sites used as parts of a single undertaking is used for purposes consisting of or including purposes falling within classes B1 and B2 in the Schedule, those classes may be treated as a single class in considering the use of that land for the purposes of this Order, so long as the area used for a purpose falling within class B2 is not substantially increased as a result'.

3.29 For B8, a common issue is whether storage and distribution is ancillary to another use. If a site takes in items, finishes them and sends them out that may be a B1 or B2 use with storage and distribution being ancillary. An online retailer's warehouse will be a B8 use. However, a shop which does a substantial amount of business by home delivery (such as a supermarket) or by postal sales (for example, a specialist retailer) will still be a shop.

3.30 Previously classes B3 to B7 comprised five special industrial groups labelled A to E. These may have continuing relevance to old planning permissions, leases or restrictive covenants. Class B3 Special Industrial Group A was:

> 'Use for any work registrable under the Alkali, etc Works Regulation Act 1906 and which is not included in any of classes B4 to B7 below'.

This was revoked from 31 March 1992 and is now *sui generis* under art 3(6)(h).

The following four use classes were revoked from 9 March 1995. These are now within the general industrial class B2 or the light industrial class B1(c), more usually the former.

---

[33] It has been held that the incidental use may be incidental to a use being carried out on a completely separate site: *Winchester City Council v Secretary of State for Communities and Local Government* [2007] EWHC 2303 (Admin), [2008] JPL 315. In that case an unusually technical process of producing pathogen-free eggs from hens isolated in buildings was held to be an industrial process rather than agriculture, as they were used for vaccine production offsite and so incidental to that industrial process.

[34] For example offices (*London Residuary Body v Secretary of State for the Environment* (1989) 58 P & CR 370 at 379 per Slade LJ) or as a 'cooking centre' for the provision of school meals (*Rael-Brook Ltd v Minister of Housing and Local Government* [1967] 2 QB 65).

Categorisation **3.33**

3.31 Class B4 Special Industrial Group B comprised:

'Use for any of the following processes, except where the process is ancillary to the getting, dressing or treatment of minerals and is carried on in or adjacent to a quarry or mine:

(a) smelting, calcining, sintering or reducing ores, minerals, concentrates or mattes;

(b) converting, refining, re-heating, annealing, hardening, melting, carburising, forging or casting metals or alloys other than pressure die-casting;

(c) recovering metal from scrap or drosses or ashes;

(d) galvanizing;

(e) pickling or treating metal in acid;

(f) chromium plating'.

3.32 Class B5 Special Industrial Group C was

'Use for any of the following processes, except where the process is ancillary to the getting, dressing or treatment of minerals and is carried on in or adjacent to a quarry or mine:

(a) burning bricks or pipes;

(b) burning lime or dolomite;

(c) producing zinc oxide, cement or alumina;

(d) foaming, crushing, screening or heating minerals or slag;

(e) processing pulverized fuel ash by heat;

(f) producing carbonate of lime or hydrated lime;

(g) producing inorganic pigments by calcining, roasting or grinding'.

3.33 Class B6 Special Industrial Group D covered:

'Use for any of the following processes:

(a) distilling, refining or blending oils (other than petroleum or petroleum products);

(b) producing or using cellulose or using other pressure sprayed metal finishes (other than in vehicle repair workshops in connection with minor repairs, or the application of plastic powder by the use of fluidised bed and electrostatic spray techniques);

(c) boiling linseed oil or running gum;

(d) processes involving the use of hot pitch or bitumen (except the use of bitumen in the manufacture of roofing felt at temperatures not exceeding 220°C and also the manufacture of coated roadstone);

(e) stoving enamelled ware;

(f) producing aliphatic esters of the lower fatty acids, butyric acid, caramel, hexamine, iodoform, napthols, resin products (excluding plastic moulding or extrusion operations and producing plastic sheets, rods, tubes, filaments, fibres or optical components produced by casting, calendering, moulding, shaping or extrusion), salicylic acid or sulphonated organic compounds;

(g) producing rubber from scrap;

(h) chemical processes in which chlorphenols or chlorcresols are used as intermediates;

3.34 *Use classes*

(i) manufacturing acetylene from calcium carbide;

(j) manufacturing, recovering or using pyridine or picolines, any methyl or ethyl amine or acrylates'.

3.34 Finally, class B7 Special Industrial Group E was:

'Use for carrying on any of the following industries, businesses or trades:

- Boiling blood, chitterlings, nettlings or soap.
- Boiling, burning, grinding or steaming bones.
- Boiling or cleaning tripe.
- Breeding maggots from putrescible animal matter.
- Cleaning, adapting or treating animal hair.
- Curing fish.
- Dealing in rags and bones (including receiving, storing, sorting or manipulating rags in, or likely to become in, an offensive condition, or any bones, rabbit skins, fat or putrescible animal products of a similar nature).
- Dressing or scraping fish skins.
- Drying skins.
- Making manure from bones, fish, offal, blood, spent hops, beans or other putrescible animal or vegetable matter.
- Making or scraping guts.
- Manufacturing animal charcoal, blood albumen, candles, catgut, glue, fish oil, size or feeding stuff for animals or poultry from meat, fish, blood, bone, feathers, fat or animal offal either in an offensive condition or subjected to any process causing noxious or injurious effluvia.
- Melting, refining or extracting fat or tallow.
- Preparing skins for working'.

Part C: residential uses

Class C1: hotel

3.35

'Use as a hotel or as a boarding or guest house where, in each case, no significant element of care is provided'.

The essence of a hotel is that it takes transient passengers[35]. There will not be (with perhaps a few exceptions) long-term residents or people making the units their homes. The premises will be staffed and catering will be provided on site, but the facilities available to residents for their own catering will be rudimentary. ODPM

---

[35] *Mayflower Cambridge Ltd v Secretary of State for the Environment* (1975) 30 P & CR 28. The term 'hotel' is widely used in statute but rarely defined. In the Hotel Proprietors Act 1956, s 1(3) provides: 'In this Act, the expression "hotel" means an establishment held out by the proprietor as offering food, drink and, if so required, sleeping accommodation, without special contract, to any traveller presenting himself who appears able and willing to pay a reasonable sum for the services and facilities provided and who is in a fit state to be received'.

Circular 03/2005 said 'These are premises which provide a room as temporary accommodation on a commercial, fee-paying basis, where meals can be provided but where residential care is not provided'[36]. A hotel is in the C1 use class, along with boarding or guest houses.

Hostel

3.36 A hostel is a *sui generis* use, taken out of the C1 use class in 1994[37]. It must, therefore, be different from a hotel, boarding or guest house. The fullest assessment of the meaning of hostel was given by Kennedy J in *Panayi v Secretary of State for the Environment*[38], concerning an alleged change from 4 self-contained flats and prior to the removal of hostels from the C1 use class. He started with the statutory definition in the Housing Act 1974, s 129 (now contained in the same terms in the Housing Act 1985, s 622)[39]:

> 'a building in which is provided, for persons generally or for a class or classes of persons residential accommodation (otherwise than in separate and self-contained sets of premises) and either board or facilities for the preparation of food adequate to the needs of those persons, or both'.

3.37 The court also cited the Greater London Council General Powers Act 1981, s 8 definition:

> '"hostel" means any premises in which there is provided on payment sleeping accommodation, whether with or without the provision of board or facilities for the preparation of food, in one or more common dormitories or other sleeping areas, if in any one of those areas four or more persons, not all being members of the same family or the same household, are accommodated at the same time'.

This definition requires dormitories or sleeping areas for people not in the same household. In *Commercial and Residential Property Development Co Ltd v Secretary of State for the Environment*[40] Glidewell J said hostel means 'a building in which people either live or stay which provides communal facilities. The sleeping accommodation is often, although not by any means always, in dormitories other than single rooms and provides shared cooking, eating and recreational facilities. It is of the essence of a hostel that its accommodation is relatively basic and inexpensive'. He drew a distinction between permanent accommodation in a hostel, which could be treated as part of the housing stock, and transient accommodation, which had many of the characteristics of a hotel. Having reviewed these cases, in *Panayi* Kennedy J decided not to try to add to these definitions of the word hostel, which was an ordinary English word in common use.

---

[36] Paragraph 59. The circular was cancelled in 2014.
[37] Town and Country Planning (Use Classes) Order 1987, art 3(6)(i).
[38] [1985] JPL 783. *Panayi* does not provide a definitive checklist of relevant factors: *Westminster City Council v Secretary of State for Communities and Local Government* [2015] EWCA Civ 482 at para 30 per Richards LJ.
[39] In *R (on the application of Hossack) v Kettering Borough Council* [2002] EWCA Civ 886, [2002] JPL 1206, the Court of Appeal were disposed to accept that the Housing Act cases on HMOs and dwelling houses applied to the interpretation of the Use Classes Order (para 25 per Simon Brown LJ).
[40] (1981) 80 LGR 443.

3.38 *Use classes*

3.38 ODPM Circular 03/2005 commented[41]:

'A hostel usually provides overnight or short-term accommodation which may be supervised, where people (including sometimes the homeless) can usually stay free or cheaply. Hostels may provide board, although some may provide facilities for self-catering. The element of supervision should not be relied upon as a determining factor but as a factor to take into account in consideration of the use class of the premises. Occasionally, hostels are used to provide longer-term accommodation, although it should be stressed that a hostel is not a residential care home, irrespective of any supervision it may have'.

There is no satisfactory definition for planning purposes of a 'hostel'. Perhaps the key elements are: (a) communal facilities, including kitchens; (b) accommodation not being self-contained; (c) on-site management and supervision; (d) limited services such as some board or cleaning.

Class C2: residential institutions

3.39 Class C2 comprises:

'Use for the provision of residential accommodation and care to people in need of care (other than a use within class C3 (dwelling houses)).

Use as a hospital or nursing home.

Use as a residential school, college or training centre'.

3.40 Care is defined in the Use Classes Order as[42]:

'personal care for people in need of such care by reason of old age, disablement, past or present dependence on alcohol or drugs or past or present mental disorder, and in class C2 also includes the personal care of children and medical care and treatment'.

It is sufficient for old age to require care, rather than a medical condition[43].

The expression 'residential development' in planning policy might extend to C2 uses as well as other residential uses and not be confined to C3 dwellinghouses[44].

Class C2A: secure residential institutions

3.41

'Use for the provision of secure residential accommodation, including use as a prison, young offenders institution, detention centre, secure training centre, custody centre, short-term holding centre, secure hospital, secure local authority accommodation or use as military barracks'.

The C2A use class was introduced as a consequence of the abolition of Crown immunity from planning law by the Planning and Compulsory Purchase Act 2004. With the exception of secure local authority accommodation, these uses were carried

---

[41] Paragraph 61. Cancelled in 2014.
[42] Town and Country Planning (Use Classes) Order 1987, art 2.
[43] *Leelamb Homes Ltd v Secretary of State for Communities and Local Government* [2009] EWHC 1926 (Admin) at para 20 per Robin Purchas QC.
[44] *Barchester Healthcare Ltd v Secretary of State for Communities and Local Government* [2010] EWHC 2784 (Admin), [2011] JPL 544.

out by the Crown on land without needing planning permission. The use class allows a former military base to become an immigration detention centre without a need for planning permission.

Class C3: dwellinghouse

3.42 The dwellinghouse category varies between the nations. Wales continues to have the original, and simpler version:

'Use as a dwellinghouse (whether or not as a sole or main residence):

(a) by a single person or by people living together as a family, or

(b) by not more than 6 residents living together as a single household (including a household where care is provided for residents)'.

3.43 In England there was an intention to separate out unrelated persons who might live together as a single household, such as students or young workers in a flatshare, from family occupiers. The C3 use class was revised in 2010 to provide:

'**Class C3: dwellinghouses**

Use as a dwellinghouse (whether or not as a sole or main residence) by:

(a) a single person or by people to be regarded as forming a single household;

(b) not more than six residents living together as a single household where care is provided for residents; or

(c) not more than six residents living together as a single household where no care is provided to residents (other than a use within Class C4).

Interpretation of Class C3

For the purposes of Class C3(a) *'single household'* shall be construed in accordance with section 258 of the Housing Act 2004.'

Also in England only is Class C4:

'**Class C4: houses in multiple occupation**

Use of a dwellinghouse by not more than six residents as a "house in multiple occupation"

Interpretation of Class C4

For the purposes of Class C4 a "house in multiple occupation" does not include a converted block of flats to which section 257 of the Housing Act 2004 applies but otherwise has the same meaning as in section 254 of the Housing Act 2004'.

3.44 In *Gravesham Borough Council v Secretary of State for the Environment* McCullough J described dwellinghouses as 'buildings that ordinarily afford the facilities required for day-to-day private domestic existence'[45]. He said that buildings which remained dwellinghouses included second homes, homes which cannot be occupied because of flooding or extensive repairs and time-share holiday cottages. In that case a building constructed with planning permission as a 'weekend and holiday chalet' subject to a condition prohibiting winter use was a dwellinghouse.

---

[45] (1984) 47 P & CR 142 at 146.

3.45 Use classes

3.45 Premises which are used as holiday accommodation might be dwellinghouses. In *Blackpool Borough Council v Secretary of State for the Environment* an inspector's conclusion that a house used by the owner as a second home for holidays by himself and his family, by members of his office staff, and by 'family groups' who paid rent was used as a dwellinghouse was upheld[46]. *Moore v Secretary of State for the Environment and New Forest District Council*[47] concerned an Inspector's finding that outbuildings to a country house which were each 'supplied with the facilities necessary for daily life, including living, sleeping and eating space, kitchens, bathrooms and WC's' but as let for short periods between a weekend and three or four months were holiday accommodation rather than dwellinghouses. The Court of Appeal disagreed, rejecting the view that holiday accommodation cannot be a dwellinghouse[48].

3.46 In a later case, *Moore v Secretary of State for Communities and Local Government and Suffolk Coastal District Council*, the Court of Appeal emphasised[49]:

> 'whether the use of a dwelling house for commercial letting as holiday accommodation amounts to a material change of use will be a question of fact and degree in each case, and the answer will depend upon the particular characteristics of the use as holiday accommodation. Neither of the two extreme propositions – that using a dwelling house for commercial holiday lettings will always amount to a material change of use, or that use of a dwelling house for commercial holiday lettings can never amount to a change of use – is correct'

In that case a country house was being let on weekend, midweek or full week terms to groups of up to 20 people who tended to have common interests (yoga or cycling groups) or for weekend parties[50]. The Court of Appeal considered they were not single households and the inspector was entitled to conclude that there had been a material change of use from a dwellinghouse.

3.47 The C3 use class had been held to include small community care homes consisting of up to six people (including resident staff)[51]. It might also include a house occupied by students as a group[52].

---

[46] (1980) 40 P & CR 104.
[47] (1999) 77 P & CR 114.
[48] At para 71.
[49] [2012] EWCA Civ 1202, [2013] JPL 192 at para 27 per Sullivan LJ.
[50] See the facts set out fully in the High Court judgment [2012] EWHC 1092 (Admin).
[51] See *R (on the application of Hossack) v Kettering Borough Council* [2002] EWCA Civ 886, [2003] 2 P & CR 34.
[52] This was considered in the housing legislation case of *Barnes v Sheffield City Council* (1995) 27 HLR 719 by Sir Thomas Bingham MR. He identified helpful factors summarised by the Court of Appeal in *Hossack* as:
 'i) the origin of the tenancy; whether the residents arrived in a single group or were independently recruited by the landlord;
 ii) the extent to which the facilities were shared;
 iii) whether the occupants were responsible for the whole house (including the common parts) or just their particular rooms;
 iv) the extent to which the residents can and do lock their doors;
 v) the responsibility for filling vacancies: whether that of the existing occupants or the landlord;
 vi) the allocation of rooms: whether by the occupants or the landlord;
 vii) the size of the establishment;
 viii) the stability of the group;
 ix) the mode of living: to what extent communal and to what extent independent.'

3.48 The C4 class had been introduced by the Labour government in 2010 to restrict student and young adults sharing accommodation. Its practical effect was reduced almost immediately by the Coalition government, who granted permitted development rights to move between the two classes[53]. So unless those rights are removed by an Article 4 direction, it is of limited importance. However it remains and the meaning of C3 and C4 is unduly complicated, as it involves different cross-referencing to parts of the Housing Act 2004. In general the C4 category is concerned with accommodation lived in by persons who do not form a single household, which is either not self-contained or is a self-contained flat[54]. A single household under the Housing Act 2004, s 258 contains persons who are all members of the same family (defined as couples or relatives)[55] or live-in staff, carers or foster parents[56]. The Housing Act is concerned with the regulation of particular types of landlord rather than land use planning, so the distinction between what is or is not a house in multiple occupation has often nothing to do with the character of the use of the land. For example, the payment of rent is required for a property to be a house in multiple occupation[57] but local authority, housing association and health service accommodation and student accommodation managed by an educational establishment are all excluded from the definition[58].

3.49 If a person uses the ground floor of a building to provide professional services, such as an estate agency or solicitors, and lives in the upper floors it is a factual question whether the building is in a dwelling house use or a dual business and residential use (either as two planning units or a mixed use)[59]. Conversely the use of a room in a house as a study would be ancillary to the residential use even if the resident did almost all of their work there[60]. That a personal assistant might come to the house to work or clients would occasionally visit might not take it outside C3.

Class D: community uses

3.50 A variety of community and recreation uses are included in the D classes

> 'Class D1: non-residential institutions
>
> Any use not including a residential use:
>
> (a) for the provision of any medical or health services except the use of premises attached to the residence of the consultant or practitioner,

---

[53] For the history of these changes see the unsuccessful challenge to the creation of the permitted development right: *R (on the application of Milton Keynes Council) v Secretary of State for Communities and Local Government* [2011] EWCA Civ 1575, [2012] JPL 728.
[54] Where the C4 issue arises, so usually only if permitted development rights have been withdrawn, there is little real alternative but to work through the Housing Act 2004, ss 254–258, to determine if the premises are within C4. Some guidance on its meaning was given in the now-revoked Circular 08/2010 *Changes to planning regulations for dwellinghouses and houses in multiple occupation.*
[55] Housing Act 2004, s 258(2)–(4).
[56] See the Licensing and Management of Houses in Multiple Occupation and Other Houses (Miscellaneous Provisions) (England) Regulations 2006, SI 2006/373 and the Licensing and Management of Houses in Multiple Occupation and Other Houses (Miscellaneous Provisions) (Wales) Regulations 2006, SI 2006/1715.
[57] Housing Act 2004, s 254(2)(e), (3)(b), (4)(f).
[58] Housing Act 2005, s 254(5) and Sch 14, paras 4, 9.
[59] See where an estate agency and residential was a dual use: *Scurlock v Secretary of State for Wales* (1977) 33 P & CR 202, followed in *Deitsch v Secretary of State for the Environment* [1993] JPL 579.
[60] As distinct from just evenings, weekends and bank holidays.

3.51 *Use classes*

    (b)   as a creche, day nursery or day centre,
    (c)   for the provision of education,
    (d)   for the display of works of art (otherwise than for sale or hire),
    (e)   as a museum,
    (f)   as a public library or public reading room,
    (g)   as a public hall or exhibition hall,
    (h)   for, or in connection with, public worship or religious instruction,
    (i)   as a law court'.

Class D2 is in England:

'Assembly and leisure

Use as:

    (a)   a cinema,
    (b)   a concert hall,
    (c)   a bingo hall,
    (d)   a dance hall,
    (e)   a swimming bath, skating rink, gymnasium or area for other indoor or outdoor sports or recreations, not involving motorised vehicles or firearms'.

Casinos are also included in the D2 use class in Wales, whereas they are *sui generis* in England.

3.51 Two important points on class D2 were raised by the contention that Twickenham stadium could be used for concerts within its existing D2 use. In *Rugby Football Union v Secretary of State for Transport, Local Government and the Regions* the High Court and the Court of Appeal held that the stadium could not be a concert hall because it did not have a roof[61]. It was not simply a matter of whether concerts where held there, but whether the premises had the characteristics of a concert hall. Second, 'recreation' in D2(e) needs to be read in its context which is dealing with physical activities rather than hobbies, interests, or recreational activities of an artistic or creative nature. Spectators are not engaging in recreation with class D2, but the D2 use of a stadium arises from the sport played there[62].

TOWN AND COUNTRY PLANNING (USE CLASSES) ORDER 1972

3.52 The long-revoked Town and Country Planning (Use Classes) Order 1972 is sometimes referenced in old leases and restrictive covenants. Its classes were differently structured and are set out below with their current 1987 order equivalents, or nearest equivalents:

---

[61] [2001] EWHC Admin 927, [2002] JPL 740 at para 21 per Ouseley J. He saw it as possible that the Millennium Stadium in Cardiff, with its retractable roof, could be a concert hall, presumably with the roof shut (para 17). The judgment was affirmed at [2002] EWCA Civ 1169, [2003] JPL 96.

[62] See paras 42–47, per Ouseley J. A limited view of recreation was also suggested in *Millington v Secretary of State for the Environment, Transport and the Regions* [2000] JPL 297 at 304–305 per Schiemann LJ.

Town and Country Planning (Use Classes) Order 1972   3.52

Use Classes Order 1972	Use Classes Order 1987 (at 2015)
Class I Use as a shop[63] for any purpose except as: (i) a shop for the sale of hot food; (ii) a tripe shop; (iii) a shop for the sale of pet animals or birds; (iv) a cats-meat shop; (v) a shop for the sale of motor vehicles	Class A1, although (ii)–(iv) are now within A1.
Class II Use as an office[64] for any purpose	Class B1(a) as part of Class B1
Class III Use as a light industrial building[65] for any purpose	Class B1(c) as part of Class B1
Class IV Use as a general industrial building for any purpose	Class B2
Class V Special Industrial Group A	Same text as Class B3, now *sui generis*
Class VI Special Industrial Group B	Same text as Class B4, now Class B2
Class VII Special Industrial Group C	Same text as Class B5, now Class B2
Class VIII Special Industrial Group D	Materially the same text as Class B6, now Class B2
Class IX Special Industrial Group E	Materially the same list of unpleasant activities as Class B7, now usually Class B2
Class X Use as a wholesale warehouse or repository[66] for any purpose	Class B8
Class XI Use as a boarding or guest house, or a hotel providing sleeping accommodation	A hotel would be Class C1, other uses might be a *sui generis* hostel or non-C3 residential boarding house.
Class XII Use as a residential or boarding school or a residential college	Within Class C2
Class XIII Use as a building for public worship or religious instruction or for the social or recreational activities of the religious body using the building	Within Class D1
Class XIV Use as a home or institution providing for the boarding, case and maintenance of children, old people or persons under disability, a convalescent home, a nursing home, a sanatorium or a hospital	Within Class C2

---

[63] 'Shop' had an extensive definition in Use Classes Order 1972, art 2(2) with the primary purpose being the selling of goods by retail subject to various exceptions.
[64] Including a bank or estate agency, building society or employment agency, but not a post office or betting office: Use Classes Order 1972, art 2(2).
[65] Light industrial building was defined in the same way as the current B1(c) use as being able to be carried on in a residential area: Use Classes Order 1972, art 2(2).
[66] In *Newbury District Council v Secretary of State for the Environment* [1981] AC 578 a 'repository' need not be used for business purposes: the storage of civil defence vehicles in hangars by the Home Office was use as a repository.

3.52 *Use classes*

Use Classes Order 1972	Use Classes Order 1987 (at 2015)
Class XV Use (other than residentially) as a health centre, a school treatment centre, a clinic, a creche, a day nursery or a dispensary, or use as a consulting room or surgery unattached to the residence of the consultant or practitioner	Within Class D1
Class XVI Use as an art gallery (other than for business purposes), a museum, a public library or reading room, a public hall, or an exhibition hall	Within Class D1
Class XVII Use as a theatre, cinema, music hall or concert hall	Within Class D2, except that theatres are now *sui generis*
Class XVIII Use as a dance hall, skating rink, swimming bath, Turkish or other vapour or foam bath, or as a gymnasium or sports hall	Within Class D2

Chapter 4

The need for planning permission

4.1 Subject to limited exceptions, planning permission is required for the carrying out of development. This chapter considers the need for planning permission for operational development and the making of a material change of use of land, the exceptions to that requirement and the circumstances in which rights to carry out operational development or use land can be lost.

THE NEED FOR PLANNING PERMISSION

4.2 Section 57(1) of the Town and Country Planning Act 1990 provides:

> 'Subject to the following provisions of this section, planning permission is required for the carrying out of any development of land'.

This subsection demonstrates that the concept of development is central to the planning system. Essentially, if development is carried out then it requires planning permission. Conversely, if what is done is not development then it does not need planning permission.

4.3 Planning permission is usually granted either following an application made to the local planning authority or under permitted development rights. The Town and Country Planning (General Permitted Development) (England) Order 2015 (GPDO 2015) and, in Wales, the Town and Country Planning (General Permitted Development) Order 1995 (GPDO 1995)[1] grant planning permission for specified classes of development subject to various conditions and, in certain cases, the approval of details. These permitted development rights can be restricted by 'Article 4 directions' made by the local planning authority under the GPDO. Planning permission may also be granted either for particular projects or specific classes of development by special development orders[2], local development orders, neighbourhood planning orders, community right to build orders, simplified planning zones or on the designation or modification of an enterprise zone[3]. Planning applications may be made to Ministers in certain circumstances[4], and where consent is granted by the Secretary of State or Welsh Ministers under particular enactments they may also grant a deemed planning permission under the Town and Country Planning Act 1990, s 90.

4.4 The development authorised by a planning permission can normally only be carried out once. For example, when planning permission was granted for a garage

---

[1] SI 2015/596 and SI 1995/418 respectively.
[2] See Town and Country Planning Act 1990, s 59(3)(b).
[3] For the list of provisions see Town and Country Planning Act 1990, s 58(1). See Chapter 26.
[4] See Chapter 18.

4.5 *The need for planning permission*

and following the construction of the garage part of it was demolished with a view to rebuilding to enable an order to be made diverting a public footpath, the permission did not authorise the rebuilding of the garage: *Hall v Secretary of State for the Environment, Transport and the Regions*[5]. Most obviously this applies where the relevant part of the development has been completed: a building is constructed and is subsequently demolished in whole or part and rebuilt. In *Hall* Nigel MacLeod QC said:

> 'it does seem to me that it is right that when a discrete and substantial part of a planning permission is completed in accordance with that permission, then that part of the permission has been completed and achieved, and is spent in so far as that aspect of the permission is concerned. To knock the garage down and rebuild it is not in my judgment authorised by this planning permission'.

4.5 A different situation may arise if, part-way through construction, some of the works have to be taken down and rebuilt, for example because they turn out to be unstable or are damaged by fire. In those circumstances the authorised building will not have been constructed until the works, including the repeated works, have been concluded.

4.6 Similarly a planning permission for a material change of use will usually be capable of being exercised only once. In *Cynon Valley Borough Council v Secretary of State for Wales*[6] planning permission had been granted to make a material change of use to a fish and chip shop (an A3 use class[7]). The use of the shop had reverted to A1 retail use (an antiques shop) under permitted development rights. It then changed to a Chinese takeaway (again, an A3 use). Both changes were material changes of use and the local planning authority enforced against the change to a takeaway. The Court of Appeal held that original planning permission was spent when the change of use to a fish and chip shop took place, and could not be used to authorise a subsequent change back to an A3 use[8].

4.7 There is, however, no reason in principle why a planning permission should not expressly authorise repeated development. This might be a seasonal use of land, changes between particular uses or a building erected and dismantled on a seasonal basis (such as a large marquee, tennis dome or agricultural polytunnels) but the consent ought to be explicit.

EXCEPTIONS TO THE NEED FOR PLANNING PERMISSION

4.8 There are several exceptions to the requirement for planning permission which are concerned with an alternative means of approval and returning to earlier uses following temporary or unlawful activity:

(i) if development consent is required as part of a nationally significant infrastructure project then no planning permission is required: s 57(1A)[9];

---

[5] [1998] JPL 1055.
[6] (1987) 53 P & CR 68.
[7] In England, hot food takeaways including fish and chip shops and Chinese takeaways are now in the A5 use class: Town and Country Planning (Use Classes) Order 1987, SI 1987/764.
[8] *Cynon Valley* at 76. The reversion to an A3 use was lawful for another reason, based on what is now the Town and Country Planning Act 1990, s 57(3) as discussed below.
[9] The requirement for development consent rather than planning permission is in the Planning Act 2008, s 33(1).

(ii) where planning permission has been 'granted for a limited period, planning permission is not required for the resumption, at the end of that period, of its use for the purpose for which it was normally used before the permission was granted': s 57(2). A permission for a limited period will most obviously include a permission for a defined period of time but may go wider. In *Westminster City Council v Davenport*[10] the Court of Appeal held that this subsection applied to a planning permission which was subject to a personal condition (in that case permission for diplomatic uses being personal to the Commissioner of particular governments). The temporary permission must be implemented for this provision to be relied upon[11]. 'Normal use' does not include any use begun in breach of planning control[12], so it is not possible to revert to the previous use of the land if that was started without planning permission even if it had become lawful by the passage of time before the temporary permission was granted. There has been debate whether it is possible to revert to the previous lawful use even if there was a supervening unlawful use[13]. Also unresolved in the courts is whether, following a series of temporary or personal permissions, it is possible to revert to the last permanent and lawful use. However what is settled is that the provision can be relied upon even if the temporary use had ceased to be carried on before or after the permission required cessation, and does not have to be carried out immediately the period expires[14];

(iii) if a development order, local development order or neighbourhood development order grants planning permission subject to limitations, planning permission is not required for the use of the land for its normal use: s 57(3)[15]. The Town and Country Planning (General Permitted Development) (England) Order 2015 grants permissions 'subject to any relevant exception, limitation or condition specified in Schedule 2' to that Order[16]. In *Cynon Valley Borough Council v Secretary of State for Wales*[17] it was held that the permitted development rights to change uses imported the limitations in the Use Classes Order. Since Class A1 of the Use Classes Order provided for use as a shop except for certain purposes, the planning permission was subject to limitations. It was therefore possible to revert to the previous use of the shop, namely class A3 hot food. The text of the Use Classes Order has subsequently changed and the particular limitation in the *Cynon Valley* case no longer arises;

(iv) s 57(4) applies to the resumption of uses following an enforcement notice:

> 'Where an enforcement notice has been issued in respect of any development of land, planning permission is not required for its use for the purpose which (in accordance with the provisions of this Part of this Act) it could lawfully have been used if that development had not been carried out'.

---

[10] [2011] EWCA Civ 458, [2011] JPL 1325.
[11] *Smith v Secretary of State for the Environment* (1984) 47 P & CR 194 at 204–205 per Woolf J.
[12] Town and Country Planning Act 1990, s 57(5). This includes any breach of planning control under the Town and Country Planning Act since the 1947 Act: Town and Country Planning Act 1990, s 57(6).
[13] In *LTSS Print and Supply Services Ltd v Hackney London Borough Council* [1976] QB 663 Cairns LJ suggested at 673 that such a reversion was possible. However the House of Lords declined to comment on this point in *Young v Secretary of State for the Environment* [1983] AC 662 at 671 per Lord Fraser of Tullybelton.
[14] *Smith v Secretary of State for the Environment* (1984) 47 P & CR 194 at 205.
[15] Community right to build orders are 'a particular type of neighbourhood development order' (Town and Country Planning Act 1990, s 61Q) so are also subject to s 57(3).
[16] SI 2015/596; in Wales the Town and Country Planning (General Permitted Development) Order 1995, SI 1995/418, art 3(2).
[17] (1987) 53 P & CR 68.

4.9 *The need for planning permission*

4.9 Where an enforcement notice has been issued s 57(4) therefore permits a reversion to the previous use if that was a lawful use. There is no right to revert to the previous lawful use if no enforcement notice has been issued. One consequence is that if two successive unlawful material changes of use take place (neither becoming lawful by passage of time) and an enforcement notice is issued against the second material change of use, then there is no right to revert to the original lawful use[18]. This applies even if the original and final uses are the same[19].

A lawful use for the purposes of s 57(4) includes uses which have become lawful by passage of time[20].

4.10 Land which was in a particular use on 1 July 1948 was able to continue in that use, subject to compliance with the previous systems of planning control[21]. This is referred to as 'existing use', but once a material change of use away from that use had occurred, there was no general right to return to the earlier use. The resumption of various uses which had been carried on before 1 July 1948 was permitted if begun before 6 December 1968[22].

4.11 If planning permission is granted for development, but is unnecessary as rights already exist, then the planning permission does not have effect: *Newbury District Council v Secretary of State for the Environment*[23].

ABANDONMENT OF A LAWFUL USE

4.12 Abandonment is one of the ways in which it may be unlawful to carry on a use of land. This applies directly where it is physically possible to resume the use, but the question is whether the use can be carried on. This was the issue in *Hartley v Minister of Housing and Local Government*[24]. Whether a use is abandoned is judged objectively, with knowledge of all the facts, including the owner's intentions. The approach in *Hartley* was simply to ask whether the use has 'not merely been suspended for a short and determined period, but has ceased with no intention to resume it'[25]. Lord Denning MR held 'when a man ceases to use a site for a particular purpose and lets it remain unused for a considerable time, then the proper inference

---

[18] *Young v Secretary of State for Environment* [1983] 2 AC 662.
[19] *Fairstate Ltd v First Secretary of State* [2004] EWHC 1807 (Admin), [2005] JPL 369 at paras 27, 28 per Sullivan J.
[20] *Hillingdon London Borough Council v Secretary of State for Communities and Local Government* [2008] EWHC 198 (Admin), [2008] JPL 1486. This is the effect of the passage of time conferring lawfulness rather than merely immunity: see Town and Country Planning Act 1990, s 191 . *LTSS Print and Supply Services Ltd v Hackney London Borough Council* [1976] 1 QB 663 on the previous legislation (which only conferred immunity) is no longer good law.
[21] The Town and Country Planning Act 1932 had allowed local authorities to introduce schemes over land, meaning that authorisation would be required. However the Town and Country Planning (Interim Development) Act 1943 provided that all land was deemed to be subject to a scheme and permitted applications for permission under interim development orders: ss 1, 2. By the Town and Country Planning Act 1947, s 77(1), planning permission was deemed to be granted for development authorised by an interim development permission which had been approved after 21 July 1943.
[22] Town and Country Planning Act 1990, s 57(7) and Sch 4.
[23] [1981] AC 578.
[24] [1970] 1 QB 413, CA.
[25] At 421 per Widgery LJ.

may be that he has abandoned the former use'[26]. In that case premises had been used as a petrol filling station and for car sales. The owners had terminated the car sales, intending not to resume them, but four years later a new owner began selling cars again. The Divisional Court and then the Court of Appeal upheld an enforcement notice on the basis that the previous car sales use had been abandoned and needed planning permission to be resumed.

4.13 Abandonment may also be part of the policy test applied in deciding whether to permit a replacement building, as was the case in *Hughes v Secretary of State for the Environment, Transport and the Regions*[27].

4.14 Usually a considerably greater period than four years is required to establish abandonment[28]. In *Castell-Y-Mynach v Secretary of State for Wales and Taff Ely Borough Council*[29] four factors relating to abandonment were identified in the High Court:

'(a) physical condition of the building;

(b) the period of non-use;

(c) whether there had been any other use; and

(d) evidence regarding the owner's intentions'.

An 18-year gap in residential use in *Castell-Mynach* was sufficient in those particular circumstances[30].

INTERVENTIONS WHICH END LAWFUL USES

4.15 Certain changes in the use or condition of law may end a lawful use. Most obviously, making a material change of use will terminate the previous use. The implementation of a planning permission can also end the existing use. In both cases issues may arise as to the planning unit of the new use and whether there are several planning units or a mixed use of the land. Where a use of land is reliant upon buildings then the demolition of the buildings may be held to destroy the use of the land[31].

4.16 There may be circumstances in which a planning permission becomes impossible to implement and build out. One situation is where there are inconsistent planning permissions on the same land: the *Pilkington v Secretary of State* situation[32]. Lord Scarman observed in *Pioneer Aggregates v Secretary of State for the Environment* 'there is no case, so far as I am aware, in which a previous planning permission has been lost by reason of subsequent development save in circumstances

---

[26] At 420. Following his comments in *Webber v Minister of Housing and Local Government* [1968] 1 WLR 29 at 33 and *Miller (TA) Ltd v Minister of Housing and Local Government* [1968] 1 WLR 992 at 996.

[27] [2000] 1 PLR 76.

[28] Another example is a gap of over 40 years in *Bramall v Secretary of State for Communities and Local Government* [2011] EWHC 1531 (Admin).

[29] [1985] JPL 40.

[30] A right to resume a use under Town and Country Planning Act 1990, s 57(2) can be abandoned: *Bramall v Secretary of State for Communities and Local Government* [2011] EWHC 1531 (Admin) at para 23 per Wyn Williams J.

[31] *Iddenden v Secretary of State for the Environment* [1972] 3 All ER 863.

[32] [1973] 1 WLR 1527.

4.17 *The need for planning permission*

giving rise to [the *Pilkington*] class of case'[33]. Lord Scarman did later compare the *Pilkington* class to cases where an existing planning use was lost by physical changes to the land, but he concluded:

> 'There is no principle in the planning law that a valid permission capable of being implemented according to its terms can be abandoned'[34].

4.17 Lord Mance in *Welwyn-Hatfield Borough Council v Secretary of State for Communities and Local Government* set out the approach on loss of existing use rights[35]:

> 'As explained by Lord Scarman in *Pioneer Aggregates (UK) Ltd v Secretary of State for the Environment* [1985] AC 132, 143f–144d , a new development sanctioned by a planning permission may extinguish the existing use rights which the land or a previous building on the land possessed: see eg *Prossor v Minister of Housing and Local Government* (1968) 67 LGR 109; *Petticoat Lane Rentals Ltd v Secretary of State for the Environment* [1971] 1 WLR 1112 , discussed in *Newbury District Council v Secretary of State for the Environment* [1981] AC 578, 598–599, per Viscount Dilhorne, pp 606e–h , per Lord Fraser of Tullybelton, pp 616–617, per Lord Scarman and pp 625a–626f , per Lord Lane. The straightforward explanation is that the planning permission, once taken up and implemented, gives rise to a new situation in which the building owner has the advantage of, but is also bound by the limitations of, the rights of use permitted by the planning permission, and no longer has the benefit of any other rights of use which may have existed prior to the new development'.

4.18 In *Jennings Motors Ltd v Secretary of State for the Environment*[36] Lord Denning MR said:

> 'In future it should no longer be thought that a new building creates a "new planning unit" which starts with a "nil use". Certainly not when it is just the replacement of an old building. The better theory is the opening of a "new chapter in the planning history". This may take place when there is a radical change in the nature of the buildings on the site or the uses to which they are put – so radical that it can be looked upon as a fresh start altogether in the character of the site. If there is such a change and the occupier applies for permission and gets it subject to conditions – and acts upon that permission – he cannot afterwards revert to any previous existing use rights'.

STATUTORY POWERS TO REMOVE THE RIGHT TO DEVELOP OR TO RETAIN DEVELOPMENT

4.19 Local planning authorities and Ministers have powers to remove the right to carry out development under planning permissions or to retain a lawful use or development. These powers under the Town and Country Planning Act 1990 are:

(i) completion notices: requiring development under a planning permission to be completed within a specified period and any further right would then be lost.

(ii) revocation or modification: which eliminates or alters planning permissions insofar as they have not been carried out;

---

[33] [1985] AC 132 at 143G.
[34] At 145G.
[35] [2011] UKSC 15, [2011] 2 AC 304 at para 23.
[36] [1982] QB 541.

Statutory powers to remove the right to develop or to retain development **4.24**

(iii) discontinuance: which requires the cessation or limitation of uses or the removal or alteration of buildings on land whether or not these are unlawful;

Completion notices

4.20 Planning permission for the carrying out of development in the future must contain a condition requiring the development to be begun within a certain period. Unless it is a temporary planning permission (granted for a limited period) the permission will state a period by the end of which the development must be completed. It is possible to build some houses on an estate and never complete the remainder or to make a very limited start and then make no more progress for many years. The right to develop under a planning permission is not lost by inaction, provided development has begun[37].

4.21 If the local planning authority[38] consider that an implemented planning permission should be built out or given up then it may give a completion notice under s 94, subject to confirmation by the Minister.

4.22 A completion notice may be used where development has begun but has not been completed for[39]:

(i) planning permissions granted by the local planning authority or the Minister after the period in which a condition requires the permission to have been implemented;

(ii) development authorised under a simplified planning zone or enterprise zone after the area has ceased to be in such a zone;

(iii) development authorised by a neighbourhood development order after the expiry of the period for commencement in that order.

4.23 The local planning authority may serve a completion notice if in its opinion 'the development will not be completed within a reasonable period'[40]. The completion notice will specify a further period, not less than 12 months after the notice takes effect, at the end of which the planning permission will cease to have effect[41]. A notice will only take effect once it is confirmed by the Minister[42], so the notice should set a period from confirmation. There is no provision for automatic confirmation of unopposed notices.

Completion notices have to be served on the owner and occupier of the land as well as any other person who in the opinion of the local planning authority will be affected by the notice[43].

4.24 The completion notice will specify a period within which the person served may exercise a right to be heard by the Secretary of State (usually by a hearing

---

[37] See *Pioneer Aggregates v Secretary of State for the Environment* [1985] AC 132.
[38] This is the district planning authority unless the planning permission was granted by the county planning authority, in which case the county and district both have the power, the latter after consultation with the county: Town and Country Planning Act 1990, Sch 1, para 10.
[39] Town and Country Planning Act 1990, s 94(1).
[40] Town and Country Planning Act 1990, s 94(2).
[41] Town and Country Planning Act 1990, s 94(2), (3).
[42] Town and Country Planning Act 1990, s 95(1).
[43] Town and Country Planning Act 1990, s 94(4).

4.25 *The need for planning permission*

or inquiry conducted by an inspector)[44]. The local planning authority will also be entitled to appear at the oral hearing (although it has no right to demand one)[45]. Ministers may confirm or decline to confirm the notice and if confirming, may extend the period at the end of which the permission expires[46]. The period will run from confirmation and the permission will become invalid at its conclusion. However this invalidity 'shall not affect any permission so far as development carried out under it before the end of the period ... is concerned'[47]. Consequently, development carried out under the permission before the completion notice is served or confirmed or in the compliance period would remain lawful. The permission itself is not affected with respect to such development, so ongoing controls (such as hours of operation) or restoration conditions will continue to have effect.

A completion notice may be withdrawn at any point before the planning permission ceases to have effect[48].

Revocation or modification

4.25 A planning permission may be revoked or modified under the Town and Country Planning Act 1990, s 97. This removes or alters a planning permission. It provides a means of exercising greater control or remedying erroneous planning decisions.

4.26 Section 97(1) provides:

'If it appears to the local planning authority that it is expedient to revoke or modify planning permission to develop land granted on an application made under this Part, the authority may by order revoke or modify the permission to such an extent as they consider expedient.'

The authority[49] shall have regard to the development plan and to other material considerations[50], so the presumption in favour of the development plan applies[51]. The potential liability to pay compensation for the loss sustained by the revocation or modification is relevant to the decision whether to make the order[52]. If land is designated as a European site (Special Protection Areas and Special Areas of Conservation) for its nature conservation interest then any existing planning permission should be reviewed under the Conservation of Habitats and Species Regulations 2010[53]. Any

---

[44] Town and Country Planning Act 1990, s 95(3). The period must be at least 28 days from service of the notice.
[45] Town and Country Planning Act 1990, s 95(3). Other persons served will be allowed to be heard.
[46] Town and Country Planning Act 1990, s 95(2).
[47] Town and Country Planning Act 1990, s 95(5).
[48] Town and Country Planning Act 1990, s 94(5). Notice of the withdrawal must be served on every party who was served with the notice (s 94(6)), which is not necessarily those who would now be served with the notice.
[49] This is the district planning authority, except for minerals planning authority matters which are exclusive to it and other county matters where the power can be exercised by either authority (subject to the district consulting the county in such cases): Town and Country Planning Act 1990, Sch 1, para 11.
[50] Town and Country Planning Act 1990, s 97(2).
[51] Planning and Compulsory Purchase Act 2004, s 38(6).
[52] *R (on the application of Health and Safety Executive) v Wolverhampton City Council* [2012] UKSC 34, [2012] 1 WLR 2264.
[53] Conservation of Habitats and Species Regulations 2010, SI 2010/490, regs 63, 69–72.

Statutory powers to remove the right to develop or to retain development **4.29**

consequent modification or revocation will then be carried out under s 97[54]. If the effect of a revocation or modification order is to authorise development to proceed then EIA may be required[55].

4.27 Revocation and modification deals with development which has not yet taken place[56]:

'The power conferred by this section may be exercised:

(a) where the planning permission relates to the carrying out of building or other operations, at any time before those operations have been completed;

(b) where the permission relates to a change of the use of any land, at any time before the change has taken place'.

A revocation or modification order of a planning permission for building or other operations does not affect so much of those operations as has been carried out[57]. However it may affect how that operational development is used (for example, by imposing conditions on hours of operation).

4.28 An order requires confirmation from the Minister unless it is able to be confirmed as an unopposed order[58].

When the order is sent to the Minister for confirmation, the local planning authority must serve notice on the landowners and occupiers of the land subject to the order and any other person who in the local planning authority's opinion will be affected by the order[59]. They may require an oral hearing by making a request to the Minister within the period specified in the notice[60].

The order may be confirmed without modification or subject to such modification as the Minister considers expedient, or Minister may decline to confirm it[61].

4.29 An order may take effect as an unopposed order if, following the making of the order, 'the owner and the occupier of the land and all persons who in the authority's opinion will be affected by the order have notified the authority in writing that they do not object to it'[62]. If such notice of an absence of objection is given then the authority must advertise the fact that the order has been made and give persons affected by the order a period to be required to be heard by the Secretary of State. The notice period must not be less than 28 days, and the order would take effect not less than 14 days after the end of that period unless a representation has been made by a

---

[54] Conservation of Habitats and Species Regulations 2010, reg 69(6).
[55] *Smout v Welsh Ministers* [2011] EWCA Civ 1750 and [2010] EWHC 3307 (Admin), [2011] Env LR 17. The Town and Country Planning (Environmental Impact Assessment) Regulations 2011, SI 2011/1824 do not cover this situation, so the Directive applies by direct effect.
[56] Town and Country Planning Act 1990, s 97(3).
[57] Town and Country Planning Act 1990, s 97(4).
[58] Town and Country Planning Act 1990, s 98(1).
[59] Town and Country Planning Act 1990, s 98(2).
[60] Town and Country Planning Act 1990, s 98(3)–(5). The period must be not less than 28 days from service of the notice.
[61] Town and Country Planning Act 1990, s 98(6).
[62] Town and Country Planning Act 1990, s 99(1).

4.30 *The need for planning permission*

person claiming to be affected by the order and the Minister has not directed that the order be submitted to him[63].

4.30 The Secretary of State and the Welsh Ministers may revoke or modify a planning permission of their own volition if they consider it expedient to do so under s 97[64]. Consequently they too must have regard to the development plan and apply the s 38(6) presumption[65]. In addition to the need for the owners, occupiers and affected persons to be able to make representations[66], the Minister must consult and notify the local planning authority before making the order[67], giving it a specified period to request an oral hearing[68]. The Ministerial approach has been to use this power very sparingly[69]:

> 'Such intervention by the Secretary of State can only be justified in exceptional circumstances. However, the Secretary of State will generally use this power only if the original decision is judged to be grossly wrong, so that damage is likely to be done to the wider public interest'.

4.31 Compensation is payable for any loss caused by a revocation or modification order[70]. If the order is made by the Minister then compensation is still payable by the local planning authority. This has caused some upset in the past[71]. Care must be taken to establish that the order caused the loss. If the developer needs another consent (such as a species licence) which would not have been granted, then any loss would not have been caused by the revocation or modification order[72].

4.32 There is no provision relating to failure to comply with a revocation or modification order. As the order has prospective effect only, the question is whether what is then done is without a necessary planning permission having regard to the order, or whether it is in breach of a condition on the relevant planning permission as modified by the order. Such a breach of planning control would then be enforced against in the usual way.

Discontinuance orders

4.33 The local planning authority is empowered to require the discontinuance of any use of land or require that buildings should be altered or removed, whether the use or buildings are lawful or unlawful. Compensation may be payable for losses

---

[63] Town and Country Planning Act 1990, s 99. The unopposed procedure may not be used on a planning permission granted or deemed to have been granted by the Minister or to an order modifying the conditions limiting the time for the commencement of development: Town and Country Planning Act 1990, s 99(8).
[64] Town and Country Planning Act 1990, s 100(1).
[65] Under the Planning and Compulsory Purchase Act 2004.
[66] Under Town and Country Planning Act 1990, s 98.
[67] Town and Country Planning Act 1990, s 100(3), (4). It is not apparent why there are duties to consult and to serve notice of the proposal to make an order. They amount to the same thing.
[68] Town and Country Planning Act 1990, s 100(5). The period specified in the notice to the authority must not be less than 28 days.
[69] Reply by the Planning Minister, Yvette Cooper MP, 443 HC Official Report (6th series), col 2444W, 16 March 2006.
[70] Town and Country Planning Act 1990, s 107.
[71] See *Alnwick District Council v Secretary of State for the Environment, Transport and the Regions* (2000) 70 P & CR 130.
[72] *MWH Associates Ltd v Wrexham County Borough Council* [2012] EWCA Civ 1884, [2013] Env LR 27.

Statutory powers to remove the right to develop or to retain development **4.38**

caused by discontinuance orders. Consequently orders tend to be used in a limited number of cases against lawful development as enforcement action can be taken without a compensation risk against unlawful development.

4.34 The power is exercised in the interests of the proper planning of the area and if it appears in the Town and Country Planning Act 1990, s 102(1):

'(a) that any use of land should be discontinued, or that any conditions should be imposed on the continuance of a use of land; or

(b) that any buildings or works should be altered or removed, [the local planning authority] may by order:

(i) require the discontinuance of that use, or

(ii) impose such conditions as may be specified in the order on the continuance of it, or

(iii) require such steps as may be so specified to be taken for the alteration or removal of the buildings or works, as the case may be'.

4.35 A discontinuance order may grant planning permission for any development of the land to which the order relates, subject to such conditions as may be specified in the order[73]. Such a planning permission may authorise development carried on up to the submission of the order to the Minister for confirmation[74] and may be permanent or temporary[75]. Similar provisions are made with respect to mineral workings in the Town and Country Planning Act 1990, s 102(8) and Sch 9 (special minerals orders).

4.36 Compensation is payable if the development is lawful[76]. However, compensation is not recoverable if the use or development is contrary to law[77] and this includes a breach of planning control which can still be the subject of enforcement action[78].

4.37 A discontinuance order may only take effect if confirmed by the Secretary of State or the Welsh Ministers, with or without modification[79]. Prior to confirmation, the owner or occupier of the land affected by the order and any other person affected by the order are entitled to a hearing[80]. A confirmed order may only be challenged by application to the High Court under the Town and Country Planning Act 1990, s 288[81]. It is not possible for the local planning authority to withdraw a discontinuance order once it has given notice of its confirmation, even if an appreciation of the scale of likely compensation means that the authority now wishes it had not made the order.

4.38 The Secretary of State or Welsh Ministers are able to make a discontinuance order[82]. Any compensation due as a result of a ministerial order is payable by the local planning authority.

---

[73] Town and Country Planning Act 1990, s 102(2).
[74] Town and Country Planning Act 1990, s 102(4).
[75] Town and Country Planning Act 1990, s 102(5).
[76] Town and Country Planning Act 1990, s 115.
[77] Land Compensation Act 1961, s 5, rule 4.
[78] *Hughes v Doncaster Metropolitan Council* [1991] 1 AC 382.
[79] Town and Country Planning Act 1990, s 103.
[80] Town and Country Planning Act 1990, s 103(4).
[81] Town and Country Planning Act 1990, ss 284(2), 288.
[82] Town and Country Planning Act 1990, s 104.

4.39 *The need for planning permission*

It is an offence to use land in breach of a discontinuance order or to contravene a condition in such an order[83].

4.39 The local planning authority can enter land and carry out the steps required under a discontinuance or special minerals order, recovering the cost from the owner (s 190).

4.40 Because of the potential liability for compensation and the fact that criminal sanctions are weaker than for enforcement notices, discontinuance orders are rarely used. The discontinuance process might be employed with enforcement notices where the undesirable activities consist of a mix of lawful and unlawful uses. Essentially the enforcement notices would deal with the unlawful uses and a discontinuance order would address the totality. That is a risky enterprise if the extent of the lawful uses is not correctly ascertained[84].

---

[83] Town and Country Planning Act 1990, s 189(1).
[84] For example, in *Jeffrey v First Secretary of State* [2007] EWCA Civ 584 and [2006] EWHC 2920 (Admin), [2007] JPL 907 the local planning authority made a discontinuance order for the use of land for siting touring caravans and tents, believing that the touring caravan part was time-limited and had expired, when it was subsequently held to be permanent.

Chapter 5

Permitted development rights

5.1 The scope of development and the consequent need for planning permission is very wide. It catches a huge number of actions. If each of those acts could only take place following the approval of an application by a public authority, the costs and delays would be considerable. Many will be perfectly innocuous. The planning system has, since 1948, included a system of granting planning permission at a national level for particular categories of development. These are permitted development rights.

5.2 The Secretary of State and the Welsh Ministers are able to provide for the granting of planning permission by development order[1]. A development order can deal with planning permission in two ways:

(i) by setting out the procedure for permission being granted on application to a local planning authority or Minister. These procedures are presently in the Town and Country Planning (Development Management Procedure) (England) Order 2015 (DMPO 2015) and the Town and Country Planning (Development Management Procedure) (Wales) Order 2012 (DMPO Wales)[2];

(ii) by itself granting planning permission for a specified development or class of development in the order[3].

5.3 This latter form of development order may cover a type of development and be nationwide, in which case it is a general development order, or may be specific to a scheme or site, usually called a special development order[4]. Permitted development rights are contained in general development orders which grant planning permission. Until 1995 there was a single general development order which covered procedural rules and permitted development rights. These functions were then split between the Town and Country Planning (General Development Procedure) Order 1995 and the Town and Country Planning (General Permitted Development) Order 1995 (GPDO 1995)[5]. The General Development Procedure Order has been replaced by separate Development Management Procedure Orders for England and Wales[6].

5.4 Permitted development rights in Wales remain in the GPDO 1995, but have been subject to numerous amendments over the years. The GPDO 1995 was replaced

---

[1] Town and Country Planning Act 1990, s 59(1).
[2] SI 2015/595 and SI 2012/801 respectively.
[3] Town and Country Planning Act 1990, s 59(2).
[4] Special development orders are addressed in Chapter 26.
[5] Known at the time as the GDPO and GPDO respectively, acronyms which were often muddled up.
[6] The first English DMPO was made in 2010 and was replaced in 2015. The Welsh DMPO was made in 2012.

5.5 *Permitted development rights*

in England by the Town and Country Planning (General Permitted Development) (England) Order 2015 (GPDO 2015)[7].

5.5 Regrettably, because of their technicality, there is no alternative but to consider the wording of the particular part of the legislation when dealing with any permitted development rights matter.

5.6 The primary legislation is in general terms, providing that the permission 'may be granted either unconditionally or subject to such conditions or limitations as may be specified in the order'[8]. In particular, the order may require the local planning authority's approval of the 'design or external appearance of the buildings'[9] as the basis for long-established prior approval procedures on agricultural buildings and telecommunications. The Town and Country Planning Act 1990 does allow for considerable flexibility in procedure, although Parliamentary sanction has been obtained for novel mechanisms. When the Secretary of State wished to provide that certain householder permitted development could take place without further approval unless a neighbour objected, in which case the local planning authority could consider the narrow question of impact on amenity of adjoining premises, the 1990 Act was amended to provide for it[10]. The Housing and Planning Bill 2015 proposes to allow permitted development rights for building operations which are generally subject to approval by the local planning authority[11]. The methods of granting a general permitted development order planning permission can therefore be extremely flexible.

5.7 Permitted development rights will authorise the carrying out of the development described in them subject to:

(i) any restrictions on the description of development, usually as 'development not included';

(ii) any conditions or limitations imposed by the GPDO;

(iii) the rights not having been withdrawn by a condition on an existing, implemented planning permission;

(iv) the lawfulness of any existing development which is the basis for the permitted development

(v) any need for Environmental Impact Assessment or EIA screening. If EIA is required then permitted development rights do not apply and a planning application must be made;

(vi) any need for approval due to likely significant effects on a European site or European offshore marine site under the Conservation of Habitats and Species Regulations 2010[12];

(vii) the withdrawal of the permitted development rights by an art 4 direction;

---

[7] SI 2015/596.
[8] Town and Country Planning Act 1990, s 60(1).
[9] Town and Country Planning Act 1990, s 60(2).
[10] Town and Country Planning Act 1990, s 60(2A)–(2C), inserted by the Growth and Infrastructure Act 2013, s 4(1).
[11] Housing and Planning Bill 2015, cl 104 proposing to insert s 60(1A) in the Town and Country Planning Act 1990. The Bill reference is as published for First Reading in the House of Commons.
[12] Conservation of Habitats and Species Regulations 2010, SI 2010/490, regs 73–76.

(viii) any requirement in the GPDO for a determination whether the prior approval by the planning authority of particular details of the development is required, and if so, the grant of such prior approval;

(ix) compliance with any conditions properly imposed on a prior approval.

PERMITTED DEVELOPMENT RIGHTS: GENERAL PRINCIPLES

5.8 Planning permission is granted by the GPDO, art 3(1)[13]:

> 'Subject to the provisions of this Order and regulations 73 to 76 of the Conservation Habitats and Species Regulations 2010 (general development orders), planning permission is hereby granted for the classes of development described as permitted development in Schedule 2'.

5.9 Schedule 2 is organised by Parts, which relate to particular types of development or development in relation to particular types of uses, and classes which are specific forms of development within each class. For example, Part 1 of Sch 2 is 'development within the curtilage of a dwellinghouse'. Part 1 contains eight classes, listed as Class A to Class H. The classes do not have a descriptive title, so are explained either by the development they permit or informally by some briefer summary. Part 1, Class A permits 'the enlargement, improvement or other alteration of a dwellinghouse'.

Some of the Parts contain additional paragraphs, with their referencing following the classes, for interpretation or procedure, for example paragraph I in Part 1 which is after Class H.

5.10 Interpretative provisions are found in some of the classes, in some of the Parts, in the GPDO 2015, art 2[14] and in the Town and Country Planning Act 1990, s 336. The art 2 and s 336 definitions apply 'unless the context otherwise requires', which gives a degree of latitude in interpretation. Definitions in the particular Parts and classes will relate only to their Parts and classes unless they otherwise reflect the actual meaning of the words.

5.11 Each class contains the development permitted and then a paragraph of any exclusions from that permitted development under the heading 'development not permitted'. Any conditions are then set out, followed by any interpretation provisions for that specific class.

Article 3 restrictions on the grant of permission

5.12 The grant of planning permission in art 3(1) (of either GPDO) is subject to particular exclusions and restrictions in art 3 and in Habitats legislation.

---

[13] GPDO 1995, art 3(1) is to the same effect but refers to the equivalent but revoked regs 60–63 of the Conservation (Natural Habitats) Regulations 1994. As a matter of language, permitted development rights grant a planning permission not a deemed planning permission. Deemed planning permission is that granted by the Secretary of State under Town and Country Planning Act 1990, s 90.

[14] For Wales, in GPDO 1995, art 1.

5.13 *Permitted development rights*

Permitted development restricted by Sch 2

5.13 The first restriction is in art 3(2) that any such permission is 'subject to any relevant exception, limitation or condition specified in Sch 2'.[15]

'Exception' in art 3(2) covers types of development which are identified as 'not permitted' for the particular class. 'Limitation' is harder to define. The remainder of the GPDO includes it in the expression 'conditions, limitations or restrictions' referring either to the remainder of the relevant Part or class[16]. That points to a limitation existing only as a restriction upon a permitted development right, most obviously in the 'development not permitted' paragraphs. In *I'm Your Man Ltd v Secretary of State for the Environment*[17] Robin Purchas QC held that there was no power to impose limitations on a grant of planning permission on application. That might be the case for most purposes, however Part 3, Class V, which allows flexibility within planning permissions, refers to limitations contained in planning permissions granted on applications, which may mean that such flexibility is confined to the description of development of such permissions. Part 17 para N(1) (mining) also refers to a 'condition or limitation' on a planning permission granted or deemed to be granted under Part III of the Town and Country Planning Act 1990. It may well be that for the operation of certain permitted development rights, a planning permission or deemed planning permission granted by the local planning authority or the Minister will contain 'limitations'.

For the purposes of art 3(2), conditions are those specified in the particular condition paragraph for the relevant class.

5.14 However they are described, the constraints imposed by Sch 2 fall into three categories:

(i) restrictions on the development permitted by its type, scale and the current nature or use or designation of the land;

(ii) requirements for determinations whether the prior approval of certain details are required and if so, obtaining that approval;

(iii) requirements for the removal of the development or restoration of the land.

Conditions on other planning permissions which withdraw permitted development rights

5.15 Article 3(4) of both GPDOs provides:

'Nothing in this Order permits development contrary to any condition imposed by any planning permission granted or deemed to be granted under Part 3 of the Act otherwise than by this Order'.

5.16 A planning permission may withdraw certain or all permitted development rights from the development which it authorises. This is best done by an explicit reference to the removal of permitted development rights for particular works or uses

---

[15] The GPDO 2015 and GPDO 1995 are identical in this paragraph.
[16] GPDO 2015, Sch 2, Part 1, para A.4(3); Part 3, para W(3).
[17] (1999) 77 P & CR 251.

Permitted development rights: general principles **5.19**

or particular classes in the GPDO. For example, model condition 51 in DoE Circular 11/95 says[18]:

> 'Notwithstanding the provisions of the Town and Country Planning (General Permitted Development) Order 1995 (or any order revoking and re-enacting that Order with or without modification), no fences, gates or walls shall be erected within the curtilage of any dwellinghouse forward of any wall of that dwellinghouse which fronts onto a road'.

5.17 Other model conditions are in a similar vein. The intention in drafting such a condition is to identify the particular operations or uses which would not be permitted and state that the prohibition arises irrespective of the current or any future permitted development rights. The alternative course is to identify the particular current permitted development rights which are to be excluded and provide that neither they nor any future version of them will apply. Identifying the particular works or uses has the benefit of giving precise consideration to what is to be excluded and this might not be the entirety of a particular class. It needs to be ensured that no developments are omitted from the prohibition by mistake in its drafting.

5.18 Permitted development rights may be implicitly excluded by a condition. However the conditions in question need to be examined with care, as an exclusion would deprive the landowner of a benefit which is given by statute. In *Dunoon Developments Ltd v Secretary of State for the Environment*[19] planning permission had been granted to erect a building for use as offices, showroom, car sales, service and maintenance. The Court of Appeal held that the following conditions did not exclude permitted development rights:

> '1 that the use of the proposed premises shall be limited to the display, sale and storage of new and used cars – together with an administrative centre and the preparation of vehicles including facilities for cleaning, polishing and for such essential auxiliaries as general routine inspection of engine, brakes, steering and lighting
>
> 2 that no heavy repairs, panel beating, cellulosing, crashed vehicle repairs or lorry repairs shall be carried on and that no machine tools or noisy plant and equipment shall be installed in these buildings'.

The conditions limited what could be done under the planning permission but did not exclude permitted development rights. 'Limited' was used to prevent bad neighbour activities under the planning permission. Farquharson LJ observed that in the absence of explicit reference to permitted development 'The question, therefore, is whether it is to be implied from the words themselves, in the context in which they are used, to so exclude them'.

The *Dunoon Developments* approach has continued to be applied, most particularly in cases involving the exclusion of the Town and Country Planning (Use Classes) Order 1987 by planning condition[20].

5.19 Removing permitted development rights by planning condition should only be done where there is a real need to do so. The National Planning Policy Framework says there should be a 'clear justification' for such conditions, drawing a comparison

---

[18] The model conditions have not been cancelled, although the rest of the circular has been.
[19] (1993) 65 P & CR 101.
[20] SI 1987/764. See the discussion in Chapter 3.

5.20 *Permitted development rights*

with its policy on the removal of such rights by an art 4 direction as being necessary to protect local amenity or the wellbeing of the area[21].

Only lawful development benefits from permitted development rights

5.20 Article 3(5) provides[22]:

'The permission granted by Schedule 2 shall not apply if:

(a) in the case of permission granted in connection with an existing building, the building operations involved in the construction of that building are unlawful;

(b) in the case of permission granted in connection with an existing use, that use is unlawful.'

5.21 Many permitted development rights concern the extension of existing buildings, operational development in support of existing uses of land or a material change of use from one particular use to another. Article 3(5) requires existing development to be lawful at the time that the permitted development rights are relied upon. The prohibitions are expressed in the present tense: 'are' or 'is' unlawful. Consequently, permitted development rights apply to buildings or uses which have now become lawful by the passage of time[23]. Lawfulness can be conclusively demonstrated by a lawful development certificate[24] but that is normally not necessary. Either an existing planning permission or the undisputed longevity of the building or use may give sufficient comfort to all concerned.

5.22 'In connection with' is concerned with the existing building or use giving rise to the permitted development right. Where the entire building or the use which would give rise to the permitted development right is unlawful then it is straightforward that the permitted development rights do not exist. In *Evans v Secretary of State for Communities and Local Government*[25] Neil Cameron QC held that if any part of the building was unlawful then no permitted development rights applied by art 3(5). However whilst a building includes part of a building, that raises the question, which part? The installation of a window opening in an unlawful rear extension would not itself have permitted development rights. However, if a house has a unlawful satellite dish in excess of the Part 1, Class H rights it would seem to be a disproportionate outcome if it consequently had no permitted development rights. Whilst a part of the building may be unlawful, the parts that enable a rear extension to be built might not be.

ENVIRONMENTAL IMPACT ASSESSMENT AND PERMITTED DEVELOPMENT RIGHTS

5.23 Environmental Impact Assessment (EIA) requires the likely significant effects of development on the environment to be identified, consulted upon and mitigation proposed before a reasoned decision is taken on whether the project

---

[21] NPPF, para 200.
[22] The text is the same in the GPDO 2015 and GPDO 1995.
[23] The time limits being in Town and Country Planning Act 1990, s 171B and lawfulness defined in s 191.
[24] Granted under Town and Country Planning Act 1990, ss 191, 192.
[25] [2014] EWHC 4111 (Admin), [2015] JPL 589 at para 37.

Environmental Impact Assessment and permitted development rights **5.25**

should proceed in the light of that material. Permitted development operates by either not requiring any individual authorisation before the project can proceed, or having a much more limited consideration of particular issues under the prior approval process. Consequently, unless the project has already been subject to the EIA process by another approval mechanism:

(i) permitted development rights do not exist for projects which require EIA;

(ii) if a planning application for that project would have required a screening decision that EIA was not required before it could proceed without EIA, then a similar screening exercise has to be carried out before the permitted development rights apply to that project;

(iii) Ministers have the same power to require EIA as for planning applications.

5.24 Therefore by art 3(10) of either GPDO, projects which are Sch 1 development or Sch 2 development under the EIA Regulations[26] are not permitted by the GPDO unless a decision has been made that EIA is not required by a screening opinion made by the local planning authority, a screening direction by the Minister or the Minister has directed that the scheme is exempted from the EIA regime[27]. If the local authority has decided that EIA is required and has not been overruled by the Minister, or if the Minister requires EIA then the project does not have permitted development rights[28].

5.25 The requirement to consider the need for EIA does not apply to various works listed in art 3(12). In the GPDO 2015 these are[29]:

(i) improvement works by drainage bodies subject to the Environmental Impact Assessment (Land Drainage Improvement Works) Regulations 1999[30];

(ii) forestry development[31], waste deposits on pre-1 July 1948 sites[32], laying of underground mains, pipes or other apparatus by gas transporters[33], certain coal mining and mineral permitted development[34], and works by the Minister or a strategic highways company under the Highways Act 1980[35];

(iii) the completion of any development begun prior to 14 March 1999[36].

---

[26] The Town and Country Planning (Environmental Impact Assessment) Regulations 2011, SI 2011/1824 in England and the Town and Country Planning (Environmental Impact Assessment) (England and Wales) Regulations 1999, SI 1999/293 in Wales.

[27] Schedule 1 development always requires EIA. Schedule 2 development requires EIA if it is determined that the particular project is likely to have a significant effect on the environment.

[28] GPDO 1995 and GPDO 2015, art 3(11).

[29] Similar provision is made by the GPDO 1995, art 3(12).

[30] SI 1999/1783.

[31] Part 6, Class E.

[32] From industrial processes under Part 7, Class K and by local authorities under Part 12, Class B.

[33] Part 15, Class A(a). These works require separate approval under the Gas Transporter Pipe-line Works (Environmental Impact Assessment) Regulations 1999, SI 1999/1672.

[34] Under Part 17, Classes D, E, F, H, I, K. Classes F, H and K are subject to provisos in art 3(12)(c).

[35] Part 9, Class B. These works are subject to the Highways (Environmental Impact Assessment) Regulations 2007, SI 2007/1062.

[36] This was when the Town and Country Planning (Environmental Impact Assessment) (England and Wales) Regulations 1999 came into force. Whilst of academic interest, this is a transposition error as EIA provisions have applied under the Directive since 1988 and a further error in the amendment itself as EIA has been introduced to permitted development in domestic legislation since the Town and Country Planning (Environmental Assessment and Permitted Development) Regulations 1995, SI 1995/417.

5.26 *Permitted development rights*

Broadly these are ones which will have been subject to EIA processes or which are longstanding uses of land. In addition there are large swathes of permitted development rights which are so limited in extent that they will not in practice amount to Sch 1 or Sch 2 development. Some works which would otherwise be permitted development may require EIA, a prominent example being the proposal to demolish terraced housing in the Welsh Streets, Liverpool, which was halted by a screening direction made by the Secretary of State in 2011.

HABITATS

5.26 A further consent is required before permitted development rights can be used to carry out development which is likely to have a significant effect on a European site, that is a site designated as a Special Protection Area under the Birds Directive or a Special Area of Conservation under the Habitats Directive[37]. The grant of planning permission in art 3(1) of the GPDO 2015 is subject to the Conservation of Habitats and Species Regulations 2010, regs 73–76[38]. Regulation 73(1) says:

'It is a condition of any planning permission granted by a general development order, whether made before or after 1st April 2010, that development which:

(a) is likely to have a significant effect on a European site or a European offshore marine site (either alone or in combination with other plans or projects), and

(b) is not directly connected with or necessary to the management of the site, must not be begun until the developer has received written notification of the approval of the local planning authority under regulation 75 (approval of local planning authority)'.

5.27 The effect is that permitted development rights will exist in such a case, but subject to the condition that approval must be given by the local planning authority under reg 75[39]. If the project is not likely to have a significant effect then no approval is required. A determination by Natural England or the Natural Resources Body for Wales that the development is not likely to have such an effect is conclusive[40].

5.28 If an application is made to the local planning authority for a reg 75 approval then the authority must assume that the development is likely to have such a significant effect[41]. If Natural England advise that there is no likely significant effect then the application will normally be withdrawn.

5.29 In considering the application the local planning authority is required to carry out an appropriate assessment[42]. It may only give the reg 75 approval 'having ascertained that it will not adversely affect the integrity of the [European] site'[43].

---

[37] Council Directive 92/43/EEC on the conservation of natural habitats and of wild fauna and flora.

[38] The regulations apply to England and Wales. As mentioned above the GPDO 1995 still refers to the long-revoked Conservation (Natural Habitats) Regulations 1994 but the new regulations apply pursuant to the Interpretation Act 1978, s 20(2).

[39] For the purpose of appeals and timescales for determination, the approval is treated as an approval required by a condition imposed on a grant of planning permission: Conservation of Habitats and Species Regulations 2010, reg 76(3).

[40] Conservation of Habitats and Species Regulations 2010, regs 74(6), 75(4), (5). The regulations use the expression 'appropriate nature conservation body', which is defined in reg 5.

[41] Conservation of Habitats and Species Regulations 2010, reg 75(2).

[42] Conservation of Habitats and Species Regulations 2010, reg 75(6).

[43] Conservation of Habitats and Species Regulations 2010, reg 75(7).

5.30 'Appropriate assessment' is not defined in the Habitats Regulations 2010 so its meaning in the Habitats Directive applies[44], where it is simply said that a 'plan or project ... shall be subject to appropriate assessment of its implications for the site in view of the site's conservation objectives'[45]. Regulation 61(1) of the Habitats Regulations 2010 echoes this language by providing that the authority 'must make an appropriate assessment of the implications for that site in view of that site's conservation objectives'[46]. Regulation 61(6) requires:

> 'In considering whether a plan or project will adversely affect the integrity of the site, the authority must have regard to the manner in which it is proposed to be carried out or to any conditions or restrictions subject to which they propose that the consent, permission or other authorisation should be given'.

5.31 The appropriate assessment under reg 75 must therefore consider the way in which the project is to be carried out and any conditions or restrictions which may be proposed. It will follow that the approval only relates to the application which is made. If the development is not carried out in accordance with the application then it will be in breach of the condition created by reg 73(1). There may be a question as to whether conditions can be imposed on a reg 75 approval. The ability to impose conditions on prior approvals under permitted development rights is a matter of some debate[47], and further complications arise on the status of reg 75 approvals.

PARTICULAR ACTS LIMITED TO PARTICULAR PERMITTED DEVELOPMENT RIGHTS

5.32 Article 3 limits certain types of operational development to particular permitted development rights even if other classes would seem, on their face, to include that development.

5.33 The following acts of development are limited to particular Parts and classes by GPDO 2015, art 3(6)[48]:

> 'The permission granted by Schedule 2 does not, except in relation to development permitted by Classes A, B, D and E of Part 9 and Class A of Part 18 of that Schedule, authorise any development which requires or involves the formation, laying out or material widening of a means of access to an existing highway which is a trunk road or classified road, or creates an obstruction to the view of persons using any highway used by vehicular traffic, so as to be likely to cause danger to such persons'.

These are classes relating to development by highway authorities or for the collection of road tolls or under local or private Acts or Orders approved by Parliament. The implication presumably is that the highway bodies will have considered safety and should not be second-guessed by the planning authorities.

---

[44] Conservation of Habitats and Species Regulations 2010, reg 3(3).
[45] Habitats Directive, art 6(3).
[46] Conservation of Habitats and Species Regulations 2010, reg 61(1). This provision is applied to reg 75 determinations by the Conservation of Habitats and Species Regulations 2010, reg 60.
[47] See paras **5.50–5.52**.
[48] GPDO 1995, art 3(6) refers to the equivalent provisions at Parts 9, 11, 13 or 30.

5.34 Permitted development rights

5.34 The only permitted development rights authorising the laying of a notifiable pipeline are such works by gas transporters under Part 15, Class A[49]. Of wider application, the only permitted development rights which authorise the demolition of a building (other than part of a building) are the specific demolition provisions in Part 11, Classes B and C[50]. In particular this limits the very wide powers of statutory undertakers.

PRIOR APPROVAL OF DETAILS

5.35 Prior approval is concerned with whether approval is required for specific details or on specific issues before development can take place under certain permitted development rights. Forms of prior approval apply to particular permitted development rights for householders (Part 1), changes of use (Part 3), film-making (Part 4), agriculture (Part 6), non-domestic alterations (Part 7), tolls (Part 9), demolition (Part 11), communications (Part 16), mining (Part 17) and local or private Acts (Part 18). The GPDO 2015 sought to give greater consistency to the time periods for these approvals in England but unfortunately the subject matter and the detailed procedures for prior approval mechanisms all vary. This discussion therefore deals with the general principles which apply. The procedure for any prior approval application requires careful consideration of the individual Part.

5.36 Until 2014 it could be said that prior approval governed certain details of permitted development where the principle of the operations or use had been determined by the existence of the permitted development right itself. Amendments made by the Growth and Infrastructure Act 2013 allowed the prior approval regime in change of use cases to consider specified matters that go to the principle of the development[51]. The permitted development rights to change agricultural buildings to state-funded schools, registered nurseries or dwellings in England are subject to the potential to require prior approval as to the sustainability of the location[52]. New rights to change from shop uses to food and drink or assembly and leisure uses are subject to prior approval in respect of the loss of services and effects on key shopping areas[53]. This ability to consider the principle of development in specified prior approvals may be extended further under Housing and Planning Bill 2015 amendments to s 60. These propose that prior approval may be required for building operations on specified issues[54].

5.37 Otherwise, the concept that prior approval is concerned with details rather than principle holds good. That said, the extent of the details depends upon the terms of the particular class and the legislative context of that form of development. For example, the siting of mobile phone masts and antennae can be a subject for prior approval of siting and design, but since electronic communications operators' powers to site apparatus is so wide, including on the highway, the decision may consider alternatives hundreds of metres away[55].

---

[49] GPDO 2015 and 1995, art 3(8). The GPDO 1995 refers to its predecessor, Part 17, Class F.
[50] GPDO 2015 and 1995, art 3(9). The demolition provisions formerly being in Part 31.
[51] Town and Country Planning Act, s 60(2A), inserted by Growth and Infrastructure Act 2013, s 4(1).
[52] Now in GPDO 2015 Sch 2, Part 3, Classes Q and S, previously GPDO 1995, Sch 2, Part 3, Classes MA and MB.
[53] GPDO 2015, Sch 2, Part 3, Classes C and J.
[54] Housing and Planning Bill 2015, cl 104 proposing to insert s 60(1A) in the Town and Country Planning Act 1990.
[55] See *Phillips v First Secretary of State* [2004] EWHC 2415 (Admin), [2004] JPL 613.

Prior approval of details **5.42**

5.38 A prior approval is concerned with the details which are reserved for that approval and cannot be used to reopen the principle of development: *Murrell v Secretary of State for Communities and Local Government*[56]. The order's description of the details which may be subject to prior approval has to be considered with care to determine whether an issue is relevant to the decision. A local planning authority or Minister may not decide the approval on any matter other than the merits of the details which have to be approved.

5.39 Prior approval usually comprises two elements:

(i) an application to, and a decision by, the local planning authority whether prior approval is required;

(ii) the decision of the local planning authority whether to grant prior approval.

Those are formally separate decisions, although the procedures may allow them to be taken at the same time. It is not uncommon, although it is unhelpful, for the local planning authority's analysis to fail to distinguish between a decision that prior approval is not required, and the grant of prior approval.

Some permitted development rights require prior approval to be granted, rather than allowing an express or deemed decision that prior approval is not required[57].

5.40 No application form is prescribed, but standard forms are available and it is most convenient to use these. Fees are payable with each application. In England these are currently £80 for changes of use, £172 for changes of use and connected building operations under Part 3, £80 for agricultural, forestry or demolition applications and £385 for electronic communications[58]. In Wales the only fees are £80 for agricultural, forestry or demolition applications and £380 for electronic communications applications[59].

5.41 Publicity requirements and practices vary. Some permitted development rights require the applicant to display a site notice (Part 6, agriculture; Part 11, demolition) or notify the owner of the land (Part 16, communications) whilst publicity and consultation requirements may be placed on the local planning authority (Part 3, change of use; Part 4, Class E temporary filming, Part 16). The timing of the publicity will also vary: a site notice is only displayed under agricultural permitted development if the authority has decided that prior approval is required[60], whilst notices are displayed under other rights when the initial application is made.

5.42 A form of prior approval applies to larger single storey rear extensions to dwellinghouses in England[61]. The applicant must serve notice on the local planning

---

[56] [2010] EWCA Civ 1367, [2011] JPL 739 at paras 45, 47. This reflects the approach to the approval of reserved matters or other details under conditions attached to a planning permission granted following an application.
[57] For example, GPDO 2015, Sch 2, Part 17, Class B developments ancillary to mining operations.
[58] Town and Country Planning (Fees for Applications, Deemed Applications, Requests and Site Visits) (England) Regulations 2012, SI 2012/2920, reg 14.
[59] Town and Country Planning (Fees for Applications, Deemed Applications and Site Visits) (Wales) Regulations 2015, reg 13(1).
[60] GPDO 2015 and GPDO 1995, Sch 2, Part 6, Class A, condition A.2(2)(iv).
[61] Those more than 4 metres and up to 8 metres from the rear wall of the original detached dwellinghouse, or more than 3 metres and up to 6 metres for terraced houses outside art 2(3) land: GPDO 2015, Sch 2, Part 1, Class A, conditions A1(f) and (g), condition A4.

5.43 *Permitted development rights*

authority, who then notify each adjoining owner or occupier. If any of those notified object then the prior approval of the local planning authority is required as to 'the impact of the proposed development on the amenity of any adjoining premises'[62].

The prior approval process must be taken to a successful conclusion prior to the development being carried out. It does not operate retrospectively[63].

Failure to give notice of a decision

5.43 Failure of the local planning authority to give notice that prior approval is required, has been granted or is not required, within a set period will mean that prior approval is not required. If no time is specified in the particular Part of Sch 2 then under GPDO 2015 it is the 'period of 8 weeks beginning with the day immediately following that on which the application is received by the authority'[64]. Other periods of 28 or 42 days are, however, used.

5.44 Unsurprisingly, the allowing of the proposed scheme by a failure to give notice has caused battles between developers, local planning authorities and third parties aggrieved by apparent mistakes. The limits of when notice is or is not in time can be set out.

5.45 An application is received by the local planning authority when it arrives in physical or electronic form. Where the electronic communication is received by the recipient outside the recipient's business hours, it is taken to have been received on the next working day[65]. To be valid the application must be accompanied by the documents required by the GPDO[66] and any necessary fee[67], and will only become valid when all the documentation is complete. It does not matter when the application is registered or validated by the planning authority – the period runs from when it was in fact received.

5.46 The start of the time period is expressed differently in the various provisions. So in Part 3 (changes of use) it is 'the expiry of 56 days following the date on which the application was received', meaning the first day of the period is the day after receipt[68]. However for communications rights notice has to be given before 'the expiry of a period of 56 days beginning with the date on which the local planning authority received the application'[69]. The first day of the period is then the date of

---

[62] GPDO 2015, Sch 2, Part 1, Class A, condition A4(7).
[63] *Airwave mm02 Ltd v First Secretary of State* [2005] EWHC 1701 (Admin), [2006] JPL 362 at para 32 per Judge Gilbart QC.
[64] GPDO 2015, art 7. That standardisation provision is not contained in the GPDO 1995.
[65] GPDO 2015, art 2(9) which provides that working day means a day which is not a Saturday, Sunday, Christmas Day, Good Friday or a day which is a Bank Holiday in England under the Banking and Financial Dealings Act 1971. Similar provision is made by GPDO 1995, art 1(10), working day meaning 'a day which is not a Saturday, Sunday, Bank Holiday or other public holiday'.
[66] A failure to specify which materials would be used rendered an application invalid in *R v Caradon District Council, ex p Lovejoy* [2000] JPL 186.
[67] *Infocus Public Networks Ltd v Secretary of State for Communities and Local Government* [2012] EWHC 3309 (Admin), [2011] JPL 1048 at para 40 per Foskett J.
[68] Paragraph W. See the authorities on time limits for bringing proceedings: *Kaur (Pritam) v S Russell & Sons Ltd* [1973] QB 336; *R (on the application of Berky) v Newport City Council* [2012] EWCA Civ 378, [2012] 2 CMLR 44.
[69] GPDO 2015, Sch 2, Part 16, Class A, condition A.3(7), and the equivalent provision in the GPDO 1995, Part 24, Class A.

receipt. The effect is that if the application was received on a Tuesday then in the first case the last day on which the local planning authority's decision should be received is the Tuesday eight weeks later, but in the second example the deadline is the day before, the Monday.

5.47 Notification of the local planning authority's decision within the period involves receipt or deemed receipt of the decision notice. Its despatch within the time limit is insufficient[70].

A local planning authority is able to agree a minor modification to a prior approval. This agreement may be without formality: see *Lever (Finance) Ltd v Westminster Corpn*[71].

A refusal of prior approval or its grant subject to conditions may be appealed to the Minister under the Town and Country Planning Act 1990, s 78(1).

The effect of a prior approval determination

5.48 A determination that prior approval is not required, or is granted or a failure to make a determination in time at all means that the prior approval requirement is dealt with. Conventionally it does not amount to a determination that the proposal complies with the particular class in terms of the development permitted or avoiding the development not permitted categories. Such certainty can only be achieved by a lawful development certificate. For example, a barn might still not be reasonably necessary for the purposes of agriculture within that unit, even though prior approval had been secured[72].

5.49 Doubt may arise because of recently introduced provisions which allow (but do not require) the application to be refused if the local planning authority considers that the proposed development does not comply with the conditions, limitations or restrictions applicable to the particular scheme or that the developer has provided insufficient information to determine that issue[73]. That allows a refusal if it is not shown that the permitted development right arises. A question, though, is whether a failure to refuse for that reason has a similar effect to a lawful development certificate in meaning that the proposal does have the benefit of those rights.

Attaching conditions to prior approvals under permitted development rights

5.50 It remains uncertain whether in general conditions may be applied by the local planning authority to a prior approval. The powers to impose conditions under the Town and Country Planning Act 1990, ss 70 and 72 are expressed to be on the determination of an application for planning permission. A prior approval is not such

---

[70] *Walsall Metropolitan Borough Council v Secretary of State for Communities and Local Government* [2012] EWHC 1756 (Admin), [2012] JPL 1502 on electronic communications permitted development rights in GPDO 1995, Part 24, now GPDO 2015, Part 16.
[71] [1971] 1 QB 222. This remains good law: see *R (on the application of Midcounties Co-operative Ltd) v Wyre Forest District Council* [2009] EWHC 964 (Admin) at paras 67–69 per Ouseley J.
[72] *Harrogate Borough Council v Crossland* [2012] EWHC 3260 (QB) at paras 68–71 per Coulson J. The point is also implicit in *Tapecrown v First Secretary of State* [2006] EWCA Civ 1744, [2007] 2 P & CR 7.
[73] For example, GPDO 2015, Sch 2, Part 1, Class A, condition A4(3), Part 3, paragraph W(3).

5.51 *Permitted development rights*

an application. However s 78(1)(c) of the Act grants a right of appeal where a local planning authority:

> 'refuse an application for any approval of that authority required under a development order a local development order or a neighbourhood development order or grant it subject to conditions'.

5.51 This must be predicated on the basis that either there is a general power to impose conditions or that development orders do, or plausibly might, set out a power to impose conditions. It presupposes that a conditional approval is possible. Case law is mixed. There is no express power to impose conditions on the grant of reserved matters approval under a planning permission, yet it is well-established by the courts that such conditions can be imposed. On the contrary, the view of Mr Justice Collins in *R (on the application of Lucchetti) v South Norfolk District Council*[74] was that local planning authorities could not impose conditions when granting prior approvals. The only conditions on such approvals were those applied by the GPDO itself, requiring compliance with the submitted details.

5.52 Sometimes the GPDO expressly allows conditions to be imposed[75]. The provisions on prior approval for certain changes of use (under Part 3) were amended in 2014 to allow the imposition of conditions 'reasonably related to the subject matter of the prior approval'[76]. Such conditions may not relate to other matters.

Planning obligations and prior approval

5.53 A planning obligation may be required before a prior approval is issued provided that it is necessary to make the details which are subject to the approval acceptable. A conventional example would be a contribution to off-site highways works to ameliorate the transport impacts of a change of use to residential. It is unlawful to refuse to grant prior approval because the applicant fails to enter into an obligation to make contributions for other purposes, such as affordable housing, education or open space contributions on a residential change of use[77].

THE EFFECT OF CHANGES TO PERMITTED DEVELOPMENT RIGHTS OR THEIR APPLICATION

5.54 The permitted development rights which apply to a particular development on a particular site may change for a variety of different reasons:

(i) the GPDO may be revoked or amended;

(ii) the permitted development rights might be withdrawn by an Article 4 Direction;

(iii) the designation of the land changing, for example it becoming a conservation area;

(iv) the underlying factual circumstances on the ground may change, such as other extensions being carried out or the use having changed.

---

[74] [2012] EWHC 3557 (Admin).
[75] An example is on development ancillary to mining operations under GPDO 2015, Sch 2, Part 17, Class B.
[76] GPDO 1995, Sch 2, Part 3, para N(11), now GPDO 2015, Sch 2, Part 3, para W(13).
[77] A view also taken in the Written Ministerial Statement by Nick Boles MP, 6 February 2014.

The effect of changes to permitted development rights or their application **5.60**

5.55 Two situations can be easily described. First, none of these changes can have a retrospective effect, making unlawful operational development or a material change of use which has already taken place, or indeed making lawful previously unlawful development. Similarly where the development has neither started in accordance with the previous permitted development right nor has completed an applicable prior approval process, it will be judged against the new permitted development rights (or their absence). More complex, affected by transitional provisions and perhaps uncertain, is the situation where prior approval has been obtained or the development has commenced but not been completed.

Changes to the GPDO

5.56 In *Williams Le Roi v Secretary of State for the Environment*[78] the General Development Order had been replaced during the course of building operations. Michael Harrison QC held that the correct time to determine which development order applied was immediately before the commencement of development rather than at a later point. This decision may have been overlooked when the Planning and Compulsory Purchase Act 2004 inserted s 61D into the 1990 Act. Section 61D(1) provides:

> 'A development order or local development order may include provision permitting the completion of development if:
>
> (a) planning permission is granted by the order in respect of the development, and
>
> (b) the planning permission is withdrawn at a time after the development is started but before it is completed'.

5.57 Permission is withdrawn by the revocation of the order or its amendment or revision so that it ceases to grant planning permission for the development or materially changes any condition or limitation applicable to it or by the issue of a direction under the order[79]. The premise of s 61D is that the original order will set out what happens in the event of revocation or modification or if a direction is made. However neither the 1995 nor 2015 GPDOs have made any such provision.

5.58 Circular 10/97 *Enforcing Planning Control* considered that in the event of a GPDO amendment if 'the proposed use is instituted or the operations are begun, the change of use remains lawful, or the operations are lawful, and may lawfully be completed, as the case may be'[80].

5.59 On balance, therefore, modifications to the GPDO do not affect development which has already commenced, and it can thus be completed.

The effect of an Article 4 direction

5.60 The government circular introducing the original Article 4 provisions in 1950 said it allowed a direction to be made 'after the development has been begun,

---

[78] [1993] JPL 1033.
[79] Town and Country Planning Act 1990, s 61D(2), (3). Section 61D applies to general or special development orders made by Ministers and to local development orders made by local planning authorities. Special or local orders are discussed in Chapter 26.
[80] Circular 10/97, para 8.30. This was cancelled with the publication of the *Planning Practice Guidance* which does not contain advice on the point.

5.61 *Permitted development rights*

provided it has not been completed'[81]. However compensation is payable for abortive expenditure or other loss or damage directly attributable to the withdrawal of the rights or revocation or modification[82]. Under the GPDO 1995 the better view has been that a direction can remove permitted development rights from projects which have started or which have passed the prior approval stage[83].

5.61 Additionally the effect of an Article 4 direction will also depend upon its terms. A variety of directions to remove permitted development rights for changes from office to residential use were modified by the Secretary of State in 2014 to protect such rights on land where the prior approval process had been completed before the art 4 direction had come into force[84].

5.62 No doubt reflecting that experience, the GPDO 2015 introduced protection in England where prior approval had been dealt with before the Article 4 direction came into force. Such a direction does not affect the carrying out of[85]:

> 'development permitted by any Class in Schedule 2 which is expressed to be subject to prior approval where, in relation to that development, the prior approval date occurs before the date on which the direction comes into force and the development is completed within a period of 3 years starting with the prior approval date'.

Changes to the designation of the land

5.63 Permitted development rights may be restricted or removed by a change to the statutory designation of the land, most commonly, it becoming a conservation area. *R (Orange Personal Communications Services Ltd) v Islington London Borough Council*[86] concerned the designation of a conservation area following a decision that prior approval was not required for the installation of telecommunications under what was then Part 24, Class A. The requisite permitted development rights did not apply in conservation areas. Upholding the High Court[87], Laws LJ held that the permitted development rights remained as the prior approval process was successfully completed prior to the designation[88]. He also considered, strictly *obiter*, that for a permitted development right which did not involve prior approval processes the relevant point was the commencement of development[89].

---

[81] MTCP Circular 87, Appendix.
[82] Town and Country Planning Act 1990, ss 107, 108.
[83] This was the *obiter* view of Crane J in *R (on the application of Orange Personal Communications Services Ltd) v Islington London Borough Council* [2005] EWHC 963 (Admin), [2006] JPL 396 at para 43.
[84] In particular directions concerning Brighton and Hove, Islington and Richmond-upon-Thames.
[85] GPDO 2015, art 4(2)(a). By GPDO 2015, art 4(5):
 "prior approval date' means the date on which:
 (a) prior approval is given;
 (b) a determination that such approval is not required is given, or
 (c) any period for giving such a determination has expired without the applicant being notified whether prior approval is required, given or refused'.
[86] [2006] EWCA Civ 157, [2006] JPL 1309.
[87] [2005] EWHC 963 (Admin), [2006] JPL 396.
[88] At paras 21–24.
[89] At paras 18–20.

Changes of the underlying circumstances on the ground

5.64 There may be circumstances in which a change to the building or land will prevent the completion under permitted development rights of works which have been commenced. These situations would include:

(i) permitted development rights for extensions rely upon there being an existing building. If the works are so substantial that the present building is lost and what happens amounts to the construction of a new building, then permitted development rights would not apply to the extensions[90];

(ii) some extension rights are limited by volume or floorspace relative to the original building[91] and it might be that the capacity available is affected by other works being carried out at the same time as the claimed permitted development (for example, under a planning permission granted on application). The actual capacity needs to be available whilst the permitted development is being carried out, and no regard is given to other development which is consented but not physically in place[92].

THE MAKING OF ARTICLE 4 DIRECTIONS

5.65 The GPDO may provide for the Secretary of State or the local planning authority to be able to direct that the permitted development rights should not apply, in whole or in part, to development in a particular area or a particular development[93]. This power has for a long time been contained in art 4 of the various GPDOs, although the procedure has been recast over the years. The GPDO 2015 significantly revises the procedure and so it is appropriate to deal with England and Wales separately.

England

5.66 The principal provision in England is the GPDO 2015, art 4(1)[94]:

'If the Secretary of State or the local planning authority is satisfied that it is expedient that development described in any Part, Class or paragraph in Schedule 2, other than Class K or M of Part 17, should not be carried out unless permission is granted for it on an application, the Secretary of State or (as the case may be) the local planning authority, may make a direction under this paragraph that the permission granted by article 3 does not apply to:

(a) all or any development of the Part, Class or paragraph in question in an area specified in the direction; or

---

[90] *Arnold v Secretary of State for Communities and Local Government* [2015] EWHC 1197 (Admin), [2015] JPL 1053 at paras 69, 70 per Dove J.
[91] For example GPDO 2015, Sch 2, Part 1, Class B, para B1(d) (householder roofs); Part 7, Class A, para A1(a) (shop extensions).
[92] *Watts v Secretary of State for the Environment, Transport and the Regions* [2002] EWHC 993 (Admin), [2002] JPL 173.
[93] Town and Country Planning Act 1990, s 60(3).
[94] Part 17, Class K is the use of land for mineral exploration and Class M the removal of material from mineral-working deposits and are dealt with by art 5 directions. The Welsh equivalent of art 4(1) is materially the same, referring to the equivalent Part 22, Class B and Part 23, Class B.

5.67 *Permitted development rights*

(b) any particular development, falling within that Part, Class or paragraph, which is specified in the direction, and the direction must specify that it is made under this paragraph'.

5.67 Certain development under permitted development rights cannot be affected by Article 4 directions, either at all or without making specific provision to remove those rights. Rights which cannot be removed at all are in Part 9, Class B (highway works by the Secretary of State or a strategic highways company), Part 18, Class A (authorised by Acts or Parliamentary orders, provided they post-date 1 July 1948), Part 19 Classes Q, R, S, T (emergency or national security development by the Crown).

5.68 Various rights of statutory undertakers to carry out the maintenance of buildings and various works connected with railways, harbours, watercourses and drainage and aerodromes are only removed if the Article 4 direction so provides[95].

5.69 Article 4 directions may be made to have effect immediately or after a period of time. Compensation is ordinarily payable by the local planning authority if planning permission is subsequently refused for development which is the subject of an Article 4 direction[96]. The planning application must be made within 12 months beginning with the date on which the rights are withdrawn[97]. However for the following classes of development compensation is not payable if notice of the withdrawal of the permitted development rights was published not less than 12 months before the Article 4 direction took effect[98]:

(i) Part 1 (development within the curtilage of a dwellinghouse);

(ii) Part 2, Classes D and E (minor operations relating to electric vehicle charging points);

(iii) Part 3, Classes C, D, J, L, M, N, O, P, Q, R, S, T and U (certain changes of use);

(iv) Part 4, Classes C, D and E (temporary uses);

(v) Part 7, Classes A to H, L, M and N (non-domestic extensions, alterations etc);

(vi) Part 14 (installation of renewable energy equipment); and

(vii) Part 16, Class A (development by electronic communications code operators) to the extent that paragraph A.2(5) of Class A disapplies certain conditions in paragraph A.3 of Class A.

Consequently Article 4 directions are often made to take effect after the 12-month notice period is up.

---

[95] GPDO 2015, art 4(3).
[96] Town and Country Planning Act 1990, s 108. Compensation is payable under s 107 for abortive expenditure and loss or damage which is directly attributable to the withdrawal of rights.
[97] Town and Country Planning Act 1990, s 108(2A) and Town and Country Planning (Compensation) (England) Regulations 2015, SI 2015/598, art 2.
[98] Town and Country Planning Act 1990, s 108(3B)(a), (3C) and Town and Country Planning (Compensation) (England) Regulations 2015, art 2.

The making of Article 4 directions **5.75**

English procedures for making Article 4 directions

5.70 A direction which does not have immediate effect will only come into force following confirmation by the local planning authority and on a date specified in the order which must be at least 28 days after the end of the statutory consultation on the direction[99]. In practice such a notice will not take effect until at least two months after it has been made.

5.71 Constitutional authority to make Article 4 directions will need to be checked. In a local authority operating executive arrangements, the making of an Article 4 direction is an executive function, not within the powers of the planning committee[100].

5.72 Statutory consultation for non-immediate Article 4 directions takes place once they are made. A local advertisement is required, along with a site notice being displayed at two locations within the area of the direction or, if it relates to a specific development, at that site, for not less than six weeks[101]. Notice has to be given to the owners and occupiers of every part of the land subject to the direction unless it is difficult to identify or locate a particular owner or occupier or the number within the area makes individual service impracticable[102]. A copy of the direction, notice and map defining the area or site must be sent to the Minister at the same time as the first publicity[103]. County and district planning authorities must notify each other of the making of a direction[104].

5.73 The content of the notice is prescribed[105] and must describe the development and area or site to which it relates with a statement of its effect. Article 4(1) must be referenced and details given of where the direction can be inspected, a minimum 21-day consultation period and the date proposed for the direction to take effect.

5.74 A non-immediate direction will only take effect once it is confirmed by the local planning authority. In confirming the direction the authority must, of course, take into account any representations made in the statutory period[106]. If a direction is confirmed then notice must be given in the same manner as notice of its making[107].

5.75 Subject to various heritage exceptions, the Secretary of State may make a direction modifying or cancelling an Article 4 direction 'at any time before or after

---

[99] GPDO 2015, Sch 3, para 1(4), (7).
[100] Local Government Act 2000, s 9D (in England) and s 13 (in Wales). The relevant functions and responsibilities regulations do not make art 4 directions non-executive functions.
[101] GPDO 2015, Sch 3, para 1(1). The site display is considered to be achieved even if the notice is removed, obscured or defaced provided this occurs without fault or intention of the local planning authority and it has taken reasonable steps for the protection of the notice, including, if need be, its replacement: GPDO 2015, Schedule 3, para 1(5).
[102] GPDO 2015, Sch 3, para 1(1)(c), (2). Notice would normally be given by sending letters addressed to the 'owner' and to the 'occupier' at the property. Difficulty with individual notice would tend to arise for properties without postal addresses or letter boxes, such as empty urban plots. Individual notice to statutory undertakers and the Crown is always required: GPDO 2015, Sch 3, para 1(3).
[103] GPDO 2015, Sch 3, para 1(6).
[104] GPDO 2015, Sch 3, para 1(8).
[105] By GPDO 2015, Sch 3, para 1(4).
[106] GPDO 2015, Sch 3, para 1(9).
[107] GPDO 2015, Sch 3, para 1(11), (12).

5.76 *Permitted development rights*

its confirmation'[108]. The direction is sent to the local planning authority who must then publicise it as it would its own decision[109]. A local planning authority may cancel any Article 4 direction made by it, repeating the procedure used for immediate effect and non-immediate effect directions[110].

5.76 A direction can be made with immediate effect if[111]:

(a)
- (i) it relates only to development permitted by Parts 1 to 4 (householder, minor operations, change of use and temporary use) or Class B or C of Part 11 (demolition); and
- (ii) 'the authority consider that the development to which the direction relates would be prejudicial to the proper planning of their area or constitute a threat to the amenities of their area'; or

(b)
- (i) the direction is within the 'whole or part of any conservation area';
- (ii) the authority consider it should have immediate effect; and
- (iii) it consists of particular development within Parts 1 (householder), 2 (minor works) and Part 11, Class C (demolition of means of enclosure)

5.77 The development which may be restricted by a 'conservation area' immediate direction is that described in[112]:

'(a) Class A of Part 1 of Schedule 2, consisting of the enlargement, improvement or other alteration of a dwellinghouse, where any part of the enlargement, improvement or alteration would front a relevant location;

(b) Class C of Part 1 of that Schedule, where the alteration would be to a roof slope which fronts a relevant location;

(c) Class D of Part 1 of that Schedule, where the external door in question fronts a relevant location;

(d) Class E of Part 1 of that Schedule, where the building or enclosure, swimming or other pool to be provided would front a relevant location, or where the part of the building or enclosure maintained, improved or altered would front a relevant location;

(e) Class F of Part 1 of that Schedule, where the hard surface would front a relevant location;

(f) Class G of Part 1 of that Schedule, consisting of the installation, alteration or replacement of a chimney on a dwellinghouse;

(g) Class H of Part 1 of that Schedule, where the part of the building or other structure on which the antenna is to be installed, altered or replaced fronts a relevant location;

---

[108] GPDO 2015, Sch 3, para 1(13). The exceptions are in Sch 3, para 2(3) (certain works under Parts 1, 2 and 11 in conservation areas) and para 2(4) (art 4 direction relating solely to a listed building, building or architectural or historic interest or development within the curtilage of a listed building). The latter sub-paragraph therefore allows the removal of permitted development rights for the demolition of non-designated heritage assets by a local planning authority without Ministerial intervention.
[109] GPDO 2015, Sch 3, para 1(15)–(18).
[110] GPDO 2015, Sch 3, para 1(13), (15).
[111] GPDO 2015, Sch 3, para 2(1).
[112] GPDO 2015, Sch 3, para 2(3).

(h) Class A of Part 2 of that Schedule, where the gate, fence, wall or other means of enclosure would be within the curtilage of a dwellinghouse and would front a relevant location;

(i) Class C of Part 2 of the Schedule, consisting of the painting of the exterior of any part of—

   (i) a dwellinghouse; or

   (ii) any building or enclosure within the curtilage of a dwellinghouse, which fronts a relevant location;

(j) Class C of Part 11 of that Schedule, where the gate, fence, wall or other means of enclosure is within the curtilage of a dwellinghouse and fronts a relevant location'.

A relevant location is a highway, waterway or open space[113].

5.78 Consultation procedures are essentially the same as non-immediate directions except that the direction will have already come into force and notice to the Secretary of State is given on the day that the notice is made[114]. The direction comes into force on the day that it is first served on the occupier of that part of the land (and in the absence of an occupier, the owner) or if service is difficult or impracticable under Sch 3, para 1(2), when it is first published or a site notice displayed[115]. It is therefore possible for a direction to come into force on different parts at different times. There is also the benefit that a direction can be quickly served in respect of land where damaging development is imminent, even if its wider dissemination may take longer.

5.79 An immediate effect direction will expire after six months starting with the day it came into force, unless confirmed by the local planning authority before the end of that period[116]. A decision to confirm may not occur until 28 days after the notice has been served or published and representations considered[117]. A decision not to confirm does not bring the effect of the direction to an end. Only the passage of time or the cancellation of the direction by a further direction will do that[118]. Notice of confirmation must be given in a similar manner to other directions, except that a copy need not be sent to the Secretary of State where the direction solely concerns listed buildings or buildings notified by the authority to the Minister as being of architectural or historic interest[119].

5.80 The National Planning Policy Framework advises[120]:

'The use of Article 4 directions to remove national permitted development rights should be limited to situations where this is necessary to protect local amenity or the wellbeing of the area (this could include the use of Article 4 directions to require planning permission for the demolition of local facilities)'.

---

[113] GPDO 2015, Sch 3, para 2(10).
[114] GPDO 2015, Sch 3, para 2(2).
[115] GPDO 2015, Sch 3, para 2(5).
[116] GPDO 2015, Sch 3, para 2(6).
[117] GPDO 2015, Sch 3, para 2(6) applying para 1(10).
[118] Cancellation taking place under GPDO 2015, Sch 3, para 1(13), (15).
[119] GPDO 2015, Sch 3, para 2(7)–(9).
[120] NPPF, para 200.

5.81 *Permitted development rights*

The NPPF also disapproves of 'blanket' Article 4 directions against communications permitted development over a wide area or a wide range of apparatus[121].

Welsh procedures for making art 4 directions

5.81 Welsh Article 4 directions are divided between those which come into force following Ministerial approval (Article 4(1) directions), a category of Article 4(1) directions affecting historic buildings which do not need approval, a further category of Article 4(1) directions which have effect for six months pending approval or disallowance by the Minister, and Article 4(2) directions in conservation areas which have immediate effect[122]. The circumstances where Article 4(2) directions can be made are very similar to those in England discussed above.

The procedure for making an Article 4(1) direction is set out in art 5, and for Article 4(2) directions in art 6.

5.82 The approval of the Welsh Ministers is required for any Article 4(1) direction except for two categories. First, approval is not required for directions which solely relate to listed buildings, land within their curtilage or any other building which the Minister has notified the local planning authority as being of architectural or historic interest[123]. Second, a direction only covering householder rights, minor operations, change of use, temporary development or demolition may be made for a six-month period without Ministerial approval[124]. However approval is required for the direction to continue after six months and it will immediately cease to have effect if disallowed by the Minister within that period[125].

5.83 Notice of an Article 4(1) direction has to be given to the owner and occupier of the land affected once the direction has been approved by the Minister or if approval is not required, once it is made[126]. If individual service is impracticable because of the numbers involved or difficulties in identifying or locating all of those to be served, a local newspaper advertisement may be used instead[127]. Directions have effect when notice is given on the individual part of the land or on advertisement[128]. Otherwise there is no statutory obligation to consult prior to making a direction or Ministerial approval, but consultation at some stage is desirable.

Article 4(1) directions may be cancelled by the local planning authority or the Minister by direction[129].

5.84 Article 4(2) directions are advertised and notice is given to owners or occupiers of the land affected unless it is impracticable to do so because of the numbers involved or identifying them[130]. The direction takes effect on service or,

---

[121] NPPF, para 44.
[122] The existence of three types of 'Article 4(1) directions' is unnecessarily complex.
[123] GPDO 1995, art 5(3).
[124] GPDO 1995, art 5(4). Approval may be with modifications: art 5(11).
[125] GPDO 1995, art 5(5), (8). Repeated directions of this nature are not permitted: GPDO 1995, art 5(6).
[126] GPDO 1995, art 5(10).
[127] GPDO 1995, art 5(12)–(14).
[128] GPDO 1995, art 5(10), (15).
[129] GPDO 1995, art 5(16). Similar publicity then occurs: art 5(17).
[130] GPDO 1995, art 6(1), (4), (5).

The making of Article 4 directions **5.86**

if that is not practicable, on local advertisement[131]. An Article 4(2) direction will cease to have effect after six months unless it is confirmed by the local planning authority[132]. A consultation period of at least 21 days will be stated in the notice[133] and any comments made will have to be taken into account in a confirmation decision[134].

Article 5 directions restricting certain mineral permitted development

5.85 In England if a mineral planning authority receives a notification of proposed development under Part 17 Class K (use of land for mineral exploration) or Class M (removal of material from mineral-working deposits) it may make a direction removing those permitted development rights in whole or in part from the development if it is expedient to do so because:

'(a) the land on which the development is to be carried out is within:

   (i) a National Park;

   (ii) an area of outstanding natural beauty;

   (iii) a site of archaeological interest, and the operation to be carried out is not one described in the Schedule to the Areas of Archaeological Importance (Notification of Operations) (Exemption) Order 1984 (exempt operations);

   (iv) a site of special scientific interest; or

   (v) the Broads;

(b) the development, either taken by itself or taken in conjunction with other development which is already being carried out in the area or in respect of which notification has been given under the provisions of Class K or M of Part 17 of Schedule 2 would cause serious detriment to the amenity of the area in which it is to be carried out or would adversely affect the setting of a Grade I listed building;

(c) the development would constitute a serious nuisance to the inhabitants of a nearby residential building, hospital or school; or

(d) the development would endanger aircraft using a nearby aerodrome'.

Similar provision is made for Part 22, Class B and Part 23, Class B rights by art 7 in Wales.

5.86 In both nations, once the direction is made, a copy must be sent as soon as reasonably practicable to the Minister and the person who gave the notice[135]. The Secretary of State has 28 days from the date on which the direction is made to disallow it[136]. An art 5 direction will come into force 29 days from the date on which notice of its making is sent to the Secretary of State. For clarity, the date of coming into force must be stated on the direction[137].

---

[131] GPDO 1995, art 6(3).
[132] GPDO 1995, art 6(7).
[133] GPDO 1995, art 6(2).
[134] GPDO 1995, art 6(8). Confirmation may not take place until at least 28 days after the final notice is given (art 6(9)). Notice of confirmation has to be given in the same way as notice of making the direction (art 6(10)).
[135] GPDO 2015, art 5(4); GPDO 1995, art 7(4).
[136] GPDO 2015, art 5(5); GPDO 1995, art 7(5). If disallowed, the mineral planning authority must give notice of that to the developer.
[137] GPDO 2015, art 5(3); GPDO 1995, art 7(3).

5.87 *Permitted development rights*

TYPES OF PERMITTED DEVELOPMENT RIGHTS

5.87 The GPDO 2015 reorganised the Parts in Sch 2, putting the various rights within 19 Parts rather than the GPDO 1995's 43 Parts. The new Parts are:

Part 1: Development within the curtilage of a dwellinghouse
Part 2: Minor operations
Part 3: Changes of use
Part 4: Temporary buildings and uses
Part 5: Caravan sites and recreational campsites
Part 6: Agricultural and forestry
Part 7: Non-domestic extensions, alterations etc
Part 8: Transport related development
Part 9: Development relating to roads
Part 10: Repairs to services
Part 11: Heritage and demolition
Part 12: Development by local authorities
Part 13: Water and sewerage
Part 14: Renewable energy
Part 15: Power related development
Part 16: Communications
Part 17: Mining and mineral exploration
Part 18: Miscellaneous development
Part 19: Development by the Crown or for national security purposes

For the most part the reduction has been achieved by reorganising the existing permitted development rights into fewer parts. The destinations of the GPDO 1995 elements (which remain in force in Wales) are:

GPDO Order 1995, Sch 2 Parts (Wales, and prior to 15 April 2015, England)	GPDO 2015, Sch 2 Parts (England only from 15 April 2015)
Part 1 Development within the curtilage of a dwelling-house:	Part 1 Development within the curtilage of a dwellinghouse
Part 2 Minor operations:	Part 2 Minor operations
Part 3 Changes of use:	Part 3 Changes of use
Part 4 Temporary buildings and uses	Part 4 Temporary buildings and uses
Part 5 Caravan sites	Part 5 Caravan sites and recreational campsites
Part 6 Agricultural buildings and operations	Part 6 Agricultural and forestry
Part 7 Forestry buildings and operations	Part 6 Agricultural and forestry
Part 8 Industrial and warehouse development	Part 7 Non-domestic extensions, alterations etc,
Part 9 Repairs to unadopted streets and private ways	Part 9 Development relating to roads
Part 10 Repairs to services	Part 10 Repairs to services
Part 11 Development under local or private Acts or orders	Part 18 Miscellaneous development, Class A
Part 12 Development by local authorities	Part 12 Development by local authorities

Types of permitted development rights **5.87**

GPDO Order 1995, Sch 2 Parts (Wales, and prior to 15 April 2015, England)	GPDO 2015, Sch 2 Parts (England only from 15 April 2015)
Part 13 Development by local highway authorities	Part 9 Development relating to roads
Part 14 Development by drainage bodies	Part 13 Water and sewerage
Part 15 Development by the Environment Agency	Part 13 Water and sewerage
Part 16 Development by or on behalf of sewerage undertakers	Part 13 Water and sewerage
Part 17 Development by statutory undertakers	Part 8 Transport related development; Part 9 Development relating to roads; Part 13 Water and sewerage; Part 15 Power related development; Part 16 Communications
Part 18 Aviation development	Part 8 Transport related development
Part 19 Developments ancillary to mining operations	Part 17 Mining and mineral exploration
Part 20 Coal mining development by the Coal authority or licensed operators	Part 17 Mining and mineral exploration
Part 21 Waste tipping at a mine	Part 17 Mining and mineral exploration
Part 22 Mineral exploration	Part 17 Mining and mineral exploration
Part 23 Removal of material from mineral-working deposits	Part 17 Mining and mineral exploration
Part 24 Developments by electronic communications code operators	Part 16 Communications
Part 25 Other telecommunications development	Part 16 Communications
Part 26 Development by English Heritage	Part 11 Heritage and demolition
Part 27 Use by members of certain recreational organisations	Part 5 Caravan sites and recreational campsites
Part 28 Development at amusement parks	Part 18 Miscellaneous development, Class B
Part 29 Driver information systems	Part 16 Communications
Part 30 Toll road facilities	Part 9 Development relating to roads
Part 31 Demolition of buildings	Part 11 Heritage and demolition
Part 32 Schools, colleges, universities and hospitals	Part 7 Non-domestic extensions, alterations etc
Part 33 Closed circuit television cameras	Part 2 Minor operations
Part 34 Development by the Crown	Part 19 Development by the Crown or for national security purposes
Part 35 Aviation Development by the Crown	Part 19 Development by the Crown or for national security purposes
Part 36 Crown Railways, Dockyards etc and Lighthouses	Part 19 Development by the Crown or for national security purposes

5.88 *Permitted development rights*

GPDO Order 1995, Sch 2 Parts (Wales, and prior to 15 April 2015, England)	GPDO 2015, Sch 2 Parts (England only from 15 April 2015)
Part 37 Emergency Development by the Crown	Part 19 Development by the Crown or for national security purposes
Part 38 Development for National Security Purposes	Part 19 Development by the Crown or for national security purposes
Part 39 Temporary Protection of Poultry and other Captive Birds	*Expired in 2009*
Part 40 Installation of Domestic Microgeneration Equipment	Part 14 Renewable energy
Part 41 Office Buildings	Part 7 Non-domestic extensions, alterations etc,
Part 42 Shops or Catering, Financial or Professional Services Establishments	Part 7 Non-domestic extensions, alterations etc,
Part 43 Installation of Non-Domestic Microgeneration Equipment	Part 14 Renewable energy

INTERPRETATION OF THE PERMITTED DEVELOPMENT RIGHTS

5.88 The permitted development rights are complex, seek to be precise, but are sometimes artfully vague. In *English Clays Lovering Pochin & Co Ltd v Plymouth Corpn* Goulding J commented[138]:

> 'It is common ground that the development order is to be construed in what has sometimes been called in argument "a broad or common sense manner", at any rate in the manner appropriate, as counsel say, to a document framed for administrative purposes rather than as an instrument couched in conveyancing language. ... I have to apply myself to the ordinary meaning of the language used by the Minister in making the development order ...'.

5.89 Perhaps the real starting point is that each GPDO is secondary legislation and is to be construed in the same way as other legislation. The ordinary meaning of the language is the best place to begin.

A few general pointers do apply:

(i) read the particular class, with its exclusions and conditions carefully. Every word does count;

(ii) consider the class in the context of the Part it is in;

(iii) remember to look for definitions of terms, whether in art 1(2) of the relevant order or in the Town and Country Planning Act 1990, s 336;

(iv) permitted development rights have been written to relate to real world construction and activity. Considering typical types of building or use will help the reader to understand what the legislation is talking about;

---

[138] [1973] 2 All ER 730 at 735.

Interpretation of the permitted development rights **5.92**

(v) government guidance can provide useful illustrations (particularly the Technical Guidance), but it does not alter what the GPDO actually means and may be less useful for non-standard situations;

(vi) there is some case law on the meaning of particular elements of the GDPO, but not a great deal.

Particular issues which arise across the classes

The meaning of building

5.90 Building has a wide meaning under the Town and Country Planning Act 1990[139] and other legislation. It can comprise some substantial elements of fixed plant and machinery. In *Barvis Ltd v Secretary of State for the Environment*[140] the Divisional Court upheld the minister's decision that the erection of a tower crane on steel track was a building.

5.91 However, in the GPDO 2015, 'building' has a narrower definition in art 2(1)[141]:

'"building":

(a) includes any structure or erection and, except in Class F of Part 2, Class B of Part 11, Classes A to I of Part 14, Classes A, B and C of Part 16 and Class T of Part 19, of Schedule 2, includes any part of a building; and

(b) does not include plant or machinery and, in Schedule 2, except in Class F of Part 2 and Class C of Part 11, does not include any gate, fence, wall or other means of enclosure'.

Consequently certain structures and erections which would be buildings under the Town and Country Planning Act 1990 and which are erected by building operations are not buildings for the purposes of the GPDO. These include walls and other means of enclosure and 'plant or machinery'.

5.92 The GPDO definitions also include[142]:

'"machinery" includes any structure or erection in the nature of machinery...

"plant" includes any structure or erection in the nature of plant'

The meaning of plant has been considered by the courts in non-planning cases. For the purposes of capital allowances under the tax regime grain silos are plant[143]. The tax cases treat plant as apparatus used for the business but not stock in trade or premises[144]. Other examples of plant for capital allowances include pipelines[145] and dry docks[146]. Silos are also plant for rating purposes, although they will usually

---

[139] By s 336(1) it 'includes any structure or erection, and any part of a building, as so defined, but does not include plant or machinery comprised in a building'.
[140] (1971) 22 P & CR 710.
[141] GPDO 1995, art 1(2) refers to the 1995 classes, but to the same effect.
[142] GPDO 2015, art 2(1), GPDO 1995, art 1(2).
[143] *Schofield v Hall* [1975] STC 353.
[144] *Yarmouth v France* (1887) 19 QBD 658.
[145] *Barclays Mercantile Business Finance Ltd v Mawson (Inspector of Taxes)* [2005] 1 AC 684.
[146] *Inland Revenue Commissioners v Barclay, Curle & Co Ltd* [1969] 1 WLR 675.

5.93 *Permitted development rights*

be included in the heriditament[147]. Of course, the meaning of an expression in tax legislation is not necessarily the same as in planning legislation.

5.93 A recent inspector's decision has also considered the meaning of plant and machinery in Part 8, Class B of the GPDO. In *Bardsea Business Park*[148] the inspector found, following an inquiry, that a concrete batching plant was plant or machinery within Class B.

5.94 Except for the permitted development rights in Part 3 to change the use of land, the term dwellinghouse does not include a flat or a building containing one or more flats[149]. A flat is a separate and self-contained dwelling which is divided horizontally from another part of the building[150].

5.95 A reference to a highway will include vehicular highways and public rights of way (byways open to all traffic, bridleways, cycleways and footpaths) unless expressly confined to vehicular highways[151].

5.96 In the GPDOs statutory undertakers are[152]:

(i) persons authorised by any enactment to carry on any railway, light railway, tramway, road transport, water transport, canal, inland navigation, dock, harbour, pier or lighthouse undertaking or any undertaking for the supply of hydraulic power and a relevant airport operator;

(ii) a universal service provider for postal services;

(iii) the Civil Aviation Authority;

(iv) an air traffic services licence holder;

(v) the Environment Agency or Natural Resources Body for Wales;

(vi) a water undertaker;

(vii) a sewerage undertaker

(viii) a gas transporter; and

(ix) an Electricity Act 1989 licence holder.

Restricted categories of land: art 2(3), (4), (5) land

5.97 Various specific areas where permitted development rights are further restricted are identified within the GPDO. These areas are known, with a lack of imagination, as art 2(3), art 2(4) or art 2(5) land and are set out in the GPDO 2015, Sch 1. Broadly they comprise:

---

[147] Valuation for Rating (Plant and Machinery) (England) Regulations 2000, Schedule, Class 4, Table 4.
[148] APP/M0933/X/00/1035902.
[149] GPDO 2015, art 2(1), GPDO 1995, art 1(2).
[150] GPDO 2015, art 2(1), GPDO 1995, art 1(2). In contrast, a terraced house is divided vertically.
[151] *R (on the application of Littman) v London Borough of Barnet* [2007] EWHC 3411 (Admin).
[152] By a combination of Town and Country Planning Act 1990, s 262 and GPDO 2015, art 2(1) or GPDO 1995, art 1(2).

(i) *art 2(3) land*: land within a National Park, area of outstanding natural beauty, a conservation area, an area specified for the purposes of the Wildlife and Countryside Act 1981, s 41(3) (enhancement and protection of the natural beauty and amenity of the countryside), the Broads and a World Heritage Site;

(ii) *art 2(4) land*: land within a National Park or the Broads and other identified land in parts of Cumbria and Derbyshire;

(iii) *art 2(5) land*: land mapped to exclude permitted development rights to change from office to residential uses[153]. These areas range from the Central Activities Zone (essentially central London), Tech City in London, the Royal Borough of Kensington and Chelsea, various parts of London's Docklands, Manchester City Centre and specified areas in Ashford (Kent), East Hampshire, Sevenoaks, Stevenage, the Vale of White Horse[154].

5.98 Equivalent areas of landscape or conservation interest are defined in the GPDO 1995 for Wales as art 1(5) land and art 1(6) land, but the office to residential provisions do not apply:

(i) *art 1(5) land*: land within a National Park, area of outstanding natural beauty, a conservation area, an area specified for the purposes of the Wildlife and Countryside Act 1981, s 41(3) (enhancement and protection of the natural beauty and amenity of the countryside), and a World Heritage Site;

(ii) *art 1(6) land*: land within a National Park or the Broads and other identified land in parts of Aberconwy and Colwyn, Caernarfonshire and Merionethshire and in Denbighshire.

THE PERMITTED DEVELOPMENT RIGHTS

5.99 The Parts and classes are listed as in the GPDO 2015. Cross references are given to the GPDO 1995 in Wales as appropriate.

Part 1 Household permitted development rights

5.100 Part 1 consists of eight classes:

Class A The enlargement, improvement or other alteration of a dwellinghouse

Class B The enlargement of a dwellinghouse consisting of an addition or alteration to its roof

Class C Any other alteration to the roof of a dwellinghouse

Class D The erection or construction of a porch outside any external door of a dwellinghouse

---

[153] These permitted development rights are now in GPDO 2015, Sch 2, Part 3, Class O (previously in England the GPDO 1995, Sch 2, Part 3, Class J). The Secretary of State's decision not to include further areas in what is now art 2(5) land was upheld in *R (Islington London Borough Council) v Secretary of State for Communities and Local Government* [2013] EWHC 4009 (Admin).
[154] It is a matter of opinion whether the most prosaic location is 'BT Building, London Road, Sevenoaks' or 'An area in London Road, Sevenoaks'.

5.101 *Permitted development rights*

Class E The provision within the curtilage of the dwellinghouse of:

(a) any building or enclosure, swimming or other pool required for a purpose incidental to the enjoyment of the dwellinghouse as such, or the maintenance, improvement or other alteration of such a building or enclosure; or

(b) a container used for domestic heating purposes for the storage of oil or liquid petroleum gas.

Class F Development consisting of:

(a) the provision within the curtilage of a dwellinghouse of a hard surface for any purpose incidental to the enjoyment of the dwellinghouse as such; or

(b) the replacement in whole or in part of such a surface.

Class G The installation, alteration or replacement of a chimney, flue or soil and vent pipe on a dwellinghouse.

Class H The installation, alteration or replacement of a microwave antenna on a dwellinghouse or within the curtilage of a dwellinghouse.

5.101 Extensive permitted development rights are provided for dwellinghouses and land within their curtilage. For this Part dwellinghouse does not include a building containing flats or a flat itself[155]. The curtilage is an area of land associated with a building[156], which can be seen as 'part and parcel' of the land comprised with the building[157]. In the urban context 'land attached to a dwelling house which is able and intended to be used in conjunction with the house (whether or not formally described as its garden) is likely to be within its curtilage'[158]. However that might not be the case for a large country house[159]. The use of the curtilage must be lawful before it can be relied upon[160].

5.102 The headline permitted development in the classes varies little between England and Wales: Class E explicitly includes raised platforms in Wales and the Welsh version does not include flue, soil or vent pipes in Class G. The development not permitted and the conditions need to be considered carefully in all situations.

5.103 Class A in particular is subject to a large list of exceptions which differ between England and Wales. Several substantive amendments were made by the GPDO 2015, prohibiting Class A extensions beyond the principal elevation of the original dwellinghouse even if they do not front a highway, and continuing the time to exercise a right for large rear extensions from 2016 to 2019[161]. The amendments

---

[155] GPDO 2015, art 2(1), GPDO 1995, art 1(2).
[156] *Skerritts of Nottingham Ltd v Secretary of State for the Environment, Transport and the Regions* [2001] QB 59.
[157] *Methuen-Campbell v Walters* [1979] 1 QB 525 at 543.
[158] *R (on the application of Sumption) v London Borough of Greenwich* [2007] EWHC 2776 (Admin), [2008] 1 P & CR 336 at para 24 per Collins J.
[159] For example in *McAlpine v Secretary of State for the Environment* [1995] 1 PLR 16 a grassed area used for recreation beyond the formal garden of a large house was held to be outside the curtilage.
[160] GPDO 2015, art 3(5).
[161] GPDO 2015, Sch 2, Part 1, Class A, para A1(e) and (g) respectively.

also altered the conditions on roof extensions, so that enlargements could be up to 20 cm from the outside edge of the eaves[162].

5.104 In Class H, a microwave antenna is a satellite or terrestrial microwave antenna[163]. Terrestrial television aerials, including for digital television, operate at different frequencies and have, with their mountings and poles, been treated as *de minimis* or not having a material effect on the external appearance of the building and so not development requiring planning permission[164].

5.105 There is relatively little useful guidance from the courts on the meaning of the householder permitted development rights. Historically few disputes were taken as far as the High Court. Part 1 was comprehensively replaced in England in 2008 and in Wales in 2013 and so the earlier case law is of limited assistance. Judgments on the old Part 1 provisions need to be considered with great care if they are to be applied to the new rules.

5.106 In *Evans v Secretary of State for Communities and Local Government*[165] it was held that what is now Class A, para A2(c) that the prohibition for art 2(3) land 'the enlarged part of the dwellinghouse would have more than a single storey and extend beyond the rear wall of the original dwellinghouse' judged the rear wall at the level of the extension, so a first floor extension on top of an existing ground floor element was not permitted.

5.107 The construction of a building within the curtilage of a house under Class E needs to be for incidental purposes. In *Peche D'Or Investments v Secretary of State for the Environment*[166] Nigel Macleod QC acknowledged that 'additions to the normal basic domestic living accommodation of a dwelling-house, such as bedrooms, would not be expected to be regarded as being "incidental to the enjoyment of a dwelling-house as such" because they were generally an integral part of the ordinary residential use as a dwelling-house'. What is incidental is a matter of judgment in each case, but includes sheds, garages and summerhouses, and might include a gym[167] or home office or studio.

Part 2 Minor operations

5.108 Part 2 comprises a variety of works which can be carried out on land in any use[168]:

'A The erection, construction, maintenance, improvement or alteration of a gate, fence, wall or other means of enclosure

B The formation, laying out and construction of a means of access to a highway which is not a trunk road or a classified road, where that access is required in connection with development permitted by any Class in this Schedule (other than by Class A of this Part).

---

[162] GPDO 2015, Sch 2, Part 1, Class B, para B2(b)(i)(bb), reversing *Waltham Forest London Borough Council v Secretary of State for Communities and Local Government* [2013] EWHC 2816 (Admin).
[163] GPDO 2015, art 2(1), GPDO 1995, art 1(2).
[164] See the former Planning Policy Guidance 8 *Telecommunications*, Appendix, para 43.
[165] [2014] EWHC 4111 (Admin), [2015] JPL 589.
[166] [1996] JPL 311. Followed in *Rambridge v Secretary of State for the Environment* (1997) 74 P & CR 126.
[167] See inspector's decision *Qureshi v London Borough of Barnet* [2014] PAD 52.
[168] GPDO 2015. Classes D and E are not contained in the Welsh version of the GPDO 1995.

5.109 *Permitted development rights*

C The painting of the exterior of any building or work.

D The installation, alteration or replacement, within an area lawfully used for off-street parking, of an electrical outlet mounted on a wall for recharging electric vehicles.

E The installation, alteration or replacement, within an area lawfully used for off-street parking, of an upstand with an electrical outlet mounted on it for recharging electric vehicles[169].

F The installation, alteration or replacement on a building of a closed circuit television camera to be used for security purposes[170].

Means of enclosure in Class A are limited to one metre in height adjacent to a highway used by vehicular traffic[171] and two metres elsewhere.

5.109 In *Nicholson v First Secretary of State*[172] Collins J held that 'highway used by vehicular traffic' was concerned with safety. He held:

'if Parliament had intended to limit the restriction on height to highways for use by vehicular traffic it could have used the word "carriageway" as defined in the Highways Act 1980. Section 329(1) of that Act defines it as a "way (other than a cycle track) over which the public have a right of way for the passage of vehicles". ... Since some highways which are not for use by vehicular traffic may be used quite extensively by vehicular traffic (for example, an access to a private club) it is not surprising that Parliament should have concerned itself with whether there was de facto use'.

Consequently the one metre limit will apply to walls adjacent to footpaths and bridleways if those ways are used by vehicles, whether motor vehicles under private rights or (perhaps) bicycles. Collins J also held that ground level would be measured from the highway side of the wall.

Part 3 Changes of use

5.110 The ability to change between particular use classes under Part 3 is one of the most important parts of the GPDO[173]. It is also one of the political tools available for promoting or restricting change. Either change can be facilitated or inhibited. By 2015 the GPDO 1995 had diverged significantly between England and Wales. Further changes were made in England by the GPDO 2015 and there was a general reordering of the classes. Set out below are the GPDO 2015 provisions, alongside any equivalent provisions in the GPDO 1995 as it existed in England in April 2015 and the current Welsh version of the GPDO 1995.

---

[169] In Wales closed security television cameras are in GPDO 1995, Sch 2, Part 33, Class A.
[170] Closed circuit television is GPDO 1995, Sch 2, Part 33, Class A in Wales.
[171] GPDO 2015 and 1995, Sch 2, Part 2, Class A, para A1, although school walls in England can be up to 2 metres high if they do not obstruct the views of highway users so as to be a danger: GPDO 2015, Sch 2, Part 2, Class A, para A1.
[172] [2005] EWHC 378 (Admin).
[173] For more discussion of this Part, see Goodall *A Practical Guide to Permitted Changes of Use* (Bath Publishing, 2015).

The permitted development rights **5.110**

GPDO 2015, Sch 2 Part 3, classes and paragraphs (England from April 2015)	GPDO 1995, Sch 2 Part 3, classes and paragraphs (England prior to April 2015)	GPDO 1995, Sch 2 Part 3, classes and paragraphs (Wales)
Class A restaurants, cafes [A3], takeaways [A5] or pubs [A4] to retail [A1 or A2]	Class A [A3, A4, A5 to A1] Class C [A3, A4, A5 to A2]	Class A food and drink (A3) to shops (A1); Class C food and drink (A3) to financial and professional services (A2)
Class B takeaways [A4] or pubs [A5] to restaurants and cafes [A3]	Class AA [A4, A5 to A3]	
Class C retail [A1, A2], betting office or pay day loan shop or casino to restaurant or café [A3]		
Class D shops [A1] to financial and professional [A2]	Class CA [A1 to deposit-taker]	
Class E financial and professional [A2] or betting office or pay day loan shop to shops [A1][174]	Class D [A2 to A1]	Class D [A2 to A1]
Class F betting offices or pay day loan shops to financial and professional [A2]		
Class G retail [A1, A2] or betting office or pay day loan shop to mixed use [as previous plus up to 2 flats]	Class F [A1, A2 to mixed use with up to two flats]	Class F [A1, A2 to mixed use with a single flat]
Class H mixed use to retail [A1/A2/betting shop/pay day loan shop and flats to A1/A2]	Class G [mixed use with up to two flats to A1, A2]	Class F [mixed use with a single flat to A1, A2]
Class I industrial and general business conversions [B2 (general industrial), B8 (storage and distribution) to B1 (office, research and development, light industry); B1, B2 to B8][175]	Class B	Class B [B2, B8 to B1; B1, B2 to B8]
Class J retail [A1 or A2] or betting office or pay day loan shop to assembly and leisure [D2]		
Class K casinos to assembly and leisure [D2]	Class H [casino to D2]	

---

[174] The building whose use is being changed must have a ground floor display window.
[175] A change to or from B8 storage and distribution is limited to 500 m² floorspace in both England and Wales.

5.111 *Permitted development rights*

GPDO 2015, Sch 2 Part 3, classes and paragraphs (England from April 2015)	GPDO 1995, Sch 2 Part 3, classes and paragraphs (England prior to April 2015)	GPDO 1995, Sch 2 Part 3, classes and paragraphs (Wales)
Class L small HMOs [C4] to dwellinghouses [C3] and vice versa [C3 to C4]	Class I [C3,C4]	
Class M retail [A1 shops, A2 financial and professional] or betting office or pay day loan shop [or mixed A1/A2/betting/pay day and residential] to dwellinghouses	Class IA [A1, A2 to C3]	
Class N specified sui generis uses [amusement arcade or centre, casino] to dwellinghouses		
Class O offices [B1(a)] to dwellinghouses	Class J [B1(a) to C3]	
Class P storage or distribution centre [B8] to dwellinghouses		
Class Q agricultural buildings to dwellinghouses	Class MB [agricultural buildings to C3]	
Class R agricultural buildings to a flexible commercial use	Class M [agricultural buildings to a flexible commercial use	
Class S agricultural buildings to state-funded school or registered nursery	Class MA [agricultural buildings to state-funded school or registered nursery	
Class T business, hotels etc to state-funded schools or registered nursery	Class K [B1, C1, C2, C2A, D2 to state-funded schools or registered nursery]	
Class U return to previous use from converted state-funded school or registered nursery	Class L [state-funded schools or registered nursery to previous use]	
Class V changes of use permitted under a permission granted on an application	Class E [flexible planning permissions]	Class E [flexible planning permissions]
Paragraph W Procedure for applications for prior approval under Part 3	Paragraph N Procedure for applications for prior approval under Part 3	

5.111 Change of use permitted development rights have seen the greatest changes in recent years with a sharp divergence between England and Wales. In England new rights have been created with the aim of encouraging development, most notably changes from office, storage, retail and agricultural to residential and from retail to food and drink. Conversely permitted development rights have been removed for development which is seen as potentially undesirable, such as the exclusion of changes to betting offices and pay day loan shops. As an illustration of the nuanced

The permitted development rights **5.115**

approach, permitted development rights to change from A4 drinking establishments (such as pubs) do not apply where they are listed as assets of community value or are subject to an outstanding nomination for such listing. Additionally notice must be given to the local planning authority for changes from A4 to allow a 56-day period for an ACV application to be made[176].

5.112 Restrictions and conditions can be quite complex. In some cases the land has to have been in the original use before the particular permitted development right was proposed by government, to avoid changes designed to take advantage of such rights[177]. The office to residential permitted development rights were introduced in 2013 on a temporary basis, with use needing to be commenced by 30 May 2016[178], but Ministers have announced that the right will be made permanent subject to completion within three years of prior approval[179].

5.113 Many of the change of use rights in England are subject to prior approval processes[180]. In some cases these extend beyond technical issues to points of principle: the effect of a change from retail on the provision of services in an area[181]; the effect on the sustainability of storage, distribution and industrial services of losing B8[182]; and whether the location or siting makes it impractical or undesirable to change from agricultural use[183].

5.114 The prior approval processes are set out in paragraph W. The application must be accompanied by[184]:

(i) a written description of the proposed development, which, in relation to development proposed under Class C, M, N or Q of this Part, must include any building or other operations;

(ii) a plan indicating the site and showing the proposed development;

(iii) the developer's contact address;

(iv) the developer's email address if the developer is content to receive communications electronically; and

(v) if the site is in flood zone 2 or 3 or in flood zone 1 and the Environment Agency has notified the Council of critical drainage problems, a site-specific flood risk assessment.

5.115 The local planning authority may refuse the application if the application does not comply with any conditions, limitations or restrictions specified in Part 3, or the developer has not provided sufficient information to establish that it does

---

[176] GPDO 2015, Sch 2, Part 3, Class A, para A1, A2, Class B, para B1, B2.
[177] For example, office to residential (Class O, para O1(b)) and agriculture to residential (Class Q, para Q1(a)).
[178] GPDO 2015, Sch 2, Part 3, Class O, para O.1(c).
[179] Press release by Minister for Housing and Planning, Brandon Lewis MP, 13 October 2015. The announcement also proposed to remove exemptions in the GPDO for specific areas in May 2019 (allowing Article 4 directions to be made). Other changes proposed would allow the demolition of offices and new building for residential use and changes of use from light industrial and launderettes to residential.
[180] GPDO 2015, Sch 2, Part 3, Classes C, J, M, N, O, P, Q, R, S, T.
[181] GPDO 2015, Sch 2, Part 3, Classes C, M.
[182] GPDO 2015, Sch 2, Part 3, Class P.
[183] GPDO 2015, Sch 2, Part 3, Classes Q, S.
[184] GPDO 2015, Sch 2, Part 3, para W(2).

5.116 *Permitted development rights*

comply[185]. Whilst it is sensible for prior approval to be refused if the proposed development does not have permitted development rights at all, to avoid any attempt to rely on the approval, the GPDO goes too far in allowing refusals for insufficient information. The result is that applicants may have to produce a considerable amount of evidence, in particular on the use of the property at particular historic dates, to avoid a summary refusal. Effectively a lawful development certificate application is required but without granting a certificate, so a prior approval will not be determinative that the rights do exist.

5.116 Consultation may be required with highway authorities and the Environment Agency[186], and the local planning authority must have a site notice displayed and serve notice on adjoining owners and occupiers[187]. Interestingly, in determining whether prior approval is required and, if so, whether to grant it, the authority is required to have considered the National Planning Policy Framework, but no mention is made of the development plan[188].

5.117 The decision whether prior approval is required and, if so, whether it should be granted should be notified within 56 days following the receipt of the application[189]. Conditions may be imposed if they are reasonably related to the subject matter of the prior approval[190].

5.118 In respect of Class G where a mixed use of A1 or A2 shopping area uses and up to two flats are referred to, the flats can be in separate planning units to the commercial uses: *Valentino Plus Ltd v Secretary of State for Communities and Local Government*[191].

Class V: flexible planning permissions

5.119

'Development consisting of a change of use of a building or other land from a use permitted by planning permission granted on an application, to another use which that permission would have specifically authorised when it was granted'.

Class V is a very different permitted development right, which allows changes between any of the uses authorised by a particular planning permission. A conventional example would be planning permission for the erection of a large shed building for B1/B2/B8 uses. Leaving aside the size limited permitted development rights to change between those uses, under Class V the entirety of the building may change repeatedly between B1, B2 and B8 uses. The relevant restrictions are that any change must take place within 10 years of the grant of planning permission and would not breach 'any condition, limitation or specification contained in that permission in relation to the use'. In England a change to use as a betting office or pay day loan shop is not permitted.

---

[185] GPDO 2015, Sch 2, Part 3, para W(3). This refusal may be appealed: para W(4).
[186] GPDO 2015, Sch 2, Part 3, para W(5), (6) respectively.
[187] GPDO 2015, Sch 2, Part 3, para W(8).
[188] GPDO 2015, Sch 2, Part 3, para W(10)(b). The development plan will be material as far as it is relevant but the Planning and Compulsory Purchase Act 2004, s 38(6) presumption does not apply.
[189] GPDO 2015, Sch 2, Part 3, para W(11).
[190] GPDO 2015, Sch 2, Part 3, para W(13).
[191] [2015] EWHC 19 (Admin), [2015] JPL 707.

The permitted development rights **5.123**

Part 4 Temporary buildings and uses

5.120 Part 4 contains a miscellany of temporary rights. Classes A and B are common to England and Wales, but the remainder apply only in England.

Class A: temporary buildings and structures

5.121

> 'The provision on land of buildings, moveable structures, works, plant or machinery required temporarily in connection with and for the duration of operations being or to be carried out on, in, under or over that land or on land adjoining that land'.

Operational development required temporarily in connection with other lawful development is permitted development under Part 4, Class A. It does not permit buildings and structures simply because they are temporary but they must be required temporarily in connection with lawful operations. Examples of temporary works are buildings, moveable structures, works, plant or machinery on the land on which the development is taking place or adjoining land. These would include temporary hardstanding or access ways for construction vehicles, fencing and building for construction compounds and alternative accesses or provision for occupants whilst works are taking place[192]. In deciding whether a building is temporary under the permitted development rights or permanent it is necessary to have regard to all of the relevant circumstances amongst which the size and means of construction of the building will be highly relevant. Size, permanence of construction and ease of removal affect whether it is genuinely 'required temporarily'. A greater explanation may be required as to why an apparently permanent building is temporary[193].

5.122 By the condition in the GPDO class any necessary planning permission must have been granted for the operations which the temporary works support. The temporary building or structure has to be removed when the operations are carried out and if the temporary works were on adjoining land then this land must as soon as reasonably practicable, be reinstated to its condition before that development was carried out. The state of the development site at the completion of the project will be set out in the planning permission for the permanent development.

5.123 The operations required are operations within the meaning of the Town and Country Planning Act 1990, s 55(1) and do not extend to a change of use[194]. However the permitted development rights do apply where operations are being carried out which do not need planning permission or where the planning permission is encompassed within a 'change of use' permission. In *North Cornwall District Council v Secretary of State for the Environment, Transport and the Regions*[195] a unit was being converted, under permitted development rights, from Class A2 to Class A1 use. Sullivan J held that a temporary stall could be erected on the forecourt for retail sales under Part 4, Class A. Operations were being carried out,

---

[192] Advertising hoardings may also be erected around a construction site under the Town and Country Planning (Control of Advertisements) (England) Regulations 2007, Sch 3, Class 8 and the Town and Country Planning (Control of Advertisements) Regulations 1992, Sch 3, Class 8.
[193] *Wilsdon v First Secretary of State* [2006] EWHC 2980 (Admin) at paras 16–22 per Sullivan J.
[194] *Sunbury-on-Thames v Mann* (1958) 9 P & CR 309; *Brown v Hayes and Harlington Urban District Council* (1963) 15 P & CR 284.
[195] [2002] EWHC 2318 (Admin), [2003] JPL 600.

5.124 *Permitted development rights*

by internal works to the shop unit. Whilst the stall was not for the carrying out of the operations it was required in connection with the operations because the unit could not be used whilst those works were being carried out. The same result would have followed if there had been no material change of use but merely the refitting of an A1 retail unit.

Class B: temporary uses

5.124

'The use of any land for any purpose for not more than 28 days in total in any calendar year, of which not more than 14 days in total may be for the purposes of:

(a) the holding of a market;

(b) motor car and motorcycle racing including trials of speed, and practising for these activities, and the provision on the land of any moveable structure for the purposes of the permitted use'.

Permitted development rights for temporary uses of up to 28 or 14 days are often useful, troublesome, controversial and misunderstood. They permit the change of use of land for these periods, which may be non-consecutive. The land benefiting from the rights may not include buildings or land within the curtilage of buildings[196], the effect of which is in practice to limit the right to agricultural and forestry land, sports grounds, parks and airfields. Uses which are not permitted are caravan sites (although camping is allowed), the use of the land for the display of an advertisement and in sites of special scientific interest motor racing and practicing, clay pigeon shooting and war games[197]. For the application of the 14-day limit, practising for motor racing or speed trials has been taken to be concerned with formal practice sessions associated with races and trials[198].

5.125 Where permission is granted by the GPDO for a limited number of days the period is taken to be a limitation[199]. The use will need to revert to the non-permitted development use for the remainder of the year[200]. The boundaries of the land will need to be established with care. It is possible that a use being carried out at different locations on one piece of land on different days could fall within a single 28-day right, rather than have separate 28-day periods[201].

---

[196] GPDO 2015, Sch 2, Part 4, Class B, para B1(b).

[197] GPDO 2015, Sch 2, Part 4, Class B, para B1(c), (e) and (d) respectively. War games are enacted, mock or imaginary battles, including paintballing, not carried out by the military: GPDO 2015, Sch 2, Part 4, para F.

[198] See *Hart District Council v Benford* [2006] EWHC 240 (QB), [2006] JPL 1318 and also *Miles v National Assembly for Wales* [2007] EWHC 10 (Admin), [2007] JPL 1235.

[199] Town and Country Planning Act 1990, s 60(4).

[200] It might revert to the other use even if permanent development in relation to the temporary use remains, as in lawful banks, depressions and jumps on land used for motorcycle scrambling/practice which were grazed by animals when not in use: *Ramsey v Secretary of State for the Environment, Transport and the Region* [2002] EWCA Civ 118, [2002] JPL 1123. This is distinct from a permanent use where the activity takes place on only a few days, such as a racecourse: *Hawes v Thornton Cleveleys Urban District Council* (1965) 17 P & CR 22 at 28 per Widgery J.

[201] *Thames Heliports plc v London Borough of Tower Hamlets* (1997) 74 P & CR 164 which raised, but did not resolve, whether a floating heliport moved between 22 locations on the Thames would have the benefit of up to 28 days in each position or one 28-day period on the entire river.

Class C

5.126 Class C permits change to a state funded school for a single academic year, to address difficulties in establishing new schools or their enlargement.

Class D

5.127 Class D is

'Development consisting of a change of use of a building and any land within its curtilage:

(a) from:

(i) a use falling within Class A1 (shops), Class A2 (financial and professional services), Class A3 (restaurants and cafes), Class A4 (drinking establishments), Class A5 (hot food takeaways), Class B1 (business), Class D1 (non-residential institutions) and Class D2 (assembly and leisure) of the Schedule to the Use Classes Order, or,

(ii) a use as a betting office or pay day loan shop,

(b) to a flexible use falling within Class A1 (shops), Class A2 (financial and professional services), Class A3 (restaurants and cafes) or Class B1 (business) of that Schedule, for a single continuous period of up to 2 years beginning on the date the building and any land within its curtilage begins to be used for the flexible use or on the date given in the notice under paragraph D.2(a), whichever is the earlier'.

Class D allows changes within these use classes for a continuous period of up to two years. Notice has to be given to the local planning authority of the initial change and any subsequent change before a reversion to the lawful use at the end of the period[202].

Use class A4 drinking establishments which are or may become assets of community value are protected from Class C or D development[203].

Class E

5.128 Class E authorises the temporary use of land for commercial film-making, including the provision of temporary structures, works, plant or machinery[204].

Part 5 Caravan sites and recreational campsites

5.129 These provisions are common to the GPDO 2015 and GPDO 1995.

---

[202] GPDO 2015, Sch 2, Part 4, Class D, para D2(a), (c), (e).
[203] GPDO 2015, Sch 2, Part 4, Class C, para C1(e), C2(f); Class D, para D1(f), D2(f).
[204] This would have made unnecessary the retrospective planning application for the construction of a replica Scottish manor house on a Surrey heathland which was approved only after it had been blown up by the makers of the Bond film *Skyfall*: Waverley Central Area Planning Committee, 29 March 2012, reference WA/2012/0178.

5.130 *Permitted development rights*

Class A: use of land as a caravan site

5.130 Class A authorises the use of land, but not buildings, as a caravan site in the following circumstances listed in the Caravan Sites and Control of Development Act 1960, Sch 1, paras 2–10. In summary these are[205]:

- a single caravan for one or two nights at a time up to 28 days a year;
- where at least 5 acres of land is in a single occupation and has not been built on, use of part of that land for up to three caravans a time up to 28 days a year;
- use by an organisation exempted by the Minister[206];
- site approved by exempted organisations for up to five caravans;
- use by an exempted organisation for a meeting of its members for not more than five days;
- seasonal occupation[207] by agricultural workers employed on land with the same occupier[208];
- seasonal occupation by forestry workers employed on land with the same occupier;
- occupation by persons employed in connection with building or engineering operations on the same or adjoining land;
- use by a certified travelling showman who is travelling for business[209].

Local authorities may ask the Minister to order that any or all of these paragraphs do not apply to specified land[210].

In any event, the use must be discontinued when the circumstances cease to exist and the caravans must be removed from the site[211].

Class B

5.131 Class B authorises development on a caravan site required by conditions on a Caravan Sites and Control of Development Act 1960 licence. A caravan sites licence,

---

[205] The full detail of the Schedule should be checked if a provision might apply.
[206] Under Caravan Sites and Control of Development Act 1960, Sch 1, para 12. Exempted organisations are essentially caravan clubs, but also include the Guide Association and the Showmen's Guild of Great Britain
[207] Seasonal does not encompass employment throughout the year: *North v Brown* (1974) 231 EG 737. Nine or ten months is longer than seasonal: *Hall Hunter v First Secretary of State* [2006] EWHC 3482 (Admin), [2007] 2 P & CR 5 at para 43 per Sullivan J.
[208] In *Hall Hunter v First Secretary of State* [2006] EWHC 3482 (Admin), [2007] 2 P & CR 5, an inspector had held that it was material, and so fatal to the right, that workers spent 17% of their time on other farms see paras 44, 45. The court did not need to resolve the point.
[209] However whilst a showman at winter quarters with his equipment between 1 October and 31 March is exempt from the licensing requirement, permitted development rights do not apply: GPDO 2015, Sch 2, Part 4, para A2.
[210] Caravan Sites and Control of Development Act 1960, Sch 1, para 13.
[211] The use might not be discontinued if the infrastructure remains in place see Sullivan J in *Hall Hunter* at para 42:
> 'When the caravans have departed, do they leave behind an agricultural field or do they leave behind an empty caravan site with all the necessary infrastructure, pathways, services et cetera waiting for them to return?'.

The permitted development rights **5.134**

issued by the district or unitary council, will prescribe the layout and facilities on a caravan site[212].

Class C

5.132 Class C authorises the use of land and the placing of tents by various recreational organisations for the purpose of recreation or instruction[213].

Part 6 Agricultural and forestry

5.133 Agriculture and forestry[214] has a particularly relaxed (or favourable) status in the planning system. The use of land for agricultural or forestry purposes is not development[215]. The carrying out of building, engineering, mining or other operations for agricultural or forestry purposes is development in the same way as works for any other purpose. However, they benefit from extensive permitted development rights, contained in England in Part 6 of the GPDO 2015 and in Wales split between Part 6 (agriculture) and Part 7 (forestry) of the GPDO 1995.

5.134 In the GPDO 2015 the categories are:

(i) Class A: agricultural development on units of five hectares or more. These works may be for the erection, extension or alteration of a building or any excavation or engineering operations 'which are reasonably necessary for the purpose of agriculture within that unit'[216];

(ii) Class B: agricultural development on units of less than five hectares. Class B contains a more detailed, and so narrower, list of permitted works than Class A (in particular excluding the erection of a building), comprising:

'(a) the extension or alteration of an agricultural building;

(b) the installation of additional or replacement plant or machinery;

(c) the provision, rearrangement or replacement of a sewer, main, pipe, cable or other apparatus;

(d) the provision, rearrangement or replacement of a private way;

(e) the provision of a hard surface;

(f) the deposit of waste; or

(g) the carrying out of any of the following operations in connection with fish farming, namely, repairing ponds and raceways; the installation of grading machinery, aeration equipment or flow meters and any associated channel; the dredging of ponds; and the replacement of tanks and nets, where the development is reasonably necessary for the purposes of agriculture within the unit';

(iii) Class C: mineral working for agricultural purposes;

---

[212] Caravan Sites and Control of Development Act 1960, s 5.
[213] The organisations are licensed by local authorities under the Public Health Act 1936, s 269; see GPDO, Sch 2, Part 5, para C2. The equivalent permitted development right in Wales is GPDO 1995, Sch 2, Part 27, Class A.
[214] For discussion of the meaning of agriculture see Chapter 2.
[215] Town and Country Planning Act 1990, s 55(2)(e).
[216] It does not include 'other operations' within the Town and Country Planning Act 1990, s 55(1).

5.135 *Permitted development rights*

(iv) Class E: forestry developments

Paragraph D contains interpretative provisions for Classes A to C. Most importantly, agricultural land must be in that use for the purpose of a trade or business prior to the development being carried out[217].

5.135 Both Classes A and B are subject to detailed lists of development which is not permitted and conditions. Those need to be considered with care in respect of any scheme. Whilst they generally relate to size, they also prohibit the use of permitted development buildings, structures, excavations and works for the accommodation of livestock or the storage of slurry, material for biomass boilers or anaerobic digestion systems or hydro-turbines within 400 metres of residential buildings which are not on agricultural units, to protect their amenity[218].

5.136 Prior approval provisions apply to certain of the agricultural and forestry rights:

(i) under Class A for the erection, extension or alteration of a building, the formation or alteration of a private way or excavations or waste deposit on more than 0.5 hectares, or placing or assembling a tank in any waters[219];

(ii) Class B: on art 2(4) land the extension or alteration of a building or provision, rearrangement or replacement of a private way;

(iii) Class E: the erection, extension or alteration of a building or formation or alteration of a private way[220].

5.137 The prior approval process is genuinely two-stage under this Part. The local planning authority has 28 days to decide whether prior approval is required and then, if it does so, the applicant must display a site notice for at least 21 days.

5.138 Agricultural permitted development rights apply to agricultural units, not land in a mixed use, one of whose elements is agriculture[221].

5.139 Whether agricultural development is 'reasonably necessary for the purposes of agriculture within that unit' depends upon whether the particular works are reasonably necessary, not whether some other building was necessary[222]. The words 'accommodating livestock' in the GDPO 1995, Sch 2, Part 6, Class A mean 'providing livestock with something suitable'. The provision of hard standing for the feeding of livestock is capable of falling within that definition[223].

---

[217] Whilst agricultural land does not include dwellings or gardens, an agricultural unit does include the farmer or farm worker's dwellings: GPDO, Sch 2, Part 6, para D(1).

[218] GPDO 2015, Sch 2, Part 6, Class A, para A1(k), condition A2(1)(a), Class B, para B1(d), condition B5(1), definition in para D(1).

[219] GPDO 2015, Sch 2, Part 6, Class A, condition A2(2), subject to limited exceptions for buildings in condition A2(3); GPDO 2015, Sch 2, Part 6, Class B, condition B5(2).

[220] GPDO 2015, Sch 2, Part 6, Class E, condition E2(1).

[221] *Lyons v Secretary of State for Communities and Local Government* [2010] EWHC 3652 (Admin), in that case a mix of agriculture and aviation.

[222] *Harrogate Borough Council v Crossland* [2012] EWHC 3260 (QB) at paras 68–70 per Coulson J. The purposes of agriculture are expanded by para D(6)–(8) in respect of fertilising, biomass boilers, anaerobic digestion and hydro-turbines for certain purposes.

[223] *Taylor & Sons (Farms) v Secretary of State for the Environment, Transport and the Regions* [2001] EWCA Civ 1254, [2002] PLCR 11.

The permitted development rights **5.140**

Part 7 Non-domestic extensions, alterations etc

5.140 Part 7 of the GPDO 2015 encompasses a whole range of building and engineering works related to particular uses of land and buildings[224]. These have been pulled from various provisions of the GPDO 1995 and are subject to a variety of exclusions and conditions, mainly relating to size and location.

The Part 7 permitted development rights are set out below, along with their equivalents in Wales in the GPDO 1995. The rights must be exercised for the purposes of those particular uses. Where the right is expressed to be limited to a particular use class, this is shown.

GPDO 2015, Part 7 (England)	GPDO 1995 (Wales)	Notes
Class A extension or alteration of a shop or financial or professional services establishment [A1, A2]	Part 42, Class A	
Class B erection or construction of a trolley store within the curtilage of a shop [A1]	Part 42, Class B	
Class C 'click and collect' erection or construction of a collection facility within the curtilage of a shop [A1]		Prior approval applies to siting, design and external appearance
Class D modification of shop loading bays [A1]		
Class E provision or replacement of hard surface within curtilage of a shop, catering or financial or professional services establishment [A1 to A5]		
Class F extension or alteration of an office building [B1(a)]	Part 41, Class A	
Class G provision or replacement of hard surface within curtilage of an office building [B1(a)]		
Class H erection, extension or alteration of an industrial building or a warehouse, including ancillary employee social, care or recreational facilities including a creche	Part 8, Class A erection, extension or alteration of an industrial building or a warehouse including ancillary employee facilities	This must be within the curtilage of an existing, non-permitted development industrial building or warehouse, size limits apply[225]

---

[224] Various definitions are in GPDO 2015, Sch 2, Part 7, para O.
[225] Also see the definitions of industrial building and warehouse in GPDO, Sch 2, Part 7, para O.

5.140 *Permitted development rights*

GPDO 2015, Part 7 (England)	GPDO 1995 (Wales)	Notes
Class I on industrial land, installation of additional or replacement plant, machinery, sewer, pipe, cable, other apparatus, private way, railway, siding or conveyor for an industrial process	Part 8, Class B	
Class J provision or replacement of hard surface within curtilage of an industrial building or warehouse	Part 8, Class C	
Class K deposit of waste on a site used for that purpose on 1 July 1948	Part 8, Class D	
Class L at a waste management facility, extension or alteration of a building, installation of replacement plant or machinery		
Class M erection, extension or alteration of a school, college, university or hospital building[226]	Part 32, Class A	Limited to various sizes no greater than 100 m² floorspace
Class N provision or replacement of hard surface within curtilage of a school, college, university or hospital		
	Part 8, Class E erection or construction of a refuse or cycle store within the curtilage of an industrial building or warehouse.	Subject to various restrictions, including not permitted on art 1(5) land
	Part 32, Class B erection or construction of a refuse or cycle store within the curtilage of a school, college, university or hospital building	Subject to various restrictions, including not permitted on art 1(5) land
	Part 41, Class B erection or construction of a refuse or cycle store within the curtilage of an office building	Subject to various restrictions, including not permitted on art 1(5) land
	Part 42, Class C erection or construction of a refuse or cycle store within the curtilage of a shop or financial or professional services establishment.	Subject to various restrictions, including not permitted on art 1(5) land

---

[226] School is defined in GPDO 2015, Sch 2, Part 7, para O.

Part 8 Transport related development

5.141 Extensive permitted development rights are provided for transport undertakers on their operational land for the purposes of their undertakings. They are often limited by the type of development, but less frequently by their size. It has sometimes been possible for quite substantial projects to be permitted development, although subject to any need for Environmental Impact Assessment and any restrictions imposed by planning conditions.

5.142 The categories of transport permitted development rights are:

GPDO 2015, Part 7 (England)	GPDO 1995 (Wales)
Class A railways (but not new railways or stations)	Part 17, Class A
Class B dock, pier, harbour, water transport, or canal or inland navigation undertakings	Part 17, Class B
Class C inland waterway	Part 17, Class C
Class D spreading of dredged material by transport undertakings	Part 17, Class D
Class E development by lighthouse authorities	Part 17, Class I
Class F development by a relevant airport operator[227] (not including a runway or sizeable passenger terminal)	Part 18, Class A
Class G air traffic services development on a relevant airport	Part 18, Class B
Class H air traffic services development within 8 km of an airport	Part 18, Class C
Class I air traffic services licence holder within an airport	Part 18, Class D
Class J air traffic services licence holder development on operational land	Part 18, Class E
Class K use of land in an emergency by an air traffic services licence holder	Part 18, Class F
Class L temporary use of moveable structures by an air traffic services licence holder	Part 18, Class G
Class M surveys or monitoring by the Civil Aviation Authority	Part 18, Class H
Class N use of airport buildings managed by relevant airport operators	Part 18, Class I

Part 9 Development relating to roads

5.143 Highway authorities are usually the county council or unitary authority, but include Transport for London in respect of 'GLA roads' in London. For motorways and trunk roads the highway authority has been the Secretary of State for Transport or the Welsh Ministers. Historically the Secretary of State has operated through an executive agency, the Highways Agency. The Infrastructure Act 2015 allows strategic highway companies to take over the Highways Agency's role in carrying out the Minister's functions and so that role has been transferred to Highways England.

Roads related permitted development rights are:

---

[227] Relevant airports are those certified by the Civil Aviation Authority as having a turnover exceeding £1 million a year and which are not owned by a local authority, and relevant airport operators is interpreted similarly: GPDO 2015, Sch 2, Part 8, para O, applying Airports Act 1986, s 57A.

5.144 *Permitted development rights*

(i) Class A: works by a highway authority within or adjoining the boundary of a road for its maintenance or improvement[228];

(ii) Class B: works by the Secretary of State or a strategic highways company in carrying out functions under the Highways Act 1980[229];

(iii) Class C: tracks, posts apparatus and development on operational land for tramway or road transport undertakings[230];

(iv) Class D: toll facilities and hard surfaces in the vicinity of a toll road subject to conditions and sometimes prior approval applications[231];

(v) Class E: the maintenance or improvement of an unadopted street or private way[232].

Part 10 Repairs to services

5.144 Part 10 (in both the 2015 and 1995 GPDO) contains just Class A, which permits 'any works for the purposes of inspecting, repairing or renewing any sewer, main, pipe, cable or other apparatus, including breaking open any land for that purpose'.

Part 11 Heritage and demolition

5.145 Not all heritage is about demolition, and not all demolition is about heritage, but each tends to be inimical to the other. Part 11 does deal with two different aspects:

(i) Class A: allows Historic England to carry out particular works for the preservation of buildings or monuments in their guardianship, ownership, control or management;

(ii) Classes B and C: deal with demolition, Class B being wider but subject to more limitations and potentially prior approval. Class B permits 'any building operation consisting of the demolition of buildings'. Excluded is 'relevant demolition' of unlisted buildings in conservation areas[233] and where 'the building has been rendered unsafe or otherwise uninhabitable by the action or inaction of any person having an interest in the land on which the building stands and it is practicable to secure safety or health by works of repair or works for affording temporary support'[234]. Additionally, permitted development rights for demolition do not apply to the proposed demolition of A4 drinking establishments which are assets of community value or nominated as such with a 56-day notice period being given for nominations to take place[235].

---

[228] GPDO 1995, Sch 2, Part 13, Class A in Wales.
[229] GPDO 1995, Sch 2, Part 13, Class B.
[230] In Wales, the GPDO 1995, Sch 2, Part 17, Class H.
[231] GPDO 1995, Sch 2, Part 30, Class A in Wales.
[232] GPDO 1995, Sch 2, Part 9, Class A in Wales. Any person may exercise the unadopted street or private way rights.
[233] In practice relevant demolition is all demolition except those no larger than 115 m³ (except pre-1925 tombstones) or post-1948 agricultural or forestry buildings: GPDO 2015, Sch 2, Part 11, Class B, para B1(b) applying Town and Country Planning Act 1990, s 196D which in turn applies directions made under the Planning (Listed Buildings and Conservation Areas) Act 1990, s 75.
[234] GPDO 2015, Sch 2, Part 11, Class B, para B1(a).
[235] GPDO 2015, Sch 2, Part 11, Class B, para B1(c), para B2(x) and interpretation in para B3.

5.146 Except for 'excluded demolition'[236], Class B is subject to a determination whether prior approval is required of the method of demolition and any proposed restoration of the site.

Class C authorises 'the demolition of the whole or any part of any gate, fence, wall or other means of enclosure' unless, in England, it is relevant demolition in a conservation area.

In Wales the demolition permitted development rights are in Part 31, Classes A and B respectively. Conservation area consent is still required in the Principality, so permitted development rights are retained in conservation areas to cater for the need for planning permission[237]. Further, the asset of community value provisions do not apply in Wales.

Part 12 Development by local authorities

5.147 In the GPDOs 1995 and 2015 Part 12 authorises certain activities by local authorities, including parish councils, and, under Class A, urban development corporations.

5.148 Class A permits the construction, maintenance, improvement or alteration of any small ancillary building[238] by those bodies or works for their functions, except as statutory undertakers, on land. Similar works may be carried out for:

> 'lamp standards, information kiosks, passenger shelters, public shelters and seats, telephone boxes, fire alarms, public drinking fountains, horse troughs, refuse bins or baskets, barriers for the control of people waiting to enter public service vehicles, electric vehicle charging points and any associated infrastructure, and similar structures or works required in connection with the operation of any public service administered by them'.

Class B authorises the deposit of waste (other than mineral waste) by a local authority on a site used for that purpose on 1 July 1948.

Part 13 Water and sewerage

5.149 Permitted development rights in respect of water and sewerage are set out separately for the different bodies involved. Water or hydraulic power undertakers have rights under Class A[239], sewerage undertakers under Class B[240], drainage works by the Environment Agency, an internal drainage board or any other body having

---

[236] Excluded demolition is that on land with planning permission for redevelopment, permitted by scheduled monument or listed building consent, required or permitted under any other enactment or required under a planning obligation: GPDO 2015, Sch 2, Part 11, Class B, para B3.
[237] *R (SAVE Britain's Heritage) v Secretary of State for Communities and Local Government* [2011] EWCA Civ 334, [2011] JPL 1016. Demolition controls in the planning process, the *SAVE* litigation and conservation area consent are discussed in Harwood *Historic Environment Law* (Institute of art and Law, 2012) pp 160–169 and its 2014 *Supplement* pp 5–9, 46–47.
[238] Small ancillary buildings or works are no higher than 4 metres and no larger than 200 m³: GPDO Sch 2, Part 12, para A1.
[239] GPDO 1995, Sch 2, Part 17, Class E in Wales.
[240] GPDO 1995, Sch 2, Part 16, Class A in Wales.

5.150 *Permitted development rights*

power to make or maintain works for the drainage of land[241] are permitted by Class C[242].

5.150 The High Court has expressed the view there was a very strong case that what is now Class C 'Development by a drainage body in, on or under any watercourse or land drainage works required in connection with the improvement, maintenance or repair of that watercourse or those works' included the construction of a new £34 million pumping station[243].

Permitted development rights for other water resources development by the Environment Agency are provided by Class D[244].

Part 14 Renewable energy

5.151 Extensive permitted development rights are provided for renewable energy installations on buildings and, at a small scale, on the ground. In England these are contained in Part 14, whilst in Wales they are split in the GPDO 1995 between domestic sites (Part 40) and non-domestic (Part 43). Subject to any further restrictions under particular classes, the rights apply to microgeneration which produces not more than 50 kilowatts of electricity or 45 kilowatts thermal for heat[245].

5.152 Domestic rights apply in England to dwellinghouses and blocks of flats, defined as buildings which consist wholly of flats[246]. In Wales the relevant definition is of 'dwellinghouse' which 'includes a building which consists wholly of flats or which is used for the purposes of a dwellinghouse'[247]. In the table below 'dwelling' is used for the dwellinghouse/flats definition in each nation. Various limitations to size and siting apply, in particular in conservation areas and World Heritage Sites.

The renewable energy permitted development rights are:

Development	GPDO 2015, Part 14 (England)	GPDO 1995, Parts 40 and 43 (Wales)
Solar PV or solar thermal on a dwelling or building within its curtilage	Class A	Part 40, Class A
Stand-alone solar within the curtilage of a dwelling	Class B	Part 40, Class B
Ground source heat pump within the curtilage of a dwelling	Class C	Part 40, Class C
Water source heat pump within the curtilage of a dwelling	Class D	Part 40, Class D

---

[241] See the definition of 'drainage body' in the Land Drainage Act 1991, s 72(1), as applied by GPDO 2015, Sch 2, Part 13, Class C, para C1.
[242] The equivalent of Part 13, Class C under the GPDO 1995 is Part 14, Class A.
[243] *Middle Level Commissioners v Atkins Ltd* [2012] EWHC 2884 (TC), [2013] JPL 356.
[244] In Wales, by the Natural Resources Body for Wales under GPDO 1995, Part 15, Class A.
[245] Energy Act 2004, s 82(6), (8) as applied by GPDO 2015, Sch 2, Part 14, para P and GPDO 1995, Sch 2, Part 40, para J.
[246] See GPDO 2015, Sch 2, Part 14, para P.
[247] GPDO 1995, Sch 2, Part 40, para J.

The permitted development rights **5.154**

Development	GPDO 2015, Part 14 (England)	GPDO 1995, Parts 40 and 43 (Wales)
Flue for a biomass heating system on a dwelling[248]	Class E	Part 40, Class E
Flue for a combine heat and power system on a dwelling	Class F	Part 40, Class F
Air source heat pump on a dwelling or within its curtilage, including on a building	Class G	Part 40, Class G
Wind turbine on a detached dwellinghouse or a detached building within the curtilage of a dwellinghouse or block of flats (English provision)	Class H	
Stand alone wind turbine within the curtilage of a dwelling	Class I	Part 40, Class H
Temporary installation of an anemometry mast within the curtilage of a dwellinghouse		Part 40, Class I
Microgeneration solar thermal, PV on a building or other solar PV equipment[249] on the roof of a building, other than a dwelling	Class J	Part 43, Class A
Stand-alone solar within the curtilage of a building other than a dwelling	Class K	Part 43, Class B
Ground source heat pump within the curtilage of a building other than a dwelling	Class L	Part 43, Class C
Water source heat pump within the curtilage of a building other than a dwelling	Class M	Part 43, Class D
Flue for a biomass heating system on a building other than a dwelling	Class N	Part 43, Class E
Flue for a combine heat and power system on a building other than a dwelling	Class O	Part 43, Class F

Part 15 Power related development

5.153 Gas transporters[250] have permitted development rights to lay underground mains, pipes or other apparatus and carry out development on operational land under Class A[251], some of which may require consent under the Gas Transporter Pipeline Works (Environmental Impact Assessment) Regulations 1999[252] in any event. Additionally the class includes the construction of boreholes in areas specified by an underground gas storage order under the Gas Act 1965.

5.154 Class B covers development by 'statutory undertakers for the generation, transmission, distribution or supply of electricity for the purposes of their

---

[248] The installation of a new heating system inside an existing building will not be development: see Town and Country Planning Act 1990, s 55(2)(a) (unless it is part of a material change of use).
[249] 'Other solar PV equipment' means that with a capacity above 50 kilowatts and is subject to prior approval.
[250] Licensed under Gas Act 1986, s 7, see Town and Country Planning Act 1990, s 336(1).
[251] In Wales, the GPDO 1995, Sch 2, Part 17, Class F.
[252] SI 1999/1672.

5.155 *Permitted development rights*

undertaking'[253]. These include the installation of electric lines[254] and buildings on operational land, subject to size restrictions and sometimes prior approval.

Part 16 Communications

5.155 Communications permitted development rights are some of the most important but also contentious. Much communications equipment, such as mobile telephone antennae, equipment cabinets and call boxes, is small scale, but numerous and on public view. The introduction of new technology, such as mobile phones and fibre optic broadband has created a need for a large number of installations[255] to be put in place quickly. Such equipment can raise concerns about visual impact, not least in the countryside and in conservation areas, and health effects of antennae has been a source of contention.

5.156 Class A gives rights to electronic communications code operators[256]:

'for the purpose of the operator's electronic communications network in, on, over or under land controlled by that operator or in accordance with the electronic communications code, consisting of:

(a) the installation, alteration or replacement of any electronic communications apparatus,

(b) the use of land in an emergency for a period not exceeding 6 months to station and operate moveable electronic communications apparatus required for the replacement of unserviceable electronic communications apparatus, including the provision of moveable structures on the land for the purposes of that use, or

(c) development ancillary to radio equipment housing'.

5.157 The electronic communications code under the Telecommunications Act 1984, Sch 2 authorises code operators (who include the telecommunications companies and water companies) to install electronic communications apparatus, including poles and lines, on land, including highway land. Planning permission is required for any of these works which are development and the GPDOs are used to confer extensive permissions.

5.158 There are a series of limitations depending upon the type of apparatus and whether it is installed on a building. These are conveniently sub-headed in the GPDO 2015, but less well laid out in the GPDO 1995[257]. As always, these need to be considered with great care. In particular, all except small antennae do not have permitted development rights in national parks, areas of outstanding natural beauty and conservation areas[258].

---

[253] GPDO 1995, Sch 2, Part 17, Class G in Wales.
[254] Unless consent for an overhead electric line is required under Electricity Act 1989, s 37(1), generally lines with a nominal voltage exceeding 20 kilovolts or serving multiple consumers (s 37(2)): see GPDO 2015, Sch 2, Part 15, Class B, para B1(a).
[255] The Mobile Operators Association estimate there are approximately 52,500 radio base stations for mobile phones in the UK: www.mobilemastinfo.com/base-stations-and-masts/ accessed 26 November 2015.
[256] The Welsh equivalent is GPDO 1995, Sch 2, Part 24, Class A which has material differences.
[257] GPDO 1995, Sch 2, Part 24, Class A.
[258] GPDO 2015, art 2(3) and Sch 16, Class A, para A1(5), GPDO 1995, art 1(5) and Sch 2, Part 24, Class A, para A.1(i).

The permitted development rights **5.164**

5.159 A prior approval process for siting[259] and design applies to development on art 2(3) land and to any masts, antennae more than six metres higher up than the building they are on, public call boxes and radio equipment housing of more than 2.5 cubic metres[260].

5.160 The prior approval process requires the developer to notify any owner or tenant of the land before making the application[261]. Once the prior approval application is received, the local planning authority must carry out publicity and consultation as if it were a planning application[262]. The local planning authority must decide whether prior approval is required and give notice whether it has been granted or refused within 56 days beginning with the date of receipt of the application[263].

5.161 Classes B and C authorise the installation, alteration and replacement on buildings of microwave antennae by any person[264]. Class B applies to buildings or structures which are 15 metres high or taller, and Class C to those below that height. Different limitations apply to the two classes.

5.162 Class D permits the installation, alteration and replacement of apparatus by a driver information systems operator, licensed to collect data on vehicle or traffic conditions and to transmit it to drivers[265].

5.163 Moving from the electronic to the physical, Class E authorises development by a universal postal service provider[266], in reality, Royal Mail. Permitted development is the installation of posting boxes (the red Royal Mail post boxes) and self-service machines, which are frequently installed on highways. Additionally development on operational land is permitted. These rights do not include the erection of a building or the reconstruction or alteration of a building where its design or external appearance would be materially affected, or plant and machinery where the height exceeds 15 metres or any existing higher equipment. For these purposes posting boxes and self-service machines will not be buildings, notwithstanding the usual wide meaning of that term[267], otherwise the benefit of the rights will be lost.

5.164 The National Planning Policy Framework emphasises that advanced, high-quality communications infrastructure is essential for sustainable economic growth[268]. Relevant to prior approval and planning applications, it points to the need

---

[259] Since the powers to install equipment under the Electronic Communications Code are wide, potential alternative sites may be hundreds of metres away: *Phillips v First Secretary of State* [2004] EWHC 2415 (Admin), [2004] JPL 613.
[260] GPDO 2015, Sch 2, Part 24, Class A, para A2(4). However, illustrating the government encouragement for new services, prior approval is not required for fixed line broadband equipment on art 2(3) land which is installed by 30 May 2018: GPDO 2015, Sch 2, Part 24, Class A, para A2(5).
[261] GPDO 2015, Sch 2, Part 24, Class A, para A3(1). Notice to aviation interests is also required if the development is within 3 km of an aerodrome: GPDO 2015, Sch 2, Part 24, Class A, para A3(2).
[262] GPDO 2015, Sch 2, Part 24, Class A, para A3(5).
[263] GPDO 2015, Sch 2, Part 24, Class A, para A3(7). Responses to publicity and consultation have to be taken into account in making these decisions: see para A3(6).
[264] GPDO 1995, Sch 2, Part 25, Classes A and B respectively in Wales.
[265] See the Road Traffic (Driver Licensing and Information Systems) Act 1989, ss 8, 10; GPDO 1995, Sch 2, Part 29, Class A in Wales.
[266] Broadly the universal postal service obligation is to deliver to every address, six days a week at an affordable, uniform tariff throughout the UK: Postal Services Act 2011, ss 30, 31. In Wales the permitted development rights are in the GPDO 1995, Sch 2, Part 17, Class J.
[267] See Town and Country Planning Act 1990, s 336(1) and GPDO 2015, art 2(1).
[268] NPPF, para 42.

5.165 *Permitted development rights*

to minimise the number of masts and sites and sympathetic design and camouflage. Information expected with prior approval applications includes the outcome of consultations with organisations with an interest in the proposed development, in particular with the relevant body where a mast is to be installed near a school or college or within a statutory safeguarding zone surrounding an aerodrome or technical site and self-certification that the cumulative exposure, when operational, will not exceed International Commission on non-ionising radiation protection guidelines. For a new mast or base station, evidence should be provided that the possibility of erecting antennae on an existing building, mast or other structure has been explored[269].

Part 17 Mining and mineral exploration

5.165 A series of permitted development rights are granted in connection with mining operations. These are subject to particularly complex limitations and conditions and in some cases prior approval so their text needs to be considered with care.

5.166 The most general right is in Class A, authorising the erection, extension, installation, rearrangement, replacement, repair or other alteration of any plant or machinery, buildings, private ways or private railways or sidings, or sewers, mains, pipes, cables or other similar apparatus, on land used as a mine[270]. This is subject to various size restrictions and the removal of the development and the restoration of the land within 24 months of the mining operations having permanently ceased.

5.167 Class B authorises the erection, installation, extension, rearrangement, replacement, repair or other alteration of any plant or machinery, buildings, or structures or erections[271]. This may be for the operation of the mine, treatment, preparation for sale, consumption or utilisation of minerals from the mine or the storage or removal of such minerals, their products or wastes. Class B applies to the mine and ancillary mining land[272]. Prior approval is required for the siting, design and external appearance of the development[273]. Approval may only be denied or granted subject to conditions if the proposed development would injure the amenity of the neighbourhood and modifications can reasonably be made or conditions reasonably imposed in order to avoid or reduce that injury; or it ought to be, and could reasonably be, sited elsewhere.

5.168 Class C concerns development for the safety and maintenance of a (non-coal) mine or disused mine or land adjacent to it[274].

---

[269] NPPF, para 45.
[270] In Wales the rights are in GPDO 1995, Sch 2, Part 19, Class A. A mine is any site on which mining operations are carried out and *'mining operations'* means the winning and working of minerals in, on or under land, whether by surface or underground working: GPDO 2015, art 2(1); GPDO 1995, art 1(2).
[271] GPDO 1995, Sch 2, Part 19, Class B in Wales.
[272] In Part 17 ancillary mining land means land adjacent to and occupied together with a mine at which the winning and working of minerals is carried out in pursuance of planning permission: GPDO 2015, Sch 2, Part 17, para N1. In a drafting error the definition is repeated for Class H: GPDO 2015, Sch 2, Part 17, Class H, para H3.
[273] GPDO 2015, Sch 2, Part 17, Class B, para B2.
[274] GPDO 2015, Sch 2, Part 17, Class C and GPDO 1995, Sch 2, Part 19, Class C in Wales. Prior approval may be required.

The permitted development rights **5.173**

5.169 Coal mining is the subject of Classes D–G[275]. Class D authorises underground mining by Coal Authority licensees in seams designated by 1993 in mines which started before 1948. A restoration scheme may have to be approved. Class E grants such rights to licensees of the British Coal Corporation, with an assumption that no restoration scheme is required. Class F grants permission for above ground development in connection with coal mining operations at existing mines, subject to some limits and certain prior approvals. Finally Class G approves safety works at existing and disused coal mines in a similar way to Class C.

5.170 Classes H and I deal with mineral waste tipping[276]. Class H authorises its deposit on mines and ancillary mining land subject to certain limits. Class I authorises the tipping of waste from coal mining on land used for such purposes prior to 1 July 1948 in accordance with a scheme approved by 1988.

5.171 Classes J and K approve certain mineral exploration[277]:

'(a) the drilling of boreholes;
(b) the carrying out of seismic surveys; or
(c) the making of other excavations,

for the purpose of mineral exploration, and the provision or assembly on that land or adjoining land of any structure required in connection with any of those operations'.

Neither class applies to the drilling of boreholes for petroleum extraction[278] (although other petroleum exploration is permitted). Class J operates for a period not exceeding 28 consecutive days and is subject to various limitations on the location, nature, extent and timing of the development. Class K permits investigations for six months, or longer if the mineral planning authority agree. It is also less constrained, for example, allowing exploration in national parks and areas of outstanding natural beauty. However 28 days' notice of the intention to carry out works under Class K must be given. This gives the mineral planning authority an opportunity to make an art 5 direction.

Restoration conditions apply under both classes.

5.172 Class L authorises the removal of any material from a stockpile, which is defined as a mineral-working deposit consisting primarily of minerals which have been deposited for the purposes of their processing or sale[279].

5.173 Class M authorises the removal of material from a mineral-working deposit other than a stockpile, for example the reclamation of a tip. Notice must be given and the works not commence until 28 days later or, if an art 5 direction is made, a further 28 days after the direction is sent to the Minister[280]. If the direction is not disallowed

---

[275] The equivalent Welsh provisions are in GPDO 1995, Sch 2, Part 20, Classes A to E.
[276] GPDO 1995, Sch 2, Part 21, Classes A and B in Wales.
[277] GPDO 1995, Sch 2, Part 22, Classes A and B in Wales.
[278] GPDO 2015, Sch 2, Part 17, Class J, para J1(a), Class K, para K1(a).
[279] The definition is in GPDO 2015, Sch 2, Part 17, para N1. The Wales equivalent to Class L is GPDO 1995, Sch 2, Part 23, Class A with stockpile defined in para C.
[280] GPDO 2015, Sch 2, Part 17, Class M, para M2(d), (3). In Wales see the GPDO 1995, Sch 2, Part 23, Class B.

5.174 *Permitted development rights*

then it will come into force, restricting or removing the Class M rights in accordance with its terms.

The authority may require the developer to submit a restoration and aftercare scheme for the site and the approved scheme must then be carried out[281].

Part 18 Miscellaneous development

5.174 Notwithstanding the imagination of the drafters in putting various uses together, some permitted development rights live on their own. Two very contrasting rights are therefore in Part 18.

5.175 Class A grants planning permission for development authorised by local or private Acts or orders which have been approved by Parliament or made under the Harbours Act 1964, ss 14 or 16, 'which designates specifically the nature of the development authorised and the land upon which it may be constructed'[282]. An Act of Parliament may grant planning permission itself, an approach followed by the Channel Tunnel Rail Link, Crossrail and High Speed rail legislation.

Prior approval is required[283] of the detailed plans and specifications of any building, bridge, aqueduct, pier or dam or means of access to a highway used by vehicular traffic.

A further restriction on these rights is introduced by art 3(7)[284] that any consent or approval under the Act or order is required before the permitted development rights apply, except where the Act was passed or the order made after 1 July 1948 and it contains provision to the contrary.

5.176 Class B authorises the erection of booths or stalls or the installation of plant or machinery at amusement parks[285].

Part 19 Development by the Crown or for national security purposes

5.177 Until 2006 the Crown was exempted from planning control and could therefore do what it liked, subject to a consultation procedure. The Planning and Compulsory Purchase Act 2004 removed that privilege[286], leading to the need for permitted development rights. These rights tend to reflect non-Crown rights but with the addition of emergency powers. The Crown also has the permitted development rights available at large under the rest of the GPDO.

5.178 Class A comprises the erection, construction, maintenance, improvement or alteration of any ancillary building, works or equipment not exceeding four metres in height or 200 m³ on Crown land and:

---

[281] GPDO 2015, Sch 2, Part 17, Class M, para M2(b), (c).
[282] In Wales, GPDO 1995, Sch 2, Part 11, Class A.
[283] Unusually the obligation is to obtain prior approval, not apply for a determination whether prior approval is required and then obtain it if it is.
[284] Since this provision applies only to Part 18, it ought to be in that part rather than in the general provisions of art 3.
[285] GPDO 1995, Sch 2, Part 28, Class A in Wales.
[286] By inserting the Town and Country Planning Act 1990, s 292A, discussed in Chapter 6.

The permitted development rights **5.187**

'lamp standards, information kiosks, passenger shelters, shelters and seats, telephone boxes, fire alarms, drinking fountains, refuse bins or baskets, barriers for the control of people and vehicles, and similar structures or works required in connection with the operational purposes of the Crown'.

5.179 Class B is the extension or alteration of any Crown building subject to various limitations.

5.180 Class C approves plant or machinery, sewers, mains, pipes, cables, other apparatus, private ways, railways, sidings or conveyors.

5.181 A hard surface within the curtilage of a Crown building is approved by Class D[287].

5.182 Class E authorises various works within an airbase[288], although not runways or more than small-scale passenger terminals. Consultation with the local planning authority is required unless it is modest development urgently required for the efficient running of the airbase[289].

5.183 Air traffic services on operational land are authorised by a variety of classes: Class F on an airbase; Class G within 8 kilometres of an airbase; Class H on operational land; Class I in an emergency; and moveable structures in Class J[290].

5.184 Class K authorises temporary surveying or investigations[291].

Reverting to airbases, Class L approves the use of buildings by or on behalf of the Crown within an airbase for purposes connected with air transport services[292] or other flying activities[293].

5.185 Class M[294] permits development on operational Crown land[295] required in connection with the movement of traffic by rail, subject to the limitations which apply to railway undertakings in Part 8, Class A.

5.186 Class N authorises development by or on behalf of the Crown or its lessees on operational Crown land which is required for the purposes of shipping or at a dock, pier, pontoon or harbour in connection with the embarking, disembarking, loading, discharging or transport of military or civilian personnel, military equipment, munitions, or other items.

5.187 The spreading of dredged material from a dock, pier, harbour, water transport, canal of inland navigation undertaking is permitted by Class O.

---

[287] Classes A–D are in the GPDO 1995, Sch 2, Part 34, Classes A to D in Wales.
[288] An airbase is a government aerodrome with the meaning of the Air Navigation Order 2009, SI 2009/3015, art 255: GPDO 2015, Sch 2, Part 19, para U.
[289] GPDO 2015, Sch 2, Part 19, Class E, paras E2, E4.
[290] In Wales see GPDO 1995, Sch 2, Part 35, Classes A–F.
[291] GPDO 1995, Sch 2, Part 35, Class G in Wales.
[292] These are the carriage by air of passengers or cargo: Airports Act 1982, s 82(1).
[293] GPDO 1995, Sch 2, Part 35, Class H in Wales.
[294] GPDO 1995, Sch 2, Part 36, Class A in Wales.
[295] Operational Crown land is Crown land used or held for operational purposes but does not include land comparable to land in general or held by the Crown Estate, the Monarch in her private capacities or the Duchies of Lancaster or Cornwall: GPDO 2015, art 2(1).

5.188 *Permitted development rights*

Lighthouses, buoys, beacons and 'all other marks and signs of the sea' are approved by Class P[296].

5.188 Class Q deals with emergency powers[297]. Development on Crown land for the purposes of preventing an emergency, reducing, controlling or mitigating its effects or taking other action in connection with an emergency is permitted subject to notifying the local planning authority as soon as possible after commencement. The right can be exercised for six months, at the end of which the use must cease, any buildings be removed and the land restored to the original or an agreed condition[298]. An emergency is an event or situation which threatens serious damage to human welfare or the environment in a place in the UK or the security of the UK[299].

5.189 Classes R, S and T deal with development on Crown land for national security purposes[300]. Means of enclosure are permitted by Class R and closed circuit television cameras with associated lighting by Class S. Class T authorises the installation of fixed or moveable electronic communications apparatus and development ancillary to radio equipment housing in, on, over or under Crown land for national security purposes. This is subject to detailed size and location limits, but not, for obvious reasons, prior approval.

Avian flu

5.190 Concern about outbreaks of avian flu in the Far East led to the grant of temporary permitted development rights for the erection of buildings for poultry and captive birds. Those rights expired on 19 February 2008 and any buildings had to be removed. The provision is therefore omitted from the GPDO 2015 but remains, with a now-passed 21 March 2009 time limit for removal, in the GPDO 1995, Sch 2, Part 39, Class A in Wales.

---

[296] GPDO 1995, Sch 2, Part 36, Classes B–D are the equivalent provisions to Classes N–P in Wales.
[297] GPDO 1995, Sch 2, Part 37, Class A in Wales.
[298] GPDO 2015, Sch 2, Part 19, Class Q, para Q1.
[299] GPDO 2015, Sch 2, Part 19, Class Q, para Q2, which contains exclusive definitions of damage to human welfare and the environment.
[300] This is GPDO 1995, Sch 2, Part 38, Classes A to C in Wales.

Chapter 6

Planning applications

6.1 Planning permission is obtained from local planning authorities by the making of a planning application. The formality of the process is important to ensure certainty as to what is applied for, that consultation and publicity take place, relevant matters are considered properly in the decision and that the decision is certain and subject to the necessary and intended controls.

6.2 Planning applications are governed, essentially, by the Town and Country Planning Act 1990, ss 65–73A and the respectively procedural development orders: the Town and Country Planning (Development Management Procedure) (England) Order 2015 (DMPO 2015) and the Town and Country Planning (Development Management Procedure) (England) Order 2012 (DMPO Wales)[1]. The DMPO 2015 replaced the Town and Country Planning (Development Management Procedure) (England) Order 2010 (DMPO 2010) from 15 April 2015, although planning applications which were current at that time will continue to be governed by the DMPO 2010 for the purpose of publicity, consultation and notice of the decision[2]. Some applications will be subject to Environmental Impact Assessment (EIA), or the need for a decision that EIA is not required, under either the Town and Country Planning (Environmental Impact Assessment) Regulations 2011 (EIA Regulations 2011) in England or the Town and Country Planning (Environmental Impact Assessment) (England and Wales) Regulations 1999 (EIA Regulations 1999) in Wales[3].

TYPES OF PLANNING APPLICATIONS

6.3 A planning application can be for any form of development: operational development; the making of a material change of use of land; or both. It may also overcome conditions on existing planning permissions, either explicitly or implicitly. However, in terms of process and procedure, planning applications fall into the following types:

(i) full otherwise called detailed applications, which contain the principal drawings for the scheme;

(ii) outline applications in which one or more of access, appearance, landscaping, layout and scale of a building are kept back for later approval as 'reserved matters';

(iii) applications for the carrying out of development approved under an earlier planning permission, but subject to different conditions (s 73 applications);

---

[1] SIs 2015/595 and 2012/801 respectively.
[2] DMPO 2015, art 47(2), (3). Consequently references are given to the DMPO 2015 and DMPO 2010.
[3] SIs 2011/1824 and 1999/293 respectively.

6.4 *Planning applications*

(iv) applications for development which has been carried out without planning permission or in breach of condition. These are retrospective applications made under s 73A;

(v) in England, applications to extend the time for beginning development under an existing planning permission[4].

6.4 All are subject to differences in procedure and approach to the decision, although the underlying principles applied are closer than differences in language might suggest. The boundaries between categories are not absolute. Planning permission on a full application may defer a great number of matters to later approval. An application may be a hybrid, for example the main road in a new housing estate being a detailed part of the application whilst the proposed houses are dealt with on an outline basis. An application might be both prospective, for future development, and retrospective for development which has already taken place.

6.5 A full or detailed planning application has no statutory definition and in reality means it is not an outline planning application, which is a defined term. The essential point with any planning permission is that it must be possible to know what is authorised by the permission, as far as any uncertainty is material in planning terms. However, not all of that detail has to be approved in the single application at one time. Various elements may be deferred to a later approval following the submission of details under conditions. A particular statutory format was devised for a particular deferral of details: the outline planning application followed by the approval of reserved matters. An outline planning permission is defined as[5]:

> 'a planning permission for the erection of a building, which is granted subject to a condition requiring the subsequent approval of the local planning authority with respect to one or more reserved matters'.

6.6 The definitions of reserved matters vary between the two nations, which says something about the benefits and difficulties that outline planning applications have at times been seen to generate. Reserved matters are defined in England as[6]:

> 'any of the following matters in respect of which details have not been given in the application:
>
> (a) access;
>
> (b) appearance;
>
> (c) landscaping;
>
> (d) layout; and
>
> (e) scale'.

These terms are all individually defined in the DMPO 2015, art 2(1).

6.7 In relation to reserved matters, access means:

---

[4] DMPO 2015, art 20; DMPO 2010, art 18.
[5] DMPO 2015, art 2(1); DMPO 2010, art 2(1) and DMPO Wales, art 2(1).
[6] DMPO 2015, art 2(1); DMPO 2010, art 2(1).

Types of planning applications **6.11**

'the accessibility to and within the site, for vehicles, cycles and pedestrians in terms of the positioning and treatment of access and circulation routes and how these fit into the surrounding access network; where "site" means the site or part of the site in respect of which outline planning permission is granted or, as the case may be, in respect of which an application for such a permission has been made'.

'To' the site means the planning application site boundary. The definition does, though, go further than just the edge of the development and includes the ways inside the site (see 'within' and 'circulation routes').

6.8 Appearance means:

'the aspects of a building or place within the development which determines the visual impression the building or place makes, including the external built form of the development, its architecture, materials, decoration, lighting, colour and texture'.

6.9 Landscaping is hard (terraces, walls) and soft (plants, water and earth):

'the treatment of land (other than buildings) for the purpose of enhancing or protecting the amenities of the site and the area in which it is situated and includes:

(a) screening by fences, walls or other means;

(b) the planting of trees, hedges, shrubs or grass;

(c) the formation of banks, terraces or other earthworks;

(d) the laying out or provision of gardens, courts, squares, water features, sculpture or public art; and

(e) the provision of other amenity features'.

6.10 Layout is defined as:

'the way in which buildings, routes and open spaces within the development are provided, situated and orientated in relation to each other and to buildings and spaces outside the development'.

6.11 Scale means the height, width and length of each building proposed within the development in relation to its surroundings.

The Welsh definition of reserved matters is the same except that the scale is 'within the upper and lower limit for the height, width and length of each building stated in the application for planning permission in accordance with article 3(4)'[7]. A Welsh application for outline planning permission must set out various parameters within which reserved matters must be sought[8]:

'(3) Where layout is a reserved matter, the application for outline planning permission must state the approximate location of buildings, routes and open spaces included in the development proposed.

(4) Where scale is a reserved matter, the application for outline planning permission must state the upper and lower limit for the height, width and length of each building included in the development proposed.

---

[7] DMPO Wales, art 2(1).
[8] DMPO Wales, art 3(3)–(5).

6.12 *Planning applications*

(5) Where access is a reserved matter, the application for outline planning permission must state the area or areas where access points to the development proposed will be situated'.

6.12 Historically both nations had allowed outline planning permissions to establish the principle of operational development (with any change of use) on land and left the details to be determined on reserved matters. For example, an outline planning permission was granted to Imperial Chemical Industries Limited by the Severn Estuary for factories on 1,000 acres, offices, warehouses and amenity uses on 545 acres and ancillary buildings on a further 1,100 acres. No further detail of the quantum of development was provided[9]. Outline planning permission could be secured over a large or small area, without the cost and effort involved in working up a detailed design and keeping flexibility for the eventual developer, who might not be the applicant for planning permission.

6.13 Whilst outline planning applications were often accompanied by an explanation of what was proposed along with illustrative drawings of what the scheme would look like, the eventual outcome might be very different. In two high profile 1990s cases neighbouring planning authorities challenged the grant of reserved matters for factory outlet centres selling discounted clothes when the schemes had been presented as large retail warehouse units for bulky goods. Both judicial reviews failed[10]. The factory outlet cases illustrated the concern that outline planning permissions were being secured for attractive proposals and the final schemes then turned out to be less welcome.

6.14 Environmental Impact Assessment case law began to develop in the late 1990s with Mr Justice Sullivan identifying in the two *Rochdale* cases the problem of how to assess an application if little is known about the scheme[11]. The solution, arrived at in the second *Rochdale* case *Milne*, was to limit the development to a range of unit numbers, floorspace, building size and locations within the site. Outline applications for EIA development therefore tended to be accompanied by masterplans indicating the scale and distribution of the development.

6.15 A wider response to both issues was provided by 2006 amendments to the then Town and Country Planning (General Development Procedure) Order 1995 to require parameters to be set out in any outline planning application in England. The changes were subsequently adopted in Wales. However, whilst the Welsh requirements remain in the DMPO Wales, set out above, the English details were revoked in 2013 to ease the application process.

LOCAL PLANNING AUTHORITIES

6.16 Planning applications are made to the local planning authority responsible for that type of development in that area. The limited ability to apply directly to the Minister is discussed in Chapter 18. Where there is a single tier of council for the

---

[9] See *Redrow Homes Ltd v First Secretary of State* [2003] EWHC 3094 (Admin), [2004] JPL 1273 at paras 5, 7.
[10] *R v Ashford Borough Council, ex p Shepway District Council* [1999] PLCR 12; *R v Bolsover District Council, ex p Ashfield District Council* (1995) 70 P & CR 507.
[11] *R v Rochdale Metropolitan Borough Council, ex p Tew* [2000] JPL 54; *R v Rochdale Metropolitan Borough Council, ex p Milne* [2001] JPL 470. This is considered further in Chapter 7.

area (excluding any town or parish council) then the local planning authority is that council or any national park authority (or the Broads Authority) for that area[12], unless the scheme is within planning responsibilities given to enterprise zone authorities[13], urban development corporations[14], Mayoral development corporations in London[15], housing action trusts[16] and the Homes and Communities Agency[17]. Greater London, the former metropolitan counties of Greater Manchester, Merseyside, South Yorkshire, West Midlands and West Yorkshire, and Wales are made up of unitary authorities. Elsewhere in England there are some unitary authorities, usually big cities, component parts of former 'new' and unlamented counties such as Humberside and some county breakups (Berkshire splitting into unitaries) or county mergers (a single council in Cornwall).

6.17 In two-tier authority areas with a county council, the district councils[18] handle all planning applications except those which relate to a county matter, which are submitted to the county council[19]. County matters are defined in the Town and Country Planning Act 1990, Sch 1 and the Town and Country Planning (Prescription of County Matters) (England) Regulations 2003[20] as[21]:

'(a) the winning and working of minerals in, on or under land (whether by surface or underground working) or the erection of any building, plant or machinery:

   (i) which it is proposed to use in connection with the winning and working of minerals or with their treatment or disposal in or on land adjoining the site of the working; or

   (ii) which a person engaged in mining operations proposes to use in connection with the grading, washing, grinding or crushing of minerals;

(b) the use of land, or the erection of any building, plant or machinery on land, for the carrying out of any process for the preparation or adaptation for sale of any mineral or the manufacture of any article from a mineral where:

   (i) the land forms part of or adjoins a site used or proposed to be used for the winning and working of minerals; or

   (ii) the mineral is, or is proposed to be, brought to the land from a site used, or proposed to be used, for the winning and working of minerals by means of a pipeline, conveyor belt, aerial ropeway, or similar plant or machinery, or by private road, private waterway or private railway;

(c) the carrying out of searches and tests of mineral deposits or the erection of any building, plant or machinery which it is proposed to use in connection with them;

(d) the depositing of mineral waste;

---

[12] Town and Country Planning Act 1990, ss 4A, 5 respectively.
[13] Town and Country Planning Act 1990, s 6.
[14] Town and Country Planning Act 1990, s 7.
[15] Town and Country Planning Act 1990, s 7A.
[16] Town and Country Planning Act 1990, s 8.
[17] Town and Country Planning Act 1990, s 8A.
[18] Districts may sometimes be styled Borough Council or City Council.
[19] Town and Country Planning Act 1990, Sch 1, para 3. Both authorities are local planning authorities: Town and Country Planning Act 1990, s 1. Consequently either can enter into planning obligations as local planning authority: *Oxfordshire County Council v Secretary of State for Communities and Local Government* [2015] EWHC 186 (Admin) at para 32 per Lang J.
[20] SI 2003/1033.
[21] Town and Country Planning Act 1990, Sch 1, para 1.

6.18 *Planning applications*

(e) the use of land for any purpose required in connection with the transport by rail or water of aggregates (that is to say, any of the following, namely:

    (i) sand and gravel;

    (ii) crushed rock;

    (iii) artificial materials of appearance similar to sand, gravel or crushed rock and manufactured or otherwise derived from iron or steel slags, pulverised fuel ash, clay or mineral waste), or the erection of any building, plant or machinery which it is proposed to use in connection with them;

(f) the erection of any building, plant or machinery which it is proposed to use for the coating of roadstone or the production of concrete or of concrete products or artificial aggregates, where the building, plant or machinery is to be erected in or on land which forms part of or adjoins a site used or proposed to be used:

    (i) for the winning and working of minerals; or

    (ii) for any of the purposes mentioned in paragraph (e) above;

(g) the erection of any building, plant or machinery which it is proposed to use for the manufacture of cement;

(h) the carrying out of operations in, on, over or under land, or a use of land, where the land is or forms part of a site used or formerly used for the winning and working of minerals and where the operations or use would conflict with or prejudice compliance with a restoration condition or an aftercare condition;

(i) the carrying out of operations in, on, over or under land, or any use of land, which is situated partly in and partly outside a National Park'.

And these operations and uses of land[22]:

'(a) (i) the use of land;

    (ii) the carrying out of building, engineering or other operations; or

    (iii) the erection of plant or machinery used or proposed to be used,

wholly or mainly for the purposes of recovering, treating, storing, processing, sorting, transferring or depositing of waste;

(b) the use of land or the carrying out of operations for any purposes ancillary to any use or operations specified in paragraph (a) above, including the formation, laying out, construction or alteration of a vehicular access to any public highway'.

The question is whether in substance the application relates to a county matter. If so, it is for the county council to determine it, even if some elements are not county matters[23]. There are mechanisms for the authorities to consult each other[24].

6.18 Applications by local planning authorities for them to develop any of their land (including jointly with another person) are to be made to that local planning authority[25]. In two-tier authority areas, such permissions will exist only for the benefit

---

[22] Town and Country Planning (Prescription of County Matters) (England) Regulations 2003, reg 2.
[23] *R v Berkingham County Council, ex p Wokingham District Council* [1997] Env LR 545 at 552 per Beldam LJ.
[24] See paras **6.130–6.132** below.
[25] Town and Country Planning Act 1990, s 316; Town and Country Planning General Regulations 1992, SI 1992/1492, regs 3, 4. If the application is solely for relevant demolition (see Town and Country Planning Act 1990, s 196D) in a conservation area then the application shall be sent to the Secretary of State for determination if Historic England objects: Town and Country Planning General Regulations 1992, reg 4A.

of that local planning authority or any other person specified in the application who is to carry out the development jointly with them, unless the authority is an urban development corporation[26]. If a local planning authority intends to obtain planning permission and then dispose of the land for it to be developed by someone else then a conventional planning application will be made to the usual planning authority, rather than one under these provisions.

6.19 If planning permission is required for development in two local planning authority areas, then separate applications will need to be made to each authority for the development in its area.

6.20 It is not a permissible ground of challenge that a planning decision should have been taken by a different local planning authority[27].

STAGES IN THE APPLICATION PROCESS

6.21 The potential stages in the planning application process, with their references to chapters in this book and the relevant legislation are:

Potential stage	Book reference	English provisions	Welsh provisions
Pre-application advice	Chapter 6		
EIA screening	Chapter 7	EIA Regulations 2011, regs 4–6	EIA Regulations 1999, regs 4–6
Pre-application consultation	Chapter 6	TCPA 1990, s 61W; DMPO 2015, arts 3, 4; DMPO 2010, arts 3A, 3B	
Notice to the owner and agricultural tenants	Chapter 6	TCPA 1990, s 65; DMPO 2015, arts 13,14; DMPO 2010, arts 11, 12	DMPO Wales, arts 10, 11
Submission of the application and supporting documents	Chapter 6	DMPO 2015, arts, 5, 7–9, 11; DMPO 2010, arts 4, 6–8, 10	DMPO Wales, arts 3, 5–9
Publicity and consultation on the application	Chapter 6	DMPO 2015, articles 15–21, 25, 26; DMPO 2010, articles 13, 14, 16–19, 23, 24	DMPO Wales, articles 12–17
Amendments, further information and further publicity	Chapter 6	DMPO 2015, arts 5, 25; DMPO 2010, arts 4(2) (reserved matters), 23 (parish councils); TCPA 1990, Sch 1, para 8	DMPO Wales, arts 3(2) (reserved matters)
Publication of a report if the decision is taken by councillors	Chapter 8	Local Government Act 1972, ss 100C, 100D, 100E	Local Government Act 1972, ss 100C, 100D, 100E

---

[26] Town and Country Planning General Regulations 1992, regs 9, 9A, 9AA.
[27] Town and Country Planning Act 1990, s 286(1). Judicial review proceedings could be brought before the application is determined, see *R v Berkshire County Council, ex p Wokingham District Council* [1997] Env LR 545.

6.22 *Planning applications*

Potential stage	Book reference	English provisions	Welsh provisions
Decision on the application	Chapter 8, 9	TCPA 1990, s 70; DMPO 2015, arts 25, 33; DMPO 2010, arts 23, 28; EIA Regulations 2011, reg 3	DMPO Wales, arts 16, 21
Imposition of conditions	Chapter 11	TCPA 1990, ss 70, 72	TCPA 1990, ss 70, 72
Planning obligations	Chapter 12	TCPA 1990, s 106	TCPA 1990, s 106
Direction by Mayor of London	Chapter 10	TCPA 1990, s 74; Mayor of London Order	
Potential referral to Ministers	Chapter 17	DMPO 2015, art 31; DMPO 2010, art 25	DMPO Wales, art 18
Issue of the decision notice	Chapter 13	DMPO 2015, art 35; DMPO 2010, art 31; EIA Regulations 2011, reg 3	DMPO Wales, art 24; EIA Regulations 1999, reg 3
Post-decision publicity	Chapter 7, 13	DMPO 2015, arts 25, 35; DMPO 2010, arts 23, 31; EIA Regulations 2011, reg 24	DMPO Wales, art 24; EIA Regulations 1999, reg 21

WORKING UP THE SCHEME

6.22 The potential applicant for planning permission has first to decide what they want to achieve, whether they can achieve it and how to do so. Ultimately planning is the control of the use and development of land in the public interest. It rarely in practice dictates what has to happen but provides a range of possibilities, including usually leaving things as they are. So the first question is what does the potential applicant want to achieve?

6.23 The most common application is an alteration or extension to an existing building to meet the needs of the current occupiers. Some of these works might not be development at all[28] or might benefit from permitted development rights[29]. The restrictions on permitted development and any need for prior approval would have to be considered with care. If some elements of the project are permitted development and some are not, it may be worth considering whether it is possible to proceed under the GPDO for part of the project and an application for planning permission for the remainder. It does not follow that a developer should try to confine a modest project to permitted development. Contrary to the general reputation of planning being contentious, over 80% of planning applications are approved, and an extension which is sensitive to its surroundings is unlikely to be difficult or expensive to obtain consent for.

6.24 The greater the scale of development or redevelopment, the larger the issues and options will be. A project does, though, need to be something which the potential

---
[28] See Chapter 2.
[29] Chapter 5. It is also worth considering whether any existing planning permissions allow the project or, by condition, restrict further what can be done.

applicant intends and is able to carry out or is able to sell on to someone who might. Obtaining planning permission for a scheme which no one would carry out is rarely a beneficial occupation: it is unlikely to provide a springboard to a further consent if the local planning authority appreciates that it is not a realistic fallback, nor add greatly to the land value.

6.25 For a larger project the potential applicant needs to think more widely, but still starting with the market. Once complete, is it saleable or lettable at an economic return? If the intention is to obtain the permission and then sell the site on to a developer, what schemes is the market interested in? What is desirable in market terms has then to be considered in the light of what may be achievable in planning terms. 'May' is used deliberately. Planning is an exercise of political judgment, albeit within a considerable amount of policy and detailed technical issues. Whilst some projects could easily be seen as acceptable or not acceptable, the boundaries of what would be consented are not firm or even easy to discern. Council officers, councillors, planning inspectors and Ministers may all take different views as to what development is acceptable in principle, let alone detail, on a particular site.

6.26 A prospective developer will need to consider what might be approved and how to tailor their aspirations to the requirements of consent. A starting point is to ask what harm might be caused to the public interest and what benefits to the public interest arise from the project. Turning to specifics, the site itself and its physical context are critical. Local and national planning policy should be considered: what is promoted or opposed? What needs to be considered and what policy tests apply? Draft local policy should be considered, both at the local planning authority (Local Plan) and neighbourhood plan levels. Do they help or hinder? Should the potential applicant take part in the process to strengthen or protect their position?

6.27 A scheme may need to take into account other regulatory constraints, such as the Environmental Permitting Regulations, Building Regulations and highways. Some matters which will require further consents may be addressed on similar principles by the planning process, such as listed buildings and licences to disturb European protected species. Private law constraints such as easements, restrictive covenants and rights of light may also need to be factored into the scheme design and viability.

6.28 The amount of development which would be acceptable on a site is rarely capable of being objectively (let alone mathematically) determined. Often the sensible course is to apply for the amount which the developer thinks is acceptable in planning terms and desirable commercially. That will be the quickest way to start building. Alternative options might be to apply for more initially and see whether that is approved and if necessary revert to a smaller scheme, alternatively to secure permission for a modest level of development and then return for a denser or higher scheme on the basis that the difference is not objectionable.

6.29 A preliminary question when preparing a scheme for new buildings is whether to apply for full or outline permission. If the applicant intends to build out the scheme and has a firm view of what it wants then it is usually better to seek full planning permission. Outline planning permission is useful where there is a desire to retain flexibility or a likelihood of selling the site or part of it onto another developer who may have their own proposals, such as house designs. Outline permissions were a useful means of deciding the principle of development without great expense, but

6.30 *Planning applications*

increased requirements to provide information with applications have eroded that benefit. It remains to be seen whether amendments made in England in 2013 to relax the detail needed has encouraged their use.

6.30 The applicant will have to consider what professionals are required. A planning application for a modest house extension might need the assistance of little more than a builder and someone to draw the plans. If an architect is being used for the project then they might handle the planning application. More complex or contentious schemes may need the assistance of planning consultants. Other consultants may be required for particular issues. It is important to identify what consultancy advice is needed at an early stage. Some investigative work may be seasonal (such as ecological surveys) or require lengthy monitoring (such as measuring wind speeds for a turbine project). Other investigations may be time consuming and expensive, for example, archaeological evaluations if important remains are likely to be found[30]. Timetabling the project will be affected by the amount of consultancy work required. Legal advice from solicitors or counsel might be required, either on specific legal issues or on strategic or tactical issues on applications which are likely to be contentious.

6.31 If the development is of any great size the applicant will need to consider whether EIA is required or whether an EIA screening decision is necessary. EIA will significantly affect the preparation of the planning application.

Any pre-application consultations will also need to be taken into account in the timetable for securing planning permission.

PRE-APPLICATION ADVICE

6.32 Many local planning authorities offer a service giving advice to developers proposing to make applications to them. At its most straightforward this may involve attending the Council offices without appointment to talk to a duty planning officer, but for a scheme of any size a more formal approach will be involved. The developer would want to submit an outline of its ideas, usually with some preliminary drawings, then hold a meeting with officers who would then advise by letter. Discussion would focus on the potential acceptability of the scheme, the relevant policies, any issues which were likely to arise and the information which would be required with any application.

6.33 The essence of pre-application advice is that it is an informal but carefully thought through view, albeit given with limited information and without public consultation. Pre-application advice is not binding upon the local planning authority, nor would it usually be seen as giving rise to a legitimate expectation. Initially, at least, the developer's proposals are likely to be confidential, although that status may change if an application is made[31]. Issues with the disclosure of the advice arise in two types of circumstance. The first is when one of the participants wishes to use notes of the meeting or the subsequent advice to say that the local planning authority is raising a new point or reneging on what it has said, or that the developer has

---

[30] It might also be best to be able to time archaeological excavations for when they do not disturb valuable crops, such as lettuces.
[31] Something is only confidential if it has a character which makes it confidential, not because one or both parties who are aware of it would like it to be treated as confidential.

ignored a warning about a particular issue. Since the discussions would not have been privileged or without prejudice (in the sense of concerning the settlement of a legal dispute) and might no longer be confidential, this is allowed unless there is a 'no knock' agreement in contract. Pre-application advice might be sought by third parties under the Environmental Information Regulations 2004[32] or the Freedom of Information Act 2000. The application of the confidentiality exceptions would need to be considered with care[33].

6.34 It has long been established that local authorities are able to give pre-application planning advice, as it 'facilitates, and is conducive and incidental to, the function of determining planning applications' under the Local Government Act 1972, s 111[34]. However, as with any local authority power to raise money, there needed to be statutory authority for charging for such advice. Whilst s 111 might provide a basis for charging for the exercise of powers in some circumstances if that can be necessarily implied into the legislation, it did not for pre-application planning advice, in particular as a charge would be incidental to the incidental[35]. A general power to charge for discretionary services was only introduced by the Local Government Act 2003, s 93[36]. A person may be charged for the provision of a service to him if the authority is authorised, but not required, by an enactment to provide the service to him, and he has agreed to its provision[37]. Charges may vary between different persons and some might not be charged at all[38]. On an annual basis the income from the charges set must not exceed the costs of providing the particular service[39], here pre-application advice.

6.35 Charges may vary greatly between authorities and types of development. Fees for advice on householder planning applications may be under £100, if charged at all. Advice on a major development may be several thousand pounds.

6.36 Pre-application advice may also be sought from other public bodies. This is particularly useful if the body is likely to respond to consultation and have views about what information should be submitted with the application. For most large schemes these will include the highways authority, and if particular interests are affected, the natural and historic environment bodies. Where the body would subsequently be consulted under the schedule in the relevant DMPO (and in certain other cases in England)[40], then any person may seek pre-application advice from them in relation to a proposed development[41]. A substantive response must be given within 21 days

---

[32] SI 2004/3391.
[33] A contract will not necessarily prevent the material having to be disclosed under the Environmental Information Regulations 2004, Freedom of Information Act 2000 or the Data Protection Act 1998.
[34] *McCarthy & Stone (Developments) Ltd v Richmond-upon-Thames London Borough Council* [1992] 2 AC 48 at 70 per Lord Lowry.
[35] *McCarthy & Stone* at 73–75 per Lord Lowry.
[36] A power to charge in circumstances identified in regulations is contained in the Local Government and Housing Act 1989, s 150.
[37] Local Government Act 2003, s 93(1). No charge may be made under this power if the authority has another charging power available or is expressly prohibited from charging for the provision of the service: s 93(2).
[38] The authority will have to act reasonably and without breaching equalities provisions.
[39] Local Government Act 2003, s 93(3), (4).
[40] In England the bodies are those consulted under DMPO 2015, art 22 and Sch 4, and under other provisions listed in DMPO, art 22. DMPO Wales, art 15A(1), applies the list of the consultees identified by art 14 and Sch 4.
[41] Planning and Compulsory Purchase Act 2004, s 54(3). The duty was introduced in England on 24 August 2005 and in Wales on 22 June 2015.

6.37 *Planning applications*

beginning with the receipt of the documents on which advice is sought (or receipt of the last of those documents)[42] or any other agreed period.

6.37 A potential applicant should consider whether it is advantageous to seek pre-application advice. For many householder and small commercial applications it is likely to be unnecessary. Such discussions do tend to be useful for larger schemes. Relatively large fees can be justified if the officers are sufficiently senior and put work into the advice. If an application might be reported to a planning committee it is worth having the views of an officer who regularly attends that committee to understand what interests or concerns those councillors.

Planning Performance Agreements

6.38 A local planning authority and a person who intends to make or who has made a planning application may enter into a Planning Performance Agreement[43]. This is now a commonplace feature at least of large developments, where it is unlikely that the statutory timetable will be met and so it is extended by agreement. It provides a bespoke timetable for the processing of the application, and governs the way the parties proceed. An agreement may explain when and how the applicant will provide information, include notification by the council of reports being made to committees or promise pre-determination discussions on conditions. No assurance can, of course, be given as to the outcome of the application process. A Planning Performance Agreement may be contractually binding – and should state whether it is or is not – and might also give rise to a legitimate expectation as to how the authority will proceed. For example, a mutual duty of 'utmost fairness and good faith' in an agreement gave rise to a legitimate expectation that the developer would be consulted upon a proposal to designate a conservation area to include the application site[44].

PRE-APPLICATION CONSULTATION

6.39 There will often be good reasons for prospective applicants for planning permission to consult to varying degrees statutory bodies, neighbours, interest groups and the public prior to submitting a planning application. Historically this has not been required before a planning application was made, but what was a growing practice for larger schemes is now subject to some legal and policy expectation. Consultation has been encouraged by some statements of community involvement made by local planning authorities. The development consent order regime for nationally significant infrastructure projects incorporates pre-application consultation as a key element of the process[45]. With that experience it was perhaps not too large a step to bring statutory pre-application consultation into the planning permission regime.

---

[42] DMPO, art 22(3); DMPO Wales, art 15A(2), being prescribed under Planning and Compulsory Purchase Act 2004, s 54(4)(a).
[43] The National Planning Policy Framework at para 195 says:

'Applicants and local planning authorities should consider the potential of entering into planning performance agreements, where this might achieve a faster and more effective application process'. See also the Planning Practice Guidance, para 20-016-20140306.

[44] *R (on the application of Trillium (Prime) Property GP Ltd) v London Borough of Tower Hamlets* [2011] EWHC 146 (Admin) at 173 per Ouseley J.
[45] Under the Planning Act 2008.

6.40 The Localism Act 2011 introduced a power by development order in England to require pre-application consultation for specified types of development. Similar powers are being introduced in Wales.

Local authority policies and pre-application consultation

6.41 Statements of community involvement set out the local planning authority's policies on the exercise of its powers for dealing with planning applications and planning policy making[46]. When these were being legislated for in 2004, the Minister disavowed any role for such statements to put consultation obligations on applicants for planning permission[47]. However in practice many SCIs have encouraged pre-application consultation.

Statutory pre-application consultation

6.42 The Localism Act 2011 introduced a duty on applicants to carry out consultation with the public prior to making a planning application for types of development specified in a development order by inserting new s 61W into the Town and Country Planning Act 1990.

6.43 Where the duty to consult under s 61W(1) arises, the intended applicant 'must publicise the proposed application in such manner as the person reasonably considers is likely to bring the proposed application to the attention of a majority of the persons who live at, or otherwise occupy, premises in the vicinity of the land'[48] and consult any specified person[49]. The publicity must set out how the intended applicant may be contacted by persons wishing to comment on, or collaborate with them on the design of, the proposed development, and provide a timetable so that comments may be made in good time[50]. In complying with the duty to consult, the intended applicant must have regard to any advice given by the local planning authority about local good practice[51].

The Planning (Wales) Act 2015 proposes to introduce a similar provision, as s 61Z of the Town and Country Planning Act 1990[52]. At the time of writing no commencement date has been announced.

6.44 The duty so far applies only to planning applications for certain wind turbines in England. The pre-application consultation duty applies to planning applications made after 17 December 2013 for[53]:

'any development involving an installation for the harnessing of wind power for energy production where:

---

[46] Planning and Compulsory Purchase Act 2004, s 18(2).
[47] 657 HL Official Report (5th series) cols 115–116, 27 January 2004.
[48] Town and Country Planning Act 1990, s 61W(2).
[49] Town and Country Planning Act 1990, s 61W(3).
[50] Town and Country Planning Act 1990, s 61W(4).
[51] Town and Country Planning Act 1990, s 61W(7).
[52] Planning (Wales) Act 2015, s 17. Explicit power for pre-application services by local planning authorities would be introduced by Planning (Wales) Act 2015, s 18 as Town and Country Planning Act 1990, ss 61Z1, 61Z2.
[53] DMPO 2015, art 3(1); DMPO 2010, art 3A(1).

6.45 *Planning applications*

(a) the development involves the installation of more than 2 turbines; or

(b) the hub height of any turbine exceeds 15 metres'.

6.45 This covers all wind turbines which must be screened to decide whether EIA is required. When consultation is required DMPO 2015, art 4 provides that:[54]

'an application for planning permission must be accompanied by particulars of:

(a) how the applicant complied with section 61W(1) of the 1990 Act;

(b) any responses to the consultation that were received by the applicant; and

(c) the account taken of those responses'.

Non-statutory pre-application consultation

6.46 The applicant will want to consider whether any non-statutory pre-application consultation should be carried out. There may be value in discussing the proposals with statutory consultees, who will inevitably be interested in the project, such as the highways authority if road movements are materially affected, Natural England or the Natural Resources Body for Wales where national nature sites are impacted, or Historic England or Cadw if the setting of scheduled monuments or Grade I or II* listed buildings might be harmed.

6.47 Neighbour or local consultation may be sensible if there is a real prospect of an impact on them or a chance to head off objections. For schemes of some interest it may also be helpful to talk to ward councillors[55], although planning committee members may be more reticent about being engaged.

THE APPLICATION PROCESS

Notice of the application to landowners and agricultural tenants

6.48 A planning application may be made by any person, including those with no legal interest in the land. Normally the applicant will be a landowner or be in dealings with the landowner, but it does sometimes happen that some or all of the owners would not be told, at least before the application is determined. Consequently the applicant is put under statutory obligations to give notice of the planning application and to certify that this has been done[56].

6.49 The relevant development order provision in England is art 13(1) of the DMPO 2015, which provides[57]:

'… an applicant for planning permission shall give requisite notice of the application to any person (other than the applicant) who on the prescribed date is an owner of the land to which the application relates, or a tenant:

---

[54] Also DMPO 2010, art 4. Made under the Town and Country Planning Act 1990, s 62(8).
[55] The involvement of elected members is encouraged by the *Planning Practice Guidance* 20-007-20140306.
[56] The requirements are imposed by the respective DMPOs, pursuant to the Town and Country Planning Act 1990, s 65(1), (3).
[57] DMPO 2010, art 11(1) and DMPO Wales, art 10 are to the same effect.

The application process **6.53**

(a) by serving the notice on every such person whose name and address is known to the applicant; and

(b) where the applicant has taken reasonable steps to ascertain the names and addresses of every such person, but has been unable to do so, by publication of the notice after the prescribed date in a newspaper circulating in the locality in which the land to which the application relates is situated'.

6.50 'Owner' means a person having a freehold interest or a leasehold interest the unexpired term of which is not less than seven years or in the case of development consisting of the winning or working of minerals, a person entitled to an interest in a mineral in the land, other than oil, gas, coal, gold or silver[58]. Tenant is defined in art 13(9) as an agricultural tenant.

6.51 The significance of notice is that the landowner is not only aware of the application but is aware that it includes his land (this point is implicit in *R (on the application of Pridmore) v Salisbury District Council*[59] where the challenger had been notified of the application as a neighbour). A certificate has to be completed in the published form, or a form substantially to like effect, confirming that this notice has been given[60].

6.52 A planning application for underground mining must encompass the underground working as well as surface development and so may extend over a very large area. Consequently notification requirements are widened in underground mining cases to include public notice as well as the notification of individual landowners and occupiers. Instead of the art 13(1) provisions, art 13(2) requires that notice is given to the owners and tenants of any land[61]:

'(a) by serving the notice on every such person whom the applicant knows to be such a person and whose name and address is known to the applicant;

(b) by publication of the notice after the prescribed date in a newspaper circulating in the locality in which the land to which the application relates is situated; and

(c) by site display in at least one place in every parish within which there is situated any part of the land to which the application relates, leaving the notice in position for not less than 7 days in the period of 21 days immediately preceding the making of the application to the local planning authority'.

6.53 These notice requirements can be onerous on applicants, although it might be thought that a landowner would want to know if someone was mining under their land. Individual notice had applied to oil and gas extraction which by directional

---

[58] DMPO 2015, Sch 2; DMPO 2010, Sch 2; DMPO Wales, Sch 2. The owner of registered land is the registered proprietor (*East Lindsey District Council v Thompson* [2001] EWHC Admin 81, (2001) 82 P 7 CR 33, which is to be preferred to *R v Surrey County Council, ex p Bridge Court Holdings Ltd* [2000] PLCR 344).

[59] [2005] EWHC 2511 (Admin), [2005] JPL 655, paras 12, 13.

[60] DMPO 2015, art 14(1); DMPO 2010 art 12; DMPO (Wales) art 11. Those persons notified will be identified on the certificate. The certificate is required where the application is made and the application is only valid once the certificate is provided: see DMPO 2015, art 34(4). Notice is therefore required to pre-date the making of the application as a correct certificate cannot otherwise be provided. The suggestion in *R (on the application of O'Brien) v West Lancashire District Council* [2012] EWHC 2376 (Admin) at paras 25, 26 per Stephen Davies that notice is not required before the application is made is incorrect.

[61] Previously DMPO 2010, art 11(2). The Welsh underground mining provisions are the same, with the replacement of parish by community: DMPO Wales, art 10(2).

6.54 *Planning applications*

drilling can extend a long way from the well site. In the debate about the introduction of unconventional hydrocarbon extraction (fracking) the government considered that it was impractical to continue this extent of notification. Consequently for 'development consisting of the winning and working of oil or natural gas (including exploratory drilling)' the requirement to serve notice under art 13(2)(a) in England is removed, a newspaper advertisement is still required, and there must be a site notice displayed in every parish (or in an area without a parish, each ward) in which the above or below ground works are intended to take place[62].

6.54 Where underground mining operations are proposed, including oil and natural gas, the site notice must 'specify a place within the area of the local planning authority to whom the application is made where a copy of the application for planning permission, and of all plans and other documents submitted with it, will be open to inspection by the public at all reasonable hours during such period as may be specified in the notice'[63]. Additionally the application and all plans and documents submitted with it must be on the local planning authority's website[64]. Where the site notice is removed within the seven-day period the applicant is treated as having complied if it 'has taken reasonable steps for [the] protection of the notice and, if need be, its replacement'[65].

6.55 The certificate of notice provided with the application in these underground mining cases has to certify compliance with all of the art 13 requirements[66]. If the site notice has been removed in the seven-day period and reliance placed on the reasonable steps provision, then the relevant circumstances must be explained[67], including steps to protect and replace the notice.

The offence of giving an inaccurate certificate of notice

6.56 The requirements under the Town and Country Planning Act 1990, s 65 to give notice to owners and agricultural tenants were seen as being of such importance that an offence has been created for issuing an inaccurate certificate. By s 65(6):

'If any person:

(a) issues a certificate which purports to comply with any requirement imposed by virtue of this section and contains a statement which he knows to be false or misleading in a material particular; or

(b) recklessly issues a certificate which purports to comply with any such requirement and contains a statement which is false or misleading in a material particular,

he shall be guilty of an offence'.

---

[62] DMPO 2015, art 13(3); DMPO 2010 art 11(2A). The Welsh provisions for oil and gas are the same as for other underground mining.
[63] DMPO 2015, art 13(4). DMPO Wales, art 10(3) is to the same effect.
[64] DMPO 2015, art 13(5). The requirement to put the application and supporting documents on the website is wider than the general obligation to give notice of planning applications on the local planning authority website: DMPO 2015, art 15(7). In Wales the obligation to put the application on the Council's website only applies if the website is used for advertising applications: DMPO Wales, art 10(4).
[65] DMPO 2015, art 13(6); DMPO Wales, art 10(5).
[66] DMPO 2015, art 14(1); DMPO Wales, art 11(1).
[67] DMPO 2015, art 14(2); DMPO Wales, art 11(2).

The application process **6.59**

The offence is triable in the magistrates' court with an unlimited fine[68]. It may take time for an inaccurate certificate to be discovered and so a prosecution may be brought at any time[69].

The planning application

6.57 An applicant[70] must submit a planning application: the local planning authority has no power to grant planning permission otherwise. The application is the completed[71] written application form itself. Historically local planning authorities had prepared their own forms, but applicants are now required to use 'a form published by the Minister (or a form to substantially like effect)'[72], except for mineral applications which still use local forms[73]. The Secretary of State and Welsh Ministers have produced a series of forms, known as 1APP, for different types of application. These are available on the Planning Portal website[74] and in a re-badged form from the particular local planning authority.

6.58 The applicant will want to provide with the form sufficient material to show what is being applied for and to justify the application. This will usually involve drawings and a written case for the scheme, often called a planning statement, and may also include expert reports. Sufficient material should be produced, but not too much, since documentation takes time and is costly.

Beyond the pragmatic need to put enough information in, there are a variety of legal duties to provide documents.

Drawings

6.59 Except where the application is to vary conditions prospectively or retrospectively under the Town and Country Planning Act 1990, ss 73 or 73A or an extension of time under the DMPO 2015[75], art 20, it must be accompanied by[76]:

---

[68] Legal Aid, Sentencing and Punishment of Offenders Act 2012 (Fines on Summary Conviction) Regulations 2015, SI 2015/664, with effect to offences committed on or after 12 March 2015. The maximum fine for earlier offences is £5,000: Town and Country Planning Act 1990, s 65(7).

[69] Town and Country Planning Act 1990, s 65(9), disapplying the Magistrates' Court Act 1980, s 127, which sets a six-month limitation period. It is uncertain how often prosecutions are brought. The practical remedies are to refuse to deal with applications or appeals with inaccurate certificates and to quash unlawfully granted consents.

[70] The applicant must be identified on the application form, but a misdescription might not lead to the court quashing a resultant planning permission: *R (on the application of Park Pharmacy Trust) v Plymouth City Council* [2008] EWHC 445 (Admin), [2008] 2 P & CR 11 at paras 12–14 per Sullivan J.

[71] The application must 'include the particulars specified or referred to in the form': DMPO 2015, art 7(1)(b), DMPO 2010, art 6(1)(b).

[72] DMPO 2010, art 6(1)(a); DMPO Wales, art 5(1)(a). The Town and Country Planning (Applications) Regulations 1988, reg 3(1) provides for a paper submission on a form provided by the local planning authority or an electronic submission on a form provided by the Minister. This is inconsistent with the newer DMPO Wales.

[73] DMPO 2015, art 7(4); DMPO 2010, art 6(4); DMPO Wales, art 5(4). In England, applications for winning and working of oil or natural gas by underground operations (including exploratory drilling) now use national forms or are exempted in the same manner as non-mining applications: DMPO 2015, art 7(5); DMPO 2010, art 6(4A).

[74] www.planningportal.gov.uk.

[75] Formerly DMPO 2010, art 18.

[76] DMPO 2015, art 7(1)(c); DMPO 2010, art 6(1)(c); DMPO Wales, art 5(1)(c).

6.60 *Planning applications*

'(i) a plan which identifies the land to which the application relates;

(ii) any other plans, drawings and information necessary to describe the development which is the subject of the application;

(iii) except where the application is made by electronic communications or the local planning authority indicate that a lesser number is required, 3 copies of the form; and

(iv) except where they are submitted by electronic communications or the local planning authority indicate that a lesser number is required, 3 copies of any plans, drawings and information accompanying the application'.

6.60 The excepted types of application will all identify the underlying planning permission on the form, so the drawings from that consent can be considered. It may be that a s 73 application to vary conditions will want to change the drawings and so new drawings will be submitted with it.

Plans or drawings which describe the development should be to an identified scale and plans should show the direction of North[77].

Planning applications may be submitted online via the Planning Portal or in paper hard copy to the local planning authority. The majority of planning applications are now submitted on the Planning Portal[78].

Crown land

6.61 An Act of Parliament is presumed not to bind the Crown except by express provision or by necessary implication. Consequently under the Town and Country Planning Act 1947 and its successors the Crown did not need planning permission to carry out development on its own land[79] or on any other land[80]. Development on Crown land which was not by or on behalf of the Crown was subject to planning control whether it was carried on by a tenant or a trespasser. However a private contractor who leased land from the Crown for the purpose of building and operating a government facility (such as a prison) did not need planning permission[81]. Whilst sometimes contentious – particularly for political reasons – the Crown did not ignore planning policies and local views, carrying out consultation under Circular 18/84[82].

6.62 A longstanding government aspiration to lift Crown immunity in planning was finally realised by the Planning and Compulsory Purchase Act 2004. The Town and Country Planning Act 1990 was therefore applied to the Crown from 7 June 2006 by the simple words[83] 'This Act binds the Crown'.

---

[77] DMPO 2015, art 7(2); DMPO 2010, art 6(2); DMPO Wales, art 5(2). Plans are drawings which show a view of a site, building, floor or roof from overhead. Additional unscaled drawings, such as artist's impressions or perspectives, can be submitted but the scaled drawings should be sufficient to explain the scheme.

[78] 438,551 applications were submitted by this route in 2014, an increase from 362,882 in 2013.

[79] *Ministry of Agriculture, Fisheries and Food v Jenkins* [1963] 2 QB 317.

[80] *Lord Advocate v Dumbarton District Council* [1990] 2 AC 580 where the Ministry of Defence had put portable workmen's cabins and other building material on a road whilst improving the perimeter fence of the Faslane submarine base.

[81] *Cherwell District Council v First Secretary of State* [2004] EWCA Civ 1420, [2005] 1 WLR 1128.

[82] Planning permission could also be obtained with a view to the development taking place following the disposal of the land and planning obligations made for those purposes: the now repealed Town and Country Planning Act 1990, ss 299 and 299A respectively.

[83] Town and Country Planning Act 1990, s 292A(1).

The application process **6.64**

6.63 The change swept away many of the specific Crown provisions[84]. In general a planning application by the Crown is treated in the same way as any other application. Crown land contains a Crown interest or a Duchy interest[85]. An application in respect of Crown land shall be accompanied by a statement that it is Crown land and if the applicant has been authorised by the appropriate authority, a copy of that authorisation[86]. No special statutory provisions apply to sensitive information in Crown applications at the planning application stage, although the usual exemptions in other legislation exist and advice on the planning register is given in the *Planning Practice Guidance*[87]. Special national security provisions may be applied to planning appeals.

Urgent applications for Crown development may be made directly to the Secretary of State[88].

Fees for planning applications

6.64 Most planning applications made to the local planning authority have to be accompanied by a fee. The fees and various exceptions and exemptions are set out in the Town and Country Planning (Fees for Applications, Deemed Applications, Requests and Site Visits) (England) Regulations 2012 and for Wales in the Town and Country Planning (Fees for Applications, Deemed Applications and Site Visits) (Wales) Regulations 2015[89]. Both sets of regulations are subject to regular amendment. The second part of Sch 1 to the particular regulations sets out various categories of application. These are at the start of the table below. Additional fees are charged for reserved matters applications, so outline fees are half those of a full application. Various types of applications are subject to different fees under the first part of Sch 1 and the main body of the regulations. Where convenient these are listed in the table, otherwise they are set out under it. The fees are current at January 2016, the latest changes being on 1 October 2015.

Application	English fee	Welsh fee
Category 1 erection of dwellinghouses (outline application)	£385 per 0.1 hectare, but if site area over 2.5 hectares, £9,527 and £115 per additional 0.1 hectare to maximum £125,000	£380 per 0.1 hectare, but if site area over 2.5 hectares, £9,500 and £100 per additional 0.1 hectare to maximum £143,750

---

[84] It did lead to the introduction of new permitted development rights and a new use class for the Crown, see Chapters 3 and 5.
[85] Town and Country Planning Act 1990, s 293(1). A Crown interest is by s 293(1):
 '(a) an interest belonging to Her Majesty in right of the Crown or in right of Her private estates;
 (b) an interest belonging to a government department or held in trust for Her Majesty for the purposes of a government department;
 (c) such other interest as the Secretary of State specifies by order'.
 A Duchy interest is an interest belonging to Her Majesty in right of the Duchy of Lancaster or belonging to the Duchy of Cornwall. By the Planning (Application to the Houses of Parliament) Order 2006, SI 2006/1469, interests of the Houses of Parliament are Crown land.
[86] DMPO 2015, art 8; DMPO 2010, art 7; DMPO Wales, art 6.
[87] See Chapter 8 for further consideration of these issues.
[88] Town and Country Planning Act 1990, s 293A.
[89] SI 2015/1522. The 2015 Welsh Regulations replaced the Town and Country Planning (Fees for Applications and Deemed Applications) Regulations 1989 from 1 October 2015.

6.64 *Planning applications*

Application	English fee	Welsh fee
Category 1 erection of dwellinghouses (full application)	£385 per dwelling if less than 50, if more than 50 dwellings £19,049 and £115 per further dwelling, to maximum £250,000	£380 per dwelling if less than 50, if more than 50 dwellings £19,000 and £100 per further dwelling, to maximum £287,500
Category 2 Erection of buildings (other than categories 1, 3, 4, 5 or 7) (outline)	As Category 1 outline	As Category 1 outline
Category 2 Erection of buildings (other than categories 1, 3, 4, 5 or 7) (full)	If no new floorspace or up to 40m² £195, otherwise £385 per 75m²; if over 3,750m² then £19,049 and £115 per additional 75m² to maximum £250,000	If no new floorspace or up to 40m² £190, otherwise £380 per 75m² to maximum £287,500
Category 3 erection of agricultural buildings (other than category 4) (outline)	As Category 1 outline	As Category 1 outline
Category 3 erection of agricultural buildings (other than category 4) (full)	Up to 40m² floorspace £80, otherwise £385 per 540m²; if over 4,215m² then £19,049 and £115 per additional 75m² to maximum £250,000	Up to 465m² floorspace £70, otherwise £380 for the first 540m² and £380 per additional 75m² to maximum £287,500
Category 4 agricultural glasshouses	Up to 465m² gross floospace £80, otherwise £2,150	Up to 465m² gross floospace £70, otherwise £2,150
Category 5 erection, alteration or replacement of plant or machinery.	£385 per 0.1 hectare, but if site area over 5 hectares, £19,049 and £115 per additional 0.1 hectare to maximum £250,000	£385 per 0.1 hectare if site area under 5 hectares, otherwise £19,000 and £100 per additional 0.1 hectare to maximum £287,500
Category 6 enlargement, improvement or other alteration of existing dwellinghouses.	One dwellinghouse £172, two or more dwellinghouses £339	One dwellinghouse £190, two or more dwellinghouses £380
Category 7 operations within curtilage of existing dwellinghouse or erection or alteration of its means of enclosure (Category 7(a) in Wales)	£172	£190
Category 8 car parks, service road or access to existing single undertaking (Category 7(b) in Wales)	£195	£190
Category 9 exploratory drilling for oil or natural gas (Category 8 in Wales)	£423 per 0.1 hectare, but if site area over 7.5 hectares, £31,725 and £126 per additional 0.1 hectare to maximum £250,000	£380 per 0.1 hectare, but if site area over 7.5 hectares, £28,500 and £100 per additional 0.1 hectare to maximum £287,500

The application process **6.64**

Application	English fee	Welsh fee
Category 9A other operations for winning and working oil or natural gas	£214 per 0.1 hectare, but if site area over 15 hectares, £32,100 and £126 per additional 0.1 hectare to maximum £65,000	[Not a separate category but in Welsh category 9(a) below]
Category 10(a) any other operations for winning and working of minerals (Category 9(a) in Wales)	£195 per 0.1 hectare, but if site area over 15 hectares, £29,112 and £115 per additional 0.1 hectare to maximum £65,000	£190 per 0.1 hectare, but if site area over 15 hectares, £28,500 and £100 per additional 0.1 hectare to maximum £74,800
Category 10(b) any other operations (Category 9(b) in Wales)	£195 per 0.1 hectare to maximum £1,690	£190 per 0.1 hectare to maximum £287,500
Category 11 change of use of a a building to dwellinghouses (Category 10 in Wales)	£385 per additional dwellinghouse, if over 50 dwellinghouses, £19,049 and £115 per further dwelling, to maximum £250,000	£380 per additional dwellinghouse, if change from single dwelling to over 50 dwellinghouses, £19,000 and £100 per further dwelling, to maximum £287,500 (if the change is from some other use to dwellings then the same figures apply for each new dwelling)
Category 12 (a) the disposal of refuse or waste materials; (b) the deposit of material remaining after minerals have been extracted from land; or (c) the storage of minerals in the open (Category 11 in Wales)	As Category 10(a)	As Welsh category 9(a)
Category 13 Any other material change of use	£385	£380
Material change of use to playing field or ancillary operations (other than a building containing floorspace) by a not-for-profit club, society or other organisation with sport or recreation objects	£385[90]	£385[91]

---

[90] Town and Country Planning (Fees for Applications, Deemed Applications, Requests and Site Visits) (England) Regulations 2012, Sch 1, para 3.
[91] Town and Country Planning (Fees for Applications, Deemed Applications and Site Visits) (Wales) Regulations 2015, Sch 1, para 3.

6.65 *Planning applications*

Application	English fee	Welsh fee
Section 73 application	£195[92]	£190[93]
Retrospective section 73A application	If development without planning permission, what the fee would have been, otherwise £195[94]	If development without planning permission, what the fee would have been, otherwise £190[95]
Applications for replacement or renewal of planning permission	A renewal under under DMPO 2015, art 20 householder £57, major development £575, any other case £195[96]	Renewal if period for commencement not expired, £190[97]

6.65 Site area is the planning application site area (that is, within the red line).[98] In England for the winning and working of oil or natural gas (including exploratory drilling) only the above ground area is counted[99]. In categories 2, 3 or 4, gross floorspace is measured externally and fractions of 75m² are rounded up[100]. If a single planning application or reserved matters application contains alternative proposals then the fee is the highest fee for any of the alternatives plus half of the sum of the other proposals' fees[101].

Where applications include development within different categories then amounts are calculated for each category and the highest fee paid, subject to adjustments between particular categories[102].

Changes to fees for different applicants

6.66 Various exceptions, exemptions and reductions are provided for particular applicants.

---

[92] Town and Country Planning (Fees for Applications, Deemed Applications, Requests and Site Visits) (England) Regulations 2012, Sch 1, para 5.
[93] Town and Country Planning (Fees for Applications, Deemed Applications and Site Visits) (Wales) Regulations 2015, Sch 1, para 5.
[94] Town and Country Planning (Fees for Applications, Deemed Applications, Requests and Site Visits) (England) Regulations 2012, Sch 1, para 6.
[95] Town and Country Planning (Fees for Applications, Deemed Applications and Site Visits) (Wales) Regulations 2015, Sch 1, para 6.
[96] Town and Country Planning (Fees for Applications, Deemed Applications, Requests and Site Visits) (England) Regulations 2012, Sch 1, para 7.
[97] Town and Country Planning (Fees for Applications, Deemed Applications and Site Visits) (Wales) Regulations 2015, Sch 1, para 7.
[98] Town and Country Planning (Fees for Applications, Deemed Applications, Requests and Site Visits) (England) Regulations 2012, Sch 1, para 11; Town and Country Planning (Fees for Applications, Deemed Applications and Site Visits) (Wales) Regulations 2015, Sch 1, para 10. Any fraction is rounded up.
[99] Town and Country Planning (Fees for Applications, Deemed Applications, Requests and Site Visits) (England) Regulations 2012, Sch 1, para 11(1A).
[100] Town and Country Planning (Fees for Applications, Deemed Applications, Requests and Site Visits) (England) Regulations 2012, Sch 1, para 12; Town and Country Planning (Fees for Applications, Deemed Applications and Site Visits) (Wales) Regulations 2015, Sch 1, para 11.
[101] Town and Country Planning (Fees for Applications, Deemed Applications, Requests and Site Visits) (England) Regulations 2012, Sch 1, para 10; Town and Country Planning (Fees for Applications, Deemed Applications and Site Visits) (Wales) Regulations 2015, Sch 1, para 9.
[102] Town and Country Planning (Fees for Applications, Deemed Applications, Requests and Site Visits) (England) Regulations 2012, Sch 1, paras 13, 14; Town and Country Planning (Fees for Applications, Deemed Applications and Site Visits) (Wales) Regulations 2015, Sch 1, paras 12, 13.

No fee applies for improvements to access for disabled persons who are or will be resident in an existing dwellinghouse or for disabled access to and within buildings to which the public are admitted[103].

6.67 No fee is payable for a planning application made solely in respect of what would have been permitted development under the relevant GPDO were it not for an Article 4 direction or a planning condition on a planning permission removing those rights[104]. Similarly planning applications for changes of use in the same use class do not carry a fee if they are required solely by a condition on a planning permission[105]. Historically fees have not been charged for conservation area consent applications for the demolition of buildings. Since conservation area consent has now been replaced in England by the need to apply for planning permission for 'relevant demolition' within conservation areas, no fee is payable for planning applications solely for such demolition[106].

6.68 Fees are not payable for applications to consolidate existing mineral permissions, provided that they do not approve any new development[107]. This presumably reflects the benefits to the local planning authority of having a single permission and set of conditions with which to manage a site.

The fee for an application by or on behalf of a parish or community council is half of the normal rate[108].

6.69 For reserved matters applications the fee is calculated on the same basis as the outline planning permission fee for that category of development[109]. So if the reserved matters application is for the whole of the site then the fee is what would be the current outline fee for that site. A reserved matters application on part of the site is charged on the area or floorspace of that part. If an applicant has made previous reserved matters applications under that permission for which the full reserved matters fee for the site has been paid and no other person has applied for reserved

---

[103] Town and Country Planning (Fees for Applications, Deemed Applications, Requests and Site Visits) (England) Regulations 2012, reg 4; Town and Country Planning (Fees for Applications, Deemed Applications and Site Visits) (Wales) Regulations 2015, reg 4.
Town and Country Planning (Fees for Applications, Deemed Applications, Requests and Site Visits) (England) Regulations 2012.
[104] Town and Country Planning (Fees for Applications, Deemed Applications, Requests and Site Visits) (England) Regulations 2012, reg 5; Town and Country Planning (Fees for Applications, Deemed Applications and Site Visits) (Wales) Regulations 2015, reg 5.
[105] Town and Country Planning (Fees for Applications, Deemed Applications, Requests and Site Visits) (England) Regulations 2012, reg 6; Town and Country Planning (Fees for Applications, Deemed Applications and Site Visits) (Wales) Regulations 2015, reg 6.
[106] Town and Country Planning (Fees for Applications, Deemed Applications, Requests and Site Visits) (England) Regulations 2012, reg 5A.
[107] Town and Country Planning (Fees for Applications, Deemed Applications, Requests and Site Visits) (England) Regulations 2012, reg 7; Town and Country Planning (Fees for Applications, Deemed Applications and Site Visits) (Wales) Regulations 2015, reg 9.
[108] Town and Country Planning (Fees for Applications, Deemed Applications, Requests and Site Visits) (England) Regulations 2012, Sch 1, para 2; Town and Country Planning (Fees for Applications, Deemed Applications and Site Visits) (Wales) Regulations 2015, Sch 1, para 2.
[109] Town and Country Planning (Fees for Applications, Deemed Applications, Requests and Site Visits) (England) Regulations 2012, Sch 1, para 1; Town and Country Planning (Fees for Applications, Deemed Applications and Site Visits) (Wales) Regulations 2015, Sch 1, para 1.

6.70 *Planning applications*

matters, any further reserved matters application they make is charged at a low flat rate[110].

Design and access statements in England

6.70 A requirement to provide design and access statements with planning applications in England was introduced by amendments to the General Development Procedure Order in 2006[111]. The object of the statement is to explain how design principles and access have been addressed in the application scheme. These reflected material which was already being submitted on larger schemes but the requirements were drawn so widely that almost every new building, and any development in conservation areas, needed a design and access statement. Statements were often consequently unnecessarily expensive or incredibly banal. Amendments to the Development Management Procedure Order in 2013 severely curtailed the requirement for these statements.

6.71 In England design and access statements are governed by art 9 of the DMPO 2015. Such statements must be submitted with planning applications for[112]:

'(a) development which is major development;

(b) where any part of the development is in a conservation area or a World Heritage Site ("a designated area"), development consisting of:

  (i) the provision of one or more dwellinghouses; or

  (ii) the provision of a building or buildings where the floor space created by the development is 100 square metres or more'.

6.72 However, statements are not required for applications for planning permission:

(i) for development the subject of a previous permission but with different conditions which has not yet taken place (a s 73 application);

(ii) the renewal of a planning permission granted before 1 October 2010 which has not yet been begun but which has not expired[113] or the renewal of an outline planning permission granted before 1 October 2010 allowing development in phases where development has begun and the time limits for implementation have not expired[114];

(iii) for engineering or mining operations;

(iv) for a material change in use of the land or buildings;

(v) for development which is waste development.

---

[110] £385 in England and Wales: Town and Country Planning (Fees for Applications, Deemed Applications, Requests and Site Visits) (England) Regulations 2012, Sch 1, para 4; Town and Country Planning (Fees for Applications, Deemed Applications and Site Visits) (Wales) Regulations 2015, Sch 1, para 4.

[111] Made pursuant to a revision of the Town and Country Planning Act 1990, s 62(5) by the Planning and Compulsory Purchase Act 2004, s 42.

[112] The duty is in art 9(1) and the exceptions in art 9(4).

[113] See DMPO 2015, art 20(1)(b).

[114] See DMPO 2015, art 20(1)(c).

The application process **6.75**

6.73 Consequently the requirement applies to the following categories of major development[115]:

'(c) the provision of dwellinghouses where:

    (i) the number of dwellinghouses to be provided is 10 or more; or

    (ii) the development is to be carried out on a site having an area of 0.5 hectares or more and it is not known whether the development falls within sub-paragraph (c)(i);

(d) the provision of a building or buildings where the floor space to be created by the development is 1,000 square metres or more; or

(e) development carried out on a site having an area of 1 hectare or more'.

For present purposes minerals and waste development is excluded from the requirement for a design and access statement so the duty applies outside designated areas to schemes of at least 10 dwelling or 0.5 hectare residential development, 1,000m² buildings or 1 hectare sites.

6.74 An English design and access statement shall[116]:

'(a) explain the design principles and concepts that have been applied to the development;

(b) demonstrate the steps taken to appraise the context of the development and how the design of the development takes that context into account;

(c) explain the policy adopted as to access, and how policies relating to access in relevant local development documents have been taken into account;

(d) state what, if any, consultation has been undertaken on issues relating to access to the development and what account has been taken of the outcome of any such consultation; and

(e) explain how any specific issues which might affect access to the development have been addressed'.

Design and access statements are also required for listed building consent applications with particular regard to the listed building's special interest[117].

Design and access statements in Wales

6.75 Requirements for design and access statements in Wales are governed by art 7 of the DMPO (Wales) and are a little different from the English provisions. Design and access statements are required for planning applications *except* those for[118]:

'(a) engineering or mining operations;

---

[115] DMPO 2015, art 2(1).
[116] DMPO 2015, art 9(3).
[117] Planning (Listed Buildings and Conservation Areas) Regulations 1990, SI 1990/1519, reg 3A (unless the application is connected with an extension of time planning application under DMPO 2015, art 20(1)(b) or (c)): Planning (Listed Buildings and Conservation Areas) Regulations 1990, reg 3(1A).
[118] DMPO Wales, art 7(1). If the change of use necessitates access by an employee or involves the provision of services to the public or a section of the public then an access statement has to be produced.

6.76 *Planning applications*

(b) development of an existing dwellinghouse, or development within the curtilage of such a dwellinghouse for any purpose incidental to the enjoyment of the dwellinghouse as such; or

(c) a material change in the use of land or buildings'.

6.76 As in England, the design and access statement must explain the design principles and concepts used and how issues relating to access have been dealt with[119]. In relation to design the Welsh statement must[120]:

'(a) explain the design principles and concepts that have been applied to the following aspects of the development:

(i) environmental sustainability;

(ii) movement to, from and within the development;

(iii) character; and

(iv) community safety; and

(b) demonstrate the steps taken to appraise the context of the development and how the design of the development takes that context into account in relation to its proposed use and each of the aspects specified in sub-paragraph (a)'.

6.77 On access, the Welsh design and access statement must explain[121]:

'(a) the policy or approach adopted as to access and how policies relating to access in the development plan have been taken into account;

(b) how any specific issues which might affect access to the development have been addressed; and

(c) how features which ensure access to the development are to be maintained'.

6.78 If no design and access statement is required but a material change of use will 'necessitate access by an employee or involves the provision of services to the public or to a section of the public, with or without payment', then an access statement must address access issues in the same way[122].

Environmental statement

6.79 If EIA of the planning application is required then the application should be accompanied or followed by an environment statement under the relevant EIA Regulations. This is discussed in Chapter 7. To avoid confusion it is best if any other

---

[119] DMPO Wales, art 7(3).
[120] DMPO Wales, art 7(4). Several of the terms used are defined in art 7(6):
"amount' ('maint') means:
(a) in relation to residential development, the number of proposed units for residential use; and
(b) in relation to all other forms of development, the proposed floor space for each proposed use forming part of the development;
'character' ('cymeriad') includes any landscaping comprised in the development and the amount, layout, scale and appearance of the development; and
'context' ('cyd-destun') means the physical, social, economic and policy context of the development'.
[121] DMPO Wales, art 7(5).
[122] DMPO Wales, art 7(1)(c). The provision of services includes 'the provision of any goods or facilities': DMPO Wales, art 7(2).

environmental reports or appraisals which are submitted on a non-EIA basis are not called environmental statements or environmental assessments.

Local lists

6.80 Developments of any real size usually require much more information to be submitted to explain what is proposed and its effects than simply an application form, drawings and design and access statement. It is desirable that such material is submitted with the application rather than put in whilst the application is being considered. Later submission of consultants' reports and the like delay the application process, pose difficulties with consultation and may be too late to stave off a refusal for lack of information.

6.81 To counter these problems, amendments were made by the Planning and Compulsory Purchase Act 2004 to enable local planning authorities to prepare local lists of documents which had to be submitted with planning applications. Coming into force in 2006, these had the side effect of requiring excessive material to be provided, sometimes at considerable expense and delay.

6.82 By the Town and Country Planning Act 1990, s 62(3) a local planning authority may require that an application for planning permission must include such particulars and evidence in support of anything in or relating to the application as it thinks necessary. These requirements may not be inconsistent with the relevant DMPO[123], which therefore prohibits demands for extra copies of documents but has less effect in reducing requirements for evidence on further matters. Such particulars or evidence could only be required if they are on a list of requirements published by the local planning authority on its website for that purpose[124]. These local lists are now subject to further limitations on their scope.

6.83 There has been a recognition that these local list requirements have caused the submission of unnecessary material, delaying projects and increasing costs. A list of documents required for an application to be valid is inevitably a blunt tool. There will have been no assessment of or consultation on the application and officers dealing with validation will have little time to think about what is required. It may lead to applications being rejected because of reports which are not actually necessary and does not avoid the risk of further information being necessary after the application has been submitted. The result has been some cutting down of the local list provisions.

6.84 Section 62(4A) of the Town and Country Planning Act 1990 provides that[125]:

'the particulars or evidence the authority require to be included in the application:

(i) are reasonable having regard, in particular, to the nature and scale of the proposed development; and

(ii) are about a matter which it is reasonable to think will be a material consideration in the determination of the application'.

---

[123] Town and Country Planning Act 1990, s 62(4).
[124] DMPO 2015, art 11(3)(a), (b); DMPO 2010, art 10(3)(a), (b); DMPO Wales, art 8(2)(b), (c).
[125] Town and Country Planning Act 1990, s 62(4A), inserted by the Growth and Infrastructure Act 2013, s 6. The text was repeated in the DMPO 2010, art 10(3)(bb), now contained in DMPO 2015, art 11(3)(c).

6.85 *Planning applications*

This provision at present applies to England only, but is to be extended to Wales by the Planning (Wales) Act 2015[126] at a date to be announced.

6.85 In both England and Wales these lists are subject to further but different restrictions in the relevant DMPO. For applications made on or after 31 July 2013 in England, the list must have been published (or republished) during the two years before the application is made[127]. In Wales, the lists only apply if the application is for major development[128].

Acknowledgment of a valid application

6.86 Once a valid application has been received, the local planning authority must send an acknowledgment to the applicant in the terms, or substantially in the terms, of the letter in the relevant DMPO, Sch 1[129]. The letter includes optional text if the validity of the application is still to be checked. If a pre-validation acknowledgment is sent, then a letter confirming validity should be sent subsequently.

The effect of a failure to give notice or submit the required documents

6.87 There is a prohibition on considering invalid planning applications. Section 327A of the Town and Country Planning Act 1990 provides that a local planning authority must not entertain an application which fails to comply with a requirement imposed by the Act or a provision[130] made under it as to:

'(a) the form or manner in which the application must be made;
(b) the form or content of any document or other matter which accompanies the application'.

6.88 Additionally the Town and Country Planning Act 1990, s 65(5) provides, in respect of the duties to notify owners and agricultural tenants of the application site and to certify to the authority that has been done:

'A local planning authority shall not entertain an application for planning permission unless any requirements imposed by virtue of this section have been satisfied'.

6.89 Section 65(5) therefore says that the local planning authority may not entertain an application unless any requirements imposed by virtue of s 65 have been complied with. Section 327A imposes a similar requirement, more generally. Since DMPO 2015, arts 13 and 14 say that an applicant 'shall' do various things in respect of notice to owners, these are requirements to which ss 65 and 327A apply.

---

[126] Planning (Wales) Act 2015, s 28, deleting reference to England.
[127] DMPO 2015, art 11(3)(d); DMPO 2010, art 10(3)(c).
[128] DMPO Wales, art 8(2)(a).
[129] DMPO 2015, art 11(2); DMPO Wales, art 8(1).
[130] In *R (on the application of Obar Camden Ltd) v London Borough of Camden* [2015] EWHC 2475 (Admin) Stewart J held that 'provision' referred to provision made under a development order (by reason of s 62(1)–(3)) and did not include a local list adopted by the local planning authority: see paras 45–47.

The application process **6.90**

6.90 The effect can be summarised as follows:

(i) the prohibition in those sections is absolute. There is no discretion for a local planning authority to determine an application where there is a breach, regardless of whether there might be prejudice to third parties;

(ii) consequently if a local planning authority becomes aware of a failure to comply at any point in the process then it cannot determine the application and must insist upon the error being corrected;

(iii) an error can be corrected part way through the application process. For example, notice can be given to owners and a correct certificate submitted prior to a permission being issued. Consultation and other processing which has already been carried out would still be taken into account and does not necessarily have to be redone[131]. The local planning authority should consider whether the production of new material required to validate the application requires consultation and publicity to be redone in whole or part;

(iv) the periods for determining applications, for the purpose of the right to appeal, run from the receipt of a valid application[132];

(v) if the validity of an application is disputed then the applicant can appeal to the Minister following the expiry of the determination period which for, these purposes, runs from the receipt of the application. If the application is valid then time ran from that point. If it is invalid then the appeal would fail;

(vi) the Minister has no power to determine an appeal on an invalid application and either the Minister or inspector should refuse to deal with it[133]. This is even if the error is only spotted in an appeal[134];

(vii) an invalidity in the application is a ground of challenge to the grant of planning permission by the local planning authority or the Minister. In those circumstances the effect of the error and the identity of the claimant may be critically important to whether the decision is quashed. For example, if an owner was not notified by the applicant, relief will be affected by whether they were aware of the application and that it included their land, whether they can be found or have a view on the application, and whether they are supporting the challenge to the decision[135]. However if a local planning authority or Minister grants permission knowing that the application is invalid in breach of s 65 or 327A, then the court should have no mercy and quash the decision. The rule of law cannot tolerate deliberate contraventions of statutory prohibitions by public authorities.

---

[131] The view expressed in *R (on the application of Pridmore) v Salisbury District Council* [2004] EWHC 2511 (Admin), [2005] JPL 655 at para 26 per Newman J that a fresh application is required is going too far.

[132] DMPO 2015, art 34(4); DMPO 2010, art 29(3); DMPO Wales, art 22(3).

[133] *Newcastle-upon-Tyne City Council v Secretary of State for Communities and Local Government* [2009] EWHC 3469 (Admin), [2010] JPL 904 at paras 34–37 per Langstaff J, which is to be preferred to the obiter indication to the contrary in *Parker v Secretary of State for Communities and Local Government* [2009] EWHC 2330 (Admin) at para 31 per Keith Lindblom QC. The court has a discretion not to quash an unlawful decision but a public authority has no discretion to act unlawfully.

[134] The classic, but real, example is a failure to complete the agricultural holdings certificate on a purely urban site in an inner London borough.

[135] See *Main v Swansea City Council* (1985) 49 P & CR 26. Similarly a misdescription of the applicant on the form might not lead to a quashing: *R (on the application of Park Pharmacy Trust) v Plymouth City Council* [2008] EWHC 445 (Admin), [2008] 2 P & CR 11 at paras 12–14 per Sullivan J.

6.91 *Planning applications*

Determining the validity of a planning application

6.91 If the local planning authority refuses to accept that an application is valid and the applicant disagrees, then the usual remedy is to appeal to the Minister against the refusal or non-determination of the application. A notice procedure has been introduced in England to challenge requirements to produce documents under local lists but the ultimate remedy remains a planning appeal.

6.92 In *R v Secretary of State for the Environment, Transport and the Regions, ex p Bath and North East Somerset Council*[136] the Court of Appeal held that where a local planning authority rejected a planning application as invalid, the applicant was able to appeal for non-determination and ask the Secretary of State to determine the validity of the application. Pill LJ held that the general scheme of the legislation meant that the local planning authority was not the sole arbiter of the validity of planning applications. An applicant was able to appeal and have the issue resolved by the Secretary of State rather than having to proceed by judicial review.

6.93 Provisions on the validity of planning applications have changed since the *BANES* decision but the ability of the Secretary of State to decide validity was maintained by the High Court in *Newcastle-upon-Tyne City Council v Secretary of State for Communities and Local Government*[137] with one important qualification (since reversed by legislation). *Newcastle* considered the Town and Country Planning Act 1990, s 62(3) which allows the local planning authority to require that an application for permission must include particulars and evidence which it thinks necessary. A valid application for development order purposes was defined as one which includes that material, taken from the authority's published local list of requirements[138]. Langstaff J held that the requirement imposed was a matter for the local planning authority (subject to judicial review) and could not be determined by the Secretary of State[139]. Consequently an appellant could contend that an authority's requirements had been met, but not that they were excessive or unnecessary.

6.94 This aspect of *Newcastle* has been reversed by the DMPO 2010 and 2015, albeit in a complicated manner. If the applicant contends that the information required by the local planning authority under its local list (as distinct from requirements of the DMPO) are not reasonable, having regard to the nature and scale of the proposed development, or are not about a matter which it is reasonable to think will be a material consideration in the determination of the application[140], then it may send a notice to the local planning authority setting out the particulars or evidence required which fail this test, with reasons, and requesting the authority to waive the requirement[141]. The authority must then either drop the requirement (a response known as a validation notice) or maintain it (a non-validation notice)[142]. The authority should respond within the time period for the determination of the planning application or in the seven working days following receipt of the applicant's notice, whichever is later[143].

---

[136] [1999] 1 WLR 1759.
[137] [2009] EWHC 3469 (Admin), [2010] 2 P & CR 5.
[138] DMPO 2010, art 29(3).
[139] *Newcastle* at paras 36, 38.
[140] See DMPO 2015, art 34(6)(c).
[141] DMPO 2015, art 12(1), (2).
[142] DMPO 2015, art 12(3).
[143] DMPO 2015, art 12(4). There is a typo in DMPO 2015, in that art 12(3) refers to the date being specified in 'paragraph (3)' when it should say 'paragraph (4)'.

A non-validation notice does not amount to a refusal of the planning application, in the sense that it could be validated if the information is provided or the requirement subsequently withdrawn.

6.95 The applicant may appeal for the non-determination of a planning application including an application where the local planning authority has served a non-validation notice[144]. Consequently a ground of appeal is that the authority ought not to have refused to validate the application on that basis. It then becomes a matter for the Secretary of State or an inspector to decide whether the requirements are reasonable in the terms of art 34(6)(c).

THE PLANNING REGISTER

6.96 Various details of planning applications and permissions must be kept on the planning register and open for 'inspection by the public at all reasonable hours'[145]. This is distinct from the totality of the material held by the local planning authority on an application, which is usually referred to as the planning file. Planning registers are kept by the local planning authority, except that in England outside Greater London or the former metropolitan counties the duty falls on any district planning authority, unitary authority or national park authority even where the planning authority for a particular application is the county council, development corporation, enterprise zone authority, housing action trust or the Homes and Communities Agency[146]. Every local planning authority keeps its own register in Wales[147].

6.97 The contents of the register are prescribed by the relevant DMPO, albeit in similar terms with respect to planning applications. The planning application section of the register has to be kept in two Parts[148]: Part 1 contains various details of applications until they are 'finally disposed of'; Part 2 is a permanent record of applications (containing some of the same material as Part 1), decisions upon them and consequential decisions. This distinction is historic, unnecessary and few registers seem to be kept in full accordance with the statutory requirements in any event.

6.98 For the purposes of the planning register Part 1 an application is finally disposed of when the time limit for appealing to the Minister has expired, any appeal or call-in has been determined without a High Court application under s 288 being made, or any such High Court proceedings have finally concluded or the planning application has been withdrawn[149].

---

[144] DMPO 2015, arts 34(1)–(3), 37(2).
[145] Town and Country Planning Act 1990, s 69(8).
[146] Town and Country Planning Act 1990, Sch 1, para 14 and DMPO 2015, art 40(1).
[147] DMPO Wales, art 29(1).
[148] DMPO 2015, art 40(2). The planning register in Wales also has two parts for planning applications see DMPO Wales, art 29(2), (3).
[149] DMPO 2015, art 40(13); DMPO Wales, art 29(15). There is no time limit for making a non-determination appeal in Wales: DMPO Wales, art 26(2), amended by the Town and Country Planning (Development Management Procedure) (Wales) (Amendment) Order 2015, art 8. If the period for appealing to the Minister against non-determination has expired, the local planning authority can still determine the application and the applicant can obtain a mandatory order in judicial review that it do so: *Bovis Homes (Scotland) Ltd v Inverclyde District Council* [1982] SLT 473.

6.99 *Planning applications*

6.99 Part 1 of the register contains any planning application and[150]:

'any application for approval of reserved matters made in respect of an outline planning permission granted on such an application, made or sent to the local planning register authority and not finally disposed of:

(a) a copy ... of the application together with any accompanying plans and drawings;

(b) a copy ... of any planning obligation or section 278 agreement proposed or entered into in connection with the application;

(c) a copy ... of any other planning obligation or section 278 agreement entered into in respect of the land the subject of the application which the applicant considers relevant; and

(d) particulars of any modification to any planning obligation or section 278 agreement included in Part 1 of the register in accordance with sub-paragraphs (b) and (c)'.

6.100 Part 2 of the register contains[151]:

'in respect of every application for planning permission relating to the local planning register authority's area:

(a) a copy ... of the application and of plans and drawings submitted in relation thereto and of any accompanying design and access statement provided in accordance with article 9;

(b) particulars of any direction given under the 1990 Act or this Order in respect of the application;

(c) the decision, if any, of the local planning authority in respect of the application, including details of any conditions subject to which permission was granted, the date of such decision and the name of the local planning authority;

(d) the reference number, the date and effect of any decision of the Secretary of State in respect of the application, whether on appeal, on an application under section 293A(2) of the 1990 Act (urgent Crown development: application) or on a reference under section 77 of the 1990 Act (reference of applications to Secretary of State);

(e) the date of any subsequent approval (whether approval of reserved matters or any other approval required) given in relation to the application;

(f) a copy ... of any planning obligation or section 278 agreement entered into in connection with any decision of the local planning authority or the Secretary of State in respect of the application;

(g) a copy ...of any other planning obligation or section 278 agreement taken into account by the local planning authority or the Secretary of State when making the decision; and

(h) particulars of any modification to or discharge of any planning obligation or section 278 agreement included in Part 2 of the register in accordance with sub-paragraphs (f) or (g) or paragraph (6) [obligations or agreements in enforcement notice appeals]'.

DECLINING TO DETERMINE APPLICATIONS

6.101 In certain circumstances local planning authorities are empowered to decline to determine planning applications if they are similar to other applications

---

[150] DMPO 2015, art 40(3). DMPO Wales, art 29(2) is to the same effect.
[151] DMPO 2015, art 40(4). DMPO Wales, art 29(3) is to the same effect.

Declining to determine applications **6.104**

which are being or have been recently determined. In England these arise in three broad categories, denoted by different provisions of the Town and Country Planning Act 1990:

(i) subsequent applications (s 70A);

(ii) overlapping applications (s 70B);

(iii) retrospective applications where an enforcement notice has been issued (s 70C).

6.102 A version of s 70A operates in Wales, but s 70B has not been introduced there. Section 70C is prospectively inserted into the Welsh legislation by the Planning (Wales) Act 2015[152] from a date to be appointed

The application must meet one of the requirements in these provisions, but even if it does, the local planning authority have a discretion whether to decline to determine the application.

6.103 Section 70A applies if one of four conditions has been met and 'the authority think there has been no significant change in the relevant considerations since the relevant event'[153]. Under s 70A the conditions relate to any of the following events occurring in the two years prior to the planning application being made:

(i) the Minister having refused a similar application made directly to the Secretary of State under section 62A or called-in[154];

(ii) the Minister having refused an appeal against the refusal or non-determination of a similar application[155];

(iii) the Minister having refused a similar application deemed to have been made in an enforcement notice appeal[156]; or

(iv) the local planning authority have refused 'more than one similar application' and there has been no appeal 'any such refusal or, if there has been such an appeal, it has been withdrawn'[157].

6.104 Section 70B deals with overlapping application when a similar application:

(i) is made on the same day as the application[158];

(ii) is under consideration by the local planning authority and the determination period has not expired[159];

(iii) is under consideration by the Minister under a s 62A application, a call-in or a s 78 appeal[160]; or

---

[152] Planning (Wales) Act 2015, s 32.
[153] Town and Country Planning Act 1990, s 70A(1), (4A).
[154] Town and Country Planning Act 1990, s 70A(2). The call-in would be under s 77 or the unused s 76A power.
[155] Town and Country Planning Act 1990, s 70A(3).
[156] Town and Country Planning Act 1990, s 70A(4A), (4B).
[157] Town and Country Planning Act 1990, s 70A(4).
[158] Town and Country Planning Act 1990, s 70B(1)(a).
[159] Town and Country Planning Act 1990, s 70B(2).
[160] Town and Country Planning Act 1990, s 70B(3). The appeal could be against refusal or the grant of planning permission subject to conditions or non-determination.

6.105 *Planning applications*

(iv) has been granted or refused by the local planning authority or not decided within the determination period and the time for appealing to the Secretary of State has not yet expired[161].

6.105 The critical definition in ss 70A and 70B is that of a 'similar application'[162]:

> 'An application for planning permission is similar to another application if (and only if) the local planning authority think that the development and the land to which the applications relate are the same or substantially the same'.

Any application on different parts of the same building might be for different land (a point which is more apparent if the building is divided into different ownerships or control). In *R(on the application of Harrison) v Richmond upon Thames London Borough Council* Nicholas Paines QC held that:

> 'when Parliament used the concept of similarity or substantial sameness in section 70A it had in mind in particular points of similarity that were relevant to the question whether the section 70A power should be used. The fact that, as in this case, a fresh application shares with the old one a characteristic that was judged fatal to the success of the previous application is, in my view, a relevant point of similarity'[163].

6.106 Even if applications are similar the authority may only refuse to determine an application if the other requirements of ss 70A or 70B are met. Under s 70A there must have been a Ministerial refusal of planning permission or more than one similar planning application have been refused by the local planning authority. Additionally under s 70A the local planning authority must consider that there has been no significant change in the relevant considerations since the previous decision. An important change to policy would be significant, as might be other planning decisions on or near the site, appeal decisions or changes in economic circumstances. Section 70B deals with overlaps in particular circumstances.

6.107 Under s 70C a local planning authority *may* decline to determine a planning application if approving the application would involve granting planning permission for the whole or part of any matters specified in pre-existing enforcement notice as a breach of planning control[164]. A 'pre-existing enforcement notice' is an enforcement notice issued before the application was received by the local planning authority[165].

6.108 For the purposes of declining to consider a planning application, the pre-existing enforcement notice would appear to have to still be in existence, without having been withdrawn or quashed, since s 70C(1) refers to 'the land to which a pre-existing enforcement notice relates'. The authority is given a discretion not to determine the application, so it must act reasonably and with regard to relevant considerations. If the applicant's motive is to delay enforcement then that is a reason for refusing to determine the application[166]. Good reasons not to decline to consider the application would include a change in circumstances, the unlawful development

---

[161] Town and Country Planning Act 1990, s 70B(4).
[162] Town and Country Planning Act 1990, ss 70A(8) and 70B(5).
[163] [2013] EWHC 1677 (Admin) at para 38. Followed in *R (on the application of Gill) v Central Bedfordshire Council* [2015] EWHC 3458 (Admin) at paras 45–47 per Lang J.
[164] Town and Country Planning Act 1990, s 70C(1).
[165] Town and Country Planning Act 1990, s 70C(2).
[166] *R (on the application of Wingrove) v Stratford-on-Avon District Council* [2015] EWHC 287 (Admin), [2015] PTSR 708. Cranston J suggested that there was 'a legislative steer in favour of exercising the discretion' not to determine an application, at para 30.

could be acceptable if planning permission were granted subject to conditions, or the planning application related only to a part of the enforcement notice subject matter which might be acceptable. If the authority does decline to consider the application then the applicant has no right of appeal to the Secretary of State but instead could only challenge the decision by judicial review.

6.109 If any of the provisions of ss 70A–70C apply the local planning authority still have a discretion whether to decline to determine the application. Advice on the use of ss 70A and 70B had been contained in circular 08/2005[167] but this was cancelled with the publication of the *Planning Practice Guidance* in March 2014[168]. In exercising the discretion, it is irrelevant that the application is retrospective and would alter or amend a building which is subject to an extant enforcement notice[169].

6.110 On the discretion under s 70A the *Planning Practice Guidance* says[170]:

> '**Must a local planning authority decline to determine repeat planning applications?**
>
> Where an authority considers that an application is similar, it is not automatically obliged to decline to determine the application. The purpose of these powers is to inhibit the use of "repeat" applications that the local planning authority believes are submitted with the intention of, over time, wearing down opposition to proposed developments. They are, however, designed to be flexible and to give local planning authorities the discretion to entertain "repeat" planning applications where they are satisfied that a genuine attempt has been made to overcome the planning objections which led to rejection of the previous proposal or there has been a material change in circumstances'.

STATEMENTS OF COMMUNITY INVOLVEMENT AND LEGITIMATE EXPECTATIONS

6.111 In addition to the requirements imposed by statute and directions, public authorities may impose requirements on themselves by their own procedural rules and policies. A council's procedural rules will usually be set out in its constitution. This will explain how decisions are to be taken. It may include planning procedures, possibly in a planning code of conduct. Authorities may promise to do more than consultation and publicity than is required by legislation. Many of these promises were contained in relatively informal documents, but the process was formalised in 2004.

6.112 Statements of community involvement are required by the Planning and Compulsory Purchase Act 2004, s 18. Section 18(2) provides, as relevant:

> 'The statement of community involvement is a statement of the authority's policy as to the involvement in the exercise of the authority's functions under sections 19, 26 and 28 of this Act and Part 3 of the principal Act of persons who appear to the authority to have an interest in matters relating to development in their area'.

The principal Act is the Town and Country Planning Act 1990, Part 3 of which is concerned with planning applications. The statement of community involvement therefore sets out the Council's policy as to the involvement of the public in planning applications.

---

[167] And criticised by the High Court in *R (on the application of Skillcrown Homes Ltd) v Dartford Borough Council* [2014] EWHC 365 (Admin), [2014] JPL 988.
[168] See CLG's List of guidance documents cancelled by the planning practice guidance suite.
[169] *Gill* at paras 22, 62 per Lang J.
[170] *Planning Practice Guidance*, para 14-058-20140306.

6.113 *Planning applications*

6.113 The status of statements of community involvement was considered by the Court of Appeal in *R (on the application of Majed) v London Borough of Camden*[171] where Sullivan LJ said:

> '14 On behalf of the respondent and the interested party, [Counsel] submitted that there was no legitimate expectation. It was submitted that, since there was a specific statutory code – the General Development Procedure Order ("GDPO") – which regulates the balance between the various interests, applicants and local residents, as to who should and who should not be notified, it would be wrong to impose some rigid requirement to notify in accordance with the terms of Annex 6. It was submitted that this would upset the balance that had been struck by the statutory requirements. It seems to me that reference to the statutory requirements is of no real assistance. Legitimate expectation comes into play when there is no statutory requirement. If there is a breach of a statutory requirement then that breach can be the subject of proceedings. Legitimate expectation comes into play when there is a promise or a practice to do more than that which is required by statute. It seems to me that the Statement is a paradigm example of such a promise and a practice. As I understood it, [Counsel for LB Camden] accepted that this appellant falls within Annex 6. ... It was submitted by the respondent and the interested party that, even though there was a clear statement that a person in the position of the appellant would be sent a letter, there was nevertheless no unequivocal assurance that they would be notified. I am quite unable to accept that submission given the clear terms of paragraph 1.3 of the Statement which tells the public that when the Statement is adopted by the council it is "required to follow what it says". It would be difficult to imagine a more unequivocal statement as to who would, and who would not, be notified.
>
> 15 There was therefore, in my judgment, a clear breach of the appellant's legitimate expectation that he would be notified of planning applications, such as the application made by the interested party, in accordance with the terms of annex 6 to the Statement'.

A legitimate expectation in this context is procedural – it will give a right as to the procedure to be followed but not as to the outcome of the application. A legitimate expectation is not binding in all cases, but there needs to be an exceptional justification for not following it. As a final matter there may be some circumstances where it is irrational for a public authority to fail to consult (or reconsult) a particular person[172].

6.114 *Majed* was followed in *R (on the application of Kelly) v London Borough of Hounslow*[173], where a letter from the local planning authority notifying interested persons of the application created a legitimate expectation that the procedure it outlined would be followed. In that case the letter had said that those making representations would be notified of any committee meeting on the application.

6.115 Legitimate expectation also led to the quashing of a planning permission on consultation and delegated authority grounds in *R (on the application of Vieira)*

---

[171] [2009] EWCA Civ 1029, [2010] JPL 621.
[172] See, in the context of conservation area designation: *R (on the application of Trillium (Prime) Property GP Ltd) v London Borough of Tower Hamlets* [2011] EWHC 146 (Admin).
[173] [2010] EWHC 1256 (Admin) at para 18 per Ian Dove QC, summary at [2010] JPL 1467. An earlier case of an unlawful failure to notify objectors of the date of a committee meeting is *R v Alnwick District Council, ex p Robson* [1997] EWHC Admin 993. Other cases where statements of community involvement have given rise to legitimate expectations include *R (on the application of Embleton Parish Council) v Northumberland County Council* [2013] EWHC 3631 (Admin), [2014] Env LR 16 at para 149 per Judge Behrens; *R (on the application of Joicey) v Northumberland County Council* [2014] EWHC 3657 (Admin), [2015] PTSR 622 at paras 43–45 per Cranston J.

Statements of community involvement and legitimate expectations **6.117**

v London Borough of Camden[174]. Next-door neighbours challenged the retention of an upper ground floor conservatory and screen. The main planning issues were overlooking from the conservatory's balcony and stairs leading to the garden, and the overbearing effect of the screen erected to try to avoid this.

6.116 The court held that the decision was unlawful on the following grounds:

(i) the Council was in breach of a legitimate expectation created by its statement of community involvement that it would consult objectors on the revised drawing;

(ii) the Council was in breach of a legitimate expectation created by the statement of community involvement and its published procedure for members briefings that reports would be made available on its website for comment prior to the Panel meetings;

(iii) the Council was in breach of a legitimate expectation created by its planning protocol, Camden Planning Development Control Members Briefing and its website in failing to consult a members briefing panel in June 2010 on whether the application should be referred to committee.

The case illustrates the breadth of publicity and consultation obligations as well as the need for care in how decisions are taken.

Examples of breaches of legitimate expectation

6.117 Examples of breaches of legitimate expectation to carry out consultation which have been created by a representation include:

(i) failing to consult at all;

(ii) failing to notify neighbours beyond the statutory requirements[175];

(iii) failing to notify objectors of amendments to applications[176];

(iv) failure to put reports on the Council's website prior to a meeting[177];

(v) sending notice of a planning committee meeting so late that it arrived on the day of the meeting or failing to inform someone of the meeting at all[178];

(vi) failing to put application documents on the Council's website[179];

(vii) making a decision before the end of the consultation period[180].

---

[174] [2012] EWHC 287 (Admin).
[175] *R (on the application of Majed) v London Borough of Camden* [2009] EWCA Civ 1029, [2010] JPL 621.
[176] *R (on the application of Vieira) v London Borough of Camden* [2012] EWHC 287 (Admin); *R (on the application of Embleton Parish Council) v Northumberland County Council* [2013] EWHC 3631 (Admin), [2014] Env LR 16 at para 149; *R (on the application of Gerber) v Wiltshire Council* [2015] EWHC 524 (Admin), [2015] JPL 1021 at paras 14, 57–62, 82 per Dove J.
[177] *Vieira*.
[178] *R (on the application of Kelly) v London Borough of Hounslow* [2010] EWHC 1256 (Admin); *R (on the application of Embleton Parish Council) v Northumberland County Council* [2013] EWHC 3631 (Admin), [2014] Env LR 16.
[179] *R (on the application of Joicey) v Northumberland County Council* [2014] EWHC 3657 (Admin); [2015] PTSR 622.
[180] *R (on the application of Silus Investments SA) v London Borough of Hounslow* [2015] EWHC 358 (Admin), [2015] BLGR 391.

6.118 *Planning applications*

CONSULTATION AND PUBLICITY

Publicity

6.118 In England the main requirements for publicity are under the DMPO 2015, art 15 and Sch 3[181]. Similar provisions are contained in the DMPO Wales, art 12 and Sch 3. Additional publicity will be required of post-application submissions of environmental statements and responses to requests for further information under the EIA Regulations.

6.119 Planning applications fall into one of three categories for publicity purposes.

The greatest level publicity is required for applications which[182]:

(i) are subject to EIA;

(ii) do not accord with the development plan; or

(iii) would affect a public footpath, bridleway, restricted byway or byway open to all traffic[183].

6.120 These applications are publicised by[184]:

(i) a site notice being displayed on or near the land for not less than 21 days; and

(ii) publication of a notice in a newspaper circulating in the locality.

6.121 Applications for major development, but which do not fall into the above category, are publicised by[185]:

(i)

    (a) a site notice being displayed on or near the land for not less than 21 days; or

    (b) serving the notice on any adjoining owner or occupier; and

(ii) publication of a notice in a newspaper circulating in the locality.

6.122 All other planning applications are publicised by[186]:

(i) a site notice being displayed on or near the land for not less than 21 days; or

(ii) serving the notice on any adjoining owner or occupier.

6.123 In England all planning applications must be publicised on the local planning authority's website[187]. Welsh planning authorities can choose whether to have a website to publicise planning applications, but if it does then notice of each

---

[181] Formerly DMPO 2010, art 13 and Sch 5.
[182] DMPO 2015, art 15(2); DMPO 2010, art 13(2); DMPO Wales, art 12(2).
[183] These are the rights of way to which the Wildlife and Countryside Act 1981, Part 3 applies, as referred to in DMPO 2015, art 15(2)(c) and DMPO Wales, art 12(2)(c).
[184] DMPO 2015, art 15(3), (7); DMPO Wales, art 12(3).
[185] DMPO 2015, art 15(4), (7); DMPO Wales, art 12(4).
[186] DMPO 2015, art 15; DMPO 2010, art 13; DMPO Wales, art 12.
[187] DMPO 2015, art 15(7); DMPO 2010, art 13(7).

application must be given on it[188]. In practice the Welsh authorities do use websites for those purposes. In England and Wales the website notice must state[189]:

'(a) the address or location of the proposed development;

(b) a description of the proposed development;

(c) the date by which any representations about the application must be made, which must not be before the last day of the period of 14 days beginning with the date on which the information is published;

(d) where and when the application may be inspected;

(e) how representations may be made about the application; and

(f) that, in the case of a householder or minor commercial application, in the event of an appeal that proceeds by way of the expedited procedure, any representations made about the application will be passed to the Secretary of State and there will be no opportunity to make further representations'.

The local advertisement, site notice and notice to neighbours (and under art 16, rail infrastructure managers) must be in the form in Sch 3 to the respective DMPO, or in a form substantially to the same effect[190].

Planning applications affecting the setting of listed buildings or conservation areas in England

6.124 Further publicity arrangements apply to certain planning applications affecting listed buildings and conservation areas in England. Under the Planning (Listed Buildings and Conservation Areas) Regulations 1990, reg 5A, publicity is required for planning applications where 'the authority ... think that the development would affect (a) the setting of a listed building; or (b) the character or appearance of a conservation area'[191]. The local planning authority is required to:[192]

'(a) publish in a local newspaper circulating in the locality in which the land is situated a notice indicating the nature of the development in question and naming a place within the locality where a copy of the application, and of all plans and other documents submitted to it, will be open to inspection by the public at all reasonable hours during the period of 21 days beginning with the date of publication of the notice;

(b) for not less than 21 days display on or near the said building a notice containing the same particulars as are required to be published in accordance with sub-paragraph (a); and

(c) for not less than 21 days publish on a website maintained by the local planning authority the following information:

---

[188] DMPO Wales, art 12(7).
[189] DMPO 2015, art 15(7); DMPO Wales, art 12(7). The expedited procedure was introduced for those appeals in Wales from 22 June 2015.
[190] DMPO 2015, art 15(10); DMPO Wales, art 12(10).
[191] Planning (Listed Buildings and Conservation Areas) Regulations 1990, SI 1990/1519, reg 5A(1). For consideration of when this applies see *R (on the application of Friends of Hethel) v South Norfolk Council* [2010] EWCA Civ 894, [2012] 1 WLR 1216; *R (on the application of Embleton Parish Council) v Northumberland County Council* [2013] EWHC 3631 (Admin), [2013] Env LR 16.
[192] Planning (Listed Buildings and Conservation Areas) Regulations 1990, reg 5A(2). The local planning authority may not determine the application until the end of all of the 21-day period for this publicity (and any related consultation with Historic England) and must take into account any representations relating to the application which are received in that period: reg 5A(4).

6.125 *Planning applications*

   (i) the address or location of the development in question;
   (ii) the nature of the development;
   (iii) the date by which any representations about the application must be made, which shall not be before the last day of the period of 21 days beginning with the date on which the information is published;
   (iv) where and when the application may be inspected; and
   (v) how representations may be made about the application'.

Statutory consultees

6.125 Legislation draws a distinction between publicity to neighbours and the public at large and consultation with particular bodies chosen for their expertise or role. The principal consultation requirements are set out in the DMPOs: art 18 and Sch 4 in England; art 14 and Sch 4 in Wales. However a number of other consultation duties are scattered through statute, regulations and directions. As mentioned above, statements of community involvement and other policies may give rise to legitimate expectations that other persons will be consulted.

6.126 Under the DMPO local planning authorities are required to consult the bodies listed in the Schedule in the relevant circumstances except where:

(i) the local planning authority is that body[193], for example where one council is both the local planning authority and the local highway authority. In those circumstances it would be irrational not to consult the council's relevant officers;

(ii) in England, the county planning authority is required to consult a district planning authority under other provisions, in which case those apply[194];

(iii) the person mentioned has advised the local planning authority that they do not wish to be consulted[195]. This exception does not apply to consultation with the Health and Safety Executive, the Environment Agency and Natural England or the Natural Resources Body for Wales on sites subject to the Control of Major Accident Hazards Directive 96/82/EC[196];

(iv) in England, the development is subject to any standing advice provided by the person to the local planning authority in relation to the category of development[197], unless the development is subject to EIA or the standing advice was issued more than two years before the date of the planning application and the advice has not been amended or confirmed as being extant within that period[198];

(v) it is an extension of time application under art 20 of the DMPO in England and not EIA development[199].

---

[193] DMPO 2015, art 18(1)(a); DMPO 2010, art 16(1)(a); DMPO Wales, art 14(1)(a).
[194] Under the Town and Country Planning Act 1990, Sch 1, para 7 or DMPO 2010, art 22: see DMPO 2015, art 18(1)(b); DMPO 2010, art 16(1)(b).
[195] DMPO 2015, art 18(1)(c); DMPO 2010, art 16(1)(b); DMPO Wales, art 14(1)(b). This may be advice specific to the application because of pre-application advice, or general advice for classes of applications.
[196] DMPO 2015, art 18(2), Sch 4, para (zb); DMPO 2010, art 16(2), Sch 5, para (zc); DMPO Wales, art 14(2), Sch 4, para (x).
[197] DMPO 2015, art 18(1)(d); DMPO 2010, art 16(1)(d).
[198] DMPO 2015, art 18(3); DMPO 2010, art 16(3).
[199] DMPO 2015, art 18(1)(e); DMPO 2010, art 16(1)(e) (which had referred to art 18 extension of time applications).

6.127 The consultation requirements in the schedules to the respective DMPOs are:

Issue	English consultee DMPO 2015, Sch 4	English consultee DMPO 2010, Sch 5	Welsh consultee, Sch 4	Observations
Likely to affect land in a National Park	(a) National Park Authority	(a)		
Likely to affect land in Greater London, metropolitan county, outside national park	(b) Local planning authority	(b)		
Likely to affect land in non-metropolitan county, outside national park	(c) District planning authority (or if unitary county, the county)	(c)		
Likely to affect land in the area of another local planning authority			(a) The local planning authority concerned	Since Welsh local planning authorities are unitary, this requirement is to the same effect as paragraphs (a)–(c) of the English DMPO
Urgent Crown development likely to affect land in parish or community	(d) The parish council	(d)	(b) the community Council	The Housing and Planning Bill proposes to extend this duty to consultation with a neighbourhood forum on applications within its area[200].

---

[200] Proposed Town and Country Planning Act 1990, Sch 1, para 8A, to be inserted by the Housing and Planning Bill 2015, cl 103 (as published following Public Bill Committee in the House of Commons).

6.127 *Planning applications*

Issue	English consultee DMPO 2015, Sch 4	English consultee DMPO 2010, Sch 5	Welsh consultee, Sch 4	Observations
Certain classes of development in areas notified by Health and Safety Executive vicinity of toxic, highly reactive, explosive or inflammable substances	(e) Health and Safety Executive	(e)	(c) Health and Safety Executive	Consider the thresholds in the DMPO
Certain classes of development in areas notified by Office for Nuclear Regulation	(f) Office for Nuclear Regulation	(ea)	(ca) Office for Nuclear Regulation	Consider the thresholds in the DMPO
Development other than minor development[201], likely to result in an adverse impact on the safety of, or queuing, on a trunk road[202]	(g) The highway authority for the trunk road			
Material increase in the volume or a material change in the character of traffic entering or leaving a trunk road		(f)(i) Secretary of State for Transport	(d)(i) The Welsh Ministers	
Likely to prejudice the improvement or construction of a trunk road	(h) The highway authority for the trunk road			
Construction, formation or laying out of access to or from a trunk road	(i) The highway authority for the trunk road			
Material increase in the volume or a material change in the character of traffic using a level crossing over a railway	(j) The railway network operator and the Secretary of State for Transport	(f)(ii)	(d)(ii) The railway network operator and the Welsh Ministers	

[201] Minor development is defined in DMPO 2015, Sch 5, para 1 as to an existing dwellinghouse, incidental development in its curtilage, extensions or alterations of non-domestic buildings by up to 250 m² floorspace.
[202] The order contains a typographical error, putting the comma after 'queuing' rather than after 'on'.

174

Consultation and publicity 6.127

Issue	English consultee DMPO 2015, Sch 4	English consultee DMPO 2010, Sch 5	Welsh consultee, Sch 4	Observations
Material increase in the volume or a material change in the character of traffic entering or leaving a classified road or proposed highway	(k) The local highway authority	(g)	(e) The local highway authority	
Likely to prejudice the improvement or construction of a classified road or proposed highway	(l) The local highway authority	(h)	(f) The local highway authority	
Formation, laying out or alteration of any means of access to a highway (other than a trunk road)	(m)(i) The local highway authority	(i)(i)	(g)(i) The local highway authority	
Construction of a highway or private means of access to premises affording access to a road in relation to which a toll order is in force	(m)(ii) The local highway authority and any concessionaire	(i)(ii)	(g)(ii) The local highway authority and any concessionaire	
Laying out or construction of a new street	(n) The local highway authority	(j)	(h) The local highway authority	
Provision of a building or pipeline in an area of coal working notified by the Coal Authority	(o) The Coal Authority	(k)	(i) The Coal Authority	
Mining operations	(p) the Environment Agency	(l)	(j) The Natural Resources Body for Wales	
Within 3 kilometres of Windsor Castle, Windsor Great Park, or Windsor Home Park, or within 800 metres of any other royal palace or park, which might affect the amenities (including security) of that palace or park	[no equivalent in DMPO 2015]	(m) English Heritage		

6.127 *Planning applications*

Issue	English consultee DMPO 2015, Sch 4	English consultee DMPO 2010, Sch 5	Welsh consultee, Sch 4	Observations
Demolition, in whole or part, or the material alteration of a Grade I or II* listed building	(r) Historic England			
Demolition, in whole or part, or the material alteration of a listed building		(n) English Heritage		
Likely to affect the site of a scheduled monument[203]	(r) Historic England	(o)	(k) The Welsh Ministers	
Likely to affect any battlefield	(s) Historic England			
Likely to affect any registered garden or park of special historic interest[204]	(s) Historic England if Grade I or II* The Garden History Society (now the Gardens Trust) for all registered parks and gardens	Consultation with the Garden History Society was required by a direction in Circular 09/95, Appendix C		
Likely to affect any Grade I or II registered garden or park of special historic interest		(p) English Heritage		
Works or operations in the bed of, or within 20 metres of the top of a bank of, a main river which has been notified by the Environment Agency as such for the purposes of this provision	(t) the Environment Agency	(q)(i)		
Culverting or control of flow of any river or stream		(q)(ii) the Environment Agency		

---

[203] See *R (on the application of Williams) v Powys County Council* (unreported, 2016).
[204] Registration of parks and gardens is under the Historic Buildings and Ancient Monuments Act 1953, s 8C.

Consultation and publicity 6.127

Issue	English consultee DMPO 2015, Sch 4	English consultee DMPO 2010, Sch 5	Welsh consultee, Sch 4	Observations
Carrying out of works or operations in the bed of or on the banks of a river or stream			(l) The Natural Resources Body for Wales	
Refining or storing mineral oils and their derivatives	(u) The Environment Agency	(r)	(m) The Natural Resources Body for Wales	
Use of land for the deposit of refuse or waste		(s) the Environment Agency	(n) The Natural Resources Body for Wales	
The retention, treatment or disposal of sewage, trade-waste, slurry or sludge[205]		(t) The Environment Agency	(o) The Natural Resources Body for Wales8	
Use of land as a cemetery	(v) The Environment Agency	(u)	(p) The Natural Resources Body for Wales	
In or likely to affect a site of special scientific interest	(w) Natural England			

---

[205] Subject to exceptions for 'the laying of sewers, the construction of pumphouses in a line of sewers, the construction of septic tanks and cesspools serving single dwellinghouses or single caravans or single buildings in which not more than 10 people will normally reside, work or congregate, and works ancillary to those matters'.

6.127 *Planning applications*

Issue	English consultee DMPO 2015, Sch 4	English consultee DMPO 2010, Sch 5	Welsh consultee, Sch 4	Observations
Development: (i) in or likely to affect a site of special scientific interest; or (ii) within an area which has been notified to the local planning authority by Natural England, and which is within 2 kilometres of a site of special scientific interest, of which notification has been given, or has effect as if given, to the local planning authority by Natural England, in accordance with the Wildlife and Countryside Act 1981, s 28		(v) Natural England	(q) The Natural Resources Body for Wales (in the description of the development in Wales, the Natural Resources Body for Wales replaces 'Natural England'	
Involving any land on which there is a theatre	(x) the Theatres Trust	(w)	(r) The Theatres Trust	

Consultation and publicity 6.127

Issue	English consultee DMPO 2015, Sch 4	English consultee DMPO 2010, Sch 5	Welsh consultee, Sch 4	Observations
Non-agricultural development which is not in accordance with the development plan involving (i) the loss of not less than 20 hectares of grades 1, 2 or 3a agricultural land which is for the time being used (or was last used) for agricultural purposes; or (ii) the loss of less than 20 hectares of grades 1, 2 or 3a agricultural land which is for the time being used (or was last used) for agricultural purposes, in circumstances in which the development is likely to lead to a further loss of agricultural land amounting cumulatively to 20 hectares or more	(y) Natural England	(x)	(s) The Welsh Ministers	
Within 250 metres of land which: (i) is or has, at any time in the 30 years before the relevant application, been used for the deposit of refuse or waste; and (ii) has been notified to the local planning authority by the Environment Agency for the purposes of this provision	(y) The Environment Agency		(t) The Natural Resources Body for Wales (in the description of the development in Wales, the Natural Resources Body for Wales replaces 'Environment Agency'	

179

6.127 *Planning applications*

Issue	English consultee DMPO 2015, Sch 4	English consultee DMPO 2010, Sch 5	Welsh consultee, Sch 4	Observations
Fish farming			(u) The Natural Resources Body for Wales	

Development which:
(i) is likely to prejudice the use, or lead to the loss of use, of land being used as a playing field; or
(ii) is on land which has been—
  (aa) Used as a playing field at any time in the 5 years before the making of the relevant application and which remains undeveloped; or
  (bb) allocated for use as a playing field in a development plan or in proposals for such a plan or its alteration or replacement; or
(iii) involves the replacement of the grass surface of a playing pitch on a playing field with an artificial, man-made or composite surface
	(z) The English Sports Council	(za)	(v) The Sports Council for Wales	

180

Consultation and publicity **6.127**

Issue	English consultee DMPO 2015, Sch 4	English consultee DMPO 2010, Sch 5	Welsh consultee, Sch 4	Observations
Likely to affect— (i) any inland waterway (whether natural or artificial) or reservoir owned or managed by the Canal & River Trust; or (ii) any canal feeder channel, watercourse, let off or culvert, which is within an area which has been notified for the purposes of this provision to the local planning authority by the Canal & River Trust	(za) The Canal & River Trust	(zb)	(w) The Canal & River Trust	
(i) Involving the siting of new establishments; (ii) Consisting of modifications to existing establishments; or (iii) New developments including transport links, locations frequented by the public and residential areas in the vicinity of existing establishments, where the siting or development is such as to increase the risk or consequences of a major accident	(zb) the COMAH competent authority; where it appears to the local planning authority that an area of particular natural sensitivity or interest may be affected, Natural England; For development within (iii) the person in control of the land on which any establishment is located, as shown by hazardous substances register or notices			Establishments are those covered by art 11, Directive 2012/18EU

6.127 *Planning applications*

Issue	English consultee DMPO 2015, Sch 4	English consultee DMPO 2010, Sch 5	Welsh consultee, Sch 4	Observations
(i) Involving the siting of new establishments; (ii) Consisting of modifications to existing establishments which could have significant repercussions on major-accident hazards; or (iii) including transport links, locations frequented by the public and residential areas in the vicinity of existing establishments, where the siting or development is such as to increase the risk or consequences of a major accident[206]		(zc) The Health and Safety Executive and the Environment Agency and, where it appears to the local planning authority that an area of particular natural sensitivity or interest may be affected, Natural England	(x) The Health and Safety Executive and the Natural Resources Body for Wales	Expressions as defined in the Control of Major Accident Hazards Directive 96/82/EC as amended by 2003/105/EC
Development, other than minor development, which is to be carried out on land: (i) in an area within Flood Zone 2 or Flood Zone 3; or (ii) in an area within Flood Zone 1 which has critical drainage problems and which has been notified for the purpose of this provision to the local planning authority by the Environment Agency	(zc) The Environment Agency	(ze)		

[206] Advice on these consultations is given in England in the *Planning Practice Guidance*, section 39, Annex A and in Wales in NAW Circular 20/01: *Planning Controls for Hazardous Substances*.

Issue	English consultee DMPO 2015, Sch 4	English consultee DMPO 2010, Sch 5	Welsh consultee, Sch 4	Observations
Major development not using a sewerage undertaker for the disposal of sewage	(zd) The Environment Agency			
Major development with surface water drainage	(ze) the Lead local flood authority			
Boring for or getting of oil and natural gas from shale	(zf) any water or sewerage undertaker whose area includes the development and where it is likely to affect water resources in any other areas, their undertakers			
Any development of land of 1 hectare or more		(zf) The Environment Agency		This consultation is for flooding purposes

Any semblance of a logical order has been lost with time.

6.128 *Planning applications*

6.128 Additional consultation duties are set out elsewhere in legislation and directions and recommended by guidance[207]:

Development	English consultee	Welsh consultee	Observations
Consultation required by legislation or directions			
Grant of planning permission for the use of land as a caravan site[208]	The local authority empowered to issue a site licence, if not already the local planning authority	The local authority empowered to issue a site licence, if not already the local planning authority	The issuing authority will be the district or unitary council[209]
Operations likely to damage any of the flora, fauna or geological or physiographical features by reason of which a site of special scientific interest is of special interest[210]	Natural England	Natural Resources Body for Wales	Applies even if the operations would not take place on land included in a site of special scientific interest[211]
Any application for planning permission or reserved matters approval which relates to land in the parish, or any alteration to that application[212]	Parish councils		The duty only arises if the parish council has asked to be notified of such applications or alterations

---

[207] There is little practical difference between a legislative requirement and a policy recommendation in these circumstances. Whilst an authority can decide not to consult, it will need to have understood the guidance and had a good reason for not contacting the relevant body. Usually it will be easier to notify that person.
[208] Town and Country Planning Act 1990, s 71(3). A site licence is one under Caravan Sites and Control of Development Act 1960, Part 1 or Mobile Homes (Wales) Act 2013, Part 2: see Town and Country Planning Act 1990, s 71(4).
[209] Caravan Sites and Control of Development Act 1960, s 29(1); Mobile Homes (Wales) Act 2013, s 6(1).
[210] Wildlife and Countryside Act 1981, s 28I(2).
[211] Wildlife and Countryside Act 1981, s 28I(3).
[212] Town and Country Planning Act 1990, Sch 1, para 8. For the making of representations pursuant to this provision, see DMPO 2015, art 25; DMPO 2010, art 23.

Development	English consultee	Welsh consultee	Observations
(a) development affecting the setting of a Grade I or II* listed; or (b) development affecting the character or appearance of a conservation area and (i) the development involves the erection of a new building or the extension of an existing building; and (ii) the area of land in respect of which the application is made is more than 1,000 square metres[213]	Historic England		
An application made by an interested planning authority to itself which relates solely to relevant demolition within a conservation area[214]	Historic England		
Mineral application on land specified by the Coal Authority as containing coal	The Coal Authority[215]	The Coal Authority[216]	
Mineral application on land specified by the Secretary of State as containing oil or gas	The Secretary of State for Energy and Climate Change[217]	The Secretary of State for Energy and Climate Change[218]	
Mineral application on land specified by the Crown Estate Commissioners as containing silver or gold	The Crown Estate Commissioners[219]	The Crown Estate Commissioners[220]	

[213] Planning (Listed Buildings and Conservation Areas) Regulations 1990, SI 1990/1519, reg 5A(3) as amended for applications made from 15 April 2015. Prior to that date Historic England had to be notified of all applications affecting listed buildings, their settings and conservation areas.
[214] Town and Country Planning General Regulations 1992, reg 4A(1).
[215] DMPO 2015, art 26(1)(a).
[216] DMPO Wales, art 17(1)(a).
[217] DMPO 2015, art 26(1)(b).
[218] DMPO Wales, art 17(1)(b).
[219] DMPO 2015, art 26(1)(c).
[220] DMPO Wales, art 17(1)(c).

6.128 *Planning applications*

Development	English consultee	Welsh consultee	Observations
The development of land forming the site of or in the neighbourhood of an aerodrome, technical site[221] or military explosives storage area for which a safeguarding map has been furnished to the authority[222]	If the map is certified by the Civil Aviation Authority, the owner or operator of the aerodrome or technical site identified on that map; or The Secretary of State for Defence if the map is certified by him	If the map is certified by the Civil Aviation Authority, the owner or operator of the aerodrome or technical site identified on that map; or The Secretary of State for Defence if the map is certified by him	
Development of land forming the site of or in the neighbourhood of a meteorological technical site (shown on a safeguarding map)[223]	The Met Office		
Consultation recommended by guidance			
Major development	The lead local flood authority[224] should be consulted on surface water drainage[225]		

---

[221] A technical site is one used or proposed to be used for air traffic services equipment.
[222] Town and Country Planning (safeguarded aerodromes, technical sites and military explosives storage areas) Direction 2002, contained in Dft/ODPM Circular 01/2003 and NAW Circular 01/03.
[223] Town and Country Planning (Safeguarding Meteorological Sites) (England) Direction 2014, para 4. A technical site uses electromagnetic radiation for acquiring or receiving information about meteorological conditions, including meteorological and wind profiling radars, satellite reception facilities and radiosondes (telemetry instruments, usually carried by weather balloons): see para 3.
[224] A county council or unitary council, see Flood and Water Management Act 2010, s 6(7).
[225] *Planning Practice Guidance* 7-045-20150323.

Development	English consultee	Welsh consultee	Observations
Development proposals that contain or are likely to affect Ancient Semi-Natural woodlands or Plantations on Ancient Woodlands Sites (PAWS)[226] (as defined and recorded in Natural England's Ancient Woodland inventory), including any development within 500 metres of an ancient semi-natural woodland or ancient replanted woodland, and where the development would involve erecting new buildings, or extending the footprint of existing buildings[227]	Forestry Commission		
Proposals that may affect the Outstanding Universal Value of a World Heritage Site[228]	Historic England (for cultural sites) or Natural England (for natural sites) and the Department of Culture, Media and Sport with a view to the World Heritage Committee being informed		The guidance says it would be 'very helpful' if these English bodies were consulted
Wind turbines 11 m to blade tip or taller, and/or has a rotor diameter of 2m or more	Ministry of Defence (usually Defence Estates)[229]		
Development in the vicinity of licensed nuclear installations	Office for Nuclear Regulation[230]		
To address crime prevention – but no particular development identified[231]	Police and Crime Commissioners		

---

[226] Defined and recorded in Natural England's Ancient Woodland inventory.
[227] *Planning Practice Guidance* 8-023-20140306.
[228] *Planning Practice Guidance* 18a-036-20140306. On the meaning of this guidance see *R (SAVE Britain's Heritage) v Liverpool City Council* (judgment January 2016).
[229] The issues tend to be effects on radar and on low flying aircraft.
[230] *Planning Practice Guidance* 39-075-20140306.
[231] *Planning Practice Guidance* 26-010-20140306. This includes counter-terrorism design in appropriate cases: 26-011-20140306.

6.129 *Planning applications*

Development	English consultee	Welsh consultee	Observations
development which might lead to: • loss of, or loss of use for sport, of any major sports facility; • the loss of use for sport of a major body of water; • creation of a major sports facility; • creation of a site for one or more playing pitches; • opportunities for sport (such as the creation of a body of water bigger than two hectares following sand and gravel extraction); • artificial lighting of a major outdoor sports facility; • a residential development of 300 dwellings or more	Sport England[232]		

6.129 A failure to give notice as required will render the decision unlawful and liable to be quashed on proceedings brought by the consultee or any other person[233]. Consultation should take place at the start of the application process, although an error can be corrected by pre-determination consultation[234]. A substantive error in a notice of an application is likely to lead to the quashing of any planning permission[235].

6.130 *R (on the application of Gibson) v Waverley Borough Council*[236] was a challenge to planning permission and listed building consent for the conversion of Sir

---

[232] *Planning Practice Guidance* 37-003-20140306.
[233] *Main v Swansea City Council* (1985) 49 P & CR 26 at 37 on notice to the Secretary of State for Transport; *R (on the application of Friends of Hethel) v South Norfolk Council* [2010] EWCA Civ 894, [2012] 1 WLR 1216 on notice to English Heritage. For another heritage decision see *R (on the application of Gerber) v Wiltshire Council* [2015] EWHC 524 (Admin), [2015] JPL 1021 at paras 38–46 per Dove J (appeal pending).
[234] *R (on the application of SAVE Britain's Heritage) v Gateshead Metropolitan Borough Council* [2014] EWHC 896 (Admin) at para 16 per Mitting J.
[235] See, for example, the decision of the Court of Appeal in *R v Lambeth London Borough Council, ex p Sharp* (1988) 55 P & CR 232 where the failure of the newspaper notice to set out the period within which representations should be made caused the quashing of a planning permission despite widespread local knowledge and campaigning about the application.
[236] [2012] EWHC 1472 (Admin).

Arthur Conan Doyle's former house from a hotel to several houses. The High Court held that the Council acted unlawfully in not following up the failure of English Heritage to respond to a consultation letter (the letter not having been received) and failing to consult English Heritage again when there was a change in material considerations (planning permission for an alternative scheme).

Consultation with county planning authorities

6.131 District and borough councils which are local planning authorities in two-tier areas are under duties to consult their county council on planning applications as set out in the Town and Country Planning Act 1990, Sch 1[237]:

(a) a development which would materially conflict with or prejudice the implementation of a relevant county policy;

(b) a development in an area in relation to which the county planning authority have given notice in writing to the district planning authority that development is likely to affect or be affected by the winning and working of minerals, other than coal;

(c) a development of land in respect of which the county planning authority have given notice in writing to the district planning authority that they propose to carry out development;

(d) a development which would prejudice a proposed development mentioned in para (c) in respect of which notice has been given as so mentioned;

(e) a development of land in relation to which the county planning authority have given notice in writing to the district planning authority that it is proposed to use the land for waste disposal; or

(f) a development which would prejudice a proposed use mentioned in para (e) in respect of which notice has been given as so mentioned.

6.132 A county policy is one in a local development document prepared under a minerals and waste development scheme which has been submitted to the Secretary of State for examination or has been adopted[238]. The consultation requirements do not apply if the county planning authority gives a direction authorising the determination of the application or a description of application without compliance with the requirements[239].

Consultation by county councils with districts

6.133 In a two-tier area, if a planning application is made to a county council then it must send a copy of the application and any accompanying plans, drawings and information to the district planning authority as soon as reasonably practicable[240]. The district then has 21 days from its receipt of the application to make recommendations[241]. The county planning authority must take any such representations into account and

---

[237] Town and Country Planning Act 1990, Sch 1, para 7.
[238] Town and Country Planning Act 1990, Sch 1, para 7(10).
[239] Town and Country Planning Act 1990, Sch 1, para 7(4), (5).
[240] DMPO 2015, art 11(4), made under the Town and Country Planning Act 1990, Sch 1, para 6.
[241] DMPO 2015, art 24(1).

6.134 *Planning applications*

may not determine the application before recommendations have been received, the district has said it will not make representations or the end of the period[242].

Consultation by National Park Authorities

6.134 National park authorities who determine any application for planning permission or for the approval of reserved matters shall consult the authority who would otherwise have been the district planning authority[243].

Consultation on s 73 applications and certain renewals

6.135 Applications may be made for the grant of planning permission subject to different conditions to those on existing permissions (under the Town and Country Planning Act 1990, s 73) or for renewals of existing permissions. If the original application process worked well, new issues should only arise on such applications if there has been a change in circumstances. There is a case for a more flexible approach to consultation in such circumstances.

6.136 Article 20 of the DMPO 2015 gives local planning authorities a discretion as to which bodies to consult within the table in Sch 4 on the following types of planning application:

(i) s 73 applications for planning permission subject to different conditions;

(ii) for development the subject of a planning permission granted on or before 1 October 2010 where development has not begun and the time for commencement has not expired[244];

(iii) for outline planning permission for development which is the subject of outline planning permission granted on or before 1 October 2010 for development which is expressly required or permitted to be implemented in phases, where development has begun and the time limits have not expired.

Advertisement, site notice, owner and neighbour consultation requirements are not affected and neither are other consultation requirements which are outside the art 18, Sch 4 list.

Consultation period with statutory bodies

6.137 Where consultation has to take place under the DMPO 2015, arts 18 or 20 in England, the local planning authority may not determine the application until 21 days after the consultation notice was given (or if the applicant served a copy of the application on the consultee, 21 days after that date) or, if earlier, the consultee has made representations or said that it does not intend to do so[245]. When consultation

---

[242] DMPO 2015, art 24(1), (2).
[243] Town and Country Planning Act 1990, Sch 1, para 4.
[244] The financial crisis which started in 2008 delayed numerous construction projects so changes were made to facilitate the renewal of pre-2010 permissions. Since time limits are usually five years for full permissions and two years to submit reserved matters, with three years following for implementation on outline permissions, this provision will soon cease to have practical importance.
[245] DMPO 2015, art 18(5), (6); DMPO 2010, art 16(5), (6).

Consultation and publicity **6.141**

with county planning authorities or parish councils takes place under the Town and Country Planning Act 1990, Sch 1, the period allowed for consultation responses is also 21 days[246].

In Wales the period for responses from statutory consultees under the DMPO Wales was increased from 14 days to 21 days for applications made from 22 June 2015[247].

6.138 Where consultation takes place with Natural England or Natural Resources Body for Wales for operations which are likely to damage a site of special scientific interest, the consultation period is 28 days, unless the nature conservation body has said that the local planning authority need not wait until then[248].

Making consultation responses

6.139 Statutory and internal local authority consultees should consider the application material in sufficient detail to form a view on the matters within their remit[249]. They should respond within the consultation period and explain whether further information is required, and if so, what that is. Any concerns should be set out with reasons and in particular whether those amount to an objection to the scheme. There may be circumstances in which a consultee will identify harm but consider that the harm might be outweighed by benefits and leave the matter to the local planning authority. The consultee needs to be careful in doing so, as the risk is that the concern is discounted by the lack of an objection, and the weight to be attached to the harm should be set out. If planning conditions are necessary to address potential impacts then these should be set out with clarity. Consultees need to think carefully whether conditions are required in the light of the material submitted with the application and the issues which might realistically arise: the unthinking recommendation of standard conditions, such as on land contamination, can impose significant costs and delays. Reasons should be provided for those conditions, including the justification for conditions to be satisfied prior to the commencement of development.

6.140 Statutory consultees should keep abreast of revisions to the scheme and further information which is provided in respect of their interests. Too often concerns are expressed about an application, the developer responds with more material and the consultee's view on the response is not known.

6.141 Concern that statutory consultees were either not replying or were taking too long to do so prompted the introduction of a duty to respond in the Planning and Compulsory Purchase Act 2004[250]. Initially applicable solely in England, it was extended to Wales in June 2015[251]. The duty applies to the bodies consulted under the DMPO except for notified landowners, occupiers and neighbours, parish councils and persons controlling hazardous substances[252]. Additionally a variety of

---

[246] DMPO 2015, arts 21, 25(1); DMPO 2010, arts 19, 23(1) respectively.
[247] DMPO Wales, art 14(4), amended by the Town and Country Planning (Development Management Procedure) (Wales) (Amendment) Order 2015, art 6.
[248] Wildlife and Countryside Act 1981, s 28I(4).
[249] It is unimpressive to have access proposals criticised by a highways officer who has not read the access part of the design and access statement.
[250] Planning and Compulsory Purchase Act 2004, s 54(2), (3).
[251] DMPO Wales, art 15A.
[252] DMPO 2015, art 22(1), (2). In Wales it is similarly confined to those consulted under DMPO Wales, art 14, see art 15A(1), (2).

6.142 *Planning applications*

consultations under the GPDO, the Town and Country Planning Act 1990 and the Planning (Listed Buildings and Conservation Areas) Act 1990 are also subject to the duty in England[253]. Substantive responses are required within 21 days of receipt of the consultation material[254], unless otherwise provided. There is, though, no sanction for a failure to respond and provided that the body was consulted the local planning authority's subsequent decision is likely to only be unlawful if it had insufficient information to form a view on the application.

6.142 Those bodies which are under a duty to respond to consultation under these provisions are required to submit an annual report to the Secretary of State or Welsh Ministers setting out how often they were consulted and responded substantively within the statutory period, giving summary reasons for any failure to comply[255].

6.143 Members of the public who are interested in the scheme should consider the application material to a reasonable degree, proportionate to their time and interest. On major schemes in particular it is unreasonable to expect someone to voluntarily go through all of the application documents. However comments based on a misunderstanding of the scheme (perhaps assuming it is the same as an earlier application) or overlooking assessments will tend to be discounted. The aim, of course, is to be persuasive to officers and members. Points can be expressed concisely, and it is helpful to refer to particular policies and references within the application documents. If concerns might be addressed by amendments to the scheme or planning conditions then these should be explained, for example, realigning an overlooking window or making it obscure glazed.

6.144 It is not necessary to instruct a planning consultant or other professional to make the representations, though that will tend to strengthen any points made. In some cases solicitors, counsel or technical consultants may be required. Whether a third party will have the resources and consider it sufficiently important to bring in professional assistance will vary.

6.145 Consultees and the public should bear in mind that their representations will be made available to the applicant and those inspecting the application files and will be sent to the Planning Inspectorate on any appeal or call-in. Depending upon the planning authority's practice, the representations may be put on the Council's website (usually with signatures, telephone numbers and e-mail addresses obscured).

6.146 Major or contentious applications may attract a large number of representations and it is unrealistic to expect all correspondents to have considered the application in detail. However, individually written letters or e-mails are far more effective than signed standard form letters or petitions.

6.147 Any representations from the public should be clear whether they support or object to the scheme and, if other points are made, whether they would amount to objections. Important points on the substance or procedure of the application should be raised[256]. If the proposal is a householder or minor commercial application then if

---

[253] DMPO 2015, art 22(1). The duty does not cover all statutory consultation with public bodies.
[254] DMPO 2015, art 22(3); DMPO Wales, art 15A(2).
[255] DMPO 2015, art 23; DMPO Wales, art 15B. The report must also explain how they have complied with their duties to respond to pre-application consultation.
[256] If a legal challenge follows it is far more attractive to say to the court that the point was raised and not addressed.

an appeal is dealt with by written representations there will be no further opportunity for third party comment, so these representations in particular need to be full.

Taking into account consultation responses

6.148 Local planning authorities should take into account the responses which they receive to publicity or a consultation. This duty arises under various statutes, as a matter of public law and as a result of promises in policies. Legislation which requires consultation or publicity to take place will often state that responses received should be considered before the decision is taken[257].

AMENDMENTS TO SCHEMES

6.149 Late amendments to a planning application or the imposition of conditions on a planning permission may not allow development which is in substance not that which was applied for. In particular, the change should not deprive those who should have been consulted on the changed development the opportunity of such consultation: *Bernard Wheatcroft Ltd v Secretary of State for the Environment*[258]. There must not be 'any possible prejudice to those who might otherwise have raised objections'[259]. Forbes J said in *Wheatcroft*:

> 'Parliament cannot have intended conditional planning permission to be used to circumvent the provisions for consultation and public participation contained in [the Planning Act]'.

6.150 Where a parish council has asked to be notified of alterations to planning or reserved matters applications relating to their area then the local planning authority must send a copy of any alteration which it accepts to the council or inform it in writing of its general effect unless the authority considers that the alteration is trivial[260].

6.151 Statements of community involvement or other published policies of the local planning authority may create a legitimate expectation that the notice is given of amendments.

---

[257] For example DMPO 2010, art 16(7); DMPO Wales, art 14(5); Wildlife and Countryside Act 1981, s 28I(5) for sites of special scientific interest; DMPO 2015, art 24(1) for districts on county applications; DMPO 2015, art 25(2) for parish councils.
[258] (1980) 43 P & CR 233.
[259] *Granada Hospitality Ltd v Secretary of State for the Environment, Transport and the Regions* (2001) 81 P & CR 36 Collins J at para 73.
[260] Town and Country Planning Act 1990, Sch 1, para 8(5).

Chapter 7

Environmental Impact Assessment

7.1 Environmental Impact Assessment (EIA) has become an integral part of the planning process for large-scale development projects[1]. It usually arises when a planning permission or other form of consent is sought.

EIA IN OUTLINE

7.2 EIA was introduced by European Directive 85/337/EEC and subsequently amended by Directive 97/11/EC, 2003/35/EC and 2009/31/EC. In 2011 the Directive was replaced by the consolidated Environmental Impact Assessment Directive 2011/92/EU. The critical obligation is contained in art 2(1):

> 'Member States shall adopt all measures necessary to ensure that, before consent is given, projects likely to have significant effects on the environment by virtue, *inter alia*, of their nature, size or location are made subject to a requirement for development consent and an assessment with regard to their effects. These projects are defined in Article 4'.

7.3 Article 4 identifies two categories of projects. Projects listed in Annex I of the Directive, such as an oil refinery, a motorway or a large power station, will automatically require EIA. These projects are described in the UK legislation as Sch 1 development. Where projects fall within Annex II member states are required to determine through a case-by-case examination or thresholds or criteria whether EIA is required. Annex II covers a wide range of projects from intensive agriculture, to mineral extraction, urban development, the food industry and flood defence works (identified in the UK regulations as Sch 2 development). The essential question is whether these projects are likely to have significant effects on the environment.

7.4 In the UK EIA has either been integrated into existing consent regimes or new regimes have been devised and in either case separate regulations have been produced. In England the regulations applying to the planning process are the Town and Country Planning (Environmental Impact Assessment) Regulations 2011 (EIA Regulations 2011). Planning matters in Wales (and those applications made in England prior to 24 August 2011) are subject to the Town and Country Planning (Environmental Impact Assessment) (England and Wales) Regulations 1999 (EIA Regulations 1999)[2]. Consents under other regimes such as highways, pipelines, harbours and electricity projects are governed by other EIA regulations. Where it takes place, EIA is usually part of the process of granting planning permission or another domestic law consent rather than a separate consent.

---

[1] The standard work on English and Welsh EIA law is Tromans *Environmental Impact Assessment: Law and Practice* (2nd edn, 2012) Bloomsbury Professional.

[2] SIs 2011/1824 and 1999/293 respectively. Planning applications made before 14 March 1999 were subject to the Town and Country Planning (Assessment of Environmental Effects) Regulations 1988.

The need for EIA **7.7**

7.5 EIA involves the following stages:

(i) deciding whether EIA is required using selection criteria (screening);

(ii) if EIA is required, considering what impacts should be subject to assessment (scoping);

(iii) the preparation of an environmental statement by the developer. The statement will explain the scheme, the environmental baseline which is capable of being affected by the scheme, the likely significant effects of the scheme, the mitigation proposed in respect of those effects and the alternatives considered by the developer. As part of the statement, a non-technical summary will be produced;

(iv) consultation of public bodies and the public on the environmental statement and any further information produced by the developer;

(v) consideration of the environmental statement, the developer's further information and the responses to the consultation by the decision-maker;

(vi) the production of a reasoned decision on the application.

THE NEED FOR EIA

7.6 The EIA Directive requires that EIA is carried out before the grant of development consent for projects falling within the ambit of the Directive which are likely to have significant effects on the environment. Development consent is the decision which authorises the developer to proceed with the project. In the planning process this is, most obviously, the grant of planning permission. However, a developer might not be able to carry out a particular scheme until reserved matters approval has been granted or details approved under various conditions prior to the start of development or the carrying out of a particular phase. An early foreshadowing of the scope of the EIA regime came in the House of Lords decision in *R v North Yorkshire County Council, ex p Brown*[3], where the review of an old mining permission was held to require EIA. Unless the review took place, the resumption of mining was not authorised. Development consent had been seen in the UK as a one-off concept: only the grant of planning permission was a development consent and the issue did not arise on later approvals[4]. In a series of judgments the European Court of Justice held that a multi-stage development consent was possible and EIA may therefore have to be carried out at all stages[5].

7.7 Consequently the EIA Regulations 1999 were amended to provide for EIA of 'subsequent applications', that is, the approval of reserved matters or approval of details under conditions that are required to enable the development to be carried out.

---

[3] [2000] 1 AC 397.
[4] *R v London Borough of Hammersmith and Fulham, ex p CPRE* [2000] Env LR 549; *R v London Borough of Bromley, ex p Barker* [2001] EWCA Civ 1766, [2002] Env LR 25. This analysis was also a factor in requiring greater detail at the planning permission stage so that all EIA could be carried out: see *R v Rochdale Metropolitan Borough Council, ex p Milne (No 1)* [2000] Env LR 1. This was only disapproved in the final decision in *R (on the application of Barker) v Bromley London Borough Council* [2006] UKHL 52, [2007] 1 AC 470.
[5] *R (on the application of Wells) v Secretary of State for Transport, Local Government and the Regions* (C-210/02) [2004] 1 CMLR 31; *R v London Borough of Bromley, ex p Barker* (C-290/03) [2006] QB 764; *Commission v United Kingdom* (C-508/03).

7.8 Environmental Impact Assessment

7.8 Usually the grant of planning permission is on an application made under the Town and Country Planning Act 1990, Part III, but other planning permissions will be subject to EIA requirements. Projects may not be carried out under permitted development rights if they need EIA and are subject to the same EIA screening requirements as planning applications[6]. If EIA is required of a scheme which would otherwise have permitted development rights then a planning application must be made for it. EIA may be required before planning permission can be granted in an enforcement notice appeal[7].

7.9 In the EIA Regulations an 'EIA application' is[8]:

'(a) an application for planning permission for EIA development; or

(b) a subsequent application in respect of EIA development'.

7.10 A 'subsequent application' is:

'an application for approval of a matter where the approval:

(a) is required by or under a condition to which a planning permission is subject; and

(b) must be obtained before all or part of the development permitted by the planning permission may be begun'.

7.11 EIA development falls into three categories. The simplest is 'Sch 1 development' which are projects within Sch 1 to the 1999 or 2011 EIA Regulations, based on those projects in Annex I of the EIA Directive. These classes of projects are reasonably self-explanatory and include modifications to such projects which meet the Sch 1 descriptions or thresholds in their own right.

7.12 The second type of EIA Development which is defined in reg 2(1) is:

'Schedule 2 development likely to have significant effects on the environment by virtue of factors such as its nature, size or location'.

Schedule 2 development is[9]:

(i) development within the first column of the table in Sch 2 to the EIA Regulations;

(ii) where:

(a) any part of the development is to be carried out in a sensitive area; or

(b) any threshold or criterion for that development (set out in the second column of the table) is respectively exceeded or met.

7.13 A sensitive area is[10]:

(i) a site of special scientific interest[11];

---

[6] See Chapter 5.
[7] See Harwood *Planning Enforcement* (2nd edn, 2013) Bloomsbury Professional, Chapter 10.
[8] EIA Regulations 2011, art 2(1); EIA Regulations 1999, art 2(1).
[9] EIA Regulations 2011, art 2(1); EIA Regulations 1999, art 2(1).
[10] EIA Regulations 2011, art 2(1); EIA Regulations 1999, art 2(1). For these purposes the proposal must be at least partly within a sensitive area, rather than outside it with the potential to affect it.
[11] Wildlife and Countryside Act 1981, s 28(1).

The need for EIA **7.16**

(ii) a National Park[12];

(iii) the Broads;

(iv) a World Heritage Site[13];

(v) a scheduled monument[14];

(vi) an area of outstanding natural beauty[15];

(vii) a European site, that is, either a Special Protection Area or a Special Area of Conservation[16].

7.14 The table in Sch 2 sets out a type of project in the first column and thresholds or criteria in the second column[17]. For example, at para 12(e) the first column contains 'permanent camp sites and caravan sites' and the corresponding entry in the second column is 'The area of the development exceeds 1 hectare'. Consequently EIA or screening must be carried out before planning permission is granted for a permanent camp or caravan site where its area exceeds 1 hectare or any part of it is in a sensitive area.

7.15 The categories in Sch 2 are taken from the EIA Directive, Annex II, with modest alterations which might extend, but more probably just clarify, individual categories. Under para 10, 'infrastructure projects' the Directive lists 'Urban development projects, including the construction of shopping centres and car parks'. The UK Regulations extend this to 'Urban development projects, including the construction of shopping centres and car parks, sports stadiums, leisure centres and multiplex cinemas'. Those additions are in practice examples of schemes which would fall inside the urban development project category in any event.

7.16 Types of projects in Schs 1 and 2 need to be construed in accordance with the Directive's 'wide scope and a broad purpose'[18]. The meaning of these categories is a matter of law, although some are sufficiently imprecise that an authority might rationally conclude that a particular project is or is not within the particular schedule[19]. The extent of 'urban development projects' in particular is wide. In *R (on the application of Goodman) v London Borough of Lewisham* the Court of Appeal held that a 'Big Yellow Warehouse' self-storage facility might be an urban development project[20]:

'"Infrastructure project" and "urban development project" are terms of wide ambit, perhaps more easily understood by those versed in planning policy than by mere lawyers

---

[12] National Parks and Access to the Countryside Act 1949.
[13] On the World Heritage List kept under the 1972 UNESCO Convention for the Protection of the World Cultural and Natural Heritage, art 11(2).
[14] Ancient Monuments and Archaeological Areas Act 1979, s 1.
[15] Countryside and Rights of Way Act 2000, s 82(1).
[16] A European site within the meaning of reg 8 of the Conservation of Habitats and Species Regulations 2010, implementing the Birds and Habitats Directives respectively.
[17] The setting of thresholds or criteria below which screening is not required is permitted under the EIA Directive, art 4, see *Berkeley v Secretary of State for Environment (No 2)* [2002] EWCA Civ 1012, [2002] Env LR 14.
[18] Case C-72/95 *Aannamaersbedrijf PK Kraaijveld BV v Gedeputeerde Staten van Zuid-Holland* [1996] ECR I-5403, para 31 (*Kraaijveld*).
[19] *R (on the application of Goodman) v London Borough of Lewisham* [2003] EWCA Civ 140, [2003] JPL 1309 at para 9 per Buxton LJ, so not a *Wednesbury* exercise of discretion.
[20] *Goodman* at para 14 per Buxton LJ.

7.17 *Environmental Impact Assessment*

... But the examples of urban development projects set out in paragraph 10(b) of the Regulation demonstrate that in this instance "infrastructure" goes wider, indeed far wider, than the normal understanding, as quoted to us from the *Shorter Oxford Dictionary*, of "the installations and services (power stations, sewers, roads, housing, etc) regarded as the economic foundations of a country". I am unable to accept that a storage and distribution facility (particularly when, as in the present case, it provides services to business and the community at large, and is not simply a private operation), however large and extensive, can never be reasonably regarded as part of the infrastructure as understood in the Regulations'.

7.17 The breadth of the definitions is also illustrated by waste disposal installation extending beyond disposal within the meaning of the Waste Directive[21] to cover 'all operations leading either to waste disposal, in the strict sense of the term, or to waste recovery'[22]. Modifications and refurbishment of installations which would be equivalent, by their size and the manner in which they are carried out, to construction may be regarded as construction projects[23].

7.18 A change to an an existing or authorised Sch 1 project will require EIA if the change itself exceeds the Sch 1 thresholds.[24] Other alterations to Sch 1 or Sch 2 projects are considered by para 13 of the table in Sch 2. In England this requires EIA screening to be carried out if the change or extension meets the equivalent threshold or criteria in Sch 2 or the development proposed may have significant adverse effects on the environment. The Welsh provisions require EIA screening if the threshold or criteria are met and the change or extension may have significant adverse effects on the environment[25].

7.19 The final category of EIA development is of projects which are within the first column of Sch 2 but are outside sensitive areas and do not meet the thresholds or criteria in Sch 2, but which the Minister directs to be EIA development[26]. For example, the Secretary of State could make a screening direction that a proposed permanent caravan site required EIA even though it was smaller than 1 hectare and outside sensitive areas.

7.20 The Sch 1 projects, which all require EIA are, in summary:

1   crude-oil refineries and installations for the gasification and liquefaction of 500 tonnes or more of coal or bituminous shale per day;

2   (a) thermal power stations and other combustion installations with a heat output of 300 megawatts or more; and

   (b) nuclear power stations and other nuclear reactors (subject to minor exceptions);

3   nuclear fuel or radioactive waste facilities;

---

[21]   2008/98/EC.
[22]   C-486/04 *Commission v Italy* at para 44.
[23]   See Case C-227/01 *Commission of the European Communities v Kingdom of Spain* [2004] ECR I-8253, para 46 and Case C-2/07 *Abraham v Région Wallonne*, 28 February 2008, para 32.
[24]   EIA Regulations 2011, Sch 1, para 21; EIA Regulations 1999, Sch 1, para 21.
[25]   EIA Regulations 1999, Sch 2, para 13. The English version, which focuses on the effects of the overall scheme, appears to better reflect the need to consider the overall effect of the project: see *R (on the application of Baker) v Bath and North East Somerset District Council* [2009] EWHC 595 (Admin), [2009] JPL 1498 at paras 41–46 per Collins J.
[26]   Under the EIA Regulations 2011, art 4(9); EIA Regulations 1999, art 4(8).

4   cast iron and steel melting works and certain non-ferrous crude metal production facilities;

5   installations producing or using defined large quantities of asbestos;

6   industrial scale integrated chemical installations;

7   (a) lines for long-distance railway traffic and airports with a 2,100 metre or longer runway;

    (b) motorways and express roads[27];

    (c) new, realigned or widened roads of four or more lanes of 10 kilometres or more;

8   (a) inland waterways and ports for inland-waterway traffic for 1,350 tonne vessels;

    (b) trading ports, piers for loading and unloading connected to land and outside ports (excluding ferry piers) for 1,350 tonne vessels;

9   waste disposal installations for the incineration, chemical treatment or landfill of hazardous waste;

10 waste disposal installations for the incineration or chemical treatment of non-hazardous waste with capacity over 100 tonnes per day;

11 groundwater abstraction or artificial groundwater recharge schemes of 10 million m³ per annum;

12 (a) transfer of 100 million m³ per annum water between river basins to prevent shortages;

    (b) transfer of water resources, other than piped drinking water, between river basins where the multi-annual average flow of the basin of abstraction exceeds 2,000 million cubic metres per year and where the amount of water transferred exceeds 5% of this flow;

13 waste water treatment plants with a capacity exceeding 150,000 population equivalent;

14 extraction of 500 tonnes per day of petroleum or 500,000 m³ of natural gas for commercial purposes;

15 dams and other installations for over 10 million m³ of water;

16 gas, oil, chemicals pipelines and those for carbon dioxide geological storage with a diameter of more than 800 millimetres and a length of more than 40 kilometres;

17 installations for the intensive rearing of more than 85,000 broilers or 60,000 hens, 3,000 production pigs (over 30 kg); or 900 sows;

18 industrial plants for:

    (a) the production of pulp from timber or similar fibrous materials;

    (b) the production of paper and board with a production capacity exceeding 200 tonnes per day;

---

[27] These may include urban roads: Case C-142/07 *Ecologistas en Acción-CODA v Ayuntamiento de Madrid* [2009] PTSR 458 at para 34.

7.21 *Environmental Impact Assessment*

19 quarries and open-cast mining sites exceeding 25 hectares, or peat extraction sites exceeding 150 hectares;

20 storage of 200,000 tonnes or more of petroleum, petrochemical or chemical products;

21 any change to or extension of development listed in the Schedule where such a change or extension in itself meets the thresholds, if any, or description of development set out in the Schedule;

22 carbon dioxide geological storage sites;

23 the capture of 1.5 megatonnes per annum of carbon dioxide for geological storage.

7.21 The Sch 2 categories and their thresholds and criteria are, in summary the following, unless they are within Sch 1[28].

1	*Agriculture and aquaculture*	
(a)	Projects for the use of uncultivated land or semi-natural areas for intensive agricultural purposes[29];	Development area over 0.5 hectare.
(b)	Water management projects for agriculture, including irrigation and land drainage projects;	Works area over 1 hectare.
(c)	Intensive livestock installations[30];	Over 500 m² of new floorspace.
(d)	Intensive fish farming;	Over 10 tonnes of dead weight fish per year.
(e)	Reclamation of land from the sea.	All development.
2	*Extractive industry*	
(a)	Quarries, open cast mining and peat extraction	All development except the construction of buildings or other ancillary structures where the new floorspace does not exceed 1,000 square metres.
(b)	Underground mining;	
(c)	Extraction of minerals by fluvial or marine dredging;	All development.
(d)	Deep drillings, in particular:	(i) Works area over 1 hectare; or

---

[28] 'Floorspace' is a commonly used threshold which is defined as 'the floorspace in a building or buildings' but extends beyond conventional floorspace to include silos and pipework: *R (on the application of Horner) v Lancashire County Council* [2007] EWCA Civ 784, [2008] JPL 209 at para 62 per Auld LJ.

[29] A local planning authority was entitled to find that 'actively managed farmland already in use for the production of soft fruit, arable crops and turf in rotation, was neither uncultivated land nor a semi-natural area': *R (on the application of Wye Valley Action Association Ltd) v Herefordshire Council* [2011] EWCA Civ 20, [2011] PTSR 1011 at para 42 per Richards LJ.

[30] 'Intensive' connotes the keeping of livestock at a density which cannot be sustained naturally and mobile' poultry units could be intensive livestock installations: *R (on the application of Save Woolley Valley Action Group) v Bath and North East Somerset Council* [2012] EWHC 2161 (Admin), [2013] Env LR 8 at paras 78–104 per Lang J.

The need for EIA **7.21**

	(i)	geothermal drilling;	(ii) for geothermal drilling and drilling for the storage of nuclear waste material, the drilling is within 100 metres of controlled waters.
	(ii)	drilling for the storage of nuclear waste material;	
	(iii)	drilling for water supplies;	
	with the exception of drillings for investigating the stability of the soil.		
(e)	Surface industrial installations for the extraction of coal, petroleum, natural gas and ores, as well as bituminous shale.		Development area over 0.5 hectare.

3 *Energy industry*

(a)	Industrial installations for the production of electricity, steam and hot water;	Development area over 0.5 hectare.
(b)	Industrial installations for carrying gas, steam and hot water;	Works area over 1 hectare.
(c)	Surface storage of natural gas;	(i) New building, deposit or structure area over 500 square metres; or
		(ii) a new building, deposit or structure is to be sited within 100 metres of any controlled waters.
(d)	Underground storage of combustible gases;	(i) new building, deposit or structure area over 500 square metres; or
		(ii) a new building, deposit or structure is to be sited within 100 metres of any controlled waters.
(e)	Surface storage of fossil fuels;	(i) new building, deposit or structure area over 500 square metres; or
		(ii) a new building, deposit or structure within 100 metres of controlled waters.
(f)	Industrial briquetting of coal and lignite;	Over 1,000 m² of new floorspace.
(g)	Installations for the processing and storage of radioactive waste;	(i) Over 1,000 m² of new floorspace; or
		(ii) the installation resulting from the development will require an authorisation or the variation of an authorisation under the Radioactive Substances Act 1993.
(h)	Installations for hydroelectric energy production;	The installation is designed to produce more than 0.5 megawatts.
(i)	Installations for the harnessing of wind power for energy production (wind farms).	(i) more than 2 turbines; or
		(ii) the hub height of any turbine or height of any other structure exceeds 15 metres.

7.21 Environmental Impact Assessment

4   *Production and processing of metals*

(a) Installations for the production of pig iron or steel (primary or secondary fusion) including continuous casting;   Over 1,000 m² of new floorspace.

(b) Installations for the processing of ferrous metals: Over 1,000 m² of new floorspace.
  (i) hot-rolling mills;
  (ii) smitheries with hammers;
  (iii) application of protective fused metal coats.

(c) Ferrous metal foundries;   Over 1,000 m² of new floorspace.

(d) Installations for the smelting, including the alloyage, of non-ferrous metals, excluding precious metals, including recovered products (refining, foundry casting, etc);   Over 1,000 m² of new floorspace.

(e) Installations for surface treatment of metals and plastic materials using an electrolytic or chemical process;   Over 1,000 m² of new floorspace.

(f) Manufacture and assembly of motor vehicles and manufacture of motor-vehicle engines;   Over 1,000 m² of new floorspace.

(g) Shipyards;   Over 1,000 m² of new floorspace.

(h) Installations for the construction and repair of aircraft;   Over 1,000 m² of new floorspace.

(i) Manufacture of railway equipment;   Over 1,000 m² of new floorspace.

(j) Swaging by explosives;   Over 1,000 m² of new floorspace.

(k) Installations for the roasting and sintering of metallic ores.   Over 1,000 m² of new floorspace.

5   *Mineral industry*   Over 1,000 m² of new floorspace

(a) Coke ovens (dry coal distillation);

(b) Installations for the manufacture of cement;

(c) Installations for the production of asbestos and the manufacture of asbestos-based products (unless included in Sch 1);

(d) Installations for the manufacture of glass including glass fibre;

(e) Installations for smelting mineral substances including the production of mineral fibres;

(f) Manufacture of ceramic products by burning, in particular roofing tiles, bricks, refractory bricks, tiles, stonewear or porcelain.

The need for EIA **7.21**

6	**Chemical industry**	
(a)	Treatment of intermediate products and production of chemicals;	Over 1,000 m² of new floorspace.
(b)	Production of pesticides and pharmaceutical products, paint and varnishes, elastomers and peroxides;	Over 1,000 m² of new floorspace.
(c)	Storage facilities for petroleum, petrochemical and chemical products.	(i) The area of any new building or structure exceeds 0.05 hectare; or
		(ii) more than 200 tonnes of petroleum, petrochemical or chemical products is to be stored at any one time.
7	**Food industry**	Over 1,000 m² of new floorspace.
(a)	Manufacture of vegetable and animal oils and fats;	
(b)	Packing and canning of animal and vegetable products;	
(c)	Manufacture of dairy products;	
(d)	Brewing and malting;	
(e)	Confectionery and syrup manufacture;	
(f)	Installations for the slaughter of animals;	
(g)	Industrial starch manufacturing installations;	
(h)	Fish-meal and fish-oil factories;	
(i)	Sugar factories.	
8	**Textile, leather, wood and paper industries**	Over 1,000 m² of new floorspace.
(a)	Industrial plants for the production of paper and board;	
(b)	Plants for the pre-treatment (operations such as washing, bleaching, mercerisation) or dyeing of fibres or textiles[31];	
(c)	Plants for the tanning of hides and skins;	
(d)	Cellulose-processing and production installations.	
9	**Rubber industry**	
	Manufacture and treatment of elastomer-based products.	Over 1,000 m² of new floorspace.

---

[31] Mechanical separation of hemp straw was not pre-treatment under this sub-paragraph: *R (on the application of Roudham and Larling Parish Council) v Breckland Council and Paul Rackham Ltd* [2008] EWCA Civ 714, [2009] LLR 545 at para 15 per Buxton LJ.

7.21 *Environmental Impact Assessment*

10 *Infrastructure projects*

(a)	Industrial estate development projects;	In England, development area over 5 hectares[32]
		In Wales, development area over 0.5 hectare.
(b)	Urban development projects, including the construction of shopping centres and car parks, sports stadiums, leisure centres and multiplex cinemas[33];	In England[34]: (i) The development includes more than 1 hectare of urban development which is not dwellinghouse development; or (ii) the development includes more than 150 dwellings; or (iii) the overall area of the development exceeds 5 hectares. In Wales, development area over 0.5 hectare.
(c)	Construction of intermodal transshipment facilities and of intermodal terminals;	Development area over 0.5 hectare.
(d)	Construction of railways;	Works area over 1 hectare.
(e)	Construction of airfields;	(i) The development involves an extension to a runway; or (ii) Works area over 1 hectare.
(f)	Construction of roads;	Works area over 1 hectare.
(g)	Construction of harbours and port installations including fishing harbours;	Works area over 1 hectare.
(h)	Inland-waterway construction, canalisation and flood-relief works[35];	Works area over 1 hectare
(i)	Dams and other installations designed to hold water or store it on a long-term basis;	Works area over 1 hectare.
(j)	Tramways, elevated and underground railways, suspended lines or similar lines of a particular type, used exclusively or mainly for passenger transport;	Works area over 1 hectare

---

[32] From 6 April 2015. If the project has already been determined to be EIA development then EIA is still required, as EIA could be insisted upon below the threshold in any event under reg 4(9): see Town and Country Planning (Environmental Impact Assessment) (Amendment) Regulations 2015, SI 2015/660, regs 4, 5.

[33] There are numerous cases on urban development projects, in particular *Goodman* (discussed above): *R (on the application of SAVE Britain's Heritage) v Secretary of State for Communities and Local Government* [2011] EWCA Civ 334, [2011] PTSR 1140 (demolition being an urban development project); *R (on the application of Warley) v Wealden District Council* [2011] EWHC 2083 (Admin), [2012] Env LR 4 per Rabinder Singh QC (floodlighting for tennis courts could be a modification to an urban development project).

[34] From 6 April 2015. As for industrial development projects, previous positive EIA decisions still arise. The raising of the threshold from 0.5 hectares is likely to lead to more requests for reg 4(9) screening directions from the Secretary of State. The revised threshold was discussed by Sullivan LJ in *Mackman v Secretary of State for Communities and Local Government* [2015] EWCA Civ 716 at paras 24–28.

[35] These include all works for retaining water and preventing floods, such as dyke construction: Case C-72/95 *Aannemersbedrijf P. K. Kraaijeveld BV v Gedeputeerde Staten Van Zuid-Holland* [1997] 3 CMLR 1.

The need for EIA 7.21

(k)	Oil and gas pipeline installations;	(i)	Works area over 1 hectare; or,
		(ii)	a gas pipeline design operating pressure exceeding 7 bar gauge.
(l)	Installations of long-distance aqueducts;	(i)	Works area over 1 hectare; or,
		(ii)	in the case of a gas pipeline, the installation has a design operating pressure exceeding 7 bar gauge.
(m)	Coastal work to combat erosion and maritime works capable of altering the coast through the construction, for example, of dykes, moles, jetties and other sea defence works, excluding the maintenance and reconstruction of such works;		All development.
(n)	Groundwater abstraction and artificial groundwater recharge schemes;		Works area over 1 hectare.
(o)	Works for the transfer of water resources between river basins;		Works area over 1 hectare.
(p)	Motorway service areas.		Development area over 0.5 hectare.

11 *Other projects*

(a)	Permanent racing and test tracks for motorised vehicles;		Development area over 1 hectare.
(b)	Installations for the disposal of waste;	(i)	incineration; or
		(ii)	Development area over 0.5 hectare; or
		(iii)	within 100 metres of controlled waters.
(c)	Waste-water treatment plants;		Development area over 1,000 square metres.
(d)	Sludge-deposition sites;	(i)	Deposit or storage area over 0.5 hectare; or
		(ii)	Deposit or storage within 100 metres of controlled waters.
(e)	Storage of scrap iron, including scrap vehicles;	(i)	Deposit or storage area over 0.5 hectare; or
		(ii)	Deposit or storage within 100 metres of controlled waters.
(f)	Test benches for engines, turbines or reactors;		New floorspace area over 1,000 square metres.
(g)	Installations for the manufacture of artificial mineral fibres;		New floorspace area over 1,000 square metres.
(h)	Installations for the recovery or destruction of explosive substances;		New floorspace area over 1,000 square metres.
(i)	Knackers' yards.		New floorspace area over 1,000 square metres.

12 *Tourism and leisure*

(a)	Ski-runs, ski-lifts and cable-cars and associated developments;	(i)	Works area over 1 hectare; or
		(ii)	building or structure height over 15 metres.

7.21 *Environmental Impact Assessment*

(b)	Marinas;	Enclosed water surface area over 1,000 square metres.
(c)	Holiday villages and hotel complexes outside urban areas and associated developments;	Development area over 0.5 hectare.
(d)	Theme parks;	Development area over 0.5 hectare.
(e)	Permanent camp sites and caravan sites;	Development area over 1 hectare.
(f)	Golf courses and associated developments.	Development area over 1 hectare.

13[36]

(a) Any change to or extension of development of a description listed in Sch 1 (other than a change or extension falling within paragraph 21 of that Schedule) where that development is already authorised, executed or in the process of being executed.

Either:

(i) The development as changed or extended may have significant adverse effects on the environment; or

(ii) in relation to development of a description mentioned in a paragraph in Sch 1 indicated below, the thresholds and criteria in column 2 of the paragraph of this table

indicated below applied to the change or extension are met or exceeded.

Paragraph in Paragraph of this table

Sch 1	
1	6(a)
2(a)	3(a)
2(b)	3(g)
3	3(g)
4	4
5	5
6	6(a)
7(a)	10(d) (in relation to railways) or 10(e) (in relation to airports)
7(b)	and (c) 10(f)
8(a)	10(h)
8(b)	10(g)
9	11(b)
10	11(b)
11	10(n)
12	10(o)
13	11(c)
14	2(e)
15	10(i)
16	10(k)
17	1(c)
18	8(a)
19	2(a)
20	6(c)

---

[36] Paragraph 13 is as set out in the EIA Regulations 2011. The Welsh version is differently expressed but intended to be to the same effect.

The need for EIA **7.23**

(b) Any change to or extension of development of a description listed in paragraphs 1 to 12 of column 1 of this table, where that development is already authorised, executed or in the process of being executed.	Either: (i) The development as changed or extended may have significant adverse effects on the environment; or (ii) in relation to development of a description mentioned in column 1 of this table, the thresholds and criteria in the corresponding part of column 2 of this table applied to the change or extension are met or exceeded.
(c) Development of a description mentioned in Sch 1 undertaken exclusively or mainly for the development and testing of new methods or products and not used for more than two years.	All development.

Screening

7.22 The process of determining whether EIA is required is screening. Unless the developer volunteers to carry out EIA by submitting an environmental statement, screening must take place. In *Berkeley v Secretary of State for the Environment* (initially in the Court of Appeal)[37] a duty to screen planning applications to decide whether EIA was required was recognised since EIA could otherwise be avoided by the public authorities failing to ask whether it was required. This obligation was explicitly contained in the Town and Country Planning (Environmental Impact Assessment) (England and Wales) Regulations 1999[38], which introduced formal screening processes. Screening decisions may either be taken by the local planning authority who would deal with the application, by adopting a screening opinion, or by the Minister making a screening direction. It will be no surprise that in the event of disagreement, a screening direction prevails over a screening opinion.

7.23 By reg 2(1) of the EIA Regulations 2011 and the 1999 regulations a '"screening opinion" means a written statement of the opinion of the relevant planning authority as to whether development is EIA development'. Provided the authority has considered whether EIA is required there is rarely a difficulty in providing a written statement of the opinion[39].

A screening opinion may be applied for before the planning application is made.

---

[37] [1998] Env LR 741.
[38] SI 1999/293.
[39] One case where the local planning authority's consideration of EIA did not amount to a screening opinion is *R (on the application of Lebus) v South Cambridgeshire District Council* [2002] EWHC 2009 (Admin), [2003] JPL 466.

7.24 *Environmental Impact Assessment*

7.24 Under reg 5 a person 'who is minded to carry out development may request the relevant planning authority to adopt a screening opinion'[40]. Regulation 5(2) requires a request for a screening opinion in relation to a proposed planning application to be accompanied by:

'(a) a plan sufficient to identify the land;

(b) a brief description of the nature and purpose of the development and of its possible effects on the environment; and

(c) such other information or representations as the person making the request may wish to provide or make.'

7.25 Consequently the development assessed in the screening opinion is that defined by the prospective developer. Screening is intended to be a fairly quick and inexpensive process. A screening request should explain the essential points of the scheme, identify any particular sensitivities arising from the project or its location and give a reasoned, if brief, explanation whether in the developer's view there are likely to be significant effects on the environment and if so on what parts. The aim is to assist the local planning authority to reach the right conclusion and to do so in a legally defensible manner.

7.26 The local planning authority may ask for any further information which it considers is needed to adopt a screening opinion[41]. The practical implication of the information not being provided may be that EIA is required because of the risk of a significant effect.

7.27 The regulations provide that the authority shall adopt a screening opinion within three weeks of the request or any longer period agreed in writing with the applicant[42]. In reality, this merely functions as an indicative timescale for a decision. Regulation 5(7) says that where an authority fails to adopt a screening opinion within that period the applicant may request a screening direction from the Minister. However the Minister can make a screening direction in any event, either on request or of his own volition[43]. All that the power to request a screening direction under reg 5(7) adds is that the Minister should make the direction within three weeks of receiving the reg 5(7) request 'or such longer period as may be reasonably required'[44].

7.28 If the local planning authority produces a positive screening opinion, so requiring EIA, or fails to adopt an opinion within the three week or any longer agreed period, the person who requested it may also ask the Secretary of State to make a screening direction under reg 5(7)[45]. In England such requests are sent to the National Planning Casework Unit. A request of the Minister under reg 5(7) shall be

---

[40] EIA Regulations 2011, reg 5(1); EIA Regulations 1999, reg 5(1). In practice requests are made by potential applicants for planning permission regardless of whether they intend to carry out the development themselves or to sell the site on with planning permission. Strictly a screening opinion may not be requested by a third party who does not want to carry out the development, but third party objectors in practice tend to ask the Minister for a screening direction.

[41] EIA Regulations 2011, reg 5(4); EIA Regulations 1999, reg 5(3).

[42] EIA Regulations 2011, reg 5(5); EIA Regulations 1999, reg 5(4).

[43] EIA Regulations 2011, reg 4(8); EIA Regulations 1999, reg 4(7); DMPO 2015, art 31(2); DMPO Wales, art 18(2). The DMPO provisions are wholly unnecessary given the respective EIA Regulations.

[44] EIA Regulations 2011, reg 6(4); EIA Regulations 1999, reg 6(4). The only sanction against ministerial delay is judicial review.

[45] In Wales these requests are under EIA Regulations 1999, reg 5(6).

accompanied by the original screening opinion request, any correspondence over further information and any screening opinion, along with any further representations which the applicant wishes to make[46]. The Minister may request further information to decide on the screening direction[47], but in practice the Minister will ask any party who may be able to help for further material or clarification of the points made in representations[48].

Screening on receipt of a planning application

7.29 Regulation 7(1) of the EIA Regulations 2011 obliges local planning authorities to consider whether EIA is required when certain planning applications are received:[49]

> 'Where it appears to the relevant planning authority that:
>
> (a) an application for planning permission which is before them for determination is a Schedule 1 application or Schedule 2 application; and
>
> (b) the development in question has not been the subject of a screening opinion or screening direction; and
>
> (c) the application is not accompanied by a statement referred to by the applicant as an environmental statement for the purposes of these Regulations,
>
> paragraphs (3) and (4) of regulation 5 shall apply as if the receipt or lodging of the application were a request made under regulation 5(1)'.

7.30 The effect is that the Council must adopt a screening opinion within three weeks of receiving a Sch 1 or Sch 2 application if it has not previously been screened and is not accompanied by an environmental statement. The planning application must therefore be for Sch 1 or 2 development to require a screening opinion.

7.31 However where the development might be Sch 1 or Sch 2 development then the local planning authority should consider whether it needs to adopt a screening opinion[50]. This prevents the EIA regime being bypassed because of planning authorities failing to ask whether it applies.

7.32 The natural meaning of the Regulations is that whether development is within Sch 2 development depends on the development referred to in the request for a screening opinion or applied for in the planning application, not on any wider development contemplated. Consequently where planning permission was sought for a new road within land which was intended to be the subject of a planning application for major redevelopment, a screening opinion was only required if the road itself met

---

[46] EIA Regulations 2011, reg 6(4); EIA Regulations 1999, reg 6(1). The request to the Minister and any further representations should be copied to the local planning authority: EIA Regulations 2011, reg 6(2); EIA Regulations 1999, reg 6(2).
[47] EIA Regulations 2011, reg 6(3); EIA Regulations 1999, reg 6(3).
[48] See for example the correspondence over screening in *R (on the application of SAVE Britain's Heritage) v Secretary of State for Communities and Local Government and Sefton Metropolitan Borough Council* [2013] EWHC 2268 (Admin), [2014] JPL 35.
[49] The Welsh reg 7(1) is in similar terms but encompasses subsequent applications as well as application for planning permission.
[50] *R (on the application of Goodman) v London Borough of Lewisham* [2003] EWCA Civ 140, [2003] JPL 1309.

7.33 *Environmental Impact Assessment*

the relevant threshold or criteria[51]. However if several planning applications are being made for an indivisible project (such as one application for anaeorobic digestion unit and another for the combined heat and power station which only it supplies with piped gas) then the wider project may have to be considered in applying the Sch 2 thresholds and criteria as being the same substantial development[52].

Below threshold screening decisions

7.33 If a planning application is for development within column 1 of Sch 2, but below the applicable threshold and outside any sensitive area, the local planning authority has no power to adopt a screening opinion or otherwise require EIA. The developer might choose to submit an environmental statement, in which case the EIA Regulations would apply[53].

7.34 Member states are permitted to adopt minimum thresholds for Annex 2 projects below which EIA cannot be required, provided that they do so having regard to the screening criteria in Annex III.[54] The UK has gone for a hybrid approach of a case-by-case examination of Annex II projects meeting thresholds or criteria, but recognising that other projects may still be likely to have a significant effect on the environment either on their own (such as a tower block) or in cumulation with other development. The Secretary of State may make a screening direction in below threshold cases under reg 4(9)[55]:

> 'The Secretary of State may direct that particular development of a description mentioned in Column 1 of the table in Schedule 2 is EIA development in spite of the fact that none of the conditions contained in sub-paragraphs (a) and (b) of the definition of "Schedule 2 development" is satisfied in relation to that development'.

Policy has in the past referred to such directions as exceptional, but whilst requirements for EIA in such circumstances will be rare, the normal test applies and the circumstances do not have to be exceptional.

7.35 The Minister may make such a direction of his own volition, however he is under no requirement to consider exercising these powers unless requested to do so. Any request must be made directly to the Minister (which in England includes a request to the National Planning Casework Unit) and asking an inspector on appeal is not sufficient[56]. Such a request must be for a screening direction and be unqualified;

---

[51] *R (on the application of Candlish) v Hastings Borough Council* [2005] EWHC 1539 (Admin), [2006] JPL 22 at paras 56, 61 per Davis J. Had screening been required then the proposed redevelopment may have needed to be considered, see paras 68, 69 citing *R v Swale Borough Council, ex p Royal Society for the Protection of Birds* [1991] JPL 39.
[52] *R (on the application of Burridge) v Breckland District Council* [2013] EWCA 228, [2013] JPL 1308 at paras 74–80 per Davis LJ.
[53] EIA Regulations 2011, reg 4(2); EIA Regulations 1999, reg 4(2)(a).
[54] EIA Directive, art 4(2), (3).
[55] A similar power exists in Wales under EIA Regulations 1999, reg 4(8).
[56] *Berkeley v Secretary of State for the Environment, Transport and the Regions Berkeley v Secretary of State for Environment (No 2)* [2002] EWCA Civ 1012, [2002] Env LR 14. Whether a request made to the inspector in a call-in application or an appeal which has been recovered by the Minister for decision is sufficient is uncertain but ought not to be relied upon. In any event, the objective would be to secure EIA at an early stage in the process. By EIA Regulations 2011, reg 2(5) references to the Secretary of State are not to be construed as references to an inspector.

asking for a screening direction if an application was called in did not require the Minister to make a direction when no call-in took place[57].

The screening decision

7.36 In adopting a screening opinion or direction the authority must take into account the relevant selection criteria in Sch 3[58]. These criteria are taken from Annex III of the EIA Directive and provide:

> 'Selection criteria for screening Schedule 2 development
>
> **Characteristics of development**
> 1. The characteristics of development must be considered having regard, in particular, to:
>   (a) the size of the development;
>   (b) the cumulation with other development;
>   (c) the use of natural resources;
>   (d) the production of waste;
>   (e) pollution and nuisances;
>   (f) the risk of accidents, having regard in particular to substances or technologies used.
>
> **Location of development**
> 2. The environmental sensitivity of geographical areas likely to be affected by development must be considered, having regard, in particular, to:
>   (a) the existing land use;
>   (b) the relative abundance, quality and regenerative capacity of natural resources in the area;
>   (c) the absorption capacity of the natural environment, paying particular attention to the following areas:
>   (i) wetlands;
>   (ii) coastal zones;
>   (iii) mountain and forest areas;
>   (iv) nature reserves and parks;
>   (v) areas designated by Member States pursuant to Council Directive 2009/147/EC on the conservation of wild birds and Council Directive 92/43/EEC on the conservation of natural habitats and of wild fauna and flora;
>   (vi) areas in which the environmental quality standards laid down in EU legislation have already been exceeded;
>   (vii) densely populated areas;
>   (viii) landscapes of historical, cultural or archaeological significance.

---

[57] *R (on the application of Threadneedle Property Investments Ltd) v London Borough of Southwark* [2012] EWHC 855, [2013] Env LR 1 at para 74 per Lindblom J.
[58] EIA Regulations 2011, reg 4(6); EIA Regulations 1999, reg 4(5).

7.37 *Environmental Impact Assessment*

Characteristics of the potential impact

3. The potential significant effects of development must be considered in relation to criteria set out under paragraphs 1 and 2 above, and having regard in particular to:

   (a) the extent of the impact (geographical area and size of the affected population);

   (b) the transfrontier nature of the impact;

   (c) the magnitude and complexity of the impact;

   (d) the probability of the impact;

   (e) the duration, frequency and reversibility of the impact'.

7.37 EIA is required if significant effects are likely, meaning they may occur or are possible[59]. 'Significant' is not defined in the EIA Directive or Regulations and finding whether effects are significant is left to the judgment of the decision-maker[60]. An environmental effect will not be significant merely because it is material to the planning decision[61], indeed many planning applications are refused because of environmental harm which is not significant in EIA terms. Some assistance may be provided by guidance from the European Commission and the UK authorities, but that needs to be approached with care. The *Planning Practice Guidance* contains indicative criteria and thresholds where EIA is more likely to be required[62]. However these need to be considered with great caution, either side of the line, as the location of the development and the impacts of the actual scheme tend to be decisive. The geographical extent of an impact is often important, but significant impacts might be localised[63].

7.38 Whether mitigation measures can be taken into account in deciding whether EIA is required can prove contentious. There is a danger in assuming that mitigation will be effective and a role of EIA is to determine what mitigation should be carried out. Conversely, there is no point in assessing significant effects if they will not happen. In *R (on the application of Lebus) v South Cambridgeshire District Council*, Sullivan J said[64]:

---

[59] The chances of the prospect arising have been variously described as more than a bare possibility but a serious possibility being sufficient *R (on the application of Bateman) v South Cambridgeshire District Council* [2011] EWCA Civ 157 at para 17 per Moore-Bick LJ; '"likely" connotes real risk and not probability'. *R (on the application of Morge) v Hampshire County Council* [2010] PTSR 1882 per Ward LJ at para 80.

[60] *R (on the application of Jones) v Mansfield District Council* [2003] EWCA Civ 1408, [2004] Env LR 391 per Dyson LJ at paras 17, 31 and per Carnwath LJ at para 61. It is not for the court to determine whether particular effects are likely to be significant and the planning authority's decision is to be considered on *Wednesbury* grounds (although as a matter of judgment rather than the exercise of a discretion): see *R (on the application of Malster) v Ipswich Borough Council* [2002] PLCR 251 at para 61 per Sullivan J; *R (on the application of Goodman) v London Borough of Lewisham* [2003] EWCA Civ 140 at para 10 per Buxton LJ; and *Bowen-West v Secretary of State for Communities and Local Government* [2012] Env LR 448 at para 39.

[61] *R (on the application of Loader) v Secretary of State for Communities and Local Government* [2012] EWCA Civ 869, [2013] PTSR 406.

[62] These replace the indicative criteria in former Circular 02/99 (which continues in Wales as Welsh Office Circular 11/99).

[63] For example, *R (on the application of Davies) v Carmarthenshire County Council* [2015] EWHC 230 (Admin) concerning the effect of a wind turbine on the setting of Dylan Thomas's house. An extremely local impact might not be an effect on the environment, such as overshadowing of a small number of houses by a football stadium: *R (on the application of Malster) v Ipswich Borough Council* [2002] PLCR 251.

[64] [2002] EWHC 2009 (Admin), [2003] JPL 466.

'45 Whilst each case will no doubt turn upon its own particular facts, and whilst it may well be perfectly reasonable to envisage the operation of standard conditions and a reasonably managed development, the underlying purpose of the Regulations in implementing the Directive is that the potentially significant impacts of a development are described together with a description of the measures envisaged to prevent, reduce and, where possible, offset any significant adverse effects on the environment. Thus the public is engaged in the process of assessing the efficacy of any mitigation measures.

46 It is not appropriate for a person charged with making a screening opinion to start from the premise that although there may be significant impacts, these can be reduced to insignificance as a result of the implementation of conditions of various kinds. The appropriate course in such a case is to require an environmental statement setting out the significant impacts and the measures which it is said will reduce their significance ...'.

7.39 *Lebus* concerned a proposed egg production unit for 12,000 free-range chickens and the judge said that it must have been obvious that with a proposal of this kind there would need to be a number of 'nonstandard planning conditions and enforceable obligations under section 106', and that these were precisely the sort of controls which should have been 'identified in a publicly-accessible way in an Environmental Statement' and:

'... it was not right to approach the matter on the basis that the significant adverse effects could be rendered insignificant if suitable conditions were imposed. The proper approach was to say that potentially this is a development which has significant adverse environmental implications: what are the measures which should be included in order to reduce or offset those adverse effects?'

7.40 These comments were endorsed by Lord Carnwath JSC in *R (on the application of Champion) v North Norfolk District Council*[65]:

'Those passages to my mind fairly reflect the balancing considerations which are implicit in the EIA Directive: on the one hand, that there is nothing to rule out consideration of mitigating measures at the screening stage; but, on the other, that the EIA Directive and the Regulations expressly envisage that mitigation measures will where appropriate be included in the environmental statement. Application of the precautionary principle, which underlies the EIA Directive, implies that cases of material doubt should generally be resolved in favour of EIA'.

7.41 The Court of Appeal's judgments on the topic were held to be on their facts and not a material departure from *Lebus*[66]. In *Champion* there was a risk that hydrocarbons would escape from a proposed lorry park, polluting a river which was a special area of conservation. Since the pollution prevention measures had not been fully identified when the planning application was submitted, EIA should have been required at the start. Subsequent reports dealt further with the mitigation risk so that the Council and Natural England were satisfied, but could not justify a later screening opinion that EIA was not required. Lord Carnwath held 'It is intrinsic to the scheme of the EIA Directive and the Regulations that the classification of the proposal is governed by the characteristics and effects of the proposal as presented to the authority, not by reference to steps subsequently taken to address those effects'[67].

---

[65] [2015] UKSC 52 at para 51.
[66] *Champion* at para 52 per Lord Carnwath citing *Gillespie v First Secretary of State* [2003] EWCA Civ 400, [2003] JPL 1287 at paras 37, 48, 49; *R (on the application of Jones) v Mansfield District Council* [2003] EWCA Civ 1408, [2004] Env LR 21 at paras 38–39; *R (on the application of Catt) v Brighton and Hove City Council* [2007] EWCA Civ 298, [2007] JPL 1517 at paras 33–35.
[67] *Champion* at para 47.

7.42 Environmental Impact Assessment

7.42 In deciding whether effects are likely to be significant (and also what should be in an environmental statement: see para **7.62**) it is necessary to consider the full extent of the project and its cumulation with other projects. A project will be wider than the particular planning application where there are other elements that must be carried out for it to be able to proceed. Cumulation concerns schemes which might or might not be connected, but which have a sufficient prospect of proceeding if the application project is built out that they ought to be considered with it. In practice it rarely matters if the other scheme is part of the same project or in cumulation with the application project; in either event its effects will be considered. Existing development should be considered in the cumulation, along with any other schemes which have planning consent (unless it can be concluded that they will not happen). It is harder to identify cumulative projects where they have not been consented. At one end of the spectrum, development which is necessary for the application project to proceed will have to be considered. For example, in *R (on the application of Brown) v Carlisle City Council*[68] a planning obligation made in connection with a freight storage and distribution centre required an upgrade of the main runway and the provision of passenger terminal facilities at Carlisle Airport for the proposal to be compliant with policy. The environmental impact of the airport works had to be considered in the EIA. Conversely, a potential future phase of development will rarely have to be considered, even if it would not happen without the current application[69]. Generally speaking, a future phase can be considered when it is applied for in the future, without needing to be anticipated in advance. Less common in practice, but more difficult to deal with, are applications which are inevitably part of a wider project which has not yet been applied for. In such cases the instant project would only be carried out if the developer or public authority concerned was sufficiently certain that it could proceed with the whole scheme (for example, consent for demolition of certain buildings within a larger area marked for demolition and redevelopment). The difficulty comes in identifying whether the works are being pursued as part of the larger project or for an independent reason[70].

7.43 It is an error of law to say that EIA is not required because the information will be provided with the application in any event[71].

In principle there may be insufficient information to lawfully screen an application, although the cases are all fact-sensitive[72].

7.44 Other errors in screening decisions have included:

---

[68] [2010] EWCA Civ 523, [2010] JPL 1571. Another example of a cumulative effect is *BAA plc v Secretary of State for Transport, Local Government and the Regions* [2002] EWHC 1920 (Admin), [2003] JPL 610. Conversely in *Davies v Secretary of State for Communities and Local Government* [2008] EWHC 2223 (Admin) a link road was separate to a proposed Park and Ride Scheme.

[69] For example, *Bowen-West v Secretary of State for Communities and Local Government* [2012] Env LR 448.

[70] For example, *R (on the application of SAVE Britain's Heritage) v Secretary of State for Communities and Local Government and Sefton Metropolitan Borough Council* [2013] EWHC 2268 (Admin), [2014] JPL 35 ('SAVE Sefton').

[71] *R (on the application of Lebus) v South Cambridgeshire District Council* [2002] EWHC 2009 (Admin), [2003] JPL 466 paras 10–13, 39 per Sullivan J.

[72] For the most thorough analysis see *Younger Homes (Northern) Ltd v First Secretary of State* [2004] JPL 950, paras 55–65 and see also *R (on the application of Noble Organisation Ltd) v Thanet District Council* [2005] EWCA Civ 782.

The need for EIA **7.47**

(i) officers failing to have delegated authority before making a screening decision[73];

(ii) considering only the significance of *adverse* effects on the environment rather than all significant effects[74].

Reasons in screening decisions

7.45 Much of the litigation of the early 2000s concerned a failure to consider screening at all, or planning authorities taking a very narrow view of the scope of the regime. It took the Court of Appeal to point out in *R (on the application of Goodman) v London Borough of Lewisham*[75] that a 'Big Yellow Warehouse' self-storage facility might be an urban development project. Screening litigation then tended to revolve around the extent to which an error could be identified in the varying amounts of explanation which might have been offered, the Court of Appeal in *R (on the application of Marson) v Secretary of State for the Environment, Transport and the Regions*[76] having decided that reasons did not have to be given. Such challenges met varying degrees of success.

7.46 Litigation took another swerve with the decision of the European Court of Justice that the reasons for not requiring an EIA had to be apparent from the material produced at the time or from an explanation provided in response to a subsequent request: *R (on the application of Mellor) v Secretary of State for Communities and Local Government*[77]:

> '59 ... effective judicial review, which must be able to cover the legality of the reasons for the contested decision, presupposes in general, that the court to which the matter is referred may require the competent authority to notify its reasons. However, where it is more particularly a question of securing the effective protection of a right conferred by Community law, interested parties must also be able to defend that right under the best possible conditions and have the possibility of deciding, with a full knowledge of the relevant facts, whether there is any point in applying to the courts. Consequently, in such circumstances, the competent national authority is under a duty to inform them of the reasons on which its refusal is based, either in the decision itself or in a subsequent communication made at their request...
>
> 60 That subsequent communication may take the form, not only of an express statement of the reasons, but also of information and relevant documents being made available in response to the request made'.

7.47 That invited a more penetrating analysis by the court of the reasoning which was actually given, for example, in *R (on the application of Bateman) v South Cambridgeshire District Council* and *R (on the application of Friends of Basildon Golf Course) v Basildon District Council*[78]. The terms of *Mellor* did, though, allow the authority's thought process to be pieced together from documents, such as any screening request and consultation responses at the screening stage[79]. This could

---

[73] *R v St Edmundsbury District Council, ex p Walton* [1999] JPL 805.
[74] *R (on the application of BT) v Gloucester City Council* [2001] EWHC Admin 1001, [2002] JPL 993.
[75] [2003] EWCA Civ 140, [2003] Env LR 28.
[76] [1999] 1 CMLR 268.
[77] C-75/08 [2010] PTSR 880, [2009] ECR I-3799, [2010] Env LR 2 at paras 59, 60.
[78] [2010] EWCA Civ 1432, [2011] Env LR 16.
[79] As in *R (on the application of Berky) v Newport City Council* [2012] EWCA Civ 378, [2012] 2 CMLR 44.

7.48 *Environmental Impact Assessment*

then be supplemented by a further explanation in response to a pre-action letter or (contrary to the intent of *Mellor*) a witness statement in litigation. There was a degree of benevolence in the willingness of the Courts to cobble together coherent and lawful reasoning from a range of documents, or to allow witness statements to explain away what were *prima facie* legal errors in the contemporaneous documents[80]. The broad trend of the post-*Mellor* cases was that if the decision-maker provided some decent amount of reasoning without clear-cut errors, then it was unlikely to find itself successfully challenged.

7.48 The ability to explain a decision later is pregnant with the possibility of what the courts call *ex post facto rationalisation*, which translates as making it up in response to the criticism raised. Since the challenge may first arise on the grant of planning permission, the position is unsatisfactory for all concerned. An explanation may be first sought two years after the screening decision and a screening opinion which relies upon much later reasoning is unreliable for all concerned, including the developer.

7.49 The Town and Country Planning (Environmental Impact Assessment) Regulations 2011 introduced a requirement in England that the screening opinion or direction 'be accompanied by a written statement giving clearly and precisely the full reasons for that conclusion'[81]. The written statement may be contained in the same document as the screening opinion or direction, but in any event must be published at the same time. Internal notes are not sufficient for this purpose.

7.50 The issues that arise are the standard expected of such reasons and whether later statements can correct omitted, unclear or defective reasoning. In *R (on the application of Embleton Parish Council) v Northumberland County Council*[82], HH Judge Behrens held that whilst a screening checklist which answered many questions with simply 'no' would have been adequate, with other material, under the 1999 Regulations post-*Mellor*:

> '[The 2011] regulations require a written statement giving "clearly and precisely" the "full" reasons for the decision. To my mind the check list is not such a statement. It does not purport to be such a statement. It does not purport to explain the reasons for the decision. It is a check list intended to help users decide whether an EIA is required'.

However he declined to quash the decision on the basis that no prejudice was caused to the claimant as it was 'possible to glean the reasons from the documents on the register' and there would be no different decision if the screening opinion was made again[83].

---

[80] See, for example, *R (on the application of Holder) v Gedling Borough Council* [2013] EWHC 1611 (Admin), [2013] JPL 1426 and the comments of Sullivan LJ in the subsequent permission hearing [2013] EWCA Civ 599; *Aston v Secretary of State for Communities and Local Government* [2013] EWHC 1936 (Admin), [2014] 2 P & CR 10.

[81] Regulation 4(7). Wales continues to use the Town and Country Planning (Environmental Impact Assessment) (England and Wales) Regulations 1999 which do not include a duty to give reasons for a negative screening decision and so are subject to the *Mellor* requirements. For post--*Mellor* consideration of EIA screening in Wales, see *R (on the application of Plant) v Pembrokeshire County Council* [2014] EWHC 1040 (Admin) and *R (on the application of Jedwell) v Denbighshire County Council* [2015] EWCA Civ 1232.

[82] [2013] EWHC 3631 (Admin), [2014] Env LR 16 at para 103.

[83] At para 106.

Scoping of proposed environmental statements **7.55**

7.51 In *Gilbert v Secretary of State for Communities and Local Government*[84], Supperstone J considered that reasons in a Secretary of State's screening direction complied with the EIA Regulations 2011, but said that these must be read together with a Planning Inspectorate screening checklist. Whilst that checklist was quickly disclosed on request, it was not part of the published statement of reasons.

Screening decisions kept on or with the planning register

7.52 In England a copy of any screening opinion or screening direction and any written statement of reasons must be made available for public inspection by the local planning authority. If a planning application has been made for that development then the decision and reasons would be on Part I of the planning register[85]. Where a screening decision precedes an application then it shall be available for inspection at the same place as the planning register for up to two years[86]. If an application is subsequently made then it will be transferred to Part 1 of the register[87]. Additionally a copy of the screening opinion and any accompanying statutory reasons shall be sent to the applicant[88].

7.53 A screening direction and any statutory reasons will be sent to the applicant and to the local planning authority who will put it with the planning register in the same way as a screening opinion[89].

However, without more, a failure to supply or make available a screening opinion will not lead to the permission being quashed[90].

Changes to the scheme post-screening

7.54 The submitted planning application might not be in full accord with the screening opinion or the application might be later amended. Lindblom J considered when a screening opinion would remain applicable in *R (on the application of CBRE Lionbrook (General Partners) Ltd) v Rugby Borough Council*[91]:

> 'the concept of a development having been the subject of a screening opinion is broad enough to include a previous screening process for an earlier version of the proposal, so long as the nature and extent of any subsequent changes to the proposal do not give rise to a realistic prospect of a different outcome if another formal screening process were to be gone through'.

SCOPING OF PROPOSED ENVIRONMENTAL STATEMENTS

7.55 An environmental statement is concerned with the main or significant effects on the environment of a project and will explain what the project is, the environment

---

[84] [2014] EWHC 1952 (Admin). The decision was upheld at [2015] EWCA Civ 314.
[85] EIA Regulations 2011, reg 23(1); EIA Regulations 1999, reg 20(1).
[86] EIA Regulations 2011, reg 23(2); EIA Regulations 1999, reg 20(2).
[87] EIA Regulations 2011, reg 23(1); EIA Regulations 1999, reg 20(1).
[88] EIA Regulations 2011, reg 5(5); EIA Regulations 1999, reg 5(5)
[89] EIA Regulations 2011, regs 6(5), 23; EIA Regulations 1999, regs 6(5), 20.
[90] *Younger Homes (Northern) Ltd v First Secretary of State and Calderdale Metropolitan Borough Council* [2004] EWCA Civ 1060, [2005] JPL 354.
[91] [2014] EWHC 646 (Admin), at para 47.

7.56 *Environmental Impact Assessment*

which might be affected, those effects, the mitigation proposed, the alternatives considered and any technical difficulties in the exercise[92]. Preparing a statement is potentially a time consuming and expensive exercise and needs to cover all the matters that the local planning authority properly requires. However it only needs to cover significant effects, not all environmental effects. There is considerable benefit in being able to ascertain what is required before preparation of the environmental statement begins.

7.56 A person who is minded to make an EIA application may ask the local planning authority for a scoping opinion setting out what information should be in the environmental statement[93]. The request should include a plan identifying the land, a brief description of the nature and purpose of the development and of its possible effects on the environment along with any other information or representations[94]. At minimum this ought to include a list of proposed topics, as the request is a chance for the prospective applicant to seek agreement to what it considers is necessary. The scoping request can be submitted with a request for a screening opinion.

7.57 Following receipt, the local planning authority should consult the applicant[95] and the consultation bodies[96]. It shall take into account the specific characteristics of the particular development and of development of the type concerned; and the environmental features likely to be affected by the development[97].

7.58 The local planning authority should adopt the scoping opinion within five weeks of the request, or within five weeks of making a screening opinion, unless longer is agreed in writing[98].

7.59 If a scoping opinion is not adopted in time then the applicant may ask the Minister to make a scoping direction[99]. A scoping direction may not be requested if the authority has adopted a scoping opinion in time, but the applicant disagrees with it. When asking for a scoping direction the Minister should be sent a copy of the request made to the local planning authority, any request for further information, any screening opinion and statement of reasons and representations[100]. The local planning authority shall be sent a copy of the request and representations[101]. The Minister may seek further information from the applicant[102], and shall consult the applicant and the

---

[92] EIA Regulations 2011, Sch 4; EIA Regulations 1999, Sch 4, discussed in more detail below.
[93] EIA Regulations 2011, reg 13(1); EIA Regulations 1999, reg 10(1).
[94] EIA Regulations 2011, reg 13(2); EIA Regulations 1999, reg 10(2).
[95] EIA Regulations 2011, reg 13(4); EIA Regulations 1999, reg 10(4). It is not apparent why the applicant needs to be consulted, since its views will be known, but dialogue between these participants is often helpful. Further information may be requested from the applicant but that does not affect the time for adopting the scoping opinion: EIA Regulations 2011, reg 13(3), (8); EIA Regulations 1999, reg 10(3), (8).
[96] EIA Regulations 2011, reg 2(1); EIA Regulations 1999, reg 2(1), defined as the public bodies consulted under the main consultation provisions of the DMPOs, the Marine Management Organisation (if relevant), any principal council, Natural England, the Environment Agency or Natural Resources Body for Wales (as appropriate) and others with statutory environmental bodies affected.
[97] EIA Regulations 2011, reg 13(6); EIA Regulations 1999, reg 10(6).
[98] EIA Regulations 2011, reg 13(4), (5); EIA Regulations 1999, reg 10(4), (5).
[99] EIA Regulations 2011, reg 13(7); EIA Regulations 1999, reg 10(7).
[100] EIA Regulations 2011, reg 14(1); EIA Regulations 1999, reg 11(1). Otherwise no formality is required and requests are usually made by letter.
[101] EIA Regulations 2011, reg 14(2); EIA Regulations 1999, reg 11(2).
[102] EIA Regulations 2011, reg 14(3); EIA Regulations 1999, reg 11(3).

consultation bodies (who will include the local planning authority if it is a council)[103]. No time limit is prescribed for the Minister's decision.

7.60 Scoping opinions and directions do not bind the local planning authority or the Minister as to what should be in the environmental statement[104]. They can subsequently take the view that more information is required. Similarly, an applicant is not bound to include the matters in the scoping opinion in its environmental statement, although it will have to argue, if necessary on appeal, why the scoping opinion overstates the requirements. In practice, therefore, the ability not to meet the scoping opinion or direction's expectations is very limited. The existence of a scoping decision provides some protection against later suggestions by third parties or public bodies that more information should have been included, but that ultimately turns on a judgment in the light of the then circumstances on how necessary that further information is.

7.61 Public bodies are under a duty to provide information to persons preparing environmental statements in what is essentially a duty to co-operate. A person intending to submit an environmental statement may serve notice[105] on the proposed recipient of the statement (the local planning authority or Minister) who will then inform the consultation bodies[106] of that proposal and pass the bodies' contact details to the applicant[107]. The local planning authority and those bodies should then, if requested, enter into consultation with the potential applicant and make relevant information available[108]. In England requests for information are to be treated as if they are made under the Environmental Information Regulations 2004[109] and so only encompass material which could have been obtained in any event. In practice, therefore, the purpose of the regulation is to encourage co-operation in identifying and assembling the information.

ENVIRONMENTAL STATEMENTS

7.62 An environmental statement means[110]:

'a statement:

(a) that includes such of the information referred to in Part 1 of Schedule 4 as is reasonably required to assess the environmental effects of the development and which the applicant can, having regard in particular to current knowledge and methods of assessment, reasonably be required to compile, but

(b) that includes at least the information referred to in Part 2 of Schedule 4'.

---

[103] EIA Regulations 2011, reg 14(4); EIA Regulations 1999, reg 11(4).
[104] EIA Regulations 2011, regs 13(9) (scoping opinions), 14(6) (scoping directions); EIA Regulations 1999, regs 10(9) and 11(6) respectively.
[105] The notice is in no particular form but shall 'include the information necessary to identify the land and the nature and purpose of the development, and shall indicate the main environmental consequences to which the person giving the notice proposes to refer in his environmental statement': EIA Regulations 2011, reg 15(2); EIA Regulations 1999, reg 12(2).
[106] As defined in EIA Regulations 2011, reg 2(1); EIA Regulations 1999, reg 2(1).
[107] EIA Regulations 2011, reg 15(1), (3); EIA Regulations 1999, reg 12(1), (3).
[108] EIA Regulations 2011, reg 15(4); EIA Regulations 1999, reg 12(4).
[109] EIA Regulations 2011, reg 15(5). The Welsh provisions do not apply the Environmental Information Regulations to any request beyond allowing authorities to decline to disclose information which is confidential under the previous Environment Information Regulations 1992: see EIA Regulations 1999, reg 15(5).
[110] EIA Regulations 2011, reg 2(1); EIA Regulations 1999, reg 2(1).

7.63 Environmental Impact Assessment

7.63 The minimum information required is therefore that in Part 2 and what in Part 1 is reasonably required and which the applicant can reasonably be required to assemble. There is a large overlap between the two parts, Part 2 being particular essential elements within Part 1.

7.64 Part 2 requires:

'1 A description of the development comprising information on the site, design and size of the development.

2 A description of the measures envisaged in order to avoid, reduce and, if possible, remedy significant adverse effects.

3 The data required to identify and assess the main effects which the development is likely to have on the environment.

4 An outline of the main alternatives studied by the applicant or appellant and an indication of the main reasons for the choice made, taking into account the environmental effects.

5 A non-technical summary of the information provided under paragraphs 1 to 4 of this Part'.

7.65 Part 1 provides:

'1 Description of the development, including in particular:

  (a) a description of the physical characteristics of the whole development and the land-use requirements during the construction and operational phases;

  (b) a description of the main characteristics of the production processes, for instance, nature and quantity of the materials used;

  (c) an estimate, by type and quantity, of expected residues and emissions (water, air and soil pollution, noise, vibration, light, heat, radiation, etc) resulting from the operation of the proposed development.

2 An outline of the main alternatives studied by the applicant or appellant and an indication of the main reasons for the choice made, taking into account the environmental effects.

3 A description of the aspects of the environment likely to be significantly affected by the development, including, in particular, population, fauna, flora, soil, water, air, climatic factors, material assets, including the architectural and archaeological heritage, landscape and the interrelationship between the above factors.

4 A description of the likely significant effects of the development on the environment, which should cover the direct effects and any indirect, secondary, cumulative, short, medium and longterm, permanent and temporary, positive and negative effects of the development, resulting from:

  (a) the existence of the development;

  (b) the use of natural resources;

  (c) the emission of pollutants, the creation of nuisances and the elimination of waste, and the description by the applicant or appellant of the forecasting methods used to assess the effects on the environment.

5 A description of the measures envisaged to prevent, reduce and where possible offset any significant adverse effects on the environment.

6 A non-technical summary of the information provided under paragraphs 1 to 5 of this Part.

7 An indication of any difficulties (technical deficiencies or lack of know-how) encountered by the applicant or appellant in compiling the required information'.

7.66 Despite these formidable lists, a few matters need to be borne in mind. The environmental statement is concerned with main or significant effects on the environment, not with all environmental effects. Consequently an environmental statement could be limited to particular topics and other environmental issues be addressed in separate reports, although the comfort of a scoping decision would assist that route. If an environmental issue is of importance there will be a need to provide information on it with the planning application in any event, so the extra work of putting that into an environmental statement is relatively modest.

7.67 A conventional structure for an environmental statement is:

(i) non-technical summary (which will also be available separately);

(ii) brief introduction, including identifying that the statement is prepared under the EIA Regulations;

(iii) description of the project;

(iv) it might be useful to have a project-wide description of the location and constraints, or this could be left to individual topics;

(v) description of the project alternatives considered by the developer;

(vi) topic-by-topic assessment, considering the aspects of the environment which may be affected within that topic, the impacts of the project, mitigation and any difficulties in investigating that topic;

(vii) any drawing together of the effects across particular topics, although the topic chapters should reflect each other's impacts where appropriate.

Publicity and consultation on the environmental statement and other material

7.68 The EIA Directive requires publicity of an application subject to EIA for the public[111]. More substantial rights are given to a narrower set of the 'public concerned', defined in the EIA Directive as 'affected or likely to be affected by, or having an interest in' the decision-making process including non governmental organisations promoting environmental protection[112]. The environmental statement has to be made available to the public concerned and they be given:

> 'early and effective opportunities to participate ... and shall ... be entitled to express comments and opinions when all options are open to the competent authority or authorities before the decision on the request for development consent is taken'[113].

The distinction between the public and the public concerned is of little practical importance in UK law since public consultation is wide and the ability to make representations is unlimited at the local planning authority level[114]. Public authorities

---
[111] EIA Directive, art 6(2).
[112] EIA Directive, art 1(2)(e).
[113] EIA Directive, art 6(3), (4).
[114] Whether someone is a member of 'the public concerned' might have a bearing if involvement is claimed which is wider than that allowed to the public at large.

7.69 *Environmental Impact Assessment*

likely to be concerned by the project by reason of their specific environmental responsibilities must also be consulted[115].

7.69 These publicity and consultation requirements are principally dealt with in England and Wales by the usual arrangements under the DMPOs. The following additions should be noted:

(i) the DMPOs require the highest category of publicity for EIA applications accompanied by environmental statements and the notice must say that the application is for EIA development and where and how copies of the environmental statement can be obtained[116];

(ii) an additional copy of the environmental statement must be provided to the local planning authority to be sent to the Secretary of State along with the planning application and any documents submitted with it[117];

(iii) the applicant or the local planning authority must send copies of the environmental statement to the 'consultation bodies'[118]. These are any bodies who the local planning authority are required to consult under the DMPOs' main consultation article[119], the Marine Management Organisation if offshore waters are likely to be affected, any principal council for the application site if not the planning authority receiving the application, Natural England and the Environment Agency (for applications in England), the Natural Resources Body (for Welsh applications), along with other bodies which by statute have specific environmental responsibilities and which the authority considers are likely to have an interest in the application[120];

(iv) the local planning authority (or on appeal or call-in, the Minister) is required to notify any person it is aware of who is likely to be affected by or has an interest in the application and who is unlikely to be aware of it by a site notice or local advertisement[121];

(v) where an environmental statement is to be submitted for the first time after the planning application has been made[122] then the applicant is required to publicise the proposed submission by a local newspaper advertisement and site

---

[115] EIA Directive, art 6(1).
[116] DMPO 2015, art 15(2); Sch 3; DMPO Wales, art 12(2), Sch 3.
[117] EIA Regulations 2011, reg 16(1). Two copies of the environmental statement must be provided for the Welsh Ministers: EIA Regulations 1999, reg 13(1).
[118] EIA Regulations 2011, reg 16; EIA Regulations 1999, reg 13. If the applicant provides the statement to the consultation body it must also send the application and drawings, saying that representations may be made and inform the local planning authority that it has done so: EIA Regulations 2011, reg 16(1), EIA Regulations 1999, reg 13(1). A minimum 14 day period for responses is provided: EIA Regulations 2011, reg 16(5), EIA Regulations 1999, reg 13(4).
[119] Under DMPO 2015, art 18 and DMPO Wales, art 14, but not under other articles of the relevant DMPO.
[120] EIA Regulations 2011, reg 2(1); EIA Regulations 1999, reg 2(1).
[121] EIA Regulations 2011, reg 16(2)(d).
[122] Including in the course of an appeal: EIA Regulations 2011, reg 17(8); EIA Regulations 1999, reg 14(8). Once the applicant indicates that it will provide an environmental statement, consideration of the application is suspended until that has been done and it may not be determined until 21 days after receipt: EIA Regulations 2011, reg 17(7); EIA Regulations 1999, reg 14(6). Suspension indicates that all consideration must stop, including any hearings, whilst the environmental statement is awaited on the basis that little could be achieved without the document.

Environmental statements **7.71**

notice[123] giving details of how the application and environment statement can be inspected, copies obtained and representations made. The applicant must certify that this has been done when submitting the environmental statement[124]. Notice must also be given to any person they have been asked by the local planning authority or Minister to inform[125];

(vi) a reasonable number of copies of the environmental statement must be available at the place where they are said to be available[126]. A 'reasonable charge reflecting printing and distribution costs' may be made for providing copies to members of the public[127]. The copies available should include paper copies, but it is commonplace to make a large environmental statement available in paper and CD-ROM form, with different charges which usually reflect the much lower costs of preparing a CD-ROM. Often environmental statements are accessed online: it is important that the document is readily navigable.

The submission of additional information

7.70 More information may be submitted in respect of the environmental statement and is required to be publicised. This falls into two categories:

(i) 'further information' which is required by the planning authority, Minister or inspector dealing with the application or appeal if they are 'of the opinion that the statement should contain additional information in order to be an environmental statement'. The material has to be requested in writing and sometimes referred to in England as a reg 22 request or reg 22 information (or in Wales by the equivalent reg 19)[128];

(ii) 'any other information' which is 'any other substantive information relating to the environmental statement' provided by the applicant or appellant[129].

7.71 Further information and any other information is subject to particular publicity requirements unless it has expressly been provided for the purpose of a public inquiry or hearing (where publicity of that event is considered to be sufficient)[130]. The local planning authority (or Secretary of State) which receives the information is required to place a local newspaper advertisement identifying the application, saying more information is available, how it can be inspected and copies

---

[123] The notice must be on application site but easily readable by members of the public off it (EIA Regulations 2011, reg 17(5)(b); EIA Regulations 1999, reg 14(4)(b)), an overcomplicated provision which means it cannot be on a lamppost by the site.
[124] EIA Regulations 2011, reg 17(6); EIA Regulations 1999, reg 14(5). It is an offence in Wales to knowingly or recklessly issue a false or misleading certificate: EIA Regulations 1999, reg 14(7).
[125] EIA Regulations 2011, reg 17; EIA Regulations 1999, reg 14.
[126] EIA Regulations 2011, reg 20; EIA Regulations 1999, reg 17.
[127] EIA Regulations 2011, reg 21; EIA Regulations 1999, reg 18.
[128] EIA Regulations 2011, regs 2(1), 22(1); EIA Regulations 1999, regs 2(1), 19(1).
[129] EIA Regulations 2011, reg 2(1); EIA Regulations 1999, reg 2(1). It has been suggested that this is not all information subsequently submitted but 'if it is substantive information provided by the applicant to ensure that the council is provided with the information required for inclusion in an environmental statement as required by Sch 4 to the EIA Regulations': *R (on the application of Corbett) v Cornwall Council* [2013] EWHC 3958 (Admin), [2014] PTSR 727 at para 71 per Lewis J.
[130] EIA Regulations 2011, reg 22(2); EIA Regulations 1999, reg 19(2).

7.72 Environmental Impact Assessment

obtained and giving a minimum of 21 days for representations to be made on it[131]. The recipient has also to send copies (provided by the applicant) to those sent the original environmental statement[132].

7.72 Where this publicity is required, determination of the application or appeal is suspended until 21 days from the newspaper advertisement or 14 days from copies of the information being sent out, whichever is the later[133]. Unlike a request for an environmental statement, where consideration of the application or appeal is suspended until it has been provided[134], the authority can continue to consider the application or appeal and only its determination is suspended whilst the information is provided.

Consideration of the environmental information

7.73 In determining the application the local planning authority is required to take into account the environmental information on the application: reg 3(4):

> 'The relevant planning authority or the Secretary of State or an inspector shall not grant planning permission or subsequent consent pursuant to an application to which this regulation applies unless they have first taken the environmental information into consideration, and they shall state in their decision that they have done so'.

7.74 Environmental information is:

> 'the environmental statement, including any further information and any other information, any representations made by anybody required by these Regulations to be invited to make representations, and any representations duly made by any other person about the environmental effects of the development'.

7.75 The requirement to say in the decision notice that the environmental information was taken into account is contained in both the EIA Regulations and the DMPOs[135]. Reference to taking into account the environmental statement is insufficient, since the environmental information is much more than that, however, mentioning the environmental statement alone is unlikely to be a fatal error unless there is doubt whether other environmental information was considered.

Subsequent applications

7.76 A 'subsequent application' is a reserved matters application or an application for the approval of details under a condition which is required before development commences or before a part of the development commences. These applications are discussed in Chapter 15 on reserved matters and approvals under conditions.

---

[131] EIA Regulations 2011, reg 22(3); EIA Regulations 1999, reg 19(3). As with the original environmental statement, a reasonable number of copies are to be available at a reasonable charge reflecting printing and distribution costs: EIA Regulations 2011, reg 22(8), (9); EIA Regulations 1999, reg 19(8).
[132] EIA Regulations 2011, reg 22(4), (5), (6); EIA Regulations 1999, reg 19(4), (5), (6).
[133] EIA Regulations 2011, reg 22(7); EIA Regulations 1999, reg 19(7).
[134] EIA Regulations 2011, reg 17(7); EIA Regulations 1999, reg 14(6).
[135] EIA Regulations 2011, reg 3(4) and the same duty is imposed by the DMPO 2015, art 35(4), DMPO 2010, art 31(2). Similar duplication arises in the Welsh regulations: the Town and Country Planning (Environmental Impact Assessment) (England and Wales) Regulations 1999, SI 1999/293, reg 3(2) and the DMPO Wales, art 24(2).

7.77 Where EIA was carried out on the original application, any subsequent application has to be publicised under the DMPO 2015, art 16 in the same way as a planning application for EIA development[136].

Publicity of EIA decisions

7.78 Planning authorities are also required to publicise the fact that they have made a decision in an EIA case and make available an explanation of the decision and of how it can be challenged, see EIA Regulations 2011, reg 24(1)[137]:

> 'Where an EIA application is determined by a local planning authority, the authority shall:
>
> (a) in writing, inform the Secretary of State of the decision;
>
> (b) inform the public of the decision, by local advertisement, or by such other means as are reasonable in the circumstances; and
>
> (c) make available for public inspection at the place where the appropriate register (or relevant section of that register) is kept a statement containing:
>
>   (i) the content of the decision and any conditions attached to it;
>
>   (ii) the main reasons and considerations on which the decision is based including, if relevant, information about the participation of the public;
>
>   (iii) a description, where necessary, of the main measures to avoid, reduce and, if possible, offset the major adverse effects of the development; and
>
>   (iv) information regarding the right to challenge the validity of the decision and the procedures for doing so'.

The importance of this publicity was emphasised in *R (on the application of Friends of Hethel) v South Norfolk Council*[138]. Informing the public by putting the material on the Council's website is insufficient[139].

---

[136] EIA Regulations 2011, reg 16(4).
[137] Similar provision is made in Wales by the EIA Regulations 1999, reg 21(1).
[138] [2009] EWHC 2856 (Admin), [2010] JPL 594 at paras 89–94 per Cranston J.
[139] See *Kendall v Rochford District Council* [2014] EWHC 3866 (Admin), [2015] Env LR 21 on similar strategic environmental assessment duties.

Chapter 8

Determining planning applications

8.1 In local planning authorities planning applications are determined either by the members of the authority or its officers. In councils, members will almost invariably decide planning applications in committees rather than in meetings of the full council. Decisions taken by officers will be known as delegated decisions. Other local planning authorities, such as national park authorities or urban development corporations, have a smaller membership so may deal with planning applications in their full meetings. This chapter is concerned with the way in which planning applications are decided at the local level. Decisions by the Mayor of London are addressed in Chapter 10.

THE DECISION-MAKING PROCESS

Decision-making

8.2 Primary legislation gives powers and duties to particular types of authorities (for present purposes, usually local planning authorities) which are then defined as being certain bodies (usually, for present purposes, local authorities). Historically, and in formal terms, a council consisted of its elected members. However it was never in practice possible for all of the authority's decisions to be taken by the members, acting together. Consequently councils have had power to make arrangements for the discharge of their functions by committees of councillors and by officers. How these arrangements worked were previously matters for the individual councils, although in practice very major decisions were made by the 'full Council' of all councillors meeting together, with the remaining important decisions being taken by committees of councillors and officers deciding other matters.

8.3 The Local Government Act 2000 required all but the smallest principal councils[1] to adopt executive arrangements. Ministers' intentions were that once a budget and policy framework was set then most political decisions would be taken by an executive consisting of a leader (or directly-elected mayor) and cabinet of councillors, with other councillors having as their main role the scrutiny of the executive. Various matters are non-excutive functions, including the handling of planning applications[2].

---

[1] Principal councils are county, district, borough or unitary councils, or in Wales, a county or county borough council: Local Government Act 1972, s 270.
[2] Local Authorities (Functions and Responsibilities) (England) Regulations 2000, SI 2000/2853, Sch 1; Local Authorities (Executive Arrangements) (Functions and Responsibilities) (Wales) Regulations 2007, SI 2007/399, Sch 1. This includes procedural matters which are calculated to facilitate or are conducive to the determination of planning applications, such as EIA screening: Local Government Act 2000, s 48(4); *R (on the application of Champion) v North Norfolk District Council* [2013] EWHC 1065 (Admin), [2013] Env LR 38. Of other planning matters, development plan making is shared between the executive and the rest of the council, other policy making is for the executive, as are conservation area designation and the making of art 4 directions. Enforcement is a non-executive function.

8.4 Decision-making on non-executive matters is governed by the Local Government Act 1972 (particularly ss 100A–101 and Sch 12). The starting point is that the powers of the local planning authority on non-executive matters remain with the full council unless arrangements are made for discharge by a committee, officers or another council.

8.5 Section 101(1), (2) of the Local Government Act 1972 provides:

'(1) Subject to any express provision contained in this Act or any Act passed after this Act, a local authority may arrange for the discharge of any of their functions:

(a) by a committee, a sub-committee or an officer of the authority; or

(b) by any other local authority.

(2) Where by virtue of this section any functions of a local authority may be discharged by a committee of theirs, then, unless the local authority otherwise direct, the committee may arrange for the discharge of any of those functions by a sub-committee or an officer of the authority and where by virtue of this section any functions of a local authority may be discharged by a sub-committee of the authority, then, unless the local authority or the committee otherwise direct, the sub-committee may arrange for the discharge of any of those functions by an officer of the authority'.

8.6 Two or more authorities can arrange for the discharge of any of their powers jointly, and may establish a joint committee to do so[3].

8.7 Consequently the full Council can delegate the exercise of powers to committees and sub-committees within the council, to its own officers, to a joint committee or to another local authority. A committee may delegate the exercise of its powers to a sub-committee or officers. Where an authority or committee has delegated decision-making downwards then it may still exercise those powers itself[4]. The difficulty, of course, is for the superior body to intervene before a decision is taken. This resumption of power can only be taken by the body who delegated it, so if the full council has delegated decisions on particular applications to officers then the planning committee cannot decide any of those applications unless the arrangements so provide.

8.8 There is a limited control on conflicts of interest within the same authority. If the local planning authority has made a planning application to itself for it to develop land (including jointly with another person)[5] then the application may not be determined[6]:

'(a) by a committee or sub-committee of the interested planning authority concerned if that committee or sub-committee is responsible (wholly or partly) for the management of any land or buildings to which the application relates; or

(b) by an officer of the interested planning authority concerned if his responsibilities include any aspect of the management of any land or buildings to which the application relates'.

---

[3] Local Government Act 1972, s 101(5).
[4] Local Government Act 1972, s 101(4).
[5] Under Town and Country Planning General Regulations 1992, SI 1992/1492, reg 3.
[6] Town and Country Planning General Regulations 1992, reg 10.

8.9 *Determining planning applications*

8.9 It is not possible under the Local Government Act 1972, s 101 to delegate the exercise of powers to an individual councillor[7]. If it is intended that a single councillor should be involved in a decision, or a small number of members be involved without meeting in committee, then the power can be delegated to an officer to be exercised after consultation with a particular member or members. This may be part of the general arrangements; for example, some authorities have delegated enforcement powers to officers in consultation with the planning committee's chairman and vice-chairman. A committee might resolve that the finalisation of a process be carried out by an officer in consultation with particular members. Examples would be delegating the approval of planning conditions or obligations to an officer subject to consultation with the committee chairman, or finalising reasons for refusal with the member who moved rejection of the application. In all such cases the decision must be that of the officer, who cannot adopt a position simply because it is the stance of the member. However, if there is a difference of view between the officer and the consulted members then it may be sensible for the application to be referred to the committee.

8.10 The s 101 arrangements as to whether planning applications are determined by which committee or by officers will usually be in the Council's constitution. These may appear in two parts: the article establishing the planning committee or committees; and the officer delegation provisions. Other procedural documents may set out procedures or policies involved in deciding the mode of determination. If these are not part of the s 101 arrangements themselves there will usually be a legitimate expectation that these will be complied with.

Common delegation arrangements

8.11 The effect of delegation arrangements is that the great majority of planning applications are determined by officers, typically some 80–90%. Of course, a very large proportion are small-scale, householder applications which do not attract any objection. Typically they would be determined by officers. Beyond those categories practices vary and reflect local experience and views. A common starting point is that officers can determine any planning application subject to specific exceptions. The types of exceptions which tend to be found include:

- *the size of the development*: it might be that all applications which are major development under the DMPO or meet some other threshold have to be determined by committee;
- *EIA schemes*: generally provide that planning applications which are subject to EIA are determined by committee because of their size, impact and potential public interest;
- *compliance with the development plan or other policies*: officers will usually not be able to allow an application which is contrary to the development plan. Normally arrangements allow officer refusals where the application contravenes planning policy;
- *whether the application is to be approved or refused*: officers may be allowed to refuse any application they wish, subject to an ability for councillors to have an application taken to committee. This may mean that agendas are dominated by

---

[7] Unlike executive functions, which can often be exercised by individual members.

applications recommended for approval and have the unintended consequence that members may feel they need to demonstrate their role by refusing a few;

- *applications by the Council*: it is often the view that applications made by the authority should be decided in public by a committee.
- *applications by councillors or officers*: it is common for planning applications made by councillors and officers in their private capacities to have to be referred to the planning committee. The reason is to promote openness so the decision is taken and has to be justified in public. If the applicant is a councillor then care needs to be taken to avoid any perception of bias. This is discussed further below;
- *objections received*: officers' powers to grant planning permission are sometimes removed if objections are made to the application. Those provisions need to be carefully drafted and construed. For example, what number of objections need to be made and should they be from people living in different properties? It may be sensible to require objections to be made before the end of the published consultation period (or any later periods), as otherwise there is a danger that an objection will be received, triggering a requirement to refer to committee, but not acted upon before permission is granted by officers. An objections trigger does mean that there will be public debate before an opposed scheme can be approved but there is a danger that acceptable schemes are delayed through weak objections;
- *requests for committee determination by councillors*: a fairly common provision is to allow a ward or divisional councillor covering the application site to insist that the application is reported to committee. The motivation may be that the application generates such interest that it ought to be decided by politicians in public. Alternatively the councillor may be concerned that the application will be approved or refused against his wishes. There is no reason why a councillor's request cannot be conditional upon the proposed outcome: for example, referring the application to committee if the officers intend to refuse it.

Another source of member referrals may be the views of members of the planning committee. This may work in a number of ways. The scheme may provide for any member of the committee to require an application to be referred to it or give that power to particular members, such as the chairman and/or vice chairman. The politicians' role might be simply consultative. A consultative panel was established by the London Borough of Camden and failures to follow its procedures were identified in *Vieira*, which is considered below at para **8.15**;

- *requests or objections by parish or town councils*: a scheme may provide that unresolved objections from a parish or town council for the application site (or a request from them) may require the application to go to committee. As with referrals triggered by objections from the public, it is sensible for a time limit to be set for a request, to avoid determination of an application in ignorance of a loss of jurisdiction.

The approval of reserved matters and details under conditions tends to be left to officers, but there is usually some ability for the largest schemes to go to committee.

Area planning committees

8.12 Some local authorities operate a system of area committees to determine planning applications. These committees would consist of some or all of the

8.13 *Determining planning applications*

councillors in the committee's particular geographical area. The reasons for adopting an area committee structure are political: a view being taken within the council that decisions should be taken more locally or powers shared amongst more councillors. Physically large council areas, such as unitary county councils, are more likely to have area committees, perhaps based on their former district structure. If an authority operates area planning committees it is still likely to have a council-wide planning committee.

8.13 Area committees give rise to several issues in practice:

(i) *the planning applications before them*: the council's constitution will identify which applications may be dealt with by an area committee. That could be all applications in the area which are sent to members for decision, or particularly large applications might have to go to the senior committee in any event;

(ii) *the relationship between area and council-wide planning committees*: there will often be a mechanism for referring planning applications from an area to the council-wide planning committee. This is usually to provide the senior committee with a degree of control. Options include referring applications at the initiative of the area committee, at the request of the senior committee, particular councillors or senior officers.

Arrangements have to be drafted and operated carefully in legal terms and with political judgment. Examples of possible schemes, and how one of them was unlawful, are given by *R (on the application of Friends of Hethel Ltd) v South Norfolk Council*[8]. In that case the Council's constitution provided that if an area planning committee rejected officer advice by less than a two-thirds majority of the members of the committee then the application was referred to the Council's district-wide committee. This contravened the Local Government Act 1972 which required decisions to be taken by 'a majority of the members of the authority present and voting'[9];

(iii) a practical issue with area committees is that in general the more councillors who are on planning committees, the lower will be the average interest, aptitude and experience of those members and the greater the chance of being overly influenced by local factors. Whilst this is not to suggest that there should not be area committees – for geographically huge councils they are a political and practical necessity – though there are quality risks which arise.

Compliance with the scheme of delegation

8.14 A decision taken by an officer, committee or group of councillors who do not have authority to make the decision is unlawful[10]. Delegation schemes need to deal carefully with the more unusual applications before a council, which might be inadvertently missed, such as relating to prior approval under permitted development rights. In *R (on the application of Grove Park Community Group) v London Borough of Lewisham*[11] the local authority accepted that the power to determine whether

---

[8] [2010] EWCA Civ 894, [2011] 1 WLR 1216 at para 19.
[9] Local Government Act 1972, Sch 12, paras 39(1), 44(1).
[10] *R (on the application of Friends of Hethel Ltd) v South Norfolk Council* [2010] EWCA Civ 894, [2011] 1 WLR 1216 at para 19.
[11] CO/7847/2011.

prior approval of the details of demolition and site restoration had not been delegated to planning officers and so an approval was unlawful.

8.15 In *R (on the application of Vieira) v London Borough of Camden*[12] the Council had established a system of members' briefings. Any planning application which was proposed for approval by officers contrary to representations was to be referred to a members briefing panel consisting of three or four councillors. They would advise whether the application should be referred to the Development Control Committee. An officer would then decide whether it should be referred. Changes had been recommended by the panel to the application in *Vieira*. The Council had said that the application had been taken back to the panel following amendment and approved. The challenge was initially, therefore, that the panel had taken the decision when they did not have power to do so. Finally the Council said that the 'panel' it had gone back to consisted of officers rather than members because it was shortly after local elections. The High Court held that the Council had made a representation that the application would be considered by the members briefing panel; that was not done and there was no justification for failing to do so.

8.16 The authority has to act in accordance with its scheme of delegation and the residual power for arrangement-making bodies to resume authority over a matter. If, for example, the number of objections received means that any approval of a planning application has to be by committee, then it must go to the committee unless officers are intending to refuse it. Often the scheme's requirements are matters of fact which can be resolved on proper investigation, such as whether a ward councillor asked for a committee decision in accordance with the scheme. The court would have no difficulty in intervening if an error has been made.

8.17 Other delegation rules would require an exercise of planning judgment, such as whether the application complies with the development plan and other policy. This would be subject to public law review by the court on relevant considerations and rationality. In *R (on the application of Carlton-Conway) v Harrow London Borough Council*[13] the Court of Appeal held that it was not rational for an officer to consider that a side and rear extension which had been subject to objection did 'not conflict with agreed policies, standards and guidelines'. Pill LJ said that the scheme of delegation[14] had to be:

> 'construed against a background that it is plainly the policy of the relevant statutory material and the circulars that there should be public participation in planning decisions, including participation by those who are affected by them. Where powers are delegated to a single individual the scope of those powers must be considered carefully. It is important that a planning officer purporting to exercise delegated powers should give careful and genuine consideration to the question whether the particular application with which he is concerned comes within the delegation. The purpose of the exception in paragraph 1.9, when a written objection has been made, is that cases may be dealt with where the relevant policies are clear and the relevant facts are clear. The policies can be applied in a straightforward manner to the facts of the particular case. The exception can only apply, in my judgment, where there is clarity as to the facts and as to the policies'.

---

[12] [2012] EWHC 287 (Admin).
[13] [2002] EWCA Civ 927, [2002] JPL 1216.
[14] At para 21.

8.18 *Determining planning applications*

However the test remains the public law one of whether it would be irrational for an officer to determine the application, and this is likely to arise relatively infrequently[15].

COMMITTEE REPORTS

8.18 A council will send an officers' report to the members of the committee and publish it at least five clear working days before the meeting[16]. The expectations upon the committee report were discussed by Judge LJ in *Oxton Farms v Selby District Council*[17] when he said:

> 'In my judgment an application for judicial review based on criticisms of the report will not normally begin to merit consideration unless the overall effect of the report significantly misleads the committee about material matters which thereafter are left uncorrected at the meeting of the planning committee before the relevant decision is taken'.

The court was emphasising the need for errors to be material, that is, capable of affecting the decision which was taken. It was not sanctioning the writing of misleading reports. Some errors in a report may be corrected elsewhere in the document or be obvious to a councillor reading it. Other errors might not matter. Errors which are spotted can be, and hopefully are, corrected at the meeting, whether by officers or members.

8.19 In *R (on the application of Lowther) v Durham County Council* Pill LJ described[18]:

> '... the duty of a planning officer in reporting to a committee. That duty is broader than a duty not actively to mislead. It includes a positive duty to provide sufficient information and guidance to enable the members to reach a decision applying the relevant statutory criteria. In the end, it is a matter of fact and degree for the members. However where, as in the present case, the decision-making body is required to apply a legal test to the facts as the members find them, it includes a duty to provide guidance as to what legal test is appropriate'.

8.20 Committee reports need to be appropriate to the audience which they are aimed at, being councillors with a degree of local knowledge and understanding of the planning system. Sullivan J said in *R v Mendip District Council, ex p Fabre*[19]:

> 'Whilst planning officers' reports should not be equated with inspectors' decision letters, it is well established that, in construing the latter, it has to be remembered that they are addressed to the parties who will be well aware of the issues that have been raised in the appeal. They are thus addressed to a knowledgeable readership and the adequacy of their reasoning must be considered against that background. That approach applies with particular force to a planning officer's report to a committee. Its purpose is not to decide the issue, but to inform the members of the relevant considerations relating to the application. It is not addressed to the world at large but to council members who, by virtue of that membership, may be expected to have substantial local and background

---

[15] See *R (on the application of Springhall) v Richmond-upon-Thames London Borough Council* [2006] EWCA Civ 19, [2006] JPL 970.
[16] Local Government Act 1972, ss 100B(3), 100E. The period is three clear working days in Wales, see para **8.33**.
[17] (18 April 1997, unreported), but frequently cited.
[18] [2001] EWCA Civ 781, [2002] JPL 197 at para 98.
[19] (2000) 80 P & CR 500 at 509.

knowledge. There would be no point in a planning officer's report setting out in great detail background material, for example, in respect of local topography, development planning policies or matters of planning history if the members were only too familiar with that material. Part of a planning officer's expert function in reporting to the committee must be to make an assessment of how much information needs to be included in his or her report in order to avoid burdening a busy committee with excessive and unnecessary detail'.

8.21 This is essentially judicial notice – what the court can take as being known in the absence of evidence on the point. What members do know has to be understood from all the circumstances, including what is said at the meeting. Councillors can be taken to appreciate what in general is seen as acceptable or harmful development and to all have a general knowledge of their authority's area. A committee operates collectively and will benefit from the greater knowledge of councillors representing that ward or division and any visits to view the application site. Assuming detailed knowledge of policies or circumstances is more difficult and may require specific evidence. Whilst judges have attributed substantial knowledge to councillors[20] in some cases that has not been possible[21].

8.22 The legal responsibility on a committee report is to ensure that members have the necessary knowledge to enable them to lawfully determine the application. Some things might not need to be said to knowledgeable members and they should not be induced into error by inaccurate or misleading reporting. Weaknesses may be corrected by officers, members or other persons allowed to make representations at the meeting. The principal question is whether the committee had regard to the material considerations. A report ought to go further and give councillors helpful advice and their officers' professional views about what the decision should be, although a report without a positive recommendation would still be lawful. The content of committee and delegated reports is not prescribed but the Housing and Planning Bill 2015 proposes to introduce a duty to refer in such reports to any financial benefits which are local finance considerations[22] or benefits of a prescribed description and which are likely to be received by the local planning authority or any other persons identified by regulations and their materiality to the determination of the application[23].

8.23 Update reports may be produced to respond to late developments (such as further correspondence sparked by the committee report) or to supplement or correct matters in the report. As Sullivan J said in *Fabre*, officer responses to late issues[24]:

'... may be given orally on the day, or it may be more helpful to set it out in writing a little time in advance. It is important that members are not "bounced" with new information that they do not have time to digest'.

---

[20] For example, in *R (on the application of Trashorfield Ltd) v Bristol City Council* [2014] EWHC 757 (Admin).

[21] In *R (on the application of McClellan) v London Borough of Lambeth* [2014] EWHC 1964 (Admin) Judge Sycamore QC was not prepared to assume that the Council's cabinet realised that a particular tree was in a conservation area.

[22] Grants from central government (presently the New Homes Bonus) and receipts which would arise under the Community Infrastructure Levy: see Town and Country Planning Act 1990, s 70(4).

[23] Proposed Town and Country Planning Act 1990, s 75ZA, which would be inserted by the Housing and Planning Bill 2015, cl 115 (as published following consideration by the Public Bill Committee in the House of Commons).

[24] *Fabre* at 515.

8.24 *Determining planning applications*

Such update reports are, by definition, not able to be provided in the s 100B period, but should be made available to the public as soon as possible after they have been circulated to members. A written report can be tabled at the meeting, but it is preferable to circulate it in advance.

ACCESS TO DOCUMENTS ON THE PLANNING APPLICATION

8.24 A variety of rights of access to documents relating to planning applications arise. These are useful for applicants who want to know what is said about their scheme and for third parties interested in understanding the project and what is said about it. Taking these in the sequence in which they tend to arise:

(i) the statutory duties to make available the planning application and any environmental statement;

(ii) the right of access to documents on request under the Environmental Information Regulations 2004[25] and the Freedom of Information Act 2000.

(iii) access to committee reports and background documents under the Local Government Act 1972 and other powers;

(iv) any legitimate expectation that documents will be available which has been created by the Council's representations, policies and practices, including its statement of community involvement[26];

(v) reasons for officer decisions under the Openness of Local Government Bodies Regulations 2014[27].

Duties of publication of planning applications themselves, including on the planning register, and environmental statements are covered in Chapters 6 and 7 respectively.

General rights of access: Environmental Information Regulations 2004, the Freedom of Information Act 2000 and the Data Protection Act 1998

8.25 Public authorities are subject to general duties to disclose information under the Environmental Information Regulations 2004, the Freedom of Information Act 2000 and the Data Protection Act 1998.

Environmental Information Regulations 2004

8.26 The Environmental Information Regulations 2004 implement Directive 2003/4/EC[28] on public access to environmental information, which is part of compliance with the Aarhus Convention on Access to Information, Public Participation in Decision-making and Access to Justice in Environmental Matters. They create a right of access to environmental information which is defined as[29]:

---

[25] SI 2004/3391.
[26] See *R (on the application of Joicey) v Northumberland County Council* [2014] EWHC 3657 (Admin), [2015] PTSR 622 at para 45.
[27] SI 2014/2095.
[28] The Directive repealed Council Directive 90/313/EEC.
[29] Directive 2003/4/EC, art 2(1); Environmental Information Regulations 2004, reg 2(1).

'any information in written, visual, aural, electronic or any other material form on:

(a) the state of the elements of the environment, such as air and atmosphere, water, soil, land, landscape and natural sites including wetlands, coastal and marine areas, biological diversity and its components, including genetically modified organisms, and the interaction among these elements;

(b) factors, such as substances, energy, noise, radiation or waste, including radioactive waste, emissions, discharges and other releases into the environment, affecting or likely to affect the elements of the environment referred to in (a);

(c) measures (including administrative measures), such as policies, legislation, plans, programmes, environmental agreements, and activities affecting or likely to affect the elements and factors referred to in (a) and (b) as well as measures or activities designed to protect those elements;

(d) reports on the implementation of environmental legislation;

(e) cost-benefit and other economic analyses and assumptions used within the framework of the measures and activities referred to in (c); and

(f) the state of human health and safety, including the contamination of the food chain, where relevant, conditions of human life, cultural sites and built structures inasmuch as they are or may be affected by the state of the elements of the environment referred to in (a) or, through those elements, by any of the matters referred to in (b) and (c)'.

The definition is wide, encompassing the state of the environment, matters that may affect it and governmental measures likely to affect the environment.

8.27 Article 3 of the 2003 Directive provides that member states shall ensure that public authorities are required to make available environmental information held by them. Article 3(1) is in these terms:

'Member states shall ensure that public authorities are required, in accordance with the provisions of this Directive, to make available environmental information held by or for them to any applicant at his request and without his having to state an interest'.

8.28 Article 4 provides that member states may provide for a request to be refused in specified cases. It states that the grounds for refusal shall be interpreted in a 'restrictive way, taking into account for the particular case the public interest served by disclosure'. In every particular case, 'the public interest served by disclosure shall be weighed against the interest served by the refusal'[30].

8.29 Consequently by reg 5 of the Environmental Information Regulations 2004, a public authority that holds environmental information shall make it available on request, 'as soon as possible and not later than 20 working days after the date of receipt of the request'[31], subject to certain exceptions. The principal exceptions are in reg 12:

'(4) ... a public authority may refuse to disclose information to the extent that:

(a) it does not hold that information when an applicant's request is received;

(b) the request for information is manifestly unreasonable;

---

[30] Summarised in *R (on the application of Evans) v Attorney General* [2015] UKSC 21, [2015] 2 WLR 813 at paras 23, 24 per Lord Neuberger of Abbotsbury PSC.
[31] Environmental Information Regulations 2004, reg 5(1), (2).

8.30 *Determining planning applications*

    (c) the request for information is formulated in too general a manner and the public authority has complied with regulation 9;

    (d) the request relates to material which is still in the course of completion, to unfinished documents or to incomplete data; or

    (e) the request involves the disclosure of internal communications.

(5) … a public authority may refuse to disclose information to the extent that its disclosure would adversely affect:

    (a) international relations, defence, national security or public safety;

    (b) the course of justice, the ability of a person to receive a fair trial or the ability of a public authority to conduct an inquiry of a criminal or disciplinary nature;

    (c) intellectual property rights;

    (d) the confidentiality of the proceedings of that or any other public authority where such confidentiality is provided by law;

    (e) the confidentiality of commercial or industrial information where such confidentiality is provided by law to protect a legitimate economic interest;

    (f) the interests of the person who provided the information where that person–

        (i) was not under, and could not have been put under, any legal obligation to supply it to that or any other public authority;

        (ii) did not supply it in circumstances such that that or any other public authority is entitled apart from these Regulations to disclose it; and

        (iii) has not consented to its disclosure; or

    (g) the protection of the environment to which the information relates'.

These are all subject to 'the public interest in maintaining the exception outweighs the public interest in disclosing the information'[32] when there is a 'presumption in favour of disclosure'[33]. In the context of a planning application, these exceptions must be addressed with an eye to whether the information will be considered when the application is determined.

The personal data of a person other than the one requesting the information is also protected in accordance with the Data Protection Act 1998[34].

The Freedom of Information Act 2000

8.30   The Freedom of Information Act 2000 applies to information which is not subject to the Environmental Information Regulations 2004[35]. Again, it contains a general right of access to information held by public authorities subject to exceptions[36]. Information is to be provided following a written request (including one by email or via a website)[37] promptly and in any event not later than the twentieth working day following the date of receipt[38]. The most relevant exemptions for documents in respect of planning applications are:

---

[32] Environmental Information Regulations 2004, reg 12(1).
[33] Environmental Information Regulations 2004, reg 12(2).
[34] See the Environmental Information Regulations 2004, reg 13.
[35] Freedom of Information Act 2000, s 39.
[36] Freedom of Information Act 2000, s 1.
[37] Freedom of Information Act 2000, s 8.
[38] Freedom of Information Act 2000, s 10.

Access to documents on the planning application **8.32**

(i) information accessible by other means[39], such as being on the Council's website already;

(ii) information intended for future publication[40];

(iii) information supplied by, or relating to, national bodies dealing with security matters[41];

(iv) safeguarding national security[42];

(v) investigations and proceedings concerned with criminal offences, civil proceedings and enforcement investigations[43];

(vi) information which would prejudice the free and frank provision of advice, or the free and frank exchange of views for the purposes of deliberation or would otherwise prejudice, or would be likely otherwise to prejudice, the effective conduct of public affairs[44];

(vii) if disclosure of the information would be an actionable breach of confidence[45];

(viii) information subject to legal professional privilege[46];

(ix) its disclosure under the Act would, or would be likely to, prejudice the commercial interests of any person[47].

Data Protection Act 1998

8.31 The Data Protection Act 1998 provides both a right of access for a living individual in respect of personal data held about them and also protection as to how that personal data is dealt with. The involvement of this legislation in the handling of planning applications is in practice limited. Personal data means[48]:

'data which relate to a living individual who can be identified:

(a) from those data, or

(b) from those data and other information which is in the possession of, or is likely to come into the possession of, the data controller, and includes any expression of opinion about the individual and any indication of the intentions of the data controller or any other person in respect of the individual'.

8.32 The right of access[49] provides a further entitlement for an individual applicant to see comments on their planning application and for a person who has made comments to see what is said about them. This is only a limited part of

---

[39] Freedom of Information Act 2000, s 21.
[40] Freedom of Information Act 2000, s 22.
[41] Freedom of Information Act 2000, s 23.
[42] Freedom of Information Act 2000, s 24. This has a particular bearing on information which may be subject to the security provisions on appeal or call-in.
[43] Freedom of Information Act 2000, ss 30, 31. This is more likely to apply to enforcement matters rather than planning applications.
[44] Freedom of Information Act 2000, s 36. An additional exemption applies to Minister's private offices: Freedom of Information Act 2000, s 35.
[45] Freedom of Information Act 2000, s 41.
[46] Freedom of Information Act 2000, s 42.
[47] Freedom of Information Act 2000, s 43.
[48] Data Protection Act 1998, s 1(1).
[49] Data Protection Act 1998, s 7.

8.33 *Determining planning applications*

the material on a file, although might be useful if other requests fail to tease out e-mails. Data controllers, including for present purposes local planning authorities, are required to process data in accordance with the data protection principles[50]. The dissemination of personal data is allowed if it is required by law or necessary for the exercising of public functions, which broadly speaking sanctions making it available when considering a planning application. However, unjustified publication may be a breach. In practice signatures and personal (but not business) telephone numbers and e-mail addresses are removed from application documents and comments which are posted on the authority's website. Unredacted originals should be made available for inspection and names should be published. The handling of sensitive personal data[51] needs to considered with care, particularly where it concerns health matters, but the need for public consideration of planning applications is a strong reason to maximise disclosure.

Access to committee reports and background documents under the Local Government Act 1972

8.33 Agendas and reports for committee meetings must be available for public inspection at least five clear working days before the meeting (three clear working days in Wales)[52]. Reports to Council committees are required to include 'a copy of a list, compiled by the proper officer, of the background papers for the report'[53]. Background papers are[54]:

'those documents relating to the subject matter of the report which:

(a) disclose any facts or matters on which, in the opinion of the proper officer, the report or an important part of the report is based, and

(b) have, in his opinion, been relied on to a material extent in preparing the report,

but do not include any published works'.

8.34 Usually on a planning application the background papers will be the planning application file. The public have a right to inspect the background papers unless the documents contain exempt or confidential information[55]. Whilst much of the background material may already be posted online by the Council, it is a useful right for applicants and interested persons to get immediate access to representations and the Council's internal paperwork[56]. If a list of background papers is not provided with the report then the right of inspection attaches to the documents which should

---

[50] Data Protection Act 1998, s 4(4).
[51] Defined in the Data Protection Act 1998, s 2.
[52] Local Government Act 1972, s 100B(3). In this legislation, clear days are interpreted as clear working days: *R v Swansea City Council, ex p Elitestone* [1993] 2 EGLR 212. If a meeting is held on Monday then three clear working days requires publication on the Tuesday before the meeting, whilst five clear working days pushes publication to the Friday a week and a half before the meeting, provided that there are no public or Bank Holidays.
[53] Local Government Act 1972, s 100D(1), applied to committees by s 100E. Similar rules apply to executive committees: see the Local Authorities (Executive Arrangements) (Meetings and Access to Information) (England) Regulations 2012, SI 2012/2089.
[54] Local Government Act 1972, s 100D(5).
[55] Local Government Act 1972, s 100D(1), (4).
[56] Access under the Freedom of Information Act 2000 or the Environmental Information Regulations 2004 may take up to 20 working days.

Access to documents on the planning application **8.38**

have been on the list[57]. The agenda and committee report need to be available on demand at the Council offices[58]. The duty is softened for background papers: a copy is taken to be open for inspection 'if arrangements exist for its production to members of the public as soon as is reasonably practicable after the making of a request to inspect the copy'[59].

8.35 Confidential information is that provided by a government department on terms which forbid disclosure to the public or information whose disclosure is prohibited by legislation or a court order[60].

8.36 Exempt information includes, as most relevant to planning applications, information relating to any individual or likely to reveal the identity of an individual, information relating to the financial or business affairs of any particular person (including the authority holding that information), that subject to legal professional privilege, information revealing that the authority proposes to give a notice imposing requirements upon any person, or make an order or direction under any enactment, or relating to any action taken or to be taken in connection with the prevention, investigation or prosecution of crime[61]. Within those categories the information can only be exempt 'if and so long, as in all the circumstances of the case, the public interest in maintaining the exemption outweighs the public interest in disclosing the information'[62].

8.37 Additionally information is not exempt information if it relates to proposed development for which the local planning authority may grant itself planning permission under the Town and Country Planning General Regulations 1992, reg 3[63].

Legitimate expectation of publication

8.38 Councils might make representations that they will publish more information on their websites than they are obliged to do by statute, or that consultation will take place on amendments or further material produced. Provided the representation is sufficiently clear there will be a legitimate expectation that it will be complied with, and which can only be departed from with good reason. Such a legitimate expectation may arise from a general policy, in particular in the Council's statement of community involvement, or by a representation on a particular matter[64]. A promise of publication involves the timely publication of the material[65].

---

[57] *R (on the application of Joicey) v Northumberland County Council* [2014] EWHC 3657 (Admin), [2015] PTSR 622 at para 44 per Cranston J.
[58] Local Government Act 1972, ss 100B(1), 100D(1).
[59] Local Government Act 1972, s 100D(5).
[60] Local Government Act 1972, s 100A(3).
[61] Local Government Act 1972, Sch 12A, Part 1, paras 1, 2, 3, 5, 6, 7.
[62] Local Government Act 1972, Sch 12A, Part 2, para 10. This public interest test was introduced by the Local Government (Access to Information) (Variation) Order 2006, SI 2006/88, which substituted a new Sch 12A.
[63] Local Government Act 1972, Sch 12A, Part 2, para 9. This provision applies to applications by the planning authority, not applications by other persons which a planning authority could have made: *R (on the application of Bedford) v Islington London Borough Council* [2002] EWHC 2044 (Admin), [2003] Env LR 22 at paras 82–84 per Ouseley J.
[64] See the discussion of legitimate expectation in Chapter 6.
[65] *R (on the application of Joicey) v Northumberland County Council* [2014] EWHC 3657 (Admin), [2015] PTSR 622 at para 47 per Cranston J.

8.39 *Determining planning applications*

Access to viability reports and sensitive material

8.39 In practice most local authorities will readily make the planning files available on request, subject to the removal of any confidential papers. Authorities vary as to how much material they publish on their website; some include all application correspondence and representations. Greater publication is helpful – the applicant and any other person can quickly see what has been produced – but readers must be alert to the possibility that an error has been made and documents missed off the website.

8.40 The Freedom of Information Act and the Environmental Information Regulations 2004 introduced a public interest test which had to be satisfied before the vast majority of material could be withheld. From 2006 this was introduced into the Local Government Act 1972. Prior to that time authorities had chosen to make available a great deal of material in planning cases which could have been treated as exempt. Difficulties only tended to arise where the applicant had provided financial information in viability or funding assessments which it did not want disclosed. One way of dealing with that was for the applicant to provide the material to consultants appointed by the local planning authority who would then report to the authority. The authority's consultants' report might then be kept by officers and summarised in any committee report. This issue arose in *R (on the application of Bedford) v Islington London Borough Council*[66] concerning Arsenal Football Club's proposed construction of a new stadium at Ashburton Grove. Some of the site was owned by the local authority and for the purpose of land negotiations Islington's consultants, DTZ, were provided with Arsenal's business plan and costs estimates. DTZ's evaluation was given to a limited number of officers. It had relevance to the price that could be paid to the Council for its land and the extent of planning benefits which the scheme could finance. Ouseley J held that it was exempt information[67] and it was not unfair for it not to be disclosed, given the lack of relevance of those points to the claimants' opposition to the scheme[68]. Additionally the councillors had managed without the DTZ report and were not in possession of information that the public had not seen[69]. The judge endorsed the approach of confidential information being given to consultants rather than directly to the authority[70].

8.41 In *R (on the application of English) v East Staffordshire Borough Council*[71] planning permission was granted for 28 houses in the open countryside to part-fill a gap in funding for a national football training centre. The developer submitted a financial report to the council, which had consultants investigate it. Neither report was provided to councillors nor to the public (despite objections) but the committee report said that the consultants had verified the figures, although members were told at the meeting that far more of the funding gap would be covered by the housing. Complaints about non-disclosure of the reports were dismissed by the court on the basis of *Bedford* and that the material was not important given the issues which arose. In *R (on the application of Perry) v Hackney London Borough Council* the applicant submitted a confidential financial assessment to justify providing less affordable housing than was sought by council policy. The court refused to order disclosure of

---

[66] [2002] EWHC 2044 (Admin), [2003] Env LR 22.
[67] At para 80.
[68] At paras 89–96.
[69] At para 98.
[70] At para 100.
[71] [2010] EWHC 2744 (Admin), [2011] JPL 586.

the material on the basis that it would prejudice the developer's discussions with third parties and the ability of local authorities to negotiate confidentially with developers was beneficial[72]. In the subsequent substantive hearing Patterson J considered that members were entitled to accept their officers' assurances about viability[73]. She held that information on the planning obligation negotiations could be withheld from members (albeit none had asked) as information relating to proposed terms in a contract (that is, a planning obligation)[74], and that the failure to disclose unredacted financial reports to the claimant was not unfair[75].

8.42 Information appeals do, however, point to greater disclosure. In *Royal Borough of Greenwich v Information Commissioner*[76] a developer sought, and obtained, a relaxation of affordable housing requirements in a signed planning obligation. The First-tier Tribunal considered whether the developer's viability report and the council's consultants' assessment should be produced in full, redacted versions having been ultimately made available. The Environmental Information Regulations 2004 were applied, with consideration of the confidentiality exception in reg 12(5)(e). This was not absolute and the tribunal said[77]:

> 'We find it particularly hard to accept that the pricing and other assumptions embedded in a viability appraisal are none of the public's business. They are the central facts determining the difference between viability and non viability. Public understanding of the issues fails at the starting line if such information is concealed, and discussion of the "point in time" nature of the viability models is frustrated'.

The tribunal pointed to how much information on prices and costs was widely available. Full disclosure of the reports was ordered, particularly given the importance of the affordable housing issue and the speed with which the developer had acquired the site and immediately sought to reduce the affordable housing contribution agreed by its predecessor.

MAKING REPRESENTATIONS TO THE COMMITTEE

8.43 The applicant, objectors and supporters may wish to make representations to the planning committee. This will usually be by writing to the committee members before the meeting or by speaking at the committee if the authority's procedures allow for this.

8.44 The best time to contact committee members is after the officer report has been published. Prior to that stage efforts should be focused on influencing the report. Councillors have many responsibilities and planning committee members are unlikely to be interested in a planning application before they have received the report unless it is in their ward or is a massive scheme. A letter written at an earlier stage might not be read, is likely not to be fully understood without a detailed report, and will probably be forgotten before the meeting takes place.

---

[72] [2014] EWHC 1721 (Admin), [2014] JPL 1329 at paras 23–36 per Patterson J.
[73] [2014] EWHC 3499 (Admin), [2015] JPL 454 at para 70.
[74] At paras 76–80.
[75] At paras 86–95. The court did not deal with the merits of an Environmental Information Regulations appeal which was proceeding over the same material: para 106.
[76] EA/2014/0122.
[77] At para 18.

8.45 *Determining planning applications*

8.45 Once the committee report is published, the opportunity arises to seek to support the officer recommendation or dissuade councillors from following it. Members will be able to consider those representations alongside the report. For written and oral representations the same basic principles apply:

(i) focus on the key points which are capable of turning councillors' minds. Bringing up a mass of technical points are likely to mean that councillors miss the critical issue. Points of detail on the report should be raised separately with the officers;

(ii) the points raised should be proper planning points which are attractive to politicians. The question is what would councillors find decisive, particularly to go against an officer recommendation? They need to be proper planning issues, which may include economic benefits. Members may detect that a plea is based on genuine but irrelevant points and officers are likely to point this out. A decision swung by an irrelevant or erroneous point might be overturned on appeal or in judicial review;

(iii) the points need to be made clearly such that they can be followed by someone who has read the committee report.

8.46 There are a few points to avoid[78]:

(i) do not assume that the members will simply follow the officer recommendation. Councillors consider, rightly, that they were elected to make decisions, not to rubberstamp the views of officers. Even worse than making the assumption is to address the councillors as if they will just do what they are advised;

(ii) do not attack the competence, honesty or integrity of the officers. Some councillors will adore their officers and consider that they are beyond personal reproach. Other councillors may consider that officers have been incompetent on a particular occasion, but may think it distasteful for someone to allege this, particularly in strong terms. What matters is whether the advice is wrong, or why it ought not be followed, rather than any motivation or ability which caused it to be wrong;

(iii) threatening the Council with an appeal, costs awards, judicial review or reporting to the local government ombudsman should be done sparingly and with great care. It can very easily look like an attempt to bully the committee and would tend to encourage councillors to resist that person's stance. The prospect of a challenge can be implicit, although there may be circumstances where it is effective to make it explicitly.

8.47 Letters should be fairly short, with two or three pages being a reasonable length. Committee meetings will usually deal with a number of applications – often more than ten – and the task of carefully reading the committee report will take some time. That preparation has to be fitted around the members' other political and personal (including work) commitments. Unless they are especially interested in the application they will not appreciate a lengthy submission, with appendices[79].

---

[78] The author is writing from the perspective of having been on the receiving end of all of these points whilst a member of a planning committee.
[79] Emailing a long document to councillors and expecting them to print it out is even less likely to be welcomed.

8.48 There is no difficulty in writing to councillors directly. Their addresses should all be available for inspection, but in some cases this will be given on websites as the council offices. Councils will have arrangements for distributing post to members and these should be checked if hard copy letters are to be sent via the council offices. Authorities' planning committee procedures may provide for correspondence to be circulated if it is received by a certain point before the meeting. In the absence of such a procedure correspondents should not assume that if they ask the planning department to circulate a letter to the committee that this will be done, or done before rather than at the meeting. Councillors' e-mail addresses are invariably on the Council website and letters can be sent that way.

8.49 If a letter is being sent to the committee it is prudent to copy it to the planning department. It is essential that applicants ensure that officers receive copies. Providing officers with copies enables them to comment on the letter. It also enables other persons to be aware of the correspondence, addressing any concern about 'secret' communications.

8.50 Other dealings with committee members in advance of a meeting should be handled with more care. Councillors should be, and generally are, concerned to avoid giving an impression that they are committed to one side before determining an application. The authority will usually have a planning code of conduct which guides such dealings. Committee members are unlikely to have meetings with parties without officers being present and may be reluctant to do so at all. Site visits for committee members should be organised with council officers (although there is no reason why members cannot view the site unaccompanied from the highway or public places).

8.51 No such restrictions apply to councillors who are not on the committee. They can be approached, in particular members representing wards or divisions which contain or are likely to be affected by the development. Such members can campaign vigorously for one side or another but it is for those individual politicians to decide what, if any, stance to take.

Oral representations to the committee

8.52 Many planning committees are prepared to hear oral representations from applicants and other persons. Whether and how this will be done will be set out in a published procedure. Invariably there will be a need to register in advance of the meeting, usually a day or so beforehand. It is vital for potential speakers to check and comply with this requirement. The committee would have a discretion to allow a late request but that cannot be relied upon. If the person finds out about the meeting at a late stage because of an error by the authority to inform them in time, then they should ask to speak out of time if they wish to do so. Where the authority has been at fault, it should treat the request as if it had been made in time.

8.53 Local authority practices reflect local experience and opinion, including whether the meeting will tend to finish at a reasonable time. Procedures vary in the following respects:

(i) the number of speakers allowed. There will be an attempt to have an equal number of speakers or amount of time on each side. Usually if there are too many speakers on one side then they will be expected to agree who will speak;

8.54 *Determining planning applications*

(ii) whether a parish, town or community council for the area is entitled to speak as of right or is treated as any other third party;

(iii) whether oral representations in support of the recommendation are allowed if there are no speakers against it. A requirement for opposition is sometimes put in place to avoid unnecessary speeches, although that may be unfortunate for an applicant whose scheme is recommended for approval and then rejected by the committee;

(iv) the time limit for each speech. These will usually be short, with three or five minutes being typical[80]. On occasion the applicant is allowed the aggregate of all the time taken by opponents;

(v) the order of speeches;

(vi) whether speakers may be questioned by the committee, and if so, for how long.

8.54 The time limits are usually ruthlessly enforced so unless the speaker is capable of extemporising a concise speech with a timer, it is sensible for the speech to be fully scripted and rehearsed against the clock. Spare time could be built into the script to allow comment on developments on the night. Speakers on the same side should coordinate their submissions to make the best use of time. If a letter has been sent to the committee before the meeting there is no point in reading this out, but the speaker may wish to make the same point in a different way[81].

8.55 Parties will need to think who should speak for them. The choice will be between the applicant/objector, the planning consultant or architect, an expert professional if a particular specialist issue arises, or a solicitor or counsel. This will often depend upon individuals' own skills and preferences, as well as the decisive issues in the case: will the committee be swayed by a heart-felt plea, or professional assurance or is there a hard issue, perhaps of law, where the committee need to be persuaded to disagree with their officers?

COMMITTEE MEETINGS

8.56 Planning committee meetings usually start with any declarations of interests and the approval of previous minutes. Applications will then be considered individually, although it is sensible for multiple applications for the same scheme to be considered together[82].

8.57 A typical format for considering an application is:

(i) introduction of the application by a planning officer. This can be quite lengthy with summaries of the issues in the report and visual presentations. The officer would be expected to update the committee on developments since the report, and including late representations and any comments on these as well as referring to any supplementary report;

(ii) any oral representations allowed from the public, other councils and the applicant;

---

[80] For very major applications authorities might arrange special committee meetings with longer presentations.
[81] Lawyers will be familiar with this advocacy technique.
[82] Such as a planning application and a listed building consent application.

(iii) representations from the ward or divisional councillor for the application site if they are not on the committee. Committee procedures invariably allow local councillors to make oral representations separately to any public speaking. These speeches should be separate to the discussion of the application by the committee itself;

(iv) officers will respond to any public or local councillor representations;

(v) the committee will then discuss and determine the application. Discussions tend to start with any questions to the officers seeking explanations or responses on matters of concern, before members turn to speeches on the merits. On some applications councillors may be content with the officer recommendation without needing any clarification, but if opponents of the recommendation have spoken or are in the public gallery then it is tactful for a member to say something in support of the recommendation;

(vi) a resolution, or resolutions will then be moved and voted upon.

8.58 Usually the officers present will be the planning officer presenting the report (this may be the case officer or a more senior officer), a Council lawyer and a committee clerk or administrator. Their role is to ensure that the committee are adequately informed about the application, have their professional views, are advised on the law in procedural and substantive terms and that the meeting is properly recorded. Advice includes briefing members on the application at the start of the item and responding to questions. It does go further to include active intervention. If issues are raised which may need assistance, such as what policy is relevant to an issue or devising a condition to address a concern, officers should volunteer comments. Similarly if a point is raised, whether by public speakers or members, which suggests a misunderstanding that needs correcting then that should be done. Most importantly, the committee should be warned if a prospective decision appears indefensible (particularly if there is a real risk of costs being awarded against the authority on appeal) or unlawful.

8.59 Planning applications will usually be considered entirely in public. Whilst there may be occasions in which the committee has to consider exempt information, which could justify that part of the item being dealt with in private, any decision should be taken with the public interest tests in mind and having regard to the open nature of planning decision-making. Sullivan J has warned that in considering any discretion to go into private session 'a local planning authority must not lose sight of the underlying requirement that what is done should be procedurally fair to the applicant for planning permission and to third parties who support or oppose the development'[83].

Resolutions

8.60 Resolutions will take the following forms:

(i) to agree the officer recommendation. If planning permission is to be granted for additional or different reasons from those in the officer reports then the mover of the motion should set these out;

---

[83] *R (on the application of Saunders) v Tendring District Council* [2003] EWHC 2977 (Admin) at para 64. There it was unlawful to deal with safety issues on a reserved matters approval in private, although counsel's advice could have been treated as exempt: paras 36–41, 50, 65, 66.

8.61 *Determining planning applications*

(ii) to reject the officer recommendation and approve or refuse planning permission. The reasons for rejecting the officer recommendation should be made clear by the member moving the motion. Several potential problems arise, and these are discussed further below;

(iii) to agree the recommendation with amendments. The amendments may be to impose different conditions or requirements for a planning obligation or additional reasons for refusal. Additionally procedural steps may be required, such as referral to the Secretary of State, amendments to the scheme or requiring the receipt of and consultation on further material. Such further stages may be subject to referral back to the committee if new issues arise or consultation with senior members of the committee prior to officers issuing a decision. For example, a committee which supported an application subject to specific concerns might resolve that it should be approved subject to amendments being made and no new issues arising out of consultation on those amendments;

(iv) to defer the application for a site visit. A committee can carry out a site visit, or appoint a sub-committee to do so and report back, however the need for this should be justified;

(v) to defer the application to a later meeting. Deferral of an application ought to be to address issues which arise. There may be a need for further information or consultation or the committee may have concerns which they wish the applicant to address. Deferral might also be required if determination of the application is premature. The fact that the committee dislike the recommendation but cannot think of a sound basis for rejecting it is not a good reason for deferring an application.

BIAS

8.61 It is useful at this point to consider the legal issue of bias in decision-making. The topic has generated a considerable amount of litigation in recent years[84], often concerning planning decisions in local government.

Principles

8.62 Concerns of bias in decision-making cover a number of different legal grounds:

(i) actual bias, which is that the decision-maker acted on a disposition for or against a person because of some personal favouritism or animosity, private interest or a public or political reason irrelevant to the purposes of the particular process, is an unlawful exercise of discretion by acting for an improper purpose or taking into account immaterial considerations;

---

[84] In addition to those discussed below, see *R (on the application of Island Farm Development Ltd) v Bridgend County Borough Council* [2006] EWHC 2189 (Admin); *Condron v National Assembly for Wales* [2006] EWCA Civ 1573, [2007] JPL 938. In two cases members of committees which had proposed council schemes (a gypsy site and a school development) had been able to take part in the planning decision: *R v Hereford and Worcester County Council, ex p Wellington Parish Council* [1996] JPL 573; *R v Derbyshire County Council, ex p Poole* [2001] PLCR 40.

(ii) pre-determination or having a closed mind is when the decision-maker has decided how to act before being fully aware of all of the circumstances and arguments. That is again an unlawful exercise of discretion, as a failure to have regard to material considerations or a failure to exercise the discretion at all;

(iii) an appearance of bias because of the real possibility that the decision was influenced by a private or irrelevant interest;

(iv) an appearance of bias because of the real possibility that the decision was pre-determined;

(v) biased advice, such as a committee report which is skewed by the omission of material or officer opinions which are not motivated by a relevant consideration of the public interest.

Complaints (i) and (ii) are part of the unlawful exercise of discretion, while (iii) and (iv) are the two main aspects of the rule against bias which is part of the public law concept of fairness. Category (v) can be characterised as having regard to immaterial considerations or failing to have regard to material considerations or the appearance of bias by a participant in the process who is not the decision-maker[85].

8.63 It is worth bearing in mind that planning is an administrative decision-making process and as such is inherently political. Planning is not a judicial or quasi-judicial process[86] and politicians are entitled to make planning decisions to advance a political agenda. However, like all administrative decisions, planning must be carried out lawfully, rationally and fairly and has a particularly detailed policy and legal underpinning which affects how applications are considered and steers their outcome. Committee members are required to have an open mind, but not an empty mind.

8.64 A discretion has to be exercised at the correct time, reasonably, in good faith and having taken into account all relevant considerations, and disregarded those which are irrelevant. The duty to have regard to relevant considerations is placed in statutory form for the consideration of planning applications by the Town and Country Planning Act 1990, s 70(2). Where a decision-maker makes up his mind before all material considerations are placed before him, or where he is influenced by an extraneous consideration which is immaterial or even a purpose other than that for which the power was enacted, he will have acted unreasonably. 'Predetermination' would have led to one or more legal errors which can all be described as broad *Wednesbury* unreasonableness. In those circumstances there would be a finding that the decision-maker had not made a reasonable and lawful decision.

8.65 Unfairness does not require an unequivocal finding that the ultimate decision was flawed. In brief it requires the decision-making process to be carried out in a fashion that the interested parties and the public at large can see as acceptable. Traditionally it involves three elements: the right to a fair hearing; the rule against bias; and compliance with procedural requirements. Despite its name, the rule against

---

[85] An example of this category is *R v Teeside Development Corpn, ex p William Morrison Supermarket plc* [1998] JPL 23 where Sedley J struck down the grant of planning permission because the development corporation's assessment had been one-sided and the advice it obtained was given with a view to supporting its scheme.

[86] The expression 'quasi-judicial' is inherently meaningless as it begs the question of what part of the process has judicial characteristics.

8.66 *Determining planning applications*

bias is not a prohibition on a person being biased – actual bias would be an exercise of power for an improper purpose or having regard to irrelevant considerations – but prohibits the appearance of bias. That is a lower threshold, and evidentially much easier to establish, than showing predetermination.

Predetermination

8.66 The essence of predetermination was set out by Ouseley J in *Bovis Homes*[87]:

> '... a Council acts unlawfully where its decision-making body has predetermined the outcome of the consideration which it is obliged to give to a matter, whether by the delegation of its decision to another body, or by the adoption of an inflexible policy, or as in effect is alleged here, by the closing of its mind to the consideration and weighing of the relevant factors because of a decision already reached or because of a determination to reach a particular decision. It is seen in a corporate determination to adhere to a particular view, regardless of the relevant factors or how they could be weighed. It is to be distinguished from a legitimate predisposition towards a particular point of view. I derive those principles from the *Kirkstall Valley Campaign Ltd*[88] case to which I have already referred, particularly at page 321G.
>
> 112 There is obviously an overlap between this requirement and the commonplace requirement to have rational regard to relevant considerations. But, in my judgment, the requirement to avoid predetermination goes further. The further vice of predetermination is that the very process of democratic decision-making, weighing and balancing relevant factors and taking account of any other viewpoints, which may justify a different balance, is evaded. Even if all the considerations have passed through the predetermined mind, the weighing and balancing of them will not have been undertaken in the manner required. Additionally, where a view has been predetermined, the reasons given may support that view without actually being the true reasons. The decision-making process will not then have proceeded from reasoning to decision, but in the reverse order. In those circumstances, the reasons given would not be true reasons but a sham'.

8.67 In *R v Secretary of State for the Environment, ex p Kirkstall Valley Campaign Ltd* Sedley J had summarised predetermination as follows[89]:

> 'The decision of a body, albeit composed of disinterested individuals, will be struck down if its outcome has been predetermined whether by the adoption of an inflexible policy or by the effective surrender of the body's independent judgment'.

Bias

8.68 The rule against bias is a long-standing principle of natural justice. However the formulation of the rule has been uncertain, with different camps preferring a 'reasonable likelihood' or 'real danger' as against a 'real possibility' of bias. The current formulation of the test, given by Lord Hope in *Porter v Magill* is[90]:

> 'The question is whether the fair-minded and informed observer, having considered the facts, would conclude that there was a real possibility that the tribunal was biased'.

---

[87] [2002] EWHC 483 (Admin) at para 111.
[88] *R v Secretary of State for the Environment, ex p Kirkstall Valley Campaign Ltd* [1996] 3 All ER 304.
[89] [1996] 3 All ER 304 at 323.
[90] [2001] UKHL 67, [2002] 2 AC 257 at 494, para 103.

Bias **8.71**

8.69 The rule against bias is concerned with the appearance rather than the fact of bias. It also relies on a full understanding of the facts, rather than a limited view. A bias can arise from a personal interest, for example the shareholding in a canal company which disqualified the Lord Chancellor from determining a case involving that company[91]. In *Bovis* and *Cummins* Ouseley J held that the source of the danger of bias had to be a personal external interest[92]. However in *Porter v Magill* the issue was whether the district auditor had created a real possibility that he might be biased when he held a press conference to make a provisional statement as liabilities of councillors. The House of Lords held that there was not, in the particular circumstances, bias. *Porter* does, however, show that bias can arise from actions or indicated views, rather than merely from interests.

8.70 Considering these cases in *R (on the application of Costas Georgiou) v London Borough of Enfield*[93] Richards J held that the *Bovis/Cummins* formulation was too narrow and that, following Porter, it is necessary to consider[94]:

'... whether, from the point of view of the fair-minded and informed observer, there was a real possibility that the planning committee or some of its members were biased in the sense of approaching the decision with a closed mind and without impartial consideration of all relevant planning issues'.

Richards J did immediately add a warning[95]:

'That is a question to be approached with appropriate caution, since it is important not to apply the test in a way that will render local authority decision-making impossible or unduly difficult. I do not consider, however, that the circumstances of local authority decision-making are such as to exclude the broader application of the test altogether'.

8.71 In *Georgiou*, three members of the planning committee had sat on their council's Conservation Advisory Group (CAG) where they had supported various planning applications. At the subsequent meeting of the planning committee nothing was said about the limited function of the CAG or about the need for those with dual membership to put on one side the support expressed in the CAG and to examine all the relevant planning issues before reaching the planning decisions. The judge concluded, with some hesitation, that there was a real possibility of bias[96]. Richards J applied *Georgiou* in *R (on the application of Ghadami) v Harlow Borough Council*[97], in which a planning permission was quashed because of views expressed by the chair of the planning committee to an objector in recorded telephone conversations.

---

[91] *Dimes v Grand Junction Canal* (1852) 3 HLC 759.
[92] *Bovis* at para 89; *R (on the application of Cummins) v London Borough of Camden* [2001] EWHC 1116 (Admin) at paras 259–260. In *R (on the application of Kelton) v Wiltshire Council* [2015] EWHC 2853 (Admin) a councillor was not disqualified by interest bias when the housing association of which he was a director was involved with a planning application as the likely (but not yet contracted) affordable housing provider and there was no direct link between the decision and personal benefit to the councillor: see para 42 per Cranston J. The decision was quashed on the basis of apparent bias: see para 50.
[93] [2004] EWHC 779 (Admin).
[94] *Georgiou* at para 31. However see comments on this paragraph in *R (on the application of Lewis) v Redcar and Cleveland Borough Council* [2008] EWCA Civ 746, [2009] 1 WLR 83 at paras 94, 95, discussed below.
[95] At para 31.
[96] At para 32.
[97] [2004] EWHC 1883 (Admin).

8.72 *Determining planning applications*

8.72 The cases were pulled together by the Court of Appeal in *R (on the application of Lewis) v Redcar and Cleveland Borough Council*[98] where a contentious planning application, in which the Council had a development interest, was approved during a local election campaign. The decision was quashed by Jackson J but reinstated by the Court of Appeal. Pill LJ explained the reversal of the High Court's decision by pointing to:

> '62 ... a more fundamental difference about the role of elected councillors in the planning process. There is no doubt that councillors who have a personal interest, as defined in the authorities, must not participate in council decisions. No question of personal interest arises in this case. The committee which granted planning permission consisted of elected members who would be entitled, and indeed expected, to have and to have expressed views on planning issues. When taking a decision councillors must have regard to material considerations, and only to material considerations, and to give fair consideration to points raised, whether in an officer's report to them or in representations made to them at a meeting of the planning committee. Sufficient attention to the contents of the proposal which on occasions will involve consideration of detail must be given. They are not, however, required to cast aside views on planning policy they will have formed when seeking election or when acting as councillors. The test is a very different one from that to be applied to those in a judicial or quasi-judicial position.
>
> 63 Councillors are elected to implement, amongst other things, planning policies. They can properly take part in the debates which lead to planning applications made by the council itself. It is common ground that in the case of some applications they are likely to have, and are entitled to have, a disposition in favour of granting permission. It is possible to infer a closed mind, or the real risk that a mind was closed, from the circumstances and evidence. Given the role of councillors, clear pointers are, in my view, required if the state of mind is to be held to have become a closed, or apparently closed, mind at the time of decision'.

8.73 The court should make its own judgment whether there is a real risk that minds are closed. Pill LJ said[99]:

> 'It is for the court to assess whether committee members did make the decision with closed minds or that the circumstances did give rise to such a real risk of closed minds that the decision ought not in the public interest to be upheld. The importance of appearances is, in my judgment, generally more limited in this context than in a judicial context'.

This question is entirely fact-specific, and turns upon whether a reasonable member of the public, neither complacent nor unduly sensitive or suspicious, would conclude that there was a real possibility that the tribunal was biased[100].

8.74 The court examined whether pre-discussion commitments or pronouncements gave rise to a perception that the decision-maker had predetermined the decision to be made through compliance with obligatory procedures[101]. Pill LJ reiterated that 'Central to such a consideration, however, must be a recognition that councillors are not in a judicial or quasi-judicial position but are elected to provide and pursue policies. Members of a planning committee would be entitled, and indeed expected, to have and to have expressed views on planning issues'[102]. Rix

---

[98] [2008] EWCA Civ 746, [2009] 1 WLR 83.
[99] *Lewis* at para 71 per Pill LJ. See also para 68.
[100] *Lawler v Northern Spirit* [2003] ICR 856 at 862 per Lord Steyn.
[101] *Bovis v New Forest District Council* [2002] EWHC 483 Admin at paras 111–112 per Ouseley J.
[102] At para 69, endorsing Woolf J in *R v Amber Valley District Council, ex p Jackson* [1985] 1 WLR 298.

LJ noted that it was common ground that 'planning context a distinction has to be made between mere predisposition, which is legitimate, and the predetermination which comes with a closed mind which is illegitimate'[103]. Questioning the dicta in *Georgiou*, he said that councillors did not have to be impartial (like the auditor in *Porter v Magill*) but to address the matters fairly, even with a predisposition[104]. There needed to be 'something which goes to the appearance of a predetermined, closed mind in the decision-making itself'[105].

The Localism Act 2011

8.75 Reflecting the number of court cases on bias issues and some spectacularly over-cautious advice given to councillors in particular instances, the Localism Act 2011 sought to protect the position of councillors. By s 25(2):

> 'A decision-maker is not to be taken to have had, or to have appeared to have had, a closed mind when making the decision just because:
> (a) the decision-maker had previously done anything that directly or indirectly indicated what view the decision-maker took, or would or might take, in relation to a matter, and
> (b) the matter was relevant to the decision'.

8.76 A decision-maker is a member or co-opted member of an authority, but not an officer[106]. The critical point is that an actual or apparent bias by predetermination cannot be found 'just because' of what a person did or said before the meeting. That reaches a similar outcome to *Lewis*. What happens at the meeting is critical, although earlier events may be relevant. A member who strongly supported a scheme before a meeting is more likely to be found to have given an appearance of a closed mind if they quickly and strongly continue that support in the meeting, but conversely might by careful questions or comments show that they are properly looking at the merits.

8.77 In *IM Properties* Patterson J held that the pre-meeting acts within s 25(2) include private statements (in that case an e-mail to fellow councillors) as well as public statements[107]. The imposition of a party whip on the adoption of local plan modifications had not given rise to predetermination[108]. However given the need for detailed, individual, up-to-the minute consideration, it does not follow that a whip will be lawful in determining planning applications. Local authority planning codes of conduct generally prohibit whipping in development control committees, with good reason.

---

[103] *Lewis* at para 89. See also Longmore LJ at paras 105–107.
[104] *Lewis* at paras 94, 95.
[105] *Lewis* at para 96 per Rix LJ. A court will weigh all such factors cumulatively to ascertain whether the requisite concern threshold is crossed, including a perusal of the actual decision-making process, and any impression conveyed thereby: *Council for National Parks Ltd v Pembrokeshire Coast National Park Authority* [2004] EWHC 2907 (Admin) at para 60 per Jack J, and *Bovis* at paras 113–114.
[106] See Localism Act 2011, s 25(4).
[107] *R (on the application of IM Properties Development Ltd) v Lichfield District Council* [2014] EWHC 2440 (Admin), [2014] PTSR 1484 at para 85.
[108] At para 86. Whips being generally permitted in local authorities provided members make up their own minds and not vote blindly in support of party policy: *R v Waltham Forest London Borough Council, ex p Baxter* [1988] QB 419.

8.78 *Determining planning applications*

Can one person taint the committee?

8.78 There are differing views as to whether a real possibility of bias by one member taints the entire body. The whole committee may be more likely to be infected if the real possibility of bias is due to an interest rather than pre-determination[109].

Summary of predetermination/bias

8.79 It is unlawful for a decision-maker:

(i) to have predetermined the outcome of a decision by delegating its decision, adopting an inflexible policy or closing its mind to the consideration and weighing of factors because of a decision already reached or because of a determination to reach a particular decision;

(ii) to lead a fair minded and informed observer, having considered the facts, to conclude that there was a real possibility of bias, either:

    1. due to a personal interest; or

    2. because the decision-maker would approach the matter with a closed mind and without impartial consideration of all relevant considerations.

8.80 It will be easier to establish a reasonable suspicion that there was closed mind bias rather than that there was in fact a closed mind. Such findings are highly fact sensitive. They must, in the particular case, be distinguished from a legitimate predisposition. So reasonable suspicion that the decision-maker has decided how to determine the application before all material considerations are available, perhaps because a party whip will be followed, will give rise to unlawfulness.

Which persons are subject to the rules on predetermination and bias?

8.81 As predetermination is a failure to lawfully exercise a discretion, any error is by the decision-maker. Again in principle the rule against bias is operative against the decision-maker, however on some occasions it will apply against advisers to the decision-maker. Advice may be partial or defective or there may be a fear that it reflects a private interest or view. There is a series of old cases where magistrates' courts clerks who have had interests (perhaps by their law firm) in a matter have vitiated the proceedings by retiring with the justices[110]. In *R v Salford Assessment Committee, ex p Ogden*[111] the clerking of a rating assessment committee by the same officer who clerked the rating committee was held by a majority decision of the Court of Appeal to give rise to bias as the rating assessment committee heard objections by the rating authority.

---

[109] For quashings on interest bias see *Kirkstall Valley* at 328A; *Bovis Homes Ltd v New Forest District Council* [2002] EWHC 483 (Admin) at paras 104, 105 per Ouseley J and in the judicial context, *R v Bow Street Metropolitan Stipendiary Magistrate, ex p Pinochet Ugarte* [2000] 1 AC 119. Any risk of pre-determination bias by a single member on a committee might be insufficient without more evidence of them influencing the rest of the committee: see *R (on the application of Berky) v Newport City Council* [2012] EWCA Civ 378, [2012] Env LR 35 at para 30 per Carnwath LJ and at paras 58, 59 per Buxton LJ.

[110] For example, *R v Sussex Justices, ex p McCarthy* [1924] 1 KB 256.

[111] [1937] 2 KB 1.

8.82 Planning officers advising a committee may be expressing views which are contrary to those of some persons interested in an application but that does not make them opposing parties. Their duty is rightly expected to be to the committee. A representative of a party ought to sit separately from the committee and not be present when the public are excluded[112].

The role of non-committee members

8.83 A planning committee will consider written objections, either in their original form or as summarised by officers, and often oral representations. Members of the local authority will often address the committee. Obviously they will not be treated in the same way as any other person allowed to speak. They will be known to the committee members, perhaps very well known. They may be senior in experience or importance in the Council or party groups to committee members. However it is perfectly proper for councillors to address the planning committee. It would be strange for everyone to be able to speak to a committee except the elected representatives of the public.

8.84 The only prohibition on other councillors speaking or attending is if they have a pecuniary interest within the Localism Act 2011[113]. If a committee adopted the position of a non-committee member for an improper reason, such as not wishing to offend the leader of the Council, that would be taking into account an immaterial consideration. It is sensible to ensure that non-committee members sit separately from the committee to ensure clarity of roles and to prevent any impression that they are part of the decision-making group.

8.85 A non-committee member speaking at the committee is likely to have taken his view on the application and the contents of his speech before the meeting. It is possible, but unusual, for the ward councillor's position to be merely reactive. He may have already made written representations on the application. If predetermination were relevant, it could commonly be said that such a councillor had predetermined his position. But that councillor would not be one of the decision-makers. If the committee weigh up all the material considerations and representations, including from other councillors, they will fairly and rationally reach a decision without any suspicion of predetermination. It is not a valid criticism of a committee decision that it receives representations from people with a particular axe to grind or whose view is formed from incomplete material. A legal challenge on the basis that a non-committee member addressing the committee was suspected of bias or predetermination would

---

[112] See by analogy *Cooper v Wilson* [1937] 2 KB 309 where a chief constable who brought disciplinary proceedings before a Watch Committee sat in on the committee's deliberations in the absence of the former police officer who was the subject of the proceedings.

[113] Localism Act 2011, ss 29–31. A member who has a 'disclosable pecuniary interest' in a matter on the agenda may not participate in the discussion or vote at that meeting (s 31(2)–(4)) without a dispensation under s 33. Whether there is an interest needs to be approached with realism. In *R (on the application of Freud) v Oxford City Council* [2013] EWHC 4613 (Admin) a councillor who was an employee of Oxford University did not have a pecuniary interest in an application made by a different part of the University to that which employed him, see paras 39–42 per Ouseley J. In *R (on the application of Kelton) v Wiltshire Council* [2015] EWHC 2853 (Admin) a councillor who was a director of a housing association was not in breach of s 31 when the association was involved with but not in contract with the applicant for planning permission: at para 45 per Cranston J. It might also be questioned whether the absence of potential financial benefit to the councillor prevented an interest arising.

8.86 *Determining planning applications*

tend to fail[114]. There might be a criticism if the presence of a member was contrary to the Code of Conduct, but such an error would have to link to the committee's decision.

Role of a disqualified member

8.86 If a non-committee member addressing the committee can have made up his mind before considering all the material, can a committee member address the committee in the same circumstances? If he dissociates himself from the committee's decision-making on that item he is in the same position as a non-committee member.

8.87 It is legitimate for a committee member with a bias/predetermination problem to speak at the same point in the item as a non-committee member. The member should make clear why he is speaking at that stage. He should not then take part in the committee's discussion on the item, propose or second motions or vote. As a vote can be entirely silent[115], it is important that the councillor is not seen to be part of the committee when the decision is made. One practice which makes this clear is for the member to speak from a position separate to those of the committee and to stay there for the item. Additionally as many of the public and applicants attending the committee will be unfamiliar with the procedures it needs to be readily apparent, even if this is slightly theatrical, that the member's status is changing for that item.

8.88 The following procedure would be lawful:

(i) non-committee members who speak at planning committee are seated separately to the committee members[116]. This helps the public understand who the committee are;

(ii) if a committee member is not taking part in the decision because of a bias/pre-determination issue, and is not barred by the Council's own Code of Conduct from participating, he should at the start of that item move to the non-committee members' seating;

(iii) either at that point or when he begins to speak he should explain that he is not taking part in the committee's decision because, for example, he has a non-pecuniary interest or has previously expressed a firm view on the application;

(iv) having spoken in the non-committee members' slot, he should take no further part in the discussion on that item;

(v) if the committee goes into a private hearing to consider exempt information, the member should withdraw along with the public.

8.89 The member would therefore have made his points but made clear that he is not one of the councillors taking the decision. There is no difference between the position of a committee member acting in this fashion and a non-committee member speaking on the item. In both cases it will be apparent that whilst they are councillors

---

[114] See *R (on the application of Bishop's Stortford Civic Federation) v East Hertfordshire District Council* [2014] EWHC 348 (Admin), [2014] PTSR 1035 at paras 16, 17, 25–36 per Cranston J.

[115] *R v Hendon Rural District Council, ex p Chorley* [1933] 2 KB 696, at 703 per Avory J.

[116] Reflecting the licensing decision of *R v London County Council, ex p Akkersdy* [1892] 1 QB 190 where members of a licensing committee who had instructed counsel to advance their view at full council should have sat with their legal team rather than with the other councillors.

they are not making the decision. They will not necessarily have any greater influence over the committee and by their position no improper influence. A non-committee member may have as much knowledge of planning as a committee member, and their views may be more respected than those of committee members.

REASONS FOR PLANNING DECISIONS

8.90 Local planning authorities have been subject to a long-standing duty to give reasons for the refusal of planning permission or for any conditions attached to a grant of permission. The statutory approach to reasons for granting permission has varied.

8.91 The English duty to give reasons for conditions and for refusing planning permission is in the DMPO 2015[117]:

'(a) where planning permission is granted subject to conditions, the notice must state clearly and precisely their full reasons:
  (i) for each condition imposed; and
  (ii) in the case of each pre-commencement condition, for the condition being a pre-commencement condition;
(b) where planning permission is refused, the notice must state clearly and precisely their full reasons for the refusal, specifying all policies and proposals in the development plan which are relevant to the decision'.

8.92 Additionally, details should be given of any direction by the Secretary of State restricting the grant of planning permission, or any views expressed by the Secretary of State or a government department that planning permission should not be granted, in whole or in part, or only be granted subject to conditions[118]. The decision notice should also explain how the local planning authority has worked with the applicant in a 'positive and proactive manner'[119] (discussed further in Chapter 14) along with the reasoning for pre-commencement conditions.

8.93 In Wales the duty on a grant of permission subject to conditions or the refusal of an application is to[120]:

'state clearly and precisely the full reasons for the refusal or for any condition imposed specifying all policies and proposals in the development plan which are relevant to the decision'.

As well as being more concise, the Welsh duty contains several differences from the English provisions. The policies and proposals in the development plan which are relevant to any condition have to be specified in the reason for that condition. Whilst this had been in the English provisions it was removed from 25 June 2013[121].

---

[117] DMPO 2015, art 35(1).
[118] DMPO 2015, art 35(1)(c).
[119] DMPO 2015, art 35(2).
[120] DMPO Wales, art 24(1).
[121] DMPO 2010, art 31(1)(a)(iii) amended by the Town and Country Planning (Development Management Procedure) (England) (Amendment) Order 2013, art 7(a).

8.94 *Determining planning applications*

Former English duty to give reasons for the grant of planning permission

8.94 Prior to 2003 the General Development Procedure Order only required reasons to be given for the refusal of permission or for the imposition of conditions. The litigation in that period is relevant to understanding the reasoning for decisions under current legislation.

8.95 The Town and Country Planning (General Development Procedure) Order 1995 was amended in England from 6 December 2003 to require where planning permission is granted, the decision notice to[122]:

> 'include a summary of their reasons for the grant together with a summary of the policies and proposals in the development plan which are relevant to the decision to grant permission'.

8.96 The intention was to give clarity as to why applications had been approved. As so often with legislative reform, many thought it was no reason to alter current practice. Consequently summary reasons were either perfunctory or entirely absent. There then followed a considerable amount of litigation to decide what the standard of reasoning should be. The first case was *R (on the application of Wall) v Brighton and Hove City Council*[123], which concerned reasoning in this form:

> 'This decision to grant Planning Permission has been taken having regard to the policies and proposals in the Brighton Borough Local and Brighton & Hove Local Plan Second Deposit Draft and to all relevant material considerations:
>
> • Brighton Borough Local Plan: ENV.1 - General principles, including amenity ...'

Sullivan J held that this was not a summary of reasons.

8.97 There was then a plethora of cases about the adequacy of summary reasons[124]. There was an 'obvious contrast between the duty to give a *summary of the reasons* for the grant of permission and the duty to give *full reasons* for each condition imposed and, in the case of a refusal, for the refusal'[125].

8.98 In *R (on the application of Ling (Bridlington) Ltd) v East Riding of Yorkshire Council* Sir Michael Harrison had said[126]:

> '47 In considering the adequacy of reasons for the grant of permission there are a number of factors which seem to me to be relevant. The first is the difference in the language of the statutory requirement relating to reasons for the grant of planning permission compared to that relating to the reasons for refusal of planning permission. In the case of a refusal, the notice has to state clearly and precisely the full reasons for the refusal, whereas in the case of a grant the notice only has to include a summary of the reasons for the grant. The difference is stark and significant. It is for that reason that I reject the claimants' contention that the standard of reasons for a grant of permission should be the same as the standard of reasons for the refusal of permission.

---

[122] Town and Country Planning (General Development Procedure) Order 1995, art 22(1)(a), (b)(i).
[123] [2004] EWHC 2582 (Admin), [2005] JPL 807.
[124] Given the abolition of the obligation, there is no need to consider these in detail.
[125] *R (on the application of Telford Trustee No 1 Ltd) v Telford and Wrekin Council* [2011] EWCA Civ 896, [2012] PTSR 935 at para 18 per Richards LJ.
[126] [2006] EWHC 1604 (Admin), [2007] JPL 396.

Reasons for planning decisions **8.100**

48 Secondly, the statutory language requires a summary of the reasons for the grant of permission. It does not require a summary of the reasons for rejecting objections to the grant of permission.

49 Thirdly, a summary of reasons does not require a summary of reasons for reasons. In other words, it can be shortly stated in appropriate cases.

50 Fourthly, the adequacy of reasons for the grant of permission will depend on the circumstances of each case. The officer's report to committee will be a relevant consideration. If the officer's report recommended refusal and the members decided to grant permission, a fuller summary of reasons would be appropriate than would be the case where members had simply followed the officer's recommendation. In the latter case, a short summary may well be appropriate'.

8.99 This advice was endorsed by Sullivan LJ in *R (on the application of Siraj) v Kirklees Metropolitan Borough Council* saying[127]:

'14 A local planning authority's obligation to give summary reasons when granting planning permission is not to be equated with the Secretary of State's obligation to give reasons in a decision letter when allowing or dismissing a planning appeal. I mention this because, although Mr Roe in his oral submissions before us recognised that there was indeed such a distinction between summary reasons and the reasons to be expected in a decision letter, the appellant's skeleton argument relied on the speech of Lord Brown in *South Bucks District Council v Porter (No 2)* [2004] UKHL 33, [2004] 1 WLR 1953 at paragraph 36. It is important to remember that that case was concerned with the adequacy of reasons in a Secretary of State's decision letter. Although a decision letter should not be interpreted in a vacuum, without regard for example to the arguments that were advanced before the inspector, a decision letter is intended to be a "stand-alone" document which contains a full explanation of the Secretary of State's reasons for allowing or dismissing an appeal. By their very nature a local planning authority's summary reasons for granting planning permission do not present a full account of the local planning authority's decision-making process.

15 When considering the adequacy of summary reasons for a grant of planning permission, it is necessary to have regard to the surrounding circumstances, precisely because the reasons are an attempt to summarise the outcome of what has been a more extensive decision-making process. For example, a fuller summary of the reasons for granting planning permission may well be necessary where the members have granted planning permission contrary to an officer's recommendation. In those circumstances, a member of the public with an interest in challenging the lawfulness of planning permission will not necessarily be able to ascertain from the officer's report whether, in granting planning permission, the members correctly interpreted the local policies and took all relevant matters into account and disregarded irrelevant matters.

16 Where on the other hand the members have followed their officers' recommendation, and there is no indication that they have disagreed with the reasoning in the report which lead to that recommendation, then a relatively brief summary of reasons for the grant of planning permission may well be adequate'.

8.100 Whilst emphasising the importance of the duty, the courts were keen to consider whether a different outcome might result on a redetermination[128]. The duty to give summary reasons for the grant of planning permission was revoked in 2013 as a

---

[127] [2010] EWCA Civ 1286; [2011] JPL 571. *Siraj* and *Ling* were then endorsed in *R (on the application of Telford Trustee No 1 Ltd) v Telford and Wrekin Council* [2011] EWCA Civ 896, [2012] PTSR 935 at paras 18–26 per Richards LJ.

[128] *R (on the application of Smith) v Cotswold District Council* [2007] EWCA Civ 1341 at paras 13–16 per May LJ, at para 18 Sir Anthony Clarke MR; *R (on the application of Park Pharmacy Trust) v Plymouth City Council* [2008] EWHC 445 (Admin), [2008] 2 P & CR 11 at paras 66–72 per Sullivan J.

8.101 *Determining planning applications*

means of reducing the workload on local planning authorities. A duty to give reasons was, though, reintroduced in an amended form for officer decisions by the Openness of Local Government Bodies Regulations 2014[129]. This is considered further below.

Why a planning decision was taken by a committee

8.101 Whilst it is correct that summary reasons for the grant of planning permission added little where the Council had simply adopted the delegated or committee report, they were of critical importance when there was a need to add to, qualify or completely depart from the report. Understanding why a planning application was determined in a particular way is necessary to provide a proper opportunity for appeal or legal challenge. The Ministers or the Mayor of London will need to be able to understand why a decision was taken to be able to decide whether to intervene. The need for reasoning is, however, even more basic. A decision-maker which does not go through the process of rationalising its decision is more likely to get it wrong. If it does not understand why it has chosen to act in a particular way, then it is less able to behave consistently in the future. The acceptability of a decision-making process depends upon participants believing that matters have been considered sensibly and rationally and that their comments have been taken into account. In planning, developers and concerned local residents alike will want to know why things turned out the way they did. The open nature of the planning process, with applications published, comments being available, decisions being taken on the basis of a disclosed report and public debate at committee all contribute to that understanding.

8.102 Where local planning authorities are not obliged to give reasons for their decisions, if they do the court can consider them in order to examine the basis in law for the decision[130]. As was explained in *Beckham* 'Reasoning advanced by the Council should be clear and unambiguous; it should not be contradictory, unsatisfactory or pregnant with possibilities of error'[131].

8.103 If the committee adopt the officer recommendation, for the officers' reasons, then the decision is no more complicated than expressing agreement, whatever trials the committee had to go through to reach that conclusion. In the absence of other evidence, it is a reasonable conclusion that a committee who have agreed an officer recommendation have done so for the reasons given by the officers in their report, any supplementary report or an oral update given at the meeting[132]. For good or ill, the council is stuck with the officers' analysis, insofar as it is adopted by the committee.

8.104 Where the committee depart from that analysis, it should be properly decided upon and recorded. A change in the reasoning might arise informally, such as a member making a point at the meeting which is accepted by officers, but this ought to be recorded in the minutes. Otherwise a change in the approach, the resolution of options given by the officers or the adoption of a position on a point left unclear in the report should be given by the mover of the motion to approve the application[133].

---

[129] SI 2014/2095.
[130] *Drexfine Holdings Ltd v Cherwell District Council* [1998] JPL 361 at 373 per Robin Purchas QC.
[131] *R v East Hertfordshire District Council, ex p Beckham* [1998] JPL 55 at 59 per Lightman J.
[132] See *R v Mendip District Council, ex p Fabre* (2000) 80 P & CR 500 at 510, 511 per Sullivan J.
[133] For an example of the latter situation, see *R (on the application of Young) v Oxford City Council* [2002] EWCA Civ 990, [2003] JPL 232 where a committee report left open whether an application should be viewed as enabling development, in which case English Heritage guidance was relevant but had been overlooked, or as acceptable in its own right and so the guidance had not been material.

Reasons for planning decisions **8.109**

8.105 More complex is when members disagree with the officer recommendation. The appropriate course is for a councillor to explain why rejection of the recommendation or approval of the contrary position is being proposed. Other members would have an opportunity to suggest additions or deletions from those reasons prior to the vote which, if the mover of the motion accepts them, could then be incorporated into that motion. There may be occasions when it is sensible for particular reasons for refusal to be subject to separate votes.

8.106 A motion proposed at a meeting is not likely to have the detail which would be contained in written reasons. There may be circumstances in which representations contain proposed reasons or can easily be adapted, but otherwise there will simply be an oral explanation of the thrust of the point. It can be dangerous for members to turn up to the meeting with pre-prepared reasons as that can suggest predetermination[134], although a member who made rough notes of possible reasons for disagreeing with the recommendation ought not to be subject to criticism if they did not have a firm view prior to the meeting[135].

8.107 Reasons proposed at a meeting are not likely to be precisely drafted or to contain the relevant policy references to go on a decision notice. The best course is for the detailed wording of the reasons to be prepared by officers in consultation with the mover of the refusal (and potentially with one or two other members). Those reasons should be a working up of the committee's reasons, rather than an opportunity to revisit why the committee made the decision it did.

8.108 Two practices should be discouraged. Some authorities require applications to be returned to committee if members have rejected the officer advice so that officers can ask members to think again. Unless something has gone so badly wrong that the decision is likely to be unlawful, that ought not to be done. Members were elected to make decisions, not to follow officer advice and the appropriate officer response to a lawful councillor decision is to implement it. The other inappropriate practice is to ask officers to report back to the next meeting with proposed reasons. The essence of the committee's reasoning should be apparent from the resolution and the debate. Whilst it might need writing up and policy references added, that can be delegated. It is not for the committee to decide to reject a recommendation and then ask officers to devise a plausible reason for doing so.

8.109 A committee decides all matters by a majority of those present and voting[136]. The chairman has a second or casting vote in the event of a tie[137]. A person who has a second or casting vote 'is clearly under a duty to exercise it honestly and in accordance with what he believes to be the best interests of those who may be affected by the vote'[138]. There is no recognised practice that chairs will cast a second vote in support of an officer recommendation or to maintain the status quo, indeed

---

[134] In *Bovis Homes Ltd v New Forest District Council* [2002] EWHC 483 (Admin) a member who proposed the rejection of an inspector's recommendation on a local plan went to the committee meeting with two pages of reasoning on acetate. This was one factor (albeit not an exclusive one) which led the court to consider that the council had adopted a closed mind.
[135] That situation is little different to a judge coming into court with notes for a judgment prior to hearing oral argument.
[136] Local Government Act 1972, Sch 12, paras 39(1), 44. Abstentions are not included in those voting for these purposes so a vote of 4 for, 3 against and 3 abstentions is a majority for the resolution.
[137] Local Government Act 1972, Sch 12, paras 39(2), 44.
[138] *R v Bradford City Council* [1990] 2 QB 363 at 371 per Neill LJ.

8.110 *Determining planning applications*

where the use of the second vote is final – rather than simply deferring a decision – following such a practice would be unlawful[139].

8.110 Other errors in the course of voting have included:

(i) in *R (on the application of Tromans) v Cannock Chase District Council*[140] members of the public had raised at the committee whether a vote at the meeting had been counted correctly. It was held to have been unfair for the Council to continue without verification or investigation;

(ii) having a constitution which required a 2/3rds majority for a committee to disagree with the officer recommendation[141];

(iii) not allowing a vote on a motion that members should carry out a site visit[142].

Recording of meetings

8.111 There will usually be an officer present with responsibility for the administration of the meeting[143]. They will be responsible for drafting the minutes so will be trying to keep a good note, although its accuracy will be affected by their understanding of planning and the agenda. The notes are a useful, if informal, record of what is said and ought to be retained until any possibility of challenge or appeal has passed.

8.112 The minutes of the meeting will be published in draft, usually with the agenda for the next meeting, and then approved by the committee. They constitute the formal published report of the meeting. Minutes will contain details of the members who attended, who declared interests and the decision on each application. Practice varies wildly as to whether the substance of oral representations and the discussion are included in the minutes. If it is, councillors and officers should ensure that it is accurate and includes any corrections or updates given to the committee and the committee's reasons.

8.113 Some local authorities webcast council and committee meetings, live and for later viewing. Some others will make an audio recording, which can be transcribed if necessary. These will provide the fullest record of the meeting, but even from a webcast it may be difficult to see which points the committee found persuasive.

8.114 Recording of meetings by the public and journalists, including bloggers, is encouraged by the Secretary of State. This includes video or audio recording and broadcasting, instantaneous reporting on social media and subsequent reporting[144].

---

[139] *R (on the application of Hewitson) v Guildford Borough Council* [2011] EWHC 3440 (Admin), [2012] JPL 951 Judge Robinson at para 39. Less persuasively, the court accepted an explanation by the chairman of the planning committee in that case that he had changed his mind on the merits in the short while between opposing the officer recommendation with his first vote and then supporting it with his second vote.

[140] [2004] EWCA Civ 1036, [2005] JPL 338.

[141] *R (on the application of Friends of Hethel Ltd) v South Norfolk District Council* [2010] EWCA Civ 894, [2011] 1 WLR 1216.

[142] *R (on the application of Hewitson) v Guildford Borough Council* [2011] EWHC 3440 (Admin), [2012] JPL 951 at paras 61–70 per Judge Robinson.

[143] This function is described as committee or democratic services.

[144] Local Government Act 1972, s 100A(7A)–(7F), (9), inserted by the Openness of Local Government Bodies Regulations 2014, SI 2014/2095, reg 4.

Reasons for officer decisions

8.115 A duty to give reasons for officer decisions on planning applications was introduced by the Openness of Local Government Bodies Regulations 2014. With effect from 6 August 2014 council officers must produce a written record of any decision which falls within reg 7(2) of these Regulations[145]. Regulation 7(2) provides:

> 'A decision falls within this paragraph if it would otherwise have been taken by the relevant local government body, or a committee, sub-committee of that body or a joint committee in which that body participates, but it has been delegated to an officer of that body either:
>
> (a) under a specific express authorisation; or
>
> (b) under a general authorisation to officers to take such decisions and, the effect of the decision is to:
>
> (i) grant a permission or licence;
>
> (ii) affect the rights of an individual; or
>
> (i) award a contract or incur expenditure which, in either case, materially affects that relevant local government body's financial position'.

8.116 Paragraph (2) covers the determination of planning applications and details as these are council functions which officers may only decide under authorisation. Where the application is to grant permission it falls within sub-para (b)(i). A refusal will invariably affect the rights of the applicant and any other person who may be the owner of the land under sub-para (b)(ii). By reg 7(3):

> 'The written record must be produced as soon as reasonably practicable after the decisionmaking officer has made the decision and must contain the following information:
>
> (a) the date the decision was taken;
>
> (b) a record of the decision taken along with reasons for the decision;
>
> (c) details of alternative options, if any, considered and rejected; and
>
> (d) where the decision falls under paragraph (2)(a), the names of any member of the relevant local government body who has declared a conflict of interest in relation to the decision'.

8.117 The recording detail could be satisfied by including reasoning on the decision notice, but would usually be achieved by an officer report on the application and explicit approval of the reasons in it by the decision-making officer. The written record, and any background papers, must be made available for inspection by members of the public at the Council offices and on its website[146]. Confidential or exempt information[147] does not have to be made available to the public[148], but all needs to be recorded and parts of the documentation which are not excluded from publication should be published.

8.118 The new requirement for officers to provide reasons for their planning decisions when no such duty applies to members may appear anomalous, although

---
[145] Openness of Local Government Bodies Regulations 2014, reg 7(1).
[146] Openness of Local Government Bodies Regulations 2014, reg 8.
[147] Within the meaning of the Local Government Act 1972, Sch 12A.
[148] Openness of Local Government Bodies Regulations 2014, reg 9.

8.119 *Determining planning applications*

member decisions are taken in public following a published officer report, so the reasons for committee resolutions are usually apparent.

Reasons for refusal

8.119 A planning obligation may be required to make a particular application acceptable. If the applicant refuses, or is unable, to enter into a satisfactory planning obligation then this may be a reason for refusal. In other cases permission may be refused for other reasons at a time when an obligation has not been made. Unless the refusal was because there was no obligation, the absence of an obligation is not a reason for refusal but the need for it can be included as informative on the decision, as was suggested by the former Costs Circular 03/09, para B26:

> 'Authorities may wish to consider using an informative note attached to the decision notice on an application for proposed development, in addition to stating a reason (or reasons) for refusal, to advise applicants that certain matters are considered to be capable of resolution by the submission of a planning obligation or by a condition. Provided that there are no objections of principle, such notes could also be used to indicate the form that a revised scheme might take in order to be regarded as acceptable'.

Reasons for rejecting advice from Natural England

8.120 Local planning authorities have a particular duty to give reasons to Natural England. If Natural England is asked by a public authority for advice on any matter relating to Natural England's general purpose[149] then it must respond[150]. Natural England may subsequently ask the public body whether the advice was rejected and that body must confirm whether that is the case and give reasons for the rejection[151].

---

[149] The general purpose is the conservation, enhancement and management of the natural environment, including nature conservation, landscape, access to the countryside and open-air recreation: Natural Environment and Rural Communities Act 2006, s 2.
[150] Natural Environment and Rural Communities Act 2006, s 4(1).
[151] Natural Environment and Rural Communities Act 2006, s 4(2), (3).

Chapter 9

Material considerations and policy

9.1 Planning decisions are taken on the merits of the particular applications which means taking into account what is relevant – otherwise described as material – to the decision and omitting anything which is immaterial. This is far from a free-for-all based on what officers or members consider to be right. In the interests of control and consistency, statute and, to a greater degree, policy points towards desirable outcomes and tests to be applied.

9.2 This chapter first considers the general requirement to take into account material considerations and the structure of policy, including the development plan. Then material considerations are addressed in two groups:

(i) substantive material considerations, being topics relevant to planning decisions, such as sustainable development, amenity, heritage and landscape;

(ii) structural material considerations, being the inter-relationship between different parts of the planning system and other planning decisions.

MATERIAL CONSIDERATIONS AND THE STRUCTURE OF POLICY

What are material considerations?

9.3 It is a basic principle of public law that a decision-maker must have regard to relevant considerations and not have regard to irrelevant considerations[1]. In the determination of planning applications and appeals, relevant considerations are described by statute as 'material considerations' and irrelevant considerations are referred to as 'immaterial considerations'. There is no difference between relevant and material considerations, Lord Carnwath JSC observing in *R (on the application of Health and Safety Executive) v Wolverhampton City Council*[2]:

---

[1] For example, as part of Lord Slynn of Hadley's summary of public law in *R (on the application of Alconbury Developments Ltd) v Secretary of State for the Environment, Transport and the Regions* [2001] UKHL 23, [2003] 2 AC 295 at para 50:

'It has long been established that if the Secretary of State misinterprets the legislation under which he purports to act, or if he takes into account matters irrelevant to his decision or refuses or fails to take account of matters relevant to his decision, or reaches a perverse decision, the court may set his decision aside. Even if he fails to follow necessary procedural steps—failing to give notice of a hearing or to allow an opportunity for evidence to be called or cross-examined, or for representations to be made or to take any step which fairness and natural justice requires—the court may interfere'.

[2] [2012] UKSC 34, [2012] 1 WLR 2264 at para 49.

9.4 Material considerations and policy

'Sufficient consistency is given to the expression if the word "material considerations" is treated as it is elsewhere in administrative law: that is, as meaning considerations material (or relevant) to the exercise of the particular power, in its statutory context and for the purposes for which it was granted'.

9.4 In England, the Town and Country Planning Act 1990, s 70(2) provides that in dealing with a planning application the local planning authority:

'shall have regard to:
(a) the provisions of the development plan, so far as material to the application,
(b) any local finance considerations, so far as material to the application, and
(c) any other material considerations'.

9.5 Local finance considerations were introduced by the Localism Act 2011 and that reference in sub-s (2)(b) does not apply to Wales[3]. The Welsh approach is therefore the time-honoured expression of regard to the provisions of the development plan, so far as material to the application, and any other material considerations.

9.6 The potential range of material considerations is wide. In *Stringer v Ministry of Housing and Local Government*[4] Cooke J said:

'It may be conceded at once that the material considerations to which the Minister is entitled and bound to have regard in deciding the appeal must be considerations of a planning nature. I find it impossible, however, to accept the view that such considerations are limited to matters relating to amenity. So far as I am aware, there is no authority for such a proposition and it seems to me wrong in principle. In principle, it seems to me that any consideration which relates to the use and development of land is capable of being a planning consideration. Whether a particular consideration falling within that broad class is material in any given case will depend on the circumstances. However, it seems to me that in considering an appeal the Minister is entitled to ask himself whether the proposed development is compatible with the proper and desirable use of other land in the area. For example, if permission is sought to erect an explosives factory adjacent to a school, the Minister must surely be entitled and bound to consider the question of safety.

... it seems to me that it would be impossible for the Minister and local planning authorities to carry out their duties as custodians of the public interest if they were precluded from considering the effect of a proposed development on a particular use of land by a particular occupier in the neighbourhood. The public interest, as I see it, may require that the interests of individual occupiers should be considered. The protection of the interests of individual occupiers is one aspect, and an important one, of the public interest as a whole. The distinction between public and private interests appears to me to be a false distinction in this context'.

Stringer concerned the effect of nearby development on the operation of the radio telescopes at Jodrell Bank[5].

---

[3] Town and Country Planning Act 1990, s 70(2A).
[4] [1971] WLR 1281, [1971] 1 All ER 65.
[5] A more down-to-earth example of interference with radio waves being material to a planning decision is the effect of tall buildings or structures on television reception: *Hunter v Canary Wharf* [1997] AC 655.

Material considerations and the structure of policy **9.10**

9.7 In *Westminster City Council v Great Portland Estates Ltd*[6] Lord Scarman observed that the test of what is a material 'consideration' is whether it serves a planning purpose, and that a planning purpose is one which relates to the character of the use of the land. But he added[7]:

> 'Personal circumstances of an occupier, personal hardship, the difficulties of businesses which are of value to the character of a community are not to be ignored in the administration of planning control. It would be inhuman pedantry to exclude from the control of our environment the human factor. The human factor is always present, of course, indirectly as the background to the consideration of the character of land use. It can, however, and sometimes should, be given direct effect as an exceptional or special circumstance. But such circumstances, when they arise, fall to be considered not as a general rule but as exceptions to a general rule to be met in special cases. If a planning authority is to give effect to them, a specific case has to be made and the planning authority must give reasons for accepting it'.

9.8 Debate about what is, or could be, a material consideration has been extensive. Lord Carnwath has observed 'in planning law the apparently innocent expression "material considerations" has acquired an impressive overburden of case law going back more than 40 years'[8].

The time when material considerations are addressed

9.9 The duty under the Town and Country Planning Act 1990, s 70(2) is to consider the development plan and other material considerations as at the time of the decision. The decision is the issue of the planning decision notice, not any committee resolution on the application. It is therefore possible for material considerations to change after the resolution and require the application to be reconsidered. Whether changes in circumstances are material and require reconsideration by a council is a matter for the court[9].

9.10 If matters change between a council resolution to grant planning permission and the actual issue of the permission then the committee must reconsider the application if those changes might have affected the decision[10]. In reality that means that it might lead to a different decision to that which had already been reached, either as to whether planning permission would be granted or that there could be a substantive difference to planning conditions or obligations. A change which would merely confirm the committee in their views would not be material[11]. The Minister or inspector on an appeal or call-in must address the material considerations which exist at the time of issuing their decision and so address any changes following

---

[6] [1985] AC 661.
[7] At 670.
[8] *R (on the application of Health and Safety Executive) v Wolverhampton City Council* [2012] UKSC 34, [2012] 1 WLR 2264 at para 49.
[9] *R (on the application of Kides) v South Cambridgeshire District Council* [2002] EWCA Civ 1370, [2003] JPL 431 at paras 121–127. In that case changes in planning policy over a five-year period between the resolution to grant and the issue of planning permission had not required a reconsideration.
[10] Carnwath LJ said in *Dry v West Oxfordshire District Council* [2010] EWCA Civ 1143, [2011] 1 P & CR 16 at para 16 'Without seeking to detract from the authority of the guidance in *Kides*, I would emphasise that it is only guidance as to what is advisable, erring on the side of caution'.
[11] It is neater to treat supportive changes as not material in the circumstances, rather than as changes in material considerations which would not lead to the quashing of the decision because the decision would have been the same.

9.11 *Material considerations and policy*

any hearing or inquiry. If a decision is quashed by the court and redetermined, the material considerations are those which exist at the date of the second decision, even if they have moved decisively for or against a party in the meantime[12].

The weight to be given to material considerations

9.11 Generally the weight to attach to a consideration is a matter for the decision-maker, subject to public law review. In *Tesco Stores v Secretary of State for the Environment*[13] Lord Hoffmann said:

> 'The law has always made a clear distinction between the question of whether something is a material consideration and the weight which it should be given. The former is a question of law and the latter is a question of planning judgment, which is entirely a matter for the planning authority. Provided that the planning authority has regard to all material considerations, it is at liberty (provided that it does not lapse into *Wednesbury* irrationality) to give them whatever weight the planning authority thinks fit or no weight at all. The fact that the law regards something as a material consideration therefore involves no view about the part, if any, which it should play in the decision-making process.
>
> This distinction between whether something is a material consideration and the weight which it should be given is only one aspect of a fundamental principle of British planning law, namely that the courts are concerned only with the legality of the decision-making process and not with the merits of the decision. If there is one principle of planning law more firmly settled than any other, it is that matters of planning judgment are within the exclusive province of the local planning authority or the Secretary of State'.

9.12 Legislation may point to particular weight being given. In *East Northamptonshire District Council v Secretary of State for Communities and Local Government*[14] Sullivan LJ correctly observed on Lord Hoffmann's *dicta*:

> 'As a general proposition, the principle is not in doubt, but *Tesco* was concerned with the application of s 70(2) of the Planning Act. It was not a case under s 66(1) or 72(1) of the Listed Buildings Act. The proposition that decision-makers may be required by either statute or planning policy to give particular weight to certain material considerations was not disputed by Mr Nardell. There are many examples of planning policies, both national and local, which require decision-makers when exercising their planning judgment to give particular weight to certain material considerations'.

Statutory duties to have regard to various matters

9.13 A statutory duty to have regard to particular matters may be specific to the handling of planning applications, to planning generally or be general obligations upon public authorities which apply to planning amongst other powers.

---

[12] See *Kingswood District Council v Secretary of State for the Environment* (1989) 57 P & CR 153 at 160 per Graham Eyre QC.
[13] [1995] 1 WLR 759 at 780. The distinction was endorsed by the Supreme Court in *R (on the application of Sainsbury's Supermarkets Ltd) v Wolverhampton City Council* [2010] UKSC 20, [2011] 1 AC 437 at para 70 per Lord Collins of Mapesbury JSC.
[14] *East Northamptonshire District Council v Secretary of State for Communities and Local Government (sub nom Barnwell Manor Wind Energy Ltd v East Northamptonshire District Council)* [2014] EWCA Civ 137, [2014] JPL 731 at para 26.

Policy

The development plan

9.14 In statutory terms the most important planning policy is the development plan, a term which may encompass several different documents. The current and historic development plan system is sketched out in Chapter 1.

9.15 The development plan for an area in England is:

(i) for unitary authorities outside Greater London, any remaining parts of the Regional Strategy for the area, the development plan documents adopted by the local planning authority for the area (including any adopted jointly), any old development plans which have not yet expired and any neighbourhood development plan for the relevant part of the area;

(ii) for areas outside Greater London with two-tier authorities, again any remaining parts of the Regional Strategy, the development plan documents adopted by the district authority (including any adopted jointly), the minerals and waste development plan documents adopted by the county council as minerals and waste planning authority, any old development plans which have not yet expired and any neighbourhood development plan for the relevant part of the area;

(iii) for areas within Greater London, the London Plan and the development plan documents adopted by the local planning authority (including any adopted jointly), any old development plans which have not yet expired and any neighbourhood development plan for the relevant part of the area.

9.16 In Wales the development plan system is simpler. Local planning authorities had each adopted a unitary development plan. Under the Planning and Compulsory Purchase Act 2004 these are to be replaced in each authority with local development plan. The Planning (Wales) Act 2015 introduces strategic development plans[15].

Approach to the development plan

9.17 Substantively, the development plan is referred to twice in the legislation on the determination of planning applications: first, as a material matter in s 70(2); and second, the creation of a presumption in favour of its policies.

9.18 Section 38(6) of the Planning and Compulsory Purchase Act 2004 provides:

'If regard is to be had to the development plan for the purpose of any determination to be made under the planning Acts the determination must be made in accordance with the plan unless material considerations indicate otherwise'.

9.19 Section 38(6) had originated in the Town and Country Planning Act 1990, s 54A, which had been inserted by the Planning and Compensation Act 1991. With an immaterial change in wording s 54A was repealed and replaced by s 38(6) in the 2004 Act. The leading authority on the presumption is *City of Edinburgh Council v*

---

[15] Planning and Compulsory Purchase Act 2004, s 60I, prospectively inserted by the Planning (Wales) Act 2015, s 6.

9.20 *Material considerations and policy*

Secretary of State for Scotland dealing with the then-equivalent Scottish provision, in which Lord Clyde commented[16]:

> 'it will obviously be necessary for the decision-maker to consider the development plan, identify any provisions in it which are relevant to the question before him and make a proper interpretation of them. His decision will be open to challenge if he fails to have regard to a policy in the development plan which is relevant to the application or fails properly to interpret it. He will also have to consider whether the development proposed in the application before him does or does not accord with the development plan. There may be some points in the plan which support the proposal but there may be some considerations pointing in the opposite direction. He will require to assess all of these and then decide whether in light of the whole plan the proposal does or does not accord with it. He will also have to identify all the other material considerations which are relevant to the application and to which he should have regard. He will then have to note which of them support the application and which of them do not, and he will have to assess the weight to be given to all of these considerations. He will have to decide whether there are considerations of such weight as to indicate that the development plan should not be accorded the priority which the statute has given to it. And having weighed these considerations and determined these matters he will require to form his opinion on the disposal of the application'.

9.20 He said that a two-stage approach of considering the priority to be given to the development plan first, before asking whether material considerations outweighed, could be adopted but was not necessary[17]. *City of Edinburgh* has been consistently followed. In *R (on the application of Hampton Bishop Parish Council) v Herefordshire Council* Richards LJ said[18]:

> 'It is up to the decision-maker how precisely to go about the task, but if he is to act within his powers and in particular to comply with the statutory duty to make the determination in accordance with the development plan unless material considerations indicate otherwise, he must as a general rule decide at some stage in the exercise whether the proposed development does or does not accord with the development plan'.

9.21 The weight to be attached to the development plan or to other material considerations is not determined by s 38(6)[19]. The s 38(6) duty remains following the introduction of the National Planning Policy Framework (NPPF), which does not displace it[20].

9.22 Section 74(1)(b) of the Town and Country Planning Act 1990 allows a development order to authorise the planning authority 'to grant planning permission for development which does not accord with the provisions of the development plan'.

---

[16] [1997] 1 WLR 1447 at 1459.
[17] At 1460.
[18] [2014] EWCA Civ 878, [2015] 1 WLR 2367 at para 28. Richards LJ continued as to the general rule 'I say "as a general rule" because there may be exceptional cases where it is possible to comply with the section without a decision on that point: I have in mind in particular that if the decision-maker concludes that the development plan should carry no weight at all because the policies in it have been overtaken by more recent policy statements, it may be possible to give effect to the section without reaching a specific decision on whether the development is or is not in accordance with the development plan'. See also paras 31–33.
[19] *Loup v Secretary of State for the Environment* (1995) 71 P & CR 175 at 186 per Glidewell LJ, approved in *City of Edinburgh* by Lord Clyde at 1458.
[20] See *Bloor Homes East Midlands Ltd v Secretary of State for Communities and Local Government* [2014] EWHC 745 (Admin) per Lindblom J; *R (on the application of Hampton Bishop Parish Council) v Herefordshire Council* [2014] EWCA Civ 878, [2015] 1 WLR 2367 at para 30 per Richards LJ.

The DMPOs make such provision[21]. This is completely unnecessary, as neither s 70(2) nor s 38(6) restrict the ability to determine applications in a way which does not accord with the development plan.

9.23 Development plan policy has passed through several incarnations. The Planning and Compulsory Purchase Act 2004 introduced development plan documents and provided for the existing development plans to expire unless 'saved' by Ministerial direction[22]. Those directions identified the policy, but not associated text. The High Court held in *R (on the application of Cherkley Campaign Ltd) v Mole Valley District Council* that the Secretary of State's direction saving a policy in a 2000 local plan also saved the reasoned justification associated with that policy[23].

9.24 In the subsequent Court of Appeal decision Richards LJ agreed with the High Court that the reasoned justification was saved as[24]:

'To blue-pencil the supporting text would risk altering the meaning of the policy, which cannot have been the legislative intention. It seems to me that the true effect of the statutory provisions was to save not just the bare words of the policy but also any supporting text relevant to the interpretation of the policy, so that the policy would continue with unchanged meaning and effect until replaced by a new policy'.

9.25 He also gave greater importance to the policies rather than the other text of a pre-2004 style development plan[25]:

'in the light of the statutory provisions and the guidance, that when determining the conformity of a proposed development with a local plan the correct focus is on the plan's detailed *policies* for the development and use of land in the area. The supporting text consists of *descriptive and explanatory matter* in respect of the policies and/or a *reasoned justification* of the policies. That text is plainly relevant to the interpretation of a policy to which it relates but it is not itself a policy or part of a policy, it does not have the force of policy and it cannot trump the policy. I do not think that a development that accorded with the policies in the local plan could be said not to conform with the plan because it failed to satisfy an additional criterion referred to only in the supporting text. That applies even where, as here, the local plan states that the supporting text indicates how the policies will be implemented'.

9.26 Statute deals expressly with conflict arising between different parts of Planning and Compulsory Purchase Act 2004 local development documents[26]:

'If to any extent a policy set out in a local development document conflicts with any other statement or information in the document the conflict must be resolved in favour of the policy'.

A conflict between policies in different development plan documents is resolved in favour of the policy in the most recent document[27].

---

[21] DMPO 2015, art 32; DMPO 2010, art 27; DMPO Wales, art 20.
[22] Planning and Compulsory Purchase Act 2004, Sch 8.
[23] [2013] EWHC 2582 (Admin), [2014] 1 P & CR 12 at paras 79–87.
[24] *R (on the application of Cherkley Campaign Ltd) v Mole Valley District Council* [2014] EWCA Civ 567, [2014] 2 EGLR 98, para 18.
[25] At para 16.
[26] Planning and Compulsory Purchase Act 2004, s 17(5).
[27] Planning and Compulsory Purchase Act 2004, s 38(5).

9.27 *Material considerations and policy*

Other local policy

9.27 Local planning authorities may produce planning policy which is not part of the development plan. Broadly speaking, this is concerned with implementing development plan policies although sometimes these policies have been used to fill gaps caused by out-of-date development plans.

9.28 In England there are three categories of documents:

(i) supplementary planning documents, adopted following statutory consultation[28];

(ii) other local development documents, which are not subject to statutory consultation[29];

(iii) supplementary planning guidance. This was the description of non-statutory planning policy adopted by local authorities prior to the implementation of the Planning and Compulsory Purchase Act 2004. It might now be used for documents in category (ii) above, and describes some of the Mayor of London's non-statutory policies.

Wales has continued to use non-statutory supplementary planning guidance.

National planning policy – England

The National Planning Policy Framework

9.29 The government's principal planning policies for England are contained in the National Planning Policy Framework, which replaced a mass of Planning Policy Statements (PPSs), Planning Policy Guidance Notes (PPGs), Mineral Planning Statements (MPSs), Mineral Policy Statements (MPGs), circulars and letters to chief planning officers in March 2012. The NPPF is concerned with the policy approach to the formulation of local policy and the determination of planning applications. It makes comment on process, such as the weight to be attached to emerging local plans. Accompanying the NPPF is the *Technical Guidance to the National Planning Policy Framework* which provides more material on flood risk and minerals policy.

9.30 National waste policies are required by the Waste Directive. Consequently the Planning Policy Statement 10: *Planning for Sustainable Waste Management* survived the publication of the NPPF pending the adoption of the National Waste Management Plan for England[30]. That plan was published in December 2013 and preserved PPS10 until the conclusion of an ongoing review. PPS10 was replaced in October 2014 by the National Planning Policy for Waste.

9.31 Provision for gypsies and travellers is subject to *Planning Policy for Traveller Sites*[31]. The main development control policy is Policy H but the whole

---

[28] Under the Town and Country Planning (Local Planning) (England) Regulations 2012, SI 2012/767, Part 5.
[29] These will be neither part of the development plan nor supplementary planning documents. Whilst no documents of this type could be adopted under the Town and Country Planning (Local Development) (England) Regulations 2004, they were created by the 2012 Regulations, very possibly by accident: see *R (on the application of RWE Npower) v Milton Keynes Council* [2013] EWHC 751 (Admin).
[30] NPPF, para 5.
[31] August 2015, replacing the original March 2012 text.

Material considerations and the structure of policy **9.35**

document will in practice be relevant to a planning application. Need, alternatives and personal circumstances are relevant, but sites are discouraged from the Green Belt and open countryside.

9.32 A final vestige of the old Planning Policy Statements was done away with in March 2015 with the cancellation of the Eco-towns Planning Policy Statement.

Remarkably the NPPF has only been amended once since it was published when changes were made to travellers policy in July 2015[32]. Otherwise clarifications have been provided by the *Planning Practice Guidance* and Ministerial statements[33].

Planning Practice Guidance

9.33 The *Planning Practice Guidance* (PPG) was first published in March 2014 and provides advice on the substance of planning policy and on planning practice. Available simply as an online document, it is regularly amended, so any text should be checked before use. Paragraph referencing is by a reference number for each category of the guidance, followed by a paragraph number and then the date on which that text was last revised. For example, the paragraph 'What planning objectives can good design help achieve?' has the reference 26-06-20140306, being category 26, paragraph 6, dating from the original publication of the PPG on 6 March 2014.

Revisions or clarification of policy tend to be announced by Ministers in written statements to Parliament, usually followed by alterations to the PPG.

National policy statements

9.34 Policy on various types of major infrastructure is contained in national policy statements adopted under the Planning Act 2008. These are principally concerned with the approval of nationally significant infrastructure projects under that Act, but may be relevant to planning applications in England[34]. Sometimes the guidance is directed at very large projects, so might need to be applied with care to smaller schemes which are the subject of planning applications.

9.35 The national policy statements are presently in three categories: energy; transport and water:

Energy NPSs:

- overarching energy (EN-1);
- fossil fuels (EN-2);

---

[32] National Planning Policy Framework: technical adjustment in a written statement by Baroness Williams of Trafford, 22 July 2015, HLWS167, amending paras 49 and 159 so that needs for travellers are assessed under the Planning Policy for Travellers. A consultation on further changes to the NPPF begun in December 2015 with a consultation period ending in February 2016.
[33] Since an alteration to the Planning Practice Guidance does not change the text of the NPPF, some revisions of government policy might be better done through an NPPF alteration: see the quashing of affordable housing revisions in *R (on the application of West Berkshire District Council and Reading Borough Council) v Secretary of State for Communities and Local Government* [2015] EWHC 2222 (Admin) (appeal pending).
[34] NPPF, para 3.

9.36 *Material considerations and policy*

- renewable energy (EN-3);
- gas supply infrastructure and gas and oil pipelines (EN-4);
- electricity networks (EN-5);
- nuclear power (EN-6).

Transport NPSs:

- ports;
- national networks[35].

Water, waste water and waste NPSs:

- hazardous waste;
- waste water treatment.

Other national policy

9.36 Various high-level government policies might be relevant to the determination of planning applications and can be taken into account if they are. For example, a 2011 Ministerial Statement *Planning for Growth* said it would be taken into account in planning decisions and so was a material consideration[36].

Cancelled guidance

9.37 Prior to 2010 a great mass of policy documents, circulars, good practice guides, letters, guides, speeches and research reports were published by the Secretary of State. It was often unclear as to what the status of the document was and whether it altered government policy. Most of this has been swept away, cancelled with the publication of the NPPF and PPG[37]. Ministers have been much better in confining policy announcements to revisions to the PPG, Written Statements to Parliament, major national policy documents and the occasional published letter to the Planning Inspectorate. This cuts down the time spent reading and debating various Ministerial utterances in appeals and the courts[38].

National planning policy – Wales

9.38 Planning policy at the Welsh national level is principally contained in non-statutory national policy adopted by the Welsh Ministers in the form of Planning Policy (Wales)[39] and Technical Advice Notes (TANs) with older circulars and the

---

[35] National networks deals with road and rail networks and strategic rail freight interchanges.
[36] *Oxford Diocesan Board of Finance v Secretary of State for Communities and Local Government* [2013] EWCA Civ 1718, [2014] JPL 530 per Sullivan LJ. However it supported rather than undermined the decision taken and the High Court's quashing ([2013] EWHC 802 (Admin), [2013] JPL 1285) was reversed.
[37] There is a list of replacements in Annex 3 of the NPPF and a list of further cancelled guidance was published alongside the PPG.
[38] Which perhaps reached its low point in *Dimsdale Developments (South East) Ltd v Secretary of State for the Environment* [1986] JPL 276 when the meaning and relevance of an after-dinner speech by the Secretary of State was argued in the High Court.
[39] Currently the 7th edn (2014).

Wales Spatial Plan adopted under the Planning and Compulsory Purchase Act 2004. National Policy Statements also apply in Wales. A National Development Framework for Wales will be introduced by the Planning (Wales) Act 2015 as a replacement for the Wales Spatial Plan.

9.39 The Technical Advice Notes are:

TAN 1 Joint Housing Land Availability Studies (2015)
TAN 2 Planning and Affordable Housing (2006)
TAN 3 Simplified Planning Zones (1996)
TAN 4 Retailing and Town Centres (1996)
TAN 5 Nature Conservation and Planning (2009)
TAN 6 Planning for Sustainable Rural Communities (2010)
TAN 7 Outdoor Advertisement Control (1996)
TAN 8 Renewable Energy (2005)
TAN 9 Enforcement of Planning Control (1997)
TAN 10 Tree Preservation Orders (1997)
TAN 11 Noise (1997)
TAN 12 Design (2014)
TAN 13 Tourism (1997)
TAN 14 Coastal Planning (1998)
TAN 15 Development and Flood Risk (2004)
TAN 16 Sport, Recreation and Open Space (2009)
TAN 18 Transport (2007)
TAN 19 Telecommunications (2002)
TAN 20 Planning and the Welsh Language (2013)
TAN 21 Waste (2014)
TAN 23 Economic Development (2014)

Other national bodies' guidance as material considerations

9.40 Guidance published by specialist public bodies might also be material, for example, advice from Historic England (formerly English Heritage) on how to deal with the effect of development upon heritage in the planning system[40].

The interpretation of policy

9.41 A policy document must be construed as a whole[41]. It may explicitly incorporate terms and meanings in other documents and may well use expressions which have a particular meaning in planning or a development context. Since planning is concerned with things in the real world, the ordinary meaning of words and how they are understood will be helpful. Considering the drafts, consultations and reports which led to the policy will not be helpful and might not be relevant. It is not appropriate to look back at the evolution of a development plan, including at the examination process and the inspector's report in determining what the plan means, given the need for the plan to be readily capable of being understood by the public.

---

[40] *R (on the application of Young) v Oxford City Council* [2002] EWCA Civ 990, [2003] JPL 232.
[41] For example, this approach is taken to the NPPF: *Bayliss v Secretary of State for Communities and Local Government* [2013] EWHC 1612 (Admin) at para 18.

9.42 *Material considerations and policy*

In *R (on the application of TW Logistics) v Tendring Borough Council*[42] the Court of Appeal deprecated the 'forensic archaeology' of looking back at the plan-making process to try to understand the meaning of a policy. A policy is a document which must be understood and applied by a large number of people, including those who were not involved in its formulation.

9.42 In the sense of being a public and self-contained document, policy has a resemblance to legislation. However there is one important difference in interpretation. Statutes have to be capable of being applied to all the relevant circumstances which might arise. Since policies do not have to be followed, it is perfectly possible, in appropriate circumstances, to conclude that the policy did not contemplate a particular situation or was not meant to apply to such a case, and the policy can be departed from.

9.43 There have been two schools of thought as to who has the final say on what a policy means. *Tesco Stores Ltd v Dundee City Council*[43] confirmed the role of the court in interpreting planning policy as a matter of law rather than leaving the meaning of policy to the decision-maker subject to a rationality review. Lord Reed JSC said:

> '18 ... The development plan is a carefully drafted and considered statement of policy, published in order to inform the public of the approach which will be followed by planning authorities in decision-making unless there is good reason to depart from it. It is intended to guide the behaviour of developers and planning authorities. As in other areas of administrative law, the policies which it sets out are designed to secure consistency and direction in the exercise of discretionary powers, while allowing a measure of flexibility to be retained. Those considerations point away from the view that the meaning of the plan is in principle a matter which each planning authority is entitled to determine from time to time as it pleases, within the limits of rationality. On the contrary, these considerations suggest that in principle, in this area of public administration as in others (as discussed, for example, in *R (Raissi) v Secretary of State for the Home Department* [2008] QB 836), policy statements should be interpreted objectively in accordance with the language used, read as always in its proper context.
>
> 19 That is not to say that such statements should be construed as if they were statutory or contractual provisions. Although a development plan has a legal status and legal effects, it is not analogous in its nature or purpose to a statute or a contract. As has often been observed, development plans are full of broad statements of policy, many of which may be mutually irreconcilable, so that in a particular case one must give way to another. In addition, many of the provisions of development plans are framed in language whose application to a given set of facts requires the exercise of judgment. Such matters fall within the jurisdiction of planning authorities, and their exercise of their judgment can only be challenged on the ground that it is irrational or perverse: *Tesco Stores Ltd v Secretary of State for the Environment* [1995] 1 WLR 759 , 780, per Lord Hoffmann. Nevertheless, planning authorities do not live in the world of Humpty Dumpty: they cannot make the development plan mean whatever they would like it to mean'.

This has encouraged challenges based on the construction of policy.

9.44 The role of the court applies to the interpretation of national policy as well as the development plan[44]. *Tesco Stores* was decided in the same month that the

---

[42] [2013] EWCA Civ 9, [2013] JPL 832.
[43] [2012] UKSC 13, [2012] PTSR 983.
[44] *Hunston Properties Ltd v Secretary of State for Communities and Local Government* [2013] EWCA Civ 1610, [2014] JPL 599.

NPPF was issued and the combination of new policy and a greater role for the court in interpreting it has prompted numerous challenges based upon disputes about its meaning. These have particularly considered housing, Green Belt and heritage policies.

SUBSTANTIVE MATERIAL CONSIDERATIONS

9.45 Since planning is concerned with the development and use of land the range of potential issues is very wide – concerns about electrical interference with radio telescope operation in *Stringer* being one of the more unusual examples. Materiality is dependent upon a relevance to land use planning and the ability to alter the decision. Sometimes these issues will be material because they have been identified in planning policy, otherwise planning policy is often important as to how they are addressed.

9.46 It may be impossible to comprehensively list all potentially relevant topics for a planning decision and it is unwise to try. The principal national documents, the NPPF and Planning Policy Wales, give the widest single compilation of issues. Instead, this section focuses on some of the major issues, particularly those which have proved litigious.

Sustainable development

9.47 The foreword to the NPPF begins 'The purpose of planning is to help achieve sustainable Development'[45]. The Welsh Assembly Government say in the first paragraph of Planning Policy Wales that it 'translates our commitment to sustainable development into the planning system'[46]. In determining planning applications in England, this objective is one in policy rather than statute[47].

9.48 With effect from 1 April 2016 the Planning (Wales) Act 2015 introduces a duty on the Welsh Ministers and local planning authorities to carry out their development control and planning policy making functions 'as part of carrying out sustainable development in accordance with the Well-being of Future Generations (Wales) Act 2015, for the purpose of ensuring that the development and use of land contribute to improving the economic, social, environmental and cultural well-being of Wales'[48]. The Well-being Act defines sustainable development as 'the process of improving the economic, social, environmental and cultural well-being of Wales by taking action, in accordance with the sustainable development principle (see section 5), aimed at achieving the well-being goals (see section 4)'[49]. The sustainable development principle is to 'act in a manner which seeks to ensure that the needs of the present are met without compromising the ability of future generations to meet their own needs'[50]. Account has to be taken of balancing short-

---

[45] The foreword is set out in Chapter 1.
[46] 7th edn, 2014, para 1.1.1.
[47] By the Planning and Compulsory Purchase Act 2004, s 39 development plan documents in England should promote sustainable development.
[48] Planning (Wales) Act 2015, s 2(2). This will be brought into force by the Planning (Wales) Act 2015 (Commencement No 2 and Transitional and Saving Provisions) Order 2015, SI/2015/1987, art 5.
[49] Well-being of Future Generations (Wales) Act 2015, s 2.
[50] Well-being of Future Generations (Wales) Act 2015, s 5(1).

9.49 *Material considerations and policy*

term and long-term needs, taking an integrated approach, involving other persons and ensuring those persons reflect the diversity of Wales or the decision-maker's part of Wales, collaboration with others and deploying resources[51]. The well-being goals are a prosperous, resilient, healthier, more equal and globally responsible Wales of cohesive communities, vibrant culture and thriving Welsh language[52].

However this does not alter[53]:

> '(a) whether regard is to be had to any particular consideration under subsection (2) of section 70 of [the Town and Country Planning Act 1990] (determination of applications for planning permission), or
>
> (b) the weight to be given to any consideration to which regard is had under that subsection'.

The effect of the sustainable development obligation in Wales on the determination of planning applications is therefore doubtful.

9.49 There is no statutory definition of sustainable development in England, and policy meanings are wide. The NPPF refers to two general definitions:

> 'Resolution 42/187 of the United Nations General Assembly defined sustainable development as meeting the needs of the present without compromising the ability of future generations to meet their own needs. The UK Sustainable Development Strategy *Securing the Future* set out five "guiding principles" of sustainable development: living within the planet's environmental limits; ensuring a strong, healthy and just society; achieving a sustainable economy; promoting good governance; and using sound science responsibly'.

For planning purposes the NPPF identifies three roles for sustainable development: economic; social and environmental[54].

9.50 Whilst explicitly recognising the presumption in favour of the development plan[55] the NPPF describes a 'presumption in favour of sustainable development' as 'a golden thread running through both plan-making and decision-taking'[56]. For the determination of planning applications and appeals this means[57]:

> - approving development proposals that accord with the development plan without delay; and
> - where the development plan is absent, silent or relevant policies are out-of-date, granting permission unless:
>   - any adverse impacts of doing so would significantly and demonstrably outweigh the benefits, when assessed against the policies in this Framework taken as a whole; or
>   - specific policies in this Framework indicate development should be restricted'.

---

[51] Well-being of Future Generations (Wales) Act 2015, s 5(2).
[52] Well-being of Future Generations (Wales) Act 2015, s 4, with further explanation in the table in that section.
[53] Planning (Wales) Act 2015, s 2(5).
[54] NPPF, para 7.
[55] In the Planning and Compulsory Purchase Act 2004, s 38(6), see NPPF, para 11, 12.
[56] NPPF, para 14.
[57] NPPF, para 14.

9.51 Where development plans are out of date, for example by not providing required housing, the policy does not mean that anything goes. The policies will remain part of the development plan although the weight to be attached to them may be reduced[58]. If the development plan is not to be followed then the presumption is in favour of sustainable development, not any development. Additionally the specific policies which indicate development should be restricted are noted as including:

> 'those policies relating to sites protected under the Birds and Habitats Directives (see paragraph 119) and/or designated as Sites of Special Scientific Interest; land designated as Green Belt, Local Green Space, an Area of Outstanding Natural Beauty, Heritage Coast or within a National Park (or the Broads Authority); designated heritage assets; and locations at risk of flooding or coastal erosion'.

That is a significant amount of land. Essentially though this means that a specific restrictive policy may be sufficient on its own to lead to the refusal of permission.

9.52 At various points the NPPF sets tests for levels of harm which would render a scheme unacceptable. Those tests have to be considered as 'other material considerations' rather than having the status of the development plan. In addition, harm which does not satisfy the NPPF tests will still be material and might individually or cumulatively cause the refusal of planning permission[59].

Effects on neighbouring land and amenity

9.53 The direct and indirect impact of development or its use on a neighbour's property is a material consideration as it relates to the use and development of land. The general proposition was stated by Pill LJ in *West Midlands Probation Committee v Secretary of State for the Environment*[60]:

> 'The impact of a proposed development upon the use of and activities upon neighbouring land may be a material consideration'.

The Court of Appeal held in that case that anti-social behaviour from the residents of a bail hostel was material. Pill LJ said 'I would not distinguish for present purposes the impact of the conduct upon the use of adjoining land from the impact of, for example, polluting discharges by way of smoke or fumes or the uses in *Finlay*[61] and *Blum*'[62]. In *Blum v Secretary of State for the Environment*[63] the effect of horse riding on the physical condition of the bridleway network near a riding school was material in deciding upon the acceptability of the school[64].

---

[58] *Crane v Secretary of State for Communities and Local Government* [2015] EWHC 425 (Admin) at paras 70–74 per Lindblom J; followed in *Wenman v Secretary of State for Communities and Local Government* [2015] EWHC 925 (Admin) at paras 61–66 per Lang J (appeal pending).
[59] *Redhill Aerodrome Ltd v Secretary of State for Communities and Local Government* [2014] EWCA Civ 1386, [2015] PTSR 274, [2015] JPL 416.
[60] (1998) 76 P & CR 589 at 597.
[61] *Finlay v Secretary of State for the Environment* [1982] JPL 802.
[62] *West Midlands Probation Committee* at 597.
[63] [1987] JPL 278.
[64] In *Finlay* the Secretary of State was entitled to consider that one factor for refusing planning permission for a private members club where sexually explicit films were to be shown was that it shared an entrance with a maisonette and was likely to discourage, and could effectively prevent, the occupation of the residential accommodation: see *West Midlands* at 594.

9.54 *Material considerations and policy*

9.54 Impacts on the amenity of occupiers and users of nearby land is perhaps the most common issue that arises on planning applications. The question for the planning authority is whether the impacts are acceptable in the public interest. That is a different question to whether there would be a private law claim by the neighbour for nuisance or interference with rights to light. Impacts which are not actionable may lead to the refusal of planning permission. Conversely, breach of private rights would not necessarily amount to harm in the public interest.

9.55 The most common neighbour impacts of concern to the planning process are:

(i) *Noise*: noise may come from a diverse range of sources such as vehicles, industrial equipment, chiller and air conditioning units, extractor fans, amplified music and human actions. Noise occurring off the site but related to it may be relevant, such as vehicles on the highway, aircraft flying to or from an airport or customers outside a bar. Noise impacts are judged in one of two ways. Some noise is assessed against standards and guidance, although these might not be designed for planning purposes. Sporadic and close-range noise might sometimes be a matter of planning judgment rather than mathematical prediction, for example vehicles manoeuvring and parking, car doors slamming and people congregating and shouting immediately adjacent to residential properties. Planning authorities and planning inspectors are capable of forming a view in those circumstances whether the impacts are likely to be disturbing;

(ii) *fumes and smells*: odour issues range from the cooking smells of a restaurant's kitchen affecting the flats above to escapes from animal rendering plants and sewage treatment works;

(iii) *daylight and sunlight*: these issues are primarily concerned with the amount of natural light reaching habitable rooms in dwellings. Local planning authorities will adopt their own standards but usually rely upon the BRE standards for daylight and sunlight. These are different to the Waldram analysis used in private rights to light claims;

(iv) *overbearing and overshadowing*: a building or structure can be so dominant as to be oppressive to neighbouring occupiers. The sensitive occupiers will almost always be residential, with particular concern about the effect on habitable rooms and outdoor amenity areas such as rear gardens and roof terraces. The impact is essentially a matter of impression and harmful development can include inconsiderate rear extensions to neighbouring dwellings, or large wind turbines[65].

9.56 As an expression, overshadowing encompasses actual shadows cast over amenity areas and gardens and overbearing effects on buildings and open areas. It is a matter of impression, unlike the more technical sunlight analysis.

---

[65] The approach to wind turbines is often called the Lavender Test, after the Inspector, David Lavender, who first used it in the Enifer Downs Farm appeal APP/X22201/A/08/2071880 at para 66:

'When turbines are present in such number, size and proximity that they represent an unpleasantly overwhelming and unavoidable presence in main views from a house or garden, there is every likelihood that the property concerned would come to be regarded as an unattractive and thus an unsatisfactory (but not necessarily uninhabitable) place in which to live. It is not in the public interest to create such living conditions where they did not exist before'.

(i) *overlooking*: views into neighbouring buildings or private areas around buildings may need to be restricted for the protection of those who may be observed. Several factors have to be considered. The first is the vulnerability of those being viewed: bedrooms are the most sensitive, followed by living rooms in homes. Bathrooms can be assumed to be obscure glazed anyway and there is some protection in the more private parts of rear gardens. Occupants of commercial buildings can be expected to put the blinds down if they need privacy. The viewpoint may also be relevant. Views directly from habitable rooms may be more intrusive than a passing view from a staircase. Overlooking from a bar may cause more concerns than from an office which would keep conventional working hours. How overt the overlooking would be is also a factor; a concern which arises with the use of balconies. Finally the nature of the location matters: privacy in rear gardens and between buildings will be less in a densely built-up urban area. For this reason local authority policies are particularly useful as a guide to what is acceptable in a particular locality;

(ii) *light pollution*: light pollution may be relevant both as an impact on the amenity of neighbours and to the area more generally. The NPPF advises authorities to 'limit the impact of light pollution from artificial light on local amenity, intrinsically dark landscapes and nature conservation'[66].

9.57 These impacts are for the most part concerned with residential amenity. Work environments and other uses may be vulnerable to noise and odours but would otherwise have to put up with their neighbours. Their sensitivity has to be judged against the more limited time that a person will spend there, what activities they will be carrying out themselves and the contrast with the expectation of quiet enjoyment of their home.

9.58 Some types of projects may have particular impacts. Large structures such as tower blocks and wind turbines may interfere with television reception[67]. Wind turbines can also generate an effect called 'shadow flicker'. Sunlight passing through the turbine blades may cause rapid flickering inside properties. That depends upon distance (the conventional rule is that the effect does not occur beyond 10 rotor diameters from the turbine),whether the sun is out, and the position of the sun and the blades (the latter affected by wind direction). Such effects occur infrequently, and are often dealt with by a condition requiring the turbine to be switched off when the sun is out and everything is in the wrong position.

Amenity effects on the occupants of the proposed development

9.59 It is not simply the amenity of neighbouring occupiers that can be important. The comfort and enjoyment of occupants and users of the development may also need protecting and may justify the refusal of permission. This may include insufficient daylight or excessive noise from external sources.

---

[66] NPPF, para 125 and section 31 of the Planning Practice Guidance are devoted to the topic. For general impacts of light pollution see *R (on the application of Warley) v Wealden District Council* [2011] EWHC 2083 (Admin), [2012] Env LR 4; *R (on the application of Embleton Parish Council) v Northumberland County Council* [2013] EWHC 3631 (Admin), [2014] Env LR 16.
[67] *Hunter v Canary Wharf Ltd* [1997] AC 655 concerned an unsuccessful allegation that interference with TV reception was a nuisance. The House of Lords considered that it should be dealt with by planning control. Mitigation measures may involve offering satellite or cable television.

9.60 *Material considerations and policy*

Extremely sensitive neighbours and users

9.60 Planning has intervened to protect very unusual and sensitive users from the impacts of development. This has given them protection which would not be available in private law but has applied solely because of a public interest in preserving the use. The classic example is *Stringer* itself, where planning permission was refused because of the risk of interference to the operation of the Jodrell Bank radio telescopes. The effect of wind turbines on radars used for air defence, air traffic control, airports and by the Met Office have been commonplace issues.

9.61 Linking all of these is a clearly-identified public interest in the protection of the facility, emphasised by its unique or essential nature and the difficulty or expense of adapting to the impact. Policy recognition of the sensitive use at national or local level is helpful, albeit not essential given the novel nature of some of the issues.

Coal mining operations

9.62 Applications for coal mines are subject to wide duties to consider impacts. A planning authority considering a planning application for coal-mining operations or the restoration of land used for coal-mining or operations incidental to such operations or restoration shall have regard to preservation of natural beauty, of the conservation of flora and fauna and geological or physiographical features of special interest and of the protection of sites, buildings, structures and objects of architectural, historic or archaeological interest and whether the reasonably practicable mitigation measures have been included in the application[68]. The duty is discrete to this narrow range of applications and illustrates the vagaries of the legislative process. These matters are dealt with, appropriately, under the Town and Country Planning Act 1990 and other legislation and this specific provision is unnecessary.

Safety and control of major accident hazards

9.63 Safety is relevant to planning decisions, albeit with due regard to other regulatory regimes. In practice planning may be more concerned with whether vulnerable users should be put in proximity with dangerous sites than with the control of the dangerous sites themselves. For example, danger to the users or occupiers of a proposed development from nearby installations will be relevant: see *R (on the application of Health and Safety Executive) v Wolverhampton City Council*[69]. Advice on considering safety is given in England in the NPPF[70] and the *Planning Practice Guidance* section 39 and in Wales in NAW Circular 20/01: *Planning Controls for Hazardous Substances*. The siting of vulnerable development, such as homes, close to installations is assessed using PADHI (Planning Advice for Developments near Hazardous Installations), addressing the risks of major accidents.[71] The PPG warns that 'advice from Health and Safety Executive that planning permission should be

---

[68] Coal Industry Act 1994, s 53(2).
[69] [2012] UKSC 34, [2012] 1 WLR 2264. *R (on the application of Saunders) v Tendring District Council* [2003] EWHC 2977 (Admin) is another example.
[70] Para 172: 'Planning policies should be based on up-to-date information on the location of major hazards and on the mitigation of the consequences of major accidents'.
[71] More advice is on the HSE's Land Use Planning website.

refused for development for, at or near to a hazardous installation or pipeline should not be overridden without the most careful consideration'[72].

9.64 The EU has adopted a series of Directives on the control of major-accident hazards involving dangerous substances. The current Directive is 2012/18/EU (known as 'SEVESO III'). The Directive requires member states to require operators to take all necessary measures to prevent major accidents and to limit their consequences. Article 13 of the SEVESO III Directive provides:

'1 Member States shall ensure that the objectives of preventing major accidents and limiting the consequences of such accidents for human health and the environment are taken into account in their land-use policies or other relevant policies. They shall pursue those objectives through controls on:

(a) the siting of new establishments;

(b) modifications to establishments covered by Article 11;

(c) new developments including transport routes, locations of public use and residential areas in the vicinity of establishments, where the siting or developments may be the source of or increase the risk or consequences of a major accident.

2 Member States shall ensure that their land-use or other relevant policies and the procedures for implementing those policies take account of the need, in the long term:

(a) to maintain appropriate safety distances between establishments covered by this Directive and residential areas, buildings and areas of public use, recreational areas, and, as far as possible, major transport routes;

(b) to protect areas of particular natural sensitivity or interest in the vicinity of establishments, where appropriate through appropriate safety distances or other relevant measures;

(c) in the case of existing establishments, to take additional technical measures in accordance with Article 5 so as not to increase the risks to human health and the environment.

3 Member States shall ensure that all competent authorities and planning authorities responsible for decisions in this area set up appropriate consultation procedures to facilitate implementation of the policies established under paragraph 1. The procedures shall be designed to ensure that operators provide sufficient information on the risks arising from the establishment and that technical advice on those risks is available, either on a case-by-case or on a generic basis, when decisions are taken.

Member States shall ensure that operators of lower-tier establishments provide, at the request of the competent authority, sufficient information on the risks arising from the establishment necessary for land-use planning purposes'.

Economy

9.65 Economical development is one of the three pillars of sustainable development, and meeting economic needs is an important part of the planning process. It can tend to be overlooked as planning applications by businesses are usually taken to be economically advantageous to them and the role of development

---

[72] ID 39-071-20140306. A similar point is made in the Welsh circular.

9.66 *Material considerations and policy*

control might be seen as deciding whether it should be allowed to proceed. The separation of economic development into a separate Planning Policy Statement (PPS4) had meant that it was not emphasised so greatly before the publication of the National Planning Policy Framework[73]. The more balanced view is that economic development is desirable, it will often need other development to enable it to happen and that carrying it out in a socially and environmentally responsible way enriches us all, in financial and human terms.

9.66 The principal locational policy for economic development has been that main town centre uses, ie retail, office and indoor leisure, should be located in town centres where possible. This has been for social reasons, the promotion of sustainable transport (that is, reducing the need to travel by car), to maintain economic activity in town and city cores and to reduce the landtake of development. A battery of assessments has grown up around this issue, in particular[74]:

(i) defining the role of particular town centres in the retail hierarchy in an area;

(ii) drawing town centre boundaries and within them, identifying primary and secondary shopping areas;

(iii) assessing the vitality and viability of town centres;

(iv) assessing the quantitative and qualitative need[75] of convenience and comparison goods (whilst need no longer has to be shown in the NPPF[76], it remains in Welsh policy[77]);

(v) applying a sequential test, of seeing if the retail development can be accommodated[78] within the defined town centre first, then edge of town centre[79] sites and finally out of centre[80].

---

[73] Now see the NPPF, paras 18–22.
[74] See NPPF, paras 23–27 and Planning Policy Wales, section 10.
[75] Quantitative need is the amount of new retail floorspace which is required to meet growing demand (if any). Qualitative need is concerned with the range and adequacy of the existing shops, and is not answered simply by asking 'Is there a Waitrose?'
[76] See *R (on the application of Warners Retail (Moreton) Ltd v Cotswold District Council* [2014] EWHC 2504 (Admin) at para 21 per Supperstone J.
[77] Planning Policy Wales, para 10.2.10.
[78] Whilst the NPPF says that 'Applicants and local planning authorities should demonstrate flexibility on issues such as format and scale' (para 24), and may include disaggregating the operator's requirements, this does not extend to requiring a quite different scheme: see *Tesco Stores Ltd v Dundee City Council* [2012] UKSC 13, [2012] PTSR 983 at para 28 per Lord Reed JSC and at para 38 per Lord Hope of Craighead DPSC; *R (on the application of Zurich Assurance Ltd t/a Threadneedle Property Investments) v North Lincolnshire Council* [2012] EWHC 3708 (Admin) at paras 61, 62 per Hickinbottom J; *R (on the application of Warners Retail (Moreton) Ltd v Cotswold District Council* [2014] EWHC 2504 (Admin) at paras 34, 35 per Supperstone J.
[79] The NPPF glossary defines 'edge of centre' as:

'For retail purposes, a location that is well connected and up to 300 metres of the primary shopping area. For all other main town centre uses, a location within 300 metres of a town centre boundary. For office development, this includes locations outside the town centre but within 500 metres of a public transport interchange. In determining whether a site falls within the definition of edge of centre, account should be taken of local circumstances'.

[80] Bottom of list are sites beyond town centres or the edge of town centres, even if they are within the urban area, so not 'out of town' in the popular sense.

Substantive material considerations **9.70**

External costs – impacts on services

9.67 Development may give rise to increased pressures on local infrastructure and public services, such as increasing the population in a locality who need schools and doctors. These were described as 'external costs' by Lord Hoffmann in *Tesco Stores v Secretary of State for the Environment*[81]. If the services could not cope with the development proposed then a contribution towards the costs (primarily the capital costs) of increasing capacity may be required. Conventional examples are the provision of new classrooms or schools for major residential development or improvising highways to cope with increased traffic flows. Less obvious examples are contributions to library services or the police. Aside from start-up costs or some open space management, the provision of revenue funding is rarely justified, as these should be met by general taxation, including from the increased population[82].

Green Belt

9.68 Green Belt is land designated in policy to prevent urban sprawl by keeping land permanently open[83]. The essential characteristics of Green Belts are their openness and their permanence. Green Belts have been identified around various cities, including London, and their very restrictive policies apply only to designated land[84]. Green Belt policy had been little changed since the 1950s, with the previous *Planning Policy Guidance Note 2* having been adopted in 1995. This was replaced by the NPPF, which brought some changes[85].

9.69 The purposes which Green Belts may serve have a bearing on the extent of the harm caused by a development. These purposes are[86]:

- to check the unrestricted sprawl of large built-up areas;
- to prevent neighbouring towns merging into one another;
- to assist in safeguarding the countryside from encroachment;
- to preserve the setting and special character of historic towns; and
- to assist in urban regeneration, by encouraging the recycling of derelict and other urban land'.

9.70 In development management decisions there are two principal Green Belt questions:

---

[81] [1995] 1 WLR 759 at 771 'consequences involving loss or expenditure by other persons or the community at large'.
[82] Funding is discussed further under Chapter 12 Planning Obligations and Chapter 27 Community Infrastructure Levy.
[83] See the NPPF, para 79.
[84] There is only one Green Belt in Wales, but Wales also has Green Wedge policies which provide similar restrictions but without the assumption that the designation will be permanent: see Planning Policy Wales, section 4.8. Metropolitan Open Land, which is designated open land within the urban area of Greater London, is subject to the same development control policies as Green Belt, see the London Plan 2015, policy 7.17.
[85] Particularly changing the meaning of inappropriate development, see below.
[86] NPPF, para 80. Paragraph 81 provides that 'Once Green Belts have been defined, local planning authorities should plan positively to enhance the beneficial use of the Green Belt, such as looking for opportunities to provide access; to provide opportunities for outdoor sport and recreation; to retain and enhance landscapes, visual amenity and biodiversity; or to improve damaged and derelict land'.

9.71 *Material considerations and policy*

(i) is the development inappropriate in the Green Belt?

(ii) if so, are there very special circumstances which clearly outweigh the harm by reason of inappropriateness and any other harm?

Appropriate and inappropriate development

9.71 If development is not inappropriate in the Green Belt then it is judged on normal planning principles, including sustainability and the countryside. Due to the restrictive tests which apply to inappropriate development, the distinction between the two categories is important.

9.72 By paras 89 and 90 of the NPPF:

'A local planning authority should regard the construction of new buildings as inappropriate in Green Belt. Exceptions to this are:

- buildings for agriculture and forestry;
- provision of appropriate facilities for outdoor sport, outdoor recreation and for cemeteries, as long as it preserves the openness of the Green Belt and does not conflict with the purposes of including land within it;
- the extension or alteration of a building provided that it does not result in disproportionate additions over and above the size of the original building;
- the replacement of a building, provided the new building is in the same use and not materially larger than the one it replaces;
- limited infilling in villages, and limited affordable housing for local community needs under policies set out in the Local Plan; or
- limited infilling or the partial or complete redevelopment of previously developed sites (brownfield land), whether redundant or in continuing use (excluding temporary buildings), which would not have a greater impact on the openness of the Green Belt and the purpose of including land within it than the existing development.

90. Certain other forms of development are also not inappropriate in Green Belt provided they preserve the openness of the Green Belt and do not conflict with the purposes of including land in Green Belt. These are:

- mineral extraction;
- engineering operations;
- local transport infrastructure which can demonstrate a requirement for a Green Belt location;
- the re-use of buildings provided that the buildings are of permanent and substantial construction; and
- development brought forward under a Community Right to Build Order'.

9.73 In *Fordent Holdings Ltd v Secretary of State for Communities and Local Government*[87] Judge Pelling QC held that paras 89 and 90 provided a closed list of operations and uses which were not inappropriate development in the Green Belt. Any material changes of use outside those lists was inevitably inappropriate development which could only be approved if there were very special circumstances, even if there

---

[87] [2013] EWHC 2844 (Admin), [2014] JPL 226.

Substantive material considerations **9.79**

was no conceivable harm to Green Belt openness or purposes. This analysis was endorsed by Richards LJ in *R (on the application of Timmins) v Gedling Borough Council* but Mitting J in the Court of Appeal doubted that para 90 was closed since it would render inappropriate desirable activities such as open air sport[88].

Outdoor sport, outdoor recreation and cemeteries

9.74 However on similar analysis to *Fordent*, a series of cases confined the exception from inappropriateness for outdoor sport, recreation and cemeteries to new buildings on existing facilities, rather than new uses.

9.75 *Newlyn Dean v Secretary of State for Communities and Local Government* concerned livery and paintballing uses in the Bournemouth Green Belt. The Court of Appeal held that the former wording in para 3.4 of Planning Policy Guidance Note 2 did not deem outdoor sport and recreation or cemeteries to be outside the categories of inappropriate development[89].

9.76 *R (on the application of Timmins) v Gedling Borough Council*[90] dealt with cemeteries under the NPPF policy. Paragraph 89 of the NPPF was held to be concerned with new buildings in cemeteries not being inappropriate, if they did not conflict with openness and purposes, not with treating a use as not inappropriate. A new cemetery was a material change of use not included in the not inappropriate development categories and so is inappropriate development and so a new cemetery can only be approved in very special circumstances.

9.77 The effect of these decisions is that new uses of land in the Green Belt, which authorities are encouraged to positively plan[91] for, will be inappropriate development. It is not obvious that this was intended by the Minister when the NPPF was adopted.

Oil and gas

9.78 Oil and gas exploration and appraisal is part of mineral extraction for the purposes of para 90 of the NPPF[92]. Consequently such operations are not inappropriate in Green Belt provided they preserve the openness of the Green Belt and do not conflict with the purposes of including land in Green Belt.

Mobile homes

9.79 Unsurprisingly, the NPPF does not include a mobile home within the term 'building'[93]. Consequently the replacement of a mobile home with a house

---

[88] [2015] EWCA Civ 10, [2015] PTSR 837 at paras 31, 32 per Richards LJ and paras 41–44 per Mitting J. Tomlinson LJ considered that the point did not need to be decided: para 40.
[89] [2014] EWCA Civ 193 at para 22. PPG2 was, if anything, more generous in what was appropriate development than the NPPF.
[90] [2015] EWCA Civ 10, [2015] PTSR 837 upholding [2014] EWHC 654 (Admin).
[91] See NPPF, para 81.
[92] *Europa Oil and Gas Ltd v Secretary of State for Communities and Local Government* [2014] EWCA Civ 825, [2014] PTSR 1471 upholding Ouseley J in [2013] EWHC 2643 (Admin), [2014] JPL 21 at para 35.
[93] *Lloyd v Secretary of State for Communities and Local Government* [2014] EWCA Civ 839, [2014] JPL 1247.

9.80 *Material considerations and policy*

(or log cabin) is not 'the replacement of a building' within the categories of building construction, which are not inappropriate development under para 89 of the NPPF.

Very special circumstances

9.80 The NPPF says, at para 87, 'inappropriate development is, by definition, harmful to the Green Belt and should not be approved except in very special circumstances'. Paragraph 88 of the NPPF is in similar terms to the former Planning Policy Guidance 2 and advises:

> 'When considering any planning application, local planning authorities should ensure that substantial weight is given to any harm to the Green Belt. "Very special circumstances" will not exist unless the potential harm to the Green Belt by reason of inappropriateness, and any other harm, is clearly outweighed by other considerations.'

9.81 There is no legal definition of very special circumstances. In *Basildon v First Secretary of State* Sullivan J said[94]:

> '... in planning, as in ordinary life, a number of ordinary factors may when combined together result in something very special. Whether any particular combination amounts to very special circumstances for the purposes of PPG2 will be a matter for the planning judgment of the decision-taker'.

The harm to be put in the balance is the harm caused by definition by inappropriate development in the Green Belt, any particular further harm to the Green Belt (such as to openness or the Green Belt's purposes) and any other planning harm[95].

9.82 The relevance of alternatives and precedent are discussed generally at paras **9.157** and **9.174** ff. As factors relevant to whether inappropriate development should be approved in the Green Belt they were considered in *R (on the application of Holder) v Gedling Borough Council*[96]. Members had been advised that on- and off-site alternatives, the precedent effect of approving the scheme, and the energy generation and efficiency of a proposed wind turbine were not material considerations. The Court of Appeal quashed the decision. On precedent, Maurice Kay LJ said that it is significant that the features said to constitute 'very special circumstances' were essentially generic features (the benefits of renewable energy generation and income for a farm) which could be claimed in relation to comparable sites[97]. Alternatives, in particular less intrusive forms of renewable energy provision, were also relevant[98].

9.83 The extent of a benefit is relevant to whether it amounts to very special circumstances. That might involve quantification of the benefit. In *Holder* the Council were[99]:

---

[94] [2004] EWHC 2759 (Admin), [2005] JPL 942 at para 17.
[95] *Redhill Aerodrome Ltd v Secretary of State for Communities and Local Government* [2014] EWCA Civ 1386, [2015] PTSR 274, [2015] JPL 416.
[96] [2014] EWCA Civ 599, [2014] JPL 1087.
[97] At para 15.
[98] At para 17.
[99] [2014] EWCA Civ 599, [2014] JPL 1087 at para 22 per Maurice Kay LJ.

'... simply wrong in [their] submission that, having regard to the full range of applicable policy, matters such as volume and efficiency are irrelevant and can be left to the working of the market. I do not accept that the Green Belt has been sold out to the market in this way. The position remains that the proposed development is, by definition, inappropriate development which can be justified only in very special circumstances. Any consideration of such circumstances must necessarily embrace assessment of the benefit which is likely to ensue. It cannot be the case that a very large but unproductive and inefficient installation ranks equally with a small but extremely efficient one when it comes to evaluating "very special circumstances". Size, efficiency and ability to meet need are all considerations relevant to the issue of "very special circumstances".'

9.84 On 1 July 2013, the Parliamentary Under-Secretary of State for Communities and Local Government said in a Written Ministerial Statement:

'The Green Belt is not always being given the sufficient protection that was the explicit policy intent of Ministers.

The Secretary of State wishes to make clear that, in considering planning applications, although each case will depend on its facts, he considers that the single issue of unmet demand, whether for Traveller sites or for conventional housing, is unlikely to outweigh harm to the Green Belt and other harm to constitute the "very special circumstances" justifying inappropriate development in the Green Belt'.

9.85 It has been suggested that the Written Ministerial Statement of 1 July 2013 does not make a relevant change to policy but can be viewed as a clarification[100]. What it does do is give greater precision to very special circumstances by establishing in policy that housing need is not on its own sufficient to outweigh harm to the Green Belt. There will usually need to be additional factors to support the development[101].

Health

9.86 The health implications of a planning permission may be material if there is a land use connection. For example, the health benefits of encouraging walking and cycling could encourage particular accesses and routes. In *R (on the application of Copeland) v London Borough of Tower Hamlets*[102] the proximity of a proposed fast food take-away to a school, and so its effect on healthy eating by schoolchildren, was capable of being material. That finding related to the physical relationship between the two uses. Cranston J said more generally[103]:

'Promoting social objectives may be a material consideration in the planning context. Planning controls in order to promote social objectives are considerations which can relate to physical land use. Whether a social objective is relevant in a particular case turns on the circumstances. As long as the promotion of the social goal is lawfully within the planning sphere it matters not that it falls elsewhere as well.'

---

[100] *Copas v Secretary of State for Communities and Local Government* [2014] EWHC 2634 (Admin), [2015] JPL 83 at paras 33, 36 per Supperstone J.
[101] See *R (on the application of Lee Valley Regional Park Authority) v Broxbourne Borough Council* [2015] EWHC 185 (Admin).
[102] [2010] EWHC 1845 (Admin), [2011] JPL 40.
[103] At para 22.

9.87 *Material considerations and policy*

Historic environment

9.87 The effect of development upon all aspects of the historic environment is material[104]. In addition specific duties are imposed when determining planning applications which directly or indirectly affect listed buildings and conservation areas.

9.88 Section 66(1) of the Planning (Listed Buildings and Conservation Areas) Act 1990 ('the Listed Buildings Act') applies to effects on listed buildings and provides that:

> 'In considering whether to grant planning permission for development which affects a listed building or its setting, the local planning authority, or, as the case may be, the Secretary of State shall have special regard to the desirability of preserving the building or its setting or any features of special architectural or historic interest which it possesses'.

9.89 The provision contains three elements. Two of these are the preservation of the building and the preservation of any features of special architectural or historic interest; both are concerned with the direct effects of development. These will usually be the carrying out of works to the listed building, which will also need listed building consent.

9.90 The final element is setting. This provides more protection to land and structures in the vicinity of the listed building: through a greater importance to saving the context of the listed building. The NPPF's glossary in Annex 2 says:

> '**Setting of a heritage asset:** The surroundings in which a heritage asset is experienced. Its extent is not fixed and may change as the asset and its surroundings evolve. Elements of a setting may make a positive or negative contribution to the significance of an asset, may affect the ability to appreciate that significance or may be neutral'.

9.91 Setting is not merely a visual concept[105], although visual relationships are usually the most important part of setting. It might include noise and odour or the experience as a traveller passes through buildings or approaches the point where a monument becomes visible. In *R (on the application of Miller) v North Yorkshire County Council* Hickinbottom J said[106]:

> 'There is no definition of "setting" in this context, but it was common ground before me that it is a matter of judgment to be determined in visual terms, with regard being had to (i) the view from the monument towards the development (ii) the view from the development towards the monument and (iii) any other relevant view which includes both the monument and the development (an approach adopted in *Revival Properties Ltd v Secretary of State for the Environment* [1996] JPL B86). In other words, the setting of a monument has to be considered "in-the-round"'.

---

[104] For more discussion of heritage in planning see Harwood *Historic Environment Law* (Institute of Art and Law, 2012 (Supplement, 2014)), Chapter 10 in particular.
[105] *Martin v Secretary of State for Communities and Local Government* [2015] EWHC 3435 (Admin) at para 104 per Lindblom LJ.
[106] [2009] EWHC 2712 at para 89.

9.92 The requirement of 'special regard' creates a strong presumption in favour of preservation. In *R (on the application of Garner) v Elmbridge Borough Council* Ouseley J held[107]:

> 'In reality it is very difficult to see how a local planning authority, having special regard to the desirability of preserving the setting of a listed building, could grant planning permission for a development which harmed it, without having strong reasons for doing so. Section 66 does not permit a local planning authority to treat the desirability of preserving the setting of a listed building as a mere material consideration to which it can simply attach what weight it sees fit in its judgment. The statutory language goes beyond that and treats the preservation of the setting of a listed building as presumptively desirable. So if a development would harm the setting of a listed building, there has to be something of sufficient strength in the merits of the development to outweigh that harm. The language of presumption against permission or strong countervailing reasons for its grant is appropriate. It is the obvious consequence of the statutory language, rather than an illegitimate substitute for it'.

9.93 The statutory duty to have special regard to listed buildings was thoroughly reviewed by the Court of Appeal in *East Northamptonshire District Council v Secretary of State for Communities and Local Government*[108]. Sullivan LJ held that[109]:

> 'Parliament's intention in enacting s 66(1) was that decision-makers should give "considerable importance and weight" to the desirability of preserving the setting of listed buildings when carrying out the balancing exercise'.

9.94 Section 72(1) of the Planning (Listed Buildings and Conservation Areas) Act 1990 imposes a general obligation in respect of conservation areas when exercising powers under the Town and Country Planning Act 1990 and certain other provisions[110] in these terms:

> 'In the exercise, with respect to any buildings or other land in a conservation area, of any functions under or by virtue of any of the provisions mentioned in subsection 2, special attention shall be paid to the desirability of preserving or enhancing the character or appearance of that area'.

9.95 The statutory duty applies to decisions with respect to buildings or land within the conservation area. Planning applications on land outside the conservation area are not subject to the section 72 duty although policy is supportive of conservation areas. The proper approach to the consideration of development in a conservation area was set out by the House of Lords in *South Lakeland District Council v Secretary*

---

[107] [2011] EWHC 86 (Admin) at para 8. This paragraph was explicitly endorsed by the Court of Appeal: [2011] EWCA Civ 891, [2012] JPL 119 at paras 4, 7 per Sullivan LJ. In *Garner* there was no expressed reference to the duty in the committee report, however the court considered that in substance the duty was applied. The Court of Appeal said at para 8 'The question is not whether a local planning authority says that it has had special regard to the desirability of preserving the setting of a listed building but whether it did in fact have special regard to the desirability of preserving the setting of the listed building in question when deciding whether or not to grant planning permission'.
[108] Sub nom *Barnwell Manor Wind Energy Ltd v East Northamptonshire District Council* [2012] EWCA Civ 137, [2015] 1 WLR 45.
[109] At para 29.
[110] The statutory provisions are listed in the Planning (Listed Building and Conservation Areas) Act 1990, s 72(2) and include the determination of planning applications and appeals.

9.96 *Material considerations and policy*

of State for the Environment[111]. Lord Bridge quoted with approval Mann LJ who had said in the Court of Appeal[112]:

> 'The statutorily desirable object of preserving the character or appearance of an area is achieved either by a positive contribution to preservation or by development which leaves character or appearance unharmed that is to say preserved'.

9.96 Lord Bridge continued:

> 'My Lords, I have no hesitation in agreeing with this construction of section [72(1)]. It not only gives effect to the ordinary meaning of the statutory language; it also avoids imputing to the legislature a rigidity of planning policy for which it is difficult to see any rational justification. We may, I think, take judicial notice of the extensive areas, both urban and rural, which have been designated as conservation areas. It is entirely right that in any such area a much stricter control over development than elsewhere should be exercised with the object of preserving or, where possible, enhancing the qualities in the character or appearance of the area which underlie its designation as a conservation area under section [69]. But where a particular development will not have any adverse effect on the character or appearance of the area and is otherwise unobjectionable on planning grounds, one may ask rhetorically what possible planning reason there can be for refusing to allow it'.

The House of Lords therefore rejected the suggestion of the High Court in *Steinberg v Secretary of State for the Environment*[113] that s 72 required a positive improvement. On the contrary, the absence of harm could be sufficient to meet the test.

9.97 If there is harm then the requirement of 'special attention' creates a strong presumption against the development. It is not simply another relevant consideration. In *South Lakeland* the House of Lords held[114]:

> 'There is no dispute that the intention of section [72] is that planning decisions in respect of development proposed to be carried out in a conservation area must give a high priority to the objective of preserving or enhancing the character or appearance of the area. If any proposed development would conflict with that objective, there will be a strong presumption against the grant of planning permission, though, no doubt in exceptional cases the presumption may be overridden in favour of development which is desirable on the ground of some other public interest. But if a development would not conflict with that objective, the special attention required to be paid to that objective will no longer stand in its way and the development will be permitted or refused in the application of ordinary planning criteria'.

This approach was endorsed in the listed building decision of *East Northamptonshire District Council v Secretary of State for Communities and Local Government*[115].

9.98 Both direct impact and the impact on the setting of other parts of the historic environment are also relevant, including on scheduled monuments[116], battlefields[117],

---

[111] [1992] 2 AC 141.
[112] *South Lakeland*, at 150. Section references have been updated from the Town and Country Planning Act 1971.
[113] [1989] 2 PLR 9.
[114] Per Lord Bridge at 146.
[115] [2014] EWCA Civ 137, [2015] 1 WLR 45.
[116] For an old case see *Hoveringham Gravels Ltd v Secretary of State for the Environment* [1975] 1 QB 754 and for a recent decision, *Pugh v Secretary of State for Communities and Local Government* [2015] EWHC 3 (Admin).
[117] *Robert Hitchen Ltd v Secretary of State for the Environment* (1995) 72 P & CR 579.

World Heritage Sites,[118] registered parks and gardens[119] and certain wrecks. Along with listed buildings and conservation areas, these are designated heritage assets under the NPPF.

9.99 The NPPF approach to designated heritage assets is:

(i) account should be taken of the desirability of sustaining and enhancing the significance of all heritage assets[120];

(ii) 'great weight' is to be given to conserving the significance of all designated heritage assets, with greater weight to more important assets[121];

(iii) any harm or loss, including harm to setting, 'should require clear and convincing justification';

(iv) Grade I and II* listed buildings, parks and gardens, scheduled monuments, protected wrecks, battlefields and World Heritage Sites are of the 'highest significance' and substantial harm or loss to them should be 'wholly exceptional';

(v) substantial harm or loss to a Grade II listed building or park or garden should be exceptional;

(vi) proposals leading to 'substantial harm to or total loss of significance of a designated heritage asset' shall be refused unless this impact is necessary to achieve substantial public benefits or four extremely demanding tests are satisfied on the asset preventing use of the site and it being impossible to fund its retention[122];

(vii) 'less than substantial harm' is to be weighed against *public* benefits of the proposal[123].

Housing policy

9.100 The NPPF expects local planning authorities to[124]:

> 'use their evidence base to ensure that their Local Plan meets the full, objectively assessed needs for market and affordable housing in the housing market area, as far as is consistent with the policies set out in this Framework ... identify and update annually a supply of specific deliverable sites sufficient to provide five years' worth of housing against their housing requirements with an additional buffer ...'

9.101 Where local plans are not up to date, the extent of the housing requirement and whether there is consequently a five-year housing supply tend to be argued out on applications. In *Hunston Properties Ltd v Secretary of State for Communities*

---

[118] *Coal Contractors Ltd v Secretary of State for the Environment* [1995] JPL 421.
[119] *R v West Dorset District Council, ex p Searle* [1999] JPL 331; *R (on the application of Lady Hart of Chilton) v Babergh District Council* [2014] EWHC 3261 (Admin), [2015] JPL 491.
[120] NPPF, para 131.
[121] Notes (ii) to (v) are from NPPF, para 132.
[122] NPPF, para 133.
[123] NPPF, para 134. This is not a simple balance, given para 132 and, often, the statutory duties in Planning (Listed Buildings and Conservation Areas) Act 1990, ss 66 and 72.
[124] NPPF, para 47.

9.102 *Material considerations and policy*

and Local Government[125] planning permission was sought for 116 dwellings on a Green Belt site in St Albans where there was no up-to-date local plan. The inspector took the government's household projections and then identified a constrained figure based on the restrictions in the area, particularly Green Belt, from the former East of England Plan. On the basis of that figure she found that there was a five-year housing land supply. The Court of Appeal upheld the High Court's quashing of the decision. The inspector ought to have considered the objectively-assessed need for housing, without taking into account constraints, in deciding whether there was a five-year supply. Sir David Keene held that she was 'mistaken to use a figure for housing requirements below the full objectively assessed needs figure until such time as the Local Plan process came up with a constrained figure'[126]. However, that was not the end of the matter. In deciding whether there are very special circumstances justifying the development, the existence of constraints which give rise to a housing shortfall are relevant. In the application process, the Green Belt was relevant to whether the shortfall should be met rather than the calculation of the housing need.

9.102 Whether there is a five-year supply affects how the development plan policies are considered. By paragraph 49 of the NPPF:

> 'Housing applications should be considered in the context of the presumption in favour of sustainable development. Relevant policies for the supply of housing should not be considered up-to-date if the local planning authority cannot demonstrate a five-year supply of deliverable housing sites'.

9.103 The effect of not having a five-year supply is two-fold. First, the application is considered against the presumption in favour of sustainable development in paragraph 14 of the NPPF and as a matter of policy that might be preferred to the development plan. Second, existing development plan policies for the supply of housing will be considered not to be up to date and so, as a matter of national policy, little weight should be attached to them. Housing policies have been interpreted in this context as including policies which specifically direct or restrict housing supply (such as those limiting development to within settlement boundaries or restricting development in the open countryside) but not those which exist for wider purposes but which have the effect of restricting residential development (such as Green Belt, Green Wedge, historic environment or nature conservation designations)[127].

Affordable housing

9.104 Affordable housing is lower cost housing for eligible households whose needs are not met by the market. There are three types[128]:

(i) social rented housing, which is let by local authorities, private registered providers (usually housing associations) or other persons in agreement with the authority or Homes and Communities Agency at guideline target rents;

---

[125] [2013] EWCA Civ 1610, [2014] JPL 599.
[126] At para 26.
[127] See *South Northamptonshire Council v Secretary of State for Communities and Local Government* [2014] EWHC 573 (Admin) at paras 46, 47 per Ouseley J; *Hopkins Homes Ltd v Secretary of State for Communities and Local Government* [2015] EWHC 132 (Admin) at paras 26–34 per Supperstone J (appeal pending); *Wenman v Secretary of State for Communities and Local Government* [2015] EWHC 925 (Admin) at paras 49–52 and 61–66 per Lang J (appeal pending).
[128] NPPF, Annex 2, Glossary.

(ii) affordable rented housing let by local authorities and private registered providers at no more than 80% of the local market rent;

(iii) intermediate housing is housing for sale and rent at below market levels, subject to criteria, and may include shared equity schemes.

9.105 Affordable housing should remain as such in perpertuity, or if sold on, the proceeds recycled into other affordable housing. Local authorities or housing associations may propose affordable housing applications themselves or buy sites on the market for that development. Affordable housing may also be required as part of a market housing development. Since policy requires affordable housing need to be met, market developments may have to contribute to affordable housing, preferably by provision on the application site[129]. Off-site provision, or a financial contribution might be provided instead, although this is usually discouraged without a sound justification.

9.106 Whilst local policies may seek affordable housing at up to 50% of the units built, requirements may be reduced if it can be shown that the scheme is not viable at that level. Where sizeable provision is made on site, the impact on the developer tends not to be so onerous. Housing associations tend to buy the units at a price which include the build cost (by the developer's contractor) and sometimes with an element for site value. Such affordable housing tends to be less profitable for a developer than an out and out subsidy. Smaller sites, even in some local planning authority areas schemes for individual dwellings or extensions, tend to be harder pressed, having to make financial contributions to off-site provision. An attempt by the government to provide a minimum threshold of ten units (five in certain rural areas) before affordable housing could be required by amending the *Planning Practice Guidance* was quashed in 2015[130].

9.107 Affordable housing requirements are unusual in that, with the exception of very large schemes, the need for affordable housing does not arise from the development permitted. It is essentially an imposition on development or, for financial contributions, a tax.

Starter homes, self-build and custom housebuilding

9.108 The Housing and Planning Bill proposes to introduce duties on local planning authorities to promote permissions for starter homes, self-build and custom housebuilding. These duties would be far-reaching.

9.109 A starter home would be[131]:

(a) a new dwelling (constructed or adapted for use as a single dwelling and not occupied since construction or adaptation);

(b) available for purchase (freehold or leasehold) only by first-time buyers under the age of 40 and meeting any other requirements in regulations;

---

[129] NPPF, para 50.
[130] *R (on the application of West Berkshire District Council and Reading Borough Council) v Secretary of State for Communities and Local Government* [2015] EWHC 2222 (Admin) (appeal pending).
[131] Housing and Planning Bill 2015, cl 2 (as published following Public Bill Committee in the House of Commons).

9.110 *Material considerations and policy*

(c) to be sold at a discount of at least 20% of the market value;

(d) to be sold for less than the price cap of £450,000 in Greater London and £250,000 elsewhere in England; and

(e) subject to any restrictions on sale or letting specified in regulations made by the Secretary of State.

9.110 Local planning authorities and the Secretary of State would have to carry out their planning application and development plan making functions 'with a view to promoting the supply of starter homes in England'[132]. Going further, regulations may provide that planning permission may only be granted for residential development of a specified description if a starter homes requirement has been met. This may be the making of a planning obligation to provide a certain starter homes or to pay a sum to be used by the authority for providing starter homes[133]. If a local planning authority has failed to carry out its functions in relation to starter homes adequately or at all then the Secretary of State may make a compliance direction that no regard is to be had to identified local policies which are inconsistent with the starter home function[134].

9.111 The Self-build and Custom Housebuilding Act 2015 will require district or borough level local authorities to keep registers of individuals and associations of individuals who wish to acquire serviced plots of land to build houses for their own occupation[135]. The registration power is not yet in force. Authorities will need to have regard to the register when carrying out their planning, housing, land disposal and regeneration functions[136]. Greater support for self-build is proposed by the Housing and Planning Bill. It would require district planning authorities to give suitable planning permission or permission in principle in respect of enough serviced plots of land to meet the demand for self-build and custom housebuilding in its area arising in each 12-month period[137].

Landscape and visual impact

9.112 The effect of development on the landscape and its visual impacts are two major considerations. These are related but separate and different concepts:[138]

> '**Landscape Impacts** are on the fabric, character and quality of the landscape. They are concerned with:
>
> • Landscape components
>
> • Landscape character – regional and local distinctiveness
>
> • Special interests, eg designations, conservation sites, cultural associations.
>
> **Visual Impacts** are the effects on people of the changes in available views through intrusion or obstruction and whether important opportunities to enjoy views may be improved or reduced'.

---

[132] Housing and Planning Bill 2015, cl 3(1).
[133] Housing and Planning Bill 2015, cl 4.
[134] Housing and Planning Bill 2015, cl 6.
[135] Self-build and Custom Housebuilding Act 2015, s 1(1).
[136] Self-build and Custom Housebuilding Act 2015, s 2.
[137] Housing and Planning Bill cl 9, proposing to insert Self-build and Custom Housebuilding Act 2015, s 2A.
[138] Taken from the Scottish National Heritage *Environmental Assessment Handbook*, Appendix 1, Landscape and Visual Impact Assessment, para 16.

Substantive material considerations **9.116**

In some cases national designations apply, bringing statutory and policy responsibilities to decision-makers.

National Parks

9.113 National Parks are extensive tracts of country that are designated because their natural beauty and the opportunities they afford for open-air recreation, given their character and position in relation to population centres, make it desirable to take necessary measures for their purposes[139]. The purposes of designation are for 'conserving and enhancing the natural beauty, wildlife and cultural heritage' of those areas and promoting the understanding and enjoyment by the public of those special areas[140]. In this context natural beauty includes wildlife and cultural heritage[141].

9.114 National Park authorities, which are the local planning authorities for their areas, 'shall seek to foster the economic and social well-being of local communities within the National Park'[142]. Public bodies and statutory undertakers are required to have regard to the National Park purposes when exercising any functions which affect land in a National Park, giving greater weight to the purpose of conserving and enhancing the natural beauty, wildlife and cultural heritage of the National Park than promoting public understanding and enjoyment in the event of conflict[143].

The Broads

9.115 Of similar status to the National Parks but with its own legal regime, is the Norfolk and Suffolk Broads. The Broads is defined by the Norfolk and Suffolk Broads Act 1988 as a particular area on the deposited map[144]. A Broads Authority is established with a general duty to manage the Broads for the purposes of[145]:

'(a) conserving and enhancing the natural beauty, wildlife and cultural heritage of the Broads;

(b) promoting opportunities for the understanding and enjoyment of the special qualities of the Broads by the public; and

(c) protecting the interests of navigation'.

9.116 The authority is under a duty to have regard to[146]:

'(a) the national importance of the Broads as an area of natural beauty and one which affords opportunities for open-air recreation;

(b) the desirability of protecting the natural resources of the Broads from damage; and

(c) the needs of agriculture and forestry and the economic and social interests of those who live or work in the Broads'.

---

[139] National Parks and Access to the Countryside Act 1949, s 5(2).
[140] National Parks and Access to the Countryside Act 1949, s 5(1).
[141] National Parks and Access to the Countryside Act 1949, s 5(2A).
[142] National Parks and Access to the Countryside Act 1949, s 11A(1).
[143] National Parks and Access to the Countryside Act 1949, s 11A(1), (2).
[144] Norfolk and Suffolk Broads Act 1988, s 2(3), subject to any variations made by or under Sch 2 to that Act.
[145] Norfolk and Suffolk Broads Act 1988, s 2(1).
[146] Norfolk and Suffolk Broads Act 1988, s 2(4).

9.117 *Material considerations and policy*

9.117 Relevant authorities include neighbouring local planning authorities and the Secretary of State. By s 17A(1)[147]:

'In exercising or performing any functions in relation to, or so as to affect, land in the Broads, a relevant authority shall have regard to the purposes of:

(a) conserving and enhancing the natural beauty, wildlife and cultural heritage of the Broads;

(b) promoting opportunities for the understanding and enjoyment of the special qualities of the Broads by the public; and

(c) protecting the interests of navigation'.

Areas of outstanding natural beauty

9.118 Areas of outstanding natural beauty are designated as areas outside national parks but which are of such outstanding natural beauty that particular provisions of the Countryside and Rights of Way Act 2000 should apply to them 'for the purpose of conserving and enhancing the natural beauty of the area[148]. Designation is carried out by Natural England or the Natural Resources Body for Wales, as appropriate. There are 38 AONBs in England and Wales and they were originally created by the National Parks and Access to the Countryside Act 1949. Some AONBs consist of multiple separate areas[149].

9.119 A duty to have regard applies to planning decisions by the Countryside and Rights of Way Act 2000, s 85(1):

'In exercising or performing any functions in relation to, or so as to affect, land in an area of outstanding natural beauty, a relevant authority shall have regard to the purpose of conserving and enhancing the natural beauty of the area of outstanding natural beauty'.

Policies on National Parks, the Broads and Areas of Outstanding Natural Beauty (AONBs)

9.120 Statutory countryside designations are National Parks, the Broads and Areas of Outstanding Natural Beauty. Paragraph 116 of the NPPF says, 'Planning permission should be refused for major developments in these designated areas except in exceptional circumstances and where it can be demonstrated they are in the public interest'. The meaning of 'major development' in this text has been considered in two cases, both in the Surrey Hills AONB in Mole Valley.

9.121 *Aston v Secretary of State for Communities and Local Government*[150] concerned a 1.94 hectare site on which planning permission was sought for 14 houses. This was 'major development' within the definition in the DMPO 2010 concerning publicity for planning applications and in the directions for reference of applications to the Secretary of State. Wyn Williams J, however, held that this meaning did not

---

[147] For consideration of the Norfolk and Suffolk Broads Act 1988, s 17A see *Howell v Secretary of State for Communities and Local Government* [2014] EWHC 3627 (Admin); affirmed [2015] EWCA Civ 1189.
[148] Countryside and Rights of Way Act 2000, s 82.
[149] For example, the Cornwall AONB has 12 separate, non-contiguous parts.
[150] [2013] EWHC 1936 (Admin), [2014] 2 P & CR 10.

Substantive material considerations **9.126**

carry over to the NPPF. Instead a normal meaning applied and the inspector was entitled to hold in that case that the scheme was not major development under para 116[151].

9.122 In *R (on the application of Cherkley Campaign Ltd) v Mole Valley District Council*[152] Haddon-Cave J held that the inclusion of a fairway and a tee within the AONB meant that a golf and hotel scheme was major development in the designated area, as para 116 'is plainly intended to include *"major developments"* which physically overlap with designated areas or visually encroach upon on them'[153].

9.123 On appeal, Richards LJ disagreed[154]:

> 'The paragraph provides that permission should be refused for major developments *"in"* an AONB or other designated area except where the stated conditions are met: the specific concern of the paragraph is with major developments in a designated area, not with developments outside a designated area, however proximate to the designated area they may be. In this case the only part of the development *in* the AONB would be the 15th fairway and 16th tee. I do not think that the creation of one fairway and one tee of a golf course could reasonably be regarded as a major development *in* the AONB, even when account is taken of the fact that they form part of a larger golf course development the rest of which is immediately adjacent to the AONB'.

Minerals

9.124 Minerals policy includes the extraction of minerals from the ground (primary minerals), the reuse or recycling of minerals[155] and transport and supply (such as railheads and depots). Minerals extend from sand and gravel, to stone or materials with specialist uses, and oil and gas. Issues in practice tend to be the extent of need, the environmental impacts of mineral development and ensuring that sites are completed and restored within suitable timescales[156].

Nature conservation

9.125 Nature conservation in planning is concerned with individual plants and animals (generally referred to as species protection) and sites of importance to plant and animal species (sites protection). In practice there may be some overlap between the two. Species and sites are characterised in terms of international and European, national or local importance, with the legal regimes and policy tests being different for all three levels.

European sites and species

9.126 The Habitats Directive 92/43/EEC and the associated Birds Directive 79/409/EEC introduce two types of European protection: designation of areas and

---

[151] At paras 93, 94.
[152] [2013] EWHC 2582 (Admin), [2014] 1 P & CR 12.
[153] At para 147.
[154] [2014] EWCA Civ 567, [2014] 2 EGLR 98 at para 44.
[155] Also called secondary minerals.
[156] Policy is principally in the NPPF, section 13, the Technical Appendix to it the *Planning Practice Guidance* section 27 and *Minerals Planning Policy Wales*.

9.127 *Material considerations and policy*

protection of species and their resting places and breeding grounds. Land may be designated by the European Commission as Special Areas of Conservation, under the Habitats Directive or Special Protection Areas under the Birds Directive.

9.127 Article 6(3), (4) of the Habitats Directive sets out the tests for the approval of plans or projects which might affect a designated area:

'3 Any plan or project not directly connected with or necessary to the management of the site but likely to have a significant effect thereon, either individually or in combination with other plans or projects, shall be subject to appropriate assessment of its implications for the site in view of the site's conservation objectives. In the light of the conclusions of the assessment of the implications for the site and subject to the provisions of paragraph 4, the competent national authorities shall agree to the plan or project only after having ascertained that it will not adversely affect the integrity of the site concerned and, if appropriate, after having obtained the opinion of the general public.

4 If, in spite of a negative assessment of the implications for the site and in the absence of alternative solutions, a plan or project must nevertheless be carried out for imperative reasons of overriding public interest, including those of a social or economic nature, the Member State shall take all compensatory measures necessary to ensure that the overall coherence of Natura 2000 is protected. It shall inform the Commission of the compensatory measures adopted.

Where the site concerned hosts a priority natural habitat type and/or a priority species, the only considerations which may be raised are those relating to human health or public safety, to beneficial consequences of primary importance for the environment or, further to an opinion from the Commission, to other imperative reasons of overriding public interest'.

These tests are applied to Birds Directive sites by art 7 of the Habitats Directive.

9.128 The Habitats Directive deals with animal species in art 12(1) which requires:

'Member States shall take the requisite measures to establish a system of strict protection for the animal species listed in Annex IV (a) in their natural range, prohibiting

(a) all forms of deliberate capture or killing of specimens of these species in the wild;

(b) deliberate disturbance of these species, particularly during the period of breeding, rearing, hibernation and migration;

(c) deliberate destruction or taking of eggs from the wild;

(d) deterioration or destruction of breeding sites or resting places'.

9.129 Article 16 permits derogations in limited circumstances which are, as relevant to development projects:

'Provided that there is no satisfactory alternative and the derogation is not detrimental to the maintenance of the populations of the species concerned at a favourable conservation status in their natural range, Member States may derogate from the provisions of Articles 12 ...

(c) in the interests of public health and public safety, or for other imperative reasons of overriding public interest, including those of a social or economic nature and beneficial consequences of primary importance for the environment'.

9.130 Whilst there are some similarities in the tests, the species tests apply only to the animals themselves, eggs, breeding sites and resting places rather than the area

Substantive material considerations **9.135**

of land which supports the species. The requirement to establish that the proposal will 'not adversely affect the integrity of the site' applies only to designated sites not species.

The UK's implementation of the Directive by the Conservation of Habitats and Species Regulations 2010 differs significantly between sites and species.

9.131 The primary protection of European designated sites is carried out through the planning process. Planning authorities are required to apply the art 6(3), (4) tests when determining planning applications[157]. However European Protected Species are primarily protected by criminal sanctions[158] and licensing by Natural England or the Natural Resources Body for Wales (including in the name of their Ministers)[159].

Sites protection

9.132 A series of tests apply to planning applications for projects which may affect European sites, whether the project is within or outside the site[160]. First, if the project[161]:

'(a) is likely to have a significant effect on a European site or a European offshore marine site (either alone or in combination with other plans or projects), and

(b) is not directly connected with or necessary to the management of that site,

[the planning authority] must make an appropriate assessment of the implications for that site in view of that site's conservation objectives'.

9.133 Subject to the exception below, planning permission may only be granted 'after having ascertained that it will not adversely affect the integrity of the European site or the European offshore marine site (as the case may be)'[162].

9.134 The exception is[163]:

- that there is no alternative solution; and
- the project must be carried out for imperative reasons of overriding public interest (which may be of a social or economic nature).

9.135 Where the site concerned hosts a priority natural habitat type or a priority species, these reasons must be either[164]:

'(a) reasons relating to human health, public safety or beneficial consequences of primary importance to the environment; or

---

[157] Conservation of Habitats and Species Regulations 2010, regs 60, 61, 62, 68.
[158] Conservation of Habitats and Species Regulations 2010, reg 41.
[159] Conservation of Habitats and Species Regulations 2010, regs 53–58.
[160] Examples of offsite development having effects will include airborne pollution from aircraft, incinerators and vehicles, waterborne pollution entering the site and residential development which may increase recreational activity in the site, disturbance by dogs and predation by domestic cats.
[161] Conservation of Habitats and Species Regulations 2010, reg 61(1), applied to planning applications by reg 68. Project includes projects within the definition in the EIA Directive: C-127/02 *Waddenzee* [2005] 2 CMLR 31, CJEU at paras 22–27.
[162] Conservation of Habitats and Species Regulations 2010, reg 61(6).
[163] Conservation of Habitats and Species Regulations 2010, reg 62(1).
[164] Conservation of Habitats and Species Regulations 2010, reg 62(2).

9.136 *Material considerations and policy*

(b) any other reasons which the competent authority, having due regard to the opinion of the European Commission, consider to be imperative reasons of overriding public interest'.

If the exception is applied then any necessary compensatory measures must be taken to ensure that the overall coherence of Natura 2000 is protected[165].

9.136 EIA and Appropriate Assessment contain some similarities but are conceptually different. EIA is a process of gathering information, consulting on it and considering that material. It does not indicate what final decision should be reached. Appropriate Assessment sets a sequence of tests to be applied which determine whether a project could be approved. The Habitats Directive and Regulations say very little about how the assessment should be carried out. As Lord Carnwath JSC said in *R (on the application of Champion) v North Norfolk District Council*[166]:

> '39 ... At least in this country the use of the term "screening" in relation to the Habitats Directive is potentially confusing, because of the technical meaning it has under the EIA Regulations. The formal procedures prescribed for EIA purposes, including "screening", preparation of an environmental statement, and mandatory public consultation, have no counterpart in the Habitats legislation.
>
> 41 ... The process envisaged by article 6(3) should not be over-complicated. ... in cases where it is not obvious, the competent authority will consider whether the "trigger" for appropriate assessment is met (and see paras 41–43 of *Waddenzee*). But this informal threshold decision is not to be confused with a formal "screening opinion" in the EIA sense. The operative words are those of the Habitats Directive itself. All that is required is that, in a case where the authority has found there to be a risk of significant adverse effects to a protected site, there should be an "appropriate assessment". "Appropriate" is not a technical term. It indicates no more than that the assessment should be appropriate to the task in hand: that task being to satisfy the responsible authority that the project "will not adversely affect the integrity of the site concerned" taking account of the matters set in the article. As the court itself indicated in *Waddenzee* the context implies a high standard of investigation'.

9.137 There are, though, a few requirements and a few practical points. The person applying for planning permission shall provide any information required to decide whether Appropriate Assessment is required[167]. If Appropriate Assessment is carried out, the planning authority must consult Natural England or the Natural Resources Body for Wales[168]. The general public may be consulted[169]. Whilst there is no explicit screening requirement to decide at an early stage whether Appropriate Assessment is required, any of the tests need to be applied with sufficient information. It would be disruptive to determine at the committee stage that Appropriate Assessment was required and then to require further investigation and consultation.

9.138 A likely significant effect 'exists if it cannot be excluded on the basis of objective information that the plan or project will have significant effects on the

---

[165] Conservation of Habitats and Species Regulations 2010, reg 66.
[166] [2015] UKSC 52, [2015] 1 WLR 3710, also citing with approval *R (on the application of Hart District Council) v Secretary of State for Communities and Local Government* [2008] EWHC 1204 (Admin), [2008] 2 P & CR 302 at para 71 per Sullivan J.
[167] Conservation of Habitats and Species Regulations 2010, reg 61(2).
[168] Conservation of Habitats and Species Regulations 2010, reg 61(3), the bodies being defined in reg 5.
[169] Conservation of Habitats and Species Regulations 2010, reg 61(4).

Substantive material considerations **9.142**

site concerned'[170]. Proposed mitigation measures can be considered when deciding whether Appropriate Assessment is required[171] but there needs to be sufficient certainty about the effectiveness of those measures. Appropriate Assessment is intended to be stringent. The effects on the site's conservation objectives 'must be identified in the light of the best scientific knowledge in the field'[172]. The 'no adverse effects on integrity' test is only satisfied if the authority is convinced it is met, that is 'no reasonable scientific doubt remains as to the absence of such effects'[173].

9.139 The exception, allowing development if an adverse effect on integrity might occur, is intentionally restrictive. Alternatives have to be considered and 'imperative reasons of overriding public interest (IROPI) are hard to satisfy and are concerned with public rather than private interests, although that might include private development[174].

Species protection in planning

9.140 In the exercise of planning powers public authorities are subject to the Conservation of Habitats and Species Regulations 2010, reg 9(5), providing that they:

> 'must have regard to the requirements of the Habitats Directive so far as they may be affected by the exercise of those functions'.

9.141 In *R (on the application of Woolley) v Cheshire East Borough Council* Judge Waksman QC held on local planning authorities' responsibilities to European Protected Species under the 1994 Habitats Regulations[175]:

> 'In my view that engagement involves a consideration by the authority of those provisions and considering whether the derogation requirements might be met. This exercise is in no way a substitute for the licence application which will follow if permission is given. But it means that if it is clear or perhaps very likely that the requirements of the Directive cannot be met because there is a satisfactory alternative or because there are no conceivable "other imperative reasons of overriding public interest" then the authority should act upon that, and refuse permission. On the other hand if it seems that the requirements are likely to be met, then the authority will have discharged its duty to have regard to the requirements and there would be no impediment to planning permission on that ground. If it is unclear to the authority whether the requirements will be met it will just have to take a view whether in all the circumstances it should affect the grant or not'.

9.142 The issue was considered by the Supreme Court in *R (on the application of Morge) v Hampshire County Council*[176], which said that the obligation on the planning authority was simply to have regard. Lord Brown of Eaton-under-Heywood held[177]:

---

[170] *Waddenzee* C-127/02 CJEU at para 44. 'Likely' means 'possible', see *Sweetman v An Bord Pleanala* C-258/11 [2013] 3 CMLR 16 Advocate General Sharpston at paras 45–47.
[171] *R (on the application of Hart District Council) v Secretary of State for Communities and Local Government* [2008] EWHC 1204 (Admin), [2008] 2 P & CR 16 at para 71 per Sullivan J.
[172] *Waddenzee* at para 54.
[173] See *Waddenzee* at paras 55–59.
[174] C-182/10 *Solvay v Region Wallonne* [2012] 2 CMLR 19 at paras 71–79 considering IROPI under art 6(4) including noting at para 77 the 'economic and social context'.
[175] [2009] EWHC 1227 (Admin), [2010] Env LR 5 at para 27.
[176] [2011] UKSC 2, [2011] 1 WLR 268.
[177] At para 29. Followed in *R (on the application of Prideaux) v Buckinghamshire County Council* [2013] EWHC 1054 (Admin), [2013] Env LR 32.

9.143 *Material considerations and policy*

> 'I cannot see why a planning permission (and, indeed, a full planning permission save only as to conditions necessary to secure any required mitigating measures) should not ordinarily be granted save only in cases where the planning committee conclude that the proposed development would both (a) be likely to offend article 12(1) and (b) be unlikely to be licensed pursuant to the derogation powers. After all, even if development permission is given, the criminal sanction against any offending (and unlicensed) activity remains available and it seems to me wrong in principle, when Natural England have the primary responsibility for ensuring compliance with the Directive, also to place a substantial burden on the planning authority in effect to police the fulfilment of Natural England's own duty'.

9.143 Consequently the responsibilities of the local planning authority, planning inspectors and the Secretary of State (when exercising planning powers) differ between the consideration of European designated sites and European Protected Species:

(i) for designated sites, the planning decision-maker is the competent authority for applying the Habitats Directive tests and no further consent is required;

(ii) for protected species, the planning decision needs only to have regard to the requirements and can consider the likelihood of them being satisfied, but the decision whether they are satisfied is to be decided by Natural England on a species licence application. That application can be informed by surveying required under a condition on a planning permission. The detail of mitigation can be worked out after the permission has been granted and if not satisfactory, a species licence can be refused. The need for a species licence provides a control on the works beyond planning permission.

One practical consequence is that more information is required by the planning decision-maker for European designated sites than for European Protected Species.

9.144 Circular 06/2005 *Biodiversity and Geological Conservation – Statutory obligations and their impact within the planning system* sets out the Secretary of State's advice on the Habitats Directive[178]. Paragraph 116 says, with reference to the 1994 Habitats Regulations:

> 'When dealing with cases where a European protected species may be affected, a planning authority is a competent authority within the meaning of regulation 6 of the Habitats Regulations, and therefore has a statutory duty under regulation 3(4) to have regard to the requirements of the Habitats Directive in the exercise of its functions. So the Directive's provisions are clearly relevant in reaching planning decisions, and these should be made in a manner which takes them fully into account. The Directive's requirements include a strict system of protection for European protected species, prohibiting deliberate killing, catching or disturbing of species, the taking of eggs etc and damage to or destruction of their breeding sites or resting places. Derogations from this strict protection are allowed only in certain limited circumstances and subject to certain tests being met (see para 112 above). Planning authorities should give due weight to the presence of a European protected species on a development site to reflect these requirements, in reaching planning decisions, and this may potentially justify a refusal of planning permission'.

---

[178] Addressing European designated sites at paras 3–55, species protection in general at paras 96–102 and licensing for European protected species at paras 112–117.

Sites of Special Scientific Interest

9.145 Local planning authorities, Ministers and Inspectors are 'section 28G authorities' for the purpose of decisions affecting sites of special scientific interest (SSSIs) under the Wildlife and Countryside Act 1981[179]. In exercising their functions so far as their exercise is likely to affect the flora, fauna or geological or physiographical features by reason of which a site of special scientific interest is of special interest, the authority is under a duty[180] to 'take reasonable steps, consistent with the proper exercise of the authority's functions, to further the conservation and enhancement of the flora, fauna or geological or physiographical features by reason of which the site is of special scientific interest'[181]. In *R (on the application of Friends of the Earth England, Wales and Northern Ireland) v Welsh Ministers* Hickinbottom J distinguished this from the listed buildings 'special regard' duty and said the question is 'not whether the Minister gave the desirability of conserving and enhancing these features particular enhanced weight, but whether she took reasonable steps to conserve and enhance those features'[182].

Biodiversity

9.146 All public authorities are required to have regard to the purpose of conserving biodiversity insofar as it is consistent with the proper exercise of their functions[183]. This includes restoring or enhancing a population of a living organism or a type of habitat[184].

Trees

9.147 Section 197 of the Town and Country Planning Act 1990 imposes a general requirement in respect of trees:

'It shall be the duty of the local planning authority:

(a) to ensure, whenever it is appropriate, that in granting planning permission for any development adequate provision is made, by the imposition of conditions, for the preservation or planting of trees; and

(b) to make such orders under section 198 as appear to the authority to be necessary in connection with the grant of such permission, whether for giving effect to such conditions or otherwise'.

---

[179] Wildlife and Countryside Act 1981, s 28G(1), (3).
[180] Wildlife and Countryside Act 1981, s 28G(1).
[181] Wildlife and Countryside Act 1981, s 28G(2).
[182] [2015] EWHC 776 (Admin), [2016] Env LR 1 at para 133.
[183] Natural Environment and Rural Communities Act 2006, s 40(1). In doing so, Ministers, but not local authorities, are expressly required to have regard to the United Nations Environmental Programme Convention on Biological Diversity of 1992: s 40(2). The duty is discussed in *R (on the application of Buglife) v Thurrock Thames Gateway Development Corpon* [2008] EWHC 475, [2008] Env LR 31 and see *Planning Practice Guidance* section 8.
[184] Natural Environment and Rural Communities Act 2006, s 40(3).

9.148 *Material considerations and policy*

Section 198 orders are tree preservation orders which can be made by local planning authorities to protect individual trees, groups of trees or woodlands if it is 'expedient in the interests of amenity'.[185]

Personal circumstances and impacts

9.148 Planning considerations are normally concerned with the character of the use of the land and not the particular personal circumstances of a particular occupier[186]. However, as Lord Scarman observed in *Westminster City Council v Great Portland Estates Ltd*[187], personal circumstances are not to be wholly ignored. The expansion needs of a particular business or adaptation of a house to assist with a person's disability may be relevant, although that cannot be pushed too far. Personal circumstances are only relevant if they engage the public interest. Planning applications will invariably be in the personal interests of the applicant but a principal purpose of the planning system is to regulate the advancement of personal interests in the public interest. Generally speaking, therefore, personal interests do not advance a planning application. The response to a business seeking to expand or a householder wanting more room for a growing family may be to move somewhere else. This assumes that going elsewhere can be achieved without too great a hardship. The more generous approach to gypsy and traveller sites in the open countryside or the Green Belt has been driven by a shortage of caravan sites in urban areas. Where occupants are already on site then the effect of moving them on health and education may be relevant, but perhaps more to justify temporary rather than permanent use.

Allied to personal circumstances are human rights and the public sector equality duty since both concern the effects on particular individuals or individuals sharing particular characteristics.

Human Rights Act 1998

9.149 The European Convention on Human Rights has some role in planning although generally only in cases involving gypsies or travellers. Section 6(1) of the Human Rights Act 1998 imposes the general duty:

> 'It is unlawful for a public authority to act in a way which is incompatible with a Convention right'.

Convention rights which more usually arise in enforcement cases are art 8 (right to respect for private and family life), art 14 (prohibition on discrimination) and art 1 of

---

[185] Town and Country Planning Act 1990, s 198(1). Tree Preservation Orders have provisional effect until a decision on confirmation or six months have expired (whichever is earlier): Town and Country Planning (Tree Preservation) (England) Regulations 2012, SI 2012/605, reg 4(2). Subject to various exceptions, it is a criminal offence to cut down, uproot, lop, top or wilfully destroy or damage a tree protected by a Tree Preservation Order or otherwise contravene such an order: s 210. There is a duty on the landowner to replace trees which are subject to a Tree Preservation Order (subject to immaterial exceptions) unless the local planning authority dispense with the requirement: s 206. In conservation areas, notice has to be given before such works are carried out on trees which are not subject to a Tree Preservation Order. The applicant is entitled to proceed with the works if the authority consents or six weeks pass unless the Council then make a tree preservation order: s 211. For further discussion of trees see Harwood *Planning Enforcement*, Bloomsbury Professional, Chapter 17.

[186] *East Barnet Urban District Council v British Transport Commission* [1962] 2 QB 491 per Lord Parker CJ.

[187] [1985] AC 661, quoted earlier in this chapter.

the First Protocol (protection of property). The procedural right to a fair trial under art 6 applies, but in planning cases has added little to the common law, apart from a requirement to deal with cases within a reasonable time[188]. Occasionally other rights are raised in planning enforcement, such as art 9 (freedom of thought, conscience and religion)[189] and art 10 (freedom of expression)[190].

'**Article 8: Right to respect for private and family life**

1   Everyone has the right to respect for his private and family life, his home and his correspondence.

2   There shall be no interference by a public authority with the exercise of this right except such as is in accordance with the law and is necessary in a democratic society in the interests of national security, public safety or the economic well-being of the country, for the prevention of disorder or crime, for the protection of health or morals, or for the protection of the rights and freedoms of others.

Article 14: Prohibition of discrimination

The enjoyment of the rights and freedoms set forth in this Convention shall be secured without discrimination on any ground such as sex, race, colour, language, religion, political or other opinion, national or social origin, association with a national minority, property, birth or other status.

Article 1: Protection of property

Every natural or legal person is entitled to the peaceful enjoyment of his possessions. No one shall be deprived of his possessions except in the public interest and subject to the conditions provided for by law and by the general principles of international law.

The preceding provisions shall not, however, in any way impair the right of a State to enforce such laws as it deems necessary to control the use of property in accordance with the general interest or to secure the payment of taxes or other contributions or penalties'.

9.150   The substantive rights (arts 8, 13, Protocol 1 art 1) which arise in planning cases are all qualified rights, in that a balance has to be struck between the right and the public interest. The Convention has been interpreted to give states a wide discretion in regulating planning matters[191].

9.151   A preliminary question is whether the rights are engaged in the particular case and in respect of which persons. A person whose land is enforced against will have their Protocol 1, art 1 rights 'engaged'. Similarly someone who is being forced out of their home (including a residential caravan) will have art 8 rights engaged. The impact of development on neighbours may be so substantial as to engage their art 8 or Protocol 1 art 1 rights, usually where there is severe environmental pollution[192].

9.152   The effect of human rights on planning decisions has been very limited. In general any effect has been to reinforce the importance of effects which were

---

[188] See *Vergos v Greece* (2005) 41 EHRR 41.
[189] See *Iskcon v United Kingdom* (1994) 18 EHRR CD 133, where a complaint against enforcement action which limited the number and size of religious festivals at a residential college was held to be inadmissible.
[190] For freedom of expression and advertising control, see *Butler v Derby City Council* [2005] EWHC 2835 (Admin), [2006] 1 WLR 1346.
[191] See *Sporrong and Lönroth v Sweden* (A/52) (1983) 5 EHRR 35 and *Hatton v United Kingdom* (36022/97) (2003) 37 EHRR 28.
[192] *Lopez Ostra v Spain* (1994) 20 EHRR 277 and *Guerra v Italy* (1998) 26 EHRR 357.

9.153 *Material considerations and policy*

already of concern. In *Lough v First Secretary of State*[193] planning permission was granted for a 20-storey tower near the Tate Modern gallery in Southwark. Local residents said their art 8 rights were engaged by a departure from the development plan involving loss of privacy, mutual overlooking, loss of a view and loss of light, coupled with temporary interference with television reception and loss of value. Whilst art 8 protected the environment of the home, any effect on amenity must be substantial for it to be engaged[194]. In that case the impacts were not so great as to engage art 8.

Public sector equality duty

9.153 Section 149 of the Equality Act 2010 provides:

'(1) A public authority must, in the exercise of its functions, have due regard to the need to:

    (a) eliminate discrimination, harassment, victimisation and any other conduct that is prohibited by or under this Act;

    (b) advance equality of opportunity between persons who share a relevant protected characteristic and persons who do not share it;

    (c) foster good relations between persons who share a relevant protected characteristic and persons who do not share it.

(2) A person who is not a public authority but who exercises public functions must, in the exercise of those functions, have due regard to the matters mentioned in subsection (1).

(3) Having due regard to the need to advance equality of opportunity between persons who share a relevant protected characteristic and persons who do not share it involves having due regard, in particular, to the need to:

    (a) remove or minimise disadvantages suffered by persons who share a relevant protected characteristic that are connected to that characteristic;

    (b) take steps to meet the needs of persons who share a relevant protected characteristic that are different from the needs of persons who do not share it;

    (c) encourage persons who share a relevant protected characteristic to participate in public life or in any other activity in which participation by such persons is disproportionately low.

(4) The steps involved in meeting the needs of disabled persons that are different from the needs of persons who are not disabled include, in particular, steps to take account of disabled persons' disabilities.

(5) Having due regard to the need to foster good relations between persons who share a relevant protected characteristic and persons who do not share it involves having due regard, in particular, to the need to:

    (a) tackle prejudice, and

    (b) promote understanding.

(6) Compliance with the duties in this section may involve treating some persons more favourably than others; but that is not to be taken as permitting conduct that would otherwise be prohibited by or under this Act.

---

[193] [2004] EWCA Civ 905, [2004] 1 WLR 2557.
[194] *Lough* at para 43(b) per Pill LJ.

(7) The relevant protected characteristics are:

age;

disability;

gender reassignment;

pregnancy and maternity;

race;

religion or belief;

sex;

sexual orientation.

(8) A reference to conduct that is prohibited by or under this Act includes a reference to—

(a) a breach of an equality clause or rule;

(b) a breach of a non-discrimination rule'.

9.154 Section 149 comprises nine needs: see *R (on the application of RB) v Devon County Council*[195]:

'They are

1) the need to eliminate discrimination;

2) the need to advance equality of opportunity between persons who share a relevant protected characteristic and persons who do not;

3) the need to remove or minimise disadvantages suffered by persons who share a relevant protected characteristic that are connected to that characteristic;

4) the need to take steps to meet needs of persons who share a relevant protected characteristic that are different from the needs from persons who do not share it;

5) in particular the need to take steps to take account of disabled person's disabilities;

6) the need to encourage persons who share any relevant protected characteristic to participate in public life or in any other activity in which participation by such persons is disproportionately low;

7) the need to foster good relations between persons who share a relevant protected characteristic and persons who do not;

8) the need to tackle prejudice, and

9) the need to promote understanding'.

9.155 There is a need to comply with the duty in substance, not in form – a failure to mention it is not in itself determinative. Conversely, it needs to be apparent how the duty has been addressed The duty must be performed with vigour and an open mind. General awareness of the duty does not amount to the necessary due regard, being a 'substantial rigorous and open-minded approach'. If a risk of adverse impact is identified, consideration should be given to measures to avoid that impact before fixing on a particular solution[196].

---

[195] [2012] EWHC 3597 (Admin), [2013] Er LR 113 at para 20 per Judge Vosper QC.
[196] *R (on the application of JM & NT) v Isle of Wight Council* [2011] EWHC 2911 (Admin) at paras 95–105.

9.156 *Material considerations and policy*

Waste

9.156 Providing facilities for dealing with waste where it is generated and for subsequent processes and disposal is an essential role of the planning process. That has been overlain by obligations in European law.

Waste and Landfill Directives

9.157 The Waste Framework Directive 2008/98/EC requires member states to take measures, which as relevant to planning applications are[197]:

'**Article 4 Waste hierarchy**

1 The following waste hierarchy shall apply as a priority order in waste prevention and management legislation and policy:

(a) prevention;

(b) preparing for re-use;

(c) recycling;

(d) other recovery, eg energy recovery; and

(e) disposal.

2 When applying the waste hierarchy referred to in paragraph 1, Member States shall take measures to encourage the options that deliver the best overall environmental outcome. This may require specific waste streams departing from the hierarchy where this is justified by life-cycle thinking on the overall impacts of the generation and management of such waste. …

Member States shall take into account the general environmental protection principles of precaution and sustainability, technical feasibility and economic viability, protection of resources as well as the overall environmental, human health, economic and social impacts, in accordance with Articles 1 and 13.

Article 10 Recovery

1 Member States shall take the necessary measures to ensure that waste undergoes recovery operations, in accordance with Articles 4 and 13.

Article 11 Re-use and recycling

1 Member States shall take measures, as appropriate, to promote the re-use of products and preparing for re-use activities, notably by encouraging the establishment and support of re-use and repair networks

Article 13 Protection of human health and the environment

Member States shall take the necessary measures to ensure that waste management is carried out without endangering human health, without harming the environment and, in particular:

(a) without risk to water, air, soil, plants or animals;

(b) without causing a nuisance through noise or odours; and

(c) without adversely affecting the countryside or places of special interest.'

---

[197] These terms are defined in art 3.

Article 16 Principles of self-sufficiency and proximity

1 Member States shall take appropriate measures ... to establish an integrated and adequate network of waste disposal installations and of installations for the recovery of mixed municipal waste collected from private households, including where such collection also covers such waste from other producers, ...

2 The network shall be designed to enable the Community as a whole to become self-sufficient in waste disposal as well as in the recovery of waste referred to in paragraph 1, and to enable Member States to move towards that aim individually, taking into account geographical circumstances or the need for specialised installations for certain types of waste.

3 The network shall enable waste to be disposed of or waste referred to in paragraph 1 to be recovered in one of the nearest appropriate installations, by means of the most appropriate methods and technologies, in order to ensure a high level of protection for the environment and public health'.

9.158 These matters have to be considered by planning authorities and 'substantial weight' should be attached to them: *R (on the application of Blewett) v Derbyshire County Council*[198]. The Waste (England and Wales) Regulations 2011 require local planning authorities to take into account the parts of arts 13 and 16 quoted above[199].

9.159 By Annex I of the Landfill Directive 1999/31/EC:

'1.1 The location of a landfill must take into consideration requirements relating to:

(a) the distances from the boundary of the site to residential and recreation areas, waterways, water bodies and other agricultural or urban sites;

(b) the existence of groundwater, coastal water or nature protection zones in the area;

(c) the geological and hydrogeological conditions in the area;

(d) the risk of flooding, subsidence, landslides or avalanches on the site;

(e) the protection of the nature or cultural patrimony in the area.

5 Nuisances and hazards

Measures shall be taken to minimise nuisances and hazards arising from the landfill through:

– emissions of odours and dust,

– wind-blown materials,

– noise and traffic,

– birds, vermin and insects,

– formation and aerosols,

– fires.

The landfill shall be equipped so that dirt originating from the site is not dispersed onto public roads and the surrounding land'.

---

[198] [2004] EWCA Civ 1508, [2005] JPL 620.
[199] Waste (England and Wales) Regulations 2011, SI 2011/988, reg 18. Regulation 19 requires planning authorities to carry out periodic inspections of waste disposal or recovery facilities.

9.160 *Material considerations and policy*

A planning authority must not grant planning permission for a landfill unless it has taken into consideration these requirements, although for para 5 'only in respect of nuisances and hazards arising from traffic beyond the site of the landfill'[200].

Welsh language

9.160 The Planning (Wales) Act 2015 will introduce into s 70(2) a duty, in Wales, to have regard to 'any considerations relating to the use of the Welsh language, so far as material to the application'[201].

STRUCTURAL MATERIAL CONSIDERATIONS

Alternatives

9.161 Planning applications are usually considered on their own merits. If a project is not harmful in policy or other terms, then it will not matter that something better could be done on that site or that the scheme would be better elsewhere. Simply causing some harm has not been seen in itself as being sufficient to require the consideration of alternatives.

9.162 The merits of an alternative proposal on an application are rarely relevant. In *R (on the application of Mount Cook) v Westminster City Council* Auld LJ held[202]:

'(1) in the context of planning control, a person may do what he wants with his land provided his use of it is acceptable in planning terms;

(2) there may be a number of alternative uses from which he could choose, each of which would be acceptable in planning terms;

(3) whether any proposed use is acceptable in planning terms depends on whether it would cause planning harm judged according to relevant planning policies where there are any;

(4) in the absence of conflict with planning policy and/or other planning harm, the relative advantages of alternative uses on the application site or of the same use on alternative sites are normally irrelevant in planning terms;

(5) where ... an application proposal does not conflict with policy, otherwise involves no planning harm and, as it happens, includes some enhancement, any alternative proposals would normally be irrelevant;

(6) even, in exceptional circumstances where alternative proposals might be relevant, inchoate or vague schemes and/or those that are unlikely or have no real possibility of coming about would not be relevant or, if they were, should be given little or no weight'.

---

[200] Waste (England and Wales) Regulations 2011, reg 20(1). Nuisances and hazards arising on site are controlled by environmental permitting. Further requirements apply to waste facilities from mineral extraction: Waste (England and Wales) Regulations 2011, reg 20(2) and Directive 2006/21/EC, arts 7(3)(b), 11(2)(a).

[201] Town and Country Planning Act 1990, s 70(2)(aa), prospectively inserted by Planning (Wales) Act 2015, s 31(2) from a date to be appointed. There should be no discrimination between individuals on linguistic grounds: Planning Policy Wales, para 4.13.3.

[202] [2003] EWCA Civ 1346, [2004] JPL 470 at para 30.

9.163 Alternatives may have to be considered either because:

(i) policy expressly requires them to be addressed; or

(ii) the planning harm from the scheme is so substantial that alternatives must be addressed.

9.164 The policy requirements may be expressed as a need to consider alternatives[203] or as a sequential approach where various land is preferred to other land. Whilst alternatives do not need to be addressed if the site is in the most preferable category, for lower ranked sites (such as retail uses proposed in out of town centre locations or land at risk of flooding) a sequential test in policy will require more preferable locations to be ruled out.

9.165 It is sometimes said that the need to consider alternatives arises only in *exceptional* circumstances, as suggested for example by Laws LJ in *R (J (a child) v North Warwickshire Borough Council*[204]. However those exceptions are quite frequent for example where[205]:

(i) there are clear planning objections to development upon a particular site, and it is submitted that the need for such a development outweighs such site-specific drawbacks;

(ii) land is identified elsewhere on which development could proceed without such adverse impacts.

9.166 Alternative sites may be relevant to whether inappropriate development should be approved in the Green Belt. In *Trusthouse Forte Hotels Ltd v Secretary of State for the Environment* Simon Brown J said[206]:

'(1) In a case where planning objections are sought to be overcome by reference to need, the greater those objections, the more material will be the possibility of meeting that need elsewhere.

(2) Although generally speaking it is desirable and preferable that a planning authority (including, of course, the Secretary of State on appeal) should identify and consider that possibility by reference to specifically identifiable alternative sites, it will not always be essential or indeed necessarily appropriate to do so.

(3) The clearer it is that the planning objections relate essentially to the development of the application site itself rather than to some intrinsically offensive aspect of the proposed development wherever it might be sited, the less likely it is to be essential to identify specific alternative sites.

---

[203] For example, mobile phone antennae under the former Planning Policy Guidance Note 8: *Phillips v First Secretary of State* [2003] EWHC 2415 (Admin), [2004] JPL 613.

[204] [2001] EWCA Civ 315, [2001] PLCR 31 at para 30 and see subsequent discussion and approval in *Laing Homes Ltd v Secretary of State for Transport, Local Government and the Regions* [2003] 1 P & CR 18 at 287–288 per Richards J. Identical reasoning was applied by Sullivan J in *R (Chelmsford Car and Commercial Limited) v Chelmsford Borough Council* [2005] EWHC 1705 (Admin), at paras 26–31.

[205] See *North Warwickshire* at paras 22–32 generally. Alternatives tend to arise if there is said to be a need for a harmful development. If a scheme is not harmful then there is no need to look for a better scheme or site. If it is harmful then in the absence of justification it would be refused.

[206] (1986) 53 P & CR 293 at 303.

9.167 *Material considerations and policy*

(4) Equally, the less specific and exacting are the requirements to be satisfied in order to meet the accepted need, the more likely is it that a planning authority could reasonably conclude that such need can be met elsewhere without reference to some identifiable preferable alternative site.

(5) Clearly, it is more difficult to make a sensible comparison in the absence of an identified alternative site and it is likely that a planning authority would be more hesitant in concluding that an accepted need could be met elsewhere if no specific alternative sites have been identified, *a fortiori* if they have been carefully searched for, identified and rejected.

(6) The extent to which it will be for the developer to establish the need for his proposed development on the application or appeal site rather than for an objector to establish that such need can and should be met elsewhere will vary. However, in cases such as this, when the green belt planning policy expressly provides that "the need for a motel on the site proposed, not merely in the area generally, has to be established in each case"[2] the burden lies squarely upon the developer. Thus in this type of case it will be the more likely that the planning authority could reasonably conclude that the need can be met elsewhere without reference to some identified more appropriate alternative site.

(7) As a matter of law it is accordingly open to a planning authority to conclude on the facts that an accepted need can and should be met elsewhere than upon the application or appeal site without reference to any specific alternative site or sites'.

9.167 In *R (on the application of Siraj) v Kirklees Metropolitan Borough Council* the Court of Appeal upheld a planning permission for an agricultural machinery workshop in the Green Belt where very special circumstances were the specialist nature of his operation, the operational requirements of customers, the difficulties of remaining in his present location and the lack of other suitable alternative sites[207].

9.168 Alternatives and precedent for inappropriate development in the Green Belt were considered in *R (on the application of Holder) v Gedling Borough Council*[208]. On a wind turbine application, members had been advised that on- and off-site alternatives, the precedent effect of approving the scheme, and the energy generation and efficiency of the proposed turbine were not material considerations. The High Court upheld the decision but this was overturned by the Court of Appeal. On precedent, Maurice Kay LJ said that it is significant that the features said to constitute 'very special circumstances' were essentially generic features (the benefits of renewable energy generation and income for a farm) which could be claimed in relation to comparable sites. Alternatives, in particular less intrusive forms of renewable energy provision, were also relevant.

Financial considerations

9.169 A potential financial benefit from a scheme for the local planning authority was generally regarded as irrelevant unless it came within the ambit of material planning obligations. From *Tesco Stores Ltd v Secretary of State for the Environment*[209] a planning obligation needed to relate to a planning application before it could be material and now as a matter of law must be necessary to be relevant, so is intended to provide for needs generated by the development. Financial

---

[207] [2010] EWCA Civ 1286, [2011] JPL 571, at paras 25–28.
[208] [2014] EWCA Civ 599, [2014] JPL 1087, in particular at paras 15, 17.
[209] [1995] 1 WLR 759.

considerations can only be taken into account in limited circumstances where they have land use consequences. That an existing or proposed use is not viable may be relevant if the consequence is that a site would be left unoccupied or run-down[210]. The use of 'enabling development' by which part of a development, which may itself be undesirable, is used to fund desirable works, such as the protection of the historic environment or the expansion of an important cultural institution, such as the Royal Opera House or a football club. Whilst considering enabling development, Kerr LJ said in *R v Westminster City Council, ex p Monahan*[211]:

> 'Financial constraints on the economic viability of a desirable planning development are unavoidable facts of life in an imperfect world. It would be unreal and contrary to common sense to insist that they must be excluded from the range of considerations which may properly be regarded as material in determining planning applications. Where they are shown to exist they may call for compromises or even sacrifices in what would otherwise be regarded as the optimum from the point of view of the public interest. Virtually all planning decisions involve some kind of balancing exercise. A commonplace illustration is the problem of having to decide whether or not to accept compromises or sacrifices in granting permission for developments which could, or would in practice, otherwise not be carried out for financial reasons. Another, no doubt rarer, illustration would be a similar balancing exercise concerning composite or related developments, ie related in the sense that they can and should properly be considered in combination, where the realisation of the main objective may depend on the financial implications or consequences of others. However, provided that the ultimate determination is based on planning grounds and not on some ulterior motive, and that it is not irrational, there would be no basis for holding it to be invalid in law solely on the ground that it has taken account of, and adjusted itself to, the financial realities of the overall situation'.

9.170 The need for the financial issues to be connected with the use and development of land was also spelled out in *Northumberland County Council v Secretary of State for the Environment*[212]. The relevance of compensation to a decision was addressed in *Alliance Against the Birmingham Northern Relief Road v Secretary of State for the Environment, Transport and the Regions*[213] where the issue was whether it was relevant to the decision of the Secretary of State on various highways orders and schemes that if he refused consent, the Highways Agency would have to pay compensation to disappointed concessionaire for the road under the New Roads and Street Works Act 1991, s 1(4). Latham J held that such liability to pay compensation was not relevant to the merits of the orders. In *Alnwick District Council v Secretary of State for the Environment, Transport and the Regions*[214] the High Court considered it to be irrelevant that a local planning authority would have to pay compensation if the Secretary of State modified a retail planning permission. The Supreme Court rejected the *Alnwick* approach for revocation and modification of planning permission under the Town and Country Planning Act 1990, s 97, in *R (on the application of Health and Safety Executive) v Wolverhampton City Council*[215]. They agreed with the Court of Appeal that the compensation implications of removing a valuable planning permission were relevant in deciding whether that should be done. This reflected the general principle that the cost of exercising a discretionary power can be taken into account. Lord Carnwarth JSC said that material considerations meant:

---

[210] For example, *Sosmo Trust Ltd v Secretary of State for the Environment* [1983] JPL 806.
[211] [1990] 1 QB 97 at 111.
[212] (1989) 59 P & CR 468.
[213] [1999] JPL 426.
[214] [2000] JPL 474.
[215] [2012] UKSC 34, [2012] 1 WLR 2264.

9.171 *Material considerations and policy*

'49 ... meaning considerations material (or relevant) to the exercise of the particular power, in its statutory context and for the purposes for which it was granted.

50 So read, the Court of Appeal's interpretation creates no inconsistency between section 70 and section 97 . The meaning is the same, but the statutory context is different. Under section 70 the planning authority has a duty to act, and it has a limited choice. It must either grant or refuse permission. Its decision must be governed by considerations material to that limited choice. Further, the decision normally has no direct cost consequences for the authority (unless exceptionally it has a direct financial interest in the development, when other constraints come into play)'.

9.171 In *R (on the application of Sainsbury's Supermarkets Ltd) v Wolverhampton City Council*[216] the Council sought to compulsorily purchase Sainsbury's land to enable a Tesco food store scheme to proceed, relying on Tesco promising to regenerate a site 850 metres away which contained listed buildings. The Supreme Court considered that the same tests applied to the relevance of the regeneration proposal for the decision to compulsorily purchase as to a planning application on the Sainsbury's site, albeit that a strict approach to the application of those principles should be taken given serious invasion of property rights involved in compulsory acquisition. Lord Collins of Mapesbury JSC said, by reference to the planning context[217]:

'First, the question of what is a material (or relevant) consideration is a question of law, but the weight to be given to it is a matter for the decision-maker. Second, financial viability may be material if it relates to the development. Third, financial dependency of part of a composite development on another part may be a relevant consideration, in the sense that the fact that the proposed development will finance other relevant planning benefits may be material. Fourth, off-site benefits which are related to or are connected with the development will be material. ... They do not ... raise questions of fact and degree. There must be a real connection between the benefits and the development'.

Local finance considerations

9.172 That allowing development might generate revenue for the local authority in terms of Council tax or business rates was traditionally seen as irrelevant (as well as financially self-defeating, as the extra costs of the new occupants were liable to exceed any extra tax). The Localism Act 2011, however, introduced explicit finance considerations into the determination of planning applications in England. It added to the s 70(2) requirement to have regard to particular matters 'any local finance considerations, so far as material to the application'[218].

9.173 By s 70(4), local finance considerations means:

'(a) a grant or other financial assistance that has been, or will or could be, provided to a relevant authority by a Minister of the Crown, or

(b) sums that a relevant authority has received, or will or could receive, in payment of Community Infrastructure Levy'.

---

[216] [2010] UKSC 20, [2011] 1 AC 437.
[217] At para 70.
[218] Town and Country Planning Act 1990, s 70(2)(b). The Housing and Planning Bill 2015 proposes to introduce a duty to refer in such reports to any financial benefits which are local finance considerations: Proposed Town and Country Planning Act 1990, s 75ZA, which would be inserted by the Housing and Planning Bill 2015, cl 115 (as published following consideration by the Public Bill Committee in the House of Commons).

Structural material considerations **9.177**

9.174 Sub-paragraph (a) concerns grants which will be received because the proposed development is allowed or takes place. At the time of the passing of the Localism Act the New Homes Bonus was being introduced as a grant from central government to local authorities where new housing was provided. The amendment proved contentious as it was encouraging the grant of planning permission because funding would go to the authority for its own purposes. It is not apparent how far this has encouraged local planning authorities to grant planning permission.

9.175 Sub-paragraph (b) is more straightforward. The intention of the Community Infrastructure Levy (CIL) is to charge development to contribute to a schedule of infrastructure works within the general area, even if the need for those works might not be directly linked to all of the developments subject to the charge. CIL does though replace many of the contributions which would have been sought under planning obligations. It was sensible therefore that the CIL contribution would be relevant in a similar manner as a planning obligation would previously have been relevant. Potentially relevant CIL contributions are not simply those from the particular development but other contributions which will be used to encourage the development of the area and so address potential issues with the individual scheme.

Interference with other legal rights

9.176 That a legal right may be infringed by a proposed development does not make the interference with that right a material consideration in the determination of a planning application. In *Brewer v Secretary of State for the Environment*[219] the High Court held that the presence or absence of private rights of light was not a material planning consideration. Planning was concerned with land use from the view point of the public interest and as a generality it was not concerned with private rights as between landowners. David Widdicombe QC, sitting as a deputy judge in that case, gave the examples of private rights of way across land or a restrictive covenant prohibiting the use applied for. As a planning permission did not override private rights, the existence of those rights was not relevant to the decision to grant permission. This principle was followed by Mr Justice Sullivan in *R v Solihull Borough Council, ex p Berkswell Parish Council*[220] in holding that the application of an Enclosure Act to a hedgerow was not material to a planning application.

9.177 As with most general principles, there are caveats and exceptions:

(i) potential harm to a private right might also be harm which is relevant in the public interest. The most obvious example is the effect of a new building on light to a room in an existing building. Planning permission might be refused because of harm to amenity caused by the reduction in light and the reduction might also be an actionable interference with rights to light. However the public interest in protecting amenity applies irrespective of the existence of private rights to light. It is worth having in mind that the methods of measuring harm to light levels in planning and rights to light are different[221]. Similarly in the Enclosure Act example, any historic landscape value of the hedgerow might bear on the planning merits of it being removed;

---

[219] [1988] JPL 480.
[220] (1998) 77 P & CR 312.
[221] Planning tends to use BRE daylight and sunlight guidance, whilst rights to light assessment is usually informed by the mapping of light levels in a Waldram analysis.

9.178 *Material considerations and policy*

(ii) the existence of a private law remedy could be a reason to consider that harm from a development will be unlikely to occur and so planning permission could be granted. In *Fitzpatrick Developments Ltd v Minister of Housing and Local Government*[222] the proposal was to build seven houses near a saw-mill. Widgery J held that the Minister on appeal was required to have regard to all the relevant circumstances and 'one could not shut one's eyes to the fact that certain rights existed at common law and by statute'. It was therefore relevant that the law of nuisance could be used to require the damage to amenities from the saw-mill to be reduced and was a material consideration in favour of granting permission. However this must be viewed with caution. Most planners would reasonably take the view that harm should be avoided by the details of the scheme, or its refusal, rather than to leave the issue to uncertain and expensive private litigation after a problem had arisen, as well as, potentially, seeking to protect the industrial use from a noise sensitive development which might compromise its operations. The existence of nuisance and statutory nuisance remedies would be relevant to the planning decision if the harm was very unlikely to occur without unreasonable conduct or defects in operations which could be readily remedied by enforcement;

(iii) the existence of third party landownership or rights, such as an easement over the development site, might give rise to a risk that the development will be carried out in part and in a harmful manner. An example would be a proposal to include car parking on land within the application site but outside the applicant's control. That would be relevant to the imposition of a condition which requires the car parking to be brought forward at an early stage to avoid the risk of the development being completed except for the car parking.

Precedent

9.178 As a general proposition, development (even if desirable in its own right) which may set a precedent for further development of that type nearby is capable of being a material consideration[223]. Precedent does not mean a binding precedent but that the decision will be relied upon in similar cases. It can be asked, given the desirability of consistency in decision-making, would officers and committee members be inclined to follow this decision in other cases? In *Poundstretcher Ltd v Secretary of State for the Environment* David Widdicombe QC said[224]:

> 'I accept Mr Hobson's proposition that where precedent is relied on, mere fear or generalised concern is not enough. There must be evidence in one form or another for the reliance on precedent. In some cases the facts may speak for themselves. For instance, in the common case of the rear extension of one of a row or terrace of dwellings, it may be obvious that other owners in the row are likely to want extensions if one is permitted. Another clear example is sporadic development in the countryside'.

9.179 *Poundstretcher* was considered in *Rumsey v Secretary of State for the Environment, Transport and the Regions* where permission was refused for extension of a bungalow in an AONB because it would make it more difficult to resist similar extensions, leading to detriment to the character and landscape value of the area. Duncan Ouseley QC held that the inspector's approach was lawful[225]:

---

[222] (1965) 194 EG 911.
[223] *Collis Radio Ltd v Secretary of State for the Environment* (1975) 29 P & CR 390.
[224] 1988] 3 PLR 69 at 74F.
[225] (2001) 81 P & CR 32 at para 16.

'I do not consider that that approach is baseless: the Council provided some written material, there was further discussion at the hearing, and above all the inspector had his planning experience, his site visit and view of the area. The reasoning of the Inspector in the decision letter is clear and adequate. *Poundstretcher* cannot be seen as providing some precise legal test as to the nature of the material which an Inspector must have before him when reaching a judgment on a precedent issue. The recognition of the inadequacy of mere fear or generalised concern is no more than saying that an Inspector must have some material on which to base his view, and the nature of what is required will vary from case to case. But just using *Poundstretcher* as a guide, the Inspector here appears to have had at least as much material as in that case went sufficiently beyond a mere fear or generalised concern. Moreover, in *Poundstretcher*, it was rightly recognised that the planning judgment as to harm by precedent can be made in circumstances where the facts speak for themselves. The Inspector here identified his concern as being with the relatively small properties in the area; his conclusions as to precedent and cumulative effect do not require greater exposition than he provided as to the material upon which they were based. The circumstances which he has identified can be treated as speaking for themselves'.

9.180 Rejecting a submission that if no harm was found in the first case, that no harm could follow from a case on all fours with it, the judge went on to say[226]:

'I consider that it is open to a planning decision-maker to reach a contrary conclusion: one development is harmless, but a second or more, each individually harmless, would lead to a harmful accumulation; thus the first might be refused, because decisions could not be taken in isolation, when in reality one decision led to another'.

Similarly it is material whether very special circumstances identified to justify development in the Green Belt will establish a precedent for future decisions[227]. This concern would be particularly well-founded where the very special circumstances relied upon may be shared by other persons[228].

Prematurity and the weight to be attached to emerging policy

9.181 Draft policy can be a material consideration although the weight to be attached to it will have to reflect the possibility that the draft will not be adopted in its current, or possibly any, form. For example, it was lawful for the Secretary of State to have regard to Ministers' intention to enact primary legislation to abolish regional strategies when local authorities were deciding upon the weight to be attached to a regional strategy when determining a planning application[229].

9.182 Advice on the weight to be given to emerging local policy is in the National Planning Policy Framework at para 216:

'From the day of publication, decision-takers may also give weight[230] to relevant policies in emerging plans according to:

---

[226] At para 17.
[227] *Doncaster Metropolitan Borough Council v Secretary of State for the Environment, Transport and the Regions* [2002] EWHC 808 (Admin), [2002] JPL 1509 at paras 32, 58–62, 68 per Sullivan J and *R (Holder) v Gedling Borough Council* [2014] EWCA Civ 599, [2014] JPL 1087 at para 17 per Maurice Kay LJ.
[228] *Doncaster* at para 62.
[229] *R (on the application of Cala Homes (South) Ltd) v Secretary of State for Communities and Local Government* [2011] EWCA Civ 639, [2011] JPL 1458 at para 25 per Sullivan LJ.
[230] Referenced as footnote 40: Unless other material considerations indicate otherwise.

9.183 *Material considerations and policy*

- the stage of preparation of the emerging plan (the more advanced the preparation, the greater the weight that may be given);
- the extent to which there are unresolved objections to relevant policies (the less significant the unresolved objections, the greater the weight that may be given); and
- the degree of consistency of the relevant policies in the emerging plan to the policies in this Framework (the closer the policies in the emerging plan to the policies in the Framework, the greater the weight that may be given)'.

9.183 Prematurity is a concept in planning policy concerning whether approval of a planning application would prejudice emerging policy. Prematurity itself is dealt with solely in the Planning Practice Guidance:

'Annex 1 of the National Planning Policy Framework explains how weight may be given to policies in emerging plans. However in the context of the Framework and in particular the presumption in favour of sustainable development – arguments that an application is premature are unlikely to justify a refusal of planning permission other than where it is clear that the adverse impacts of granting permission would significantly and demonstrably outweigh the benefits, taking the policies in the Framework and any other material considerations into account. Such circumstances are likely, but not exclusively, to be limited to situations where both:

a) the development proposed is so substantial, or its cumulative effect would be so significant, that to grant permission would undermine the plan-making process by predetermining decisions about the scale, location or phasing of new development that are central to an emerging Local Plan or Neighbourhood Planning; and

b) the emerging plan is at an advanced stage but is not yet formally part of the development plan for the area.

Refusal of planning permission on grounds of prematurity will seldom be justified where a draft Local Plan has yet to be submitted for examination, or in the case of a Neighbourhood Plan, before the end of the local planning authority publicity period. Where planning permission is refused on grounds of prematurity, the local planning authority will need to indicate clearly how the grant of permission for the development concerned would prejudice the outcome of the plan-making process'.

9.184 The starting point is the advice that prematurity is unlikely to justify the refusal of an application unless it is clear that the scheme is unacceptable in its own right. This is based on the test for sustainable development in the absence of an up-to-date development plan in para 14 of the NPPF. The guidance then says that refusal on prematurity grounds is unlikely to be justified unless granting permission would undermine the plan making process and the emerging plan is at an advanced stage. The advice on the merits of the application is new to the PPG, previous guidance on prematurity having focused on potential prejudice.

9.185 Where a planning application is in accordance with an emerging plan and constitutes sustainable development under the NPPF, it is still material that approving the scheme would pre-empt the development plan examination. However, that does not prohibit the local planning authority from granting permission. Mr Justice Ouseley observed in *R (on the application of Bedford) v London Borough of Islington*[231]:

---

[231] [2002] EWHC 2044 (Admin), [2003] Env LR 22 at paras 35–39.

Structural material considerations **9.188**

'35 Second, there is no reason in law why a Local Planning Authority cannot determine applications while a [Unitary Development Plan] is progressing. The fact that it might do so in a way which pre-empted the independent scrutiny which a UDP Inspector's views might provide is a relevant factor for the Local Planning Authority to consider in relation to the exercise of its s 70 powers. But it is perfectly clear on the authorities that even where an Inquiry Inspector is seized of the matter as a proposal, the Local Planning Authority can nonetheless grant permission and so pre-empt any recommendation either way by the Local Plan Inspector. The mere fact that a UDP review is going through its processes does not mean that a major proposal, which, subject to timing, could form part of the UDP review, must be included in the plan or, failing that, that an inquiry must under some guise (statutory or non-statutory) be held into the proposal.

38 If it be the case that a Local Planning Authority can grant permission for a proposal when the Local Plan Inspector is seized of an objection or proposal in the plan related to it, even more so can the Local Planning Authority do it where the matter is not actually before the UDP Inspector.

39 Third, in order for a complaint about the way in which a policy or proposal has been dealt with in the plan-making process, to constitute a basis upon which the grant of planning permission for it can be challenged, it is the discretion in relation to that latter decision-making process which has to be attacked; it would have to be shown that there was a failure to consider the possible advantages of the proposal first going through the UDP process, or that the only rational decision would have been a refusal of planning permission on the grounds of prematurity. There is no statutory obligation to reach that conclusion; the only issue is whether that material factor was considered. But no such basis has been shown for saying that the Local Planning Authority's exercise of its s.70 functions was unlawful. It was well aware of the position; it considered the relationship to the UDP; it reached a reasonable view on it. It was a view which the UDP Inspector supported. This was made clear to the councillors and they accepted it'.

9.186 In *Larkfleet Ltd v Secretary of State for Communities and Local Government and South Kesteven District Council*[232] Kenneth Parker J observed 'Prematurity … is not a bar or practically insuperable hurdle to the grant of planning permission'. Frances Patterson QC said in *Truro City Council v Cornwall City Council*[233]:

'The essence of a successful claim of prematurity is that the development proposed predetermines and pre-empts a decision which ought to be taken in the Development Plan process by reason of its scale, location and/or nature or that there is real risk that it might do so'.

9.187 Those cases were all based on previous guidance which emphasised prejudice to the development plan if the permission was granted. The *Planning Practice Guidance* has moved the emphasis onto whether the planning application accords with the NPPF and so seeks to avoid delaying desirable development because of an emerging plan. The observations in *Truro City Council* do not fully reflect the present guidance. A desirable development may still be approved even if it does pre-determine an emerging development plan.

9.188 A local planning authority should have regard to the fact that determining an application may pre-empt the inspector's views and to that extent frustrate those who wished to oppose the scheme in the examination process. However there is no right to a development plan examination (or equivalent process) before even a very major scheme can be approved.

---

[232] [2012] EWHC 3592.
[233] [2013] EWHC 2525 (Admin) at para 64.

9.189 *Material considerations and policy*

9.189 An intention to change or revoke a planning policy could be a material consideration, although the justification for attaching much weight to this would need careful consideration. In *R (on the application of Cala Homes (South) Ltd) v Secretary of State for Communities and Local Government*[234] Sullivan LJ held that weight could be given to the government's intention to bring forward legislation to revoke Regional Strategies, but given the uncertainties in the process, including the need for strategic environmental assessment of each revocation, very clear and cogent reasons should be given for attaching significant weight. Where revocation faces fewer obstacles then it may be easier to attach weight to the intention.

PLANNING USES AND PLANNING DECISIONS

9.190 What is there, what else could be there and what it has previously been said could be there might all be material to the determination of a particular application. A planning decision is taken within a context of rights, powers and history and may be affected by these. This section discusses the general relationships between these. Particular topics arising from what is on site, such as nature conservation or the historic environment, are discussed above under substantive material considerations.

The fallback position

9.191 The notion of the 'fallback position' in planning is not set out in legislation and is ultimately a pragmatic response. It is an example of planning decisions reflecting their circumstances. The concept, though, has become over-lawyered and is being seen as talismanic in some cases.

9.192 The fallback position is what could happen on the land if the planning application was not approved. That might be the continuation of the existing use, or development carried out under an existing planning permission or under permitted development rights. A fallback position may be taken into account by the local planning authority even if the prospect of it occurring is 'very slight indeed': see *Samuel Smith Old Brewery (Tadcaster) v Secretary of State for Communities and Local Government*[235]. Whilst a theoretical possibility – which will not happen – cannot be material as a fall back, the weight to be attached to a fallback position is a matter for the decision-maker. A possibility that a further planning application might be made for a different scheme is not strictly a fallback, but might be viewed in a similar light. However the possibility that unlawful development will take place or continue is not a fallback: the working assumption is that planning control will be enforced.

Previous planning decisions

9.193 A previous planning decision of the local planning authority, a Minister, an inspector or even (conceivably) another planning authority are all capable of being

---

[234] [2011] EWCA Civ 639, [2011] JPL 1458 at para 35.
[235] [2009] EWCA Civ 333, [2009] JPL 1326 at para 21 per Sullivan LJ, explaining *Brentwood Borough Council v Secretary of State for the Environment* (1996) 72 P & CR 61 and contrast the High Court in *PF Ahern (London) Ltd v Secretary of State for the Environment* [1996] Env LR 189 at 196. Followed in *Gambone v Secretary of State for Communities and Local Government* [2014] EWHC 952 (Admin) at para 26 per Ian Dove QC and *R (on the application of Kverndal) v London Borough of Hounslow* [2015] EWHC 3084 (Admin) at para 49 per Supperstone J.

Planning uses and planning decisions **9.196**

material considerations in the determination of a planning application. Whether it is depends upon whether it could rationally influence the decision.

9.194 In *North Wiltshire District Council v Secretary of State for the Environment* Mann LJ said[236]:

> 'It was not disputed in argument that a previous appeal decision is capable of being a material consideration. The proposition is in my judgment indisputable. One important reason why previous decisions are capable of being material is that like cases should be decided in a like manner so that there is consistency in the appellate process. Consistency is self-evidently important to both developers and development control authorities. But it is also important for the purpose of securing public confidence in the operation of the development control system. I do not suggest and it would be wrong to do so, that like cases *must* be decided alike. An inspector must always exercise his own judgment. He is therefore free upon consideration to disagree with the judgment of another but before doing so he ought to have regard to the importance of consistency and to give his reasons for departure from the previous decision.
>
> To state that like cases should be decided alike presupposes that the earlier case is alike and is not distinguishable in some relevant respect. If it is distinguishable then it usually will lack materiality by reference to consistency although it may be material in some other way. Where it is indistinguishable then ordinarily it must be a material consideration. A practical test for the inspector is to ask himself whether, if I decide this case in a particular way am I necessarily agreeing or disagreeing with some critical aspect of the decision in the previous case? The areas for possible agreement or disagreement cannot be defined but they would include interpretation of policies, aesthetic judgments and assessment of need. Where there is disagreement then the inspector must weigh the previous decision and give his reasons for departure from it. These can on occasion be short, for example in the case of disagreement on aesthetics. On other occasions they may have to be elaborate'.

9.195 'Indistinguishable' is putting the test a bit high and the Court of Appeal in *R v Secretary of State for the Environment, ex p Baber*[237] suggested that sufficiently closely related would be enough to make it material. In some cases the relevance will be the way in which a particular issue has been addressed, although the two cases may be different in other respects. This reflects the question of precedent, discussed above.

9.196 The approach has been applied to the relevance of decisions by local planning authorities[238]. Allied to the relevance of other decisions is the need for consistency in the making of planning decisions. As Lindblom J said in *Pertemps* it 'is not strictly a principle of law. It is a principle of good practice in development control which the court has recognized'[239].

Consistency is a guard against capricious, biased, ill-judged and random decision-making, but it is not an obligation. It is not better to be consistent than correct.

---

[236] (1993) 65 P & CR 137 at 145. The case law is discussed in *St Albans District Council Secretary of State for Communities and Local Government* [2015] EWHC 655 (Admin) at paras 66–126 per Holgate J.
[237] [1996] JPL 1034 at 1040 per Glidewell LJ.
[238] For example, in determining whether the needs of a business to expand were very special circumstances in the Green Belt: *Pertemps Investments Ltd v Secretary of State for Communities and Local Government* [2015] EWHC 2308 (Admin).
[239] *Pertemps* at para 52.

9.197 *Material considerations and policy*

9.197 A distinction applies in practice between decisions on that site and decisions on other sites which might be said to be relevant because they concern similar issues in the locality or because they raise a point of principle.

9.198 A planning authority or inspector will not be expected to search for other decisions which are relevant. The local planning authority can be expected to consider the planning history of the application site and it is good practice to list the previous decisions on the site unless they are irrelevant to the current application. A planning inspector ought to be aware of concurrent appeals on the site, particularly to avoid the risk of inconsistent decisions. If the main parties to an appeal fail to inform the inspector of a relevant previous decision on the appeal site then this may justify quashing[240]. The mention of a recent or ongoing appeal in the other proceedings may be sufficient[241]. There is, though, no expectation that the Minister will be aware of appeal decisions on other sites: it is for the parties to raise those in the appeal[242].

9.199 The extent to which reasoning in an inspector or Ministerial decision should distinguish the other decision will vary. On some occasions, the answer given to the current case would be sufficient to explain it. Other times, the previous decision does need to be referred to and some explanation given as to why it is departed from. Where the inconsistency is stark and fundamental, an explanation is more likely to be required[243].

The unlawfulness of a previous decision

9.200 In general, a decision will stand unless and until it is quashed by the court. Once quashed, a decision will be considered never to have had any effect[244]. However a person subject to a decision may challenge its lawfulness as a defence to proceedings unless statute bars this, so a landowner is entitled to resist an unlawfully imposed condition. The unlawfulness of a condition may be relevant to a future planning decision, as in *Earthline Ltd v Secretary of State for the Environment, Transport and the Regions* where the inspector should have recognised that a previous minerals review had unlawfully reduced the period of extraction below the 2042 date imposed by statute[245].

The protection of existing or proposed uses and users of land

9.201 The loss of an existing or authorised use of land may be material to the determination of the planning application, although the displacement of a particular existing user will rarely be material.

---

[240] *Hounslow v Secretary of State for Communities and Local Government* [2009] EWHC 1055 (Admin) at para 17 per Collins J.
[241] See *Hounslow* at paras 19–21; *Dear v Secretary of State for Communities and Local Government* [2015] EWHC 29 (Admin) at para 32.
[242] *Grantchester Retail Parks plc v Secretary of State for Transport, Local Government and the Regions* [2003] EWHC 92 (Admin) at para 26 per Jackson J. The suggestion to the contrary in *Dear* at para 32 goes too far and appears to have been raised without citation of *Grantchester*.
[243] See *JJ Gallagher Ltd v Secretary of State for Transport, Local Government and the Regions* [2002] EWHC 1812 (Admin), [2002] 4 PLR 32 at para 58 per George Bartlett QC, followed by *Fox Strategic Land and Property Ltd v Secretary of State for Communities and Local Government* [2012] EWCA Civ 1198, [2013] 1 P & CR 6 at paras 14, 30, 34 per Pill LJ.
[244] See *Mossell (Jamaica) Ltd (t/a Digicel) v Office of Utilities Regulations* [2010] UKPC 1 at para 44.
[245] See *Earthline Ltd v Secretary of State for the Environment, Transport and the Regions* [2002] EWCA Civ 1599, [2003] 1 P & CR 24.

9.202 For example, in *Westminster City Council v British Waterways Board* the Council leased land at the Paddington Basin of the Grand Union Canal which they used as a street cleansing depot. BWB resisted the grant of a new lease on the basis that they intended to occupy the premises for their own business, as part of a proposed marina use[246]. The Council, who also happened to be the local planning authority, contended that planning permission for the change of use would be refused because it would involve the loss of the street cleansing depot.

9.203 The House of Lords accepted that the desirability of preserving an existing use of land may by itself afford a valid planning reason for refusing permission for a change of use[247]. In doing so they endorsed *Clyde & Co v Secretary of State for the Environment*[248], which held that a legitimate reason for refusing planning permission to change the use of a building to office use was that the change would prevent the building from being used for residential purposes in accordance with an extant, but unimplemented, planning permission.

9.204 There is no requirement as a matter of law to balance competing needs for uses on the site; it has been held that the desirability of preserving an existing use of land is a material consideration to be taken into account, provided there is a reasonable probability that such use will be preserved if permission for the new use is refused[249].

Existing unlawful development

9.205 Generally, a developer should not gain an advantage from having carried out development unlawfully as otherwise that would encourage development without planning permission. The NPPF makes that point explicitly in refusing to take into account the deteriorated state of heritage assets which have been deliberately neglected or damaged.[250] An application for retrospective planning permission ought usually, therefore, to be considered in the same way as an application for prospective development. However the impacts of development which has taken place can be judged from what has happened. There might also be circumstances where what has been erected is not precisely what would have been permitted, but is not so objectionable that the authority would consider it disproportionate to require it to be removed. In those relatively limited circumstances a local planning authority could consider existence of the unlawful development to be a factor weighing in favour of granting retrospective planning permission. Planning policy was changed in England so that intentional unauthorised development would be a material consideration for planning applications and appeals made from 31 August 2015[251]. This was, of course, potentially relevant in any event, but the policy would tend to apply only if someone was seeking to rely on the unauthorised development having taken place to justify permission, in which case they should not benefit if this was intentional.

---

[246] The Council had a right to a new lease under the Landlord and Tenant Act 1954, Part II unless that could be resisted on the basis of one of the exceptions, here s 30(1)(g).
[247] Lord Bridge at 682.
[248] [1977] 1 WLR 926.
[249] *London Residuary Body v Lambeth London Borough Council* [1990] 1 WLR 744 at 751–752 per Lord Keith. Reasonable probability should be understood as sufficient prospect to be material, the degree of probability more properly being seen as a matter for the planning authority when assessing the weight to be given to it.
[250] NPPF, para 130.
[251] Chief Planner's letter, 31 August 2015; Written Ministerial Statement, 17 December 2015.

9.206 *Material considerations and policy*

The effect of a planning application on an existing planning permission

9.206 The effect of a planning application on development permitted by an existing permission is material. The relationship between a planning application and an existing permission was considered by Ouseley J in *R (on the application of Bibb) v Bristol City Council*[252]:

> '40. In my judgment, where a planning permission cannot be implemented, whether because of a financial impediment which a particular operator may face, or because a condition proves overly restrictive for an operator, or some other unhelpful circumstance has arisen which a further planning permission may overcome, the benefits of implementing the first planning permission may be relevant to the grant of the second. If the benefits of implementing the first planning permission are relevant to the grant of the second, then so too must be its impacts. If relevant, they could lead to the refusal of the further permission. Circumstances or policies might have changed so that implementation or further implementation of the first permission was no longer desirable, and the impacts of implementation enabled by any necessary further planning permission would be relevant to its grant. The grant of planning permission A does not mean that planning permission B should be granted simply because it is necessary to enable planning permission A to be implemented, or to be operated in a particular way which the developer would wish. Planning permission B could therefore lawfully be refused on the grounds that it would enable an extant planning permission A to be reactivated undesirably, eg if a new road were necessary to enable an old quarry to be reopened. Similarly, if a planning permission was necessary to enable a permitted use, granted without constraints, to be fully exploited in a way which was undesirable, it could be refused eg if permission for a caravan site covered a large field, but half could not be used in practice without a further facilities block, that block could be refused permission because it would enable the permitted but undesirable intensification of the use to occur.
>
> 41. There is therefore no legal bar to considering the effect which granting planning permission B would have in enabling planning permission A to be implemented or to be operated in a particular way, albeit according to its terms. That effect is not irrelevant merely because planning permission A has been granted, whether or not the particular impact now alleged to be of importance was taken into account when it was granted.
>
> 42. However, before this effect can be material, the local planning authority has to accept the factual premise that without the grant of planning permission B, planning permission A would not be implemented, or would only be operated in a materially different way from that proposed with permission B. But it cannot stop there. As Mr Wills recognised, it is the impact which would occur without the grant of planning permission B, the fallback position, which is the real baseline against which the significance of the grant of planning permission B to the implementation of planning permission A has to be judged. It is the difference between the two which is material. He defined the relevant baseline as the worse case impact likely to ensue without the grant of further planning permissions. There might be no difference between the impacts with and without the further permission'.

The effect of other regulatory regimes on a planning decision

9.207 The existence and operation of other controls can be taken into account in making a planning decision but that does not render the impacts addressed by those controls immaterial: *Gateshead Metropolitan Borough Council v Secretary of State*

---
[252] [2011] EWHC 3057 (Admin), [2012] JPL 565.

for the Environment[253]. The planning authority are not obliged to leave matters to other controls[254].

9.208 The existence of other potential remedies (such as a right to compensation under the Party Wall etc Act 1996) does not render the harm immaterial to the planning decision. For example, dust and noise at issue in *Hopkins Developments Ltd v First Secretary of State* or odours in *Harrison v Secretary of State for Communities and Local Government*[255] were not immaterial because action could be taken against them by the affected neighbours (in private or statutory nuisance) or regulators (under environmental permits). That neighbours can recover damages for nuisance does not render the possibility that a development will cause a nuisance irrelevant to the determination of a planning application for that development. On the contrary, such a proposal is likely to be refused planning permission because of the risk of that impact.

Housing technical standards

9.209 One area of overlap has been between planning requirements on housing and Building Regulations made under the Building Act 1984. The current emphasis is on the use of those Building Regulations to control the detail of development of housing along with national technical standards in planning policy[256]. Building Regulations have historically been mandatory for new development. Planning conditions may trigger optional requirements in the Building Regulations[257]. To do so, the planning permission must specify that option requirement by reference to the Building Regulations and make it a condition that the requirement must be complied with[258]. These include accessible and wheelchair use dwellings[259]. National technical standards are set for water efficiency, access and internal space in new dwellings. From 2016 it is envisaged that energy performance standards for dwellings will be those in Building Regulations, rather than the higher standards which development plan policies could allow[260].

The risks on appeal

9.210 The local planning authority are entitled to take into account the difficulties which they may face in an appeal[261]. In *R v Royal Borough of Kensington and Chelsea, ex p Stoop*[262] Otton J held that officers had been entitled to advise the committee 'The chances of the success on appeal were remote and there was a distinct possibility of a substantial amount of costs being awarded against the council'.

---

[253] [1995] Env LR 37 at 43.
[254] For example, *Hopkins Developments Ltd v First Secretary of State* [2006] EWHC 2823 (Admin), [2007] Env LR 14 and *Harrison v Secretary of State for Communities and Local Government* [2009] EWHC 3382 (Admin), [2010] Env LR 17.
[255] [2009] EWHC 3382 (Admin), [2010] Env LR 17.
[256] See the Written Ministerial Statement, 25 March 2015.
[257] See the Building Act 1984, s 2B inserted by Deregulation Act 2015, s 42.
[258] Building Regulations 2010, SI 2010/2214, reg 4(1B).
[259] Building Regulations 2010, Sch 1, Part M.
[260] The specific authorisation for higher standards in development plans (from the Planning and Energy Act 2008, s 1(1)(c)) will be removed in England by proposed Planning and Energy Act 2008, s 1(1A), to be inserted by the Deregulation Act 2015, s 43.
[261] *R v Aylesbury Vale District Council, ex p Chaplin* (1998) 76 P & CR 207 at 212 per Pill LJ.
[262] [1992] 1 PLR 58.

Chapter 10

London

10.1 The planning of London is vexed, as might be expected. Not only is there tension between the power of London (which here means Greater London) against national government but also between London government and the borough councils. Both the Greater London Authority and the boroughs see themselves as more powerful and important than the county and district councils who enjoy two-tier relationships in many other parts of the country.

10.2 Prior to the abolition of the Greater London Council in 1986 there was a Greater London Development Plan. This was replaced by strategic (or regional, depending on taste) planning guidance produced by Ministers. The re-introduction of an elected London government in 2000, in the form of the Greater London Authority, saw the creation of new planning powers. Uniquely for local government, those planning powers reside in one person, the Mayor of London. The Greater London Assembly has no powers over planning, nor are the powers farmed out to a separate body with mayoral, assembly and local representation. Planning is one area where the Mayor has power as distinct from just influence[1].

10.3 The Mayor's planning powers are two-fold:

(i) to adopt, review and revise the London Plan (known formally in legislation as the Spatial Development Strategy), which is part of the development plan[2] for all of the Council areas in Greater London. He also informally produces supplementary planning guidance and local 'opportunity area planning frameworks';

(ii) to be able to take over and determine, alternatively to direct the refusal of, certain planning applications of potential strategic importance.

10.4 The Greater London Authority and the position of the Mayor of London were established by the Greater London Authority Act 1999. The 1999 Act contains the London Plan provisions and made amendments to the Town and Country Planning Act 1990 to enable the Mayor to direct the refusal of planning applications. Further amendments to these development management powers were made by the Greater London Authority Act 2007, which enabled the Mayor to become the local planning authority for particular applications and sought to address concerns about how the Mayor's planning powers were exercised. Consequently the primary legislation is more detailed for the newer 'take over' power than the directed refusal provisions.

---

[1] The Mayor's powers are exercised personally, with some delegation to the deputy mayor responsible for planning and officers. Planning codes of conduct have been adopted in addition to the code governing the Mayor, deputy mayors and officers generally.

[2] Planning and Compulsory Purchase Act 2004, s 38.

The Mayor of London's powers over applications **10.8**

The detail and mechanics of the development management powers are contained in the Town and Country Planning (Mayor of London) Order 2008[3].

These powers do not affect the right of appeal to the Secretary of State nor the ability of Ministers to call in planning applications.

THE MAYOR OF LONDON'S POWERS OVER APPLICATIONS

10.5 Due to the history that the Mayor was given a power to direct local planning authorities to refuse applications in 2000 before being empowered to take over applications (in 2008), the powers are set out separately.

10.6 For directed refusals, a development order may enable the Mayor of London to direct the local planning authority for a London borough to refuse a planning application, may prohibit the authority from acting on the direction and may make related modifications to appeal provisions[4]. The power to direct refusal was introduced for planning applications of potential strategic importance in Greater London made on or after 3 July 2000[5]. Potential strategic importance has been defined in the relevant orders.

10.7 The mayoral power to take over applications is contained in the Town and Country Planning Act 1990, ss 2A–2F[6]. It applies to *certain* categories of applications of potential strategic importance received on or after 6 April 2008. Some post-April 2008 applications of potential strategic importance may, therefore, be the subject of a directed refusal but may not be taken over by the Mayor. Powers to direct refusal or to take over applications apply to planning applications including s 73 applications (for permission subject to different conditions from those on an existing planning permission)[7]. The power extends to the Mayor becoming the planning authority for applications made directly to the Secretary of State under the Town and Country Planning Act 1990, s 62A[8].

Applications of potential strategic importance

10.8 Applications of potential strategic importance are defined in the Sch 1 to the Mayor of London Order 2008 and set out in four Parts. The Mayor may only become the planning authority for applications within Parts 1 and 2[9].

---

[3] SI 2008/580.
[4] Town and Country Planning Act 1990, s 74(1B), inserted by Greater London Authority Act 1999, s 344(9).
[5] Initially under the Town and Country Planning (Mayor of London) Order 2000 and now under the Town and Country Planning (Mayor of London) Order 2008.
[6] Inserted by the Greater London Authority Act 2007, s 31.
[7] Town and Country Planning Act 1990, s 2A(1) (for taking over applications); and Mayor of London Order 2008, art 1(2), unless the s 73 application derives from a planning permission whose application was received before 6 April 2008: Mayor of London Order 2008, art 1(3).
[8] Town and Country Planning Act 1990, s 2A(1B). The Mayor may not exercise the power against Mayoral development corporations (Town and Country Planning Act 1990, s 2A(1A)), presumably because he does not need to.
[9] Mayor of London Order, Sch 1, para 1(2). Ministers propose to allow the order to prescribe applications of potential strategic importance by reference to the London Plan and London Borough's Local Plans: see proposed amendments to the Town and Country Planning Act 1990, ss 2A, 74 in Housing and Planning Bill 2015, cl 110 (as published following Public Bill Committee in the House of Commons).

10.9 London

Applications of potential strategic importance which may be refused or taken over

10.9 The Schedule covers:

Part 1 Large Scale Development

- Category 1A the provision of more than 150 houses, flats, or houses and flats;
- Category 1B development (other than purely residential development) which comprises or includes the erection of a building or buildings:

    (a) in the City of London with more than 100,000 m² floorspace[10];

    (b) in Central London[11] (other than the City of London) with more than 20,000 m² floorspace; or

    (c) outside Central London with more than 15,000 m² floorspace;

- Category 1C the erection of a building:

    (a) more than 25 metres high adjacent to the River Thames[12];

    (b) more than 150 metres high in the City of London;

    (c) more than 30 metres high outside the City of London;

- Category 1D an increase in the height of an existing building by more than 15 metres where the resulting building would be in Category 1C.

Part 2 Major Infrastructure

- Category 2A mining operations, by surface or underground working, where the development occupies more than 10 hectares;
- Category 2B Waste development[13] to provide an installation with capacity for a throughput of more than:

    (a) 5,000 tonnes per annum of hazardous waste; or

    (b) 50,000 tonnes per annum of waste;

    produced outside the land in respect of which planning permission is sought, or Waste development on more than 1 hectare;

- Category 2C Development to provide:

    (a) an aircraft runway;

    (b) a heliport (including a floating heliport or a helipad on a building);

    (c) an air passenger terminal at an airport;

---

[10] Floorspace means total floorspace including the width of external walls: Mayor of London Order, Sch 1, para 4.

[11] Central London is shown on a map (Category 1B, para 2) available on the www.london.gov.uk website. It roughly corresponds to the Central Activities Zone and comprises the City of London, Westminster from the City to Paddington and Hyde Park, nearby parts of adjoining boroughs and the south side of the Thames to Battersea Power Station.

[12] A building is adjacent to the Thames if it is wholly or partly within the Thames Policy Area shown on a development plan or the Thames Policy Area map adopted for the Order (Category 1C, para 2). These heights do not include any part of the building below ground level (Category 1C, para 3).

[13] Waste development is 'wholly or mainly for ... treating keeping, storing, processing, recovering or disposing of waste' Mayor of London Order, Sch 1, para 4.

The Mayor of London's powers over applications **10.10**

- (d) a railway station or a tram station;
- (e) a tramway, an underground, surface or elevated railway, or a cable car;
- (f) a bus or coach station;
- (g) an installation for a use within Class B8 (storage or distribution) of the Schedule to the Use Classes Order where the development occupies more than 4 hectares;
- (h) a crossing over or under the River Thames; or
- (i) a passenger pier on the River Thames;

- The keeping or storage of buses or coaches for more than 70 such vehicles or on more than 0.7 hectares[14].
- Various alterations are also included in Category 2C:
  - Alterations to increase the capacity of an air passenger terminal by more than 500,000 passengers per year.
- Category 2D Waste development which does not accord with one or more provisions of the development plan[15] and which:

  (a) occupies more than 0.5 hectares;

  (b) is development to provide an installation with a capacity for a throughput of more than:

  (i) 2,000 tonnes per annum of hazardous waste; or

  (ii) 20,000 tonnes per annum of waste.

10.10 Development which may be the subject of a direction to refuse permission, but which may not be taken over by the Mayor is in Parts 3 and 4 of Sch 1.

Part 3 covers development which may affect strategic policies. Much of these concern the loss of particular uses. Unusually, land is treated as being used for a purpose if that was its last use or it is allocated for that use in an adopted or emerging development plan[16].

- Category 3A Development likely to result in the loss of more than 200 homes (irrespective of whether new homes will be built) or prejudice the use of more than four hectares of land in residential use (as defined). In this latter case the prejudice might arise from off-site development;
- Category 3B Development on more than four hectares of B1, B2, B8 use land or which is likely to prejudice the use of that land for any such purpose;
- Category 3C Development likely to prejudice the use of more than two hectares of land used as a playing field[17] at the time of the application or at any point in the previous five years;

---

[14] This area includes connected maintenance, administrative and staff facilities: Category 2C, para 4.
[15] Non-compliance with any provision of the development plan is sufficient to bring the application within Category 2D even if it complies with the development plan as a whole.
[16] Mayor of London Order, Sch 1, Part 3, para 1.
[17] A playing field is as defined in what is now the Development Management Procedure Order.

10.11 *London*

- Category 3D Construction of a building exceeding 1000 m² floorspace, or a material change in the use of such a building in the Green Belt or on Metropolitan Open Land;
- Category 3E Development which does not accord with one or more provisions of the development plan and involves the provision of more than 2,500 m² of class A1, A2, A3, A4, A5, B1, B2, B8, C1, C2, D1 or D2 floorspace;
- Category 3F Non-residential development providing more than 200 car parking spaces;
- Category 3G A material change of use of a site used or designed for waste development, not according with one or more provisions of the development plan and either on more than 0.5 hectares, with an annual capacity of 2,000 tonnes of hazardous waste or 20,000 tonnes of waste;
- Category 3H Residential development which does not accord with one or more provisions of the development plan and is adjacent to a waste site with an annual capacity of 2,000 tonnes of hazardous waste or 20,000 tonnes of waste;
- Category 3I A material change of use of a site used or designed for keeping or storing more than 70 buses or coaches or over 0.7 hectares and used for those purposes, the application not according with one or more provisions of the development plan.

Under Part 4, if the Mayor must be consulted because of a direction made by the Secretary of State under the Development Management Procedure Order then the Mayor has the power to direct refusal.

10.11 The Order seeks to stop mayoral scrutiny being avoided by schemes being split up. If the local planning authority receives an application for planning permission for development, which it considers forms part of more substantial proposed development, on the same land or adjoining land, it must treat that application as an application for planning permission for the more substantial development[18].

Time for exercising the powers

10.12 The power to direct refusal and the power to become the local planning authority for a particular application may be exercised in a 14-day period after the local planning authority has informed the Mayor of the decision it intends to take on the application. Additionally the Mayor may become the planning authority within 14 days of the applicant's request provided that the local planning authority has failed to notify the Mayor of its proposed decision within the time period for determining the application in the Development Management Procedure Order 2015[19].

---

[18] Mayor of London Order, Sch 1, para 2. In considering whether it is part of more substantial development, the local planning authority must (Sch 1, para 3) ' take into account other development of the same land or adjoining land:
  (a) in respect of which an application for planning permission has been made but not finally determined on the date the relevant application is received by the local planning authority;
  (b) in respect of which planning permission has been granted within the period of five years immediately preceding that date;
  (c) substantially completed within the period of five years immediately preceding that date'.

[19] Mayor of London Order 2008, art 7(5), (6).

The Mayor of London's powers over applications **10.17**

Pre-application consultation

10.13 If a proposed application is of potential strategic importance then it is sensible for the developer's team to engage in pre-application consultation with the Mayor's office, in particular the Planning Decisions Unit[20].

Initial consultation on a planning application

10.14 Whilst formal intervention tends to be at a late stage, the Mayor is consulted on all applications of potential strategic importance following their submission. The local planning authority will notify the Mayor of these proposals when they are received (a 'Stage 1 referral'), sending a copy of the application, any connected application, and any plans, drawings or other documents submitted by the applicant in support of these applications[21]. The Mayor will then say within six weeks[22]:

'(a) whether he considers that the PSI application complies with the spatial development strategy; and

(b) his reasons for taking that view'.

If the Mayor has no concerns about the scheme he may take the opportunity to inform the authority that he does not wish to be consulted at the subsequent post-resolution stage[23].

Consultation prior to the decision being issued

10.15 The local planning authority may not determine an application of potential strategic importance without first sending to the Mayor a copy of all representations received and the committee report, along with a statement of the proposed decision and any draft conditions and draft planning obligation, unless the Mayor has previously said he does not wish to be consulted (a 'Stage 2 referral')[24]. Under the 2000 Order, referrals were confined to situations where the authority intended to grant permission[25], but since the Mayor became able to take over an application which was going to be refused, it has been applied to all relevant applications. However, this does mean that referrals are made when it is proposed to refuse Part 3 and 4 applications of potential strategic importance which the Mayor cannot take over.

10.16 In practice because of the size of these schemes, local planning authority decisions to approve the applications will be taken at committee. It is possible that such a large scheme might be refused by officers if the merits were considered to be sufficiently clear cut. In any event the Stage 2 referral arises once the authority has decided how it will determine the application.

10.17 The Mayor will then inform the local planning authority in writing of the date on which he received the documents. The local planning authority cannot issue

---

[20] An application form for pre-application advice and a list of charges are on the Mayor's website.
[21] Mayor of London Order 2008, art 4(1). Simply referring the Mayor to the local authority's website with the application details is not sufficient.
[22] Mayor of London Order 2008, art 4(2).
[23] Mayor of London Order 2008, art 5(2).
[24] Mayor of London Order 2008, art 5.
[25] Mayor of London Order 2000, art 4.

10.18 London

the decision until 14 days have elapsed beginning with that date[26] or the Mayor has said that he is content for the authority to determine the application in accordance with their statement and any proposed conditions and obligation. Of course, the decision cannot be issued as intended if the Mayor directs refusal or decides to become the local planning authority for the application. These powers operate in different ways and require separate consideration.

Directions to refuse planning permission

10.18 The Mayor may only direct refusal if the application would be contrary to the Spatial Development Strategy or prejudicial to its implementation, or be contrary to good strategic planning in Greater London[27]. In considering this matter the Mayor must have regard to the London Plan and the remainder of the development plan so far as material[28]. The duty to have regard to the relevant development plan triggers the presumption to make decisions in accordance with the development plan unless material considerations indicate otherwise[29].

10.19 Additionally the Mayor must have regard to the following matters[30]:

(a) the principal purposes of the Greater London Authority;

(b) the effect that permission would have on:

  (i) the health of persons in Greater London;

  (ii) the achievement of sustainable development in the UK;

(c) national policies and such international obligations as notified by the Secretary of State as matters to be considered by the Mayor in preparing or revising his strategies[31];

(d) the London Plan and any guidance issued by the Secretary of State so far as it relates to Greater London;

(e) any regional strategy relating to adjoining areas;

(f) the desirability of promoting and encouraging the use of the River Thames safely, in particular passenger transport services and freight transportation;

(g) the national waste management plan;

(h) duties under the Control of Major Accident Hazards Directive.

10.20 When the mayoralty was introduced in 2000 the practice was that the Mayor would receive a report from his officers which he would consider in a fortnightly Mayoral Planning and Spatial Development Strategy meeting. Attending would be the Mayor, the Deputy Mayor, mayoral and deputy mayoral advisers, and officers

---

[26] The date of receipt is included in the 14 days, so if the documents are received on a Tuesday, the authority may issue its decision on the Tuesday two weeks later.

[27] Mayor of London Order, art 6(1).

[28] Town and Country Planning Act 1990, s 74(1C). Specific provision was required in the 1990 Act because when directing refusal the Mayor is not the local planning authority so is not subject to the Town and Country Planning Act 1990, s 70(2).

[29] Planning and Compulsory Purchase Act 2004, s 38(6).

[30] Mayor of London Order, art 6(2).

[31] Under Greater London Authority Act 1999, s 41(5)(a).

The Mayor of London's powers over applications **10.24**

from GLA Policy and Partnerships, Legal, the London Development Agency and Transport for London. The meetings were held in private, with the public and Assembly Members excluded. Agenda papers would only be published following the meeting, along with the decisions taken[32].

10.21 The private nature of the process has been subject to considerable criticism, not least by the Greater London Assembly[33]. Whilst it has not changed, apart from meetings now being more frequent, a public hearing process has been introduced for when the Mayor becomes the local planning authority.

10.22 Any direction to refuse should be accompanied by a statement of reasons[34], which are contained in the Mayor's letter. A copy of the direction must be sent to the Secretary of State at the same time[35] and in practice the direction is also sent to the applicant and published on the Mayor's website.

A decision not to direct refusal is susceptible to judicial review[36].

10.23 The local planning authority is obliged to refuse the application 'as soon as reasonably practical after receiving a direction'[37] but events tend not to follow at that speed. The Mayor's direction may be countermanded by a direction from the Secretary of State[38] so the local planning authority or the applicant could try to pursue that avenue. More significantly in practice, the Mayor is empowered to cancel a direction by a further direction prior to the local planning authority issuing the decision notice[39]. From the start mayoral directions to refuse have been made with suggestions as to what compromises would be required to secure the cancellation of the direction. Under Mr Livingstone these tended to involve increased affordable housing contributions. Rather than being a direction to be obeyed immediately, mayoral refusals have often been a further stage in the application process.

10.24 The power of direction enables the Mayor to overturn local planning authority decisions to grant planning permission. It is also entirely independent of the Secretary of State's power to call in applications. Structurally, the Mayor is empowered and required to form his own view on the acceptability of strategic developments.

---

[32] *R (on the application of Gopie) v Mayor of London* [2002] EWHC 656 (Admin) at para 9 per George Bartlett QC.
[33] In a report, *Behind Closed Doors, Scrutiny of the Mayor's Planning Decisions*, June 2002.
[34] Mayor of London Order 2008, art 6(4). There is no corresponding duty to give reasons for not directing refusal (*R (on the application of Gopie) v Mayor of London* [2002] EWCA Civ 1186 at para 25 per Laws LJ), although in practice such reasons will be disclosed by the Mayor's letter and officer report on the Stage 2 consultation.
[35] Mayor of London Order 2008, art 6(6).
[36] As in *R (on the application of Gopie) v Mayor of London* [2002] EWHC 656 (Admin), where the criticism was that the Mayor had relied upon a resolution to grant planning permission on a previous application as establishing the principle of development, when that resolution was challenged by judicial review and withdrawn. The defendants should be the Mayor and if a consequential quashing of a planning permission is sought, the local planning authority: [2002] EWHC 656 (Admin) at para 36 per George Bartlett QC. However on appeal Laws and May LJJ doubted whether proceedings could be effective given the 14-day time limit for a mayoral direction: *R (on the application of Gopie) v Mayor of London* [2002] EWCA Civ 1186 at paras 29 and 34.
[37] Mayor of London Order 2008, art 6(7).
[38] Mayor of London Order 2008, art 6(7), (8). Copies of the direction must be included with the decision notice refusing planning permission and placed on Part 2 of the planning register: Mayor of London Order 2008, art 6(7)(b), (10).
[39] Mayor of London Order 2008, art 6(5).

10.25 *London*

THE POWER TO BECOME THE LOCAL PLANNING AUTHORITY FOR AN APPLICATION

10.25 The Mayor is able to direct that he is the local planning authority for particular applications of potential strategic importance which are within the Mayor of London Order 2008, Sch, Parts 1 or 2. If such a direction is made then the Mayor will also become the local planning authority or hazardous substances authority for any listed building consent or hazardous substances consent applications which are connected with that application[40]. Other planning applications associated with the potentially strategically important application will not be connected applications, but the local planning authority might treat them as part of the more substantial development and so applications of potential strategic importance[41].

10.26 The Mayor may give a direction if he considers that[42]:

'(a) the development or any of the issues raised by the development to which the PSI application relates is of such a nature or scale that it would have a significant impact on the implementation of the spatial development strategy;

(b) the development or any of the issues raised by the development to which the application relates has significant effects that are likely to affect more than one London Borough; and

(c) there are sound planning reasons for issuing a direction'.

10.27 All three criteria must be satisfied, except that sub-para (b) does not apply to Category 1A development (more than 150 residential units)[43]. In deciding whether to give a direction the Mayor must take into account[44]:

(a) in Category 1A cases the extent to which the borough is achieving, and has achieved the applicable development plan targets for new housing, including affordable housing;

(b) in all cases, the extent to which the borough is achieving, and has achieved any other relevant targets set out in the development plan.

10.28 A direction will state that the Mayor is becoming the local planning authority for the application and any connected application[45]. Included in the direction will be the Mayor's reasons[46], in particular, how development plan targets affected his decision[47]. The direction will be given to the local planning authority and copied to the Secretary of State and the applicant[48].

---

[40] Town and Country Planning Act 1990, s 2B(4)–(7).
[41] Mayor of London Order 2008, Sch 1, para 2.
[42] Mayor of London Order 2008, art 7(1).
[43] Mayor of London Order 2008, art 7(4).
[44] Mayor of London Order 2008, art 7(3). As at December 2015, the Mayor's decision to become the local planning authority for the Norton Folgate scheme in Tower Hamlets is the subject of judicial review proceedings: *R (on the application of the Spitalfields Trust) v Mayor of London*.
[45] Mayor of London Order 2008, art 7(2).
[46] Town and Country Planning Act 1990, s 2B(2).
[47] Mayor of London Order 2008, art 7(7).
[48] Town and Country Planning Act 1990, s 2B(3). The direction should be put on Part 2 of the planning register: Mayor of London Order 2008, art 7(8).

10.29 After a direction has been made the local planning authority should provide any further relevant information about the application and any connected applications to the Mayor as soon as reasonably practicable[49].

10.30 Once the Mayor becomes the local planning authority for the purpose of the application he is subject to the usual duties on such an authority, in particular to have regard to the development plan and other material considerations[50], and to determine the application in accordance with the development plan unless material considerations indicate otherwise[51]. The Mayor will also have what is described as 'the function of agreeing a planning obligation related to the application'[52]. This is a curious expression as s 106 does not give a local planning authority a function of agreeing an obligation. It may enter into a planning obligation by agreement, or a person interested in the land may make an obligation unilaterally which the authority might take into account in determining a planning application. In reality unilateral planning obligations usually involve some element of negotiation.

10.31 The reason for the provision seems to be that the Mayor does not become the local planning authority for all purposes relating to the application site and so is not the local planning authority under s 106. The Mayor must consult the local planning authority if a planning obligation is agreed under these provisions and any such obligation is enforceable by the Mayor and the local planning authority[53].

10.32 Following criticism of the Mayor's private meetings whilst directing refusals and under pressure from the Opposition, the government introduced requirements for representation hearings when the Mayor determines planning applications. The applicant and the local planning authority are entitled to make oral representations at such a hearing[54]. Other persons who may make representations and the procedure to be followed in advance and at the meeting are set out by the Mayor[55]. The Mayor's procedure allows an 'individual or organisation that has previously made a written representation about the application either to the relevant local planning authority or directly to the GLA will be given an opportunity to speak'[56]. The applicant, local planning authority and all those persons who may be allowed to speak are given at least 14 days' notice of the hearing[57]. The local planning authority (or authorities) for the application site will each be allowed to speak for five minutes and then 15 minutes is allowed in total for speakers supporting the application and the same time for opponents[58]. Finally the applicant will have five minutes to address objections[59]. Anyone wishing to speak should submit a detailed statement of the issues to be raised seven clear days in advance of the hearing[60]. The representation hearing is open

---

[49] Mayor of London Order 2008, art 8.
[50] Town and Country Planning Act 1990, s 70(2).
[51] Planning and Compulsory Purchase Act 2004, s 38(6).
[52] Town and Country Planning Act 1990, s 2E(2).
[53] Town and Country Planning Act 1990, s 2E(4), (5).
[54] Town and Country Planning Act 1990, s 2F(2).
[55] *Procedure for Representation Hearings at the Greater London Authority ('GLA')* made as required by the Town and Country Planning Act 1990, s 2F(3).
[56] *Procedure for Representation Hearings at the Greater London Authority ('GLA')*, para 4.1. This includes those who have sent standard letters, but not signatories on petitions.
[57] Town and Country Planning Act 1990, s 2F(4).
[58] *Procedure for Representation Hearings at the Greater London Authority ('GLA')*, paras 4.4, 5.6.
[59] *Procedure for Representation Hearings at the Greater London Authority ('GLA')*, para 5.9.
[60] *Procedure for Representation Hearings at the Greater London Authority ('GLA')*, para 4.6.

10.33 *London*

to the public and subject to access to information rules[61]. The Mayor's decision will either be given at the meeting, possibly after retiring privately with the Deputy Mayor for Planning and a legal adviser, or announced later[62].

Procedures for site visits are set out in the Mayor's note[63].

The Secretary of State is still able to call-in the planning application which the Mayor has taken over and determined, prior to the decision notice on the application being issued[64].

DETERMINATION OF RESERVED MATTERS

10.33 If the Mayor grants outline planning permission then he may direct that a subsequent application for the approval of reserved matters be determined by the borough council which would have been the local planning authority[65]. A similar direction may be made in respect of the approval of details under conditions on any connected listed building consents granted by the Mayor[66]. However these provisions leave a lacuna for the approval of details under conditions on full planning permissions or which are not reserved matters. In practice these appear to have been determined by the London borough council concerned.

APPEALS INVOLVING MAYORAL DECISIONS

10.34 If the Mayor becomes the local planning authority for the application then he will have that status in any appeal or call-in of it. He will be subject to the normal rules on the production of statements of case and be entitled to appear at any hearing or inquiry. Where the Mayor has directed refusal then the appeal rules are modified to make the Mayor a party, with the same rights and responsibilities as the local planning authority[67].

The Mayor is not otherwise entitled to be heard in appeals or call-ins but in practice, of course, will be allowed to be heard and take part if he wishes to intervene.

10.35 Costs awards in planning appeals and call-ins may only be made against parties to the proceedings[68], so the Town and Country Planning Act 1990 has provided that costs may be ordered against the Mayor if he acted unreasonably in directing the

---

[61] Under the Local Government Act 1972, as modified: Town and Country Planning Act 1990, s 2F(5) and Mayor of London Order 2008, art 9.
[62] *Procedure for Representation Hearings at the Greater London Authority ('GLA')*, section 6.
[63] *Procedure for Representation Hearings at the Greater London Authority ('GLA')*, section 3.
[64] Town and Country Planning Act 1990, s 77(1).
[65] Town and Country Planning Act 1990, s 2C(1).
[66] Town and Country Planning Act 1990, s 2C(3).
[67] Town and Country Planning (Inquiries Procedure) (England) Rules 2000, SI 2000/1624, r 23; Town and Country Planning Appeals (Determination by Inspectors) (Inquiries Procedure) (England) Rules 2000, SI 2000/1625, r 24; Town and Country Planning (Hearings Procedure) (England) Rules 2000, SI 2000/1626, r 20; Town and Country Planning (Appeals) (Written Representations Procedure) (England) Regulations 2009, SI 2009/452, reg 18.
[68] See Local Government Act 1972, s 250(4), (5); Town and Country Planning Act 1990, ss 321, 322, 322A.

refusal of planning permission and has not become a party to the appeal[69]. This provision failed to anticipate the modifications to the appeal rules and regulations which make the Mayor a party if he directed refusal and so the primary legislation is unnecessary. When the Mayor is a party to the appeal then costs may be awarded for or against him. On one occasion costs were awarded against the Mayor when he unreasonably directed refusal for reasons which did not raise strategic issues[70].

DIRECTIONS TO CONSULT THE MAYOR ON PLANNING APPLICATIONS

10.36 Separately to the Mayor's power to direct refusal or to take over applications of potential strategic importance, the Mayor must be consulted on developments within safeguarded wharves and within protected vistas. These directions are made under the Secretary of State's general direction making power[71].

10.37 Some 50 wharves in Greater London are subject to individual safeguarding directions. These require the local planning authority to consult the Mayor prior to granting planning permission for any development within the wharf as defined in the direction.

10.38 Thirteen particular views are subject to the Secretary of State for Communities and Local Government Directions relating to Protected Vistas[72]. The views are of St Paul's Cathedral from Alexandra Palace, Parliament Hill, Kenwood, Primrose Hill, Greenwich Park, Blackheath Point, Westminster Pier, Richmond Park, of the Palace of Westminster from Parliament Hill, Primrose Hill and the bridge over the Serpentine in Hyde Park and of the Tower of London from The Queen's Walk at City Hall. In those, planning applications for developments within certain views, except for material changes of use, must be the subject of consultation with Historic England, the Mayor of London and named local planning authorities.

THE MAYOR'S INVOLVEMENT IN PLANNING GENERALLY

10.39 The Mayor is able to comment on planning applications which are before local authorities or Ministers for determination, and has been represented at planning appeals and call-in inquiries.

MAYORAL DEVELOPMENT ORDERS

10.40 The Mayor has power to grant planning permission by order, with the agreement of the council who are the local planning authority for the area or areas, by means of a Mayoral Development Order. These are discussed further in Chapter 26.

---

[69] Town and Country Planning Act 1990, s 322B.
[70] Upheld in *R (on the application of Mayor of London) v First Secretary of State* [2008] EWHC 631 (Admin). Ironically planning permission was refused on appeal because of harm to neighbours' amenity.
[71] Town and Country Planning Act 1990, s 74(1)(c). The Housing and Planning Bill 2015 proposes to introduce a specific power for the Mayor of London Order to require consultation with the Mayor on planning applications and proposed permission in principle: proposed amendment to Town and Country Planning Act 1990, s 74(1B) in cl 110 (Bill as published following Public Bill Committee in the House of Commons).
[72] Made 15 March 2012.

Chapter 11

Planning conditions

11.1 Planning permission may be granted subject to conditions which regulate the carrying out of the development. Conditions are imposed by the planning authority, or on appeal the minister or inspector, without requiring the agreement of the applicant.

11.2 Conditions may:

- require further details of the development to be submitted and approved;
- require certain matters to have been done, whether on- or off-site, before the development begins or progresses beyond a certain point;
- control the use of the development, for example, opening hours or noise levels;
- impose a time limit for the commencement of development;
- require the cessation of the development after a certain time or limit the benefits of the permission to a particular person or type of person.

THE POWER TO IMPOSE CONDITIONS

11.3 The general powers to include conditions in the grant of planning permission are contained in the Town and Country Planning Act 1990, ss 70 and 72.

Section 70(1) provides:

'Where an application is made to a local planning authority for planning permission:

(a) subject to sections 91 and 92, they may grant planning permission, either unconditionally or subject to such conditions as they think fit; or

(b) they may refuse planning permission'.

11.4 Section 72(1), (2) provide:

'(1) Without prejudice to the generality of section 70(1), conditions may be imposed on the grant of planning permission under that section:

(a) for regulating the development or use of any land under the control of the applicant (whether or not it is land in respect of which the application was made) or requiring the carrying out of works on any such land, so far as appears to the local planning authority to be expedient for the purposes of or in connection with the development authorised by the permission;

(b) for requiring the removal of any buildings or works authorised by the permission, or the discontinuance of any use of land so authorised, at the end of a specified period, and the carrying out of any works required for the reinstatement of land at the end of that period.

(2) A planning permission granted subject to such a condition as is mentioned in subsection (1)(b) is in this Act referred to as "planning permission granted for a limited period"'.

11.5 Section 70 is the broader power and it is not constrained by the specific provisions of s 72. In *Davenport v London Borough of Hammersmith & Fulham* Richards J said[1]:

> 'section [72] confers an express power to impose certain kinds of condition in relation to land under the control of the applicant. It does not, however, purport to cut down the generality of the power in section [70] as to the imposition of conditions'.

Section 72(1)(a) refers to conditions regulating or requiring works on land under the control of the applicant. Subsection (1)(b) concerns temporary permissions, where the development must be discontinued at the end of a specified period. These provisions are therefore simply examples of planning conditions.

THE LEGAL TESTS FOR PLANNING CONDITIONS

11.6 The authority's power under s 70 to impose 'such conditions as they think fit' are constrained by the purpose of planning legislation and public law. In *Newbury District Council v Secretary of State for the Environment*[2] Lord Fraser of Tullybelton said that these words:

> '... would appear on their face to confer an unlimited power, but it is plain that the power is subject to certain limitations ... In order to be valid, a condition must satisfy three tests. First, it must have a planning purpose. It may have other purposes as well as its planning purpose. But if it is imposed solely for some other purpose or purposes, such as furtherance of the housing policy of the local authority, it will not be valid as a planning condition: see *R v Hillingdon London Borough Council, ex p Royco Homes Ltd*[3]. Second, it must relate to the permitted development to which it is annexed. The best known statement of these two tests is that by Lord Denning in *Pyx Granite Co Ltd v Ministry of Housing and Local Government* which has been followed and applied in many later cases. Lord Denning said[4]:
>
>> "Although the planning authorities are given very wide powers to impose 'such conditions as they think fit,' nevertheless the law says that those conditions, to be valid, must fairly and reasonably relate to the permitted development. The planning authority are not at liberty to use their powers for an ulterior object, however desirable that object may seem to them to be in the public interest."
>
> ... Thirdly, the condition must be "reasonable" in the rather special sense of *Associated Provincial Picture Houses Ltd v Wednesbury Corporation*[5]'.

11.7 The *Newbury* tests are therefore that a condition must:

---

[1] [1999] JPL 1122 The judge was referring to the equivalent provisions in the Town and Country Planning Act 1971, ss 29 and 30. The section numbers have been updated in this quotation.
[2] [1981] AC 578 at 607–608.
[3] [1974] QB 720.
[4] [1958] 1 QB 554 at 572.
[5] [1948] 1 KB 223, 229.

11.8 *Planning conditions*

(a) serve a planning purpose;

(b) fairly and reasonably relate to the development permitted;

(c) not be unreasonable in the public law 'irrationality' sense.

Planning purpose

11.8 A planning purpose is one which concerns the wide range of matters in land use planning[6].

Fairly and reasonably relate

11.9 The need for a planning condition to fairly and reasonably relate to the development permitted is a narrower test than the requirement for a planning purpose. The relationship is between the development which is actually authorised and the effect of the condition.

Usually it is permissible to regulate how the authorised development is carried out, but controlling or requiring other development will require closer consideration. A condition limiting flying hours could be imposed in a planning permission which expanded an existing airport because of the greater use which would arise from the works[7]. As another example, to impose a condition that required the refurbishment of other buildings on the land controlled by the applicant could properly relate to permission for new buildings if the new build was made acceptable by the wider improvements. Alternatively, if planning permission is granted for an extension to a retail building, care would have to be taken in applying a condition restricting the type of goods which could be sold in the original part of the building. Such a condition might be justified by the effect of a larger store, but that will depend upon the circumstances[8].

11.10 Requirements to demolish buildings as a consequence of a change of use have posed difficulties. In *Newbury* itself planning permission had been granted for the use of existing aircraft hangers for storage subject to a condition that the buildings were removed at the end of the period. The House of Lords held that the Secretary of State was entitled to find that the condition was unlawful as it did not fairly and reasonably relate to the development permitted, suggesting that it was rare than any such condition could be lawful[9].

Unreasonable

11.11 Unreasonableness encompasses the full range of public law unreasonableness. A condition may be unlawful because it has been adopted overlooking a material matter or because of a misinterpretation of policy. Unreasonableness in this situation

---

[6] See Chapter 9 on material considerations.
[7] *British Airports Authority v Secretary of State for Scotland* 1979 SLT 197.
[8] Clear drafting is required to make it easy to understand whether the condition applies to the extension or the whole of the building.
[9] [1981] AC 578 at 602 per Lord Edmund-Davies, at 608–609 per Lord Fraser of Tullybelton, at 619–620 per Lord Scarman. This was followed in another demolition case, *Delta Design and Engineering Ltd v Secretary of State for the Environment, Transport and the Regions* (2000) 80 P & CR 76.

is not confined to the narrow perversity sense: that no reasonable authority, properly directing itself, could have made that decision.

THE GEOGRAPHICAL EXTENT OF PLANNING CONDITIONS

11.12 Planning conditions may impose requirements with respect to:

(i) the application site;

(ii) land outside the application site but under the applicant's control;

(iii) other land, provided it is reasonable for the applicant to comply with the condition.

These are essentially aspects of the legal requirement for conditions to be rational in a *Wednesbury* sense. A condition which fell outside these parameters would not be reasonable. Of course, a condition applying within these geographical limits will not necessarily be reasonable.

The application site

11.13 Planning permission may be granted subject to conditions[10] and such conditions will in broad terms be for regulating the permission. It follows that a planning authority must be able to impose conditions which apply to all (or any part) of the application site. This is irrespective of whether the applicant controls that land. In the absence of a personal condition, a planning permission is an authorisation for any person to carry out development, not a licence for a particular person. Conditions must therefore be capable of applying to any person who might in future implement the permission. Most of the time the applicant will control the land[11]. However permission may be granted on land which the developer seeks to acquire by compulsory purchase or by agreement and may include works on public land (such as highway improvements) which it intends to achieve by later agreement. Planning conditions can provide for detailed regulation in such cases where use of a planning obligation (which only binds the land of the person making it) may not be possible.

11.14 Whether the applicant owns or controls the application site is rarely material when deciding what conditions to impose on a planning permission. There may, though, be cases where critical elements are on parts of the site outside the current control of the applicant (such as car parking or landscaping). The authority may then need to ensure that other parts of the development which rely on those elements for acceptability are not able to proceed until the steps are taken on the non-controlled land.

Other land under the applicant's control

11.15 Section 72 says that conditions may be imposed on land outside the application site but under the applicant's control. As discussed below, this is also a consequence of the general power to impose conditions if it is reasonable to expect compliance with them.

---

[10] Under the general power in s 70(1).
[11] Whether as owner, lessee or by virtue of an option or conditional contract.

11.16 *Planning conditions*

Other land under the applicant's control should be indicated in the application as blue-lined land, but the power is not confined to that shown in the application. The land will usually be adjoining and whilst it might be separate must be sufficiently close for the condition to fairly and reasonably relate to the development.

The classic example of the use of this power is to require landscaping on blue land adjacent to the development. If more substantial works are ordered, particularly if they are proposed in the application, it may be that they should be encompassed within a larger application site[12].

Land outside the application site or the applicant's control

11.16 Whilst s 72(1)(a) says that conditions may be attached to land under the control of the applicant, it is unnecessary as s 70 is sufficiently wide to cover land under the applicant's control and, in certain circumstances, other land: *Davenport v London Borough of Hammersmith and Fulham*[13].

Davenport – the scope of planning conditions

11.17 The decision of the Divisional Court in *Davenport* concerned failure to comply with breach of condition notices. The brothers ran a motor vehicle repair business at the end of a cul-de-sac named Tasso Road. Condition 8 of the permission provided:

> 'No vehicles which have been left with or are in the control of the applicant shall be stored or parked in Tasso Road'.

It was not in issue that the business's owners and staff had been parking customers' vehicles in the road.

11.18 Mr Justice Richards identified the relevant principle on the scope of the condition as:

> 'the reason why a condition requiring the carrying out of works on land not within the control of the applicant is invalid is the operation of a broader principle, namely that one cannot lawfully impose a condition requiring a person to secure a result that it does not lie wholly within his power to secure.
>
> ... There is nothing to show that a condition relating to land outside the application site and outside the control of the applicant is invalid unless that condition requires the carrying out of works on such land or is otherwise one with which the applicant could not be assured of securing compliance. Although Condition 8 regulates the use of land outside the application site and outside the applicant's control, it imposes a requirement which lies wholly within the applicant's power to comply'.

11.19 There was no issue that a condition may be imposed on land within the application site but outside the applicant's control. Richards J noted that Circular 11/95 included, in para 7 of an appendix containing examples of conditions which are unacceptable, the following:

---

[12] This may have implications for EIA screening and planning application fees.
[13] [1999] 2 PLR 96.

'To require that loading and unloading, and the parking of vehicles, shall not take place on the highway at the front of the premises. This condition purports to exercise control in respect of the public highway, which is not under the control of the applicant'.

He said that if this part of the guidance was lawful 'It may be that the particular condition given by way of example in the appendix is unlawful for the reasons that I have already touched upon, namely that the applicant is not able to secure that all loading and unloading or all parking of vehicles, including parking by customers, does not take place on the highway in front of the premises'.

The court also considered that the condition was for a planning purpose and construed it to relate solely to vehicles controlled in connection with the repair premises.

A condition which might involve actions, such as noise monitoring, on third party land may still be lawful on *Davenport* principles if it could be expected that access would be granted[14].

It might be unreasonable to impose a condition providing that uses are carried out in a manner which is outside the control of the developer and the local planning authority, being regulated by a third party[15].

POSITIVE AND NEGATIVE CONDITIONS

11.20 Conditions may require things to be done in a certain way, such as works being carried out in accordance with particular details. They may, alternatively, prohibit certain activities.

It may be necessary for something to be done by a certain point in the course of a development, such as having particular details approved or a car park open for use. However planning permissions do not require a development to have reached a certain point at a certain time, so a permission for prospective development cannot have a condition requiring the car park to be completed by 23 July 2017. The development might not even have started by that point, or it could be long completed. Conditions may, therefore, be used to set triggers at different stages of the development which require certain steps to have been carried out before they can be passed.

11.21 The common formats for these conditions are to prohibit a particular step in the development until something has happened or provide that something must have happened prior to a particular stage taking place, for example[16]:

- development shall not begin until details of the junction between the proposed service road and the highway have been approved in writing by the local planning authority; and the building shall not be occupied until that junction has been constructed in accordance with the approved details;

---

[14] *R (on the application of Friends of Hethel Ltd) v South Norfolk District Council* [2009] EWHC 2856 (Admin), [2010] JPL 594 at paras 84, 85 per Cranston J.
[15] *British Airports Authority v Secretary of State for Scotland* 1979 SLT 197. There a condition on an airport extension provided 'As far as technically and legally practicable, take off and landing to be to the north, so as to avoid overflying built-up areas, and also the routing of helicopter movements and the planning of helicopter operations generally in such a way as to avoid built-up areas as far as possible'. This was found to be unreasonable as the Civil Aviation Authority controlled aircraft routing.
[16] Taken from Circular 11/95, Appendix A.

11.22 *Planning conditions*

- before the development hereby permitted commences on the site, a soil survey of the site shall be undertaken and the results provided to the local planning authority.

11.22 'Prior to the commencement of development' is another common formulation. All of these conditions are known as 'negative' or 'Grampian' conditions[17]. The steps required are usually either entirely within the developer's control (the carrying out of one part of the project by the time another part has been delivered) or capable of being secured by the developer within the planning system. The latter includes the developer having to submit details to the local planning authority and having secured its approval, with an ability to appeal if approval is not granted, or the carrying out of off-site highways works which the developer will expect to fund or carry out in agreement with the highway authority. More rarely, a negative condition will prohibit development until an event occurs which is outside the developer's control or material influence. It might be that the traffic impacts of a scheme are so substantial in the context of existing problems that the development cannot proceed until a motorway has been widened but there is no expectation that the development could fund those works. It is in principle possible to impose a Grampian condition prohibiting the use of the development until that has occurred. This is even if there are no reasonable prospects that the event will occur[18]. However imposing a condition which does not have a reasonable chance of being able to be complied with may be tantamount to refusing permission and that could be the better course, not least to avoid unusable permissions piling up. Ministerial policy is 'Such conditions should not be used where there are no prospects at all of the action in question being performed within the time-limit imposed by the permission'[19].

11.23 Planning permissions granted by local planning authorities in England must now contain reasons why requirements in any planning conditions are 'pre-commencement' requirements[20]. This is to discourage excessive use of such conditions which can delay the start of development. Authorities should consider whether details or events are only needed at a later stage in the project.

Conditions restricting or controlling matters which are not otherwise subject to planning control

11.24 Conditions may impose controls on matters which would not otherwise require planning consent. This is where conditions apply to future activity or operations, in particular:

(i) controls over the conduct of a use, such as opening hours;

(ii) prohibitions on future works which are not operational development, such as preventing the future sub-division of a building which would be internal works exempted under s 55(2)(a);

---

[17] The latter description coming from the House of Lords decision in *Grampian Regional Council v City of Aberdeen District Council* (1984) 47 P & CR 633 where a condition prevented development from proceeding until a road had been stopped up.

[18] *British Railways Board v Secretary of State for the Environment* [1993] 3 PLR 125.

[19] Planning Practice Guidance 21a-009-20140306. The Welsh guidance is 'These conditions should not be imposed if there is no reasonable prospect of the required action being performed within the time limit imposed by the permission': Circular WGC 016/2014 The Use of Planning Conditions for Development Management, para 3.47.

[20] Town and Country Planning (Development Management Procedure) (England) Order 2015, SI 2015/595, art 35(1)(a)(ii).

(iii) preventing the carrying out of activities which are within the same use class, for example, a condition controlling the type of goods which can be sold from retail premises[21];

(iv) removing permitted development rights, either generally or in particular respects.

Since s 70(1) is in wide terms there can be no objection in principle to a condition which imposes control over matters which would not otherwise require planning permission. The justification for such a condition has to meet the *Newbury* tests in law and ought to be considered on the basis of policy in the NPPF and *Planning Practice Guidance* or the 2014 Welsh circular *The Use of Planning Conditions for Development Management*. However as a matter of principle planning permission might only be appropriate if the use is carried out in a particular way or the building is not extended further without a new planning application. Whether restrictions are imposed is a matter of considering the public interest need for control against the restriction on a party's freedom of action.

Conditions removing permitted development and use class order rights

11.25 The benefits of the Town and Country Planning (Use Classes) Order 1987 and the General Permitted Development Orders can be removed by planning condition[22]. Removal may be by implication (such as providing that use be for a certain purpose and 'for no other use')[23].

In *R (on the application of Wilkinson) v Rossendale Borough Council* a planning condition read[24]:

'The premises shall be used solely for the sewing, making up and repairing of tarpaulins and for no other purpose'.

Sullivan J held that this impliedly excluded the operation of the Use Classes Order to what was otherwise a B1 use.

Conditions affecting existing lawful uses

11.26 It is possible, as a matter of law, to require the surrender of existing lawful use rights by a planning condition or obligation in connection with the grant of a new permission[25]. However, such surrenders are rare and have to be justified in law by *Wednesbury* reasonableness and as a matter of policy by necessity to enable the consented scheme to proceed. The reason why lawful uses are rarely terminated by condition or planning obligation is that if they are on the same site they will usually

---

[21] An example of planning conditions restricting the type of goods to be sold and sub-division is *Stevenage Borough Council v Secretary of State for Communities and Local Government* [2010] EWHC 1289 (Admin).
[22] See on use classes *City of London Corpn v Secretary of State for the Environment* (1971) 23 P & CR 169 and for permitted development rights *Dunoon Development Ltd v Secretary of State for the Environment* [1992] JPL 1936. The cases on these issues are discussed further in Chapters 3 and 5.
[23] *Rugby Football Union v Secretary of State for the Environment, Transport and the Regions* [2001] EWHC Admin 927, [2002] JPL 740 at para 57
[24] [2002] EWHC 1204 (Admin), [2003] JPL 82 at paras 4, 75.
[25] *Kingston-Upon-Thames London Borough Council v Secretary of State for the Environment* [1973] 1 WLR 1549.

11.27 *Planning conditions*

be superseded by a new planning permission for a particular use, and if on adjacent or nearby land the surrender requires considerable justification.

LIMITS AS TO WHETHER CONDITIONS CAN AFFECT THE SUBSTANCE OF A PLANNING PERMISSION

11.27 A condition may not cause a fundamental alteration in the development approved by the permission[26]. The effect of a conditional planning permission must not be to allow development that was in substance not that for which permission had been applied for[27]. In *Cadogan v Secretary of State for the Environment*[28] Glidewell LJ said 'it was established that a condition on a planning permission would not be valid if it altered the extent or indeed the nature of the development permitted'[29].

Conditions which did deprive the developer of the substance of its permission were imposed in *R v Hillingdon London Borough Council, ex p Royco Homes Ltd*[30] where the council had granted planning permission for Royco's housing scheme but subject to conditions which required it to be built to council housing standards and costs and occupied by persons chosen from the Council's waiting list with security of tenure. They were held to be unreasonable in *Wednesbury* terms[31]. Essentially the application for a private housing development had been turned into planning permission for a council housing estate.

Conditions providing for later approval of details

11.28 Conditions can provide for the later approval of details by the local planning authority. The decision maker must consider it appropriate to defer the determination of those matters to a later stage. Any later approval must be within the confines of the permission which has been granted and it is not possible to go back on the principle of the permission at that stage. There is a tension in the authorities between the wide scope of later approval of details under conditions and the narrow approach, discussed below, taken to conditions allowing the later variation of details which had previously been approved. Their reconciliation may be conscious and public deferral of details in the former case as against an unheralded relaxation of what had been previously consulted upon.

Conditions providing for later variations to approved details

11.29 Conditions sometimes provide that approved details may be varied with the agreement of the local planning authority. Such variations must be immaterial, otherwise the formal procedures for planning applications, including for varied

---

[26] *R v Coventry City Council, ex p Arrowcroft Group plc* [2001] PLCR 113.
[27] *Granada Hospitality Ltd v Secretary of State for the Environment, Transport and the Regions* [2001] PLCR 81 at 97 (para 57) per Collins J.
[28] [1993] JPL 664.
[29] See also *Richmond-upon-Thames London Borough Council v Secretary of State for the Environment* [1974] 1 All ER 193.
[30] [1974] QB 720.
[31] See Lord Widgery CJ at 732.

Limits to whether conditions affect the substance of a planning permission **11.33**

conditions under s 73, would be bypassed[32]. The ambit of such variations in domestic law is very narrow and concerns expressed about such conditions sidestepping EIA[33] ought to not now arise.

Policy tests for planning conditions

11.30 The National Planning Policy Framework continues the approach to planning conditions contained in earlier policy by saying[34]:

> 'Planning conditions should only be imposed where they are necessary, relevant to planning and to the development to be permitted, enforceable, precise and reasonable in all other respects'.

The requirement of relevance arises from the first two *Newbury* tests. Enforceability, precision and reasonableness may be aspects of *Wednesbury* irrationality but operate in a broader sense. Necessity is a policy rather than a legal requirement, as in law a condition can be imposed if its inclusion is rational even if not necessary.

11.31 Similar policy tests are contained in the 2014 Welsh circular *The Use of Planning Conditions for Development Management*[35]. This circular also contains useful practical advice on drafting and agreeing conditions[36].

Model conditions for England are contained in Annex A to Circular 11/95[37] and in some other topic based guidance, and for Wales in the Appendix to the Welsh circular.

Conditions requiring the transfer of land or the making of payments

11.32 In *Attorney-General v Wilts United Dairies Ltd*[38] it was held that statutory authority was required before the executive could make any charge, even if it was expressed in the form of an agreement. Consequently a planning condition cannot require a payment to be made to the local planning authority or anyone else.

11.33 A condition is unlawful if it requires the landowner to dedicate land as a highway: see *Hall & Co Ltd v Shoreham-by-Sea Urban District Council*[39]. There, a planning condition required a road to be constructed on the applicant's land and allowed to be used by the public. The decision in *Hall* on this point has been consistently followed[40]. Lord Hoffmann in *Tesco Stores Ltd v Secretary of State for*

---

[32] *R (on the application of Midcounties Co-operative Ltd) v Wyre Forest District Council* [2009] EWHC 96 (Admin) at para 70 per Ouseley J. This decision has been followed in a series of cases, analysed in *R (on the application of Treagus) v Suffolk County Council* [2013] EWHC 950 (Admin), [2013] Env LR 36. A condition which permits 'minor variations' may be permissible: *Midcounties* at para 79.
[33] *Smith v Secretary of State* [2003] EWCA Civ 262, [2003] JPL 1316, at paras 43–44 per Waller LJ.
[34] NPPF, para 206.
[35] Circular WGC 016/2014, at para 3.1.
[36] See section 4.
[37] This Annex survived the publication of the *Planning Practice Guidance*.
[38] (1921) 37 TLR 884 (Court of Appeal); (1922) 38 TLR 781 (House of Lords). A licence was granted to deal in milk, but subject to a charge of 2 pence per gallon.
[39] [1964] 1 WLR 240 at 251.
[40] See *City of Bradford Metropolitan Council v Secretary of State for the Environment* (1987) 53 P & CR 55 and *Tesco Stores Ltd v Secretary of State for the Environment* [1995] 1 WLR 759.

11.34 *Planning conditions*

the Environment[41] identified planning obligations requiring the ceding of land or payment of money as matters that would be unreasonable in a condition under *Hall*.

11.34 The position is also reflected in the Planning Practice Guidance[42]

> 'Conditions requiring land to be given up: Conditions cannot require that land is formally given up (or ceded) to other parties, such as the Highway Authority'.

Planning conditions requiring agreements

11.35 A practice had developed in some local authorities of granting planning permission subject to conditions which require a planning obligation or Highways Act 1980, s 278 agreement to be entered into, or which expressly prevent development being carried out until an agreement has been made[43]. This was used to speed up the grant of planning permission or avoid land ownership problems from hindering the signing of an agreement at the time.

11.36 In now cancelled text DoE Circular 11/95 (the use of conditions in planning permissions) said that permission should not be granted subject to a condition that requires the parties to enter into a planning obligation. It also said that no payment of money could be required when granting a planning permission except where there is specific statutory authority. The *Planning Practice Guidance* now advises that conditions positively requiring an agreement should not be used and negatively worded conditions, limiting development until a planning obligation or highways agreement has been made are unlikely to be appropriate in the majority of cases, although might on some occasions be justified[44].

11.37 This issue has had little direct judicial consideration. In *R (on the application of Carroll) v South Somerset District Council* Collins J briefly mentioned, but did not express a conclusion on, the possibility of a condition preventing development before a planning obligation is entered into. He noted that there may be arguments that such a condition is too vague to be enforceable[45].

11.38 There are three points to bear in mind:

(i) a condition must be precise and enforceable, so a negative condition ought to state a result to be achieved (for example, particular highways improvements) rather than require an obligation or agreement to be made. The terms of the obligation or agreement will inevitably be vague to some degree. Even if an obligation can be made unilaterally, the question will be whether it complies. Achieving the result might require an agreement, but that is not the test in determining whether there is a breach of planning control;

(ii) applications for approvals under condition ought to be capable of being appealed, if at all possible. A condition which requires a planning obligation to be entered

---

[41] [1995] 1 WLR 759 at 776.
[42] *Planning Practice* Guidance, para 21a-006-20140306.
[43] The practice was supported by George Chesman in a *Journal of Planning Law* article *Conditions in planning permissions requiring the subsequent completion of planning obligations* [2004] JPL 1649. The article provoked spirited correspondence: [2005] JPL 298 and 753.
[44] I21a-010-20140306.
[45] [2008] EWHC 104 (Admin), [2008] JPL 991.

into in a form which must be by agreement rather than unilateral undermines the right to appeal to the Minister;

(iii) a positive or negative requirement to enter into an obligation or agreement must not violate the principle that payments cannot be required without statutory authority, which conditions do not contain. There is no difference between a condition which requires a payment of £10,000, one requiring a planning obligation to be entered into containing a payment of £10,000 and a negative condition prohibiting development until an obligation has been entered into to pay £10,000. In all cases the planning permission is requiring a payment for its grant.

This does not alter the lawfulness of a condition which requires an off-site event to have occurred before development commencements (such as a road closure or the provision of ways) even if in practice this will be achieved by the developer entering into a s 278 or s 106 agreement.

The GPDO 2015 expressly assumes that planning conditions can require entry into planning obligations[46].

CONDITIONS AND HIGHWAYS AGREEMENTS

11.39 It is common to impose negative conditions which limit the development until off-site highway improvements have been carried out. Often those improvements would be carried out or paid for by the developer under an agreement with the highway authority under the Highways Act 1980, s 278. Such conditions may not be used to require such agreements with local highway authorities for infrastructure which is in any Community Infrastructure Levy infrastructure list for the area, see the Community Infrastructure Levy Regulations 2010, reg 123(2A)[47]:

'... a condition falling within either of the following descriptions may not be imposed on the grant of planning permission:

(a) a condition that requires a highway agreement for the funding or provision of relevant infrastructure to be entered into;

(b) a condition that prevents or restricts the carrying out of development until a highway agreement for the funding or provision of relevant infrastructure has been entered into'.

A condition can still be used to restrict development until highway works have been carried out if those works are not in the list.

THE TIME FOR IMPLEMENTING PLANNING PERMISSION

11.40 Planning permissions for development which has not been carried out must include conditions specifying the period within which the development must be

---

[46] DMPO 2015, Sch 6, para 9.
[47] Restrictions on the pooling of no more than five planning obligations for a particular infrastructure project or type of infrastructure do not apply to highway agreements or conditions requiring highway agreements: see Community Infrastructure Levy Regulations 2010, SI 2010/948, reg 123(3).

11.41 *Planning conditions*

begun. If conditions are those included in the permission itself, then such conditions, with standard periods, are deemed to be imposed. For outline planning permissions, two periods are provided: the first for applying for reserved matters approval; and the second the time following such approval within which the development must commence. These conditions do not apply to retrospective or temporary planning permissions[48].

Full planning permissions

11.41 A full planning permission is subject to the Town and Country Planning Act 1990, s 91, which provides in sub-ss (1)–(3) in England:

> '(1) Subject to the provisions of this section, every planning permission granted or deemed to be granted shall be granted or, as the case may be, be deemed to be granted, subject to the condition that the development to which it relates must be begun not later than the expiration of:
>
> (a) three years beginning with the date on which the permission is granted or, as the case may be, deemed to be granted; or
>
> (b) such other period (whether longer or shorter) beginning with that date as the authority concerned with the terms of planning permission may direct.
>
> (2) The period mentioned in subsection (1)(b) shall be a period which the authority consider appropriate having regard to the provisions of the development plan and to any other material considerations.
>
> (3) If planning permission is granted without the condition required by subsection (1), it shall be deemed to have been granted subject to the condition that the development to which it relates must be begun not later than the expiration of three years beginning with the date of the grant'.

In Wales the three-year default period is changed to five years. Following a slow-down in the commencement of schemes during the financial crisis which started in 2008, it has become more common in England to apply a five-year period.

Outline planning permissions

11.42 An outline planning permission is subject to the Town and Country Planning Act 1990, s 92, which provides in sub-ss (1)–(3) in England:

> '(1) In this section and section 91 "outline planning permission" means planning permission granted, in accordance with the provisions of a development order, with the reservation for subsequent approval by the local planning authority or the Secretary of State of matters not particularised in the application ("reserved matters").
>
> (2) Subject to the following provisions of this section, where outline planning permission is granted for development consisting in or including the carrying out of building or other operations, it shall be granted subject to conditions to the effect:
>
> (a) that, in the case of any reserved matter, application for approval must be made not later than the expiration of three years beginning with the date of the grant of outline planning permission; and
>
> (b) that the development to which the permission relates must be begun not later than:

---

[48] Town and Country Planning Act 1990, s 91(4)(b), (c).

(ii) the expiration of two years from the final approval of the reserved matters or, in the case of approval on different dates, the final approval of the last such matter to be approved.

(3) If outline planning permission is granted without the conditions required by subsection (2), it shall be deemed to have been granted subject to those conditions'.

In Wales in addition to these periods in sub-s (2), an alternative period for commencing development is five years from the date of the grant of the outline planning permission[49]. The Welsh version avoids the anomaly that an early approval of reserved matters might lead to the period under para (b)(ii) expiring less than three years after the grant of the outline planning permission and so a fresh reserved matters application being required within the three year period.

Phasing is expressly accommodated in both nations so it is possible for different periods to apply to different parts of the development[50].

Extensions of time if the consent is challenged

11.43 There is a limited, but automatic, extension of time for implementing full permissions in England if a High Court challenge is brought to the planning permission. Section 91(3A), (3B) provides:

'(3A) Subsection (3B) applies if any proceedings are begun to challenge the validity of a grant of planning permission or of a deemed grant of planning permission.

(3B) The period before the end of which the development to which the planning permission relates is required to be begun in pursuance of subsection (1) or (3) must be taken to be extended by one year'.

11.44 This extension, of course, only matters if the challenge is unsuccessful and fails to quash the permission. It was introduced by the Planning and Compulsory Purchase Act 2004 when the standard implementation period was reduced to three years. It has rarely been needed, and with the Planning Court being able to dispose of significant planning cases within six months of the start of proceedings, most proceedings would be dealt with within a year.

No change is made to the implementation period for an outline planning permission because the period is in practice longer.

MINERALS PLANNING CONDITIONS

11.45 Mineral extraction poses a number of challenges. It is essential as part of a functioning economy, yet carrying it out causes harm. There is a limit to the amount of mineral which can be worked from a site, so extraction (as distinct from subsequent transfer or processing) must at least in theory have a limited duration. However that duration will depend upon how quickly the site is worked, which is a combination of market conditions and the operator's own inclinations. There is a danger that harmful operations will carry on for much longer than was originally

---

[49] Town and Country Planning Act 1990, s 92(2)(b)(i).
[50] Town and Country Planning Act 1990, s 92(5).

11.46 *Planning conditions*

envisaged and that might or might not be the operator's choice. A mineral site will require a considerable amount of clean up to enable it to be used for a different purpose in the future, whether it is a quarry, the pit head for an underground mine or an oil or gas wellhead. Some of that restoration work will have to take place after the mining has ceased, by which point the site will have little value to the operator.

11.46 Particular conditions can, and sometimes must, be imposed on mineral planning permissions. All planning permissions for the winning and working of minerals or involving the depositing of mineral waste shall be subject to a condition on the duration of the winning and working of minerals or the depositing of mineral waste[51]. In the absence of an expressly imposed condition this is deemed to be 60 years[52], but it is conventional for mineral permissions to limit the works to the period proposed in the application. A duration condition may be appealed to the Minister[53].

11.47 A restoration condition is one providing for the restoration of the site by the using of soil, topsoil and/or soil-making material[54]. If there is a restoration condition then an aftercare condition may require the land to be brought to the required standard for agriculture, forestry[55] or amenity uses[56]. An aftercare condition may specify the steps required or require an aftercare scheme to be approved by the mineral planning authority[57]. Unusually, the mineral planning authority has the power to modify an aftercare scheme submitted to it[58], rather than to simply refuse an unsatisfactory scheme, to avoid the possibility of no submitted scheme being approved. An aftercare period will be specified in the aftercare condition and no steps, such as planting, cultivating, fertilising, watering, draining or otherwise treating the land, may be required after that period[59].

11.48 The aftercare standards are either to bring the site back to its previous agricultural quality if this has been identified by the Minister[60] or, if not, to a reasonably fit use for the agriculture or forestry proposed. Amenity uses are required to be suitable for sustaining trees, shrubs or other plants[61], although it is not uncommon for planning obligations to provide for greater facilities for public access. The mineral planning authority is required to consult the Minister prior to imposing an aftercare condition requiring agriculture and the Forestry Commission in England or the Natural Resources Body for Wales before requiring forestry[62].

---

[51] Town and Country Planning Act 1990, Sch 5, para 1(1).
[52] Town and Country Planning Act 1990, Sch 5, para 1(2), (3). Prior to 22 February 1982 mineral permissions did not need to have a duration limit and a 60-year limit was imposed on all existing permissions on the basis that the present value of a right to extract for 60 years was the same as a permanent right.
[53] Town and Country Planning Act 1990, Sch 5, para 1(6).
[54] Town and Country Planning Act 1990, Sch 5, para 2(1), (2)(a).
[55] In this provision, forestry means the growing of a utilisable crop of timber: Town and Country Planning Act 1990, Sch 5, para 2(9). Other tree planting may be for amenity purposes.
[56] Town and Country Planning Act 1990, Sch 5, para 2(1), (2)(b).
[57] Town and Country Planning Act 1990, Sch 5, para 2(3).
[58] Town and Country Planning Act 1990, Sch 5, para 2(4),
[59] Town and Country Planning Act 1990, Sch 5, para 2(5)–(7).
[60] The Department for the Environment, Food and Rural Affairs or the Welsh Assembly Government.
[61] Town and Country Planning Act 1990, Sch 5, para 3.
[62] Town and Country Planning Act 1990, Sch 5, para 4. Consultation is also required prior to the approval of details.

CONDITION DELAYING THE START OF OPERATIONS LIKELY TO DAMAGE A SITE OF SPECIAL SCIENTIFIC INTEREST

11.49 If Natural England or Natural Resources Wales advise against permitting operations which are likely to damage a site of special scientific interest, or advise that certain conditions should be attached, but the local planning authority does not follow that advice, it[63]:

(a) shall give notice of the permission, and of its terms, to the conservation body including a statement of how the authority has taken account of that advice; and

(b) hall not grant a planning permission which would allow the operations to start before the end of the period of 21 days beginning with the date of that notice.

The 21-day period is after the grant of planning permission and the giving of notice[64], so a condition should be included preventing development from commencing until after the end of that period.

PERMISSIONS IN PART

11.50 It is lawful for the decision maker to decide of his own motion to grant a lesser permission[65], but care must be taken if that course is considered appropriate. The *Planning Practice Guidance* considers that this should not be used for more than a minor modification of a proposal[66]. Questions of fairness arise in respect of the applicant and third parties. It may be sensible to confine such partial approvals to situations where part of the development is acceptable and is capable of being carried out in its own right. On appeal the Minister or inspector may 'reverse or vary any part of the decision of the local planning authority'[67] and are able to grant permission for part of the scheme. That power is not given to local planning authorities, when it would be useful for that provision to be available, where an application can be split up[68]. An amendment to give such a power was proposed by Stephen Hammond MP to the Housing and Planning Bill, but at the time of writing has not been adopted by Ministers[69].

DETERMINING CONDITIONS

11.51 Conditions are imposed by the person granting the planning permission, whether this is the local planning authority or an inspector or Minister. There is no requirement that the terms of the conditions should be agreed with the applicant. However, it is sensible to seek to have the conditions in an agreed form, even if there is a disagreement about the need for some of them. Depending upon the time available, it is prudent for local planning authorities to discuss conditions with applicants, at least to the point of sending a draft to them in advance. Any comments

---

[63] Wildlife and Countryside Act 1981, s 28I(6).
[64] See Circular 05/06, para 66.
[65] *Kent County Council v Secretary of State for the Environment* (1976) 33 P & CR 70.
[66] 21a-013-20140306.
[67] Town and Country Planning Act 1990, s 79(1)(a).
[68] See the Joint Planning Law Conference paper by Kiely [2015] JPL OP39 at OP45–46.
[69] See Public Bill Committee, 8 December 2015 (am).

11.52 *Planning conditions*

on the conditions proposed in a committee report – from whatever source – should be considered. Some conditions may be proposed by consultees, such as highways, environmental health, contamination and archaeology. The planning authority must take responsibility for deciding whether any conditions sought by public bodies should be included or amended or omitted. If it proposes not to follow a statutory consultee's advice on conditions it is prudent to give that consultee a warning and opportunity to respond, unless the change is one made at the committee meeting.

11.52 On appeal or call-in, the applicant and the local planning authority should attempt to agree a list of conditions, in conjunction with any relevant statutory consultee. If possible, the draft should be included in the statement of common ground (noting any disagreements) and if not, should be made available to third parties who are interested. At a hearing or inquiry there will then be a discussion, led by the inspector, into conditions in which all parties are able to take part.

Chapter 12

Planning obligations

12.1 One means of controlling activity on land is by an agreement between the landowner and the local planning authority. Agreements which bind the land and are for planning purposes have been known as planning agreements and since the 1991 reforms are more broadly called planning obligations. Whilst these do not have any necessary connection with planning applications they are usually entered into to secure a grant of planning permission.

12.2 The need for legislation is two-fold. First, a public authority must always act with statutory authority and entering into agreements for a public purpose needs to have a sound legal base. Second, a local authority, which takes restrictive covenants from a land owner in its area for public purposes, cannot enforce those covenants against a successor in title of the original covenantor, because it possesses no land entitled to the benefit of the covenant[1]. Consequently planning legislation since the Town and Country Planning Act 1990 has included agreement- or obligation-making powers which bind successors in title.

SECTION 106 PLANNING OBLIGATIONS

12.3 Persons interested in land may enter into a planning obligation under the Town and Country Planning Act 1990, s 106 requiring them to do or refrain from doing various matters on site or to make payments for off-site activity. A planning obligation is contained in a deed made by a person interested in land in the area of a local planning authority[2]:

'(a) restricting the development or use of the land in any specified way;

(b) requiring specified operations or activities to be carried out in, on, under or over the land;

(c) requiring the land to be used in any specified way; or

(d) requiring a sum or sums to be paid to the authority (or, in a case where section 2E applies, to the Greater London Authority) on a specified date or dates or periodically'.

The obligation may either be signed by those involved in the land alone (a unilateral obligation) or in addition signed by the local planning authority (a planning

---

[1] *London County Council v Allen* [1914] 3 KB 642. The Council had entered into a covenant purportedly binding the landowner, his heirs and assigns and other persons claiming under him not to build on a particular plot without the Council's consent, as part of the authority approving the laying out of a new street on the land under the London Building Act 1894.

[2] Town and Country Planning Act 1990, s 106(1).

12.4 *Planning obligations*

agreement)[3]. The documents are often referred to as s 106 obligations or also, in the latter case, as s 106 agreements.

An obligation may only be made by a person who is interested in land within the area of the local planning authority. It will only bind that interest and do so in respect of the land which is identified in the obligation.

Separate legal issues arise as to whether a document is a lawful planning obligation and whether it is relevant to the determination of a planning application.

Planning obligations contained in a deed

12.4 Whilst the deed made under s 106 is commonly referred to as the planning obligation, the obligation is an individual requirement within s 106(1) contained in the deed[4]. The probable position, therefore, is that a deed can contain several different planning obligations. Usually the distinction between the whole deed and individual planning obligations within the deed does not matter – and is irrelevant when a new obligation/deed is made – but can have significance when an obligation is to be enforced, modified or discharged, as different obligations in the same deed may be enforceable against different people.

The limits of planning obligations

12.5 A requirement is only a planning obligation if it contains one or more of the matters in s 106(1). The first three sub-paragraphs of the section either require things to be done on the land subjected to the obligation or prohibit their being done. Sub-paragraph (d) concerns the payment of money to the authority.

12.6 Section 106(1) does have limitations. An obligation on the owner of a proposed flat not to apply for a residents permit to park on the street, to surrender any such permit, to advertise the property as not having permits and to prohibit applications for such permits in leases were held to be outside sub-s (1) and so not a planning obligation[5].

12.7 The subsection does not refer to the transfer of land, whether to the local planning authority or another person. However a land transfer may be included or required by a planning obligation if it is part of meeting one or more of the sub-paragraphs. For example, the transfer of proposed public open space to a council may be part of ensuring that the land is used as public open space. In *R v South Northamptonshire District Council, ex p Crest Homes plc*[6] a planning agreement fell within s 106(1)(a) and (c) where it required land to be leased to trustees 'in

---

[3] In two-tier local government areas, district and county councils can sign as local planning authorities regardless of which authority determines any related planning application: see *Oxfordshire County Council v Secretary of State for Communities and Local Government* [2015] EWHC 186 (Admin), [2015] JPL 846 at paras 32–34 per Lang J.
[4] Town and Country Planning Act 1990, s 106(4) refers to the 'instrument by which a planning obligation is entered into'.
[5] *Westminster City Council v Secretary of State for Communities and Local Government* [2013] EWHC 690 (Admin) at paras 21–23 per Belinda Bucknall QC.
[6] [1994] 3 PLR 47 at 64 per Henry LJ. Endorsed in *Tesco Stores v Secretary of State for the Environment* [1995] 1 WLR 749.

order to make suitable provision for public open space within the development and to provide suitable amenities for future occupiers of the development'. The critical question may be whether any of a particular obligation is within the section and if so, then elements which are part of achieving that objective are lawful. This can be contrasted with *Westminster*, where none of the parking permit restriction was within s 106. Provided that the object of the planning obligation is within s 106, ancillary provisions which help to give effect to it might also be permitted by the authority's general powers: *R (on the application of Millgate Developments Ltd) v Wokingham Borough Council* per Pill LJ[7]:

'Councils have powers to conduct contractual negotiations. The undertaking is enforceable by way of private law principles. In any event, without full argument, it appears to me that a repayment would be incidental in circumstances such as these to the planning powers of the council (section 111, Local Government Act 1972)'.

12.8 In addition, a planning obligation must be made for a planning purpose and not be irrational in a *Wednesbury* sense. For the obligation to be lawful it does not have to fairly and reasonably relate to particular development which has been permitted, unlike a planning condition[8]. In *Good v Epping Forest District Council* the Court of Appeal held that the previous regime of agreements under the Town and Country Planning Act 1971, s 52 was not controlled by the limits on the power to impose conditions: it needed simply to be for the purpose of restricting or regulating the development or use of land (as s 52 provided) and be made with due regard to relevant considerations and not be *Wednesbury* unreasonable[9].

12.9 However, whether an obligation is lawful is a separate question from whether it is material to a particular planning application; for the latter situation see *Tesco Stores v Secretary of State for the Environment*[10] and the Community Infrastructure Levy Regulations 2010, regs 122 and 123, which are discussed further below.

Unilateral imposition of land or obligations

12.10 A planning obligation may not impose an obligation on a person who is neither a party to its making nor who derives their title from such a person. It is therefore not possible for a unilateral obligation to impose any obligations or restrictions upon a local planning authority, whilst an agreement which the authority has signed can do so. For example, a unilateral obligation may not require a local planning authority to act reasonably in determining works of maintenance[11]. It was suggested, *obiter*, by the High Court in *Wimpey Homes Holdings Ltd v Secretary of State for the Environment*[12] that a unilateral obligation could not compel a local planning authority to accept land. The court did consider that an obligation to pay money to the authority could be unilateral[13].

---

[7] [2011] EWCA Civ 1062, [2012] JPL 25 at para 35.
[8] For planning conditions see *Newbury District Council v Secretary of State for the Environment* [1981] AC 578 at 618 per Lord Scarman.
[9] [1994] 1 WLR 376 at 386 per Ralph Gibson LJ, endorsing decisions of Roch J in *R v Gillingham Borough Council, ex p Parham Ltd* (1987) 58 P & CR 73 and Popplewell J in *R v Wealden District Council, ex p Charles Church South East Ltd* (1989) 59 P & CR 73.
[10] [1995] 1 WLR 749.
[11] *Smith v Secretary of State for the Environment, Transport and the Regions* [2003] EWCA Civ 262, [2003] JPL 1316 at para 62 per Sedley LJ.
[12] [1993] JPL 919.
[13] *Wimpey* at 921.

12.11 Planning obligations

12.11 However whilst a unilateral obligation can provide for the payment of money to a local planning authority, it cannot require the authority to spend that money for a particular purpose or in a particular way. Consequently if the payment is required to overcome a planning object to an application, it cannot be established that the money will be used to overcome the objection. Developers may attempt to address this difficulty by making the payment conditional upon the Council agreeing to spend the money in a particular way, and perhaps to repay the money with interest if it is not spent. Of course, if the authority is not willing to use the money for those purposes then the planning harm will not be overcome. Additionally where a land transfer is involved the obligation is incomplete, as it depends on such an agreement which will not then be in place[14].

12.12 The following provisions, which commonly appear in obligations, are not able to be used unilaterally:

- any requirement for the local planning authority to carry out works or to spend sums received on particular works or for particular purposes;
- any requirement to pay back sums received under the planning obligation if they are not spent for particular purposes in a specified time;
- clauses requiring disputes to be referred to arbitration or any other dispute resolution mechanism, such as mediation;
- any requirement on the authority to act reasonably or within a particular time, such as when approving details under the obligation. Whilst an authority must always exercise a discretion reasonably in *Wednesbury* terms, it cannot be unilaterally bound to act reasonably in a contractual sense

12.13 Obligations can provide for payments to the local planning authority on the basis of the authority subsequently agreeing to their use for a particular purpose, backed if necessary by a negative term in the obligation restricting an element of the development until there has been agreement on its use or the money has been spent.

Unlawful elements of planning obligations are in principle capable of being excised[15].

These problems can all be avoided if the obligation is entered into by agreement with the Council.

Interests in land

12.14 To be a planning obligation the document must bind an interest in the land to which the obligation relates. If no parties to the deed have an interest in relevant land then it is not a planning obligation at all. Such an agreement would be contractually binding but it would not fall within s 106. A planning obligation may have some parties who do not have an interest in that land; they will be bound in

---

[14] See *Wimpey* at 921 on land transfers.
[15] *R v Somerset County Council and ARC Southern Ltd* [1998] Env LR 111 at 125 per Sedley J. One approach is of blue-pencilling only 'so much as exceeds the law-maker's power' if it 'leaves in place a valid text which is capable of operating and was evidently intended to operate independently of the invalid text': *DPP v Hutchinson* [1990] 2 AC 783 at 811 per Lord Bridge.

contract[16]. However such general contractual obligations do not bind such parties' successors in title[17]. A planning obligation could be made by a person who owns an interest in any land within the authority's area, even if it is not relevant land under the proposed planning permission[18], but that raises the question of the value of such an obligation.

12.15 The meaning of 'interested in the land' varies depending upon the statutory context and has never been finally identified in planning obligations. The Court of Appeal held in *Pennine Raceway* that 'person interested in the land' for the right to compensation for the revocation of planning permission extended to a person with a licence and beyond those with a conveyancing interest[19]. Eveleigh LJ suggested, *obiter*, in that case that such a wider approach might be taken to the forerunner to planning obligations, s 52 agreements[20]. The debate, however, is of limited practical significance, which may explain the lack of a resolution to the point. Unless a planning obligation binds the interests which might develop the land then it will not be acceptable. Consequently an obligation is not likely to be made solely by a mere licensee. A problem which does arise in practice is whether a planning obligation may be made by a local planning authority as landowner which would be enforceable by itself. The general view has been that an authority may not contract with itself. In two-tier areas, authorities have sometimes made obligations which would be enforceable by the other local planning authority. Where land is being disposed of, contracts with the subsequent purchasers have been used to contain what would be in planning obligations, but at best this latter approach lacks transparency. An amendment to the Housing and Planning Bill to give local planning authorities an express power to make planning obligations as landowner, enforceable by themselves, was proposed by Stephen Hammond MP to the Housing and Planning Bill, but at the time of writing has not been adopted by Ministers[21].

12.16 The obligation must identify 'the land in which the person entering into the obligation is interested'[22]. This is the land which is to be subject to the obligation, not any other land in the authority's area in which the person has an interest. The identification of the land must be unambiguous and will usually be by its name or description, a plan and any Land Registry title numbers. As with any identification of land in a document, there needs to be clarity as to whether the description or the plans prevail. The plans should be carefully checked and signed by the parties, as they have a habit of becoming separated from the text.

12.17 Then the obligation must also identify the person entering into the obligation and state what his interest in the land is[23]. Again, the identity of the parties should be

---

[16] *Southampton City Council v Hallyard Ltd* [2008] EWHC 916 (Ch), [2008] JPL 1440 at para 54 per Morgan J. In that case a planning obligation required the developer of one site to pay an affordable housing contribution to the developer of another site. The latter developer agreed to only spend the money on providing additional affordable housing on that site. The obligation only applied to the first site and so the receiving developer was bound in contract, not under s 106. The court left open the possibility that the recipient might be subject to a *Quistclose* trust (*Barclays Bank Ltd v Quistclose Investments Ltd* [1970] AC 567), see *Hallyard* at para 62.
[17] *Hallyard* at para 61.
[18] See *Hallyard* at para 63.
[19] *Pennine Raceway Ltd v Kirklees Metropolitan Borough Council* [1983] QB 382.
[20] At 389.
[21] See Public Bill Committee, 8 December 2015 (am).
[22] Town and Country Planning Act 1990, s 109(b).
[23] Town and Country Planning Act 1990, s 106(9)(c).

12.18 Planning obligations

correct and unambiguous. The most common problem is the naming of companies. Often the landowner will be a different company to the applicant for planning permission, even if both are in the same group. The correct names must be used and, for example, the omission of 'limited' might make it unclear who the party actually is. It is helpful for company registration numbers to be included, along with the country of any non-British companies and an address for service. It is vital that the current Land Register entries for the land are checked by the local planning authority or that title is demonstrated for unregistered land. It has been known for 'planning obligations' to be submitted by persons who do not have an interest in the land or whose legal identity is unclear.

12.18 An obligation ought to bind all the interests against whom it might have to be enforced. Conventionally this will include the freeholder, any long leaseholder and any mortgagee of the property. An existing mortgagee will not be bound by the obligation unless they have agreed to it, a problem which would arise if they go into possession. There may be circumstances in which an obligation will still work sufficiently if only some of the interests are bound, but these need to be considered on a case-by-case basis. For example, if the applicant only controls part of a site, then an obligation might be agreed on the part which she owns (or whose owners she can get to agree). If that is the only part of the site which requires works under the obligation, then that might be effective. Similarly, an obligation to pay money could bind part of the site provided that the remainder cannot in practice be developed under the planning permission without that part. If an obligation controls a temporary development it might be sufficient for a long leaseholder to be a party without the freeholder. In all such cases, planning obligations need to be considered with care to ensure that the planning authority's objectives can be achieved.

FORMAL REQUIREMENTS

12.19 Several formal requirements apply to the making of planning obligations. Whilst formal, a failure to comply may have important consequences.

Deed

12.20 First, a planning obligation 'may not be entered into except by an instrument executed as a deed'[24].

Identification of the nature of the obligation

12.21 The obligation must state that it 'is a planning obligation for the purposes of' the Town and Country Planning Act 1990, s 106[25]. There may be a question as to whether a deed could as a matter of construction be a planning obligation even if this statement is omitted. A complication is that a planning obligation is a public document and ought not to be construed by reference to private documents or knowledge.

---

[24] Town and Country Planning Act 1990, s 106(9).
[25] Town and Country Planning Act 1990, s 109(9)(a).

Formal requirements **12.27**

12.22 If the obligation is a development consent obligation, made in connection with a development consent order authorising a nationally significant infrastructure project, it should say so[26].

12.23 A planning obligation is binding only if it is executed. A planning obligation is required to be entered into by 'an instrument executed as a deed' which[27]:

'(a) states that the obligation is a planning obligation for the purposes of this section;

(b) identifies the land in which the person entering into the obligation is interested;

(c) identifies the person entering into the obligation and states what his interest in the land is; and

(d) identifies the local planning authority by whom the obligation is enforceable'.

12.24 A deed must comply with the Law of Property (Miscellaneous Provisions) Act 1989, s 1(2):

'An instrument shall not be a deed unless:

(a) it makes it clear on its face that it is intended to be a deed by the person making it or, as the case may be, by the parties to it (whether by describing itself as a deed or expressing itself to be executed or signed as a deed or otherwise); and

(b) it is validly executed as a deed by that person or, as the case may be, one or more of those parties'.

12.25 If a deed is made by an individual it is only validly executed if[28]:

'(a) it is signed:

(i) by him in the presence of a witness who attests the signature; or

(ii) at his direction and in his presence and the presence of two witnesses who each attest the signature; and

(b) it is delivered as a deed by him or a person authorised to do so on his behalf'.

12.26 A company will execute a deed either by affixing its common seal to the document, or the document being signed by a director and the company secretary or by two directors of the company, alternatively is signed by a single director in the presence of a witness who attests the signature[29]. Where the director or secretary is a partnership, the signature may be from an individual authorised by the firm to sign on its behalf[30]. Delivery of the deed is required but this is presumed on execution, unless the contrary is shown[31].

12.27 A planning obligation which provides for the transfer of land must comply with the Law of Property (Miscellaneous Provisions) Act 1989, s 2[32]. This requires all the terms agreed to be incorporated in the obligation or documents referred to in

---

[26] Town and Country Planning Act 1990, s 106(9)(aa).
[27] Town and Country Planning Act 1990, s 106(9).
[28] Law of Property (Miscellaneous Provisions) Act 1989, s 1(3).
[29] Companies Act 2006, s 44. Where the director is itself a company, the authority of the person signing for that company needs to be established.
[30] Companies Act 2006, s 44(7).
[31] Companies Act 2006, s 46(1), (2).
[32] *Jelson Ltd v Derby City Council* [1999] 3 EGLR 91.

12.28 *Planning obligations*

the obligation. Where a planning obligation provides for the transfer of an interest in land to a third party, such as a registered social landlord, there is no need for that third party to be a party to the planning obligation. Section 2 requires the signature of the parties to the contract (here the obligation) not future parties to a conveyance proposed by the contract[33].

12.28 An obligation may be entered into on a counterparty basis, that is, various copies may collectively contain the signatures or seals of the different parties but there is no single document which contains all the signatures or seals. In such cases the originals of all of the versions should be delivered to the local planning authority. Whilst the Planning Inspectorate discourages the use of counterparty documents[34], they are a common and permissible commercial practice.

12.29 As a matter of practice, any obligation must be executed before the planning decision is issued[35]. Whilst a landowner could enter into the obligation at a later date, there is no leverage to force that to be done, short of bringing judicial review proceedings against the grant of planning permission due to the absence of a planning obligation.

Publicity and consultation on planning obligations

12.30 A planning obligation is usually negotiated between the landowner/developer parties and the local planning authority, even if it is made unilaterally. Where the Mayor of London has become the local planning authority for a planning application he has the function of agreeing the planning obligation, in the sense of determining whether it is acceptable[36]. However, before doing so the Mayor must consult the local planning authority[37].

12.31 Fairness may require that other persons are given an opportunity to comment on the proposed terms of a planning obligation. In *R (on the application of Lichfield Securities Ltd) v Lichfield District Council*[38] the claimant had paid over £3 million towards local road improvements under planning obligations. It objected to a planning application on a neighbouring site unless that scheme made an appropriate contribution to those road costs. Such a contribution would ultimately affect the level of Lichfield Securities' contribution. Despite several meetings, the Council refused to let Lichfield Securities know the formula and level of contribution being discussed until after the obligation was made and the permission granted. The Court of Appeal held that it was unfair to Lichfield Securities to exclude them from the decision

---

[33] *R G Kensington Management Co Ltd v Hutchinson IDH Ltd* [2003] 2 P & CR 13 at paras 56–58 per Neuberger J, followed for planning obligations in *Milebush Properties Ltd v Tameside Metropolitan Borough Council* [2010] EWHC 1022 (Ch), [2010] JPL 1303 at 1317 per Arnold J.
[34] *Procedural Guide Planning appeals – England* para N.5.4. The Inspectorate's approach has been criticised by David Brock *Why do we need the Planning Inspectorate's guidance on planning agreements?* www.localgovernmentlawyer.co.uk, 5 February 2014.
[35] It has happened that the text of a planning obligation has been agreed, planning permission issued but the obligation never entered into. See, for example, *R (on the application of Carroll) v South Somerset District Council* [2008] EWHC 104 (Admin), [2008] JPL 991, where the local planning authority had to arrange for its leader to judicially review the grant of permission as the obligation had not been made.
[36] Town and Country Planning Act 1990, s 2E(2).
[37] Town and Country Planning Act 1990, s 2E(4).
[38] [2001] EWCA Civ 304, [2001] PLCR 32.

Legality and the relationship with planning permission **12.34**

which affected them and that the formula and sum had been agreed between the Council and developer before those meetings[39].

Local policy or representations may give rise to a legitimate expectation that other persons would be consulted upon a proposed obligation.

12.32 Part I of the planning register must contain a 'copy of any planning obligation or section 278 agreement [under the Highways Act 1980] proposed or entered into in connection with the [planning] application'[40]. A proposed obligation is in this context a draft, but does not have to await the draft reaching its final form prior to execution[41]. Ouseley J has commented[42]:

> 'The section 106 agreement is not a private agreement to be revealed only when it is concluded, any more than conditions are a matter exclusively for private negotiation and debate, to the exclusion of the public. I accept there may be room for debate as to whether every draft needs to be registered for the terms and purpose of the legislation to be complied with, although all significant changes should be. I do not rule out that there may be some parts of the draft which may involve negotiations akin to without prejudice negotiations which for a while it may be legitimate not to publicise. I recognise that a new draft does not come into existence with each change made by an officer for his own internal purposes before it is sent out to the other side, where undoubtedly it would become a new draft. Not every proposed change to a clause may create a new draft, but for all that the judgment which the District Council is required to exercise is one which is intended to enable public participation and comment on a draft before it is set and executed. It is a question of judgment which must be exercised with the purpose of the statute in mind'.

LEGALITY AND THE RELATIONSHIP WITH PLANNING PERMISSION

12.33 As mentioned above, there are two separate questions of legality which can arise:

(i) whether the obligation is lawful;

(ii) whether, if lawful, the obligation can be taken into account in the determination of a particular planning application.

A planning obligation will be lawful if it complies with the formalities in s 106 and those of deeds, is for a planning purpose and is not *Wednesbury* unreasonable.

12.34 Planning obligations are usually made in connection with the grant of planning permission. The courts have displayed some caution about the relevance of planning obligations to planning applications. Lord Keith of Kinkel said in *Tesco Stores Ltd v Secretary of State for the Environment*[43]:

---

[39] See paras 4–6, 18–27.
[40] Town and Country Planning (Development Management Procedure) (England) Order 2015, SI 2015/595, art 40(3)(b). Once planning permission is issued a copy of any completed planning obligation or s 278 agreement shall be put on part 2 of the register: DMPO 2015, art 40(4)(f).
[41] *R (on the application of Midcounties Co-operative Ltd) v Wyre Forest District Council* [2009] EWHC 964 (Admin) at para 87 per Ouseley J.
[42] *Midcounties* at para 90.
[43] [1995] 1 WLR 759 at 770. There is a very useful discussion of the policy and case law background in Lord Hoffmann's speech at 771–783.

12.35 *Planning obligations*

'An offered planning obligation which has nothing to do with the proposed development, apart from the fact that it is offered by the developer, will plainly not be a material consideration and could be regarded only as an attempt to buy planning permission. If it has some connection with the proposed development which is not de minimis, then regard must be had to it'.

Regulation 122

12.35 The content of a planning obligation (or proposed obligation) must satisfy the tests in regulation 122(2) of the Community Infrastructure Levy Regulations 2010 to be relevant to the determination of a planning application[44]:

'A planning obligation may only constitute a reason for granting planning permission for the development if the obligation is:

(a) necessary to make the development acceptable in planning terms;

(b) directly related to the development; and

(c) fairly and reasonably related in scale and kind to the development'.

12.36 The necessity test had previously just been contained in policy[45]. Being directly related and fairly and reasonably related in scale and kind were, in substance, existing legal tests[46]. As Bean J observed in *R (on the application of Welcome Break Group Ltd) v Stroud District Council* 'There is nothing novel in regulation 122 except the fact that it is contained in a statutory instrument'[47]. Whether an obligation is necessary is a matter for the planning decision maker, subject to public law review by the court[48]. Richards LJ said in *R (on the application of Hampton Bishop Parish Council) v Herefordshire Council*[49] 'regulation 122 can be seen as part of a codification of principles developed in the case law'.

12.37 A classic example of an offer that cannot properly be taken into account as a material consideration was given in *R v Westminster Council, ex p Monahan*[50], where a developer wished to erect an office building at one end of the town and offered to build a swimming-pool at the other end. Staughton LJ described this as being little different from offering the planning authority a cheque so that it can build the swimming-pool for itself provided the developer has permission for his office development. In that case there is no real connection between the benefits and the development[51].

---

[44] Statutory guidance on the operation of the CIL Regulations is given in the *Planning Practice Guidance*, see Planning Act 2008, s 221.
[45] Circular 05/05 *Planning Obligations*, para B5. This circular was revoked by the National Planning Policy Framework, Annex 3.
[46] *Tesco Stores Ltd v Secretary of State for the Environment* [1995] 1 WLR 759, HL.
[47] [2012] EWHC 140 (Admin) at para 48.
[48] See *Tesco Stores* per Lord Hoffmann, applied to reg 122 in *Welcome Break* at para 50.
[49] [2014] EWCA Civ 878, [2015] 1 WLR 2367 at para 46. A more interesting question would be whether the transfer, which contained no restrictions on use of the ground, fell within s 106(1). For another case relating development to sports grounds see *R (on the application of Derwent Holdings Ltd) v Trafford Borough Council* [2011] EWCA Civ 832 (concerning Old Trafford Cricket Ground).
[50] [1990] 1 QB 87 at 122C.
[51] *R (Sainsbury's Supermarkets Ltd) v Wolverhampton City Council* [2010] UKSC 20, [2011] 1 AC 437 at para 70 per Lord Collins of Mapesbury.

12.38 A direct connection was found between the grant of planning permission for a new rugby ground, funded by housing, and the transfer of the existing ground to the local planning authority for nominal consideration in *Hampton Bishop Parish Council*[52] since the future of the old ground was a land use consequence of the move.

12.39 In *Oxfordshire County Council v Secretary of State for Communities and Local Government*[53] Lang J upheld an inspector's decision that a fee for the monitoring, assessment and enforcement of a planning obligation was not necessary under reg 122. It had been a standardised fee for straightforward payments and whether such fees were recoverable in other situations was left open.

12.40 There may be dispute about whether various obligations, in particular financial contributions, are required. On a planning appeal a developer may put forward the obligation which it considers appropriate. However, if that is thought to be insufficient then an inspector will ordinarily dismiss the appeal[54]. To address that risk a developer may put forward an obligation with a 'blue pencil' clause that various requirements will have, or not have, effect depending upon the inspector's conclusions. A potential clause is[55]:

> 'If the Planning Inspector, in this Decision Letter, concludes that any of the planning obligations set out in the Deed are incompatible with any one of the tests for planning obligations set out at Regulation 122 of the CIL Regulations, and accordingly attached no weight to that obligation in determining the appeal then the relevant obligation shall, from the date of the decision letter, cease to have effect and the Owner and the Developer shall be under no obligation to comply with them'.

Regulation 123

12.41 Regulation 123 imposes two restrictions on the materiality of planning obligations as part of the introduction of the Community Infrastructure Levy. The first is in reg 123(2) where planning permission is granted after the relevant charging authority's first charging schedule takes effect[56]:

> 'A planning obligation may not constitute a reason for granting planning permission for the development to the extent that the obligation provides for the funding or provision of relevant infrastructure'.

12.42 'Relevant infrastructure' is defined as[57]:

> '(a) where a charging authority has published on its website a list of infrastructure projects or types of infrastructure that it intends will be, or may be, wholly or partly funded by CIL (other than CIL to which regulation 59E or 59F applies), those infrastructure projects or types of infrastructure, or
>
> (b) where no such list has been published, any infrastructure'.

---

[52] [2014] EWCA Civ 878, [2015] 1 WLR 2367 at para 50.
[53] [2015] EWHC 186 (Admin), [2015] JPL 846 at para 53.
[54] On a call-in or recovered appeal the Minister might issue an interim decision that he is 'minded to' grant planning permission if the draft obligation is changed or a completed obligation supplemented.
[55] Used in the planning obligation in *Oxfordshire County Council v Secretary of State for Communities and Local Government* [2015] EWHC 186 (Admin), [2015] JPL 846 see para 9.
[56] Community Infrastructure Levy Regulations 2010, SI 2010/948, reg 123(1), (4) defines the relevant date for these purposes.
[57] Community Infrastructure Levy Regulations 2010, reg 123(4). Regulations 59E and 59F concern funding that would have gone to local councils.

12.43 *Planning obligations*

12.43 The intention of reg 123(2) is to prevent a planning obligation and a CIL charge from covering the same matters, what is sometimes referred to as 'double-dipping'. Regulation 123(2A) similarly prohibits the use of planning conditions which by positive or negative terms require the making of highways agreements under the Highways Act 1980, s 278 for the funding or carrying out of works in a highway[58]. In regs 122 and 123 'a reason for granting planning permission' includes an obligation which would otherwise be seen as being necessary to overcome a reason for refusal. Since an obligation which offered an unnecessary benefit would be irrelevant under reg 122, reg 123 is concerned with obligations which would otherwise be necessary to overcome a planning objection.

12.44 Second, reg123(3) discourages the use of a series of planning obligations to finance a particular project or type of infrastructure:

'A planning obligation ("obligation A") may not constitute a reason for granting planning permission to the extent that—

(a) obligation A provides for the funding or provision of an infrastructure project or type of infrastructure; and

(b) five or more separate planning obligations that:

(i) relate to planning permissions granted for development within the area of the charging authority; and

(ii) which provide for the funding or provision of that project, or type of infrastructure,

have been entered into on or after 6th April 2010'.

Paragraph (3) applies either if a CIL charging schedule has been adopted or from 6 April 2015, whichever is the earlier date.[59]

12.45 Both provisions refer to the 'funding or provision of relevant infrastructure'. 'Funding' is defined as 'the provision of that infrastructure by way of funding'[60]. This is much narrower than the potential use of CIL charges for 'funding the provision, improvement, replacement, operation or maintenance of infrastructure' as is permitted by the Planning Act 2008, s 216(1). In contrast, reg 123 not only refers solely to provision but confines funding to 'provision'. Whilst provision would encompass improvement or replacement, the latter two simply need there to be something there already, it is different to operation or maintenance. Operational or maintenance funding is therefore outside reg 123[61].

12.46 References to projects or types of infrastructure are used in reg 123(3) and the definition of relevant infrastructure in reg 123(4). Infrastructure projects and types are alternatives. As a matter of ordinary language an infrastructure project will be within one or more types of infrastructure, so the reference to projects in the list will be otiose unless the use of 'or' means that they are separate. If a list says that CIL will be spent on improving pedestrian and cycle provision then that is a

---

[58] Unless the highway agreement would be with the Minister or Transport for London: Community Infrastructure Levy Regulations 2010, reg 123(2B).
[59] Community Infrastructure Levy Regulations 2010, reg 123(1), (4).
[60] Community Infrastructure Levy Regulations 2010, reg 123(4).
[61] To take a common example, site access and management measures for Special Areas of Conservation or Special Protection Areas.

type of infrastructure, but the identification of a particular route to be improved for pedestrians and cyclists will be an infrastructure project

12.47 It is long established that whilst planning policy has encouraged the use of conditions in preference to obligations[62], it is lawful to enter into an obligation when a condition could be used[63]. The inclusion of the necessity test in reg 122 does not undermine this principle: what the obligation provides may be necessary even though it was not necessary to use an obligation to require it.

Submission of planning obligations and heads of terms in planning applications

12.48 It is sensible for applicants to discuss potential planning obligations at an early stage and they may wish to have an understanding of the likely requirements in pre-application advice[64]. Draft heads of terms could only be required to be submitted with a planning application if they satisfy the applicable local list provisions[65]. It is hard to see how it can be a reasonable requirement to insist upon a draft or completed planning obligation to be submitted with an application which might not be approved. Draft heads of terms ought to be settled (and hopefully agreed with council officers) prior to the decision whether to approve the application. Committee members and the public need to know what in substance the developer is proposing and what officers consider is necessary, prior to a resolution on the application. If there is disagreement, that might be a reason for refusal.

12.49 A model planning obligation has been prepared by the Law Society's Planning and Environmental Law Committee. This contains standard boilerplate text for the structure of an obligation as well as wording for particular contributions. The current version is the second edition, prepared in 2010[66]. The model may be of assistance, although it needs to be used with care[67].

Submission of planning obligations and heads of terms in planning appeals

12.50 The Planning Inspectorate's guidance deadlines for the receipt of planning obligations, including drafts are:

(i) written representations cases: an executed and certified copy to be received no later than seven weeks from the start date[68];

---

[62] And continues to do so, see the National Planning Policy Framework, para 203, *Planning Practice Guidance* 21a-011-20140306.
[63] On s 52 agreements, see *Good v Epping Forest District Council* [1994] 1 WLR 376 at 386 per Ralph Gibson LJ.
[64] This is encouraged by the *Planning Practice Guidance*, para 23b-025-20150326.
[65] See Chapter 6, above. The *Planning Practice Guidance* advises at para 14-042-20140306:

> 'So while it can be good practice to submit information about a proposed planning obligation alongside an application, it should not normally be a requirement for validation of a planning application. If they are to go on the local list, the local planning authority should be able to justify their inclusion in relation to any particular development'.

[66] Available on the Law Society website.
[67] It does not reflect subsequent case law, in particular the *Westminster* decision on residents' parking permits which is discussed above.
[68] *Procedural Guide Planning appeals – England*, 31 July 2015, para N.2.1.

12.51 *Planning obligations*

(ii) hearings and inquiries: a final draft, ideally agreed by all parties, not later than ten working days before the hearing or inquiry opens[69]. The obligation should normally be executed before the hearing or inquiry closes, without the need for an adjournment, but if this is not practicable then arrangements for the receipt of the executed obligation will be agreed at the hearing[70]. It will be difficult to settle the terms of and execute an obligation during a one day hearing or inquiry.

Executed or draft obligations may be received later, but in written representation cases there is a risk that the appeal will be determined without regard to a late obligation and late documentation may complicate or delay the conclusion of a hearing.

12.51 Only copies of the executed planning obligation should be sent to the Inspectorate, not the original obligation. The Inspectorate asks for a council officer, usually its solicitor, to certify the submitted copy[71]. Certification by the local planning authority is necessary for written representations cases as the obligation will only take effect on delivery, so that needs to be shown. If a copy of the executed obligation is handed to the inspector in a hearing or inquiry then oral confirmation from the authority that it has received the obligation is sufficient. If counterpart documents are used (so no document contains all of the necessary signatures) then certified copies of each counterpart should be provided[72].

12.52 Title needs to be demonstrated to the inspector's satisfaction. If a copy of the executed obligation is provided in or before the hearing or inquiry then the local planning authority's confirmation that it has checked the title is sufficient. If the obligation is provided after the close of the hearing or inquiry then the authority should be asked to confirm that title is satisfactory and that there are no new issues on the executed form of the obligation. In written representation appeals the appellant should provide evidence of title to the inspector unless the authority is able to confirm that it has checked the title on the day of execution.

12.53 Even where the developer and the local planning authority agree that the proposed obligation meets the tests in the Community Infrastructure Levy Regulations 2010, regs 122 and 123 that must still be demonstrated to the inspector. That this may be common ground has not in practice been taken to be sufficient and so the parties should refer to relevant local policy and explain, concisely, why the tests are satisfied. The Inspectorate advise that this evidence is likely to be needed[73]:

'• the relevant development plan policy or policies, and the relevant sections of any supplementary planning document or supplementary planning guidance;

• quantified evidence of the additional demands on facilities or infrastructure which are likely to arise from the proposed development;

• details of existing facilities or infrastructure, and up-to-date, quantified evidence of the extent to which they are able or unable to meet those additional demands;

---

[69] The *Procedural Guide Planning appeals – England*, para N.2.4 suggests an agreed draft but the following paragraph recognises that it might be revised as result of discussion at the hearing or inquiry.
[70] *Procedural Guide Planning appeals – England*, para N.2.5.
[71] *Procedural Guide Planning appeals – England*, para N.4.3.
[72] *Procedural Guide Planning appeals – England*, para N.5.5. The Inspectorate dislikes the use of counterparts: para N.5.4.
[73] *Procedural Guide Planning appeals – England*, para N.3.3.

- the methodology for calculating any financial contribution necessary to improve existing facilities or infrastructure, or provide new facilities or infrastructure, to meet the additional demands;
- details of the facilities or infrastructure on which any financial contribution will be spent'.

THE INTERPRETATION OF PLANNING OBLIGATIONS

12.54 The principles of contractual interpretation were summarised by Lord Hoffmann in *Investors Compensation Scheme Ltd v West Bromwich Building Society*[74]:

'The principles may be summarised as follows.

(1) Interpretation is the ascertainment of the meaning which the document would convey to a reasonable person having all the background knowledge which would reasonably have been available to the parties in the situation in which they were at the time of the contract.

(2) The background was famously referred to by Lord Wilberforce as the "matrix of fact", but this phrase is, if anything, an understated description of what the background may include. Subject to the requirement that it should have been reasonably available to the parties and to the exception to be mentioned next, it includes absolutely anything which would have affected the way in which the language of the document would have been understood by a reasonable man.

(3) The law excludes from the admissible background the previous negotiations of the parties and their declarations of subjective intent. They are admissible only in an action for rectification. The law makes this distinction for reasons of practical policy and, in this respect only, legal interpretation differs from the way we would interpret utterances in ordinary life. The boundaries of this exception are in some respects unclear. But this is not the occasion on which to explore them.

(4) The meaning which a document (or any other utterance) would convey to a reasonable man is not the same thing as the meaning of its words. The meaning of words is a matter of dictionaries and grammars; the meaning of the document is what the parties using those words against the relevant background would reasonably have been understood to mean. The background may not merely enable the reasonable man to choose between the possible meanings of words which are ambiguous but even (as occasionally happens in ordinary life) to conclude that the parties must, for whatever reason, have used the wrong words or syntax: see *Mannai Investments Co Ltd v Eagle Star Life Assurance Co Ltd* [1997] AC 749.

(5) The "rule" that words should be given their "natural and ordinary meaning" reflects the common sense proposition that we do not easily accept that people have made linguistic mistakes, particularly in formal documents. On the other hand, if one would nevertheless conclude from the background that something must have gone wrong with the language, the law does not require judges to attribute to the parties an intention which they plainly could not have had. Lord Diplock made this point more vigorously when he said in *Antaios Compania Naviera SA v Salen Rederierna AB* [1985] AC 191, 201:

"if detailed semantic and syntactical analysis of words in a commercial contract is going to lead to a conclusion that flouts business commonsense, it must be made to yield to business commonsense."'

---
[74] [1998] 1 WLR 896 at 912–913.

12.55 *Planning obligations*

12.55 These principles have been applied to the interpretation of written grants of easements[75] (which are similarly documents which run with the land) and to planning obligations[76]. More recently, Lord Neuberger of Abbotsbury PSC said in the context of interpreting a service charge provision in a lease[77]:

> 'When interpreting a written contract, the court is concerned to identify the intention of the parties by reference to "what a reasonable person having all the background knowledge which would have been available to the parties would have understood them to be using the language in the contract to mean", to quote Lord Hoffmann in *Chartbrook Ltd v Persimmon Homes Ltd* [2009] AC 1101, para 14. And it does so by focussing on the meaning of the relevant words, in this case clause 3(2) of each of the 25 leases, in their documentary, factual and commercial context. That meaning has to be assessed in the light of (i) the natural and ordinary meaning of the clause, (ii) any other relevant provisions of the lease, (iii) the overall purpose of the clause and the lease, (iv) the facts and circumstances known or assumed by the parties at the time that the document was executed, and (v) commercial common sense, but (vi) disregarding subjective evidence of any party's intentions'.

12.56 He emphasised:

> '17 First, the reliance placed in some cases on commercial common sense and surrounding circumstances ... should not be invoked to undervalue the importance of the language of the provision which is to be construed. The exercise of interpreting a provision involves identifying what the parties meant through the eyes of a reasonable reader, and, save perhaps in a very unusual case, that meaning is most obviously to be gleaned from the language of the provision. Unlike commercial common sense and the surrounding circumstances, the parties have control over the language they use in a contract. And, again save perhaps in a very unusual case, the parties must have been specifically focussing on the issue covered by the provision when agreeing the wording of that provision.
>
> 18 Secondly, when it comes to considering the centrally relevant words to be interpreted, I accept that the less clear they are, or, to put it another way, the worse their drafting, the more ready the court can properly be to depart from their natural meaning. That is simply the obverse of the sensible proposition that the clearer the natural meaning the more difficult it is to justify departing from it. However, that does not justify the court embarking on an exercise of searching for, let alone constructing, drafting infelicities in order to facilitate a departure from the natural meaning...
>
> 19 The third point I should mention is that commercial common sense is not to be invoked retrospectively. The mere fact that a contractual arrangement, if interpreted according to its natural language, has worked out badly, or even disastrously, for one of the parties is not a reason for departing from the natural language. ...
>
> 20 Fourthly, while commercial common sense is a very important factor to take into account when interpreting a contract, a court should be very slow to reject the natural meaning of a provision as correct simply because it appears to be a very imprudent term for one of the parties to have agreed, even ignoring the benefit of wisdom of hindsight. The purpose of interpretation is to identify what the parties have agreed, not what the court thinks that they should have agreed ....
>
> 21 The fifth point concerns the facts known to the parties. When interpreting a contractual provision, one can only take into account facts or circumstances which existed at the

---

[75] *Davill v Pull* [2009] EWCA Civ 1309, [2010] 1 P & CR 23 at para 28 per Rimer LJ.
[76] *Milebush Properties Ltd v Tameside Metropolitan Borough Council* [2010] EWHC 1022 (Ch), [2010] JPL 1303 at 1309.
[77] *Arnold v Britton* [2015] UKSC 36, [2015] 2 WLR 1593 at para 15.

time that the contract was made, and which were known or reasonably available to both parties. Given that a contract is a bilateral, or synallagmatic, arrangement involving both parties, it cannot be right, when interpreting a contractual provision, to take into account a fact or circumstance known only to one of the parties.

22 Sixthly, in some cases, an event subsequently occurs which was plainly not intended or contemplated by the parties, judging from the language of their contract. In such a case, if it is clear what the parties would have intended, the court will give effect to that intention ...'

12.57 Care should be taken with the use of material outside the planning obligation for its interpretation to reflect not only that it may bind persons who were not party to the original negotiations but there is an interest for the public at large to be able to understand its meaning and whether it addresses planning matters sufficiently. A planning obligation is similar to a planning permission in being a public document which regulates land use in the public interest. It is not a private arrangement. The relationship between the principles of contractual interpretation applicable to deeds and the more restrictive approach to the interpretation of planning permission[78] have not been fully worked through. However it might be thought that the text used in the obligation is of even greater importance and that any surrounding circumstances which are used for interpretation should be readily ascertainable from documents to which the public would be given access.

ENFORCEMENT OF PLANNING OBLIGATIONS

12.58 A planning obligation is enforceable by the appropriate authority (usually the local planning authority) in contract and also by statutory injunction or by going onto the land to carry out works[79]. Where the obligation has been entered into in relation to a planning application which is granted by the Mayor of London then both the Mayor and the local planning authority may enforce it[80].

MODIFICATION OR DISCHARGE OF PLANNING OBLIGATIONS

12.59 A planning obligation may be modified or discharged either by an agreement by all parties to it and the appropriate authority, or on an application made to that authority. The appropriate authority is the local planning authority or Mayor of London who are able to enforce it, or the Secretary of State for a development consent obligation[81]. Whilst a planning obligation is a deed binding land, the power of the Upper Tribunal (Lands Chamber) to discharge or modify restrictive covenants affecting land under the Law of Property Act 1925, s 84 does not apply to planning obligations made since the Planning and Compensation Act 1991 amendments[82].

---

[78] Discussed in Chapter 28.
[79] Town and Country Planning Act 1990, s 106(5), (6). For consideration of the power to enforce see *R (on the application of Millgate Developments Ltd) v Wokingham Borough Council* [2011] EWCA Civ 1062, [2012] JPL 258; *R (on the application of Renaissance Habitat Ltd) v West Berkshire Council* [2011] EWHC 434 (Admin), [2011] JPL 1209. The enforcement of planning obligations is discussed in Harwood *Planning Enforcement* (Bloomsbury Professional), Chapter 19.
[80] Town and Country Planning Act 1990, s 2E(5).
[81] Town and Country Planning Act 1990, s 106A(11). A development consent obligation is one made in connection with a development consent order for a nationally significant infrastructure project under the Planning Act 2008.
[82] Town and Country Planning Act 1990, s 106A(10).

12.60 *Planning obligations*

Modification or discharge by agreement

12.60 Modification or discharge by agreement may take place at any time. The agreement must be between the appropriate authority and 'the person or persons against whom the obligation is enforceable': s 106A(1).

Any agreement must be contained in a deed[83]. A practical complication may be for the agreement to include all the persons against whom the obligation is enforceable. On a site which has been partially developed there may be a number of new owners. That could require a large number of signatures on the variation agreement, however it is worth considering with care against whom the obligation is enforceable. Some new owners, such as purchasers of residential property, may be excluded from enforcement by the terms of the obligation. However an obligation is here an agreement and an agreement can ordinarily only be varied with the consent of all of the parties bound by it. A change in respect of one person or one part of the site may directly or indirectly affect other parties and so it will be difficult to say that an obligation is only enforceable against one person on one part of the site so the consent of other landowners is not required[84].

12.61 There is no statutory test set out for a modification or discharge by agreement. However the appropriate authority's exercise of discretion must be in accordance with public law principles[85]. The tests for applications to modify or discharge, discussed below, on the discharge of an obligation if it no longer serves a useful purpose and modification if it would serve that useful purpose equally well if modified, may be relevant.[86] It may be unreasonable for an authority to refuse to agree a modification which it will be obliged to make on a later application.

Applications for the modification or discharge of a planning obligation

12.62 Separately from modification or discharge by agreement, an application for the modification or discharge may be made by any person against whom the obligation can be enforced. Two sets of provisions deal with these applications, one general and one born out of the 2008 financial crisis.

12.63 The two powers allowing applications to be made to the appropriate authority to amend or discharge planning obligations are:

(i) an application under s 106A made after a certain period since the obligation was entered into, on a no useful purpose test;

---

[83] Town and Country Planning Act 1990, s 106A(2).
[84] See the discussion, albeit on a judicial review permission hearing, in *R (on the application of Symphony Ltd) v Reigate and Banstead Borough Council* (unreported, 17 December 2015) per Lang J.
[85] See *R (on the application of Batchelor Enterprises Ltd) v North Dorset District Council* [2003] EWHC 3006 (Admin), [2004] JPL 1222. There is no statutory duty to have regard to the development plan and so the presumption in favour of the development plan in Planning and Compulsory Purchase Act 2004, s 38(6) does not apply to the modification or discharge of a planning obligation: *R (on the application of Millgate Developments Ltd) v Wokingham Borough Council* [2011] EWCA Civ 1062, [2012] JPL 259 at para 29 per Pill LJ.
[86] See the debate in *R (on the application of Renaissance Habitat Ltd) v West Berkshire Council* [2011] EWHC 242 (Admin), [2011] JPL 1209 at paras 10, 11.

(ii) in England, an application under s 106BA, made at any time, on the basis that affordable housing contributions required by the obligation render the development unviable.

The appropriate authority is the one who is able to enforce the obligation, whether the Mayor of London, the local planning authority or, for obligations in connection with development consent orders, the Secretary of State[87].

Section 106A modification or discharge applications

12.64 These applications are governed by s 106A for the application, s 106B for appeals with various procedural requirements being in the Town and Country Planning (Modification and Discharge of Planning Obligations) Regulations 1992[88] (Planning Obligations Regulations).

12.65 An application may be made by 'a person against whom a planning obligation is enforceable'[89]. Such an application 'may not specify a modification imposing an obligation on any other person against whom the obligation is enforceable'[90] to avoid transferring or placing obligations on any other person. It is implicit that the modification may not make the obligation enforceable against additional persons. If two parties to a planning obligation wish to shift or change obligations between themselves then they can make a joint application under s 106A.

12.66 The period which must elapse before an application to modify or discharge a planning obligation under s 106A is the period prescribed by regulations or, in the absence of regulations, five years[91]. For many years no alternative period was prescribed, and this remains the case in Wales, but with a limited change in England. It might or might not be coincidence that development would have had to be begun under an associated planning permission prior to an application being made. Section 106A was therefore mainly used to try to amend or lift restrictions on land once a planning permission had been built out.

12.67 To address planning obligations made during economically stronger times, greater flexibility was introduced in 2013 to obligations which were only enforceable in England. Amendments were made to the Planning Obligations Regulations to this effect:

(i) where the planning obligation was entered into on or before 6 April 2010, a s 106A application could be made after 28 March 2013 if it was not already possible under the previous five-year rule;[92]

(ii) for planning obligations made after 6 April 2010, an application could be made five years after the date of the obligation.

---

[87] Town and Country Planning Act 1990, s 106A(11)
[88] SI 1992/2832.
[89] Town and Country Planning Act 1990, s 106A(3).
[90] Town and Country Planning Act 1990, s 106A(5).
[91] Town and Country Planning Act 1990, s 106A(3), (4).
[92] This is the result of the convoluted approach of reg 2A of the Planning Obligations Regulations (added by the Town and Country Planning (Modification and Discharge of Planning Obligations) (Amendment) (England) Regulations 2013, reg 3). The prescribed period for these obligations was set as one month after the 2013 amendments came into force, so applications could be made from that point.

12.68 *Planning obligations*

12.68 A s 106A application is subject to considerable formality. It must be made on a form provided by the appropriate authority which must contain[93]:

'(a) the name and address of the applicant;

(b) the address or location of the land to which the application relates and the nature of the applicant's interest in that land;

(c) sufficient information to enable the authority to identify the planning obligation which the applicant wishes to have modified or discharged;

(d) the applicant's reasons for applying for the modification or discharge of that obligation; and

(e) such other information as the authority consider necessary to enable them to determine the application'.

There is no prescribed or standard form, so each authority will produce its own form. An application cannot presently be submitted via the Planning Portal.

The application will also include a map identifying the land to which the obligation relates and any other information the applicant considers relevant[94].

12.69 Publicity and notification arrangements are similar to those arising for planning applications. The applicant must notify 'any person (other than the applicant) against whom, on the day 21 days before the date of the application, the planning obligation is enforceable'[95]. Reasonable steps are to be taken to identify those persons and if they are not known then a local newspaper advertisement must be placed[96]. The notice given to persons and in advertisements must be in the prescribed form[97] and the application must be accompanied by a certificate, again in the prescribed form, that notice has been given[98]. The notice will invite representations to be made to the local planning authority within 21 days.

12.70 The authority must publicise the application but unusually they have a choice between posting a site notice or serving notice on the owners[99] and occupiers of adjoining land or placing a newspaper advertisement[100]. The notice must be in the prescribed form and allow representations either within 21 days from the posting or service of the notice or 14 days from the advertisement[101]. The application and the 'relevant part' of the deed which created the planning obligation will be open for public inspection during the consultation period[102].

12.71 On an application the authority may determine[103]:

---

[93] Planning Obligations Regulations 1992, reg 3(1).
[94] Planning Obligations Regulations 1992, reg 3(2).
[95] Planning Obligations Regulations 1992, reg 4(1).
[96] Planning Obligations Regulations 1992, reg 4(3).
[97] Planning Obligations Regulations 1992, reg 4(4) and the Sch, Part 1.
[98] Planning Obligations Regulations 1992, reg 4(5) and the Sch, Part 2.
[99] The owner is the owner of the fee simple or a tenant with at least seven years remaining: Planning Obligations Regulations 1992, reg 5(4).
[100] Planning Obligations Regulations 1992, reg 5(1).
[101] Planning Obligations Regulations 1992, reg 5(2). The form is in Part 3 of the Schedule to the regulations.
[102] Planning Obligations Regulations 1992, reg 5(3).
[103] Town and Country Planning Act 1990, s 106A(6).

'(a) that the planning obligation shall continue to have effect without modification;

(b) if the obligation no longer serves a useful purpose, that it shall be discharged; or

(c) if the obligation continues to serve a useful purpose, but would serve that purpose equally well if it had effect subject to the modifications specified in the application, that it shall have effect subject to those modifications'.

12.72 It may be that a useful purpose must be a land use planning purpose[104]. It is said that a planning purpose is necessarily implied[105]:

'since the agreement could only be made in the first place for a planning purpose ... and could only be enforced by a public body acting for a public purpose under the Planning Acts. It was not exercising some private power or purely contractual power'.

12.73 Ouseley J in *Renaissance Habitat* accepted this proposition for the purpose of the case but queried whether some other public purpose or even a private purpose might suffice. He also drew attention to 'may determine' which was not an express obligation to discharge but which might be interpreted as such[106]. If the requirement of the relevant sub-paragraph is met, there may only be limited circumstances in which an authority may reasonably decline to modify or discharge the obligation.

12.74 The useful purpose is not constrained by any original development or planning permission which it was made in connection with.[107] If the original rationale has fallen away, the appropriate authority must take care before deciding whether another purpose is served, whether arising from an underlying objective (such as protecting the openness of land) or changed circumstances.

12.75 The appropriate authority is not able to amend the application: the discharge or modification must either be allowed as applied for, or the application refused[108]. Of course, the authority could agree a different modification, provided that the other parties were willing to sign a variation of the deed. One further effect of the inability of the authority to amend the application is that the application must be precise and set out the text of the modifications sought.

12.76 Understandably the application may only be determined following the end of the consultation period[109]. Notice of the decision should be given within eight weeks of the receipt of the application, unless the period is extended by written agreement between the applicant and the authority.[110] If the application is refused then the decision notice must state clearly and precisely the reasons for the decision and set out the right to appeal to the Minister[111].

---

[104] See *Batchelor* at para 26 and former Circular 05/05 para A20.
[105] *R (on the application of Renaissance Habitat Ltd) v West Berkshire Council* [2011] EWHC 242 (Admin), [2011] JPL 1209 per Ouseley J at para 10.
[106] *Renaissance Habitat* at para 11.
[107] *Renaissance Habitat* at para 32.
[108] *R (on the application of Garden and Leisure Group Ltd) v North Somerset Council* [2003] EWHC 1605 (Admin), [2004] JPL 232 at para 29 per Richards J. That this is the effect of the power of determination (s 106A(6)) is reinforced by the right of appeal not including situations where the application is approved with modifications.
[109] Planning Obligations Regulations 1992, reg 6(1).
[110] Town and Country Planning Act 1990, s 106A(7); Planning Obligations Regulations 1992, reg 6(2).
[111] Planning Obligations Regulations 1992, reg 6(3).

12.77 *Planning obligations*

12.77 The applicant may appeal if the authority has decided that the obligation should not be modified or has failed to give notice of the decision within the time for determination[112]. The appeal must be brought within six months of the authority's decision or the expiry of the determination period, subject to the ability of the Minister to allow a longer time in any particular case[113]. Any appeal must be on the form produced by the Minister[114], include the information specified on the form and be accompanied by a copy of[115]:

'(i) the application made to the local planning authority which has occasioned the appeal;

(ii) the certificate which accompanied the application in accordance with regulation 4(5);

(iii) the instrument by which the planning obligation which is the subject of the application was entered into;

(iv) any correspondence with the authority relating to the application; and

(v) the notice of decision, if any'.

12.78 Appellants and the appropriate authority have a right to be heard and so the Minister cannot insist on written representations[116]. Appeals are determined by inspectors, although the Minister is able to take over the final decision by recovering jurisdiction[117]. None of the appeal rules and regulations apply to s 106B appeals, although it would be expected the principles for planning appeals would be applied. Some s 106B appeals would run in parallel with planning appeals in any event.

Section 106BA affordable housing modification or discharge applications

12.79 One consequence of the financial crisis which began in 2008 was a dramatic reduction in residential development because developers lacked the incentive or the resources to do so. A concern of government was that affordable housing contributions, agreed in better economic times, were rendering projects unviable. A further mechanism for applying for variations to obligations was introduced in England to address this situation by s 106BA, inserted by the Growth and Infrastructure Act 2013[118]. This is additional to an agreed variation or an application to modify or discharge under s 106A. The emergency nature of the provision is underlined by these provisions in ss 106BA–106BC automatically expiring on 30 April 2016, unless their duration is extended by the Secretary of State by order[119]. In November 2015 the government set out its intention to extend these powers to 2018[120].

---

[112] Town and Country Planning Act 1990, s 106B(1).
[113] Planning Obligations Regulations 1992, reg 7(1).
[114] Planning Obligations Regulations 1992, reg 7(2)(a). Available on the Planning Portal website.
[115] Planning Obligations Regulations 1992, reg 7(2)(c). A copy of the appeal form should be sent to the appropriate authority at the time as the appeal is made: reg 7(3).
[116] Town and Country Planning Act 1990, s 106B(4). This right of appeal is not subject to the Secretary of State's ability to determine between the three modes in s 319A.
[117] Town and Country Planning Act 1990, s 106B(7), Sch 6; Planning Obligations Regulations 1992, reg 8.
[118] Town and Country Planning Act 1990, s 106BA, inserted by the Growth and Infrastructure Act 2013, s 7(1).
[119] Growth and Infrastructure Act 2013, s 7(4), (5).
[120] Spending Review and Autumn Statement 2015, para 3.109.

Section 106BA applications

12.80 An affordable housing requirement is 'a requirement relating to the provision of housing that is or is to be made available for people whose needs are not adequately served by the commercial housing market (and it is immaterial for this purpose where or by whom the housing is or is to be provided)'[121]. A person against whom an affordable housing requirement in a planning obligation is enforceable may apply under s 106BA for the requirement to be modified, replaced, removed or, if the obligation only contains affordable housing requirements, for the obligation to be discharged[122]. As with s 106A, applications are made to the appropriate authority by whom the obligation is enforceable, whether the Mayor of London, the local planning authority or the Secretary of State. However, this right does not apply if the related planning permission was granted wholly or partly on the basis of a policy for the provision of housing on rural exception sites[123], which are entirely or majority affordable housing sites on land which would not otherwise be permitted for housing[124].

If refused or not determined, such applications may be appealed to the Secretary of State, although usually for determination by an inspector[125].

12.81 Unusually the approach to an application varies depending upon whether it is the first of a subsequent application in respect of that obligation and with further variations depending upon whether it is being considered by the local planning authority or on appeal.

12.82 The test to be applied by the authority and on appeal for the first application made under s 106BA is whether 'the affordable housing requirement means that the development is not economically viable, the authority must deal with the application … so that the development becomes economically viable'[126]. Policy guidance on the test is[127]:

> 'The test for viability is that the evidence indicates that the *current* cost of building out the entire site (at today's prices) is at a level that would enable the developer to sell all the *market* units on the site (in today's market) at a rate of build out evidenced by the developer, and make a competitive return to a willing developer and a willing landowner'. (*original emphasis*)

12.83 Whilst regard must be had to this policy[128], it does not alter the statutory text. The policy does, though, emphasise a point in the legislation: that the viability test concerns current costs and values rather than speculation about future figures. Applicants will need to produce a viability appraisal, showing that the scheme could not proceed on the current affordable housing figures and what, if any, level of

---

[121] Town and Country Planning Act 1990, s 106BA(13). This definition, which is a more concise but essentially overlapping term to the NPPF, Annex 2 definition of affordable housing, can be amended by the Secretary of State by order: s 106BA(14).
[122] Town and Country Planning Act 1990, s 106BA(2).
[123] Town and Country Planning Act 1990, s 106BA(12).
[124] See NPPF, para 54 and Annex 2: Glossary.
[125] Town and Country Planning Act 1990, s 106BC.
[126] Town and Country Planning Act 1990, s 106BA(3).
[127] *Section 106 affordable housing requirements Review and appeal*, para 10. Published by the Secretary of State in April 2013 and referenced by the *Planning Practice Guidance* para 23b-009-20140306.
[128] Town and Country Planning Act 1990, s 106BA(8).

12.84 *Planning obligations*

affordable housing could be afforded. If one was produced with the original planning application then encouragement is given to revise that assessment, explaining the differences[129].

12.84 Application procedure is dealt with to a limited degree in the primary legislation and then in the statutory guidance[130]. Applications are made in writing, without any prescribed form. The guidance says that notice should be given by the applicant to the signatories to the obligation, and the application advertised if that is not possible, with the notification evidenced to the authority[131]. The authority has discretion how to publicise and consult upon the proposal which the guidance suggested should be 'limited and proportionate'[132]. Of course, it does need to be recognised that the level of affordable housing in a scheme could be contentious locally and both council members and the public may wish to be involved in any variation.

12.85 When the Mayor of London is determining a s 106BA application he must consult the local planning authority[133]. Similarly, if the Mayor of London had to be consulted upon the original planning application but did not take it over himself, then he must be consulted by the local planning authority on any s 106BA application[134]. A tight consultation timescale is set out: the application must be copied to the Mayor within one working day of receipt, the Mayor has seven days to say whether representations will be made and any representations must be made within 14 days of the authority's receipt of the application[135].

12.86 If the viability test is satisfied on the first application the local planning authority must do one of the following:

'(a) determine that the requirement is to have effect subject to modifications,

(b) determine that the requirement is to be replaced with a different affordable housing requirement,

(c) determine that the planning obligation is to be modified to remove the requirement, or

(d) where the planning obligation consists solely of one or more affordable housing requirements, determine that the planning obligation is to be discharged'.

12.87 Unlike s 106A applications, the authority's powers are not limited to making the modification which has been applied for. The authority may make a different modification[136], but any change on a first application, whether suggested by the applicant or not, is subject to the restrictions that it[137]:

---

[129] *Section 106 affordable housing requirements Review and appeal*, paras 7, 16–21 and Annex A.
[130] Whilst a power exists to make procedural regulations, it has not been exercised: Town and Country Planning Act 1990, s 106BA(11).
[131] *Section 106 affordable housing requirements Review and appeal*, Annex B, para 3. In practice, notice ought to be given to those against whom the obligation is enforceable.
[132] *Section 106 affordable housing requirements Review and appeal*, Annex B, para 4.
[133] Town and Country Planning Act 1990, s 106BA(16).
[134] Town and Country Planning Act 1990, s 106BB. The Mayor's role in planning applications of potential strategic importance is discussed in Chapter 10.
[135] Town and Country Planning Act 1990, s 106BB(2)–(4).
[136] Town and Country Planning Act 1990, s 106BA(6)(a).
[137] Town and Country Planning Act 1990, s 106BA(6).

'(b) may not have the effect that the obligation as modified is more onerous in its application to the applicant than in its unmodified form, and

(c) may not have the effect that an obligation is imposed on a person other than the applicant or that the obligation as modified is more onerous in its application to such a person than in its unmodified form'.

Sub-paragraph (b) avoids the applicant putting themselves in jeopardy and reflects, in different terms, the provision in s 106A that a modification may not impose an obligation on any other person[138].

12.88 The approach required of the local planning authority is changed for a second or subsequent application in relation to that planning obligation[139]:

(i) the economic viability test in s 106BA(3) does not have to be applied;

(ii) there is no duty to make a change (consequent on that or any other test), merely a discretion to do so;

(iii) the provision 'that the obligation as modified is more onerous in its application to the applicant than in its unmodified form'[140] does not apply, but the new determination 'may not have the effect that the development becomes economically unviable'[141].

12.89 Any discretion must be exercised reasonably, which must mean having regard to the viability of the development. However, the authority might take the view that the scheme is likely to become viable in the future or that it would be unacceptable without a certain level of affordable housing even if insisting upon that means that it does not proceed. These changes also introduce an element of risk for applicants, that the resulting obligation may be more onerous than the original or modified one which is the subject of the application.

The Ministerial policy advises that reasons should be given for any decision on an application[142].

Section 106BC appeals

12.90 The applicant may appeal to the Secretary of State under s 106BC if the appropriate authority[143]:

(a) fails to give notice within 28 days beginning with the day the application was received[144], or 35 days if the Mayor of London has to be notified by the authority[145] or any longer period agreed by the applicant and the authority;

(b) decides that the obligation will continue to have effect without any modification;

(c) modifies the obligation in a different manner to that proposed in the application.

---

[138] Compare Town and Country Planning Act 1990, s 106A(5).
[139] For points (i) and (ii), see Town and Country Planning Act 1990, s 106BA(4).
[140] Town and Country Planning Act 1990, s 106BA(6)(b).
[141] Town and Country Planning Act 1990, s 106BA(7).
[142] *Section 106 affordable housing requirements Review and appeal*, Annex B, para 5.
[143] Town and Country Planning Act 1990, s 106BC(1).
[144] Town and Country Planning Act 1990, s 106BA(9).
[145] Town and Country Planning Act 1990, s 106BB(5).

12.91 *Planning obligations*

12.91 An appeal may be brought within six months of the expiry of the determination period or of the decision[146]. No regulations have been made setting out an appeal procedure, so they are conducted under s 106BC and the statutory guidance. Appeals are determined under the same criteria and powers as first and subsequent s 106BA applications are by appropriate authorities[147], subject to two exceptions. The first is that the planning obligation cannot be discharged by the appeal, even if the affordable housing requirement is removed and there are no other obligations left[148].

12.92 Second, the ability to lift or relax the affordable housing obligation on appeal is temporary. Any modification must provide that 'if the development has not been completed before the end of [three years from notification of the decision on the appeal], the obligation is treated as containing the affordable housing requirement or requirements it contained immediately before the first application under section 106BA'[149]. The developer has therefore to get on with the scheme, no doubt reflecting that possibility that viability will have changed in time. Of course, it may be that the development is underway, possibly with some units completed and so the modifications must reflect that moving situation. The modifications made must therefore include

'(a) the modifications necessary to ensure that, if the development has been commenced before the end of the relevant period, the requirement or requirements apply only in relation to the part of the development that is not commenced before the end of that period, and

(b) such other modifications as the Secretary of State considers necessary or expedient to ensure the effectiveness of the requirement or requirements at the end of that period'.

12.93 This potential reversion to an affordable housing requirement only has to arise on appeal: the appropriate authority could provide a permanent lifting of the obligation, although the limited nature of an appeal decision could prompt a time-limited relaxation. In an appeal the parties should ensure that proposed modifications are submitted to provide for the various possibilities of the development not having started, or not having been completed within the three-year period.

12.94 It is therefore necessary on appeal to modify the obligation[150]:

(a) to reinstate the affordable housing obligation if the development is not completed within three years;

(b) so it only applies to parts of the development which have not commenced within the three year period

(c) to make any other changes necessary to ensure the effectiveness of the affordable housing requirement at the end of the period.

---

[146] Town and Country Planning Act 1990, s 106BC(4). No other period has been prescribed under s 106BC(3).
[147] See Town and Country Planning Act 1990, s 106BC(6). The first appeal, by Hopkins Homes Ltd on Land off Station Road, Framlingham, Suffolk, was allowed, with the affordable housing requirement being lifted entirely: reference APP/J3530/Q/14/2217963.
[148] Town and Country Planning Act 1990, s 106BC(9).
[149] Town and Country Planning Act 1990, s 106BC(11), with the period defined in sub-s (13).
[150] Whilst the Framlingham appeal decision was limited to three years, the need for modifications in respect of partial works was entirely overlooked.

12.95 The legislation seems to envisage that the affordable housing requirement will be reinstated but reduced by reference to the extent of the scheme which has not been started. Each 'part' of the development is not defined in the legislation and it is prudent for the modifications to set that out for the particular scheme, whether by reference to phases, or in smaller parcels. The effect of partial development on the quantum of affordable housing has to be considered, along with the manner of its delivery. A pro rata reduction may be appropriate. If an affordable housing obligation revives partway through the development it may be more sensible to provide for a commuted payment rather than changes to the design and layout which may be caused by a late introduction of onsite affordable housing.

AVOIDING A NEED FOR EARLY MODIFICATION OF ANY PLANNING OBLIGATION

12.96 The difficulties which arise trying to change or dispose of a planning obligation show the need for care in drafting. A developer on a planning appeal should only submit a signed planning obligation once the requirements are known with as much certainty as possible and they are content with its wording. Once the signed obligation has been handed to the local planning authority it has legal effect and cannot be modified or discharged except under the mechanisms in the Act. The developer cannot informally replace one unilateral obligation with another one. Consequently any problems with a submitted obligation would have to be resolved by a planning agreement with the authority, the making of a further planning obligation or by the imposition of planning conditions. A second obligation would need to be drafted to dovetail in with the first obligation, for example, if it was needed to increase a contribution from £10,000 to £20,000 the obligations must total £20,000, not £30,000. It may be harder to use a second unilateral obligation to alter practical controls over the use of land, as the new requirements would have to be additional to the original provisions, rather than replacing them.

A PLANNING OBLIGATION IS NOT DISCHARGED BY A BREACH

12.97 A breach of contract cannot give rise to a repudiation or the determination of a planning obligation whether by a landowner or the local planning authority[151]. The Town and Country Planning Act 1990 provides the mechanism for the discharge of obligations and that has to be followed.

PRE-1991 ACT PLANNING AGREEMENTS

12.98 The first form of planning obligation were agreements made under the Town and Country Planning Act 1932, s 34. The effect of these agreements has been preserved[152] and despite their considerable antiquity some remain in force[153]. The Town and Country Planning Act 1947 introduced a form of planning agreement which remained essentially unchanged until 1992. These agreements are most

---

[151] *Patel v Brent London Borough Council* [2005] EWCA Civ 644.
[152] See Town and Country Planning Act 1971, Sch 24, para 88.
[153] For an example see *Attorney-General (ex rel Scotland) v Barratt Manchester Ltd and Bolton Metropolitan Borough Council* (1992) 63 P & CR 179.

12.99 *Planning obligations*

commonly s 52 agreements under the Town and Country Planning Act 1971. Section 106 agreements made prior to 25 October 1991 are under the original form of s 106 and are changed and enforced in the same way as s 52 agreements.

12.99 Section 52 of the Town and Country Planning Act 1971 provided for planning agreements:

'(1) A local planning authority may enter into an agreement with any person interested in land in their area for the purpose of restricting or regulating the development or use of the land, either permanently or during such period as may be prescribed by the agreement; and any such agreement may contain such incidental and consequential provisions (including provisions of a financial character) as appear to the local planning authority to be necessary or expedient for the purposes of the agreement.

(2) An agreement made under this section with any person interested in land may be enforced by the local planning authority against persons deriving title under that person in respect of that land, as if the local planning authority were possessed of adjacent land and as if the agreement had been expressed to be made for the benefit of such land'.

12.100 Section 52 planning agreements can only be amended by the agreement of all parties to the deed (as with any deed) or by the Upper Tribunal (Lands Chamber) following an application on the limited grounds in the Law of Property Act 1925, s 84.

12.101 Planning agreements made prior to the changes made by the Planning and Compensation Act 1991 are enforced by contractual remedies. These would be by an injunction, specific performance or damages. The local planning authority need not use other enforcement powers before seeking to use contractual remedies[154]. There are no statutory remedies available to the local planning authority.

These earlier agreements do run with the land so can be enforced against successors in title.

12.102 The pre-1992 planning agreements can be modified or discharged by agreement of the parties (as contractual provisions) or by the Upper Tribunal (Lands Chamber) under the Law of Property Act 1925, s 84. Section 84 provides as relevant:

'(1) The Upper Tribunal shall (without prejudice to any concurrent jurisdiction of the court) have power from time to time, on the application of any person interested in any freehold land affected by any restriction arising under covenant or otherwise as to the user thereof or the building thereon, by order wholly or partially to discharge or modify any such restriction on being satisfied:

(a) that by reason of changes in the character of the property or the neighbourhood or other circumstances of the case which the Upper Tribunal may deem material, the restriction ought to be deemed obsolete; or

(aa) that in a case falling within subsection (1A) below the continued existence thereof would impede some reasonable user of the land for public or private purposes or, as the case may be, would unless modified so impede such user; or

(b) that the persons of full age and capacity for the time being or from time to time entitled to the benefit of the restriction, whether in respect of estates in fee simple or any lesser estates or interests in the property to which the benefit of the restriction is

---

[154] *Avon County Council v Millard* (1985) 50 P & CR 275.

annexed, have agreed, either expressly or by implication, by their acts or omissions, to the same being discharged or modified; or

(c) that the proposed discharge or modification will not injure the persons entitled to the benefit of the restriction:

and an order discharging or modifying a restriction under this subsection may direct the applicant to pay to any person entitled to the benefit of the restriction such sum by way of consideration as the Tribunal may think it just to award under one, but not both, of the following heads, that is to say, either:

(i) a sum to make up for any loss or disadvantage suffered by that person in consequence of the discharge or modification; or

(ii) a sum to make up for any effect which the restriction had, at the time when it was imposed, in reducing the consideration then received for the land affected by it.

(1A) Subsection (1) (aa) above authorises the discharge or modification of a restriction by reference to its impeding some reasonable user of land in any case in which the Upper Tribunal is satisfied that the restriction, in impeding that user, either:

(a) does not secure to persons entitled to the benefit of it any practical benefits of substantial value or advantage to them; or

(b) is contrary to the public interest; and that money will be an adequate compensation for the loss or disadvantage (if any) which any such person will suffer from the discharge or modification.

(1B) In determining whether a case is one falling within subsection (1A) above, and in determining whether (in any such case or otherwise) a restriction ought to be discharged or modified, the Upper Tribunal shall take into account the development plan and any declared or ascertainable pattern for the grant or refusal of planning permissions in the relevant areas, as well as the period at which and context in which the restriction was created or imposed and any other material circumstances.

(1C) It is hereby declared that the power conferred by this section to modify a restriction includes power to add such further provisions restricting the user of or the building on the land affected as appear to the Upper Tribunal to be reasonable in view of the relaxation of the existing provisions, and as may be accepted by the applicant; and the Upper Tribunal may accordingly refuse to modify a restriction without some such addition'.

It does not follow that because a planning application or appeal has been allowed which is inconsistent with the planning agreement that the agreement should be discharged or modified[155]. The test for obsolescence in s 84(1)(a) is whether the restriction is still capable of fulfilling its original purpose[156].

OTHER FORMS OF AGREEMENTS AND POWERS

The use of planning conditions to require payments

12.103 A planning condition cannot require the payment of money or require an agreement to be made in such terms. Statutory authority is always required before

---

[155] *In re Martins' Application* (1988) 57 P & CR 119 at 124–125 per Fox LJ. For recent consideration see *Re Rasbridge's Application* [2012] UKUT 246 (LC), [2012] JPL 1521.
[156] *Re Truman, Hanbury, Buxton and Co Ltd's Application* [1956] 1 QB 261 at 272 per Romer LJ.

12.104 *Planning obligations*

a public authority can charge[157]. The scope of planning conditions does not extend to requiring payments. Whilst a negative condition can be imposed on a planning permission requiring an off-site event to have occurred and the off-site event might in practice only occur if the applicant makes a contribution under a planning obligation, this cannot be elevated into a negative condition which is subject to a payment. Such a condition would be *Wednesbury* unreasonable, and contrary to the purpose of the legislation if it was sought to be used to bypass the Community Infrastructure Levy Regulations 2010.

The general power in the Localism Act 2011, s 1

12.104 Payments should be secured by planning obligations. The general power of competence in s 1 of the Localism Act 2011 cannot be used to require a developer or landowner to enter into an agreement to make payments in return for the grant of planning permission, any detailed approval under a condition or in relation to prior approval under the General Permitted Development Order or approval under the Conservation of Habitats and Species Regulations 2010, reg 75[158]. By s 3(2) of the Localism Act:

> 'The general power confers power to charge the person for providing the service to the person only if:
>
> (a) the service is not one that a statutory provision requires the authority to provide to the person,
>
> (b) the person has agreed to its being provided ...'

Similar restrictions apply to the power to charge in the Local Government Act 2003, s 93. To the extent that the determination of applications can be described as a service, statute requires the authority to provide it. Consequently no charge can be levied nor provided for in a non-s 106 agreement.

Contractual agreements under the Local Government Act 1972 and other provisions

12.105 A local authority may enter into contractual agreements pursuant to its other statutory powers. For example, the power to dispose of land will involve the making of an agreement. By the Local Government Act 1972, s 111(1) a local authority may do anything 'which is calculated to facilitate, or is conducive or incidental to, the discharge of any of their functions' but that must be incidental to its powers. Contractual agreements are enforceable only between the parties to them, whereas planning control usually has to run with the land.

12.106 Restrictive covenants may be included on the disposal of land but if imposed as an incident of the authority's land ownership can only be enforced against subsequent owners if the authority retains land which benefits from the covenant.

---

[157] *Attorney-General v Wilts United Dairies Ltd* (1921) 37 TLR 884 (Court of Appeal); (1922) 38 TLR 781 (House of Lords). It is for the local authority to show that it has the right to charge: *R v Richmond-upon-Thames London Borough Council, ex p McCarthy & Stone (Developments) Ltd* [1992] 2 AC 48 at 68.
[158] SI 2010/490.

Covenants imposed under statutory powers may be enforceable more generally but are limited in their purposes[159].

12.107 The Local Government (Miscellaneous Provisions) Act 1982, s 33 does allow covenants by a person interested in land to be enforced by local authorities against successors in title where the deed is expressed to be subject to that provision. The deed must be one which:

'(a) is executed for the purpose of securing the carrying out of works on land in the council's area in which the other person has an interest, or

(b) is executed for the purpose of regulating the use of or is otherwise connected with land in or outside the council's area in which the other person has an interest,

and which is neither executed for the purpose of facilitating nor connected with the development of the land in question'.

It can therefore be used for requiring works or regulating the use of land, but may not be facilitating nor connected with the development of that land. Its role where planning permission is being obtained is therefore very limited.

12.108 In Greater London undertakings and agreements made by deed in connection with land are enforceable against successors in title provided they are expressed to be given or made pursuant to the Greater London Council (General Powers) Act 1974, s 16. These agreements are not subject to the limitations in the Local Government (Miscellaneous Provisions) Act 1982.

---

[159] For example, a covenant could not restrict the use of a right to buy home to a single dwelling if the intention was for the housing authority to benefit from any increase in the value of the land due to planning permission for the construction of a second house within the plot: *R v Braintree District Council, ex p Halls* (2000) 80 P & CR 266.

Chapter 13

Planning permission for variations, retrospective and replacement consents

13.1 There are a number of planning applications which are described differently in the legislation:

(i) applications for the carrying out of development approved under an earlier planning permission, but subject to different conditions (s 73 applications);

(ii) applications for development which has been carried out without planning permission or in breach of condition. These are retrospective applications made under s 73A;

(iii) applications for a replacement planning permission in England subject to a different time limit under the Town and Country Planning (Development Management Procedure) (England) Order 2015[1], art 20 or the renewal of a planning permission in Wales.

13.2 These give rise to some procedural differences and some difference in the approach to decision making. However it is important not to overstate any alterations in the matters considered when deciding these applications. They are at heart planning applications, subject to the usual requirements to have regard to the development plan and other material considerations, where the major change is that there may be a fallback – an existing permission which can be relied upon if the planning application is refused.

SECTION 73 VARIATIONS

13.3 Section 73 of the Town and Country Planning Act 1990 provides as relevant:

'(1) This section applies, subject to subsection (4), to applications for planning permission for the development of land without complying with conditions subject to which a previous planning permission was granted.

(2) On such an application the local planning authority shall consider only the question of the conditions subject to which planning permission should be granted, and:

(a) if they decide that planning permission should be granted subject to conditions differing from those subject to which the previous permission was granted, or that it should be granted unconditionally, they shall grant planning permission accordingly, and

---

[1] SI 2015/595.

(b) if they decide that planning permission should be granted subject to the same conditions as those subject to which the previous permission was granted, they shall refuse the application'.

13.4 A s 73 planning permission is one for the same description of development but subject to different conditions. A condition could be imposed in a s 73 planning permission if it could have been imposed on the original grant of planning permission: *R v Coventry City Council, ex p Arrowcroft Group plc*[2]. Conditions are able to change the development proposed provided it is not a fundamental alteration to the proposal[3]. Whether an alteration is fundamental has to be considered in the light of the individual proposal.

As Sullivan J explained in *Arrowcroft*[4]:

'... the council is able to impose different conditions upon a new planning permission, but only if they are conditions which the council could lawfully have imposed upon the original planning permission in the sense that they do not amount to a fundamental alteration of the proposal put forward in the original application'.

13.5 The scope of permissible changes is wide and a condition may have the effect of modifying the development proposed (even to the point of making the permission different from the description of development in some cases[5]). The essential constraints on the scope of planning conditions are that they must not nullify the permission granted[6] nor must they deprive those who should have been consulted upon the change of the opportunity to comment[7]. *Arrowcroft* is itself an example of a fundamental alteration, as the original planning permission was for several buildings including '1 variety superstore' and the new condition sought to authorise up to six non-food variety stores which introduced a fundamental inconsistency with the description of development. However Sullivan J identified permissible s 73 conditions in that case as including changes to the overall floor space and altering the balance of floorspace between different retail types[8]:

'providing the floor space remaining is sufficient to accommodate what can fairly be described as a "variety superstore" ... Thus, in practice, section 73 confers a great deal of flexibility on the Council'.

The breadth of the s 73 consideration

13.6 Section 73(2) requires local planning authorities to 'consider only the question of the conditions subject to which planning permission should be granted'. However the effect of changing the conditions may be substantial, and in some cases may enable a project to proceed when it would not otherwise happen. The

---

[2] [2001] PLCR 7 at para 33 per Sullivan J.
[3] For example, *Richmond-upon-Thames London Borough Council v Secretary of State for the Environment* [1974] 1 All ER 193 and applied to s 73 applications in *Arrowcroft*.
[4] [2001] PLCR 7 at para 33.
[5] For example, the exclusion of an access road from planning permission for an oil refinery: *Kent County Council v Secretary of State for the Environment* (1977) 33 P & CR 70. The ability of conditions to alter what is applied for is also discussed at paras **11.27** and **11.50** above.
[6] See also *Kent County Council v Secretary of State for the Environment* (1977) 33 P & CR 70.
[7] On the latter point, see *Wheatcroft v Secretary of State for the Environment* (1982) 43 P & CR 233.
[8] *Arrowcroft* at para 24.

13.7 *Planning permission for variations, retrospective and replacement consents*

considerations which are material to the application will therefore depend upon the substantive effect of granting the application.

13.7 The scope of the exercise prompted a series of judgments dealing with the situation, which was then possible, for a s 73 application to be used to extend the time for implementing a planning permission or submitting reserved matters so allowing development to be carried out when it would not otherwise take place. In *R v London Docklands Development Corpn, ex p Sister Christine Frost*[9] Keene J held that the local planning authority could consider conditions other than those which were the subject of the application and impose new conditions[10]. He also considered that where a s 73 application sought to extend the period for submitting reserved matters 'the scope of matters to be considered in relation to conditions will be defined, in effect, by the question: should this planning permission be allowed to continue in force for a period of time beyond the original dates contemplated?' and so government policy on the renewal of planning permissions which advised that changes in material considerations be addressed was relevant[11]. However in *Allied London Property Investment Ltd v Secretary of State for the Environment*[12] Christopher Lockhart-Mummery QC decided that 'the purpose of the relevant powers is to consider the acceptability of existing and proposed conditions; those powers cannot be exercised for the ulterior purpose which is involved in considering the question of the acceptability of the development as a matter of principle' and so the policy was not relevant[13]. Both judgments were considered by Sullivan J in *Pye v Secretary of State for the Environment*[14]. He explained[15]:

> 'Whilst section 73 applications are commonly referred to as applications to "amend" the conditions attached to a planning permission, a decision under section 73(2) leaves the original planning permission intact and unamended. That is so whether the decision is to grant planning permission unconditionally or subject to different conditions under paragraph (a), or to refuse the application under paragraph (b), because planning permission should be granted subject to the same conditions.
>
> In the former case the applicant may choose whether to implement the original planning permission or the new planning permission; in the latter case, he is still free to implement the original planning permission. Thus, it is not possible to "go back on the original planning permission" under section 73. It remains as a baseline, whether the application under section 73 is approved or refused, in contrast to the position that previously obtained ...
>
> Considering only the conditions subject to which planning permission should be granted will be a more limited exercise than the consideration of a "normal" application for planning permission under section 70, but as Keene J pointed out at page 207 of the *Frost* case, how much more limited will depend on the nature of the condition itself. If the condition relates to a narrow issue, such as hours of operation or the particular materials to be employed in the construction of the building, the local planning authority's consideration will be confined within a very narrow compass.

---

[9] (1997) 73 P & CR 199.
[10] At 207 to 208. The same approach was subsequently taken in *R v Leicester City Council, ex p Powergen UK plc* [2000] JPL 1037 at para 31 per Schiemann LJ.
[11] At 207.
[12] (1996) 72 P & CR 327.
[13] At 339. *Allied London* was decided six weeks after *Sister Frost* but without reference to it. In those far off days, transcripts were not available on the internet (if anyone used it at all), and so judgments were not widely known unless and until they were reported.
[14] [1999] PLCR 28. As Jeremy Sullivan QC he had been counsel for the successful defendant in *Sister Frost*.
[15] At 45–46.

Since the original planning permission will still be capable of implementation, the local planning authority looking at the practical consequences of imposing a different condition, as to hours or materials, will be considering the relative merit or harm of allowing the premises to remain open until, say, 10 o'clock rather than 8 o'clock in the evening, or to be tiled rather than slated.

Equally, if an application is made under section 73 within the original time-limit for the submission of reserved matters, whilst implementation of the planning permission is still possible and is not precluded by the provisions of section 93(4), for a modest extension of time for the submission of reserved matters, the local planning authority's role in considering only the question of conditions subject to which planning permission should be granted will be more confined than in a normal section 70 case. The practical effect of submitting details one year later than would otherwise be allowed may be very limited ...

The local planning authority has to have regard to the factual circumstances as they exist at the time and to have regard to the facts that exist at the time of its decision. If at that time the original planning permission is incapable of implementation by reason of section 93(4), I can see no basis in the statutory code for requiring the local planning authority to ignore that important fact'.

The Court of Appeal addressed these cases in *R v Leicester City Council, ex p Powergen UK plc*, endorsing the analysis of Sullivan J in *Pye*[16].

13.8 The *Pye* and *Powergen* approaches have continued to be applied. In *Lawson Builders Ltd v Secretary of State for Communities and Local Government*, Pitchford LJ said[17]:

'it would be a mistake to assume that a section 73 examination of conditions will never involve the study of wider planning considerations. Although the planning merits of the development in general will not be under consideration, the conditions may have been imposed so as to ensure compliance with an important aspect of policy. The task of the planning authority and the planning inspector under section 73 is "*only*" to judge whether the conditions originally imposed should be adhered to or varied but that task may require, depending upon the purpose of the condition, a wide ranging enquiry'.

This is an application of the fallback: what could the developer do if the current application was not approved? If the developer could lawfully and in practical terms proceed under the original permission then the relevant question is what is the difference between the new application and that permission? However if the development will not take place under the first permission, or will not do so to its full extent, then the principle of allowing that development to finally proceed must be addressed on an application which is designed to do so.

The need for an extant planning permission

13.9 Where the original planning permission is prospective, for future development, s 73 application can only be made if the time limit for beginning the development has not expired without implementation of the permission. The restriction is expressed in s 73(4) as not allowing s 73 to be used if the 'time has expired without the development having been begun'.

---

[16] [2000] JPL 1037 at para 29 per Schiemann LJ and see the conclusion in that case at para 43.
[17] [2015] EWCA Civ 122, [2015] JPL 896 at para 31.

13.10 *Planning permission for variations, retrospective and replacement consents*

13.10 In *R v Secretary of State for the Environment, ex p Corby Borough Council*[18] Pill J held that sub-s (4) applied only to the time period for starting the development, not the period for applying for reserved matters. Consequently a s 73 application could be made after the reserved matters application period had expired, whether or not reserved matters had been applied for or obtained.

Extension of time for implementation and reserved matters applications

13.11 Section 73 had conventionally been used to alter the conditions on existing planning permissions which impose time limits for the beginning of development and any applications for reserved matters. Rather than apply for a new planning permission in the conventional form, an application would be made for what was often described as a 'variation of condition' under s 73.

13.12 In part the practice of using s 73 evolved from a belief (or perhaps more accurately, misunderstanding) that it would vary the original permission so the permission would become one with the new, later, time limit. There was also the perception that the consideration of the application would be more constrained and so was less likely to be refused or amended in other ways. That view arose from the opening lines of sub-s (2) that the authority 'shall consider only the question of the conditions subject to which planning permission should be granted'. At issue was how the merits of whether there should be a new planning permission was considered.

13.13 A s 73 application only covers development or matters which would contravene planning conditions which have not yet occurred. If the breach of planning control has already taken place then the application is retrospective under s 73A, at least for those elements. A failure to appreciate this when making the application, or indeed the development proceeding whilst the application is being considered, does not prevent a permission being granted, but any such permission will be under s 73A[19].

13.14 A s 73 application may not be made 'if the previous planning permission was granted subject to a condition as to the time within which the development to which it related was to be begun and that time has expired without the development having been begun'[20]. A fresh planning application would have to be made under s 70. This restriction applies if the time for commencing development has passed, not if the time for reserved matters applications has expired without applications having been made. In such cases s 73 applications were often made to allow more time for details to be submitted.

13.15 The use of s 73 to resurrect a permission whose implementation would be out of time, or to simply extend the time for submitting details or implementation was prohibited in England by an amendment in the Planning and Compulsory Purchase Act 2004. This inserted s 73(5) which provides:

> 'Planning permission must not be granted under this section to the extent that it has effect to change a condition subject to which a previous planning permission was granted by extending the time within which:

---

[18] (1994) 68 P & CR 544.
[19] See *Lawson Builders Ltd v Secretary of State for Communities and Local Government* [2015] EWCA Civ 122, [2015] JPL 896 at paras 25, 27 per Pitchford LJ.
[20] Town and Country Planning Act 1990, s 73(4).

(a) a development must be started;

(b) an application for approval of reserved matters (within the meaning of section 92) must be made'.

This provision does not apply in Wales. However, the Planning (Wales) Act 2015 seeks to reach the same result by a different means. It proposes that any s 73 permission shall be deemed to have been granted subject to a condition that the development must be begun within the period specified in the original planning permission[21] and, if it is an outline planning permission, that any application for reserved matters must have been made in the original time period[22].

Reserved matters

13.16 In England a s 73 permission cannot extend the period for submitting a reserved matters application: see s 73(5)(b). That therefore brings into focus two issues: whether previously approved reserved matters can be relied upon in a s 73 permission; and whether a reserved matters approval or any conditions on such an approval can be changed.

13.17 A s 73 application is solely in respect of a new planning permission subject to different conditions from that on an earlier permission. It cannot vary the conditions on a reserved matters approval as this is not itself a planning permission. If changes to reserved matters conditions are sought then the developer should make a further reserved matters application if it is within time to do so.

13.18 A s 73 permission cannot extend the time for applying for reserved matters approval[23] so the only way of effecting a change by a s 73 application is for the new permission to be a detailed permission encompassing the reserved matters details (with any modifications). The existing reserved matters approval would not then apply to the new s 73 permission. The complication is whether a condition could be included which provides, in essence, for a full rather than outline planning permission given the description of development as 'all matters reserved'. A s 73 permission cannot make a fundamental alteration to the original consent. In principle it ought to be possible to approve new details – although it may be contentious – as the benefit of s 73 following the grant of reserved matters approval is lost if a new permission cannot simply adopt the approved reserved matters plans – or alter those plans. In *R v Leicester City Council, ex p Powergen plc*[24] Schiemann LJ held that a s 73 planning permission can allow reference to previously approved details or alterations to them, in rejecting the argument that a developer would have:

'to resubmit details which had already been approved. Sometimes the alteration of a condition which is asked for will involve alterations as to previously approved details, sometimes it will not. In those cases where it does not there is no difficulty in referring to

---

[21] For full planning permissions the Town and Country Planning Act 1990, s 91(3ZA)–(3ZD), prospectively inserted by the Planning (Wales) Act 2015, s 35(4) and for outline permissions the Town and Country Planning Act 1990, s 92(3C)–(3D), prospectively inserted by the Planning (Wales) Act 2015, s 36(4) from a date to be appointed.

[22] Town and Country Planning Act 1990, s 92(3A)–(3B), prospectively inserted by the Planning (Wales) Act 2015, s 36(4) from a date to be appointed.

[23] See Town and Country Planning Act 1990, s 73(5)(b) in England and the proposals in the Planning (Wales) Act 2015, discussed above.

[24] [2000] JPL 1037.

13.19 *Planning permission for variations, retrospective and replacement consents*

the old plans and it may well be that the Authority will be inhibited by the opening words of section 73(2) from considering their merits'.

13.19 This observation appears to involve the s 73 permission changing conditions from 'details to be submitted' to being in accordance with identified details which had previously been approved. What may though happen in practice is that details had already been approved under the original planning permission but the s 73 permission again requires the approval of details. If those details have to be different because of other changes in the permission, then a fresh application is required. Where the details would be unchanged, it may still be reading too much into the new consent to treat an earlier approval as being under that consent. However it would rarely be the case that those earlier approvals could be said to no longer be acceptable (if the scheme is unchanged) and it may be irrational therefore to enforce against a failure to apply for a further approval of those details. In practice the issue has been glossed over, possibly for this latter reason.

RETROSPECTIVE PLANNING APPLICATIONS UNDER s 73A

13.20 Retrospective planning permission is addressed in the Town and Country Planning Act 1990, s 73A. By s 73A(1) the planning permission which may be granted on an application made to a local planning authority 'includes planning permission for development carried out before the date of the application'.

13.21 This power[25]:

'applies to development carried out:

(a) without planning permission;

(b) in accordance with planning permission granted for a limited period; or

(c) without complying with some condition subject to which planning permission was granted'.

13.22 The permission may not simply legitimise that development for the future but retrospectively approve what had taken place, see s 73A(3):

'Planning permission for such development may be granted so as to have effect from:

(a) the date on which the development was carried out; or

(b) if it was carried out in accordance with planning permission granted for a limited period, the end of that period'.

13.23 However, if the unlawful development or breach of condition was in respect of demolition within a conservation area[26] then a retrospective planning permission does not affect any criminal liability which has already been incurred[27].

---

[25] Town and Country Planning Act 1990, s 73A(2). Retrospective consents for building works have a long history, for example the licence granted by Edward III in 1359 in respect of Edington Priory, Wiltshire 'Pardon, at the asking of William de Edyndon, bishop of Winchester to him and the rector and brethren of the house of the order of St Augustine, Edyndon, founded by him, for crenellating the manse of the rector and brethren without the king's licence and licence for them to retain the manor crenellated'.

[26] Defined as 'relevant demolition' in Town and Country Planning Act 1990, s 196D(3).

[27] Town and Country Planning Act 1990, s 196D(9).

13.24 The scope of the issues on a s 73A retrospective application is similar to those on a s 73 application. Sullivan J said in *R (on the application of Wilkinson) v Rossendale Borough Council*[28]:

'I can see no difference in principle between refusing to grant planning permission under section 73 subject to a different (extended) time limit, because to do so would have the effect of enabling an unacceptable development to be carried out; and refusing to grant a planning permission under section 73A (or section 73) without a personal condition, because to do so would have the effect of enabling an unacceptable development to be continued (or commenced)'.

13.25 Section 73A can be used to enable a partially completed development to be built out in an amended form by altering the plans in the conditions. In that way the new permission will be for the whole scheme, comprising built and proposed development[29]. As a s 73A consent it will not be subject to a condition limiting the period for the commencement of development. Such a permission has a dual nature, in that it is retrospective and prospective. However the retrospective element means that no time limit for implementation arises – the development does not have to be begun following the grant of planning permission because the permission applies to some development which is already there[30].

13.26 Retrospective planning permissions may require the submission of further details for the local planning authority's approval and their subsequent implementation. Since the development will have already taken place, these will require submission within a certain, short period from the grant of permission, with a further period for any appeal to be submitted on the details and then a period for any necessary implementation (either specified in the condition or to be in the details submitted). A condition will then provide that if the details are not submitted, approved or carried out within the period then the use will have to cease and any operational development be removed with restoration works carried out[31].

'Minor material amendments'

13.27 There is sometimes reference to s 73 applications as 'minor material amendment' applications but that expression has no legal status or effect. The CLG guidance *Greater flexibility for planning permissions* introduced the term but said that these applications are made under s 73 on the usual form[32]. The *Planning Practice Guidance* refers to 'Amending the conditions attached to a permission including seeking minor material amendments (application under Section 73 TCPA 1990)', recognising that it is simply a s 73 application[33]. There is no need for the change proposed in a s 73 application to be minor: it just needs to be within the parameters discussed above. The expression 'minor material amendments' is best avoided.

---

[28] [2002] EWHC 1204 (Admin), [2003] JPL 82, para 57.
[29] *Taylor Wimpey (South West Thames) Ltd v Secretary of State for Communities and Local Government* [2011] EWHC 2090 (Admin) at para 33.
[30] See *Lawson Builders Ltd v Secretary of State for Communities and Local Government* [2015] EWCA Civ 122, [2015] JPL 896 at paras 20, 23, 26 per Pitchford LJ.
[31] Strictly the permission would not lapse but continuation would be in breach of a condition.
[32] *Greater flexibility for planning permissions*, paras 60 and 67. This was cancelled with the publication of the *Planning Practice Guidance*.
[33] ID 17a-013-20140306.

13.28 *Planning permission for variations, retrospective and replacement consents*

Interpretation issues

13.28 A s 73 or 73A permission is a standalone planning permission, so should contain all of its conditions. If it is described as a variation to an existing consent and only the altered conditions are included then it may be possible to interpret the permission as incorporating the missing elements. In *Reid v Secretary of State for Transport, Local Government and the Regions*[34] a s 73 planning permission was described as the retention of a use of land without compliance with condition 2 of a previous planning permission but contained no conditions itself. The reference to the particular condition required the earlier consent to be considered and so brought in the other previous conditions by reference[35].

Section 73 or 73A application?

13.29 Whether a planning application is under s 73 or 73A depends upon whether the development or the departure from the condition has already taken place. If there is an existing breach then the application or consequent permission is retrospective[36]. It is implicit in ss 73 and 73A, that a local planning authority considering an application under s 73 for planning permission to proceed with a development without complying with conditions attached to an existing permission may grant, under s 73A, retrospective planning permission for a development already carried out, subject to conditions imposed under s 70[37].

REPLACEMENT PLANNING PERMISSIONS IN ENGLAND

13.30 A simplified procedure applies in England to certain planning applications to replace existing planning permissions with later time limits for commencement. These comprise applications for development where:

(i) full or outline planning permission for that development had been granted on or before 1 October 2010 subject to a time limit for the commencement of development which had not yet expired and the development has not yet begun[38]; or

(ii) outline planning permission had been granted on or before 1 October 2010 subject to a time limit for the commencement of development which had not yet expired and that permission allowed or required the development to be implemented in phases.

13.31 These are 'replacement planning permissions' for the purposes of the DMPO. As the 2010 reference suggests, they are intended to provide a different and easier procedure to renew planning permissions where projects had been stalled by the financial crisis which begun in 2008. The development must have been approved by the earlier planning permission but might be simply part rather than the whole of the original approval, for example, because part of the development had already

---

[34] [2002] EWHC 2174 (Admin).
[35] *Reid* at paras 55–58 per Sullivan J.
[36] See *Lawson Builders Ltd v Secretary of State for Communities and Local Government* [2015] EWCA Civ 122 at paras 22–27 per Pitchford LJ.
[37] *Lawson Builders* at para 36 per Pitchford LJ.
[38] See DMPO 2015, art 20(1)(b).

been carried out. Otherwise this is not a mechanism for the approval of a different scheme. The previous permission must still be within its original time limits for implementation, implying that its planning merits had been subject to recent consideration, and so justifying a simplified procedure.

13.32 The determination of a replacement planning application is subject to the same duties to have regard to the development plan and other material considerations and the presumption in favour of the development plan as other applications[39]. Changes in circumstances, in particular to planning policy, must therefore be taken into account. As with s 73 and 73A applications, the decision is heavily affected by the fallback position. If the development could still in practice be carried out pursuant to the underlying permission, then the scope for refusal because the planning merits were no longer with the scheme, or the implementation of more adverse conditions, is greatly reduced. Conversely, if at the time of determination the original permission cannot be built out because the implementation period has since passed without the commencement of development or is unlikely to be built out because of an inconvenient condition, then the current planning merits will have greater and possibly decisive weight[40].

RENEWAL APPLICATIONS IN WALES

13.33 Applications to renew planning permissions in Wales are subject to the same procedures as conventional planning applications[41].

If the period for commencement under a planning permission has not expired then a lower, standard fee is charged. Applications for renewal should be determined in accordance with the up to date policies[42].

PROCEDURES FOR s 73 AND REPLACEMENT PLANNING APPLICATIONS

13.34 The starting point is that applications for s 73 permissions and replacement permissions are still planning applications and, unless excluded, are subject to the same processes as any other planning application. However they benefit from some simplified procedures because the original permissions will have recently been subject to consideration. No such leeway applies to retrospective planning applications under s 73A as some of these will not have an underlying permission.

13.35 Section 73 and replacement permission applications are dealt with in these ways:

---

[39] Under Town and Country Planning Act 1990, s 70(2) and Planning and Compulsory Purchase Act 2004, s 38(6).
[40] See the discussion of the s 73 cases above.
[41] There is an inconsistency in the Welsh legislation that the DMPO Wales, SI 2012/801, art 5 requires all planning applications to be made on the Welsh Minister's form (or one to similar effect) but the Town and Country Planning (Applications) Regulations 1988, SI 1988/812, reg 3(3) allows s 73, s 73A and renewal applications to simply be made in writing giving sufficient information to enable the authority to identify the permission and any condition in question. Prudent practice is to use the form.
[42] *Planning Policy Wales* (2014), para 3.1.2 and for town centre uses, para 10.3.16.

13.36 *Planning permission for variations, retrospective and replacement consents*

(i) statutory pre-application consultation is not required[43];

(ii) a 1APP form is used, although a specific 'minor material amendment' form is used for s 73 applications[44];

(iii) there is no need to file a plan identifying the land, or any other plans, drawings and information necessary to describe the development[45], unless of course those details have changed from the original approval;

(iv) design and access statements are not required[46];

(v) notice to owners (including long leaseholders) and agricultural tenants is given in the same way as for any other applications[47];

(vi) screening for EIA and EIA itself may be required[48], the application being considered as a modification to a project which has already been approved;

(vii) publicity requirements are unaltered[49];

(viii) provided that it is not EIA development[50], consultation under the table in the DMPO is only required to the extent that the local planning authority consider appropriate[51]. Other consultation requirements are unaltered;

(ix) provisions for the issue of decisions, time limits for decision making and appeals are the same as other planning applications.

PROCEDURES FOR RETROSPECTIVE PLANNING APPLICATIONS

13.36 Retrospective planning applications under s 73A are dealt with almost exactly the same way as a prospective, non-s 73, application. An exception is that a retrospective application for non-compliance with a condition attaching to a previous permission does not have to be accompanied by a site plan or any other plans, drawings and information necessary to describe the development[52]. This is because those details are already known, however in practice any proposed altered drawings will have to be submitted, along with an explanation for the application.

13.37 If an application is a hybrid s 73 and s 73A application when it is made, then the more onerous procedures (which are those for retrospective consents) ought to be applied. If development is begun, unlawfully, after a s 73 application is submitted but prior to determination, so that the application becomes partially retrospective, then the better course may be to keep to the s 73 procedures.

---

[43] DMPO 2015, art 3(2).
[44] DMPO 2015, art 7(1)(a), (b); DMPO Wales, art 5(1)(a), (b).
[45] DMPO 2015, art 7(1)(c), (5); DMPO Wales, art 5(1)(c).
[46] DMPO 2015, art 9(4).
[47] DMPO 2015, arts 13, 14.
[48] Section 73 applications had been omitted from the EIA regime in the Town and Country Planning (Assessment of Environmental Effects) Regulations 1988, but this was reversed in the Town and Country Planning (Environmental Impact Assessment) (England and Wales) Regulations 1999. See *R (on the application of Hautot) v London Borough of Wandsworth* [2003] EWHC 900 Admin; *R (on the application of Prokopp) v London Underground Ltd* [2003] EWCA Civ 961, [2004] JPL 44 at paras 17, 43, 44.
[49] DMPO 2015, art 15 and Planning (Listed Buildings and Conservation Areas) Regulations 1990, SI 1990/1519, reg 5A.
[50] See DMPO 2015, art 18(1)(e).
[51] DMPO 2015, art 20(2).
[52] DMPO 2015, art 7(1)(c); DMPO Wales, art 5(1)(c).

FEES PAYABLE

13.38 The planning application fees for ss 73, 73A, replacement and renewal applications are:

	England	Wales
Section 73 application	£195[53]	£190[54]
Retrospective s 73A application	If development without planning permission, what the fee would have been, otherwise £195[55]	If development without planning permission, what the fee would have been, otherwise £190[56]
Applications for replacement or renewal of planning permission	A renewal under DMPO 2015, Article 20 householder £57, major development £575, any other case £195[57]	Renewal if period for commencement not expired, £190[58]

---

[53] Town and Country Planning (Fees for Applications, Deemed Applications, Requests and Site Visits) (England) Regulations 2012, Sch 1, para 5.
[54] Town and Country Planning (Fees for Applications, Deemed Applications and Site Visits) (Wales) Regulations 2015, Sch 1, para 5.
[55] Town and Country Planning (Fees for Applications, Deemed Applications, Requests and Site Visits) (England) Regulations 2012, Sch 1, para 6.
[56] Town and Country Planning (Fees for Applications, Deemed Applications and Site Visits) (Wales) Regulations 2015, Sch 1, para 6.
[57] Town and Country Planning (Fees for Applications, Deemed Applications, Requests and Site Visits) (England) Regulations 2012, Sch 1, para 7.
[58] Town and Country Planning (Fees for Applications, Deemed Applications and Site Visits) (Wales) Regulations 2015, Sch 1, para 7.

Chapter 14

The issuing of planning permission

14.1 A planning application is only finally determined by a local planning authority when the decision notice is prepared and sent to the applicant. Several formalities apply to the issue and publication of the decision.

14.2 A number of matters may take up time between the local planning authority deciding to grant planning permission and issuing the permission. There may be a need to refer the application to the Minister or the Minister may put a direction in place whilst considering whether to call-in the application. Applications of potential strategic importance in Greater London may need to be referred to the Mayor of London. A planning obligation may have to be drafted and completed. On some occasions there may be detailed issues to resolve on the drafting of conditions. These issues affect a minority of applications. The great majority of decisions are issued within a day of the decision. Refusals of planning permission come out quickly, unless perhaps it is decided to consult members or return to committee to settle the reasons for refusal.

THE ISSUE OF A PLANNING PERMISSION

14.3 A grant of planning permission occurs when notification is given of the decision to grant planning permission. This was the conclusion reached by Woolf J in *R v West Oxfordshire District Council, ex p C H Pearce Homes Ltd*[1], after an extensive review of the authorities. It has been followed in practice since, being adopted (without dispute) by the House of Lords in *R (on the application of Burkett) v London Borough of Hammersmith and Fulham*[2].

14.4 Those decisions accord with the then and current legislative regime. Local planning authorities are required to 'give the applicant notice of their decision' within specified time periods[3]. Time periods for submitting planning appeals run 'from the date of the notice of the decision or determination' and from 'the date of the notice or determination'[4].

Consequently there is no planning permission before the decision notice is sent out.

---

[1] (1985) 26 RVR 156.
[2] [2002] UKHL 23, [2002] 1 WLR 1592.
[3] Town and Country Planning (Development Management Procedure) (England) Order 2015, SI 2015/595 (DMPO 2015), art 34(1); Town and Country Planning (Development Management Procedure) (England) Order 2010 (DMPO 2010), art 29(1); Town and Country Planning (Development Management Procedure) (Wales) Order 2012, SI 2012/801 (DMPO Wales), art 22(1).
[4] DMPO 2015, art 37(2)(a); DMPO 2010, art 33(2). DMPO Wales, art 26(2)(b) works from the date of the notice of the decision or determination.

Events between a resolution and decision notice

14.5 There may be a number of matters to deal with between the resolution and the decision notice:

(i) a planning obligation may need to be made, although its substance ought to be before the committee;

(ii) conditions may need to be drafted, but usually only if particular issues still require resolution or the committee voted to approve the application against officer advice;

(iii) in Greater London, applications of potential strategic importance may have to be referred to the Mayor of London;

(iv) the application may need to be referred to Ministers for a decision whether to call it in;

(v) occasionally, and this is not good practice, a resolution may be made before a consultation period has expired but the authority should be astute to ensure that the application is taken back to committee if any new matters are then raised;

(vi) particularly bad practice is to resolve to grant permission and then realise that a consultee has been omitted and then consulting them[5].

14.6 The events of Greenside provide a salutary lesson to landowners who move too quickly on a resolution to grant permission. The owner of the Grade II listed Modern Movement house on the Wentworth Estate in Surrey obtained a resolution to grant listed building consent for its demolition and planning permission for the construction of a mock-Jacobean house on the site. That day a councillor visiting the property had noticed men carrying furniture down the stairs but thought little of it. At the meeting officers said that the applications had to be referred to the Secretary of State. Over the following weekend the house was demolished. Soon after, in the resulting uproar, the Minister called in both applications. Following a public inquiry, the Secretary of State decided that listed building consent for demolition would not have been granted if the building was still standing, would not be approved because of an unlawful demolition and so no planning permission for a replacement dwelling would have been given. The owner was left with a flat above the garage, an open air swimming pool and a nice view of the 17th Green[6].

CONTENT OF THE DECISION NOTICE

Generally

14.7 There is no national prescribed or model form for a decision notice, although the Planning (Wales) Act 2015 proposes to set one out in a development order[7].

---

[5] For example *R (on the application of SAVE Britain's Heritage) v Gateshead Metropolitan Borough Council* [2014] EWHC 896 (Admin).
[6] Planning Inspectorate reference APP/Q3630/V/04/1145659.
[7] Town and Country Planning Act 1990, s 71ZA(1) prospectively inserted by the Planning (Wales) Act 2015, s 33(2) which would provide:

'A development order may include provision as to—
(a) the form of decision notices,
(b) the manner in which decision notices are to be given, and
(c) the particulars to be contained in decision notices'.
This provision is not yet in force.

14.8 *The issuing of planning permission*

Local planning authorities will have their own standard formats, identifying the applicant/agent, the land, the description of development, the planning application by reference number. The permission must say what it does such as to grant planning permission for the development in the application. Prospective planning permissions for different conditions (s 73) or retrospective application (s 73A) should be identified as such. Other decision notices, such as reserved matters approvals need to say clearly what they are for. The authority may wish to expressly incorporate the application and plans in its decision, by a formulation such as 'grant planning permission in accordance with the application and plans'.

Several particular points arise on the form and content of the decision notice.

Date of the decision

14.8 The date of the decision should be stated on the notice itself. The date is critical to the operation of any time period for implementing a permission and also for identifying the period for bringing an appeal to Ministers or judicial review proceedings in the High Court.

The notice ought to be dated when it is sent[8]. Giving an earlier date, such as the date of the resolution to grant planning permission can lead to confusion as to when the permission was granted and will cut down (albeit often marginally) on the time for the developer to implement the permission.

Even where the period between the resolution to grant permission and the issue of the notice is very short, such as a notice being sent out the day after an evening committee meeting, the correct approach is still to give the permission the date of despatch. In that example a planning permission will not have come into existence on the evening of the committee meeting but the following day, when the decision notice is sent out.

Conditions and notes

14.9 A planning permission should separately headline the conditions and any notes. Notes may be useful but do not have the status of planning conditions. They might help with interpretation or be informative about non-planning requirements, but a failure to comply with a note is neither a breach of condition nor the carrying out of development without planning permission.

14.10 Where planning permission is granted the notice must state 'clearly and precisely' the full reasons for each condition imposed[9]. Additionally the DMPO 2015 introduced in England a requirement for the decision notice to include the full reasons 'in the case of each pre-commencement condition, for the condition being a pre-commencement condition'[10]. A pre-commencement condition is[11]:

---

[8] The cases on local authority grants of planning permission do not address whether the permission comes into existence when the notice is sent or when it is received. Secretary of State decisions on s 78 planning appeals come into existence when they are sent.

[9] DMPO 2015, art 35(1)(a)(i); DMPO 2010, art 31(1)(a); DMPO Wales, art 24(1)(a).

[10] DMPO 2015, art 35(1)(a)(ii). This is to discourage the excessive use of pre-commencement conditions which hold up the start of the works.

[11] DMPO 2015, art 35(5).

'a condition imposed on the grant of a planning permission which must be complied with:

(a) before any building or other operation comprised in the development is begun; or

(b) where the development consists of a material change in the use of any buildings or other land, before the change of use is begun'.

The requirement to justify why conditions require compliance pre-commencement was born of a concern that such negative conditions were imposed too frequently and delayed the start of works by requiring the approval of details which were either unnecessary or which could be approved at a later stage.

In Wales in addition to stating 'clearly and precisely' the full reasons for each condition imposed, the policies and proposals in the development plan which are relevant to each condition must be set out[12], an obligation removed in England in 2013.

Refusals

14.11 A decision notice refusing permission shall 'state clearly and precisely their full reasons for the refusal, specifying all policies and proposals in the development plan which are relevant to the decision'[13]. Full reasons can be concise, but ought to explain clearly what point is being made in each reason. A common weakness in reasoning is referring to a policy which raises a number of potential issues without stating what the particular concern or concerns under that policy are.

14.12 Less commonly, where the Minister has given a direction restricting the grant of planning permission for the development for which application is made; or the Minister or a government Department has expressed the view that the permission should not be granted (either wholly or in part) or should be granted subject to conditions, the notice shall give details of the direction or of the view expressed[14].

Drawings

14.13 Approved drawings should be identified in the decision notice: it is particularly important that revisions to the drawings are identified and superseded documents omitted. It is a matter of judgment whether a condition requires the drawings to be complied with. Drawings which are approved but not the subject of conditions are part of the parameters of what has been approved, but there will be a materiality test as to whether a departure from the drawings means that the development is carried out without planning permission.

Prospective amendments in Wales will require decision notices to 'specify any plans or other documents in accordance with which the development to which it relates is to be carried out' and there will be a deemed condition that the development has to be carried out in accordance with these[15].

---

[12] DMPO Wales, art 24(1)(a).
[13] DMPO 2015, art 35(1)(b); DMPO 2010, art 31(1)(b). The Welsh obligation is to the same effect: DMPO Wales, art 24(1)(a).
[14] DMPO 2015, art 35(1)(c); DMPO 2010, art 31(1)(c); DMPO Wales, art 24(1)(b).
[15] Town and Country Planning Act 1990, s 71ZA(2), (3), prospectively inserted by the Planning (Wales) Act 2015, s 33. This is not yet in force.

14.14 *The issuing of planning permission*

The positive working statement in England

14.14 In England, where planning permission is granted subject to conditions or refused 'the notice shall include a statement explaining how, in dealing with the application, the local planning authority have worked with the applicant in a positive and proactive manner based on seeking solutions to problems arising in relation to dealing with a planning application'[16]. This provision was introduced to encourage co-operation in the application process rather than a simple refusal of the submitted application if there were difficulties with it.

14.15 The statement must explain how the authority had worked with the applicant in relation to that application and must therefore be specific to the application. It is insufficient to apply a standard text to all planning decisions (or one for approvals and one for refusals) and the officer must consider what is appropriate for the particular decision. However, common wording can often be used. Some planning permissions, such as straightforward householder applications, may need no discussion between the authority and the applicant and so formulaic text can be used. On the other hand, if there has been pre-application advice or communications from the authority in the course of the application to resolve matters, this should be mentioned, albeit briefly.

Duty to give notice of the commencement of development in Wales

14.16 The Planning (Wales) Act 2015 proposes to introduce a duty to give notice (in a specified manner) to the local planning authority prior to the commencement of development under particular planning permissions and to display a copy of the permission at or near the site when the development is being carried out[17]. Where this applies, the decision notice must set out these duties[18]. This provision is not yet in force.

EIA planning permission

14.17 If the planning application was subject to EIA under the relevant regulations and planning permission is granted then the decision notice must say that the environmental information has been taken into account[19].

The appeal notification

14.18 Where planning permission is refused or granted subject to conditions the decision notice must be accompanied by a notice explaining the rights of appeal to

---

[16] DMPO 2015, art 35(2); DMPO 2010, art 31(1)(cc). The duty was introduced by the Town and Country Planning (Development Management Procedure) (England) (Amendment No 2) Order 2012, SI 2012/2274, art 2(3) from 1 December 2012. It does not apply if the permission is granted unconditionally, which in practice can only arise on retrospective applications. No positive working duty applies in Wales.

[17] Town and Country Planning Act 1990, s 71ZB, prospectively inserted by the Planning (Wales) Act 2015, s 34.

[18] Town and Country Planning Act 1990, s 71ZB(4), prospectively inserted by the Planning (Wales) Act 2015, s 34.

[19] In England the Town and Country Planning (Environmental Impact Assessment) Regulations 2011, SI 2011/1824, reg 3(4). For no good reason the same duty is imposed by the DMPO 2015, art 35(4); DMPO 2010, art 31(2). Similar duplication arises in the Welsh secondary legislation: the Town and Country Planning (Environmental Impact Assessment) (England and Wales) Regulations 1999, reg 3(2) and the DMPO Wales, art 24(2).

the Minister, including the timescale for submitting an appeal and the right to serve a purchase notice[20]. This notice is to be in the terms (or substantially in the terms) set out in the DMPO[21]. Care needs to be taken with the notice to include the correct 6-month or 12-week period for appealing[22].

PUBLICITY OF PLANNING DECISIONS

14.19 The decision notice must be sent to the applicant for planning permission. Additionally if an owner or agricultural tenant on any part of the application site who was served with notice of the application makes representations then they must also be given notice of the decision[23]. A county planning authority shall notify the district planning authority of any decision[24]. Where a parish council has asked to be notified of applications relating to its area, it must be notified of the terms of the decision on any such planning application or reserved matters approval[25]. In Wales community councils are entitled to be notified of the terms of the decision on any planning application within their area which the authority has been required to consult them on[26].

A copy of the decision and any related planning obligation or s 278 agreement (under the Highways Act 1980) is to be put on part 2 of the planning register kept by the local planning authority[27].

Further reasoning and publicity is required for decisions on applications which have been subject to EIA[28].

If Natural England believes that its advice has been rejected by the local planning authority, it may require the authority to explain in writing whether that is the case and if so, why[29].

Local planning authorities are advised to notify the Health and Safety Executive of all decisions on planning applications on which the HSE has been consulted[30] and the Environment Agency where it has objected on flood risk grounds[31].

---

[20] A purchase notice requires the local planning authority to acquire the land if it is not and cannot be put in a reasonably beneficial state because of the refusal of planning permission or its grant subject to conditions.
[21] DMPO 2015, art 35(3), Sch 5; DMPO 2010, art 31(1)(d) and Sch 6; DMPO Wales, art 2(1)(c), Sch 5.
[22] The 12-week period applies to householder and minor commercial appeals in England and Wales: see DMPO 2015, art 37(2); DMPO 2010, art 33(2); DMPO Wales, art 26(2).
[23] DMPO 2010, art 28(2).
[24] DMPO 2015, art 24(3)(b); DMPO 2010, art 22(3)(a), made under the Town and Country Planning Act 1990, Sch 1, para 6(2).
[25] DMPO 2015, art 25(3)(a); DMPO 2010, art 23(3)(a), DMPO Wales, art 26 (noting the introduction of the householder and minor commercial appeals 12-week time limits in Wales from 22 June 2015).
[26] DMPO Wales, art 16(3).
[27] DMPO 2015, art 40(4); DMPO Wales, art 29(3).
[28] EIA Regulations 2011, reg 24(1) and in Wales the EIA Regulations 1999, reg 21. This requirement is set out and discussed in Chapter 7.
[29] Natural Environment and Rural Communities Act 2006, s 4(2), (3).
[30] *Planning Practice Guidance* 39-072-20140306; NAW Circular 20/01: *Planning Controls for Hazardous Substances*.
[31] *Planning Practice Guidance* 7-043-20150415.

14.20 *The issuing of planning permission*

INABILITY TO ISSUE A SECOND DECISION NOTICE

14.20 Once the decision notice has been sent out the local planning authority is not able to withdraw or replace the planning permission. It can only be disposed of by revocation under the Town and Country Planning Act 1990, s 97 or by a quashing order in judicial review proceedings.

The courts have for a long time suggested that local planning authorities were not able to issue a second planning decision on one application[32]. Those comments were *obiter*.

However in two judgments in 2013, the courts held that local planning authorities could not withdraw and re-issue decision notices to correct errors. In *R (on the application of Holder) v Gedling Borough Council*[33] the Council had decided to grant planning permission for a wind turbine subject to maximum noise levels at identified properties. By mistake the table setting out the properties and noise limits in a condition was omitted. Various conditions contained draft cross-references (for example to condition B) rather than referring to the correct numbered conditions. Following receipt of a judicial review pre-action letter from a local residents group the Council issued a replacement decision notice, bearing the date of the original, which attempted to correct these errors[34]. The second decision notice was quashed by the High Court as the Council had no power to issue it[35].

14.21 The issue was more fully considered by the Scottish Court of Session (Outer House) in *Archid Architecture and Interior Design v Dundee City Council*[36]. The Council had issued a notice which said it granted planning permission subject to conditions, but contained no conditions and under the reason for the decision set out what was plainly a reason for refusal. Six months later the Council said that the decision notice was incorrect and sent out a new notice which stated that planning permission was refused. Lord Glennie reviewed the English and Scottish authorities extensively (although not including *Holder*) and held that the first notice was valid unless and until the court ruled otherwise. The Council had no power to issue a further decision until that had been done. In a similar vein, the Court of Appeal held in *R (on the application of Gleeson Developments Ltd) v Secretary of State for Communities and Local Government*[37] that the Secretary of State could not withdraw a planning permission once it had been issued by a planning inspector, except by using the revocation procedure under the Town and Country Planning Act 1990, ss 97–100. Compensation is payable if a permission is revoked under those powers[38].

---

[32] For example *R v Yeovil Borough Council, ex p Trustees of Elim Pentecostal Church, Yeovil* (1972) 23 P & CR 39 at 44 per Lord Widgery CJ; *Heron Corpn Ltd v Manchester City Council* (1977) 33 P & CR 268 at 271–272 per Sir Douglas Frank QC.
[33] [2013] EWHC 1611 (Admin), [2013] JPL 1426.
[34] In fact it only partially corrected the mistakes, still leaving out part of the noise condition.
[35] *Holder* at para 54 per Kenneth Parker J.
[36] [2013] CSOH 137, [2014] JPL 336.
[37] [2014] EWCA Civ 1118, [2014] PTSR 1226, [2014] JPL 1386.
[38] Town and Country Planning Act 1990, s 107.

POTENTIAL REMEDIES FOR ERRONEOUS DECISION NOTICES

14.22 Where a decision notice has been sent out in error, either because it contains mistakes or there was no authority to issue the decision, the local planning authority will need to consider how to proceed.

The first question is whether the document which has been issued was actually a planning permission or refusal. A document may be so defective on its face as to not be a decision at all. An example would be a decision notice which is obviously missing a page or which does not say whether planning permission is granted or refused. A document which had no legal effect was the 'Permission for Development' issued in response to a lawful development certificate application in *James Hay Pension Trustees Ltd v First Secretary of State*[39]. Ward LJ put the point emphatically[40]:

> 'the Council used the wrong piece of paper. That, in my judgment, is an end to the matter. ...
>
> Looking at this certificate, one is totally at a loss to know whether it is a grant of permission or a Certificate of Lawfulness of proposed use. An interested party should not be expected to trawl through the file to discover what may have been intended. The Act specifies more precision. This certificate did not provide it'.

14.23 If the document is a planning grant or refusal, it may be possible to interpret it to the intended effect. The document has, however, to be interpreted within its own terms along with any documents expressly or necessarily incorporated in it, unless an ambiguity allows consideration of extrinsic material. The intention of the local planning authority in making the decision is irrelevant unless the evidence of that intention can be legitimately considered in contemporaneous extraneous material[41].

14.24 If the document was unauthorised or contains an error which cannot be dealt with by interpretation then a planning permission or other approval could be negated by revocation (with a prior agreement that it would be unopposed and no compensation would be claimed), a planning obligation being made by the landowner that the consent would not be implemented, or by a judicial review being brought. Traditionally these have been arranged with a councillor claimant, funded by the local authority, although there is no logical reason why the authority cannot apply to the High Court to quash its own unlawful act if there is no other ready alternative.

---

[39] [2006] EWCA Civ 1387, [2007] 1 P & CR 23. The document read:

> 'South Gloucestershire Council in pursuance of powers under the above-mentioned Act hereby PERMIT the details included in the first schedule on 13 July 2001 in accordance with the application and accompanying plans.
>
> Area Planning Manager
> On behalf of South Gloucestershire Council
> Date: 19th November 2001
>
> **First Schedule**
> (1) That the 1964 planning permission (SG 7789) is not a personal consent to the Bristol Avon River Board; and
> (2) that the store and class X use referred to in the planning permission SG 7789 is now covered by the reference to storage in the Use Class B8.
>
> **Second Schedule**
> Land at Winterbourne Station Yard ...'

[40] *James Hay* at paras 27 and 31.
[41] See Chapter 28.

Chapter 15

Non-material amendments to planning permissions

15.1 There are many reasons for wanting to make modest changes to a planning permission once it has been granted. Different ideas may emerge as the scheme proceeds, particular detailed doors or windows might not be available, the opportunity of the building works might be taken to make further alterations, a new developer or future occupier may come forward with different needs or designs. Provided the changes are not capable of affecting the acceptability of the scheme it ought to be reasonably straightforward to be able to make minor changes.

15.2 There are three mechanisms for allowing changes:

(i) immaterial variations which might or might not require informal approval;

(ii) changes approved under planning permissions;

(iii) non-material amendments approved under the Town and Country Planning Act 1990, s 96A.

THE IMPLICIT ABILITY TO MAKE IMMATERIAL CHANGES

15.3 A planning permission covers work which is specified in the detailed plans and any immaterial variation therein: *Lever (Finance) Ltd v Westminster City Council*[1]. In *Lever Finance*, Lord Denning MR said[2]:

'It is obvious that, as the developer proceeds with the work, there will necessarily be variations from time to time. Things may arise which were not foreseen. It should not be necessary for the developers to go back to the planning committee for every immaterial variation. The permission covers any variation which is not material. But then the question arises: Who is to decide whether a variation is material or not? In practice it has to be the planning officer'.

15.4 Some doubt was cast over this practice following the decision of the House of Lords in *Sage v Secretary of State for the Environment, Transport and the Regions*[3]. That case concerned a building constructed without any planning permission whatsoever and the issue was whether and if so, when, it had been substantially completed to start the time running for lawfulness[4]. In the course of his speech, Lord Hobhouse said[5]:

---

[1] [1971] 1 QB 222.
[2] At 230.
[3] [2003] UKHL 22, [2003] 1 WLR 983.
[4] Under Town and Country Planning Act 1990, s 171B(1).
[5] At para 23.

The implicit ability to make immaterial changes **15.6**

'When an application for planning consent is made for permission for a single operation, it is made in respect of the whole of the building operation. There are two reasons for this. The first is the practical one that an application for permission partially to erect a building would, save in exceptional circumstances, fail. The second is that the concept of final permission requires a fully detailed building of a certain character, not a structure which is incomplete. This is one of the differences between an outline permission and a final permission: section 92 of the Act. As counsel for Mr Sage accepted, if a building operation is not carried out, both externally and internally, fully in accordance with the permission, the *whole* operation is unlawful. She contrasted that with a case where the building has been completed but is then altered or improved. This demonstrates the fallacy in Mr Sage's case. He comes into the first category not the second'.

15.5 This has been interpreted in some quarters as not allowing any departure from the approved plans. That is to take *Sage* far from its context, which is when time runs to protect a building constructed without planning permission. Instead, the better approach is that, in accordance with *Lever Finance*, there is some scope for minor amendments that do not take the development wholly outside the scope of the planning permission. In *R (on the application of Midcounties Co-Operative Ltd) v Wyre Forest District Council* Ouseley J followed *Lever Finance* saying[6]:

'the starting point for Lord Denning's analysis was that a planning permission actually covered what was specified in it and immaterial variations. The source of the power to permit immaterial variations was not a private law estoppel but the proper construction of the planning permission itself'.

In that context, the appropriate question to ask should be what amounts to a minor or immaterial amendment? As stated above, this is a matter for the planning officer and the local planning authority to decide, subject to review by the courts, and there is a lack of guidance as to what immaterial means.

15.6 A few principles can be suggested:

(i) in *Lever Finance* Lord Denning expressly said he was not applying a *de minimis* test (that is, the change is so small that it does not matter). The power to approve changes does extend beyond the merely trivial;

(ii) materiality relates to materiality in planning terms, that is whether the change has an effect on planning considerations;

(iii) the effect on planning considerations must be of some substance for the change to be impermissible, or put another way, there must be the potential for the change to be refused on its planning merits. That will vary considerably from case to case: for example, changes to the fenestration of new buildings on a proposed housing estate might be unimportant, but minor changes to the plans on a historic building in a conservation area might require a fresh application;

(iv) the individual and cumulative effect of the changes must be considered. For example a series of small alterations to a detached house might create a much larger and differently proportioned building.

Conditions attached to planning permissions may provide for minor variations, subject to the similar (and possibly the same) constraints as changes under *Lever Finance*[7].

---

[6] [2009] EWHC 964 (Admin) at para 67.
[7] See *Midcounties* at para 70 per Ouseley J, discussed in Chapter 11.

15.7 *Non-material amendments to planning permissions*

TOWN AND COUNTRY PLANNING ACT 1990, s 96A

15.7 Non-material amendments can be made to planning permissions following an application made under the Town and Country Planning Act 1990, s 96A[8]. The effect of a non-material amendment under this section is to alter the existing planning permission, so the permission would only remain in its amended form. This is unlike a s 73 planning application which creates a new planning permission, subject to different conditions. Section 96A was inserted by the Planning Act 2008 because of concerns that *obiter* comments by Lord Hobhouse in *Sage v Secretary of State* meant that informal variations or departures from planning permissions were not permitted. As explained above, that concern was misplaced, but many local authorities had been refusing to approve minor changes to schemes.

15.8 The local planning authority is given power to make 'a change to any planning permission relating to land in their area if they are satisfied that the change is not material'[9]. As well as permissions granted by the local authority itself, the planning permission may be one granted on appeal or call in by the Secretary of State, by the Mayor of London or under permitted development rights. Section 96A can be used to amend a prior approval of details, or details submitted under prior notification processes, under the General Permitted Development Order as these are planning permissions, provided that the altered consent remains within the permitted development right. As with other planning decisions, responsibility is divided between district, county and other planning authorities[10].

15.9 An amendment may change the description of development, the approved drawings or conditions. By s 96A(3) the local planning authority's power includes the power:

'(a) to impose new conditions;

(b) to remove or alter existing conditions'.

It can therefore be used to change conditions, unlike the *Lever Finance* informal amendments which are solely concerned with drawings. It is possible to change the description of development under s 96A but such changes will have to be very modest.

15.10 The guiding question is whether the change is material. A cumulative approach is taken to a series of non-material amendments as by s 96A(2):

'In deciding whether a change is material, a local planning authority must have regard to the effect of the change, together with any previous changes made under this section, on the planning permission as originally granted'.

15.11 Materiality is not otherwise defined and in reality cannot be. Material in this context relates to whether the change is material in planning terms in the sense that it is capable of affecting the merits of the scheme. Non-material amendments are

---

[8] Originally introduced in England by the Planning Act 2008, s 190(2), the power was extended to Wales by the Town and Country Planning (Non-Material Changes and Correction of Errors) (Wales) Order 2014, SI 2014/1770, art 2(2) from 1 September 2014.
[9] Town and Country Planning Act 1990, s 96A(1).
[10] Town and Country Planning Act 1990, s 5, Sch 1, para 3(1)(b) make specific reference to s 96A.

Procedure for non-material amendments under s 96A **15.14**

intended to be resolved without requiring consultation or detailed consideration of evidence. For example, the introduction of a new window might be material if there is the possibility of creating overlooking but immaterial if it is some distance away from other users. Moving a proposed building by one metre may have no effect in a field but a potential impact next to an adjoining dwelling. The judgment relates to potential planning effects rather than the extent of the change from the approved scheme, so the materiality of altering a layby will not depend upon whether it is part of a short stretch of access road or a 10 kilometre bypass.

15.12 The power to apply is confined to 'a person with an interest in the land to which the planning permission relates' because the existing consent is changed[11]. A landowner could otherwise find that they are not able to carry out the development they obtained planning permission for because another person, who might be a prospective purchaser or a troublemaker, has had the consent changed. Whilst the modification may only affect the land in which the applicant has an interest[12], the section does not in terms prevent an enlargement of the application site. If the landowner only has an interest in part of the land to which the planning permission relates, the application may only be made in respect of that part[13]. For example, a developer which has sold parts of the site to other housebuilders may only make a s 96A application on the land it has retained.

15.13 There has been limited case law on s 96A. In *Corrie v Suffolk County Council*[14] a condition on a planning permission limited the throughput of waste at a transfer site to 95,000 tonnes a year, of which 5,000 tonnes could be hazardous waste. Following the commencement of judicial review proceedings, the hazardous waste limit was reduced to 800 tonnes under s 96A. A challenge to the ability to make this change was rejected on the basis that the lower figure reflected what had always been the anticipated actual operation of the facility[15].

PROCEDURE FOR NON-MATERIAL AMENDMENTS UNDER s 96A

15.14 An application for a non-material amendment under s 96A must be made in writing to the local planning authority on a form published by the Minister (or a form substantially to the like effect)[16]. A standard form is available on the Planning Portal and the application may be submitted electronically. A fee is payable, presently £28

---

[11] In Wales, but not in England, s 96A(10) provides that 'a person has an interest in land only if in relation to that land (or any mineral in, on or under it) the person:
 (a) is the estate owner of the fee simple;
 (b) is entitled to a tenancy granted or extended for a term of years certain of which not less than two years remain unexpired;
 (c) is the mortgagee of any interest or estate in the land; or
 (d) is a party to an estate contract within the meaning of section 2(4) of the Land Charges Act 1972'.
[12] Town and Country Planning Act 1990, s 96A(4) and (7) respectively.
[13] Town and Country Planning Act 1990, s 96A(6), (7).
[14] [2014] EWHC 2490 (Admin), [2015] Env LR 5.
[15] See Cranston J at para 71 and for context, paras 45–51, 66.
[16] In England under the Town and Country Planning (Development Management Procedure) (England) Order 2015 (DMPO 2015), art 10(2) formerly Town and Country Planning (Development Management Procedure) (England) Order 2010 (DMPO 2010), art 9(2); Town and Country Planning (Development Management Procedure) (Wales) Order 2012 (DMPO Wales), art 28A(2) all made under Town and Country Planning Act 1990, s 96A(5).

15.15 *Non-material amendments to planning permissions*

for householder applications and £195 in any other case in England[17]. Welsh fees are £30 for householder applications and otherwise £95[18].

15.15 At the same time as making the application, an applicant in England must notify any other owner of the land to which the application relates or agricultural tenant, stating[19]:

'(a) what the application is for and where the person can view a copy of it; and

(b) that any representations about the application must be made to the local planning authority within 14 days of the date when the notice is given'.

15.16 Any representations by another owner or agricultural tenant within that period must be taken into account by the local planning authority[20]. Where the proposed amendment affects only part of a development site which is in multiple ownership, the issue may arise as to whether the owners of other land within the planning permission site should be notified. Since the qualification for being able to make an application depends upon having an interest in the land on which the modification is proposed, rather than elsewhere on the planning permission site, the application would relate to the area identified within it, which may be less than the total planning permission site. In such circumstances there would be no need to notify owners elsewhere on the site.

15.17 There is no requirement in s 96A to consult the public or other bodies. The planning register must contain a copy of the application and any accompanying plans and drawings, along with any decision on the application including its date and the authority making the determination[21]. However whilst the register may be put on the Council's website, there is no obligation to do so[22]. Welsh local planning authorities are authorised to display a site notice or give notice to adjoining owners or occupiers if they wish[23]. They may also consult any person who was consulted under art 14 of the DMPO Wales on the planning application[24]. A consequence of the statutory power is that if they do consult under these, then a minimum 14-day period has to be given and representations received in that period considered[25]. It is good practice to publish non-material amendment applications on the authority's website and authorities might wish to consider whether some consultation is required in particular cases. An issue may well arise as to whether the amendment is non-material and that is partly a matter of judgment in the circumstances but also affected by whether people might have something to say about it.

---

[17] Town and Country Planning (Fees for Applications, Deemed Applications, Requests and Site Visits) (England) Regulations 2012, SI 2012/2920, reg 17.

[18] Town and Country Planning (Fees for Applications, Deemed Applications and Site Visits) (Wales) Regulations 2015, SI 2015/1522, reg 16. No fee is payable in Wales for alterations for disabled access or where the development would have been permitted development but for an art 4 direction or condition imposed on another planning permission: regs 4, 5.

[19] DMPO 2015, art 10(3); DMPO 2010, art 9(3). There is no equivalent requirement in the DMPO Wales.

[20] DMPO 2015, art 10(4); DMPO 2010, art 9(4). The 14-day period is beginning with the date when the notice was given, so includes that date. Consequently if notice is given on a Tuesday, the consultation period expires on the Monday two weeks later.

[21] DMPO 2015, art 40(5); DMPO Wales, art 29(3A).

[22] DMPO 2015, art 40(14); DMPO Wales, art 29(16).

[23] DMPO Wales, art 28A(3).

[24] DMPO Wales, art 28A(5).

[25] DMPO Wales, art 28A(6).

The decision

15.18 The local planning authority must determine a s 96A application by giving notice within 28 days of the receipt of the application or any longer period agreed with the applicant.[26] However there is no deemed approval of the application if the period is not complied with.

15.19 It does not necessarily follow that because an amendment is non-material it has to be approved, but it is difficult to see how a change which is immaterial could be unacceptable in planning terms. It might be that the purpose of the amendment is non-material but the local planning authority considers that it should be expressed differently in a condition or that further changes are required to conditions to make the alteration work. There is no expressed duty to have regard to the development plan (and so the presumption in favour of the plan does not apply) but policy is of assistance in deciding whether the alteration is non-material.

15.20 An issue arises whether it is possible for the local planning authority to make a different change to that applied for. The power is exercisable only on an application but is not expressed to be confined to approving the application made. Unlike creating a new planning permission, including by a s 73 or 73A application, the non-material amendment changes the existing permission such that the development can only be carried out in the amended form. A developer may therefore lose existing rights without any benefit if the authority changes the permission in a different way to that proposed. The prudent approach at least is for the local planning authority to suggest any alternative to the applicant for agreement before making it. Alterations may go to form or drafting style rather than substance. Substantive alterations or a view that certain elements are non-material changes but others are material and so the application might be allowed in part ought to be discussed before being made, or the application refused. Finally, it needs to be recognised that any amendment must arise out of the application, changes cannot be made to address other issues (perhaps underlying drafting problems) which occur to the local planning authority.

Challenges to local planning authority decisions

15.21 The Planning Practice Guidance considers that there is no right of appeal against the refusal of a s 96A application[27]. Rights of appeal to the Secretary of State include where the local planning authority 'refuse an application for any approval of that authority required under a development order'[28]. The DMPO sets out requirements for non-material amendments, including the timescale for the authority's determination of the application, but these are procedural rather than the duty to decide the application.

15.22 In the absence of a right of appeal to the Minister, an applicant disappointed by a refusal or a failure to determine the application has the remedy of judicial review. An application for a planning permission could be made, including under ss 73 or 73A, although the issues to be considered would then be wider. It is not an alternative remedy which means that an application for judicial review cannot be made.

---

[26] DMPO 2015, art 10(5), DMPO 2010, art 9(5); DMPO Wales, art 28A(7).
[27] Para 7a-011-20140306.
[28] Town and Country Planning Act 1990, s 78(1)(c).

15.23 *Non-material amendments to planning permissions*

Third parties who are disgruntled by a non-material amendment application being allowed may bring judicial review proceedings.

USE OF NON-MATERIAL AMENDMENTS

15.23 Non-material amendments are most obviously useful for minor changes to schemes. Use has though been more inventive.

A two-stage approach has sometimes been adopted to allow changes to approved plans. Section 73 planning applications may only change conditions, rather than the description of development. So if a condition on a planning permission requires compliance with the application drawings, whether or not they are identified in the condition, a s 73 application could be used to change the drawings. Changing the drawings may be more complicated where they were only approved as part of the grant of permission, but are not in the conditions. Whilst a s 73 application could introduce a condition which changes approved plans, that might be limited to the conditions which could have been imposed on the original application, and it is not possible under s 73 to alter the description of development. These complications can be avoided by a two stage approach. First, a s 96A non-material amendment application is made to incorporate the original plans in a condition, and potentially make the description of development more general, but not altering the development which can be carried out. Second, a s 73 application would then be made to change the condition listing the drawings so that new or revised drawings are approved[29].

15.24 In several cases s 96A amendments have been made to correct errors or possible weaknesses in planning permissions when judicial review proceedings are threatened or have been brought[30]. The extent to which such changes are non-material needs to be considered with care, particularly if the effect of amendment is to remove a potentially fatal problem in the permission.

---

[29] An approach taken, without criticism, in *R (on the application of Daniel) v East Devon District Council* [2013] EWHC 4114 (Admin) at paras 10–13 per Judge Birtles.
[30] For example, in *R (on the application of Barr) v North Somerset Council* [2015] EWHC 1735 (Admin) at paras 22, 23 per Holgate J.

Chapter 16

Reserved matters and the approval of details under conditions

16.1 Conditions on a planning permission may defer particular matters to a later submission and approval by the local planning authority. These may be in two forms:

- reserved matters pursuant to an outline planning permission;
- details which are required by a planning condition to be submitted and approved.

16.2 Conceptually there ought to be little difference between reserved matters and other approvals under conditions but separate formalities apply and outline/ reserved matters is a particular way of dealing with a planning consent that is so long established that it cannot really be treated all as one.

The grant of planning permission in outline form or subject to conditions has been addressed above. This chapter is concerned with the submission and approval of such details.

SCOPE OF DETAILS UNDER RESERVED MATTERS OR CONDITIONS

16.3 Common principles do apply to reserved matters and other details submitted under conditions. These consents operate within the parameters of the parent planning permission. Two important and interrelated constraints therefore arise:

(a) the details submitted must be within the terms already approved by the planning permission;

(b) the principles established in the planning permission have to be accepted when the details are assessed.

Put simply, the developer cannot go beyond the planning permission and the planning authority cannot go back on it.

16.4 An outline planning permission establishes the principle of the development permitted and at the reserved matters stage the principle cannot be questioned[1]. The planning authority cannot go back on what has been approved. As Lord Morris said in *Kingsway Investments v Kent County Council*[2]:

---

[1] *Camden London Borough Council v Secretary of State for the Environment* [1993] JPL 466 at 470 per Lionel Read QC.
[2] [1971] AC 72 at 96A.

16.5 *Reserved matters and the approval of details under conditions*

'So if permission is granted after an outline application the applicant clearly knows that that permission is conditional and that it will not be of use to him until he is able to submit details as to siting and design and the like which are acceptable. It must, of course, be assumed that the authority will act in good faith. They must not misuse their functions so as indirectly and without paying compensation to achieve what would amount to a revocation or modification of a permission already given'.

16.5 These propositions have been illustrated in a series of cases. In *Shemara Ltd v Luton Corpn*[3] outline permission had been granted for 'sixty one-roomed flatlets and sixty-four garages' and by condition the reserved matters had to incorporate the principles shown in sketch details, which had included three five-storey blocks. The subsequent details, showing four four-storey blocks, were not within the outline permission because they did not incorporate the sketch's principles[4]. Commercial projects have gone outside the description of development, such as a supermarket which was not within 'warehouse for wholesale and retail distribution of foodstuffs and household goods'[5] or which exceeded that comprised in a local centre[6]. Conversely, some outline permissions have been sufficiently flexible for reserved matters to accommodate new forms of retailing, such as retail warehouse consents envisaged for bulky goods being used for factory outlet centres selling discounted goods[7].

16.6 Precise details may be set in the outline permission. For example, in *R v Newbury District Council, ex p Chieveley Parish Council*[8] a floorspace figure given in an outline planning permission application form was held to be part of the outline permission (albeit not in a condition) and so restricted the floorspace at reserved matters to 'development on that scale, subject to minimal changes and to such adjustments as can reasonably be attributed to siting, design and external appearance'. Pill LJ said in *Chieveley*[9]:

'An outline application which specifies the floor area, as this one does, commits those concerned to a development on that scale, subject to minimal changes and to such adjustments as can reasonably be attributed to siting, design and external appearance'.

16.7 Conversely, if an outline planning permission residential development does not contain a number of dwellings (whether a particular figure or an upper or lower limit) then the number of dwellings on the site will be determined at reserved matters as part of the siting, design and landscaping: *R (on the application of Saunders) v Tendring District Council*[10].

---

[3] (1967) 18 P & CR 520, HC.
[4] At 529 per Diplock LJ. Another example is *R v Castle Point District Council, ex p Brooks* [1985] JPL 473 where outline planning permission was granted for a bungalow and a reserved matters approval for a very substantial house was quashed.
[5] *Calcaria Construction Co (York) Ltd v Secretary of State for the Environment* (1974) 27 P & CR 435.
[6] *Braintree District Council v Secretary of State for the Environment* (1995) 71 P & CR 323. Conversely the superstore proposed in *R (on the application of Belgrave Land) v Secretary of State* [2001] EWHC Admin 1127 was within the scope of a 'district centre'.
[7] *R v Bolsover District Council, ex p Ashfield District Council* (1995) 70 P & CR 507; *R v Ashford Borough Council, ex p Shepway District Council* [1999] PLCR 12.
[8] [1999] PLCR 51.
[9] At 60. The case is referred to as *Chieveley* to distinguish it from all of the other cases on conditions involving the former Newbury District Council.
[10] [2003] EWHC 2977 (Admin) at para 57 per Sullivan J.

Scope of details under reserved matters or conditions **16.10**

If the scale of development is to be qualified, it cannot be governed at the reserved matters stage except insofar as it can properly be judged at that stage having regard to the 'reserved matters'[11].

16.8 The merits of reserved matters applications must be considered by the planning authorities within the parameters of what had already been approved in the outline. In *Medina Borough Council v Proberun* details of the access had been refused by the local planning authority and appeal inspector on the basis that the only satisfactory access would be over third-party land. Glidewell LJ held, with reference to *Kingsway*[12]:

> 'In my opinion if a planning authority, perhaps because it regrets that outline planning permission has been granted, refuses to approve detailed proposals for access within the boundaries of the site, and makes it clear that only a scheme for access which involves the developer acquiring rights outside the land currently under its control will be approved, it is, to adopt Lord Morris's wording, misusing its function so as to achieve, without compensation, what would amount to a revocation or modification of a permission already given. Such a misuse of power patently is unlawful'.

16.9 Other matters of principle cannot be revisited. A refusal of reserved matters approval for office development on the ground that it provided more floorspace than was needed to make the development viable was unlawful[13].

16.10 The considerations which are relevant at the reserved matters stage depend upon the latitude given to that decision by the outline permission. So if the number of units or the size of the development is left at large, then all matters relevant to that should be considered. Sullivan J said, in respect of residential development where the number of houses was left to reserved matters[14]:

> 'In deciding what density is appropriate on a particular site, the relationship of that site to adjoining land uses, both residential and non-residential, is plainly relevant. Thus, if there was a noisy or a smelly use adjoining the northern boundary of the site the local planning authority might seek at the reserved matters stage to ensure that there was a layout which kept dwellings as far to the south of the site as possible, and, for example, placed the landscaping on the northern boundary. If reducing the number of dwellings or relocating the dwellings on the site would reduce the risks of an incident by making evacuation easier, I can see no reason whatsoever why the local planning authority should be precluded from considering such a factor at the reserved matters stage. Similarly, the effect of a proposed layout on adjoining land uses will be a relevant consideration. If placing too great a number of dwellings on a site would cause harm to the amenities of adjoining occupiers by reason of, for example, overlooking, or unnecessary loss of sunlight or daylight or undue visual intrusion (always bearing mind that the site is accepted as being suitable in principle for some form of residential development), then there is no reason why such factors cannot be considered at the approval of details stage'.

In that case the proximity of the scheme to a hazardous installation was relevant to the amount of housing proposed.

---

[11] *R v Newbury District Council, ex p Chieveley Parish Council* [1999] PLCR 51 at 60 per Carnwath J.
[12] At 85.
[13] *Camden London Borough Council v Secretary of State for the Environment* [1993] JPL 466 at 471 per Lionel Read QC.
[14] *R (on the application of Saunders) v Tendring District Council* [2003] EWHC 2977 (Admin) at para 62.

16.11 *Reserved matters and the approval of details under conditions*

16.11 The development plan and national planning policy will be relevant to issues which have not already been resolved in the outline permission, for example, design and neighbour amenity. The presumption in favour of the development plan in the Planning and Compulsory Purchase Act 2004, s 38(6) applies to the determination of reserved matters applications. In *St George Developments v Secretary of State for the Environment*[15] the High Court held that the predecessor, the Town and Country Planning Act 1990, s 54A, governed the Secretary of State's determination of appeals on approvals required by conditions and said this seemed to apply also to the local planning authority's determination.

OMISSION OF APPROVED ELEMENTS

16.12 Several, rather dated, cases have dealt with whether a reserved matters for the whole site can omit elements which are in the outline permission. In *Heron Corpn Ltd v Manchester City Council*[16] the complete demolition of the site and its redevelopment had been envisaged but following the grant of outline planning permission six houses on the site were listed and listed building consent for demolition was then refused. The Court of Appeal held that complete demolition had been envisaged but was not required and so reserved matters could omit the listed buildings[17]. Bridge LJ emphasised that the developer had originally omitted from the project the main building which was then listed, then included it at the local authority's request to facilitate a new highway. The listing frustrated the local authority's road scheme but he thought it unreasonable to frustrate the redevelopment[18].

16.13 In *R v Hammersmith and Fulham London Borough Council, ex p Greater London Council*[19] a bus garage which had been included in the description of development of an outline planning permission was abandoned at reserved matters stage. The GLC, which had objected to the garage at the outline stage, then challenged the reserved matters approval as non-compliant with the outline because the garage was not included. Against that unattractive background the Court of Appeal held the reserved matters approval to be valid. It considered that the exclusion of the bus garage was a planning advantage. Whilst the GLC's position looked opportunistic, the outcome is problematic given the role of public consultation in the planning process. A bus station might have been seen as necessary by some considering the planning application or the quantum of other development which could subsequently be achieved by its omission seen as excessive. It may turn on the interpretation of the planning permission which ought to reflect the application made. A planning application which provides for a range of potential uses, not all of which may be brought forward, is acceptable as a concept. Conversely, permission ought not to be obtained on the basis that the project will have particular elements and then they are omitted and replaced by other development within the original description.

16.14 What outline planning permissions require has to be looked at with care and permissions are usually much more detailed in the present day, with application documents being incorporated, numerous conditions and often EIA. The degree of

---

[15] [1996] JPL 35, [1994] 3 PLR 33.
[16] [1978] 1 WLR 937.
[17] Per Lord Denning MR at 944.
[18] At 948.
[19] (1985) 51 P & CR 120.

flexibility found in the *Heron Corporation* and *GLC* consents is less likely to arise in modern permissions.

16.15 Reserved matters or the details submitted under a condition may be required by condition to be in accordance with or have regard to a masterplan, development brief or other document. The wording of the requirement is critical. Compliance with that document may be expressly required[20] but lesser terms such as 'have regard to' or 'take full account of' do not require slavish adherence and a measure of flexibility is permissible[21].

CONDITIONS ON RESERVED MATTERS APPROVALS

16.16 Conditions may be applied to a reserved matters approval: *R v Newbury District Council, ex p Stevens and Partridge*[22]. Roch J also held in that case that such conditions may not materially derogate from the outline planning permission already granted. The derogation issue, an aspect of the *Kingsway Investments* principle set out above, as was also considered by Sullivan J in *Redrow Homes Ltd v First Secretary of State*[23]. In 1957 planning permission for a very large industrial estate had authorised accesses to existing public highways at particular points, with the precise location and details of those accesses to be approved under conditions. These details came to be approved in 2001 when the area and the highway network had been transformed[24]. The Minister approved the details, imposing a condition restricting the use of one of the accesses to public service vehicles only. The court held that the accesses approved in 1957 were for all purposes and so the condition had the unlawful effect of modifying the permission[25]. Sullivan J said[26]:

'A condition may lawfully be imposed upon an approval of details, but its effect must not be such as to amount to a revocation or modification of the "parent" outline planning permission'.

Consequently in that case[27]:

'... the Secretary of State's power was limited to securing the best (or the least worst) form of all-purpose access onto the B4055 that could be achieved within the limits imposed by the 1957 planning permission'.

16.17 The restrictions on the conditions which can be imposed go wider, in that the conditions must relate to the reserved matters or details which are being approved. In *Tesco Stores Ltd v North Norfolk District Council*[28] the parties agreed, and the court

---

[20] Such as 'shall comply with' or 'shall be in accordance with'.
[21] *R (on the application of Belgrave Land) v Secretary of State* [2001] EWHC Admin 1127, paras 61, 62 per Sullivan J.
[22] (1993) 65 P & CR 438 at 447 per Roch J. Yet another Newbury conditions case and so best known as *Stevens and Partridge*. The conditions point had been raised but not decided in *Chelmsford Corpn v Secretary of State for the Environment and Homes East Anglia Ltd* (1971) 22 P & CR 880.
[23] [2003] EWHC 3094 (Admin), [2004] JPL 1273.
[24] *Redrow* at para 10.
[25] At para 57.
[26] [2004] JPL 1273 at para 44.
[27] At para 61 per Sullivan J, following *Proberun Ltd v Secretary of State for the Environment* (1991) 61 P & CR 77.
[28] [1998] PLCR 183 at 191 per Judge Langan QC. The unlawful condition could be severed from the reserved matters approval and so did not affect its lawfulness.

16.18 *Reserved matters and the approval of details under conditions*

accepted, that the addition of an archaeological works condition in a reserved matters approval was unlawful when the outline planning permission had been silent on the issue. Similarly, attempts in reserved matters approvals to impose hours of operation conditions or to change the period for implementing the planning permission would also be unlawful.

APPLICATIONS FOR RESERVED MATTERS APPROVAL

16.18 In England an application for the approval of reserved matters[29]:

'(a) must be made in writing to the local planning authority and give sufficient information to enable the authority to identify the outline planning permission in respect of which it is made;

(b) must include such particulars, and be accompanied by such plans and drawings, as are necessary to deal with the matters reserved in the outline planning permission'.

16.19 There is no requirement to use a standard form, although one is available. If the application and plans are submitted in hard form, they must be accompanied by three copies[30]. The application is made to the local planning authority[31]. If the planning permission was granted by the Mayor of London then the reserved matters application would be made to the London borough council concerned, unless the Mayor has directed otherwise[32].

The Welsh provisions are similar except that a standard form must be used[33], drawings and plans must be to an identifiable scale and plans must indicate the direction of North[34].

In practice applications must include whatever is necessary to justify the details, bearing in mind the more limited nature of the exercise compared to a planning application.

16.20 An application for full planning permission cannot also be a reserved matters application. The decision in *Etheridge v Secretary of State for the Environment*[35] that a full planning permission can also be a grant of reserved matters approval under a pre-existing outline planning permission should not be followed. It concerned approvals granted in the 1960s where the court suggested that it did not matter whether 'the requirement as to details ... should be fulfilled on an application for full planning permission rather than an application for approval of details alone'[36]. Application procedures and the role of public consultation have become much more important. The approval of an application needs to reflect the scheme as applied for

---

[29] Town and Country Planning (Development Management Procedure) (England) Order 2015 (DMPO 2015), SI 2015/595, art 6.
[30] DMPO 2015, art 6(c).
[31] DMPO 2015, art 11(1).
[32] Town and Country Planning Act 1990, s 2C(1).
[33] Town and Country Planning (Development Management Procedure) (Wales) Order 2012 (DMPO Wales), SI 2012/801, art 4(1).
[34] DMPO Wales, art 4(2). That requirement applies to planning applications in England (DMPO 2015, art 7(2)) and is good practice in any event.
[35] (1983) 48 P & CR 35.
[36] At 39, 40.

Publicity and consultation on reserved matters and approvals of details **16.22**

and on which people would have understood they had the opportunity to comment, ensuring consideration of planning matters in the public interest[37].

As with planning applications, the local planning authority must acknowledge the receipt of valid reserved matters applications[38]. If they subsequently decide that the application is invalid then they must promptly inform the applicant[39].

FEES FOR RESERVED MATTERS APPLICATIONS

16.21 For reserved matters applications the fee is calculated on the same basis as a full planning permission fee for the category of development which has been authorised by the outline planning permission[40]. So if the reserved matters application is for the whole of the site then the fee is what would be the current outline fee for that site. A reserved matters application on part of the site is charged on the area or floorspace of that part. However, if an applicant has made previous reserved matters applications under that permission for which the full reserved matters fee for the site has been paid and no other person has applied for reserved matters, any further reserved matters application they make is charged at a low flat rate[41]. Reserved matters fees are refunded if the application has not been determined within 26 weeks of the receipt of a valid application unless that period has been extended by agreement[42].

PUBLICITY AND CONSULTATION ON RESERVED MATTERS AND APPROVALS OF DETAILS

16.22 In general there is no statutory requirement for applications for the approval of reserved matters or of details under conditions to be publicised or consulted upon[43], unless it is subject to the EIA requirements discussed below. However county planning authorities are required to send copies of the application, plans, drawings and any accompanying information to the relevant district planning authority[44] and national park authorities who determine any application for the approval of reserved matters shall consult the authority who would otherwise have been the district planning authority[45].

---

[37] This approach to procedural compliance is illustrated by *Henry Boot Homes Ltd v Bassetlaw District Council* [2002] EWCA Civ 983, [2003] JPL 1030 at 46–54 per Keene LJ.
[38] DMPO 2015, art 11(2); DMPO Wales, art 8(1).
[39] DMPO 2015, art 11(5); DMPO Wales, art 8(3).
[40] Town and Country Planning (Fees for Applications, Deemed Applications, Requests and Site Visits) (England) Regulations 2012, SI 2012/2920, Sch 1, Part 1, para 1 and Part 2; Town and Country Planning (Fees for Applications, Deemed Applications and Site Visits) (Wales) Regulations 2015, SI 2015/1522, Sch 1, Part 1, para 1 and Part 2. The scale of fees for buildings is divided between applications for outline planning permission and 'other cases', the latter including reserved matters. See also the *Planning Practice Guidance* para 22-013-20141017.
[41] £385 in England and Wales: Town and Country Planning (Fees for Applications, Deemed Applications, Requests and Site Visits) (England) Regulations 2012, Sch 1, para 4; Town and Country Planning (Fees for Applications, Deemed Applications and Site Visits) (Wales) Regulations 2015, Sch 1, para 4. See *Planning Practice Guidance* para 22-015-20141017.
[42] Town and Country Planning (Fees for Applications, Deemed Applications, Requests and Site Visits) (England) Regulations 2012, reg 9A.
[43] See DMPO 2015, arts 15, 27; DMPO 2010, arts 13, 30.
[44] DMPO 2015, art 11(4).
[45] Town and Country Planning Act 1990, Sch 1, para 4.

16.23 *Reserved matters and the approval of details under conditions*

Reserved matters applications and any accompanying plans and drawings are placed on Part 1 of the Planning Register[46]. The date of any approval must be included in Part 2 of the Planning Register[47]. A promise might be made by the local planning authority in its statement of community involvement, or in handling the outline application, that later reserved matters applications or particular approvals of details will be consulted upon. Any such promise is likely to give rise to a legitimate expectation that it will be followed[48].

EIA AND SUBSEQUENT APPLICATIONS

16.23 If development was, or could have been, subject to EIA when planning permission was originally granted, then the EIA regime applies to reserved matters and certain approvals of details under conditions which are required before a stage in the development can proceed. Pursuant to the EIA Regulations, 'subsequent application' means:[49]

'an application for approval of a matter where the approval:
(a) is required by or under a condition to which a planning permission is subject; and
(b) must be obtained before all or part of the development permitted by the planning permission may be begun'.

16.24 Where EIA was carried out on the original planning application, the planning authorities must take into account any further environmental statement submitted and if none is, the original environmental statement as far as it is relevant[50] along with any other environmental information[51]. If the planning authority does not consider that the original statement is sufficient for the present purposes and it has not been supplemented, then it may require further information to be submitted[52].

16.25 If the local planning authority could have required EIA of the original planning application (that is, it was Sch 1 or Sch 2 development under the EIA Regulations) but no EIA was carried out at that time, then a screening opinion or direction must be adopted for any subsequent application or an environmental statement submitted[53].

16.26 Any subsequent application which requires EIA has to be publicised under the DMPO 2015, art 16 or the DMPO Wales, art 12 in the same way as a planning application for EIA development, with the notice referring to a 'subsequent application in respect of'[54].

---

[46] DMPO 2015, art 40(3)(a); DMPO Wales, art 29(2)(a).
[47] DMPO 2015, art 40(4)(e); DMPO Wales, art 29(3)(e).
[48] See paras **6.110–6.116**.
[49] In England under the Town and Country Planning (Environmental Impact Assessment) Regulations 2011 (EIA Regulations 2011), SI 2011/1824, art 2(1); in Wales under the Town and Country Planning (Environmental Impact Assessment) (England and Wales) Regulations 1999 (EIA Regulations 1999), SI 1999/293, art 2(1).
[50] EIA Regulations 2011, reg 8(2).
[51] EIA Regulations 2011, reg 3(4); EIA Regulations 1999, reg 3(2). The environmental information will include the environmental statement: see reg 2(1).
[52] In England EIA Regulations 2011, reg 8(3) says that the power in reg 22 to require further information should be used. A similar power is available in Wales: EIA Regulations 1999, reg 19.
[53] EIA Regulations 2011, reg 9; EIA Regulations 1999, reg 7(1).
[54] EIA Regulations 2011, reg 16(4); EIA Regulations 1999, reg 13(3A).

Applications for the approval of details under conditions **16.30**

Where EIA is carried out on a subsequent application, it is processed, considered and the outcome publicised in a similar manner to a planning application for EIA development.

MULTIPLE APPLICATIONS AND APPROVALS

16.27 Reserved matters can be applied for in their totality in a single application or in multiple applications covering different types of matters or different parts of the site or indeed several applications over the same ground[55]. The local planning authority will have to consider whether part can be approved on its merits without knowing other details of the site, but that is a question of whether the application should be refused rather than whether it is valid[56]. If the permission expressly allows approvals in phases then those phases must be able to be considered independently, although it would be common to have an overall masterplan. Overlaps and inconsistent reserved matters can be approved, but the scheme only built out once. Reserved matters applications do have to be made in accordance with the time allowed by a condition. Determination of a reserved matters application may take place after that period.

16.28 It is also possible to amend a reserved matters application, even after the time for submitting a further reserved matters application has expired, provided it does not in substance amount to a new application: *Inverclyde District Council v Lord Advocate* per Lord Keith[57]:

> 'The planning authority must simply deal with the application procedurally in a way which is just to the applicant in all the circumstances. That being so, there is no good reason why amendment of the application should not be permitted at any stage, if that should prove necessary in order that the whole merits of the application should be properly ascertained and decided upon. There is, however, one obvious limitation upon this freedom to amend, namely that after the expiry of the period limited for application for approval of reserved matters … an amendment which would have the effect of altering the whole character of the application, so as to amount in substance to a new application, would not be competent'.

16.29 However applications to amend reserved matters approvals may only be made within the time limit for a reserved matters application, unless they are non-material amendments which are permissible on a *Lever Finance* basis[58]. The s 96A non-material amendment procedure does not apply and there is no mechanism short of a new planning permission which will extend time for another reserved matters application.

APPLICATIONS FOR THE APPROVAL OF DETAILS UNDER CONDITIONS

16.30 An application for agreement under a condition is not an application for planning permission. It must be made writing[59] and any approval must be given in

---

[55] *Heron Corpn Ltd v Manchester City Council* [1978] 1 WLR 937 at 943–944 per Lord Denning MR, at 946 per Orr LJ and at 946–947 per Bridge LJ.
[56] *Heron Corpn* at 947 per Bridge LJ.
[57] (1982) 43 P & CR 375 at 397.
[58] *Lever Finance v Westminster City Council* [1971] 1 QB 222 and see Chapter 15.
[59] DMPO 2015, art 27(1). There is no explicit requirement for a written application in Wales, but it must be 'received' by the local planning authority (DMPO Wales, art 23) and an approval which must be in writing (see *Flintshire* below) could not be understood without a written application.

16.31 *Reserved matters and the approval of details under conditions*

writing[60]. The application must include 'such particulars, and be accompanied by such plans and drawings, as are necessary to deal with the application'[61]. No form is prescribed for such application and they are often made informally by letter or e-mail. There may be circumstances in which an application and approval of reserved matters includes approvals under other conditions, even if this is not explicit: see *Tesco Stores Ltd v North Norfolk District Council*[62]. However, all applications for approvals should be clear as to which conditions or parts of conditions are the subject of the application, whether all or particular parts of the scheme are in the application and which documents are being submitted for approval. Drawing numbers and report titles and dates should be set out in the application. There is otherwise a danger of an application being overlooked or it being unclear what was approved. All of this can be troublesome in deciding whether the permission can be or has been implemented.

16.31 Fees have been introduced for applications for the approval of details under conditions, albeit this is curiously expressed in England as being when a 'request is made to a local planning authority for written confirmation of compliance with a condition or conditions'[63]. In Wales it is more straightforwardly called an application made under art 23 of the DMPO Wales[64]. For approvals relating to works to existing dwellinghouses, their boundaries or within their curtilages, the fee for each request is £28 in England and £30 in Wales. Otherwise the fee is £97 in England and £95 in Wales[65]. The fee is for each request (or application), not for each condition. Consequently the same fee is changed for a letter submitting details under one condition or six.

16.32 The fee is refunded if the decision is not made within 12 weeks of receipt of the request in England[66] or eight weeks in Wales[67].

16.33 The date of any subsequent approval, but not the contents of the approval nor the mere fact of an application, have to be placed on the Planning Register[68]. Some local planning authorities usefully go beyond this requirement and include applications for the approval of details and decisions on their websites.

16.34 The approval of details under a condition on a planning permission must have regard to all material considerations, including the statutory duties upon the local planning authority under planning legislation and planning policy. However an approval cannot be used 'to achieve what would amount to a revocation or modification of a permission already given'[69]. The question for the authority

---

[60] *R v Flintshire County Council, ex p Somerfield Stores* [1998] PLCR 336.
[61] DMPO 2015, art 27(1)(b).
[62] [1998] PLCR 183 (High Court), [1999] JPL 920 (Court of Appeal).
[63] Town and Country Planning (Fees for Applications, Deemed Applications, Requests and Site Visits) (England) Regulations 2012, reg 16(1).
[64] Town and Country Planning (Fees for Applications, Deemed Applications and Site Visits) (Wales) Regulations 2015, reg 15(1).
[65] Town and Country Planning (Fees for Applications, Deemed Applications, Requests and Site Visits) (England) Regulations 2012, reg 16(1); Town and Country Planning (Fees for Applications, Deemed Applications and Site Visits) (Wales) Regulations 2015, reg 15(1). By a quirk of drafting, car parks and service roads are also subject to the lower fee in Wales.
[66] Town and Country Planning (Fees for Applications, Deemed Applications, Requests and Site Visits) (England) Regulations 2012, reg 16(2).
[67] Town and Country Planning (Fees for Applications, Deemed Applications and Site Visits) (Wales) Regulations 2015, reg 15(2).
[68] DMPO 2015 art 40(4)(e); DMPO Wales, art 29(3)(e).
[69] *Kingsway Investments v Kent County Council* [1971] AC 72 at 96A per Lord Morris.

considering an application for the approval of details which would cause planning harm is whether they are the best scheme that can be approved within the terms of the planning permission that has been granted[70].

16.35 The local planning authority should have regard to the development plan insofar as it is material to the determination of an approval under a condition, and apply the presumption in favour of the plan in the Planning and Compulsory Purchase Act 2004, s 38(6).

16.36 Where an aftercare condition specifies a use for agriculture, the mineral planning authority shall consult the Secretary of State for Environment, Food and Rural Affairs or the Welsh Ministers before approving an aftercare scheme. Similarly if the specified use is for forestry then the Forestry Commission or the Natural Resources Body for Wales must be consulted[71].

16.37 A person interested in land which is subject to an aftercare scheme under a minerals planning permission may ask the mineral planning authority to certify that the condition has been complied with[72].

DEEMED DISCHARGE OF DETAILS UNDER CONDITIONS

16.38 A process whereby a failure to determine details under a condition imposed on a grant of planning permission[73] leads to its deemed approval has been introduced in England by the Town and Country Planning Act 1990, s 74A and the GPDO 2015. In brief, the applicant can give the local planning authority notice that unless an outstanding application is determined within a certain period it will be deemed to have been approved.

16.39 This deemed discharge is not available where the applicant and the local planning authority have agreed in writing that it does not apply and in the following categories of conditions in the DMPO 2015, Sch 6:

- development which requires EIA or is likely to have a significant effect on a Special Protection Area or Special Area of Conservation or would require such assessment or have such an effect if not for the condition. This latter element may be harder to identify;

- those intended to manage the risk of flooding;

---

[70] *Proberun Ltd v Secretary of State for the Environment and Medina Borough Council* (1991) 61 P & CR 77.
[71] Town and Country Planning Act 1990, Sch 5, para 4.
[72] Town and Country Planning Act 1990, Sch 5, para 5. An unusual intervention of the planning system in private rights it is worth noting in Sch 5, para 6:

'A person who has complied with an aftercare condition but who has not himself won and worked minerals or deposited refuse or waste materials shall be entitled, subject to any condition to the contrary contained in a contract which is enforceable against him by the person who last carried out such operations, to recover from that person any expenses reasonably incurred in complying with the aftercare condition'.

[73] The procedure is not available for the approval of details under conditions imposed by a reserved matters approval.

16.40 *Reserved matters and the approval of details under conditions*

- planning permissions on sites of special scientific interest which are likely to have significant effects on the site or would be likely to do so save for the condition;
- conditions relating to identifying or remediating contaminated land;
- archaeological investigations;
- access to the highway or conditions requiring highway agreements[74];
- the approval of reserved matters[75];
- conditions requiring planning obligations to be entered into;
- conditions attached to planning permissions granted by development order[76], special development order[77], local development order, neighbourhood development order, simplified planning zone, enterprise zone scheme or deemed planning permission[78].

Additionally deemed discharge is only available if the application for the planning permission which contains the condition was made on or after 15 April 2015[79].

16.40 If the deemed discharge mechanism is available, the developer must first make an application for the approval of details under the particular condition. It may then give a 'deemed discharge notice' to the local planning authority not earlier than six weeks after receipt of the application[80] or any shorter period agreed with the local planning authority[81]. There is no prescribed form for a deemed discharge notice and so it could be in letter or e-mail form rather than a 'notice' style but it must:

- provide details of the application for the approval under the condition and identify that planning condition;
- if the time for appealing for non-determination has arisen, confirm that no appeal has been submitted; and
- specify the date on which the deemed discharge is to take effect.

The deemed discharge date must be no earlier than the day when the right to appeal for non-determination arises or 14 days starting the day after the deemed discharge notice is received by the local planning authority[82].

16.41 Deemed discharge takes place on the date in the notice unless the local planning authority have given notice of their decision before that date[83]. Consequently if the notice is given on Thursday 1, deemed discharge can take place on Thursday 15.

---

[74] For the carrying out or funding of works in the highway under Highways Act 1980, s 278.
[75] Reserved matters are excluded twice, in DMPO 2015, art 27(3)(a) and Sch 6, para 8.
[76] This includes planning permission granted by the General Permitted Development Order and under a special development order.
[77] Under Town and Country Planning Act 1990, s 264.
[78] Under Town and Country Planning Act 1990, ss 90, 293A.
[79] DMPO 2015, art 47(5) in accordance with Town and Country Planning Act 1990, s 74A(9).
[80] DMPO 2015, art 29(2). The six-week period starts the day after the application is received.
[81] Such an agreement could be in a Planning Performance Agreement.
[82] DMPO 2015, art 29(4).
[83] DMPO 2015, art 28(2).

APPEALS ON RESERVED MATTERS APPLICATIONS OR APPLICATIONS FOR THE APPROVAL OF DETAILS

16.42 The applicant may appeal to the Secretary of State or the Welsh Ministers if the local planning authority 'refuse an application for any consent, agreement or approval of that authority required by a condition imposed on a grant of planning permission or grant it subject to conditions'[84] or fail to determine it within the prescribed period or any longer period agreed in writing[85]. In England the prescribed period for reserved matters involving major development is 13 weeks and in other reserved matters cases, eight weeks[86]. The Welsh reserved matters period is eight weeks[87]. For approvals of details under other conditions the prescribed period is eight weeks[88]. If the condition refers to details being approved by the local planning authority, an appeal can still be brought and the words 'or approved by the Minister' being read in[89]. Such appeals proceed in the same way as an appeal on a planning application, recognising the limits on determinations discussed in this chapter.

REVISION OF PLANNING PERMISSION DECISION NOTICES IN WALES

16.43 In Wales it is proposed to revise the original planning permission's decision notice if any consent, agreement or approval is given under a condition on that permission or the condition is imposed, removed or altered[90]. This change, made by the Planning (Wales) Act 2015, has not come into force at present.

---

[84] Town and Country Planning Act 1990, s 78(1)(b).
[85] Town and Country Planning Act 1990, s 78(2).
[86] In England the time periods for determining reserved matters begin on the day following the receipt of the application: DMPO 2015, art 34(2).
[87] The Welsh time period begins with the date on which the application is received, so will end one day before the English eight week period: Town and Country Planning (Development Management Procedure) (Wales) Order 2012, art 22(2).
[88] The eight week period is in DMPO 2015, art 34 and DMPO Wales, art 23. However as with reserved matters, the Welsh period begins on the day the application is received, whilst the English period starts the following day.
[89] *Kingsway Investments Ltd v Kent County Council* [1971] AC 72 at 89 per Lord Reid.
[90] Town and Country Planning Act 1990, s 71ZA(4), (5), prospectively inserted by the Planning (Wales) Act 2015, s 33.

Chapter 17

Call-ins and the role of Ministers

17.1 Whilst some decisions are taken by council officers, civil servants or planning inspectors, the planning process is ultimately one of decision-making by democratically elected politicians. The House of Lords endorsed the role of politicians in making planning decisions in *R (on the application of Alconbury) v Secretary of State for the Environment, Transport and the Regions*[1]. In that case Lord Nolan said[2]:

'In the relatively small and populous island which we occupy, the decisions made by the Secretary of State will often have acute social, economic and environmental implications. A degree of central control is essential to the orderly use and development of town and country. Parliament has entrusted the requisite degree of control to the Secretary of State, and it is to Parliament which he must account for his exercise of it. To substitute for the Secretary of State an independent and impartial body with no central electoral accountability would not only be a recipe for chaos: it would be profoundly undemocratic'.

17.2 The Law Lords were there considering the argument that it was contrary to the right to a hearing before an independent and impartial tribunal under article 6 of the European Convention on Human Rights that the final decisions on planning merits could be taken by a Minister rather than a planning inspector or, indeed, a judicial body. They recognised that planning is a political process and that the political decision-making does not stop with the formulation of policy. Determining planning applications is not a mechanistic application of planning policy nor, to put the point more politely, is giving effect to policy simply a matter of professional judgment on which expert men and women should be capable of agreeing, or in default of agreement having the matter decided by another expert. At the smallest scale, whether a house extension has an unacceptably harmful impact on neighbouring property or the character and appearance of an area, is a matter on which any person can reach a judgment, albeit that it should be informed by technical analysis and professional assessment.

17.3 Householder planning applications rarely end up in the red box of even a Parliamentary Under Secretary of State at the Department of Communities and Local Government. The applications which do, and which may cross the Secretary of State's desk, tend to be far more substantial and far more political. They may commonly include very large commercial developments, housing in the Green Belt, gypsy and traveller sites, tall towers and wind turbines. Some of these projects are so substantial with potentially considerable positive and negative effects that general policies cannot provide an answer to a particular application. The individual

---

[1] [2003] 2 AC 295.
[2] At 323.

decision is inherently a matter of personal judgment and the political authorities can decide that they should determine it, rather than officials. In some cases Ministers have taken control of particular types of application to demonstrate to the Planning Inspectorate how they consider their policy should be applied. This is a clear and effective way of ensuring that inspectors understand how Ministers would balance competing factors.

MINISTERIAL POWERS OF INTERVENTION

17.4 The powers of Ministers to intervene in planning and similar applications are:

(i) directing the local planning authority not to determine a particular application for a specified period or until the direction is lifted;

(ii) directing local planning authorities to refer particular classes of applications to him before granting permission so that he can consider whether to call in an application;

(iii) taking an application or development order out of the local planning authority's jurisdiction so it can be determined by the Minister (a call-in);

(iv) determining a planning appeal himself rather than leaving it to an inspector to determine (known as the Minister 'recovering jurisdiction');

(v) an extant, but unused power to constitute a Planning Inquiry Commission to consider a called-in application or planning appeal.

17.5 In certain underperforming council areas planning applications may be made directly to Ministers[3]. These may be determined by inspectors or the Minister may direct that he will determine an application himself.

17.6 Planning appeals are made to the Secretary of State in England or the Welsh Ministers but are transferred to inspectors to determine. However, the Minister may decide to take over the responsibility of determining the appeal by recovering jurisdiction over it. The decision to recover jurisdiction shares some similarities with call-ins and is discussed in this chapter.

17.7 Finally Ministers have the power to grant planning permission without a planning application having been made, either for a class of development (by a general development order) or a particular development (by a special development order). A deemed planning permission may be granted for development which requires certain other ministerial authorisations[4].

---

[3] In England see the Town and Country Planning Act 1990, s 62A and a similar power is intended to be introduced in Wales as Town and Country Planning Act 1990, s 62M, inserted by the Planning (Wales) Act 2015, s 23. It is also proposed that applications for nationally significant development will have to be made directly to the Welsh Ministers (Town and Country Planning Act 1990, s 62D, inserted by the Planning (Wales) Act 2015, s 19). These provisions are discussed in Chapter 18.

[4] Town and Country Planning Act 1990, s 90. For special development orders and deemed planning permission see Chapter 26.

17.8 *Call-ins and the role of Ministers*

DIRECTIONS PREVENTING THE DETERMINATION OF APPLICATIONS (ARTICLE 31 DIRECTIONS)

17.8 The Secretary of State and the Welsh Ministers are empowered by their respective Development Management Procedure Orders to make directions restricting the grant of planning permission or other approvals by local planning authorities[5].

17.9 By the Town and Country Planning (Development Management Procedure) (England) Order 2015, art 31(1), in England[6]:

> 'The Secretary of State may give directions restricting the grant of permission by a local planning authority, either indefinitely or during such a period as may be specified in the directions, in respect of any development or in respect of development of any class so specified'.

17.10 The Welsh powers are in the same terms, under art 18 of the Town and Country Planning (Development Management Procedure) (Wales) Order 2012[7]. The power may be exercised generally, in respect of classes of development, or for a particular application. A general direction may relate to all local planning authorities. General directions are used to require local planning authorities to refer particular classes of application to Ministers if they are minded to grant planning permission and to prevent the authorities determining those applications within a particular period whilst the Minister decides whether to call-in the applications. These are discussed further below.

17.11 Directions made in respect of individual applications are referred to in England as Article 31 directions[8]. Article 31 directions are generally made:

(i) to give the Minister more time to consider whether to call-in an application following the expiry of the automatic stay in a general direction;

(ii) if there is concern within government, often following a third party representation, that the Minister might wish to call-in an application which would not otherwise be referred to him under a general direction.

Article 31 directions therefore tend to be used on applications which might be called in. They have also been used for other purposes, such as preventing the determination of applications on major sites until a development plan inspector has reported on those proposals. This would be to provide an inspector review of the principle of the proposal and, potentially, to avoid prejudice to the plan process.

17.12 An Article 31 direction will usually contain an indefinite stay to allow a decision to be made on call-in. Ministers should still seek to decide whether to call in the application or revoke the direction expeditiously. A large and potentially desirable scheme will be held up until a decision is made.

---

[5] The development orders are made under the Town and Country Planning Act 1990, s 74(1)(a).
[6] Local planning authorities are required to give effect to such directions: DMPO 2015, SI 2015/595, art 31(3).
[7] SI 2012/801.
[8] Under the predecessor Town and Country Planning (General Development Procedure) Order 1995 and DMPO 2010 they were again known by their respective articles as Article 14 or Article 25 directions respectively.

Persuading a Minister to make a direction

17.13 If the application will not have to be referred to the Minister under the relevant general direction then a person who would want the application to be called in if the local planning authority are minded to approve it would need to get the Minister to make a direction quickly. Any request for a direction should be made before the Council resolve to grant planning permission. It may make sense to alert central government whilst the application is being consulted upon. A request should certainly be made as soon as the committee report is published if there is a recommendation to approve or a chance that the committee will vote to approve it. The Minister is unlikely to have been aware of the scheme previously, so relevant details and links should be provided. An explanation should be given of why the Minister should be concerned about the scheme, in particular any conflict with national policy. The party's representations on the application should be provided, along with any critical statutory consultee comments. The committee report should be sent, either with the request or when it is available. Civil servants should be told of the committee meeting's date and time so that a direction can be made before it takes place.

Persuading a Minister to lift a direction

17.14 Explaining why an application should not be called in is discussed further below. However another aspect is the delay from an Article 31 direction remaining in force. The applicant and the local planning authority can make the point that a decision should be made speedily, particularly if the direction is the only matter which is holding up the issue of a planning permission. It is not uncommon for a committee resolution to set time limits for the completion of a planning obligation, requiring the application to be refused or returned to committee if the obligation is not finalised and the permission issued by a particular date. An Article 31 direction might delay the issue of the decision notice until that date is passed and the application has to be reconsidered by members. That causes further delay and a degree of uncertainty. If there is a risk of such a timing problem occurring then the Minister can be asked to make a decision within that timescale. It would be prudent to make the request several weeks before the deadline.

DUTIES TO REFER APPLICATIONS TO THE MINISTER

17.15 Relying on the use of directions on a case-by-case basis to enable Ministers to decide whether to call in applications is fraught with the risks of schemes being missed entirely, directions being made too late and encouraging an excessive number of requests. Directions have therefore been made to require all applications in certain classes to be referred to the Minister if the local planning authority proposes to grant planning permission.

Town and Country Planning (Consultation) (England) Direction 2009

17.16 The main direction requiring the referral of planning applications to the Minister in England is the Town and Country Planning (Consultation) (England) Direction 2009. The Direction applies to any application for planning permission falling within the defined categories of 'Green Belt development, development outside town centres, World Heritage Site development, playing field development

17.16 *Call-ins and the role of Ministers*

or flood risk area development'. Previous directions had focused on whether the application was a departure from the development plan[9]. That is no longer part of the tests for consultation.

The relevant categories are defined extensively in the Direction and are in turn:

(1) *Green Belt development* means inappropriate development on land allocated as Green Belt in an adopted development plan which includes:

   (a) the provision of a building or buildings where the new floor space is 1,000 m² or more; or

   (b) any other development which, by reason of its scale or nature or location, would have a significant impact on the openness of the Green Belt[10];

(2) *development outside town centres* consists of or includes retail, leisure or office use in an edge-of-centre, out-of-centre or out-of-town location, which is not in accordance with one or more provisions of the development plan which will create 5,000 m² of floorspace[11] or extensions or new development of 2,500 m² which when aggregated with existing development of that type would exceed 5,000 m² in total within a 1 km radius[12]. Edge of centre means 'for retail purposes, a location that is well connected to and within easy walking distance (ie up to 300 metres) of the primary shopping area and, for all other main town centre uses, is likely to be within 300 metres of a town centre boundary'[13]. Town centres and primary shopping areas are not defined in the Direction, but the areas designated in the relevant development plan should be used. A point to note on town centre uses is that the duty to refer arises if the proposal does not accord with any provision of the development plan, even if it accords with the plan as a whole.

(3) *World Heritage Sites* are designated by UNESCO and include the Tower of London, Stonehenge and the City of Bath. 'World Heritage Site development' means development which would have an adverse impact on the outstanding universal value, integrity, authenticity and significance of a World Heritage Site or its setting, including any buffer zone or its equivalent, which is subject to an outstanding objection from Historic England, implicitly for that reason[14]. It might be disputed whether there is an adverse impact, but the prudent approach is to treat the provision as applying if Historic England considers that is the case.

---

[9] Circular 07/99: The Town and Country Planning (Development Plans and Consultation) (Departures) Directions 1999.

[10] Town and Country Planning (Consultation) (England) Direction 2009, para 4.

[11] Floorspace is gross floorspace measured externally: Town and Country Planning (Consultation) (England) Direction 2009, para 2. In *R (on the application of Lady Hart of Chilton) v Babergh District Council* [2014] EWHC 3261 (Admin), [2015] JPL 491 Sales J held at paras 74–79 that the development simply had to include retail, leisure or office use and provided this use was not immaterial, the remainder of the building could be in another use and its floorspace still be counted within this part of the Direction.

[12] Town and Country Planning (Consultation) (England) Direction 2009, para 5(1). Existing floor space is already provided, has been substantially completed, applied for or approved within the five years before the current application was made: para 5(2). 'Provided' and the other categories appear to be alternatives so the existing building may have been provided more than five years ago.

[13] Town and Country Planning (Consultation) (England) Direction 2009, para 2. 'Out-of-centre' and 'out-of-town' are given their usual planning meanings in para 2.

[14] Town and Country Planning (Consultation) (England) Direction 2009, para 6. In this context, setting is defined as 'the area around a World Heritage Site (including any buffer zone or its equivalent) in which development is capable of having an adverse impact on the World Heritage Site, including an adverse impact on views to and from the World Heritage Site': para 2.

Duties to refer applications to the Minister **17.16**

(4) Playing field development is development which[15]:

(i) is likely to prejudice the use, or lead to the loss of use, of land being used as a playing field[16]; or

(ii) is on land which has been:

(aa) used as a playing field at any time in the five years before the making of the relevant application and which remains undeveloped; or

(bb) allocated for use as a playing field in a development plan or in proposals for such a plan or its alteration or replacement; or

(iii) involves the replacement of the grass surface of a playing pitch on a playing field with an artificial, man-made or composite surface; and

(a) the land (or any part of the land) which is the subject of the application:

(i) is land of a local authority; or

(ii) is currently used by an educational institution as a playing field; or

(iii) has at any time in the five years before the application is received been used by an educational institution as a playing field; and

(b) the English Sports Council ('Sport England') has been consulted pursuant to art 10(1) of the Order, and has made representations objecting to the whole or part of the development on one or more of the following grounds:

(i) that there is a deficiency in the provision of playing fields in the area of the local authority concerned;

(ii) that the proposed development would result in such a deficiency; or

(iii) that where the proposed development involves a loss of a playing field and an alternative or replacement playing field is proposed to be provided, that alternative or replacement does not match (whether in quantity, quality or accessibility) that which would be lost;

(5) *'flood risk area development'* means 'major development in a flood risk area to which the Environment Agency has made an objection that it has not been able to withdraw even after discussions with the local planning authority'[17]. A flood risk area is either within zones 2 or 3 (so with a 1 in 1000 year chance of flooding) or zone 1 with critical drainage problems which the Environment Agency has notified to the local planning authority under the DMPO. Major development is given a different definition than in the DMPO, being residential development of 10 units or 0.5 hectares or non-residential development with gross external floorspace of 1,000m² or a site area of 1 hectare or more[18].

---

[15] Town and Country Planning (Consultation) (England) Direction 2009, para 6 which incorporates those playing fields which are the subject of consultation under the DMPO 2015, Sch 5, Table, para (z).
[16] Playing field is defined as the whole of a site which encompasses at least one playing pitch. A playing pitch is a delineated area, which together with any run-off area is of at least 0.2 hectares and is used for the playing of association football, American football, rugby, cricket, hockey, lacrosse, rounders, baseball, softball, Australian football, Gaelic football, shinty, hurling, polo or cycle polo: Town and Country Planning (Consultation) (England) Direction 2009, para 2, applying the definition which is now in the DMPO 2015, Sch 5, para 1(j).
[17] Town and Country Planning (Consultation) (England) Direction 2009, para 8.
[18] Town and Country Planning (Consultation) (England) Direction 2009, para 2.

17.17 *Call-ins and the role of Ministers*

17.17 A duty to consult the Secretary of State arises when the local planning authority 'does not propose to refuse an application for planning permission' which is within any of the categories[19]. Since the authority's powers are to grant or refuse planning applications, the duty arises when it decides to grant planning permission (usually by a committee resolution).

17.18 Where consultation with the Secretary of State is required, the local planning authority shall as soon as practicable send[20]:

'(a) a copy of the application (including copies of any accompanying plans, drawings and any appropriate flood risk assessment) and supporting information;

(b) a copy of the requisite notice;

(c) a copy of any representations made to the authority in respect of the application;

(d) a copy of any report on the application prepared by an officer of the authority;

(e) unless contained in a report supplied pursuant to sub-paragraph (d), a statement of the material considerations which the authority consider indicate a departure application should be determined otherwise than in accordance with s 38(6) of the Planning and Compulsory Purchase Act 2004'.

The documents are to be sent to:

National Planning Casework Unit
5 St Philip's Place
Colmore Row
Birmingham
B3 2PW

npcu@communities.gsi.gov.uk

Requests for Ministers to call-in applications can be made to the National Planning Casework Unit.

17.19 The local planning authority may not grant planning permission until the expiry of 21 days beginning with the date of the Minister's confirmation that the specified material has been received[21] unless the Minister informs the authority within that period that the application will not be called in[22]. In practice, if the 21-day period will pass without a ministerial decision then an Article 31 direction is likely to be made to extend the bar on issuing a planning permission.

WGC: 07/2012: The Town and Country Planning (Notification) (Wales) Direction 2012

17.20 The Town and Country Planning (Notification) (Wales) Direction 2012 contains the principal referral provisions in Wales, replacing various earlier directions. Where the local planning authority does not propose to refuse planning permission for

---

[19] Town and Country Planning (Consultation) (England) Direction 2009, para 9.
[20] Town and Country Planning (Consultation) (England) Direction 2009, para 10.
[21] Town and Country Planning (Consultation) (England) Direction 2009, para 11.
[22] Town and Country Planning (Consultation) (England) Direction 2009, para 12.

'notification development' it must give notice to the Welsh Ministers[23]. Notification development consists of five categories: flood risk area development; significant residential; minerals; waste; and aggregates extraction within National Parks or areas of outstanding natural beauty[24].

- *flood risk area development* has a different meaning to that in England. It applies to zone C2 land which are areas of flood plain without significant flood defence infrastructure[25] and so to a narrower category of land than over the border. Development which triggers the requirement is emergency services development (sites which need to be operational and accessible at all times including: hospitals, ambulance stations, fire stations, police stations, coastguard stations, command centres, emergency depots or buildings used to provide emergency shelter in time of flood) and highly vulnerable development (unless that is of fewer than 10 dwellings). Highly vulnerable development is that relating to 'residential premises (including hotels and caravan parks), public buildings such as schools, libraries and leisure centres; industrial development where there would be a risk to the public and the water environment if the site is inundated such as power stations, chemical plants and incinerators; and waste disposal sites';
- *significant residential development* is more than 150 dwellings on a site of more than 6 hectares which does not accord with the provisions of the development plan. Non-accordance appears to be with the development plan as a whole, rather than any individual policy;
- *minerals development* consists of or includes the winning and working of minerals whether at a new site or an extension to an existing site which does not accord with the development plan;
- *waste development* is wholly or mainly for the deposit of waste into or on to land and again not in accordance with the development plan;
- the final category consists of the extraction of aggregates (but not other minerals) from new or existing sites within a National Park or an Area of Outstanding Natural Beauty

17.21 Planning permission may not be granted until the expiry of 21 days beginning with the day the Welsh Ministers received the notification unless the Minister has said that the application will not be called in or is not considered to be notification development[26]. As in England, if the Minister needs more time, a direction will be made, in this case under the DMPO Wales, art 18.

17.22 The Ministers must be provided with a copy of the planning application, drawings and supporting information, notice of the application, representations received, any officer report, EIA screening opinion and appropriate assessment. If the application is proposed to be determined other than in accordance with the development plan the authority should provide a statement explaining why[27].

---

[23] Town and Country Planning (Notification) (Wales) Direction 2012, para 4.
[24] Town and Country Planning (Notification) (Wales) Direction 2012, para 2. These terms are all defined in para 2.
[25] Flood plain is shown definitively on a map kept by the Welsh Assembly Government rather than being assessed on a case-by-case basis.
[26] Town and Country Planning (Notification) (Wales) Direction 2012, paras 6, 7.
[27] Town and Country Planning (Notification) (Wales) Direction 2012, para 5.

17.23 *Call-ins and the role of Ministers*

Town and Country Planning (Safeguarded aerodromes, technical sites and military explosives storage areas) Direction 2002

17.23 In England and Wales local planning authorities are required to consult the owners and operators of aerodromes on safeguarding maps approved by the Civil Aviation Authority and the Secretary of State for Defence for certain establishments certified by that Minister[28].

17.24 If a local planning authority proposes to grant permission contrary to the advice of that consultee, it must notify both the Civil Aviation Authority and the consultee; or the Secretary of State for Defence, as appropriate[29]. The application may not be determined until 28 days after such notification, unless the Secretary of State for Communities and Local Government or the Welsh Ministers have said they will not call-in the application.

Town and Country Planning (Safeguarding Meteorological Sites) (England) Direction 2014

17.25 If a local planning authority resolves to approve development within a safeguarding area established to protect Met Office technical sites contrary to the recommendation of the Met Office, then the Met Office must be notified of that intention[30]. Planning permission may not then be granted before the expiry of 28 days from the date of notification unless the Secretary of State has said that the application will not be called in[31].

Safeguarding directions

17.26 Directions may be made to protect proposed transport routes, for example, High Speed 2 and the two Crossrail schemes. Such a direction will prevent the grant of planning permission on land shown as safeguarded on a plan with the direction until the Minister has had an opportunity to decide whether to call-in the application.

17.27 A safeguarding direction does not amount to a plan or programme which supports whatever project it is intended to protect. Consequently it is not subject to the requirements of the Strategic Environmental Assessment Directive[32].

Health and safety

17.28 If the local planning authority proposes to grant planning permission contrary to the advice of the Health and Safety Executive then it is advised to give the HSE notice of that intention and not to issue the decision until 21 days have passed, to enable the HSE to seek a call-in[33].

---

[28] Town and Country Planning (Safeguarded aerodromes, technical sites and military explosives storage areas) Direction 2002.
[29] Town and Country Planning (Safeguarded aerodromes, technical sites and military explosives storage areas) Direction 2002, para 9.
[30] Town and Country Planning (Safeguarding Meteorological Sites) (England) Direction 2014, para 7.
[31] Town and Country Planning (Safeguarding Meteorological Sites) (England) Direction 2014, paras 9, 10.
[32] *R (on the application of HS2 Action Alliance) v Secretary of State for Transport* [2014] EWHC 2759 (Admin), upheld at [2014] EWCA Civ 1578.
[33] Circular 04/00: *Planning controls for hazardous substances*, Annex A, para A5 and in Wales, NAW Circular 20/01: *Planning Controls for Hazardous Substances*.

Other referral provisions

17.29 If the Lee Valley Regional Park Authority considers that a local planning authority's proposed determination of a planning application would conflict with its statutory park plan then it may require the authority to refer the application to the Secretary of State who can decide to call it in[34].

CALL-INS

17.30 The Secretary of State and the Welsh Ministers have the power to 'call-in' planning applications and other applications for their own decision. Call-ins of planning applications can be carried out under two alternative provisions of the Town and Country Planning Act 1990:

(i) s 77 contains a general power to call in any planning application or application for approval under an order;

(ii) in England, s 76A provides a more specific power intended for major infrastructure projects which leads to altered inquiries rules.

Section 77, however, remains the commonly used call-in power and the procedural rules for s 76A call-ins were revoked in 2015.

Section 77

17.31 By s 77(1) of the Town and Country Planning Act 1990:

'The Secretary of State may give directions requiring applications for planning permission, or for the approval of any local planning authority required under a development order, a Mayoral development order, a local development order or a neighbourhood development order, to be referred to him instead of being dealt with by local planning authorities'.

17.32 The power is most usually exercised on planning applications, but it can also be deployed on prior approval applications under the Town and Country Planning (General Permitted Development) Order 1995[35] and approvals proceeding under extant local development, Mayoral development or neighbourhood development orders. The ability of Ministers to intervene in the making of such orders is dealt with separately in the Planning Acts.

17.33 The call-in power may only be exercised by a direction. Such a direction[36]:

'(a) may be given either to a particular local planning authority or to local planning authorities generally; and

(b) may relate either to a particular application or to applications of a class specified in the direction'.

---

[34] Lee Valley Regional Park Act 1966, s 14(8).
[35] SI 1995/419.
[36] Town and Country Planning Act 1990, s 77(2).

17.34 *Call-ins and the role of Ministers*

17.34 Since Ministers like to keep control over which applications they do call in, in practice directions are made in respect of particular applications. There are no directions providing for automatic call-in of classes of applications or operating on particular local planning authorities.

17.35 Unlike directions by Ministers to recover jurisdiction over planning appeals from inspectors, no formality is prescribed for a call-in direction. However it needs to be given to the local planning authority and in reality this must be done before the decision notice is issued by the authority.

An important constraint is that the power can only be exercised against applications. If the application has been determined, most obviously by a planning permission being issued, then it cannot be called in.

Call-in policy

17.36 Historically Ministerial policy on the calling-in of planning applications has been announced to Parliament. The longstanding guidance was the 'Caborn' principles announced on 16 June 1999[37]. The policy was revised on 26 October 2012 to explain[38]:

> 'The policy is to continue to be very selective about calling in planning applications. We consider it only right that as Parliament has entrusted local planning authorities with the responsibility for day-to-day planning control in their areas, they should, in general, be free to carry out their duties responsibly, with the minimum of interference. ...
>
> The Secretary of State will, in general, only consider the use of his call-in powers if planning issues of more than local importance are involved. Such cases may include, for example, those which in his opinion:
>
> - may conflict with national policies on important matters;
> - may have significant long-term impact on economic growth and meeting housing needs across a wider area than a single local authority;
> - could have significant effects beyond their immediate locality;
> - give rise to substantial cross-boundary or national controversy;
> - raise significant architectural and urban design issues; or
> - may involve the interests of national security or of foreign Governments.
>
> However, each case will continue to be considered on its individual merits'.

Planning applications involving the extraction of gas from shale have been added to the call in criteria[39].

---

[37] By the then Planning Minister Richard Caborn MP, 494 HC Official Report (6th series), col 138W, 16 June 1999.

[38] 551 HC Official Report (6th series), cols 71–72WS, 26 October 2012, by the Parliamentary Under-Secretary of State for Communities and Local Government (Nick Boles MP).

[39] News release by DCLG and DECC, 13 August 2015. The speed of determination of onshore oil and gas applications is monitored by the Secretary of State with active consideration of calling in applications before authorities which have failed to determine more than half of such applications within the time limits: Written Ministerial Statement by the Secretary of State for Communities and Local Government by Greg Clark, 599 HC Official Report (6th series), col WS201, 16 September 2015.

Call-ins **17.42**

17.37 A call-in might arise following consideration of an application referred to the Minister under a general direction. Alternatively the potential for a call-in may be raised with the Minister by interested persons.

17.38 The factors which can be considered in exercising the discretion are wide and may include entitling third parties to put their objections at an inquiry[40].

17.39 A person seeking a call-in should write to the Minister. In England this can be done to the Secretary of State for Communities and Local Government at the London headquarters[41] or at the Department's National Planning Casework Unit[42]. The request should explain why the application should be called in with reference to the examples in the call-in policy where possible. Conflict with national policy is the most common basis for calling in an application and any claimed conflict should be set out. Whilst not part of the call-in criteria, the criteria upon which a Minister might recover jurisdiction over an appeal from an inspector may also be a useful indicator and can be referred to[43]. Any novel aspects of the case, in particular the application of national policy, should be identified.

17.40 Call-ins normally take place once the local planning authority has resolved to grant planning permission (hence the need for a direction to prevent the permission being issued). If the authority proposes to refuse planning permission then the Minister will usually await the refusal and any appeal rather than call-in the application. Occasionally call-ins take place earlier in the application's consideration. This may be because the project is so large, important and controversial that it ought to be dealt with at national level following an inquiry. Sometimes applications are called-in so that they can be dealt with alongside a competing scheme, such as a major retail development or a motorway service area, which is going to appeal. Either developer may see advantages in having both schemes before the Minister at the same time.

17.41 Usually, of course, a developer who has local planning authority support for its scheme will not want the application called in. A call-in causes delay, cost and a risk of refusal. The applicant and any local planning authority resisting a call-in will want to explain why the application is compliant with national policy and that it has been properly considered at the local authority level. Whilst some of this can be explained in correspondence, the committee report ought to be cogent and clear as to why the application should be approved, if that was the officer view.

Challenges to decisions whether or not to call-in applications

17.42 The call-in criteria are broad and it is very much a matter of judgment as to whether the Minister wishes to intervene in a particular application. Such decisions are subject to judicial review, but unlawfulness is very difficult to

---

[40] *R (on the application of Adlard) v Secretary of State for the Environment, Transport and the Regions* [2002] EWCA Civ 735, [2002] 1 WLR 2515 at paras 39–41 per Auld LJ.
[41] 2 Marsham Street, London SW1P 4DF.
[42] National Planning Casework Unit, 5 St Philip's Place, Colmore Row, Birmingham B3 2PW; npcu@communities.gsi.gov.uk.
[43] In para **17.60**.

17.43 *Call-ins and the role of Ministers*

establish[44]. The reason is that a decision whether or not to call-in an application is a reasonably unlimited discretion and is both highly political and highly unpredictable in practice. There are few, if any, applications which really are certain to be called in, and there are many which might or might not be. Whilst the government agreed to give reasons for not calling in applications in the Planning Green Paper[45] which preceded the Planning and Compulsory Purchase Act 2004, those reasons have not greatly increased the prospects of a successful challenge.

17.43 A rare, and possibly unique, instance of a successful challenge to a failure to call-in a planning application is *Lakin Ltd v Secretary of State for Scotland*[46]. Lakin were promoting a retail development at Corbiewood which was refused on appeal alongside another scheme called Broadleys Farm. The sites were in competition, with only one likely to be approved. Lakin and the Broadleys Farm developers both reapplied for planning permission. Lakin were refused again and lodged an appeal. The council resolved to approve a second application for Broadleys Farm and the Secretary of State declined to call it in, having considered, amongst other things, whether Lakin's site was a better alternative than Broadleys Farm. The Court of Session agreed with Lakin's complaint that this was unfair and the Minister had pre-empted their appeal. On those particularly unusual facts the decision not to call-in was quashed.

17.44 A more traditional outcome occurred in *R (on the application of Persimmon Homes Ltd) v Secretary of State for Communities and Local Government*[47] where one housebuilder's attempt to challenge the refusal to call-in a rival's scheme failed. Sullivan J observed that the Minister must be entitled to carry out a preliminary assessment of the planning merits to judge, for example, whether there may be a conflict with national policy on an important matter[48].

17.45 In *Westminster City Council v Secretary of State for Communities and Local Government* Collins J held that it was not irrational for the Secretary of State to decline to call-in the redevelopment of the Elizabeth House site by Waterloo railway station notwithstanding the risk that the nearby Westminster World Heritage Site would be endangered. Despite a badly-drafted letter saying that the application would not be called in, the briefing note given to Ministers showed that they had been correctly advised and understood their policy[49].

---

[44] The power to call-in applications is not part of a supervisory duty that, for example, requires the Minister to ensure that local authorities act lawfully, and a decision whether to call-in an application does not itself engage the right to a fair hearing under art 6 of the European Convention on Human Rights: *R (on the application of Adlard) v Secretary of State for the Environment, Transport and the Regions* [2002] EWCA Civ 735, [2002] 1 WLR 2515 at para 36 per Auld LJ.

[45] *Planning: Delivering a Fundamental Change* (2001):

'6.18 At the moment, we state the reasons for calling in a planning application for the Secretary of State's decision and place on the DTLR planning web site both copies of letters calling in applications and notifying applicants of Ministers' final decision. We have not given reasons for not calling in a planning application. In the interests of greater transparency, we will now, as from today, give reasons for not calling in individual cases and to put copies of these letters on the Department's web site'.

[46] 1988 SLT 780.
[47] [2007] EWHC 1985 (Admin), [2008] JPL 323. A challenge also failed in *R v Secretary for the Environment, ex p Middlesbrough Borough Council* [1988] 3 PLR 52.
[48] See para 34.
[49] [2014] EWHC 708 (Admin) at paras 17–21, 36–38.

These cases both proceeded on the basis that the Secretary of State was not required to give reasons when deciding whether to call-in an application[50].

Section 76A and major infrastructure projects in England

17.46 The Town and Country Planning Act 1990, s 76A has its origin in continuing political disquiet at the time taken to approve major projects in the planning process and in particular the lengthy Heathrow Terminal 5 inquiry of the 1990s. The result has been a series of initiatives, some productive and some left to languish on the statute book. Section 76A is one of the latter ones[51]. It was introduced by the Planning and Compulsory Purchase Act 2004 and whilst in place, has not been used in practice and with the revocation of its procedural rules in April 2015 is destined for oblivion.

17.47 Under s 76A(1) the power applies to an application for planning permission or for the approval of a local planning authority required under a development order 'if the Secretary of State thinks that the development to which the application relates is of national or regional importance'. Whilst the section is entitled 'Major infrastructure projects', those words are not in the text of the section. They are not the test for its applicability and neither expand nor restrict the ambit of 'national or regional importance'. Regional relates to the list of regions in the now repealed Regional Development Agencies Act 1998[52]. There are no statutory criteria for determining whether the development is sufficiently important.

17.48 If the application is of national or regional importance then the Secretary of State has a discretion whether to call it in under s 76A[53]. The Minister may decide to leave it with the local planning authority or indeed to call it in but under s 77. If an application is called in under s 76A the Minister may also direct that any connected application made under or for the purposes of the Planning Acts is called in[54]. Such applications would include planning applications for small elements in the project which would not themselves be of national or regional importance[55] or applications for listed building, conservation area or hazardous substances consent[56].

17.49 As a result of a s 76A direction, the application is referred to the Secretary of State, who must appoint an inspector to consider it[57]. The inspector may be directed to consider prescribed matters and make recommendations to the Minister[58]. Since the general duties on planning authorities in the determination of applications apply to s 76A call-ins[59], there is a need for the Minister to consider all material matters, although the direction can draw attention to specific areas of interest. One

---

[50] *Persimmon* at para 40; *Westminster* at para 14. However, neither case considered the Planning Green Paper and whether that gave rise to a legitimate expectation that reasons would be given.
[51] Section 76A does not apply to the development of land in Wales: Town and Country Planning Act 1990, s 76A(12). The earlier initiative of the Planning Inquiry Commission is discussed below.
[52] Town and Country Planning Act 1990, s 76A(9), referring to Regional Development Agencies Act 1998, Sch 1.
[53] Town and Country Planning Act 1990, s 76A(2).
[54] Town and Country Planning Act 1990, s 76A(3).
[55] For example, major off-site highway improvements required by the scheme.
[56] These applications could be called in anyway under their own legislation: Planning (Listed Buildings and Conservation Areas) Act 1990, s 12; Planning (Hazardous Substances) Act 1990, s 20.
[57] Town and Country Planning Act 1990, s 76A(4).
[58] Town and Country Planning Act 1990, s 76B(2).
[59] Town and Country Planning Act 1990, ss 70, 72(1) and (5), 73 and 73A as applied by s 76A(10).

17.50 *Call-ins and the role of Ministers*

of the innovations intended in the s 76A process was for several Inspectors to be appointed who may look at different matters and report back to the lead inspector. Having several inspectors or an inspector sitting with one or more assessors was not uncommon for complex inquiries. However one intention behind s 76A was to speed up inquiries by holding concurrent sessions on different topics. The Secretary of State was empowered to appoint additional Inspectors, after considering any recommendations of the lead inspector[60], who would then be instructed by and report to the lead Inspector[61].

Additionally, once a direction is made the applicant must prepare an economic impact report[62].

17.50 Procedures for call-in inquiries under s 76A were contained in the Town and Country Planning (Major Infrastructure Project Inquiries Procedure) (England) Rules 2005[63]. These were revoked without replacement on 6 April 2015[64]. Consequently it is not in practice possible to determine a s 76A call-in by inquiry, and so at all. The 2005 Rules are therefore of historical interest but did contain a number of innovations which might be borne in mind in future inquiry procedures:

(i) registration of participants once the inquiry has been announced, including whether they wished to play a major role[65];

(ii) the appointment of technical advisers to the inquiry. Unlike an assessor who sits with and provides a report to the inspector which is only published with the final decision and the inspector's report, the technical adviser would assess evidence in consultation with parties and report in writing to the inspector. That report would include a description of any areas of disagreement between the parties and shall state his view of the significance of each such disagreement and be published during the inquiry. The technical adviser would give evidence on the report and be open to cross-examination[66];

(iii) the Secretary of State could appoint a mediator to try to resolve, define and narrow disagreements. The mediator would send a report to the inquiry, but not give evidence[67];

(iv) outline statements of case would have to identify any disagreement with the applicant's environmental statement[68].

---

[60] Town and Country Planning Act 1990, s 76B(3).
[61] Town and Country Planning Act 1990, s 76B(4).
[62] Town and Country Planning Act 1990, s 76A(5). The contents of an economic impact report and the submission and publicity requirements were set out in DMPO 2010, art 15 but are omitted from the DMPO 2015.
[63] The Town and Country Planning (Inquiries Procedure) (England) Rules 2000, SI 2000/1624 do not apply to s 76A call-ins, see r 3 of those Rules.
[64] By the Town and Country Planning (Hearings and Inquiries Procedure) (England) (Amendment and Revocation) Rules 2015, r 7, Sch 1.
[65] Former Town and Country Planning (Major Infrastructure Project Inquiries Procedure) (England) Rules 2005, r 5.
[66] Former Town and Country Planning (Major Infrastructure Project Inquiries Procedure) (England) Rules 2005, r 7.
[67] Former Town and Country Planning (Major Infrastructure Project Inquiries Procedure) (England) Rules 2005, r 8.
[68] Former Town and Country Planning (Major Infrastructure Project Inquiries Procedure) (England) Rules 2005, r 9(5).

Revocation of a decision to call-in an application

17.51 In *R (on the application of Trustees of the Friends of the Lake District) v Secretary of State for the Environment*[69] the High Court held that it was implicit that a decision to call-in a planning application under s 77 could be revoked by the Secretary of State. A decision to call-in an application is simply a procedural step and does not give rise to a substantive legitimate expectation that the Minister will not change his mind and return the application to the local planning authority's jurisdiction[70].

There is an explicit power for the Secretary of State to vary or revoke a direction calling in an application under s 76A[71].

THE CALL-IN PROCESS

17.52 Decisions to call-in applications are taken by Ministers. In England this may be by the Secretary of State for Communities and Local Government or by one of the other Ministers in that department. Advice will be given by officials, with reference to the call-in criteria, but the decision is ultimately one for the politician.

17.53 By s 77(2) a call-in direction is given to the local planning authority. In practice the call-in direction will be sent to the applicant for planning permission and any person who requested the call-in, in addition to the local planning authority.

17.54 Even though the applicant will probably already be aware of a call in, the local planning authority has to send them a notice[72]:

'(a) setting out the terms of the direction and any reasons given by the Secretary of State for issuing it;

(b) stating that the application has been referred to the Secretary of State'.

17.55 Where a parish council has asked to be notified of applications relating to its area, it must be informed by the local planning authority of the date of any call-in and the terms of the Secretary of State's determination of the application[73]. A county planning authority must give similar notice to any district planning authority for the site if an application made to it is called in[74].

17.56 In England the applicant and the local planning authority are entitled to appear before and be heard by an inspector[75] so the Secretary of State is not able to insist that the call-in is dealt with by written representations. Call-ins are almost always dealt with following a public inquiry with the inspector reporting to the

---

[69] [2001] EWHC Admin 281, [2002] JPL 72 at paras 37–38 per Harrison J.
[70] *Lake District* at paras 43–45.
[71] Town and Country Planning Act 1990, s 76A(7).
[72] DMPO 2015, art 17, replacing with amendment DMPO 2010, art 14. DMPO Wales, art 13 is in similar terms, with the replacement of 'Secretary of State' by 'Welsh Ministers'. Since the applicant's contact details are on the planning application form, the obligation of notifying the applicant could be placed on the Minister to avoid the usually unnecessary further notice being given.
[73] DMPO 2015, art 25(3), replacing DMPO 2010, art 23(3).
[74] DMPO 2015, art 24(3).
[75] Town and Country Planning Act 1990, s 77(5).

17.57 *Call-ins and the role of Ministers*

Minister. The right to a hearing in Wales has been removed, but it remains to be seen whether this will affect practice[76].

PLANNING APPLICATIONS MADE DIRECTLY TO THE SECRETARY OF STATE OR THE WELSH MINISTERS

17.57 Where local planning authorities have been designated for not dealing with applications adequately, planning applications for major development may be submitted directly to the Secretary of State under the Town and Country Planning Act 1990, s 62A. Similar procedures are being introduced in Wales, along with a requirement for applications for nationally significant development to be made to the Welsh Ministers. These processes are considered in Chapter 18.

RECOVERY OF APPEALS

17.58 Planning appeals are made to the Secretary of State or Welsh Ministers, as appropriate but the power to determine appeals has been generally transferred to individual planning inspectors[77], subject to the ability of Ministers to take over a particular appeal by recovering jurisdiction. That Ministerial power is exercised by direction[78].

17.59 Most of the recovery criteria in England were set out in a written ministerial statement in 2008[79], which as updated by the *Planning Practice Guidance* are[80]:

- proposals for development of major importance having more than local significance;
- proposals giving rise to substantial regional or national controversy;
- proposals which raise important or novel issues of development control, and/or legal difficulties;
- proposals against which another Government department has raised major objections or has a major interest;
- proposals of major significance for the delivery of the Government's climate change programme and energy policies;

---

[76] Town and Country Planning Act 1990, s 77(6A), inserted by Town and Country Planning (Determination of Procedure) (Wales) Order 2014, Sch 1, para 2.

[77] In England by the Town and Country Planning (Determination of Appeals by Appointed Persons) (Prescribed Classes) Regulations 1997, SI 1997/420, reg 3(1), made under Town and Country Planning Act 1990, Sch 6, para 1. Classes of cases may be excluded in the regulations or by direction made by the Minister: Town and Country Planning Act 1990, Sch 6, para 1(2). Consequently certain appeals by statutory undertakers are determined by Ministers rather than inspectors: see Town and Country Planning Act 1990, s 266 and Town and Country Planning (Determination of Appeals by Appointed Persons) (Prescribed Classes) Regulations 1997, reg 4. The Town and Country Planning (Determination of Appeals by Appointed Persons) (Prescribed Classes) (Wales) Regulations 2015, SI 2015/1822 apply to Welsh appeals made from 16 December 2015.

[78] Town and Country Planning Act 1990, Sch 6, para 3(1).

[79] By the Parliamentary Under-Secretary of State for Communities and Local Government Parmjit Dhanda, 478 HC Official Report (6th series) col 44WS, 30 June 2008.

[80] Para 16-005-20140728.

Recovery of appeals **17.63**

- proposals for residential development of over 150 units or on sites of over 5 hectares, which would significantly impact on the Government's objective to secure a better balance between housing demand and supply and create high quality, sustainable, mixed and inclusive communities;
- proposals which involve any main town centre use or uses where that use or uses comprise(s) over 9,000m² gross floorspace (either as a single proposal or as part of or in combination with other current proposals) and which are proposed on a site in an edge of centre or out of centre location that is not in accordance with an up-to-date development plan document;
- proposals for significant development in the Green Belt;
- major proposals involving the winning and working of minerals;
- proposals which would have an adverse impact on the outstanding universal value, integrity, authenticity and significance of a World Heritage Site.

17.60 In addition the recovery criteria were extended to traveller sites in the Green Belt (whether or not they were significant development) in 2013[81]. Also added to the recovery criteria were 'proposals for residential development over 10 units in areas where a qualifying body has submitted a neighbourhood plan proposal to the local planning authority or where a neighbourhood plan has been made'[82]. Planning applications involving the extraction of gas from shale have been introduced to the recovery criteria for a period of two years from 16 September 2015[83]. Whilst not an additional criterion, appeals concerning unauthorised development in the Green Belt might be considered for recovery to so that the Secretary of State could illustrate how his policy of considering intentional unauthorised development is to be applied[84].

17.61 The power of the Minister to recover jurisdiction over an appeal, and so have it decided by a minister rather than an inspector, is an important tool in the political machinery. Whilst used relatively rarely, it is not simply for the massive or exceptional projects. As with the ability to call-in an application, the recovery power is a reminder that ultimately the planning system is political.

17.62 Recovery can be used where Ministers are concerned that the Planning Inspectorate are not properly reflecting their approach to policy and decisions. Where the political approach to an issue moves, it may take time for officialdom to catch up. Recovering appeals is one way of asserting the political view.

17.63 It has been apparent from the renewable energy and traveller changes to the recovery criteria that by 2013 Ministers were concerned whether the Planning Inspectorate's application of policy accorded with their own. As a result, a swathe of

---

[81] Parliamentary Under-Secretary of State for Communities and Local Government, Brandon Lewis: 565 HC Official Report (6th series) col 41WS, 1 July 2013, extended by a written ministerial statement at 573 HC Official Report (6th series) col 35WS, 17 January 2014.
[82] Under-Secretary of State for Communities and Local Government, Nick Boles, 584 HC Official Report (6th series) col 2-25WS, 10 July 2014, continued by Minister for Housing and Planning, Brandon Lewis: 598 HC Official Report (6th series) col 7WS, 9 July 2015.
[83] News release by DCLG and DECC, 13 August 2015 and Written Ministerial Statement the by Secretary of State for Communities and Local Government by Greg Clark, 599 HC Official Report (6th series) col HCWS201, 16 September 2015.
[84] Chief Planner's letter, 31 August 2015.

17.64 *Call-ins and the role of Ministers*

such appeals were recovered and Ministers have been prepared to differ from their inspectors' recommendations. In *Moore v Secretary of State for Communities and Local Government* the High Court found that the Minister's practice of recovering very large numbers of caravan site appeals in the Green Belt was indirectly discriminatory[85] as it affected gypsies and travellers and that Ministers had neither justified that interference as proportionate nor considered the Public Sector Equality Duty[86]. The lengthier period for determining recovered jurisdiction cases was also seen as a breach of the right to a fair hearing within a reasonable time under art 6 of the European Convention on Human Rights[87].

Recovery procedure

17.64 A direction to recover jurisdiction shall be reasoned[88]. The direction is to be served on the inspector (if already appointed), the appellant, the local planning authority and any person who has made in the time period for statutory consultation or publicity[89]. No valid direction exists at least until it has been served on any inspector[90]. In *R (on the application of Gleeson Developments Ltd) v Secretary of State for Communities and Local Government*[91] the Minister had decided that an appeal should be recovered and the Minister's Private Secretary informing the Planning Inspectorate of that decision. The Inspectorate then started preparing the letters which would be sent out but erroneously the inspector's decision was sent out before that happened. No direction had been made and the inspector had power to determine the appeal when his decision was issued[92].

17.65 The Minister must give the appellant, local planning authority and those others notified an opportunity to make further representations if the reasons for the direction raise matters which they have not dealt with previously[93]. These may include requesting that the mode of determination be changed[94].

MINISTERIAL CONDUCT OF PLANNING MATTERS

17.66 The handling of planning matters by the Secretary of State for Communities and Local Government and other ministers in his department is governed by the

---

[85] Under the Equality Act 2010, s 19.
[86] Despite this the reality is that gypsy and traveller cases do raise different issues as to very special circumstances in the Green Belt to 'bricks and mortar' applications, so a difference in treatment is explicable.
[87] At para 149 per Gilbart J. However, the periods of delay caused by recovery were very modest compared to other cases: see *Lafarge Redland Aggregates Ltd v Scottish Ministers* [2000] SLT 1361.
[88] Town and Country Planning Act 1990, Sch 6, para 3(2).
[89] Town and Country Planning Act 1990, Sch 6, para 3(2).
[90] *R (on the application of Gleeson Developments Ltd) v Secretary of State for Communities and Local Government* [2014] EWCA Civ 1118, [2014] PTSR 1226, [2014] JPL 1386 at para 14 per Sullivan LJ. The court left open whether service on other persons was required for the direction to be effective and did not in that case have to consider the minimum requirement for service before an inspector was appointed.
[91] [2014] EWCA Civ 1118, [2014] PTSR 1226, [2014] JPL 1386.
[92] At paras 15–19 per Sullivan LJ.
[93] Town and Country Planning Act 1990, Sch 6, para 3(5A), (5B).
[94] *Gleeson* at para 12 per Sullivan LJ.

Ministerial Code of Conduct which applies to all their actions and *Guidance on Planning Propriety Issues*[95]. These Planning Ministers[96]:

> 'should take no part in making a planning decision in which they have or might be perceived to have a private or constituency interest. That includes decisions in respect of planning matters with which he or she has previously been associated, as an MP or in a private capacity. Nor should Planning Ministers use their ministerial position to influence such a decision'.

Such Ministers may make representations, including to other Ministers, on matters affecting their constituents' interests but will not then be involved in the decision[97].

17.67 Representations which are made to Ministers should be directed to the relevant planning casework official[98]. Whilst meetings on planning applications and appeals are discouraged, a degree of informal 'button-holing' of Ministers by MPs may well take place. This can take place as long as that is dealt with in accordance with the guidance[99].

Parliamentary Private Secretaries to DCLG Ministers are subject to the same guidance[100].

PLANNING INQUIRY COMMISSION

17.68 A Planning Inquiry Commission is a half-forgotten and possibly mythical creature which Ministers may appoint to consider a called-in planning application or appeal. Originally introduced by the Town and Country Planning Act 1968[101], its role and constitution is in the Town and Country Planning Act 1990, s 101 and Sch 8. The Secretary of State may constitute a Planning Inquiry Commission to inquire into and report into any called-in application, planning appeal, proposed deemed planning permission for development by a local authority, National Park authority or by statutory undertakers or any development by a government department[102].

17.69 A Commission may be established if the Minister considers it expedient that there[103]:

---

[95] The current edition was published by the Department for Communities and Local Government in February 2012.
[96] *Guidance on Planning Propriety Issues*, para 8.
[97] *Guidance on Planning Propriety Issues*, para 9. As an example of the correct handling of a recovered appeal when the Secretary of State had objected as the constituency MP see *Ball v Secretary of State for Communities and Local Government* [2014] EWCA Civ 372, [2014] JPL 1016.
[98] *Guidance on Planning Propriety Issues*, para 11.
[99] See *Broadview Energy Developments Limited v Secretary of State for Communities and Local Government* [2015] EWHC 1743 (Admin) at paras 35–41 per Cranston J drawing on his experience as a former MP and Minister (having been Solicitor General from 1998–2001).
[100] *Guidance on Planning Propriety Issues*, para 20. The guidance was revised after Alan Meale MP, the then PPS to the Secretary of State for Environment, Transport and the Regions, John Prescott, had lobbied the Minister in support of two planning applications in Barnet, 140 miles from his Mansfield constituency: see HC Official Report (6th series) col WA310, 2 November 1998.
[101] Town and Country Planning Act 1968, ss 61–63 and Sch 6.
[102] Town and Country Planning Act 1990, s 101(2).
[103] Town and Country Planning Act 1990, s 101(3). A reference to a commission can be made at any time prior to the determination of the application or grant of deemed planning permission, even if a call-in or planning appeal inquiry has been held: Sch 8, para 4(2), (3).

17.70 *Call-ins and the role of Ministers*

'should be the subject of a special inquiry on either or both of the following grounds:

(a) that there are considerations of national or regional importance which are relevant to the determination of that question and require evaluation, but a proper evaluation of them cannot be made unless there is a special inquiry for the purpose;

(b) that the technical or scientific aspects of the proposed development are of so unfamiliar a character as to jeopardise a proper determination of that question unless there is a special inquiry for the purpose'.

17.70 A Planning Inquiry Commission would consist of a chairman and between two and four further members, all appointed by the Minister[104]. The Commission could deal with multiple applications or appeals if they relate to development for similar purposes on different sites and they could be asked by the Minister to look at alternative sites[105]. It would be required to[106]:

'(a) identify and investigate the considerations relevant to, or the technical or scientific aspects of, that matter which in their opinion are relevant to the question whether the proposed development should be permitted to be carried out, and

(b) assess the importance to be attached to those considerations or aspects'.

17.71 The applicant, local planning authority and any person who made representations in accordance with the Development Management Procedure Order consultation timescales are entitled to be heard at an inquiry by one or more members of the commission[107]. Unusually, the commission would be able to carry out or commission its own research[108]. It would then report to the Minister, who would decide whether to grant permission.

17.72 Whilst Planning Inquiry Commissions were intended to address complex and major infrastructure projects, they have never been used and were not part of the government's thinking in the two attempts to deal with major infrastructure in the Planning and Compulsory Purchase Act 2004 and the Planning Act 2008. During the debates on the Bill which became the 2008 Act, the Opposition spokesman, Mrs Jacqui Lait MP, moved amendments to repeal the Commission provisions as redundant. The Minister, Mr Dhanda MP, resisted saying[109]:

'I accept that there has never been a planning inquiry commission. Indeed, there is no prospect of one either. I sympathise with the thrust of the amendment, although we would have to check whether any consequential changes were needed before considering it further. As the provision in the 1990 Act is effectively harmless, its removal is not a priority and there are other pressures on parliamentary time'.

The Planning Inquiry Commission concept is so unloved that not only has it not been used, but Ministers have not even been bothered enough to repeal it.

---

[104] Town and Country Planning Act 1990, Sch 8, para 1(1).
[105] Town and Country Planning Act 1990, Sch 8, para 2.
[106] Town and Country Planning Act 1990, Sch 8, para 3(1).
[107] Town and Country Planning Act 1990, Sch 8, paras 3(2), 5. This has been understood as a two stage process of investigation by the commission followed by an inquiry (see Grant *Urban Planning Law*, pp 604–605), but the legislation does not require separate (or consecutive) stages provided the process is carried out fairly.
[108] Town and Country Planning Act 1990, Sch 8, para 3(4).
[109] Planning Bill 2008, Public Bill Committee 5 February 2008, col 652.

Chapter 18

Planning applications made directly to the Minister

18.1 Historically planning applications have been made to the local planning authorities. The Secretary of State has presided over appeals against the local decisions (or failures to make decisions) and has been able to call-in applications for his own determination. Ministers have been able to grant planning permission for particular schemes themselves by a special development order or an enterprise zone scheme. Additionally they can grant deemed planning permission whilst determining consents under other infrastructure powers[1]. The development consent order provisions of the Planning Act 2008 transferred certain schemes which would have been the subject of application to the local planning authority to a new Ministerial approval[2]. The deemed planning permission or development consent order processes lead to planning permission or an equivalent consent, but are not planning applications themselves.

18.2 A limited ability to make a planning application directly to the Secretary of State in England was introduced by the Localism Act 2011 and planning permission can be obtained urgently from Ministers for Crown development. Once the Planning (Wales) Act 2015 comes into force there will be four mechanisms by which planning applications may be made directly to Ministers under the Town and Country Planning Act 1990:

(i) applications to the Secretary of State in England under s 62A in the areas of underperforming local planning authorities;

(ii) applications to the Welsh Ministers under s 62M in the areas of underperforming local planning authorities;

(iii) applications for developments of national significance which must be made to the Welsh Ministers under s 62D;

(iv) urgent Crown development applications made to the Secretary of State or the Welsh Ministers under s 293A.

THE RIGHT TO APPLY TO THE SECRETARY OF STATE IN ENGLAND UNDER THE TOWN AND COUNTRY PLANNING ACT 1990, s 62A

18.3 Apart from the urgent Crown development provisions[3], introduced in 2006, it had not been possible to apply directly to Ministers for planning permission

---

[1] These orders, schemes and deemed planning permissions are discussed in Chapter 26 below.
[2] For example, airports and waste water treatment works. Some other development consent matters would have been subject to applications to Ministers in any event.
[3] Discussed from para **18.29**.

18.4 *Planning applications made directly to the Minister*

or reserved matters approval. Developers had to try for a local decision first and either appeal or await call-in. Some planning applications do spend a long time before the local authority awaiting determination, sometimes for good reasons and sometimes for bad, sometimes due to the applicant and sometimes to the authority. An ability to make applications directly to the Secretary of State was introduced by the Growth and Infrastructure Act 2013 for the promoters of large schemes in areas where the local planning authority had been designated because it was slow to determine applications. Section 62A applications are to be determined within 13 weeks, or 16 weeks for EIA development, or any longer period agreed in writing by the Secretary of State[4]. This promises a quick decision.

18.4 In such areas applying to the Secretary of State is discretionary: the developer has the option to apply to the local authority in the usual way. The option needs to be chosen with care. Whilst a decision will be obtained quicker than by appealing against a refusal or non-determination, it would be slower and more expensive than a rapidly determined local application and the developer only has one bite of the cherry. It cannot try to persuade the local authority and then if that fails ask the Minister to support it. The risks involved became apparent in the first and so far only s 62A application to be made, a scheme for 220 homes which was then refused by the inspector[5].

18.5 There is a wider political angle to the power. By allowing developers to apply directly to Ministers on important schemes where local authority timeliness is poor, Parliament was encouraging those authorities to speed up their decision-making. No council would want the embarrassment of major schemes being taken entirely out of their hands.

18.6 The direct application regime is in the Town and Country Planning Act 1990, ss 62A–62C and 76C–76E with the Town and Country Planning (Section 62A Applications) (Procedure and Consequential Amendments) Order 2013, the Town and Country Planning (Section 62A Applications) (Written Representations and Miscellaneous Provisions) Regulations 2013 and the Town and Country Planning (Section 62A Applications) (Hearings) Rules 2013[6].

18.7 Section 62A of the Town and Country Planning Act 1990[7] allows applications for planning permission (except s 73 applications for development subject to different conditions) and applications for the approval of reserved matters[8] to be made to the Secretary of State for major development in the areas of designated local planning authorities.

18.8 Major development is defined for these purposes as[9]:

'any development involving one or more of the following:

(a) the provision of dwellinghouses where:

---

[4] Town and Country Planning (Section 62A Applications) (Procedure and Consequential Amendments) Order 2013, SI 2013/2140, art 23.
[5] S62A/2014/0001/Hospital Lane Blaby.
[6] SIs 2013/2140, 2013/2142 and 2013/2141 respectively. The Procedure Order has been amended by SIs 2013/2932, 2013/3194, 2014/1532, 2015/797.
[7] Inserted by the Growth and Infrastructure Act 2013, s 1.
[8] Collectively defined as 'relevant applications': Town and Country Planning Act 1990, s 62A(2)(b).
[9] Town and Country Planning (Section 62A Applications) (Written Representations and Miscellaneous Provisions) Regulations 2013, reg 3, made under Town and Country Planning Act 1990, s 62A(2).

The right to apply to the Secretary of State **18.10**

      (i)   the number of dwellinghouses to be provided is 10 or more; or

      (ii)   the development is to be carried out on a site having an area of 0.5 hectares or more and it is not known whether the development falls within sub-paragraph (a)(i);

  (b)   the provision of a building or buildings where the floor space to be created by the development is 1,000 square metres or more;

  (c)   development carried out on a site having an area of 1 hectare or more'.

18.9 Before designating local planning authorities the Secretary of State must set out criteria for designation and for revoking designation in a document laid before Parliament and published[10]. The document is subject to the negative resolution procedure, allowing either House to vote it down within 40 days[11]. The current criteria are in *Improving planning performance: Criteria for designation (revised 2015)*[12] and are whether:

(a)   50% or fewer of the applications for major development in the last two years have been determined within the statutory period (13 weeks, or 16 weeks for EIA development) or any extended period agreed in writing with the local planning authority[13]; or

(b)   20% or more of their decisions on major development applications are overturned on appeal[14].

18.10 The Secretary of State may designate an authority if by reference to those criteria, the Secretary of State considers that there are respects in which the authority is not adequately performing its function of determining applications[15]. Consequently the criteria are not decisive as to whether the authority is not adequately performing its functions. Failure to achieve the criteria might be excused and conceivably an authority which met the wording of the criteria might be found to be inadequate if it operated so as to make the criteria unworkable[16]. Any decision to designate an authority, or subsequently to revoke the designation must be published[17].

---

[10]   Town and Country Planning Act 1990, s 62B(1), (2).
[11]   Town and Country Planning Act 1990, s 62B(2)–(4).
[12]   These replaced criteria documents laid before Parliament in 2013 and 2014.
[13]   *Criteria*, paras 12–16. This is a further incentive for local planning authorities to agree extensions of time for determination. It might be that separate criteria are adopted for oil and gas applications: see DECC/DCLG news release *Faster decision making on shale gas for economic growth and energy security*, 13 August 2015.
[14]   *Criteria*, paras 17–22. Applications which were granted by the authority or refusals which were not appealed are included in the total against which successful appeals are calculated. Penalties are applied to the speed and quality scores if data is not provided by the local planning authority concerned: see Annex A.
[15]   Town and Country Planning Act 1990, s 62B(1). The applications are under the Town and Country Planning Act 1990, Part III, so will essentially be planning applications, reserved matters approval and details under conditions, but might include planning obligation modifications. The Minister may not designate the Homes and Communities Agency, the Mayor of London, a Mayoral development corporation or an urban development corporation (Town and Country Planning Act 1990, s 62B(5)) so the designation power may only be exercised over councils and national park authorities. Ministers have direct powers over non-Mayoral bodies.
[16]   Examples would be an authority which delayed running time for determination of applications until they had been validated and delayed the validation decision, or was improperly refusing to validate applications. Exceptional circumstances for not designating may be raised by authorities which fail to meet the thresholds: *Criteria* para 23.
[17]   Town and Country Planning Act 1990, s 62B(6).

18.11 *Planning applications made directly to the Minister*

The s 62A application process

18.11 The application process is principally contained in the Town and Country Planning (Section 62A Applications) (Procedure and Consequential Amendments) Order 2013 (the 2013 Order), which is essentially an altered version of the Town and Country Planning (Development Management Procedure) (England) Order 2010. Written representation and hearing procedures are in the Town and Country Planning (Section 62A Applications) (Written Representations and Miscellaneous Provisions) Regulations 2013 and the Town and Country Planning (Section 62A Applications) (Hearings) Rules 2013.

18.12 The processes have many similarities to applications made and then appealed to the Secretary of State so the discussion of conventional applications will tend to be relevant. The table below sets out the s 62A stages, their legislative basis, the equivalent provisions for applications made to local planning authorities and consideration of those matters in this book. Particular points on the s 62A regime are then addressed.

Potential stage	s 62A provisions	LPA application provisions	Book reference to LPA applications
Pre-application advice	Fees for this advice are set under Town and Country Planning (Fees for Applications, Deemed Applications, Requests and Site Visits) (England) Regulations 2012, reg 2A		Chapter 6
EIA screening	EIA Regulations 2011, reg 10A	EIA Regulations 2011, regs 4–6	Chapter 7
Pre-application consultation	2013 Order, arts 3A, 3B	Town and Country Planning Act 1990, s 61W; DMPO arts 3A, 3B	Chapter 6
Notice to the owner and agricultural tenants	2013 Order, arts 9, 10	Town and Country Planning Act 1990, s 65; DMPO 2015, arts 11, 12	Chapter 6
Submission of the application and supporting documents	2013 Order, arts 4–8	DMPO 2015, arts 4, 6–8, 10	Chapter 6
Publicity and consultation on the application	Town and Country Planning Act 1990, s 62C (parish councils); 2013 Order, arts 11–14A, 17–21; Planning (Listed Buildings and Conservation Areas) Regulations 1990, reg 5A(2A)–(2C)	Town and Country Planning Act 1990, Sch 1, para 8; DMPO 2015, arts 13, 14, 16–19, 24	Chapter 6

The right to apply to the Secretary of State **18.14**

Potential stage	s 62A provisions	LPA application provisions	Book reference to LPA applications
Amendments, further information and further publicity		DMPO 2015, art 4(2) (reserved matters)	Chapter 6
Publication of a report if the decision is taken by councillors		Local Government Act 1972, ss 100C, 100D, 100E	Chapter 8
Decision on the application	Town and Country Planning Act 1990, s 70; 2013 Order, art 24; EIA Regulations 2011, reg 3	TCPA s 70; DMPO 2015, arts 23, 28; EIA Regulations 2011, reg 3	Chapters 8, 9
Imposition of conditions	Town and Country Planning Act 1990, ss 70, 72, applied by s 77	Town and Country Planning Act 1990, ss 70, 72	Chapter 11
Planning obligations		Town and Country Planning Act 1990, s 106	Chapter 12
Direction by Mayor of London	Not applicable	Town and Country Planning Act 1990, s 74; Mayor of London Order	Chapter 10
Potential referral to Ministers	Not applicable	DMPO 2015, art 25	Chapter 17
Issue of the decision notice	2013 Order, art 24	DMPO 2015, art 31; EIA Regulations 2011, reg 3	Chapter 13
Post-decision publicity	2013 Order, art 25; EIA Regulations 2011, reg 24	DMPO 2015, art 31; EIA Regulations 2011, reg 24	Chapters 7, 13

18.13 When a s 62A application is made to the Secretary of State an application for listed building consent which is connected to that application may also be made to the Secretary of State[18]. If the Secretary of State considers that that application is not connected then he may direct that it be treated as having been made to the local planning authority and is then to be determined by them[19]. A procedure for making listed building consent applications under these arrangements is also set out[20].

18.14 Application fees are paid to the Secretary of State at the same level as if the planning application had been made to the local planning authority[21]. Various exemptions arise for applications made in the 12 months following the approval or

---

[18] Town and Country Planning Act 1990, s 62A(3). The applicants need not be the same person.
[19] Town and Country Planning Act 1990, s 62A(4).
[20] Town and Country Planning (Section 62A Applications) (Procedure and Consequential Amendments) Order 2013, arts 28–49.
[21] Town and Country Planning (Fees for Applications, Deemed Applications, Requests and Site Visits) (England) Regulations 2012, reg 11A(1)–(3).

18.15 *Planning applications made directly to the Minister*

refusal of an earlier application or the receipt of a subsequently withdrawn application[22]. Pre-application advice is charged at hourly rates set for planning inspectors and planning officers (who in this case are staff at the Planning Inspectorate)[23].

The Minister is able to decline to determine the application on any of the grounds relating to repΩeat and duplicate applications in the Town and Country Planning Act 1990, ss 70A–70C[24].

18.15 A s 62A planning or reserved matters application which relates to land in a parish, or any alteration to that application, must be notified to the parish council if it has asked the local planning authority to inform it of applications[25].

18.16 Section 62A applications are determined by a Planning Inspector appointed by the Secretary of State[26], unless the Minister decides to determine it personally[27]. The appointment of the inspector by the Minister is personal – that is, the Minister may revoke the appointment and ask another inspector to act[28]. Applications may be determined on written representations or following a hearing. Whilst there is no provision for an inquiry to be held, the hearing procedure is flexible. The applicant, local planning authority, ward councillor, any statutory consultee and any person who requested to be heard when making representations is entitled to appear[29].

THE RIGHT TO APPLY TO THE WELSH MINISTERS UNDER s 62M

18.17 The Planning (Wales) Act 2015 will introduce a similar mechanism to s 62A applications (albeit with some differences in the detail) as the Town and Country Planning Act 1990, ss 62M–62O[30]. Beyond the power to make secondary legislation, these provisions are not yet in force.

A planning or reserved matters application will be able to be made to the Welsh Ministers if the local planning authority for the area has been designated by the Ministers and the development is of a description prescribed in regulations[31]. Whilst the description of development is left at large by the Act, it is likely to be the definition of major development in the DMPO Wales[32].

18.18 The designation of a local planning authority by the Welsh Ministers can only take place on the basis of criteria which have been the subject of consultation

---

[22] Town and Country Planning (Fees for Applications, Deemed Applications, Requests and Site Visits) (England) Regulations 2012, reg 11A(4)–(7).
[23] Town and Country Planning (Fees for Applications, Deemed Applications, Requests and Site Visits) (England) Regulations 2012, reg 2A.
[24] Town and Country Planning Act 1990, s 76C(1). See the discussion of these powers in Chapter 6.
[25] Town and Country Planning Act 1990, s 62C, applying the requirements of Sch 1, para 8.
[26] Town and Country Planning Act 1990, s 76D(1).
[27] Under Town and Country Planning Act 1990, s 76E.
[28] Town and Country Planning Act 1990, s 76D(2).
[29] Town and Country Planning (Section 62A Applications) (Hearings) Rules 2013, r 6(2). Third parties commenting on s 62A applications should include a request to be heard.
[30] Inserted by the Planning (Wales) Act 2015, s 23. In force from 6 September 2015 for the purposes of making secondary legislation only. This had been proposed in *Positive Planning: A consultation on proposals to reform the planning system in Wales* (2013).
[31] Town and Country Planning Act 1990, s 62M. These applications do not include s 73 applications unless the regulations provide for them: Town and Country Planning Act 1990, s 62M(5), (6).
[32] DMPO Wales, art 2(1), see the Explanatory Notes to the Planning (Wales) Act 2015, para 100.

with local authorities, then laid before the National Assembly for Wales and published without being voted down[33]. The power to designate or to revoke a designation is exercisable by written notice to the authority[34].

18.19 If an application is made to the Welsh Ministers, then a connected application may be made on the same day. These applications will be prescribed in regulations, but can be expected to include listed building, conservation area and hazardous substances consent.

18.20 The procedure for s 62M is expected to be set out in a development order[35] and any further regulations. As a preliminary point, a community council must be notified of an application in its area if it has previously asked the local planning authority to inform it of applications of that description[36].

APPLICATIONS FOR NATIONALLY SIGNIFICANT DEVELOPMENT IN WALES UNDER s 62D

18.21 The ability to apply to the Minister under ss 62A or 62M is merely an option given to developers of major schemes in the areas of poorly performing local authorities. The English experience to date has been that it operates more as a threat to local planning authorities, encouraging faster decision making, than as a common route for applicants. The other new mechanism proposed by the Planning (Wales) Act 2015 is of more obvious practical significance. Beyond the ability to make secondary legislation to implement these powers, this regime is not yet in force.

18.22 Section 62D will provide that any 'nationally significant development application is to be made to the Welsh Ministers instead of to the local planning authority'[37]. This is an application for planning permission where the development to which it relates[38]:

(i) meets criteria in regulations as being of national significance; or

(ii) the National Development Framework for Wales specifies it as being of national significance.

18.23 Section 73 applications (for development subject to different conditions) are only within this definition if prescribed by the regulations[39]. Applications for outline planning permission are excluded from s 62D[40], an interesting omission, as the largest residential and commercial consents tend to be sought in outline.

18.24 'Secondary consents' will also have to be sought from the Welsh Ministers. A secondary consent is a consent or notice given under legislation which relates

---

[33] Town and Country Planning Act 1990, s 62N.
[34] Town and Country Planning Act 1990, s 62N(7). The notice must then be published: s 62N(8).
[35] Made under the Town and Country Planning Act 1990, s 62R.
[36] Town and Country Planning Act 1990, s 62Q.
[37] Town and Country Planning Act 1990, s 62D(1), inserted by the Planning (Wales) Act 2015, s 19.
[38] Town and Country Planning Act 1990, s 62D(3), (4).
[39] Town and Country Planning Act 1990, s 62D(6), (7).
[40] Town and Country Planning Act 1990, s 62D(5). Unlike s 62M, reserved matters applications may not be made under s 62D, the process being concerned with control over the scheme itself, rather than speeding up the approval of details.

18.25 *Planning applications made directly to the Minister*

to or is connected with the development or use of land in Wales[41]. Such consents must be within the legislative competence of the National Assembly and concern bodies' public functions[42] rather than private rights. To be connected to the s 62A application the consent would be required for the s 62A application development to be carried out, 'would facilitate the carrying out of that development or facilitate the re-development or improvement, or the achievement of any other purpose, carried out in relation to land in connection with that development'[43]. It is for the Welsh Ministers to decide whether a secondary consent is connected and they have then to consider whether that consent should be determined by them[44]. Connected secondary consents would most obviously include planning applications for elements away from the main site, such as highway works, and listed building or conservation area consent applications. However the potential scope of these consents is wider.

18.25 A secondary consent application may be dealt with by the Ministers if it is made at the same time or after the s 62D application or has already been made, but not determined, when that application is submitted[45].

Section 62D application procedure

18.26 Secondary legislation will set out the full procedures for s 62D applications[46] but a few elements are in the primary legislation. Pre-application notice must be given to the Welsh Ministers and the local planning authority in a prescribed form[47]. Once an application is made, the Welsh Ministers must give notice to the local planning authority for the application site requiring it to prepare and submit a local impact report[48] which gives details of the likely impact on that body's area[49]. Community councils are to be consulted if they have requested notification of applications[50].

18.27 In determining the s 62D application, the Welsh Ministers must have regard to the local impact report which they have requested and any similar reports voluntarily submitted by other local planning authorities or community councils[51].

18.28 Section 62D applications are to be determined within 36 weeks beginning with the date of acceptance of the application by the Welsh Ministers, but Ministers may suspend the period by notice[52].

---

[41] Town and Country Planning Act 1990, s 62H(1).
[42] Town and Country Planning Act 1990, s 62H(2).
[43] Town and Country Planning Act 1990, s 62F(6).
[44] Town and Country Planning Act 1990, s 62F(1).
[45] Town and Country Planning Act 1990, s 62F(3). The detail of the secondary consent application regime is to be determined by regulations and directions: Town and Country Planning Act 1990, s 62G.
[46] See the order making power in Town and Country Planning Act 1990, s 62R.
[47] Town and Country Planning Act 1990, s 62E.
[48] Town and Country Planning Act 1990, s 62I. This echoes provisions in the Planning Act 2008 for development consent orders for nationally significant infrastructure projects.
[49] Town and Country Planning Act 1990, s 62K.
[50] See Town and Country Planning Act 1990, s 62Q, applying Town and Country Planning Act 1990, Sch 1A, para 2.
[51] Town and Country Planning Act 1990, s 62J(2), (3).
[52] Town and Country Planning Act 1990, s 62L.

URGENT CROWN DEVELOPMENT

18.29 Up to 2006, central government (as the Crown) was able to carry out development without obtaining planning permission, albeit usually subject to an informal consultation process. Amendments made by the Planning and Compulsory Purchase Act 2004 removed the Crown's exemption from planning control. Generally planning permission is now obtained by the government in the usual way, by a planning application to the local planning authority or by permitted development rights. However Ministerial concern remained where a project was required urgently. Permitted development rights would assist in some urgent cases[53], but it was considered there was a need for an urgency procedure to allow applications to be made directly to the Secretary of State. This is contained in the Town and Country Planning Act 1990, s 293A.

18.30 Applications are made by the appropriate authority. This is usually the government department concerned or the Crown Estate Commissioners[54]. If the authority certifies that the development is of national importance and that it is necessary that it is carried out as a matter of urgency[55] then it may make the planning application to the Secretary of State or Welsh Ministers. Publicity and consultation requirements are contained in s 293A and the relevant Development Management Procedure Order.

18.31 Prior to making the application the appropriate authority must publish a local newspaper advertisement describing the development and saying that it proposes to make an application to the Minister[56]. The application must comply, if necessary, with the relevant EIA Regulations[57] and must include a statement of the grounds for making the application[58]. The Development Management Procedure Order requirements as to the content of planning applications do not appear to apply: they refer to applications made to the local planning authority. Interestingly the *Planning Practice Guidance* says that an application must be made on the form provided by the local planning authority[59], but whilst this may make practical sense, there seems to be no statutory basis for such a requirement. Further information may be required by the Minister[60].

In England a fee is payable to the Secretary of State for applications for urgent Crown development at the same rate as if the application had been made to the local planning authority[61].

---

[53] Town and Country Planning (General Permitted Development) Order 2015, Sch 2, Part 19, Classes E and I.
[54] Town and Country Planning Act 1990, s 293(2). Appropriate authorities less likely to require urgent approvals include those representing the Duchies of Lancaster and Cornwall and parts of the Palace of Westminster.
[55] Town and Country Planning Act 1990, s 293A(1). The *Planning Practice Guidance* says that the procedure may be invoked if it is likely that the application will be refused by the local planning authority (para 44-028-20140306). However the likelihood that an appeal would be needed is not a basis for certification: the proposed development must be urgently required.
[56] Town and Country Planning Act 1990, s 293A(3).
[57] Town and Country Planning Act 1990, s 293A(4)(a), applying the Town and Country Planning (Environmental Impact Assessment) Regulations 2011 and the Town and Country Planning (Environmental Impact Assessment) (England and Wales) Regulations 1999 as appropriate.
[58] Town and Country Planning Act 1990, s 293A(4)(b).
[59] *Planning Practice Guidance* para 44-029-20140306. This paragraph also sets out the addresses to which the application must be submitted.
[60] Town and Country Planning Act 1990, s 293A(6).
[61] Town and Country Planning (Fees for Applications, Deemed Applications, Requests and Site Visits) (England) Regulations 2012, reg 12. No equivalent fee is contained in the Welsh fees regulations.

18.32 *Planning applications made directly to the Minister*

18.32 Public bodies must be consulted by the Minister on the urgent application as they would have been if the application had been made to the local planning authority[62] as well as the local planning authority itself[63]. The Minister must also make the application and supporting documents available for public inspection in the locality, unless they are subject to a national security direction[64]. There appears to be no express requirement for the Minister to advertise the application or the place of inspection, since the Development Management Procedure Order provisions relate to applications made to the local planning authority, but a right to inspect in the locality is meaningless if the public are not told of the application and where it can be seen.

18.33 Urgent Crown development applications are treated as if they have been called-in by the Minister under s 77 in terms of the duty to have regard to the development plan, the power to impose conditions and the right of the application and local planning authority to a hearing[65]. Any Ministerial decision on a s 293A application is challengeable by an application to the High Court under s 288 of the Act[66].

---

[62] Town and Country Planning (Development Management Procedure) (England) Order 2015, art 19; Town and Country Planning (Development Management Procedure) (Wales) Order 2012, art 15.
[63] Town and Country Planning Act 1990, s 293A(9)(a).
[64] Town and Country Planning Act 1990, s 293A(7), (10).
[65] Town and Country Planning Act 1990, s 293A(11).
[66] Town and Country Planning Act 1990, ss 284(1)(f), (3)(i), 288.

Chapter 19

Planning appeals: preliminaries and tactics

19.1 The applicant for planning permission may appeal to the Secretary of State in England or the Welsh Assembly Government against a local planning authority's refusal of its planning application or application for the approval of reserved matters or details under conditions on a planning permission or development order, or against the grant of such consent subject to conditions or the failure to determine the application within a prescribed period (an appeal against non-determination). Appeals are decided by the Secretary of State or a Minister in the Welsh Assembly Government (if Ministers have recovered jurisdiction over the appeal) or by a planning inspector (a transferred appeal).

19.2 There is no right of appeal against the refusal of applications made to the Minister, called-in planning applications or deemed planning permission since these are already decided by Ministers or inspectors.

19.3 Appeals may be determined by written representations (with a simplified procedure for appeals against the refusal of householder and minor commercial applications) or following a hearing or inquiry. In 2014/2015 16,042 appeals were received in England. Of these, 34% were to be dealt with under the householder and minor commercial appeals service, with about 58% under the other written representations procedure. Inquiries constituted about 3% of the planning appeals and hearings about 5%[1].

THE ENTITLEMENT TO APPEAL

19.4 The applicant is entitled to appeal to the Minister against a refusal of the application or its grant subject to conditions under the Town and Country Planning Act 1990, s 78(1):

'Where a local planning authority:

(a) refuse an application for planning permission or grant it subject to conditions;

(b) refuse an application for any consent, agreement or approval of that authority required by a condition imposed on a grant of planning permission or grant it subject to conditions; or

(c) refuse an application for any approval of that authority required under a development order, a local development order or a neighbourhood development order or grant it subject to conditions,

the applicant may by notice appeal to the Secretary of State'.

---

[1] Planning Inspectorate Statistical Report: England 2014/15, table 1.3 contains the main figures. The proportion of inquiries is slightly understated as the percentages exclude 113 appeals recovered by the Secretary of State, of which a high proportion will have been determined following an inquiry.

19.5 *Planning appeals: preliminaries and tactics*

19.5 An appeal can be made against the non-determination of such applications under s 78(2)[2]:

'(2) A person who has made such an application *to the local planning authority* may also appeal to the Secretary of State if the local planning authority have done none of the following:

(a) given notice to the applicant of their decision on the application;

(aa) given notice to the applicant that they have exercised their power under section 70A *or 70B* or 70C to decline to determine the application;

(b) given notice to him that the application has been referred to the Secretary of State in accordance with directions given under section 77,

within such period as may be prescribed by the development order or within such extended period as may at any time be agreed upon in writing between the applicant and the authority'.

19.6 The right of appeal against refusal or the grant of the consent subject to conditions extends to: (a) applications for planning permission; (b) applications for the approval of reserved matters or details under conditions on planning permissions; and (c) prior approval and other applications for approval under the Town and Country Planning (General Permitted Development) (England) Order 2015[3] or in Wales the Town and Country Planning (General Permitted Development) Order 1995[4], any special development order, local development order or neighbourhood development order. A community right to build order is 'a particular type of neighbourhood development order'[5] so the right of appeal will apply to details under it. A simplified planning zone has the effect of granting planning permission, so might allow appeals within sub-para (b).

If a grant of planning permission subject to conditions is appealed then the whole consent is in issue in the appeal: it is possible for the inspector to refuse it entirely.

19.7 The right to appeal against non-determination arises when the local planning authority fails to give notice of its decision on the application within the prescribed period, or any extended period which has been agreed in writing between the parties. These applications are all those subject to the sub-s (1) right, except that a non-determination of an application for a decision whether prior approval of details is required under the General Permitted Development Order operates as an automatic approval of those details, so no right of appeal is required.

19.8 The right to appeal for non-determination does not arise, or expires, if the authority:

(a) provides its decision notice granting or refusing the application;

(b) gives notice that it has declined to determine the application under:

(i) s 70A (power to decline to determine subsequent application);

(ii) s 70B (power to decline to determine an overlapping application in England);

---

[2] Italicised text applies to England only.
[3] SI 2015/596.
[4] SI 1995/418.
[5] Town and Country Planning Act 1990, s 61Q.

(iii) s 70C (power to decline to determine a retrospective application to which a pre-existing enforcement notice relates)[6];

(c) gives notice that the application has been called-in by the Minister: referral to the Minister under a direction for consideration whether the application should be called-in does not prevent an appeal against non-determination.

19.9 Even if the right to appeal against non-determination has arisen, the local planning authority may still determine the application provided that an appeal has not already been submitted. Conversely, once the appeal has been submitted, the local planning authority has no power to decide the application, even if it would have approved it, subject to the dual jurisdiction powers available in Wales[7].

19.10 An appeal may only be brought by the applicant for planning permission, not by a successor in title or another person who has an interest in the land. Whilst a planning permission will run with the land, a planning application has to be made and continued by a person. There is a dearth of authority on changes to the appellant but it would seem that joint applicants must make a joint appeal. Successors ought to be dealt with in a pragmatic fashion: a person who takes over another's rights and responsibilities, such as an executor of the deceased or the administrator of an insolvent company should be able to bring or continue an appeal in that capacity[8]. A subsequent purchaser of or successor to the property who was not the applicant would be not able to appeal. However, they could take over the conduct of the appeal in the applicant's name by agreement with the applicant. The costs of the appeal and liabilities for any costs awards would need to be agreed between those persons.

19.11 There is no ability for a non-applicant to appeal against the grant of planning permission. The only way to remove the planning permission would be by a challenge to its lawfulness by judicial review[9] or by persuading the local planning authority or the Minister to revoke the planning permission[10].

THE ROLE OF THE APPEAL

19.12 In an appeal the Minister or the inspector will consider the merits of the planning application and decide it as they consider appropriate. The appeal is not a review, confined to considering the lawfulness or reasonableness of the local planning authority's decision. On an appeal the decision-maker may[11]:

'(a) allow or dismiss the appeal, or

(b) reverse or vary any part of the decision of the local planning authority (whether the appeal relates to that part of it or not),

and may deal with the application as if it had been made to him in the first instance'.

---

[6] Section 70C is prospectively inserted in Wales by the Planning (Wales) Act 2015, s 32. No commencement date has yet been announced.
[7] See para **19.36**.
[8] More problematic is where a corporate applicant has been dissolved and so has ceased to exist.
[9] See Chapter 25 on High Court challenges.
[10] Town and Country Planning Act 1990, ss 97–101.
[11] Town and Country Planning Act 1990, s 79(1).

19.13 *Planning appeals: preliminaries and tactics*

19.13 The requirement to have regard to the development plan and other material considerations in the Town and Country Planning Act 1990, s 70(2) applies[12], and consequently so does the presumption in favour of the development plan in the Planning and Compulsory Purchase Act 2004, s 38(6)[13]. Statutory duties to have regard or special regard to particular matters, such as nature conservation or historic environment designations, apply to Ministers and inspectors as they do to local planning authorities. Similarly European law duties, such as those under the Habitats, Birds, Environmental Impact Assessment and Waste Directives, apply at the appeal stage. Everything which the authority should have or did consider must be taken into account in the planning appeal. Ministers and inspectors have the local planning authority's powers to grant planning permission subject to conditions and to grant it with varied conditions from an earlier permission (s 73), retrospectively (s 73A) or subject to the special minerals provisions in Sch 5[14]. They may also grant permission or consent in part[15].

19.14 All the relevant matters have to be considered in the appeal and an appeal can therefore be dismissed on the basis of points taken by the local planning authority, third parties or those raised by the Minister or inspector on their own initiative. An appeal is therefore not simply confined to the contentions of the respective parties.

19.15 However, the appeal process is designed not only to enable the parties to raise their arguments but to focus on the issues in dispute with the aim of refining and analysing those issues. Whilst the appellate body may raise points which are not contentious between the parties, it must do so fairly. Ministers and their inspectors are not able to introduce evidence themselves.

TIME LIMITS FOR APPEALING

19.16 The notice of appeal must be served on the Minister within the time prescribed by a development order[16]. In England, the time limits specified in the DMPO 2015, art 37(2) are six months from the date of the notice or decision giving rise to the appeal, from the service of a notice by the local planning authority requiring further information under art 4(2) (if that information is not provided) or from the expiry of the period for determination or any longer period agreed in writing between the applicant and the local planning authority[17]. Where EIA is required the period for determination is 16 weeks beginning with the day after the receipt of the application or the determination that EIA is required, if that is later[18]. For non-EIA major development the determination period is 13 weeks and for all other applications, eight weeks[19]. The six-month period in England is subject to these exceptions:

---

[12] Town and Country Planning Act 1990, s 79(4).
[13] See Chapter 8 for discussion of the development plan and material considerations.
[14] Town and Country Planning Act 1990, s 79(4).
[15] Town and Country Planning Act 1990, s 79(1).
[16] Town and Country Planning Act 1990, s 78(3). The prescribed period must not be less than 28 days from the date of notification of the decision or the expiry of the period for determination: s 78(4).
[17] DMPO 2015, art 37(2)(d), formerly DMPO 2010, art 33(2)(d).
[18] Town and Country Planning (Environmental Impact Assessment) Regulations 2011, SI 2011/1824, reg 61.
[19] DMPO 2015, art 34(2)(a), (b). 'Major development' is defined in DMPO 2015, art 2(1). The authority have the full period, so if a non-major, non-EIA application is submitted on Wednesday 1 July, the eight-week period begins on 2 July and the last day for determination within the period is Wednesday 26 August. An appeal for non-determination could be made on Thursday 27 August.

Time limits for appealing **19.19**

(i) where a copy of an enforcement notice was served in respect of substantially the same development on substantially the same land at a time between two years before the application was made and either the determination of the appeal or the expiry of the period for determination (a Type A appeal) the appeal must be made within 28 days from notice of the decision or the expiry of the specified period for the determination of the application[20]. This brings the appeal period forward to discourage further delay to the enforcement of planning control;

(ii) where a copy of an enforcement notice is served in respect of substantially the same development on substantially the same land on or after the date of notice of the decision or the expiry of the statutory determination period (a Type B appeal) the period is reduced to 28 days from the service of the copy of the notice if more than that time for appealing remained[21]. A planning appeal will therefore run quite close in time to an enforcement notice appeal;

(iii) an appeal against the refusal of planning permission on a householder or minor commercial application is to be brought within 12 weeks of notice of the decision, unless it is a Type A or B appeal in which case the shorter timescales apply[22]. Appeals against the grant of permission subject to conditions or against the non-determination of a householder or minor commercial application are subject to the usual six-month timescale.

19.17 A 'householder application' means[23]:

'(a) an application for planning permission for development of an existing dwellinghouse, or development within the curtilage of such a dwellinghouse for any purpose incidental to the enjoyment of the dwellinghouse; or

(b) an application for any consent, agreement or approval required by or under a planning permission, development order or local development order in relation to such development,

but does not include an application for change of use or an application to change the number of dwellings in a building'.

19.18 And 'minor commercial application' means:

'(a) an application for planning permission for development of an existing building or part of a building currently in use for any of the purposes set out in Schedule 1A, or

(b) an application for any consent, agreement or approval required by or under a planning permission, development order or local development order in relation to such development,

where such an application does not include a change of use, a change to the number of units in a building, or development that is not wholly at ground floor level or that would increase the gross internal area of a building'.

19.19 For planning applications made prior to 22 June 2015 the time for appealing in Wales was the more straightforward six months from the date of the notice or decision giving rise to the appeal, from the service of a notice by the local planning

---

[20] DMPO 2015, art 37(2)(b), (8), formerly DMPO 2010, art 33(2)(b), (7).
[21] DMPO 2015, art 37(2)(c), (8), formerly DMPO 2010, art 33(2)(c), (7).
[22] DMPO 2015, art 37(2)(a), formerly DMPO 2010, art 33(2)(a).
[23] DMPO 2015 and formerly 2010, art 2(1) define both terms. Their meaning is discussed further in Chapter 20 on Householder and minor commercial appeals.

19.20 *Planning appeals: preliminaries and tactics*

authority requiring further information under art 4(2) (if that information is not provided) or from the expiry of the period for determination or any longer period agreed in writing[24].

19.20 Two changes were introduced in Wales for applications made to the local planning authority on or after 22 June 2015[25]:

- the period for appealing for non-determination was removed, so a non-determination appeal can be brought at any time after the determination period (as set or extended by agreement) has expired;
- the introduction of a householder and minor commercial appeals service, along the same lines as the English system resulted in the period for appealing the refusal of planning permission for such an application being reduced to 12 weeks from the decision notice.

19.21 The scope of householder and minor commercial applications[26] in Wales does differ from the English provisions. Their meaning in each nation is discussed in Chapter 20.

An appeal may be submitted after the expiry of these time periods if the Minister allows in a particular case[27].

Inability to appeal for non-determination for timing reasons

19.22 An applicant for planning permission may only appeal for non-determination if they are within the given period for non-determination appeals in England or the Secretary of State allows a late appeal. Applicants should therefore seek extensions of the determination period from the local planning authority in writing if there is a risk that the right to appeal might expire. The local planning authority is though under a duty to deal with the application notwithstanding the expiry of the period for determination and for appeal for non-determination[28]. Consequently the authority can be ordered by judicial review to determine the application, which would then give the possibility of an appeal against refusal.

THE NOTICE OF APPEAL AND ACCOMPANYING DOCUMENTS IN ENGLAND

19.23 In 2013 the planning appeal procedures were reformed in England with the aim of speeding up the process. One change was to require the appellant to deploy their full case when initiating the appeal, rather than using relatively short grounds of appeal and presenting their arguments and documents at a later stage.

---

[24] DMPO Wales, art 26(2), prior to 22 June 2015.
[25] DMPO Wales, art 26(2), as amended by the Town and Country Planning (Development Management Procedure) (Wales) (Amendment) Order 2015, SI 2015/1330, art 8(2)(b).
[26] Defined in DMPO Wales, art 2(1).
[27] DMPO 2015, art 37(1)(a)(ii); DMPO Wales, art 26(2).
[28] *Bovis Homes (Scotland) Ltd v Inverclyde District Council* 1982 SLT 473, followed in *Billings v First Secretary of State* [2005] EWHC 2274 (Admin), [2006] JPL 693 at para 26 per Sir Michael Harrison.

19.24 By the English DMPO 2015, art 37, the appellant must submit a completed appeal form (which will include grounds of appeal), obtained from the Secretary of State, and the following documents as far as relevant to the appeal[29].

19.25 For a householder or minor commercial appeal:

'(i) a copy of the application which was sent to the local planning authority which has occasioned the appeal;

(ii) any other plans, documents or drawings relating to the application which were not sent to the authority, except any plans, documents or drawings relating to amendments to the application proposed after the authority have made their determination; and

(iii) the notice of the decision or determination'.

19.26 The Inspectorate will obtain the planning application drawings and supporting documents from the local planning authority in these simplified cases. In these appeals the only opportunity for further comment is with the appeal form, so the appellant needs to ensure that its case is fully set out.

19.27 The material requirements in other cases are more substantial:

'(i) a copy of the application which was sent to the local planning authority which has occasioned the appeal;

(ii) all plans, drawings and documents sent to the authority in connection with the application;

(iii) all correspondence with the authority relating to the application;

(iv) any certificate provided to the authority under article 14;

(v) any other plans, documents or drawings relating to the application which were not sent to the authority, except any plans, documents or drawings relating to amendments to the application proposed after the authority have made their determination;

(vi) the notice of the decision or determination, if any;

(vii) if the appeal relates to an application for approval of certain matters in accordance with a condition on a planning permission, the application for that permission, the plans submitted with that application and the planning permission granted;

(viii) subject to paragraph (4), the applicant's full statement of case (if they wish to make additional representations);

(ix) subject to paragraph (4), a statement of which procedure (written representations, a hearing or an inquiry) the applicant considers should be used to determine the appeal; and

(x) subject to paragraph (4), a draft statement of common ground if the applicant considers that the appeal should be determined through a hearing or an inquiry'.

19.28 The full statement of case is a 'written statement which contains full particulars of the case which a person proposes to put forward and copies of any documents which that person intends to refer to or put in evidence'[30]. That is an

---

[29] The requirement arises under DMPO 2015, art 37(1) and the list of documents is in art 36(3).
[30] DMPO 2015, art 37(8).

19.29 *Planning appeals: preliminaries and tactics*

onerous obligation, although its nature does vary between the different procedures. These are discussed further in the particular chapters.

19.29 Paragraph (4) provides that these three categories of documents are not required for appeals subject to national security directions, urgent Crown appeals and type A or B appeals concerning enforcement matters.

19.30 The appeal form should also be served on the local planning authority along with a copy of the documents which it will not already have, namely the documents which had not been submitted in the application process and for non-householder/minor commercial appeals, the full statement of case, proposed procedure and, if required, draft statement of common ground[31]. This should be served on the authority as soon as reasonably practicable and so does not have to be provided within the time limit[32].

19.31 Where an environmental statement has been submitted in connection with the application, a copy of the statement and any further information submitted under the EIA Regulations must be sent to the Secretary of State by the applicant[33].

The notice of appeal and accompanying documents in Wales

19.32 Article 26 of the DMPO Wales requires the appellant to submit a completed appeal form (which again includes grounds of appeal), obtained from the Welsh Ministers, and the following documents as far as relevant to the appeal[34]. For householder and minor commercial appeals which are subject to the new appeals regime, the documents to be provided are[35]:

'(i) a copy of the application which was sent to the local planning authority which has occasioned the appeal;

(ii) any other plans, documents or drawings relating to the application which were not sent to the local planning authority, except any plans, documents or drawings relating to amendments to the application proposed after the local planning authority have made their determination; and

(iii) the notice of the decision or determination'.

19.33 For other appeals the appellant should provide[36]:

'(i) the application made to the local planning authority which has occasioned the appeal;

(ii) all plans, drawings and documents sent to the authority in connection with the application;

(iii) all correspondence with the authority relating to the application;

(iv) any certificate provided to the authority under article 11;

---

[31] DMPO 2015, art 37(1)(b).
[32] Compare DMPO 2015, art 36(1)(a) and (b).
[33] Town and Country Planning (Environmental Impact Assessment) Regulations 2011, reg 18. In Wales three copies of the material must be sent to the Welsh Ministers: Town and Country Planning (Environmental Impact Assessment) (England and Wales) Regulations 1999, SI 1999/293, reg 15.
[34] The requirement arises under DMPO Wales, art 26(1).
[35] DMPO Wales, art 26(3)(a).
[36] DMPO Wales, art 26(3)(b).

Dual jurisdiction: Determining applications after they have been appealed **19.37**

    (v) any other plans, documents or drawings relating to the application which were not sent to the authority;

    (vi) the notice of the decision or determination, if any;

    (vii) if the appeal relates to an application for approval of certain matters in accordance with a condition on a planning permission, the application for that permission, the plans submitted with that application and the planning permission granted'.

19.34 The appeal form should also be served on the local planning authority along with a copy of any other plans, documents or drawings relating to the application which were not sent to the authority with the application[37]. This is to be done as soon as reasonably practicable.

Notice of the appeal for owners and agricultural tenants

19.35 The appellant must give notice of the appeal to any other person who is an owner of the land (that is, a freeholder or leaseholder with more than seven years' interest remaining) or an agricultural tenant in the same way as notice is given of a planning application. The certificates in respect of notice to the owners and agricultural tenants must also be completed[38].

A failure to correctly give the notice and certificate at the application or appeal stage would invalidate the appeal[39].

DUAL JURISDICTION: DETERMINING APPLICATIONS AFTER THEY HAVE BEEN APPEALED IN WALES

19.36 The inability of local planning authorities to determine applications which had been appealed prompted the government to include a dual jurisdiction provision in the Planning and Compulsory Purchase Act 2004. A new s 78A was to be inserted into the Town and Country Planning Act 1990 to allow authorities an 'additional period' from the submission of an appeal against non-determination to issue a decision on the appealed application. If the decision was to grant permission subject to conditions then the appellant could decide whether to proceed with the appeal, perhaps on revised grounds. If the application was refused then the appeal would proceed as an appeal against refusal, potentially with revised grounds of appeal or mode of determination. The Minister could not issue the appeal decision until the end of the additional period. That additional period would be prescribed by a development order and so was never set out, but two months was being contemplated.

19.37 Dual jurisdiction received a lukewarm response at the time and has never been brought into force in England. It has been introduced in Wales from 22 June 2015. If an appeal is brought against the non-determination of a planning application[40]

---

[37] DMPO Wales, art 26(1).
[38] DMPO 2015, art 36 applying arts 13 and 14 respectively; DMPO Wales, art 25 applying arts 10 and 11. Notice and certification is discussed under planning applications in Chapter 6.
[39] This is even if a problem is not plausible. Appeals in London boroughs which contain no agricultural land at all have been invalidated because of a failure to complete the agricultural tenancy certificate.
[40] This does not include applications for the approval of details under conditions or for an approval under a development or local development order as the provision is confined to applications within s 78(1)(a): see Town and Country Planning Act 1990, s 78A(1).

19.38 *Planning appeals: preliminaries and tactics*

then the local planning authority has an 'additional period' of 28 days[41] starting with the date of the appeal in which it may issue a decision notice. There is no obligation on the authority to make such a decision.

19.38 If the local planning authority issues a refusal then the appeal proceeds as one under s 78(1) against refusal and the appellant is given an opportunity to revise the grounds of the appeal[42]. Section 78A allows the appellant to make a different choice of mode of determination of the appeal[43] even though the right to a hearing was removed following the enactment of s 78A[44]. In practice the appellant should be allowed to give a different view and reasons on how the appeal should be determined given the decision. If permission is granted subject to conditions then the appellant will have the opportunity to continue the appeal because of the conditions and revise its grounds of appeal and comments on mode of determination accordingly[45].

THE DECISION TO APPEAL

Refusals

19.39 One of the options if a planning application is refused is to appeal, but it is only one of the options, other possibilities being to submit an amended or different scheme, resubmit the same scheme but with different evidence or arguments or to abandon the aim of developing the site. A further application can be pursued at the same time as an appeal unless the local planning authority is empowered to refuse to determine the application under the Town and Country Planning Act 1990, ss 70A or 70B and does so[46].

19.40 Important factors in deciding whether to appeal may be:

- what are the prospects of success? In particular, how might an inspector (or if the case is recovered for his decision, the Minister) consider the issues? They might take a more or less favourable approach to certain issues;

- are any difficulties with the scheme capable of being resolved by amendment, planning condition or planning obligation at the appeal stage? If not, a further application would have to be brought;

- how much better could an appeal outcome be compared to a new application?

- might an unsuccessful appeal still resolve important points in the appellant's favour or might it establish that the proposal causes harm in principle?

- what are the costs and timescales of an appeal?

- if the applicant has an option or conditional contract to acquire the land or some form of development agreement there may be a requirement to appeal against

---

[41] The period is prescribed by the DMPO Wales, art 26A.
[42] Town and Country Planning Act 1990, s 78A(3).
[43] Town and Country Planning Act 1990, s 78A(4)(c).
[44] By Town and Country Planning Act 1990, ss 319A, 319B in England and Wales respectively, inserted by the Planning Act 2008, s 196 and the Town and Country Planning (Determination of Procedure) (Wales) Order 2014.
[45] Town and Country Planning Act 1990, s 78A(4).
[46] See Chapter 6.

a refusal of permission or such an appeal is necessary to keep a contract alive. Decisions to appeal due to contracts may depend upon views as to the prospects on appeal, for example from a senior planning lawyer.

Grant of permission subject to conditions

19.41 Where the applicant has the planning permission but dislikes one or more of the conditions, the two potential courses of action are to make a s 73 planning application for a new permission with different conditions or to appeal against the planning permission[47]. Such an appeal puts the merits of the whole planning application up for determination: it is possible for the Minister or the inspector to refuse to grant any permission. For this reason, appeals against a grant subject to conditions are relatively infrequent. There may be circumstances in which a condition makes a development incapable of being carried out for practical or economic reasons and an appeal is necessary. Some planning applications may just be about the conditions, such as a s 73 application, and with an existing underlying planning permission it may be sensible to appeal altered, but still unacceptable, conditions on the basis that there is still a permission. Again conditional contracts or options may require there to be a satisfactory planning permission and possibly appeal if the permission is unsatisfactory.

Non-determination

19.42 An appeal against non-determination takes the application out of the local planning authority's hands and delivers it to an inspector or the Secretary of State. Factors to be considered in deciding whether to bring such an appeal include:

- what is the prospect that the local planning authority will approve the application?
- how do those chances compare with the prospect on appeal? Is this a form of development which Ministers and Inspectors seem to favour more than the local planning authority, or in general are the chances better with the authority?
- when are the authority likely to determine the application? If there is a delay, what is its cause?
- if a non-determination appeal is brought, will the local planning authority resist it?
- will an appeal, particularly if it proceeds by inquiry, strengthen the position of third-party objectors such as commercial rivals, statutory consultees and local groups?
- is the detail of the application sufficiently good for an appeal? Is amendment required or more information?
- is there an issue of principle with the local planning authority which will only be resolved by an appeal?
- what are the timescales for an appeal to be determined? In terms of the applicant's objectives, is there a timescale in which a decision has to be received? How does awaiting the authority's decision and then appealing if necessary compare to that timescale?

---

[47] Simply putting up with the unsatisfactory permission is a course of inaction.

19.43 *Planning appeals: preliminaries and tactics*

- is there an appeal already running and is this application to be joined in with it?
- is there benefit in appealing against non-determination and then making a further planning application? In England, what are the prospects that the authority will decline to determine the further application under the Town and Country Planning Act 1990, s 70B(3)?

Other avenues and further applications

19.43 Alongside any decision to appeal, the developer should consider whether to make a further planning application as an alternative or in addition to an appeal. A further application might be identical, if it is thought that a further opportunity to consider the scheme might produce a different outcome, perhaps with additional supporting material. Alternatively, a second application might seek to revise the scheme to address the reasons for refusal, or take an entirely different tack.

AMENDMENT OF SCHEMES ON APPEAL

19.44 There is a limited ability to amend an application during the course of an appeal. A need for an amendment may arise as a means of addressing a reason for refusal or another objection made, or to reflect a changing aspiration or market. However, such changes should not mean that the scheme is in substance not that which was applied for. In particular, the change should not deprive those who should have been consulted on the changed development the opportunity of such consultation: *Bernard Wheatcroft Ltd v Secretary of State for the Environment*[48]. In *Wheatcroft* a planning application had been made for 420 dwellings on 35 acres and the Minister's refusal to consider the appellant's alternative scheme of 250 dwellings on 25 acres was quashed. Forbes J considered the test to be 'is the effect of the conditional planning permission to allow development that is in substance not that which was applied for?'[49]. In doing so he considered whether the amendment could be imposed by 'a condition the effect of which is to allow the development but which amounts to a reduction on that proposed in the application can legitimately be imposed so long as it does not alter the substance of the development for which permission was applied for'. The Secretary of State had erred in considering that a reduced scheme could only be approved if it was severable from the remainder of the development. The judge emphasised the limits of the flexibility[50]:

'Parliament cannot have intended conditional planning permission to be used to circumvent the provisions for consultation and public participation contained in [the Planning Act]'.

19.45 A later decision has warned that there must not be 'any possible prejudice to those who might otherwise have raised objections'[51]. The limitations on amendments are greater in an appeal than when the application is before the local planning authority. The appeal process is focussed on those who have taken part at the application stage, rather than the potentially wider consultation on a planning application, and so a change might affect someone who is unaware of the appeal

---

[48] (1980) 43 P & CR 233.
[49] At 241.
[50] At 239.
[51] *Granada Hospitality Ltd v Secretary of State for the Environment, Transport and the Regions* (2001) 81 P & CR 36 at para 73 per Collins J.

or considered it not to impact on their interests. Even those already involved in the process have only defined opportunities to comment, particularly on written representations and so may be unaware of or unable to deal with a late change. In householder and minor commercial appeals there is no facility for further comments by the local planning authority or third parties, so any amendment would have to be confined to one which could have been unilaterally imposed by a planning condition, for example, installing obscured glazing and limited opening on a window.

19.46 An amendment is more likely to be acceptable if it reduces the scale of the scheme or a particular impact, provided it does not raise further issues. Enlargements to the scheme might be possible[52]. Any amendments should be proposed at the earliest possible opportunity, ideally with the submission of the appeal. Whether it is fair to make an amendment will be affected by whether other parties have been given an opportunity to comment in the appeal process. In *Carroll v Secretary of State for Communities and Local Government* a change in the description of the development by the inspector to reflect a change in the appellant's case was unlawful because third parties had no opportunity to comment[53]. The appellant might want to consider consulting on their amendment, but that may be more effective if specific persons need to be consulted and then respond, such as a public body or neighbour. A widely circulated invitation by the developer to comment might not be certain of drawing in representations from all involved.

The Inspectorate's advice gives limited encouragement to the use of amendments, but is too restrictive in saying that their use is exceptional[54].

WITHDRAWAL OF AN APPEAL

19.47 An appeal may be withdrawn by the appellant. However once withdrawn it cannot be reinstated[55]. A withdrawal of an appeal without good reason may give rise to a costs award against the appellant for unreasonable behaviour.

DECIDING UPON THE MODE OF DETERMINATION

19.48 Whether a planning appeal is to be determined by written representations or following a hearing or inquiry is a matter for the Minister, in practice the Planning Inspectorate. Historically appellants and local planning authorities in a planning appeal have had 'an opportunity of appearing before and being heard by a person appointed by the Secretary of State for the purpose'[56]. This meant that either could insist on the appeal being dealt with by one of a hearing or a public inquiry. They could not dictate which, but could veto the written representations route.

19.49 The Inspectorate would ask the main parties for their views but were willing to require an appeal to proceed through a more searching route, for example, by

---

[52] *Breckland District Council v Secretary of State for the Environment* (1992) 65 P & CR 34.
[53] [2015] EWHC 316 (Admin) at paras 69–71 per Supperstone J.
[54] *Procedural Guide: Planning appeals – England* (31 July 2015), Annex M; *Procedural Guidance Planning appeals and called-in planning applications – Wales* (July 2015), Annex I.
[55] *R (on the application of Corbett) v First Secretary of State* [2005] EWHC 2433 (Admin), [2006] JPL 505.
[56] Town and Country Planning Act 1990, s 78(2), as originally enacted.

19.50 *Planning appeals: preliminaries and tactics*

inquiry rather than a hearing, if they considered it necessary. The nature of the processes is, however, that dealing with an appeal at a hearing will normally take up more inspector time than by written representations and an inquiry will usually be longer in duration and writing up time than a hearing.

19.50 The Planning Act 2008 allowed the removal of the appellant and local planning authority's right to a hearing, giving the Minister the ability to decide whether an appeal or call-in should be dealt with by written representations, hearing or inquiry. These have been implemented by different provisions in England and Wales.

Mode of determination in England

19.51 In England the Secretary of State is empowered by the Town and Country Planning Act 1990, s 319A to decide the mode of determination of planning appeals, planning applications to the Minister under s 62A and s 106BC affordable housing viability appeals on planning obligations[57]. A right to be heard is retained for s 106B planning obligation appeals[58] and for listed building consent appeals in England[59]. The Secretary of State must decide on the mode of determination within seven working days from the receipt of a valid appeal[60]. At any point in the appeal process, the Secretary of State can decide that an appeal should be determined by a different means[61].

19.52 The mode of determination has to be decided by the application of published criteria[62], presently contained in the Inspectorate's procedural guidance[63]:

'The criteria for each procedure cannot be fully prescriptive or entirely determinative: they require judgement to be applied using common sense. More than one criterion may apply.

Written representations - written representations would be appropriate if:

- the planning issues raised or, in an enforcement appeal, the grounds of appeal, can be clearly understood from the appeal documents and a site inspection (if required [footnote 13 A small number of appeals do not require a site visit and can be dealt with on the basis of the appeal documents]); or

- the issues are not complex and the Inspector is not likely to need to test the evidence by questioning or to clarify any other matters; or

- in an enforcement appeal the alleged breach, and the requirements of the notice, are clear.

---

[57] Other appeals included are those on enforcement notices. The provision may also be extended to s 77 call-ins, lawful development certificates and tree replacement notices but has not yet been brought into force for these purposes: Planning Act 2008, s 196; Planning Act 2008 (Commencement No 1 and Savings) Order 2009, SI 2009/400, art 3(j).
[58] Town and Country Planning Act 1990, s 106B(4).
[59] Planning (Listed Buildings and Conservation Areas) Act 1990, s 22(2). Whilst provision is made in s 88D of that Act for control over mode of determination this has not been brought into force for other than order making powers: Planning Act 2008, s 196; Planning Act 2008 (Commencement No 1 and Savings) Order 2009, art 3(j).
[60] Town and Country Planning Act 1990, s 319A(3); Town and Country Planning (Determination of Appeal Procedure) (Prescribed Period) (England) Regulations 2009, SI 2009/454, reg 2(1).
[61] Town and Country Planning Act 1990, s 319A(4).
[62] Town and Country Planning Act 1990, s 319A(6).
[63] *Procedural Guide: Planning appeals – England* (31 July 2015), Annex K.

Deciding upon the mode of determination **19.52**

Hearing - a hearing would be appropriate if:

- the Inspector is likely to need to test the evidence by questioning or to clarify matters [footnote 14 For example where detailed evidence on housing land supply needs to be tested by questioning]; or

- the status or personal circumstances of the appellant are at issue [footnote 15 For example whether in traveller appeals the definition in Annex 1 of DCLG's planning policy for traveller sites is met, or in agricultural dwelling appeals.]; or

- there is no need for evidence to be tested through formal questioning by an advocate or given on oath; or

- the case has generated a level of local interest such as to warrant a hearing [footnote 16 Where the proposal has generated significant local interest a hearing or inquiry may need to be considered. In such circumstances the local planning authority should indicate which procedure it considers would be most appropriate taking account of the number of people likely to attend and participate at the event. We will take that advice into account in reaching the decision as to the appropriate procedure.]; or

- it can reasonably be expected that the parties will be able to present their own cases (supported by professional witnesses if required) without the need for an advocate to represent them; or

- in an enforcement appeal, the grounds of appeal, the alleged breach, and the requirements of the notice, are relatively straightforward.

Inquiry - an inquiry would be appropriate if:

- there is a clearly explained need for the evidence to be tested through formal questioning by an advocate [footnote 17 This does not preclude an appellant representing themselves as an advocate.]; or

- the issues are complex [footnote 18 For example where large amounts of highly technical data are likely to be provided in evidence]; or

- the appeal has generated substantial local interest to warrant an inquiry as opposed to dealing with the case by a hearing [footnote 19 Where the proposal has generated significant local interest a hearing or inquiry may need to be considered. In such circumstances the local planning authority should indicate which procedure it considers would be most appropriate taking account of the number of people likely to attend and participate at the event. We will take that advice into account in reaching the decision as to the appropriate procedure.]; or

- in an enforcement appeal, evidence needs to be given on oath [footnote 20 For example where witnesses are giving factual evidence about how long the alleged unauthorised use has been taking place.]; or

- in an enforcement appeal, the alleged breach, or the requirements of the notice, are unusual and particularly contentious.

Note - It is considered that the prospect of legal submissions being made is not, on its own, a reason why a case would need to be conducted by inquiry. Where a party considers that legal submissions will be required (and are considered to be complex such as to warrant being made orally), the Inspectorate requires that the matters on which submissions will be made are fully explained – including why they may require an inquiry – at the outset of the appeal or otherwise at the earliest opportunity'.

Parties should refer to these criteria when making representations to the Inspectorate on the mode of determination. Particularly where a hearing or inquiry is sought,

19.53 *Planning appeals: preliminaries and tactics*

parties should explain, usually relatively briefly, why one is necessary[64]. A third party who disagrees with the procedure should raise the point in the appeal rather than leave it to a later court challenge[65].

Mode of determination in Wales

19.53 Town and Country Planning Act 1990, s 319B empowers the Welsh Ministers to decide the mode of determination of s 77 call-ins, planning appeals, enforcement notice appeals, lawful development certificate appeals and tree replacement notice[66]. The processes are in substance those in England, with a determination within seven working days[67] on the basis of published criteria[68]. Annex H of the Procedural Guidance sets out the criteria, which are the same as those in England apart from excluding cases involving costs applications from written representations[69]. The Ministers are able to change the procedure at any point prior to the determination of the appeal or application[70].

---

[64] See *Sea Estates Ltd v Secretary of State for Communities and Local Government* [2012] EWHC 2252 (Admin) at paras 41–43 per Simon J; *Riza v Secretary of State for Communities and Local Government* [2014] EWHC 909 (Admin) at para 16 per Judge Robinson.
[65] *Bluebell Cemetery Ltd v Secretary of State for Communities and Local Government* [2015] EWHC 2339 (Admin) at paras 56–59 per Holgate J.
[66] Inserted by the Town and Country Planning (Determination of Procedure) (Wales) Order 2014, SI 2014/2773, art 2, made under Planning Act 2008, s 203.
[67] Town and Country Planning Act 1990, s 319B(3); Town and Country Planning (Determination of Procedure) (Prescribed Period) (Wales) Regulations 2014, reg 2.
[68] Town and Country Planning Act 1990, s 319B(6).
[69] *Procedural Guidance Planning appeals and called-in planning applications – Wales* (July 2015).
[70] Town and Country Planning Act 1990, s 319B(4).

Chapter 20

Householder and minor commercial appeals

20.1 A simplified procedure for determining householder appeals against the refusal of consent by written representations was introduced in England in 2009 and then extended to minor commercial and advertising appeals in October 2013. A similar procedure was introduced in Wales in June 2015. Essentially, a planning inspector will consider the material which was in front of the local planning authority, the comments of the appellant on the authority's determination, carry out a site visit and then write a decision. This procedure changes from the previous exchange of representations in the appeal itself between the appellant, local planning authority and interested parties. It is therefore critical for all potential participants to have said what they want to say in the planning application process. The simplified procedure does not apply to non-determination appeals or appeals against planning permissions granted subject to conditions. Additionally in Wales it does not include appeals on applications for the approval of details under conditions on planning permissions or details under a development order or local development order.

The simplified procedure has been widely used, even when it was only available for householder appeals, it was still used in over 30% of planning appeals[1].

20.2 Simplified written representations are dealt with under the Town and Country Planning (Appeals) (Written Representations Procedure) (England) Regulations 2009, Part 1 (the Written Representations Regulations) and the Town and Country Planning (Referrals and Appeals) (Written Representations Procedure) (Wales) Regulations 2015, Part 1 (the Welsh Written Representations Regulations)[2]. Advice is given in the *Procedural Guide Planning appeals – England* (31 July 2015) in particular at Annex C. In Wales this simplified procedure applies to householder and minor commercial planning applications submitted on or after 22 June 2015[3]. The Planning Inspectorate's Welsh guidance *Procedural Guidance Planning appeals and called-in planning applications – Wales* (July 2015) deals with the simplified procedure at Annex B.

20.3 The stages in a simplified written representations case, and the relevant legislation (with references to the written representations regulations unless indicated otherwise) are as follows:

---

[1] Planning Inspectorate Statistical Report: England 2013–2014, table 1.2 showing 4,374 householder appeals determined by that process.
[2] SIs 2009/452 and 2015/1331 respectively.
[3] Welsh Written Representations Regulations 2015, reg 22(2). Earlier applications are dealt with by the Town and Country Planning (Referrals and Appeals) (Written Representations Procedure) (Wales) Regulations 2003, SI 2003/395.

20.4 *Householder and minor commercial appeals*

Stage	England	Wales
Submission of appeal		
Submission of the appellant's notice of appeal and documents	With the appeal form: see DMPO 2015, art 33	With the appeal form: see DMPO Wales, art 26
Notice of the appeal having been received and decision on mode of determination	Sent by Secretary of State as soon as practicable after determination to proceed by written representations under Part 1: reg 4. This is the starting date[4]	Sent by Welsh Ministers as soon as practicable after determination to proceed by written representations under Part 1: reg 4. This is the starting date[5]
Local authority questionnaire	Within five working days of starting date: reg 5	Within five working days of starting date: reg 5
Local authority to provide notice of the appeal to those consulted in accordance with legislation and those who made representations	Within five working days of starting date: reg 6(1)	Within five working days of starting date: reg 6(1)
Site visit		
Decision made	Regulation 10	Decision and reasons notified in writing: reg 11

HOUSEHOLDER, ADVERTISEMENT AND MINOR COMMERCIAL APPEALS

20.4 The simplified regime applies to a householder appeal, advertisement consent or minor commercial appeal where the Minister has decided that the appeal should be determined by written representations[6]. The Minister could alternatively have decided that the particular appeal be dealt with by hearing or inquiry. When announcing the procedure the regulations require the Minister to apply the simplified regime rather than the conventional written representations procedure, in Part 2 of the Written Representations Regulations to one of these appeals[7]. However, it is possible for the Minister at any time to transfer the appeal to the conventional written representations procedure[8]. That decision could be taken when the mode of determination is decided upon.

---

[4] Written Representations Regulations 2009, reg 2(1). The regulations are modified in the frankly implausible event that the written representations appeal is into an application of potential strategic importance and its refusal has been directed by the Mayor of London: Written Representations Regulations 2009, reg 18.

[5] Welsh Written Representations Regulations 2015, reg 2(1).

[6] Written Representations Regulations 2009, reg 3(2); Welsh Written Representations Regulations 2015, reg 3(2) In England the householder planning application must have been submitted to the local planning authority on or after 6 April 2009, and the advertising or minor commercial application submitted on or after 1 October 2013. In Wales a householder, minor commercial or advertising consent appeal is only subject to the simplified procedure if the application was made on or after 22 June 2015. The reason for the new procedure applying from the date of the application (not the date of the appeal) is that it requires all parties to have had ample warning that they needed to make all of their representations at the application stage.

[7] See Written Representations Regulations 2009, reg 3(2), (3) and the Wales Written Representations Regulations 2015, reg 3(2), (3) which set out two exclusive regimes depending upon the categorisation of the application.

[8] Written Representations Regulations 2009, reg 9(1); Wales Written Representations Regulations 2015, reg 9(1).

20.5 Simplified procedure appeals may be against the refusal of the permission or consent but not against the grant of permission subject to conditions or the non-determination of the application[9]. A grant subject to conditions may raise new issues and in the case of non-determination there will be no existing local authority reasoning or report for the appellant to respond to or the Inspector to consider.

SCOPE OF THE ENGLISH SIMPLIFIED WRITTEN REPRESENTATIONS

20.6 In England a householder application means[10]:

'(a) an application for planning permission for development of an existing dwellinghouse, or development within the curtilage of such a dwellinghouse for any purpose incidental to the enjoyment of the dwellinghouse, or

(b) an application for any consent, agreement or approval required by or under a planning permission, development order or local development order in relation to such development, but does not include:

(i) an application for change of use,

(ii) an application to change the number of dwellings in a building'.

Paragraph (a) therefore applies to planning applications and para (b) the approval of reserved matters, details under conditions and prior approval including under householder permitted development rights. The ambit is alterations or extensions to an existing dwelling or the construction of ancillary structures within its curtilage[11]. Any change of use is excluded. Most obviously an application to change from a dwellinghouse use would fall under the conventional written representations regime. However, the change of use does not have to be a material change. For example, the discharge of an occupancy condition to break the link between an annex and the main house would also be a change of use[12]. The creation of a new dwelling within the curtilage of an existing dwellinghouse would also be outside the simplified system.

20.7 The inference from the context is that the application must relate to a single dwellinghouse. Given the restricted nature of the simplified procedure, it is not intended to apply to an application that covers multiple properties. In this situation the singular does not include the plural.

20.8 A minor commercial application means[13]:

'(a) an application for planning permission for development of an existing building or part of a building currently in use for any of the purposes set out in the Schedule to these Regulations, or

---

[9] See the definitions of the appeals in Written Representations Regulations 2009, reg 2(1). The appeal must be under the Town and Country Planning Act 1990, s 78(1), which applies to applications which have been determined, rather than s 78(2) which allows non-determination appeals where the authority's view on the application will be unknown.
[10] Written Representations Regulations 2009, reg 2(1).
[11] The demolition of an entire dwellinghouse would be outside the provisions as it would be a change of use or a change in the number of dwellings.
[12] *Arun District Council v Secretary of State* [2006] EWCA Civ 1172, [2007] 1 WLR 523 concerning the four-year time limit for change of use to residential by breach of a condition limiting occupation of a granny annex.
[13] Written Representations Regulations 2009, reg 2(1).

20.9 *Householder and minor commercial appeals*

(b) an application for any consent, agreement or approval required by or under a planning permission, development order or local development order in relation to such development,

where such an application does not include a change of use, a change to the number of units in a building, or development that is not wholly at ground floor level or that would increase the gross internal area of a building'.

20.9 The schedule sets out in full the text of the use classes A1–A5 from the Town and Country Planning (Use Classes) Order 1987[14]. These relate to retail (A1), professional and financial services for visiting members of the public (A2), restaurants and cafes (A3), drinking establishments (A4) and hot food takeaways (A5). It does not take account of the exclusion of *sui generis* uses from the use classes[15], so applies to car sales. Use is for any of the purposes in the categories, and a mixed use within those categories must be included (such as a mixed retail/ café use). The simplified regime does not apply to the business use classes, such as offices, industry or storage and distribution.

20.10 As with the householder appeal regime, these appeals include appeals against the refusal or non-determination of planning applications or on the approval of details under orders or conditions. The simplified regime applies only to commercial development at the ground floor of the building which does not increase the internal area, change the use or the number of units. This is a narrow category, the most obvious examples being the installation of security shutters or other external alternations to the shop frontage.

20.11 Publicity of the original planning application by the local planning authority should have warned that in the event of an appeal which proceeds by way of the expedited procedure, any representations made about the application will be passed to the Secretary of State and there will be no opportunity to make further representations[16]. This does, though, highlight a problem with the English simplified system, which the Welsh regime avoids. It might be thought that issues on the approval of reserved matters or details under conditions would be natural objects for a simplified procedure which relied upon the material before the local planning authority. However, there is no requirement to publicise reserved matters or details applications, unless EIA applies, and so whether anyone outside the local planning authority would have had the opportunity to make representations is, generally, doubtful[17]. Local planning authorities might put applications on their websites, and some more controversial applications might be the subject of consultation or publicity or committee decision. However, there is the real possibility that interested parties, including neighbours who would have commented if they had known of the application, would have wished to comment on any appeal. That is relevant to whether the Secretary of State should change a particular appeal from the simplified to conventional written representations.

20.12 The simplified regime also extends to advertisement appeals which are against the refusal of an application for consent under the Town and Country Planning

---

[14] SI 1987/764.
[15] Town and Country Planning (Use Classes) Order 1987, art 3(6).
[16] Town and Country Planning (Development Management Procedure) Order 2015, art 15(7).
[17] See Chapter 15. Applications for the approval of details under conditions do not even have to be on the Planning Register.

(Control of Advertisements) (England) Regulations 2007 or the Town and Country Planning (Control of Advertisements) Regulations 1992 in Wales[18].

SCOPE OF THE WELSH SIMPLIFIED WRITTEN REPRESENTATIONS

20.13 Since the Welsh regime deals only with planning applications, rather than reserved matters or details under conditions, the scope of the appeals regime is differently expressed but there are also some other changes. 'Householder application' means an application for[19]:

'(a) planning permission for the enlargement, improvement or other alteration of a dwellinghouse, or development within the curtilage of such a dwellinghouse, or

(b) change of use to enlarge the curtilage of a dwelling house,

for any purpose incidental to the enjoyment of the dwellinghouse but does not include:

(i) any other application for change of use,

(ii) an application for erection of a dwellinghouse, or

(iii) an application to change the number of dwellings in a building'.

20.14 Unlike England, the procedure may be used in Wales for a change of use to enlarge the curtilage of a dwellinghouse (for example, to expand a garden into a field). It explicitly excludes the erection of a dwellinghouse, albeit that was not obviously within the Welsh definition of 'enlargement, improvement or other alteration' in the first place, although for the English provision 'development of an existing dwellinghouse' this might be more debatable.

20.15 A minor commercial application is[20]:

'an application for planning permission for the enlargement, improvement or other alteration of an existing building of no more than 250 square metres gross external floor space at ground floor level, or part of that building, currently in use for any of the purposes set out in the Schedule to these Regulations which is an application for:

(a) the change of use from any of the purposes set out at paragraph 1 in the Schedule to these Regulations to any of the purposes set out in either paragraph 2 or paragraph 3 of that Schedule;

(b) the change of use from any of the purposes set out at paragraph 2 in the Schedule to these Regulations to any of the purposes set out in paragraph 3 of the Schedule; or

(c) the carrying out of building or other operations to a shop front'.

20.16 This is quite different to the English version, which allows any operational development to A class uses, but not changes of use. The Welsh provisions deal with appeals for changes of use from A1 use class shops (and *sui generis* retail)[21] to A2 use class financial and professional services or from retail or A2 to A3 food and

---

[18] SIs 2007/783 and 1992/666 respectively.
[19] Wales Written Representations Regulations 2015, reg 2(1). Sub-paragraph (b) refers to an application for change of use rather than an application for planning permission but it is difficult to imagine such an application being other than an application for planning permission.
[20] Wales Written Representations Regulations 2015, reg 2(1).
[21] Paragraphs 1, 2 and 3 respectively in the Schedule.

20.17 *Householder and minor commercial appeals*

drink[22]. Operational development is limited, unlike in England, to alterations to the shop fronts of buildings which are no larger than 250 m² gross internal floorspace.

THE SIMPLIFIED PROCEDURE

20.17 Any householder or minor commercial appeal must be brought within '12 weeks from the date of the notice of the decision or determination giving rise to the appeal'[23], unless it is a Welsh appeal accompanied by an enforcement notice or listed building or conservation area consent appeal when the conventional six months period applies for the planning appeal[24]. Such periods may be extended by the Minister[25].

20.18 The appeal starts with the appellant's submission of its completed appeal form and supporting documents to the Planning Inspectorate[26]. These are taken as the appellant's representations on the appeal in the simplified procedure[27]. The documents are[28]:

(i) a copy of the application;

(ii) any other plans, documents or drawings relating to the application which were not sent to the authority; and

(iii) the decision notice (if there is one).

20.19 The documents which have to be provided exclude 'any plans, documents or drawings relating to amendments to the application proposed after the authority have made their determination'[29]. Whilst this provision also applies to other appeals and is expressed as an exception to what must be produced rather than a prohibition on amending the application, the simplified procedure is not suitable for amendments which would require any further comment. Application plans are not to be provided to the Inspectorate by the appellant, but subsequently by the local planning authority. This should ensure that the inspector has copies of the drawings which the authority considered, rather than earlier or later versions.

The appeal form and any additional plans, documents or drawings should be sent by the appellant to the local planning authority as soon as reasonably practicable thereafter[30].

---

[22] Many of these changes are permitted development in England, but still subject to a prior approval process which may lead to conventional, rather than simplified, written representations appeals.

[23] DMPO 2015, art 37(2)(a); DMPO Wales, art 26(2)(a). As 'from' the 12-week period starts the day after the notice. In case of dispute about the date of the notice, it is prudent to take it from the date on the notice, unless same-day despatch and receipt can be shown by e-mail or fax.

[24] See DMPO Wales, art 26(7).

[25] DMPO 2015, art 37(1); DMPO Wales, art 26(2).

[26] DMPO 2015, art 37; DMPO Wales, art 26. Certification that notice of the appeal has been given to the owner of the land is also required on the appeal form: DMPO 2015, art 36; DMPO Wales, art 25.

[27] Written Representations Regulations 2009, reg 7(1); Wales Written Representations Regulations 2015, reg 7(1).

[28] DMPO 2015, art 37(3)(a); DMPO Wales, art 26(3)(a). If a Welsh householder or minor commercial appeal is accompanied by an enforcement notice or listed building or conservation area consent appeal then the conventional appeal document requirements apply, as discussed in Chapter 19.

[29] DMPO, art 37(3)(a)(ii); DMPO Wales, art 26(3)(a)(ii).

[30] DMPO, art 37(1)(b); DMPO Wales, art 26(1)(b). The English and Welsh Written Representations Regulations, reg 7(3) require the Minister to copy the appellant's appeal form and the documents submitted to the local planning authority but this is unnecessary as the authority should either have received the documents from the appellant or already have them. It is important that the parties know what documents have been submitted by the other side and have copies of them.

The simplified procedure **20.25**

20.20 The time limits and document requirements for the submission of householder and minor commercial appeals apply irrespective of the mode of determination. They do not apply only where the simplified procedure is to be used, because the definitions of such appeals in the respective DMPOs do not refer to the written representations procedure[31].

20.21 Submission of the appeal is the appellant's sole opportunity to make representations to the inspector. The chance should therefore be taken to respond to any reasons for refusal, any likely objections from the authority in the event of a non-determination appeal, any other matters raised by third parties which need comment, and possible conditions.

20.22 Once the Secretary of State has decided upon the procedure, notice of this will be given to the appellant and local planning authority[32]. The date of the notice is the starting date[33].

20.23 The local planning authority must send its questionnaire with a copy of the documents referred to in it to the Secretary of State and the appellant within five working days of the starting date[34]. Again, these are the authority's representations on the appeal[35]. On the questionnaire the authority will be asked for its views on the appropriate mode of determination and ought to take the opportunity to say if the simplified procedure is not appropriate[36].

20.24 The authority must also give information about the appeal to any person who was notified or consulted upon the application in accordance with the Town and Country Planning Act 1990 or a development order[37] or who sent in representations on the application[38]. The notice does not invite representations to be made: it simply tells them about the appeal and that any representations which they made on the planning application would be considered by the inspector unless withdrawn within four weeks of the starting date[39]. The Planning Inspectorate has a standard form letter which can be used.

20.25 Further information may be required by the Minister from the appellant, local planning authority or interested parties[40]. If so, a time limit for responding will be set. Such a request would not be a general opportunity for comment, although a

---

[31] See DMPO 2015, arts 2(1), 37(8); DMPO Wales, arts 2(1), 26(7).
[32] Written Representations Regulations 2009, reg 4; Wales Written Representations Regulations 2015, reg 4.
[33] Written Representations Regulations 2009, reg 2(1); Wales Written Representations Regulations 2015, reg 2(1).
[34] Written Representations Regulations 2009, reg 5; Wales Written Representations Regulations 2015, reg 5.
[35] Written Representations Regulations 2009, reg 7(2); Wales Written Representations Regulations 2015, reg 7(2).
[36] See *Procedural Guide Planning appeals – England* (31 July 2015), para C.7.1; *Procedural Guidance Planning appeals and called-in planning applications – Wales* (July 2015), para B.6.1.
[37] This therefore excludes persons notified under other regulations, directions or the local authority's own practices or policies, but they should, if interested, have previously made representations.
[38] Written Representations Regulations 2009, reg 6(1); Wales Written Representations Regulations 2015, reg 6(1).
[39] Written Representations Regulations 2009, reg 6(2); Wales Written Representations Regulations 2015, reg 6(2).
[40] Written Representations Regulations 2009, reg 8(1); Wales Written Representations Regulations 2015, reg 8(1).

20.26 *Householder and minor commercial appeals*

party will want to ensure that any wider implications for the appeal of the matters raised are addressed.

Site visits

20.26 The inspector will normally carry out a site visit. Indeed, if any judgment has to be formed of the site in its context then a site visit is inevitable. If the site is sufficiently visible from the road or other public viewpoints then the visit will be carried out unaccompanied[41]. A shop front alteration or changes to the frontage of a house are obvious examples.

20.27 Where the inspector needs to have access to the site then the visit will take place with notice to and in the presence of the appellant or its representative. The local planning authority will not attend. Arrangements may also be made to view the site from neighbouring property where that is considered to be necessary. In the appeal questionnaire the local planning authority ought to indicate whether the inspector should visit nearby properties. If on a site visit (including an unaccompanied visit) the inspector decides that she does need to go onto private land then she may ask the occupants. In all cases the role of the person present is simply to let the inspector onto the land. Unlike traditional accompanied site visits they should not point things out to the inspector and in addition there should be no discussion about the case[42].

20.28 The simplified procedure site visit is therefore very different to the historic approach that an inspector going onto private property had to be accompanied by representatives of the main parties to ensure that nothing untoward happened. When introduced, there was some concern about the breaking of this cardinal rule. That it does not appear to have been problematic in practice is probably due to the good sense of inspectors and in the inability of other parties to find out if anything has gone wrong.

20.29 The guidance *Procedural Guide Planning appeals – England* refers to a site visit by the inspector 'or his/her representative'. What has started to happen is that sometimes a planning officer from the Planning Inspectorate has been sent to conduct the site visit and then reported to the inspector who made the decision[43]. Planning officers in this context are Inspectorate staff with some planning qualifications (so not simply administrative) but with neither the planning experience nor the training of inspectors. The use of planning officers for these purposes was endorsed in that particular case by the High Court in *Harris*

---

[41] *Procedural Guide Planning appeals – England* para C.9.2; *Procedural Guidance Planning appeals and called-in planning applications – Wales* (July 2015), para B.8.2.
[42] *Procedural Guide Planning appeals – England* paras C.9.3–C.9.8. The guidance refers to a site visit by the inspector 'or his/her representative' but it is difficult to see how or why an Inspector would delegate that function. The *Procedural Guidance Planning appeals and called-in planning applications – Wales* (July 2015), para 8.6 refers simply to not allowing any discussion about the case with anyone at the site visit.
[43] See *Harris v Secretary of State for Communities and Local Government* [2014] EWHC 3740 (Admin) at para 35 per Judge David Cooke; Planning Inspectorate Annual Report and Accounts 2014–2015, p 14.

v Secretary of State for Communities and Local Government[44] on the basis that the written representation regulations did not require a site visit at all and so it was a matter of judgment for the inspector whether and how one was conducted. However it is unsatisfactory for a site visit to be carried out by anyone other than the inspector. Whilst council committee members and local authority planning managers might rely on site visits by case officers or other councillors, they will be familiar with the area and may have passed the property. Ministers will rarely conduct site visits, but will have a considerable amount of material on which to make a decision. Householder and minor commercial appeals are, of course, determined on the application documentation which for a modest scheme will tend to be much less substantial than even a conventional written representations appeal. These appeals will usually turn on their effect on the locality, rather than technical or policy issues. There is a considerable danger that the perceived (and actual) quality of the decision-making will be reduced by inspectors delegating site visits to other officers. That quality is critical to the operation of the appeal system: not only are inspectors seen as independent, but they are also regarded as expert and experienced. There is also the legal risk that the inspector might be considered not to have had sufficient information to determine the appeal.

FURTHER REPRESENTATIONS AND ISSUES

20.30 The essence of the simplified procedure is that the appeal will be determined on the basis of the material which was in front of the local planning authority at the application stage, the authority's consideration of the application, the appellant's response to that material and the inspector's site visit. The assumption is that the local planning authority and third parties would have said everything they needed to say during the application and do not need to reply to the appellant's statement. Third parties, including any statutory consultees, should therefore ensure that their comments on the application are full. Authorities should ensure that their decision is clear and persuasive, when read with any committee or delegated officer report or committee minute[45].

20.31 The appellant is the sole person entitled to respond to the decision on the application. That is a necessary fairness and it will also be the first formal opportunity to comment on third-party representations (comments might have been made informally). An appellant has the chance to deal with the reasons for refusal as fully as necessary, however should be cautious about how the material is handled. For example, if an expert noise report is supplied for the first time with the appeal then it is likely that the local planning authority and third parties should be given an

---

[44] [2014] EWHC 3740 (Admin) at paras 39–41 per Judge David Cooke, in particular at para 40:

'It cannot, in my view, be said to be a material error of procedure if he does not in every case make the site visit himself. In some cases it may be necessary for him to do so, in others, and it must be a matter for his judgment, it is perfectly acceptable it seems to me for him to delegate that to somebody within his service to make and report back to him, in the same way he would be entitled to delegate somebody in his service to review documents and to produce a report for his benefit on the basis of which he can make his decision'.

[45] The *Procedural Guide Planning appeals – England* para C.7.2 and *Procedural Guidance Planning appeals and called-in planning applications* – Wales, para C.6.2 draw attention to the importance of clear minutes when the committee disagree with the officer recommendation.

20.32 *Householder and minor commercial appeals*

opportunity to comment on it[46]. The appellant and local planning authority need to be alert to the possibility that new evidence may mean that the appeal should be switched to the conventional written representations procedure or to a hearing or inquiry. The Planning Inspectorate and the inspector will have to consider whether continuing to use the simplified procedure is appropriate.

20.32 A straightforward amendment which might be imposed by condition could be raised on appeal for the first time, for example the use of obscure glazing and limited opening in a window where a concern has been raised about overlooking. That is unlikely to require further consultation. However amendments which would need consultation are unlikely to be accepted by the Planning Inspectorate in this type of appeal. It may be more sensible for the disappointed applicant to reapply with an amended scheme.

---

[46] See for comparison *Ashley v Secretary of State for Communities and Local Government* [2012] EWCA Civ 559, [2012] JPL 1235, discussed in Chapter 21 on written representations.

Chapter 21

Written representations

21.1 Written representations remain the most common means of determining a planning appeal. Such appeals in England and Wales are now split into two different procedures: what can be called the conventional written representations; and the simplified householder and minor commercial appeals procedure. The latter procedure is considered in Chapter 20.

21.2 Following the preliminary stages in the Town and Country Planning (Development Management Procedure) (England) Order 2015 (DMPO 2015) and the Town and Country Planning (Development Management Procedure) (Wales) Order 2012 (DMPO Wales)[1], conventional written representations are dealt with under the Town and Country Planning (Appeals) (Written Representations Procedure) (England) Regulations 2009, Part 2 (the Written Representations Regulations) and the Town and Country Planning (Referrals and Appeals) (Written Representations Procedure) (Wales) Regulations 2015, Part 2 (the Welsh Written Representations Regulations 2015)[2]. Where the application was made in Wales prior to 22 June 2015 any written representations appeal (whether made before or after that date) will be governed by the Town and Country Planning (Referrals and Appeals) (Written Representations Procedure) (Wales) Regulations 2003 (Welsh Written Representations Regulations 2003)[3]. Guidance on these appeals is contained in the *Procedural Guide: Planning appeals – England*[4] and the *Procedural Guidance Planning appeals and called-in planning applications – Wales*[5].

21.3 The stages in a conventional written representations case, and the relevant regulations, are as follows (references are to the English or Welsh Written Representations Regulations unless otherwise indicated).

Stage	England	Wales
	English Written Representations Regulations 2009, Part 2	Welsh Written Representations Regulations 2015, Part 2
Submission of appeal	See DMPO 2015, art 37	See DMPO Wales, art 26
Submission of the appellant's full statement of case	With the appeal form: see DMPO 2015, art 37	Statement of case at six week point – see below

---

[1] SIs 2015/595 and 2012/801 respectively.
[2] SIs 2009/452 and 2015/1331 respectively.
[3] Welsh Written Representations Regulations 2015, reg 22. If an appeal decision under the 2003 Regulations is subsequently quashed by the court it will be redetermined under Part 2 of the 2015 Regulations: see Welsh Written Representations Regulations 2015, reg 22(3).
[4] 31 July 2015, in particular, Annex D.
[5] July 2015, in particular, Annex C.

21.3 Written representations

Stage	England	Wales
Decision on mode of determination	Within seven working days from the receipt of the appeal: Town and Country Planning Act 1990, s 319A(3); Town and Country Planning (Determination of Procedure) (Prescribed Period) (England) Regulations 2009, reg 2	Within seven working days from the receipt of the appeal: Town and Country Planning Act 1990, s 319B(3); Town and Country Planning (Determination of Procedure) (Prescribed Period) (Wales) Regulations 2014, reg 2
Notice of the appeal having been received and decision on mode of determination	Sent by Secretary of State as soon as practicable after determination to proceed by written representations: reg 11. This is the starting date	Sent by Welsh Ministers as soon as practicable after determination to proceed by written representations: reg 12. This is the starting date
Local authority questionnaire	Within one week of starting date: reg 12	Within two weeks of starting date: reg 13(1)
Local authority to provide notice of the appeal to those consulted in accordance with legislation and those who made representations	Within one week of starting date: reg 13(1)	Within two weeks of starting date: reg 14(1)
Submission of the appellant's further representations	Sent with appeal form (see above)	Within six weeks of the starting date: reg 15(4)
Local planning authority's statement of case/ representations	Within five weeks of the starting date: reg 14(3)	Within six weeks of the starting date: reg 15(3)
Third party representations	Within five weeks of the starting date for those notified: reg 15(1)	Within six weeks of the starting date for statutory parties and those who made representations on the application: reg 16(3)
Statements of case and representations circulated by Planning Inspectorate	As soon as practicable after receipt: regs 14(5), 15(2)(a)	As soon as practicable after receipt: reg 15(5), 16(2)(a)
Comments by the appellant and local planning authority on other main party representations,	By the appellant only within seven weeks of the starting date: reg 14(7)	Within nine weeks of the starting date: reg 15(7)
Comments by the appellant and local planning authority on third party representations,	Within seven weeks of the starting date (or any earlier date specified for commenting on third party representations): reg 15(2)(b)	Within a period of not less than two weeks specified by the Welsh Ministers: reg 16(2)(b)
Notice of decision	Regulation 16	Regulations 17, 18 (including duty to give reasons)

THE PROCEDURE IN ENGLAND UNDER THE 2013 AMENDMENTS

21.4 The start of the appeals process is the submission of the appellant's full statement of case with its appeal notice in accordance with the DMPO 2015, art 37. That statement is the appellant's opportunity to put its whole case and to positively promote its case[6]. The only later opportunity which the appellant has is to comment on what others have said. Consequently, at the outset of the appeal the appellant must pull its case together and present any new evidence. Whilst the inspector will have all of the application documentation, that may be a considerable amount of material. The removal of the right to a hearing and a caution by parties about the costs of hearings has meant that larger cases are being dealt with by written representations. On occasion schemes subject to EIA are being determined by the conventional written procedure. Inspectors have limited time to deal with each case; usually dealing with four to five written representations appeals a week[7], including carrying out the necessary site visits. Whilst more time can be sought by Inspectors for particular cases, guiding the inspector around the material and enabling her to focus on the critical issues will be a considerable help.

21.5 The full statement of case does not, therefore, need to repeat large amounts of material which were in the application but its author should ask the question which all written submissions must do: what is the best way of explaining the case to a person who is entirely new to it? In part it can guide the inspector through the paperwork. The submissions would also need to neatly put the appellant's case on the overall merits of the scheme and the response to any reasons for refusal. Matters raised by third parties should also be addressed, even if they were not adopted by the local planning authority. It may be that they are covered by the supporting documents to the planning application or by the authority's committee or delegated report. Any changes in circumstances not previously addressed by the appellant should be covered in the full statement of case, such as a change in policy.

The starting date

21.6 Following the validation of the appeal the Secretary of State will decide whether to proceed by written representations and set the starting date by sending out notice of its decision to the appellant and local planning authority[8]. That notice will also contain the appeal reference and details of the case officer at the Inspectorate who will deal with correspondence.

Notice to third parties

21.7 Within one week of the starting date the local planning authority is required to give notice of the appeal to any person who was consulted under the Town and Country Planning Act 1990 or the relevant DMPO and any other person who made

---

[6] Written Representations Regulations 2009, reg 14(1) reinforces the point describing the notice of appeal and accompanying documents as 'the appellant's representations in relation to the appeal'.
[7] *Planning Inspector Band 1 Recruitment 2015/16 Guidance notes for applicants.*
[8] Written Representations Regulations 2009, reg 11. The regulations are modified in the unlikely event that the written representations appeal is into an application of potential strategic importance and its refusal has been directed by the Mayor of London: Written Representations Regulations 2009, reg 18.

21.8 *Written representations*

representations about the application[9]. This does not include bodies who had to be notified under other provisions[10] if they did not make representations following the consultation.

21.8 The notice shall[11]:

'(a) describe the application;

(b) state the starting date;

(c) set out the matters notified to the appellant and the local planning authority [by the Minister] under regulation 11;

(f) state that any representations made to the local planning authority in relation to the application, before it was determined, will be sent to the Secretary of State and the appellant by the local planning authority and will be considered by the Secretary of State when determining the appeal unless they are withdrawn, in writing, within 5 weeks of the starting date; and

(g) state that further written representations may be sent to the Secretary of State within 5 weeks of the starting date'.

Questionnaire

21.9 The local planning authority must also return its questionnaire and a copy of the documents referred to in it within one week of the starting date[12]. When sending in the questionnaire the local planning authority should say whether the questionnaire and the supporting documents constitute its representations on the appeal[13]. If so, it is not entitled to make any further representations in the appeal.

21.10 If the planning application was refused or granted subject to conditions then there should be a committee or delegated report which sets out the officer analysis of the merits of the scheme. Provided the decision was in accordance with the report, it should be reasonably informative as to why the decision was taken. Such a report might or might not explain why a contentious condition was imposed. The questionnaire will also append consultation responses and, for example, a highways consultation response might contain all that needs to be said on a traffic objection.

21.11 The local planning authority will need to consider whether any report and accompanying material is sufficient to effectively put over its case. The appeal form will be accompanied by its response to the authority's decision and it is likely that something will need to be said about this. There may be more information with the appeal or the authority's earlier analysis might need expanding to put the points more effectively in the appeal context.

---

[9] Written Representations Regulations 2009, reg 13(1). The one-week period is a reduction from the two-week period which applied prior to October 2013.

[10] Such as Historic England under the Planning (Listed Buildings and Conservation Areas) Regulations 1990, reg 5A(3) or an airport operator under the Town and Country Planning (safeguarded aerodromes, technical sites and military explosives storage areas) Direction 2002, unless they made representations on the application.

[11] Written Representations Regulations 2009, reg 13(2).

[12] Written Representations Regulations 2009, reg 12.

[13] Written Representations Regulations 2009, reg 14(2).

If an appeal is against non-determination there will invariably be no pre-approved report and so further explanation from the authority will be required.

Five-week representations by the local planning authority

21.12 The local planning authority's principal opportunity to make new representations is within five weeks of the starting date[14]. This period was reduced from six weeks in 2013, in changes which also removed the appellant's right to make representations at this point. The full statement of case comprises 'a written statement which contains full particulars of the case which a person proposes to put forward and copies of any documents which that person intends to refer to or put in evidence'[15]. Any statement at this stage should set out the local planning authority's case and add to the assessment in any report on the application, otherwise it is not worth doing. That said, there is no benefit in repeating material from the earlier committee or delegated report and there may be an advantage in being able to refer to that report to show the soundness of the authority's initial consideration of the application. The statement should be careful to respond to the appeal case so that the inspector can see precisely how it is answered.

21.13 Many relevant documents will have been provided with the questionnaire, so only additional material should be provided. The Inspectorate advises that 'These should not normally include new evidence or additional technical data'[16]. However whilst the material with the questionnaire should be complete, this is the proper opportunity for the authority to produce material, particularly for later developments or in response to the appellant's case. New material at this stage might require a further consultation.

Third party representations

21.14 Third parties may also make representations within five weeks of the starting date[17]. There are a few points to bear in mind. The inspector will have the original representations made on the planning application, although not a record of any oral representations made to the authority's planning committee nor necessarily anything sent to councillors. There is a value in responding anyway, to emphasise that the proposal is still taken seriously, whether supporting or objecting. However, reference can simply be made to the earlier representations unless further or better submissions are to be made. A third party should check how the application has developed since they made their original representations to the authority: has the application been amended? What more information has been produced by the applicant or comments made by consultees? How did the authority analyse the application? What has

---

[14] Written Representations Regulations 2009, reg 14(3). Two copies must be provided if the representations are submitted in paper form.
[15] Written Representations Regulations 2009, reg 2(1).
[16] *Procedural Guide: Planning appeals – England*, para D.5.1 and *Procedural Guidance Planning appeals and called-in planning applications – Wales*, para C.5.2.
[17] Written Representations Regulations 2009, reg 15(1). The regulation refers to representations by the persons notified of the appeal by the local planning authority under reg 13(1), but in practice representations from any person will be taken into account provided they are made within that period. Only one copy of the representation is required by the regulations, although the Inspectorate in England asks for three hard copies if they are not submitted electronically: *Procedural Guide: Planning appeals – England*, para 6.2.

21.15 *Written representations*

been submitted on the appeal? The case may well have moved on since the initial consultation and publicity on the application. Often, and hopefully, such new material will be on the Council's website but some authorities choose to publish more than others, and even more dangerously, some are haphazard in adding later documents. A physical check on the planning file may be necessary.

21.15 Representations on the appeal should deal with any developments, even if it is simply a matter of confirming that original representations are not altered. They may choose to adopt arguments raised by other persons. Subject to the usefulness of simply referring to the original representations, third party representations should set out that person's view of the application.

Responses to the five-week representations

21.16 A copy of the local planning authority's five-week statement will be sent to the appellant by the Planning Inspectorate[18]. Third party representations are copied by the Inspectorate to the appellant and the authority[19]. The appellant may send comments on the authority's five-week statement within seven weeks of the starting date[20]. The appellant and the local planning authority may also comment on the third party representations within a period specified by the Planning Inspectorate, which is not later than within seven weeks of the starting date[21].

21.17 There is no further right to comment, although the Secretary of State may request further information[22]. The inspector and the main parties should be alert to a need for comment or further consultation as a matter of fairness if new issues or evidence is raised in these stages[23]. The appeal decision has to be based on the material considerations which exist at the time the appeal is determined, so it may be necessary to update the inspector outside the formal representation rights[24]. The Inspectorate advises[25]:

---

[18] Written Representations Regulations 2009, reg 14(5).
[19] Written Representations Regulations 2009, reg 15(2)(a).
[20] Written Representations Regulations 2009, reg 14(6). If submitted in hard form, two copies must be sent.
[21] Written Representations Regulations 2009, reg 15(2)(b). The flexibility in setting the timescale does allow an earlier deadline for comments on third party representations if they are made relatively early in the five-week period, but the utility in demanding an earlier response is limited as other representations can be made at the end of the five-week period and two weeks is in practice a tight period for responding. It is usually more sensible to be able to reply to all comments in a single document. There is no requirement in the regulations for multiple hard copies of these comments. This is because they do not have to circulated to the other main party, although they are copied by the Inspectorate to that party in practice. The Inspectorate does though ask for two copies if the comments are not circulated electronically *Procedural Guide: Planning appeals – England*, para D.7.1; *Procedural Guidance Planning appeals and called-in planning applications – Wales*, para C.7.1.
[22] Written Representations Regulations 2009, reg 14(7), (7A).
[23] 'However, if the appellant or Local Planning Authority has provided new or revised evidence as part of their evidence for the appeals; and it has only recently been prepared and was not considered at application stage, interested persons will be invited to comment on the contents of the new evidence'.
[24] See *Carroll v Secretary of State for Communities and Local Government* [2015] EWHC 316 (Admin) at para 77 per Supperstone J.
[25] *Procedural Guide: Planning appeals – England*, para B.2.1; *Procedural Guidance Planning appeals and called-in planning applications – Wales*, para J.2.1.

'If:

- a decision has been made, or enforcement action taken, on a local similar development since the appealed application was decided, (either by the local planning authority or on appeal);

- there has been a change in circumstances (eg new or emerging legislation or Government policy or guidance or local policy) since the local planning authority's decision ...

the local planning authority must alert us in writing, as soon as possible (copying their correspondence to the appellant), to the decision or the change in circumstances. The appellant may also do this'.

Whilst this duty to inform is a general principle, it is most important that parties are alert to this in written representations where there is not the opportunity to update the inspector at a hearing.

21.18 Time limits can be enforced strictly. The regulations authorise the Secretary of State to disregard representations which are made late[26]. A curious provision is that if no written representations are made by the local planning authority or third parties (and so there is no opportunity for the main parties to respond) the Secretary of State may determine the appeal if there is sufficient material to do so and provided that notice has been given to the appellant and local planning authority that he will do so[27]. Since the Minister would be expected to get on with determining the appeal whether or not submissions had been made, the purpose of this notice requirement is not apparent.

WRITTEN REPRESENTATIONS IN WALES AND THOSE IN ENGLAND PRIOR TO THE 2013 AMENDMENTS

21.19 The Welsh written representations procedures and those for English appeals made prior to October 2013 provide for simpler grounds of appeal, representations by the appellant, local planning authority and third parties at the six-week point and responses by the appellant and local planning authority by nine weeks. The 2015 Welsh Regulations introduced the householder and minor commercial appeals in Part 1 but retained the existing process for all other written representations appeals in the form of the new Part 2.

21.20 As the regulations now operate in Wales, these provide for interested persons (those notified of the original application or who had made representations on it) to be informed of the appeal[28] and be able to make representations within six weeks of the starting date[29]. The local planning authority and appellant have the same six-week period to send in their written representations[30] and a further period to comment on other parties' representations (strictly to the end of nine weeks for the other main party[31] and a specified period of at least two weeks for other representations)[32]. By

---

[26] Written Representations Regulations 2009, regs 14(7), (7A), 16(1).
[27] Written Representations Regulations 2009, reg 16(2).
[28] Welsh Written Representations Regulations 2015, reg 14.
[29] Welsh Written Representations Regulations 2015, reg 16(2).
[30] Welsh Written Representations Regulations 2015, reg 16(3), (4) respectively.
[31] Welsh Written Representations Regulations 2015, reg 15(7).
[32] Welsh Written Representations Regulations 2015, reg 16(2)(b). As mentioned on the English regulations, the deadline for commenting on local authority and third party representations should be standardised to a fixed point in the timetable.

21.21 *Written representations*

reg 15(7), 'The Welsh Ministers may disregard further information from the appellant and the local planning authority which is not received within 9 weeks of the starting date unless that further information has been requested by the Secretary of State'. A more curious provision is that if the local planning authority has failed to notify third parties in accordance with the regulations[33], the Welsh Ministers may disregard any comments which the local authority has on the third party representations which are made in the appeal[34].

21.21 The Welsh Ministers, or the inspector, must send their reasoned decision to the appellant, local planning authority, any persons who made representations and requested to be notified of the decision and any other person who asked to be notified and whom it is reasonable to notify[35].

21.22 The Welsh Written Representations Regulations 2003 govern all written representations appeals which relate to planning applications made before 22 June 2015[36]. These operate in the same way as Part 2 of the 2015 Regulations. Notice is given that the appeal is to be dealt with by written representations[37]. The local planning authority will notify third parties and submit its questionnaire within two weeks of the starting date[38]. All parties may make representations at the six-week point[39], with the appellant and the local planning authority then being able to comment on those representations[40].

21.23 Prior to the 1 October 2013 amendments in England two week periods for questionnaires and notification and six-week periods for representations applied. Additionally the appellant was able to submit further representations at the six-week point and consequently both main parties were able to comment on each other's representations. Those representations had to be made within nine weeks of the starting date[41].

21.24 The process only requires the appellant to make their main submissions at the six-week period. This poses a danger of unfairness to third parties if it is not handled with care by appellants and the Planning Inspectorate. If a new issue or new evidence is raised at the six-week point there will be no opportunity under the regulations for third parties to deal with it. These problems are considered under fairness below.

FAIRNESS

21.25 The general approach to fairness in planning appeals is discussed in Chapter 23 on inquiries. The principles of natural justice do arise in written representations appeals, in particular[42]:

---

[33] In accordance with reg 14.
[34] Welsh Written Representations Regulations 2015, reg 16(3).
[35] Welsh Written Representations Regulations 2015, reg 18.
[36] See the transitional provisions in Welsh Written Representations Regulations 2015, reg 22(2). If a written representations appeal decision under the 2003 Regulations is quashed by the court then the decision will be redetermined under Part 2 of the 2015 Regulations: reg 22(3).
[37] Welsh Written Representations Regulations 2003, regs 3, 4.
[38] Welsh Written Representations Regulations 2003, regs 5, 6.
[39] Welsh Written Representations Regulations 2003, regs 7, 8.
[40] Welsh Written Representations Regulations 2003, regs 7(7), 8(2)(b).
[41] Written Representations Regulations 2009, reg 14(4), (6), (7) (as originally made).
[42] Taken from *Hopkins Development Ltd v Secretary of State for Communities and Local Government* [2014] EWCA Civ 470, [2014] JPL 1000 at para 62 in the planning inquiry context, see Chapter 23.

(i) any party ... is entitled (a) to know the case which he has to meet and (b) to have a reasonable opportunity to adduce evidence and make submissions in relation to that opposing case.

(ii) if there is procedural unfairness which materially prejudices a party to a planning inquiry that may be a good ground for quashing the inspector's decision.

21.26 The courts have for a long time emphasised that the rules of natural justice apply to planning appeals by written representations[43]. That an appeal is dealt with by written representations is not a ground for any relaxation of the standards laid down by the courts for appeal decisions under the Town and Country Planning Act 1990[44].

21.27 The rules of natural justice in written representations appeals were neatly summarised in *Ball v Secretary of State for the Environment, Transport and the Regions* by Nigel Macleod QC[45]:

'(1) The rules of natural justice apply to planning appeals, including appeals by written representations (*London Borough of Southwark v Secretary of State for the Environment* [1987] JPL 36).

(2) That an appeal is dealt with by written representations is not a ground for any relaxation of the standards laid down by the Court of Appeal decisions under the Town and Country Planning Act 1990 (*Westminster City Council v Secretary of State for the Environment* [1984] JPL 27).

(3) All cases in which principles of natural justice are invoked must depend on the particular circumstances of the case but a question is whether the appellant has had "a fair crack of the whip" (*Fairmount Ltd v Secretary of State for the Environment* [1976] 1 WLR 1255 at 1265H–1266A).

(4) It is necessary to show substantial prejudice to constitute a breach of natural justice. The appropriate test to identify such a breach is: would a reasonable person, viewing the matter objectively, and knowing all the facts known to the court, consider that there was a risk that the procedure adopted by the Secretary of State has resulted in injustice or unfairness? (*Robert Hitchin Ltd v Secretary of State for the Environment* (1995) 72 P & CR 579 at 586–587).

(5) The question, whether there has been a breach of natural justice, applying that test, is a matter of fact and degree according to the circumstances of the case (see *Robert Hitchin Ltd* at page 587)'.

21.28 A particular problem which arises in written representation appeals is the restriction on third party comments to a five- or six-week period after the start date. They are not entitled under the regulations to comment on any later appeal representations by the appellant. It is important, therefore, that a non-statutory reconsultation is added to the process if appeal representations raise new issues or important new evidence that third parties should be able to comment on. These are illustrated by the decisions in *Phillips v First Secretary of State*[46], *Ashley v Secretary of State for Communities and Local Government*[47], and *Carroll v Secretary for Communities and Local Government*[48].

---

[43] *London Borough of Southwark v Secretary of State for the Environment* [1987] JPL 36.
[44] *Westminster City Council v Secretary of State for the Environment* [1984] JPL 27.
[45] [2000] PLCR 299 at 304. Bearing in mind Jackson LJ's dislike of the 'fair crack of the whip' metaphor in *Hopkins Development*.
[46] [2004] EWHC 2415 (Admin), [2004] JPL 613.
[47] [2012] EWCA Civ 559, [2012] JPL 1235.
[48] [2015] EWHC 316 (Admin).

21.29 *Written representations*

21.29 In *Phillips* a new point arose in that the telecommunications operator set out a larger area of search for alternative sites in its written representation appeal submissions. Richards J held that the public should have been able to comment on this new point[49]:

'The need to invite further representations in the interests of fairness is likely to arise very infrequently. The sequence of representations provided for in the regulations will normally be sufficient to achieve fairness. But the opportunity to make additional representations can and should be given if a new point is raised which the inspector ought to take into consideration and which cannot fairly be taken into consideration without giving such an opportunity. Whether fairness requires it depends entirely on the particular facts of the case'.

21.30 The issue in *Ashley v Secretary of State for Communities and Local Government*[50] was that the appellant had submitted potentially contentious expert evidence on noise just before the close of the period for public comments on the appeal. The inspector's decision was quashed, as an opportunity for comment should have been given. Pill LJ rejected the argument that the claimant should have visited the Council's offices to inspect the file after the six-week submission date[51]. Similarly in *Carroll v Secretary for Communities and Local Government*[52] the appellant in a B1 (office) to residential conversion said at the six-week point (under the pre-2013 Regulations) that the existing use was B8 (storage) rather than office so seeking to avoid policy restrictions on loss of office uses. Then, following the close of representations, she sent to the inspector a council committee report on a subsequent application on the site which said that the use was B8 and that there was no policy objection to a change from B8 to C3 (residential). It was unfair not to have consulted objecting neighbours on each change and the inspector also failed to have regard to material considerations because he was not told that the Council committee had refused the second application raising a policy objection to change from B8 to C3 (and indeed had done prior to the appellant's letter with the committee report being sent)[53].

21.31 These three cases all took place under the regulations prior to the 2013 amendments in England. The risk of substantive new material being produced late by the appellant in English cases is reduced by the requirement to file its case with the appeal notice. The Welsh position for six-week representations is unaltered[54]. Even in England, a late change of circumstances (whether actual or apparent) may require consultation, as *Carroll* shows.

Other new issues might arise in even later representations which require wider consultation.

---

[49] *Phillips* at para 55.
[50] [2012] EWCA Civ 559, [2012] JPL 1235.
[51] At para 33, see also Kitchen LJ at paras 48, 50.
[52] [2015] EWHC 316 (Admin).
[53] The appellant's response to the judgment was to paint the front of the building with red stripes, prompting considerable press comment.
[54] The *Procedural Guidance Planning appeals and called-in planning applications – Wales*, does warn (at what by a typographical error is the second para C.5.2):

'However, if the appellant or Local Planning Authority has provided new or revised evidence as part of their evidence for the appeals; and it has only recently been prepared and was not considered at application stage, interested persons will be invited to comment on the contents of the new evidence'.

21.32 Fresh points might occur to the inspector and, if so, the parties should be given an opportunity to comment on them. In *Grant v Secretary of State for the Environment*[55] the High Court quashed the dismissal of a planning appeal determined on written representations because the inspector relied on a new issue, the effect on a nearby property, and failed to give the parties an opportunity to make representations about it.

SITE VISITS

21.33 There are two forms of site visits in conventional written representations cases:

(i) if the site can be seen adequately from the highway or other vantage points open to the public then an unaccompanied site visit may take place[56]. The inspector[57] will view the site from whatever public locations are thought to be helpful, without giving any notice;

(ii) an accompanied site visit, where the inspector is accompanied by representatives of the appellant and the local planning authority. The inspector will go onto the appeal site, view the site from public vantage points and may, with the occupiers' permission, go onto third party land. The parties may point features out to the inspector, but there should be no discussion of the case.

21.34 On an unaccompanied site visit the inspector is not able to go onto private property, even at the occupier's request, as the main parties will not be represented (unlike in the simplified procedure for householder and minor commercial appeals). An inspector on an unaccompanied site visit will aim to be fairly inconspicuous, but smartly dressed persons standing in the street and looking at buildings whilst holding large drawings tend to get noticed[58]. If asked, the inspector will explain who they are but will not be drawn into any discussion of the case.

21.35 In *Tait v Secretary of State for Communities and Local Government*[59] an inspector's decision was remitted where an accompanied site visit was arranged, the appellant did not attend and the inspector carried on in the presence of only the Council officer. There was found to be a real risk of prejudice to the appellant.

---

[55] [1990] JPL 110.
[56] *Procedural Guide: Planning appeals – England*, para D.8.2. Where an appeal raises a pure legal point then a site visit might not be required.
[57] The Inspectorate's guidance allows for the site visit to be conducted by a planning officer working in the Planning Inspectorate rather than by the inspector who determines the appeal: *Procedural Guide: Planning appeals – England*, para D.8.3. That is discussed in Chapter 20.
[58] Just a personal observation.
[59] [2012] EWHC 643 (Admin).

Chapter 22

Hearings

22.1 A hearing is an inspector-led structured discussion of the issues in the appeal followed by a site visit at which the discussion may continue. The virtues of the hearing format are that it is relatively quick and allows parties' positions to be clarified and explained succinctly. It is also more informal than an inquiry but still in a disciplined environment. Hearings are not suitable formats for cross-examination, so the ability to test a party's case is constrained. The hearing format can accommodate detailed legal submissions.

22.2 There are fewer preparatory stages for hearings than for inquiries, in particular there is no stage for the production of proofs or statements of evidence. All of a party's evidence, which may include expert reports or proofs/statements from witnesses, should be produced with their case.

22.3 The English procedures for hearings are contained in the Town and Country Planning (Hearings Procedure) (England) Rules 2000 (the English Hearings Rules)[1]. In Wales the rules are in Town and Country Planning (Hearings Procedure) (Wales) Rules 2003 (the Welsh Hearings Rules)[2]. Changes to the English procedures in 2013 mean that there are now significant differences in the procedural timetables in the two countries. Parties, of course, need to have the relevant rules in mind. The principal guidance is in *Procedural Guide Planning appeals – England* (31 July 2015), Annex E and *Procedural Guidance Planning appeals and called in planning applications – Wales* (July 2015), Annex D.

22.4 The stages in a hearing, and the relevant rules are as follows

Stage	England	Wales
Submission of appeal		
Submission of the appellant's full statement of case	With the appeal form: see DMPO 2015, art 37	Statement of case at six-week point: see below
Notice of the appeal having been received		Sent by Welsh Ministers as soon as practicable after all the documents have been received: r 3A
Decision on mode of determination	Sent by Secretary of State as soon as practicable after determination to hold hearing: r 3A	Sent by Welsh Ministers as soon as practicable after determination to hold hearing: r 4(A)

---

[1] SI 2000/1626.
[2] SI 2003/1271.

Stage	England	Wales
'Starting date' notice of hearing	The starting date runs from the date of the r 3A notice: r 2(1)	The starting date runs from the date of the r 3A or 4(A) notice, whichever is later: r 2(1)
Local authority to provide details of statutory parties	'forthwith' on receipt of the Secretary of State's notice: r 4(1)	'forthwith' on receipt of the Welsh Ministers' notice: r 4(1)
Appellant provides full statement of case to statutory parties	As soon as practicable after receiving details of the statutory parties: r 6(1)	
Local authority questionnaire	Within one week of starting date: r 4(2)	Within two weeks of starting date: r 4(2)
Local authority to provide notice of the appeal to statutory parties and those who made representations	Within one week of starting date: r 4(2)	Within two weeks of starting date: r 4(2)
Submission of the appellant's statement of case	Sent with appeal form (see above)	Within six weeks of the starting date: r 6(1)
Local planning authority's statement of case	Within five weeks of the starting date: r 6(1A)	Within six weeks of the starting date: r 6(1)
Third party representations	Within five weeks of the starting date for statutory parties and those who made representations on the application: r 6(3)	Within six weeks of the starting date for statutory parties and those who made representations on the application: r 6(3)
Statements of case and representations circulated by Planning Inspectorate	As soon as practicable after receipt: r 6(5), (7)	As soon as practicable after receipt: r 6(5), (7)
Comments by the appellant and local planning authority on other main party and third party representations, sent to Inspectorate and statutory parties	No provision in the rules	Within nine weeks of the starting date: r 6(4)
Statement of common ground	To be agreed within five weeks of the starting date: r 6A(1)	No provision in the rules
Notice of the hearing	At least four weeks' notice unless agreed with appellant and local planning authority: r 7(2)	At least four weeks' notice unless agreed with appellant and local planning authority: r 7(2)
Hearing	Not later than 10 weeks after the starting date, unless impracticable: r 7(1)	Not later than 12 weeks after the starting date, unless impracticable: r 7(1)

22.5 Hearings

PROCEDURE

Submission of the appeal

22.5 The English provisions require the appellant to submit its 'full statement of case' with the notice of appeal. Since there is no further opportunity for the appellant to submit documents in an English case, the material must be fully deployed at this state. In a Welsh appeal, the notice need simply set out the grounds of appeal[3].

Decision on mode of determination

22.6 The Secretary of State or the Welsh Ministers will then decide how the case is to be determined[4].

'Starting date' notice of hearing and preliminaries

22.7 Appeal timetables run from the starting date. This is the date of the notice from the Minister which gives the mode of determination of the appeal[5]. The notice will state the starting date and the timetable which will then be followed.

22.8 The local authority will 'forthwith' provide details of statutory parties to the appellant[6]. A statutory party is any owner or long leaseholder or agricultural tenant of the application site who was served with notice of the application[7]. If any other statutory parties make representations to the Minister then the Planning Inspectorate will inform the appellant and local planning authority of their names and addresses[8]. In England the appellant must provide a copy of its full statement of case to those statutory parties as soon as practicable after being given their details[9].

22.9 The local planning authority will complete the appeal questionnaire and send it to the Minister and the appellant, along with copies of the documents referred to in it. In England this must be done within one week of the starting date, whilst two weeks are allowed in Wales[10].

Statements of case and third-party representations

22.10 An appellant in England will have submitted its statement of case with the appeal form. The local planning authority will have to submit its full statement of case

---

[3] For the requirements with the notice of appeal, see Chapter 19.
[4] See Chapter 19.
[5] See English and Welsh Hearings Rules, r 2(1). In the Welsh rules the starting date is the later of the date of the notice that all documents necessary for the appeal have been received (the r 3A notice) or the notice that a hearing is to be held (the relevant notice). In practice the notice that a hearing will be held is sent after notification that an appeal has been received.
[6] English and Welsh Hearings Rules, r 4(1).
[7] In the English and Welsh Hearings Rules, r 2(1) the definition of statutory party applies the categories of person whose representations must be taken into account in the (now revoked) Town and Country Planning (General Development Procedure) Order 1995, art 19.
[8] English and Welsh Hearings Rules, r 4(1).
[9] English Hearings Rules, r 6(1).
[10] English Hearings Rules, r 4(2) and Welsh Hearings Rules, r 4(2), respectively.

within five weeks of the starting date. Read in conjunction with the questionnaire, this should be a comprehensive statement of the authority's position and should put in front of the inspector all of the necessary documents which have not already been submitted in the appeal process[11]. There is no need to duplicate documents which have already been sent by any party to the inspector.

22.11 If submitted in hard copy[12], two copies of the full statement of case must be received by the Inspectorate within the period. The local planning authority must also send copies to the statutory parties[13].

Statutory parties, persons who made representations on the application or who were notified about the application[14], are required to make any comments in writing in the same five-week period[15]. The regulations make no mention of representations by any other person, but they ought to make representations within that period and if they do so, the representations would be considered by the inspector or Minister.

22.12 In Wales the hearing statements of the appellant and the local planning authority should be received by the Inspectorate and statutory parties within six weeks of the starting date[16]. Statutory parties, persons who made representations on the application or who were notified about the application have six weeks to make written representations[17].

22.13 The statements of case and representations will be circulated by the Planning Inspectorate to the appellant/local planning authority and the inspector as soon as practicable following their receipt[18]. They are to be made available, along with the questionnaire response for inspection and copying by any person[19]. This can be by physical inspection or on a website[20]. The arrangements for inspection, including the place and time for hard copies or the website address, where on the website it can be accessed and how, must be specified in the local planning authority's statement[21]. If the website alone is being relied upon, a person has an opportunity if they are notified of how to access the information on the website. That notice would have to be separate to the statement of case and so it is sensible for the local planning authority's notice of the appeal to explain how information will be made available.

---

[11] 'Full statement of case' is defined for these purposes as 'a written statement which contains full particulars of the case which a person proposes to put forward and copies of any documents which that person intends to refer to or put in evidence': English Hearings Rules, r 2(1).
[12] Where multiple copies are required by the Rules, a single, electronic copy will suffice: English and Welsh Hearings Rules, r 2(4), (8).
[13] English Hearings Rules, r 6(1A).
[14] The rules do not address why the person was notified, so a person who was sent non-statutory notice by the local planning authority (perhaps because they occupy in the locality) would be within this provision.
[15] English Hearings Rules, r 6(3). If submitting hard copies, three copies are required (with one each being sent by the Inspectorate to the appellant and the local planning authority).
[16] Welsh Hearings Rules, r 6(1).
[17] Welsh Hearings Rules, r 6(3).
[18] English and Welsh Hearings Rules, r 6(5), (7).
[19] English and Welsh Hearings Rules, r 6(6).
[20] English and Welsh Hearings Rules, r 6(6A).
[21] English and Welsh Hearings Rules, r 6(6), (6A).

22.14 Hearings

Further information and representations

22.14 The Minister may in writing require the appellant and the local planning authority to provide further information about the matters contained in their statement of case within a set period[22].

22.15 Under the English rules there is no provision for anyone to comment in writing on the five-week statements. Any response would, on that basis, be left to the hearing itself. In Wales the appellant and the local planning authority may comment in writing on the other's hearing statement, any representations submitted to the Minister by third parties and 'comments made to them by any other person' within nine weeks of the starting date[23].

22.16 The provision for nine-week comments was dropped from the English system because these tended not to add much and are less important now that the appellant had to produce their full case with the appeal form. In Wales, where nine-week comments are still available, a party must always consider whether anything needs to be submitted and if so, what. The best way to approach the question is to have in mind that the inspector will read the documents which have already been submitted in one go, so there is no need to remind her of matters she will have just read. Any further comments must add to what has already been said and a failure to comment is not a concession of the other side's points. There may be something new to say or it may be helpful to refer the inspector to the relevant parts of reports which have already been submitted.

22.17 The *Procedural Guide Planning appeals – England* is discouraging of any submissions outside the time limits, saying they will normally be returned, unseen by the inspector[24]. Late evidence may only be produced at the hearing itself exceptionally[25], but if new material has to be provided, it is better this is done before the hearing rather than on the day. Any further written submission to the Inspectorate should explain why it is being made at this time and, as far as possible, why it could not have been made earlier. The evidence should be copied to the other main and statutory parties so that at least they have it in advance of the hearing. Of course, some new material might be necessitated by changes in circumstances, such as new policy or decisions, or by the resolution of issues between the main parties.

Statement of common ground

22.18 The English rules require an agreed statement of common ground to be submitted to the Secretary of State and any statutory party within five weeks of the starting date[26]. There is no mention of statements of common ground in the Welsh rules, although it may be helpful to produce one.

---

[22] English and Welsh Hearings Rules, r 6(2).
[23] Welsh Hearings Rules, r 6(4).
[24] *Procedural Guide Planning appeals – England* (31 July 2015), para 1.6; *Procedural Guidance Planning appeals and called in planning applications – Wales* (July 2015), para 1.7.1.
[25] *Procedural Guide Planning appeals – England*, para E.9.2; *Procedural Guidance Planning appeals and called in planning applications – Wales*, para D.8.2 This is discussed further below.
[26] English Hearings Rules, r 6A(1).

Potential to change the mode of determination

22.19 If the appellant or the local planning authority consider that the hearings procedure is inappropriate then they may raise this with the Minister in writing prior to the hearing, or with the inspector at the hearing[27]. At the hearing if the inspector considers that cross-examination is required then the appellant and the local planning authority must be consulted on whether the hearing should be closed and an inquiry held instead[28]. Whilst not in the rules, the inspector can raise the question of the suitability of proceeding by a hearing at any time after receiving details of the appeal.

22.20 In England the decision whether to change the mode of determination is vested in the Secretary of State, not the inspector[29]. If the inspector considers at the hearing that an inquiry is required then he will need to consider whether to adjourn the hearing part-heard or to continue with the hearing and conclude it that day against the possibility that it will not be converted into an inquiry. It is, of course, difficult for a tribunal to continue with what it considers to be the wrong procedure. Following the issue arising at a hearing the inspector will report whether the mode of determination should be changed, along with the views of the parties. If a main party requests a change prior to the hearing, the Secretary of State must consult the other party before altering the mode of determination[30].

22.21 In Wales the Ministers will decide on any change to the mode of determination prior to the hearing, but the inspector is able to decide to close the hearing and arrange an inquiry instead following a request or on his own initiative[31].

THE HEARING

Appearances at the hearing

22.22 Entitled to appear at the hearing are the appellant, the local planning authority and any statutory party[32]. The inspector may permit any other person to appear and 'such permission shall not be unreasonably withheld'[33]. In practice, that person would have been expected to have made representations on the application or in the written part of the appeal process or be able to explain why they have come later to the appeal.

The hearing date

22.23 In England hearings should be held within 10 weeks of the starting date unless that is impracticable and otherwise at the earliest practicable date[34]. The equivalent period in Wales is 12 weeks[35].

---

[27] English Hearings Rules, r 8(3) and Welsh Hearings Rules, r 8(1).
[28] English and Welsh Hearings Rules, r 11(3).
[29] Due to Town and Country Planning Act 1990, s 319A(4).
[30] English Hearing Rules, r 8(4).
[31] Welsh Hearings Rules, r 8(1), (2).
[32] English and Welsh Hearings Rules, r 9(1).
[33] English and Welsh Hearings Rules, r 9(2).
[34] English Hearings Rules, r 7(1).
[35] Welsh Hearings Rules, r 7(1).

22.24 Hearings

Notice of the hearing date

22.24 Unless a shorter period is agreed by the Minister with the appellant and the local planning authority, not less than four weeks' notice of the date, time and place of the hearing shall be given to every person entitled to attend the hearing[36]. The Inspectorate and the parties entitled to take part in the appeal may agree to notice being given via a website[37]. The date, time or place for the hearing may be varied. Four weeks' notice of a new date is required, unless otherwise agreed by the main parties. Reasonable notice is required for other changes[38].

22.25 The Minister may require the local planning authority to publish a notice of the hearing in a local newspaper not less than two weeks before the hearing date and provide other notice of the hearing[39]. The notice shall contain[40]:

(a) a clear statement of the date, time and place of the hearing and of the powers enabling the Minister or inspector to determine the appeal in question;

(b) a written description of the land sufficient to identify approximately its location;

(c) a brief description of the subject matter of the appeal; and

(d) details of where and when copies of the local planning authority's completed questionnaire and documents sent by and copied to the authority may be inspected.

Hearing venue

22.26 The accommodation for the hearing should be informal with the inspector and the parties sitting around a table. In the past the use of small committee rooms in the council offices has been recommended. There does need to be sufficient place to accommodate the third parties who are likely to turn up, both potential participants (who should be at the table) and spectators. The inspector will often wish to sit at the same table as the parties, rather than apart from them.

The rigour of a hearing

22.27 Hearings are intended to be an inspector-led discussion, however the exercise must be carried out with sufficient rigour to test and resolve the matters which need to be decided. In *Dyason v Secretary of State for the Environment, Transport and the Regions* Pill LJ warned[41]:

> 'Planning permission having been refused, conflicting propositions and evidence will often be placed before an Inspector on appeal. Whatever procedure is followed, the strength of a case can be determined only upon an understanding of that case and by

---

[36] English and Welsh Hearings Rules, r 7(2).
[37] English and Welsh Hearings Rules, r 7(2A).
[38] English and Welsh Hearings Rules, r 7(3), (4).
[39] English and Welsh Hearings Rules, r 7(5).
[40] English and Welsh Hearings Rules, r 7(6).
[41] [1998] JPL 778 at 784. Following *Dyason*, Dove J observed in *King's Lynn and West Norfolk Borough Council v Secretary of State for Communities and Local Government* [2015] EWHC 2464 (Admin) at para 49 'it is for the Inspector to be on top of matters and ultimately if he cannot discharge his inquisitorial duty because of late material, then he must adjourn or regulate the procedure accordingly'.

testing it with reference to propositions in the opposing case. At a public local inquiry the Inspector, in performing that task, usually has the benefit of cross-examination on behalf of the other party. If cross-examination disappears, the need to examine propositions in that way does not disappear with it. Further, the statutory right to be heard is nullified unless, in some way, the strength of what one party says is not only listened to by the tribunal but is assessed for its own worth and in relation to opposing contentions.

There is a danger, upon the procedure now followed by the Secretary of State of observing the right to be heard by holding a "hearing", that the need for such consideration is forgotten. The danger is that the "more relaxed" atmosphere could lead not to a "full and fair" hearing but to a less than thorough examination of the issues. A relaxed hearing is not necessarily a fair hearing. The hearing must not become so relaxed that the rigorous examination essential to the determination of difficult questions may be diluted. The absence of an accusatorial procedure places an inquisitorial burden upon an inspector.

... if there is any suggestion that the requirements at a "hearing" are fundamentally different from those at a "public local inquiry" that suggestion is to be resisted. A fair and thorough investigation can in my judgment be expected by a party who has the right to be heard whichever procedure is followed'.

Procedure at a hearing

22.28 At the start, the inspector will explain that the hearing will take the form of a discussion[42] which he will lead. He will review the case as he sees it and outline the main issues and matters that require further explanation[43]. Usually the inspector will produce a written agenda on the day. This does not prevent parties from raising other issues[44].

22.29 The appellant or his agent will start the discussion. Questions may be asked informally during the proceedings, provided they are relevant and the discussion is orderly. Interested third parties may be present and may join in the discussion. The discussion is intended to be 'inspector-led' and inquisitorial, but the rules of natural justice must be observed[45].

22.30 If it becomes apparent that cross-examination is required, then the inspector will need to decide, having consulted the main parties, whether to close the hearing and hold (or ask the Secretary of State to hold) an inquiry (on a different occasion) instead[46]. It is still possible to cross-examine, with the inspector's permission, in a hearing[47].

22.31 The rules refer to evidence being called[48] but in practice there is no formal calling of evidence. Where a party has an advocate and one or more expert or factual witnesses, then there can be a rough distinction between evidence and submissions. Where a party's main representation also provides their sole or main evidence (such as a planning consultant or planning officer), the role of advocate and witness is essentially merged.

---

[42] It is provided that 'A hearing shall take the form of a discussion': English and Welsh Hearings Rules, r 11(2).
[43] English and Welsh Hearings Rules, r 11(4).
[44] English and Welsh Hearings Rules, r 11(5).
[45] *Rydon Homes v Secretary of State for the Environment* (1995) 70 P & CR 657.
[46] See paras **22.19–22.21** above.
[47] English and Welsh Hearings Rules, r 11(2).
[48] English and Welsh Hearings Rules, r 11(6).

22.32 Hearings

22.32 A party is entitled to be represented by any other person[49], and so can attend with a solicitor or counsel. However, for many years the Planning Inspectorate thought it odd for lawyers to appear at hearings. That view has changed[50], particularly because the Inspectorate have been pushing cases down to hearings which would previously have been dealt with by inquiries. Parties consequently often consider they need to have professional advocates as well as witnesses. Using an advocate and a witness or witnesses can be effective in hearings, particularly where there are legal or merits based submissions to make or several witnesses to marshall. In the hearing it is useful to distinguish between points best made by submission or by an expert explaining their professional view. The Planning Inspectorate has asked that the other side is told in advance if a party intends to be represented at the hearing by a lawyer.

Third parties may take part, at the inspector's discretion, although if many other people want to speak then it may be more suitable to hold an inquiry.

The appellant will have the last word.

22.33 The discussion about conduct at inquiries in Chapter 23 generally remains good for hearings. Parties remain seated and refer to each other formally. Whilst a discussion is less structured than a formal hearing, parties will often be asked to comment in turn. Speakers should only be interrupted with care – when it helps in understanding or addressing an issue – and parties will be given the chance to say what they want to say. Discussions with inspectors outside the hearing sessions should be limited and ideally in the other parties' hearing. Recording of and reporting on hearings is now encouraged[51].

Late evidence at the hearing

22.34 Ideally all evidence should be submitted with the statements of case or third party representations. The Hearing Rules do allow those persons entitled to take part to call evidence allow the inspector may refuse to permit the giving or production of evidence or any other presentation which is irrelevant or repetitious[52]. The inspector otherwise has a discretion as to the calling of evidence, however if he refuses to allow oral evidence then the person refused may submit any evidence or other matter in writing before the close of the hearing.[53] The *Procedural Guide Planning appeals – England* is discouraging of late evidence being given at the hearing. Without considering the rights conferred by the Rules it takes the view that inspectors have a discretion to accept such evidence but this should be exercised exceptionally[54]:

'E.9.3 Before deciding whether, exceptionally, to accept it, the Inspector will require:
- an explanation as to why it was not received by us in accordance with the rules; and
- an explanation of how and why the material is relevant; and

---

[49] English and Welsh Hearings Rules, r 9(3).
[50] The use of advocates at hearings, including testing evidence by questioning (but not cross-examination), is acknowledged in *Procedural Guidance Planning appeals and called-in planning applications – Wales* (July 2015), Annex H.
[51] See para **23.123**.
[52] English and Welsh Hearings Rules, r 11(6), (7).
[53] English and Welsh Hearings Rules, r 11(7). A person required to leave the hearing for acting in a disruptive manner is also able to make written submissions prior to the close of the hearing: r 11(8).
[54] The same text is in the *Procedural Guidance Planning appeals and called in planning applications – Wales* (July 2015, paras D.8.2 and D.8.3 with the omission of the third bullet point in para E.9.4.

Adjournment of the hearing to site or a site visit **22.36**

- the opposing party's views on whether it should be accepted.

E.9.4 The Inspector will refuse to accept late evidence unless fully satisfied that:
- it is not covered in the evidence already received; and
- it is directly relevant and necessary for his or her decision;
- it would not have been possible for the party to have provided the evidence when they sent us their full statement of case; and
- it would be procedurally fair to all parties (including interested people) if the late evidence were taken into account'.

TACTICS AND PREPARATION

22.35 A hearing will run to the inspector's agenda and the opportunity for formal submissions will be limited. Preparation addresses how to deal with matters orally. The following questions might be worth focusing on:

- What is the inspector likely to identify as the main issues?
- What is our case on these?
- Are there any procedural issues which will arise at the outset?
- Are there issues we need to raise which might not be on the inspector's agenda?
- What points do we want to bring out which might not be apparent or as obviously important on the papers?
- Are there points we want the other side to clarify – such as what part of their scheme is or the rationale for a reason for refusal? What is the best way of getting this out?
- On what points might our case be questioned? What is the response to these?
- Might third parties attend? If so, who, what will they say and how would they want to do it?
- Are there any issues on conditions?
- Is there to be a planning obligation? What is its current status and what material does the inspector need?
- Who is best to deal with particular points: the advocate; the planning officer/consultant; another expert; the client?

In terms of dividing up the speaking, matters of professional judgment are best explained by the relevant professional. An advocate can deal with the overall case, legal submissions (including policy interpretation), procedural points and any quick response (whether by question or comment) to the other side.

ADJOURNMENT OF THE HEARING TO SITE OR A SITE VISIT

22.36 A hearing may be adjourned to the site for the discussion to be concluded if the inspector is satisfied that[55]:

---

[55] English and Welsh Hearings Rules, r 12(1).

22.37 *Hearings*

(i) one or more matters would be more satisfactorily resolved by adjourning the hearing to the appeal site;

(ii) the hearing would proceed satisfactorily and that no party would be placed at a disadvantage;

(iii) all parties present at the hearing would have the opportunity to attend the adjourned hearing; and

(iv) the local planning authority, the appellant or any statutory party has not raised reasonable objections to it being continued at the appeal site.

22.37 Adjournment of the hearing to the site allows issues to be discussed with the relevant buildings and land in view. However, the discussion needs to be possible with the inspector and the parties standing around, holding at most a few drawings, in whatever are the current weather conditions. It is usually sensible for the issues to have all been discussed in the hearing room, with particular detailed points and general observations addressed on site. The number of participants is an important constraint. It needs to be possible for everyone to hear what is being said on site. Advocates may attend a hearing which has been adjourned to the site, whereas usually they will not be present at the inspector's site visit.

22.38 Alternatively the inspector may close the hearing and may then hold a site visit at his initiative and shall conduct a site visit if requested by the appellant or local planning authority[56]. The appellant and local planning authority are able to attend if they wish to[57]. Other persons entitled to, permitted or who did appear at the hearing may attend the site visit at the inspector's discretion[58]. The differences in practice are that if the hearing is adjourned to the site then discussion will continue, but on a site inspection the merits of the appeal are not discussed and the parties are confined to pointing out things they have already referred to. An inspector ought to be careful to explain whether the hearing is adjourned to the site or is being closed and a site visit being conducted and the implications of that decision[59].

22.39 The effect of the rules is that there must be a site visit, if requested, either in the form of an inspection or in the form of an adjourned hearing[60]. If it is not possible for all of the parties who wish to attend on site to be present, then the hearing cannot be adjourned and a site visit must be carried out instead. This would be the case if a party was unavailable, a party would be unwelcome on another's property or the physical arrangements (such as being on top of a silo) made it impractical for everyone to be present at the same time.

The inspector is required to go onto the appeal site in the adjourned hearing or site visit[61] unless the relevant parties agree that there is no need to do so.

---

[56] English and Welsh Hearings Rules, r 12(2).
[57] English and Welsh Hearings Rules, r 12(4)(a).
[58] English and Welsh Hearings Rules, r 12(4)(b).
[59] The inspector's decision was muddled in *Payne v Secretary of State for Communities and Local Government* [2010] EWHC 3528 (Admin), [2011] JPL 767 at para 2 per Burton J.
[60] *Payne* at para 19.
[61] *Payne* at paras 14–19.

Chapter 23

Inquiries

23.1 An inquiry is a formal process where parties appear before an inspector, making submissions and calling and cross-examining witnesses. Its purpose is to enable evidence and cases to be rigorously examined, enabling parties to put their cases whilst dealing with issues efficiently.

23.2 The English procedures for inquiries into call-ins and appeals recovered by the Secretary of State are contained in the Town and Country Planning (Inquiries Procedure) (England) Rules 2000 (the English Inquiries Rules)[1]. Inquiries for appeals determined by inspectors are governed by the Town and Country Planning Appeals (Determination by Inspectors) (Inquiries Procedure) (England) Rules 2000 (the English Inspectors Inquiries Rules)[2]. In Wales the rules are in the Town and Country Planning (Inquiries Procedure) (Wales) Rules 2003 (for Ministerial decisions) (the Welsh Inquiries Rules)[3] and Country Planning Appeals (Determination by Inspectors) (Inquiries Procedure) (Wales) Rules 2003 (the Welsh Inspectors Inquiries Rules)[4]. The reforms of English appeal procedures in 2013 mean that there are now significant differences in the procedural timetables in the two countries. Parties, of course, need to have the relevant rules in mind.

Guidance on call-ins and appeals dealt with by inquiry is contained in the *Procedural Guide: Planning appeals – England*[5] and the *Procedural Guidance Planning appeals and called-in planning applications – Wales*[6].

23.3 The stages in an inquiry and the relevant dates are below. These dates are subject to any changes contained in a bespoke timetable. The similarities between the four sets of rules are more notable than the differences but substance and references do vary between the nations and between Ministerial and inspector decisions. References in the table are to the relevant rules unless otherwise indicated. For simplicity, in Ministerial cases applicant includes appellants.

---

[1] SI 2000/1624.
[2] SI 2000/1625.
[3] SI 2003/1266.
[4] SI 2003/1267.
[5] 31 July 2015, in particular, Annex G for Secretary of State recovered appeals and Annex F for transferred appeals determined by an inspector.
[6] July 2015, in particular, Annex E for inquiries generally.

23.3 Inquiries

Stage	England: Secretary of State	England: inspectors	Wales: Welsh Ministers	Wales: inspectors
	Inquiries Rules	Inspectors Inquiries Rules	Welsh Inquiries Rules	Welsh Inspectors Inquiries Rules
Call in	TCPA 1990, s 77		TCPA 1990, s 77	
Notice of call-in given to applicant and parish council	By local planning authority: DMPO 2015, arts 17, 25			
Submission of appeal	DMPO 2015, arts 36, 37	DMPO 2015, arts 36, 37	DMPO Wales, arts 25, 26	DMPO Wales, arts 25, 26
Submission of the appellant's full statement of case	In appeals, with the appeal form: see DMPO 2015, art 37 (but see later requirement)	With the appeal form: see DMPO 2015, art 37		
Decision on mode of determination	Within seven working days from the receipt of the appeal: TCPA 1990, s 319A(3); Town and Country Planning (Determination of Procedure) (Prescribed Period) (England) Regulations 2009, reg 2	Within seven working days from the receipt of the appeal: TCPA 1990, s 319A(3); Town and Country Planning (Determination of Procedure) (Prescribed Period) (England) Regulations 2009, reg 2	Within seven working days from the receipt of the appeal: TCPA 1990, s 319B(3); Town and Country Planning (Determination of Procedure) (Prescribed Period) (Wales) Regulations 2014, reg 2	Within seven working days from the receipt of the appeal: TCPA 1990, s 319B(3); Town and Country Planning (Determination of Procedure) (Prescribed Period) (Wales) Regulations 2014, reg 2
'Starting date' notice of hearing	Sent by Secretary of State as soon as practicable after determination to hold inquiry (if appeal) or after receipt of documents (for call-in/listed building appeal): r 3A	Sent by Secretary of State as soon as practicable after determination to hold inquiry (if appeal) or after receipt of documents (for listed building appeal): r 3A	Sent by Ministers as soon as practicable after receipt of documents (r 3A) or notice of intention to hold inquiry (r 4(A)). Starting date is the later of these two events	Sent by Ministers as soon as practicable after receipt of documents (r 3A) or notice of intention to hold inquiry (r 4(A)). Starting date is the later of these two events

Inquiries **23.3**

Stage	England: Secretary of State	England: inspectors	Wales: Welsh Ministers	Wales: inspectors
Local authority to provide details of statutory parties who made representations	'forthwith' on receipt of the Secretary of State's notice: r 4(1)	'forthwith' on receipt of the Secretary of State's notice: r 4(1)	'forthwith' on receipt of the Ministers' notice: r 4(1)	'forthwith' on receipt of the Ministers' notice: r 4(1)
Minister to inform local authority and appellant of statutory parties who made representations to Minister	As soon as practicable after receiving authority's list: r 4(1)	As soon as practicable after receiving authority's list: r 4(1)	As soon as practicable after receiving authority's list: r 4(1)	As soon as practicable after receiving authority's list: r 4(1)
Local planning authority to inform Ministers and Historic England (if made direction) and DMPO consultees who made representations and they must respond	Forthwith after the starting date: r 4(2), (3)	Forthwith after the starting date: r 4(2), (3)	Forthwith after the starting date (other than Historic England): r 4(2), (3)	Forthwith after the starting date (other than Historic England): r 4(2), (3)
Local authority questionnaire to Minister and appellant	Within two weeks of starting date: r 4(4) Not required in call-in cases: r 4(5)	Within one week of the starting date: r 4(4)	Within two weeks of starting date: r 4(4) Not required in call-in cases: r 4(5)	Within two weeks of the starting date: r 4(4)
Local authority to notify statutory parties and those who made representations of the inquiry	Within two weeks of the starting date: r 4(4). Not required in call-in cases: r 4(5)	Within one week of the starting date: r 4(4)	Within two weeks of the starting date: r 4(4). Not required in call-in cases: r 4(5)	Within two weeks of the starting date: r 4(4)
Minister holding pre-inquiry meeting (discretionary)	Held within 16 weeks of starting date: r 5(6)		Held within 16 weeks of starting date: r 5(6)	

23.3 Inquiries

Stage	England: Secretary of State	England: inspectors	Wales: Welsh Ministers	Wales: inspectors
Outline statement of case	If pre-inquiry meeting called by Secretary of State, by applicant and local planning authority within eight weeks of starting date: r 5(2); other persons, within four weeks of requirement: r 5(5)		If pre-inquiry meeting called by Minister, by applicant and local planning authority within eight weeks of starting date: r 5(2); other persons, within four weeks of requirement: r 5(5)	
Provision of information requested at Ministerial pre-inquiry meeting	Within four weeks of meeting: r 5(10)		Within four weeks of meeting: r 5(10)	
Local planning authority's statement of case	Within six weeks of the starting date or four weeks of conclusion of Ministerial pre-inquiry meeting: r 6(1)	Full statement of case within five weeks of the starting date: r 6(1)	Within six weeks of the starting date or four weeks of conclusion of Ministerial pre-inquiry meeting: r 6(1)	Within six weeks of the starting date: r 6(1)
Applicant produces statement of case	Within six weeks of the starting date or four weeks of conclusion of Ministerial pre-inquiry meeting: r 6(3)	With appeal form (see above)	Within six weeks of the starting date or four weeks of conclusion of Ministerial pre-inquiry meeting: r 6(3)	Within six weeks of the starting date: r 6(3)
Appellant provides full statement of case to statutory parties		As soon as practicable after receiving details of the statutory parties: r 6(3)		
Statements of case circulated by PINS	As soon as practicable after receipt: r 6(4)	As soon as practicable after receipt: r 6(4)	As soon as practicable after receipt: r 6(4)	As soon as practicable after receipt: r 6(4)
Third party representations	Informally requested within six weeks of the starting date	Informally requested within five weeks of the starting date	Informally requested within six weeks of the starting date	Informally requested within six weeks of the starting date

Inquiries 23.3

Stage	England: Secretary of State	England: inspectors	Wales: Welsh Ministers	Wales: inspectors
'Rule 6' parties to provide statements of case	Within four weeks of requirement: r 6(6)	Full statement of case within four weeks of requirement: r 6(6)	Within four weeks of requirement: r 6(6)	Within four weeks of requirement: r 6(6)
Minister or inspector requiring further information about statement of case	r 6(8)	rr 6(8), 13	r 6(8)	r 6(8)
Comments by local planning authority and applicant on each other's statement of case			Within nine weeks of the starting date or seven weeks of the pre-inquiry meeting: r 6(14)	Within nine weeks of the starting date or seven weeks of the pre-inquiry meeting: r 6(14)
Comments by rule 6 parties on any other statements of case			At least four weeks before the inquiry: r 6(15)	Within nine weeks of the starting date: r 6(15)
Inspector's statement of matters		Optional, but within ten weeks of the starting date: r 7(1)		Optional, but within 12 weeks of the starting date: r 7(1)
Inspector may hold pre-inquiry meeting	Power if not called by the Minister: r 7(1). Two weeks' notice required: r 7(2)	Rule 7(1). Two weeks' notice required: r 7(2)	Power if not called by the Minister: r 7(1). Two weeks' notice required: r 7(2)	Rule 7(2). Two weeks' notice required: r 7(3)
Timetable prepared by inspector	Required if r 5 pre-inquiry meeting or eight-day inquiry: r 8(1)	Required if eight-day inquiry: r 8(1)	Required if r 5 pre-inquiry meeting or eight-day inquiry: r 8(1)	Required if r 5 pre-inquiry meeting or eight-day inquiry: r 8(1)
Provision of information requested at inspector's pre-inquiry meeting		Within 4 weeks of meeting: rule 7(5)		Within four weeks of meeting: rule 7(5)

23.3 Inquiries

Stage	England: Secretary of State	England: inspectors	Wales: Welsh Ministers	Wales: inspectors
Statement of common ground	To be agreed within six weeks of the starting date: r 14	To be agreed within five weeks of the starting date: r 15(1)	To be agreed not less than four weeks before the inquiry: r 14(1)	To be agreed not less than four weeks before the inquiry: r 15(1)
Notice of appointment of assessor	Rule 9	Rule 9	Rule 9	Rule 9
Production of proofs of evidence and summaries	Four weeks before the inquiry or any date in the bespoke timetable: r 13(3)	Four weeks before the inquiry or any date in the bespoke timetable: r 14(3)	Statements of evidence four weeks before the inquiry or any date in the bespoke timetable: r 13(3)	Four weeks before the inquiry or any date in the bespoke timetable: r 14(3)
Notice of the inquiry by Inspectorate	At least four weeks' notice unless agreed with applicant and local planning authority: r 10(3)	At least four weeks' notice unless agreed with appellant and local planning authority: rule 10(2)	At least four weeks' notice unless agreed with applicant and local planning authority: r 10(3)	At least four weeks' notice unless agreed with applicant and local planning authority: r 10(2)
Requests for government department to attend	At least four weeks before the inquiry: r 12	At least four weeks before the inquiry: r 12	At least four weeks before the inquiry: r 12	At least four weeks before the inquiry: r 12
Publicity of the inquiry on Minister's requirements	Rule 10(6), (7)	Rule 10(5), (6)	Rule 10(6), (7)	Rule 10(5), (6)
Submission of draft planning obligations (guidance only)				
Inquiry	Not later than 22 weeks after the starting date or eight weeks after r 5 pre-inquiry meeting unless impracticable: r 10(1)	Not later than 16 weeks after the starting date unless impracticable: r 10(1)	Not later than 22 weeks after the starting date or eight weeks after r 5 pre-inquiry meeting unless impracticable: r 10(1)	Not later than 20 weeks after the starting date unless impracticable: r 10(1)
Procedure	Inquiry procedure: r 15; site inspections, r 16	Inquiry procedure: r 16; site inspections, r 17	Inquiry procedure: r 15; site inspections, r 16	Inquiry procedure: r 16; site inspections, r 17

Stage	England: Secretary of State	England: inspectors	Wales: Welsh Ministers	Wales: inspectors
Post-inquiry steps/report to the Minister	Rule 17	Post-inquiry steps: r 18	Rule 17	Post-inquiry steps: r 18
Decision	Rule 18	Rule 19	Rule 18	Rule 19
Post-decision publicity	In EIA cases: EIA Regulations 2011, reg 24	In EIA cases: EIA Regulations 2011, reg 24	In EIA cases: EIA Regulations 1999, reg 21	In EIA cases: EIA Regulations 1999, reg 21

THE START OF THE PROCESS

23.4 The process leading to an inquiry will begin either with the decision of the Minister to call in the planning application or the submission of an appeal. In England and Wales the Minister (albeit usually the Planning Inspectorate) will then decide whether to hold an inquiry. If it is an appeal case, then a decision might be taken around the same time whether the Minister will recover jurisdiction. Decisions to recover appeals are taken personally by Ministers. However, recovery may take place at any point prior to the issue of the appeal decision.

23.5 A called-in application or recovered appeal is subject to the Inquiries Rules in the relevant nation, whilst the Inspectors Rules apply to transferred appeals. Differences between Ministerial and inspector cases are the timescales for statements of case (in England), the Minister's ability to call a pre-inquiry meeting, target dates for the inquiry, the need for the inspector to write a report to the Minister and the post-inquiry process.

All the timetables, however, begin with the starting date. This varies slightly between the four sets of rules and between appeals and call-ins.

23.6 In English Ministerial cases the starting date is the date that the Secretary of State gives notice that a s 78 planning appeal is to be dealt with by inquiry or sufficient documents have been received by the Minister to enable the call-in or listed building consent appeal to proceed, see r 3A[7].

23.7 Similarly, in English inspector cases the starting date is the date that the Secretary of State gives notice that a s 78 planning appeal is to be dealt with by inquiry or sufficient documents have been received by the Minister to enable the listed building consent appeal to proceed[8].

23.8 For Welsh Ministerial cases the starting date is the date that they give notice that they have sufficient documents to determine the appeal or call-in, or they give notice that the appeal is to be determined by inquiry, whichever is the later[9].

---

[7] English Inquiries Rules, rr 2(1), 3A.
[8] English Inspectors Inquiries Rules, rr 2(1), 3A.
[9] Welsh Inquiries Rules, rr 2(1), 3A, 4(A).

23.9 *Inquiries*

23.9 Again, in Welsh inspector cases, the starting date is the date that the Welsh Ministers give notice that they have sufficient documents to determine the appeal or notice that the appeal is to be determined by inquiry, whichever is the later[10].

TIMETABLING

23.10 The timescales in the relevant rules apply subject to any permitted alterations. Ministers – in practice the Planning Inspectorate – have the power to extend the time for any step to be taken, including the submission of statements of case and evidence[11]. It is also possible for the inquiry inspector to set a timetable for the submission of proofs and for the conduct of the inquiry itself[12]. The Inspectorate's practice in England is to arrange a bespoke programme for inquiries which are expected to sit for three or more days[13]. In those cases the main parties are encouraged to prepare a draft timetable including two possible hearing dates before the submission of the appeal[14]. Bespoke programmes may not always keep within the statutory deadlines for holding inquiries, but need to justify being much later[15]. A bespoke programme will ultimately be set by the Inspectorate, following consultation. Often the effect of a bespoke timetable is to give further time for statements of case and include provision for rebuttal proofs. The timescales discussed below have to be considered in the light of any timetable or programme which has been established.

Initial publicity of the appeal or call in inquiry

23.11 On being notified that an inquiry will be held, the local planning authority must inform the Minister and the applicant of the name and address of any statutory party[16] who has made representations to them; and the Inspectorate shall, as soon as practicable thereafter, inform the applicant and the local planning authority in writing of the name and address of any statutory party who has made representations to it[17]. The authority shall also give notice of the appeal to any Minister, government department, county or district council, enterprise zone authority, the Broads Authority or housing action trust for the application site who advised that there should be a refusal or approval subject to conditions, and any consultee under the DMPO who made representations on the application[18].

23.12 In appeal cases the local planning authority will complete the appeal questionnaire and send it to the Minister and the appellant, along with copies of the documents referred to in it. They must also notify any statutory party or person who made representations on the application of the appeal. In England this must be done within one week of the starting date in inspector appeals, whilst two weeks are

---

[10] Welsh Inspectors Inquiries Rules, rr 2(1), 3A, 4(A).
[11] English and Welsh Inquiries Rules, r 20; English and Welsh Inspectors Inquiries Rules, r 21.
[12] English and Welsh Inquiries Rules, r 8; English and Welsh Inspectors Inquiries Rules, r 8.
[13] *Procedural Guidance: Planning appeals - England*, para 2.1.4 and Annex H. On possible hearing dates see Annex S.
[14] There needs to be a sufficient steer by the Inspectorate as to the range of dates that might be realistic.
[15] *Procedural Guidance: Planning appeals - England*, para H.2.7.
[16] A freeholder or leaseholder with more than seven years remaining, in minerals cases a person interested in a mineral in the land, other than oil, gas, coal, gold or silver or an agricultural tenant.
[17] English and Welsh Inquiries Rules, r 4(1); English and Welsh Inspectors Inquiries Rules, r 4(1).
[18] English and Welsh Inquiries Rules, r 4(2), (3); English and Welsh Inspectors Inquiries Rules, r 4(2), (3).

allowed for appeals decided by Ministers and all inquiries in Wales[19]. These duties of notification and provision of an appeal statement do not apply in call-in cases[20].

Ministerial cases – pre-inquiry meetings and outline statements of case

23.13 Where the inquiry arises from a call-in or is a recovered appeal the Minister is able to call a pre-inquiry meeting at a relatively early stage. The provision is expressed as a duty to hold a pre-inquiry meeting if he expects the inquiry to last eight days or more, unless he considers it unnecessary and a power to hold such a meeting for shorter inquiries if it appears to be necessary to do so[21]. In practice this amounts to a discretion to hold a pre-inquiry meeting if the Minister thinks it is required.

23.14 An early pre-inquiry meeting of this nature is useful for very major inquiries where there is a need to establish who will be the major participants, what are the major issues and the arrangements for a lengthy inquiry.

23.15 In Wales notice of the intention to hold a pre-inquiry meeting is expected to be sent to the local planning authority with the 'relevant notice' that an inquiry is to be held[22]. The English provisions also require notice of this intention to be given with the 'relevant notice' but that term was otherwise revoked in the English Inquiries Rules in 2009[23]. It appears that it should be a reference to the notice given under r 3A. Accompanying this notice will be a statement of matters that the Minister particularly wishes to be informed of about the application or appeal, along with any statement by a Minister or government department that the application should not be granted or that it should only be approved subject to conditions[24]. The notice at this stage is of the intention to hold a pre-inquiry meeting, not necessarily of the date, time and venue of the meeting.

The local planning authority shall place a local newspaper advertisement containing the notice of the intention to hold a pre-inquiry meeting and the Minister's statement of matters[25].

23.16 Where a Ministerial pre-inquiry meeting is to be held, outline statements of case must be provided by the local planning authority and the applicant/appellant within eight weeks of the starting date[26]. The Minister may require any other person who has given notice to them of an intention or wish to take part in the inquiry to send an outline statement of case to the Minister, the local planning authority and the applicant within four weeks of the Minister's request.

---

[19] English and Welsh Inquiries Rules, r 4(4); English and Welsh Inspectors Inquiries Rules, r 4(4).
[20] English and Welsh Inquiries Rules, r 4(5).
[21] English and Welsh Inquiries Rules, r 5(1).
[22] Welsh Inquiries Rules, r 5(2). Relevant notice means the notice of the intention to hold an inquiry: r 2(1).
[23] Town and Country Planning (Hearings and Inquiries Procedures) (England) (Amendment) Rules 2009, SI 2009/455, r 4.
[24] English and Welsh Inquiries Rules, r 5(2)(a)(ii). Any such statement will be copied to the Minister or department concerned.
[25] English and Welsh Inquiries Rules, r 5(2)(c).
[26] English and Welsh Inquiries Rules, r 5(2)(d). If sent as hard copies, two copies should be provided so that one can be passed on to the other main party: see r 5(2)(d), (3).

23.17 *Inquiries*

23.17 An outline statement of case is 'a written statement of the principal submissions which a person proposes to put forward at an inquiry'[27]. It is therefore a relatively short pleading of the case, rather than a document which contains evidence.

23.18 The pre-inquiry meeting itself must be held within 16 weeks of the starting date. At least three weeks' written notice of the meeting, that is, the where and when, must be given to the applicant, the local planning authority, any person known to be entitled to appear at the inquiry[28] and any other person whose presence appears to the Minister to be desirable. This last category covers anyone who appears likely to wish to appear at the inquiry. The local planning authority may be required to publicise the pre-inquiry meeting by local newspaper advertisement, notice to particular persons or classes of persons or by the display of a site notice[29].

The inspector who is appointed to conduct the inquiry will preside.

Statements of case in inquiries

23.19 A Welsh statement of case must comprise the 'full particulars of the case' which the party intends to put forward and a list of the documents which it intends to refer to or to put in evidence[30]. The same requirements apply to statements of case in English Secretary of State cases[31] but in English appeals (including recovered appeals) more detailed full statements of case will already have been filed.

Appellant's statement of case

23.20 In English planning appeals a full statement of case will have been submitted by the appellant with the appeal form[32]. Of course, at the equivalent start of a call-in process there will be no statement of case. In English and Welsh Ministerial cases the appellant's statement of case has to be submitted within six weeks of the starting date or if a pre-inquiry meeting is called by a Minister then within four weeks of its conclusion[33]. This allows an English appellant to submit a further statement of case as well as a called-in applicant to do so for the first time. In Welsh Inspector cases the appellant's statement of case must be submitted within six weeks of the starting date[34].

23.21 In Welsh cases the appellant must submit its statement of case within six weeks of the starting date or, if the Minister calls a pre-inquiry meeting in a Ministerial case, within four weeks of the conclusion of that meeting[35].

---

[27] English and Welsh Inquiries Rules, r 2(1).
[28] For persons entitled to appear see English and Welsh Inquiries Rules, r 11(1), discussed below.
[29] English and Welsh Inquiries Rules, r 5(7).
[30] Welsh Inquiries Rules, r 2(1); Welsh Inspectors Inquiries Rules, r 2(1). Guidance is given in *Procedural Guidance Planning appeals and called-in planning applications – Wales* para E.9.3.
[31] English Inquiries Rules, r 2(1).
[32] DMPO 2015, art 37(3)(b)(viii). Advice on the content of a full statement of case is given in *Procedural Guide Planning appeals – England* (31 July 2015), Appendix J, with a suggestion that their length should not normally exceed 3,000 words: para J.2.4.
[33] English Inquiries Rules, r 6(3).
[34] Welsh Inspectors Rules, r 6(3).
[35] Welsh Inquiries Rules, r 6(3); Welsh Inspectors Inquiries Rules, r 6(3).

Local planning authority's statement of case

23.22 Local planning authorities are required to file their statements of case[36]:

(i) within six weeks of the starting date, except that for English appeals determined by inspectors this period is reduced to five weeks; except that

(ii) if the Minister (but not the inspector) calls a pre-inquiry meeting, within four weeks of the close of the meeting.

Mayor of London

23.23 If the Mayor of London had taken over the planning application as the local planning authority then he has that status in any appeal or call-in. If the Mayor directed the London borough to refuse permission then the rules are modified to give him the same status as the applicant/appellant and the local planning authority. In particular, the Mayor has the same responsibilities to prepare outline statements of case, statements of case and proofs of evidence as those two parties[37].

Third parties and rule 6 status

23.24 A third party who intends to play a very active role in the inquiry, including cross-examining witnesses, ought to seek what is informally referred to as rule 6 status. This requires them to serve a statement of case (for planning appeals this is under rule 6 of the Inquiries Rules, hence the name) within four weeks of being required to do so and produce proofs of evidence to the same timescale as the main parties. They are then entitled to appear and, more importantly, are seen as having a more formal role in the proceedings.

23.25 A person can only become a r 6 party with the Minister's agreement, so merely volunteering a statement of case will not be enough. In some cases the Minister will impose r 6 status on a party, usually if they appear to be preparing a substantial case which the parties and Inspectorate need to know about in advance. Consequently the Minister may require any other person who has informed him of an intention to appear at the inquiry to serve a statement of case within four weeks on him and any person specified by the Minister[38].

The Minister or an inspector may require that third party to provide further information and copy it to the persons served with the statement of case[39].

---

[36] English and Welsh Inquiries Rules, r 6(1); English and Welsh Inspectors Inquiries Rules, r 6(1)
[37] English Inquiries Rules, r 23; English Inspectors Inquiries Rules, r 24.
[38] English and Welsh Inquiries Rules, r 6(6), English and Welsh Inspectors Inquiries Rules, r 6(6). If provided in hard copy, three copies should be sent to the Planning Inspectorate to allow copies to be sent to the appellant and local planning authority and the person providing the statement of case must also send copies to any other statutory party: also r 6(6). In the English Inspectors Inquiries Rules the statement of case is a 'full statement of case'.
[39] English and Welsh Inquiries Rules, r 6(8), (10), English and Welsh Inspectors Inquiries Rules, r 6(8), (10).

23.26 *Inquiries*

Copies of statements of case and referenced documents

23.26 Two copies should be sent by the appellant and the local planning authority to the Secretary of State (unless transmitted electronically) and one copy to all of the statutory parties (owners, long leaseholders and agricultural tenants notified of the application)[40]. If not using electronic means, r 6 parties have to send three hard copies to the Inspectorate and one to each statutory party[41]. Copies of the listed documents do not have to be submitted in Welsh cases or English call-ins and recovered appeals, albeit that the appellant and local planning authority may require the other, in writing, to provide documents they refer to[42]. The introduction of 'full statements of case' in 2013 in England means that the appellant's notice of appeal should be accompanied by those documents[43] and the documents must be sent with the statements of case submitted by the local planning authority or r 6 parties in inspectors' cases[44].

Further information

23.27 The Minister may require any person who has served a statement of case to provide further information about the matters in the statement and should (but is not obliged to) specify a period for doing so[45]. This is primarily a mechanism for seeking clarification about a party's case and the request will often be initiated by another party. A party who does not understand what case the opposition are going to advance should first try to clarify it in correspondence and if that fails, might ask the Minister to make a request.

Pre-inquiry meetings called by inspectors

23.28 A pre-inquiry meeting is a procedural meeting intended to enable the inspector to explain how the inquiry will run, obtain information from the parties to assist with programming and to allow the parties to raise procedural issues. Pre-inquiry meetings are only held for long inquiries.

23.29 For call-ins or the appeals to be determined by the Minister, the Minister shall hold a pre-inquiry meeting if the inquiry is expected to last for eight days or more (unless the meeting is considered unnecessary) and for any shorter inquiry where a meeting is considered necessary.[46] In inspector-determined appeals, the inspector is subject to the similar duties to consider calling a pre-inquiry meeting[47]. In a Ministerial decision case, if the Minister has not called a pre-inquiry meeting, the inspector may do so[48].

---

[40] English and Welsh Inquiries Rules, r 6(1), (3); English and Welsh Inspectors Inquiries Rules, r 6(1), (3).
[41] English and Welsh Inquiries Rules, r 6(6); English and Welsh Inspectors Inquiries Rules, r 6(6).
[42] English and Welsh Inquiries Rules, r 6(5); Welsh Inspectors Inquiries Rules, r 6(5).
[43] DMPO 2015, art 37(8).
[44] See the definition in English Inspectors Inquiries Rules, r 2(1).
[45] English and Welsh Inquiries Rules, r 6(8); English and Welsh Inspectors Inquiries Rules, r 6(8).
[46] English and Welsh Inquiries Rules, r 5(1). As formulated, the rules mean that a pre-inquiry meeting is held if the Minister thinks it is necessary, but subject to a presumption for calling one for longer inquiries.
[47] English and Welsh Inspectors Inquiries Rules, r 7(2).
[48] English and Welsh Inquiries Rules, r 7(1).

Timetabling **23.35**

23.30 If the Minister calls a pre-inquiry meeting, the applicant/appellant and local planning authority must produce an outline statement within eight weeks of the starting date[49]. The Minister may also require any other person who intends to take part in the appeal to produce an outline statement with four weeks of any request[50]. In Ministerial cases, the Minister will give not less than three weeks' notice and the authority will then advertise it[51]. Where an inspector calls a pre-inquiry meeting, the Planning Inspectorate will give not less than two weeks' notice to the applicant/appellant, the local planning authority, any person entitled to appear and any other person whose attendance at the pre-inquiry meeting appears desirable[52]. Unlike Ministerial pre-inquiry meetings, there is no requirement for local advertisement of the event.

23.31 The inspector will preside at any pre-inquiry meeting and will decide the matters to be discussed and the procedure[53]. An agenda may be circulated by the inspector in advance, and if not, is likely to be available at the meeting[54].

23.32 Pre-inquiry meetings should resolve the order in which evidence is to be heard, which parties make opening statements and the detail of document numbering and arrangement. Venue arrangements should be clarified where possible (finding the venue being the responsibility of the local planning authority). The main parties should be able to indicate the number of witnesses they will have and the topics they will cover. For programming purposes, the inspector may ask how long the parties will take to call their witnesses in chief. However, the critical programming matter is how long cross-examination will take, and that is difficult to judge until the evidence has been seen.

23.33 It is also an opportunity for the parties to raise any procedural points. These tend to be requests for clarification of statements of case or attempts to obtain documents. If a party wishes to raise a particular issue at the pre-inquiry meeting it might want to write to the inspector about it beforehand.

23.34 Conventionally the inspector will subsequently circulate a note of the meeting. This is important to set out the procedural expectations which the inspector has, any rulings and to inform those who were not present of how the inquiry will be conducted.

23.35 Neither the inspector nor the Secretary of State are able to set aside requirements of the Rules at a pre-inquiry meeting or otherwise, although they are able to relax the timescales in them, by agreeing to accept proofs of evidence and other material after the deadlines in the Rules. It was unlawful for an inspector at a call-in inquiry into redevelopment at the Shell Centre in London to dispense with the requirements on the main parties to provide statements of case and summaries of their proofs of evidence[55].

---

[49] English and Welsh Inquiries Rules, r 5(2)(d).
[50] English and Welsh Inquiries Rules, r 5(5).
[51] English and Welsh Inquiries Rules, r 5(2)(a), (c), (7).
[52] English and Welsh Inquiries Rules, r 7(2); English and Welsh Inspectors Inquiries Rules, r 7(3).
[53] English and Welsh Inquiries Rules, rr 5(8), 7(3); English and Welsh Inspectors Inquiries Rules, r 7(4). The inspector also has the management powers to require any person present who is acting in a disruptive manner to leave and may refuse to permit them to return to attend any further pre-inquiry meeting or may set conditions for doing so.
[54] Good practice is to put copies of the agenda alongside an attendance list for signing in at the entrance to the meeting room.
[55] *Turner v Secretary of State for Communities and Local Government* [2015] EWHC 375 (Admin) at paras 46–51 per Collins J.

23.36 *Inquiries*

Statement of matters

23.36 If the appeal is being determined by the minister then he must send a statement of the matters about which he particularly wishes to be informed in considering the appeal either with notice of any pre-inquiry meeting he calls or within 12 weeks of the starting date[56]. An inspector may produce a statement of matters in a delegated inquiry case[57].

Timetable

23.37 If an inquiry is expected to last for eight days or more or the Minister has called a pre-inquiry meeting, the inspector is required to prepare a timetable for the proceedings[58]. A timetable can be prepared for shorter inquiries[59] and the timetable may be changed at any time[60]. This timetable may alter the dates for sending proofs and statements of evidence[61].

23.38 The timetable for the hearing does not set absolute deadlines for particular stages, but the inspector would wish to try to keep to the schedule. It may be particularly useful for parties who do not intend to attend throughout the hearing, so they know when they will be involved.

PERSONS ENTITLED TO APPEAR AT THE INQUIRY OR HEARING

23.39 In England, the following persons are entitled to appear as of right at the inquiry[62]:

(a) the appellant/applicant;

(b) the local planning authority[63];

(c) the following if the site is in their area:

    (i) a county or a district council;

    (ii) an enterprise zone authority;

    (iii) the Broads Authority;

    (iv) a housing action trust;

(d) if in an area previously designated as a new town, the Homes and Communities Agency;

---

[56] English and Welsh Inquiries Rules, rr 5(2)(a)(ii), 6(12).
[57] English and Welsh Inspectors Inquiries Rules, r 7(1). In England the inspector may do this within 10 weeks of the starting date and in Wales within 12 weeks of that date.
[58] English and Welsh Inquiries Rules, r 8(1); English and Welsh Inspectors Inquiries Rules, r 8(1).
[59] English and Welsh Inquiries Rules, r 8(2); English and Welsh Inspectors Inquiries Rules, r 8(2).
[60] English and Welsh Inquiries Rules, r 8(3); English and Welsh Inspectors Inquiries Rules, r 8(3).
[61] English and Welsh Inquiries Rules, r 13(3); English and Welsh Inspectors Inquiries Rules, r 14(3).
[62] English Inquiries Rules, r 11(1); English Inspectors Inquires Rules, r 11(1). Historic England are also entitled to appear in listed building consent appeals where they have been notified of the application under the Planning (Listed Buildings and Conservation Areas) Act 1990, s 14.
[63] The local planning authority might be a national park authority or an urban development corporation.

Persons entitled to appear at the inquiry or hearing **23.44**

(e) any statutory party, which is a freeholder or leaseholder with more than seven years remaining, in minerals cases a person interested in a mineral in the land, other than oil, gas, coal, gold or silver or an agricultural tenant[64];

(f) any parish council for the application site which made representations on the application

(g) any other person who has served a statement of case or outline statement having been required to do so by the Secretary of State in accordance with the rules.

23.40 The Welsh inquiry provisions are the same except for the geographical differences that county and country borough councils are entitled to appear, there are community rather than parish councils in Wales and the Broads Authority is in Norfolk[65]. The Welsh legislation still refers to the Commission for the New Towns as having a right to appear for areas previously designated as a new town, but it has been abolished and its functions transferred to the Welsh Ministers.

23.41 The right to appear is given to certain locally-based public authorities concerned with land use. Government departments and agencies, such as the Department for the Environment, Food and Rural Affairs or the Environment Agency, are not entitled to appear as of right. It would, though, be remarkable for such bodies not to be allowed to play a full role, subject to preparing outline statements, statement of case and proofs as required under the rules. The Mayor of London may have directed that he be the local planning authority and so has that status for the appeal, but is also entitled to appear as a statutory party if he was notified of the application under the Town and Country Planning (Mayor of London) Order 2008[66].

23.42 Neighbourhood fora, tasked with neighbourhood planning outside areas within parish councils, are not entitled to appear but ought normally to be allowed to do so. If they wish to do more than read out a statement they might wish to seek r 6 status.

23.43 The inspector may permit any other person, including government departments, to appear at the inquiry or hearing 'and such permission shall not be unreasonably withheld'[67]. In practice, inspectors will permit anyone with something to say that appears relevant to speak. The inspector will normally ask at the start of the inquiry who wishes to speak. If other persons indicate during the inquiry that they wish to speak they will normally be heard, but all third parties must speak before the appellant's closing submissions.

Representatives of government departments at the inquiry

23.44 Usually if a public body intends to take an active role critical of a scheme at inquiry it will make its own representations, often becoming a r 6 party and attending. The local planning authority may also call witnesses from other public authorities in support of its case. However provision is made in the rules to deal with the possibility that an authority will make a decisive intervention without wishing to attend the

---

[64] English Inquiries Rules, r 2(1); English Inspectors Inquiries Rules, r 2(1) both applying what is now DMPO 2015, art 13(1) and Sch 2.
[65] Welsh Inquiries Rules, r 11(1); Welsh Inspectors Inquiries Rules, r 11(1).
[66] SI 2008/580. English Inquiries Rules, r 23(3); English Inspectors Inquiries Rules 2000, r 24(3).
[67] English and Welsh Inquiries Rules, r 11(2); English and Welsh Inspectors Inquiries Rules, r 11(2).

23.45 *Inquiries*

inquiry. The appellant is able to require attendance so that the body's stance can be challenged.

23.45 The appellant may require a representative of a Minister of the Crown or other authority to attend the inquiry and give evidence if[68]:

(i) the Minister (or, in listed building consent cases, Historic England) has directed that the permission or consent should not be granted; or

(ii) a Minister, department or a county or district council, enterprise zone authority, the Broads Authority or housing action trust whose area includes the application site has expressed a view on the application or appeal in writing to the local planning authority that permission should not be granted or should be granted subject to conditions and the local planning authority refers to that view in its statement of case; or

(iii) another Minister has said that permission should be refused or granted subject to conditions and that has been referred to in the Secretary of State's or Welsh Ministers' list of matters.

23.46 For example, the Department for the Environment, Food and Rural Affairs may have expressed concern about the effects of the development on best and most versatile agricultural land. The attendance must be requested in writing to the Secretary of State who is determining the appeal at least four weeks before the date of the inquiry[69]. The Secretary of State will then provide a representative or pass the request to the Minister or department concerned who will provide the representative[70]. Similar provisions apply in Wales, where the request is made to the Welsh Ministers and a representative of the Welsh Ministers or the UK Minister or government department would be required to attend[71].

The representative shall give the reasons for the expressed view and is subject to cross-examination in the usual way[72].

23.47 This provision is rarely invoked. If a government department has supported the authority's decision on an important issue then it is likely to appear with its own advocate and witnesses or provide one or more witnesses for the local planning authority.

DATE OF THE INQUIRY

23.48 Various deadlines are set in the rules for the start of an inquiry, subject to whether the dates are impracticable. In a ministerial case in England or Wales the inquiry will be held not later than 22 weeks after the starting date or eight weeks after the conclusion of the pre-inquiry meeting unless the Minister considers that that would be impractical, in which case it will be held at the earliest practical date[73]. In practice the appellant and local planning authority are offered a date, with each party

---

[68] English and Welsh Inquiries Rules, r 12(1); English and Welsh Inspectors Inquiries Rules, r 12(1).
[69] English and Welsh Inquiries Rules, r 12(1); English and Welsh Inspectors Inquiries Rules, r 12(1).
[70] English Inquiries Rules, r 12(2); English Inspectors Inquiries Rules, r 12(2).
[71] Welsh Inquiries Rules, r 12; Welsh Inspectors Inquiries Rules, r 12.
[72] English and Welsh Inquiries Rules, r 12(3); English and Welsh Inspectors Inquiries Rules, r 12(3).
[73] English and Welsh Inquiries Rules, r 10(1), (2).

Date of the inquiry **23.53**

being entitled to one refusal. If the appeal is being determined by an inspector, the inquiry should be held within 16 weeks of the starting date in England or within 20 weeks in Wales, or the earliest practical date if later[74].

The Minister can vary the date, time or place of the inquiry[75].

23.49 A decision on the date of an inquiry is amenable to judicial review, but such an application would be exceptional[76]. There would need to be some very strong basis for considering it would be unfair to proceed on the proposed date.

Notification of the inquiry or hearing date

23.50 Notice of the making of the appeal and the arrangements for any pre-inquiry meetings have been discussed earlier in this chapter.

Parties and the public at large also need to know when and where the hearing or inquiry will take place.

23.51 Unless a lesser period of notice has been agreed with the appellant/applicant and the local planning authority, the Planning Inspectorate shall give not less than four weeks' written notice of the date, time and place of the inquiry or hearing to every person entitled to appear[77]. Similar notice, unless otherwise agreed, must be given if the date of the inquiry is varied[78]. The Inspectorate and the parties entitled to take part in the appeal may agree to notice being given via a website[79].

If the time or place of the inquiry is varied, the Minister must give reasonable notice[80].

23.52 The Minister may require the local planning authority to do any of the following in inquiry cases[81]:

'(a) not less than 2 weeks before the date fixed for the inquiry, to publish a notice of the inquiry in one or more newspapers circulating in the locality in which the land is situated;

(b) to send a notice of the inquiry on such persons or classes of persons as he may specify, within such period as he may specify;

(c) to post a notice of the inquiry in a conspicuous place near to the land, within such period as he may specify'.

23.53 Where the subject land is under the appellant's/applicant's control, the Minister may require him to fix a notice of the inquiry 'firmly' to the land or an object on or near the land. The notice must be readily visible to, and legible by, the public. The appellant must not remove it, or cause or permit it to be removed, for such period before the inquiry as the Minister may specify[82].

---

[74] English and Welsh Inspectors Inquiries Rules, r 10(1).
[75] English and Welsh Inquiries Rules, r 10(4), (5); English and Welsh Inspectors Inquiries Rules, r 10(4).
[76] *R v Secretary of State for the Environment, ex p Leeds City Council* [1995] JPL B61.
[77] English and Welsh Inquiries Rules, r 10(3); English and Welsh Inspectors Inquiries Rules, r 10(2).
[78] English and Welsh Inquiries Rules, r 10(4); English and Welsh Inspectors Inquiries Rules, r 10(3).
[79] English and Welsh Inquiries Rules, r 10(3A); English and Welsh Inspectors Inquiries Rules, r 10(2A).
[80] English and Welsh Inquiries Rules, r 10(5); English and Welsh Inspectors Inquiries Rules, r 10(4).
[81] English and Welsh Inquiries Rules, r 10(6); English and Welsh Inspectors Inquiries Rules, r 10(5).
[82] English and Welsh Inquiries Rules, r 10(7), English and Welsh Inspectors Inquiries Rules, r 10(6).

23.54 *Inquiries*

23.54 Any notices of the inquiry shall contain[83]:

'(a) a clear statement of the date, time and place of the inquiry and of the powers enabling the [Minister or inspector] to determine the appeal in question;

(b) a written description of the land sufficient to identify approximately its location;

(c) a brief description of the subject matter of the appeal;

(d) details of where and when copies of the local planning authority's completed questionnaire and any document sent by and copied to the authority pursuant to rule 6 may be inspected'.

23.55 It is a matter for ministerial discretion as to whether the authority and appellant have to give notice. Consequently these parties should be alert for any direction being given and ensure that it is complied with. At the start of the hearing or inquiry the inspector will usually ask the local planning authority's advocate or representative if the notice requirements have been complied with. In response the authority should have a copy of any direction and certification of notices and advertisements available for the inspector. If it appears that notice has not been given correctly and there may be people who would have wished to take part or simply attend but who are not present or are unable to play a proper role because of the error, then it is likely that the hearing will be adjourned.

23.56 If such a notification error is not corrected then the appeal decision is likely to be quashed if substantial prejudice arises[84]. However, a failure to provide additional notice, even if it was intended to do so, will probably not justify the quashing of the decision[85]. Where there has been a representation that notice will be given (whether by the Planning Inspectorate or the local planning authority) then failure to give such notice would be a breach of a legitimate expectation[86].

23.57 The Planning Inspectorate will notify those entitled to appear of the name of the inspector and any assessor and the matters on which the assessor is to advise the inspector[87]. If a replacement inspector is appointed, the Planning Inspectorate will, if practicable, notify this before the inquiry begins. The inspector will, in any event, give his name at the start of the inquiry.

It is useful to know what the inspector's professional background is (such as planner, architect, engineer or solicitor) and the inspector's previous decisions can be examined.

ADVOCATES AND WITNESSES

23.58 The roles of advocates and witnesses are distinctly different. The responsibility of a witness is to give relevant evidence. That evidence should be truthful. Witness evidence is of two types: evidence of fact and expert evidence. Evidence of fact is evidence of what happened or what the position is or, sometimes,

---

[83] English and Welsh Inquiries Rules, r 10(8), English and Welsh Inspectors Inquiries Rules, r 10(7).
[84] *R v London Borough of Lambeth Council, ex p Sharp* (1986) 55 P & CR 232, CA.
[85] *R v Secretary of State for the Environment, ex p Kent* [1988] 3 PLR 17.
[86] *R (on the application of Majed) v London Borough of Camden* [2009] EWCA Civ 1029, [2010] JPL 621; *R (on the application of Vieira) v London Borough of Camden* [2012] EWHC 287 (Admin).
[87] English and Welsh Inquiries Rules, rr 5, 9, English and Welsh Inspectors Inquiries Rules, rr 5, 9.

what a party intends to do. Expert evidence is the professional view of an expert on a matter within their professional expertise. For example, a highways consultant in an appeal might give evidence of the acceptability of an access to a site. The consultant's evidence should be the consultant's own opinion, rather than running whatever argument is best for his client. Hopefully if the client is listening to his experts, conflict does not arise.

23.59 In planning appeals, views on the merits of the scheme are likely to be presented by individuals without professional expertise. Those views can be given as evidence and in inquiries can be tested in cross-examination. They will often be right. An intelligent layperson is quite capable of exposing flaws in expert evidence and it is a mistake, made sometimes but too often, to assume that local residents cannot contribute on technical matters.

23.60 The role of the advocate is quite different from that of a witness. An advocate's task is to put his client's case as effectively as it can be put. An advocate is not giving evidence or expressing their own opinion, even on matters within their expertise, such as the law.

23.61 The advocate's conduct of the case is constrained by professional rules. An advocate may not say something which they know to be untrue or to mislead the tribunal, they must not put an argument which is so poor as to be unarguable and should ensure that the tribunal is aware of any case which contradicts their submissions. Whilst promoting their client's interests, advocates should contribute to the effective management of the case. Questioning of witnesses can be robust but is most effective if put politely, and advocates should not raise irrelevant matters or subject a witness to ridicule or abuse. They should avoid criticising third parties who are not before the tribunal where possible and should only criticise a witness if they have taken the opportunity to put that criticism to the witness.

THE INQUIRY

Assessors

23.62 An assessor may be appointed to assist an inquiry inspector on particular matters[88].

The assessor will normally be a member of the Planning Inspectorate and will have expertise in a particular aspect of the case, such as heritage or technically complex topics such as oil and gas. In the inquiry the assessor will sit and retire with the inspector. An assessor may ask questions. Conventionally in a case decided by Ministers the assessor will produce his own report, which will be appended to the inspector's report and taken into account by the inspector in preparing his own report[89]. The inspector will identify whether they accept the assessor's views and the reasons for any disagreement[90]. However the formal recommendation to the Minister will be from the inspector. In inspector decisions the statutory obligation is simply

---

[88] The Minister shall notify in writing every person entitled to appear of the appointment of an assessor: English and Welsh Inquiries Rules, r 9; English and Welsh Inspectors Inquiries Rules, r 9.
[89] English and Welsh Inquiries Rules, r 17(2).
[90] English and Welsh Inquiries Rules, r 17(3).

23.63 *Inquiries*

for the inspector to say whether the assessor made a report to him[91] although it would be prudent to publish the report.

In practice the inspector and assessor will have been working together closely in the inquiry process and it would be uncommon for them to disagree on the matters within the assessor's area of expertise.

Proofs and statements of evidence

23.63 A proof of evidence is a statement from a witness setting out his evidence. A proof must be submitted in advance where a party who is entitled to appear (so including the appellant, local planning authority or r 6 party) intends to give evidence by reading from a statement.

23.64 In Wales the parties are required to prepare statements of evidence, but these are exactly the same as proofs of evidence. In the rest of this chapter, the term proofs of evidence will include statements of evidence.

23.65 A proof will frequently be 'taken as read' at the inquiry with the summary only read out, along with any supplementary questions in examination in chief. Planning inquiries have not moved as far as the civil courts in simply asking a witness to confirm their written statement with very limited room for further questions in chief. In part this reflects the absence of a formal mechanism for written response to the other side's proof and the need for the public to be able to follow the proceedings, but also a more relaxed approach by inspectors so they can see how witnesses explain their evidence.

23.66 The proof should concisely but comprehensively set out the witness's evidence. It should be clearly structured. If a planning witness is dealing with all the issues on the appeal then the headings may be along these lines:

Introduction: witness's qualifications
Site location and description
Planning history
Relevant planning policies
The issues:
Conclusions

Guidance on the contents of proofs or statements in inquiries is given in the Inspectorate guidance[92].

23.67 The Inspectorate's aim is for the length of a proof to be limited[93]. In the past excessively lengthy and expensive proofs have been the bane of inquiry proceedings.

---

[91] English and Welsh Inspectors Inquiries Rules, rr 18(1), 19(1).
[92] *Procedural Guidance: Planning appeals - England*, sections F.11, G.12; *Procedural Guidance: Planning appeals and called-in planning applications – Wales*, para E.10.
[93] *Procedural Guidance: Planning appeals – England*, paras F.11.5, G.12.4; *Procedural Guidance: Planning appeals and called-in planning applications – Wales*, para E.10.4. The aspiration that proofs be no longer than 3,000 words has been abandoned: cf *Procedural Guidance: Planning appeals and called-in planning applications* PINS 01/2009, para 6.8.3.

With a 60, 80 or even 100-page proof it is difficult to remember where a point is dealt with, let alone what the witness was trying to say about it. Extensive quotation of policies can usually be avoided because the full text will be available elsewhere, but it may be useful to quote the particular point that the witness wishes to draw attention to.

23.68 A summary should be produced if the proof is more than 1,500 words long[94]. It should itself be fewer than 1,500 words and should summarise the evidence in the proof. It must not contain new material, even in the form of conclusions, nor merely state the topics that are covered by the proof.

23.69 Expert evidence (including the views of local authority officers on the merits of schemes) should include an endorsement that the evidence is the professional opinion of the witness. Some professional bodies use a set format, alternatively the Planning Inspectorate recommends[95]:

> 'The evidence which I have prepared and provide for this appeal reference APP/xxx (in this proof of evidence, written statement or report) is true [and has been prepared and is given in accordance with the guidance of my professional institution] and I confirm that the opinions expressed are my true and professional opinions'.

23.70 Whilst not required by Inspectorate guidance, it is appropriate for proofs or statements on factual matters to contain a statement of truth that the maker of the statement believes that the facts stated in the document are true.

23.71 The pages and paragraphs should be numbered. Appendices should be provided in a separate, paginated bundle, preferably in A4 size although some plans and photographs may be best seen in A3. Proofs should also cross-reference to other documents in a convenient format: first, by using any core document numbers and then by referring to the relevant part of the document (such as to the particular paragraph of Historic England's setting guidance rather than to the document generally). As with any presentation, thought should be given to how it can be best understood by the recipient, who is the inspector but also the other side and the public.

23.72 If a person entitled to be heard at the inquiry proposes to call a witness giving evidence by reading a proof (or in Wales, a statement), copies of the proof and any summary should be sent to the Planning Inspectorate at least four weeks before the inquiry, or as specified in any timetable arranged by the inspector[96]. If provided in hard form, two copies are to be provided by the appellant and local planning authority, with three copies from other persons entitled to be heard. Copies would then be circulated by the Planning Inspectorate, if the parties had not already supplied copies to each other. A person required to submit a proof or statement has also to send it to any other statutory party (that is, owner, long leaseholder or agricultural tenant). The duties to provide copies are therefore something of a mess. The appellant and local planning authority receive proofs and statements via the Planning Inspectorate. All parties submitting proofs have to send copies to statutory parties, whether or

---

[94] English and Welsh Inquiries Rules, r 13(1), (2), English and Welsh Inspectors Inquiries Rules, r 14(1), (2). *Procedural Guidance: Planning appeals – England*, paras F.11.5, F.11.6, G.12.4, G.12.5, *Procedural Guidance: Planning appeals and called-in planning applications – Wales*, para E.10.4

[95] *Procedural Guidance: Planning appeals – England*, para O.2.1; *Procedural Guidance: Planning appeals and called-in planning applications – Wales*, para L.2.1.

[96] English and Welsh Inquiries Rules, r 13(1), (3), English and Welsh Inspectors Inquiries Rules, r 14(1), (3).

23.73 *Inquiries*

not those persons are intending to take part in the inquiry. Rule 6 parties have no right to receive copies of proofs and strictly are only entitled to inspect them at the local planning authority's offices and take copies. The potential problems of acting solely in accordance with the rules are often overcome by inspector's timetables and programmes providing for copies to be provided to r 6 parties and direct exchange. More often common sense, and a desire for orderly preparation for the inquiry mean that the parties co-operate in the service of proofs. Direct supply of copies is more convenient than waiting for the Planning Inspectorate to circulate them and realism over the number of copies required by a party will help. At the very minimum a party's advocate will need copies of all of the proofs whilst a witness will need to see the proof of the opposing witness and any other witness whose evidence bears on his. Particularly where proofs contain complex, coloured appendices it may be sensible for the parties to provide multiple copies. It would be more sensible if the rules provided for copies to be circulated between those entitled to and intending to appear.

23.73 Requests from non-r 6 parties for copies of proofs and other inquiry documentation should be acceded to as soon as practicable, subject perhaps to providing electronic copies in lieu of very large printed bundles.

Producing evidence at the inquiry for the first time tends to lead to delay as it is read and possible adjournment whilst matters are investigated.

23.74 There is no provision in the rules for supplementary proofs dealing with matters raised in other parties' proofs. It might be agreed at a pre-inquiry meeting that these can be produced, but usually the opportunity to respond to the other side's evidence is in examination in chief. Supplementary proofs can be useful if the response is so technical or detailed that it is useful to have it available in writing. These should be sent to the other parties and the inspector as soon as possible.

23.75 Third parties (other than those entitled to be heard) are not obliged to serve proofs. As a matter of practice they should if the evidence is detailed or amounts to expert evidence. They are entitled to copy proofs received by the local planning authority under the Rules.

Statement of common ground in inquiries

23.76 The appellant and local planning authority are required to provide an agreed statement of common ground. In the rules such a statement is to contain 'agreed factual information about the proposal'[97]. Its role is in fact much wider. The statement will usually try to set out a description of the site, the application scheme (including listing the application plans and any agreed amendments), the planning history, identify the relevant policies, the matters not in dispute between the main parties and those which are in dispute and contain a draft list of conditions[98]. A model format is on the Planning Portal website.

23.77 There is now a significant difference between English and Welsh requirements for the timing of statements of common ground. In England, a draft

---
[97] English and Welsh Inquiries Rules, r 2(1); English and Welsh Inspectors Inquiries Rules, r 2(1).
[98] *Procedural Guidance: Planning appeals – England*, para T.2.5.

The inquiry **23.80**

statement of common ground must be filed by the appellant with the appeal if it considers that determination should be following a hearing or inquiry[99]. Where an appeal or call-in does proceed to an inquiry then the agreed statement of common ground must be received by the Secretary of State and any statutory party within six weeks of the starting date in Ministerial cases and five weeks in inspector cases[100].

In Wales the agreed statement of common ground must be received by the Welsh Ministers and any statutory party four weeks before the inquiry[101].

23.78 Whilst the statement is required to be produced by the same time as the proofs of evidence, it is more useful if it can be worked up by the parties before the proofs are written. That way, the parties can avoid including descriptive material in their proofs and the statement of common ground.

23.79 The statement of common ground is not required to be agreed with third parties, although there may be occasions when this would be useful. For example, it may be possible to agree a statement of common ground on highways matters between the appellant, local planning authority and the highway authority. Whilst separate to statements of common ground, in inquiries of any great size it is useful to agree a common referencing for documents, weed out duplication of material and in some cases produce a core documents bundle. To be useful, this needs to be done before proofs or statements are finalised.

Requiring the production of documents or the attendance of witnesses

23.80 The inspector is able to issue a summons requiring persons to attend to produce documents or to give evidence. The power is contained in the Local Government Act 1972, s 250(2)[102]:

> 'For the purpose of any such local inquiry, the person appointed to hold the inquiry may by summons require any person to attend, at a time and place stated in the summons, to give evidence or to produce any documents in his custody or under his control which relate to any matter in question at the inquiry, and may take evidence on oath, and for that purpose administer oaths:
>
> Provided that:
>
> (a) no person shall be required, in obedience to such summons, to attend to give evidence or to produce any such documents, unless the necessary expenses of this attendance are paid or tendered to him; and
>
> (b) nothing in this section shall empower the person holding the inquiry to require the production of the title, or of any instrument relating to the title, of any land not being the property of a local authority'.

---

[99] DMPO 2015, art 37(3)(b)(x), subject to exceptions for national security, urgent Crown development and type A or B appeals: art 37(4), see Chapter 19. The Inspectorate encourage discussion of the draft statement prior to submission of the appeal: *Procedural Guidance: Planning appeals – England*, para T.1.2.
[100] English Inquiries Rules, r 14(1); English Inspectors Inquiries Rules, r 15(1) respectively.
[101] Welsh Inquiries Rules, r 14(1); Welsh Inspectors Inquiries Rules, r 15(1).
[102] Applied by the Town and Country Planning Act 1990, s 320(2).

23.81 *Inquiries*

23.81 It is an offence to refuse or deliberately fail to attend or to suppress or destroy documents[103]. The existence of the power is often overlooked[104] and indeed is rarely raised in inquiries[105]. Even if an application might be unsuccessful, the ability to ask has some value. It provides a basis for raising a dispute about the production of documents in a formal manner with the inspector: that is, asking the inspector to make a decision rather than simply draw an adverse inference. This can provide some leverage for the production of the material in advance of an inquiry. If the material or witness sought is seen as of assistance to the inquiry, the inspector might encourage that evidence to be provided whilst declining, or deferring a decision on a summons.

THE INQUIRY PROCEEDINGS

23.82 It is a basic principle that at any planning inquiry 'oral evidence shall be heard in public and documentary evidence shall be open to public inspection' subject to limited exceptions for national security and security measures for premises or property: Town and Country Planning Act 1990, s 321(3). The exceptions, which are rarely invoked, are considered below.

Inquiry venues

23.83 Planning inquiries are referred to in legislation as local inquiries[106]. The local nature of an inquiry is important: it should be easy for those in the locality interested to attend to take part or simply to observe proceedings[107]. Since a site visit will be required at some point it is useful to be close by. Inquiries will invariably be held within the local authority's administrative area or close to it.

23.84 How close the inquiry venue is to the site will depend upon the availability of suitable accommodation and local administrative convenience and practice. Finding a room to hold the inquiry in is the responsibility of the local planning authority, which will be expected to meet any costs involved. Inquiries tend to be held at council offices but can sometimes take place in village halls. It is desirable for there to be continuity in the venue, rather than moving between rooms, so conference centres or hotels may be used for long inquiries.

23.85 The essential requirement is for a suitable room in which to hold the inquiry, which is capable of accommodating everyone present in comfort. Other practical

---

[103] Local Government Act 1972, s 250(3):

'Every person who refuses or deliberately fails to attend in obedience to a summons issued under this section, or to give evidence, or who deliberately alters, suppresses, conceals, destroys, or refuses to produce any book or other document which he is required or is liable to be required to produce for the purposes of this section, shall be liable on summary conviction to a fine not exceeding level 3 on the standard scale or to imprisonment for a term not exceeding six months, or to both'.

[104] For example, by the Planning Inspectorate in *Turner v Secretary of State for Communities and Local Government* [2015] EWHC 375 (Admin) at paras 18, 19.

[105] In *South Oxfordshire District Council v Secretary of State for the Environment* (1994) 68 P & CR 551 at 561 the inspector said that he would have to be asked to issue a summons, but having said that he was unlikely to do so, no application was made.

[106] Town and Country Planning Act 1990, s 320.

[107] This is more likely to be an issue for county councils or geographically large unitary authorities whose main offices could be a considerable distance from the site.

The inquiry proceedings **23.88**

requirements, in a rough order of importance, are access to copying facilities, a room for the inspector to retire to, rooms for the main parties to meet in and proximity to somewhere that sells or serves a quick lunch. If the inquiry is to last for more than one day it is preferable for parties and the inspector to be able to leave papers at their desks, otherwise it must be convenient to store papers elsewhere in the inquiry room or at the venue[108].

23.86 The venue should be available from at least 9 am to enable parties to set up and confer and to accommodate the possibility of a 9.30 am start after the first day. Whilst inquiries will usually adjourn at 5 pm, they may sit later to finish a witness, keep up to programme or to finish the hearing. It is preferable for the room to be available until 6 pm (and potentially later) to give some flexibility. Having to vacate the room on the dot of 5 pm is not appreciated by inspectors. One of the persons present from the party who organised the accommodation (usually the local authority) should be able to inform the inquiry when the room is available to that evening and whether papers can be left on participants' desks overnight.

Procedure at the inquiry

23.87 Procedure at the inquiry is essentially a matter for the inspector. The normal form is set out below.

The inspector will introduce himself by name and qualifications and explain the procedure to be followed, such as sitting times.

The inspector will ask who wishes to appear, starting with the main parties. The advocates present will state who they are, in the case of counsel who instructs them and their professional client's address, the name and address of the party they represent and the witnesses they propose to call[109]. Any person appearing on their own behalf will give their name and address.

Journalists present are then asked to give the name and address of their organisation so that a copy of the decision letter can be sent to them.

The local planning authority will be asked to show that the formalities for publicising the inquiry have been carried out. The authority's advocate should therefore have copies of any letter from the Inspectorate setting out publicity requirements and any consequent site notices, letters to interested persons, list of such persons and newspaper advertisements for the inspector.

23.88 Again as a preliminary matter, the inspector will check what the application drawings are, usually by reading from a list. The parties should ensure that they have their plans and, ideally, a list of those plans, to hand. This will also be an opportunity for the inspector to say whether there are any amendments which the appellant proposes to make, although it may be best to postpone any debate on such amendments until after opening speeches.

---

[108] Where Council chambers or committee rooms are used then papers may need to be put out of the way whilst evening meetings are held.
[109] The advocate can simply say that the addresses will be in the papers. A note can be handed up with these details to save the inspector's writing.

23.89 *Inquiries*

23.89 The inspector will set out what he considers to be the main issues to be considered and any matters requiring further explanation[110]. This statement is important in practice as an indication of what the inspector has understood about the case from pre-reading. However, it does not prevent parties from raising any issues they consider to be relevant[111]. Unless the inspector invites discussion of what are the main issues at that point, the parties can set our their views of the main issues in opening.

23.90 The appellant will start with an opening speech setting out their case. The Inspectorate preference is for short, 5–10 minute openings, except in major inquiries where longer speeches may be helpful. Practice varies as to whether the local planning authority and any r 6 parties also make opening statements. If the inquiry is likely to last for several days (or longer) or there are reasonable numbers of members of the public present then it is useful for those parties to deliver short openings. The main utility of an opening is to set out what the party considers the main issues to be and why its case is right on those issues. It is a way of cutting through what is likely to be a large amount of material. The first morning of an inquiry usually attracts the greatest public and press attention (if there is any). If press coverage is anticipated, openings should be given with an eye on that wider reporting. Where a one-day inquiry only involves the appellant and local authority, a local authority or other opening may be unnecessary.

23.91 There is no obligation to provide written skeleton arguments or draft submissions for opening or closing speeches, except for closing submissions in inquiries which the Minister expected to last eight or more days[112]. However, it may be useful to the inspector and the parties and save time note-taking. If media reporting is likely or desired then parties may want a written opening, or extracts from it, to circulate. Inspectors will often request written closings for cases that last more than one day[113]. The High Court has encouraged the use of skeleton arguments in inquiries where there are points of law that may go to the courts on appeal[114].

23.92 The rules provide that 'unless in any particular case the inspector otherwise determines, the local planning authority shall begin and the appellant shall have the final right of reply; and other persons entitled or permitted to appear shall be heard in such order as the inspector may determine'[115]. This is taken as meaning that the authority should call their evidence first – not that they make the first opening statement.

23.93 Following openings, the local planning authority will call their witnesses. In appeals against the refusal or non-determination of planning applications, the local planning authority is expected to call its evidence first to focus discussion on the actual or proposed reasons for refusal. Evidence in chief is subject to the normal rule against leading questions. The restrictions on admissibility of evidence in criminal or civil proceedings do not apply. The inspector will give appropriate weight to the evidence: if it is hearsay, then less reliance is likely to be placed upon it.

---

[110] English and Welsh Inquiries Rules, r 15(2); English and Welsh Inspectors Inquiries Rules, r 16(2).
[111] English and Welsh Inquiries Rules, r 15(4); English and Welsh Inspectors Inquiries Rules, r 16(4).
[112] English and Welsh Inquiries Rules, r 15(14); English and Welsh Inspectors Inquiries Rules, r 16(14).
[113] Sometimes acknowledging the substantial workload that imposes upon advocates.
[114] *P G Vallance Ltd v Secretary of State for the Environment* [1993] 1 PLR 74 at 78 per Henry J.
[115] English and Welsh Inquiries Rules, r 15(4); English and Welsh Inspectors Inquiries Rules, r 16(4).

The inquiry proceedings **23.97**

23.94 On the usual basis that the inspector and the other parties have had sufficient opportunity to read the proof, the summary only will be read out[116]. If the only persons present are the main parties then the inspector might not need summaries to be read out. The main proof will then be taken as read and considered as part of the witness's evidence. Questions may be asked in chief to highlight areas in the main proof or to address matters in the other side's evidence or new developments[117].

23.95 Witnesses at planning inquiries are normally not examined on oath. But if factual disputes are likely to arise then witnesses on those issues will be sworn or affirmed by the inspector under the Local Government Act 1972, s 250[118].

23.96 The witness will then be open to cross-examination by the appellant. This cross-examination may include questions on any relevant matters which the witness can be expected to give factual or expert evidence on. This will include parts of the proof that were not read out. The inspector may then permit cross-examination by other parties supporting the appeal. The appellant, local planning authority and any statutory party are entitled to cross-examine (implicitly witnesses they disagree with)[119]. Other public authorities and r 6 parties are not given the statutory right to cross-examine but are entitled to appear and call evidence[120]. Cross-examination by those and any other persons is said to be at the inspector's discretion. However that discretion has to be exercised fairly. It is inconceivable that a r 6 party or other person entitled to appear would not be able to cross-examine witnesses whose evidence they were challenging.

23.97 The inspector has a discretion to allow third parties to cross-examine but has to exercise that in accordance with the rules of natural justice and fairly: *Nicholson v Secretary of State for Energy*[121]. In that case the claimant had objected to an open cast mining application by the National Coal Board. He had been allowed to cross-examine an NCB witness but the inspector prevented him from cross-examining council officers who had given evidence adverse to his case. Sir Douglas Frank held:

> 'a reasonable person, viewing the matter objectively, would consider that there was a risk that injustice or unfairness would result if a person considering himself to be directly affected by a proposal was denied the opportunity to cross-examine a witness who had given evidence contrary to his case. Cross examination was not to be used for the purpose of a "fishing expedition" but the plaintiff had been denied the right to cross-examine the very evidence upon which his own case turned. An inspector was entitled to refuse to hear, or at least to stop cross-examination by objectors who intentionally engaged in irrelevancies and repetition …'.

---

[116] English and Welsh Inquiries Rules, r 13(5); English and Welsh Inspectors Inquiries Rules, r 14(5) require only the summary to be read out unless the inspector permits or requires otherwise. Where the issues are well known to the parties and the public are not present then the inspector and the parties may agree that summaries do not need to be read out.

[117] The approach asking supplementary questions in examination in chief is not as restrictive as the conventional approach in civil proceedings where further questions are discouraged.

[118] As applied by the Town and Country Planning Act 1990, s 320(2). Following civil practice, witnesses of fact are not excluded from the inquiry hearing before they have given their evidence. In any courts the parties to proceedings and their experts are never excluded: *R (on the application of Elvington Park Ltd) v York Crown Court* [2011] EWHC 2213 (Admin), [2012] Env LR 10. Different rules apply to national security aspects of planning inquiries.

[119] English and Welsh Inquiries Rules, r 15(5); English and Welsh Inspectors Inquiries Rules, r 16(5).

[120] English and Welsh Inquiries Rules, r 15(5); English and Welsh Inspectors Inquiries Rules, r 16(5).

[121] 76 LGR 693, [1978] 1 EGLR 111. These decisions are very fact sensitive: see *Aston v Secretary of State for Communities and Local Government* [2013] EWHC 1936 (Admin), [2014] 2 P & CR 10 at paras 78–89 per Wyn Williams J.

23.98 *Inquiries*

23.98 The inspector may refuse to permit the giving of evidence, cross-examination or submissions which he considers to be irrelevant or repetitious[122]. That allows proper control over the proceedings, but the inspector must be careful to act fairly and not to exclude relevant matters. Any such error could leave the decision vulnerable to challenge.

The witness can then be re-examined by the authority's advocate. Re-examination can only cover matters raised in cross-examination and should not be leading.

23.99 The inspector may then question the witness (some inspectors do this before re-examination). If the inspector raises new points, the authority's advocate (and sometimes the appellant's advocate), with the inspector's permission, may ask further questions on those points. This further questioning is relatively rare. The inspector's role is more inquisitorial than that of a judge in adversarial court proceedings. However the inspector's interventions must be fair and not show a risk of bias. Inspectors can raise questions with witnesses whilst they are being examined by advocates, but those are best confined to ensuring that questions are answered and that the inspector understands the answers. An inspector should not take over the examination of a witness or disrupt an advocate's questions more than is necessary[123].

The authority will then call their remaining witnesses, following the same procedure.

23.100 The timing of other objectors' evidence is a matter for the inspector's discretion. The usual practice is for organised objectors, such as r 6 parties, to give evidence immediately following the local authority's case. Objectors who are simply attending as individuals may be asked to give evidence at that point or the inspector may allow them to speak after the appellant's witnesses. Whenever they appear, objectors may be cross-examined by the appellant and, at the inspector's discretion, other supporters of the appeal. The inspector may also ask them questions. Whether a person who is not entitled to be heard is allowed to give evidence is a matter for the inspector's discretion, acting reasonably and fairly, but if a person is not allowed to give oral evidence on a point then they are entitled to submit any evidence or other matter in writing before the close of the inquiry[124]. Any written representations received by the inspector before or during an inquiry should be disclosed to the parties at the inquiry[125].

23.101 Following the local authority's evidence and that of any other objectors who are being heard immediately afterwards, the appellant will call its witnesses. Their evidence will be given in the same fashion. Cross-examination will be begun by the local planning authority and any other r 6 parties who have objected will be allowed to cross-examine. Cross-examination by non-r 6 parties is at the discretion of the inspector.

23.102 Cross-examination of a third party by another third party will rarely be permitted, as there should normally be a main party to take up the issue.

---

[122] English and Welsh Inquiries Rules, r 15(6); English and Welsh Inspectors Inquiries Rules, r 16(6).
[123] Discussed further at paras **23.136–23.137**.
[124] English and Welsh Inquiries Rules, r 15(6); English and Welsh Inspectors Inquiries Rules, r 16(6). For discussion of the submission of evidence at the inquiry see *Anderson v Secretary of State for Communities and Local Government* [2015] EWHC 3005 (Admin).
[125] English and Welsh Inquiries Rules, r 15(12); English and Welsh Inspectors Inquiries Rules, r 16(12).

23.103 Conditions to be imposed in the event of planning permission being granted will usually be discussed after the evidence has been heard. The local planning authority will propose any conditions it wants (without prejudice to its opposition to the grant of planning permission). These will be discussed in a more informal session[126] along with any proposals by the appellant and third parties. Even if conditions are agreed between the parties, the inspector is likely to still have questions about them. If there are major factual or judgment issues about potential conditions then these should be addressed in the witnesses' evidence. Any planning obligation will also be discussed in that session, usually beginning with an explanation of its terms by the appellant's advocate or solicitor.

23.104 Closing submissions will then be made. Any third parties who are making closings will speak first, followed by the local planning authority and the appellant is entitled to the final word unless otherwise agreed[127]. Inspectors will often request a written text of the closing to be handed up when it is delivered[128]. Where the inspector is reporting to the Secretary of State a full written text is essential as this will provide the basis of the inspector's summary of the party's case in the report and will also be available to the Minister[129]. Even where a written text is produced, the closing will still be delivered orally, allowing the inspector to make notes of further submissions.

23.105 There are several points to note about the practice of closing submissions. Even if there is the opportunity to do so, it has not been common practice to circulate written closings until the advocate starts to speak. However there may be an advantage in circulating written closings in advance if there is an adjournment of the proceedings. Where this has taken place it has been found useful. It allows the parties to make the oral presentation by reference to the text, rather than by having to read it all out, more in the manner of courtroom submissions. If there are significant legal issues which have not been canvassed earlier in the proceedings then prior notice of those points (if not the whole closing) is helpful. This would enable the other parties to consider the point and research legislation and case law in advance, rather than risking adjournment during the hearing or a need for further written submissions.

After the closing speeches, applications for costs can be made[130].

23.106 The inspector will then close the inquiry. Unless otherwise agreed, further material or submissions may not be made after this point. An accompanied site visit will usually take place at this point, although it may have occurred at an earlier break in the proceedings[131].

---

[126] Advocates and witnesses tend to make comments in these sessions without the formality of giving evidence. Third parties are able to take part in these discussions and copies of the proposed conditions should be made available to them.

[127] English and Welsh Inquiries Rules, r 15(4); English and Welsh Inspectors Inquiries Rules, r 16(4).

[128] It is essential to have copies for the other advocates and desirable to have sufficient copies for those attending the session, including members of the public.

[129] It will usually be helpful to the inspector's writing of the report to the Minister to provide by email to the case officer at the Planning Inspectorate a Word file of the closing as well as a hard copy.

[130] Costs are discussed in Chapter 24.

[131] In some cases it may be helpful for the inspector to go onto the site before hearing evidence, but an accompanied site visit has to be announced in advance at the inquiry so can only take place following the start of the inquiry: English and Welsh Inquiries Rules, r 16(2), (3); English and Welsh Inspectors Inquiries Rules, r 17(2), (3) and para **23.124**.

23.107 *Inquiries*

23.107 Inquiries may be adjourned from day to day, at which point the inspector will announce where and when the inquiry is resuming. If an inquiry does go into further days, each day is likely to start with the inspector asking for any procedural or housekeeping points to be dealt with. This is often a convenient time for the parties to hand in any further documents which the inspector has requested or been promised or which they consider should be produced. It is also an opportunity to deal with programming or other news[132].

Inquiry conduct

23.108 Inquiries are run in a formal manner, akin to court or tribunal proceedings, rather than a committee or public meeting. In practice that means that the person who is entitled to speak at that moment should not be interrupted, unless an intervention is required on an important point, either to prevent an inappropriate step (such as answer being sought to an improper question) or in extreme helpfulness (for example, pointing out that a matter is agreed).

23.109 Inquiries are now almost always conducted with the participants remaining seated. Until the turn of the century the practice was for the advocates to stand when speaking (except during a discussion of conditions), whilst witnesses remained seated. The Planning Inspectorate then introduced a practice of advocates being seated whilst examining witnesses for a trial period on the basis that this would be less intimidating for witnesses. The practice continued and spread to the remaining parts of the inquiry process[133]. The only circumstances in which an advocate might stand whilst making submissions would be for reasons of visibility and audibility in a particularly large room.

23.110 The inspector should be addressed as 'Sir' or 'Madam'[134]. Other persons should be addressed or referred to by title ('Mister', 'Miss', 'Doctor'). Practice varies as to whether councillors are referred to as such, although if they were acting or are appearing as a councillor then it is appropriate to do so ('Councillor Smith').

23.111 In the event of disturbance to the proceedings the inspector may require any person appearing or present at an inquiry who, in his opinion, is behaving in a disruptive manner to leave; and refuse to permit that person to return; or permit him to return only on specified conditions but any such person may submit to him any evidence or other matter in writing before the close of the inquiry[135].

23.112 Comments made at a planning inquiry are at least subject to qualified privilege, in that a person cannot be sued in libel for defamatory comments if they

---

[132] On a long-running inquiry it is permissible to announce the birth of children or grandchildren for inquiry participants at this point, provided the baby's weight is given in metric units.
[133] Unlike courts or tribunals it has never been the practice in planning inquiries to stand when the inspector enters the room. Indeed, the inspector is normally seated before the inquiry is due to start.
[134] There is no gender neutral mode of address, although on one occasion a recently-appointed QC did inadvertently address the inspector in an inquiry as 'Darling'.
[135] English and Welsh Inquiries Rules, r 15(9); English and Welsh Inspectors Inquiries Rules, r 16(9).

act without express malice[136]. Qualified but not absolute privilege was found for correspondence to an inspector in a planning enforcement appeal[137], although the point might not be beyond debate as some tribunals and inquiries are subject to absolute privilege so a person cannot be sued even if they have acted maliciously[138]. An inspector should, though, intervene to stop irrelevant or merely offensive comments and professional participants are subject to their own codes of conduct. Comments by the inspector in a decision or report, and their reporting of participants' submissions, will at the very least be subject to qualified privilege. Another occasional complaint raised at inquiries is the copyright of documents, however 'Copyright is not infringed by anything done for the purposes of the proceedings of a ... statutory inquiry'[139].

Communication with the inspector outside the formal hearing

23.113 As a general rule any discussion with the inspector about the inquiry should take place openly in the formal session, so that all people attending are able to hear what is being said. This includes discussion of procedural or programming matters. There may be occasions when for reasons of giving advanced warning or sensitivity a matter should be raised during an adjournment[140]. Even so, those discussions should take place in the presence of representatives of the main parties and any third party affected by the issue. If a problem arises then it may be appropriate to warn the inspector as soon as possible if the inspector is at the inquiry venue[141].

23.114 Generally speaking the substance of any informal discussion between the main parties and the inspector should be explained in the next formal session of the inquiry by the inspector or an advocate, and certainly if it has any bearing on the conduct of the inquiry. The merits of the appeal or call-in should never be discussed informally with the inspector, even in the presence of the other main party, as that will exclude the present or notional public. This reflects the statutory requirement for evidence to be heard in public[142].

23.115 There will be a degree of informal contact with the inspector at the inquiry venue[143]. Parties should be polite and can say 'Good morning, Sir/Madam' (as appropriate). They should not discuss the merits of the case and it is best to leave to

---

[136] In *Royal Aquarium And Summer And Winter Garden Society v Parkinson* [1892] 1 QB 431 at 443 Lord Esher MR held that where 'a body of persons are engaged in the performance of the duty imposed upon them, of deciding a matter of public administration, which interests not themselves, but the parties concerned and the public, it seems to me clear that the occasion is privileged'. In that case a county council meeting on licensing was held to have qualified but not absolute privilege.

[137] *Richards v Cresswell* (1987) Times, 24 April.

[138] The purpose of absolute privilege is that a person can act 'free from any fear of being harassed by an action of an allegation, whether true or false, that they acted from malice': *Trapp v Muckie* [1979] 1 WLR 377 at 379 per Lord Diplock. The principal considerations as to whether a tribunal or inquiry is subject to absolute privilege are discussed in *Trapp*.

[139] Copyright, Designs and Patents Act 1988, s 46(1). 'Statutory inquiry' means an inquiry held or investigation conducted in pursuance of a duty imposed or power conferred by or under an enactment (s 46(4)), which would include an inquiry, hearing or written representations appeal or call in.

[140] For example, that the appellant's counsel would quite like an early finish today because his wife has gone into labour and it would be a good idea if he got back from South Wales soon-ish.

[141] Such as a need to adjourn because the next planning witness was last seen being stretchered into an ambulance having had a fall.

[142] Town and Country Planning Act 1990, s 321(3).

[143] Unlike court and tribunal judges, inspectors will not be separated from the parties although they may have their own room. They might therefore be in the same queue for the council canteen or the same toilets.

23.116 *Inquiries*

the inspector to initiate any general conversation. Some inspectors are quite chatty, but many are quite properly not. If there is a discussion it is still best for someone from the other party to be within earshot.

23.116 A similar need for care arises if the inspector is staying at the same hotel as some of the participants. Whilst inspectors have been known to change hotel when this occurs that is usually unnecessary. Normally all that is required is for the inspector and the other guests not to talk to each other at the hotel (beyond the normal courtesies) and for the parties to avoid discussing the case (particularly over dinner) within earshot of the inspector. That may require moving to a different table or staggering dinner times but is perfectly practicable.

Interests of inspectors

23.117 Sometimes a personal interest of an inspector may disqualify them from taking part in a particular appeal or call-in. Planning inspectors have always been careful to be seen to be independent from parties to an appeal. Everyone has a past and inspectors are drawn from professionals practising in the planning field. Some are part-time, acting also as consultants or local government offices. Their previous (and occasionally, current) employers will still be active in planning appeals. Inspectors therefore have had a list of areas of the country in which they will not be appointed, relating to their residence and any former local authority employers. This does make the charting of inspectors' casework more difficult.

23.118 The Inspectorate's Conflict of Interest policy generally avoids inspectors working in the same postcode as their home or relatively close to it and care is taken with financial interests. Previous or concurrent employment may pose difficulties.

23.119 In *Ortona v Secretary of State for Communities and Local Government* an appeal decision was quashed due to a real possibility of bias because the case involved local transport policies which the inspector had been responsible for formulating and implementing when he worked at the County Council. Sullivan LJ emphasised that his mere former employment by the County Council was not sufficient to prevent him hearing the case[144].

Inspector conduct generally

23.120 Inspectors are subject to a code of conduct, setting out the following principles:

'Principles of Conduct

Inspectors should make their decisions and recommendations fairly and in the public interest.

–   Inspectors should take decisions and recommendations solely in terms of the public interest and not in order to gain financial or other benefits for themselves, their family or their friends.

Decisions and recommendations should be made solely on merit.

---

[144] [2009] EWCA Civ 863, [2010] JPL 361 at paras 32, 35, 36.

Inspectors should not be fettered with pre-determined views and should not judge cases before they have considered the evidence.

– Inspectors may hold tentative views on the merits of individual cases but they should be open to persuasion and alternative points of view. Therefore they should not reach their final conclusions on any case until they have considered all the evidence and representations.

Inspectors should not be influenced by irrelevant considerations or outside influences when making their decisions and recommendations.

– Inspectors' decisions and recommendations should be based on the relevance and substance of the evidence and arguments put to them by the parties and not by the identity, status or personality of those providing that evidence or argument.

– Inspectors should at no time deal privately with one party in the absence of the other parties.

Inspectors must register any offers of gifts, hospitality and other benefits offered by parties who have an interest in a case in accordance with the Acceptance of Gifts, Benefits and Hospitality Policy

– Inspectors should be honest. They should never act in a way that could give the impression that they may or have in fact been influenced by gifts, hospitality or other benefits to show favour or disfavour to a particular party.

Inspectors should treat each person with dignity and respect.

– Inspectors should behave at all times with courtesy, patience and understanding, whilst at the same time ensuring that cases are conducted efficiently and effectively.

Inspectors should not discriminate against people because of their race, sex, sexuality, marital status, religion, disability or age.

– Inspectors should treat everyone the same and consider evidence on its merits regardless of whose evidence it is.

Inspectors should avoid unnecessary delay in reaching their decisions and recommendations.

– Inspectors should not be dilatory in completing cases assigned to them and, where not governed by a statutory timetable, should make every reasonable effort to ensure that decisions and recommendations are made as soon as possible after the relevant evidence has been considered.

Inspectors should be responsible for their decisions and recommendations.

– Except where functions may lawfully be allocated to other inspectors, inspectors should not delegate their responsibilities to anyone else. Nor should they allow anyone to usurp their responsibilities'.

These principles codify some of the approaches in case law and practice, but also apply personally principles of good administration and independence to the role of individual inspectors

In addition to the code, inspectors may be subject to codes of conduct by their own membership of professional bodies.

23.121   *Inquiries*

Recording inquiries and hearings

23.121   The inspector will make notes for his or her own use. The Inspectorate does not normally arrange for either the audio recording of an inquiry or hearing or the taking of a transcript of the proceedings[145]. Consequently parties will need to ensure that they have their own good note of the proceedings[146].

23.122   Historically whilst journalists have been able to be present during an inquiry it has been rare for filming or photography to take place during the sessions. In large part this was due to an absence of demand from television companies for live coverage. Some television footage and still photography might take place just before the start of an inquiry if it was particularly newsworthy[147]. The ability of anyone to place footage on the web and to blog and tweet has made real time reporting of inquiries a practical and frequent occurrence. This has been supported by the Secretary of State in England[148]. The Procedural Guide advises[149]:

> 'Provided that it does not disrupt proceedings, anyone will be allowed to report, record and film proceedings including the use of digital and social media. Inspectors will advise people present at the start of the event that the proceedings may be recorded and/or filmed, and that anyone using social media during or after the end of the proceedings should do so responsibly'.

Anyone wishing to record with equipment larger than a compact camera or tablet is encouraged to discuss the arrangements with the local planning authority and the Inspectorate in advance[150].

Site visits

23.123   Almost all planning appeals require a site visit before they can be sensibly decided[151].

Prior to a hearing or inquiry the inspector will usually try to view the site from the highway or other land on which the public have a right of access. Such a visit will be informal and unaccompanied. Unaccompanied visits might also take place at other times, for example, to see peak hour traffic. The inspector will normally inform the parties at the hearing if an informal visit has taken place and if there was anything particular to note.

---

[145] Recording and the production of transcripts has occasionally taken place at very large inquiries. Audio recordings of development consent examinations are routinely made and placed on the examination website although they are not officially transcribed.

[146] Advocates should be able to keep a good note but not when they themselves are speaking. Someone in the team will need to take a thorough note when their advocate is cross-examining.

[147] Following one inquiry a junior counsel was ribbed for being photographed in the national press appearing to write in his notebook when: (a) he was wearing a garland of flowers from his client; and (b) whilst he was holding his pen halfway down the page, the sheet was obviously blank.

[148] See press release 22 August 2013 https://www.gov.uk/government/news/eric-pickles-opens-up-planning-appeals-and-lays-down-challenge.

[149] *Procedural Guide Planning appeals – England* (31 July 2015), para 3.5.1; *Procedural Guidance Planning appeals and called-in planning applications - Wales* (July 2015), para 3.6.1.

[150] *Procedural Guide Planning appeals – England*, para 3.5.2; in Wales, para 3.6.2. The inspector may give witnesses and opportunity to say whether they wish to be filmed whilst giving evidence. In smaller inquiry venues the positioning of camera tripods and microphone booms can be awkward.

[151] Exceptions would be cases that turn solely on points of law.

23.124 During an inquiry or after its close the inspector may carry out an accompanied site visit and has to do so if requested by the appellant or local planning authority[152]. Since the date and time of the proposed accompanied site visit has to be announced at the inquiry[153], an accompanied inspection can only take place after the inquiry has been opened[154].

23.125 If the inspector needs to enter private property, or a party wants to point out something particular and he agrees, the site visit will be accompanied. Representatives of the appellant (or the appellant himself), the local planning authority and any statutory parties are entitled to attend[155] and other participants will usually be allowed to do so.

23.126 An accompanied site inspection is not a further opportunity to argue the case, so the parties' role is confined to pointing out matters and ensuring fair play. Where an inspector and the local planning authority attended for an accompanied site visit but the appellant's representative was not present, it was unfair for the inspector to proceed accompanied by the planning officer[156]. It is not possible to adjourn the discussion of an appeal from the inquiry session to the site, unlike the provision under the hearing rules[157].

23.127 Inspecting the land under the inquiries rules requires the inspector to go onto the appeal site. Simply viewing the appeal site from the road is insufficient[158], although that might be excused with the willing consent of the parties.

23.128 It is important that the inspector sees sufficient to decide the case with regard to all relevant matters. In *Chichester District Council v First Secretary of State*[159] the local planning authority contended that a building which had been unlawfully constructed on a farm was a new dwelling. The inspector granted planning permission for the building, conditioned to use as an agricultural workshop and feedstore. Having carried out an unaccompanied site visit in the written representations appeal, the inspector failed to look inside the property, even though the authority had asked for this to be done. The decision was remitted for redetermination.

THE FAIRNESS OF INQUIRY PROCEEDINGS

23.129 Whilst not setting out a new approach some general principles on fairness were identified by Jackson LJ in *Hopkins Developments v Secretary of State for Communities and Local Government*[160]:

---

[152] English and Welsh Inquiries Rules, r 16(2); English and Welsh Inspectors Inquiries Rules, r 17(2).
[153] English and Welsh Inquiries Rules, r 16(3); English and Welsh Inspectors Inquiries Rules, r 17(3).
[154] *Anderson v Secretary of State for Communities and Local Government* [2015] EWHC 3005 (Admin) at paras 59–63 per Judge Behrens. As the name suggests, a pre-inquiry meeting is not the start of the inquiry.
[155] English and Welsh Inquiries Rules, r 16(2); English and Welsh Inspectors Inquiries Rules, r 17(2).
[156] *R (on the application of Tait) v Secretary of State for Communities and Local Government* [2012] EWHC 643 (Admin).
[157] English and Welsh Hearings Rules, r 12(2).
[158] *Payne v Secretary of State for Communities and Local Government* [2010] EWHC 3528 (Admin), [2011] JPL 767.
[159] [2006] EWHC 1876 (Admin), [2007] JPL 389.
[160] [2014] EWCA Civ 470, [2014] PTSR 1145 at para 62. An illustration of point (v) is that an appellant in a public inquiry should have addressed a written representation by a flying club about aviation safety without being warned by the inspector that he might rely on it: *Ecotricity Ltd v Secretary of State for Communities and Local Government* [2015] EWHC 801 (Admin).

23.130 *Inquiries*

'i) Any party to a planning inquiry is entitled (a) to know the case which he has to meet and (b) to have a reasonable opportunity to adduce evidence and make submissions in relation to that opposing case.

ii) If there is procedural unfairness which materially prejudices a party to a planning inquiry that may be a good ground for quashing the inspector's decision.

iii) The [Town and Country Planning Appeals (Determination by Inspectors) (Inquiries Procedure) (England) Rules 2000] are designed to assist in achieving objective (i), avoiding pitfall (ii) and promoting efficiency. Nevertheless the Rules are not a complete code for achieving procedural fairness.

iv) A rule 7 statement or a rule 16 statement identifies what the inspector regards as the main issues at the time of his statement. Such a statement is likely to assist the parties, but it does not bind the inspector to disregard evidence on other issues. Nor does it oblige him to give the parties regular updates about his thinking as the Inquiry proceeds.

v) The inspector will consider any significant issues raised by third parties, even if those issues are not in dispute between the main parties. The main parties should therefore deal with any such issues, unless and until the inspector expressly states that they need not do so.

vi) If a main party resiles from a matter agreed in the statement of common ground prepared pursuant to rule 15, the inspector must give the other party a reasonable opportunity to deal with the new issue which has emerged'.

23.130 He emphasised[161]:

'The Rules provide a framework, within which both the inspector and the parties operate. It remains the duty of the inspector to conduct the proceedings so that each party has a reasonable opportunity to adduce evidence and make submissions on the material issues, whether identified at the outset or emerging during the course of the hearing'.

Jackson LJ also expressed the view that the 'crack of the whip' metaphor, repeated ever since *Fairmount Investments Ltd v Secretary of State for the Environment*[162] was of little assistance.

23.131 In *Hopkins* the issue had been sufficiently ventilated – both main parties having submitted evidence on the point – so the inspector's handling of it was fair.

23.132 In *Bushell v Secretary of State for the Environment*, Lord Diplock said this of inquiries into motorway schemes[163]:

'fairness requires that the objectors should have an opportunity of communicating to the minister the reasons for their objections to the scheme and the facts on which they are based. ... Fairness, as it seems to me, also requires that the objectors should be given sufficient information about the reasons relied on by the department as justifying the draft scheme to enable them to challenge the accuracy of any facts and the validity of any arguments upon which the departmental reasons are based'.

23.133 Considering the duties of an inspector in *Castleford Homes Ltd v Secretary of State for the Environment, Transport and the Regions* Ouseley J stated[164]:

---

[161] At para 61.
[162] [1976] 1 WLR 1255 at 1265H–1266A per Lord Russell of Killowen.
[163] [1981] 1 AC 75 at 96.
[164] [2001] EWHC Admin 77, [2001] PLCR 29 at para 53.

'It is obviously helpful if an inspector does flag up issues which the parties do not appear to have fully appreciated or explored. The point at which a failure to do so, amounts to a breach of the rules of natural justice and becomes unfair, is a question of degree, there being no general requirement for an inspector to reveal any provisional thinking. It involves a judgment being made as to what is fair or unfair in a particular case'.

23.134 In *RWE Npower Renewables Ltd v Welsh Ministers*[165] *Pill LJ pointed out that the inspector 'was* not required to tell the witnesses that he might not accept their opinions. That was, or should have been, obvious and the respondents had every opportunity to put their case to him and to put on it the best face they could'.

The inspector's role during the giving of evidence

23.135 The classic description of the role of a judge in a civil trial was given by Denning LJ in *Jones v National Coal Board*[166]:

'In the system of trial which we have evolved in this country, the judge sits to hear and determine the issues raised by the parties, not to conduct an investigation or examination on behalf of society at large, as happens, we believe, in some foreign countries. Even in England, however, a judge is not a mere umpire to answer the question "How's that?" His object, above all, is to find out the truth, and to do justice according to law; and in the daily pursuit of it the advocate plays an honourable and necessary role. Was it not Lord Eldon LC who said in a notable passage that "truth is best discovered by powerful statements on both sides of the question"?: see *Ex parte Lloyd* (1822) Mont 70, 72n and Lord Greene MR who explained that justice is best done by a judge who holds the balance between the contending parties without himself taking part in their disputations? If a judge, said Lord Greene, should himself conduct the examination of witnesses, "he, so to speak, descends into the arena and is liable to have his vision clouded by the dust of conflict": see *Yuill v Yuill* [1945] P 15.

Yes, he must keep his vision unclouded. It is all very well to paint justice blind, but she does better without a bandage round her eyes. She should be blind indeed to favour or prejudice, but clear to see which way lies the truth: and the less dust there is about the better. Let the advocates one after the other put the weights into the scales – the "nicely calculated less or more" – but the judge at the end decides which way the balance tilts, be it ever so slightly. So firmly is all this established in our law that the judge is not allowed in a civil dispute to call a witness whom he thinks might throw some light on the facts. He must rest content with the witnesses called by the parties: see *In re Enoch & Zaretzky, Bock & Co* [1910] 1 KB 327. So also it is for the advocates, each in his turn, to examine the witnesses, and not for the judge to take it on himself lest by so doing he appear to favour one side or the other: see *R v Cain* (1936) 25 Cr App r 204, *R v Bateman* (1946) 31 Cr App r 106, and *Harris v Harris*, The Times, Apr 9, 1952 by Birkett LJ especially and it is for the advocate to state his case as fairly and strongly as he can, without undue interruption, lest the sequence of his argument be lost: see *R v Clewer* (1953) 37 Cr App r 37. The judge's part in all this is to hearken to the evidence, only himself asking questions of witnesses when it is necessary to clear up any point that has been overlooked or left obscure; to see that the advocates behave themselves seemly and keep to the rules laid down by law; to exclude irrelevancies and discourage repetition; to make sure by wise intervention that he follows the points that the advocates are making and can assess their worth; and at the end to make up his mind where the truth lies. If he goes beyond this, he drops the mantle of a judge and assumes the robe of an advocate; and the change does not become him well. Lord Chancellor Bacon spoke right when he said that (Essays or Counsels Civil and Moral. Of Judicature): "Patience and gravity of hearing is an essential part of justice; and an over-speaking judge is no well-tuned cymbal"'.

---

[165] [2012] EWCA Civ 311, [2012] Env LR 39 at para 33.
[166] [1957] 2 QB 55 at 63–64.

23.136 *Inquiries*

Given the need for a planning appeal to consider the material considerations as a whole, a planning inspector's role is not quite the same. The inspector must be able to investigate matters which are not being pursued by the parties, but the need for the parties and witnesses to have a fair hearing remains.

23.136 In *Turner v Secretary of State for Communities and Local Government*[167] Sales LJ put the role of planning inspectors conducting inquiries into this context:

'The notional fair-minded observer would appreciate a number of aspects of the present context: (i) an inspector's role has a strong inquisitorial dimension, investigating matters in a way which will enable him to report helpfully to the relevant decision-maker, the Secretary of State; with that end in view, it is fair and appropriate for an inspector to seek to focus debate at an inquiry by making interventions to ensure that he is provided with material to assist him in his task; (ii) an inspector has to manage efficiently the conduct of an inquiry within a limited time-frame and involving a range of parties wishing to give evidence, make submissions and participate in cross-examination of witnesses; this may require robust case management in the interests of all participants; (iii) an inspector is entitled to expect, and may legitimately seek to encourage, focused questioning and short and focused answers in the course of cross-examination of witnesses; (iv) the inquiry process provides an inspector with relevant information through a range of media, including written opening statements, examination of plans and the making of detailed closing submissions, as well as through the evidence of witnesses (both by witness statement and orally in cross-examination), and an inspector is expected to have done a good deal of preparation before an inquiry commences and is entitled to seek to focus debate on particular issues in the form which is most likely to provide clarity about what is at stake and assistance for him in writing a report; and (v) as part of his inquiry-management function, and to encourage a focus on what is most likely to assist him in his reporting task, an inspector is entitled to give indications in the course of an inquiry of points which appear to him to be unrealistic or bad and to require concentration on what appear to him to be the real substantive points of contention or where continued debate will be most helpful to him. It is of course possible that an inspector may go too far in robust inquiry management or in closing down debate, so as to give an appearance of bias. But given the expectation that an inspector should be actively managing the inquiry process to ensure that it is efficient, effective and fair to all interested parties, it will be a rare case, as Woolf J observed[168], in which it is likely that robust inquiry management will be found to have done so'.

Reference to material not produced by the parties

23.137 An inspector may be aware of case law in the courts or decisions by Ministers or inspectors which have not been referred to by the parties. If these are to be considered then the parties usually ought to be given an opportunity for comment unless these authorities could not alter the decision either way. First, there is the possibility that the decision-maker gets the law wrong in reliance upon these cases, either because the decisions are wrong or are misapplied. Second, the case law might prompt the parties to put their cases differently, with new evidence or submissions. Nigel Macleod QC warned in *Ball v Secretary of State for the Environment, Transport and the Regions*[169]:

---

[167] [2015] EWCA Civ 582, [2015] CP Rep 38 at para 18.
[168] Author's note: in *Halifax Building Society v Secretary of State for the Environment* [1983] JPL 816.
[169] [2000] PLCR 299 at 310. The written representations decision in that case was quashed as the inspector relied upon High Court and appeal decisions which had not been referred to the parties.

'There will, however, be cases where the inspector's reliance upon case law, not referred to by the parties, does not give rise to illegality but still gives rise to a legitimate complaint. Such a case would be one where the inspector's correct understanding of the law, based on his own researchers, indicates that an issue, not treated by the parties as a principal one to which they devoted significant weight in their representations, is in fact a decisive issue in the appeal. In such a case, there could be a real risk that the parties would have more to draw to the inspector's attention in respect of the facts and circumstances relevant to that issue; and that a failure to give them the opportunity to do would cause substantial prejudice. In such a case, therefore, the inspector's correct reliance upon the relevant case law would not of itself give grounds for review by the court; but his decision based upon analysis of the facts and circumstances of the appeal in the light of that case law would be open to challenge unless he gave the parties the opportunity to address him further on the consequences of his understanding of the law in the circumstances of the instant appeal'.

23.138 If the additional material or any submissions it may have prompted would not have altered the eventual decision then there is no need to seek comments upon it. There may be value in referring to it in the decision – particularly if it is an important judgment or new policy document which post-dates any hearing or representations – so that all parties are aware that it was considered.

23.139 In *Jory v Secretary of State for Transport, Local Government and the Regions* it was unfair for an inspector to consult the appellant and the local planning authority on the wording of conditions following a hearing, but not to consult local residents where 'the extent to which any harm to the living conditions enjoyed by local residents could be mitigated and controlled by conditions was of central importance in the inspector's reasoning'[170].

23.140 It is ordinarily necessary to show substantial prejudice to constitute a breach of natural justice. An appropriate test to identify such a breach is[171]:

'Would a reasonable person viewing the matter objectively and knowing all the facts known to the court consider that there was a risk that the procedure adopted by the Secretary of State has resulted in injustice or unfairness?'

23.141 The maxim is that justice must not only be done but must be seen to be done or, put another way, appearances matter. Generally speaking a procedural or fairness error must have the potential to affect the final decision for there to be a breach of natural justice or for a remedy to be granted (either analysis amounts to the same outcome in practice). There may be some proceedings which are so grossly unfair that they must be quashed even if the outcome would have been the same. If a party was shut out from the proceedings, by for example, not being told of them when they should have been informed, then it is offensive for the decision to stand even if the court could be satisfied that anything that person had to say would not have affected the outcome.

---

[170] *Jory v Secretary of State for Transport, Local Government and the Regions* [2002] EWHC 2724, [2003] JPL 549 at para 28 per Sullivan J. He accepted that in the 'great majority' of cases it would not be unfair to consult on the precise terms of conditions (at para 26).
[171] *Robert Hitchin Ltd v Secretary of State for the Environment* (1995) 72 P & CR 579 at 586–587 per Harrison J.

23.142 *Inquiries*

NATIONAL SECURITY CASES

23.142 The general principle is that at a planning inquiry 'oral evidence shall be heard in public and documentary evidence shall be open to public inspection'[172]. This has been subject to a long standing power of the Secretary of State to direct that particular evidence may only be heard or inspected by specified persons if that evidence was likely to disclose matters of national security or measures to ensure the security of any premises or property and that public disclosure of that information would be contrary to the national interest[173]. Of course, if parties are excluded from part of the evidence it is difficult to effectively scrutinise the case and it is presumptively unfair on those parties.

23.143 How inquiries would be conducted in those circumstances became of more immediate concern with the extension of planning control to the Crown in the Planning and Compulsory Purchase Act 2004. Those reforms allowed the Attorney General or the Consul General to the Welsh Government to appoint persons to represent those who would be excluded from dealing with that evidence[174]. The legislation envisages the appointed representative to be a 'special advocate'. A special advocate is a barrister in independent practice on a government list who has undergone security vetting. A special advocate will take instructions from those who are interested but excluded from the closed evidence prior to the advocate seeing that material. Once the advocate has seen the closed evidence then they cannot receive further instructions or discuss the case with those persons because of the risk of disclosing the closed evidence. The special advocate will then deal with procedural matters, cross-examine and make submissions on the closed evidence and attend any closed site visit[175].

23.144 Any person may request the Minister[176] to make a national security direction applying these procedures[177]. The receipt of such a request has to be publicised and an opportunity given for written representations as to whether the direction should be made[178]. The Minister will consider whether to make the direction on written representations or following a hearing[179]. A special advocate may be appointed to make written or oral submissions as to whether a direction should be made in respect of what at that point is still 'potentially closed evidence'[180]. Notice of the Minister's

---

[172] Town and Country Planning Act 1990, s 321(2).
[173] Town and Country Planning Act 1990, s 321(3), (4).
[174] Town and Country Planning Act 1990, ss 321(5), (6), 321B(2). The costs of those persons may be paid by the government or any person interested in the inquiry in relation to the security issues that the Secretary of State directs: s 321(9). These costs provisions are applied in non-inquiry cases by s 321A.
[175] See in the planning context Planning (National Security Directions and Appointed Representatives) (England) Rules 2006, SI 2006/1284, r 4; Planning (National Security Directions and Appointed Representatives) (Wales) Rules 2006, SI 2006/1387, r 4.
[176] The Minister is a Secretary of State in England but in Wales the power is exercised concurrently by the Welsh Ministers and a Secretary of State.
[177] Planning (National Security Directions and Appointed Representatives) (England) Rules 2006, r 5; Planning (National Security Directions and Appointed Representatives) (Wales) Rules 2006, r 5.
[178] Planning (National Security Directions and Appointed Representatives) (England) Rules 2006, r 6; Planning (National Security Directions and Appointed Representatives) (Wales) Rules 2006, r 6.
[179] Planning (National Security Directions and Appointed Representatives) (England) Rules 2006, rr 8–11; Planning (National Security Directions and Appointed Representatives) (Wales) Rules 2006, rr 8–11.
[180] Planning (National Security Directions and Appointed Representatives) (England) Rules 2006, r 4(1); Planning (National Security Directions and Appointed Representatives) (Wales) Rules 2006, r 4(1).

National security cases **23.148**

decision has to be given to those who made representations but no reasons can be given which would result in the public disclosure of closed evidence[181]. Such national security directions can be made at any time, including prior to the submission of an appeal.

23.145 Appeal and call in procedures are modified where a national security direction is in place. These alterations however assume that the person introducing the closed evidence is the applicant or appellant; they cater less well for the situation that a government agency is raising a concern about another development which might interfere with communications or overlook a restricted site[182].

23.146 If a national security direction is in force then an appeal form does not have to be accompanied by a statement of case, statement of proposed procedures or draft statement of common ground, unlike the usual English position[183]. In inquiry cases the applicant is expected to produce open and closed versions of any outline statements and statements of case[184]. Open versions go to all parties including the local planning authority, whilst the closed version is seen by the inspector and the appointed representative. Rule 6 parties are required to provide open statements of case, the implication being that a closed statement may be produced outside the rules. If the application or appeal is made by or on behalf of the Crown then the applicant and the special advocate will agree a closed statement of common ground. Any party entitled to appear who proposes to call closed evidence shall produce two versions of the proof, one with and one without the closed evidence. The open version will be sent to the local planning authority and the applicant (if it is not from the applicant), whilst the special advocate will have the closed version. The closed evidence will be heard in sessions involving the body producing it, the special advocate, the inspector and any assessor but with other parties and the public excluded.

23.147 The status of an applicant who is not acting for the Crown is somewhat inconsistent in the modified rules. They are not entitled to see the closed submissions or proofs, but are entitled to attend any site visit which involves closed evidence[185]. Following the inquiry the inspector and any assessor will produce separate open and closed reports and the Minister's decision will contain reasons in closed and open sections.

23.148 The use of a closed material procedure is inherently controversial as it means that parties are denied access to part of the case and evidence against them, are not allowed to challenge that and are not allowed to know some of the reasons why a decision is made against them. The ability of a special advocate to represent a party who is unaware of the case being made is limited and the advocates may need experts of their own, particularly to advise on technical matters. Closed evidence processes must be exceptional and used only to the most limited degree possible, maximising the ability to deal with the issues in open evidence. The extent to which a

---

[181] Planning (National Security Directions and Appointed Representatives) (England) Rules 2006, r 14; Planning (National Security Directions and Appointed Representatives) (Wales) Rules 2006, r 14.
[182] Both examples given by the Minister for Housing and Planning, Keith Hill, in the passage of the Bill: Standing Committee A, 14 October 2003, col 37.
[183] DMPO 2015, art 37(4).
[184] See modifications made by the English Inquiries Rules, r 23A and Sch 1, Part 1; the Welsh Inquiries Rules, r 22B and Sch 1, Part 1. There is no equivalent provision in the Inspectors Rules so the assumption must be that security cases will be determined by the Minister.
[185] English and Welsh Inquiries Rules, r 16(2A) as modified by Sch 1, Part 1, para 7.

23.149 *Inquiries*

party excluded from the closed hearing is entitled to know the gist of the case against it does depend upon the effect of the proceedings, with more disclosure required where individual liberty is at stake[186].

URGENT CROWN DEVELOPMENT

23.149 Inquiries into urgent Crown development are subject to a modified procedure[187]. These reduce the time scales for the submission of statements of case and proofs and for the holding of pre-inquiry meetings and the inquiry itself.

---

[186] See *Tariq v Home Office* [2011] UKSC 35, [2012] 1 AC 452; *CF v Ministry of Defence* [2014] EWHC 3171 (QB).

[187] English Inquiries Rules, r 23A(2) and Sch 1, Part 2; Welsh Inquiries Rules, r 22B(2) and Sch 1, Part 2.

Chapter 24

Decisions and costs in appeals and call-ins

24.1 Following the close of any inquiry or hearing and the end of the site visit in an appeal or call-in, the determination processes become similar.

The powers and duties of inspectors in determining the appeal are the same across the inquiry, hearing and written representations procedures. Ministerial decisions in call-in and recovered jurisdiction cases will usually in practice take place following an inquiry.

MINISTERIAL DECISION-MAKING

24.2 Call-in or recovered appeal decisions in England are taken by the Secretary of State for Communities and Local Government unless a joint determination process arises for statutory undertakers. Applications are jointly determined by the Secretary of State for Communities and Local Government and the Minister responsible for the statutory undertaker if the planning application is made by a statutory undertaker on their operational land or land they propose to acquire and one of the Ministers so directs following a call-in or appeal[1]. In such cases the inspector will report to both Ministers. Welsh Ministerial decisions are taken by a variety of ministers, currently the Minister for Natural Resources and the Minister for Housing and Regeneration, or by officials.

24.3 Where the appeal is being decided by the Minister, the inspector will write a report setting out procedural matters, summarising the notices, identifying policy, summarising the parties' submissions and making recommendations. The report, along with all of the inquiry documentation, will be sent to civil servants. They will then send the report to the Minister, with a briefing note containing the civil service recommendation, along with any key documents. The Minister will decide upon the outcome and a decision letter will be drafted, to be signed by a Minister or civil servant.

24.4 The procedural rules for ministerial consideration following an inquiry are in rr 17 and 18 of the Town and Country Planning (Inquiries Procedure) (England) Rules 2000 (the English Inquiries Rules) and the Town and Country Planning (Inquiries Procedure) (Wales) Rules 2003 (the Welsh Inquiries Rules)[2]. The English and Welsh procedures are identical in legislative terms. The Town and Country Planning (Hearings Procedure) (England) Rules 2000 (the English Hearings Rules) and the Town and Country Planning (Hearings Procedure) (Wales) Rules 2003 (the

---

[1] Town and Country Planning Act 1990, s 266. The appropriate Minister is defined in s 265.
[2] SIs 2000/1629 and 2003/1266 respectively.

24.5 *Decisions and costs in appeals and call-ins*

Welsh Hearings Rules)[3] deal with the post-hearings procedures for Ministerial decisions at r 13. The written representations regulations in both nations do not distinguish between Ministerial and inspector decisions.

24.5 Following the inquiry the inspector is required to make a report in writing which shall include his 'conclusions and his recommendations or his reasons for not making any recommendations'[4]. It will be extremely rare for an inspector to fail to include a recommendation. Even if there are important legal matters which the inspector will leave to the Minister, a planning judgment will usually have to be made once the law is decided. The inspector would be expected to make a recommendation as to whether the planning decision in the law was found to be X or found to be Y.

24.6 In practice the inspector's report will be set out in a chapter format. It will usually begin by setting out any procedural matters, summarising the scheme and perhaps the site and locality. There will be a chapter identifying the relevant policy and then chapters summarising the parties' submissions. The summaries will usually be edited versions of the parties' closings[5] along with any particular points which the inspector considers arose of the evidence. A cogent, written closing from the main parties is therefore essential[6]. The critical part of the report is the inspector's assessment of the appeal and recommendation to the Minister, which will be contained in a further chapter. The inspector will also report on any submitted planning obligation and on the conditions which ought to be imposed if the application or appeal is allowed.

24.7 If an assessor has been appointed, any assessor's report will be appended to the inspector's report and the inspector's report will state how far he agrees or disagrees with it and the reasons for any disagreement[7]. Whilst an assessor could simply advise the inspector on matters to incorporate on his report, it is normal practice for the assessor to write a report. That report essentially goes to the inspector who will take it into account in writing his report and then send both reports to the Minister.

24.8 An inspector's report is the inspector's own work and view. Sometimes inspectors will ask other inspectors to read the draft report to check for clarity and obvious errors, but the Planning Inspectorate has no control over the report.

24.9 The inspector's report will be sent with all the appeal or call-in documents and any assessors' report to the Minister's department. In England the papers will go to the National Planning Casework Unit of the Department of Communities and Local Government. The civil servants will consider the report and material with a view to making a recommendation to their Minister. Legal advice on any aspects may be taken at that point. It is possible, albeit rare, for the inspector to be asked to prepare an addendum report if there are matters that officials consider need to be addressed further.

---

[3] SIs 2000/1626 and 2003/1271 respectively.
[4] English Inquiries Rules, r 17(1). The Welsh r 17(1) is materially identical.
[5] Omitting most of the jokes and occasionally toning down the language.
[6] The inspector will usually ask for a Word version of the closing to be e-mailed to the Inspectorate to form the basis of the report. Unless otherwise agreed, this should be identical to the printed version handed to the inspector and not amended to reflect the 'as delivered' closing or further refined.
[7] English and Welsh Inquiries Rules, r 17(2), (3). As in earlier chapters, where the English and Welsh references are identical The sets of rules or regulations are referred to collectively.

24.10 Usually the Minister will be provided with a briefing report from civil servants, containing a recommendation, the inspector's report and the more important document from the appeal or call-in. The Minister may request any other documents which were in front of the inspector. Sometimes the content of the briefing will be important. The lawfulness of a decision taken by a Minister depends on the Minister's personal knowledge and if the Minister has been incorrectly briefed then the decision will be in error[8]. The briefing note to the Minister will usually have to be disclosed following the decision under the Environmental Information Regulations 2004[9] or the Freedom of Information Act 2000[10].

24.11 If the Minister differs from the inspector on a material matter of fact or takes into account any new evidence or new fact (other than changing government policy) and consequently is disposed to disagree with the inspector's recommendation, then notice must be given to the persons who were entitled to appear at the inquiry and did so appear[11]. They must be told of the disagreement and the reasons for it, and given an opportunity to make written representations on the point within a three-week period. If the notice is because of new evidence or a new matter of fact, the appellant or local planning authority may require the inquiry to be reopened to address those matters[12].

24.12 The Minister is, however, entitled to disagree with the inspector's judgments and does not have to refer such matters back to the parties for comment, unless he raises a new point which the parties could not have been expected to deal with. There is no need for the Minister to conduct a site visit[13], or commission a civil servant to do so, even when disagreeing with the inspector on matters which could be informed by such a visit, such as visual or landscape impact or the setting of heritage assets[14]. The test is 'is whether the Secretary of State had sufficient material before him on which he was reasonably able to make a judgment on the issue'[15]. A considerable amount of evidence on these topics, including photographs, will inevitably be in the papers available to the Minister. If officials advise a Minister to grant planning permission for a proposed development and the Minister disagrees with that advice and wishes to refuse planning permission, officials will then draft a decision letter

---

[8] *R (National Association of Health Stores) v Secretary of State for Health* [2005] EWCA Civ 154 at paras 71–74 per Keene LJ.
[9] SI 2004/3391.
[10] *Lord Baker of Dorking v Information Commissioner* EA/2006/0043 where the former Cabinet Minister Kenneth Baker obtained the release of the briefing given to the Deputy Prime Minister on the Vauxhall Tower scheme.
[11] English Inquiries Rules, r 17(5), (6); Welsh Inquiries Rules, r 17(5), (6). Similar rules apply in the very rare event of a hearing being determined by a Minister: English and Welsh Hearings Rules, r 13.
[12] English and Welsh Inquiries Rules, r 17(7).
[13] The *Guidance on Planning Propriety Issues* for Ministers envisages that site visits can be carried out.
[14] *R v Secretary of State for the Environment ex p Gosport Borough Council* [1992] JPL 476 at 479–480 per Popplewell J; *Campaign for the Protection of Rural Wales v Secretary of State for Wales* (unreported, 7 April 2000) at para 13 per Nigel Macleod QC; *De Mulder v First Secretary of State* [2005] EWHC 2640 (Admin) at para 30 per Crane J; *Novalong Ltd v Secretary of State for Communities and Local Government* [2008] EWHC 2136 (Admin) at paras 25–28, 57 per Sullivan J; *Searle v Secretary of State for Communities and Local Government* [2012] EWHC 2269 (Admin) at paras 43–51 per Edwards-Stuart J; *Wind Prospect Developments Ltd v Secretary of State for Communities and Local Government* [2014] EWHC 4041 (Admin) at para 54 per Lang J; *Ecotricity (Next Generation) Ltd v Secretary of State for Communities and Local Government* [2014] EWHC 2699 (Admin) at para 22 per Mitting J, upheld [2015] EWCA Civ 657 at para 34 per Sullivan LJ.
[15] *Ecotricity (Next Generation) Ltd v Secretary of State for Communities and Local Government* [2015] EWCA Civ 657 at para 35 per Sullivan LJ.

24.13 *Decisions and costs in appeals and call-ins*

setting out what they understand to be the Minister's reasons for wishing to refuse planning permission[16].

24.13 The decision will be contained in a decision letter, usually accompanied by the inspector's report. The decision letter may be sent with a statement of the inspector's conclusion and recommendation and a copy of the report may be requested from the Minister in writing[17]. In practice decision letters and reports are usually e-mailed to the main parties and those who requested them. They are also immediately published on the Minister's websites.

'Minded to' letters

24.14 Ministers are able to write provision decision letters saying that they are 'minded to' decide the application or appeal in a certain way if or unless a particular step is taken. The Minister might consider that a scheme would be acceptable if it included more affordable housing or starter homes, a greater contribution to particular works or was amended in a certain way. If the change could not be brought about by a condition, this could only be achieved by a new or altered planning obligation or by a formal amendment to the scheme. The purpose of a 'minded to' letter is to give the developer an opportunity to make the change. Minded to letters have the benefit of enabling a generally desirable and usually large scheme to be approved in line with the Minister's view, rather than refused and left to a second application to the local planning authority, where the issues might not be confined to the point of concern to the Minister.

INSPECTOR'S DECISION-MAKING

24.15 The inspector will write up his decision having considered any assessor's report. If the inspector proposes to take into account any new evidence or new matter of fact then notice must be given to the parties who were entitled to and did appear, allowing them three weeks to make written representations or request a re-opening of the inquiry or hearing[18]. In such cases the inquiry or hearing must be re-opened at the appellant or local planning authority's request[19].

New matters following the close of an inquiry or hearing

24.16 Practice is that an inspector will not take into account any representations received after the close of the inquiry unless he has specifically requested them to address particular points. The Minister has a discretion whether to take into account any later material[20] but that must be exercised fairly and ensuring that the Minister has regard to all material matters. In practice, the parties should say everything they need to say to the inspector and only make representations to the Minister on later developments.

---

[16] *Ball v Secretary of State for Communities and Local Government* [2014] EWCA Civ 372, [2014] JPL 1016 at para 25 per Sullivan LJ.
[17] English and Welsh Inquiries Rules, r 18(2).
[18] English and Welsh Inspectors Inquiries Rules, r 18(3), (4); English and Welsh Inspectors Hearings Rules, r 14(3).
[19] English and Welsh Inspectors Inquiries Rules, r 18(4); English and Welsh Inspectors Hearings Rules, r 14(4).
[20] English and Welsh Inquiries Rules, r 17(4).

If post-inquiry correspondence takes place, Ministers must be careful to ensure that there is a fair opportunity to comment on new points made which are subsequently relied upon[21].

24.17 The Minister must have regard to the material considerations at the time of deciding the appeal or call-in[22] and so may need to consult on these. However, it is only changes which might alter the decision which could require further debate. There would be no point consulting upon a change which simply strengthened the Minister's view.

Split decisions

24.18 The Minister and inspector are able to allow or dismiss the appeal or 'reverse or vary any part of the decision of the local planning authority (whether the appeal relates to that part of it or not)'[23]. Consequently they may grant permission for part and to refuse permission for part. Whether the approved part is severable or substantially different from the scheme applied for are factors in deciding whether this ought to be done. As Ouseley J observed in *Johnson v Secretary of State for Communities and Local Government*[24] these tests are 'endeavouring to express the concern that a permission granted in part only should not be significantly different, in its context were it to be implemented, from the basis upon which it was applied for, consulted upon and considered'. In some circumstances it may be appropriate for the decision-maker to suggest that a split decision is possible if it has not already been raised by a party.

REASONS

24.19 Whether the appeal is decided following an inquiry or hearing, Ministerial or inspectorial decisions must be accompanied by written reasons[25]. There is a statutory duty to give reasons in Welsh written representations cases[26]. Whilst no such statutory duty applies in English written representations[27], conventionally reasons

---

[21] For example, *Reading Borough Council v Secretary of State for the Environment* (1986) 52 P & CR 385.
[22] In a similar manner to the obligation on local planning authorities in *R (on the application of Kides) v South Cambridgeshire District Council* [2002] EWCA Civ 1370, [2003] JPL 431 at paras 121–127 per Jonathan Parker LJ.
[23] Town and Country Planning Act 1990, s 79(1).
[24] [2007] EWHC 1839 (Admin) at para 25.
[25] English and Welsh Inquiries Rules, r 18(1); English and Welsh Inspectors Inquiries Rules, r 19(1); English and Welsh Hearings Rules, r 15(2), 16(2).
[26] Town and Country Planning (Referrals and Appeals) (Written Representations Procedure) (Wales) Regulations 2015, SI 2015/1331, regs 11 (for householder and minor commercial cases) and 18 (for all other written representations appeals).
[27] A general duty to give reasons under Tribunals and Inquiries Act 1992, s 10 (and referred to in the inspector provisions in the Town and Country Planning Act 1990, Sch 6, para 8) only applies where the person concerned could have required an inquiry to be heard. Whilst this had been the position (see *North Wiltshire District Council v Secretary of State for the Environment* (1993) 65 P & CR 137 at 142–143 per Mann LJ), it is no longer the case following the Planning Act 2008: see Town and Country Planning Act 1990, ss 78(2), (3) and 319A. There is no relevant general duty at common law (see *R (on the application of Hasan) v Secretary of State for Trade and Industry* [2008] EWCA Civ 1312). But the duty to give reasons derives either from the principles of procedural fairness applied in the statutory context of a written representations appeal or from the legitimate expectation generated by the Secretary of State's long-established practice of giving reasons in such cases, or both: see *Martin v Secretary of State for Communities and Local Government* [2015] EWHC 3435 (Admin) at para 51 per Lindblom LJ.

24.20 *Decisions and costs in appeals and call-ins*

are given. In practice the reasons are contained in the same document. The Ministerial decision letter will contain the Minister's reasons. The letter will explicitly adopt the inspector's reasons or set out where the Minister disagrees with the inspector and why. An inspector's decision will set out the entirety of the reasoning, although it will be much shorter than a report. A decision is aimed primarily at the parties, who know what has happened at the inquiry or hearing and what is in the appeal papers, whereas a report has to explain the case to Ministers and civil servants.

24.20 The decision with its reasons must be sent[28] to the appellant, the local authority, those who were entitled to and did take part in the inquiry or hearing, along with anyone who did take part in the inquiry or hearing and had asked to be sent a copy of the decision[29].

Reasons for ministerial and inspector decisions

24.21 The adequacy of reasons in planning decisions and other contexts has generated a mass of case law. Since a reasons challenge is inherently fact-sensitive it is unproductive to search the cases for too many detailed rules[30]. What may be an acceptable omission in one case might not be acceptable in another. The most useful, and most often quoted, summary of the court's approach to reasons was given by Lord Brown of Eaton-under-Heywood in *South Buckinghamshire District Council v Porter (No 2)*[31]:

> 'The reasons for a decision must be intelligible and they must be adequate. They must enable the reader to understand why the matter was decided as it was and what conclusions were reached on the "principal important controversial issues", disclosing how any issue of law or fact was resolved. Reasons can be briefly stated, the degree of particularity required depending entirely on the nature of the issues falling for decision. The reasoning must not give rise to a substantial doubt as to whether the decision-maker erred in law, for example by misunderstanding some relevant policy or some other important matter or by failing to reach a rational decision on relevant grounds. But such adverse inference will not readily be drawn. The reasons need refer only to the main issues in the dispute, not to every material consideration. They should enable disappointed developers to assess their prospects of obtaining some alternative development permission, or, as the case may be, their unsuccessful opponents to understand how the policy or approach underlying the grant of permission may impact upon future such applications. Decision letters must be read in a straightforward manner, recognising that they are addressed to parties well aware of the issues involved and the arguments advanced. A reasons challenge will only succeed if the party aggrieved can satisfy the court that he has genuinely been substantially prejudiced by the failure to provide an adequately reasoned decision'.

---

[28] Traditionally this has been by post, but may be by e-mail or by informing participants that the documents have been put on a website and how to access them.

[29] English and Welsh Inquiries Rules, r 21; English and Welsh Inspectors Inquiries Rules, r 20; English and Welsh Hearings Rules, rr 15, 16.

[30] See the comments to similar effect in *Mordue v Secretary of State for Communities and Local Government* [2015] EWCA Civ 1243 at para 27 per Sales LJ: 'Reading other decision letters (and the judgments in relation to them) can take up considerable time and effort without adding value for the determination of the particular case before the court. The relevant principles in relation to the giving of reasons are well-established and very well known, and it should be sufficient for a judge to be reminded of them and taken to the reasons in the case before him or her to assess them in light of those principles, without any need for exegetical comparison with reasons given in relation to other planning decisions'.

[31] [2004] UKHL 33, [2004] 1 WLR 1953 at para 36.

24.22 In an appeal from the Upper Tribunal (Lands Chamber) *Thomas Newall Ltd v Lancaster City Council* Rimer LJ provided a neat explanation as to why reasons should be given[32]:

> 'A tribunal should always give reasons for its decisions, however briefly. If it does not, the parties do not know why they have respectively won and lost, and the losing party is at a disadvantage in that he cannot know whether such reasoning, if any, as did result in the tribunal's decision might properly be the subject of challenge on an appeal. The articulation of reasons for a decision is anyway an essential part of the intellectual discipline that every tribunal and court should always go through, since such articulation is the best possible check as to the correctness of the decision. There can be few judges or tribunals who have not arrived at a conclusion that the answer to a particular question is X, only to realise that their attempt to provide a reasoned explanation of such answer reveals to them its obvious error'.

24.23 The general statements apply across the board: there is no particular higher standard of reasoning required, for example, in listed building cases[33]. Some particular situations have been usefully examined. If a Minister or inspector 'is going to depart from the policy, it must give clear reasons for not doing so in order that the recipient of its decision will know why the decision is being made as an exception to the policy and the grounds upon which the decision is taken': see *Gransden & Co Ltd v Secretary of State for the Environment*[34]. A difference from statutory consultees should be identified and explained, see Beatson J in *Shadwell Estates Ltd v Breckland District Council*[35]:

> 'a decision-maker should give the views of statutory consultees, in this context the "appropriate nature conservation bodies", "great" or "considerable" weight. A departure from those views requires "cogent and compelling reasons": see *R (Hart DC) v Secretary of State for Communities and Local Government* [2008] EWHC 1204 (Admin) per Sullivan J at [49] and *R (Akester) v DEFRA* [2010] EWHC 232 (Admin) per Owen J. at [112], [115]'.

24.24 There is no particularly higher standard of reasoning required where the Minister or inspector disagrees with the views of expert witnesses. The decision-maker needs to give adequate and intelligible reasons for the decision, but that does not necessarily require a rebuttal of the evidence of particular expert witnesses[36].

DECISIONS SUBJECT TO ENVIRONMENTAL IMPACT ASSESSMENT

24.25 Where a planning application or appeal subject to EIA (an EIA application) is determined by the Secretary of State, Welsh Ministers or an inspector, the decision must say that the 'environmental information' has been taken into account[37]. Since

---

[32] [2013] EWCA Civ 802, [2013] JPL 1531 at para 53.
[33] *Mordue v Secretary of State for Communities and Local Government* [2015] EWCA Civ 1243 at para 26 per Sales LJ.
[34] (1987) 54 P & CR 86 at 94 per Woolf J.
[35] [2013] EWHC 12 (Admin) at para 72.
[36] *RWE Npower Renewables Ltd v Welsh Ministers* [2012] EWCA Civ 311 per Pill LJ at paras 22–28; *Tegni Cymru Cyf v Welsh Ministers* [2010] EWCA Civ 1635 per Pitchford LJ at para 27; and see the misgivings of Lang J in *Macarthur v Secretary of State for Communities and Local Government* [2013] EWHC 3 (Admin) at paras 56–63.
[37] In England by the Town and Country Planning (Environmental Impact Assessment) Regulations 2011, SI 2011/1824, reg 3(4); in Wales, under the Town and Country Planning (Environmental Impact Assessment) (England and Wales) Regulations 1999, SI 1999/293, reg 3(2).

24.26 *Decisions and costs in appeals and call-ins*

the environment information includes additional information produced by the applicant and representations from third parties[38] it is insufficient simply to say that the environmental statement has been taken into account.

24.26 Once an EIA application is determined by the Secretary of State, Welsh Ministers or an inspector, the Minister shall notify the local planning authority of the decision and provide it with a statement of:

'(i) the content of the decision and any conditions attached to it;

(ii) the main reasons and considerations on which the decision is based including, if relevant, information about the participation of the public;

(iii) a description, where necessary, of the main measures to avoid, reduce and, if possible, offset the major adverse effects of the development; and

(iv) information regarding the right to challenge the validity of the decision and the procedures for doing so'[39].

24.27 This requirement is almost invariably met by the conventional reasoned decision and the accompanying note on how it can be challenged. Where the EIA legislation goes further than the conventional decision taking obligations is that the local planning authority is required to publicise the EIA decision. As with its own determinations of EIA applications, it must 'inform the public of the decision, by local advertisement, or by such other means as are reasonable in the circumstances' and make the Minister's statement (so in practice the decision and note on challenges) available for inspection with the planning register[40]. This publicity must be given 'as soon as reasonably practicable' after receiving the decision.

Placing the decision on the authority's own website where it can be found under the planning application reference is insufficient[41].

COSTS IN PLANNING APPEALS AND CALL-INS

24.28 Usually parties in planning appeals and call-ins meet their own costs, however the Minister or the inspector may order one party to pay some or all of another party's costs of the appeal or call-in. Such costs are only awarded if one party has acted unreasonably[42] and that unreasonable behaviour has caused the other party to waste costs of the appeal. Unreasonable in this context has its ordinary meaning[43], rather than the more extreme level of public law unreasonableness or

---

[38] See reg 2(1) of the 2011 and 1999 EIA Regulations.
[39] In England by the Town and Country Planning (Environmental Impact Assessment) Regulations 2011, reg 24(1)(c), (2); in Wales, under the Town and Country Planning (Environmental Impact Assessment) (England and Wales) Regulations 1999, reg 21(1)(c), (2).
[40] Town and Country Planning (Environmental Impact Assessment) Regulations 2011, reg 24(3) applying (1)(b), (c); Town and Country Planning (Environmental Impact Assessment) (England and Wales) Regulations 1999, reg 21(3) applying (1)(c), (2).
[41] See on the inadequacy of a website alone to meet the requirement of the Environmental Assessment of Plans and Programmes Regulations 2004, SI 2004/1633, to 'take such steps as it considers appropriate to bring the preparation of the relevant documents to the attention of the persons': *Kendall v Rochford District Council* [2014] EWHC 3866 (Admin), [2015] Env LR 21 at paras 79–94, 127 per Lindblom J.
[42] A different approach applies in compulsory purchase and analogous orders where a successful landowner will recover its costs.
[43] *Manchester City Council v Secretary of State for the Environment* [1988] JPL 774.

perversity. Unreasonable behaviour may be substantive or procedural. Substantively unreasonable conduct would include bringing an appeal which is bound to fail, or unreasonably refusing a planning application. An individual ground of appeal or reason for refusal may also be unreasonable and attract a partial costs award. An example of unreasonable procedural behaviour would be the submission of late evidence which causes the adjournment of the hearing.

24.29 The power to award costs in inquiries originated in the Local Government Acts and is presently contained in the Local Government Act 1972, s 250(5):

> 'The Secretary of State may make orders as to the costs of the parties at the inquiry and as to the parties by whom the costs are to be paid, and every such order may be made a rule of the High Court on the application of any party named in the order'.

That provision applies to inquiries held under the 1972 Act[44]. Conventionally costs powers are granted in other inquiries and proceedings by applying s 250(5). So the provision is applied to an inquiry which the Minister causes to be held for his functions under the Town and Country Planning Act 1990 by s 320(2). It is also applied to written representation and hearing cases[45].

24.30 The essential elements of any costs award are:

- the paying party (that is, the person against whom the award is made) has acted unreasonably;

- that unreasonable conduct has caused unnecessary or wasted expenditure by the receiving party;

- an application for costs is made at the appropriate time or initiated by the inspector.

English costs guidance is primarily contained in the *Planning Practice Guidance*[46] whilst in Wales it is still in Welsh Office Circular 23/93[47].

Unreasonable conduct

24.31 Unreasonableness is used as an ordinary word, so without its public law meanings. A party's position may be unreasonable where there is no justification offered for the position or where any justification is not only found to be wrong but was so poor or weak as to be unreasonable. For example, a reason for refusal may be unreasonable if it is withdrawn late or no evidence or submissions are offered in favour of it, or it is maintained but the evidence and submissions are so weak as to be unreasonable. It is best not to try to put a gloss on the word 'unreasonable' in this context: there is no particular threshold for how bad a point has to be. Of course,

---

[44] There is also a separate power for the Minister to direct parties to pay the Minister's costs (s 250(4)) but that has not been used in planning appeal or call in inquiries. This power is modified for planning purposes in England to allow a portion of the costs to be ordered: Town and Country Planning Act 1990, s 320(3).
[45] Town and Country Planning Act 1990, s 322. The power to award costs in written representations cases was extended to Wales from 11 November 2014, by s 322(1AA) inserted by the Town and Country Planning (Determination of Procedure) (Wales) Order 2014, SI 2014/2773.
[46] ID 16-027 to 16-056.
[47] There is also *Costs Awards in Planning Appeals: a guide for applicants* covering England and Wales.

24.32 *Decisions and costs in appeals and call-ins*

there may be good reasons for the late withdrawal of a reason for refusal, perhaps because the issue has been settled.

24.32 Costs applications can be divided between complaints about the merits of a party's case (substantive) and about their conduct of the appeal (procedural). Conduct of the application process is treated as a substantive complaint.

24.33 An award of costs for adopting a substantively unreasonable decision is 'not envisaged' in call-in cases[48] as there has been neither a decision to appeal nor a reason for refusal, prior to the call-in.

24.34 The *Planning Practice Guidance* provides the following examples of substantively unreasonable behaviour by local planning authorities[49]:

'by unreasonably refusing or failing to determine planning applications, or by unreasonably defending appeals. ...

- preventing or delaying development which should clearly be permitted, having regard to its accordance with the development plan, national policy and any other material considerations.
- failure to produce evidence to substantiate each reason for refusal on appeal
- vague, generalised or inaccurate assertions about a proposal's impact, which are unsupported by any objective analysis.
- refusing planning permission on a planning ground capable of being dealt with by conditions risks an award of costs, where it is concluded that suitable conditions would enable the proposed development to go ahead
- acting contrary to, or not following, well-established case law
- persisting in objections to a scheme or elements of a scheme which the Secretary of State or an inspector has previously indicated to be acceptable
- not determining similar cases in a consistent manner
- failing to grant a further planning permission for a scheme that is the subject of an extant or recently expired permission where there has been no material change in circumstances
- refusing to approve reserved matters when the objections relate to issues that should already have been considered at the outline stage
- imposing a condition that is not necessary, relevant to planning and to the development to be permitted, enforceable, precise and reasonable in all other respects, and thus does not comply with the guidance in the National Planning Policy Framework on planning conditions and obligations
- requiring that the appellant enter into a planning obligation which does not accord with the law or relevant national policy in the National Planning Policy Framework, on planning conditions and obligations
- refusing to enter into pre-application discussions, or to provide reasonably requested information, when a more helpful approach would probably have resulted in either the appeal being avoided altogether, or the issues to be considered being narrowed, thus reducing the expense associated with the appeal

---

[48] *Planning Practice Guidance* para 16-034-20140306.
[49] *Planning Practice Guidance* para 16-049-20140306. If the Mayor of London has directed refusal of the application then he will be treated in the same way as the local planning authority.

- not reviewing their case promptly following the lodging of an appeal against refusal of planning permission (or non-determination), or an application to remove or vary one or more conditions, as part of sensible on-going case management.
- if the local planning authority grants planning permission on an identical application where the evidence base is unchanged and the scheme has not been amended in any way, they run the risk of a full award of costs for an abortive appeal which is subsequently withdrawn'.

24.35 Substantively unreasonable behaviour by appellants includes[50]:

- 'the development is clearly not in accordance with the development plan, and no other material considerations such as national planning policy are advanced that indicate the decision should have been made otherwise, or where other material considerations are advanced, there is inadequate supporting evidence
- the appeal follows a recent appeal decision in respect of the same, or a very similar, development on the same, or substantially the same site where the Secretary of State or an inspector decided that the proposal was unacceptable and circumstances have not materially changed in the intervening period
- lack of co-operation on any planning obligation'.

24.36 Procedural failures by appellants or local planning authorities would include[51]:

- lack of co-operation with the other party or parties
- delay in providing information or other failure to adhere to deadlines
- only supplying relevant information at appeal when it was previously requested, but not provided, at application stage
- not agreeing a statement of common ground in a timely manner or not agreeing factual matters common to witnesses of both principal parties
- introducing fresh and substantial evidence at a late stage necessitating an adjournment, or extra expense for preparatory work that would not otherwise have arisen
- prolonging the proceedings by introducing a new reason for refusal [local planning authorities]
- prolonging the proceedings by introducing a new ground of appeal or issue [appellants]
- withdrawal of any reason for refusal [local planning authorities]
- failing to provide relevant information within statutory time limits, resulting in an enforcement notice being quashed without the issues on appeal being determined
- failing to attend or to be represented at a site visit, hearing or inquiry without good reason
- ...
- providing information that is shown to be manifestly inaccurate or untrue
- deliberately concealing relevant evidence at planning application stage or at subsequent appeal

---

[50] *Planning Practice Guidance* para 16-053-20140306.
[51] Types of procedural unreasonableness are often common to both parties: *Planning Practice Guidance* para 16-047-20140306 and 16-052-20140306.

24.37 *Decisions and costs in appeals and call-ins*

- failing to notify the public of an inquiry or hearing, where this leads to the need for an adjournment [local planning authorities, although site notice errors might apply to the appellant]
- withdrawal of an appeal without good reason [appellant].

Additionally, a failure of a local planning authority to determine an application prior to a non-determination appeal without substantive reasons for the delay may be unreasonable[52].

24.37 The Welsh Office Circular 23/93 provides similar examples of procedural unreasonableness in Annex 2 and substantive unreasonableness in Annex 3.

Unnecessary or wasted expenditure

24.38 Wasted expenditure is that which would not have been incurred were it not for the unreasonable conduct. This may be the cost of bringing the appeal if the refusal was unreasonable, or of defending an unreasonable appeal. Where a ground of appeal or reason for refusal was unreasonable then the costs directly referable to that issue could be considered wasted, unless the point had to be addressed in any event. Procedural conduct might give rise to identifiable costs, such as an adjournment.

24.39 The applying party need only show the inspector that there would be some wasted expenditure: its quantification is a matter for later assessment by the court. Whether an application for a partial award of costs is worth making is affected by how much might be recovered. For example, a late abandoned and bad reason for refusal might not have taken much effort to address.

Making a costs application in time

24.40 It is good practice to give early warning of an intention to make a costs application and to produce a skeleton of the submissions. This should be done once a firm intention to apply has been settled, so in some cases the skeleton will be in advance of the hearing. If the decision to apply arises out of events at the hearing or inquiry or is crystallised there, then it is preferable to produce a short skeleton if practicable. There is, however, no advantage in premature warnings of costs applications which might not materialise. Those tend to be a distraction for all parties. A written response may be submitted to any costs skeleton provided before an inquiry or hearing.

24.41 The timescales set in guidance for costs applications are[53]:

- in householder or minor commercial written representations appeals an appellant should make any costs application when the appeal is submitted, whilst any local planning authority application should be made within 14 days of the starting date. It should be remembered that since no merits submissions are allowed, local planning authority costs in such appeals should be minimal;

---

[52] *Planning Practice Guidance* para 16-048-20140306.
[53] *Planning Practice Guidance* para 16-035-20140306.

Costs in planning appeals and call-ins **24.46**

- in other written representations cases, costs should be applied for at or before the final comments stage, unless they relate to events at the site visit, in which case they should be within seven days of that event;
- costs applications in hearings and inquiries should be made after closing submissions and before the hearing or inquiry has closed or before the hearing is adjourned to the site visit;
- where an appeal is withdrawn or otherwise settled, within four weeks of that event.

24.42 The Planning Inspectorate is prepared to consider applications made after this time (even sometimes after the issue of the decision) if good reason is shown, in which case the application will be dealt with by the Costs and Decisions Branch of the Planning Inspectorate rather than by the inspector. That has been seen by the Inspectorate as a two-stage process to decide whether to allow the application to be made and then to consider the costs application itself. However, fairness should allow the target of the costs application to comment on whether a late application should be allowed to proceed if the Inspectorate is minded to entertain it.

24.43 The ability for costs applications to be made following the withdrawal of an appeal or following the close of an inquiry or hearing means that parties should be careful to document any agreement that a costs application will not be made. Where an appeal is withdrawn, it is prudent to seek to agree whether costs may be sought.

24.44 In English cases the inspector or the Secretary of State may order any party to pay another's costs even if an application for costs has not been made[54]. An opportunity for comment will be given if an inspector is considering initiating a costs award against a person[55], and the same must hold where the Secretary of State proposes to make an order of his own initiative. It may be appropriate for the potential receiving party to be able to comment as well.

Making a costs application

24.45 Whether made in writing or orally, a costs application should identify the alleged unreasonable behaviour and the nature of the unnecessary or wasted expense. The unreasonable conduct can sometimes be explained quite shortly or by reference to the party's submissions on the merits of the appeal. In other cases, particularly where procedural error is alleged, the claim may have to set out the relevant history and correspondence. It is useful to refer to examples of unreasonable behaviour in the *Planning Practice Guidance* or circular, emphasising that they are only examples. There may be some unreasonable behaviour which is quite different but still justifying a costs award.

24.46 The application should say whether it is for the full costs of the appeal or a partial award (and an application may be on alternative bases). The scope of a proposed partial award needs to be set out clearly so that it is able to be replied to and also assessed by the court.

---

[54] *Planning Practice Guidance* para 16-036-20140306. This has been introduced for planning appeals made or applications called-in from 1 October 2013.
[55] *Planning Practice Guidance* para 16-038-20140306.

24.47   *Decisions and costs in appeals and call-ins*

24.47   In an oral application the usual format would be for the applicant for costs to make their submissions, the other party to respond and the applicant to have a final response. Any further costs applications are usually best dealt with as a separate set of oral submissions. A written procedure will run in a similar order.

24.48   Documentation relevant to costs is best introduced in the evidence or submissions in the normal way, rather than retained for the costs application itself. Oral evidence might be relevant to costs applications, particularly on substantive complaints although sometimes for procedural issues, although it is best not to spend any more time than is necessary cross-examining on costs issues rather than the merits of the appeal or call-in.

A suggested form for making an application has been produced by the Planning Inspectorate but that does not need to be used.

Costs and interested parties

24.49   Interested parties may obtain or be subject to awards of costs. However in Wales and historically in England, as a matter of guidance this will only arise in exceptional circumstances[56]. This is considered to be more likely for procedural unreasonableness 'for example where an unnecessary adjournment of a hearing or inquiry is caused by unreasonable conduct'[57]. The *Planning Practice Guidance* now distinguishes between those third parties who 'who choose to be recognised as Rule 6 parties under the inquiry procedure rules', who seem to be subject to the principal parties approach, and other interested parties whose costs rights and liabilities are still subject to exceptional circumstances.

24.50   Costs will not be awarded to any interested parties where the merits of one of the principal parties' case was substantively unreasonable[58], although the guidance is silent on the lack of merit of a third party's case. In practice a public authority or well-resourced commercial rival might be at risk for running an unmeritorious case which causes additional expense, but local residents ought not to be.

Assessing costs

24.51   Costs awards are enforced by a party named in the order making them a rule of the High Court[59]. An award is made an order of the court by being sent to the Administrative Court Office referring to s 250(5). If the amount to be paid under a costs award is not agreed by the payer and payee then an application can be made if it is to be assessed by a Senior Courts Costs Judge as with any other costs order of the court. Recoverable costs are confined to those legal or professional costs of the appeal, or the relevant part of it. These would seem to include the time of an appellant if they were fulfilling the agent's role of conducting the appeal, in a similar fashion to a litigant in person[60], but not their time as the 'client'. Costs do not include any costs

---

[56]   WO Circular 23/93, Annex 4, para 2 and the equivalent DoE Circular 08/93 in England.
[57]   *Planning Practice Guidance*, ID 16-056-20140306 and to the same effect WO Circular 23/93, Annex 4, para 2.
[58]   See the *Planning Practice Guidance*, ID 16-056-20140306 and WO Circular 23/93, Annex 4, para 2.
[59]   Local Government Act 1972, s 250(5).
[60]   See for comparison CPR 46.5 and Practice Direction 46, para 3.4 (any provable loss of time or £19 per hour).

of the application process before the local planning authority nor any consequential losses, such as holding costs during delays to a development or loss of trade due to a lack of permission.

24.52 The High Court's decision on planning appeal costs in *Scrivens v Secretary of State for Communities and Local Government*[61] contains two salutary lessons. The first is that submitting an excessive amount of material might be considered unreasonable and subject to a partial award of costs. The second is the need for a costs award to be sufficiently certain to be capable of detailed assessment by the High Court. An award of costs 'so far as they related to the quantity of material submitted' did not give a costs judge much to go on and the Secretary of State ultimately agreed to its quashing on that basis. Parties seeking partial awards of costs and inspectors need to think how a potential costs award would be capable of being worked out. It may be that points to costs for a particular time period, on discrete elements of the evidence and submissions or just a rough and ready proportion of the costs. That will not necessarily be easy or seem scientific but, like a trial judge, the appeal inspector is in the best position to determine what the effect of unnecessary or excessive evidence is.

CORRECTION OF ERRORS IN DECISIONS

24.53 A decision, once issued, is final subject to challenge in the courts. It confers rights, ends processes or imposes liabilities on parties. It is not implicit that even obvious errors can be corrected by administrative means, a point finally confirmed in the *Gleeson* litigation discussed below. Whilst a planning permission could be revoked or modified by the Minister, that is a slow and expensive procedure which may result in compensation being paid for loss caused by the change.

The Planning and Compulsory Purchase Act 2004 introduced a statutory slip rule for most planning appeals and call-in decisions[62].

24.54 Where a decision issued by a Minister or an inspector contains a 'correctable error' the decision maker has the power to issue a fresh decision[63]. Decisions listed in the 2004 Act as subject to the powers are decisions on applications made to the Secretary of State under the Town and Country Planning Act 1990, s 62A, applications referred to the Minister under ss 76A or 77, planning appeals[64], decisions to confirm a completion notice, enforcement notice appeal decisions, purchase notice decisions, lawful development certificate appeals, decisions relating to applications for consent under the tree preservation or advertising regulations, tree preservation enforcement notice appeals, decisions on urgent Crown development[65], listed building consent appeals and call-in decisions, listed building purchase notice confirmation decisions, listed building enforcement notice appeals, conservation area consent appeals and call-ins, and hazardous substances consent appeal and call-in decisions[66].

---

[61] [2013] EWHC 3549 (Admin), [2014] JPL 521 at para 36 per Collins J.
[62] Planning and Compulsory Purchase Act 2004, s 59(4). Listed building, conservation area and hazardous substances appeal decisions may also be corrected under the slip rule.
[63] Planning and Compulsory Purchase Act 2004, s 56.
[64] Under Town and Country Planning Act 1990, s 78.
[65] Town and Country Planning Act 1990, s 293A.
[66] Planning and Compulsory Purchase Act 2004, s 59(4).

24.55 *Decisions and costs in appeals and call-ins*

24.55 A correctable error is an error[67]:

'(a) which is contained in any part of the decision document which records the decision, but

(b) which is not part of any reasons given for the decision'.

This power can only be exercised if a request to make a correction has been received or the Minister or inspector have informed the applicant or appellant that they are considering making a correction within the High Court challenge period[68]. The local planning authority must be informed by the decision-maker of the request or the statement[69]. Corrections tend to be initiated by a complaint being made to the Planning Inspectorate (in England, to its Quality Assurance Unit). The complainant might request that a correction be made or it may be that the Inspectorate will identify an error whilst considering a complaint and decide that a correction is appropriate. That might not be an error which was the subject of the complaint. It would be possible for the Planning Inspectorate to identify an error on its own and then start the correction process but that will have rarely, if ever, happened. Additionally further categories of decision may be specified by order.

24.56 Despite the long list of decisions subject to the slip rule, various Ministerial and inspector decisions are outside this regime. In particular, costs decisions are not included, nor are appeals on planning obligation modification or discharge applications[70].

24.57 The legislative intention is that a correctable error is a formal, but potentially important, slip such as a mistake in the description of development, list of approved drawings or in a condition[71]. It would need to be apparent what the correction should be. In such cases the legal decision does not correctly reflect the decision-maker's intention. The slip rule is not an opportunity for the decision-maker to change their mind or strengthen weak reasoning.

24.58 From the start, however, the slip rule has been used for minor, but unnecessary changes, such as adding omitted speakers to the list of appearances or correcting obvious typos in the summary of the appeal or in the reasoning. Given the delay to the decision, such changes are not worth making.

In Wales corrections require the consent of the appellant and any other person who owns the land[72].

24.59 A correction is made by issuing a correction notice[73] which will be the decision as corrected with an introductory paragraph saying that it is a correction notice. The original decision's paragraph numbering will be retained.

---

[67] Planning and Compulsory Purchase Act 2004, s 59(5).
[68] Planning and Compulsory Purchase Act 2004, s 56(4). This does not include any potential extension of time for appealing.
[69] Planning and Compulsory Purchase Act 2004, s 56(3)(b).
[70] Under the Town and Country Planning Act 1990, ss 106B, 106BC.
[71] See the Advisory Panel on Standards for the Planning Inspectorate, 13th Report, 2007, para 54.
[72] Planning and Compulsory Purchase Act 2004, s 56(3)(c), (6).
[73] Planning and Compulsory Purchase Act 2004, s 57(1).

24.60 A correction notice becomes the determination of the appeal. Time for bringing High Court proceedings consequently runs from the date of the correction notice[74]. If proceedings have already been brought against the original decision then it is safer to bring fresh proceedings against the correction notice[75]. An application to amend the first proceedings would seek to challenge the new decision and if permission to amend was refused a claimant is likely to be out of time to bring a new claim. The first proceedings would then be academic except in respect of their costs. A reasonable approach to costs would be that an ultimately successful claimant will recover the costs of both proceedings. If the correction notice resolves a ground raised by the claimant then the claimant might recover some costs of the first proceedings even if the other grounds fail in the second claim. The Minister is unlikely to have incurred any significant costs on the first claim before the corrected decision is issued and challenged, but would be hard-pressed to justify recovering extra because a government mistake forced two claims to be brought.

24.61 Appellants and local planning authorities should read decisions carefully on receipt to check that here are no problems which ought to be corrected under the slip rule. It is a useful tool to deal with errors in lists of drawings or conditions which may prove troublesome in due course. A correction might, occasionally, head off a legal challenge or dispose of a technical but good point in such a claim. Care should, though, be taken by parties and the Planning Inspectorate not to make corrections which are pointless. If a person was missed off the list of appearances then an apology in a letter will suffice, without needing to delay the final decision.

INABILITY OF MINISTERS TO WITHDRAW ISSUED DECISIONS

24.62 The courts have for a long time suggested that local planning authorities were not able to issue a second planning decision on one application, a point finally confirmed in *Archid Architecture and Interior Design v Dundee City Council*[76].

24.63 The same approach applies to the Secretary of State, only more so. In *R (Gleeson Developments Ltd) v Secretary of State for Communities and Local Government*[77] the Minister had decided to recover jurisdiction over a planning appeal. Later that same day the inspector's decision allowing the appeal was issued by the Planning Inspectorate. The Minister then purported to withdraw the planning permission and issue a refusal. It is not obvious what was the most astonishing: the decision of the Department that it could simply rip up a planning permission by letter; or the High Court's judgment that this was lawful. The developer, Gleeson, appealed. The Court of Appeal did not feel the need to call on the appellant, Sullivan LJ holding that the Secretary of State could not withdraw a planning permission once it had been issued:

---

[74] Planning and Compulsory Purchase Act 2004, s 58.
[75] This was done in *Mid-Suffolk District Council v Secretary of State for Communities and Local Government* [2009] EWHC 369 (Admin) at paras 33–35, 76–78. The successful claimant recovered the costs of both proceedings from the Secretary of State.
[76] [2013] CSOH 137, [2014] JPL 336. See also *R v Yeovil Borough Council, ex p Trustees of Elim Pentecostal Church, Yeovil* 70 LGR 142, (1972) 23 P & CR 39 at 44; *Heron Corpn Ltd v Manchester City Council* (1977) 33 P & CR 268 at 271–272; *R (on the application of Holder) v Gedling Borough Council* [2013] EWHC 1611 (Admin), [2013] JPL 1426 discussed in Chapter 12 above.
[77] [2014] EWCA Civ 1118, [2014] PTSR 1226, [2014] JPL 1386.

24.64 *Decisions and costs in appeals and call-ins*

'22 If a planning permission has been granted, whether on appeal by the Secretary of State or by an appointed person, or on an application for planning permission by a local planning authority, there is no power to "withdraw" that planning permission on the basis that there has been an administrative error at some stage in the decision making process. Once granted, a planning permission may be revoked only under the procedure contained in ss 97–100 of the Act. Although [Leading Counsel for the Secretary of State] criticised the appellant's reliance on the well known proposition that the Planning Acts form what has been described as "a comprehensive code", there can no doubt that they do comprise a very detailed and highly prescriptive legislative code. The code prescribes how planning permissions, once granted, can be revoked, and in ss 56 and 59 of the Planning and Compulsory Act 2004 it describes the extent to which and the manner in which errors in planning decisions can be corrected under the "slip rule".

24 ... A planning permission confers a substantive right, often a very valuable substantive right, and it is therefore by its very nature irrevocable, save under the procedure which is contained in ss 97–100 of the Act which make provision for compensation'.

24.64 Lord Justice Sullivan had also held that the inspector had still had the power to issue the decision, since the direction to recover jurisdiction had to contain the reasons it was being made and be served on the inspector[78]. What had happened prior to the inspector's decision being issued was that Communities and Local Government had informed the Planning Inspectorate's casework unit of the Minister's desire to recover the appeal and asked PINS to arrange the necessary letters. The recovery letter was sent out, by the Inspectorate, two days later. So, the Court of Appeal concluded, the inspector still had the power to determine the appeal when his decision was issued. There was an administrative error in that the decision was issued as the Minister had decided to recover the case – obviously the issue of the decision should have been stopped whilst the recovery letter was prepared.

24.65 The Court of Appeal's conclusion that the inspector still had the power to act fed into its analysis that there was no power to withdraw the permission. They distinguished an Australian decision, relied upon by the High Court, on the ability of their Immigration Review Tribunal to reopen a decision taken when it was unaware of an application for an adjournment[79]. Sullivan LJ said:

'25 In the present case there was no error on the part of the decision taker. In the absence of any direction under para.3 prior to the issue of his decision, the inspector, as the appointed person, had authority to issue his decision. He intended to allow the appeal and to grant planning permission, and he did so. While an administrative error did occur elsewhere within the Planning Inspectorate, to confer on the Secretary of State a power to 'withdraw' a planning permission that has been lawfully granted, on the basis of some administrative error at some stage in the process by a person other than the decision taker cannot, by any stretch of the imagination, be described as "an implicit auxiliary power" which facilitates the exercise of any of the powers that are expressly conferred by the Act'.

24.66 The court did not, therefore, have to go further into any claimed withdrawal of an unlawfully granted decision, but given the approach in the local authority cases and the Town and Country Planning Act 1990, s 284 which prevents a challenge to the validity of planning appeal decision except by application to the High Court, an unlawful decision cannot simply be withdrawn. It can be challenged by a s 288

---

[78] See Town and Country Planning Act 1990, Sch 6, para 3(2).
[79] *Minister for Immigration v Bhardwaj* (2002) High Court of Australia 11.

application[80]. There may be occasions when a decision is so obviously defective on its face as to not be a decision: pages may be clearly missing, or it may fail to identify the application or say whether it is granted or refused.

24.67 Subsequently in *Mulvenna v Secretary of State for Communities and Local Government* Cranston J put the point simply[81]:

'The Secretary of State has no power to review a decision already taken on an appeal under section 78, or a prior recovery direction in the event of a decision on a section 78 appeal. Nor does the legislation afford him a power to revoke a decision to dismiss an appeal under section 78. This conclusion follows whether the Secretary of State's prior recovery direction is lawful or not. Under the legislation, his determination on these appeals remains lawful and valid unless set aside by the court'.

---

[80] Although in the *Gleeson* case there was the further complication that the Town and Country Planning Act 1990, Sch 6, para 2(8) provides: 'It shall not be a ground of application to the High Court under section 288 ... that an appeal ought to have been determined by the Secretary of State and not by an appointed person, unless the appellant or the local planning authority challenge the appointed person's power to determine the appeal before his decision on the appeal is given'.
[81] [2015] EWHC 3494 (Admin) at para 59.

Chapter 25

High Court challenges

25.1 The exercise of public law powers is subject to review by the courts. Historically this power has vested in the Queen's Bench Division[1] of the High Court. Within the Queen's Bench Division public law responsibilities were given to the Crown Office. In 2000 the Crown Office was renamed the Administrative Court to make more obvious what it was about. Since 6 April 2014 challenges to planning and related decisions have been heard in the Planning Court, which is administered from the Administrative Court Office.

25.2 At common law a public law challenge could be brought by an ordinary action or by judicial review. Prior to the reform of the Rules of the Supreme Court in 1977 public law challenges tended to be ordinary actions rather than judicial review. From that time onwards these challenges have had to be brought by judicial review unless – importantly in the planning context – statute provides for another form of proceedings or the point arises by way of a defence in other proceedings (a collateral challenge). Where statute provides an alternative means of challenging the decision in the High Court then that route has to be taken rather than judicial review.

25.3 Decisions to grant or refuse planning permission or related planning decisions are challenged by an application under the Town and Country Planning Act 1990, s 288 (in respect of Secretary of State or inspector decisions on planning appeals or call-ins) or by judicial review. The most common form of planning judicial review is a challenge to the grant of planning permission by a local planning authority. Major changes are made to the s 288 procedure by the Criminal Justice and Courts Act 2015.

This chapter deals with the legal grounds of challenge to planning decisions, the court's exercise of its powers, the rules for bringing a challenge and the practice of the Planning Court.

PUBLIC LAW GROUNDS OF REVIEW

25.4 The grounds on which public law decisions can be reviewed by the High Court are essentially derived from judicial decisions and so the terminology used varies according to fashion and taste. It is also possible for a single substantive error to be characterised as a variety of different legal errors. There are three main categories of challenge.

---

[1] The King's Bench Division when the monarch is male.

Illegality

25.5 This ground, historically known as an error going to jurisdiction, comes into two categories:

(i) error of law: if the decision-maker makes an error of law in coming to the decision then it will be outside the decision maker's power and so *ultra vires*. These errors include misunderstanding legal powers and duties and a misinterpretation of policy can be characterised as an error of law;

(ii) error of fact: traditionally this has been viewed narrowly only allowing the court to consider errors going to the decision maker's jurisdiction, that is a fact essential to the decision-maker's ability to exercise his power is correct. For example, the court can determine whether the site is within the local planning authority's area. However, a broader approach is now taken to a mistake of fact giving rise to unfairness. In *E v Secretary of State for the Home Department* the Court of Appeal held[2]:

> 'First, there must have been a mistake as to an existing fact, including a mistake as to the availability of evidence on a particular matter. Secondly, the fact or evidence must have been "established", in the sense that it was uncontentious and objectively verifiable. Thirdly, the appellant (or his advisers) must not have been responsible for the mistake. Fourthly, the mistake must have played a material (not necessarily decisive) part in the tribunal's reasoning'.

Unreasonableness

25.6 This ground, also called irrationality, is concerned with defects in the way the decision was thought through. Usually this is concerned with the exercise of discretion, although similar principles are applied when the court is reviewing the lawfulness of a judgment formed by a public authority (such as a decision that there are not likely to be significant effects and so EIA is not required). Unreasonableness in its broad sense includes acting for an improper purpose; failing to take account of relevant considerations (known by the Town and Country Planning Act 1990, s 70 as material considerations); taking account of immaterial considerations; opposing the policy of Parliament; and making a finding of fact on no evidence.

25.7 Unreasonableness in its narrow sense means making a decision that no reasonable person could have come to. This is often known as '*Wednesbury* unreasonableness'[3], or sometimes as perversity. The premise of this narrow category is that, having been unable to identify another specific error, the overall decision was not one that the decision-maker could have come to if they had been approaching their task properly. This narrow category is hard to demonstrate, particularly in planning cases where the courts are concerned not to be seen to be deciding the planning merits of the scheme. Sullivan J emphasised in *Newsmith Stainless Ltd v Secretary of State for the Environment, Transport and the Regions*[4]:

---

[2] [2004] EWCA Civ 49, [2004] QB 1044 at para 66.
[3] From Lord Greene MR's judgment in *Associated Provincial Picture Houses Ltd v Wednesbury Corpn* [1948] 1 KB 223 at 229. The categories of unlawfulness identified in *Wednesbury* do encompass the full range of legal error in the exercise of discretion and so *Wednesbury* unreasonableness also needs to be understood in a broad sense.
[4] [2001] EWHC Admin 74 at paras 6–8.

25.8 High Court challenges

'An allegation that an inspector's conclusion on the planning merits is *Wednesbury* perverse is, in principle, within the scope of a challenge under section 288, but the court must be astute to ensure that such challenges are not used as a cloak for what is, in truth, a rerun of the arguments on the planning merits.

7 In any case, where an expert tribunal is the fact finding body the threshold of *Wednesbury* unreasonableness is a difficult obstacle for an applicant to surmount. That difficulty is greatly increased in most planning cases because the inspector is not simply deciding questions of fact, he or she is reaching a series of planning judgments. For example: is a building in keeping with its surroundings? Could its impact on the landscape be sufficiently ameliorated by landscaping? Is the site sufficiently accessible by public transport? et cetera. Since a significant element of judgment is involved there will usually be scope for a fairly broad range of possible views, none of which can be categorised as unreasonable.

8 Moreover, the inspector's conclusions will invariably be based not merely upon the evidence heard at an inquiry or an informal hearing, or contained in written representations but, and this will often be of crucial importance, upon the impressions received on the site inspection. Against this background an applicant alleging an inspector has reached a *Wednesbury* unreasonable conclusion on matters of planning judgment, faces a particularly daunting task'.

Natural justice

25.8 This ground, which is also known as procedural impropriety, is concerned with errors in the way the decision was made and comprises three categories:

(i)   failure to comply with procedural requirements: these requirements may be set out in statute or in rules or regulations, for example, how notice is given of a hearing. This will include a failure to give adequate and intelligible reasons when required to do so;

(ii) failure to give a fair hearing: even if any procedural requirements have been met, the decision-maker may have failed to give a party a fair opportunity to state his case and challenge any opposing case;

(iii) the appearance of bias: this is a real danger, from his interests or from his behaviour, that the decision-maker is biased against a party[5].

25.9 Whilst public law challenges, including planning cases, are concerned with the legality of decision-making rather than its merits, the decisive issues between the parties tend to be how the facts are understood rather than what the law is. Some cases do turn on major points of legal principle, such as the scope of development or duties to give reasons for EIA screening, but even in some of the major, quotable judgments the law was relatively uncontroversial. The outcome of most cases is determined by the interpretation of the facts: what did the committee report mean; did the inspector understand the position or explain his conclusion? Since these cases are almost always resolved by submissions on documentary evidence, sometime supplemented by witness statements, disputes are rarely about what was said to or by the decision-maker, but about what those words meant and whether in all of the circumstances the approach was permissible.

25.10 In respect of any ground therefore, the claimant needs to closely analyse what the decision-maker knew, said or what happened in the process to identify

---

[5] This principle and its application to local planning authorities is discussed in Chapter 8.

the error or errors of law and their consequences for the decision. In preparing grounds it is usually useful to think what went wrong in non-technical terms: an issue was overlooked or misunderstood; someone did not get a chance to deal with new material. Such substantive errors might be characterised in a number of legal ways – and pleaded as such – but at heart there is often a simple error which can be summarised in very human terms.

HIGH COURT CHALLENGES TO PLANNING DECISIONS

25.11 The lawfulness of decisions of public bodies is generally able to be challenged in the High Court. This will be by judicial review unless a statutory right of appeal or application to the court is expressed to be exclusive or the court considers that an alternative remedy is effective and convenient[6].

25.12 Three different mechanisms apply to challenge decisions to approve or refuse planning permission[7]:

(i) application to the High Court under the Town and Country Planning Act 1990, s 288; this includes most challenges on planning appeals and call ins;

(ii) application to the High Court under the Town and Country Planning Act 1990, s 287 on the making of simplified planning zones or their alteration;

(iii) judicial review proceedings in the High Court.

Changes in 2015 have done much to standardise the different procedures but there are still important differences. It is important, therefore, to identify the correct process to be used. There is an overwhelming case for legislative reform to deal with all planning challenges by judicial review, subject to statutory time limits where appropriate.

25.13 Section 284 of the Town and Country Planning Act 1990 sets out various decisions which can only be challenged by applications to the High Court under Part XII of the Act. These include actions on the part of the Secretary of State or Welsh Ministers[8] of the following descriptions, with explanations in square brackets[9]:

(ya) any decision on an application made to the Secretary of State under s 62A [planning applications made directly to the Secretary of State][10];

(za) any decision on an application referred to the Secretary of State under s 76A [major infrastructure planning applications called in];

(a) any decision on an application referred to him under s 77 [call-ins];

---

[6] *R v Chief Constable of the Merseyside Police, ex p Calveley* [1986] 1 QB 424.
[7] Challenges to enforcement notice appeal decisions are made under the Town and Country Planning Act 1990, s 289 and are discussed in Harwood *Planning Enforcement* (Bloomsbury, 2015), Chapter 8.
[8] See Town and Country Planning Act 1990, s 284(1)(f).
[9] Town and Country Planning Act 1990, s 284(3).
[10] The prohibition on challenge except under s 288 is also set out in Town and Country Planning Act 1990, s 76D(5). A challenge to the decision that an appointed person should determine a s 62A application rather than the Minister must be brought by s 288 application prior to the determination of the application (Town and Country Planning Act 1990, s 76D(6)), the implication being that time runs from the appointment or possibly any refusal by the Minister to take over the application.

25.14 *High Court challenges*

(b) any decision on an appeal under s 78 [planning appeals];

(d) any decision to confirm a completion notice under s 95;

(e) any decision to grant planning permission under paragraph (a) of s 177(1) or to discharge a condition or limitation under paragraph (b) of that section [grant of planning permission in an enforcement notice appeal];

(f) any decision to confirm or not to confirm a purchase notice including:

   (i) any decision not to confirm such a notice in respect of part of the land to which it relates, or

   (ii) any decision to grant any permission, or give any direction, instead of confirming such a notice, either wholly or in part;

(g) any decision on an appeal under s 195(1) [lawful development certificate appeal];

(h) any decision relating:

   (i) to an application for consent under tree preservation regulations [a consent required under a tree preservation order];

   (ii) to an application for consent under any regulations made in accordance with s 220 or 221; or

   (iii) to any certificate or direction under any such order or regulations,

   whether it is a decision on appeal or a decision on an application referred to the Secretary of State for determination in the first instance [advertising consent];

(i) any decision on an application for planning permission under s 293A [urgent Crown development].

In addition, the validity of an inspector's determination of an appeal may only be challenged under this Part[11].

25.14 All of these decisions may be challenged by an application to the High Court under s 288 of the Act. Simplified planning zone schemes or their alterations are challenged under the Town and Country Planning Act 1990, s 287 by an identical procedure.

Other than by way of a challenge under that Part, these decisions 'shall not be questioned in any legal proceedings whatsoever'[12].

25.15 Certain Ministerial or inspector decisions on planning applications or appeals may not be challenged under s 288 and so are said to have to be the subject of judicial review. These include:

(i) the making or lifting of an art 25 direction to prevent the issue of planning decision or the failure to take such steps;

(ii) a decision whether to call-in a planning application;

---

[11] Town and Country Planning Act 1990, Sch 6, para 2(7).
[12] Town and Country Planning Act 1990, s 284(1).

(iii) a decision by the Minister to recover or not to recover jurisdiction over a planning appeal[13];

(iv) a decision on the mode of determination of an appeal or call-in[14];

(v) a Ministerial refusal or failure to make a decision which if taken would be challenged under s 288 since the court's existing jurisdiction is explicitly retained[15], so including a refusal to accept an appeal as valid or an unreasonable or unfair delay in the determination of an appeal;

(vi) ministerial policy both in respect of the substance of planning decisions and how procedural decisions should be made[16].

25.16 Some of these are not directly part of the process which produces a decision challengeable under s 288. However, decisions on the mode of determination and the recovery of jurisdiction are particular procedural decisions in the course of an appeal, which are not necessarily adverse to a particular potential claimant. They may find that they win the appeal anyway, so requiring an earlier judicial review would be a waste of everyone's resources. Additionally, if the final decision is issued during the course of the judicial review proceedings then a s 288 challenge to the determination of the appeal must be able to rely on the alleged recovery or mode of determination error, which would bring it within the s 288 jurisdiction. There is a difference between an ability to bring judicial review against a step or decision partway through an appeal process and having to take the point by judicial review at an early stage rather than awaiting the final decision.

25.17 Prior to October 2015, decisions whether to order a party to pay the costs of a planning appeal or call-in had to be challenged by judicial review on the basis that they were not a 'decision on' an appeal[17]. Since costs challenges are usually

---

[13] *Connors v Secretary of State for Communities and Local Government* [2014] EWHC 2358 (Admin), [2015] JPL 196 at para 135 per Lewis J; *R v Secretary of State for the Environment, ex p Allied London Property Investments Ltd* [1991] JPL 637. By Town and Country Planning Act 1990, Sch 6, para 2(8) a s 288 application may not be brought on the basis that 'an appeal ought to have been determined by the Secretary of State and not by an appointed person, unless the appellant or the local planning authority challenge the appointed person's power to determine the appeal before his decision on the appeal is given'. This would appear to cover a rare case where the inspector did not have transferred jurisdiction (see *Mulvenna v Secretary of State for Communities and Local Government* [2015] EWHC 3494 (Admin) at para 74 per Cranston J), but its applicability to an allegedly unlawful failure to recover jurisdiction may be doubted. Whilst a s 288 application could be brought in such cases if a challenge is made, it is unclear what is meant by 'challenge': it cannot be a s 288 application as that can only occur after the substantive decision. An unlawful decision to recover jurisdiction was held in *Mulvenna* not to render the determination of the appeal unlawful: at para 76 per Cranston J.

[14] See the obiter comments in *Westerleigh Group Ltd v Secretary of State for Communities and Local Government* [2014] EWHC 4313 (Admin) at para 23 per Wyn Williams J; *Bluebell Cemetery Ltd v Secretary of State for Communities and Local Government* [2015] EWHC 2339 (Admin) at paras 60–66 per Holgate J.

[15] See Town and Country Planning Act 1990, s 284(4):

'Nothing in this section shall affect the exercise of any jurisdiction of any court in respect of any refusal or failure on the part of the Secretary of State to take any such action as is mentioned in subsection (3)'.

[16] For example, the Ministerial approach to recovering jurisdiction over appeals: *Connors v Secretary of State for Communities and Local Government* [2014] EWHC 2358 (Admin) at para 135 per Lewis J.

[17] *North Kesteven District Council v Secretary of State for the Environment* [1989] JPL 445. Conversely challenges to costs decisions in enforcement notice appeals could be brought under s 289: *Botton v Secretary of State for the Environment* [1992] 1 PLR 1.

25.18 *High Court challenges*

brought alongside a claim against the substantive decision, this resulted in two sets of proceedings having to be brought, with different procedural rules. The Criminal Justice and Courts Act 2015 removes this duplication by allowing a 'relevant costs order' to be challenged under s 288[18]. A relevant costs order is 'an order made under the Local Government Act 1972, s 250(5) (orders as to costs of parties), as applied by virtue of any provision of this Act'[19] made in connection with a decision or action challengeable under s 288[20].

25.18 Various decisions on related, but non-planning application, provisions are governed entirely by judicial review:

(i) the grant of planning permission, reserved matters, approval under a condition or prior approval by a local planning authority;

(ii) a local planning authority's agreement to modify or discharge a planning obligation whether by agreement or pursuant to an application under the Town and County Planning Act 1990, ss 106A or 106B;

(iii) a local planning authority refusal to modify or discharge a planning obligation by agreement where the person concerned is not able to make a formal application and then appeal under ss 106A or 106BA

(iv) appeals seeking the modification or discharge of a planning obligation under ss 106A or 106BA;

(v) judicial review is the appropriate mechanism for challenging a refusal of the Secretary of State to hear a planning appeal[21];

(vi) the grant or refusal of a deemed planning permission under the Town and Country Planning Act 1990, s 90[22];

(vii) other decision-making processes which give rise to planning permission: the making of general and special development orders and enterprise zone schemes, local development orders, neighbourhood development orders and community right to build orders;

(viii) development consent order decisions under the nationally significant infrastructure provisions of the Planning Act 2008[23].

25.19 Some decisions may be challenged either by judicial review at the time or be the subject of a challenge to the lawfulness of the eventual decision under s 288, for example:

(i) an interim ruling of an inspector on a matter which goes to the substance of the case. In *R (on the application of Belgrave Land Ltd) v Secretary of State for the*

---

[18] Town and Country Planning Act 1990, s 288(1A), inserted by Criminal Justice and Courts Act 2015, Sch 16, para 4. This change, which will avoid duplication of proceedings, was proposed by Bob Neill MP.
[19] Town and Country Planning Act 1990, s 284(3A), inserted by Criminal Justice and Courts Act 2015, Sch 16, para 2.
[20] See Town and Country Planning Act 1990, s 284(1)(g), inserted by Criminal Justice and Courts Act 2015, Sch 16, para 2.
[21] See Town and Country Planning Act 1990, s 284(4) and the similar approach to enforcement notice appeals in *Lenlyn v Secretary of State for the Environment* (1984) 50 P & CR 129.
[22] Town and Country Planning Act 1990, s 90(3) and *R (on the application of Samuel Smith Old Brewery (Tadcaster)) v Secretary of State for Energy and Climate Change* [2012] EWHC 46 (Admin).
[23] See Planning Act 2008, s 118.

Environment, Transport and the Regions[24] an inspector on a reserved matters appeal had ruled on the interpretation of the underlying planning permission at the start of the inquiry. The inquiry was then adjourned whilst the High Court determined the meaning of the permission and so the lawfulness of the reserved matters application;

(ii) a procedural decision, such as a refusal to adjourn or postpone the hearing, to require further evidence or allow cross-examination;

(iii) the adoption of an EIA screening direction can be the subject of judicial review at the time[25] or form part of a later challenge to the final decision as the absence of a lawful screening decision would render any planning permission unlawful[26]. The later challenge would be by judicial review or s 288, depending upon its nature.

25.20 Steps in an application process before a local planning authority, such as the validity of the EIA screening opinion[27], may be challenged either at the time of the particular step or when the final adverse grant of consent occurs. There is no need to bring judicial review proceedings challenging the resolution to grant permission, although such a challenge could be brought[28]. If an earlier decision is attacked any extension of time would be judged on the basis that the ultimate issue of a permission could be challenged.

25.21 A challenge to the reasons adopted in an appeal decision, which does not seek to challenge the underlying decision may be brought by judicial review[29]. However the courts will only entertain such a challenge in exceptional circumstances. In *R (on the application of Redditch Borough Council) v First Secretary of State*[30] the High Court refused to allow the council to challenge an inspector's interpretation of policies for an area of restraint when the appeal had been refused on highways grounds. The inspector's interpretation did not bind the council and Wilson J said[31]:

'The trouble is that a presentation of this issue to the court now is academic; it is hypothetical. The possible further application, whether by this developer or otherwise, referable to this site may never materialise. This court has enough difficulty in despatching the work which it is required to do in relation to live issues. What is wrong, asks Mr Coppel on behalf of the Secretary of State, with a situation where a further application refused by the local authority is the subject of a successful appeal and where there is then a live issue which can be brought to this court by way of application/appeal under s 288 of the Act of 1990?'

---

[24] [2001] EWHC Admin 1127.
[25] For example, *R (on the application of Commercial Estates Group) v Secretary of State for Communities and Local Government* [2014] EWHC 3089 (Admin), [2015] JPL 350; *R (on the application of Gilbert) v Secretary of State for Communities and Local Government* [2015] EWCA Civ 314.
[26] See *R (on the application of Burkett) v London Borough of Hammersmith and Fulham* [2002] UKHL 23, [2002] 1 WLR 1593; *Younger Homes (Northern) Ltd v First Secretary of State* [2003] EWHC 3058 (Admin), [2004] JPL 950; *R (on the application of Catt) v Brighton and Hove City Council* [2007] EWCA Civ 298, [2007] JPL 1517. In *R (on the application of Champion) v North Norfolk District Council* [2015] UKSC 52, [2015] 1 WLR 3710 at para 63 Lord Carnwath JSC reserved his position on the point.
[27] See *Burkett* and *R (on the application of Catt) v Brighton and Hove City Council* [2007] EWCA Civ 298, [2007] Env LR 32.
[28] *R (on the application of Burkett) v London Borough of Hammersmith and Fulham* [2002] UKHL 23, [2002] 1 WLR 1593.
[29] *Greater London Council v Secretary of State for the Environment* [1985] JPL 868.
[30] [2003] EWHC 650 (Admin), [2003] JPL 21.
[31] At para 28.

25.22 High Court challenges

25.22 A disgruntled victor is in a bind. If the inspector's reasoning discloses a legal error, the legality of that position can be challenged if the point arises again in a further appeal. If the concern is about the inspector's view on the planning merits, then a legal challenge ought not to succeed in any event. However in the meantime, other parties may rely on the decision and the victor may have to prepare to re-argue its rejected stance before an inspector, facing threats of costs applications for unreasonable behaviour.

25.23 There are two further categories of decisions on planning applications by bodies other than local planning authorities which could be challenged:

(i) any decision of the Mayor of London on a stage 2 referral not to direct the refusal of the application or alternatively to direct that he be the local planning authority for the application[32]. This probably is a free-standing challenge – so time would run from the decision[33]. There has been some debate whether a challenge to a failure to refuse has utility due to whether the Mayor could subsequently decide to refuse permission[34];

(ii) any decision of the Minister to call-in or to decline to call-in the planning application. Again, time probably runs from the Minister's decision. Such decisions are notoriously hard to challenge[35]. The imposition of a holding direction by the Minister or a later refusal to lift such a direction is amenable to judicial review, but the discretion to make a direction is broad.

Alternative remedies

25.24 In general, judicial review should not be brought where the potential claimant has an alternative remedy. For example, a disappointed applicant for planning permission has a right of appeal to the Secretary of State so judicial review can only be brought in the 'most exceptional circumstances': *R (on the application of Taylor) v Maidstone Borough Council*[36]. One factor is on whether 'the real issue' can be determined in the alternative proceedings[37], although that might not be enough on its own. In *Taylor* the claimant complained about the fairness of the Council's consideration of his application but the court considered that the real issue was whether planning permission should be granted. Sullivan J concluded[38]:

> 'In essence the claimant complains that because of the faulty procedure, the defendant refused planning permission when it should have adhered to its first inclination which was to grant planning permission. The real issue is whether the defendant was right to change its mind on the planning merits. Since that question will be answered by the inspector, it would not be right to grant judicial review of the process which led the defendant to its decision to refuse planning permission'.

---

[32] See Chapter 10.
[33] These decisions are taken under the Town and Country Planning Act 1990, so are subject to a six-week period for proceedings to be brought, subject to any possible extension or ability to challenge a later decision on the application.
[34] See the Court of Appeal permission judgments in *R (on the application of Gopie) v Mayor of London* [2002] EWCA Civ 1186 discussed in Chapter 10.
[35] See the discussion in Chapter 17.
[36] [2004] EWHC 257 (Admin) per Sullivan J at para 10.
[37] *Taylor* quoting Latham J in *R v Leeds City Council, ex p Hendry* (14 December 1993, unreported).
[38] *Taylor* at para 25.

25.25 An exceptional case where judicial review was allowed is *R v Hillingdon London Borough Council, ex p Royco Homes Ltd*[39] where the council had granted planning permission for Royco's housing scheme but subject to conditions which required it to be built to council housing standards and occupied by persons chosen from the Council's waiting list with security of tenure. The developer sought to quash the permission as the conditions were ultra vires. Lord Widgery CJ said[40]:

> 'that it is speedier and cheaper than the other methods, and in a proper case, therefore, it may well be right to allow it to be used in preference to them. I would, however, define a proper case as being one where the decision in question is liable to be upset as a matter of law because on its face it is clearly made without jurisdiction or in consequence of an error of law'.

If a similar case arose now it would be dangerous to assume that the developer would be allowed to proceed by judicial review rather than by appeal to the Minister.

CHALLENGES TO COSTS DECISIONS IN PLANNING APPEALS

25.26 The Secretary of State, Welsh Ministers or a planning inspector may order a party to pay all or part of the costs incurred by another party in a planning appeal[41]. Those costs decisions may be challenged on public law grounds in the High Court. The procedure to be adopted depends on the nature of the appeal before the inspector or Minister.

25.27 Where the costs decision on a planning appeal or call-in is made after 26 October 2015 it may be challenged by a s 288 application along with any challenge to the substantive s 77 or 78 decision[42]. Earlier costs decisions in appeals (or call-ins) on a planning application fall outside s 288, as those proceedings concern a 'decision on an appeal' which was held to mean the substantive decision only[43]. They can therefore only be challenged by judicial review.

25.28 The merits of challenging a costs decision are affected by the wider context of the case. For example, a costs award may have been made on substantive grounds against a party who is also seeking to challenge the substantive outcome. The flaw in the inspector's substantive decision is likely to have infected the costs decision and the costs grounds can include reliance on the substantive challenge[44]. If a claimant's substantive appeal to the Secretary of State had failed as did its application for costs, it might be that the costs decision ought to be quashed if the substantive s 288 application succeeds. In that latter case a claimant will need to show why redetermination of the substantive appeal might affect the costs decision or identify separate legal errors in the costs decision.

---

[39] [1974] QB 720.
[40] At 729.
[41] See Chapter 24.
[42] See para **25.17**.
[43] *North Kesteven District Council v Secretary of State for the Environment* [1989] JPL 445; *Golding v Secretary of State for Communities and Local Government* [2012] EWHC 1656 (Admin).
[44] For one of many examples, see *Mid-Suffolk District Council v Secretary of State for Communities and Local Government* [2009] EWHC 3649 (Admin).

25.29 *High Court challenges*

Consequently if the substantive appeal decision is being challenged in the High Court it will often be sensible and relatively straightforward to challenge the costs decision as well.

25.29 Different issues arise if the sole challenge is to the costs decision to award or not to award costs. Since costs decisions are an exercise of discretion and based primarily on the inspector's view of what was reasonable conduct, the court will give a fair degree of latitude to the decision-maker if the substantive appeal decision was lawful. Additionally the courts have on occasion expressed concern at challenges being brought where the costs of the High Court proceedings will equal or exceed the likely quantum of the costs award. Sullivan J said in *R v Secretary of State for the Environment, ex p Ealing London Borough Council*[45]:

> 'The decision whether or not to make an award of costs is pre-eminently a discretionary matter, and the inspector who actually heard the evidence is in the best position to judge, not merely whether or not the evidence is well-founded in terms of the planning merits of the matter, but also whether or not a party has or has not acted unreasonably. Only very rarely will it be proper for this court to intervene and strike down such an exercise of discretion. Where one has the position that the costs of investigating the exercise of discretion are likely to be equal to if not more than the costs the subject of the award, parties should think long and hard before deciding to seek leave to move for judicial review'.

PROCEDURES FOR HIGH COURT CHALLENGES

25.30 Section 288 applications are made under the Civil Procedure Rules 1998 Part 8, whilst judicial review is carried out under a highly modified form of the Part 8 procedure under Part 54. Whilst the legal tests applied have been the same, the processes have historically operated very differently. The introduction of a requirement to obtain permission to apply to the court under s 288 for decisions taken on or after 26 October 2015 gave rise to new Part 8 procedures for planning challenges which are for the most part identical to judicial review[46].

There are important differences in the documentation to commence the proceedings, standing and time limits and these are discussed first, before the common processes for conducting the cases are assessed.

APPLICATION TO THE HIGH COURT UNDER s 288

25.31 The largest proportion of non-judicial review planning challenges are brought by applications under s 288, including the determination of s 77 call-ins and s 78 planning appeals.

Grounds of challenge

25.32 The s 288 application is on the grounds[47]:

---

[45] 22 April 1999 (unreported).
[46] Amendments inserted by the Criminal Justice and Courts Act 2015, s 91 and Sch 16 and brought into force by the Criminal Justice and Courts Act 2015 (Commencement No 3 and Transitional Provisions) Order 2015, art 3 with transitional provisions in art 4.
[47] Town and Country Planning Act 1990, s 288(1).

'(i) that the action is not within the powers of this Act, or

(ii) that any of the relevant requirements have not been complied with in relation to that action.'

The relevant requirements are those under the Act and the Tribunals and Inquiries Act 1992 and of orders, regulations and rules made under those Acts[48].

25.33 The tests are those in judicial review: see *Seddon Properties Ltd v Secretary of State for the Environment*[49] and *Ashbridge Investments Ltd v Minister of Housing and Local Government*[50]. These include errors of law, unreasonableness in acting without evidence, taking into account irrelevant considerations or failing to take into account relevant considerations, or failure to comply with the statutory procedures or the principles of natural justice.

25.34 The High Court may quash the grant of planning permission if it is satisfied that it[51]:

'is not within the powers of this Act, or that the interests of the applicant [to the Court] have been substantially prejudiced by a failure to comply with any of the relevant requirements in relation to it'.

Standing to bring s 288 applications

25.35 Standing is the right of a person to bring proceedings which in s 288 applications is given to a 'person aggrieved'[52]. A person is aggrieved in the ordinary sense of the word for a s 288 application[53]. This has generally been viewed widely, but not as widely as the sufficient interest test in judicial review. A claimant may be directly affected, such as the unsuccessful appellant or the disturbed next-door neighbour. The reasons for a wide approach were put by Lord Hope of Craighead DPSC in *Walton v Scottish Ministers*[54]:

'152 I think, with respect, that this is to take too narrow a view of the situations in which it is permissible for an individual to challenge a scheme or order on grounds relating to the protection of the environment. An individual may be personally affected in his private interests by the environmental issues to which an application for planning permission may give rise. Noise and disturbance to the visual amenity of his property are some obvious examples. But some environmental issues that can properly be raised by an individual are not of that character. Take, for example, the risk that a route used by an osprey as it moves to and from a favourite fishing loch will be impeded by the proposed erection across it of a cluster of wind turbines. Does the fact that this proposal cannot reasonably be said to affect any individual's property rights or interests mean that it is not open to an individual to challenge the proposed development on this ground? That would seem to be contrary to the purpose of environmental law, which proceeds on the basis that the quality of the natural environment is of legitimate concern to everyone. The osprey has no means of taking that step on its own behalf, any more than any other wild creature. If its interests are to be protected someone has to be allowed to speak up on its behalf.

---

[48] Town and Country Planning Act 1990, s 288(9).
[49] (1978) 41 P & CR 26.
[50] [1965] 1 WLR 1320.
[51] Town and Country Planning Act 1990, s 288(5).
[52] Town and Country Planning Act 1990, s 288(1).
[53] *Times Investment Ltd v Secretary of State for the Environment* (1990) Times, 21 June.
[54] [2012] UKSC 44, [2013] PTSR 51.

25.36 *High Court challenges*

153 Of course, this must not be seen as an invitation to the busybody to question the validity of a scheme or order under the statute just because he objects to the scheme of the development. Individuals who wish to do this on environmental grounds will have to demonstrate that they have a genuine interest in the aspects of the environment that they seek to protect, and that they have sufficient knowledge of the subject to qualify them to act in the public interest in what is, in essence, a representative capacity. ….'

25.36 In cases where EIA has been carried out or an issue arises as to whether EIA should have been required, the person aggrieved test must be applied in a way which gives effect to art 11(1) of the EIA Directive:

'Member states shall ensure that, in accordance with the relevant national legal system, members of the public concerned:

(a) having a sufficient interest, or alternatively;

(b) maintaining the impairment of a right, where administrative procedural law of a member state requires this as a precondition'.

Under the Directive 'sufficient interest and impairment of a right shall be determined by the member states, consistently with the objective of giving the public concerned wide access to justice'[55]. The public concerned mean the public affected or likely to be affected by, or having an interest in, the EIA processes and include non-governmental organisations promoting environmental protection meeting requirements of national law[56].

25.37 A person aggrieved will include:

(i) those who made representations against the decision which was finally taken[57];

(ii) those who would have made representations had they been aware of the process, usually being mislead or not being informed by error[58];

(iii) someone whose interests have been prejudicially affected by the decision, whether they had taken part in the process or not[59].

25.38 Third party pressure groups have been allowed to challenge planning permissions[60]. Broadly speaking, a claimant must show that they took part in the appeal proceedings, were not told about the appeal and would have taken part if they had known, or are directly affected by the proposal[61]. A failure to take an opportunity to make representations may mean that a person does not have standing[62]. In *Ashton* a person who did not object but was a member of the local residents' company which

---

[55] Environmental Impact Assessment Directive, art 11(3).
[56] Environmental Impact Assessment Directive, art 1(2)(e).
[57] For example, *Turner v Secretary of State for the Environment* (1973) 28 P&CR 123; *Times Investments Ltd; and Walton v Scottish Ministers* [2012] UKSC 44, [2013] PTSR 51 per Lord Reed JSC at paras 86–88.
[58] For example, *Wilson v Secretary of State for the Environment* [1973] 1 WLR 1083 where an inaccurate notice misled the public about which land was affected by a proposal.
[59] *Ashton v Secretary of State for Communities and Local Government* [2010] EWCA Civ 600, [2010] JPL 1645.
[60] Eg *Save Britain's Heritage v Secretary of State for the Environment* [1991] 2 All ER 10.
[61] See *Walton v Scottish Ministers* [2012] UKSC 44, [2013] PTSR 51; *Ashton v Secretary of State for Communities and Local Government* [2010] EWCA Civ 600, [2010] JPL 1645 and the Aarhus Convention on Access to Environmental Justice, art 9.
[62] *Lardner v Renfrewshire District Council* [1997] SCLR 454 per Lord Rodger (Lord President) at 457.

Application to the High Court under s 288 **25.40**

appeared at the inquiry (having asked them to make representations on his behalf) and who attended part of inquiry did not have standing[63]. Two claimants were found not to have standing in *Crawford-Brunt v Secretary of State for Communities and Local Government*[64]. Whilst living in separate properties adjoining the site, neither had made representations on the appeal. However, one of the claimants had made representations on the planning application and the judgment overlooked that those representations would have been sent to the Inspectorate by the local planning authority with the appeal questionnaire and would have been considered and rejected by the inspector[65]. Representations on a planning application are also representations on any appeal which follows and in respect of that claimant, the decision is in error.

25.39 Person aggrieved status has also been refused in a number of cases where claimants become interested at the time of the decision and not before[66]. Care may need to be taken to identify the claimant. In *Eco-Energy (GB) Ltd v First Secretary of State* a consortium called Eco-Energy Group had applied for planning permission and appealed to the Minister but the High Court proceedings were brought by a company related to a party in the consortium. They were not a person aggrieved, although they might have been if an option in the land had been transferred to them. Whilst an interest in land can be transferred, enabling a person to apply to the High Court, an interest in a planning application or the right to bring proceedings as a person aggrieved cannot be transferred[67]. In another unusual case, an objector who withdrew their objections, believing that planning permission would give them a ransom strip, did not have standing when that turned out not to be the case[68].

The local planning authority is entitled to apply to the court under s 288.

Standing in judicial review proceedings

25.40 A person may bring judicial review proceedings if they have 'sufficient interest' in the matter[69]. A wide approach to standing was explained by Sedley J in *R v Somerset County Council, ex p Dixon*[70]:

---

[63] *Ashton* per Pill LJ at para 54.
[64] [2015] EWHC 3580 (Admin).
[65] See the Inspectorate's *Guide to taking part in planning, listed building and conservation area consent appeals proceeding by an inquiry – England* (6 March 2014), para 5.1 which promises that these will be 'fully considered by the Inspector who decides the appeal'. Third parties are only encouraged to send comments on the appeal if they have something to add: 'If you did not write at application stage, or you did write and now have something new to say, you can send us your representations about the appeal' (para 5.2).
[66] In *Morbaine Ltd v First Secretary of State* [2004] EHWC 1708 (Admin), [2005] JPL 377 one claimant was a rival developer who had taken no part in the appeal process and so did not have standing.
[67] *Eco-Energy* per Buxton LJ at 21.
[68] *JB Trustees Ltd v Secretary of State for Communities and Local Government* [2013] EWHC 3555 (Admin), [2014] JPL 656 per Lindblom J at paras 45, 46. An objector who withdrew on the basis that a particular condition would be included or obligation made might be a person aggrieved if that event does not happen.
[69] Standing has been taken generously at the permission stage, excluding a claimant who 'has no interest whatsoever and is, in truth, no more than a meddlesome busybody': *R v Monopolies and Mergers Commission, ex p Argyll Group* [1986] 1 WLR 763 at 773 per Lord Donaldson MR. The extent of a person's interest may be relevant to whether they should be granted substantive relief at the end of the case. Since the likelihood of a remedy is relevant to whether permission should be granted, this may now have greater importance at the permission stage: see Senior Courts Act 1981, s 31(2A)–(2C), (3C)–(3F).
[70] [1997] JPL 1030 at 1037.

25.41 *High Court challenges*

'Public law is not at base about rights, even though abuses of power may and often do invade private rights; it is about wrongs – that is to say misuses of public power; and the courts have always been alive to the fact that a person or organisation with no particular stake in the issue or the outcome may, without in any sense being a mere meddler, wish and be well placed to call the attention of the court to an apparent misuse of public power. If an arguable case of such misuse can be made out on an application for leave, the court's only concern is to ensure that it is not being done for an ill motive. It is if, on a substantive hearing, the abuse of power is made out that everything relevant to the applicant's standing will be weighed up, whether with regard to the grant or simply to the form of relief'.

Once a person has standing to bring proceedings then they may challenge the decision on any grounds if they are issues which they do not have a personal interest in[71]. However a lack of interest in the particular issue might affect whether the court's discretion to quash is exercised in their favour.

The commencement of s 287 and 288 proceedings

25.41 The procedure is set out in CPR Part 8 and Practice Direction 8C. The Part 8 claim form[72] will identify the decision to be challenged and set out the grounds of challenge (or have those grounds appended to it). The Claim form and grounds should be marked 'Planning Court'[73]. Conventionally, the Secretary of State for Communities and Local Government or Welsh Ministers will be the first defendant if the challenge is to a Ministerial or inspector decision[74]. The appellant/applicant and the local planning authority will be added as defendants if they are not a claimant.

25.42 With or on the claim form the claimant must give[75]:

'(a) the name and address of any person that the claimant considers must be served in accordance with paragraph 4.1;

(b) that the claimant is requesting permission to proceed with a claim for planning statutory review;

(c) a detailed statement of the claimant's grounds for bringing the claim for planning statutory review;

(d) a statement of the facts relied on;

(e) any application for directions; and

(f) the remedy being claimed (including any interim remedy)'.

25.43 Usually the claim form will be accompanied by details of claim which set out the facts and grounds of the application. A claim which lacks any grounds will

---

[71] *R (on the application of Kides) v South Cambridgeshire District Council* [2003] 1 P&CR 19, applied to s 288 in *Ashton v Secretary of State for Communities and Local Government* [2010] EWCA Civ 600, [2010] JPL 1645 per Pill LJ at para 37.

[72] Form N208. If the application made in the wrong form, such as by a judicial review claim form or s 289 appeal, then the court can allow an amendment to the correct form or for the erroneous document to stand as an application: *R v Secretary of State for the Environment, Transport and the Regions and the National Assembly for Wales* (CO/3109/99, 24 November 1999); *Thurrock Borough Council v Secretary of State for the Environment, Transport and the Regions and Holding* [2001] CP Rep 55.

[73] Practice Direction 54E, para 2.2.

[74] The defendant is never the Planning Inspectorate (which simply acts as part of the Minister's department) nor the individual inspector.

[75] Practice Direction 8C, para 2.2.

Application to the High Court under s 288 **25.46**

not be valid and is incapable of correction by amendment outside the time limit. Also, and more formally, the details should say that the application is brought under the Town and Country Planning Act 1990, s 288 and CPR Part 8[76].

25.44 Details in s 288 cases have historically tended to be pleaded quite fully, explaining the facts and law, the headline of the grounds and reasoning why they are made out. In part this has been to seek to persuade the defendants to give in. With the introduction of a requirement for permission from the Court to bring the claim, details need to be detailed as they need to be persuasive to a judge reading the papers in an hour when faced with likely responses from the defendants.

Various other documents need to be failed with the claim and since these are identical to those required for judicial review, they are considered below.

Time for commencing proceedings

25.45 As a consequence of amendments made by the Criminal Justice and Courts Act 2015[77] the period for challenging decisions under the Town and Country Planning Act 1990 has been standardised as six weeks beginning with the day after the relevant event, reflecting the long-established position under s 288. Consequently if a decision is dated on a Tuesday then the claim must be made on or before the Tuesday six weeks later[78]. There are, though, some differences relating to the event which triggers the running of time and whether the court can extend the time limit.

25.46 The rules on time limits are:

- *s 288 applications* must be brought within six weeks from the date of the decision[79]. This time limit cannot be extended[80];

- *s 287 applications* on simplified planning zone schemes must be filed within six weeks from the date of the publication of the first notice of the approval of the scheme[81]. Again, this cannot be extended

- *judicial review proceedings* on neighbourhood development orders and community right to build orders may be brought within six weeks of various stages in the processes[82]. These stages are: the decision whether to take the draft order to a referendum following the examiner's report[83]; the conduct of the referendum

---

[76] CPR 8.2.
[77] Criminal Courts and Justice Act 2015, ss 91, 92 and Sch 16. These follow amendments proposed by Bob Neill MP.
[78] There is authority that the claim form needs to be with the court office by close of business on the final day rather than delivered to the court building after the office has closed: *Barker v Hambleton District Council* [2011] EWHC 1707 (Admin). The point was left open by the Court of Appeal in that case: [2012] EWCA Civ 610, [2013] 1 P & CR 1.
[79] Town and Country Planning Act 1990, s 288(3).
[80] See the similar development plan challenge provisions considered in *Barker v Hambleton District Council* [2012] EWCA Civ 610, [2013] 1 P & CR 1 and judicial review of development consent orders in *R (on the application of Blue Green London Plan) v Secretary of State for the Environment, Food and Rural Affairs* [2015] EWHC 495 (Admin) and *R (on the application of Williams) v Secretary of State for Energy and Climate Change* [2015] EWHC 1202 (Admin).
[81] Town and Country Planning Act 1990, s 287(4), (5)(b).
[82] Town and Country Planning Act 1990, s 61N.
[83] Town and Country Planning Act 1990, s 61N(2).

25.47 *High Court challenges*

(within six weeks of the declaration of the result[84]; and finally the making or declining to make the order following a referendum[85]. The stepped approach to judicial review raises the issue as to the extent to which errors earlier in the process can be challenged on the final making of the order. This may depend upon the grounds raised but potential claimants should be alert to the possibility of having to challenge the consideration of the examiner's report rather than waiting until a later stage. A six-week period is also applied to challenges to the making or refusal of development consent orders from the publication of any order and the reasons for the decision[86]. These periods cannot be extended;

- *other judicial review proceedings under the Town and Country Planning Act 1990* must be filed within six weeks of the decision by CPR 54.5(5). This is a change from the conventional judicial review time limit that[87]:

'The claim form must be filed:

(a) promptly; and

(b) in any event not later than 3 months after the grounds to make the claim first arose'.

25.47 Given the desire of developers to proceed with projects and the sums at stake, the promptness requirement generated a large amount of debate in planning cases. This was mostly fruitless as in virtually no planning judicial review was permission refused to bring an arguable case because it had not been brought promptly[88]. At best, lateness may have encouraged judges to find weak cases to be unarguable.

25.48 The period for challenges under the 'Planning Acts' was changed to six weeks, with no promptness requirement, for decisions made from 1 July 2013[89]. Civil Procedure Rule 54.5(5) provides:

'Where the application for judicial review relates to a decision made by the Secretary of State or local planning authority under the Planning Acts, the claim form must be filed not later than six weeks after the grounds to make the claim first arose'.

25.49 The Planning Acts are as defined in the Town and Country Planning Act 1990: Town and Country Planning Act 1990, the Planning (Listed Buildings and Conservation Areas) Act 1990, the Planning (Hazardous Substances) Act 1990 and the Planning (Consequential Provisions) Act 1990[90]. The Secretary of State will include the Welsh Ministers and is likely to be taken to include planning inspectors[91]. The small number of decisions under these Acts which are potentially subject to judicial review but which are not taken by Ministers or local planning authorities are subject to the conventional 'promptly and within three months' requirement.

---

[84] Town and Country Planning Act 1990, s 61N(3).
[85] Town and Country Planning Act 1990, s 61N(1).
[86] Planning Act 2008, s 118.
[87] CPR 54.5(1). The CPR time limit does not apply if statute provides for a shorter period: CPR 54.5(4), for example the Planning Act 2008, s 118.
[88] For some of the numerous cases on the topic see *R (on the application of Burkett) v London Borough of Hammersmith and Fulham* [2002] UKHL 23, [2002] 1 WLR 1593; *Finn-Kelcey v Milton Keynes Borough Council* [2008] EWCA Civ 1067, [2009] JPL 493.
[89] CPR 54.5(1) which contains the promptness requirement is disapplied entirely in Planning Act cases: CPR 54.5(4).
[90] Town and Country Planning Act 1990, s 336(1), applied by CPR 54.5(A1).
[91] A judicial review of an inspector's decision as opposed to a s 288 application or judicial review of an Inspectorate administrative decision made in the name of the Minister would be rare.

25.50 The final time for bringing such a challenge runs from the issue of the decision notice[92]. The judicial review formulation 'after the grounds ... arose' mean that the six weeks start to be counted from the day after the decision. So if the decision was issued on a Tuesday then the period expires on the Tuesday six weeks later[93].

Since bringing a planning statutory application or judicial review involves the filing of the claim form with the court office, this can only be done on a day that the court is open. Consequently if the period would expire on a weekend or a public or Bank Holiday then filing may take place on the next working day[94].

The six-week time limit has been held to be compatible with the right to a fair hearing under art 6 of the European Convention on Human Rights and access to environmental justice under European law[95].

25.51 The court may grant an extension of time for bringing judicial review proceedings where the time limit is in the CPR rather than an Act of Parliament, but extensions would only be granted in exceptional circumstances[96]. It should not be assumed that an extension would be granted. Long extensions of time have been granted in planning cases where there has been a failure to notify a neighbour of a planning application for example, two years and eight months from the decision in *R (on the application of Gavin) v London Borough of Haringey*[97], although the delay may mean that only declaratory relief is given.

PRE-ACTION PROCESSES

25.52 Judicial reviews in planning cases have been taken as being subject to the Judicial Review Pre-Action Protocol, although in its terms it does not apply if the decision-maker is unable to revisit its decision without the intervention of the court. Where a decision notice has been issued, the planning authority will not in practice be able to revoke it so on that strict view the protocol would not apply to most planning cases. However, even prior to the protocol the courts had said that warning of planning judicial reviews should be given[98]. As a matter of practice it is useful to send a pre-action letter giving sufficient time (ideally two weeks) for a substantive response to be received. This will, at the least, allow any challenge to be better informed and focused. It might lead the local planning authority into agreeing to submit to judgment upon proceedings being brought.

---

[92] *R (on the application of Burkett) v London Borough of Hammersmith and Fulham* [2002] UKHL 23, [2002] 1 WLR 1593.
[93] *R (on the application of Berky) v Newport City Council* [2012] EWCA Civ 378, [2012] 2 CMLR 44.
[94] *Nottingham City Council v Calverton Parish Council* [2015] EWHC 503 (Admin) following *Kaur v S Russell & Sons Ltd* [1973] QB 336.
[95] See *Barker v Hambleton District Council* and *R (on the application of Blue Green London Plan) v Secretary of State for the Environment, Food and Rural Affairs* [2015] EWHC 495 (Admin) on analogous provisions and, for human rights, *Matthews v Secretary of State for the Environment* [2002] 2 P & CR 34 per Sullivan J at para 33 on s 288 applications.
[96] A lack of awareness of the matter until long after the decision, caused by an unlawful failure to be consulted, is the best justification for an extension of time. Efforts to resolve the matter by other means and its importance might be held to justify an extension of time: eg *R (on the application of Gerber) v Wiltshire Council* [2015] EWHC 514 (Admin), [2015] Env LR 33 per Dove J at paras 82–87 (appeal pending).
[97] [2003] EWHC 2591 (Admin).
[98] *R v Cotswold District Council, ex p Barrington Parish Council* (1998) 75 P & CR 515 at 528 per Keene J.

25.53 *High Court challenges*

25.53 The pre-action protocol sets out a list of matters to be included in pre-action letters and recommends a standard format. Most importantly the letter should identify the decision and the proposed grounds along with any information being requested. Formally, it should also identify the claimant and their legal team along with the proposed defendant and any interested parties. The defendant ought to reply substantively within the requested period. As a matter of practice, interested parties who wish to take part in any proceedings ought to do so as well, although the protocol does not require that.

25.54 The reduced period of six weeks for bringing almost all planning judicial reviews means that it is harder to comply with the pre-action procedures. The Pre-Action Protocol for Judicial Review now provides[99]:

> 'This protocol may not be appropriate in cases where one of the shorter time limits in Rules 54.5(5) or (6) applies. In those cases, the parties should still attempt to comply with this protocol but the court will not apply normal cost sanctions where the court is satisfied that it has not been possible to comply because of the shorter time limits'.

Section 288 applications are not subject to any pre-action protocol. Whilst formally the Practice Direction – Pre-Action Conduct and Protocols would apply and encourage a pre-action letter, such correspondence has not traditionally been sent. The view of central government has tended to be that a final decision will have been made and so any dispute could only be resolved in the courts.

SECTION 288 AND JUDICIAL REVIEW PROCEEDINGS FROM COMMENCEMENT

25.55 Once proceedings have been filed, the 2015 planning statutory review procedures are almost identical to the well-established judicial review processes. Reviews under s 288 are dealt with by CPR Practice Direction 8C, which is based on CPR Part 54 and Practice Direction 54A which are used for judicial review.

Documentation filed with the proceedings

25.56 In addition to the claim form, detailed grounds[100] and application fee, the claim form must be accompanied by[101]:

> '(a) any written evidence in support of the claim;
>
> (b) a copy of any decision, order, relevant document or action that the claimant seeks to have quashed;
>
> (c) copies of any documents on which the claimant proposes to rely;
>
> (d) copies of any relevant statutory material; and
>
> (e) a list of essential documents for advance reading by the court (with page references to the passages relied on)'.

---

[99] Paragraph 6.
[100] Usually called Details of Claim in planning statutory reviews and a Statement of Facts and Grounds in judicial review.
[101] Planning reviews: Practice Direction 8C, para 2.3. The judicial review requirements are to the same effect: Practice Direction 54A, para 5.7.

It is also helpful to include any judgments which the judge will need to refer to at the permission stage. The bundle must be paginated[102].

The commencement of the proceedings

25.57 The proceedings should be filed with the relevant documents and fee in the Administrative Court Office at the Royal Courts of Justice or the relevant regional Administrative Court Office in the District Registry of the High Court at Cardiff, Birmingham, Leeds or Manchester[103].

If the claimant considers that the case should be categorised as a significant planning case this should be indicated in a covering letter[104].

Service of proceedings

25.58 Section 287 or 288 proceedings should be served within the six-week period but judicial review proceedings are to be served within seven days of their commencement. In either case the court may extend time for service[105].

25.59 In s 288 proceedings against Minister's or inspector's decisions, the claim must always be served on the Minister[106]. In addition it would be served on the local planning authority (if it is not the claimant). The Practice Direction also provides that if the authority is the claimant then the claim must be served on anyone who would be entitled to apply to the court if they were aggrieved, which includes those who would be aggrieved by a different outcome. This gives rise to the problem that the number of third parties who might be persons aggrieved could run into the hundreds and occasionally thousands. If an interested person is the claimant then the Practice Direction only requires them to serve the Minister and the local planning authority, but is silent as to serving the applicant for planning permission. In practice the claimant ought to always serve the Minister, the local planning authority and the applicant/appellant. There might be circumstances where other persons ought to be notified, but it should be left to interested persons to ask to join in the proceedings. It might be that a parish council, local action group or commercial rival has played such a role in the appeal that it should be allowed into the proceedings. Such persons could be added on application to the court.

---

[102] It is useful to include a gap in the pagination between the grounds and the evidence to allow other pleadings and orders to be included in a trial bundle without upsetting the existing pagination.
[103] Practice Direction 54D. Filing the claim in the wrong office but in the right building can be excused: *Cala Homes (South) Ltd v Chichester District Council* (2000) 79 P & CR 430 (claim filed in Central office of the High Court rather than what was then the Crown Office), approved by in *San Vicente v Secretary of State for Communities and Local Government* [2013] EWCA Civ 817, [2014] 1 WLR 966 at para 52 per Beatson LJ.
[104] Practice Direction 54E, para 3.3.
[105] For the principles on extending time for service in statutory applications such as s 288 see *Corus UK Ltd v Erewash Borough Council* [2006] EWCA Civ 1175.
[106] Practice Direction 8C, para 4.1. Under Practice Direction 66 Crown Proceedings, claims against the Secretary of State for Communities and Local Government are served on the Treasury Solicitor, One Kemble Street, London WC2B 4TS (and helpfully close to the Royal Courts of Justice). Service on the Welsh Ministers is effected on The Director of Legal Services to the Welsh Assembly Government, Cathays Park, Cardiff CF10 3NQ.

25.60 *High Court challenges*

In judicial review the claim form must be served on the defendant and any person whom the claimant considers to be an interested party[107].

Acknowledgments of service and summary grounds

25.60 Since permission to proceed is required from the court in judicial review and now in planning statutory reviews, a judge needs to form a view at an early stage whether there is an arguable case. The 2000 judicial review reforms had changed the application for permission (previously called leave) from a 'without notice' procedure (where the first the planning authority might know of the claim was on receipt of the permission decision) into a 'with notice' process where the relevant parties expected to comment on merits from the beginning. This has been continued, almost in the same terms, in the new procedures for s 288 and similar applications.

25.61 A person served with the claim who wishes to take part in the proceedings must file an acknowledgment of service and if intending to contest it, must provide summary grounds of resistance[108]. Summary grounds ought to be kept short, as Carnwath LJ explained 'The purpose of the 'summary of grounds' is not to provide the basis for full argument of the substantive merits, but rather ... to assist the judge in deciding whether to grant permission, and if so on what terms'[109]. They might need to do little more than refer back to any pre-action correspondence and could make their points in a few pages. In some cases, of course, the claimant's explanation of the facts may be so unclear or incomplete from the defendant's perspective that a lengthier explanation is required. There is no provision for the production of evidence by defendants or interested parties at this stage, but it may be submitted[110]. This is best confined to critical issues going to whether permission should be granted.

25.62 Acknowledgments and summary grounds must be filed not more than 21 days after service of the claim form and then served on the claimant and the other parties as soon as practicable and, in any event, not later than seven days after filing[111]. No provision is made for any reply by the claimant, but that may be done. Any reply should be short and confined to making new and essential points arising from the summary grounds.

Consideration of permission

25.63 The permission application will then be considered by a judge on the papers[112]. In significant planning cases the target is for this to be done within three weeks of receipt of the expiry of the acknowledgment of service deadline[113]. A reasoned decision whether to grant or refuse permission will usually be given,

---

[107] CPR 54.7.
[108] Planning reviews: Practice Direction 8C, para 5.2, 5.5; judicial review: CPR 54.8(1), (4).
[109] *R (on the application of Ewing) v Office of the Deputy Prime Minister* [2005] EWCA Civ 1583, [2006] 1 WLR 1260 at para 43. In *R (on the application of Davey) v Aylesbury Vale District Council* [2007] EWCA Civ 1166, [2008] 1 WLR 878 at 33, Sir Anthony Clarke MR said that the court at the permission stage should 'decline to look at anything which goes beyond the "summary of grounds" described in *Ewing*'s case'.
[110] The requirement in CPR 8.5(3), (4) to serve evidence with an acknowledgement of service to a Part 8 claim is disapplied by Practice Direction 8C, para 12.3.
[111] Planning reviews: Practice Direction 8C, para 5.3; judicial review: CPR 54.8(2).
[112] Planning reviews: Practice Direction 8C, para 7.1; judicial review: CPR 54.8(2).
[113] Practice Direction 54E, para 3.4(a); judicial review; Practice Direction 54A, para 8.4.

Section 288 and judicial review proceedings from commencement 25.67

and it is possible to grant permission only on certain grounds. Occasionally the judge may decide that the application should be referred to a 'rolled-up' hearing to consider whether permission should be granted and, if so, whether the claim should succeed.

25.64 If permission is refused then the application may be renewed (with short grounds) to an oral hearing unless the judge records it to be totally without merit. In this latter case the claimant may only appeal to the Court of Appeal. Any request for reconsideration by the High Court or appeal to the Court of Appeal must be filed within seven days after service of the order and its reasons[114].

25.65 Oral hearings will usually be listed for 30 minutes unless a longer listing has been requested[115]. There is no requirement to file skeleton submissions and the parties will need to consider what assists the court given the submissions which will already be in[116]. A claimant may wish to respond to reasons for refusal given on the papers and it might be helpful to shortly guide the judge through the paperwork. Sometimes there is value in preparing a skeleton which is a revision of the grounds, picking up the issues as they have subsequently developed[117].

25.66 On either the papers or following an oral hearing the judge may make directions. If the case is particularly urgent then expedition may be ordered, potentially with a hear by date, and if it may need to be heard in August or September then it should be certified as fit for vacation business. If permission is refused then the court will usually order the unsuccessful claimant to pay the costs of the decision maker's acknowledgment of service and summary grounds but will not usually allow the decision maker to recover the costs of attending any renewal hearing[118].

Post-permission

25.67 The defendant and anyone else served with the claim form who wishes to defend the claim or support it on additional grounds must file and serve detailed grounds and any written evidence within 35 days after service of the order giving permission[119]. Any other evidence can only be submitted with the permission of the court (or the agreement of the parties) and directions may provide time either in

---

[114] Planning reviews: Practice Direction 8C, para 7.5 (reconsideration), CPR 52.15B(3) (appeal); judicial review: CPR 54.13(4) (reconsideration), CPR 52.15(2) (appeal).

[115] How long the hearing actually takes is down more to the judge and the number of cases in the list that day, followed by the extent of the issues and the nature of the parties' submissions.

[116] The court does, though, informally request parties to file any skeletons one week before the hearing (or indicate that it is not proposed to file a skeleton). If further cases or legislation are to be cited then an authorities' bundle (ideally agreed) ought to be filed.

[117] As with any written submissions, the objective is to find the most helpful and persuasive way of explaining the case to the judge given the material which is already before the court.

[118] Costs for the acknowledgment of service and summary grounds should generally be awarded: *R (on the application of Mount Cook Ltd) v Westminster City Council* at para 74, 76(1) per Auld LJ (but query whether more than one set of costs should be awarded unless justified under *Bolton Metropolitan Borough Council v Secretary of State for the Environment (Practice Note)* [1995] 1 WLR 1176 – see para 25.95-25.96 below). For the award of costs of permission hearings see for planning reviews Practice Direction 8C, para 8.2 and for judicial review Practice Direction 54A, para 8.6: 'Where the defendant or any party does attend a hearing, the court will not generally make an order for costs against the claimant'. Defendant's costs of attending permission hearings should only be recovered in exceptional circumstances, some of which are identified in *Mount Cook* at para 76(5).

[119] Planning reviews: Practice Direction 8C, para 12.1; judicial review: CPR 54.14(1).

25.68 *High Court challenges*

which the claimant is entitled to submit evidence in replay or to apply to be able to submit such evidence.

THE FORMER s 288 PROCEDURE

25.68 Planning decisions made prior to 26 October 2015 and challenged under s 288 or other statutory applications to the High Court were subject to a different procedure under CPR Part 8 and the Part 8 Practice Direction, para 22. Leave to apply to the court was not required. The claimant would file a Part 8 claim form with details of claim. A defendant was required to file an acknowledgment of service within 14 days of receiving the claim form if it wished to take part in the hearing[120]. The acknowledgment would simply say whether the defendant was resisting the proceeding and whether it would file evidence. There was no requirement to provide any grounds of resistance or for the defendant to explain its case in any way. Whilst any evidence had to be filed at an early stage, it was rarely necessary for the Secretary of State to produce evidence, as he was simply defending the Minister or inspector's reasoned decision and most potentially relevant material was usually put in by the claimant. Consequently claimants did not know the case they had to meet until they received the Minister's skeleton argument. There was also a real danger that the government did not consider the merits of a challenge properly at an early stage. It was too common for the Minister when his skeleton was being prepared for evidence to be filed or the Secretary of State to concede the case at the last minute.

25.69 This was the source of some disquiet, although an attempt by the Administrative Court to introduce summary grounds of resistance into s 288 applications by handing down a judgment was rejected by the Court of Appeal in *Bovale Ltd v Secretary of State for Communities and Local Government*[121] who said that a formal practice direction was required. In 2014 the Practice Direction 54E said[122]:

> 'The Planning Court may make case management directions, including a direction to any party intending to contest the claim to file and serve a summary of his grounds for doing so'.

This was overtaken by the new leave requirement in 2015 and the consequent Practice Direction 8C.

25.70 Evidence was to be filed and served by the claimant within 14 days of serving the claim form and by the defendants 21 days after service of that evidence[123]. Skeletons were in practice required from the claimant three weeks before the hearing and from the defendant a week later.

EVIDENCE IN STATUTORY APPLICATIONS AND JUDICIAL REVIEW

25.71 Evidential matters are dealt with in a similar manner in judicial review and the equivalent statutory applications and appeals, such as under s 288. First of all, the

---

[120] CPR 8(3). If there has been a failure to acknowledge service then the permission of the court is required to take part in the hearing: CPR 8(4).
[121] [2009] EWCA Civ 171, [2009] 1 WLR 2274.
[122] Practice Direction 54E, para 3.5.
[123] Practice Direction 8A, paras 22.8–22.10.

court is concerned with the lawfulness of the decision or the decision-making process and so the evidence will usually just include what was in front of the decision-maker and what actually happened. That evidence must bear on the grounds which are raised. For example, if a challenge is confined to the lawfulness of the inspector handling of ecology then the ecological evidence in the application and appeal is likely to need to be before the court, but the highways evidence is unlikely to be relevant[124].

25.72 Material which was not in the decision-making process is rarely relevant, the exceptions generally being:

- if a complaint is that the claimant was not informed of the appeal or of some evidence then they may wish to indicate what would have been said about the matter;
- anything which as a matter of law had to be considered but was not, for example, parts of the development plan relevant to the grounds raised;
- subsequent developments but only if they materially assist in the exercise of the court's discretion if the decision was unlawful. Discretion is primarily focused on the position at the date of the unlawful decision, so it would be rare for the court to conclude that on the circumstances of that time the decision should be quashed but later events (such as policy changes or other planning decisions) mean that a quashing order should not now be made.

25.73 For the most part evidence can be dealt with by exhibiting documents. The course of events will be described in the grounds, with a statement of truth, and a witness statement only needs to expand on matters if they are not in the contemporaneous documents. Witness evidence therefore tends to be required if there is criticism of what happened at a committee meeting, site visit, appeal hearing or inquiry. A claimant might need to explain their interest in the matter or that they were unaware of an application until it was too late to be involved.

Evidence about the inspector or Minister's reasoning

25.74 As the Minister and the inspector are required to give a reasoned decision, their reasoning cannot be supplemented by witness evidence. In *Rumsey v Secretary of State for the Environment, Transport and the Regions*[125] it was found to be wrong for witness statements to be used to supplement or clarify the reasoning in an inspector's decision as opposed to explaining what material was before the inspector. The point was reinforced in *Ioannou v Secretary of State for Communities and Local Government* by Mr Justice Ouseley[126]:

> '51 I add that I would strongly discourage the use of witness statements from inspectors in the way deployed here. The statutory obligation to give a decision with reasons must be fulfilled by the decision letter, which then becomes the basis of challenge. There is no provision for a second letter or for a challenge to it. A witness statement should not be a backdoor second decision letter. It may reveal further errors of law. In my view, the statement is not admissible, elucidatory or not.

---

[124] Whilst it might sometimes be useful to place the decision in an early and separate tab, evidential documents should otherwise be organised chronologically.
[125] (2000) 81 P & CR 32.
[126] [2013] EWHC 3945 (Admin), [2014] JPL 608 at paras 51–53.

25.75 *High Court challenges*

52 However, if that is wrong, the question whether the statement elucidates or contradicts the reasoning in the decision letter, and so is admissible or inadmissible on *Ermakov* principles, can only be resolved once the decision letter has been construed without it. To the extent that a court concludes that the reasoning is legally deficient in itself, or shows an error of law for example in failing to deal with a material consideration, it is difficult to see how the statement purporting to resolve the issue could ever be merely elucidatory. A witness statement would also create all the dangers of rationalisation after the event, fitting answers to omissions into the already set framework of the decision letter, risking demands for the inspector to be cross-examined on his statement, and creating suspicions about what had actually been the reasons, all with the effect of reducing public and professional confidence in the high quality and integrity of the Inspectorate.

53 Inspectors could be required routinely to produce witness statements when a reasons challenge was brought or when it was alleged that a material consideration had been overlooked, since the challenging advocate would be able to say that, in its absence, there was nothing to support the argument put forward by counsel for the Secretary of State, when there so easily could have been, and he must therefore be flying kites of his own devising. This is not the same as an inspector giving evidence of fact about what happened before him, which can carry some of the same risks, but if that is occasionally necessary, it is for very different reasons'.

The Court of Appeal adopted these comments[127].

Disclosure

25.75 There is no automatic disclosure in judicial review or statutory applications. In planning cases a great deal of the necessary evidence will already be available to the parties, published on websites or in files which are open to public inspection. There are circumstances, more usually on challenges to local authority decisions, where internal notes and e-mails are required. Occasionally an issue may arise on a claimant's involvement, knowledge or interest in a matter which requires documents.

25.76 Public law cases should be fought with all of the parties being in possession of the relevant material. All parties are under a duty of candour to make a full and frank disclosure of relevant facts to the court[128]. Issues of the claimant's knowledge of the matter may be relevant to timing of the proceedings and standing and should be fully disclosed where they arise. The decision-making process may need to be honestly and fully explained by the defendant. As Sir John Donaldson MR pointed out in *R v Lancashire County Council, ex p Huddleston*[129] judicial review is:

'a process which falls to be conducted with all the cards face upwards on the table and the vast majority of the cards will start in the authority's hands'.

25.77 The obligation to make full and frank disclosure to the court is particularly onerous where an application is made without notice to the other side, although in judicial reviews this will only in practice arise in urgent injunction applications. Where all parties are aware of published documents a party need only put before the

---

[127] [2014] EWCA Civ 1432 per Sullivan LJ at para 41.
[128] See for application to the claimant: *Cocks v Thanet District Council* [1983] 2 AC 286 at 294G per Lord Bridge and for defendants and interested parties: *Belize Alliance of Conservation Non-Governmental Organisations v Department of the Environment* [2004] UKPC 6, [2004] Env LR 761 at paras 86, 87 per Lord Walker of Gestingthorpe.
[129] [1986] 2 All ER 941.

Evidence in statutory applications and judicial review **25.80**

court the documents which it considers to be relevant to the claim as put. The other parties can put other documents in if they wish, although it is prudent for any party to ensure that the unhelpful documents are produced and addressed.

25.78 A party seeking documents should request them in the context of the proceedings (to avoid potential delays if requests to public bodies are dealt with under the Freedom of Information Act/Environmental Information Regulations). An application for specific disclosure can be made. If documentation has been refused prior to the commencement of proceedings then a disclosure application can be included in the claim form, to be dealt with by the permission judge.

Cross-examination in statutory applications and judicial review

25.79 Cross-examination may be ordered in s 288 or judicial review proceedings[130]. In *Jones v Secretary of State for Wales*[131] the Court of Appeal ordered cross-examination of a planning inspector after a dispute about a conversation with a participant during an adjournment of the inquiry. Balcombe LJ said 'The principle is clear – that cross-examination will be allowed when the justice of the case requires and the decision whether justice so requires is a matter for the discretion of the judge'[132].

25.80 Cross-examination in Administrative Court and Planning Court cases is very rare[133]. Lord Neuberger of Abbotsbury MR warned on judicial review in *Bubb v Wandsworth London Borough Council*[134]:

'for reasons of both principle and practice, such a course should only be taken in the most exceptional case. As its name suggests, judicial review involves a judge reviewing a decision, not making it; if the judge receives evidence so as to make fresh findings of fact for himself, he is likely to make his own decision rather than to review the original decision. Also, if judges regularly allow witnesses and cross-examination in judicial review cases, the court time and legal costs involved in such cases will spiral'.

There may be factual issues as to what was done or said which can only be resolved by live witnesses being heard and questioned. One example is if an explanation of the authority's thinking is given in a witness statement and the issue is raised, in the absence of contemporaneous documents, as to whether that is accurate and whether it was in the authority's mind at the time of the decision or is an ex post facto rationalisation[135].

Oral expert evidence is rarely of assistance in a s 288 application or planning judicial review[136].

---

[130] CPR 8.6(2), (3), in judicial review cases as applied by CPR 54.1.
[131] [1995] 2 PLR 26.
[132] *Jones* at 30.
[133] One such example is cross-examination ordered of a council officer as to whether consideration was given to publishing an advertisement of an application due to potential effects on a listed building: *R (on the application of Embleton Parish Council) v Northumberland County Council* [2013] EWHC 3631 (Admin), [2014] Env LR 16 at paras 113–118 per Judge Behrens.
[134] [2011] EWCA Civ 1285, [2012] PTSR 1011 at paras 24, 25.
[135] *R (on the application of Jedwell) v Denbighshire County Council* [2015] EWCA Civ 1232 at paras 48–60 per Lewison LJ.
[136] See the comments of Dove J in *R (on the application of Groves) v Boston Borough Council* [2014] EWHC 3950 (Admin) at paras 22, 23 where the enforceability of a noise condition on a wind turbine planning permission was in issue. The judge did derive some benefit from a joint statement of experts which crystallised the issues.

25.81 *High Court challenges*

Interim orders

25.81 Under s 288 the High Court may suspend a challenged planning permission by interim order until the final determination of proceedings[137], although this is rarely if ever done. Judicial review has a wider range of remedies. If the lawfulness of a planning decision or a failure to enforce is challenged then an interim injunction may be granted against the developer or landowner to prevent irreversible harm, such as the demolition of a historic building or the destruction of natural habitat[138].

THE HEARING OF THE CASE

25.82 The Practice Directions require the filing of a trial bundle of the necessary documents, skeleton submissions and an agreed bundle of authorities. The Practice Directions require a skeleton argument from the claimant not less than 21 working days before the hearing and from the defendant and any other party 14 working days before the hearing[139] although these periods have often been shortened by judges at the judicial review permission stage[140]. Under the Practice Directions skeleton arguments must contain[141]:

(1) a time estimate for the complete hearing, including delivery of judgment;

(2) a list of issues;

(3) a list of the legal points to be taken (together with any relevant authorities with page references to the passages relied on);

(4) a chronology of events (with page references);

(5) a list of essential documents for the advance reading of the court (with page references) and a time estimate for that reading; and

(6) a list of persons referred to.

It may be useful for the parties to agree statement of agreed factual matters, legal propositions and chronologies[142]. This may save time where the facts are complex and potentially contentious, such as there being multiple witness statements about events at a planning inquiry[143].

25.83 It is conventional for the bundle of authorities to include relevant legislation and published national policy. Parties are not required to file national policy documents

---

[137] Town and Country Planning Act 1990, s 288(5).
[138] *R (on the application of Prokopp) v London Underground Ltd* [2003] EWHC 960 (Admin) per Collins J at para 15. For the discharge of such an injunction see *R (on the application of SAVE Britain's Heritage) v Gateshead Metropolitan Borough Council* [2010] EWHC 2919 (Admin), [2011] JPL 339.
[139] For statutory reviews, Practice Direction 8C, para 15; judicial review, Practice Direction 54A, paras 15.1, 15.2.
[140] Periods of 3 and 2 or 2 and 1 weeks are practical.
[141] In practice the issues and legal points need to be clearly identified, albeit not mechanistically listed. Chronologies tend to be useful, but lists of persons are rarely essential in planning cases.
[142] The production of these documents in significant planning cases are encouraged by the Planning Court judges Dame Frances Patterson and Sir Ian Dove in their article 'The Planning Court: future directions' [2015] JPL 1118.
[143] As was, for example, done in *Anderson v Secretary of State for Communities and Local Government* [2015] EWHC 3005 (Admin).

as evidence, although it is again conventional to include local policy within evidence, in part because of a need to be satisfied of its relevance, completeness and status.

25.84 The case is usually heard by a single judge, either a High Court or Deputy High Court Judge[144]. In the absence of orders for cross-examination of witnesses, the hearing will simply involve submissions, with the usual order being the claimant's advocate, any party supporting the claim, the principal defendant (the Minister or the local planning authority) and any other defendants or interested parties opposing the claim, with the claimant having a final right of reply.

REMEDIES

25.85 In s 288 applications the court is given the power to quash the decision if it is unlawful. No other power is set out in the legislation and there is room for argument as to whether any other remedies can be ordered[145]. For judicial review the court's powers are extremely flexible, encompassing quashing mandatory and prohibitory orders, injunctions, damages and declarations.

25.86 The starting point is that the discretion of the court to do other than quash the relevant decision where excessive exercise of power is shown is very narrow[146]. The normal response to an unlawfully granted planning permission is to quash it[147]. The decision in *Berkeley v Secretary of State for the Environment*[148] that the scope to decline to quash in European law cases was narrowed to those where there had been substantial compliance with the relevant Directive was effectively disapproved in *Walton v Scottish Ministers*[149] and *R (on the application of Champion) v North Norfolk District Council*[150].

25.87 Under s 288 applications there is a power to quash either if the action 'is not within the powers of this Act' or 'the interests of the applicant have been substantially prejudiced by a failure to comply with any of the relevant requirements in relation to' the decision[151]. 'Relevant requirements' are those of the Town and Country Planning Act 1990, the Tribunals and Inquiries Act 1992 or any order, regulations or rules made under either of those Acts. This division in the powers is often seen as being between substantive legal errors (error of law, unlawful exercise of discretion) and breaches of procedural requirements. However even procedural errors may be outside

---

[144] Up to the 1970s many planning cases were dealt with by the Divisional Court of the High Court, consisting of the Lord Chief Justice or a Lord Justice and one or two High Court judges. The Divisional Court now just deals with criminal appeals by case stated and the most sensitive judicial reviews. A Lord or Lady Justice may occasionally sit as a single judge in the High Court.

[145] A declaration was made in *Wiltshire Council v Secretary of State for Communities and Local Government* [2015] EWHC 1459 (Admin) although there was no discussion of the jurisdictional basis for such a remedy.

[146] *Berkeley v Secretary of State for the Environment* [2001] 2 AC 603 at 608 per Lord Bingham of Cornhill.

[147] *R (on the application of Tata) v Newport City Council* [2010] EWCA Civ 1626; followed in *R (on the application of Plunkett) v Sefton Borough Council* [2011] EWHC 368 (Admin); *R (on the application of Holder) v Gedling Borough Council* [2014] EWCA Civ 599, [201] JPL 1087.

[148] [2001] 2 AC 603 at 608 per Lord Bingham of Cornhill and at 615–617 per Lord Hoffmann.

[149] [2012] UKSC 44, [2013] PTSR 51 at paras 124–138 per Lord Carnwath JSC.

[150] [2015] UKSC 52, [2015] 1 WLR 3710 at paras 54–61 per Lord Carnwath JSC.

[151] Town and Country Planning Act 1990, s 288(5)(b).

25.88 *High Court challenges*

the powers of the Act[152]. Whether substantial prejudice is actually required in respect of the particular error is in practice unimportant. The court has a discretion whether to quash under either head and would be reluctant to quash if there was no potential harm, mischief or different outcome.

25.88 The general approach to the exercise of discretion was set out in *Simplex GE (Holdings) v Secretary of State for the Environment*[153] that, if there has been an error in a decision letter, then the court has to be satisfied, if it is not to quash the decision, that the same decision would, not might, be reached by the decision taker notwithstanding the error. There may be circumstances where the court is satisfied that even an unlawful failure to consult would not have produced a different outcome[154]. However a developer who chooses to carry on development with knowledge of the proceedings is unlikely to receive much sympathy from the court[155]. Where there has been undue delay in the proceedings, and so they are brought with an extension of time, then prejudice caused in the meantime to a developer who was unaware of a potential challenge may count against a quashing. This is relevant to discretion and also the application of the Senior Courts Act 1981, s 31(6) which provides[156]:

'(6) Where the High Court considers that there has been undue delay in making an application for judicial review, the court may refuse to grant:

(a) leave for the making of the application; or

(b) any relief sought on the application,

if it considers that the granting of the relief sought would be likely to cause substantial hardship to, or substantially prejudice the rights of, any person or would be detrimental to good administration'.

25.89 The virtual certainty of an unchanged decision is now altered in judicial review proceedings by the Senior Courts Act 1981, s 31 to a refusal of permission to apply for judicial review or of relief if 'it appears to the court to be highly likely that the outcome for the applicant would not have been substantially different if the conduct complained of had not occurred'[157]. In those circumstances the court must

---

[152] For example on EIA screening: *Younger Homes (Northern) Ltd v First Secretary of State* [2003] EWHC 3058 (Admin); [2004] JPL 950 at paras 71–73 per Ouseley J. A failure to provide adequate reasons will usually be a failure to comply with the relevant requirements, requiring substantial prejudice, but because there is not statutory duty to give reasons in English written representations cases, a failure in reasoning will be 'not within the powers of the Act': see *Martin v Secretary of State for Communities and Local Government* [2015] EWHC 3435 (Admin) at para 51 per Lindblom LJ.

[153] (1989) 57 P & CR 306.

[154] For two examples, for different reasons, see *R (on the application of Majed) v London Borough of Camden* [2009] EWCA Civ 1029, [2010] JPL 621 at para 31 per Sullivan LJ; *R (on the application of Wainwright) v London Borough of Richmond-upon-Thames* [2001] EWCA Civ 2062 at para 55 per Clarke LJ.

[155] *R (on the application of Holder) v Gedling Borough Council* [2014] EWCA Civ 599, [201] JPL 1087 at paras 28–31 per Maurice Kay LJ.

[156] The detrimental to good administration limb is less likely to help a defendant. As the Court of Appeal observed in *R (on the application of Burkett) v London Borough of Hammersmith and Fulham* [2001] 3 PLR 1 at 13: 'Administration beyond law is bad administration. The courts exist to protect the former as jealously as to stop the latter, but they cannot know which they are dealing with unless they can hear out, and decide, viable challenges to the legality of administrative acts'.

[157] Senior Courts Act 1981, s 31(3D) (at the permission stage) and s 31(2A) (at the substantive hearing). This applies only to proceedings brought from 13 April 2015: see Criminal Justice and Courts Act 2015 (Commencement No 1, Saving and Transitional Provisions) Order 2015, SI 2015/778, art 4, Sch 2, para 6.

refuse permission or substantive relief unless there are reasons of exceptional public interest[158]. It remains to be seen how much practical difference this makes.

25.90 An issue may arise as to what extent new material needs to be produced showing that there might have been a different outcome so that, where appropriate, substantial prejudice had occurred and, in terms of discretion, that there was a real possibility of a different decision. A claimant who was unable to make representations because of a consultation error ought to indicate the nature of the comments which they would have made. In some circumstances expert evidence could be produced, although Collins J in *R v Bolsover District Council, ex p Paterson*[159] was of the view that this would be an excessive requirement upon claimants.

The court must have in mind that it is not qualified to determine planning merits which combine matters of professional judgment and political opinion.

Severance of unlawful parts of decisions

25.91 In judicial review it is possible in principle to quash only the unlawful part of a decision. This can be useful, particularly if the problem is confined to a discrete element or condition. The power to quash under s 288 is only capable of being exercised against the whole decision.

25.92 Whether an unlawful condition or the unlawful part of a decision can be quashed and the remainder survive depends upon whether the unlawful part is severable from the rest of the consent. Severability has been considered in a range of cases, including *Hall & Co Ltd v Shoreham-by-Sea Urban District Council*[160] with debate as to whether conditions were important or trivial. The Court of Appeal in *Pedgrift v Oxfordshire County Council*[161] identified a test: is the condition which has been held to be invalid essential to or at least an important part of the planning permission?[162].

25.93 It may well be that the real test is whether there might have been any change to the decision other than the simple deletion of the unlawful text had that error not been made. This was indicated by Mr Justice Ouseley in *R (on the application of MidCounties Co-operative Ltd) v Wyre Forest District Council*[163]:

> '72 ... This tailpiece is linguistically severable, and after severance the condition requires no further amendment nor the insertion of any other words to make linguistic and planning sense. The substance of the condition would not be altered. It retains the floorspace limits which are at the heart of the condition and are what the condition aims to achieve. It reflects exactly what was applied for, assessed and contemplated in the officer's report, by the committee and approved by it. It is not, in my judgment, an important part of the planning condition, let alone of the planning permission. Its excision merely prevents the District Council doing what it would have been unlawful for it to do any way.

---

[158] Senior Courts Act 1981, s 31(3E) and s 31(2B) respectively.
[159] [2001] JPL 211 at paras 15, 16.
[160] [1964] 1 WLR 240.
[161] (1991) 63 P & CR 246, also reported as *Mouchel Superannuation Fund Trustees v Oxfordshire County Council* [1992] 1 PLR 97.
[162] At 257 per Glidewell LJ.
[163] [2009] EWHC 964 (Admin). For the application of severability see *R (on the application of Treagus) v Suffolk County Council* [2013] EWHC 950 (Admin), [2013] Env LR 36 at paras 67–76 per Lord Carlile of Berriew QC.

25.94 High Court challenges

74 ... severance does not involve substituting a court decision for one not made by the Council, let alone for one that it is possible the Council may not have made if it knew the tailpiece to be unlawful. The condition would have been issued without that tailpiece had attention been paid to its lawfulness ...'

COSTS OF HIGH COURT APPEALS AND APPLICATIONS

25.94 Costs are in the discretion of the court. However, the general rule is that 'the unsuccessful party will be ordered to pay the costs of the successful party'[164]. Consequently the winner of the final hearing will usually recover its costs. Some exceptions do arise. There is a value in establishing unlawful acts by public authorities even if a substantive remedy is refused in the exercise of the court's discretion. Lord Toulson JSC held in *R (on the application of Hunt) v North Somerset Council*[165]:

'If a party who has been given leave to bring a judicial review claim succeeds in establishing after fully contested proceedings that the defendant acted unlawfully, some good reason would have to be shown why he should not recover his reasonable costs'.

In any proceedings some apportionment of costs might also arise. A party who has been ultimately successful but failed on a significant number of its arguments might not recover its full costs.

25.95 However, the losing party in judicial review or a statutory application or appeal will not normally be expected to pay more than one set of costs, for example to both the Secretary of State and the respondent developer, unless this is justified by the case. Following conflicting case law, the House of Lords in *Bolton Metropolitan District Council v Secretary of State for the Environment (Practice Note)*[166] set out tests for these cases. Lord Lloyd said[167]:

'Where there is multiple representation, the losing party will not normally be required to pay more than one set of costs, unless the recovery of further costs is justified in the circumstances of the particular case'.

25.96 He continued:

'What then is the proper approach? As in all questions to do with costs, the fundamental rule is that there are no rules. Costs are always in the discretion of the court, and a practice, however widespread and longstanding, must never be allowed to harden into a rule. But the following propositions may be supported

(1) The Secretary of State, when successful in defending his decision, will normally be entitled to the whole of his costs. He should not be required to share his award of costs by apportionment, whether by agreement with other parties, or by further order of the court. ....

(2) The developer will not normally be entitled to his costs unless he can show that there was likely to be a separate issue on which he was entitled to be heard, that is to say an issue not covered by counsel for the Secretary of State; or unless he

---

[164] CPR 44.3(2)(a).
[165] [2015] UKSC 51, [2015] 1 WLR 3575 at para 16.
[166] [1995] 1 WLR 1176.
[167] At 1178.

has an interest which requires separate representation. The mere fact that he is the developer will not of itself justify a second set of costs in every case.

(3) A second set of costs is more likely to be awarded at first instance, than in the Court of Appeal or House of Lords, by which time the issues should have crystallised, and the extent to which there are indeed separate interests should have been clarified'.

25.97 The *Bolton* approach has been applied to judicial review and applications to the High Court under planning legislation. The starting point remains a presumption that only one set of costs will be awarded to a successful side. It may be that additional costs may be awarded in part, for example, where the developer helpfully put in evidence on a particular point.

Costs protection for parties

25.98 The final hearing of a Planning Court challenge will usually take one or two days. It would be rare for a case to take three or four days to argue and anything more would be exceptional. Parties do not rack up hundreds of thousands or millions of pounds in costs. Costs are, though, significant in any normal terms and whilst for the developer of a major project such costs may be unwelcome but manageable, for others they may be prohibitive. The greatest concerns tend to be expressed by local resident or pressure group claimants fearing liability for the other parties' costs. Whilst the prospect of paying the developer's costs is slim, those sums are potentially large.

Consequently in certain circumstances costs protection may be applied, limiting the claimant's liability to adverse costs orders and, in return, restricting the claimant's potential to recover costs (a cross-cap). There are at present three categories of costs protection.

Aarhus Convention claims in judicial review

25.99 The Aarhus Convention on Access to Information, Public Participation in Decision-making and Access to Justice in Environmental Matters provides for access to court proceedings to review access to environmental information (art 9(1)), EIA (art 9(3)) and acts and omissions which 'contravene provisions of [the member state's] national law relating to the environment' (art 9(3)). In all cases the proceedings must 'provide adequate and effective remedies, including injunctive relief as appropriate, and be fair, equitable, timely and not prohibitively expensive' (art 9(4)).

25.100 A claimant who brings judicial review proceedings within art 9, paras (1)–(3) is able to have the case categorised as an Aarhus Convention claim under CPR 45.41. In such circumstances the claimant's liability is capped to £5,000 where the claimant is claiming only as an individual and not as, or on behalf of, a business or other legal person and in all other cases, £10,000. The defendant's liability in such cases is limited to £35,000[168]. In *Venn v Secretary of State for Communities and Local Government*[169] the Court of Appeal identified the breadth of art 9(3) of the Aarhus Convention in the context of planning cases, as including alleged breaches of planning policies concerned with protecting the environment[170]. It also ruled that the

---

[168] The figures are in Practice Direction 45, paras 5.1, 5.2.
[169] [2014] EWCA Civ 1539, [2015] 1 WLR 2328.
[170] Para 18 per Sullivan LJ.

25.101 *High Court challenges*

CPR 45.41 procedure applied only to judicial review and not to statutory applications to the High Court, in that case, under the Town and Country Planning Act 1990, s 288[171]. However this omission was in breach of the Aarhus Convention[172].

25.101 On the CPR as presently drafted, Aarhus Convention status can be claimed by any claimant, not just a member of the public and therefore includes large local authorities: *R (HS2 Action Alliance, London Borough of Hillingdon) v Secretary of State for Transport*[173]. The government is consulting on an amendment to the CPR to confine claimants to members of the public, but there is still uncertainty as to who are members of the public for these purposes[174].

Protective costs orders generally

25.102 Where the claim is outside the Aarhus Convention claim rules being either non-environmental or brought under s 288, then a protective costs order (PCO) may be granted. The standard criteria to be applied are those in *R (on the application of Corner House Research) v Secretary of State for Trade and Industry*[175] which as subsequently applied are:

(i) the issues raised are of general public importance;

(ii) the public interest requires that those issues be resolved;

(iii) having regard to the financial resources of the applicant and the respondent(s) and to the amount of costs that are likely to be involved, it is fair and just to make the order;

(iv) if the order is not made the applicant will probably discontinue the proceedings and will be acting reasonably in so doing.

Protective costs orders in Environmental Impact Assessment or Industrial Emissions Directive cases

25.103 The Environmental Impact Assessment Directive and the Industrial Emissions Directives provide that the public concerned in a decision may apply for a review of its legality. Reflecting the Aarhus Convention, this procedure shall not be prohibitively expensive[176]. In decisions subject to these Directives the public importance and public interest tests under *Corner House* are considered always to be satisfied, whether or not the ground of challenge relates to the Directives[177].

---

[171] Para 33 per Sullivan LJ.
[172] Paras 34, 35 per Sullivan LJ.
[173] [2015] EWCA Civ 203, [2015] 2 Costs LR 411.
[174] is some authority that parish or community councils could be members of the public: *R (on the application of Halebank Parish Council) v Halton Borough Council* [2012] EWHC 1889 (Admin), [2013] JPL 56 where a protective costs order was made in favour of a parish council in an EIA case although its basis is not recorded in the judgment *Avich and Kilchrenan Community Council* (Aarhus Convention Compliance Committee: ACCC/2012/68).
[175] [2005] EWCA Civ 192, *[2005] 1 WLR 2600*.
[176] See the EIA Directive, art 11(4).
[177] *R (on the application of Garner) v Elmbridge Borough Council* [2010] EWCA Civ 1006, [2012] PTSR 250 at para 39 per Sullivan LJ. For the potential considerations in European law cases see *R (on the application of Edwards) v Environment Agency* (C-260/11) [2013] 1 WLR 2914 and [2013] UKSC 78, [2014] 1 WLR 55.

25.104 There is no automatic right cost-capping in s 288 applications or other statutory applications or appeals to the Planning Court, as distinct from the Aarhus Convention claims procedure available for judicial reviews. In September 2015 the Ministry of Justice issued a consultation paper on Planning Court proceedings which proposed extending automatic costs protection to statutory reviews and appeals brought by members of the public which fell within the Environmental Impact Assessment or Industrial Emissions Directives, but did not propose to extend the automatic protection to other Aarhus cases.

APPEALING TO THE COURT OF APPEAL IN JUDICIAL REVIEW AND s 288 CASES

25.105 Where a s 288 application or judicial review proceedings have gone to a final hearing either because permission to apply had been granted or the s 288 application predates the leave requirement, then permission to appeal is required and may be sought from the High Court or the Court of Appeal. Whilst there is no requirement to apply for permission from the High Court before an application for permission to appeal can be made to the Court of Appeal, it is conventional to ask the High Court judge who decided the case for permission first. There is little to be lost from making the application and it is possible that permission to appeal will be granted. At the least it provides a first opportunity to think through the grounds of appeal before applying to the Court of Appeal.

The appellants' notice, ground and skeleton submissions must be filed in the Civil Appeals Office within 21 days from the decision in the High Court unless altered by the High Court judge.

25.106 Where permission to apply under s 288 or judicial review has been refused either following an oral hearing or by a judge on the papers who has certified that the application is totally without merit then permission to appeal can only be sought from the Court of Appeal[178]. In those cases the appellants' notice, ground and skeleton submissions must be filed in the Civil Appeals Office within seven days from the hearing or the receipt of the written decision[179]. These are technically 'applications for permission to appeal the refusal of permission to apply for' planning statutory review or judicial review. Whilst the Court of Appeal can grant permission to appeal and then hold a full hearing to decide whether permission to apply under s 288 or for judicial review should be granted it is common for the court to simply grant permission to bring the statutory review or judicial review rather than permission to appeal[180]. Such cases will usually be returned to the High Court for a substantive hearing[181] but may be retained in the Court of Appeal, usually if the facts are all in front of the court and there has been a detailed High Court judgment which has clarified the circumstances and the issues.

25.107 In any of these appeals the rule for the grant of permission to appeal is in CPR 52.3(6):

---

[178] For s 288 applications see CPR 52.15B(1), (2).
[179] For s 288 applications see CPR 52.15B(3).
[180] It is empowered to do this for planning reviews by CPR 52.15B(4) and for judicial review by CPR 52.15(3).
[181] See for planning reviews CPR 52.15B(5) and for judicial review CPR 52.15(4).

25.108 *High Court challenges*

'Permission to appeal may be given only where:

(a) the court considers that the appeal would have a real prospect of success; or

(b) there is some other compelling reason why the appeal should be heard'.

Ordinarily the appellant would have taken an active part in the High Court proceedings, however a person who could have taken part in the lower court but did not do so can appeal[182].

THE EFFECT OF QUASHING

25.108 The effect of a quashing order is that the decision never had any legal effect[183]. Additionally the reasoning in an appeal decision would not stand if it was quashed: *Kingswood District Council v Secretary of State for the Environment*[184] Graham Eyre QC held 'the Secretary of State has to start again *de novo* with a clean sheet'.

The redetermination of an appeal or call-in following a quashing

25.109 The effect of a successful challenge under s 288 or occasionally on judicial review is that the appeal returns to the Minister for redetermination following a quashing. There will then be a need to re-determine the appeal unless the appeal or application is withdrawn.

25.110 Where a decision taken following a planning inquiry or hearing has been quashed the rules set out the initial procedure for redetermination. The Minister will send a written statement of those matters on which further representations are requested to those persons entitled to appear who did appear. Those persons, usually simply the appellant, local planning authority and any r 6 party, can make representations on the substance of the appeal or call-in, or seek the holding of a re-opened or new inquiry or hearing. That may be in front of a different inspector[185]. Any such representations are to be made within three weeks. There is no equivalent redetermination provision in the written representations regulations in England or Wales but a similar procedure will be followed.

---

[182] *George Wimpey UK Ltd v Tewkesbury Borough Council* [2012] EWCA Civ 12, [2008] 1 WLR 1649. An example would be a developer leaving the defence of a permission in the High Court to the Secretary of State and seeking to appeal when the Minister has been unsuccessful. It would though invariably be better for a party to take part in the High Court rather than to try to salvage the position on appeal.

[183] 'Incapable of having any legal effect upon the rights and duties of the parties to the proceedings': Lord Diplock in *Hoffmann-Le Roche v Secretary of State for Trade and Industry* [1975] AC 295 at 365. The point has been put more simply 'it will be treated as never having had any legal effect at all': *R (on the application of H) v Ashworth Special Hospital Authority* [2002] EWCA Civ 923, [2003] 1 WLR 127 at para 46 per Dyson LJ. See also *Mossell (Jamaica) Ltd (t/a Digicel) v Office of Utilities Regulations* [2010] UKPC 1 at para 44.

[184] (1989) 57 P & CR 153 at 162.

[185] Town and Country Planning (Inquiries Procedure) (England) Rules 2000, SI 2000/1624, r 19; Town and Country Planning Appeals (Determination by Inspectors) (Inquiries Procedure) (England) Rules 2000, SI 2000/1625, r 20; Town and Country Planning (Hearings Procedure) (England) Rules 2000, SI 2000/1626, r 17; Town and Country Planning (Inquiries Procedure) (Wales) Rules 2003, SI 2003/1269, r 19; Town and Country Planning Appeals (Determination by Inspectors) (Inquiries Procedure) (Wales) Rules 2003, SI 2003/1270, r 20; Town and Country Planning (Hearings Procedure) (Wales) Rules 2003, SI 2003/1271, r 17.

The effect of quashing **25.114**

25.111 In practice following any quashing the Minister will ask for representations on any matters arising out of the litigation and any changes in material considerations since the original decision as well as proposing the mode of redetermination and whether it shall involve the same inspector. The claimant should be consulted even if they were not entitled to appear in the appeal. It is common for the Minister to propose that the original inspector reconsider the case, for the successful claimant to reject that proposal and for the Minister to then give way.

25.112 Effectively a bespoke timetable has to be worked up for a redetermination. The material which was before the original decision maker remains in the process and sometimes it is simply a matter of allowing supplementary proofs or submissions. In other cases fresh statements of case or proofs/statements of evidence will be required. This is most common if the mode of determination is changed to a hearing or inquiry, the quashing was on wide-ranging issues or there have been significant changes in other considerations.

The costs to the parties of that redetermination are not part of the costs of the High Court proceedings and so not recoverable under a court order.

25.113 Where the redetermination arises because of an error by an inspector, the Planning Inspectorate or a Minister then the Inspectorate practice has been that the reasonable costs of redetermination will be paid as *ex gratia* compensation. In the 1970s the Inspectorate would pay the costs which had been incurred on the initial appeal hearing or inquiry. In the 1980s the practice changed to pay the costs of the redetermination rather than the initial hearing. The practice of making *ex gratia* payments was well-known amongst participants and professionals in the planning system although for many years the Inspectorate did not publicise it. It was dealt with in internal Inspectorate guidance before being set out in the 2009 Good Practice Advice Note 15 *Challenges and complaints*. This scheme was scrapped (without announcement) in April 2011. Compensation arrangements were resurrected in 2012 following two judicial reviews, which the Secretary of State conceded, and severe criticism by the Parliamentary Ombudsman[186]. Compensation arrangements are set out in the Planning Inspectorate's procedural guidance, saying that requests should normally be made within six months of the error or of the redetermination of the appeal[187].

Redetermination of a planning application which was before the local planning authority

25.114 If a planning permission, reserved matters approval or details under a condition granted by a local planning authority is quashed then the application will revive and be back before the authority for a decision. This will be the same application and should retain the same reference. Details submitted and representations made originally will remain for consideration, unless they are withdrawn.

---

[186] *R (on the application of Koumis) v Secretary of State for Communities and Local Government*; *R (on the application of Payne) v Secretary of State for Communities and Local Government* CO/8053/2011. The Parliamentary Ombudsman published *A false economy?* in October 2012.
[187] *Procedural Guide – Planning appeals and called-in planning applications – England* (31 July 2015) Annex Q paras Q.6.4 and Q.6.5 and see *Procedural Guidance Planning appeals and called-in planning applications – Wales* (July 2015) para N.6.3.

25.115 High Court challenges

It is sensible for the local planning authority to reconsult and republicise the application prior to redetermination.

DECLARATIONS AS TO THE PLANNING STATUS OF LAND

25.115 Ordinarily a developer who wishes to establish that a particular development is or would be lawful on the land should make an application for a lawful development certificate[188]. A declaration that a situation is not or would not be lawful may, however, be granted as the statutory process of a lawful development certificate cannot be pursued as that is only conclusive of the lawfulness of a situation, not that it is unlawful[189]. The planning status of land is a continuing state of affairs (eg a permission has lapsed or a condition is or will be breached) and so the time for bringing judicial review proceedings does not run from the point that situation first came about[190]. A flexible and commonsense approach should be taken and it may be more sensible for issues to be determined at the present time rather than left for the future[191].

THE PLANNING COURT: STRUCTURE AND ORGANISATION

The Planning Court

25.116 Historically the power of the courts to control the actions of public authorities was exercised by the King's or Queen's Bench Division. This evolved to be the responsibility of the Crown Office list within that Division. The Bowman reforms updated Crown Office practice and procedure, creating the Administrative Court in 2000.

25.117 From April 2014 the Planning Court became a specialist list within the Queen's Bench Division[192]. To what extent the running of the Planning Court is separate from the Administrative Court is a matter of opinion[193]. Planning Court claims are issued in the Administrative Court Office, either in the Royal Courts of Justice or one of its regional/national centres (Cardiff, Birmingham, Leeds or Manchester)[194]. Such claims are stamped 'Planning Court' but as with cases in the Administrative Court cases are given a Crown Office number (CO/number/year) and an Administrative Court stamp[195]. The court is an evolution of the Planning Fast

---

[188] See *R v East Sussex County Council, ex p Reprotech (Pebsham) Ltd* [2002] UKHL 8, [2002] JPL 821 and Harwood *Planning Enforcement* (2013) Chapter 21.
[189] *R (on the application of Hammerton) v London Underground Ltd* [2002] EWHC 2307 (Admin) at para 187 per Ouseley J.
[190] *Hammerton* at para 197.
[191] *Hammerton* at para 199.
[192] CPR 54.22(1) inserted by the Civil Procedure (Amendment No 3) Rules 2014, SI 2014/610, r 3.
[193] The Planning Court was at least to have its own letterhead (*Explanatory Memorandum to the Civil Procedure (Amendment No 3) Rules 2014* para 9.1) although the suggestion that its heraldic supporters should be a JCB digger and a Great Crested Newt was not taken up. The letterhead simply says 'Planning Court, Administrative Court Office'.
[194] Practice Direction 54E, para 2.1.
[195] The first claim to be filed in the Planning Court was *R (on the application of Campaign for Real Ale) v Bradford Metropolitan Borough Council*. This concerned a grant of listed building consent for works to a public house. In pre-action correspondence the Council had agreed to submit to judgment, having previously submitted to judgment on an earlier consent. The claimant's solicitors were Susan Ring and Heather Hamilton of Richard Buxton and counsel was Richard Harwood QC.

The Planning Court: structure and organisation **25.120**

Track which was introduced into the Administrative Court in July 2013. The aim of the Fast Track was to ensure that important planning cases were heard quickly before specialist judges[196].

25.118 A Lead Judge is in charge of the Planning Court specialist list[197]. Mr Justice Lindblom (formerly planning silk Keith Lindblom QC) was appointed as the Planning Liaison Judge for the Planning Fast Track and was appointed as the first Lead Judge of the Planning Court. Following her promotion to the Court of Appeal in 2015, Mrs Justice Patterson was appointed as the Lead Judge. Again she is a former planning silk and also served as a Law Commissioner[198].

Jurisdiction

25.119 CPR 54.21(2) sets the jurisdiction of the Planning Court by defining a 'Planning Court claim' as:

'a judicial review or statutory challenge which:
(a) involves any of the following matters:
 (i) planning permission, other development consents, the enforcement of planning control and the enforcement of other statutory schemes;
 (ii) applications under the Transport and Works Act 1992;
 (iii) wayleaves;
 (iv) highways and other rights of way;
 (v) compulsory purchase orders;
 (vi) village greens;
 (vii) European Union environmental legislation and domestic transpositions, including assessments for development consents, habitats, waste and pollution control;
 (viii) national, regional or other planning policy documents, statutory or otherwise; or
 (ix) any other matter the judge appointed under rule 54.22(2) considers appropriate; and
(b) has been issued or transferred to the Planning Court'.

25.120 As expected, the Planning Court has jurisdiction over certain judicial reviews. Statutory challenges are not defined in the Civil Procedure Rules, and the expression appears to be new to the CPR. It would include applications to the High Court to challenge the validity of various decisions, actions or orders and appeals which challenge validity, such as appeals under the Town and Country Planning Act 1990, s 289, against enforcement notice appeal decisions. Open for debate is whether it includes civil or criminal appeals by way of case stated or a judicial review of a criminal case, in practice these still appear to be dealt with by the Divisional Court

---

[196] For a discussion of the evolution of the Planning Court proposals see *The High Court's New Planning Court* by Richard Harwood QC (February 2014).
[197] CPR 54.22(2).
[198] Very useful extra-judicial papers on practice in the Planning Court have been written by the lead judges: Sir Keith Lindblom 'The Planning Court: one year on' [2015] JPL OP3; Dame Frances Patterson and Sir Ian Dove 'The Planning Court: future directions' [2015] JPL 1118.

25.121 *High Court challenges*

or the Administrative Court. The Planning Court's jurisdiction does not extend to other civil proceedings which collaterally raise matters within these topics. Planning injunctions (under the Town and Country Planning Act 1990, s 187B) are outside its remit.

25.121 The court covers a wide range of topics, reflecting the traditional compass of the Planning Bar, including highways, compulsory purchase and village greens. The breadth of the court's role was illustrated by the first case it heard. On 7 April 2014 Mr Justice Lindblom granted permission to apply for judicial review of English Heritage's decision not to designate land at Germany Beck, York on the Battlefields Register as the site of the 1066 Battle of Fulford, a case that could only come under 'any other matter the judge ... considers appropriate'[199].

25.122 The approach to the court's jurisdiction on environmental law is interesting. The Planning Court deals with EU environmental law and its domestic transpositions but does not automatically have jurisdiction over non-European environmental law. So a challenge to an environmental permit for a waste or Industrial Emissions Directive installation which falls in part under EU law is within the remit, but a purely domestic environmental permit matter is not. Similarly Part IIA contaminated land or statutory nuisance proceedings are not automatically for the Planning Court.

25.123 The Planning Liaison Judge is able to transfer other cases to the Planning Court. Most, if not all, Administrative Court cases on planning matters were transferred to the Planning Court in the week commencing 7 April 2014.

25.124 A Planning Court claim will only be one which has been issued in or transferred to the Planning Court[200]. The Practice Direction requires Planning Court claims to be issued or lodged in the Administrative Court Office and marked by the claimant as 'Planning Court', but it does not in terms say that any case within the category must be a Planning Court claim. It would make sense to bring such cases in the Planning Court to make use of the expertise which should be available.

Significant cases and timetabling

25.125 The Planning Liaison Judge is able to categorise Planning Court claims as 'significant'[201]. It may be that this can be done by class as well as individually. According to the Practice Direction, significant Planning Court claims include claims which[202]:

'a) relate to commercial, residential, or other developments which have significant economic impact either at a local level or beyond their immediate locality;

b) raise important points of law;

---

[199] *R (on the application of Jones) v English Heritage* CO/1932/2013. Leading counsel for the claimant, and so the first advocate to speak in the Planning Court, was Ian Dove QC. He led James Corbet Burcher, and the claimant's solicitor was Lisa Foster of Richard Buxton. Counsel for English Heritage was Emma Dring and their solicitor Trevor Griffiths of Sharpe Pritchard.

[200] CPR 54.21(2)(b).

[201] Practice Direction 54E, para 3.1. Categorisation involves a judicial decision, but whilst noted on the file, it is not contained in an order or routinely notified to the parties. It would be helpful if such notice was given.

[202] Practice Direction 54E, para 3.2.

The Planning Court: structure and organisation 25.128

c) generate significant public interest; or

d) by virtue of the volume or nature of technical material, are best dealt with by judges with significant experience of handling such matters'.

25.126 Parties may make representations as to whether a matter should be characterised as significant on issuing the claim or lodging an acknowledgment of service. To be identified and dealt with promptly it is best if this is done in a separate document. One implication of being identified as significant is that the case should come before a specialist judge. The other consequence is that tight timescales apply to the handling of the case. By para 3.4 of the Practice Direction target timescales for hearing significant cases are:

> '(a) applications for permission to apply for judicial review or planning statutory review are to be determined within three weeks of the expiry of the time limit for filing of the acknowledgment of service;
>
> (b) oral renewals of applications for permission to apply for judicial review or planning statutory review are to be heard within one month of receipt of request for renewal;
>
> (c) applications for permission under section 289 of the Town and Country Planning Act 1990 are to be determined within one month of issue;
>
> (d) planning statutory reviews are to be heard within six months of issue; and
>
> (e) judicial reviews are to be heard within ten weeks of the expiry of the period for the submission of detailed grounds by the defendant or any other party as provided in rule 54.14'.

This would mean that a judicial review substantive hearing should take place within six months of the claim being filed if permission to apply is granted by the Planning Court at a hearing.

25.127 The Planning Liaison Judge is able to direct the expedition of any Planning Court claim if it is necessary to deal with the case justly[203].

25.128 The target timescales are subject to the overriding objective of the interests of justice but the parties should be prepared to meet them. In *London & Henley (Middle Brook Street) Ltd v Secretary of State for Communities and Local Government*[204] Mr Justice Lindblom agreed to the adjournment of a two-day substantive hearing of a compulsory purchase order challenge in 'truly exceptional circumstances' on the basis that it was effectively settled. He emphasised the loss of court time which had been caused by the late adjournment and took[205]:

> 'this opportunity to remind parties in proceedings such as these of the new targets for planning cases in the Administrative Court, which have been published on its website, and in particular the guidance given on listing. The guidance makes it clear that parties will be consulted before substantive hearings are listed, but – and this is important for parties to note – listing will respect the general timetable and targets. Dates may be imposed and counsel's availability will not be a reason for hearing a case significantly outside the target timetable'.

---

[203] Practice Direction 54E, para 3.6.
[204] [2013] EWHC 4207 (Admin).
[205] At para 17.

25.129 High Court challenges

Judges

25.129 One objective of government is for the Planning Court to be staffed by specialist judges. At present a large number of High Court judges are able to sit in the Administrative Court, along with circuit judges, recorders and others as deputy High Court judges. When efforts were being made to reduce a backlog of claims the result was that few planning cases came before specialist judges. In 2012 around 40 judges heard 120 substantive planning cases in the Administrative Court, most hearing only one case each[206]. Of those only a small number of High Court judges and a smaller number of circuit judges had real planning expertise from their former legal practices.

25.130 The President of the Queen's Bench Division is responsible for the nomination of specialist planning judges to deal with significant Planning Court claims and also of other judges to deal with other cases in the Planning Court[207]. Following the first hearing in the court before Mr Justice Lindblom, the second hearing was conducted by a planning silk, Mr Rhodri Price Lewis QC, sitting as a Deputy High Court Judge on 8 April. Mr Justice Lewis (formerly Clive Lewis QC) also sat in the Planning Court in its first week.

25.131 The judges dealing with Planning Court cases are mainly full High Court judges with substantial planning or public law experience in their previous practice or certain High Court judges who have built up experience through longevity in the Administrative Court or cases being directed their way, along with certain circuit judges and several planning silks who sit as deputy High Court Judges. The list is far narrower than the 40 judges dealing with planning cases in 2012, now numbering about 17 judges.

---

[206] *Judicial Review: Proposals for further reform* (Ministry of Justice, September 2013), para 39 citing indicative management information from the Administrative Court. The paper describes these as 'High Court judges' but appears to include deputies.
[207] CPR 54.22(3).

Chapter 26

The grant of planning permission by orders and other means

26.1 Planning permission may be granted by several mechanisms other than an application to the local planning authority or reliance on the General Permitted Development Order. The UK planning system has essentially operated by a case-by-case consideration of proposals or nationally set permitted development rights. Plan-making has been to establish policies which can be applied when case-by-case applications are determined. This is distinct from a zoning approach, where an area-wide document will grant permission for development of certain classes in certain locations. Proposals which do not accord with the zone may be permitted on an individual application. Whilst the zone might establish the principle of the use up to certain dimensions, the detail of the scheme is likely to require individual approval. Zoning in these terms is adopted widely in Europe, the United States and some former British colonies, including Hong Kong.

26.2 Zoning has occasionally appealed as a concept with the result that there are now seven mechanisms for granting planning permission by zones or local orders of some kind:

(i) the making of a special development order by the Secretary of State under the Town and Country Planning Act 1990, s 59;

(ii) local development orders initiated by the local planning authority under the Town and Country Planning Act 1990, s 61A;

(iii) neighbourhood development orders initiated by a parish council or designated neighbourhood forum under the Town and Country Planning Act 1990, s 61E;

(iv) community right to build orders made by community organisations under the Town and Country Planning Act 1990, s 61Q;

(v) mayoral development orders in London under the Town and Country Planning Act 1990, ss 61DA–61DE;

(vi) simplified planning zones made by the local planning authority under the Town and Country Planning Act 1990, s 82;

(vii) designation of an enterprise zone under the Local Government, Planning and Land Act 1980, Sch 32 and by the Town and Country Planning Act 1990, s 88;

Such orders may consent development of certain descriptions, in a particular defined area or across a council area. They may also be used to approve a very particular scheme.

26.3 *The grant of planning permission by orders and other means*

26.3 Additionally the Secretary of State or Welsh Ministers may grant deemed planning permission under s 90 where authorisation for the development is given under other mechanisms, such as the Transport and Works Act 1992[1].

Development consent orders under the Planning Act 2008 are required for nationally significant infrastructure projects rather than planning permission[2].

Mechanisms for granting planning permission in principle are proposed for England in the Housing and Planning Bill 2015. These are considered at the end of this chapter.

SPECIAL DEVELOPMENT ORDERS

26.4 A special development order is 'applicable only to such land or descriptions of land as may be specified in the order' in distinction to a general development order which authorises development on all land subject to any exclusions[3]. The order 'may be granted either unconditionally or subject to such conditions or limitations as may be specified in the order'[4]. A particular use was to grant planning permission for proposals made by urban development corporations[5].

26.5 Whilst special development orders were used decades ago, the procedure has fallen into disuse. However the Town and Country Planning (Operation Stack) Special Development Order 2015[6] was made to grant temporary planning permission for the stationing of goods vehicles, the provision of temporary structures and the use of an existing building for coordination at Manston Airport, to accommodate HGVs stuck due to disruption at the Channel ports and the Channel Tunnel[7].

26.6 There are no EIA procedures for these orders. Additionally, special development orders may not be made where appropriate assessment is required under the Conservation of Habitats and Species Regulations 2010[8].

LOCAL DEVELOPMENT ORDERS

26.7 Local development orders (LDOs) are made by the local planning authority by order under the Town and Country Planning Act 1990, s 61A[9]. An LDO may grant planning permission for development specified in the order or development

---

[1] Town and Country Planning Act 1990, s 90.
[2] The development consent order regime is considered in the *National Infrastructure Planning Handbook 2015* by Michael Humphries QC (Bloomsbury Professional).
[3] Town and Country Planning Act 1990, s 59(3).
[4] Town and Country Planning Act 1990, s 60(1).
[5] Local Government, Planning and Land Act 1980, s 148(1), (2), for example the Town and Country Planning (London Docklands Urban Development Area) Special Development Order 1981, SI 1981/1082.
[6] SI 2015/1635.
[7] The only other recent use was to amend publicity requirements for planning applications in Camden as part of a trial of different means of public engagement: Town and Country Planning (London Borough of Camden) Special Development Order 2004, SI 2004/2355 and the Town and Country Planning (London Borough of Camden) Special Development (Amendment and Revocation) Order 2010, SI 2010/569.
[8] Conservation of Habitats and Species Regulations 2010, SI 2010/490, reg 77.
[9] Inserted by the Planning and Compulsory Purchase Act 2004, s 40.

of any specified class on all of the land in the authority's area, part of it or on a specified site[10]. Such an order can therefore function as a local version of the General Permitted Development Order or to authorise a particular scheme, like a special development order. Obvious uses include the approval of particular classes of works within an area which has a particular characteristic, such as commercial frontages within a shopping area, particular types of extensions to a common style of housing in an estate, or giving greater flexibility in large business estates. This would allow a general consent to be used by a variety of different owners, occupiers and developers. Local development orders are, however, a complex means of approving a particular scheme compared to making a planning application.

26.8 Planning permission granted by local development orders is additional to the General Permitted Development Order and any permission granted on application. An LDO may not remove existing rights to develop. It is, though, a matter of interpretation of the individual right whether it can be used as well as carrying out development under another planning permission. An LDO permission may be unconditional or subject to conditions or limitations which are specified in the order[11]. Where the order authorises development 'of a specified description' it may include provision allowing the local planning authority to direct that permission does not apply to development in a particular area or any particular development[12]. Since LDOs can be for 'development specified in the order' and 'development of any class so specified' this potential power of direction may be limited to only certain rights. Any direction making power will need to be contained in the LDO itself with its ambit set out.

26.9 In Wales an LDO may not authorise development which has to be subject to EIA[13]. English LDOs can be subject to EIA (unless they fall within Sch 1 to those Regulations)[14] and their environmental statements are to be publicised and available for inspection[15]. Additionally in both nations, LDOs may not be made where appropriate assessment is required under the Conservation of Habitats and Species Regulations 2010[16]. Similarly LDOs may not affect a listed building[17].

The LDO-making process

26.10 An LDO must first be prepared by the local planning authority in draft with a statement of reasons[18]. The statement of reasons must describe the development which the order would permit and contain a plan or statement identifying the land[19]. This is a curious requirement, since both of these would have to be in the order in any event. The purpose may be to ensure that the statement of reasons is comprehensible on its own, in a non-technical manner, without a need to study the draft order.

---

[10] Town and Country Planning Act 1990, s 61A(2). An order may contain different provisions for different areas of land: s 61A(4).
[11] Town and Country Planning Act 1990, s 61C(1).
[12] Town and Country Planning Act 1990, s 61C(2).
[13] DMPO Wales, art 27(13).
[14] DMPO 2015, art 38(12)(b), referring to the Town and Country Planning (Environmental Impact Assessment) (England and Wales) Regulations 2011, SI 2011/1824, Sch 1.
[15] DMPO 2015, art 38(6).
[16] Conservation of Habitats and Species Regulations 2010, reg 78.
[17] DMPO 2015, art 38(12)(a); DMPO Wales, art 27(13)(a).
[18] DMPO 2015, art 38(1); DMPO Wales, art 27(1).
[19] DMPO 2015, art 38(2); DMPO Wales, art 27(2).

26.11 *The grant of planning permission by orders and other means*

26.11 In England the local planning authority is required to consult the following bodies if it considers that its interests would be affected by the proposed order[20]:

(a) if the local planning authority is a London borough council, the Mayor of London;

(b) a local planning authority, county council or parish council whose area is in or adjoins the area of the local planning authority;

(c) Natural England;

(d) the Environment Agency;

(e) Historic England;

(f) where the Secretary of State is the highway authority for any highway in the area of the local planning authority, the Secretary of State for Transport;

(g) a strategic highways company any part of whose area is in or adjoins the area of the local planning authority;

(h) any electronic communications code operator who owns or controls electronic communications apparatus in the authority's area;

(i) any of the following persons who exercise functions in any part of the area of the local planning authority:

    (i) a clinical commissioning group;

    (ii) the National Health Service Commissioning Board;

    (iii) a person authorised to supply electricity;

    (iv) a licensed gas transporter;

    (v) a sewerage undertaker;

    (vi) a water undertaker;

(j) voluntary bodies some or all of whose activities benefit any part of the local planning authority's area;

(k) bodies which represent the interests of persons who share a protected characteristic under the Equality Act 2010 in the authority's area;

(l) bodies which represent the interests of persons carrying on business in the area.

26.12 The Welsh list of consultees is similar, omitting the English bodies and adding community councils, Local Health Boards, the Natural Resources Body for Wales and the Welsh Ministers[21]. Rather than persons with protected characteristics under the Equality Act, the Welsh consultees are those bodies representing the interests of different racial, ethnic, national or religious groups or the interests of disabled persons[22].

26.13 In addition the authority must consult anyone else whom it would have been required to consult on an application for planning permission for that development[23].

---

[20] DMPO 2015, art 38(3).
[21] DMPO Wales, art 27(3).
[22] DMPO Wales, art 27(3)(h)–(j).
[23] DMPO 2015, art 38(4); DMPO Wales, art 27(4).

This would include consultees (as opposed to the recipients of publicity) under the relevant Development Management Procedure Order and those required to be consulted under regulations or directions[24]. The draft order and statement of reasons must be sent to the consultee with a consultation period of at least 28 days being set[25].

26.14 The draft order and statement of reasons must be published by local newspaper advertisement setting out how they can be inspected and with a minimum 28-day period being set for representations[26]. The documents will be published on the authority's website and made available for inspection at their principal office during normal working hours and at any other places the authority considers appropriate[27].

26.15 Where development is specified in the order it will be a scheme on a particular site. At least one site notice must be displayed and notice served by the authority on any person known to be an owner or tenant of the site[28].

26.16 Any representations received within the consultation period must be considered by the local planning authority before deciding whether to make the order, with or without modifications[29]. Any LDO is to be made by a resolution of the local planning authority[30].

26.17 The Welsh Ministers may call-in an LDO for their own approval at any time before it is adopted by the local planning authority[31]. The power of intervention is exercised by a direction, which may be in respect of only part of a proposed order[32]. Once the local planning authority has considered the representations made on its draft order it must send a copy of the draft order and statement of reasons with any modifications it proposes to those documents to the Welsh Ministers[33]. The order may not be adopted until the Minister has said that a direction will not be made or until a period of 21 days (which the Minister may extend) has elapsed[34]. If the Welsh Ministers direct then they may approve or reject the proposed order (or part of it) or direct the local planning authority to modify it, giving reasons for their decision[35]. A local planning authority must comply with a modification direction and not adopt the order unless the Minister has by notice said that he or she is satisfied with the modification[36]. This leaves it open to the local planning authority to withdraw the proposed order if it is dissatisfied with the modification required.

---

[24] See Chapter 6.
[25] DMPO 2015, art 38(5); DMPO Wales, art 27(5). Representations made within that period have to be considered.
[26] DMPO 2015, art 38(6); DMPO Wales, art 27(6). This publicity should take place during the period for consulting particular bodies on the proposed order.
[27] DMPO 2015, art 38(6)(a), (b); DMPO Wales, art 27(6)(a), (b).
[28] DMPO 2015, art 38(7); DMPO Wales, art 27(7). Again, a minimum consultation period of 28 days is allowed. If necessary, reasonable steps should be taken to protect or replace the site notice: DMPO 2015, art 38(8); DMPO Wales, art 27(8).
[29] DMPO 2015, art 38(9), (10); DMPO Wales, art 27(9).
[30] Town and Country Planning Act 1990, Sch 4A, para 3.
[31] Town and Country Planning Act 1990, s 61B(1). Once the direction is given the local planning authority may take no further steps on the proposed LDO and the order can have no effect until authorised by the Minister.
[32] Town and Country Planning Act 1990, s 61B(1).
[33] DMPO Wales, art 27(10).
[34] DMPO Wales, art 27(11), (12).
[35] Town and Country Planning Act 1990, s 61B(5), (6).
[36] Town and Country Planning Act 1990, s 61B(7).

26.18 *The grant of planning permission by orders and other means*

26.18 The power of the Secretary of State in England to call in or direct the modification of draft local development orders was repealed from December 2013[37]. An English local planning authority must submit a copy of the LDO, statement of reasons and any environmental statement to the Secretary of State as soon as reasonably practicable following adoption[38].

26.19 The National Planning Policy Framework advises on the use of LDOs[39]:

> 'Local planning authorities should consider using Local Development Orders to relax planning controls for particular areas or categories of development, where the impacts would be acceptable, and in particular where this would promote economic, social or environmental gains for the area, such as boosting enterprise'.

Welsh Government Circular 003/2012 *Guidance on Using a Local Development Order* suggests 'an LPA may wish to make an LDO to assist in the regeneration of an employment area or industrial estate or guide development in [to?] areas where significant change is anticipated. It could also encourage the provision of housing on a particular site'[40].

26.20 The local planning authority may revoke a local development order at any time[41]. It must publicise any revocation by them on their website, by local advertisement and by written notice to anyone consulted on the order[42]. The Secretary of State and the Welsh Ministers may revoke a local development order if it thinks it is expedient to do so and must give reasons for that decision[43]. Prior to a Ministerial revocation notice must be given to the local planning authority providing it with an opportunity to request a hearing[44]. A hearing or inquiry would then be held if sought by the authority.

26.21 A development order or an LDO may set out whether development which has been started can be completed if the order is revoked, amended or a direction is made restricting development[45].

26.22 Local planning authorities may prepare revisions of LDOs at any time[46]. They must do so if directed by the Minister and in accordance with any timetable set down[47].

Register of LDOs

26.23 The planning register kept by each local planning authority must contain in Part 3 details of any LDOs[48]. The first section of the part will contain copies

---

[37] By the Growth and Infrastructure Act 2013, s 5(2) providing that Town and Country Planning Act 1990, s 61B(1)–(7) ceased to apply in England.
[38] Town and Country Planning Act 1990, s 61B(7A), DMPO 2015, art 38(11).
[39] NPPF, para 199.
[40] The '[to?]' is original to the text.
[41] Town and Country Planning Act 1990, s 61A(6).
[42] DMPO 2015, art 38(13); DMPO Wales, art 27(13).
[43] Town and Country Planning Act 1990, s 61B(8).
[44] Town and Country Planning Act 1990, s 100(3)–(6), as applied by s 61B(9).
[45] Town and Country Planning Act 1990, s 61D.
[46] Town and Country Planning Act 1990, Sch 4A, para 2(1).
[47] Town and Country Planning Act 1990, Sch 4A, para 2(2), (3).
[48] DMPO 2015, art 41; DMPO Wales, art 29(5).

of draft LDOs which have been prepared by the authority but not adopted, along with its statement of reasons[49]. If an order is made then it is placed in the second section of Part 3 along with its statement of reasons and the details of any subsequent revocation or revision[50].

NEIGHBOURHOOD PLANNING

26.24 Neighbourhood planning was introduced by the Localism Act 2011. Its essence is the devolution of planning powers below the district or borough council level and comprises the following elements:

(i) the establishment of Neighbourhood Areas;

(ii) the giving of certain planning powers to the parish council or a neighbourhood forum;

(iii) the making of a Neighbourhood Development Plan;

(iv) the granting of planning permission by Neighbourhood Development Orders or Community Right to Build Orders.

This section focuses on the final element, the orders which actually grant planning permission.

Neighbourhood Areas

26.25 Neighbourhood Areas are designated by local planning authorities under the Town and Country Planning Act 1990, s 61G following an application by a parish council or organisation or body capable of becoming a neighbourhood forum[51].

Parish councils and neighbourhood forums

26.26 If there is a parish council for the neighbourhood area then it will take the neighbourhood planning responsibilities[52]. Where there is no parish council the local planning authority may designate a neighbourhood forum which is a body established for the 'express purpose of promoting or improving the social, economic and environmental wellbeing' with at least 21 members from the locality[53].

---

[49] DMPO 2015, art 41(2)(a), (5); DMPO Wales, art 29(5)(a). The draft order must be placed on the register when it is sent for consultation: DMPO 2015, art 41(3); DMPO Wales, art 29(6).

[50] DMPO 2015, art 41(2)(b), (5); DMPO Wales, art 29(5)(b), (7), (8). The order must be on the second section of the register within 14 days of its adoption: DMPO 2015, art 41(4); DMPO Wales, art 29(7).

[51] Under the procedure in the Neighbourhood Planning (General) Regulations 2012, SI 2012/637, regs 5–7. Local planning authorities have a fair amount of discretion about the boundaries of neighbourhood areas: *R (on the application of Daws Hill Neighbourhood Forum) v Wycombe District Council* [2014] EWCA Civ 228, [2014] 1 WLR 1362.

[52] Town and Country Planning Act 1990, s 61F(1).

[53] Town and Country Planning Act 1990, s 61F(4)–(6). The designation procedures are in the Neighbourhood Planning (General) Regulations 2012, regs 8–12.

26.27 *The grant of planning permission by orders and other means*

Neighbourhood development plans

26.27 In practice the first task in neighbourhood planning has been to prepare a neighbourhood development plan. Once made, this is part of the development plan[54].

All neighbourhood processes involve the preparation of the plan or order by the parish council or neighbourhood forum, its submission to an independent examination, followed by a referendum and finally the making of the plan by the local planning authority.

Neighbourhood development orders and community right to build orders

26.28 These orders can grant planning permission for specified development (eg a building) or for a class of development[55]. A neighbourhood development order may relate to all land or part of the land of neighbourhood area or a site or sites[56]. It may not grant permission for a particular case where planning permission already exists or apply to more than one neighbourhood area[57]. The orders cannot authorise excluded development[58] which is[59]:

- minerals-related county matters[60];
- waste development[61];
- development for which EIA is mandatory under Annex 1 of the EIA Directive;
- development that is wholly or partly a nationally significant infrastructure project under the Planning Act 2008.

26.29 A neighbourhood development order is a community right to build order if made pursuant to a proposal by a community organisation and grants permission for a specified development on a specified site[62].

Orders may be subject to conditions or limitations, including providing for approvals by the local planning authority and limiting the duration of the rights[63].

26.30 A neighbourhood development order may be promoted by a qualifying body, that is, a parish or town council, neighbourhood forum or a defined community

---

[54] Planning and Compulsory Purchase Act 2004, s 38(2), (3). The main provisions for making the plans are the Planning and Compulsory Purchase Act 2004, ss 38A–38C which apply the procedures for Neighbourhood Development Orders in ss 61F, 61I, 61M–61P and Sch 4B, Town and Country Planning Act 1990 and the Neighbourhood Planning (General) Regulations 2012, regs 14–20. Provisions for referenda are in the Neighbourhood Planning (Referendums) Regulations 2012, SI 2012/3031, and the Neighbourhood Planning (Prescribed Dates) Regulations 2012, SI 2012/2030.
[55] Town and Country Planning Act 1990, s 61E.
[56] Town and Country Planning Act 1990, s 61J(1).
[57] Town and Country Planning Act 1990, s 61J(4), (5).
[58] Town and Country Planning Act 1990, s 61J(2).
[59] Town and Country Planning Act 1990, s 61K. Other development may be excluded by regulation.
[60] As set out in the Town and Country Planning Act 1990, Sch 1, para 1(a)–(h).
[61] As defined in the Town and Country Planning (Prescription of County Matters) (England) Regulations 2002, SI 2002/1033, reg 2.
[62] Town and Country Planning Act 1990, Sch 4C, para 2.
[63] Town and Country Planning Act 1990, s 61L(1), (2), (5). Regulations may allow for the order to provide that details are approved by a parish council instead of the local planning authority but no such provision has yet been made.

organisation[64]. Prior to submitting the proposal to the local planning authority this body must carry out consultation and publicity. It is required to publicise in a manner that is likely to bring it to the attention of people who live, work or carry on business in the neighbourhood area[65]:

(i) details of the proposals;

(ii) where and when the proposals may be inspected;

(iii) how to make representations; and

(iv) the final date for the receipt of the representations, not less than six weeks from the first publicity.

26.31 They must also consult any electronic communications code operator, clinical commissioning group, the National Health Service Commissioning Board, any electricity or gas licence holder or water or sewerage undertaker, any parish council for the area or for an adjoining neighbourhood area, or, in the case of a neighbourhood development order (but not a community right to build order), a neighbourhood forum for an adjoining area, in all cases where their interests may be affected by the proposals[66]. Historic England must be consulted on all proposals and other bodies consulted if they would be consulted under the table in Sch 5 to the Town and Country Planning (Development Management Procedure) (England) Order 2015[67]. The Civil Aviation Authority and NATS Holdings Limited must be consulted on proposals in the neighbourhood of a civil aerodrome or air traffic services site[68]. The Secretary of State for Defence is to be consulted on proposals in the neighbourhood of military aerodromes, air traffic sites or explosives sites or involving the construction of highways or changes to their accesses within 300 metres of a military aerodrome. Proposals which affect registered parks or gardens are to be notified to the Garden History Society and development in areas subject to the Protected Vistas Directions in London require consultation with the Mayor of London[69]. The highway authority also has to be consulted on development which includes the construction, formation or laying out of access to or from a trunk road. The owner and any tenant of the land to be developed under the proposed order are also to be consulted[70].

A copy of the proposals must also be sent to the local planning authority as part of this pre-submission consultation[71].

26.32 Following this consultation the order proposals are then finalised and submitted to the local planning authority. The proposal must include[72]:

---

[64] Neighbourhood Planning (General) Regulations 2012, reg 3 applying Town and Country Planning Act 1990, s 61E(6) and Sch 4C, para 4(2). Community organisations must meet the requirements in the Town and Country Planning Act 1990, s 61E(6) and Sch 4C, para 3 and the Neighbourhood Planning (General) Regulations 2012, reg 13. More than half of the members of the community organisation must live in the neighbourhood area: Town and Country Planning Act 1990, Sch 4C, para 4. The order making procedure is in the Neighbourhood Planning (General) Regulations 2012, regs 21–27.
[65] Neighbourhood Planning (General) Regulations 2012, reg 21(a).
[66] Neighbourhood Planning (General) Regulations 2012, reg 21(b)(i) applying Sch 1, para 2(1)(a)–(c).
[67] SI 2015/595. Neighbourhood Planning (General) Regulations 2012, reg 21(b)(ii) and for the table see Chapter 6.
[68] NATS run the UK civil air traffic control.
[69] And for the vista of the Tower of London from outside City Hall, the Historic Royal Palaces Trust.
[70] Neighbourhood Planning (General) Regulations 2012, reg 21(b)(ii).
[71] Neighbourhood Planning (General) Regulations 2012, reg 21(c).
[72] Neighbourhood Planning (General) Regulations 2012, reg 22(1).

26.33 *The grant of planning permission by orders and other means*

(a) a map identifying the order land;

(b) a consultation statement giving details of the consultation process, the main issues raised and how they were considered and whether they are addressed in the proposed order;

(c) the proposed neighbourhood development order or community right to build order;

(d) if appropriate, following consultation with Historic England, an archaeology statement based on a review of the historic environment record;

(e) a statement explaining how the 'basic conditions' are met; and

(f) the removal of any housing tenant enfranchisement rights in a proposed community right to build order.

26.33 There are specific Habitats and Environmental Impact Assessment provisions. A neighbourhood development order may authorise development within Sch 2 to the Town and Country Planning (Environmental Impact Assessment) Regulations 2011 if it has been subject to a screening decision that EIA is not required or EIA has been carried out[73]. However, this is subject to a prohibition on a community right to build order being made if EIA is required[74]. The habitats regime is more restrictive. A neighbourhood development plan may not grant planning permission for development which is likely to have a significant effect on a European site or a European offshore marine site (either alone or in combination with other plans or projects) and is not directly connected with or necessary to the management of the site[75].

26.34 The local planning authority has a discretion to decline to consider an order proposal if it considers it is a repeat of one proposed and dismissed in the previous two years[76]. If it considers that the draft order does not comply with the statutory requirements on its content or that consultation to date has not been carried out in accordance with the regulations then it must refuse the proposal and give reasons for doing so[77].

26.35 The authority is then required to publicise the order proposal on its website and in other ways to bring it to the attention of those living, working or carrying on business in the neighbourhood area and notify those consultation bodies who had been consulted previously[78]. A minimum six-week consultation is carried out at this stage[79]. If EIA takes place then newspaper and site notices are also required[80].

26.36 An examiner will usually be appointed by the local planning authority with the qualifying body's consent[81]. The examiner must be independent of the qualifying

---

[73] Town and Country Planning (Environmental Impact Assessment) Regulations 2011, reg 29A which applies the EIA Regulations with modifications.
[74] Town and Country Planning Act 1990, Sch 4C, para 6(1)(a).
[75] Conservation of Habitats and Species Regulations 2010, reg 78A; and for a community right to build order, Town and Country Planning Act 1990, Sch 4C, para 6(1)(b).
[76] Town and Country Planning Act 1990, Sch 4B, para 5. The authority can also decline to consider a competing community right to build order proposal: Town and Country Planning Act 1990, Sch 4C, para 4(5).
[77] Town and Country Planning Act 1990, Sch 4B, para 6.
[78] Neighbourhood Planning (General) Regulations 2012, reg 23(1).
[79] Neighbourhood Planning (General) Regulations 2012, reg 23(1)(a)(v).
[80] Neighbourhood Planning (General) Regulations 2012, reg 23(2).
[81] Town and Country Planning Act 1990, Sch 4B, para 7(4), and in default of agreement the Secretary of State may appoint an examiner: Sch 4B, para 7(5).

body and the authority, without any interest in land that may be affected by the draft order and have 'appropriate qualifications and experience'[82]. Whilst examiners can be employees of central government or other local planning authorities, they tend to be private planning consultants[83]. The examiner is provided with the submitted documents and copies of the representations made in the consultation[84].

26.37 The examiner must consider[85]:

(i) whether the draft neighbourhood development order meets the basic conditions (see sub-para (2));

(ii) whether the draft order is for development specified or of a class specified in the order, is not prohibited from being in an order and any conditions or limitations are lawful and appropriate[86];

(iii) whether the referendum should be held over a larger area than the neighbourhood area.

26.38 The basic conditions in sub-para (2) are[87]:

'(a) having regard to national policies and advice contained in guidance issued by the Secretary of State, it is appropriate to make the order,

(b) having special regard to the desirability of preserving any listed building or its setting or any features of special architectural or historic interest that it possesses, it is appropriate to make the order,

(c) having special regard to the desirability of preserving or enhancing the character or appearance of any conservation area, it is appropriate to make the order,

(d) the making of the order contributes to the achievement of sustainable development,

(e) the making of the order is in general conformity with the strategic policies contained in the development plan for the area of the authority (or any part of that area),

(f) the making of the order does not breach, and is otherwise compatible with, EU obligations, and

(g) prescribed conditions are met in relation to the order and prescribed matters have been complied with in connection with the proposal for the order'.

26.39 The examiner may only consider these matters and compatibility with the European Convention on Human Rights[88]. Examinations are generally carried out on written representations[89] but the examiner must hold a hearing on a particular

---

[82] Town and Country Planning Act 1990, Sch 4B, para 7(6).
[83] The Neighbourhood Planning Independent Examiner Referral Service keeps a list of examiners but they do not have to be used.
[84] Neighbourhood Planning (General) Regulations 2012, reg 24.
[85] Town and Country Planning Act 1990, Sch 4B, para 8(1). Other matters may be prescribed.
[86] Pursuant to Town and Country Planning Act 1990, ss 61E(2), 61J, 61L; and for community right to build orders, the requirements on their scope in Sch 4C, para 2, see Sch 4C, para 8.
[87] Town and Country Planning Act 1990, Sch 4B, para 8(2).
[88] Town and Country Planning Act 1990, Sch 4B, para 8(6). The Basic Conditions are not the same as the test of soundness for development plan examinations (under the Planning and Compulsory Purchase Act 2004, s 20) and the 'limited role' of the examiner has to be appreciated: *BDW Trading Ltd (t/a Barratt Homes) v Cheshire West and Chester Borough Council* [2014] EWHC 1470 (Admin) per Supperstone J at para 81. How limited that role will need further consideration – questions of appropriateness and sustainable development within the basic conditions are potentially quite wide.
[89] Town and Country Planning Act 1990, Sch 4B, para 9(1).

26.40 *The grant of planning permission by orders and other means*

issue if he or she considers it to be 'necessary to ensure adequate examination of the issue or a person has a fair chance to put a case'[90]. If a hearing is held then the qualifying body, local planning authority are entitled to be heard and if the hearing was convened to give a person a fair chance to put a case, then so is that person[91]. At a hearing the principle is that questioning should be done by the examiner unless another person should do it to ensure adequate examination of particular issues or to give a fair chance to put a case[92].

26.40 The examiner will provide a reasoned report recommending whether the draft order is submitted to a referendum, with any modifications necessary to ensure it complies with the tests or to correct errors[93]. It is then for the local planning authority to consider, in the light of the examiner's report, whether the basic conditions and the other legal requirements are met, or would be met if the order were modified[94]. However a narrower area of judgment is left to the authority in respect of a community right to build order: the authority does not consider the basic conditions and can only make its own modifications to comply with EU or human rights obligations or to correct errors[95]. If the authority proposes to make a different decision from that recommended by the examiner because of new evidence, new facts or a different view on a particular fact, then it must carry out a consultation and may refer the issue to examination[96].

26.41 If the authority decides that the order should proceed, a referendum would then be held amongst local authority electors in the neighbourhood area, or any larger area determined by the local planning authority[97]. If the neighbourhood area has been designated as a business area[98] then an additional referendum would be held amongst non-domestic ratepayers[99].

26.42 The local planning authority must make the order if a majority of those voting in the referendum have voted in favour[100] unless this would breach or be incompatible with any EU obligation or rights under the European Convention on Human Rights[101]. If separate referenda are held because the order relates to a business area, then the authority has a discretion to make the order if one referendum

---

[90] Town and Country Planning Act 1990, Sch 4B, para 9(2)(a). Regulations may prescribe other circumstances in which hearings must be held.
[91] Town and Country Planning Act 1990, Sch 4B, para 9(3).
[92] Town and Country Planning Act 1990, Sch 4B, para 9(6).
[93] Town and Country Planning Act 1990, Sch 4B, para 10.
[94] Town and Country Planning Act 1990, Sch 4B, para 12. The decision must be published with reasons: Neighbourhood Planning (General) Regulations 2012, reg 25. The Housing and Planning Bill proposes to allow the Secretary of State to impose time limits for the authority's consideration and any subsequent consultation by regulation: proposed Town and Country Planning Act 1990, Sch 4B, para 13A, proposed to be inserted by Housing and Planning Bill 2015, cl 101(1) (as published following Public Bill Committee in the House of Commons). If the authority fails to make a decision or to follow the examiner's recommendation or they make a modification not required by law then it is proposed that the Secretary of State can intervene in the process: proposed Town and Country Planning Act 1990, Sch 4B, paras 13B, 13C, proposed to be inserted by Housing and Planning Bill 2015, cl 102(1).
[95] Town and Country Planning Act 1990, Sch 4C, para 10.
[96] Town and Country Planning Act 1990, Sch 4B, para 12.
[97] Town and Country Planning Act 1990, Sch 4B, para 14. The referendum procedure is governed by the Neighbourhood Planning (Referendums) Regulations 2012 and the Neighbourhood Planning (Prescribed Dates) Regulations 2012.
[98] Under Town and Country Planning Act 1990, s 61H.
[99] Town and Country Planning Act 1990, Sch 4B, para 15.
[100] Town and Country Planning Act 1990, s 61E(4).
[101] Town and Country Planning Act 1990, s 61E(8).

supports it[102]. The order will only come into effect on being made by the local planning authority[103].

26.43 As might be expected, the initial focus has been on making neighbourhood development plans rather than orders[104]. The first order made was the Cockermouth Neighbourhood Development Order 2014 which authorises various changes of use or minor works to buildings in specified areas.

Policy on neighbourhood development orders and community right to build orders

26.44 Neighbourhood planning is an important part of the government's localism agenda and so there is considerable encouragement for its use. The NPPF says[105]:

> 'Neighbourhood Development Orders and Community Right to Build Orders require the support of the local community through a referendum. Therefore, local planning authorities should take a proactive and positive approach to proposals, working collaboratively with community organisations to resolve any issues before draft orders are submitted for examination. Policies in this Framework that relate to decision-taking should be read as applying to the consideration of proposed Neighbourhood Development Orders, wherever this is appropriate given the context and relevant legislation'.

Some guidance on neighbourhood development orders is also given in the *Planning Practice Guidance*[106].

Register of neighbourhood development orders and community right to build orders

26.45 Part 4 of the Planning Register kept by each local planning authority in England contains details of any neighbourhood development orders including community right to build orders[107]. The first section of the part contains copies of draft neighbourhood development orders which have been submitted to the authority and not finally disposed of, along with a copy of any plan or statement identifying the land, any other accompanying plans or drawings and any made or proposed planning obligation or s 278 agreement[108]. Additionally in the case of a draft community right to build order, the register contains details of any enfranchisement rights which the qualifying body proposes are not exercisable, and the properties, or types of

---

[102] Town and Country Planning Act 1990, s 61E(5), implicitly of course subject to compliance with the law. The Housing and Planning Bill proposes that making is to be 'as soon as reasonably practicable after the referendum is held' within a period set by regulations: proposed amendments to Town and Country Planning Act 1990, s 61E(4)(b), made by Housing and Planning Bill 2015, cl 101(2).

[103] The making of the order is published under Neighbourhood Planning (General) Regulations 2012, reg 26.

[104] The case law tends to relate to matters specific to plans rather than orders. The first quashing of a plan decision was of the Loxwood Neighbourhood Plan referendum since the local planning authority officer concerned did not have authority to determine that strategic environmental assessment was not required: *R (Crownhall Estates Ltd) v Chichester District Council* CO/3299/2014. A second referendum was cancelled because another officer did not have authority to make that subsequent decision: *R (Crownhall Estates Ltd) v Chichester District Council* CO/2669/2015.

[105] NPPF, para 202.

[106] Section 41, paras 10–13.

[107] DMPO 2015, art 42.

[108] DMPO 2015, art 42(2). For the meaning of 'not finally disposed of' see art 42(3).

26.46 *The grant of planning permission by orders and other means*

properties, in relation to which those rights are not exercisable[109]. If an order is made then it is placed in the second section of Part 4. The documents required in respect of draft orders must be included along with the made order (omitting any draft documents), the details of any subsequent revocation and the date of any subsequent approval given under the order[110].

MAYORAL DEVELOPMENT ORDERS

26.46 The Infrastructure Act 2015 proposes to introduce a power for the Mayor of London to grant planning permission by a Mayoral development order but, importantly, only with the agreement of the local planning authority. These provisions will be inserted as ss 61DA–61DE, with various consequential amendments also being made[111]. The power to make regulations or orders for these purposes came into force on 12 February 2015, but commencement provisions have not otherwise been published at the time of writing.

26.47 A Mayoral development order will grant planning permission for specified development 'on one or more sites specified in the order'[112]. The site or sites may be in the areas of one or more local planning authorities in Greater London[113], providing a potentially useful mechanism for projects which require works in more than one borough. However, the reference to planning permission on sites rather than in areas is significant. Mayoral orders are concerned with approving specific schemes rather than granting a general consent for specified development on land with particular types of buildings or uses.

26.48 Amendments to the Development Management Procedure Order will be expected to set out the procedures to be followed, including public consultation[114]. It would be a reasonable assumption that this would reflect the local development order processes. Three provisions are put in place by the Act to ensure that Mayoral development orders are agreed by the local planning authorities (the London Borough or City of London Corporation) for the sites they cover:

(a) an order 'may be made only in response to an application to the Mayor of London by each relevant local planning authority'[115];

(b) a proposed order 'may be consulted on only with the consent of each relevant local planning authority'[116];

(c) such an order 'may not be made unless the order has been approved, in the form in which it is made, by each relevant local planning authority'[117].

26.49 The role of the Secretary of State in the order making process will be clearer when secondary legislation is made. As with local development orders, the Town and Country Planning Act 1990 itself does not provide for confirmation of an order

---

[109] DMPO 2015, art 42(2)(d).
[110] DMPO 2015, art 42(4).
[111] The amendments are provided for by the Infrastructure Act 2015, s 30 and Sch 4.
[112] Proposed Town and Country Planning Act 1990, s 61DA(1).
[113] Proposed Town and Country Planning Act 1990, s 61DA(2).
[114] See proposed Town and Country Planning Act 1990, s 61DC(1), (2).
[115] Proposed Town and Country Planning Act 1990, s 61DC(3).
[116] Proposed Town and Country Planning Act 1990, s 61DC(4).
[117] Proposed Town and Country Planning Act 1990, s 61DC(5).

by the Minister. It is simply made by the Mayor and a copy subsequently sent to the Secretary of State[118]. The Secretary of State is, however, empowered to revoke a Mayoral development order by order[119] or direct the Mayor to revise it[120]. The ability of a Minister to revoke a Mayoral development order may suggest a central government role in the making of the order, even if only as a consultee to try to avoid the need for a revocation.

The content of a Mayoral development order

26.50 A Mayoral development order may grant planning permission unconditionally or subject to conditions or limitation specified in the order[121]. A condition in the planning permission granted by the order may provide for the submission and approval of details by the Mayor or a relevant local planning authority[122]. A refusal or conditional approval of an application under a condition may be appealed to the Secretary of State, as may a failure to determine it[123]. However, it is also possible for the Secretary of State to provide in a development order (as distinct from the Mayoral development order itself) that if the approval is not given 'within a specified period, that consent, agreement or approval may be sought from a specified person'[124].

26.51 If a developer does not wish to comply with the conditions in the Mayoral development order, or is unable to do so, then it may apply for planning permission in the usual way. The Secretary of State may provide for a planning application to be made for permission to develop without complying with a condition in the order. In effect this would be a s 73 application for some of the development permitted by the Mayoral development order but subject to different conditions[125].

Revocation and revision

26.52 The Mayor may revoke or revise a Mayoral development order with the approval of each local planning authority[126]. Procedures for the revision or revocation of an order will be set out by the government in a development order[127]. The Secretary of State may direct the Mayor to revise an order, without local planning authority consent, or may by order revoke a Mayoral development order[128]. Similarly the steps to be taken before a Ministerial direction or order is made for these purposes may be set out by the Secretary of State in a development order[129].

---

[118] Proposed Town and Country Planning Act 1990, s 61DC(6).
[119] Proposed Town and Country Planning Act 1990, s 61DD(3), (4). Reasons need to be given by the Minister for making a revocation order: s 61DD(5).
[120] Proposed Town and Country Planning Act 1990, s 61DD(2).
[121] Proposed Town and Country Planning Act 1990, s 61DB(1).
[122] Proposed Town and Country Planning Act 1990, s 61DB(2), (3).
[123] Town and Country Planning Act 1990, s 78(1)(c) as proposed to be amended by Infrastructure Act 2015, Sch 4, para 12. Local planning authority in s 78 will include the Mayor for these purposes, see generally proposed Town and Country Planning Act 1990, s 61DB(8).
[124] Proposed Town and Country Planning Act 1990, s 61DB(4). The person or their description being specified in the Secretary of State's development order: s 61DB(5).
[125] Proposed Town and Country Planning Act 1990, s 61DB(6), (7). Any such provision would be in the Secretary of State's development order
[126] Proposed Town and Country Planning Act 1990, s 61DD(1). If the Mayor is directed by the Secretary of State to revise the order then local planning authority approval is not required: s 61DD(2).
[127] Proposed Town and Country Planning Act 1990, s 61DD(6)(b), (7).
[128] Proposed Town and Country Planning Act 1990, s 61DD(2)–(4).
[129] Proposed Town and Country Planning Act 1990, s 61DD(6)(a), (7).

26.53 *The grant of planning permission by orders and other means*

26.53 If a Mayoral development order is revoked or revised to withdraw planning permission at a time that development under it has been started but not completed then the development may be completed unless it is determined otherwise[130]. The decision preventing the continuation of the development will be contained in a Mayoral determination accompanying his revocation of the order, in the Secretary of State's revocation order or in the revised Mayoral development order, as appropriate[131]. An issue which may arise in any event is the scope of the development which has been started but not completed. If, as is likely, an order authorises a variety of buildings and uses on a site, but it is not likely to be constructed in one tranche, or even by one developer, the question may be whether a start on one building allows the development of others following withdrawal of the planning permission. That is likely to depend on the circumstances, but a Mayoral or Ministerial decision ought to be clear as to what rights to continue to develop, if any, remain.

SIMPLIFIED PLANNING ZONES

26.54 Another mechanism for granting a general planning permission over a defined area is a simplified planning zone, originally introduced by the Housing and Planning Act 1986. These are currently dealt with by the Town and Country Planning Act 1990, ss 82–87 and Sch 7 and the Town and Country Planning (Simplified Planning Zones) Regulations 1992[132]. Guidance on the use of simplified planning zones in Wales is given in Technical Advice Note 3 (TAN3).

26.55 A simplified planning zone scheme will grant planning permission for development specified in the scheme or development of a specified class in a simplified planning zone or a specified part of it[133]. Such permissions may be unconditional or subject to such conditions, limitations or exceptions as may be specified in the scheme[134]. Simplified planning zones are made and altered by the local planning authority for the area[135]. A simplified planning zone scheme consists of a map and written statement with any appropriate 'diagrams, illustrations and descriptive matter'[136]. The scheme must specify[137]:

'(a) the development or classes of development permitted by the scheme,

(b) the land in relation to which permission is granted, and

(c) any conditions, limitations or exceptions subject to which it is granted'.

26.56 A local planning authority who decide to make a simplified planning zone scheme shall notify the Minister[138]. Decisions to promote simplified planning zones are, however, not solely a matter for the local authority. Any person may ask the

---

[130] Proposed Town and Country Planning Act 1990, s 61DE(3).
[131] Proposed Town and Country Planning Act 1990, s 61DE(4)–(7).
[132] SI 1992/2414. Various amendments to the simplified planning zone provisions are proposed by the Planning and Compulsory Purchase Act 2004, s 45 but like a number of sections of that Act it has not been brought into force.
[133] Town and Country Planning Act 1990, s 82(2).
[134] Town and Country Planning Act 1990, s 82(3).
[135] Town and Country Planning Act 1990, s 82(2). In two tier areas, this will be the district planning authority: Town and Country Planning Act 1990, Sch 1, para 9.
[136] Town and Country Planning Act 1990, Sch 7, para 1(1).
[137] Town and Country Planning Act 1990, Sch 7, para 1(2).
[138] Town and Country Planning Act 1990, Sch 7, para 2(1).

authority to make or alter a scheme and if it refuses to do so, or fails to decide within three months of the request, may refer the matter to the Minister[139]. The Minister must consider representations from the proposer and the local planning authority and may carry out further consultations[140]. At the end of this the Minister may give a simplified planning zone direction requiring the authority to make or alter a scheme over land which includes some or all of the land the subject of the request[141].

26.57 The local planning authority is required to consult the Highways Agency, any County Council for its area, parish councils, the landowners within the area and any persons who would be consulted under the Town and Country Planning (Development Management Procedure) (England) Order 2015 or the Welsh 2012 Order for a planning application covering the same matters[142]. Following that consultation, the authority is required to publish the proposed scheme or alterations for a six-week consultation period[143].

26.58 Objections may be considered following a local inquiry, hearing or on written representations, at the local planning authority's discretion[144]. Any inquiry or hearing will be held by an inspector appointed by the Minister and written representations may be considered by an inspector or just by the authority. After considering the objections and any report by an inspector, the local planning authority may adopt the proposed scheme, whether as originally prepared or subject to modifications[145]. Further consultation is required on any modifications which will materially affect the content of the scheme[146]. Adoption has to be publicised by a local advertisement and the serving of notice on remaining objectors[147]. A scheme will last for ten years beginning with the date of its adoption or approval[148]. Alterations to adopted schemes are made by the same process. Any additions to the area of the scheme, the range of permission granted or the withdrawal or relaxation of conditions, limitations or restrictions will take place immediately on adoption or approval[149]. However, changes which reduce or limit the right to develop, by removing land, withdrawing planning

---

[139] Town and Country Planning Act 1990, Sch 7, para 3(1). No reference may be made if a scheme was adopted, approved or altered over the whole of the proposed area in the previous 12 months: Town and Country Planning Act 1990, Sch 7, para 3(2).
[140] Town and Country Planning Act 1990, Sch 7, para 3(3), (4).
[141] Town and Country Planning Act 1990, Sch 7, para 4.
[142] Town and Country Planning Act 1990, Sch 7, para 5 and the Town and Country Planning (Simplified Planning Zones) Regulations 1992, reg 3.
[143] Town and Country Planning Act 1990, Sch 7, para 6 and the Town and Country Planning (Simplified Planning Zones) Regulations 1992, regs 4, 5.
[144] Town and Country Planning Act 1990, Sch 7, para 8(1) and Town and Country Planning (Simplified Planning Zones) Regulations 1992, reg 7. The Secretary of State may direct that an inquiry or hearing be held, or the objections considered by an Inspector: Town and Country Planning Act 1990, Sch 7, para 8(2).
[145] Town and Country Planning Act 1990, Sch 7, para 9(1), (2). A statement of the decisions reached in the light of the objections and any report has to be prepared by the authority, giving reasons for their decisions: Town and Country Planning (Simplified Planning Zones) Regulations 1992, regs 8, 9. The Minister may direct the authority to make modifications if the proposals are unsatisfactory: Town and Country Planning Act 1990, Sch 7, para 9(3).
[146] Town and Country Planning (Simplified Planning Zones) Regulations 1992, reg 12. Advertisement of the six week consultation period is required (reg 12) and a further inquiry, hearing or consideration by an Inspector may be required (reg 13).
[147] Town and Country Planning (Simplified Planning Zones) Regulations 1992, reg 11.
[148] Town and Country Planning Act 1990, s 85(1). At the end of this period the planning permission granted by the scheme shall cease to have effect except where the development authorised by it has been begun: s 85(2).
[149] Town and Country Planning Act 1990, s 86(2)–(4).

26.59 *The grant of planning permission by orders and other means*

permission or imposing new or more stringent conditions, limitations or restrictions have delayed effect, coming into force a year after adoption or approval[150].

26.59 Simplified planning zones may not include land within particular designations: national parks, conservation areas, the Broads, areas of outstanding natural beauty, land identified in the development plan as Green Belt and sites of special scientific interest[151]. A simplified planning zone may not grant planning permission for development which requires EIA, that is, development within the Town and Country Planning (Environmental Impact Assessment) Regulations 2011, Sch 1, or Sch 2 development which does not benefit from a negative screening opinion or direction[152]. Further, a simplified planning zone may not be made where appropriate assessment is required under the Conservation of Habitats and Species Regulations 2010[153].

ENTERPRISE ZONES

26.60 An enterprise zone scheme may grant planning permission for development specified in it. A scheme would be made by an order under the Local Government, Planning and Land Act 1980, Sch 32. On the date on which the designation order takes effect, planning permission is granted for development specified in the scheme or for development of any class so specified: Town and Country Planning Act 1990, s 88(1)[154]. The planning permission 'shall be subject to such conditions or limitations as may be specified in the scheme or modified scheme or, if none is specified, shall be unconditional'[155]. These conditions may require the approval of details by the enterprise zone authority[156]. The authority may direct that the permission does not apply to specified development, classes of development or classes of development in particular areas[157], however such directions need the approval of the Secretary of State[158]. Enterprise zone schemes may not grant planning permission for development requiring EIA or for development requiring EIA screening (that is, within Sch 2 to the relevant regulations) unless that grant is made subject to the prior adoption of a screening opinion or prior making of a screening direction that the particular proposed development is not EIA development[159]. As with other orders and schemes, planning permission may not be granted by an enterprise zone scheme where appropriate assessment is required under the Conservation of Habitats and Species Regulations 2010[160].

Planning permission may be granted in an enterprise zone by any of the other available means, such as application for planning permission, permitted development and development order[161].

---

[150] Town and Country Planning Act 1990, s 86(5). If an alteration both widened and restricted rights then care would need to be taken as to whether one part would come into force on its own, or whether changes needed to be considered as a whole.
[151] Town and Country Planning Act 1990, s 87(1).
[152] Town and Country Planning (Environmental Impact Assessment) Regulations 2011, regs 27, 28.
[153] Conservation of Habitats and Species Regulations 2010, reg 79.
[154] A modified scheme will grant planning permission from the day on which the modification takes effect: Town and Country Planning Act 1990, s 88(2).
[155] Town and Country Planning Act 1990, s 88(3).
[156] Town and Country Planning Act 1990, s 88(6).
[157] Town and Country Planning Act 1990, s 88(4).
[158] Town and Country Planning Act 1990, s 88(5).
[159] Town and Country Planning (Environmental Impact Assessment) Regulations 2011, reg 28.
[160] Conservation of Habitats and Species Regulations 2010, reg 80.
[161] Town and Country Planning Act 1990, s 88(8).

DEEMED PLANNING PERMISSION

26.61 Deemed planning permission is a mechanism for a minister to grant a planning approval in the process of giving consent under another statutory regime. These are for matters which constitute development but which are neither given planning permission by that other consent nor are exempted from the need for planning permission by that consent. The general power to make a direction granting planning permission is in the Town and Country Planning Act 1990, s 90(1):

> 'Where the authorisation of a government department is required by virtue of an enactment in respect of development to be carried out by a local authority or National Park authority, or by statutory undertakers who are not a local authority or National Park authority, that department may, on granting that authorisation, direct that planning permission for that development shall be deemed to be granted, subject to such conditions (if any) as may be specified in the direction'.

26.62 Authorisation by a government department arises if it[162]:

(i) grants any consent, authority or approval to or for the development under an enactment;

(ii) confirms a compulsory purchase order;

(iii) grants consent for the acquisition or appropriation of land;

(iv) authorises the borrowing or application of money for that purpose;

(v) undertakes to pay grant in accordance with an enactment.

26.63 Specific provision is made for deemed planning permission where consent is given for an electricity generating station (of 50 MW or greater) or an electric line (of nominal voltage exceeding 20 kilovolts) under ss 36 or 37 respectively of the Electricity Act 1989[163]. Deemed planning permission may be granted, subject to conditions, as specified in the direction for[164]:

> '(a) so much of the operation or change of use to which the consent relates as constitutes development;
>
> (b) any development ancillary to the operation or change of use to which the consent relates'.

Sub-paragraph (a) is self-evidently necessary in that planning permission is only required for operations or uses which constitute development. Sub-paragraph (b) extends the power to approve ancillary development which does not itself require an Electricity Act consent, but this must be directly related to the generation of electricity by that station[165].

---

[162] Town and Country Planning Act 1990, s 90(4).
[163] Town and Country Planning Act 1990, s 90(2). The procedures for these applications are in the Electricity (Applications for Consent) Regulations 1990, SI 1990/455, Electricity Works (Environmental Impact Assessment) (England and Wales) Regulations 2000, SI 2000/1927, and Electricity Generating Stations and Overhead Lines (Inquiries Procedure) (England and Wales) Rules 2007, SI 2007/841.
[164] Town and Country Planning Act 1990, s 90(2).
[165] Town and Country Planning Act 1990, s 90(5).

26.64 *The grant of planning permission by orders and other means*

26.64 A variation of a s 36 or 37 Electricity Act consent may be accompanied by a deemed planning permission or a direction varying an existing deemed planning permission[166].

26.65 The Electricity Act provisions have their own duties of publicity and consultation[167]. However, these are not as full as the requirements for planning applications. Some statutory considerations arise as for these consents the applicant[168]:

'(a) shall have regard to the desirability of preserving natural beauty, of conserving flora, fauna and geological or physiographical features of special interest and of protecting sites, buildings and objects of architectural, historic or archaeological interest; and

(b) shall do what he reasonably can to mitigate any effect which the proposals would have on the natural beauty of the countryside or on any such flora, fauna, features, sites, buildings or objects'.

The Minister shall have regard to the desirability of (a) and the extent to which there is compliance with (b)[169].

26.66 Similarly, on making a Transport and Works order[170] which includes provision for development, the Secretary of State may direct that planning permission for that development shall be deemed to be granted, subject to such conditions (if any) as may be specified in the direction[171].

26.67 In *R (on the application of Samuel Smith Old Brewery (Tadcaster)) v Secretary of State for Energy and Climate Change* the view was taken that a direction to grant deemed planning permission is not a determination under the Town and Country Planning Act 1990 and so is not subject to the s 70(2) duty to have regard to the development plan or the presumption in favour of the development plan in the Planning and Compulsory Purchase Act 2004, s 38(6)[172]. The Town and Country Planning Act 1990 applies to any planning permission deemed to have been granted by a direction made under s 90 as if it had been granted on s 77 call-in, aside from the provisions on the validity of a permission[173]. In *Samuel Smith* it was considered that this concerned the position following the grant of permission rather than the process of directing that deemed permission is granted[174].

PLANNING PERMISSION IN PRINCIPLE UNDER THE HOUSING AND PLANNING BILL 2015

26.68 The Housing and Planning Bill 2015 proposes to introduce planning 'permission in principle' granted either automatically upon the inclusion of proposals

---

[166] Town and Country Planning Act 1990, s 90(2ZA).
[167] See for example the Electricity (Applications for Consent) Regulations 1990, SI 1990/455, regs 5–9.
[168] Electricity Act 1989, Sch 9, para 1(1).
[169] Electricity Act 1989, Sch 9, para 1(2). For discussion, see *Sustainable Shetland v Scottish Ministers* [2015] UKSC 4, [2015] Env LR 23 and *R (Samuel Smith Old Brewery (Tadcaster)) v Secretary of State for Energy and Climate Change* [2012] EWHC 46 (Admin), [2012] 2 All ER 849.
[170] Under the Transport and Works Act 1992, s 1 or 3.
[171] Town and Country Planning Act 1990, s 90(2A).
[172] [2012] EWHC 46 (Admin), [2012] 2 All ER 849 at para 75 per Edwards-Stuart J.
[173] Town and Country Planning Act 1990, s 90(3). These decisions are challenged by means of judicial review rather than a s 288 application to the High Court.
[174] At para 79 per Edwards-Stuart J.

in particular planning documents or by an application to the local planning authority in respect of particular sites and uses identified in planning policy. It is by no means certain that these provisions will be passed or passed without amendment, or indeed whether they will then be brought into force[175]. The proposals apply to England only.

26.69 Much of the detail of the regime would be in a development order or regulations and its scope, in terms of the types of development and locations, is not in the Bill. The general concepts are, though, set out in the Bill.

Permission in principle would be followed by a 'technical details consent', which together would be the equivalent of a full planning permission. Planning conditions would be imposed at the technical details consent stage.

Permission in principle could derive from two routes: grant by a development order or grant on application to the local planning authority.

Grant of planning permission in principle by development order

26.70 The first route is for permission in principle to be granted by a development order in relation to land which is allocated for development in a qualifying document[176]. A 'qualifying document' would be a 'plan, register or other document ... made, maintained or adopted' by a local planning authority, of a prescribed description, which 'indicates that the land in question is allocated for development for the purposes of this section' and which contains 'prescribed particulars in relation to the land allocated and the kind of development for which it is allocated'[177]. 'Adopted' can encompass a local plan, whilst neighbourhood development plans are 'made' by the local planning authority. 'Maintained' is envisaged for registers of land which could be required under a proposed new section: the Planning and Compulsory Purchase Act 2004, s 14A[178].

26.71 Under proposed s 14A, local planning authorities would be required to prepare, maintain and publish a register of land which is of a prescribed description or which satisfies prescribed criteria[179]. Regulations would prescribe when land has to be included and also where local planning authorities have a discretion whether to include it, or indeed any power to exclude land which would otherwise be included[180]. In compiling the register, the local planning authority is required to have regard to the development plan and national policies and advice[181].

26.72 It is envisaged that the registration duty would require the creation of a brownfield register of previously developed land which is suitable for housing

---

[175] The passage and implementation of the Planning and Compulsory Purchase Act 2004 illustrates provisions withdrawn entirely (statements of development principles) and enacted but never brought into force (planning contributions).
[176] See proposed Town and Country Planning Act 1990, s 59A(1)(a), to be inserted by Housing and Planning Bill 2015, cl 111(2). References are to the Bill following Public Bill Committee in the House of Commons.
[177] Proposed Town and Country Planning Act 1990, s 59A(2).
[178] To be inserted by Housing and Planning Bill 2015, cl 112(1).
[179] Proposed Planning and Compulsory Purchase Act 2004, s 14A(1).
[180] Proposed Planning and Compulsory Purchase Act 2004, s 14A(4).
[181] Proposed Planning and Compulsory Purchase Act 2004, s 14A(7).

26.73 *The grant of planning permission by orders and other means*

development[182]. As presently drafted, the register provisions do not include any mechanism for independent examination, appeal or Ministerial intervention.

26.73 In addition to the brownfield register, it is anticipated that automatic planning permission in principle would be granted by development order to allocations within particular categories in local plans or neighbourhood plans. The document would have to allocate the land for the purposes of permission in principle[183], so existing allocations will not have that effect.

26.74 A number of consequences flow for the preparation of the brownfield register, local plans and neighbourhood development plans.

Consultation and publicity requirements will need to apply to the immediate locality of a proposed allocation as well as across the plan area. At present the local plan and neighbourhood plan processes require area-wide publicity but not notification to individual properties. The owners of allocated sites have no right to be consulted, although they are in practice consulted in plan making to judge the availability of the land. More importantly, plan making does not presently involve neighbour notification or the display of site notices. That would need to be changed.

26.75 The automatic grant of planning permission by reason of the status of land in a document means that the document itself is a development consent under the EIA Directive. It authorises the developer to proceed, as part of a multi-stage consent process[184]. Consequently the document must contain sufficient detail to enable a decision to be taken as to whether EIA is required and, if so, to carry it out sufficiently for the details approved at the planning permission in principle stage[185]. This will involve consideration of the mitigation proposed, even though that will not be secured until the technical details stage. Most local and neighbourhood plans are, though, presently subject to Strategic Environmental Assessment.

26.76 As well as what is proposed, a decision whether to permit a development may involve consideration of what is lost. Careful consideration is required as to whether the permission in principle will authorise demolition, whether certain existing uses are protected and with regard to designated heritage assets, such as listed buildings and conservation areas, and undesignated assets such as locally listed buildings and assets of community value. Sufficient information would need to be available at the document making stage to determine the principle and extent of what is proposed and the extent of what, if anything, would be lost.

Grant of planning permission in principle on application

26.77 The second route is for a grant on application to the local planning authority for permission in principle for development of a prescribed description[186]. Such applications will be determined having regard to the development plan and any

---
[182] Explanatory Notes to Housing and Planning Bill 2015, First Reading, House of Commons, para 262.
[183] Proposed Town and Country Planning Act 1990, s 59A(2).
[184] Environmental Impact Assessment Directive, art 1(2).
[185] See the requirements of the EIA Directive, Annex 4.
[186] Proposed Town and Country Planning Act 1990, s 59A(1)(b), inserted by Housing and Planning Bill 2015, cl 111(2).

other material considerations[187], and so applying the presumption in favour of the development plan[188]. Applications would be determined under the proposed new s 70(1A) of the Town and Country Planning Act 1990[189]:

> 'Where an application is made to a local planning authority for permission in principle:
> (a) they may grant permission in principle; or
> (b) they may refuse permission in principle'.

Unlike s 70(1) this does not permit the imposition of conditions. These are to be left to the technical details consent. The authority will have to be satisfied that that development can be carried out in an acceptable manner in accordance with the permission in principle. There may therefore need to be assessments of the impact of the scheme and whether conditions can be imposed on a later technical details consent which would satisfactorily address both the construction and operation of the scheme.

26.78 Applications for permission in principle will be subject to the usual rules on notice being given to landowners, powers to decline to determine repeat applications, call-ins and appeals as apply to planning applications[190].

The government's current intention is to allow this to be used to approve the creation of fewer than 10 homes[191].

Technical details consent

26.79 If planning permission in principle is granted, whether automatically or following an application, then a full planning permission is achieved by the approval of a technical details consent. Any application for technical details consent must be within the matters approved by the permission in principle and contain sufficient details to be a full, but not outline, planning application, see proposed s 70(2ZB):

> 'An application for technical details consent is an application for planning permission that:
> (a) relates to land in respect of which permission in principle is in force,
> (b) proposes development all of which falls within the terms of the permission in principle, and
> (c) particularises all matters necessary to enable planning permission to be granted without any reservations of the kind referred to in section 92'.

---

[187] Proposed Town and Country Planning Act 1990, s 70(2), as to be amended by Housing and Planning Bill 2015, Sch 9, para 11(2).
[188] In Planning and Compulsory Purchase Act 2004, s 38(6).
[189] To be inserted by Housing and Planning Bill 2015, cl 111(3)(a).
[190] See amendments in Housing and Planning Bill 2015, Sch 9. Permissions in principle are expected to be recorded on the planning register, whether they are automatic or granted on application: proposed Town and Country Planning Act 1990, ss 59A(7), 69(1)(aza), to be inserted by Housing and Planning Bill 2015, cl 111(2), Sch 9, para 10 respectively. Applications could also be made directly to the Secretary of State under Town and Country Planning Act 1990, s 62A, see Housing and Planning Bill 2015, cl 114.
[191] Explanatory Notes to Housing and Planning Bill 2015, First Reading, House of Commons, para 254.

26.80 *The grant of planning permission by orders and other means*

26.80 Unless the permission in principle is out of date, the local planning authority should have to determine the application in accordance with the permission in principle, see proposed s 70(2ZA):

'The authority must determine an application for technical details consent in accordance with the relevant permission in principle'.

A permission would be out of date if it has been in force for longer than a prescribed period and there has been a material change in circumstances since it came into force[192].

26.81 The requirements that the technical details application accords with the permission in principle and that the authority cannot go back on the principle which has been established reflect the case law on reserved matters and the approval of details under conditions[193]. A technical details application could relate to only part of the site of a permission in principle, although might be refused if a more comprehensive application was considered necessary or it would prejudice the development of the remainder of the site.

26.82 The government intention is that whether permission in principle has been granted automatically or on application, conditions may be imposed in the technical details consent[194]. However the Bill does not at present include such provision (there being no equivalent of s 70(1) or s 72 for technical details consent). Whilst it might be intended to include this in the development order, the better approach would be to provide for the imposition of conditions on the face of the Act. Such conditions could not derogate from the permission in principle but otherwise would be subject to the normal principles for planning conditions.

---

[192] Proposed Town and Country Planning Act 1990, s 70(2ZC).
[193] See Chapter 16.
[194] Explanatory Notes, para 259.

Chapter 27
Community Infrastructure Levy

27.1 Financial contributions towards the costs of infrastructure to meet the needs of development have been collected in the planning system through s 106 obligations. That has, at times, been seen by government as too slow and generating insufficient funds from too small a proportion of developments. Parallel to that debate, but logically separate from it, has been the idea of taxation of the increased value of land caused by the grant of planning permission. That latter concept of a betterment tax has been introduced in one form or other by every Labour government since the Second World War and repealed by every Conservative government which replaced them. It remains to be seen whether the Community Infrastructure Levy (CIL) will ultimately escape or conform to the lessons of history.

27.2 The governments of Tony Blair and Gordon Brown spent a great deal of time considering whether and how to replace or supplement planning obligations. The Planning and Compulsory Purchase Act 2004 contained provisions for planning contributions which were never brought into force. Kate Barker's *Review of Housing Supply: Delivery Stability: Securing our Future Housing Needs*, published by the Treasury in 2004, proposed a planning gain supplement ('PGS'). Extensive consultation was carried out on PGS and the Planning-gain Supplement (Preparations) Act 2007 was passed to allow ministers to incur expenditure to prepare PGS. Whilst the subsequent Planning White Paper[1] said relatively little on the topic, the Housing White Paper of July 2007 said that the government's preference was for PGS but floated other possibilities including a planning charge[2].

27.3 However the Planning Act 2008 introduced the CIL[3], brought into force by the Community Infrastructure Levy Regulations 2010[4]. Under the Coalition Government of 2010 to 2015 these were subject to annual, major amendments to find ways of making them work.

This chapter concentrates on determining when CIL is payable on development and how it is applied to a particular scheme.

THE PURPOSE OF CIL

27.4 CIL is a charge made on the carrying out of certain development for the purpose of supporting development by funding the provision, improvement,

---

[1] *Planning for a Sustainable Future*, May 2007.
[2] *Homes for the future: more affordable, more sustainable*.
[3] Some of the thinking behind CIL was explained in the DCLG publications *Community Infrastructure Levy – Initial Impact Assessment* (November 2007) and *The Communities Infrastructure Levy* (January 2008).
[4] SI 2010/948.

27.5 *Community Infrastructure Levy*

replacement, operation or maintenance of infrastructure[5]. CIL is levied by the charging authority for the area[6] which is the local planning authority and in addition the Mayor of London[7] (the local planning authority also being the collecting authority)[8]. CIL may not be charged before the authority has adopted a charging schedule setting out the rates or other criteria to be applied[9]. CIL rates are set having regard to the actual and expected costs of infrastructure to support the development of its area, the desirability of funding this from CIL, the economic viability of development across its area, other actual and expected sources of funding for infrastructure and the administrative costs of CIL[10]. The effect of exemptions and exceptions to liability for CIL must also be taken into account both in how much is raised and also in the rates levied on paying development.

27.5 Different rates may be set for different zones, intended uses, intended gross internal areas or the number of dwelling or units proposed[11]. This may include a different rate per square metre for developments over a certain size (such as larger rates for superstores than for smaller retail units) and nil rates can be set for particular types of development or zones.

27.6 A draft charging schedule is subject to consultation and an examiner appointed by the charging authority will consider whether the schedule complies with the legislative requirements[12]. If any failures cannot be resolved by modifications then the examiner must make a binding recommendation that the schedule be rejected. Otherwise the authority must consider the examiner's report and if any non-compliance is identified by the examiner then the schedule may only be approved with modifications (whether their own or the examiner's) which remedy this. They may incorporate any other modifications proposed by the examiner[13]. An approved charging schedule may not take effect until it has been published by the charging authority[14].

LIABILITY TO PAY CIL

27.7 There are three elements to whether a person is liable to pay CIL and if so, how much:

(i) the nature of the development;

(ii) the timing of the planning permission or the development in relation to CIL schedules;

(iii) the assumption and transfer of liability.

---

[5] See Planning Act 2008, s 216(1).
[6] Planning Act 2008, s 206(1).
[7] Planning Act 2008, s 206(2), (3)(a). The Mayor of London adopted a CIL charging schedule to contribute towards the costs of the Crossrail project before most of the London boroughs had adopted their own schedules.
[8] CIL Regulations 2010, reg 10.
[9] Planning Act 2008, s 211(1).
[10] Planning Act 2008, s 211(2), Community Infrastructure Levy Regulations 2010, reg 14.
[11] CIL Regulations, reg 13(1).
[12] Planning Act 2008, s 212.
[13] Planning Act 2008, s 213.
[14] Planning Act 2008, s 214(1). Publication takes place under CIL Regulations 2010, reg 25.

Liability to pay CIL **27.11**

The nature of the development

27.8 There are certain forms of development which are not subject to CIL at all, or which benefit from mandatory or discretionary exemptions or reliefs. Some of the exemptions and reliefs have to be claimed.

The starting point is to consider what is covered by the charging schedule: if it is not included, then it is not liable. Even if it appears to be included then liability may be excluded by one means or another.

Development categories subject to CIL

27.9 For the purposes of liability, development is limited to 'anything done by way of or for the purpose of the creation of a building' or 'anything done to or in respect of an existing building'[15]. Anything done in respect of an existing building may include a change of use[16]. The meaning of development for CIL purposes can be altered by the CIL Regulations, but only to exclude works or changes of use or to add development which relates to structures[17]. CIL cannot, therefore, apply to development which does not involve the erection, extension, alteration or change of use of a building. The CIL Regulations exclude from 'development' buildings into which people do not normally go or into which they only go intermittently for the purpose of inspecting or maintaining fixed plant or machinery[18]. CIL is also not chargeable in respect of increases in the internal floorspace of buildings which would only be development under the Town and Country Planning Act 1990, s 55(2A)[19]. The change of use of a building previously used as a single dwellinghouse to two or more separate dwellinghouses is not development for CIL purposes[20].

27.10 Whilst not spelt out in the Planning Act 2008, CIL liability is tied to development which requires planning permission[21], so actions or changes of use which are not development under the Town and Country Planning Act 1990, s 55 are also not subject to CIL[22].

Exemptions and reliefs

27.11 A variety of exemptions and reliefs apply. Some of these must be claimed by notice on the correct form to the collecting authority prior to the commencement of the chargeable development.

---

[15] Planning Act 2008, s 209(1).
[16] See Planning Act 2008, s 209(2)(a).
[17] Planning Act 2008, s 209(2).
[18] CIL Regulations 2010, reg 6(1)(a), (b), (2).
[19] This is an increase in retail floorspace over 200 m²: Town and Country Planning (Development Management Procedure) (England) Order 2015, art 44; Town and Country Planning (Development Management Procedure) (Wales) Order 2012, art 2A: see Chapter 2.
[20] CIL Regulations 2010, reg 6(1)(d). Building might include part of a building: although this definition in Town and Country Planning Act 1990, s 336(1) is not applied to the CIL provisions by the interpretation section of the Planning Act 2008 (s 235(1)).
[21] See CIL Regulations 2010, reg 9(1).
[22] Also excluded are the acts of development which do not require planning permission under Town and Country Planning Act 1990, s 57: see Chapter 4.

27.12 Community Infrastructure Levy

Minor development

27.12 CIL does not arise if the gross internal area of new buildings and enlargements to existing buildings will be less than 100 m² unless the development will comprise one or more dwellings[23].

Residential annexes or extensions by owner occupiers and long leaseholders

27.13 The owner or long leaseholder[24] of a dwelling who occupies it as their sole or main residence is exempt from paying CIL for the development of a new dwelling (a residential annex) within the curtilage of the main dwelling or an enlargement (a residential extension) of the main dwelling[25]. CIL will, however, become payable if the main dwelling is used for any purpose other than as a single dwelling, the residential annex is let; or the main dwelling or annex are sold separately within the clawback period[26] which is within three years of the final Buildings Regulations certificate[27].

27.14 A claim for exemption must be made to and determined by the collecting authority before the chargeable development is commenced[28]. The claim must be submitted on a completed form published by the Secretary of State (or one substantially to the same effect) accompanied by the documents required by the form[29]. Even with the exemption in their hand, reg 42B(6) requires that person to submit a commencement notice prior by the day before the chargeable development is commenced otherwise the exemption is lost[30]. There is, however, a conflict in the regulations, since reg 67(1A)(aa) says that no commencement notice is required for development 'in relation to which no CIL is payable because an exemption for residential extensions was granted'. The inconsistency needs to be resolved by amendment, but in the meantime it may be prudent to submit a commencement notice. Commencement notices are required for residential annexes.

Charities

27.15 An exemption applies for material interests held solely by charities where the chargeable development will be used wholly or mainly for charitable purposes, whether by that person or another[31]. A charging authority may publish a policy setting out when it will allow discretionary charitable relief[32]. This relief may be available to charitable institutions who will between them hold the whole or the major part of the chargeable development as investments with the profits to be used

---

[23] CIL Regulations 2010, reg 42. There is no requirement to give notice of this exemption.
[24] The requirement is to have a material interest, which is a freehold estate or at least seven years remaining on the lease when planning permission first permits chargeable development: CIL Regulations 2010, reg 4(2).
[25] CIL Regulations 2010, reg 42A.
[26] CIL Regulations 2010, reg 42C.
[27] The clawback period is defined in CIL Regulations 2010, reg 2(1).
[28] CIL Regulations 2010, reg 42B(1), (2)(a), (3).
[29] CIL Regulations 2010, reg 42B(2).
[30] CIL Regulations 2010, reg 42B(6).
[31] CIL Regulations 2010, reg 43(1), (2). Use for charitable purposes may include leaving it unoccupied: reg 43(3). If this automatic relief is prohibited as a state aid then discretionary charitable relief can still be claimed if it is available in the area: reg 45.
[32] CIL Regulations 2010, reg 46.

Liability to pay CIL **27.17**

for charitable purposes[33]. However it is not available if it is to be used for trading other than the sale of donated goods for the charity's funds or the material interest is owned by the charity jointly with someone other than a charitable institution[34]. Charitable relief must be claimed by notice to the collecting authority and determined prior to the commencement of the development[35].

Social housing

27.16 Five categories of existing or proposed dwellings are eligible for relief from CIL liability as social housing under reg 49:

(i) local authority housing let on a demoted, introductory or secure tenancy[36];

(ii) shared ownership housing which was leased with not more than 75% of the equity sold[37];

(iii) private registered providers of social housing in England let on an assured tenancy, assured agricultural occupancy or demoted tenancy[38];

(iv) registered social landlords in Wales let on an assured tenancy, assured agricultural occupancy or demoted tenancy at no more than 80% of market rent[39];

(v) intermediate rented housing let on an assured tenancy or assured agricultural occupancy[40] to a person 'whose needs are not adequately served by the commercial housing market', the rent is no more than 80% of the market rent (including service charges) and this is secured by a planning obligation[41].

Discretionary social housing relief may be granted to properties sold for no more than 80% of their market value[42].

27.17 Relief under these categories also extends to qualifying communal development which is for the benefit of occupiers of more than one qualifying dwelling even if it also benefits other occupants of the development authorised by the permission[43]. However such communal development may not include dwellings themselves, nor may it be wholly or mainly for use by the general public nor for

---

[33] CIL Regulations 2010, reg 4(1).
[34] CIL Regulations 2010, reg 44(2)–(4).
[35] CIL Regulations 2010, reg 47(1)–(3). The published form must be used.
[36] This is condition 1: CIL Regulations 2010, reg 49(3) and also includes what would be a secure tenancy but for the Housing Act 1985, Sch 1, para 4ZA or 12. The definitions in the Housing Acts of 1985, 1988 and 1998 apply to the various means of letting in this regulation: see reg 49(11).
[37] CIL Regulations 2010, reg 49(4) (condition 2). The initial annual rent must be not more than 3% of the value of the remainder of the equity and may not increase more than the retail price index plus 0.5%.
[38] Condition 3: CIL Regulations 2010, reg 49(5) and including arrangements which would be assured tenancies or agricultural occupancies but for the Housing Act 1985, Sch 1, para 12(1)(h) or 12ZA. The rents must be regulated or not more than 80% of the market rate: see the details in CIL Regulations 2010, reg 49(6).
[39] CIL Regulations 2010, reg 49(7) and including arrangements which would be assured tenancies or agricultural occupancies but for the Housing Act 1985, Sch 1, para 12(1)(h) or 12ZA (condition 4).
[40] Condition 5 under CIL Regulations 2010, reg 49(7A) and including arrangements which would be assured tenancies or agricultural occupancies but for the Housing Act 1985, Sch 1, para 12(1)(h).
[41] Made under the Town and Country Planning Act 1990, s 106.
[42] CIL Regulations 2010, reg 49A. Publicity arrangements on the adoption of such a policy are in reg 49B and include a policy on the allocation of relief to particular developments.
[43] CIL Regulations 2010, regs 49(1), 49C(2); see also the definition of relevant development in reg 49C(5).

27.18 *Community Infrastructure Levy*

the benefit of the occupants of development outside the planning permission nor be wholly or mainly for commercial purposes[44]. Relief is granted on the proportion of the gross internal area of the development represented by the qualifying dwellings[45].

27.18 A claim for social housing relief must be made in advance of the commencement of the chargeable development (so under the scheme or its phase), with a 'relief assessment' calculating the amount due and the relevant floorspaces[46].

Social housing relief may be lost by the disposal of the land before qualifying dwellings are made available for occupation[47].

27.19 If a dwelling ceases to comply with any of the qualifying conditions for relief within the clawback period then the relief may be lost[48]. The clawback period is seven years from the commencement of the chargeable development or, for intermediate rented housing, seven years from its first letting[49]. Relief will, however, not be lost if the proceeds are spent on another qualifying dwelling or (broadly) transferred within the public sector[50].

Self-build housing

27.20 A further exemption applies to self-build housing and self-build communal housing. Self-build housing is 'a dwelling built by [a person] (including where built following a commission by [that person]) and occupied by [them] as [their] sole or main residence'[51]. The self-builder does not need to carry out the work personally, but needs to have commissioned it. The term is not further defined in the CIL Regulations but the Housing and Planning Bill 2015 proposes to define 'self-build and custom housebuilding' in the Self-build and Custom Housebuilding Act 2015 as[52]:

'the building or completion by:

(a) individuals,

(b) associations of individuals, or

(c) persons working with or for individuals or associations of individuals,

of houses to be occupied as homes by those individuals'.

27.21 In the proposed definition there would not be included 'the building of a house on a plot acquired from a person who builds the house wholly or mainly to plans or specifications decided or offered by that person'[53]. There must be a dividing

---

[44] CIL Regulations 2010, reg 49C(3).
[45] CIL Regulations 2010, reg 49C(4).
[46] CIL Regulations 2010, reg 51. The indexation of the liability is set out in reg 50.
[47] CIL Regulations 2010, reg 52. The collecting authority may seek information about eligibility for social housing relief and whether it is lost by serving an information notice: CIL Regulations 2010, reg 54.
[48] CIL Regulations 2010, reg 53.
[49] CIL Regulations 2010, reg 2(1).
[50] CIL Regulations 2010, reg 53(3).
[51] CIL Regulations 2010, reg 54A(2). The inserts replace 'P' which means 'a person': see reg 54A(1).
[52] Proposed Self-build and Custom Housebuilding Act 2015, s 1(A1), to be inserted by Housing and Planning Bill 2015, cl 8(1) (as published following Public Bill Committee in the House of Commons).
[53] Proposed Self-build and Custom Housebuilding Act 2015, s 1(A2), to be inserted by Housing and Planning Bill 2015, cl 8(1).

line between a self-built house commissioned by its future occupant and a house being sold off plan by a developer, perhaps with adjustments for individual purchasers.

27.22 Self-build communal development is also exempted in the same manner as for social housing communal development[54]. A person or persons benefiting from the self-build housing exemption must assume liability for the communal development (and may do so jointly with the developer of the rest of the site) before the self-build communal exemption can be claimed[55]. It cannot be claimed simply by the overall developer of the site.

27.23 Claims for exemptions for self-build housing must be made by the person who intends to build or commission and occupy the dwelling, having assumed liability for it[56]. They must then submit the necessary form and particulars and obtain the authority's decision prior to the commencement of chargeable development[57]. Within six months of the date of the Building Regulations compliance certificate for the exempted development, the relevant form must be submitted to the collecting authority confirming that it is self-build housing or communal development[58].

The exemption is lost if, before the end of the three-year clawback period, the development ceases to qualify as self-build or is let out or sold[59].

Exceptional circumstances relief because of an unacceptable impact on economic viability

27.24 Charging authorities have a discretion to grant relief in exceptional circumstances if the chargeable amount would have an unacceptable impact on the economic viability of the development[60]. Before doing so it must have decided to make such relief available in its area[61]. Relief may only be granted to developments which are also subject to a planning obligation[62].

27.25 Relief must be applied for before the commencement of the chargeable development. In particular though the details must include the claimant's explanation why the charge has an unacceptable impact on the economic viability of the scheme and include an independent person's assessment of its economic viability[63]. This person must be appointed by the claimant with the agreement of the charging authority[64], however it is not a joint appointment. Where there is more than one material interest in the land, the claimant must provide an apportionment assessment explaining how liability is split up[65].

---

[54] CIL Regulations 2010, reg 54A(3)–(6).
[55] CIL Regulations 2010, reg 54A(8).
[56] CIL Regulations 2010, reg 54B(2)(a).
[57] CIL Regulations 2010, reg 54B(2), (3).
[58] CIL Regulations 2010, regs 54C, 54D(2)(b). The collecting authority must give notice of the default giving a date, in at least 28 days' time, by which the form must be submitted to retain the exemption: reg 54D(5), (6).
[59] CIL Regulations 2010, reg 54D(2).
[60] CIL Regulations 2010, reg 55(1), (3).
[61] CIL Regulations 2010, reg 55(3)(a). This decision must be publicised in accordance with reg 56.
[62] CIL Regulations 2010, reg 55(3)(b). There is no requirement that the planning obligation itself affects the viability of the development.
[63] CIL Regulations 2010, reg 57(4)(d)(ii), (iii).
[64] CIL Regulations 2010, reg 57(5).
[65] CIL Regulations 2010, reg 57(4)(d)(iv). This is calculated by the share of the value in the site: see reg 34, applied by reg 41.

27.26 *Community Infrastructure Levy*

Exclusion of retained and replacement floorspace

27.26 CIL is not charged where 'in-use buildings' are retained or replaced or other buildings are put or kept in a use which was already lawful. The objective is to avoid CIL being applied in most circumstances to the quantum of existing floorspace and it tending to be applied to additional floorspace. For all of these purposes the building must have been on the site when planning permission permitted the chargeable development[66].

27.27 An 'in-use' building is such a building which 'contains a part that has been in lawful use for a continuous period of at least six months within the period of three years ending on the day planning permission first permits the chargeable development'[67]. In this context 'use' requires actual activity rather than merely the existence of a lawful planning use[68]. The actual carrying on of a lawful business use would be sufficient, and would include any holiday periods, as would be a period where the building was being refurbished for the purposes of that use. However, closing down the business with a view to redevelopment or with no real prospect of the activity resuming would not be continuing a lawful use for these purposes, even if equipment remained on the premises[69]. A lawful use in part of the building would be sufficient, such as a couple of rooms in a large office building, however the continuation of an ancillary activity may raise issues as to the current use and whether it is lawful (such as car parking in the basement of an otherwise empty office building). Very low levels of ancillary activity, such as security patrols, might raise issues both of the nature of the use and whether it is too small to matter.

27.28 Where development is carried out under a general consent[70] the three-year period is counted back from the date on which notice of chargeable development is given, so the timing of that notice needs to be considered with care[71].

27.29 Excluded from CIL liability is[72]:

(i) the retained parts of in-use buildings;
(ii) for buildings which are not 'in-use' any retained parts which would be used in the new development for a purpose which they could lawfully have been used without the planning permission for that development. This will include a continuation of the previous use, any other use which is not a material change of use from that use or a use which benefits from another planning permission (however it has been granted)[73];

---

[66] See the definition of 'relevant land' in CIL Regulations 2010, reg 40(11).
[67] CIL Regulations, regulation 40(11).
[68] *R (on the application of Hourhope Ltd) v Shropshire Council* [2015] EWHC 518 (Admin), [2015] PTSR 933 at paras 18–24 per Judge David Cooke.
[69] See *Hourhope* at paras 27, 28 per Judge David Cooke.
[70] A general consent is permission under a special or general development order, local development order, neighbourhood development order, simplified planning zone scheme, deemed planning permission under Town and Country Planning Act 1990, s 90 or an enterprise zone scheme: CIL Regulations 2010, reg 5(3).
[71] CIL Regulations 2010, regs 8(7), 64.
[72] CIL Regulations 2010, reg 40(7).
[73] The regulations do not explicitly resolve the situation where the prior approval process must be gone through before it is known whether permitted development rights for the use are able to be exercised.

(iii) an amount of floorspace equal to the gross internal areas of in-use buildings which are to be demolished.

Where CIL liability on a project applies in stages, the formulae are drafted to avoid double counting of exemptions.

Development not subject to CIL for timing reasons

27.30 A development is not subject to CIL if there was no charging schedule in effect when planning permission was granted for it following an application or under a special planning zone, neighbourhood development order or community right to build order[74]. If permission is granted by a General Permitted Development Order, a special development order, local development order or enterprise zone scheme then CIL liability does not arise if the development was commenced before 6 April 2013 or on a later date when there was no charging schedule in effect[75].

27.31 If a charging schedule comes into effect after a planning permission is granted but before a subsequent s 73 planning permission (for development subject to different conditions) is granted, then CIL liability arises only for any additional sum which is due to the s 73 permission (whether by increased floorspace or a different use)[76]. Where planning permission was granted to replace a pre-1 October 2010 permission[77] then no CIL is payable[78].

THE CIL RATES APPLIED

27.32 The CIL rates applied to a particular development are[79]:

'... taken from the charging schedules which are in effect:

(a) at the time planning permission first permits the chargeable development; and

(b) in the area in which the chargeable development will be situated'.

CIL rates for development under planning permission granted on an application

27.33 Where a planning application has been made, planning permission first permits the chargeable development[80]:

(i) when it is granted;

(ii) if it is a phased planning permission[81]:

---

[74] CIL Regulations 2010, reg 128(1).
[75] CIL Regulations 2010, reg 128(2), (3).
[76] CIL Regulations 2010, reg 128A.
[77] Under the procedure in the Town and Country Planning (General Development Procedure) (England) Order 2010, art 18(1)(b), (c).
[78] CIL Regulations 2010, reg 128B.
[79] CIL Regulations 2010, reg 40(4).
[80] CIL Regulations 2010, reg 8.
[81] That is, a permission which expressly provides for the development to be carried out in phases: CIL Regulations 2010, reg 2(1).

27.34 *Community Infrastructure Levy*

(a) when final approval is given for the last reserved matter associated with a phase which has been approved in outline or, if earlier and agreed in writing by the collecting authority, when final approval is given under any pre-commencement condition associated with that phase[82];

(b) if the phase is not in outline, then when final approval is given under any pre-commencement condition associated with that phase or if there are no such conditions, when permission is granted;

(iii) if it is an outline permission which is not phased, when the final reserved matters approval is granted.

Consequently the CIL charging rates may depend upon when details are approved under outline or phased permissions and vary on different parts of the scheme.

CIL rates for development under a general consent

27.34 Where permission arises under a general consent (a special or general development order, local development order, neighbourhood development order, simplified planning zone scheme, deemed planning permission or an enterprise zone scheme)[83] planning permission first permits development[84]:

'(a) on the day on which the collecting authority receives a notice of chargeable development submitted to it in accordance with regulation 64 in respect of that development; or

(b) if no notice of chargeable development is submitted in accordance with regulation 64, the day on which the last person is served with a notice of chargeable development in accordance with regulation 64A(3)'.

The notice of chargeable development must be submitted before the development is commenced[85]. Consequently it is possible in a general consent case to fix the CIL contribution by serving a notice of chargeable development at any time in advance of the commencement of the development.

The calculation of the chargeable amount

27.35 Different rates may apply to different parts of the development and need to be calculated separately before being added up. The deemed net chargeable area is multiplied by the rate, indexed by the change in the national All-in Tender Price Index published by the Building Cost Information Service[86] between 1 November of the year the charging schedule took effect and the year in which planning permission was granted[87]. The 'deemed net chargeable area' is the gross internal area which is

---

[82] This text does not therefore apply to 'full' permission phases in a hybrid permission which contains a mix of full and outline phases.
[83] CIL Regulations 2010, reg 5(3).
[84] CIL Regulations 2010, reg 8(7).
[85] CIL Regulations 2010, reg 64(2).
[86] Of the Royal Institution of Chartered Surveyors.
[87] CIL Regulations 2010, reg 40(5). This throws up an anomaly in that the charging schedule is applied as it stands when 'planning permission first permits the chargeable development', yet the planning permission might be granted in a different, earlier, year which might pre-date that version of the charging schedule.

subject to that particular rate less the exclusions applied under reg 40 which have not previously been applied[88].

Apportionment and assumption of liability

27.36 The default position is that liability to pay CIL is apportioned between the owners of material interests (freeholds or leases with at least seven years remaining) pro rata according to the value of those interests[89]. However a person may assume liability to pay CIL by giving notice in an approved form to the collecting authority prior to the commencement of the development[90]. This assumed liability may be transferred to another person, by notice, at any point prior to the day on which the final payment of CIL is due[91]. Ultimately if the collecting authority is unable, after making all reasonable efforts, to recover CIL from the person who had assumed liability, then it may transfer the liability to the owners of the land[92].

The collecting authority must serve a demand notice, in an approved form, on each person who is liable to pay CIL[93].

APPEALS

27.37 Appeals may be brought against certain decisions on CIL liability. Those circumstances are relatively limited and other decisions can then only be challenged by judicial review or as a defence to proceedings to enforce CIL liabilities. Any appeal must usually be determined before the development is commenced[94].

27.38 A person who has assumed liability, submitted the relevant planning application or owns land on which development takes place under a general consent where there had been no notice of chargeable development may ask the collecting authority for a review of the chargeable amount within 28 days of the issue of the liability notice[95]. The request must include written representations in support and the authority must determine the review within 14 days[96]. The person who made the request may then appeal[97].

27.39 The owner of a material interest may appeal within 28 days of the issue of the demand notice[98]. A person who claimed charitable relief or assumed liability in respect of that development may appeal if the relief is granted but they contend that the collecting authority has incorrectly determined the value of the interest in the land[99].

---

[88] CIL Regulations 2010, reg 40(5), (7), (8). The word 'deemed' is superfluous.
[89] CIL Regulations 2010, regs 33, 34.
[90] CIL Regulations 2010, reg 31.
[91] CIL Regulations 2010, reg 32.
[92] CIL Regulations 2010, reg 36. This is potentially an important issue for subsequent purchasers.
[93] CIL Regulations 2010, reg 69.
[94] CIL Regulations 2010, regs 114(4), 116(3), 116A(3), 116B(3). This runs the risk of either delaying desirable development or discouraging meritorious appeals. An exception is an appeal against the apportionment of liability under reg 115.
[95] CIL Regulations 2010, reg 113(1), (2).
[96] CIL Regulations 2010, reg 113(3), (7).
[97] CIL Regulations 2010, reg 114.
[98] CIL Regulations 2010, reg 115.
[99] CIL Regulations 2010, reg 116.

27.40 *Community Infrastructure Levy*

27.40 Regulation 116A says:

'An interested person [that is, a person granted an exemption][100] who is aggrieved at the decision of a collecting authority to grant an exemption for residential annexes may appeal to the appointed person on the ground that the collecting authority has incorrectly determined that the development is not wholly within the curtilage of the main dwelling'.

Since the exemption would be refused if the development is not wholly within the curtilage[101], the text does not make sense. It may be that this is intended to be a right of appeal against a refusal to grant an exemption.

27.41 Where an exemption for self-build housing has been granted, an appeal may be brought by the person with the exemption against the value given to the exemption[102].

All of these appeals are made to a valuation officer or district valuer[103], who are appointed by HM Revenue and Customs.

Appeals may be made to the Secretary of State against surcharges[104], determinations of deemed commencement dates[105] and CIL stop notices[106].

27.42 All CIL appeals are determined under a written representations procedure. An appeal form must be submitted and include the appellant's representations[107]. Any interested parties, essentially the collecting or charging authorities and other landowners or persons liable[108], must make representations within 14 days of the acknowledgment of receipt of the appeal or any longer period given by the appointed person[109]. There is then a further 14 days (which may be extended) for the parties to comment on each other's representations[110]. The appointed person must give a written decision with reasons[111]. Parties' costs may be awarded against each other[112].

Any appeal decision may be challenged in the High Court by judicial review.

PAYMENT

27.43 A liability notice must be issued by the Council as soon as practicable after planning permission first permits development[113]. The notice is to be served on the person who applied for planning permission or who submitted a notice of chargeable development, any person who assumed liability and each owner of the land[114].

---

[100] CIL Regulations 2010, reg 112(2)(c).
[101] CIL Regulations 2010, reg 42A(2).
[102] CIL Regulations 2010, reg 116B.
[103] CIL Regulations 2010, reg 112(1).
[104] CIL Regulations 2010, reg 117.
[105] CIL Regulations 2010, reg 118.
[106] CIL Regulations 2010, reg 119. Surcharges and CIL stop notices are discussed in Harwood *Planning Enforcement* (Bloomsbury Professional, 2013), Chapter 22.
[107] CIL Regulations 2010, reg 120(1), (4).
[108] These are defined in CIL Regulations 2010, reg 112(3).
[109] CIL Regulations 2010, regs 112(1), 120(5).
[110] CIL Regulations 2010, reg 120(7).
[111] CIL Regulations 2010, reg 120(9).
[112] CIL Regulations 2010, reg 121.
[113] CIL Regulations 2010, reg 65(1).
[114] CIL Regulations 2010, reg 65(3), (12).

27.44 However CIL only becomes payable once the development has started (the developer having served a commencement notice or the authority having calculated a deemed commencement date)[115]. A commencement notice must be served unless the minor development or residential extension exemptions apply, or the chargeable amount calculated under reg 40 is zero[116]. Payment is due at the end of the period of 60 days beginning with the intended commencement date, or any later date set by an instalment policy[117].

27.45 Payment may be made in money or by the transfer of land which is to be used to provide or facilitate the provision of infrastructure to support the development of the charging authority's area[118].

---

[115] CIL Regulations 2010, regs 67, 68. A deemed commencement date is calculated if no commencement notice has been received or the collecting authority has reason to believe development was commenced earlier than the intended commencement date given in the commencement notice.
[116] CIL Regulations 2010, reg 67(1), (1A). A commencement notice must therefore be served in respect of many exempt developments.
[117] CIL Regulations 2010, reg 70.
[118] CIL Regulations 2010, reg 72, 73.

Chapter 28

The effect and interpretation of planning permission

28.1 Having obtained a planning permission by one of the various means discussed so far in this book, the developer or landowner may be disappointed to find that there might be an issue as to what it means or what can be done with it. These can be considered under the overlapping questions of the effect of a planning permission and its interpretation.

THE EFFECT OF PLANNING PERMISSION

28.2 Most obviously, planning permission is granted for the development contained in the permission, subject to the conditions (and if permitted development, any limitations) contained in it. Some development may be necessarily implicit in a permission. In *R v Basildon District Council, ex p Martin Grant Homes Ltd*[1] Mr Justice McCowan observed in the context of whether a residential planning permission allowed a raising of land levels to facilitate drainage, that it:

> 'seems to me to make good sense to say that the planning authority must have intended that all necessary and reasonable works for the implementation of the permission were being incorporated within the general grant of consent'.

28.3 A permission will have certain effects which are not stated on the face of the permission. It makes no sense for a planning permission to be granted for something to be constructed but not to allow it to be used. Section 75(2) and (3) of the Town and Country Planning Act 1990 address this issue in the context of buildings:

> '(2) Where planning permission is granted for the erection of a building, the grant of permission may specify the purposes for which the building may be used.
>
> (3) If no purpose is so specified, the permission shall be construed as including permission to use the building for the purpose for which it is designed'.

28.4 The use of a new building may therefore be specified in the permission either as a building for a particular purpose or by reason of its description, for example, the erection of a dwellinghouse. If so, the permission authorises the use of the house as a dwelling as well as its construction. Section 75(3) authorises use for the purpose for which the building is designed if the use is not described in the permission. Building is interpreted widely including, for example, a basin used for mooring boats[2].

---

[1] (1987) 53 P & CR 397 at 409.
[2] *Wood v Secretary of State for Communities and Local Government* [2015] EWHC 2368 (Admin) at para 51 per Lindblom J.

Designed in this context means 'intended' rather than architecturally designed, so s 75(3) applies to buildings in outline permissions as well as full consents[3]. The intention may be disclosed by the application documents[4].

28.5 In seeking to apply s 75 any permission has to be considered with care. The grant of planning permission for alterations to a building may not carry with it by s 75 planning permission for a use of the building. In *R (on the application of Peel Land and Property Investments plc) v Hyndburn Borough Council*[5] planning permissions for works to existing retail warehouse units had variously included external works, the internal sub-division and re-configuration and the insertion of a mezzanine floor. Peel argued that by s 75 these constituted new planning permissions for the retail use of the existing retail units, bypassing restrictions in planning obligations on the types of goods which could be sold. The Court of Appeal disagreed, holding that they were not permissions for a material change of use but only related to physical works[6].

Planning permission benefits the land unless specified otherwise

28.6 A planning permission is in principle a consent for development to be carried out on land by anyone rather than an authorisation for a particular person. Section 75(1) of the Town and Country Planning Act 1990 provides:

> '... any grant of planning permission to develop land shall (except in so far as the permission otherwise provides) enure for the benefit of the land and of all persons for the time being interested in it'.

28.7 The person carrying out a development need not be the applicant. Similarly the conditions on a permission may be enforced against persons other than the applicant. Where conditions refer to 'the applicant' – as in 'development shall not commence until the applicant has submitted a scheme for ...' – that can be satisfied by any person. The exceptions are:

(i) If the permission provides that it does not enure for the benefit of the land. This will usually be where a condition gives the benefit of the permission to a particular person (a personal condition);

(ii) Where the permission is applied for by the local planning authority under the Town and Country Planning Act 1990, s 316 and the Town and Country Planning General Regulations 1992 and is personal to the authority by reason of reg 9. The question will arise as to the effect of such a permission on a subsequent

---

[3] *Wilson v West Sussex County Council* [1963] 2 QB 764 at 783 per Diplock LJ ('Set apart for,' 'destine' or 'intend'), see also Danckwerts LJ at 780. In *Trinder v Sevenoaks Rural District Council* (1967) 204 EG 803, Ungoed-Thomas J held that 'including' in what is now s 75(3) meant that the permission was solely authorising that use.
[4] *Mid Suffolk District Council v Clarke* [2005] EWHC 3099 (QB) at paras 10, 18–22 per Newman J where a planning permission for a 'replacement cooking plant' was to operate as part of, and so ancillary to, an existing pig farm, as explained in *R (on the application of Mid Suffolk District Council) v Secretary of State for Communities and Local Government* [2009] EWHC 3649 (Admin) at paras 14, 15 per Mitting J.
[5] [2013] EWCA Civ 1680.
[6] Judgment of the court, at paras 142, 143 per Sir John Mummery. The contrary decision in similar circumstances in *R (Prudential Assurance Co Ltd) v Sunderland City Council and Peel Investments (UK) Ltd* [2010] EWHC 1771 (Admin), [2011] JPL 322 must be considered with caution.

28.8 *The effect and interpretation of planning permission*

owner or occupier. If the development has been carried out then another person may be able to continue the use.

INTERPRETATION OF A PLANNING PERMISSION

28.8 The interpretation of a planning permission is a matter of law: *Redrow Homes Ltd v Secretary of State*[7]. The classic summary of the principles applicable to the interpretation of planning permissions was given by Keene J in *R v Ashford Borough Council, ex p Shepway District Council*[8]:

'1 The general rule is that in construing a planning permission which is clear, unambiguous and valid on its face, regard may only be had to the planning permission itself, including the conditions (if any) on it and the express reasons for those conditions: see *Slough Borough Council v Secretary of State for the Environment* (1995) JPL 1128, and *Miller-Mead v Minister of Housing and Local Government* [1963] 2 QB 196.

2 This rule excludes reference to the planning application as well as to other extrinsic evidence, unless the planning permission incorporates the application by reference. In that situation the application is treated as having become part of the permission. The reason for normally not having regard to the application is that the public should be able to rely on a document which is plain on its face without having to consider whether there is any discrepancy between the permission and the application: see *Slough Borough Council v Secretary of State (ante); Wilson v West Sussex County Council* [1963] 2 QB 764; and *Slough Estates Limited v Slough Borough Council* [1971] AC 958.

3 For incorporation of the application in the permission to be achieved, more is required than a mere reference to the application on the face of the permission. While there is no magic formula, some words sufficient to inform a reasonable reader that the application forms part of the permission are needed, such as "… in accordance with the plans and application …" or "… on the terms of the application …", and in either case those words appearing in the operative part of the permission dealing with the development and the terms in which permission is granted. These words need to govern the description of the development permitted: See *Wilson* (ante); *Slough Borough Council v Secretary of State for the Environment* (ante).

4 If there is an ambiguity in the wording of the permission, it is permissible to look at extrinsic material, including the application, to resolve that ambiguity: see *Staffordshire Moorlands District Council v Cartwright* [1992] JPL 138 at 139; *Slough Estates Limited v Slough Borough Council (ante); Creighton Estates Limited v London County Council* (1958) The Times, 20th March 1958.

5 If a planning permission is challenged on the ground of absence of authority or mistake, it is permissible to look at extrinsic evidence to resolve that issue: *see Slough Borough Council v Secretary of State* (ante); *Co-operative Retail Services v Taff-Ely Borough Council* (1979) 39 P & CR 223 affirmed (1981) 42 P & CR 1'[9].

28.9 This statement applies to outline planning permissions and is subject to important qualifications. A planning application must include all the drawings and details necessary to describe the development to be authorised. In *Barnett v Secretary of State for Communities and Local Government*[10] Sullivan J pointed out

---

[7] [2003] EWHC 3094 (Admin), [2004] JPL 1273 at para 45 per Sullivan J.
[8] [1999] PLCR 12 at 19. A more recent summary of the case law was given by Beatson J in *Telford and Wrekin Council v Secretary of State for Communities and Local Government* [2013] EWHC 79 (Admin), [2013] JPL 865 at para 33.
[9] Paragraph 5 is about the lawfulness of planning permissions, rather than their interpretation.
[10] [2008] EWHC 1601 (Admin), [2009] JPL 243 at para 24.

Interpretation of a planning permission **28.11**

that the cases cited in *Ashford* and *Ashford* itself did not deal with detailed planning permissions:

> 'If it is plain on the face of a permission that it is a full permission for the construction, erection or alteration of the building, the public will know that, in addition to the plan which identifies the site, there will be plans and drawings which will describe the building works which have been permitted precisely because the permission is not, on its face, an outline planning permission. In such a case those plans and drawings describing the building works were as much a part of the description of what has been permitted as the permission notice itself. It is not a question of resolving an "ambiguity". On its face, a grant of full planning permission for building operations is incomplete without the approved plans and drawings showing the detail of what has been permitted. In the absence of any indication to the contrary, those plans and drawings will be the plans listed in the application for permission. If the local planning authority does not wish to approve the plans submitted with the application and wishes to approve amended plans, then it can include a statement to that effect in the decision notice. Absent any such statement, the reasonable inference, against the statutory background provided by Section 62 of the Act and the 1988 Regulations, is that a grant of full planning permission approves the application drawings'.

These observations were followed by the Court of Appeal in that case, in particular by Keene LJ[11]. Consequently application drawings are approved in full planning permissions, whether or not this is stated expressly.

28.10 From 2006 outline planning applications were required to state the approximate location of buildings, routes and open spaces, and the upper and lower dimensions for buildings, along with the location of access points to the development even when layout, scale and access were reserved. Those requirements have now been removed in England (other than for access) but remain in Wales[12]. If those provisions applied to the planning application at the relevant time then those parameters would be approved[13].

28.11 Laws LJ explained in *R (on the application of Mid-Counties Co-operative Ltd) v Wyre Forest District Council*[14]:

> 'A planning permission is a public document likely to affect in varying degrees third party rights and the public at large. In consequence the materials that may be referred to for the purpose of its interpretation are quite strictly confined. In *Carter Commercial Developments Ltd (In Administration) v Secretary of State for Transport, Local Government and the Regions* [2002] EWCA Civ 1994 Arden L.J. observed (at [27]), basing her remarks on what had been said by Keene J in *R v Ashford BC, ex p Shepway DC* [1999] PLCR 12; [1998] JPL 1073, that a permission is not to be construed like a commercial document, but "is to be given the meaning that a reasonable reader would give to it, having available to him only the permission" [and any documents incorporated by reference, such as in this case the application documents]. Extrinsic material may otherwise only be admitted in order to resolve an ambiguity in the permission, or to address a challenge advanced on the ground of absence of authority or mistake (see per Keene J in *R v Ashford BC, ex p Shepway DC* at propositions (3) and (4)).

---

[11] *Barnett v Secretary of State for Communities and Local Government* [2009] EWCA Civ 476, [2009] JPL 1597 at paras 17–22.

[12] The revision to bare outlines was made to the Town and Country Planning (Development Management Procedure) (England) Order 2010, art 4 from 31 January 2013 and now in Town and Country Planning (Development Management Procedure) (England) Order 2015, art 5. The Welsh provision is the Town and Country Planning (Development Management Procedure) (Wales) Order 2012, art 3.

[13] Discussed in *R (on the application of Wrenn) v Wiltshire Council* [2011] EWHC 2198 (Admin).

[14] [2010] EWCA Civ 841, [2011] JPL 173 at para 10.

28.12 The effect and interpretation of planning permission

11 It is worth noting ... that a mere *ambiguity* in a planning permission will by no means necessarily suffice to render the permission void for *uncertainty*. In *Fawcett Properties Ltd v Buckingham CC* [1961] AC 636, 678, Lord Denning was at pains to emphasise the fact that the courts' daily task is to resolve ambiguities of language in legal documents, and to do so without striking down the document; but:

> "a planning condition is only void for uncertainty if it can be given no meaning or no sensible or ascertainable meaning"'.

28.12 As the first *Ashford* principle shows, the planning permission must be construed as a whole. The description of development, whilst important, is not the totality of the permission, and the document as a whole, along with material incorporated in it, must be considered[15].

28.13 Whether there is an ambiguity must be considered with caution. Discussing ambiguity in *Ashford*, Keene J said 'As a matter of principle, if the words ... can be understood from the permission itself and can have a sensible meaning attached to them without a need to resort to the application, then no such resort should be permissible'[16]. If an ambiguity arises, extrinsic evidence may only be used to resolve that ambiguity and not for any other purpose[17].

28.14 An example of a need to consider extrinsic evidence arose in *Campbell Court Property v Secretary of State for the Environment, Transport and the Regions*[18] where a site for the demolition of terraced houses and its redevelopment for flats was insufficiently described by the address in circumstances where there was no site plan. In that case the applicant's registered title was not of significant assistance, with planning documents being more use[19]. It was suggested that the way in which a permission is implemented on the ground can be extrinsic evidence of what the permission means, if there was no complaint about a breach of planning control over many years[20]. Extrinsic evidence ought to be directed at dealings between the applicant and the planning authority[21], and it might be thought that it should be material which the public, searching diligently, could obtain. Facts known by only one party cannot be relevant to the exercise: if the planning authority does not know them it cannot affect its decision; if the applicant does not know them then it cannot understand the permission which it has been given[22]. How a permission was subsequently implemented cannot resolve an ambiguity in the permission itself (as it can at best only show how someone chose to resolve the ambiguity) although it might, as in *Campbell Court*, provide evidence of the content of missing documents. In a similar vein, extrinsic evidence is admissible to identify the approved plans when they are not identified in a planning permission or to determine which of two drawings (different but carrying the same number) were approved[23].

---

[15] See *Mid-Suffolk District Council v Clarke* [2005] EWHC 3099 (QB) per Newman J at paras 12–15.
[16] At 21.
[17] *Ashford* per Keene J at 24.
[18] [2001] EWHC Admin 102, [2002] PLCR 4 per Sullivan J at para 50.
[19] *Campbell Court* per Sullivan J at para 52. If a committee report is to be considered it must be viewed as a whole: para 55. That is a useful precaution given the potential for errors or ambiguities in such reports.
[20] *Campbell Court* per Sullivan J at paras 58–60 (recognising that such evidence could not be conclusive), *Wood* per Lindblom J at paras 43, 44.
[21] *Campbell Court* per Sullivan J at para 69.
[22] A similar approach is taken to contractual interpretation: *Arnold v Britton* [2015] UKSC 36, [2015] 2 WLR 1593 per Lord Neuberger of Abbotsbury PSC at para 21.
[23] *Koumis v Secretary of State for Communities and Local Government* [2014] EWCA Civ 1723, [2015] JPL 682 at paras 45–48 per Sullivan LJ.

Interpretation of a planning permission **28.17**

28.15 Whilst a planning permission is to be interpreted within a narrow range of documentation, certain terms may have particular meanings in planning practice and planning guidance may be referred to in interpreting that term when used in a planning permission[24]. Otherwise, as in statutory interpretation, ordinary meanings of words are adopted unless the result is absurdity or inconvenience such that it could not have been intended[25].

28.16 Interpretation of a planning permission takes place within the framework of the law governing the grant of the permission. It is reasonable to seek to interpret a particular permission in a way which is lawful rather than to give a meaning which renders the permission unlawful. However that must still be within the confines of what the words in the permission are able to mean, and avoid giving a meaning to the permission which is absurd or ineffectual. It was suggested in *R (on the application of Gregan) v Hartlepool Borough Council* that where an environmental impact assessment has been carried out the planning permission should not be interpreted, where possible, to allow development outside that assessed in the environmental statement. The point was not resolved but Sullivan J observed[26]:

> 'the underlying approach to the interpretation of an Environmental Statement, having regard to its statutory function, should be that if an activity is proposed to be carried out it will have been described, and the environmental implications of carrying it out will have been assessed in the Statement. If an activity is not described or assessed in an Environmental Statement, the proper inference to be drawn (absent any indication to the contrary) must be that it does not form part of the proposed development'.

28.17 Broader principles have sometimes been relied upon. In *Newark and Sherwood District Council v Secretary of State for Communities and Local Government*[27] a planning application had been made for a wind turbine with documents showing a two-bladed machine. The inspector granted planning permission with a condition which required a three-bladed turbine. It was held that the condition could be interpreted as referring to two rather than three blades. Stephen Morris QC, sitting as a Deputy High Court Judge, relied upon these general principles:

> 'General principles of construction
>
> 18 General principles of construction fall to be considered. In appropriate circumstances, it is permissible, as a matter of construction, to read documentary provisions as being subject to addition, omission or even substitution. As regards substitution, Lord Reid in *Federal Steam Navigation Co Ltd v Department of Trade and Industry* [1974] 1 WLR 505 at 509B stated as follows:
>
>> "Cases where it has properly been held that a word can be struck out of a deed or statute and another substituted can as far as I am aware be grouped under three heads: where without such substitution the provision is unintelligible or absurd or totally unreasonable; where it is unworkable; and where it is totally irreconcilable with the plain intention shown by the rest of the deed or statute."
>
> This is an approach applicable to a "unilateral" document (deed or statute), as in this case.

---

[24] *Green v Secretary of State for Communities and Local Government* [2010] EWCA Civ 64, [2010] JPL 1022; *R (on the application of Belgrave Land Ltd) v Secretary of State for the Environment, Transport and the Regions* [2001] EWHC (Admin) 1127.
[25] *River Wear Commissioners v Adamson* [1877] 2 AC 743.
[26] [2003] EWHC 3278 (Admin), [2004] JPL 1088 at para 76. See also paras 77, 78.
[27] [2013] EWHC 2162 (Admin).

28.18 *The effect and interpretation of planning permission*

19 As regards a contractual document, where there is a mistake, rectification is not necessary and in certain circumstances the mistake can be dealt with by way of construction: *Chitty on Contracts* (31st edn) Vol 1 para 5-113, citing Brightman LJ in *East v Pantiles Plant Hire Ltd* (1982) EGLR 111 at 112:

> "It is clear on the authorities that a mistake in a written instrument can, in limited circumstances, be corrected as a matter of construction without obtaining a decree in an action for rectification. Two conditions must be satisfied: first, there must be a clear mistake on the face of the instrument; secondly, it must be clear what correction ought to be made in order to cure the mistake".

In *Chartbrook Ltd v Persimmon Homes Ltd* [2009] UKHL 38, [2009] AC 1101, [2009] 4 All ER 677 Lord Hoffmann (at 1114 paras 22 to 25) cited and approved this passage in *East*, subject to two qualifications: first, that correction of mistake by construction is just part of a single task of interpreting the agreement in context, in order to get as close as possible to the meaning which the parties intended. Second, in deciding whether there is a clear mistake, the court is not confined to reading the 'face of the instrument', without regard to the background and context, which must always be taken into consideration. He went on to state that:

> "there is no limit to the amount of red ink or verbal rearrangement or correction which the court is allowed. All that is required is that it should be clear that something has gone wrong with the language and that it should be clear what a reasonable person would have understood the parties to have meant'".

28.18 In identifying the error and what the correct position was, the court did, however, seek to keep within the *Ashford/Barnett* rules on what was relevant to interpretation.

28.19 Occasionally perverse interpretations have been sanctioned. In *R (on the application of Prokopp) v London Underground Ltd*, a listed building consent application had been made. The local authority issued what purported to be a planning permission, but one which gave the reason for the time of implement condition as the Planning (Listed Buildings and Conservation Areas) Act 1990, s 18. Collins J said the consent was a listed building consent, not a planning permission[28]. However, in the Court of Appeal, Buxton LJ said the decision was a planning permission, saying the document was not ambiguous or incomprehensible[29]. Since the document on its face referred to the Town and Country Planning Act and the Listed Buildings Act this was an obvious example of ambiguity which could be resolved in favour of listed building consent by considering the application.

Interpretation of conditions

28.20 The documents considered in interpreting a planning condition are the same as for the planning permission as a whole. Principles for interpreting conditions were set out by Elias LJ in *Hulme v Secretary of State for Communities and Local Government* at paras 13 and 14[30]:

---

[28] [2003] EWHC 960 (Admin), para 25.
[29] [2003] EWCA Civ 961, [2004] JPL 44.
[30] [2011] EWCA Civ 638.

Interpretation of a planning permission **28.23**

'a) The conditions must be construed in the context of the decision letter as a whole.

b) The conditions should be interpreted benevolently and not narrowly or strictly: see *Carter Commercial Development Limited v Secretary of State for the Environment* [2002] EWHC 1200 (Admin) para 49, per Sullivan J, as he was.

c) A condition will be void for uncertainty only "if it can be given no meaning or no sensible or ascertainable meaning, and not merely because it is ambiguous or leads to absurd results" per Lord Denning in *Fawcett Properties v Buckingham County Council* [1961] AC 636 , 678. This seems to me to be an application of the benevolent construction principle.

d) There is no room for an implied condition (although for reasons I discuss more fully below, the scope of this principle needs careful analysis). This principle was enunciated by Widgery LJ, as he then was, in *Trustees of Walton on Thames Charities v Walton and Weighbridge District Council* [1970] 21 P & CR 411 at 497, in the following terms:

> "I have never heard of an implied condition in a planning permission and I believe no such creature exists. Planning permission ... is not simply a matter of contract between the parties. There is no place, in my judgment, within the law relating to planning permission for an implied condition. Conditions should be expressed, they should be clear, they should be in the document containing the permission."

14 Accordingly, whilst there must be a limit to the extent to which conditions should be rewritten to save them from invalidity, if they can be given a sensible and reasonable interpretation when read in context, they should be'.

28.21 The question of implied conditions had also arisen in *Sevenoaks District Council v First Secretary of State*[31] where the failure to include a requirement in a condition that details of engineering works be carried out as approved meant that the developer did not have to comply with the approved details. The High Court rejected the submission requirements could be implied into the condition. Sullivan J said[32]:

> 'If conditions are to be included in a public document such as a planning permission, they should be clearly and expressly imposed, so that they are plain for all to read. There is no room for implication'.

28.22 It is said that the interpretation of a condition should be benevolent and neither too narrow nor too strict[33]. However benevolence should only extend as far as trying to make the condition work rather than tilting in favour of the local planning authority or the landowner. A condition imposes restrictions which it might be expensive, inconvenient and time-consuming to comply with and criminal penalties may follow from a breach. Conversely a condition should cover a matter of importance which is to be secured or protected in the public interest.

28.23 Care needs to be taken as to whether a condition controls only the initial characteristics of the development or restricts future changes. For example, in *Northampton Borough Council v First Secretary of State*[34] a condition limiting non-

---

[31] [2004] EWHC 771, [2005] JPL 116.
[32] At para 45.
[33] For example, *R (on the application of Groves) v Boston Borough Council* [2014] EWHC 3950 (Admin) at para 35.
[34] [2005] EWHC 168 (Admin). The transcript erroneously describes the first defendant as the Home Secretary. See also the discussions on the removal of rights under the Use Classes Order and permitted development rights by condition in Chapters 3 and 5.

28.23 *The effect and interpretation of planning permission*

food retail floorspace on an entire site was considered to have a continuing effect. Conversely in *Knott v Secretary of State for the Environment*[35] planning permission for the erection of a house was conditioned to be solely for the benefit of named individuals. The High Court held that this restricted who could have the house built, but not the identity of future residential occupiers.

---

[35] (1998) 75 P & CR 65.

Chapter 29

Implementation of planning permission

29.1 A planning permission confers a right, but a right which only authorises and controls what happens on land when it is exercised. Implementation is starting to use the rights contained in a planning permission.

29.2 For these purposes, planning permissions can be divided into two types: prospective and retrospective. A prospective permission authorises development which has not yet begun. Retrospective permissions authorise development which has taken place. It is possible to have a permission which is part prospective and part retrospective.

29.3 A retrospective planning permission will come into effect immediately and will therefore not contain a time limit within which the permission must be begun. A prospective permission will have to be implemented by doing some act under the permission within the implementation period. That period will be set out in a condition included on the permission, and if not a condition will apply by reason of the Town and Country Planning Act 1990, ss 91 and 92. In England the implementation period for a full planning permission is extended by one year in the event of an unsuccessful High Court challenge to the lawfulness of the permission[1].

INITIATED, BEGUN AND COMMENCED

29.4 The Town and Country Planning Act 1990 contains definitions of when development is initiated, begun or commenced:

(a) by s 56(1) development is 'initiated' when the operations are begun or the material change of use is instituted, or at the earliest of those two actions;

(b) by s 56(2) development is begun for the purpose of listed provisions 'on the earliest date on which any material operation comprised in the development begins to be carried out'. These listed sections do not include s 56(1);

(c) s 72(3) applies to permissions subject to a condition that development be commenced not later than a specified time and provides that building or other operations commenced after that time are not authorised. This provision does not however apply to the time limits for the commencement of development which have to be imposed on permissions by ss 91 and 92[2].

---

[1] See Town and Country Planning Act 1990, s 91(3A), (3B). No change is made to the time to implement an outline planning permission.
[2] Town and Country Planning Act 1990, s 72(4).

29.5 *Implementation of planning permission*

The provision which is of importance is s 56(2). Indeed it is not apparent what ss 56(1) and 72(3) add to the planning system[3].

IMPLEMENTATION OF PROSPECTIVE PLANNING PERMISSIONS

29.5 The legislative intention is that planning permission is obtained before development takes place. By the Town and Country Planning Act 1990, ss 91 and 92 a planning permission for prospective development granted on an application by the local planning authority or on appeal is subject to a condition requiring that the development must be begun within a specified period, unless the permission is itself granted for a limited period[4].

29.6 There are two elements to implementation:

(i) carrying out material operations or the material change of use comprised in the permission;

(ii) compliance with the conditions on the permission, subject to limited exceptions.

These are considered in turn below and then the role of intention in carrying out the works is discussed.

Material operations

29.7 For the purpose of meeting the condition in a planning permission requiring development to be begun within a certain period, the Town and Country Planning Act 1990, s 56(2) provides that:

'development shall be taken to be begun on the earliest date on which any material operation comprised in the development begins to be carried out'.

By s 56(4):

'In subsection (2) "material operation" means:

(a) any work of construction in the course of the erection of a building;

(aa) any work of demolition of a building;

(b) the digging of a trench which is to contain the foundations, or part of the foundations, of a building;

(c) the laying of any underground main or pipe to the foundations, or part of the foundations, of a building or to any such trench as is mentioned in paragraph (b);

(d) any operation in the course of laying out or constructing a road or part of a road;

(e) any change in the use of any land which constitutes material development'.

---

[3] In the absence of a useful purpose, ss 56(1) and 72(3), (4) should be repealed at the next convenient opportunity.
[4] Permissions granted for a limited period are not subject to the time limit: see Town and Country Planning Act 1990, s 91(4)(c).

29.8 Section 56(4) does include actions which are insufficient in themselves to be development, such as pegging out the line of a road[5]. These pegs do not have to be permanent[6], although they would need to be part of the development. Following the general approach to interpretation, building includes part of a building[7].

The amount of works carried out does not need to be large.

29.9 In minerals cases, s 56(2) is modified to read[8]:

> 'For the purpose of sections 91, 92 and 94, development consisting of the winning and working of minerals shall be taken to be begun on the earliest date on which the winning and working of minerals to which the relevant grant of planning permission relates begins'.

The Court of Appeal in *English Clays v Plymouth Corpn* suggested that 'to 'win' a mineral is to make it available or accessible to be removed from the land, and to 'work' a mineral is (at least initially) to remove it from its position in the land'[9].

29.10 Development may be begun by works which are not material operations in the list: *Field v First Secretary of State*[10]. In *Field* a cottage had been demolished in the 1960s long before the category of material operations had included demolition, sub-para (aa) on demolition being inserted by the Planning and Compensation Act 1991. Mr Justice Sullivan held that the definition of material operations was not exclusive, as some planning permissions would not involve any of these actions. It must be possible to implement any type of planning permission, such as consent for the construction of embankments, and so material operations must be wider than the listed operations or changes of use.

Works which are not in exact accord with the permission

29.11 It will sometimes be the case that works are carried out within categories in s 56(4), such as digging a trench, but they are carried out in the wrong place or not entirely in accordance with the approved plans.

29.12 The effect of these works depends upon whether they, or some of them, were 'comprised in the development'. It is not necessary for the works to be in exact accordance with the approved scheme to still be comprised in the development. In *Spackman v Wiltshire County Council*[11] Willis J held that the construction of a soakaway 35 feet from the nearest one shown on the plans and a deviation in an

---

[5] See *Malvern Hills District Council v Secretary of State for the Environment* (1983) 46 P & CR 58 where what is now sub-s (4)(d) was considered to refer to any working activity on the land in the course of laying out a road, whether or not that activity resulted in a change in the character of the land or in anything that might be called development: see Eveleigh LJ at 69.
[6] *Aerlink Leisure Ltd (in liquidation) v First Secretary of State* [2004] EWHC 3198 (Admin), [2005] 2 P & CR 15 at para 31 per Davis J.
[7] Town and Country Planning Act 1990, s 336(1).
[8] Town and Country Planning (Minerals) Regulations 1995, SI 1995/2863, Sch 1, para 1. The remainder of s 56 is omitted.
[9] [1974] 1 WLR 72 at 746H per Russell LJ, giving the judgment of the court. This was adopted in *Bleaklow Industries Ltd v Secretary of State for Communities and Local Government* [2009] EWCA Civ 206, [2009] JPL 1477 at para 29 per Keene LJ.
[10] [2004] JPL 1286.
[11] (1976) 33 P & CR 430.

29.13 *Implementation of planning permission*

access way position did not prevent those works constituting the commencement of development.

29.13 In *Thayer v Secretary of State for the Environment*[12] a 12-foot-wide access had been made in a hedge. This was half the size of the access authorised by the planning permission. The Court of Appeal considered that the question was whether the works were referable to the planning permission. The Court of Appeal in *Staffordshire County Council v Riley*[13] held that the effect of stripping topsoil on implementation of a minerals planning permission was not affected by the stripping not coinciding with the planning permission boundary and some of the works being outside the site. However in the particular case the works were not 'an unequivocal act pursuant to the planning permission' and there was ambivalence, because the stripping of topsoil could have been distinct from working minerals beneath it. In *Handoll v Warner Goodman and Streat*[14] a house had been constructed 90 feet from the approved position and outside the planning application site. There was no difficulty in finding this was not under the permission. McCowan LJ agreed with submissions that[15]:

> 'a building constructed otherwise than in accordance with the terms of a planning permission (including any details properly approved pursuant to a condition imposed on that permission) is not authorised by it and therefore [the building] was built without planning permission. The planning permission granted did not authorise the building constructed and accordingly the works involved were not permitted and were unlawful'.

He then agreed[16]:

> 'If a permission does not apply, then the condition subject to which it was granted has no application'.

Peter Gibson LJ said[17]:

> 'If a development does not comply in a material respect, or to a material extent, with the planning permission which has been granted, I cannot see how an occupancy condition attached to the permission for the development which was not carried out can have application to the unauthorised development which was carried out'.

29.14 The issue was also considered by Ouseley J in *Commercial Land Ltd v Secretary of State for Transport, Local Government and the Regions*[18]. Planning permission had been granted for the erection of an additional storey on a block of flats to provide four further flats. Two walls were erected, but not in accordance with the plans. The walls contained door openings in the wrong places (some 2.8 to 3.8 metres out) and failed to include window openings. On a lawful development certificate appeal the inspector considered that the permission had not been implemented. The court held that 'the question of whether a material operation is or is not 'comprised in the development' cannot necessarily be answered by asking simply if there is

---

[12] [1992] JPL 264.
[13] [2001] EWCA Civ 257, [2002] PLCR 75.
[14] (1994) 70 P & CR 627.
[15] At 633–634.
[16] At 634.
[17] Sir John May agreed with both judgments.
[18] [2003] JPL 358.

a difference between the approved plans and the actual operations relied on'[19]. Ouseley J relied on *Spackman* and *Riley*. He continued[20]:

> '33 It is, in my judgment, necessary for an Inspector dealing with this sort of problem to consider not just the existence of differences between the plans and the operations relied on, but also to consider the significance of those differences. ... Consideration of the similarities, or degree of compliance of the operations relied upon, with the approved plans is also relevant, together with the substantial usability of those works in the permitted development, and the degree of alteration required to them in order for them to be effective to that end.
>
> 35 I consider that the question of whether the operations done were comprised within the development involves looking at what has been done as a whole and reaching a judgment as a matter of fact and degree upon that whole. It does not entail any artificial process of ignoring part of what has been done. I reach that view even where it is not contended that the works are different functionally from the planning permission which has been granted, or are ambivalent in nature and so not unequivocally referable to the planning permission in question'.

29.15 The comments of Lord Hobhouse in *Sage v Secretary of State for the Environment, Transport and the Regions*[21] have sometimes been thought to suggest that absolute compliance was required:

> 'When an application for planning consent is made for permission for a single operation, it is made in respect of the whole of the building operation. There are two reasons for this. The first is the practical one that an application for permission partially to erect a building would, save in exceptional circumstances, fail. The second is that the concept of final permission requires a fully detailed building of a certain character, not a structure which is incomplete. This is one of the differences between an outline permission and a final permission (see s 92 of the 1990 Act). As counsel for Mr Sage accepted, if a building operation is not carried out, both externally and internally, fully in accordance with the permission, the *whole* operation is unlawful. She contrasted that with a case where the building has been completed but is then altered or improved. This demonstrates the fallacy in Mr Sage's case. He comes into the first category not the second'.

The comments on carrying out development in accordance with a planning permission were obiter as Mr Sage did not have a planning permission. The ratio of *Sage* is that the construction of building is not substantially complete until internal works are substantially completed. No authority is referred to for the concession on carrying out works in accordance with the permission and the cases discussed above are ample authority that a permission may be implemented by works which are not in full accordance with it.

29.16 An early deviation from approved plans might mean that a permission was not implemented[22]. In *Silver v Secretary of State for Communities and Local Government* Supperstone J followed *Commercial Land* in holding that it was a matter of looking at what had been done as a whole[23]. In *Silver* what was done

---

[19] Para 31.
[20] This approach was approved in *Green v Secretary of State for Communities and Local Government* [2013] EWHC 3980 (Admin) at para 30 per Cranston J and *Silver v Secretary of State for Communities and Local Government* [2014] EWHC 2729 (Admin), [2015] JPL 154 at para 44 per Supperstone J.
[21] [2003] 2 All ER 689 at para 23.
[22] *Green v Secretary of State for Communities and Local Government* [2013] EWHC 3980 (Admin) per Cranston J at para 30.
[23] [2014] EWHC 2729 (Admin), [2015] JPL 154 at para 44.

29.17 *Implementation of planning permission*

at expiration of the permission was ambiguous, and therefore it was necessary to consider what happened next and to what extent it was capable of being comprised in the development[24]. Both cases concerned developments with single elements. If a scheme comprises a number of buildings, a failure to construct all of the authorised development does not alter the lawfulness of those buildings which have been erected[25]. Similarly if one building is constructed in accordance with the permission, the permission will remain implemented even if other buildings are then constructed under other consents or without permission.

29.17 Of course, the importance of a mis-sited building may vary greatly. Placing the structure 1.5 metres out in a field may be irrelevant for all practical purposes, but such an error in a closely built up area could cause substantial adverse overshadowing[26].

Conditions on the planning permission

29.18 As a general principle the implementation of a planning permission must be in accordance with its conditions. In *Whitley & Sons Co Ltd v Secretary of State for Wales* Woolf LJ said[27]:

> 'As I understand the effect of the authorities to which I am about to refer, it is only necessary to ask the single question: are the operations (in other situations the question would refer to the development) permitted by the planning permission read together with its conditions? The permission is controlled by and subject to the conditions. If the operations contravene the conditions they cannot be properly described as commencing the development authorised by the permission. If they do not comply with the permission they constitute a breach of planning control and for planning purposes will be unauthorised and thus unlawful'.

29.19 That principle has been subject to exceptions, not least in *Whitley* itself where details under the relevant conditions had been applied for before the consent had to be implemented and were then approved. The various exceptions have been explained as part of a general principle that the permission would have been implemented if it would have been irrational (and so unlawful in public law) for the planning authority to have enforced against the breach[28]. Irrationality of enforcement action is an extremely high hurdle for a developer to satisfy. It would only be in very rare situations that it would be unlawful to enforce a properly-drafted condition. However, in a number of recent decisions the courts have indicated a softer approach, asking whether the condition breached was fundamental or went to the heart of the permission[29].

---

[24] At para 40.
[25] *R (on the application of Robert Hitchins Ltd) v Worcestershire County Council* [2015] EWCA Civ 1060 at para 49 per Richards LJ.
[26] Where a planning permission provides for multiple buildings, some of which are built in accordance with the permission and some of which are not, those built in accordance with the permission might be subject to the permission's conditions: see *Morland v Secretary of State for Communities and Local Government* [2009] EWHC 310 (Admin), [2010] JPL 176.
[27] (1992) 64 P & CR 296 at 302. Following *Oakimber v Elmbridge Borough Council* (1991) 62 P & CR 594 and *R v Elmbridge Borough Council, ex p Health Care Corpn* (1991) 63 P & CR 260.
[28] *R (on the application of Hammerton) v London Underground Ltd* [2002] EWHC 2307 (Admin), [2003] JPL 984 at para 127 per Ouseley J; *Norris v First Secretary of State* [2006] EWCA Civ 12, [2006] JPL 1574. This approach has been confirmed in the *Hart Aggregates* and *Greyfort* decisions.
[29] *Greyfort Properties Ltd v Secretary of State for Communities and Local Government* [2011] EWCA Civ 908, [2012] JPL 40 following *R (on the application of Hart Aggregates Ltd) v Hartlepool Borough Council* [2005] EWHC 840 (Admin), [2005] JPL 1602 and *Bedford Borough Council v Secretary of State for Communities and Local Government* [2008] EWHC 2304 (Admin), [2009] JPL 604.

29.20 There were said to be three exceptions to the *Whitley* principle, identified in *Leisure Great Britain plc v Isle of Wight Council*[30]:

(i) where approval has subsequently been given so that work done before the deadline was made lawful: see *Whitley* where details had been applied for before the permission had to be implemented but were approved long afterwards[31]. Therefore mining had been lawfully commenced by the time subsequent enforcement action was taken;

(ii) where the local planning authority have agreed that development could commence without full compliance with the relevant conditions: see *Agecrest Ltd v Gwynedd County Council*[32] where Collins J held that a council had later agreed to staged approvals under a 1960s permission; and

(iii) where the condition had in substance been complied with but the formalities, including a written notice of approval, had not been completed before work started on the site: see *R v Flintshire County Council, ex p Somerfield Stores Ltd*[33].

Twenty-first century approaches to the issue have been characterised by two countervailing trends. The first is the formalisation of planning processes and a reluctance to allow informal exceptions. The second is a softening of approach, allowing certain non-compliance.

29.21 In *R (on the application of Reprotech (Pebsham) Ltd) v East Sussex County Council*[34] the House of Lords had held that informal representations by public authorities did not give rise to an estoppel and sought to turn away from private law concepts being used as solutions for public law problems. This was quickly followed in the implementation case of *R (on the application of Henry Boot) v Bassetlaw District Council*[35]. Outline planning permission had been granted for the development of 315 houses. The developer sought a declaration that development had commenced prior to the expiry of the permission, the issue arising because details required to be submitted and approved under conditions before the commencement of development had not been submitted, or in some cases approved. In correspondence Henry Boot's solicitors told the Council:

> 'We believe that your Council has had all the information required to enable the satisfaction of these conditions. It may be that there was some procedural informality but this reflected the practice of your Council in other matters relating to this development as well as other developments elsewhere'.

They then did apply for approvals under the outstanding conditions but some were refused by the council and Henry Boot's appeal was rejected by the Inspectorate

---

[30] [2000] PLCR 88 at 379–380 per Keene J.
[31] The exception applies with even more force if the application for approval is made before the works are commenced and the approval is granted after commencement but before the time limit for implementation had expired: *R (on the application of Ellaway) v Cardiff County Council* [2014] EWHC 836 (Admin), [2015] Env LR 19 at paras 55–58 per Wyn Williams J. This exception was also applied in *R (on the application of the Government of the Republic of France) v Royal Borough of Kensington and Chelsea* [2015] EWHC 3437 (Admin) at paras 83, 85 per Holgate J.
[32] [1998] JPL 325.
[33] [1998] PLCR 336.
[34] [2002] UKHL 8, [2002] JPL 821.
[35] [2002] EWHC 546 (Admin), [2002] JPL 1224.

29.22 *Implementation of planning permission*

because certain documents were not provided. Sullivan J rejected the approach of *R v Secretary of State for the Environment, ex p Percy Bilton Industrial Properties Ltd*[36] that an outline planning permission could be implemented where reserved matters had been approved for only part of the development even though the permission did not refer to a phased or staged implementation. The statutory code was now radically different and the wording of the conditions was different. Similarly Sullivan J confined the flexibility allowed in *Agecrest* to old planning permissions where public consultation and procedures to change conditions were less advanced. The judge observed, 'It is important at all times to remember the public nature of Town and Country Planning. It is not a matter for private agreement between developers and Local Planning Authorities'[37]. He was prepared to assume for the purposes of the case that a local planning authority could conduct itself in such a way as to give rise to a legitimate expectation that a development will be treated as having been lawfully commenced despite the fact that there has been no compliance with conditions precedent, but expressed great scepticism about it. He held that the application failed on its facts.

29.22 The Court of Appeal upheld Sullivan J in *Henry Boot Homes Ltd v Bassetlaw District Council*[38]. Keene LJ noted the more comprehensive mechanisms in planning legislation, such as s 73 applications for planning permission subject to different conditions which had been introduced in 1986. That procedure imported 'the safeguards for third parties and the public generally which apply to applications for planning permission under the Act' such as publicity and inclusion in the planning register. Keene LJ then commented:[39]

> 'In those circumstances, the scope for such variation or discharge to be achieved by some other non-statutory method, bypassing the statutory safeguards for the public, must be extremely limited. Such a change is not simply a matter for bilateral agreement between the developer and the local planning authority'.

29.23 Citing *Reprotech* Keene LJ said:[40]

> 'Even more than many areas of public law which concern an individual and a public body, planning law is likely to have to reflect the fact that third parties and the public generally may have interests in any decision. ... The scope, therefore, for waiver by non-statutory means of the need to comply with a condition must be extremely limited. That is so, whether one is concerned with an alleged waiver of a condition in total or with an allegation that the local planning authority has allowed development to take place in a phased manner, contrary to a condition'.

The developer raised before the Court of Appeal a new argument based on legitimate expectation. It was roundly dismissed. Keene LJ held:[41]

> 'The issue whether the works carried on in breach of condition amounted to a start to "the development to which the permission relates" within the meaning of section 92(2) of the Act was and is essentially a legal one, to be determined in the last resort by the courts. It is not simply a matter for the local planning authority, and it means that any view expressed

---

[36] (1975) 31 P & CR 154.
[37] At para 140.
[38] [2002] EWCA Civ 983, [2003] JPL 1030.
[39] At para 51.
[40] At para 52.
[41] At para 58.

on it by the local planning authority is in a very different category from the normal case of a legitimate expectation that a public body will exercise its powers in a particular way'.

29.24 The public law based approach was exemplified by Richards J in *Coghurst Wood Leisure Ltd v Secretary of State*[42] when he commented:

'It is obvious that the judgments in *Powergen* and *Reprotech* mark an important change in direction in this area of planning law. Looked at together, they emphasise not just the need to apply public law concepts rather than private law concepts but also the importance attached in public law to a statutory body's powers and duties in the wider public interest. It cannot be assumed that exceptions previously found to exist will still apply. Substantial reappraisal is required'.

29.25 An attempt to pull the cases together was undertaken in *R (on the application of Hammerton) v London Underground Ltd*[43]. Approval for the construction of the East London Line Northern Extension (ELLX) had been given by a Transport and Works Order and a deemed planning permission. The deemed permission had to be implemented by February 2002. London Underground carried out certain limited works in the face of judicial reviews by commercial occupiers of Bishopsgate Goods Yard which was to be largely demolished for the scheme. Part of the Goods Yard (the 1838 Braithwaite Viaduct) was listed in March 2002. The court held that London Underground's works were in breach of a negative condition which required the laying out of exchange land before works commenced. After reviewing these authorities Ouseley J stated at paras 127, 128 that:

'the principle discernable in Woolf LJ's judgment [in *Whitley v Secretary of Wales* (1992) 3 PLR 72] that it would be unlawful in accordance with public law principles to take enforcement action to prevent development proceeding, the development albeit in breach of planning control is nevertheless effective to commence development .... I also consider the decisions in *Agecrest* and *Flintshire* can be seen as fitting that analysis. Certainly Keene J in *Leisure Great Britain* saw both decisions as "being in accord with normal legal principles" ... Whether *Agecrest* is analysed as legitimate expectation or as an abuse of power in the light of what in 1967 would be seen as permissible managerial discretion in public and planning law, it would be harsh indeed if its facts provided no public law remedy against a planning authority taking enforcement proceedings. *Flintshire* can also be similarly analysed. Once the jurisprudential basis for the Whitley case is clear, other cases can be seen as further illustrations of the application of the principle rather than further ad hoc exceptions to the statutory code'.

The court considered that reasonableness of enforcement action depended upon whether the relevant parts of the Goods Yard could be demolished without a further consent[44].

29.26 In the subsequent case on the East London Line Extension, *R (on the application of Prokopp) v London Underground Ltd,* Collins J considered that *Hammerton* had expressed the principle too widely, certainly where the unlawfulness

---

[42] [2002] EWHC 1091 (Admin), [2003] JPL 206 at para 56.
[43] [2002] EWHC 2307 (Admin), [2003] JPL 984.
[44] This hinged in that case on whether the Goods Yard was a single building or several structures as the Town and Country Planning (Demolition – Description of Building) Direction 1995 permitted demolition of entire buildings not parts of buildings. Following the subsequent *R (on the application of SAVE Britain's Heritage) v Secretary of State for Communities and Local Government* [2011] EWCA Civ 334, [2011] JPL 1016 all of the demolition would have required planning permission in any event.

29.27 *Implementation of planning permission*

of a decision to enforce is said to flow from a breach of a legitimate expectation[45]. However Buxton LJ in the Court of Appeal in *Prokopp* agreed with the *Hammerton* analysis that the irrationality of enforcement action was an exception to the *Whitley* principle[46].

29.27 In *Norris v First Secretary of State* the Court of Appeal rejected a challenge to the Secretary of State's decision to bring into operation a compulsory purchase order. The court held that whether a planning permission was still in effect was irrelevant to this decision, so its comments on the implementation of the planning permission were expressly *obiter*[47]. Whilst no mention was made of *Hart Aggregates* Laws LJ followed *Hammerton* and *Prokopp* and formulated the principle as[48]:

> 'unlawful operations cannot amount to the commencement of development under a planning permission. ... The reason why operations in breach of condition will not ordinarily suffice to commence development is that a developer (like anyone else) should not be advantaged by his own unlawful act. But a breach of condition will not be treated as unlawful for this purpose if it would be irrational, or otherwise legally objectionable, to enforce against it. As it seems to me the true principle, therefore, is that *unlawful* operations cannot amount to the commencement of development'. (original emphasis)

29.28 *Whitley* did not draw any distinction between conditions which said 'no development shall take place' and 'prior to the commencement of development'. In *Tesco Stores v North Norfolk District Council*[49] a condition required the submission and approval of drainage details 'prior to the commencement of development'. The Court of Appeal held that there had been a failure to comply with the condition as drainage details had not been submitted and consequently the permission was not implemented in accordance with *Whitley*.

29.29 In *R (on the application of Hart Aggregates) v Hartlepool Borough Council*[50] Sullivan J suggested that the *Whitley* principle might apply simply to 'no development' conditions rather than 'prior to commencement' conditions. In the former case the carrying out of development was prohibited and the latter formulation simply provided a timetable for the submission of particular details. Those comments were followed by the High Court in *Bedford Borough Council v Secretary of State for Communities and Local Government*[51]. However *Tesco Stores v North Norfolk* is binding and was not referred to in either the *Hart* or *Bedford* judgments. *Greyfort* rejected the *Hart Aggregates* suggestion and held that the formulations were equivalent and required compliance before works were usually lawfully commenced[52].

29.30 There was suggestion in *Hart Aggregates* that the importance of the breach would affect whether the failure meant that implementation had not taken place. The Council had referred to 'conditions precedent (ie conditions that go to the heart

---

[45] [2003] EWHC 960 (Admin) at para 9.
[46] *R (on the application of Prokopp) v London Underground Ltd* [2003] EWCA Civ 961, [2004] JPL 44 at paras 81–85.
[47] *Norris* at para 29.
[48] At para 40.
[49] (1999) 78 P & CR 359.
[50] [2005] EWHC 840 (Admin), [2005] JPL 1602.
[51] [2008] EWHC 2304 (Admin), [2009] JPL 604 at paras 35 and 44 per Judge Waksman QC.
[52] *Greyfort Properties Ltd v Secretary of State for Communities and Local Government* [2011] EWCA Civ 908, [2012] JPL 40 at paras 29–34 per Richards LJ.

of the permission and without whose discharge there could not be a lawful start on site)'[53] although these appeared to be all conditions precedent. Argument hinged on condition 10 which required the approval of the details of restoration levels. Sullivan J held[54]:

'Condition 10 is a "condition precedent" in the sense that it requires something to be done before extraction is commenced, but it is not a "condition precedent" in the sense that it goes to the heart of the planning permission, so that failure to comply with it will mean that the entire development, even if completed and in existence for many years, or in the case of a minerals extraction having continued for 30 years, must be regarded as unlawful'.

29.31 Much of Sullivan J's analysis had rested on the 'no development/prior to commencement' distinction which was subsequently rejected in *Greyfort*[55] but he continued:

'66 ... what happens if there is not an outline but a detailed planning permission and if all the conditions of that detailed planning permission are complied with, save for one, which requires approval of some particular aspect of the development before any development commences? Is the resulting unlawfulness confined to that particular aspect of the development, or does it render the entire development unlawful?

67 For the reasons set out above, I believe that the statutory purpose is better served by drawing a distinction between those cases where there is only a permission in principle because no details whatsoever have been submitted, and those cases where the failure has been limited to a failure to obtain approval for one particular aspect of the development. In the former case, common sense suggests that the planning permission has not been implemented at all. In the latter case, common sense suggests that the planning permission has been implemented, but there has been a breach of condition which can be enforced against. I appreciate that these are two opposite ends of a spectrum. Each case will have to be considered upon its own particular facts, and the outcome may well depend upon the number and the significance of the conditions that have not been complied with. Provided that the Court applies *Wednesbury* principles when considering these issues, there is no reason why it should usurp the responsibilities of the local planning authority'.

So he suggested that different outcomes would follow for different conditions, but in a public law review context although it was unclear whether this was an application of the irrationality exception to *Whitley* or merely the Court's review of the public authority decision whether the permission had been implemented. Had the *Whitley* principle applied to the condition then it would have been irrational to enforce in any event as quarrying had been allowed to take place for 34 years and the restoration scheme had been superseded by later consents[56].

29.32 *Bedford Borough Council v Secretary of State for Communities and Local Government*[57] upheld an Inspector's view that details of landscaping and boundary treatment did not go to the heart of the permission and so the failure to obtain those approvals did not prevent implementation. Whilst permission to appeal had been granted in *Greyfort Properties Ltd v Secretary of State for Communities and Local Government* by Sullivan LJ specifically to allow consideration of whether his

---

[53] *Hart Aggregates* at para 16.
[54] Para 61.
[55] See *Hart Aggregates* at paras 50–52, 58–60.
[56] At para 90.
[57] [2008] EWHC 2304 (Admin), [2009] JPL 604.

29.33 *Implementation of planning permission*

judgment in *Hart Aggregates* had been correct, the parties proceeded on the basis that *Hart Aggregates* was correctly decided, and that the substance of Sullivan J's observations on the *Whitley* principle was correct[58]. Consequently the Court of Appeal proceeded on that basis for the purposes of the appeal[59]. It held that a condition requiring the prior approval of levels was sufficiently important that the permission was not implemented[60].

29.33 The implications of the *Hart Aggregates* approach, as altered by *Greyfort* are:

(i) as a general proposition, development must be carried out in accordance with the planning permission read with its conditions to implement the permission;

(ii) whether a breach of a condition which relates to actions or approvals before the start of development is capable of preventing implementation depends upon what in broad terms might be called the importance of the condition;

(iii) whether such a condition explicitly prohibits development prior to the act or approval or just requires the act or approval to take place prior to the commencement of development does not matter;

(iv) if the condition is sufficiently important then the permission will be implemented if it would be irrational to take enforcement action when that issue arises, that is, it falls within the *Whitley* exceptions as later explained.

29.34 In *Dunsford Park Ltd v Secretary of State for Communities and Local Government*[61] a developer had sought to argue that its failure to comply with vehicle movement management and monitoring conditions meant that two permissions had not been implemented. The inspector's view that these conditions did not go to the heart of the permission was said to be within a 'fact and degree' decision with a margin of judgment[62]. Conversely in *Green v Secretary of State for Communities and Local Government* a failure to have external materials approved, on a building in the countryside, rendered implementation unlawful[63]. *Greyfort* was also followed in rejecting the implementation of planning permission because of a failure to discharge landscape conditions in *Glenholme Developments Ltd v Welsh Ministers*[64].

29.35 In implementation situations conditions need to be interpreted with care. A condition which prohibits the commencement of development before the approval of reserved matters may require details of all of the site to be submitted and approved[65]. There is no general principle allowing development to proceed under partial reserved matters unless provided for by a condition.

---

[58] *Greyfort* at para 18 per Richards LJ.
[59] At para 19.
[60] At paras 40–44.
[61] [2013] EWHC 1878 (Admin), [2013] JPL 1568.
[62] Per Foskett J at para 73. In *Silver v Secretary of State for Communities and Local Government* [2014] EWHC 2729 (Admin), [2015] JPL 154 Supperstone J reviewed the inspector's decision on whether a condition went to the heart of a permission on irrationality grounds, see paras 47–53.
[63] [2013] EWHC 3980 (Admin) at paras 37–44 per Cranston J.
[64] [2013] EWHC 3679 (Admin).
[65] *R v Leicester City Council, ex p Powergen Ltd* [2000] JPL 629 at 635 per Dyson J; upheld by the Court of Appeal [2000] JPL 1037 at paras 22, 34 per Schiemann LJ.

No need for an intention to implement

29.36 As a general proposition, whether a planning permission has been implemented is to be judged objectively from the facts on the ground and the compliance of what has been done with the permission and its conditions. Whether the developer intended to build out the permission or was simply seeking to keep the permission alive does not matter. There may still be room for considering intention where implementation may be of one of several planning permissions or works were carried out for a different reason: these issues are considered further below.

29.37 Whether there was an intention to build out the permission or just to keep the permission alive, and whether the latter intention was sufficient, was referred to as 'colourability'. It was said in some cases that implementation was 'colourable' and so ineffective if there was insufficient intention. This issue first arose in *Spackman v Secretary of State for the Environment* where it was simply observed that the construction of trenches and a soakaway were not a 'colourable operation'[66]. In *Malvern Hills District Council v Secretary of State for the Environment* Watkins LJ noted that the developer had manifested an intention to begin development within the permitted time and proceed until completion[67]. Potential importance to the issue, as distinct from it merely being an aside, arose when Eveleigh LJ said in respect of the Town and Country Planning Act 1971, s 43 which is the predecessor to s 56[68]:

> 'Section 43 seeks some earnest of intention to develop. The specified operations are not necessarily very extensive. Very little need be done to satisfy the section. That which is done, however, must genuinely be done for the purpose of carrying out the development. Section 43 is a benevolent section that aims at avoiding hardship to a developer who is genuinely undertaking the development'[69].

29.38 These observations were followed in *Thayer v Secretary of State for the Environment*[70] *and R v Inland Revenue Commissioners, ex p Harrow London Borough Council*[71]. A spate of cases arose of out works carried out shortly before 6 April 1967 to avoid betterment levy being applied to development projects with existing planning permissions[72]. This was at a time when it was also being contemplated that time limits for the implementation of planning permissions would be introduced[73]. In *Agecrest Ltd v Gwynedd County Council* Collins J said[74]:

> 'There must be an intention to develop when the operation is carried out, but it need not be immediate. The longer the time that elapses the less chance there will be that a court will accept that there was an intention to develop at the material time or that what was done was genuinely done for the purpose of carrying out the development'.

---

[66] [1977] 1 All ER 257 at 260 per Willis J.
[67] (1982) 46 P & CR 58 at 72.
[68] At 70.
[69] *Malvern Hills* at 70.
[70] [1992] JPL 264.
[71] [1988] STC 246.
[72] Under the Land Commission Act 1967.
[73] The time limits were subsequently included in the Town and Country Planning Act 1968. They applied to current as well as future planning permissions, giving a five year period for existing permissions to be implemented.
[74] [1998] JPL 325 at 333.

29.39 *Implementation of planning permission*

29.39 Buxton J in *R v Arfon Borough Council, ex p Walton Commercial Group Ltd* went further, saying that works which were intended only to preserve the planning permission would not suffice[75]:

> 'It was artificial to say that development was commenced by an act done by a person who, after that act, intended himself to do nothing further. It was not enough to say, as was argued before me, that the intent was or may have been to sell the land as "development land" ... where the purpose for which the work was done was simply to preserve a permission, or (as here) to seek to fix the value of land for the statutory purposes, rather than to commence the actual development, then that act could not count as "beginning development"'.

The *Arfon* dicta were doubted in *Tesco Stores Ltd v North Norfolk District Council* by Judge Langan QC[76] and by Judge Rich QC in *South Gloucestershire Council v Secretary of State for the Environment*[77].

29.40 However the tide first turned decisively against the colourability doctrine north of the border in *East Dunbartonshire Council v Secretary of State for Scotland*. An Extra Division of the Court of Session held[78]:

> 'There is authority that the work which is alleged to constitute specified operations must be work done pursuant to the planning permission in question (see, eg *R v Secretary of State for the Environment, ex p Percy Bilton Industrial Properties Ltd*, per Lord Widgery CJ at *(1975) 31 P & CR, pp 158–159* ; *Etheridge v Secretary of State for the Environment*, per Woolf J at *(1984) 48 P & CR, pp 40–41*). The work done must not merely be *some* development but must be part of the development covered by the planning permission in question (*Campbell v Argyll and Bute District Council*). ... nothing ... supports the argument that there is some requirement that the specified operations there defined must be undertaken with some particular intention. ... the statute prescribes time limits and also prescribes the circumstances in which planning permissions are to continue in force beyond those time limits, and does so without any requirement as to intention. It seems to us therefore that to add a requirement as to intention would clearly go beyond what the statute prescribes'.

29.41 The court continued[79]:

> 'It is, no doubt, natural to feel that it would be unsatisfactory if the person entitled to the benefit of a planning permission could keep it in being by carrying out some work which could be regarded as a mere token or pretence. It seems to us however that the solution to that problem, if it is a problem, is more likely to be found by applying an objective approach and considering first, whether what has been done has been done in accordance with the relevant planning permission and, secondly, whether it is material, in the sense of not being de minimis'.

29.42 The English High Court in *Riordan Communications Ltd v South Buckinghamshire District Council*[80] then 'entirely agreed' with *East Dunbartonshire*. Finally the *East Dunbartonshire* principle was endorsed by the Court of Appeal in *Staffordshire County Council v Riley*[81].

---

[75] [1997] JPL 237 at 251.
[76] [1998] PLCR 183 at 208.
[77] [1999] JPL B99.
[78] 1999 SLT 1088 at 1092. Opinion of the court delivered by Lord Coulsfield.
[79] At 1094.
[80] [2000] JPL 594 at 603 per David Vaughan QC.
[81] [2001] EWCA Civ 257, [2002] PLCR 5 at para 28 per Pill LJ.

Duty to give and display notice of the commencement of development in Wales

29.43 The Planning (Wales) Act 2015 proposes to introduce a duty to give notice to the local planning authority prior to the commencement of development under particular planning permissions and to display a copy of the permission at or near the site when the development is being carried out[82]. These requirements will be a condition deemed to be on the planning permission[83]. A development order will identify the types of planning permission to which this will apply[84].

Since the requirement to give notice to the local planning authority before beginning development will be a condition, the issue will arise whether a failure to give notice means that development has not commenced.

Planning obligations

29.44 Planning obligations may provide for various things to be done or approved prior to the commencement of development. A contravention of such a requirement will be a breach of the obligation (and capable of being enforced against as such) but will not affect the implementation of the planning permission. The permission and obligation are separate documents.

29.45 An obligation may contain a definition of the commencement of development to identify when liabilities will start to arise under it. For example, groundworks for archaeology or contamination or the demolition of buildings might be excluded from commencement under the obligation. This will not affect whether development has begun under the planning permission.

RETROSPECTIVE PERMISSIONS

29.46 A retrospective permission authorises development which has already been carried out and is not subject to time limits on implementation by reason of the Town and Country Planning Act 1990, s 91[85]. A permission might though encompass retrospective and prospective elements. It could be conditioned to impose a time limit on the commencement of the prospective element even if the developed part was authorised in any event.

CARRYING OUT CONFLICTING PLANNING PERMISSIONS

29.47 It is possible for there to be more than one planning permission authorising development on a particular piece of land but it is not possible to develop under

---

[82] Town and Country Planning Act 1990, s 71ZB, prospectively inserted by the Planning (Wales) Act 2015, s 34. No commencement order has yet been made. The notices must be in a form specified by a development order and, where appropriate, displayed as required by it: prospective Town and Country Planning Act 1990, s 71ZB(3).
[83] Town and Country Planning Act 1990, s 71ZB(5), prospectively inserted by the Planning (Wales) Act 2015, s 34.
[84] Town and Country Planning Act 1990, s 71ZB(6), prospectively inserted by the Planning (Wales) Act 2015, s 34.
[85] It is not possible to have a retrospective outline planning permission as the full details of the development are physically in place.

29.48 *Implementation of planning permission*

inconsistent planning permissions[86]. To do so could create a different form of development from that envisaged, even potentially doubling the built volume. For example it would not be possible to build out the site under the totality of each of an original permission and a subsequent s 73 permission. Conflicts between different permissions might prevent one scheme from being implemented at all or mean that one or both could only be carried out in part.

29.48 The classic case, which has become the shorthand description for the issue, is *Pilkington v Secretary of State for the Environment*[87]. *Pilkington* was a factually straightforward example where two planning permissions had been granted: the first for a bungalow in the northernmost part of the site and the remainder used as a smallholding; the second had a bungalow in the middle of the site, with the remainder being within its curtilage. The second permission was subject to a condition that the bungalow would be the only dwelling erected on the site. The bungalow in the second permission was constructed, as was a further bungalow under a third planning permission. Mr Pilkington then began to construct the bungalow from the first permission and the local planning authority served an enforcement notice. The Divisional Court said that inconsistent permissions could be sought and granted and such applications should be dealt with on their own merits unless one application deliberately and expressly refers to or incorporates another[88]. The present question was whether the development contemplated in the first permission could be carried out consistently with that approved by the implemented second permission. Lord Widgery CJ said[89]:

> 'One looks first of all to see the full scope of that which has been done or can be done pursuant to the permission which has been implemented. One then looks at the development which was permitted in the second permission, now sought to be implemented, and one asks oneself whether it is possible to carry out the development proposed in that second permission, having regard to that which was done or authorised to be done under the permission which has been implemented'.

He emphasised that 'I base my decision on the physical impossibility of carrying out that which was authorised' under the first permission and not on the condition in the second permission[90].

29.49 *Pilkington* was approved by the Court of Appeal in a compensation case, *Hoveringham Gravels Ltd v Chiltern District Council*[91], and then in a planning decision, *Durham County Council v Secretary of State for the Environment* where Neill LJ held[92]:

> 'The question for consideration in cases involving a permission for operational development is: is it possible to carry out the development covered by the permission on

---

[86] The need to choose between permissions at the point at which they become inconsistent has been emphasised in the s 73 cases: *Pye v Secretary of State for the Environment* [1999] PLCR 28 at 44 per Sullivan J and *R v Leicester City Council ex p Powergen UK plc* [2000] JPL 1037 at para 27 per Schiemann LJ, applied to inconsistency in *R (on the application of Robert Hitchins Ltd) v Worcestershire County Council* [2014] EWHC 3809 (Admin) at para 48 per Hickinbottom J.
[87] [1973] 1 WLR 1527.
[88] At 1531 per Lord Widgery CJ.
[89] At 1532.
[90] At 1532–1533. The court followed dicta of Erskine Simes QC in the Lands Tribunal in *Ellis v Worcestershire County Council* (1961) 12 P&CR 178 at 183.
[91] (1978) 35 P & CR 295.
[92] (1989) 60 P & CR 507 at 513.

which it is now sought to rely having regard to that which has been done or authorised to be done under the permission which has already been implemented'.

29.50 *Staffordshire County Council v NGR Land Developments Ltd*[93] further endorsed the *Pilkington* approach. Jonathan Parker LJ held:

'55 In *Pilkington* Lord Widgery CJ made it abundantly clear, as I read his judgment, that in considering whether an earlier permission was still valid, it was irrelevant that the carrying out of the permitted development might breach a condition attached to a later permission; rather, the correct test was whether it was physically possible to carry out that development in accordance with the terms of the earlier permission. This is a theme which runs through the entirety of Lord Widgery CJ's exposition on page 1532 of *Pilkington* (quoted earlier), and at the foot of that page Lord Widgery CJ says in terms that his conclusions:

"… do not in any way depend on the fact that the building on site A may have been a breach of the condition in number 756." [Ie the later permission].

56 The ratio of the decision in *Pilkington*, in my judgment, is that development pursuant to the earlier permission could not be carried out in accordance with its terms since the earlier permission contemplated that the remainder of the site would consist of a smallholding, whereas development carried out in implementation of the later permission – ie the building of a house on the centre of the site – had (to use Lord Scarman's word in *Pioneer* at page 145A) "destroyed" the smallholding. I respectfully agree with the observations of Buxton J in *Arfon* on the concept of physical impossibility in the context of *Pilkington*. It was physically possible to build the bungalow on site A, since that part of the site remained vacant. But it was not possible to carry out the physical development permitted by the earlier permission in a manner which accorded with the terms of that permission.

57 I also agree with the conclusion and reasoning of Mr Spence QC in *Prestige*. In particular, I agree with him that in using the expression "incapable of implementation" in *Pioneer* (see ibid. page 145A and C) Lord Scarman was doing no more than express the doctrine established in *Pilkington* in (as Mr Spence put it at page 133E) "virtually the same words". As Mr Spence QC rightly said, the true doctrine in *Pilkington* is that where there are inconsistent planning permissions the question to be addressed is, to use the words of Lord Scarman at page 145C:

"… whether development has been carried out which renders one or other of the planning permissions incapable of implementation."

58 And that in turn means seeing whether it is still possible to carry out the development authorised by the relevant permission in accordance with the terms of that permission, and not by reference to conditions attached to another permission'.

29.51 Consequently it was accepted that planning permissions may overlap on a piece of land without one permission displacing the other. There is no principle that the more recent permission prevails. The issue may be whether the carrying out of development under one permission renders the other incapable of being carried out[94]. In *Staffordshire County Council* planning permissions for the extraction of clay and coal overlapped. Extraction had begun under the earlier clay permission, then planning permission for coal was granted, the coal extracted and restoration carried out in accordance with the coal permission. Under examination was whether clay extraction could be continued, destroying the restoration carried out under the coal permission.

---

[93] [2003] JPL 56.
[94] See *Pilkington v Secretary of State for the Environment* [1973] 1 WLR 1527.

29.52 *Implementation of planning permission*

29.52 Applying the *Pilkington* approach in practice is often not straightforward[95]. In *Lobb v Secretary of State for the Environment*[96] outline planning permission had been granted for six houses. A subsequent outline planning permission was granted, and details approved, for the construction of one house on 20% of the overall site. Details had been approved for, at most, only one of the houses under the original planning permission. Woolf J considered that the house approved under the second permission could not be deducted from the six allowed under the first provision and it would be inconsistent, in *Pilkington* terms, to construct seven houses under the two consents.

29.53 *F Lucas & Sons Ltd v Dorking and Horley Rural District Council*[97] preceded the decision in *Pilkington*. Planning permission had been granted for the construction of 28 houses around a new cul-de-sac off Hogspudding Lane, Newdigate, there being 14 houses on each side. A subsequent planning permission for the same total site authorised the construction of 6 houses fronting onto Hogspudding Lane. Two of those houses were built on one side. The court granted a declaration that 14 houses could be built under the original permission on the other side. Winn J considered that the original permission authorised the construction of any one of the 28 houses and they did not all need to be built out.

29.54 In the 2010 decision of *Singh v Secretary of State for Communities and Local Government*[98], planning permission had been granted for an extension (comprising a family room and double garage) to a house and the construction of a new driveway. Planning permission was then granted for a new house on land which included part of the proposed driveway. Hickinbottom J emphasised that sometimes the question was not whether one permission could be implemented following the carrying out of another but whether that permission could be completed. There the earlier permission could not be separated into independent parts, unlike in *Lucas*, and so none of the extension permission could be lawfully carried out[99].

29.55 If development commences under a planning permission for a particular scheme and then a second planning permission is granted for the same scheme but subject to different conditions or planning obligation, then the developer is able to change from the first to the second permission part way through the development[100].

29.56 Ultimately the outcomes are pragmatic responses to the circumstances of the individual cases. Two permissions should be made to fit together if that was envisaged but unplanned doubling up of development is prohibited.

---

[95] Perhaps the decision closest to *Pilkington* on the facts is *Wealden District Council v Taylor* [1992] 1 PLR 42 where two planning permissions proposed a replacement dwelling on different parts of the site and could not both be carried out.
[96] [1984] JPL 336.
[97] (1964) 17 P & CR 111.
[98] [2010] EWHC 1621 (Admin).
[99] See paras 18–25 in particular.
[100] *R (on the application of Robert Hitchins Ltd) v Worcestershire County Council* [2015] EWCA Civ 1060.

Town and Country Planning Act 1990

PART III CONTROL OVER DEVELOPMENT

Meaning of development

55 Meaning of 'development' and 'new development'

(1) Subject to the following provisions of this section, in this Act, except where the context otherwise requires, 'development,' means the carrying out of building, engineering, mining or other operations in, on, over or under land, or the making of any material change in the use of any buildings or other land.

[(1A) For the purposes of this Act 'building operations' includes—
   (a) demolition of buildings;
   (b) rebuilding;
   (c) structural alterations of or additions to buildings; and
   (d) other operations normally undertaken by a person carrying on business as a builder.]

(2) The following operations or uses of land shall not be taken for the purposes of this Act to involve development of the land—
   (a) the carrying out for the maintenance, improvement or other alteration of any building of works which—
      (i) affect only the interior of the building, or
      (ii) do not materially affect the external appearance of the building,

      and are not works for making good war damage or works begun after 5th December 1968 for the alteration of a building by providing additional space in it underground;
   (b) the carrying out on land within the boundaries of a road by a ... highway authority of any works required for the maintenance or improvement of the road [but, in the case of any such works which are not exclusively for the maintenance of the road, not including any works which may have significant adverse effects on the environment];
   (c) the carrying out by a local authority or statutory undertakers of any works for the purpose of inspecting, repairing or renewing any sewers, mains, pipes, cables or other apparatus, including the breaking open of any street or other land for that purpose;
   (d) the use of any buildings or other land within the curtilage of a dwellinghouse for any purpose incidental to the enjoyment of the dwellinghouse as such;
   (e) the use of any land for the purposes of agriculture or forestry (including afforestation) and the use for any of those purposes of any building occupied together with land so used;
   (f) in the case of buildings or other land which are used for a purpose of any class specified in an order made by the Secretary of State under this

section, the use of the buildings or other land or, subject to the provisions of the order, of any part of the buildings or the other land, for any other purpose of the same class;

[(g) the demolition of any description of building specified in a direction given by the Secretary of State to local planning authorities generally or to a particular local planning authority.]

[(2A) The Secretary of State may in a development order specify any circumstances or description of circumstances in which subsection (2) does not apply to operations mentioned in paragraph (a) of that subsection which have the effect of increasing the gross floor space of the building by such amount or percentage amount as is so specified.

(2B) The development order may make different provision for different purposes.]

(3) For the avoidance of doubt it is hereby declared that for the purposes of this section—

(a) the use as two or more separate dwellinghouses of any building previously used as a single dwellinghouse involves a material change in the use of the building and of each part of it which is so used;

(b) the deposit of refuse or waste materials on land involves a material change in its use, notwithstanding that the land is comprised in a site already used for that purpose, if—

(i) the superficial area of the deposit is extended, or

(ii) the height of the deposit is extended and exceeds the level of the land adjoining the site.

(4) For the purposes of this Act mining operations include—

(a) the removal of material of any description—

(i) from a mineral-working deposit;

(ii) from a deposit of pulverised fuel ash or other furnace ash or clinker; or

(iii) from a deposit of iron, steel or other metallic slags; and

(b) the extraction of minerals from a disused railway embankment.

[(4A) Where the placing or assembly of any tank in any part of any inland waters for the purpose of fish farming there would not, apart from this subsection, involve development of the land below, this Act shall have effect as if the tank resulted from carrying out engineering operations over that land; and in this subsection—

'fish farming' means the breeding, rearing or keeping of fish or shellfish (which includes any kind of crustacean and mollusc);

'inland waters' means waters which do not form part of the sea or of any creek, bay or estuary or of any river as far as the tide flows; and

'tank' includes any cage and any other structure for use in fish farming.]

(5) Without prejudice to any regulations made under the provisions of this Act relating to the control of advertisements, the use for the display of advertisements of any external part of a building which is not normally used for that purpose shall be treated for the purposes of this section as involving a material change in the use of that part of the building.

(6) ....

Part III Control over Development

Amendment

Sub-s (1A): inserted by the Planning and Compensation Act 1991, s 13(1).

Sub-s (2): in para (b) word omitted repealed by the Planning and Compulsory Purchase Act 2004, ss 118(1), 120, Sch 6, paras 1, 2, Sch 9. Date in force: 7 June 2006: see SI 2006/1281, art 2(e), (f)(i)).

Sub-s (2): in para (b) words from 'but, in' to 'the environment' in square brackets inserted by SI 1999/293, reg 35(1) (14 March 1999).

Sub-s (2): para (g) inserted by the Planning and Compensation Act 1991, s 13(2).

Sub-ss (2A), (2B): inserted by the Planning and Compulsory Purchase Act 2004, s 49(1); for effect see s 49(2)–(4) thereof. Date in force (for the purpose of making, or making provision by means of, subordinate legislation): 6 August 2004: see SI 2004/2097, art 2. Date in force (in relation to England for remaining purposes): 10 May 2006: see SI 2006/1061, art 2(b). Date in force (in relation to Wales for remaining purposes): 22 June 2015: see SI 2015/340, art 2(a).

Sub-s (4A): inserted by the Planning and Compensation Act 1991, s 14.

Sub-s (6): repealed by the Planning and Compensation Act 1991, ss 31, 84, Sch 6, para 9, Sch 19, Parts I, II.

56 Time when development begun

(1) Subject to the following provisions of this section, for the purposes of this Act development of land shall be taken to be initiated—

   (a) if the development consists of the carrying out of operations, at the time when those operations are begun;

   (b) if the development consists of a change in use, at the time when the new use is instituted;

   (c) if the development consists both of the carrying out of operations and of a change in use, at the earlier of the times mentioned in paragraphs (a) and (b).

(2) For the purposes of the provisions of this Part mentioned in subsection (3) development shall be taken to be begun on the earliest date on which any material operation comprised in the development begins to be carried out.

(3) The provisions referred to in subsection (2) are sections [61L(5) and (7),] 85(2), 86(6), 87(4), [89], 91, 92 [, 94 and 108(3E)(c)(i)].

(4) In subsection (2) 'material operation' means—

   (a) any work of construction in the course of the erection of a building;

   [(aa) any work of demolition of a building;]

   (b) the digging of a trench which is to contain the foundations, or part of the foundations, of a building;

   (c) the laying of any underground main or pipe to the foundations, or part of the foundations, of a building or to any such trench as is mentioned in paragraph (b);

   (d) any operation in the course of laying out or constructing a road or part of a road;

   (e) any change in the use of any land which constitutes material development.

(5) In subsection (4)(e) 'material development' means any development other than—

   (a) development for which planning permission is granted by a general development order [*or a local development order*] [, a local development order or a Mayoral development order] for the time being in force and

Town and Country Planning Act 1990

which is carried out so as to comply with any condition or limitation subject to which planning permission is so granted;

[(b) development of a class specified in paragraph 1 or 2 of Schedule 3;] and

(c) development of any class prescribed for the purposes of this subsection.

(6) In subsection (5) 'general development order' means a development order (within the meaning of section 59) made as a general order applicable (subject to such exceptions as may be specified in it) to all land in England and Wales.

Amendment

Sub-s (3): words '61L(5) and (7),' in square brackets inserted by the Localism Act 2011, s 121, Sch 12, paras 1, 2(a). Date in force (in so far as it confers power on the Secretary of State to make regulations or publish documents setting standards): 15 November 2011: see the Localism Act 2011, s 240(5)(j). Date in force (for certain purposes): 15 January 2012: see SI 2012/57, art 4(1)(h). Date in force (for certain purposes): 6 April 2012: see SI 2012/628, art 8(a). Date in force (for certain purposes): 3 August 2012: see SI 2012/2029, arts 2, 3(a); for transitional provisions and savings see art 5 thereof. Date in force (for remaining purposes): 6 April 2013: see SI 2013/797, arts 1(2), 2.

Sub-s (3): reference to '89' in square brackets inserted by the Planning and Compensation Act 1991, s 32, Sch 7, para 10(1).

Sub-s (3): words ', 94 and 108(3E)(c)(i)' in square brackets substituted by the Localism Act 2011, s 121, Sch 12, paras 1, 2(b). Date in force (in so far as it confers power on the Secretary of State to make regulations or publish documents setting standards): 15 November 2011: see the Localism Act 2011, s 240(5)(j). Date in force (for certain purposes): 15 January 2012: see SI 2012/57, art 4(1)(h). Date in force (for certain purposes): 6 April 2012: see SI 2012/628, art 8(a). Date in force (for certain purposes): 3 August 2012: see SI 2012/2029, arts 2, 3(a); for transitional provisions and savings see art 5 thereof. Date in force (for remaining purposes): 6 April 2013: see SI 2013/797, arts 1(2), 2.

Sub-s (4): para (aa) inserted by the Planning and Compensation Act 1991, s 32, Sch 7, para 10(2).

Sub-s (5): in para (a) words 'or a local development order' in square brackets inserted by the Planning and Compulsory Purchase Act 2004, s 40(2)(a). Date in force (for the purpose of making, or making provision by means of, subordinate legislation): 6 August 2004: see SI 2004/2097, art 2. Date in force (in relation to England for remaining purposes): 10 May 2006: see SI 2006/1061, art 2(a). Date in force (in relation to Wales for remaining purposes): 30 April 2012: see SI 2012/1100, art 2.

Sub-s (5): in para (a) words 'or a local development order' in italics repealed and subsequent words in square brackets substituted by the Infrastructure Act 2015, s 30(1), Sch 4, Pt 2, paras 2, 3. Date in force (for certain purposes): 12 February 2015: see the Infrastructure Act 2015, s 57(5)(d)(i). Date in force (for remaining purposes): to be appointed: see the Infrastructure Act 2015, s 57(5)(d)(ii).

Sub-s (5): para (b) substituted by the Planning and Compensation Act 1991, s 31, Sch 6, para 10.

Requirement for planning permission

57 Planning permission required for development

(1) Subject to the following provisions of this section, planning permission is required for the carrying out of any development of land.

[(1A) Subsection (1) is subject to section 33(1) of the Planning Act 2008 (exclusion of requirement for planning permission etc for development for which development consent required).]

(2) Where planning permission to develop land has been granted for a limited period, planning permission is not required for the resumption, at the end of that period, of its use for the purpose for which it was normally used before the permission was granted.

(3) Where by a development order[, a local development order[, a Mayoral development order] or a neighbourhood development order] planning permission to develop land has been granted subject to limitations, planning permission is not required for the use of that land which (apart from its use in accordance with that permission) is its normal use.

(4) Where an enforcement notice has been issued in respect of any development of land, planning permission is not required for its use for the purpose for which (in accordance with the provisions of this Part of this Act) it could lawfully have been used if that development had not been carried out.

(5) In determining for the purposes of subsections (2) and (3) what is or was the normal use of land, no account shall be taken of any use begun in contravention of this Part or of previous planning control.

(6) For the purposes of this section a use of land shall be taken to have been begun in contravention of previous planning control if it was begun in contravention of Part III of the 1947 Act, Part III of the 1962 Act or Part III of the 1971 Act.

(7) Subsection (1) has effect subject to Schedule 4 (which makes special provision about use of land on 1st July 1948).

Amendment

Sub-s (1A): inserted by the Planning Act 2008, s 36, Sch 2, paras 34, 35. Date in force: 1 March 2010: see SI 2010/101, art 2; for savings see art 6 thereof.

Sub-s (3): words ', a local development order or a neighbourhood development order' in square brackets substituted by the Localism Act 2011, s 121, Sch 12, paras 1, 3. Date in force (for certain purposes): 15 January 2012: see SI 2012/57, art 4(1)(h). Date in force (for certain purposes): 6 April 2012: see SI 2012/628, art 8(a). Date in force (for certain purposes): 3 August 2012: see SI 2012/2029, arts 2, 3(a); for transitional provisions and savings see art 5 thereof. Date in force (for remaining purposes): 6 April 2013: see SI 2013/797, arts 1(2), 2.

Sub-s (3): words ', a Mayoral development order' in square brackets inserted by the Infrastructure Act 2015, s 30(1), Sch 4, Pt 2, paras 2, 4. Date in force (for certain purposes): 12 February 2015: see the Infrastructure Act 2015, s 57(5)(d)(i). Date in force (for remaining purposes): to be appointed: see the Infrastructure Act 2015, s 57(5)(d)(ii).

58 Granting of planning permission: general

(1) Planning permission may be granted—

   (a) by a development order[, a local development order[, a Mayoral development order] or a neighbourhood development order];

   (b) by the local planning authority (or, in the cases provided in this Part, by the Secretary of State) on application to the authority [(or, in the cases provided in this Part, on application to the Secretary of State)] in accordance with a development order;

   (c) on the adoption or approval of a simplified planning zone scheme or alterations to such a scheme in accordance with section 82 or, as the case may be, section 86; or

Town and Country Planning Act 1990

(d) on the designation of an enterprise zone or the approval of a modified scheme under Schedule 32 to the Local Government, Planning and Land Act 1980 in accordance with section 88 of this Act.

(2) Planning permission may also be deemed to be granted under section 90 (development with government authorisation).

(3) This section is without prejudice to any other provisions of this Act providing for the granting of permission.

Amendment

Sub-s (1): in para (a) words ', a local development order or a neighbourhood development order' in square brackets substituted by the Localism Act 2011, s 121, Sch 12, paras 1, 4. Date in force (for certain purposes): 15 January 2012: see SI 2012/57, art 4(1)(h). Date in force (for certain purposes): 6 April 2012: see SI 2012/628, art 8(a). Date in force (for certain purposes): 3 August 2012: see SI 2012/2029, arts 2, 3(a); for transitional provisions and savings see art 5 thereof. Date in force (for remaining purposes): 6 April 2013: see SI 2013/797, arts 1(2), 2.

Sub-s (1): in para (a) words ', a Mayoral development order' in square brackets inserted by the Infrastructure Act 2015, s 30(1), Sch 4, Pt 2, paras 2, 5. Date in force (for certain purposes): 12 February 2015: see the Infrastructure Act 2015, s 57(5)(d)(i). Date in force (for remaining purposes): to be appointed: see the Infrastructure Act 2015, s 57(5)(d)(ii).

Sub-s (1): in para (b) words '(or, in the cases provided in this Part, on application to the Secretary of State)' in square brackets inserted by the Growth and Infrastructure Act 2013, s 1(2), Sch 1, paras 1, 3. Date in force (in relation to England for the purposes of making regulations or orders): 9 May 2013: see SI 2013/1124, art 2. Date in force (for remaining purposes): 1 October 2013: see SI 2013/2143, art 2(1)(a).

Development orders

59 Development orders: general

(1) The Secretary of State shall by order (in this Act referred to as a 'development order') provide for the granting of planning permission.

(2) A development order may either—

(a) itself grant planning permission for development specified in the order or for development of any class specified; or

(b) in respect of development for which planning permission is not granted by the order itself, provide for the granting of planning permission by the local planning authority (or, in the cases provided in the following provisions, by the Secretary of State) on application to the authority [(or, in the cases provided in the following provisions, on application to the Secretary of State)] in accordance with the provisions of the order.

(3) A development order may be made either—

(a) as a general order applicable, except so far as the order otherwise provides, to all land, or

(b) as a special order applicable only to such land or descriptions of land as may be specified in the order.

Amendment

Sub-s (2): in para (b) words '(or, in the cases provided in the following provisions, on application to the Secretary of State)' in square brackets inserted by the Growth and

Part III Control over Development

Infrastructure Act 2013, s 1(2), Sch 1, paras 1, 4. Date in force (in relation to England for the purposes of making regulations or orders): 9 May 2013: see SI 2013/1124, art 2. Date in force (for remaining purposes): 1 October 2013: see SI 2013/2143, art 2(1)(a).

60 Permission granted by development order

(1) Planning permission granted by a development order may be granted either unconditionally or subject to such conditions or limitations as may be specified in the order.

(2) Without prejudice to the generality of subsection (1), where planning permission is granted by a development order for the erection, extension or alteration of any buildings, the order may require the approval of the local planning authority to be obtained with respect to the design or external appearance of the buildings.

[(2A) Without prejudice to the generality of subsection (1), where planning permission is granted by a development order for development consisting of a change in the use of land in England, the order may require the approval of the local planning authority, or of the Secretary of State, to be obtained—

(a) for the use of the land for the new use;

(b) with respect to matters that relate to the new use and are specified in the order.

(2B) Without prejudice to the generality of subsection (1), a development order may include provision for ensuring—

(a) that, before a person in reliance on planning permission granted by the order carries out development of land in England that is a dwelling house or is within the curtilage of a dwelling house—

(i) a written description, and a plan, of the proposed development are given to the local planning authority,

(ii) notice of the proposed development, and of the period during which representations about it may be made to the local planning authority, is served by the local planning authority on the owner or occupier of any adjoining premises, and

(iii) that period has ended, and

(b) that, where within that period an owner or occupier of any adjoining premises objects to the proposed development, it may be carried out in reliance on the permission only if the local planning authority consider that it would not have an unacceptable impact on the amenity of adjoining premises.

(2C) In subsection (2B) 'adjoining premises' includes any land adjoining—

(a) the dwelling house concerned, or

(b) the boundary of its curtilage.]

(3) Without prejudice to the generality of subsection (1), where planning permission is granted by a development order for development of a specified class, the order may enable the Secretary of State or the local planning authority to direct that the permission shall not apply either—

(a) in relation to development in a particular area, or

(b) in relation to any particular development.

(4) Any provision of a development order by which permission is granted for the use of land for any purpose on a limited number of days in a period specified

Town and Country Planning Act 1990

in that provision shall (without prejudice to the generality of references in this Act to limitations) be taken to be a provision granting permission for the use of land for any purpose subject to the limitation that the land shall not be used for any one purpose in pursuance of that provision on more than that number of days in that period.

Amendment

Sub-ss (2A)–(2C): inserted by the Growth and Infrastructure Act 2013, s 4(1). Date in force: 25 April 2013: see the Growth and Infrastructure Act 2013, s 35(2).

61 Development orders: supplementary provisions

(1) A general development order may make different provision with respect to different descriptions of land.

(2) For the purpose of enabling development to be carried out in accordance with planning permission, or otherwise for the purpose of promoting proper development in accordance with the development plan, a development order may direct that any pre 1947 Act enactment, or any regulations, orders or byelaws made at any time under any such enactment—

 (a) shall not apply to any development specified in the order, or

 (b) shall apply to it subject to such modifications as may be so specified.

(3) In subsection (2) 'pre 1947 Act enactment' means—

 (a) any enactment passed before 6th August 1947 (the date of the passing of the 1947 Act), and

 (b) any enactment contained in the Highways Act 1980 which—

  (i) is an enactment derived from the Highways Act 1959, and

  (ii) re-enacts (with or without modifications) any such enactment as is mentioned in paragraph (a).

[Local development orders]

[61A Local development orders]

[(1) ...

(2) [A local planning authority may by order (a local development order)] grant planning permission—

 (a) for development specified in the order;

 (b) for development of any class so specified.

(3) A local development order may relate to—

 (a) all land in the area of the relevant authority;

 (b) any part of that land;

 (c) a site specified in the order.

(4) A local development order may make different provision for different descriptions of land.

(5) But a development order may specify any area or class of development in respect of which a local development order must not be made.

(6) A local planning authority may revoke a local development order at any time.

Part III Control over Development

(7)   Schedule 4A makes provision in connection with local development orders.]

Amendment
Inserted by the Planning and Compulsory Purchase Act 2004, s 40(1). Date in force (for the purpose of making, or making provision by means of, subordinate legislation): 6 August 2004: see SI 2004/2097, art 2. Date in force (in relation to England for remaining purposes): 10 May 2006: see SI 2006/1061, art 2(a). Date in force (in relation to Wales for remaining purposes): 30 April 2012: see SI 2012/1100, art 2.

Sub-s (1): repealed by the Planning Act 2008, ss 188(1), (2), 238, Sch 13. Date in force (in relation to England): 23 June 2009: see SI 2009/1303, art 2, Schedule. Date in force (in relation to Wales): 30 April 2012: see SI 2012/802, art 2(a), (c), Schedule.

Sub-s (2): words 'A local planning authority may by order (a local development order)' in square brackets substituted by the Planning Act 2008, s 188(1), (3). Date in force (in relation to England): 23 June 2009: see SI 2009/1303, art 2(a). Date in force (in relation to Wales): 30 April 2012: see SI 2012/802, art 2(a).

[61B Intervention by Secretary of State or National Assembly]

[(1)   At any time before a local development order is adopted by a local planning authority [in Wales,] the appropriate authority may direct that the order (or any part of it) is submitted to it for its approval.

(2)   If the appropriate authority gives a direction under subsection (1)—

  (a)   the authority must not take any step in connection with the adoption of the order until the appropriate authority gives its decision;

  (b)   the order has no effect unless it (or, if the direction relates to only part of an order, the part) has been approved by the appropriate authority.

(3)   In considering an order or part of an order submitted under subsection (1) the appropriate authority may take account of any matter which it thinks is relevant.

(4)   It is immaterial whether any such matter was taken account of by the local planning authority.

(5)   The appropriate authority—

  (a)   may approve or reject an order or part of an order submitted to it under subsection (1);

  (b)   must give reasons for its decision under paragraph (a).

(6)   If the appropriate authority thinks that a local development order [being prepared by a local planning authority in Wales] is unsatisfactory—

  (a)   it may at any time before the order is adopted by the local planning authority direct them to modify it in accordance with the direction;

  (b)   if it gives such a direction it must state its reasons for doing so.

(7)   The local planning authority—

  (a)   must comply with the direction;

  (b)   must not adopt the order unless the appropriate authority gives notice that it is satisfied that they have complied with the direction.

[(7A) Where a local development order is adopted by a local planning authority in England, that authority must submit a copy of the order to the appropriate authority as soon after the order's adoption as is reasonably practicable.]

Town and Country Planning Act 1990

(8) The appropriate authority—

(a) may at any time by order revoke a local development order if it thinks it is expedient to do so;

(b) must, if it revokes a local development order, state its reasons for doing so.

(9) Subsections (3) to (6) of section 100 apply to an order under subsection (8) above as they apply to an order under subsection (1) of that section and for that purpose references to the Secretary of State must be construed as references to the appropriate authority.

(10) The appropriate authority is—

(a) the Secretary of State in relation to England;

(b) the National Assembly for Wales in relation to Wales.]

Amendment

Inserted by the Planning and Compulsory Purchase Act 2004, s 40(1). Date in force (for the purpose of making, or making provision by means of, subordinate legislation): 6 August 2004: see SI 2004/2097, art 2. Date in force (in relation to England for remaining purposes): 10 May 2006: see SI 2006/1061, art 2(a). Date in force (in relation to Wales for remaining purposes): 30 April 2012: see SI 2012/1100, art 2.

Sub-s (1): words 'in Wales,' in square brackets inserted by the Growth and Infrastructure Act 2013, s 5(1), (3)(a). Date in force: 9 December 2013: see SI 2013/2878, art 2; for transitional and saving provisions see art 3 thereof.

Sub-s (6): words 'being prepared by a local planning authority in Wales' in square brackets inserted by the Growth and Infrastructure Act 2013, s 5(1), (3)(b). Date in force: 9 December 2013: see SI 2013/2878, art 2; for transitional and saving provisions see art 3 thereof.

Sub-s (7A): inserted by the Growth and Infrastructure Act 2013, s 5(1), (4). Date in force: 9 December 2013: see SI 2013/2878, art 2; for transitional and saving provisions see art 3 thereof.

[61C Permission granted by local development order]

[(1) Planning permission granted by a local development order may be granted—

(a) unconditionally, or

(b) subject to such conditions or limitations as are specified in the order.

(2) If the permission is granted for development of a specified description the order may enable the local planning authority to direct that the permission does not apply in relation to—

(a) development in a particular area, or

(b) any particular development.]

Amendment

Inserted by the Planning and Compulsory Purchase Act 2004, s 40(1). Date in force (for the purpose of making, or making provision by means of, subordinate legislation): 6 August 2004: see SI 2004/2097, art 2. Date in force (in relation to England for remaining purposes): 10 May 2006: see SI 2006/1061, art 2(a). Date in force (in relation to Wales for remaining purposes): 30 April 2012: see SI 2012/1100, art 2.

[61D Effect of revision or revocation of development order on incomplete development]

[(1) A development order or local development order may include provision permitting the completion of development if—

Part III Control over Development

      (a) planning permission is granted by the order in respect of the development, and

      (b) the planning permission is withdrawn at a time after the development is started but before it is completed.

(2) Planning permission granted by a development order is withdrawn—

      (a) if the order is revoked;

      (b) if the order is amended so that it ceases to grant planning permission in respect of the development or materially changes any condition or limitation to which the grant of permission is subject;

      (c) by the issue of a direction under powers conferred by the order.

(3) Planning permission granted by a local development order is withdrawn—

      (a) if the order is revoked under section 61A(6) or 61B(8);

      (b) if the order is revised in pursuance of paragraph 2 of Schedule 4A so that it ceases to grant planning permission in respect of the development or materially changes any condition or limitation to which the grant of permission is subject;

      (c) by the issue of a direction under powers conferred by the order.

(4) The power under this section to include provision in a development order or a local development order may be exercised differently for different purposes.]

Amendment

Inserted by the Planning and Compulsory Purchase Act 2004, s 41. Date in force (for the purpose of making, or making provision by means of, subordinate legislation): 6 August 2004: see SI 2004/2097, art 2. Date in force (in relation to England for remaining purposes): 10 May 2006: see SI 2006/1061, art 2(a). Date in force (in relation to Wales for remaining purposes): 30 April 2012: see SI 2012/1100, art 2.

[Mayoral development orders]

[61DA Mayoral development orders]

[(1) The Mayor of London may by order (a Mayoral development order) grant planning permission for development specified in the order on one or more sites specified in the order.

(2) The site or sites must fall within—

      (a) the area of a local planning authority in Greater London, or

      (b) the areas of two or more local planning authorities in Greater London.

(3) The Secretary of State may by development order specify an area or class of development in respect of which a Mayoral development order must not be made.]

Amendment

Inserted by the Infrastructure Act 2015, s 30(1), Sch 4, Pt 1, para 1. Date in force (for certain purposes): 12 February 2015: see the Infrastructure Act 2015, s 57(5)(d)(i). Date in force (for remaining purposes): to be appointed: see the Infrastructure Act 2015, s 57(5)(d)(ii).

Town and Country Planning Act 1990

[61DB Permission granted by Mayoral development order]

[(1) Planning permission granted by a Mayoral development order may be granted—
   (a) unconditionally, or
   (b) subject to such conditions or limitations as are specified in the order.

(2) A condition imposed by a Mayoral development order may provide for the consent, agreement or approval to a matter specified in the condition to be given by one or more persons specified in the condition.

(3) A person specified in a condition must be the Mayor of London or a relevant local planning authority.

(4) The Secretary of State may by development order provide that, if the consent, agreement or approval of a person required by a condition imposed by a Mayoral development order is not given within a specified period, that consent, agreement or approval may be sought from a specified person.

(5) In subsection (4) 'specified' means specified, or of a description specified, in the development order.

(6) The Secretary of State may by development order make provision for a person to apply for planning permission for the development of land without complying with a condition imposed on the grant of planning permission by a Mayoral development order.

(7) A development order under subsection (6) may, in particular make provision similar to that made by section 73, subject to such modifications as the Secretary of State thinks appropriate.

(8) So far as the context requires, in relation to—
   (a) an application for the consent, agreement or approval of the Mayor of London to a matter specified in a condition imposed by a Mayoral development order, or
   (b) the determination of such an application,

   any reference in an enactment to a local planning authority (however expressed) includes a reference to the Mayor.

(9) For the purposes of this Act a local planning authority is a relevant local planning authority in relation to a Mayoral development order or proposed Mayoral development order if a site or part of a site to which the order or proposed order relates is within the authority's area.]

Amendment

Inserted by the Infrastructure Act 2015, s 30(1), Sch 4, Pt 1, para 1. Date in force (for certain purposes): 12 February 2015: see the Infrastructure Act 2015, s 57(5)(d)(i). Date in force (for remaining purposes): to be appointed: see the Infrastructure Act 2015, s 57(5)(d)(ii).

[61DC Preparation and making of Mayoral development order]

[(1) The Secretary of State may by development order make provision about the procedure for the preparation and making of a Mayoral development order.

(2) A development order under subsection (1) may in particular make provision about—

(a) notice, publicity and inspection by the public;

(b) consultation with and consideration of views of such persons and for such purposes as are specified in the order;

(c) the making and consideration of representations.

(3) A Mayoral development order may be made only in response to an application to the Mayor of London by each relevant local planning authority.

(4) A proposed Mayoral development order may be consulted on only with the consent of each relevant local planning authority.

(5) A Mayoral development order may not be made unless the order has been approved, in the form in which it is made, by each relevant local planning authority.

(6) If the Mayor of London makes a Mayoral development order, the Mayor must send a copy to the Secretary of State as soon as is reasonably practicable after the order is made.]

Amendment
Inserted by the Infrastructure Act 2015, s 30(1), Sch 4, Pt 1, para 1. Date in force (for certain purposes): 12 February 2015: see the Infrastructure Act 2015, s 57(5)(d)(i). Date in force (for remaining purposes): to be appointed: see the Infrastructure Act 2015, s 57(5)(d)(ii).

[61DD Revision or revocation of Mayoral development order]

[(1) The Mayor of London may at any time revise or revoke a Mayoral development order with the approval of each relevant local planning authority.

(2) The Mayor of London must revise a Mayoral development order if the Secretary of State directs the Mayor to do so (and the requirement for the approval of each relevant local planning authority does not apply in those circumstances).

(3) The Secretary of State may at any time revoke a Mayoral development order if the Secretary of State thinks it is expedient to do so.

(4) The power under subsection (3) is to be exercised by order made by the Secretary of State.

(5) If the Secretary of State revokes a Mayoral development order the Secretary of State must state the reasons for doing so.

(6) The Secretary of State may by development order make provision about—

(a) the steps to be taken by the Secretary of State before giving a direction or making an order under this section;

(b) the procedure for the revision or revocation of a Mayoral development order.

(7) A development order under subsection (6) may in particular make provision about—

(a) notice, publicity and inspection by the public;

(b) consultation with and consideration of views of such persons and for such purposes as are specified in the order;

(c) the making and consideration of representations.]

Town and Country Planning Act 1990

Amendment

Inserted by the Infrastructure Act 2015, s 30(1), Sch 4, Pt 1, para 1. Date in force (for certain purposes): 12 February 2015: see the Infrastructure Act 2015, s 57(5)(d)(i). Date in force (for remaining purposes): to be appointed: see the Infrastructure Act 2015, s 57(5)(d)(ii).

[61DE Effect of revision or revocation on incomplete development]

[(1) This section applies if planning permission for development granted by a Mayoral development order is withdrawn at a time when the development has been started but not completed.

(2) For this purpose planning permission for development granted by a Mayoral development order is withdrawn—

    (a) if the order is revoked under section 61DD, or

    (b) if the order is revised under that section so that it ceases to grant planning permission for the development or materially changes any condition or limitation to which the grant of permission is subject.

(3) The development may, despite the withdrawal of the permission, be completed, subject as follows.

(4) If the permission is withdrawn because the Mayoral development order is revoked by the Mayor of London, the Mayor may make a determination that subsection (3) is not to apply in relation to development specified in the determination.

(5) A determination under subsection (4) must be published in such manner as the Mayor of London thinks appropriate.

(6) If the permission is withdrawn because the Mayoral development order is revoked by an order made by the Secretary of State under section 61DD, the order under that section may provide that subsection (3) is not to apply in relation to development specified in that order.

(7) If the permission is withdrawn because the order is revised as mentioned in subsection (2)(b), the revised order may provide that subsection (3) is not to apply in relation to development specified in the order.

(8) The power under this section to include provision in an order under section 61DD or a Mayoral development order may be exercised differently for different purposes.]

Amendment

Inserted by the Infrastructure Act 2015, s 30(1), Sch 4, Pt 1, para 1. Date in force (for certain purposes): 12 February 2015: see the Infrastructure Act 2015, s 57(5)(d)(i). Date in force (for remaining purposes): to be appointed: see the Infrastructure Act 2015, s 57(5)(d)(ii).

[Neighbourhood development orders]

[61E Neighbourhood development orders]

[(1) Any qualifying body is entitled to initiate a process for the purpose of requiring a local planning authority in England to make a neighbourhood development order.

(2) A 'neighbourhood development order' is an order which grants planning permission in relation to a particular neighbourhood area specified in the order—

Part III Control over Development

    (a) for development specified in the order, or

    (b) for development of any class specified in the order.

(3) Schedule 4B makes provision about the process for the making of neighbourhood development orders, including—

    (a) provision for independent examination of orders proposed by qualifying bodies, and

    (b) provision for the holding of referendums on orders proposed by those bodies.

(4) A local planning authority to whom a proposal for the making of a neighbourhood development order has been made—

    (a) must make a neighbourhood development order to which the proposal relates if in each applicable referendum under that Schedule more than half of those voting have voted in favour of the order, and

    (b) if paragraph (a) applies, must make the order as soon as reasonably practicable after the referendum is held.

(5) If—

    (a) there are two applicable referendums under that Schedule (because the order relates to a neighbourhood area designated as a business area under section 61H), and

    (b) in one of those referendums (but not the other) more than half of those voting have voted in favour of the order,

the authority may (but need not) make a neighbourhood development order to which the proposal relates.

(6) A 'qualifying body' means a parish council, or an organisation or body designated as a neighbourhood forum, authorised for the purposes of a neighbourhood development order to act in relation to a neighbourhood area as a result of section 61F.

(7) For the meaning of 'neighbourhood area', see sections 61G and 61I(1).

(8) The authority are not to be subject to the duty under subsection (4)(a) if they consider that the making of the order would breach, or would otherwise be incompatible with, any EU obligation or any of the Convention rights (within the meaning of the Human Rights Act 1998).

(9) Regulations may make provision as to the procedure to be followed by local planning authorities in cases where they act under subsection (8).

(10) The regulations may in particular make provision—

    (a) for the holding of an examination,

    (b) as to the payment by a local planning authority of remuneration and expenses of the examiner,

    (c) as to the award of costs by the examiner,

    (d) as to the giving of notice and publicity,

    (e) as to the information and documents that are to be made available to the public,

    (f) as to the making of reasonable charges for anything provided as a result of the regulations,

Town and Country Planning Act 1990

      (g) as to consultation with and participation by the public, and

      (h) as to the making and consideration of representations (including the time by which representations must be made).

(11) The authority must publish in such manner as may be prescribed—

      (a) their decision to act under subsection (4) or (8),

      (b) their reasons for making that decision, and

      (c) such other matters relating to that decision as may be prescribed.

(12) The authority must send a copy of the matters required to be published to—

      (a) the qualifying body that initiated the process for the making of the order, and

      (b) such other persons as may be prescribed.

(13) A local planning authority must publish each neighbourhood development order that they make in such manner as may be prescribed.]

Amendment

Inserted by the Localism Act 2011, s 116(1), Sch 9, Pt 1, paras 1, 2. Date in force (for certain purposes): 15 November 2011: see the Localism Act 2011, s 240(5)(j). Date in force (for certain purposes): 6 April 2012: see SI 2012/628, art 8(a); for transitional provisions see arts 9, 12 thereof. Date in force (for certain purposes): 3 August 2012: see SI 2012/2029, arts 2, 3(a); for transitional provisions and savings see art 5 thereof. Date in force (for remaining purposes): 6 April 2013: see SI 2013/797, arts 1(2), 2.

[61F Authorisation to act in relation to neighbourhood areas]

[(1) For the purposes of a neighbourhood development order, a parish council are authorised to act in relation to a neighbourhood area if that area consists of or includes the whole or any part of the area of the council.

(2) If that neighbourhood area also includes the whole or any part of the area of another parish council, the parish council is authorised for those purposes to act in relation to that neighbourhood area only if the other parish council have given their consent.

(3) For the purposes of a neighbourhood development order, an organisation or body is authorised to act in relation to a neighbourhood area if it is designated by a local planning authority as a neighbourhood forum for that area.

(4) An organisation or body may be designated for a neighbourhood area only if that area does not consist of or include the whole or any part of the area of a parish council.

(5) A local planning authority may designate an organisation or body as a neighbourhood forum if the authority are satisfied that it meets the following conditions—

      (a) it is established for the express purpose of promoting or improving the social, economic and environmental well-being of an area that consists of or includes the neighbourhood area concerned (whether or not it is also established for the express purpose of promoting the carrying on of trades, professions or other businesses in such an area),

      (b) its membership is open to—

          (i) individuals who live in the neighbourhood area concerned,

Part III Control over Development

        (ii) individuals who work there (whether for businesses carried on there or otherwise), and

        (iii) individuals who are elected members of a county council, district council or London borough council any of whose area falls within the neighbourhood area concerned,

    (c) its membership includes a minimum of 21 individuals each of whom—

        (i) lives in the neighbourhood area concerned,

        (ii) works there (whether for a business carried on there or otherwise), or

        (iii) is an elected member of a county council, district council or London borough council any of whose area falls within the neighbourhood area concerned,

    (d) it has a written constitution, and

    (e) such other conditions as may be prescribed.

(6) A local planning authority may also designate an organisation or body as a neighbourhood forum if they are satisfied that the organisation or body meets prescribed conditions.

(7) A local planning authority—

    (a) must, in determining under subsection (5) whether to designate an organisation or body as a neighbourhood forum for a neighbourhood area, have regard to the desirability of designating an organisation or body—

        (i) which has secured (or taken reasonable steps to attempt to secure) that its membership includes at least one individual falling within each of sub-paragraphs (i) to (iii) of subsection (5)(b),

        (ii) whose membership is drawn from different places in the neighbourhood area concerned and from different sections of the community in that area, and

        (iii) whose purpose reflects (in general terms) the character of that area,

    (b) may designate only one organisation or body as a neighbourhood forum for each neighbourhood area,

    (c) may designate an organisation or body as a neighbourhood forum only if the organisation or body has made an application to be designated, and

    (d) must give reasons to an organisation or body applying to be designated as a neighbourhood forum where the authority refuse the application.

(8) A designation—

    (a) ceases to have effect at the end of the period of 5 years beginning with the day on which it is made but without affecting the validity of any proposal for a neighbourhood development order made before the end of that period, and

    (b) in the case of the designation of an unincorporated association, is not to be affected merely because of a change in the membership of the association.

(9) A local planning authority may withdraw an organisation or body's designation as a neighbourhood forum if they consider that the organisation or body is no longer meeting—

    (a) the conditions by reference to which it was designated, or

Town and Country Planning Act 1990

      (b) any other criteria to which the authority were required to have regard in making the designation;

    and, where an organisation or body's designation is withdrawn, the authority must give reasons to the organisation or body.

(10) A proposal for a neighbourhood development order by a parish council or neighbourhood forum may not be made at any time in relation to a neighbourhood area if there is at that time another proposal by the council or forum in relation to that area that is outstanding.

(11) Each local planning authority must make such arrangements as they consider appropriate for making people aware as to the times when organisations or bodies could make applications to be designated as neighbourhood forums for neighbourhood areas.

(12) Regulations—

      (a) may make provision in connection with proposals made by qualifying bodies for neighbourhood development orders, and

      (b) may make provision in connection with designations (or withdrawals of designations) of organisations or bodies as neighbourhood forums (including provision of a kind mentioned in section 61G(11)(a) to (g)).

(13) The regulations may in particular make provision—

      (a) as to the consequences of the creation of a new parish council, or a change in the area of a parish council, on any proposal made for a neighbourhood development order,

      (b) as to the consequences of the dissolution of a neighbourhood forum on any proposal for a neighbourhood development order made by it,

      (c) suspending the operation of any duty of a local planning authority under paragraph 6 or 7 of Schedule 4B in cases where they are considering the withdrawal of the designation of an organisation or body as a neighbourhood forum,

      (d) for determining when a proposal for a neighbourhood development order is to be regarded as outstanding, and

      (e) requiring a local planning authority to have regard (in addition, where relevant, to the matters set out in subsection (7)(a)) to prescribed matters in determining whether to designate an organisation or body as a neighbourhood forum.]

Amendment

Inserted by the Localism Act 2011, s 116(1), Sch 9, Pt 1, paras 1, 2. Date in force (for certain purposes): 15 November 2011: see the Localism Act 2011, s 240(5)(j). Date in force (for certain purposes): 6 April 2012: see SI 2012/628, art 8(a); for transitional provisions see arts 9, 12 thereof. Date in force (for certain purposes): 3 August 2012: see SI 2012/2029, arts 2, 3(a); for transitional provisions and savings see art 5 thereof. Date in force (for remaining purposes): 6 April 2013: see SI 2013/797, arts 1(2), 2.

[61G Meaning of 'neighbourhood area']

[(1) A 'neighbourhood area' means an area within the area of a local planning authority in England which has been designated by the authority as a neighbourhood area; but that power to designate is exercisable only where—

Part III Control over Development

    (a) a relevant body has applied to the authority for an area specified in the application to be designated by the authority as a neighbourhood area, and

    (b) the authority are determining the application (but see subsection (5)).

(2) A 'relevant body' means—

    (a) a parish council, or

    (b) an organisation or body which is, or is capable of being, designated as a neighbourhood forum (on the assumption that, for this purpose, the specified area is designated as a neighbourhood area).

(3) The specified area—

    (a) in the case of an application by a parish council, must be one that consists of or includes the whole or any part of the area of the council, and

    (b) in the case of an application by an organisation or body, must not be one that consists of or includes the whole or any part of the area of a parish council.

(4) In determining an application the authority must have regard to—

    (a) the desirability of designating the whole of the area of a parish council as a neighbourhood area, and

    (b) the desirability of maintaining the existing boundaries of areas already designated as neighbourhood areas.

(5) If—

    (a) a valid application is made to the authority,

    (b) some or all of the specified area has not been designated as a neighbourhood area, and

    (c) the authority refuse the application because they consider that the specified area is not an appropriate area to be designated as a neighbourhood area,

the authority must exercise their power of designation so as to secure that some or all of the specified area forms part of one or more areas designated (or to be designated) as neighbourhood areas.

(6) The authority may, in determining any application, modify designations already made; but if a modification relates to any extent to the area of a parish council, the modification may be made only with the council's consent.

(7) The areas designated as neighbourhood areas must not overlap with each other.

(8) A local planning authority must publish a map setting out the areas that are for the time being designated as neighbourhood areas.

(9) If the authority refuse an application, they must give reasons to the applicant for refusing the application.

(10) In this section 'specified', in relation to an application, means specified in the application.

(11) Regulations may make provision in connection with the designation of areas as neighbourhood areas; and the regulations may in particular make provision—

    (a) as to the procedure to be followed in relation to designations,

    (b) as to the giving of notice and publicity in connection with designations,

Town and Country Planning Act 1990

  (c) as to consultation with and participation by the public in relation to designations,

  (d) as to the making and consideration of representations about designations (including the time by which representations must be made),

  (e) as to the form and content of applications for designations,

  (f) requiring an application for a designation to be determined by a prescribed date,

  (g) entitling or requiring a local planning authority in prescribed circumstances to decline to consider an application for a designation, and

  (h) about the modification of designations (including provision about the consequences of modification on proposals for neighbourhood development orders, or on neighbourhood development orders, that have already been made).]

Amendment

Inserted by the Localism Act 2011, s 116(1), Sch 9, Pt 1, paras 1, 2. Date in force (for certain purposes): 15 November 2011: see the Localism Act 2011, s 240(5)(j). Date in force (for certain purposes): 6 April 2012: see SI 2012/628, art 8(a); for transitional provisions see arts 9, 12 thereof. Date in force (for certain purposes): 3 August 2012: see SI 2012/2029, arts 2, 3(a); for transitional provisions and savings see art 5 thereof. Date in force (for remaining purposes): 6 April 2013: see SI 2013/797, arts 1(2), 2.

[61H Neighbourhood areas designated as business areas]

[(1) Whenever a local planning authority exercise their powers under section 61G to designate an area as a neighbourhood area, they must consider whether they should designate the area concerned as a business area.

(2) The reference here to the designation of an area as a neighbourhood area includes the modification under section 61G(6) of a designation already made.

(3) The power of a local planning authority to designate a neighbourhood area as a business area is exercisable by the authority only if, having regard to such matters as may be prescribed, they consider that the area is wholly or predominantly business in nature.

(4) The map published by a local planning authority under section 61G(8) must state which neighbourhood areas (if any) are for the time being designated as business areas.]

Amendment

Inserted by the Localism Act 2011, s 116(1), Sch 9, Pt 1, paras 1, 2. Date in force (for certain purposes): 15 November 2011: see the Localism Act 2011, s 240(5)(j). Date in force (for certain purposes): 6 April 2012: see SI 2012/628, art 8(a); for transitional provisions see arts 9, 12 thereof. Date in force (for certain purposes): 3 August 2012: see SI 2012/2029, arts 2, 3(a). Date in force (for remaining purposes): 6 April 2013: see SI 2013/797, arts 1(2), 2.

[61I Neighbourhood areas in areas of two or more local planning authorities]

[(1) The power to designate an area as a neighbourhood area under section 61G is exercisable by two or more local planning authorities in England if the area falls within the areas of those authorities.

(2) Regulations may make provision in connection with—

  (a) the operation of subsection (1), and

Part III Control over Development

(b) the operation of other provisions relating to neighbourhood development orders (including sections 61F to 61H) in cases where an area is designated as a neighbourhood area as a result of that subsection.

(3) The regulations may in particular make provision—

(a) modifying or supplementing the application of, or disapplying, any of the provisions mentioned in subsection (2)(b),

(b) applying (with or without modifications) any provision of Part 6 of the Local Government Act 1972 (discharge of functions) in cases where the provision would not otherwise apply,

(c) requiring local planning authorities to exercise, or not to exercise, any power conferred by any provision of that Part (including as applied by virtue of paragraph (b)), and

(d) conferring powers or imposing duties on local planning authorities.]

Amendment

Inserted by the Localism Act 2011, s 116(1), Sch 9, Pt 1, paras 1, 2. Date in force (for certain purposes): 15 November 2011: see the Localism Act 2011, s 240(5)(j). Date in force (for certain purposes): 6 April 2012: see SI 2012/628, art 8(a); for transitional provisions see arts 9, 12 thereof. Date in force (for certain purposes): 3 August 2012: see SI 2012/2029, arts 2, 3(a); for transitional provisions and savings see art 5 thereof. Date in force (for remaining purposes): 6 April 2013: see SI 2013/797, arts 1(2), 2.

[61J Provision that may be made by neighbourhood development order]

[(1) A neighbourhood development order may make provision in relation to—

(a) all land in the neighbourhood area specified in the order,

(b) any part of that land, or

(c) a site in that area specified in the order.

(2) A neighbourhood development order may not provide for the granting of planning permission for any development that is excluded development.

(3) For the meaning of 'excluded development', see section 61K.

(4) A neighbourhood development order may not grant planning permission for any development in any particular case where planning permission is already granted for that development in that case.

(5) A neighbourhood development order may not relate to more than one neighbourhood area.

(6) A neighbourhood development order may make different provision for different cases or circumstances.]

Amendment

Inserted by the Localism Act 2011, s 116(1), Sch 9, Pt 1, paras 1, 2. Date in force (for certain purposes): 15 November 2011: see the Localism Act 2011, s 240(5)(j). Date in force (for certain purposes): 6 April 2012: see SI 2012/628, art 8(a); for transitional provisions see arts 9, 12 thereof. Date in force (for certain purposes): 3 August 2012: see SI 2012/2029, arts 2, 3(a); for transitional provisions and savings see art 5 thereof. Date in force (for remaining purposes): 6 April 2013: see SI 2013/797, arts 1(2), 2.

[61K Meaning of 'excluded development']

[The following development is excluded development for the purposes of section 61J—

Town and Country Planning Act 1990

(a) development that consists of a county matter within paragraph 1(1)(a) to (h) of Schedule 1,

(b) development that consists of the carrying out of any operation, or class of operation, prescribed under paragraph 1(j) of that Schedule (waste development) but that does not consist of development of a prescribed description,

(c) development that falls within Annex 1 to Council Directive 85/337/EEC on the assessment of the effects of certain public and private projects on the environment (as amended from time to time),

(d) development that consists (whether wholly or partly) of a nationally significant infrastructure project (within the meaning of the Planning Act 2008),

(e) prescribed development or development of a prescribed description, and

(f) development in a prescribed area or an area of a prescribed description.]

Amendment
Inserted by the Localism Act 2011, s 116(1), Sch 9, Pt 1, paras 1, 2. Date in force (for certain purposes): 15 November 2011: see the Localism Act 2011, s 240(5)(j). Date in force (for certain purposes): 6 April 2012: see SI 2012/628, art 8(a); for transitional provisions see arts 9, 12 thereof. Date in force (for certain purposes): 3 August 2012: see SI 2012/2029, arts 2, 3(a); for transitional provisions and savings see art 5 thereof. Date in force (for remaining purposes): 6 April 2013: see SI 2013/797, arts 1(2), 2.

[61L Permission granted by neighbourhood development orders]

[(1) Planning permission granted by a neighbourhood development order may be granted—

(a) unconditionally, or

(b) subject to such conditions or limitations as are specified in the order.

(2) The conditions that may be specified include—

(a) obtaining the approval of the local planning authority who made the order but not of anyone else, and

(b) provision specifying the period within which applications must be made to a local planning authority for the approval of the authority of any matter specified in the order.

(3) Regulations may make provision entitling a parish council in prescribed circumstances to require any application for approval under subsection (2) of a prescribed description to be determined by them instead of by a local planning authority.

(4) The regulations may in particular make provision—

(a) as to the procedure to be followed by parish councils in deciding whether to determine applications for approvals (including the time by which the decisions must be made),

(b) requiring parish councils in prescribed circumstances to cease determining applications for approvals,

(c) conferring powers or imposing duties on local planning authorities,

(d) treating parish councils as local planning authorities (instead of, or in addition to, the authorities) for the purposes of the determination of

Part III Control over Development

applications for approvals (subject to such exceptions or modifications in the application of any enactment as may be prescribed),

(e) applying any enactment relating to principal councils within the meaning of section 270 of the Local Government Act 1972 for those purposes (with or without modifications), and

(f) disapplying, or modifying the application of, any enactment relating to parish councils for those purposes.

(5) A neighbourhood development order may provide for the granting of planning permission to be subject to the condition that the development begins before the end of the period specified in the order.

(6) Regulations may make provision as to the periods that may be specified in neighbourhood development orders under subsection (5).

(7) If—

(a) planning permission granted by a neighbourhood development order for any development is withdrawn by the revocation of the order under section 61M, and

(b) the revocation is made after the development has begun but before it has been completed,

the development may, despite the withdrawal of the permission, be completed.

(8) But an order under section 61M revoking a neighbourhood development order may provide that subsection (7) is not to apply in relation to development specified in the order under that section.]

Amendment

Inserted by the Localism Act 2011, s 116(1), Sch 9, Pt 1, paras 1, 2. Date in force (for certain purposes): 15 November 2011: see the Localism Act 2011, s 240(5)(j). Date in force (for certain purposes): 6 April 2012: see SI 2012/628, art 8(a); for transitional provisions see arts 9, 12 thereof. Date in force (for certain purposes): 3 August 2012: see SI 2012/2029, arts 2, 3(a); for transitional provisions and savings see art 5 thereof. Date in force (for remaining purposes): 6 April 2013: see SI 2013/797, arts 1(2), 2.

[61M Revocation or modification of neighbourhood development orders]

[(1) The Secretary of State may by order revoke a neighbourhood development order.

(2) A local planning authority may, with the consent of the Secretary of State, by order revoke a neighbourhood development order that they have made.

(3) If a neighbourhood development order is revoked, the person revoking the order must state the reasons for the revocation.

(4) A local planning authority may at any time by order modify a neighbourhood development order that they have made for the purpose of correcting errors.

(5) If the qualifying body that initiated the process for the making of that order is still authorised at that time to act for the purposes of a neighbourhood development order in relation to the neighbourhood area concerned, the power under subsection (4) is exercisable only with that body's consent.

(6) A modification of a neighbourhood development order is to be done by replacing the order with a new one containing the modification.

(7) Regulations may make provision in connection with the revocation or modification of a neighbourhood development order.

Town and Country Planning Act 1990

(8) The regulations may in particular make provision—
(a) for the holding of an examination in relation to a revocation proposed to be made by the authority,
(b) as to the payment by a local planning authority of remuneration and expenses of the examiner,
(c) as to the award of costs by the examiner,
(d) as to the giving of notice and publicity in connection with a revocation or modification,
(e) as to the information and documents relating to a revocation or modification that are to be made available to the public,
(f) as to the making of reasonable charges for anything provided as a result of the regulations,
(g) as to consultation with and participation by the public in relation to a revocation, and
(h) as to the making and consideration of representations about a revocation (including the time by which representations must be made).]

Amendment
Inserted by the Localism Act 2011, s 116(1), Sch 9, Pt 1, paras 1, 2. Date in force (for certain purposes): 15 November 2011: see the Localism Act 2011, s 240(5)(j). Date in force (for certain purposes): 6 April 2012: see SI 2012/628, art 8(a); for transitional provisions see arts 9, 12 thereof. Date in force (for certain purposes): 3 August 2012: see SI 2012/2029, arts 2, 3(a); for transitional provisions and savings see art 5 thereof. Date in force (for remaining purposes): 6 April 2013: see SI 2013/797, arts 1(2), 2.

[61N Legal challenges in relation to neighbourhood development orders]

[(1) A court may entertain proceedings for questioning a decision to act under section 61E(4) or (8) only if—
(a) the proceedings are brought by a claim for judicial review, and
(b) the claim form is filed before the end of the period of 6 weeks beginning with [the day after] the day on which the decision is published.

(2) A court may entertain proceedings for questioning a decision under paragraph 12 of Schedule 4B (consideration by local planning authority of recommendations made by examiner etc) only if—
(a) the proceedings are brought by a claim for judicial review, and
(b) the claim form is filed before the end of the period of 6 weeks beginning with [the day after] the day on which the decision is published.

(3) A court may entertain proceedings for questioning anything relating to a referendum under paragraph 14 or 15 of Schedule 4B only if—
(a) the proceedings are brought by a claim for judicial review, and
(b) the claim form is filed [before the end of] the period of 6 weeks beginning with [the day after] the day on which the result of the referendum is declared.]

Amendment
Inserted by the Localism Act 2011, s 116(1), Sch 9, Pt 1, paras 1, 2. Date in force (for certain purposes): 15 November 2011: see the Localism Act 2011, s 240(5)(j). Date in force (for certain purposes): 6 April 2012: see SI 2012/628, art 8(a); for transitional provisions see arts 9, 12 thereof. Date in force (for certain purposes): 3 August 2012: see SI 2012/2029,

arts 2, 3(a); for transitional provisions and savings see art 5 thereof. Date in force (for remaining purposes): 6 April 2013: see SI 2013/797, arts 1(2), 2.

Sub-s (1): in para (b) words 'the day after' in square brackets inserted by the Criminal Justice and Courts Act 2015, s 92(1)(a). Date in force: 13 April 2015: see SI 2015/778, art 3, Sch 1, para 71.

Sub-s (2): in para (b) words 'the day after' in square brackets inserted by the Criminal Justice and Courts Act 2015, s 92(1)(a). Date in force: 13 April 2015: see SI 2015/778, art 3, Sch 1, para 71.

Sub-s (3): in para (b) words 'before the end of' in square brackets substituted by the Criminal Justice and Courts Act 2015, s 92(1)(b)(i). Date in force: 13 April 2015: see SI 2015/778, art 3, Sch 1, para 71.

Sub-s (3): in para (b) words 'the day after' in square brackets inserted by the Criminal Justice and Courts Act 2015, s 92(1)(b)(ii). Date in force: 13 April 2015: see SI 2015/778, art 3, Sch 1, para 71.

[61O Guidance]

[Local planning authorities must have regard to any guidance issued by the Secretary of State in the exercise of any function under any provision relating to neighbourhood development orders (including any function under any of sections 61F to 61H).]

Amendment

Inserted by the Localism Act 2011, s 116(1), Sch 9, Pt 1, paras 1, 2. Date in force (for certain purposes): 15 November 2011: see the Localism Act 2011, s 240(5)(j). Date in force (for certain purposes): 6 April 2012: see SI 2012/628, art 8(a); for transitional provisions see arts 9, 12 thereof. Date in force (for certain purposes): 3 August 2012: see SI 2012/2029, arts 2, 3(a); for transitional provisions and savings see art 5 thereof. Date in force (for remaining purposes): 6 April 2013: see SI 2013/797, arts 1(2), 2.

[61P Provision as to the making of certain decisions by local planning authorities]

[(1) Regulations may make provision regulating the arrangements of a local planning authority for the making of any prescribed decision under any provision relating to neighbourhood development orders (including under any of sections 61F to 61H).

(2) The provision made by the regulations is to have effect despite provision made by any enactment as to the arrangements of a local planning authority for the exercise of their functions (such as section 101 of the Local Government Act 1972 or section 13 of the Local Government Act 2000).]

Amendment

Inserted by the Localism Act 2011, s 116(1), Sch 9, Pt 1, paras 1, 2. Date in force (for certain purposes): 15 November 2011: see the Localism Act 2011, s 240(5)(j). Date in force (for certain purposes): 6 April 2012: see SI 2012/628, art 8(a); for transitional provisions see arts 9, 12 thereof. Date in force (for certain purposes): 3 August 2012: see SI 2012/2029, arts 2, 3(a); for transitional provisions and savings see art 5 thereof. Date in force (for remaining purposes): 6 April 2013: see SI 2013/797, arts 1(2), 2.

[61Q Community right to build orders]

[Schedule 4C makes provision in relation to a particular type of neighbourhood development order (a community right to build order).]

Amendment

Inserted by the Localism Act 2011, s 116(1), Sch 9, Pt 1, paras 1, 2. Date in force (for certain purposes): 15 November 2011: see the Localism Act 2011, s 240(5)(j). Date in force

Town and Country Planning Act 1990

(for certain purposes): 6 April 2012: see SI 2012/628, art 8(a); for transitional provisions see arts 9, 12 thereof. Date in force (for certain purposes): 3 August 2012: see SI 2012/2029, arts 2, 3(a); for transitional provisions and savings see art 5 thereof. Date in force (for remaining purposes): 6 April 2013: see SI 2013/797, arts 1(2), 2.

[Consultation before applying for planning permission]

[61W Requirement to carry out pre-application consultation]

[(1) Where—

(a) a person proposes to make an application for planning permission for the development of any land in England, and

(b) the proposed development is of a description specified in a development order,

the person must carry out consultation on the proposed application in accordance with subsections (2) and (3).

(2) The person must publicise the proposed application in such manner as the person reasonably considers is likely to bring the proposed application to the attention of a majority of the persons who live at, or otherwise occupy, premises in the vicinity of the land.

(3) The person must consult each specified person about the proposed application.

(4) Publicity under subsection (2) must—

(a) set out how the person ('P') may be contacted by persons wishing to comment on, or collaborate with P on the design of, the proposed development, and

(b) give such information about the proposed timetable for the consultation as is sufficient to ensure that persons wishing to comment on the proposed development may do so in good time.

(5) In subsection (3) 'specified person' means a person specified in, or of a description specified in, a development order.

(6) Subsection (1) does not apply—

(a) if the proposed application is an application under section 293A, or

(b) in cases specified in a development order.

(7) A person subject to the duty imposed by subsection (1) must, in complying with that subsection, have regard to the advice (if any) given by the local planning authority about local good practice.]

Amendment

Inserted by the Localism Act 2011, s 122(1). Date in force (in so far as this provision requires or authorises the making of provision in a development order): 15 November 2011: see the Localism Act 2011, s 240(5)(l). Date in force (for remaining purposes): 17 December 2013: see SI 2013/2931, art 2; for effect see the Localism Act 2011, s 122(3), (4).

[61X Duty to take account of responses to consultation]

[(1) Subsection (2) applies where a person—

(a) has been required by section 61W(1) to carry out consultation on a proposed application for planning permission, and

Part III Control over Development

(b) proposes to go ahead with making an application for planning permission (whether or not in the same terms as the proposed application).

(2) The person must, when deciding whether the application that the person is actually to make should be in the same terms as the proposed application, have regard to any responses to the consultation that the person has received.]

Amendment

Inserted by the Localism Act 2011, s 122(1). Date in force (in so far as this provision requires or authorises the making of provision in a development order): 15 November 2011: see the Localism Act 2011, s 240(5)(l). Date in force (for remaining purposes): 17 December 2013: see SI 2013/2931, art 2; for effect see the Localism Act 2011, s 122(3), (4).

[61Y Power to make supplementary provision]

[(1) A development order may make provision about, or in connection with, consultation which section 61W(1) requires a person to carry out on a proposed application for planning permission.

(2) The provision that may be made under subsection (1) includes (in particular)—
   (a) provision about, or in connection with, publicising the proposed application;
   (b) provision about, or in connection with, the ways of responding to the publicity;
   (c) provision about, or in connection with, consultation under section 61W(3);
   (d) provision about, or in connection with, collaboration between the person and others on the design of the proposed development;
   (e) provision as to the timetable (including deadlines) for—
      (i) compliance with section 61W(1),
      (ii) responding to publicity under section 61W(2), or
      (iii) responding to consultation under section 61W(3);
   (f) provision for the person to prepare a statement setting out how the person proposes to comply with section 61W(1);
   (g) provision for the person to comply with section 61W(1) in accordance with a statement required by provision under paragraph (f).

(3) Provision under subsection (1) may be different for different cases.]

Amendment

Inserted by the Localism Act 2011, s 122(1). Date in force (in so far as this provision requires or authorises the making of provision in a development order): 15 November 2011: see the Localism Act 2011, s 240(5)(l). Date in force (for remaining purposes): 17 December 2013: see SI 2013/2931, art 2; for effect see the Localism Act 2011, s 122(3), (4).

Applications for planning permission

[62 Applications for planning permission]

[(1) A development order may make provision as to applications for planning permission made to a local planning authority.

(2) Provision referred to in subsection (1) includes provision as to—
   (a) the form and manner in which the application must be made;
   (b) particulars of such matters as are to be included in the application;

(c) documents or other materials as are to accompany the application.

[(2A) In subsections (1) and (2) references to applications for planning permission include references to[—

(a) applications for consent, agreement or approval as mentioned in section 61DB(2), and

(b)] applications for approval under section 61L(2).]

(3) The local planning authority may require that an application for planning permission must include—

(a) such particulars as they think necessary;

(b) such evidence in support of anything in or relating to the application as they think necessary.

(4) But a requirement under subsection (3) must not be inconsistent with provision made under subsection (1).

[(4A) Also, a requirement under subsection (3) in respect of an application for planning permission for development of land in England—

(a) must be reasonable having regard, in particular, to the nature and scale of the proposed development; and

(b) may require particulars of, or evidence about, a matter only if it is reasonable to think that the matter will be a material consideration in the determination of the application.]

(5) A development order must require that an application for planning permission of such description as is specified in the order must be accompanied by such of the following as is so specified—

(a) a statement about the design principles and concepts that have been applied to the development;

(b) a statement about how issues relating to access to the development have been dealt with.

(6) The form and content of a statement mentioned in subsection (5) is such as is required by the development order.]

[(7) In subsection (8) 'a relevant application' means the application for planning permission in a case where a person—

(a) has been required by section 61W(1) to carry out consultation on a proposed application for planning permission, and

(b) is going ahead with making an application for planning permission (whether or not in the same terms as the proposed application).

(8) A development order must require that a relevant application be accompanied by particulars of—

(a) how the person complied with section 61W(1),

(b) any responses to the consultation that were received by the person, and

(c) the account taken of those responses.]

Amendment

Substituted by the Planning and Compulsory Purchase Act 2004, s 42(1). Date in force (for the purpose of making, or making provision by means of, subordinate legislation): 6 August 2004: see SI 2004/2097, art 2. Date in force (in relation to England for remaining

Part III Control over Development

purposes): 10 August 2006: see SI 2006/1061, art 3(a). Date in force (in relation to Wales for remaining purposes): 30 June 2007: see SI 2007/1369, art 2(a).

Sub-s (2A): inserted by the Localism Act 2011, s 121, Sch 12, paras 1, 5. Date in force (for certain purposes): 15 January 2012: see SI 2012/57, art 4(1)(h). Date in force (for certain purposes): 6 April 2012: see SI 2012/628, art 8(a). Date in force (for certain purposes): 3 August 2012: see SI 2012/2029, arts 2, 3(a); for transitional provisions and savings see art 5 thereof. Date in force (for remaining purposes): 6 April 2013: see SI 2013/797, arts 1(2), 2.

Sub-s (2A): words from '—(a) applications for' to '61DB(2), and (b)' in square brackets inserted by the Infrastructure Act 2015, s 30(1), Sch 4, Pt 2, paras 2, 6. Date in force (for certain purposes): 12 February 2015: see the Infrastructure Act 2015, s 57(5)(d)(i). Date in force (for remaining purposes): to be appointed: see the Infrastructure Act 2015, s 57(5)(d)(ii).

Sub-s (4A): inserted by the Growth and Infrastructure Act 2013, s 6. Date in force: 25 June 2013: see SI 2013/1488, art 3(c).

Sub-ss (7), (8): inserted by the Localism Act 2011, s 122(2); for effect see s 122(3), (4) thereof. Date in force (in so far as they require or authorise the making of provision in a development order): 15 November 2011: see the Localism Act 2011, s 240(5)(l). Date in force (for remaining purposes): 17 December 2013: see SI 2013/2931, art 2; for effect see the Localism Act 2011, s 122(3), (4).

[62A When application may be made directly to Secretary of State]

[(1) A relevant application that would otherwise have to be made to the local planning authority may (if the applicant so chooses) be made instead to the Secretary of State if the following conditions are met at the time it is made—

(a) the local planning authority concerned is designated by the Secretary of State for the purposes of this section; and

(b) the development to which the application relates (where the application is within subsection (2)(b)(i)), or the development for which outline planning permission has been granted (where the application is within subsection (2)(b)(ii)), is major development.

(2) In this section—

(a) 'major development' means development of a description prescribed by the Secretary of State;

(b) 'relevant application' means—

(i) an application for planning permission for the development of land in England, other than an application of the kind described in section 73(1); or

(ii) an application for approval of a matter that, as defined by section 92, is a reserved matter in the case of an outline planning permission for the development of land in England.

(3) Where a relevant application is made to the Secretary of State under this section, an application under the planning Acts—

(a) that is—

(i) an application for listed building consent, or for conservation area consent, under the Planning (Listed Buildings and Conservation Areas) Act 1990, or

(ii) an application of a description prescribed by the Secretary of State,

(b) that is considered by the person making the application to be connected with the relevant application,

Town and Country Planning Act 1990

(c) that would otherwise have to be made to the local planning authority or hazardous substances authority,

(d) that is neither a relevant application nor an application of the kind described in section 73(1), and

(e) that relates to land in England,

may (if the person so chooses) be made instead to the Secretary of State.

(4) If an application ('the connected application') is made to the Secretary of State under subsection (3) but the Secretary of State considers that it is not connected with the relevant application concerned, the Secretary of State may—

(a) refer the connected application to the local planning authority, or hazardous substances authority, to whom it would otherwise have been made; and

(b) direct that the connected application—

(i) is to be treated as having been made to that authority (and not to the Secretary of State under this section), and

(ii) is to be determined by that authority accordingly.

(5) The decision of the Secretary of State on an application made to the Secretary of State under this section shall be final.

(6) The Secretary of State may give directions requiring a local planning authority or hazardous substances authority to do things in relation to an application made to the Secretary of State under this section that would otherwise have been made to the authority; and directions under this subsection—

(a) may relate to a particular application or to applications more generally; and

(b) may be given to a particular authority or to authorities more generally.]

Amendment

Inserted by the Growth and Infrastructure Act 2013, s 1(1). Date in force (for the purpose of enabling the Secretary of State to make regulations or orders): 9 May 2013: see SI 2013/1124, art 2. Date in force (in so far as relating to sub-ss (1), (2), (5), (6) for remaining purposes): 1 October 2013: see SI 2013/2143, art 2(1)(a). Date in force (for remaining purposes): 1 October 2014: see SI 2014/1531, art 2.

[62B Designation for the purposes of section 62A]

[(1) An authority may be designated for the purposes of section 62A only if—

(a) the criteria that are to be applied in deciding whether to designate the authority are set out in a document to which subsection (2) applies,

(b) by reference to those criteria, the Secretary of State considers that there are respects in which the authority are not adequately performing their function of determining applications under this Part, and

(c) the criteria that are to be applied in deciding whether to revoke a designation are set out in a document to which subsection (2) applies.

(2) This subsection applies to a document if—

(a) the document has been laid before Parliament by the Secretary of State,

(b) the 40-day period for the document has ended without either House of Parliament having during that period resolved not to approve the document, and

(c) the document has been published (whether before, during or after the 40-day period for it) by the Secretary of State in such manner as the Secretary of State thinks fit.

(3) In this section 'the 40-day period' for a document is the period of 40 days beginning with the day on which the document is laid before Parliament (or, if it is not laid before each House of Parliament on the same day, the later of the two days on which it is laid).

(4) In calculating the 40-day period for a document, no account is to be taken of any period during which—

(a) Parliament is dissolved or prorogued, or

(b) both Houses of Parliament are adjourned for more than four days.

(5) None of the following may be designated for the purposes of section 62A—

(a) the Homes and Communities Agency;

(b) the Mayor of London;

(c) a Mayoral development corporation;

(d) an urban development corporation.

(6) The Secretary of State must publish (in such manner as the Secretary of State thinks fit)—

(a) any designation of an authority for the purposes of section 62A, and

(b) any revocation of such a designation.]

Amendment

Inserted by the Growth and Infrastructure Act 2013, s 1(1). Date in force: 25 April 2013: see the Growth and Infrastructure Act 2013, s 35(2).

[62C Notifying parish councils of applications under section 62A(1)]

[(1) If an application is made to the Secretary of State under section 62A(1) and a parish council would be entitled under paragraph 8 of Schedule 1 to be notified of the application were it made to the local planning authority, the Secretary of State must notify the council of—

(a) the application, and

(b) any alteration to the application accepted by the Secretary of State.

(2) Paragraph 8(4) and (5) of Schedule 1 apply in relation to duties of the Secretary of State under subsection (1) as they apply to duties of a local planning authority under paragraph 8(1) of that Schedule.

(3) An authority designated for the purposes of section 62A must comply with requests from the Secretary of State for details of requests received by the authority under paragraph 8(1) of Schedule 1.]

Amendment

Inserted by the Growth and Infrastructure Act 2013, s 1(1). Date in force (for the purpose of enabling the Secretary of State to make regulations or orders): 9 May 2013: see SI 2013/1124, art 2. Date in force (for remaining purposes): 1 October 2013: see SI 2013/2143, art 2(1)(a).

63 ...

...

Town and Country Planning Act 1990

Amendment

Repealed by the Planning and Compensation Act 1991, ss 32, 84(6), Sch 7, paras 8, 11, 12, Sch 19, Pt I.

64 ...

...

Amendment

Repealed by the Planning and Compensation Act 1991, ss 32, 84(6), Sch 7, paras 8, 11, 12, Sch 19, Pt I.

Publicity for applications

[65 Notice etc of applications for planning permission]

[(1) A development order may make provision requiring—

    (a) notice to be given of any application for planning permission, and

    (b) any applicant for such permission to issue a certificate as to the interests in the land to which the application relates or the purpose for which it is used,

and provide for publicising such applications and for the form, content and service of such notices and certificates.

(2) Provision shall be made by a development order for the purpose of securing that, in the case of any application for planning permission, any person (other than the applicant) who on such date as may be prescribed by the order is an owner of the land to which the application relates, or [an agricultural tenant of that land], is given notice of the application in such manner as may be required by the order.

(3) A development order may require an applicant for planning permission to certify, in such form as may be prescribed by the order, or to provide evidence, that any requirements of the order have been satisfied.

[(3A) In subsections (1) and (3) references to any application for planning permission or any applicant for such permission include references to[—

    (a) any application for consent, agreement or approval as mentioned in section 61DB(2) or any applicant for such consent, agreement or approval, and

    (b)] any application for approval under section 61L(2) or any applicant for such approval.]

(4) A development order making any provision by virtue of this section may make different provision for different cases or different classes of development.

(5) A local planning authority shall not entertain an application for planning permission unless any requirements imposed by virtue of this section have been satisfied.

(6) If any person—

    (a) issues a certificate which purports to comply with any requirement imposed by virtue of this section and contains a statement which he knows to be false or misleading in a material particular; or

    (b) recklessly issues a certificate which purports to comply with any such requirement and contains a statement which is false or misleading in a material particular,

he shall be guilty of an offence.

Part III Control over Development

(7) A person guilty of an offence under this section shall be liable on summary conviction to a fine not exceeding level 5 on the standard scale.

(8) In this section—

['agricultural tenant', in relation to any land, means any person who—

(a) is the tenant, under a tenancy in relation to which the Agricultural Holdings Act 1986 applies, of an agricultural holding within the meaning of that Act any part of which is comprised in that land; or

(b) is the tenant, under a farm business tenancy (within the meaning of the Agricultural Tenancies Act 1995), of land any part of which is comprised in that land;] and

'owner' in relation to any land means any person who—

(a) is the estate owner in respect of the fee simple;

(b) is entitled to a tenancy granted or extended for a term of years certain of which not less than seven years remain unexpired; or

(c) in the case of such applications as may be prescribed by a development order, is entitled to an interest in any mineral so prescribed,

and the reference to the interests in the land to which an application for planning permission relates includes any interest in any mineral in, on or under the land.

(9) Notwithstanding section 127 of the Magistrates' Courts Act 1980, a magistrates' court may try an information in respect of an offence under this section whenever laid.]

Amendment

Substituted for ss 65–68, as originally enacted, by the Planning and Compensation Act 1991, s 16(1).

Sub-s (2): words in square brackets substituted by the Agricultural Tenancies Act 1995, s 40, Schedule, para 35(2).

Sub-s (3A): inserted by the Localism Act 2011, s 121, Sch 12, paras 1, 6. Date in force (for certain purposes): 15 January 2012: see SI 2012/57, art 4(1)(h). Date in force (for certain purposes): 6 April 2012: see SI 2012/628, art 8(a). Date in force (for certain purposes): 3 August 2012: see SI 2012/2029, arts 2, 3(a); for transitional provisions and savings see art 5 thereof. Date in force (for remaining purposes): 6 April 2013: see SI 2013/797, arts 1(2), 2.

Sub-s (3A): words from '—(a) any application' to 'approval, and (b)' in square brackets inserted by the Infrastructure Act 2015, s 30(1), Sch 4, Pt 2, paras 2, 7. Date in force (for certain purposes): 12 February 2015: see the Infrastructure Act 2015, s 57(5)(d)(i). Date in force (for remaining purposes): to be appointed: see the Infrastructure Act 2015, s 57(5)(d)(ii).

Sub-s (8): definition 'agricultural tenant' substituted for definition 'agricultural holding' as originally enacted, by the Agricultural Tenancies Act 1995, s 40, Schedule, para 35(3).

66 ...

...

Amendment

Substituted, together with ss 65, 67, 68, by new s 65, by the Planning and Compensation Act 1991, s 16(1).

67 ...

...

Town and Country Planning Act 1990

Amendment
Substituted, together with ss 65, 66, 68, by new s 65, by the Planning and Compensation Act 1991, s 16(1).

68 ...

...

Amendment
Substituted, together with ss 65–67, by new s 65, by the Planning and Compensation Act 1991, s 16(1).

[69 Register of applications etc]

[(1) The local planning authority must keep a register containing such information as is prescribed as to—
   (a)   applications for planning permission;
   [(aa) applications for non-material changes to planning permission under section 96A;]
   (b)   ...
   (c)   local development orders;
   [(cza) Mayoral development orders;]
   [(ca) neighbourhood planning matters;]
   (d)   simplified planning zone schemes.

(2) The register must contain—
   (a) information as to the manner in which applications mentioned in subsection (1)(a) [and (aa)] and requests mentioned in subsection (1)(b) have been dealt with;
   (b) such information as is prescribed with respect to any local development order[, [Mayoral development order,] neighbourhood planning matter] or simplified planning zone scheme in relation to the authority's area.

[(2A) For the purposes of subsections (1) and (2) 'neighbourhood planning matters' means—
   (a) neighbourhood development orders;
   (b) neighbourhood development plans (made under section 38A of the Planning and Compulsory Purchase Act 2004); and
   (c) proposals for such orders or plans.]

(3) A development order may require the register to be kept in two or more parts.

(4) Each part must contain such information as is prescribed relating to the matters mentioned in subsection (1)(a)[, (aa)] and (b).

(5) A development order may also make provision—
   (a) for a specified part of the register to contain copies of applications or requests and of any other documents or material submitted with them;
   (b) for the entry relating to an application or request (and everything relating to it) to be removed from that part of the register when the application (including any appeal arising out of it) or the request (as the case may be) has been finally disposed of.

Part III Control over Development

(6) Provision made under subsection (5)(b) does not prevent the inclusion of a different entry relating to the application or request in another part of the register.

(7) The register must be kept in such manner as is prescribed.

(8) The register must be kept available for inspection by the public at all reasonable hours.

(9) Anything prescribed under this section must be prescribed by development order.]

Amendment

Substituted by the Planning and Compulsory Purchase Act 2004, s 118(1), Sch 6, paras 1, 3. Date in force (for the purpose of making, or making provision by means of, subordinate legislation): 6 August 2004: see SI 2004/2097, art 2. Date in force (for remaining purposes): 22 February 2010: see SI 2010/321, art 2.

Sub-s (1): para (aa) inserted by the Planning Act 2008, s 190(1), (4)(a). Date in force: 6 April 2010: see SI 2010/566, art 3(b).

Sub-s (1): para (b) repealed by the Localism Act 2011, s 237, Sch 25, Pt 18. Date in force: 6 April 2012: see SI 2012/628, art 8(e).

Sub-s (1): para (cza) inserted by the Infrastructure Act 2015, s 30(1), Sch 4, Pt 2, paras 2, 8(1), (2). Date in force (for certain purposes): 12 February 2015: see the Infrastructure Act 2015, s 57(5)(d)(i). Date in force (for remaining purposes): to be appointed: see the Infrastructure Act 2015, s 57(5)(d)(ii).

Sub-s (1): para (ca) inserted by the Localism Act 2011, s 121, Sch 12, paras 1, 7(1), (2). Date in force (for certain purposes): 15 January 2012: see SI 2012/57, art 4(1)(h). Date in force (for certain purposes): 6 April 2012: see SI 2012/628, art 8(a). Date in force (for certain purposes): 3 August 2012: see SI 2012/2029, arts 2, 3(a); for transitional provisions and savings see art 5 thereof. Date in force (for remaining purposes): 6 April 2013: see SI 2013/797, arts 1(2), 2.

Sub-s (2): in para (a) words 'and (aa)' in square brackets inserted by the Planning Act 2008, s 190(1), (4)(b). Date in force: 6 April 2010: see SI 2010/566, art 3(b).

Sub-s (2): in para (b) words ', neighbourhood planning matter' in square brackets inserted by the Localism Act 2011, s 121, Sch 12, paras 1, 7(1), (3). Date in force (for certain purposes): 15 January 2012: see SI 2012/57, art 4(1)(h). Date in force (for certain purposes): 6 April 2012: see SI 2012/628, art 8(a). Date in force (for certain purposes): 3 August 2012: see SI 2012/2029, arts 2, 3(a); for transitional provisions and savings see art 5 thereof. Date in force (for remaining purposes): 6 April 2013: see SI 2013/797, arts 1(2), 2.

Sub-s (2): in para (b) words 'Mayoral development order,' in square brackets inserted by the Infrastructure Act 2015, s 30(1), Sch 4, Pt 2, paras 2, 8(1), (3). Date in force (for certain purposes): 12 February 2015: see the Infrastructure Act 2015, s 57(5)(d)(i). Date in force (for remaining purposes): to be appointed: see the Infrastructure Act 2015, s 57(5)(d)(ii).

Sub-s (2A): inserted by the Localism Act 2011, s 121, Sch 12, paras 1, 7(1), (4). Date in force (for certain purposes): 15 January 2012: see SI 2012/57, art 4(1)(h). Date in force (for certain purposes): 6 April 2012: see SI 2012/628, art 8(a). Date in force (for certain purposes): 3 August 2012: see SI 2012/2029, arts 2, 3(a); for transitional provisions and savings see art 5 thereof. Date in force (for remaining purposes): 6 April 2013: see SI 2013/797, arts 1(2), 2.

Sub-s (4): reference to ', (aa)' in square brackets inserted by the Planning Act 2008, s 190(1), (4)(c). Date in force: 6 April 2010: see SI 2010/566, art 3(b).

Determination of applications

70 Determination of applications: general considerations

(1) Where an application is made to a local planning authority for planning permission—

Town and Country Planning Act 1990

      (a) subject to sections 91 and 92, they may grant planning permission, either unconditionally or subject to such conditions as they think fit; or

      (b) they may refuse planning permission.

(2) In dealing with such an application the authority shall have regard [to—

      (a) the provisions of the development plan, so far as material to the application,

      (b) any local finance considerations, so far as material to the application, and

      (c) any other material considerations].

[(2A) Subsection (2)(b) does not apply in relation to Wales.]

(3) Subsection (1) has effect subject to [section 65] and to the following provisions of this Act, to sections 66, 67, 72 and 73 of the Planning (Listed Buildings and Conservation Areas) Act 1990 and to section 15 of the Health Services Act 1976.

[(4) In this section—

'local finance consideration' means—

      (a) a grant or other financial assistance that has been, or will or could be, provided to a relevant authority by a Minister of the Crown, or

      (b) sums that a relevant authority has received, or will or could receive, in payment of Community Infrastructure Levy;

'Minister of the Crown' has the same meaning as in the Ministers of the Crown Act 1975;

'relevant authority' means—

      (a) a district council;

      (b) a county council in England;

      (c) the Mayor of London;

      (d) the council of a London borough;

      (e) a Mayoral development corporation;

      (f) an urban development corporation;

      (g) a housing action trust;

      (h) the Council of the Isles of Scilly;

      (i) the Broads Authority;

      (j) a National Park authority in England;

      (k) the Homes and Communities Agency; or

      (l) a joint committee established under section 29 of the Planning and Compulsory Purchase Act 2004.]

Amendment

Sub-s (2): words from 'to— (a) the' to the end in square brackets substituted by the Localism Act 2011, s 143(1), (2). Date in force: 15 January 2012: see the Localism Act 2011, s 240(1)(i); for transitional provision see s 143(5) thereof.

Sub-s (2A): inserted by the Localism Act 2011, s 143(1), (3). Date in force: 15 January 2012: see the Localism Act 2011, s 240(1)(i); for transitional provision see s 143(5) thereof.

Sub-s (3): words in square brackets substituted by the Planning and Compensation Act 1991, s 32, Sch 7, para 14.

Sub-s (4): inserted by the Localism Act 2011, s 143(1), (4). Date in force: 15 January 2012: see the Localism Act 2011, s 240(1)(i); for transitional provision see s 143(5) thereof.

Part III Control over Development

[70A *Power of local planning authority to decline to determine applications*]
[70A Power to decline to determine subsequent application]

[(1) A local planning authority may decline to determine an application for planning permission for the development of any land if—
  (a) within the period of two years ending with the date on which the application is received, the Secretary of State has refused a similar application referred to him under section 77 or has dismissed an appeal against the refusal of a similar application; and
  (b) in the opinion of the authority there has been no significant change since the refusal or, as the case may be, dismissal mentioned in paragraph (a) in the development plan, so far as material to the application, or in any other material considerations.

(2) For the purposes of this section an application for planning permission for the development of any land shall only be taken to be similar to a later application if the development and the land to which the applications relate are in the opinion of the local planning authority the same or substantially the same.

(3) The reference in subsection (1)(a) to an appeal against the refusal of an application includes an appeal under section 78(2) in respect of an application.]

([1) A local planning authority may decline to determine a relevant application if—
  (a) any of the conditions in subsections (2) to (4) is satisfied, and
  (b) the authority think there has been no significant change in the relevant considerations since the relevant event.

(2) The condition is that in the period of two years ending with the date on which the application mentioned in subsection (1) is received the Secretary of State has refused a similar application [made to the Secretary of State under section 62A or] referred to him under section 76A or 77.

(3) The condition is that in that period the Secretary of State has dismissed an appeal—
  (a) against the refusal of a similar application, or
  (b) under section 78(2) in respect of a similar application.

(4) The condition is that—
  (a) in that period the local planning authority have refused more than one similar application, and
  (b) there has been no appeal to the Secretary of State against any such refusal [or, if there has been such an appeal, it has been withdrawn].

[(4A) A local planning authority in England may also decline to determine a relevant application if—
  (a) the condition in subsection (4B) is satisfied, and
  (b) the authority think there has been no significant change in the relevant considerations since the relevant event.

(4B) The condition is that—
  (a) in the period of two years ending with the date on which the application mentioned in subsection (4A) is received the Secretary of State has refused a similar application,

Town and Country Planning Act 1990

      (b) the similar application was an application deemed to have been made by section 177(5), and

      (c) the land to which the application mentioned in subsection (4A) and the similar application relate is in England.]

(5) A relevant application is—

      (a) an application for planning permission for the development of any land;

      (b) an application for approval in pursuance of section 60(2)[, (2A) or (2B)].

(6) The relevant considerations are—

      (a) the development plan so far as material to the application;

      (b) any other material considerations.

(7) The relevant event is—

      (a) for the purposes of subsections (2) [, (4) and (4B)] the refusal of the similar application;

      (b) for the purposes of subsection (3) the dismissal of the appeal.

(8) An application for planning permission is similar to another application if (and only if) the local planning authority think that the development and the land to which the applications relate are the same or substantially the same.]

Amendment

Inserted by the Planning and Compensation Act 1991, s 17(1).

Substituted, by new ss 70A, 70B, by the Planning and Compulsory Purchase Act 2004, s 43(1); for effect see s 43(5) thereof. Date in force (in relation to England): 24 August 2005: see SI 2005/2081, art 2(a). Date in force (in relation to Wales): to be appointed: see the Planning and Compulsory Purchase Act 2004, s 121(1), (2)(b), (3A), (3B) (as amended by the Planning Act 2008, s 187, Sch 7, para 7).

Sub-s (2) (as substituted by the Planning and Compulsory Purchase Act 2004): words 'made to the Secretary of State under section 62A or' in square brackets inserted by the Growth and Infrastructure Act 2013, s 1(2), Sch 1, paras 1, 6. Date in force (in relation to England for the purposes of making regulations or orders): 9 May 2013: see SI 2013/1124, art 2. Date in force (for remaining purposes): 1 October 2013: see SI 2013/2143, art 2(1)(a).

Sub-s (4) (as substituted by the Planning and Compulsory Purchase Act 2004): in para (b) words 'or, if there has been such an appeal, it has been withdrawn' in square brackets inserted by the Planning Act 2008, s 187, Sch 7, paras 1, 2(1), (2). Date in force (in relation to England): 6 April 2009: see SI 2009/400, art 5(b). Date in force (in relation to Wales): to be appointed: see the Planning Act 2008, s 241(3), (4)(a), (b), (8).

Sub-ss (4A), (4B): inserted by the Planning Act 2008, s 187, Sch 7, paras 1, 2(1), (3). Date in force: 6 April 2009: see SI 2009/400, art 3(n).

Sub-s (5) (as substituted by the Planning and Compulsory Purchase Act 2004): words ', (2A) or (2B)' in square brackets inserted by the Growth and Infrastructure Act 2013, s 4(2). Date in force: 25 April 2013: see the Growth and Infrastructure Act 2013, s 35(2).

Sub-s (7) (as substituted by the Planning and Compulsory Purchase Act 2004): in para (a) words ', (4) and (4B)' in square brackets substituted by the Planning Act 2008, s 187, Sch 7, paras 1, 2(1), (4). Date in force: 6 April 2009: see SI 2009/400, art 3(n).

[70B Power to decline to determine overlapping application]

[(1) A local planning authority may decline to determine an application for planning permission for the development of any land which is[—

      (a) made on the same day as a similar application, or

Part III Control over Development

(b)] made at a time when any of the conditions in subsections (2) to (4) applies in relation to a similar application.

(2) The condition is that a similar application is under consideration by the local planning authority and the determination period for that application has not expired.

(3) The condition is that a similar application is under consideration by the Secretary of State in pursuance of section [62A,] 76A or 77 or on an appeal under section 78 and the Secretary of State has not issued his decision.

(4) The condition is that a similar application—

(a) has been granted by the local planning authority,

(b) has been refused by them, or

(c) has not been determined by them within the determination period,

and the time within which an appeal could be made to the Secretary of State under section 78 has not expired.

[(4A) A local planning authority in England may also decline to determine an application for planning permission for the development of any land in England which is made at a time when the condition in subsection (4B) applies in relation to a similar application.

(4B) The condition is that—

(a) a similar application is under consideration by the Secretary of State,

(b) the similar application is an application deemed to have been made by section 177(5), and

(c) the Secretary of State has not issued his decision.]

(5) An application for planning permission is similar to another application if (and only if) the local planning authority think that the development and the land to which the applications relate are the same or substantially the same.

(6) The determination period is—

(a) the period prescribed by the development order for the determination of the application, or

(b) such longer period as the applicant and the authority have agreed for the determination of the application.

[(7) If a local planning authority exercise their power under subsection (1)(a) to decline to determine an application made on the same day as a similar application, they may not also exercise that power to decline to determine the similar application.]]

Amendment

Substituted, together with s 70A, for s 70A, by the Planning and Compulsory Purchase Act 2004, s 43(1); for effect see s 43(5) thereof. Date in force (in relation to England): 6 April 2009: see SI 2009/384, art 2(a). Date in force (in relation to Wales): to be appointed: see the Planning and Compulsory Purchase Act 2004, s 121(1), (2)(b), (3A), (3B) (as amended by the Planning Act 2008, s 187, Sch 7, para 7).

Sub-s (1): para (a) inserted and para (b) numbered as such by the Planning Act 2008, s 187, Sch 7, paras 1, 3(1), (2). Date in force (in relation to England): 6 April 2009: see

Town and Country Planning Act 1990

SI 2009/400, art 5(b). Date in force (in relation to Wales): to be appointed: see the Planning Act 2008, s 241(3), (4)(a), (b), (8).

Sub-s (3): reference to '62A,' in square brackets inserted by the Growth and Infrastructure Act 2013, s 1(2), Sch 1, paras 1, 7. Date in force (in relation to England for the purposes of making regulations or orders): 9 May 2013: see SI 2013/1124, art 2. Date in force (for remaining purposes): 1 October 2013: see SI 2013/2143, art 2(1)(a).

Sub-ss (4A), (4B): inserted by the Planning Act 2008, s 187, Sch 7, paras 1, 3(1), (3). Date in force: 6 April 2009: see SI 2009/400, art 3(n).

Sub-s (7): inserted by the Planning Act 2008, s 187, Sch 7, paras 1, 3(1), (4). Date in force (in relation to England): 6 April 2009: see SI 2009/400, art 5(b). Date in force (in relation to Wales): to be appointed: see the Planning Act 2008, s 241(3), (4)(a), (b), (8).

[70C Power to decline to determine retrospective application]

[(1) A local planning authority in England may decline to determine an application for planning permission for the development of any land if granting planning permission for the development would involve granting, whether in relation to the whole or any part of the land to which a pre-existing enforcement notice relates, planning permission in respect of the whole or any part of the matters specified in the enforcement notice as constituting a breach of planning control.

(2) For the purposes of the operation of this section in relation to any particular application for planning permission, a 'pre-existing enforcement notice' is an enforcement notice issued before the application was received by the local planning authority.]

Amendment

Inserted by the Localism Act 2011, s 123(1), (2). Date in force: 6 April 2012: see SI 2012/628, art 8(b); for transitional provisions see arts 9, 13(1) thereof.

71 Consultations in connection with determinations under s 70

[(1) A development order may provide that a local planning authority shall not determine an application for planning permission before the end of such period as may be prescribed.

(2) A development order may require a local planning authority—

(a) to take into account in determining such an application such representations, made within such period, as may be prescribed; and

(b) to give to any person whose representations have been taken into account such notice as may be prescribed of their decision.

[(2ZA) In subsections (1) and (2) references to an application for planning permission include references to[—

(a) an application for consent, agreement or approval as mentioned in section 61DB(2), and

(b)] an application for approval under section 61L(2).]

(2A) A development order making any provision by virtue of this section may make different provision for different cases or different classes of development.]

(3) Before a local planning authority grant planning permission for the use of land as a caravan site, they shall, unless they are also the authority with power to issue a site licence for that land, consult the local authority with that power.

[(3A) Subsection (3) does not apply in relation to planning permission granted by [a Mayoral development order or] a neighbourhood development order.]

(4) In this section—

['prescribed' means prescribed by a development order]; and

'site licence' means a licence under Part 1 of the Caravan Sites and Control of Development Act 1960 authorising the use of land as a caravan site [or under Part 2 of the Mobile Homes (Wales) Act 2013 authorising the use of the land as a site for mobile homes (within the meaning of that Act)].

Amendment

Sub-ss (1), (2), (2A): substituted for sub-ss (1), (2), as originally enacted, by the Planning and Compensation Act 1991, s 16(2).

Sub-s (2ZA): inserted by the Localism Act 2011, s 121, Sch 12, paras 1, 8(1), (2). Date in force (for certain purposes): 15 January 2012: see SI 2012/57, art 4(1)(h). Date in force (for certain purposes): 6 April 2012: see SI 2012/628, art 8(a). Date in force (for certain purposes): 3 August 2012: see SI 2012/2029, arts 2, 3(a); for transitional provisions and savings see art 5 thereof. Date in force (for remaining purposes): 6 April 2013: see SI 2013/797, arts 1(2), 2.

Sub-s (2ZA): words from '—(a) an application' to '61DB(2), and (b)' in square brackets inserted by the Infrastructure Act 2015, s 30(1), Sch 4, Pt 2, paras 2, 9(1), (2). Date in force (for certain purposes): 12 February 2015: see the Infrastructure Act 2015, s 57(5)(d)(i). Date in force (for remaining purposes): to be appointed: see the Infrastructure Act 2015, s 57(5)(d)(ii).

Sub-s (3A): inserted by the Localism Act 2011, s 121, Sch 12, paras 1, 8(1), (3). Date in force (for certain purposes): 15 January 2012: see SI 2012/57, art 4(1)(h). Date in force (for certain purposes): 6 April 2012: see SI 2012/628, art 8(a). Date in force (for certain purposes): 3 August 2012: see SI 2012/2029, arts 2, 3(a); for transitional provisions and savings see art 5 thereof. Date in force (for remaining purposes): 6 April 2013: see SI 2013/797, arts 1(2), 2.

Sub-s (3A): words 'a Mayoral development order or' in square brackets inserted by the Infrastructure Act 2015, s 30(1), Sch 4, Pt 2, paras 2, 9(1), (3). Date in force (for certain purposes): 12 February 2015: see the Infrastructure Act 2015, s 57(5)(d)(i). Date in force (for remaining purposes): to be appointed: see the Infrastructure Act 2015, s 57(5)(d)(ii).

Sub-s (4): definition 'prescribed' substituted for original definitions 'agricultural holding' and 'owner' by the Planning and Compensation Act 1991, s 32, Sch 7, para 15.

Sub-s (4): in definition 'site licence' words from 'or under Part 2' to 'of that Act)' in square brackets inserted by the Mobile Homes (Wales) Act 2013, s 58(1), Sch 4, para 6(1), (2). Date in force: 1 October 2014: see SI 2014/11, arts 3(2), 4; for transitional provisions see the Mobile Homes (Wales) Act, s 58(2), Sch 5 thereto.

[71A Assessment of environmental effects]

[(1) The Secretary of State may by regulations make provision about the consideration to be given, before planning permission for development of any class specified in the regulations is granted, to the likely environmental effects of the proposed development.

(2) The regulations—

(a) may make the same provision as, or provision similar or corresponding to, any provision made, for the purposes of any [EU] obligation of the United Kingdom about the assessment of the likely effects of development on the environment, under section 2(2) of the European Communities Act 1972; and

(b) may make different provision for different classes of development.

(3) Where a draft of regulations made in exercise both of the power conferred by this section and the power conferred by section 2(2) of the European

Town and Country Planning Act 1990

Communities Act 1972 is approved by resolution of each House of Parliament, section 333(3) shall not apply.]

Amendment

Inserted by the Planning and Compensation Act 1991, s 15.

Sub-s (2): in para (a) reference to 'EU' in square brackets substituted by SI 2011/1043, art 6(1)(e). Date in force: 22 April 2011: see SI 2011/1043, art 2; for transitional savings see art 3(3) thereof.

72 Conditional grant of planning permission

(1) Without prejudice to the generality of section 70(1), conditions may be imposed on the grant of planning permission under that section—

   (a) for regulating the development or use of any land under the control of the applicant (whether or not it is land in respect of which the application was made) or requiring the carrying out of works on any such land, so far as appears to the local planning authority to be expedient for the purposes of or in connection with the development authorised by the permission;

   (b) for requiring the removal of any buildings or works authorised by the permission, or the discontinuance of any use of land so authorised, at the end of a specified period, and the carrying out of any works required for the reinstatement of land at the end of that period.

(2) A planning permission granted subject to such a condition as is mentioned in subsection (1)(b) is in this Act referred to as 'planning permission granted for a limited period'.

(3) Where—

   (a) planning permission is granted for development consisting of or including the carrying out of building or other operations subject to a condition that the operations shall be commenced not later than a time specified in the condition; and

   (b) any building or other operations are commenced after the time so specified,

   the commencement and carrying out of those operations do not constitute development for which that permission was granted.

(4) Subsection (3)(a) does not apply to a condition attached to the planning permission by or under section 91 or 92.

(5) Part I of Schedule 5 shall have effect for the purpose of making special provision with respect to the conditions which may be imposed on the grant of planning permission for development consisting of the winning and working of minerals [or involving the depositing of refuse or waste materials], and subsection (2) has effect subject to paragraph 1(6)(a) of that Schedule.

Amendment

Sub-s (5): words in square brackets inserted by the Planning and Compensation Act 1991, s 21, Sch 1, para 2.

73 Determination of applications to develop land without compliance with conditions previously attached

(1) This section applies, subject to subsection (4), to applications for planning permission for the development of land without complying with conditions subject to which a previous planning permission was granted.

Part III Control over Development

(2) On such an application the local planning authority shall consider only the question of the conditions subject to which planning permission should be granted, and—

(a) if they decide that planning permission should be granted subject to conditions differing from those subject to which the previous permission was granted, or that it should be granted unconditionally, they shall grant planning permission accordingly, and

(b) if they decide that planning permission should be granted subject to the same conditions as those subject to which the previous permission was granted, they shall refuse the application.

(3) ...

(4) This section does not apply if the previous planning permission was granted subject to a condition as to the time within which the development to which it related was to be begun and that time has expired without the development having been begun.

[(5) Planning permission must not be granted under this section to the extent that it has effect to change a condition subject to which a previous planning permission was granted by extending the time within which—

(a) a development must be started;

(b) an application for approval of reserved matters (within the meaning of section 92) must be made.]

Amendment

Sub-s (3): repealed by the Planning and Compulsory Purchase Act 2004, ss 42(2), 120, Sch 9. Date in force: 6 August 2004: see SI 2004/2097, art 2.

Sub-s (5): inserted by the Planning and Compulsory Purchase Act 2004, s 51(3); for further effect see s 51(6) thereof. Date in force (in relation to England): 24 August 2005: see SI 2005/2081, art 2(c); for savings see art 4(2) thereof. Date in force (in relation to Wales): to be appointed: see the Planning and Compulsory Purchase Act 2004, s 121(1), (2)(b).

[73A Planning permission for development already carried out]

[(1) On an application made to a local planning authority, the planning permission which may be granted includes planning permission for development carried out before the date of the application.

(2) Subsection (1) applies to development carried out—

(a) without planning permission;

(b) in accordance with planning permission granted for a limited period; or

(c) without complying with some condition subject to which planning permission was granted.

(3) Planning permission for such development may be granted so as to have effect from—

(a) the date on which the development was carried out; or

(b) if it was carried out in accordance with planning permission granted for a limited period, the end of that period.]

Amendment

Inserted by the Planning and Compensation Act 1991, s 32, Sch 7, para 16.

Town and Country Planning Act 1990

74 Directions etc as to method of dealing with applications

(1) Provision may be made by a development order for regulating the manner in which applications for planning permission to develop land are to be dealt with by local planning authorities, and in particular—

- (a) for enabling the Secretary of State to give directions restricting the grant of planning permission by the local planning authority, either indefinitely or during such period as may be specified in the directions, in respect of any such development, or in respect of development of any such class, as may be so specified;
- (b) for authorising the local planning authority, in such cases and subject to such conditions as may be prescribed by the order or by directions given by the Secretary of State under it, to grant planning permission for development which does not accord with the provisions of the development plan;
- (c) for requiring that, before planning permission for any development is granted or refused, local planning authorities prescribed by the order or by directions given by the Secretary of State under it shall consult with such authorities or persons as may be so prescribed;
- (d) for requiring the local planning authority to give to any applicant for planning permission, within such time as may be prescribed by the order, such notice as may be so prescribed as to the manner in which his application has been dealt with;
- (e) for requiring the local planning authority to give any applicant for any consent, agreement or approval required by a condition imposed on a grant of planning permission notice of their decision on his application, within such time as may be so prescribed;
- (f) for requiring the local planning authority to give to the Secretary of State, and to such other persons as may be prescribed by or under the order, such information as may be so prescribed with respect to applications for planning permission made to the authority, including information as to the manner in which any such application has been dealt with.

[(1ZA) In subsection (1)—

- (a) in paragraph (c) the reference to planning permission for any development includes a reference to[—
    - (i) a consent, agreement or approval as mentioned in section 61DB(2), and
    - (ii)] an approval under section 61L(2), and
- (b) in paragraph (f) references to applications for planning permission include references to[—
    - (i) applications for consent, agreement or approval as mentioned in section 61DB(2), and
    - (ii)] applications for approvals under section 61L(2).]

[(1A) Provision may be made by a development order—

- (a) for determining the persons to whom applications under this Act are to be sent; and
- (b) for requiring persons to whom such applications are sent to send copies to other interested persons.]

[(1B) Provision may be made by a development order—

(a) for enabling the Mayor of London in prescribed circumstances, and subject to such conditions as may be prescribed, to direct the local planning authority for a London borough to refuse an application for planning permission of a prescribed description in any particular case;

(b) for prohibiting a local planning authority to which any such direction is given from implementing the direction in prescribed circumstances or during prescribed periods; and

(c) for modifying any provision of this Act relating to an appeal against a refusal of planning permission (and, in particular, any such provision concerning parties or costs) in its application in relation to a refusal in compliance with such a direction;

and in the preceding provisions of this subsection 'prescribed' means prescribed by, or by directions made under, a development order.

(1C) In determining whether to exercise any power under subsection (1B) to direct a local planning authority to refuse an application, the Mayor of London shall have regard to—

(a) the development plan, and

(b) the spatial development strategy prepared and published under Part VIII of the Greater London Authority Act 1999,

so far as material to the application.]

(2) Subsection (1) is subject to the provisions of … sections 67(7) and 73(1) of the Planning (Listed Buildings and Conservation Areas) Act 1990.

Amendment

Sub-s (1A): inserted by the Planning and Compensation Act 1991, s 19(1).

Sub-s (1ZA): inserted by the Localism Act 2011, s 121, Sch 12, paras 1, 9. Date in force (for certain purposes): 15 January 2012: see SI 2012/57, art 4(1)(h). Date in force (for certain purposes): 6 April 2012: see SI 2012/628, art 8(a). Date in force (for certain purposes): 3 August 2012: see SI 2012/2029, arts 2, 3(a); for transitional provisions and savings see art 5 thereof. Date in force (for remaining purposes): 6 April 2013: see SI 2013/797, arts 1(2), 2.

Sub-s (1ZA): in para (a) words from '—(i) a consent' to '61DB(2), and (ii)' in square brackets inserted by the Infrastructure Act 2015, s 30(1), Sch 4, Pt 2, paras 2, 10(a). Date in force (for certain purposes): 12 February 2015: see the Infrastructure Act 2015, s 57(5)(d)(i). Date in force (for remaining purposes): to be appointed: see the Infrastructure Act 2015, s 57(5)(d)(ii).

Sub-s (1ZA): in para (b) words from '—(i) applications for' to '61DB(2), and (ii)' in square brackets inserted by the Infrastructure Act 2015, s 30(1), Sch 4, Pt 2, paras 2, 10(b). Date in force (for certain purposes): 12 February 2015: see the Infrastructure Act 2015, s 57(5)(d)(i). Date in force (for remaining purposes): to be appointed: see the Infrastructure Act 2015, s 57(5)(d)(ii).

Sub-ss (1B), (1C): inserted by the Greater London Authority Act 1999, s 344(1), (9). Date in force (in so far as these subsections confer the power to make orders): 11 November 1999: see the Greater London Authority Act 1999, s 425(2). Date in force (for remaining purposes): 12 January 2000: see SI 1999/3434, art 2.

Sub-s (2): words omitted repealed by the Planning and Compensation Act 1991, ss 32, 84, Sch 7, para 17, Sch 19, Part I.

[74A Deemed discharge of planning conditions]

[(1) The Secretary of State may by development order make provision for the deemed discharge of a condition to which this section applies.

Town and Country Planning Act 1990

(2) This section applies to a condition which—

   (a) has been imposed on the grant of planning permission for the development of land in England, and

   (b) requires the consent, agreement or approval of a local planning authority to any matter.

(3) Deemed discharge of a condition means that the local planning authority's consent, agreement or approval to any matter as required by the condition is deemed to have been given.

(4) A development order which makes provision for deemed discharge of a condition must provide that the condition is deemed to be discharged only if—

   (a) a person ('the applicant') has applied to the local planning authority for the consent, agreement or approval required by the condition,

   (b) the period for the authority to give notice of their decision on the application has elapsed without that notice having been given, and

   (c) the applicant has taken such further steps (if any) as are prescribed under subsection (5).

(5) The Secretary of State may by development order make provision about the procedure for the deemed discharge of a planning condition and, in particular, provision—

   (a) allowing or requiring steps to be taken by the applicant or the local planning authority;

   (b) as to the time at which or period within which a step may or must be taken;

   (c) as to the time at which the deemed discharge takes effect (including for this to be determined by the applicant, subject to such limitations as may be prescribed);

   (d) for a time or period within paragraph (b) or (c) to be modified by agreement between the applicant and the local planning authority;

   (e) as to the form or content of any notice which may or must be given as part of the procedure, and as to the means by which it may or must be given.

(6) The Secretary of State may by development order provide that provision for deemed discharge of a condition does not apply—

   (a) in relation to a condition of a prescribed description;

   (b) in relation to a condition imposed on the grant of planning permission of a prescribed description;

   (c) in relation to a condition imposed on the grant of planning permission for development of a prescribed description;

   (d) in other prescribed circumstances.

(7) The power in subsection (6)(d) includes power to provide that provision for deemed discharge of a condition does not apply where an applicant for planning permission and the local planning authority to whom the application is made agree, before or after planning permission is granted, that it should not apply in relation to a condition imposed on the grant of permission.

(8) The Secretary of State may by development order make provision for section 78(2) (appeals to the Secretary of State) not to apply, or to apply with modifications, where—

(a) a person has applied for the consent, agreement or approval of a local planning authority required by a condition imposed on a grant of planning permission,

(b) the local planning authority have not given notice to that person of their decision on the application within the period mentioned in section 78(2), and

(c) the person has taken such further steps (if any) as are prescribed to bring about the deemed discharge of the planning condition.

(9) A development order which makes provision for deemed discharge of a condition must limit the application of that provision to a condition imposed on the grant of planning permission following an application made after the development order comes into force.

(10) In this section—

'condition' includes a limitation;

'prescribed' means prescribed by development order made by the Secretary of State.]

Amendment

Inserted by the Infrastructure Act 2015, s 29. Date in force: 12 February 2015: see the Infrastructure Act 2015, s 57(5)(c).

75 Effect of planning permission

(1) Without prejudice to the provisions of this Part as to the duration, revocation or modification of planning permission, any grant of planning permission to develop land shall (except in so far as the permission otherwise provides) enure for the benefit of the land and of all persons for the time being interested in it.

(2) Where planning permission is granted for the erection of a building, the grant of permission may specify the purposes for which the building may be used.

(3) If no purpose is so specified, the permission shall be construed as including permission to use the building for the purpose for which it is designed.

76 ...

...

Amendment

Repealed by the Planning and Compulsory Purchase Act 2004, ss 118(1), 120, Sch 6, paras 1, 4, Sch 9. Date in force (in relation to England): 10 August 2006: see SI 2006/1061, art 3(b). Date in force (in relation to Wales): 30 June 2007: see SI 2007/1369, art 2(b).

Secretary of State's powers as respects planning applications and decisions

[76A Major infrastructure projects]

[(1) This section applies to—

(a) an application for planning permission;

(b) an application for the approval of a local planning authority required under a development order,

if the Secretary of State thinks that the development to which the application relates is of national or regional importance.

Town and Country Planning Act 1990

(2) The Secretary of State may direct that the application must be referred to him instead of being dealt with by the local planning authority.

(3) If the Secretary of State gives a direction under subsection (2) he may also direct that any application—

   (a) under or for the purposes of the planning Acts, and

   (b) which he thinks is connected with the application mentioned in subsection (1),

   must also be referred to him instead of being dealt with by the local planning authority.

(4) If the Secretary of State gives a direction under this section—

   (a) the application must be referred to him;

   (b) he must appoint an inspector to consider the application.

(5) If the Secretary of State gives a direction under subsection (2) the applicant must prepare an economic impact report which must—

   (a) be in such form and contain such matter as is prescribed by development order;

   (b) be submitted to the Secretary of State in accordance with such provision as is so prescribed.

(6) For the purposes of subsection (5) the Secretary of State may, by development order, prescribe such requirements as to publicity and notice as he thinks appropriate.

(7) A direction under this section or section 76B may be varied or revoked by a subsequent direction.

(8) The decision of the Secretary of State on any application referred to him under this section is final.

(9) Regional relates to a region listed in Schedule 1 to the Regional Development Agencies Act 1998 (c 45).

(10) The following provisions of this Act apply (with any necessary modifications) to an application referred to the Secretary of State under this section as they apply to an application which falls to be determined by a local planning authority—

   (a) section 70;

   (b) section 72(1) and (5);

   (c) section 73;

   (d) section 73A.

(11) A development order may apply (with or without modifications) any requirements imposed by the order by virtue of section 65 or 71 to an application referred to the Secretary of State under this section.

(12) This section does not apply to an application which relates to the development of land in Wales.]

Amendment

Inserted by the Planning and Compulsory Purchase Act 2004, s 44. Date in force (for the purpose of making, or making provision by means of, subordinate legislation): 6 August

2004: see SI 2004/2097, art 2. Date in force (in relation to England for remaining purposes): 24 August 2005 (except in relation to an application received by a local planning authority before that date): see SI 2005/2081, arts 2(b), 4(1). Date in force (in relation to Wales for remaining purposes): to be appointed: see the Planning and Compulsory Purchase Act 2004, s 121(1), (2)(b).

[76B Major infrastructure projects: inspectors]

[(1) This section applies if the Secretary of State appoints an inspector under section 76A(4)(b) (the lead inspector).

(2) The Secretary of State may direct the lead inspector—

(a) to consider such matters relating to the application as are prescribed;

(b) to make recommendations to the Secretary of State on those matters.

(3) After considering any recommendations of the lead inspector the Secretary of State may—

(a) appoint such number of additional inspectors as he thinks appropriate;

(b) direct that each of the additional inspectors must consider such matters relating to the application as the lead inspector decides.

(4) An additional inspector must—

(a) comply with such directions as to procedural matters as the lead inspector gives;

(b) report to the lead inspector on the matters he is appointed to consider.

(5) A copy of directions given as mentioned in subsection (4)(a) must be given to—

(a) the person who made the application;

(b) the local planning authority;

(c) any other person who requests it.

(6) If the Secretary of State does not act under subsection (3) he must direct the lead inspector to consider the application on his own.

(7) In every case the lead inspector must report to the Secretary of State on—

(a) his consideration of the application;

(b) the consideration of the additional inspectors (if any) of the matters mentioned in subsection (3)(b).

(8) The function of the lead inspector in pursuance of subsection (2)—

(a) may be exercised from time to time;

(b) includes making recommendations as to the number of additional inspectors required from time to time.

(9) The power of the Secretary of State under subsection (3) to appoint an additional inspector includes power to revoke such an appointment.]

Amendment

Inserted by the Planning and Compulsory Purchase Act 2004, s 44. Date in force (for the purpose of making, or making provision by means of, subordinate legislation): 6 August 2004: see SI 2004/2097, art 2. Date in force (in relation to England for remaining purposes): 24 August 2005 (except in relation to an application received by a local planning authority before that date): see SI 2005/2081, arts 2(b), 4(1). Date in force (in relation to Wales for

Town and Country Planning Act 1990

remaining purposes): to be appointed: see the Planning and Compulsory Purchase Act 2004, s 121(1), (2)(b).

[76C Provisions applying to applications made under section 62A]

[(1) Sections 62(3) and (4), 65(5), 70 to 70C, 72(1) and (5) and 73A apply, with any necessary modifications, to an application for planning permission made to the Secretary of State under section 62A as they apply to an application for planning permission which is to be determined by the local planning authority.

(2) Any requirements imposed by a development order by virtue of section 62, 65 or 71 or paragraph 8(6) of Schedule 1 may be applied by a development order, with or without modifications, to an application for planning permission made to the Secretary of State under section 62A.

(3) Where an application is made to the Secretary of State under section 62A(3) instead of to the authority to whom it would otherwise have been made, a development order may apply, with or without modifications, to the application any enactment that relates to applications of that kind when made to that authority.]

Amendment
Inserted by the Growth and Infrastructure Act 2013, s 1(2), Sch 1, paras 1, 5. Date in force (in relation to England for the purposes of making regulations or orders): 9 May 2013: see SI 2013/1124, art 2. Date in force (for remaining purposes): 1 October 2013: see SI 2013/2143, art 2(1)(a).

[76D Deciding applications made under section 62A]

[(1) An application made to the Secretary of State under section 62A ('a direct application') is to be determined by a person appointed by the Secretary of State for the purpose instead of by the Secretary of State, subject to section 76E.

(2) Where a person has been appointed under subsection (1) or this subsection to determine a direct application then, at any time before the person has determined the application, the Secretary of State may—

 (a) revoke the person's appointment; and

 (b) appoint another person to determine the application instead.

(3) A person appointed under this section to determine an application for planning permission made to the Secretary of State under section 62A has the same powers and duties that the Secretary of State has under section 76C.

(4) Where a direct application is determined by a person appointed under this section, the person's decision is to be treated as that of the Secretary of State.

(5) Except as provided by Part 12, the validity of that decision is not to be questioned in any proceedings whatsoever.

(6) It is not a ground of application to the High Court under section 288 that a direct application ought to have been determined by the Secretary of State and not by a person appointed under this section unless the applicant challenges the person's power to determine the direct application before the person's decision on the direct application is given.

(7) Where any enactment (other than this section and section 319A)—

Part III Control over Development

(a) refers (or is to be read as referring) to the Secretary of State in a context relating to or capable of relating to an application made under section 62A (otherwise than by referring to the application having been made to the Secretary of State), or

(b) refers (or is to be read as referring) to anything (other than the making of the application) done or authorised or required to be done by, to or before the Secretary of State in connection with any such application,

then, so far as the context permits, the enactment is to be read, in relation to an application determined or to be determined by a person appointed under this section, as if the reference to the Secretary of State were or included a reference to that person.]

Amendment

Inserted by the Growth and Infrastructure Act 2013, s 1(2), Sch 1, paras 1, 5. Date in force (in relation to England for the purposes of making regulations or orders): 9 May 2013: see SI 2013/1124, art 2. Date in force (for remaining purposes): 1 October 2013: see SI 2013/2143, art 2(1)(a).

[76E Applications under section 62A: determination by Secretary of State]

[(1) The Secretary of State may direct that an application made to the Secretary of State under section 62A ('a direct application') is to be determined by the Secretary of State instead of by a person appointed under section 76D.

(2) Where a direction is given under subsection (1), the Secretary of State must serve a copy of the direction on—

(a) the person, if any, appointed under section 76D to determine the application concerned,

(b) the applicant, and

(c) the local planning authority.

(3) Where a direct application is to be determined by the Secretary of State in consequence of a direction under subsection (1)—

(a) in determining the application, the Secretary of State may take into account any report made to the Secretary of State by any person previously appointed to determine the application, and

(b) subject to that, the provisions of the planning Acts which are relevant to the application apply to it as if section 76D had never applied to it.

(4) The Secretary of State may by a further direction revoke a direction under subsection (1) at any time before the determination of the direct application concerned.

(5) Where a direction is given under subsection (4), the Secretary of State must serve a copy of the direction on—

(a) the person, if any, previously appointed under section 76D to determine the application concerned,

(b) the applicant, and

(c) the local planning authority.

(6) Where a direction is given under subsection (4) in relation to a direct application—

Town and Country Planning Act 1990

(a) anything done by or on behalf of the Secretary of State in connection with the application which might have been done by a person appointed under section 76D to determine the application is, unless the person appointed under section 76D to determine the application directs otherwise, to be treated as having been done by that person, and

(b) subject to that, section 76D applies to the application as if no direction under subsection (1) had been given in relation to the application.]

Amendment
Inserted by the Growth and Infrastructure Act 2013, s 1(2), Sch 1, paras 1, 5. Date in force (in relation to England for the purposes of making regulations or orders): 9 May 2013: see SI 2013/1124, art 2. Date in force (for remaining purposes): 1 October 2013: see SI 2013/2143, art 2(1)(a).

77 Reference of applications to Secretary of State

(1) The Secretary of State may give directions requiring applications for planning permission, or for the *approval* [consent, agreement or approval] of any local planning authority required under a development order[, a local development order[, a Mayoral development order] or a neighbourhood development order], to be referred to him instead of being dealt with by local planning authorities.

(2) A direction under this section—

(a) may be given either to a particular local planning authority or to local planning authorities generally; and

(b) may relate either to a particular application or to applications of a class specified in the direction.

(3) Any application in respect of which a direction under this section has effect shall be referred to the Secretary of State accordingly.

(4) Subject to subsection (5), where an application for planning permission is referred to the Secretary of State under this section, sections [70, 72(1) and (5), 73 and 73A] shall apply, with any necessary modifications, as they apply to such an application which falls to be determined by the local planning authority [and a development order may apply, with or without modifications, to an application so referred any requirements imposed by such an order by virtue of section 65 or 71].

(5) Before determining an application referred to him under this section, the Secretary of State shall, if either the applicant or the local planning authority wish, give each of them an opportunity of appearing before, and being heard by, a person appointed by the Secretary of State for the purpose.

(6) *Subsection (5) does not apply to an application for planning permission referred to a Planning Inquiry Commission under section 101.*

[(6) Subsection (5) does not apply to—

(a) an application for planning permission referred to a Planning Inquiry Commission under section 101; or

(b) an application referred to the Secretary of State under this section instead of being dealt with by a local planning authority in England.]

[(6A) Subsection (5) does not apply to an application referred to the Welsh Ministers under this section instead of being dealt with by a local planning authority in Wales.]

Part III Control over Development

(7) The decision of the Secretary of State on any application referred to him under this section shall be final.

Amendment

Sub-s (1): word 'approval' in italics repealed and subsequent words in square brackets substituted by the Infrastructure Act 2015, s 30(1), Sch 4, Pt 2, paras 2, 11(a). Date in force (for certain purposes): 12 February 2015: see the Infrastructure Act 2015, s 57(5)(d)(i). Date in force (for remaining purposes): to be appointed: see the Infrastructure Act 2015, s 57(5)(d)(ii).

Sub-s (1): words ', a local development order or a neighbourhood development order' in square brackets substituted by the Localism Act 2011, s 121, Sch 12, paras 1, 10. Date in force (for certain purposes): 15 January 2012: see SI 2012/57, art 4(1)(h). Date in force (for certain purposes): 6 April 2012: see SI 2012/628, art 8(a). Date in force (for certain purposes): 3 August 2012: see SI 2012/2029, arts 2, 3(a); for transitional provisions and savings see art 5 thereof. Date in force (for remaining purposes): 6 April 2013: see SI 2013/797, arts 1(2), 2.

Sub-s (1): words ', a Mayoral development order' in square brackets inserted by the Infrastructure Act 2015, s 30(1), Sch 4, Pt 2, paras 2, 11(b). Date in force (for certain purposes): 12 February 2015: see the Infrastructure Act 2015, s 57(5)(d)(i). Date in force (for remaining purposes): to be appointed: see the Infrastructure Act 2015, s 57(5)(d)(ii).

Sub-s (4): first words in square brackets substituted, and final words in square brackets inserted, by the Planning and Compensation Act 1991, s 32, Sch 7, para 18.

Sub-s (6): substituted by the Planning Act 2008, s 196(4), Sch 10, paras 1, 2. Date in force: to be appointed: see the Planning Act 2008, s 241(8).

Sub-s (6A): inserted, in relation to Wales, by SI 2014/2773, art 3, Sch 1, paras 1, 2. Date in force: 11 November 2014: see SI 2014/2773, art 1(2).

78 Right to appeal against planning decisions and failure to take such decisions

(1) Where a local planning authority—

   (a) refuse an application for planning permission or grant it subject to conditions;

   (b) refuse an application for any consent, agreement or approval of that authority required by a condition imposed on a grant of planning permission or grant it subject to conditions; or

   (c) refuse an application for any approval of that authority required under a development order[, a local development order[, a Mayoral development order] or a neighbourhood development order] or grant it subject to conditions,

   the applicant may by notice appeal to the Secretary of State.

(2) A person who has made such an application [to the local planning authority] may also appeal to the Secretary of State if the local planning authority have [done none of the following]—

   (a) given notice to the applicant of their decision on the application;

   [(aa) given notice to the applicant that they have exercised their power under section 70A [or 70B] [or 70C] to decline to determine the application;]

   (b) given notice to him that the application has been referred to the Secretary of State in accordance with directions given under section 77,

   within such period as may be prescribed by the development order or within such extended period as may at any time be agreed upon in writing between the applicant and the authority.

Town and Country Planning Act 1990

(3) Any appeal under this section shall be made by notice served within such time and in such manner as may be prescribed by a development order.

(4) The time prescribed for the service of such a notice must not be less than—

(a) 28 days from the date of notification of the decision; or

(b) in the case of an appeal under subsection (2), 28 days from the end of the period prescribed as mentioned in subsection (2) or, as the case may be, the extended period mentioned in that subsection.

[(4A) A notice of appeal under this section must be accompanied by such information as may be prescribed by a development order.

(4B) The power to make a development order under subsection (4A) is exercisable by—

(a) the Secretary of State, in relation to England;

(b) the Welsh Ministers, in relation to Wales.

(4C) Section 333(5) does not apply in relation to a development order under subsection (4A) made by the Welsh Ministers.

(4D) A development order under subsection (4A) made by the Welsh Ministers is subject to annulment in pursuance of a resolution of the National Assembly for Wales.]

(5) For the purposes of the application of sections *79(1)* [79(1) and (3)], 253(2) (c), 266(1)(b) *and 288(10)(b)* [, 288(10)(b)] [, 319A(7)(b) and 319B(7)(b)] in relation to an appeal under subsection (2), it shall be assumed that the authority decided to refuse the application in question.

Amendment

Sub-s (1): in para (c) words ', a local development order or a neighbourhood development order' in square brackets substituted by the Localism Act 2011, s 121, Sch 12, paras 1, 11. Date in force (for certain purposes): 15 January 2012: see SI 2012/57, art 4(1)(h). Date in force (for certain purposes): 6 April 2012: see SI 2012/628, art 8(a). Date in force (for certain purposes): 3 August 2012: see SI 2012/2029, arts 2, 3(a); for transitional provisions and savings see art 5 thereof. Date in force (for remaining purposes): 6 April 2013: see SI 2013/797, arts 1(2), 2.

Sub-s (1): in para (c) words ', a Mayoral development order' in square brackets inserted by the Infrastructure Act 2015, s 30(1), Sch 4, Pt 2, paras 2, 12. Date in force (for certain purposes): 12 February 2015: see the Infrastructure Act 2015, s 57(5)(d)(i). Date in force (for remaining purposes): to be appointed: see the Infrastructure Act 2015, s 57(5)(d)(ii).

Sub-s (2): words 'to the local planning authority' in square brackets inserted by the Growth and Infrastructure Act 2013, s 1(2), Sch 1, paras 1, 8. Date in force (in relation to England for the purposes of making regulations or orders): 9 May 2013: see SI 2013/1124, art 2. Date in force (for remaining purposes): 1 October 2013: see SI 2013/2143, art 2(1)(a).

Sub-s (2): words 'done none of the following' in square brackets substituted by the Planning and Compensation Act 1991, s 17(2).

Sub-s (2): para (aa) substituted by the Planning and Compensation Act 1991, s 17(2).

Sub-s (2): in para (aa) words 'or 70B' in square brackets inserted by the Planning and Compulsory Purchase Act 2004, s 43(2); for effect see s 43(5) thereof. Date in force (in relation to England): 6 April 2009: see SI 2009/384, art 2(b). Date in force (in relation to Wales): to be appointed: see the Planning and Compulsory Purchase Act 2004, s 121(1), (2) (b), (3A), (3B) (as amended by the Planning Act 2008, s 187, Sch 7, para 7).

Sub-s (2): in para (aa) words 'or 70C' in square brackets inserted by the Localism Act 2011, s 123(1), (3). Date in force: 6 April 2012: see SI 2012/628, art 8(b); for transitional provisions see arts 9, 13(1) thereof.

Part III Control over Development

Sub-ss (4A)–(4D): inserted by the Planning Act 2008, s 197, Sch 11, paras 1, 2. Date in force (in relation to England): 6 April 2009: see SI 2009/400, art 5(d). Date in force (in relation to Wales): 30 April 2012: see SI 2012/802, art 2(b).

Sub-s (5): reference to '79(1)' in italics repealed and subsequent words in square brackets substituted by the Planning Act 2008, s 196(4), Sch 10, paras 1, 3(a). Date in force (for certain purposes): 6 April 2009: see SI 2009/400, art 3(j); for savings see art 6(2) thereof. Date in force (for remaining purposes): to be appointed: see the Planning Act 2008, s 241(8).

Sub-s (5): words 'and 288(10)(b)' in italics repealed and subsequent words in square brackets substituted by the Planning Act 2008, s 196(4), Sch 10, paras 1, 3(b). Date in force (for certain purposes): 6 April 2009: see SI 2009/400, art 3(j); for savings see art 6(2) thereof. Date in force (for remaining purposes): to be appointed: see the Planning Act 2008, s 241(8).

Sub-s (5): words ', 319A(7)(b) and 319B(7)(b)' in square brackets substituted by SI 2014/2773, art 3, Sch 1, paras 1, 3. Date in force: 11 November 2014: see SI 2014/2773, art 1(2).

[78A Appeal made: functions of local planning authorities]

[(1) This section applies if a person who has made an application mentioned in section 78(1)(a) appeals to the Secretary of State under section 78(2).

(2) At any time before the end of the additional period the local planning authority may give the notice referred to in section 78(2).

(3) If the local planning authority give notice as mentioned in subsection (2) that their decision is to refuse the application—

　(a) the appeal must be treated as an appeal under section 78(1) against the refusal;

　(b) the Secretary of State must give the person making the appeal an opportunity to revise the grounds of the appeal;

　(c) the Secretary of State must give such a person an opportunity to change any option the person has chosen relating to the procedure for the appeal.

(4) If the local planning authority give notice as mentioned in subsection (2) that their decision is to grant the application subject to conditions the Secretary of State must give the person making the appeal the opportunity—

　(a) to proceed with the appeal as an appeal under section 78(1) against the grant of the application subject to conditions;

　(b) to revise the grounds of the appeal;

　(c) to change any option the person has chosen relating to the procedure for the appeal.

(5) The Secretary of State must not issue his decision on the appeal before the end of the additional period.

(6) The additional period is the period prescribed by development order for the purposes of this section and which starts on the day on which the person appeals under section 78(2).]

Amendment

Inserted by the Planning and Compulsory Purchase Act 2004, s 50(1); for effect see s 50(3), (4) thereof. Date in force (for the purpose of making, or making provision by means of, subordinate legislation): 6 August 2004: see SI 2004/2097, art 2. Date in force (in relation to Wales for remaining purposes): 22 June 2015: see SI 2015/340, art 2(b). Date in force (in relation to England for remaining purposes): to be appointed: see the Planning and Compulsory Purchase Act 2004, s 121(1), (2)(b).

Town and Country Planning Act 1990

79 Determination of appeals

(1) On an appeal under section 78 the Secretary of State may—

(a) allow or dismiss the appeal, or

(b) reverse or vary any part of the decision of the local planning authority (whether the appeal relates to that part of it or not),

and may deal with the application as if it had been made to him in the first instance.

(2) Before determining an appeal under section 78 the Secretary of State shall, if either the appellant or the local planning authority so wish, give each of them an opportunity of appearing before and being heard by a person appointed by the Secretary of State for the purpose.

(3) *Subsection (2) does not apply to an appeal referred to a Planning Inquiry Commission under section 101.*

[(3) Subsection (2) does not apply to—

(a) an appeal referred to a Planning Inquiry Commission under section 101; or

(b) an appeal against a decision of a local planning authority in England.]

[(3A) Subsection (2) does not apply to an appeal to the Welsh Ministers.]

(4) Subject to subsection (2), the provisions of sections [70, 72(1) and (5), 73 and 73A] and Part I of Schedule 5 shall apply, with any necessary modifications, in relation to an appeal to the Secretary of State under section 78 as they apply in relation to an application for planning permission which falls to be determined by the local planning authority [and a development order may apply, with or without modifications, to such an appeal any requirements imposed by a development order by virtue of section 65 or 71].

(5) The decision of the Secretary of State on such an appeal shall be final.

(6) If, before or during the determination of such an appeal in respect of an application for planning permission to develop land, the Secretary of State forms the opinion that, having regard to the provisions of sections 70 and 72(1), the development order and any directions given under that order, planning permission for that development—

(a) could not have been granted by the local planning authority; or

(b) could not have been granted otherwise than subject to the conditions imposed,

he may decline to determine the appeal or to proceed with the determination.

[(6A) If at any time before or during the determination of such an appeal it appears to the Secretary of State that the appellant is responsible for undue delay in the progress of the appeal, he may—

(a) give the appellant notice that the appeal will be dismissed unless the appellant takes, within the period specified in the notice, such steps as are specified in the notice for the expedition of the appeal; and

(b) if the appellant fails to take those steps within that period, dismiss the appeal accordingly.]

(7) Schedule 6 applies to appeals under section 78, including appeals under that section as applied by or under any other provision of this Act.

Part III Control over Development

Amendment

Sub-s (3): substituted by the Planning Act 2008, s 196(4), Sch 10, paras 1, 4. Date in force (for certain purposes): 6 April 2009: see SI 2009/400, art 3(j); for savings see art 6(2) thereof. Date in force (for remaining purposes): to be appointed: see the Planning Act 2008, s 241(8).

Sub-s (3A): inserted, in relation to Wales, by SI 2014/2773, art 3, Sch 1, paras 1, 4. Date in force: 11 November 2014: see SI 2014/2773, art 1(2).

Sub-s (4): first words in square brackets substituted, and final words in square brackets inserted, by the Planning and Compensation Act 1991, s 32, Sch 7, para 19.

Sub-s (6A): inserted by the Planning and Compensation Act 1991, s 18.

80 ...

...

Amendment

Repealed by the Planning and Compensation Act 1991, ss 31(4), 84(6), Sch 6, paras 8, 11, Sch 19, Pt II.

81 ...

...

Amendment

Repealed by the Planning and Compensation Act 1991, ss 31(4), 84(6), Sch 6, paras 8, 11, Sch 19, Pt II.

Simplified planning zones

82 Simplified planning zones

(1) A simplified planning zone is an area in respect of which a simplified planning zone scheme is in force.

(2) The adoption or approval of a simplified planning zone scheme has effect to grant in relation to the zone, or any part of it specified in the scheme, planning permission—

(a) for development specified in the scheme, or

(b) for development of any class so specified.

(3) Planning permission under a simplified planning zone scheme may be unconditional or subject to such conditions, limitations or exceptions as may be specified in the scheme.

83 Making of simplified planning zone schemes

(1) Every local planning authority shall consider, as soon as practicable after 2nd November 1987, the question for which part or parts of their area a simplified planning zone scheme is desirable, and then shall keep that question under review.

(2) If as a result of their original consideration or of any such review a local planning authority decide that it is desirable to prepare a scheme for any part of their area they shall do so; and a local planning authority may at any time decide—

(a) to make a simplified planning zone scheme, or

(b) to alter a scheme adopted by them, or

(c) with the consent of the Secretary of State, to alter a scheme approved by him.

(3) Schedule 7 has effect with respect to the making and alteration of simplified planning zone schemes and other related matters.

[(5) In this section and in Schedule 7 references to a regional strategy are to a regional strategy under Part 5 of the Local Democracy, Economic Development and Construction Act 2009.]

Amendment

Sub-s (5): inserted by the Local Democracy, Economic Development and Construction Act 2009, s 85(1), Sch 5, paras 1, 2(1), (3). Date in force: 1 April 2010: see SI 2009/3318, art 4(cc), (gg).

Sub-s (5): repealed by the Localism Act 2011, s 237, Sch 25, Pt 16. Date in force: to be appointed: see the Localism Act 2011, s 240(2).

84 Simplified planning zone schemes: conditions and limitations on planning permission

(1) The conditions and limitations on planning permission which may be specified in a simplified planning zone scheme may include—

(a) conditions or limitations in respect of all development permitted by the scheme or in respect of particular descriptions of development so permitted, and

(b) conditions or limitations requiring the consent, agreement or approval of the local planning authority in relation to particular descriptions of permitted development.

(2) Different conditions or limitations may be specified in a simplified planning zone scheme for different cases or classes of case.

(3) Nothing in a simplified planning zone scheme shall affect the right of any person—

(a) to do anything not amounting to development, or

(b) to carry out development for which planning permission is not required or for which permission has been granted otherwise than by the scheme.

(4) No limitation or restriction subject to which permission has been granted otherwise than under the scheme shall affect the right of any person to carry out development for which permission has been granted under the scheme.

85 Duration of simplified planning zone scheme

(1) A simplified planning zone scheme shall take effect on the date of its adoption or approval and shall cease to have effect at the end of the period of 10 years beginning with that date.

(2) When the scheme ceases to have effect planning permission under it shall also cease to have effect except in a case where the development authorised by it has been begun.

86 Alteration of simplified planning zone scheme

(1) This section applies where alterations to a simplified planning zone scheme are adopted or approved.

Part III Control over Development

(2) The adoption or approval of alterations providing for the inclusion of land in the simplified planning zone has effect to grant in relation to that land, or such part of it as is specified in the scheme, planning permission for development so specified or of any class so specified.

(3) The adoption or approval of alterations providing for the grant of planning permission has effect to grant such permission in relation to the simplified planning zone, or such part of it as is specified in the scheme, for development so specified or development of any class so specified.

(4) The adoption or approval of alterations providing for the withdrawal or relaxation of conditions, limitations or restrictions to which planning permission under the scheme is subject has effect to withdraw or relax the conditions, limitations or restrictions immediately.

(5) The adoption or approval of alterations providing for—
   (a) the exclusion of land from the simplified planning zone,
   (b) the withdrawal of planning permission, or
   (c) the imposition of new or more stringent conditions, limitations or restrictions to which planning permission under the scheme is subject,

has effect to withdraw permission, or to impose the conditions, limitations or restrictions, with effect from the end of the period of 12 months beginning with the date of the adoption or approval.

(6) The adoption or approval of alterations to a scheme does not affect planning permission under the scheme in any case where the development authorised by it has been begun.

87 Exclusion of certain descriptions of land or development

(1) The following descriptions of land may not be included in a simplified planning zone—
   (a) land in a National Park;
   (b) land in a conservation area;
   (c) land within the Broads;
   (d) land in an area designated under [section 82 of the Countryside and Rights of Way Act 2000] as an area of outstanding natural beauty;
   (e) land identified in the development plan for the district as part of a green belt;
   [(f) land within a site of special scientific interest (within the meaning of the Wildlife and Countryside Act 1981)].

(2) Where land included in a simplified planning zone becomes land of a description mentioned in subsection (1), that subsection does not operate to exclude it from the zone.

(3) The Secretary of State may by order provide that no simplified planning zone scheme shall have effect to grant planning permission—
   (a) in relation to an area of land specified in the order or to areas of land of a description so specified, or
   (b) for development of a description specified in the order.

Town and Country Planning Act 1990

(4) An order under subsection (3) has effect to withdraw such planning permission under a simplified planning zone scheme already in force with effect from the date on which the order comes into force, except in a case where the development authorised by the permission has been begun.

Amendment

Sub-s (1): in para (d) words 'section 82 of the Countryside and Rights of Way Act 2000' in square brackets substituted by the Countryside and Rights of Way Act 2000, s 93, Sch 15, Pt I, para 10. Date in force (in relation to England): 1 April 2001: see SI 2001/114, art 2(2) (e). Date in force (in relation to Wales): 1 May 2001: see SI 2001/1410, art 2(g).

Sub-s (1): para (f) substituted by the Countryside and Rights of Way Act 2000, s 76(1), Sch 10, Pt II, para 7. Date in force: 30 January 2001: see the Countryside and Rights of Way Act 2000, s 103(2).

Enterprise zone schemes

88 Planning permission for development in enterprise zones

(1) An order designating an enterprise zone under Schedule 32 to the Local Government, Planning and Land Act 1980 shall (without more) have effect on the date on which the order designating the zone takes effect to grant planning permission for development specified in the scheme or for development of any class so specified.

(2) The approval of a modified scheme under paragraph 11 of that Schedule shall (without more) have effect on the date on which the modifications take effect to grant planning permission for development specified in the modified scheme or for development of any class so specified.

(3) Planning permission so granted shall be subject to such conditions or limitations as may be specified in the scheme or modified scheme or, if none is specified, shall be unconditional.

(4) Subject to subsection (5), where planning permission is so granted for any development or class of development the enterprise zone authority may direct that the permission shall not apply in relation—

   (a) to a specified development; or

   (b) to a specified class of development; or

   (c) to a specified class of development in a specified area within the enterprise zone.

(5) An enterprise zone authority shall not give a direction under subsection (4) unless—

   (a) they have submitted it to the Secretary of State, and

   (b) he has notified them that he approves of their giving it.

(6) If the scheme or the modified scheme specifies, in relation to any development it permits, matters which will require approval by the enterprise zone authority, the permission shall have effect accordingly.

(7) The Secretary of State may by regulations make provision as to—

   (a) the procedure for giving a direction under subsection (4); and

   (b) the method and procedure relating to the approval of matters specified in a scheme or modified scheme as mentioned in subsection (6).

Part III Control over Development

(8) Such regulations may modify any provision of the planning Acts or any instrument made under them or may apply any such provision or instrument (with or without modification) in making any such provision as is mentioned in subsection (7).

(9) Nothing in this section prevents planning permission being granted in relation to land in an enterprise zone otherwise than by virtue of this section (whether the permission is granted in pursuance of an application made under this Part or by a development order[, a local development order[, a Mayoral development order] or a neighbourhood development order]).

(10) Nothing in this section prejudices the right of any person to carry out development apart from this section.

Amendment

Sub-s (9): words ', a local development order or a neighbourhood development order' in square brackets substituted by the Localism Act 2011, s 121, Sch 12, paras 1, 12. Date in force (for certain purposes): 15 January 2012: see SI 2012/57, art 4(1)(h). Date in force (for certain purposes): 6 April 2012: see SI 2012/628, art 8(a). Date in force (for certain purposes): 3 August 2012: see SI 2012/2029, arts 2, 3(a); for transitional provisions and savings see art 5 thereof. Date in force (for remaining purposes): 6 April 2013: see SI 2013/797, arts 1(2), 2.

Sub-s (9): words ', a Mayoral development order' in square brackets inserted by the Infrastructure Act 2015, s 30(1), Sch 4, Pt 2, paras 2, 13. Date in force (for certain purposes): 12 February 2015: see the Infrastructure Act 2015, s 57(5)(d)(i). Date in force (for remaining purposes): to be appointed: see the Infrastructure Act 2015, s 57(5)(d)(ii).

89 Effect on planning permission of modification or termination of scheme

(1) Modifications to an enterprise zone scheme do not affect planning permission under the scheme in any case where the development authorised by it has been begun before the modifications take effect.

(2) When an area ceases to be an enterprise zone, planning permission under the scheme shall cease to have effect except in a case where the development authorised by it has been begun.

Deemed planning permission

90 Development with government authorisation

(1) Where the authorisation of a government department is required by virtue of an enactment in respect of development to be carried out by a local authority [or National Park authority], or by statutory undertakers who are not a local authority [or National Park authority], that department may, on granting that authorisation, direct that planning permission for that development shall be deemed to be granted, subject to such conditions (if any) as may be specified in the direction.

[(2) On granting or varying a consent under section 36 or 37 of the Electricity Act 1989 in relation to a generating station or electric line in England or Wales, the Secretary of State may give a direction for planning permission to be deemed to be granted, subject to such conditions (if any) as may be specified in the direction, for—

(a) so much of the operation or change of use to which the consent relates as constitutes development;

Town and Country Planning Act 1990

      (b) any development ancillary to the operation or change of use to which the consent relates.

(2ZA) On varying a consent under section 36 or 37 of the Electricity Act 1989 in relation to a generating station or electric line in England or Wales, the Secretary of State may give one or more of the following directions (instead of, or as well as, a direction under subsection (2))—

      (a) a direction for an existing planning permission deemed to be granted by virtue of a direction under subsection (2) (whenever made) to be varied as specified in the direction;

      (b) a direction for any conditions subject to which any such existing planning permission was deemed to be granted to be varied as specified in the direction;

      (c) a direction for any consent, agreement or approval given in respect of a condition subject to which any such existing planning permission was deemed to be granted to be treated as given in respect of a condition subject to which a new or varied planning permission is deemed to be granted.]

[(2A) On making an order under section 1 or 3 of the Transport and Works Act 1992 which includes provision for development, the Secretary of State may direct that planning permission for that development shall be deemed to be granted, subject to such conditions (if any) as may be specified in the direction.]

(3) The provisions of this Act (except [Part] XII) shall apply in relation to any planning permission deemed to be granted by virtue of a direction under this section as if it had been granted by the Secretary of State on an application referred to him under section 77.

(4) For the purposes of this section development is authorised by a government department if—

      (a) any consent, authority or approval to or for the development is granted by the department in pursuance of an enactment;

      (b) a compulsory purchase order is confirmed by the department authorising the purchase of land for the purpose of the development;

      (c) consent is granted by the department to the appropriation of land for the purpose of the development or the acquisition of land by agreement for that purpose;

      (d) authority is given by the department—

           (i) for the borrowing of money for the purpose of the development, or

           (ii) for the application for that purpose of any money not otherwise so applicable; or

      (e) any undertaking is given by the department to pay a grant in respect of the development in accordance with an enactment authorising the payment of such grants;

and references in this section to the authorisation of a government department shall be construed accordingly.

[(5) In subsection (2), the reference to ancillary development, in the case of a consent relating to the extension of a generating station, does not include any development which is not directly related to the generation of electricity by that station.

Part III Control over Development

(6) In this section, references to England or Wales include—

(a) waters adjacent to England or Wales up to the seaward limits of the territorial sea, and

(b) a Renewable Energy Zone, except any part of a Renewable Energy Zone in relation to which the Scottish Ministers have functions.

(7) In this section 'electric line', 'extension', 'generating station' and 'Renewable Energy Zone' have the same meanings as in Part 1 of the Electricity Act 1989.]

Amendment

Sub-s (1): words in square brackets inserted by the Environment Act 1995, s 78, Sch 10, para 32(4).

Sub-ss (2), (2ZA): substituted, for sub-s (2) as originally enacted, by the Growth and Infrastructure Act 2013, s 21(1), (2). Date in force: 31 July 2013: see SI 2013/1488, art 5(b).

Sub-s (2A): inserted by the Transport and Works Act 1992, s 16(1).

Sub-s (3): word in square brackets substituted by the Planning and Compensation Act 1991, s 31, Sch 6, para 12.

Sub-ss (5)–(7): substituted, for sub-s (5) as originally enacted, by the Growth and Infrastructure Act 2013, s 21(1), (3). Date in force: 31 July 2013: see SI 2013/1488, art 5(b).

Duration of planning permission

91 General condition limiting duration of planning permission

(1) Subject to the provisions of this section, every planning permission granted or deemed to be granted shall be granted or, as the case may be, be deemed to be granted, subject to the condition that the development to which it relates must be begun not later than the expiration of—

(a) *five years* [three years] beginning with the date on which the permission is granted or, as the case may be, deemed to be granted; or

(b) such other period (whether longer or shorter) beginning with that date as the authority concerned with the terms of planning permission may direct.

(2) The period mentioned in subsection (1)(b) shall be a period which the authority consider appropriate having regard to the provisions of the development plan and to any other material considerations.

(3) If planning permission is granted without the condition required by subsection (1), it shall be deemed to have been granted subject to the condition that the development to which it relates must be begun not later than the expiration of *five years* [three years] beginning with the date of the grant.

[(3A) Subsection (3B) applies if any proceedings are begun to challenge the validity of a grant of planning permission or of a deemed grant of planning permission.

(3B) The period before the end of which the development to which the planning permission relates is required to be begun in pursuance of subsection (1) or (3) must be taken to be extended by one year.

(3C) Nothing in this section prevents the development being begun from the time the permission is granted or deemed to be granted.]

(4) Nothing in this section applies—

Town and Country Planning Act 1990

    (a) to any planning permission granted by a development order[, a local development order[, a Mayoral development order] or a neighbourhood development order];

    (b) to any planning permission [granted for development carried out before the grant of that permission];

    (c) to any planning permission granted for a limited period;

    [(d) to any planning permission for development consisting of the winning and working of minerals or involving the depositing of mineral waste which is granted (or deemed to be granted) subject to a condition that the development to which it relates must be begun before the expiration of a specified period after—

        (i) the completion of other development consisting of the winning and working of minerals already being carried out by the applicant for the planning permission; or

        (ii) the cessation of depositing of mineral waste already being carried out by the applicant for the planning permission;]

    (e) to any planning permission granted by an enterprise zone scheme;

    (f) to any planning permission granted by a simplified planning zone scheme; or

    (g) to any outline planning permission, as defined by section 92.

Amendment

Sub-s (1): in para (a) words 'five years' in italics repealed and subsequent words in square brackets substituted by the Planning and Compulsory Purchase Act 2004, s 51(1)(a); for effect see s 51(6) thereof. Date in force (in relation to England): 24 August 2005: see SI 2005/2081, art 2(c). Date in force (in relation to Wales): to be appointed: see the Planning and Compulsory Purchase Act 2004, s 121(1), (2)(b).

Sub-s (3): words 'five years' in italics repealed and subsequent words in square brackets substituted by the Planning and Compulsory Purchase Act 2004, s 51(1)(b); for effect see s 51(6) thereof. Date in force (in relation to England): 24 August 2005: see SI 2005/2081, art 2(c). Date in force (in relation to Wales): to be appointed: see the Planning and Compulsory Purchase Act 2004, s 121(1), (2)(b).

Sub-ss (3A)–(3C): inserted by the Planning and Compulsory Purchase Act 2004, s 51(1); for effect see s 51(6) thereof. Date in force (in relation to England): 24 August 2005: see SI 2005/2081, art 2(c). Date in force (in relation to Wales for certain purposes): 22 June 2015: see SI 2015/340, art 3. Date in force (in relation to Wales for remaining purposes): to be appointed: see the Planning and Compulsory Purchase Act 2004, s 121(1), (2)(b).

Sub-s (4): in para (a) words ', a local development order or a neighbourhood development order' in square brackets substituted by the Localism Act 2011, s 121, Sch 12, paras 1, 13. Date in force (for certain purposes): 15 January 2012: see SI 2012/57, art 4(1)(h). Date in force (for certain purposes): 6 April 2012: see SI 2012/628, art 8(a). Date in force (for certain purposes): 3 August 2012: see SI 2012/2029, arts 2, 3(a); for transitional provisions and savings see art 5 thereof. Date in force (for remaining purposes): 6 April 2013: see SI 2013/797, arts 1(2), 2.

Sub-s (4): in para (a) words ', a Mayoral development order' in square brackets inserted by the Infrastructure Act 2015, s 30(1), Sch 4, Pt 2, paras 2, 14. Date in force (for certain purposes): 12 February 2015: see the Infrastructure Act 2015, s 57(5)(d)(i). Date in force (for remaining purposes): to be appointed: see the Infrastructure Act 2015, s 57(5)(d)(ii).

Part III Control over Development

Sub-s (4): in para (b) words 'granted for development carried out before the grant of that permission' in square brackets substituted by the Planning and Compensation Act 1991, s 32, Sch 7, para 20.

Sub-s (4): para (d) substituted by the Planning and Compensation Act 1991, s 21, Sch 1, para 3.

92 Outline planning permission

(1) In this section and section 91 'outline planning permission' means planning permission granted, in accordance with the provisions of a development order, with the reservation for subsequent approval by the local planning authority or the Secretary of State of matters not particularised in the application ('reserved matters').

(2) Subject to the following provisions of this section, where outline planning permission is granted for development consisting in or including the carrying out of building or other operations, it shall be granted subject to conditions to the effect—

   (a) that, in the case of any reserved matter, application for approval must be made not later than the expiration of three years beginning with the date of the grant of outline planning permission; and

   (b) that the development to which the permission relates must be begun not later than—

   (i) *the expiration of five years from the date of the grant of outline planning permission; or*

   (ii) *if later*, the expiration of two years from the final approval of the reserved matters or, in the case of approval on different dates, the final approval of the last such matter to be approved.

(3) If outline planning permission is granted without the conditions required by subsection (2), it shall be deemed to have been granted subject to those conditions.

(4) The authority concerned with the terms of an outline planning permission may, in applying subsection (2), substitute, or direct that there be substituted, for the periods of three years, *five years* or two years referred to in that subsection such other periods respectively (whether longer or shorter) as they consider appropriate.

(5) They may also specify, or direct that there be specified, separate periods under paragraph (a) of subsection (2) in relation to separate parts of the development to which the planning permission relates; and, if they do so, the condition required by paragraph (b) of that subsection shall then be framed correspondingly by reference to those parts, instead of by reference to the development as a whole.

(6) In considering whether to exercise their powers under subsections (4) and (5), the authority shall have regard to the provisions of the development plan and to any other material considerations.

Amendment

Sub-s (2): para (b)(i) repealed by the Planning and Compulsory Purchase Act 2004, s 51(2)(a); for effect see s 51(6) thereof. Date in force (in relation to England): 24 August 2005: see SI 2005/2081, art 2(c). Date in force (in relation to Wales): to be appointed: see the Planning and Compulsory Purchase Act 2004, s 121(1), (2)(b), (g).

Town and Country Planning Act 1990

Sub-s (2): in para (b)(ii) words 'if later' in italics repealed by the Planning and Compulsory Purchase Act 2004, s 51(2)(b); for effect see s 51(6) thereof. Date in force (in relation to England): 24 August 2005: see SI 2005/2081, art 2(c). Date in force (in relation to Wales): to be appointed: see the Planning and Compulsory Purchase Act 2004, s 121(1), (2)(b), (g).

Sub-s (4): words 'five years' in italics repealed by the Planning and Compulsory Purchase Act 2004, s 51(2)(c); for further effect see s 51(6) thereof. Date in force (in relation to England): 24 August 2005: see SI 2005/2081, art 2(c). Date in force (in relation to Wales): to be appointed: see the Planning and Compulsory Purchase Act 2004, s 121(1), (2)(b), (g).

93 Provisions supplementary to ss 91 and 92

(1) The authority referred to in section 91(1)(b) or 92(4) is—

   (a) the local planning authority or the Secretary of State, in the case of planning permission granted by them,

   (b) in the case of planning permission deemed to be granted under section 90(1), the department on whose direction planning permission is deemed to be granted, and

   (c) in the case of planning permission deemed to be granted under section 90(2), the Secretary of State.

(2) For the purposes of section 92, a reserved matter shall be treated as finally approved—

   (a) when an application for approval is granted, or

   (b) in a case where the application is made to the local planning authority and on an appeal to the Secretary of State against the authority's decision on the application the Secretary of State grants the approval, when the appeal is determined.

(3) Where a local planning authority grant planning permission, the fact that any of the conditions of the permission are required by the provisions of section 91 or 92 to be imposed, or are deemed by those provisions to be imposed, shall not prevent the conditions being the subject of an appeal under section 78 against the decision of the authority.

(4) In the case of planning permission (whether outline or other) which has conditions attached to it by or under section 91 or 92—

   (a) development carried out after the date by which the conditions require it to be carried out shall be treated as not authorised by the permission; and

   (b) an application for approval of a reserved matter, if it is made after the date by which the conditions require it to be made, shall be treated as not made in accordance with the terms of the permission.

94 Termination of planning permission by reference to time limit: completion notices

(1) This section applies where—

   (a) by virtue of section 91 or 92, a planning permission is subject to a condition that the development to which the permission relates must be begun before the expiration of a particular period, that development has been begun within that period, but that period has elapsed without the development having been completed; or

Part III Control over Development

    (b) development has been begun in accordance with planning permission under a simplified planning zone scheme but has not been completed by the time the area ceases to be a simplified planning zone; or

    (c) development has been begun in accordance with planning permission under an enterprise zone scheme but has not been completed by the time the area ceases to be an enterprise zone[; or

    (d) a planning permission under a neighbourhood development order is subject to a condition that the development to which the permission relates must be begun before the expiration of a particular period, that development has been begun within that period, but that period has elapsed without the development having been completed].

(2) If the local planning authority are of the opinion that the development will not be completed within a reasonable period, they may serve a notice ('a completion notice') stating that the planning permission will cease to have effect at the expiration of a further period specified in the notice.

(3) The period so specified must not be less than 12 months after the notice takes effect.

(4) A completion notice shall be served—

    (a) on the owner of the land,

    (b) on the occupier of the land, and

    (c) on any other person who in the opinion of the local planning authority will be affected by the notice.

(5) The local planning authority may withdraw a completion notice at any time before the expiration of the period specified in it as the period at the expiration of which the planning permission is to cease to have effect.

(6) If they do so they shall immediately give notice of the withdrawal to every person who was served with the completion notice.

Amendment

Sub-s (1): para (d) and word '; or' immediately preceding it inserted by the Localism Act 2011, s 121, Sch 12, paras 1, 14. Date in force (for certain purposes): 15 January 2012: see SI 2012/57, art 4(1)(h). Date in force (for certain purposes): 6 April 2012: see SI 2012/628, art 8(a). Date in force (for certain purposes): 3 August 2012: see SI 2012/2029, arts 2, 3(a); for transitional provisions and savings see art 5 thereof. Date in force (for remaining purposes): 6 April 2013: see SI 2013/797, arts 1(2), 2.

95 Effect of completion notice

(1) A completion notice shall not take effect unless and until it is confirmed by the Secretary of State.

(2) In confirming a completion notice the Secretary of State may substitute some longer period for that specified in the notice as the period at the expiration of which the planning permission is to cease to have effect.

(3) If, within such period as may be specified in a completion notice (which must not be less than 28 days from its service) any person on whom the notice is served so requires, the Secretary of State, before confirming the notice, shall give him and the local planning authority an opportunity of appearing before and being heard by a person appointed by the Secretary of State for the purpose.

Town and Country Planning Act 1990

(4) If a completion notice takes effect, the planning permission referred to in it shall become invalid at the expiration of the period specified in the notice (whether the original period specified under section 94(2) or a longer period substituted by the Secretary of State under subsection (2)).

(5) Subsection (4) shall not affect any permission so far as development carried out under it before the end of the period mentioned in that subsection is concerned.

96 Power of Secretary of State to serve completion notices

(1) If it appears to the Secretary of State to be expedient that a completion notice should be served in respect of any land, he may himself serve such a notice.

(2) A completion notice served by the Secretary of State shall have the same effect as if it had been served by the local planning authority.

(3) The Secretary of State shall not serve such a notice without consulting the local planning authority.

[Non-material changes to planning permission]

[96A Power to make non-material changes to planning permission]

[(1) A local planning authority *in England* may make a change to any planning permission relating to land in their area if they are satisfied that the change is not material.

(2) In deciding whether a change is material, a local planning authority must have regard to the effect of the change, together with any previous changes made under this section, on the planning permission as originally granted.

(3) The power conferred by subsection (1) includes power—

 (a) to impose new conditions;

 (b) to remove or alter existing conditions.

(4) The power conferred by subsection (1) may be exercised only on an application made by or on behalf of a person with an interest in the land to which the planning permission relates.

(5) An application under subsection (4) [to a local planning authority in England] must be made in the form and manner prescribed by development order.

[(5A) A development order may provide that an application under subsection (4) to a local planning authority in Wales must be made—

 (a) in the form prescribed by the order or in a form published by the Welsh Ministers; and

 (b) in the manner prescribed by the order.]

(6) Subsection (7) applies in relation to an application under subsection (4) made by or on behalf of a person with an interest in some, but not all, of the land to which the planning permission relates.

(7) The application may be made only in respect of so much of the planning permission as affects the land in which the person has an interest.

(8) A local planning authority [in England] must comply with such requirements as may be prescribed by development order as to consultation and publicity in relation to the exercise of the power conferred by subsection (1).]

Part III Control over Development

[(9) A development order may make provision about how a local planning authority in Wales are to deal with an application under subsection (4) (including provision imposing requirements as to consultation and publicity and as to when steps specified in the order are to be taken).

(10) For the purposes of this section as it applies in relation to Wales, a person has an interest in land only if in relation to that land (or any mineral in, on or under it) the person—

  (a) is the estate owner of the fee simple;

  (b) is entitled to a tenancy granted or extended for a term of years certain of which not less than two years remain unexpired;

  (c) is the mortgagee of any interest or estate in the land; or

  (d) is a party to an estate contract within the meaning of section 2(4) of the Land Charges Act 1972.]

Amendment

Inserted by the Planning Act 2008, s 190(1), (2). Date in force: 1 October 2009: see SI 2009/2260, art 3.

Sub-s (1): words 'in England' in italics repealed, in relation to Wales, by SI 2014/1770, art 2(1), (2). Date in force: 1 September 2014: see SI 2014/1770, art 1.

Sub-s (5): words 'to a local planning authority in England' in square brackets inserted, in relation to Wales, by SI 2014/1770, art 2(1), (3). Date in force: 1 September 2014: see SI 2014/1770, art 1.

Sub-s (5A): inserted, in relation to Wales, by SI 2014/1770, art 2(1), (4). Date in force: 1 September 2014: see SI 2014/1770, art 1.

Sub-s (8): words 'in England' in square brackets inserted, in relation to Wales, by SI 2014/1770, art 2(1), (5). Date in force: 1 September 2014: see SI 2014/1770, art 1.

Sub-ss (9), (10): inserted, in relation to Wales, by SI 2014/1770, art 2(1), (6). Date in force: 1 September 2014; see SI 2014/1770, art 1.

Revocation and modification of planning permission

97 Power to revoke or modify planning permission

(1) If it appears to the local planning authority that it is expedient to revoke or modify any permission to develop land granted on an application made under this Part, the authority may by order revoke or modify the permission to such extent as they consider expedient.

(2) In exercising their functions under subsection (1) the authority shall have regard to the development plan and to any other material considerations.

(3) The power conferred by this section may be exercised—

  (a) where the permission relates to the carrying out of building or other operations, at any time before those operations have been completed;

  (b) where the permission relates to a change of the use of any land, at any time before the change has taken place.

(4) The revocation or modification of permission for the carrying out of building or other operations shall not affect so much of those operations as has been previously carried out.

Town and Country Planning Act 1990

(5) References in this section to the local planning authority are to be construed in relation to development consisting of the winning and working of minerals as references to the mineral planning authority, ...

[(6) Part II of Schedule 5 shall have effect for the purpose of making special provision with respect to the conditions that may be imposed by an order under this section which revokes or modifies permission for development—

(a) consisting of the winning and working of minerals; or

(b) involving the depositing of refuse or waste materials.]

Amendment

Sub-s (5): words omitted repealed by the Planning and Compensation Act 1991, ss 21, 84, Sch 1, para 4, Sch 19, Part I.

Sub-s (6): inserted by the Planning and Compensation Act 1991, s 21, Sch 1, para 4.

98 Procedure for s 97 orders: opposed cases

(1) Except as provided in section 99, an order under section 97 shall not take effect unless it is confirmed by the Secretary of State.

(2) Where a local planning authority submit such an order to the Secretary of State for confirmation, they shall serve notice on—

(a) the owner of the land affected,

(b) the occupier of the land affected, and

(c) any other person who in their opinion will be affected by the order.

(3) The notice shall specify the period within which any person on whom it is served may require the Secretary of State to give him an opportunity of appearing before, and being heard by, a person appointed by the Secretary of State for the purpose.

(4) If within that period such a person so requires, before the Secretary of State confirms the order he shall give such an opportunity both to him and to the local planning authority.

(5) The period referred to in subsection (3) must not be less than 28 days from the service of the notice.

(6) The Secretary of State may confirm an order submitted to him under this section either without modification or subject to such modifications as he considers expedient.

99 Procedure for s 97 orders: unopposed cases

(1) This section applies where—

(a) the local planning authority have made an order under section 97; and

(b) the owner and the occupier of the land and all persons who in the authority's opinion will be affected by the order have notified the authority in writing that they do not object to it.

(2) Where this section applies, instead of submitting the order to the Secretary of State for confirmation the authority shall advertise in the prescribed manner the fact that the order has been made, and the advertisement must specify—

(a) the period within which persons affected by the order may give notice to the Secretary of State that they wish for an opportunity of appearing

Part III Control over Development

before, and being heard by, a person appointed by the Secretary of State for the purpose; and

(b) the period at the expiration of which, if no such notice is given to the Secretary of State, the order may take effect by virtue of this section without being confirmed by the Secretary of State.

(3) The authority shall also serve notice to the same effect on the persons mentioned in subsection (1)(b).

(4) The period referred to in subsection (2)(a) must not be less than 28 days from the date the advertisement first appears.

(5) The period referred to in subsection (2)(b) must not be less than 14 days from the expiration of the period referred to in subsection (2)(a).

(6) The authority shall send a copy of any advertisement published under subsection (2) to the Secretary of State not more than three days after the publication.

(7) If—
   (a) no person claiming to be affected by the order has given notice to the Secretary of State under subsection (2)(a) within the period referred to in that subsection, and
   (b) the Secretary of State has not directed within that period that the order be submitted to him for confirmation,

the order shall take effect at the expiry of the period referred to in subsection (2)(b), without being confirmed by the Secretary of State as required by section 98(1).

(8) This section does not apply—
   (a) to an order revoking or modifying a planning permission granted or deemed to have been granted by the Secretary of State under this Part or Part VII, or
   (b) to an order modifying any conditions to which a planning permission is subject by virtue of section 91 or 92.

100 Revocation and modification of planning permission by the Secretary of State

(1) If it appears to the Secretary of State that it is expedient that an order should be made under section 97, he may himself make such an order.

(2) Such an order which is made by the Secretary of State shall have the same effect as if it had been made by the local planning authority and confirmed by the Secretary of State.

(3) The Secretary of State shall not make such an order without consulting the local planning authority.

(4) Where the Secretary of State proposes to make such an order he shall serve notice on the local planning authority.

(5) The notice shall specify the period (which must not be less than 28 days from the date of its service) within which the authority may require an opportunity of appearing before and being heard by a person appointed by the Secretary of State for the purpose.

(6) If within that period the authority so require, before the Secretary of State makes the order he shall give the authority such an opportunity.

Town and Country Planning Act 1990

(7) The provisions of this Part and of any regulations made under this Act with respect to the procedure to be followed in connection with the submission by the local planning authority of any order under section 97 and its confirmation by the Secretary of State shall have effect, subject to any necessary modifications, in relation to any proposal by the Secretary of State to make such an order and its making by him.

[(8) Subsections (5) and (6) of section 97 apply for the purposes of this section as they apply for the purposes of that.]

Amendment
Sub-s (8): substituted by the Planning and Compensation Act 1991, s 21, Sch 1, para 5.

References to Planning Inquiry Commission

101 Power to refer certain planning questions to Planning Inquiry Commission

(1) The Secretary of State may constitute a Planning Inquiry Commission to inquire into and report on any matter referred to them under subsection (2) in the circumstances mentioned in subsection (3).

(2) The matters that may be referred to a Planning Inquiry Commission are—

(a) an application for planning permission which the Secretary of State has under section 77 directed to be referred to him instead of being dealt with by a local planning authority;

(b) an appeal under section 78 (including that section as applied by or under any other provision of this Act);

(c) a proposal that a government department should give a direction under section 90(1) that planning permission shall be deemed to be granted for development by a local authority [or National Park authority] or by statutory undertakers which is required by any enactment to be authorised by that department;

(d) a proposal that development should be carried out by or on behalf of a government department.

(3) Any of those matters may be referred to any such commission under this section if it appears expedient to the responsible Minister or Ministers that the question whether the proposed development should be permitted to be carried out should be the subject of a special inquiry on either or both of the following grounds—

(a) that there are considerations of national or regional importance which are relevant to the determination of that question and require evaluation, but a proper evaluation of them cannot be made unless there is a special inquiry for the purpose;

(b) that the technical or scientific aspects of the proposed development are of so unfamiliar a character as to jeopardise a proper determination of that question unless there is a special inquiry for the purpose.

(4) Part I of Schedule 8 shall have effect as respects the constitution of any such commission and its functions and procedure on references to it under this section, and the references in subsection (3) and in that Schedule to 'the responsible Minister or Ministers' shall be construed in accordance with Part II of that Schedule.

Part III Control over Development

(5) In relation to any matter affecting both England and Wales, the functions of the Secretary of State under subsection (1) shall be exercised by the Secretaries of State for the time being having general responsibility in planning matters in relation to England and in relation to Wales acting jointly.

Amendment

Sub-s (2): words in square brackets inserted by the Environment Act 1995, s 78, Sch 10, para 32(4).

Other controls over development

102 Orders requiring discontinuance of use or alteration or removal of buildings or works

(1) If, having regard to the development plan and to any other material considerations, it appears to a local planning authority that it is expedient in the interests of the proper planning of their area (including the interests of amenity)—

   (a) that any use of land should be discontinued or that any conditions should be imposed on the continuance of a use of land; or

   (b) that any buildings or works should be altered or removed,

they may by order—

   (i) require the discontinuance of that use, or

   (ii) impose such conditions as may be specified in the order on the continuance of it, or

   (iii) require such steps as may be so specified to be taken for the alteration or removal of the buildings or works,

as the case may be.

(2) An order under this section may grant planning permission for any development of the land to which the order relates, subject to such conditions as may be specified in the order.

(3) Section 97 shall apply in relation to any planning permission granted by an order under this section as it applies in relation to planning permission granted by the local planning authority on an application made under this Part.

[(4) The planning permission which may be granted by an order under this section includes planning permission, subject to such conditions as may be specified in the order, for development carried out before the date on which the order was submitted to the Secretary of State under section 103.

(5) Planning permission for such development may be granted so as to have effect from—

   (a) the date on which the development was carried out; or

   (b) if it was carried out in accordance with planning permission granted for a limited period, the end of that period.]

(6) Where the requirements of an order under this section will involve the displacement of persons residing in any premises, it shall be the duty of the local planning authority, in so far as there is no other residential accommodation suitable to the reasonable requirements of those persons available on reasonable terms, to secure the provision of such accommodation in advance of the displacement.

Town and Country Planning Act 1990

(7) Subject to section 103(8), in the case of planning permission granted by an order under this section, the authority referred to in sections 91(1)(b) and 92(4) is the local planning authority making the order.

(8) The previous provisions of this section do not apply to the use of any land for development [consisting of the winning and working of minerals or involving the depositing of refuse or waste materials] except as provided in Schedule 9, and that Schedule shall have effect for the purpose of making provision as respects land which is or has been so used.

Amendment

Sub-ss (4), (5): substituted by the Planning and Compensation Act 1991, s 32, Sch 7, para 21.

Sub-s (8): words in square brackets substituted by the Planning and Compensation Act 1991, s 21, Sch 1, para 6.

103 Confirmation by Secretary of State of s 102 orders

(1) An order under section 102 shall not take effect unless it is confirmed by the Secretary of State, either without modification or subject to such modifications as he considers expedient.

(2) The power of the Secretary of State under this section to confirm an order subject to modifications includes power—

(a) to modify any provision of the order granting planning permission, as mentioned in subsections (2) to (5) of section 102;

(b) to include in the order any grant of planning permission which might have been included in the order as submitted to him.

(3) Where a local planning authority submit an order to the Secretary of State for his confirmation under this section, they shall serve notice—

(a) on the owner of the land affected,

(b) on the occupier of that land, and

(c) on any other person who in their opinion will be affected by the order.

(4) The notice shall specify the period within which any person on whom it is served may require the Secretary of State to give him an opportunity of appearing before, and being heard by, a person appointed by the Secretary of State for the purpose.

(5) If within that period such a person so requires, before the Secretary of State confirms the order, he shall give such an opportunity both to him and to the local planning authority.

(6) The period referred to in subsection (4) must not be less than 28 days from the service of the notice.

(7) Where an order under section 102 has been confirmed by the Secretary of State, the local planning authority shall serve a copy of the order on the owner and occupier of the land to which the order relates.

(8) Where the Secretary of State exercises his powers under subsection (2) in confirming an order granting planning permission, he is the authority referred to in sections 91(1)(b) and 92(4).

104 Power of the Secretary of State to make s 102 orders

(1) If it appears to the Secretary of State that it is expedient that an order should be made under section 102, he may himself make such an order.

(2) Such an order made by the Secretary of State shall have the same effect as if it had been made by the local planning authority and confirmed by the Secretary of State.

(3) The Secretary of State shall not make such an order without consulting the local planning authority.

(4) Where the Secretary of State proposes to make such an order he shall serve notice on the local planning authority.

(5) The notice shall specify the period within which the authority may require an opportunity of appearing before and being heard by a person appointed by the Secretary of State for the purpose.

(6) If within that period the authority so require, before the Secretary of State makes the order he shall give the authority such an opportunity.

(7) The period referred to in subsection (5) must not be less than 28 days from the date of the service of the notice.

(8) The provisions of this Part and of any regulations made under this Act with respect to the procedure to be followed in connection with the submission by the local planning authority of any order under section 102, its confirmation by the Secretary of State and the service of copies of it as confirmed shall have effect, subject to any necessary modifications, in relation to any proposal by the Secretary of State to make such an order, its making by him and the service of copies of it.

105 ...

...

Amendment
Repealed by the Environment Act 1995, ss 96(4), 120(3), Sch 24.

[106 Planning obligations]

[(1) *Any person interested in land in the area of a local planning authority may, by agreement or otherwise, enter into an obligation (referred to in this section and sections 106A [to 106C] as 'a planning obligation'), enforceable to the extent mentioned in subsection (3)—*
- *(a) restricting the development or use of the land in any specified way;*
- *(b) requiring specified operations or activities to be carried out in, on, under or over the land;*
- *(c) requiring the land to be used in any specified way; or*
- *(d) requiring a sum or sums to be paid to the authority [(or, in a case where section 2E applies, to the Greater London Authority)] on a specified date or dates or periodically.*

[(1A) *In the case of a development consent obligation, the reference to development in subsection (1)(a) includes anything that constitutes development for the purposes of the Planning Act 2008.*]

Town and Country Planning Act 1990

(2) *A planning obligation may—*
   (a) *be unconditional or subject to conditions;*
   (b) *impose any restriction or requirement mentioned in subsection (1)(a) to (c) either indefinitely or for such period or periods as may be specified; and*
   (c) *if it requires a sum or sums to be paid, require the payment of a specified amount or an amount determined in accordance with the instrument by which the obligation is entered into and, if it requires the payment of periodical sums, require them to be paid indefinitely or for a specified period.*

(3) *Subject to subsection (4) a planning obligation is enforceable by the authority identified in accordance with subsection (9)(d)—*
   (a) *against the person entering into the obligation; and*
   (b) *against any person deriving title from that person.*

(4) *The instrument by which a planning obligation is entered into may provide that a person shall not be bound by the obligation in respect of any period during which he no longer has an interest in the land.*

(5) *A restriction or requirement imposed under a planning obligation is enforceable by injunction.*

(6) *Without prejudice to subsection (5), if there is a breach of a requirement in a planning obligation to carry out any operations in, on, under or over the land to which the obligation relates, the authority by whom the obligation is enforceable may—*
   (a) *enter the land and carry out the operations; and*
   (b) *recover from the person or persons against whom the obligation is enforceable any expenses reasonably incurred by them in doing so.*

(7) *Before an authority exercise their power under subsection (6)(a) they shall give not less than twenty-one days' notice of their intention to do so to any person against whom the planning obligation is enforceable.*

(8) *Any person who wilfully obstructs a person acting in the exercise of a power under subsection (6)(a) shall be guilty of an offence and liable on summary conviction to a fine not exceeding level 3 on the standard scale.*

(9) *A planning obligation may not be entered into except by an instrument executed as a deed which—*
   (a) *states that the obligation is a planning obligation for the purposes of this section;*
   [(aa) *if the obligation is a development consent obligation, contains a statement to that effect;*]
   (b) *identifies the land in which the person entering into the obligation is interested;*
   (c) *identifies the person entering into the obligation and states what his interest in the land is; and*
   (d) *identifies the local planning authority by whom the obligation is enforceable [and, in a case where section 2E applies, identifies the Mayor of London as an authority by whom the obligation is also enforceable].*

Part III Control over Development

(10) A copy of any such instrument shall be given to the [local planning authority so identified and, in a case where section 2E applies, to the Mayor of London].

(11) A planning obligation shall be a local land charge and for the purposes of the Local Land Charges Act 1975 the authority by whom the obligation is enforceable shall be treated as the originating authority as respects such a charge.

(12) Regulations may provide for the charging on the land of—

(a) any sum or sums required to be paid under a planning obligation; and

(b) any expenses recoverable by a local planning authority [or the Mayor of London] under subsection (6)(b),

and this section and sections 106A [to 106BC] shall have effect subject to any such regulations.

(13) In this section 'specified' means specified in the instrument by which the planning obligation is entered into and in this section and section 106A 'land' has the same meaning as in the Local Land Charges Act 1975.

[(14) In this section and section 106A 'development consent obligation' means a planning obligation entered into in connection with an application (or a proposed application) for an order granting development consent.]]

Amendment

Substituted, together with ss 106A, 106B, for s 106 as originally enacted, by the Planning and Compensation Act 1991, s 12(1).

Repealed by the Planning and Compulsory Purchase Act 2004, ss 118(1), 120, Sch 6, paras 1, 5, Sch 9. Date in force: to be appointed: see the Planning and Compulsory Purchase Act 2004, s 121(1), (2)(f), (g).

Sub-s (1): words 'to 106C' in square brackets substituted by the Growth and Infrastructure Act 2013, s 7(2), Sch 2, paras 1, 3(1), (2). Date in force: 25 April 2013: see the Growth and Infrastructure Act 2013, s 35(2); for transitional provisions see s 7(3) thereof.

Sub-s (1): in para (d) words from '(or, in a' to 'Greater London Authority)' in square brackets inserted by the Greater London Authority Act 2007, s 33(1), (2). Date in force: 6 April 2008: see SI 2008/582, art 2(a).

Sub-s (1A): inserted by the Planning Act 2008, s 174(1), (2)(a). Date in force: 1 March 2010: see SI 2010/101, art 3(k); for savings see art 6 thereof.

Sub-s (9): para (aa) inserted by the Planning Act 2008, s 174(1), (2)(b). Date in force: 1 March 2010: see SI 2010/101, art 3(k); for savings see art 6 thereof.

Sub-s (9): in para (d) words from 'and, in a' to 'is also enforceable' in square brackets inserted by the Greater London Authority Act 2007, s 33(1), (3). Date in force: 6 April 2008: see SI 2008/582, art 2(a).

Sub-s (10): words from 'local planning authority' to 'Mayor of London' in square brackets substituted by the Greater London Authority Act 2007, s 33(1), (4). Date in force: 6 April 2008: see SI 2008/582, art 2(a).

Sub-s (12): in para (b) words 'or the Mayor of London' in square brackets inserted by the Greater London Authority Act 2007, s 33(1), (5). Date in force: 6 April 2008: see SI 2008/582, art 2(a).

Sub-s (12): words 'to 106BC' in square brackets substituted by the Growth and Infrastructure Act 2013, s 7(2), Sch 2, paras 1, 3(1), (3). Date in force: 25 April 2013: see the Growth and Infrastructure Act 2013, s 35(2); for transitional provisions see s 7(3) thereof.

Sub-s (14): inserted by the Planning Act 2008, s 174(1), (2)(c). Date in force: 1 March 2010: see SI 2010/101, art 3(k); for savings see art 6 thereof.

Town and Country Planning Act 1990

[106A Modification and discharge of planning obligations]

[(1) A planning obligation may not be modified or discharged except—

    (a) by agreement between [the appropriate authority (see subsection (11))] and the person or persons against whom the obligation is enforceable; or

    (b) in accordance with [—]

        [(i)] this section and section 106B [, or

        (ii) sections 106BA and 106BC].

(2) An agreement falling within subsection (1)(a) shall not be entered into except by an instrument executed as a deed.

(3) A person against whom a planning obligation is enforceable may, at any time after the expiry of the relevant period, apply to [the appropriate authority] for the obligation—

    (a) to have effect subject to such modifications as may be specified in the application; or

    (b) to be discharged.

(4) In subsection (3) 'the relevant period' means—

    (a) such period as may be prescribed; or

    (b) if no period is prescribed, the period of five years beginning with the date on which the obligation is entered into.

(5) An application under subsection (3) for the modification of a planning obligation may not specify a modification imposing an obligation on any other person against whom the obligation is enforceable.

(6) Where an application is made to an authority under subsection (3), the authority may determine—

    (a) that the planning obligation shall continue to have effect without modification;

    (b) if the obligation no longer serves a useful purpose, that it shall be discharged; or

    (c) if the obligation continues to serve a useful purpose, but would serve that purpose equally well if it had effect subject to the modifications specified in the application, that it shall have effect subject to those modifications.

(7) The authority shall give notice of their determination to the applicant within such period as may be prescribed.

(8) Where an authority determine [under this section] that a planning obligation shall have effect subject to modifications specified in the application, the obligation as modified shall be enforceable as if it had been entered into on the date on which notice of the determination was given to the applicant.

(9) Regulations may make provision with respect to—

    (a) the form and content of applications under subsection (3);

    (b) the publication of notices of such applications;

    (c) the procedures for considering any representations made with respect to such applications; and

Part III Control over Development

(d) the notices to be given to applicants of determinations under subsection (6).

(10) Section 84 of the Law of Property Act 1925 (power to discharge or modify restrictive covenants affecting land) does not apply to a planning obligation.]

[(11) In this section 'the appropriate authority' means—

(a) the Mayor of London, in the case of any planning obligation enforceable by him;

[(aa) the Secretary of State, in the case of any development consent obligation ...;

(ab) ...]

(b) in the case of any other planning obligation, the local planning authority by whom it is enforceable.

(12) The Mayor of London must consult the local planning authority before exercising any function under this section.]

Amendment

Substituted, together with ss 106, 106B, for s 106 as originally enacted, by the Planning and Compensation Act 1991, s 12(1).

Repealed by the Planning and Compulsory Purchase Act 2004, ss 118(1), 120, Sch 6, paras 1, 5, Sch 9. Date in force: to be appointed: see the Planning and Compulsory Purchase Act 2004, s 121(1), (2)(f), (g).

Sub-s (1): in para (a) words 'the appropriate authority (see subsection (11))' in square brackets substituted by the Greater London Authority Act 2007, s 34(1), (2). Date in force: 6 April 2008: see SI 2008/582, art 2(a).

Sub-s (1): para (b)(i) numbered as such by the Growth and Infrastructure Act 2013, s 2(1), Sch 2, paras 1, 4(1), (2)(a). Date in force: 25 April 2013: see the Growth and Infrastructure Act 2013, s 35(2).

Sub-s (1): para (b)(ii) and word ', or' immediately preceding it inserted by the Growth and Infrastructure Act 2013, s 7(2), Sch 2, paras 1, 4(1), (2)(b). Date in force: 25 April 2013: see the Growth and Infrastructure Act 2013, s 35(2); for transitional provisions see s 7(3) thereof.

Sub-s (3): words 'the appropriate authority' in square brackets substituted by the Greater London Authority Act 2007, s 34(1), (3). Date in force: 6 April 2008: see SI 2008/582, art 2(a).

Sub-s (8): words 'under this section' in square brackets inserted by the Growth and Infrastructure Act 2013, s 7(2), Sch 2, paras 1, 4(1), (3). Date in force: 25 April 2013: see the Growth and Infrastructure Act 2013, s 35(2); for transitional provisions see s 7(3) thereof.

Sub-ss (11), (12): inserted by the Greater London Authority Act 2007, s 34(1), (4). Date in force: 6 April 2008: see SI 2008/582, art 2(a).

Sub-s (11): paras (aa), (ab) inserted by the Planning Act 2008, s 174(1), (3). Date in force: 1 March 2010: see SI 2010/101, art 3(k); for savings see art 6 thereof.

Sub-s (11): in para (aa) words omitted repealed by the Localism Act 2011, ss 128(2), 237, Sch 13, Pt 2, para 77(1), (2)(a), Sch 25, Pt 20. Date in force: 1 April 2012: see SI 2012/628, art 7.

Sub-s (11): para (ab) repealed by the Localism Act 2011, ss 128(2), 237, Sch 13, Pt 2, para 77(1), (2)(b), Sch 25, Pt 20. Date in force: 1 April 2012: see SI 2012/628, art 7.

[106B Appeals [in relation to applications under section 106A]]

[(1) Where [an authority] [(other than the Secretary of State ...)]—

Town and Country Planning Act 1990

      (a) fail to give notice as mentioned in section 106A(7); or

      (b) determine [under section 106A] that a planning obligation shall continue to have effect without modification,

    the applicant may appeal to the Secretary of State.

(2) For the purposes of an appeal under subsection (1)(a), it shall be assumed that the authority have determined that the planning obligation shall continue to have effect without modification.

(3) An appeal under this section shall be made by notice served within such period and in such manner as may be prescribed.

(4) Subsections (6) to (9) of section 106A apply in relation to appeals to the Secretary of State under this section as they apply in relation to applications to authorities under that section.

(5) Before determining the appeal the Secretary of State shall, if either the applicant or the authority so wish, give each of them an opportunity of appearing before and being heard by a person appointed by the Secretary of State for the purpose.

(6) The determination of an appeal by the Secretary of State under this section shall be final.

(7) Schedule 6 applies to appeals under this section.]

[(8) In the application of Schedule 6 to an appeal under this section in a case where the authority mentioned in subsection (1) is the Mayor of London, references in that Schedule to the local planning authority are references to the Mayor of London.]

Amendment

Substituted, together with ss 106, 106A, for s 106 as originally enacted, by the Planning and Compensation Act 1991, s 12(1)

Section heading: words 'under section 106A' in square brackets inserted by the Growth and Infrastructure Act 2013, s 7(2), Sch 2, paras 1, 5(1), (2). Date in force: 25 April 2013: see the Growth and Infrastructure Act 2013, s 35(2).

Repealed by the Planning and Compulsory Purchase Act 2004, ss 118(1), 120, Sch 6, paras 1, 5, Sch 9. Date in force: to be appointed: see the Planning and Compulsory Purchase Act 2004, s 121(1), (2)(f), (g).

Sub-s (1): words 'an authority' in square brackets substituted by the Greater London Authority Act 2007, s 34(5), (6). Date in force: 6 April 2008: see SI 2008/582, art 2(a).

Sub-s (1): words in square brackets beginning with the words '(other than the Secretary of State' inserted by the Planning Act 2008, s 174(1), (4). Date in force: 1 March 2010: see SI 2010/101, art 3(k); for savings see art 6 thereof.

Sub-s (1): words omitted repealed by the Localism Act 2011, ss 128(2), 237, Sch 13, Pt 2, para 77(1), (3), Sch 25, Pt 20. Date in force: 1 April 2012: see SI 2012/628, art 7.

Sub-s (1): in para (b) words 'under section 106A' in square brackets inserted by the Growth and Infrastructure Act 2013, s 7(2), Sch 2, paras 1, 5(1), (3). Date in force: 25 April 2013: see the Growth and Infrastructure Act 2013, s 35(2); for transitional provisions see s 7(3) thereof.

Sub-s (8): inserted by the Greater London Authority Act 2007, s 34(5), (7). Date in force: 6 April 2008: see SI 2008/582, art 2(a).

[106BA Modification or discharge of affordable housing requirements]

[(1) This section applies in relation to an English planning obligation that contains an affordable housing requirement.

Part III Control over Development

(2) A person against whom the affordable housing requirement is enforceable may apply to the appropriate authority—
   (a) for the requirement to have effect subject to modifications,
   (b) for the requirement to be replaced with a different affordable housing requirement,
   (c) for the requirement to be removed from the planning obligation, or
   (d) in a case where the planning obligation consists solely of one or more affordable housing requirements, for the planning obligation to be discharged.

(3) Where an application is made to an authority under subsection (2) and is the first such application in relation to the planning obligation—
   (a) if the affordable housing requirement means that the development is not economically viable, the authority must deal with the application in accordance with subsection (5) so that the development becomes economically viable, or
   (b) if paragraph (a) does not apply, the authority must determine that the affordable housing requirement is to continue to have effect without modification or replacement.

(4) Where an application is made to an authority under subsection (2) and is the second or a subsequent such application in relation to the planning obligation, the authority may—
   (a) deal with the application in accordance with subsection (5), or
   (b) determine that the affordable housing requirement is to continue to have effect without modification or replacement.

(5) The authority may—
   (a) determine that the requirement is to have effect subject to modifications,
   (b) determine that the requirement is to be replaced with a different affordable housing requirement,
   (c) determine that the planning obligation is to be modified to remove the requirement, or
   (d) where the planning obligation consists solely of one or more affordable housing requirements, determine that the planning obligation is to be discharged.

(6) A determination under subsection (5)(a), (b) or (c)—
   (a) may provide for the planning obligation to be modified in accordance with the application or in some other way,
   (b) may not have the effect that the obligation as modified is more onerous in its application to the applicant than in its unmodified form, and
   (c) may not have the effect that an obligation is imposed on a person other than the applicant or that the obligation as modified is more onerous in its application to such a person than in its unmodified form.

(7) Subsection (6)(b) does not apply to a determination in response to the second or a subsequent application under this section in relation to the planning obligation; but such a determination may not have the effect that the development becomes economically unviable.

(8) In making a determination under this section the authority must have regard to—

(a) guidance issued by the Secretary of State, and

(b) where the determination relates to an application to which section 106BB applies, any representations made by the Mayor of London in accordance with that section.

(9) The authority must give notice of their determination to the applicant—

(a) within such period as may be prescribed by the Secretary of State, or

(b) if no period is prescribed under paragraph (a) (and subject to section 106BB(5)), within the period of 28 days beginning with the day on which the application is received, or such longer period as is agreed in writing between the applicant and the authority.

(10) Where an authority determine under this section that a planning obligation is to have effect subject to modifications, the obligation as modified is to be enforceable as if it had been entered into on the date on which notice of the determination was given to the applicant.

(11) The Secretary of State may by regulations make provision with respect to—

(a) the form and content of applications under subsection (2), and

(b) the notices to be given to applicants of determinations under subsection (9).

(12) This section and section 106BC do not apply in relation to an English planning obligation if planning permission for the development was granted wholly or partly on the basis of a policy for the provision of housing on rural exception sites.

(13) In this section and section 106BC—

'affordable housing requirement' means a requirement relating to the provision of housing that is or is to be made available for people whose needs are not adequately served by the commercial housing market (and it is immaterial for this purpose where or by whom the housing is or is to be provided);

'the appropriate authority' has the same meaning as in section 106A;

'the development', in relation to a planning obligation, means the development authorised by the planning permission to which the obligation relates;

'English planning obligation' means a planning obligation that—

(a) identifies a local planning authority in England as an authority by whom the obligation is enforceable, and

(b) does not identify a local planning authority in Wales as such an authority.

(14) The Secretary of State may by order amend this section so as to modify the definition of 'affordable housing requirement' in subsection (13).

(15) An order under subsection (14) may have effect for the purposes of planning obligations entered into before (as well as after) its coming into force.

(16) The Mayor of London must consult the local planning authority before exercising any function under this section.]

Amendment

Inserted by the Growth and Infrastructure Act 2013, s 7(1). Date in force: 25 April 2013: see the Growth and Infrastructure Act 2013, s 35(2); for transitional provisions see s 7(3), (4) thereof.

Part III Control over Development

[106BB Duty to notify the Mayor of London of certain applications under section 106BA]

[(1) This section applies to an application under section 106BA(2) in relation to a planning obligation where—
   (a) the application for the planning permission to which the planning obligation relates was an application to which section 2A applied (applications of potential strategic importance relating to land in Greater London),
   (b) the application for planning permission was not determined by the Mayor of London, and
   (c) pursuant to an order under section 2A or a development order, the local planning authority that determined the application for planning permission were required to consult the Mayor of London in relation to that determination.

(2) A local planning authority that receive an application to which this section applies must send a copy of the application to the Mayor of London before the end of the next working day following the day on which the application was received.

   In this subsection, 'working day' means a day which is not a Saturday, Sunday, Bank Holiday or other public holiday.

(3) The Mayor of London must notify the local planning authority before the end of the period of 7 days beginning with the day on which the application was received by the authority whether the Mayor intends to make representations about the application.

(4) Where pursuant to subsection (3) the Mayor of London notifies the local planning authority that the Mayor intends to make representations, those representations must be made before—
   (a) the end of the period of 14 days beginning with the day on which the application was received by the authority, or
   (b) the end of such longer period as may be agreed in writing between the authority and the Mayor.

(5) Where this section applies, section 106BA(9)(b) applies as if it required an authority to give notice of their determination to an applicant within—
   (a) the period of 35 days beginning with the day on which the application was received by the authority, or
   (b) such longer period as is agreed in writing between the applicant and the authority.]

Amendment

Inserted by the Growth and Infrastructure Act 2013, s 7(1). Date in force: 25 April 2013: see the Growth and Infrastructure Act 2013, s 35(2); for transitional provisions see s 7(3), (4) thereof.

[106BC Appeals in relation to applications under section 106BA]

[(1) Where an authority other than the Secretary of State—
   (a) fail to give notice as mentioned in section 106BA(9),
   (b) determine under section 106BA that a planning obligation is to continue to have effect without modification, or

Town and Country Planning Act 1990

  (c) determine under that section that a planning obligation is to be modified otherwise than in accordance with an application under that section,

the applicant may appeal to the Secretary of State.

(2) For the purposes of an appeal under subsection (1)(a), it is to be assumed that the authority have determined that the planning obligation is to continue to have effect without modification.

(3) An appeal under this section must be made by notice served within such period as may be prescribed by the Secretary of State.

(4) If no period is prescribed under subsection (3), an appeal under this section must be made—

  (a) in relation to an appeal under subsection (1)(a), within the period of 6 months beginning with the expiry of the period mentioned in section 106BA(9) that applies in the applicant's case, or

  (b) otherwise, within the period of 6 months beginning with the date on which notice of the determination is given to the applicant under section 106BA(9).

(5) An appeal under this section must be made by notice served in such manner as may be prescribed by the Secretary of State.

(6) Subsections (3) to (8), (10) and (11) of section 106BA apply in relation to an appeal under this section as they apply in relation to an application to an authority under that section, subject to subsections (7) to (15) below.

(7) References to the affordable housing requirement or the planning obligation are to the requirement or obligation as it stood immediately before the application under section 106BA to which the appeal relates.

(8) References to the first, the second or a subsequent application in relation to a planning obligation are to an appeal under this section against a determination on the first, the second or a subsequent application in relation to the obligation (whether or not it is the first such appeal).

(9) Section 106BA(5)(d) (discharge of affordable housing requirement) does not apply in relation to an appeal under this section.

(10) Subsection (11) applies if, on an appeal under this section, the Secretary of State—

  (a) does not uphold the determination under section 106BA to which the appeal relates (if such a determination has been made), and

  (b) determines that the planning obligation is to be modified in accordance with section 106BA(5)(a), (b) or (c).

(11) The Secretary of State must also determine that the planning obligation is to be modified so that it provides that, if the development has not been completed before the end of the relevant period, the obligation is treated as containing the affordable housing requirement or requirements it contained immediately before the first application under section 106BA in relation to the obligation, subject to the modifications within subsection (12).

(12) Those modifications are—

  (a) the modifications necessary to ensure that, if the development has been commenced before the end of the relevant period, the requirement or

Part III Control over Development

requirements apply only in relation to the part of the development that is not commenced before the end of that period, and

(b) such other modifications as the Secretary of State considers necessary or expedient to ensure the effectiveness of the requirement or requirements at the end of that period.

(13) In subsections (11) and (12) 'relevant period' means the period of three years beginning with the date when the applicant is notified of the determination on the appeal.

(14) Section 106BA and this section apply in relation to a planning obligation containing a provision within subsection (11) as if—

(a) the provision were an affordable housing requirement, and

(b) a person against whom the obligation is enforceable were a person against whom that requirement is enforceable.

(15) If subsection (11) applies on an appeal relating to a planning obligation that already contains a provision within that subsection—

(a) the existing provision within subsection (11) ceases to have effect, but

(b) that subsection applies again to the obligation.

(16) The determination of an appeal by the Secretary of State under this section is to be final.

(17) Schedule 6 applies to appeals under this section.

(18) In the application of Schedule 6 to an appeal under this section in a case where the authority mentioned in subsection (1) is the Mayor of London, references in that Schedule to the local planning authority are references to the Mayor of London.]

Amendment

Inserted by the Growth and Infrastructure Act 2013, s 7(1). Date in force: 25 April 2013: see the Growth and Infrastructure Act 2013, s 35(2); for transitional provisions see s 7(3), (4) thereof.

[106C Legal challenges relating to development consent obligations]

[(1) A court may entertain proceedings for questioning a failure by the Secretary of State ... to give notice as mentioned in section 106A(7) [or 106BA(9)] only if—

(a) the proceedings are brought by a claim for judicial review, and

(b) the claim form is filed [before the end of] the period of 6 weeks beginning with [the day after] the day on which the period prescribed under section 106A(7) [or 106BA(9)] ends.

[(1A) If no period is prescribed under section 106BA(9), the period of 6 weeks referred to in subsection (1)(b) that applies in relation to proceedings for failure to give notice as mentioned in subsection (9) of section 106BA begins with [the day after] the expiry of the period mentioned in that subsection that applies in the applicant's case.]

(2) A court may entertain proceedings for questioning a determination by the Secretary of State ... that a planning obligation shall continue to have effect without modification only if—

755

Town and Country Planning Act 1990

    (a) the proceedings are brought by a claim for judicial review, and

    (b) the claim form is filed [before the end of] the period of 6 weeks beginning with [the day after] the day on which notice of the determination is given under section 106A(7) [or 106BA(9)].]

[(3) A court may entertain proceedings for questioning a determination by the Secretary of State on an application under section 106BA that a planning obligation shall be modified otherwise than in accordance with the application only if—

    (a) the proceedings are brought by a claim for judicial review, and

    (b) the claim form is filed [before the end of] the period of 6 weeks beginning with [the day after] the day on which notice of the determination is given under section 106BA(9).]

Amendment

Inserted by the Planning Act 2008, s 174(1), (5). Date in force: 1 March 2010: see SI 2010/101, art 3(k); for savings see art 6 thereof.

Sub-s (1): words omitted repealed by the Localism Act 2011, ss 128(2), 237, Sch 13, Pt 2, para 77(1), (4), Sch 25, Pt 20. Date in force: 1 April 2012: see SI 2012/628, art 7.

Sub-s (1): words 'or 106BA(9)' in square brackets in the first place they occur inserted by the Growth and Infrastructure Act 2013, s 7(2), Sch 2, paras 1, 6(1), (2). Date in force: 25 April 2013: see the Growth and Infrastructure Act 2013, s 35(2); for transitional provisions see s 7(3) thereof.

Sub-s (1): in para (b) words 'before the end of' in square brackets substituted by the Criminal Justice and Courts Act 2015, s 92(2)(a)(i). Date in force: 13 April 2015: see SI 2015/778, art 3, Sch 1, para 71.

Sub-s (1): in para (b) words 'the day after' in square brackets inserted by the Criminal Justice and Courts Act 2015, s 92(2)(a)(ii). Date in force: 13 April 2015: see SI 2015/778, art 3, Sch 1, para 71.

Sub-s (1): in para (b) words 'or 106BA(9)' in square brackets inserted by the Growth and Infrastructure Act 2013, s 7(2), Sch 2, paras 1, 6(1), (2). Date in force: 25 April 2013: see the Growth and Infrastructure Act 2013, s 35(2); for transitional provisions see s 7(3) thereof.

Sub-s (1A): inserted by the Growth and Infrastructure Act 2013, s 7(2), Sch 2, paras 1, 6(1), (3). Date in force: 25 April 2013: see the Growth and Infrastructure Act 2013, s 35(2); for transitional provisions see s 7(3) thereof.

Sub-s (1A): words 'the day after' in square brackets inserted by the Criminal Justice and Courts Act 2015, s 92(2)(b). Date in force: 13 April 2015: see SI 2015/778, art 3, Sch 1, para 71.

Sub-s (2): words omitted repealed by the Localism Act 2011, ss 128(2), 237, Sch 13, Pt 2, para 77(1), (4), Sch 25, Pt 20. Date in force: 1 April 2012: see SI 2012/628, art 7.

Sub-s (2): in para (b) words 'before the end of' in square brackets substituted by the Criminal Justice and Courts Act 2015, s 92(2)(c)(i). Date in force: 13 April 2015: see SI 2015/778, art 3, Sch 1, para 71.

Sub-s (2): in para (b) words 'the day after' in square brackets inserted by the Criminal Justice and Courts Act 2015, s 92(2)(c)(ii). Date in force: 13 April 2015: see SI 2015/778, art 3, Sch 1, para 71.

Sub-s (2): in para (b) words 'or 106BA(9)' in square brackets inserted by the Growth and Infrastructure Act 2013, s 7(2), Sch 2, paras 1, 6(1), (4). Date in force: 25 April 2013: see the Growth and Infrastructure Act 2013, s 35(2); for transitional provisions see s 7(3) thereof.

Sub-s (3): inserted by the Growth and Infrastructure Act 2013, s 7(2), Sch 2, paras 1, 6(1), (5). Date in force: 25 April 2013: see the Growth and Infrastructure Act 2013, s 35(2); for transitional provisions see s 7(3) thereof.

Sub-s (3): in para (b) words 'before the end of' in square brackets substituted by the Criminal Justice and Courts Act 2015, s 92(2)(c)(i). Date in force: 13 April 2015: see SI 2015/778, art 3, Sch 1, para 71.

Sub-s (3): in para (b) words 'the day after' in square brackets inserted by the Criminal Justice and Courts Act 2015, s 92(2)(c)(ii). Date in force: 13 April 2015: see SI 2015/778, art 3, Sch 1, para 71.

284 Validity of development plans and certain orders, decisions and directions

(1) Except in so far as may be provided by this Part, the validity of—

    (a) ...

    (b) a simplified planning zone scheme or an alteration of such a scheme, whether before or after the adoption or approval of the scheme or alteration; or

    (c) an order under any provision of Part X except section 251(1), whether before or after the order has been made; or

    (d) an order under section 277, whether before or after the order has been made; or

    (e) any such order as is mentioned in subsection (2), whether before or after it has been confirmed; or

    (f) any such action on the part of the Secretary of State as is mentioned in subsection (3), [or—

    (g) a relevant costs order made in connection with an order mentioned in subsection (2) or an action mentioned in subsection (3),]

shall not be questioned in any legal proceedings whatsoever.

(2) The orders referred to in subsection (1)(e) are—

    (a) any order under section 97 or under the provisions of that section as applied by or under any other provision of this Act;

    (b) any order under section 102;

    (c) any tree preservation order;

    (d) any order made in pursuance of section 221(5);

    (e) any order under paragraph 1, 3, 5 or 6 of Schedule 9.

(3) The action referred to in subsection (1)(f) is action on the part of the Secretary of State of any of the following descriptions—

    [(ya) any decision on an application made to the Secretary of State under section 62A;]

    [(za) any decision on an application referred to the Secretary of State under section 76A;]

    (a) any decision on an application *for planning permission* referred to him under section 77;

    (b) any decision on an appeal under section 78;

    (c) ...

    (d) any decision to confirm a completion notice under section 95;

    (e) any decision to grant planning permission under paragraph (a) of section 177(1) or to discharge a condition or limitation under paragraph (b) of that section;

Town and Country Planning Act 1990

(f) any decision to confirm or not to confirm a purchase notice including—
  (i) any decision not to confirm such a notice in respect of part of the land to which it relates, or
  (ii) any decision to grant any permission, or give any direction, instead of confirming such a notice, either wholly or in part;
(g) any decision ... on an appeal under section 195(1);
(h) any decision relating—
  (i) to an application for consent under *a tree preservation order* [tree preservation regulations],
  (ii) to an application for consent under any regulations made in accordance with section 220 or 221, or
  (iii) to any certificate or direction under any such order or regulations,

whether it is a decision on appeal or a decision on an application referred to the Secretary of State for determination in the first instance;

[(i) any decision on an application for planning permission under section 293A].

[(3A) In this section, 'relevant costs order' means an order made under section 250(5) of the Local Government Act 1972 (orders as to costs of parties), as applied by virtue of any provision of this Act.]

(4) Nothing in this section shall affect the exercise of any jurisdiction of any court in respect of any refusal or failure on the part of the Secretary of State to take any such action as is mentioned in subsection (3).

Amendment

Sub-s (1): para (a) repealed by the Planning and Compulsory Purchase Act 2004, ss 118(1), 120, Sch 6, paras 1, 8, Sch 9. Date in force (in relation to England): 28 September 2004: see SI 2004/2202, arts 2(h), (k), 3(c), (d), Sch 1, Pt 1; for transitional provisions and savings see art 4, Sch 2 thereto. Date in force (in relation to Wales): 15 October 2005: see SI 2005/2847, art 2(e), (g), Sch 1; for savings see art 3(3), Sch 2 thereto.

Sub-s (1): para (g) and word 'or—' immediately preceding it inserted by the Criminal Justice and Courts Act 2015, s 91, Sch 16, paras 1, 2(a). Date in force: 26 October 2015: see SI 2015/1778, art 3(b); for transitional provisions see art 4.

Sub-s (3): para (ya) inserted by the Growth and Infrastructure Act 2013, s 1(2), Sch 1, paras 1, 9. Date in force (in relation to England for the purposes of making regulations or orders): 9 May 2013: see SI 2013/1124, art 2. Date in force (for remaining purposes): 1 October 2013: see SI 2013/2143, art 2(1)(a).

Sub-s (3): para (za) inserted by the Planning Act 2008, s 191(1), (2). Date in force: 6 April 2009: see SI 2009/400, art 3(g); for savings see art 6(1) thereof.

Sub-s (3): in para (a) words 'for planning permission' in italics repealed by the Planning Act 2008, ss 191(1), (3), 238, Sch 13. Date in force (in relation to England): 6 April 2009: see SI 2009/400, art 5(c), (g), Schedule, Pt 2; for savings see art 6(1) thereof. Date in force (in relation to Wales): to be appointed: see the Planning Act 2008, s 241(3), (4)(a), (d)(i). (8).

Sub-s (3): para (c) repealed by the Planning and Compensation Act 1991, ss 31, 84, Sch 6, para 24, Sch 19, Pt II.

Sub-s (3): in para (g) words omitted repealed by the Planning and Compensation Act 1991, ss 32, 84, Sch 7, para 41, Sch 19, Pt I.

Sub-s (3): in para (h)(i) words 'a tree preservation order' in italics repealed and subsequent words in square brackets substituted by the Planning Act 2008, s 192(8), Sch 8, paras 7, 17. Date in force (in relation to England): 6 April 2012: see SI 2012/601, art 2(a). Date in force (in relation to Wales): to be appointed: see the Planning Act 2008, s 241(3), (4)(a), (c).

Part III Control over Development

Sub-s (3): para (i) inserted by the Planning and Compulsory Purchase Act 2004, s 82(2). Date in force (for the purpose of making, or making provision by means of, subordinate legislation): 6 August 2004: see SI 2004/2097, art 2. Date in force (for remaining purposes): 7 June 2006: see SI 2006/1281, art 2(a).

Sub-s (3A): inserted by the Criminal Justice and Courts Act 2015, s 91, Sch 16, paras 1, 2(b). Date in force: 26 October 2015: see SI 2015/1778, art 3(b); for transitional provisions see art 4.

288 Proceedings for questioning the validity of other orders, decisions and directions

(1) If any person—

    (a) is aggrieved by any order to which this section applies and wishes to question the validity of that order on the grounds—

        (i) that the order is not within the powers of this Act, or

        (ii) that any of the relevant requirements have not been complied with in relation to that order; or

    (b) is aggrieved by any action on the part of the Secretary of State [or the Welsh Ministers] to which this section applies and wishes to question the validity of that action on the grounds—

        (i) that the action is not within the powers of this Act, or

        (ii) that any of the relevant requirements have not been complied with in relation to that action,

he may make an application to the High Court under this section.

[(1A) If a person is aggrieved by a relevant costs order made in connection with an order or action to which this section applies and wishes to question its validity, the person may make an application to the High Court under this section (whether or not as part of an application made by virtue of subsection (1)) on the grounds—

    (a) that the relevant costs order is not within the powers of this Act, or

    (b) that any of the relevant requirements have not been complied with in relation to the order.]

(2) Without prejudice to subsection (1) [or (1A)], if the authority directly concerned with any order to which this section applies, or with any action on the part of the Secretary of State [or the Welsh Ministers] to which this section applies, [or with any relevant costs order,] wish to question the validity of that order or action on any of the grounds mentioned in subsection (1) [or (1A) (as the case may be)], the authority may make an application to the High Court under this section.

(3) ...

(4) This section applies to any such order as is mentioned in subsection (2) of section 284 and to any such action on the part of the Secretary of State [or the Welsh Ministers] as is mentioned in subsection (3) of that section.

[(4A) An application under this section may not be made without the leave of the High Court.

(4B) An application for leave for the purposes of subsection (4A) must be made before the end of the period of six weeks beginning with the day after—

Town and Country Planning Act 1990

    (a) in the case of an application relating to an order under section 97 that takes effect under section 99 without confirmation, the date on which the order takes effect;

    (b) in the case of an application relating to any other order to which this section applies, the date on which the order is confirmed;

    (c) in the case of an application relating to an action to which this section applies, the date on which the action is taken;

    (d) in the case of an application relating to a relevant costs order, the date on which the order is made.

(4C) When considering whether to grant leave for the purposes of subsection (4A), the High Court may, subject to subsection (6), make an interim order suspending the operation of any order or action the validity of which the person or authority concerned wishes to question, until the final determination of—

    (a) the question of whether leave should be granted, or

    (b) where leave is granted, the proceedings on any application under this section made with such leave.]

(5) On any application under this section the High Court—

    (a) may, subject to subsection (6), by interim order suspend the operation of [any order or action], the validity of which is questioned by the application, until the final determination of the proceedings;

    (b) if satisfied that [any such order or action] is not within the powers of this Act, or that the interests of the applicant have been substantially prejudiced by a failure to comply with any of the relevant requirements in relation to it, may quash that order or action.

[(6) The High Court may not suspend a tree preservation order under subsection (4C) or (5)(a).]

(7) In relation to a tree preservation order, or to an order made in pursuance of section 221(5), the powers conferred on the High Court by subsection [(4C) or] (5) shall be exercisable by way of quashing or (where applicable) suspending the operation of the order either in whole or in part, as the court may determine.

(8) References in this section to the confirmation of an order include the confirmation of an order subject to modifications as well as the confirmation of an order in the form in which it was made.

[(9) In this section—

'relevant costs order' has the same meaning as in section 284;

'the relevant requirements'—

    (a) in relation to any order or action to which this section applies, means any requirements of this Act or of the Tribunals and Inquiries Act 1992, or of any order, regulations or rules made under either of those Acts, which are applicable to that order or action;

    (b) in relation to a relevant costs order, means any requirements of this Act, of the Local Government Act 1972 or of the Tribunals and Inquiries Act 1992, or of any order, regulations or rules made under any of those Acts, which are applicable to the relevant costs order.]

(10) Any reference in this section to the authority directly concerned with any order or action to which this section applies—

Part III Control over Development

(a) in relation to any such decision as is mentioned in section 284(3)(f), is a reference to the council on whom the notice in question was served and, in a case where the Secretary of State *has modified* [or the Welsh Ministers have modified] such a notice, wholly or in part, by substituting another local authority or statutory undertakers for that council, includes a reference to that local authority or those statutory undertakers;

(b) in any other case, is a reference to the authority who made the order in question or made the decision or served the notice to which the proceedings in question relate, or who referred the matter to the Secretary of State [or the Welsh Ministers], or, where the order or notice in question was made or served by *him* [the Secretary of State or the Welsh Ministers], the authority named in the order or notice.

[(11) References in this Act to an application under this section do not include an application for leave for the purposes of subsection (4A).]

Amendment

Sub-s (1): in para (b) words 'or the Welsh Ministers' in square brackets inserted by the Planning (Wales) Act 2015, s 27, Sch 4, paras 1, 16(1), (2). Date in force (for certain purposes): 6 September 2015: see the Planning (Wales) Act 2015, s 58(2)(b). Date in force (for remaining purposes): to be appointed: see the Planning (Wales) Act 2015, s 58(4)(b).

Sub-s (1A): inserted by the Criminal Justice and Courts Act 2015, s 91, Sch 16, paras 1, 4(1), (2). Date in force: 26 October 2015: see SI 2015/1778, art 3(b); for transitional provisions see art 4.

Sub-s (2): words 'or (1A)' in square brackets inserted by the Criminal Justice and Courts Act 2015, s 91, Sch 16, paras 1, 4(1), (3)(a). Date in force: 26 October 2015: see SI 2015/1778, art 3(b); for transitional provisions see art 4.

Sub-s (2): words 'or the Welsh Ministers' in square brackets inserted by the Planning (Wales) Act 2015, s 27, Sch 4, paras 1, 16(1), (3). Date in force (for certain purposes): 6 September 2015: see the Planning (Wales) Act 2015, s 58(2)(b). Date in force (for remaining purposes): to be appointed: see the Planning (Wales) Act 2015, s 58(4)(b).

Sub-s (2): words ' or with any relevant costs order,' in square brackets inserted by the Criminal Justice and Courts Act 2015, s 91, Sch 16, paras 1, 4(1), (3)(b). Date in force: 26 October 2015: see SI 2015/1778, art 3(b); for transitional provisions see art 4.

Sub-s (2): words 'or (1A) (as the case may be)' in square brackets inserted by the Criminal Justice and Courts Act 2015, s 91, Sch 16, paras 1, 4(1), (3)(c). Date in force: 26 October 2015: see SI 2015/1778, art 3(b); for transitional provisions see art 4.

Sub-s (3): repealed by the Criminal Justice and Courts Act 2015, s 91, Sch 16, paras 1, 4(1), (4). Date in force: 26 October 2015: see SI 2015/1778, art 3(b); for transitional provisions see art 4.

Sub-s (4): words 'or the Welsh Ministers' in square brackets inserted by the Planning (Wales) Act 2015, s 27, Sch 4, paras 1, 16(1), (4). Date in force (for certain purposes): 6 September 2015: see the Planning (Wales) Act 2015, s 58(2)(b). Date in force (for remaining purposes): to be appointed: see the Planning (Wales) Act 2015, s 58(4)(b).

Sub-ss (4A)–(4C): inserted by the Criminal Justice and Courts Act 2015, s 91, Sch 16, paras 1, 4(1), (5). Date in force: 26 October 2015: see SI 2015/1778, art 3(b); for transitional provisions see art 4.

Sub-s (5): in para (a) words 'any order or action' in square brackets substituted by the Criminal Justice and Courts Act 2015, s 91, Sch 16, paras 1, 4(1), (6)(a). Date in force: 26 October 2015: see SI 2015/1778, art 3(b); for transitional provisions see art 4.

Sub-s (5): in para (b) words 'any such order or action' in square brackets substituted by the Criminal Justice and Courts Act 2015, s 91, Sch 16, paras 1, 4(1), (6)(b). Date in force: 26 October 2015: see SI 2015/1778, art 3(b); for transitional provisions see art 4.

Town and Country Planning Act 1990

Sub-s (6): substituted by the Criminal Justice and Courts Act 2015, s 91, Sch 16, paras 1, 4(1), (7). Date in force: 26 October 2015: see SI 2015/1778, art 3(b); for transitional provisions see art 4.

Sub-s (7): words '(4C) or' in square brackets inserted by the Criminal Justice and Courts Act 2015, s 91, Sch 16, paras 1, 4(1), (8). Date in force: 26 October 2015: see SI 2015/1778, art 3(b); for transitional provisions see art 4.

Sub-s (9): substituted by the Criminal Justice and Courts Act 2015, s 91, Sch 16, paras 1, 4(1), (9). Date in force: 26 October 2015: see SI 2015/1778, art 3(b); for transitional provisions see art 4.

Sub-s (10): in para (a) words 'has modified' in italics repealed and subsequent words in square brackets substituted by the Planning (Wales) Act 2015, s 27, Sch 4, paras 1, 16(1), (5)(a). Date in force (for certain purposes): 6 September 2015: see the Planning (Wales) Act 2015, s 58(2)(b). Date in force (for remaining purposes): to be appointed: see the Planning (Wales) Act 2015, s 58(4)(b).

Sub-s (10): in para (b) words 'or the Welsh Ministers' in square brackets inserted by the Planning (Wales) Act 2015, s 27, Sch 4, paras 1, 16(1), (5)(b)(i). Date in force (for certain purposes): 6 September 2015: see the Planning (Wales) Act 2015, s 58(2)(b). Date in force (for remaining purposes): to be appointed: see the Planning (Wales) Act 2015, s 58(4)(b).

Sub-s (10): in para (b) word 'him' in italics repealed and subsequent words in square brackets substituted by the Planning (Wales) Act 2015, s 27, Sch 4, paras 1, 16(1), (5)(b)(ii). Date in force (for certain purposes): 6 September 2015: see the Planning (Wales) Act 2015, s 58(2)(b). Date in force (for remaining purposes): to be appointed: see the Planning (Wales) Act 2015, s 58(4)(b).

Sub-s (11): inserted by the Criminal Justice and Courts Act 2015, s 91, Sch 16, paras 1, 4(1), (10). Date in force: 26 October 2015: see SI 2015/1778, art 3(b); for transitional provisions see art 4.

PART XV MISCELLANEOUS AND GENERAL PROVISIONS

[Determination of procedure]

Amendment

Inserted by the Planning Act 2008, s 196(1). Date in force (for certain purposes): 6 April 2009: see SI 2009/400, art 3(j); for savings see art 6(2) thereof. Date in force (for remaining purposes): to be appointed: see the Planning Act 2008, s 241(8).

[319A Determination of procedure for certain proceedings][: England]

[(1) The Secretary of State must make a determination as to the procedure by which proceedings to which this section applies are to be considered.

(2) A determination under subsection (1) must provide for the proceedings to be considered in whichever of the following ways appears to the Secretary of State to be most appropriate—

   (a) at a local inquiry;

   (b) at a hearing;

   (c) on the basis of representations in writing.

(3) The Secretary of State must make a determination under subsection (1) in respect of proceedings to which this section applies before the end of the prescribed period.

(4) A determination under subsection (1) may be varied by a subsequent determination under that subsection at any time before the proceedings are determined.

Part XV Miscellaneous and General Provisions

(5) The Secretary of State must notify the appellant or applicant (as the case may be) and the local planning authority of any determination made under subsection (1).

(6) The Secretary of State must publish the criteria that are to be applied in making determinations under subsection (1).

(7) This section applies to—

[(za) an application made to the Secretary of State under section 62A;]

(a) an application referred to the Secretary of State under section 77 instead of being dealt with by a local planning authority in England;

(b) an appeal under section 78 against a decision of a local planning authority in England;

[(ba) an appeal under section 106BC (appeals in relation to applications for modification or discharge of affordable housing requirements);]

(c) an appeal under section 174 against an enforcement notice issued by a local planning authority in England;

(d) an appeal under section 195 against a decision of a local planning authority in England; and

(e) an appeal under section 208 against a notice under section 207(1) issued by a local planning authority in England.

(8) But this section does not apply to proceedings if they are referred to a Planning Inquiry Commission under section 101; and on proceedings being so referred, any determination made in relation to the proceedings under subsection (1) of this section ceases to have effect.

(9) The Secretary of State may by order amend subsection (7) to—

(a) add proceedings to, or remove proceedings from, the list of proceedings to which this section applies, or

(b) otherwise modify the descriptions of proceedings to which this section applies.

(10) An order under subsection (9) may—

(a) contain incidental, supplementary, consequential, transitional and transitory provision and savings;

(b) amend, repeal or revoke any provision made by or under this Act or by or under any other Act.]

Amendment

Inserted by the Planning Act 2008, s 196(1). Date in force (for certain purposes): 6 April 2009: see SI 2009/400, art 3(j); for savings see art 6(2) thereof. Date in force (for remaining purposes): to be appointed: see the Planning Act 2008, s 241(8).

Section heading: word 'England' in square brackets inserted by SI 2014/2773, art 2(1). Date in force: 11 November 2014: see SI 2014/2773, art 1(2).

Sub-s (7): para (za) inserted by the Growth and Infrastructure Act 2013, s 1(2), Sch 1, paras 1, 11. Date in force (in relation to England for the purposes of making regulations or orders): 9 May 2013: see SI 2013/1124, art 2. Date in force (for remaining purposes): 1 October 2013: see SI 2013/2143, art 2(1)(a).

Sub-s (7): para (ba) inserted by the Growth and Infrastructure Act 2013, s 7(2), Sch 2, paras 1, 7. Date in force: 25 April 2013: see the Growth and Infrastructure Act 2013, s 35(2); for transitional provisions see s 7(3) thereof.

[319B Determination of procedure for certain proceedings: Wales]

[(1) The Welsh Ministers must make a determination as to the procedure by which proceedings to which this section applies are to be considered.

(2) A determination under subsection (1) must provide for the proceedings to be considered in such one or more of the following ways as appear to the Welsh Ministers to be appropriate—
   (a) at a local inquiry;
   (b) at a hearing;
   (c) on the basis of representations in writing.

(3) The Welsh Ministers must make a determination under subsection (1) in respect of proceedings to which this section applies before the end of the prescribed period.

(4) A determination under subsection (1) may be varied by a subsequent determination under that subsection at any time before the proceedings are determined.

(5) The Welsh Ministers must notify the appellant or applicant (as the case may be) and the local planning authority of any determination made under subsection (1).

(6) The Welsh Ministers must publish the criteria which are to be applied in making determinations under subsection (1).

(7) This section applies to—
   (a) an application referred to the Welsh Ministers under section 77;
   (b) an appeal to the Welsh Ministers under section 78;
   (c) an appeal to the Welsh Ministers under section 174;
   (d) an appeal to the Welsh Ministers under section 195; and
   (e) an appeal to the Welsh Ministers under section 208.

(8) But this section does not apply to proceedings if they are referred to a Planning Inquiry Commission under section 101; and on proceedings being so referred, any determination made in relation to the proceedings under subsection (1) ceases to have effect.

(9) The Welsh Ministers may by order amend subsection (7) to—
   (a) add proceedings to, or remove proceedings from, the list of proceedings to which this section applies, or
   (b) otherwise modify the descriptions of proceedings to which this section applies.

(10) An order under subsection (9) may—
   (a) contain incidental, supplementary, consequential, transitional and transitory provision and savings;
   (b) amend, repeal or revoke any provision made by or under this Act or by or under any other Act.

(11) No order may be made under subsection (9) unless a draft of the instrument containing the order has been laid before and approved by resolution of the National Assembly for Wales.]

Amendment

Inserted by SI 2014/2773, art 2(1). Date in force: 11 November 2014: see SI 2014/2773, art 1(2).

Local inquiries and other hearings

320 Local inquiries

(1) The Secretary of State may cause a local inquiry to be held for the purposes of the exercise of any of his functions under any of the provisions of this Act.

(2) Subsections (2) to (5) of section 250 of the Local Government Act 1972 (local inquiries: evidence and costs) apply to an inquiry held by virtue of this section.

[(3) In its application by subsection (2) to an inquiry held in England, section 250(4) of that Act has effect as if—

(a) after 'the costs incurred by him in relation to the inquiry' there were inserted ', or such portion of those costs as he may direct,', and

(b) after 'the amount of the costs so incurred' there were inserted 'or, where he directs a portion of them to be paid, the amount of that portion'.]

Amendment

Sub-s (3): inserted by the Growth and Infrastructure Act 2013, s 2(1). Date in force: 1 October 2013: see SI 2013/2143, art 2(1)(b).

321 Planning inquiries to be held in public subject to certain exceptions

(1) This section applies to any inquiry held under section 320(1), paragraph 6 of Schedule 6 or paragraph 5 of Schedule 8.

(2) Subject to subsection (3), at any such inquiry oral evidence shall be heard in public and documentary evidence shall be open to public inspection.

(3) If the Secretary of State is satisfied in the case of any such inquiry—

(a) that giving evidence of a particular description or, as the case may be, making it available for inspection would be likely to result in the disclosure of information as to any of the matters mentioned in subsection (4); and

(b) that the public disclosure of that information would be contrary to the national interest,

he may direct that evidence of the description indicated in the direction shall only be heard or, as the case may be, open to inspection at that inquiry by such persons or persons of such descriptions as he may specify in the direction.

(4) The matters referred to in subsection (3)(*a*) are—

(a) national security; and

(b) the measures taken or to be taken to ensure the security of any premises or property.

[(5) If the Secretary of State is considering giving a direction under subsection (3) the Attorney General may appoint a person to represent the interests of any person who will be prevented from hearing or inspecting any evidence at a local inquiry if the direction is given.

(6) If before the Secretary of State gives a direction under subsection (3) no person is appointed under subsection (5), the Attorney General may at any time appoint a person as mentioned in subsection (5) for the purposes of the inquiry.

Town and Country Planning Act 1990

(7) The Lord Chancellor may by rules make provision—

(a) as to the procedure to be followed by the Secretary of State before he gives a direction under subsection (3) in a case where a person has been appointed under subsection (5);

(b) as to the functions of a person appointed under subsection (5) or (6).

(8) Rules made under subsection (7) must be contained in a statutory instrument subject to annulment in pursuance of a resolution of either House of Parliament.

(9) If a person is appointed under subsection (5) or (6) (the appointed representative) the Secretary of State may direct any person who he thinks is interested in the inquiry in relation to a matter mentioned in subsection (4) (the responsible person) to pay the fees and expenses of the appointed representative.

(10) If the appointed representative and the responsible person are unable to agree the amount of the fees and expenses, the amount must be determined by the Secretary of State.

(11) The Secretary of State must cause the amount agreed between the appointed representative and the responsible person or determined by him to be certified.

(12) An amount so certified is recoverable from the responsible person as a civil debt.]

Amendment

Sub-ss (5)–(12): inserted by the Planning and Compulsory Purchase Act 2004, s 80(1). Date in force (for the purpose of making, or making provision by means of, subordinate legislation): 6 August 2004: see SI 2004/2097, art 2. Date in force (for remaining purposes): 7 June 2006: see SI 2006/1281, art 2(a).

[321A Appointed representative: no inquiry]

[(1) This section applies if—

(a) a person is appointed under subsection (5) or (6) of section 321, but

(b) no inquiry is held as mentioned in subsection (1) of that section.

(2) Subsections (9) to (12) of section 321 apply in respect of the fees and expenses of the person appointed as if the inquiry had been held.

(3) For the purposes of subsection (2) the responsible person is the person to whom the Secretary of State thinks he would have given a direction under section 321(9) if an inquiry had been held.

(4) This section does not affect section 322A.]

Amendment

Inserted by the Planning and Compulsory Purchase Act 2004, s 80(2). Date in force (for the purpose of making, or making provision by means of, subordinate legislation): 6 August 2004: see SI 2004/2097, art 2. Date in force (for remaining purposes): 7 June 2006: see SI 2006/1281, art 2(a).

[321B Special provision in relation to planning inquiries: Wales]

[(1) This section applies if the matter in respect of which a local inquiry to which section 321 applies is to be held relates to Wales.

(2) The references in section 321(5) and (6) to the Attorney General must be read as references to the Counsel General to the [Welsh Assembly Government].

Part XV Miscellaneous and General Provisions

(3) The Assembly may by regulations make provision as mentioned in section 321(7) in connection with a local inquiry to which this section applies.

(4) If the Assembly acts under subsection (3) rules made by the Lord Chancellor under section 321(7) do not have effect in relation to the inquiry.

(5) ...

(6) Section 333(3) does not apply to regulations made under subsection (4).]

Amendment

Inserted by the Planning and Compulsory Purchase Act 2004, s 81(1). Date in force (for the purpose of making, or making provision by means of, subordinate legislation): 6 August 2004: see SI 2004/2097, art 2. Date in force (for remaining purposes): 7 June 2006: see SI 2006/1281, art 2(a).

Sub-s (2): words 'Welsh Assembly Government' in square brackets substituted by the Government of Wales Act 2006, s 160(1), Sch 10, para 35(a). Date in force: this amendment came into force on 25 May 2007 being the date on which the initial period ended (following the appointment of the First Minister): see the Government of Wales Act 2006, ss 46, 161(4), (5).

Sub-s (5): repealed by the Government of Wales Act 2006, ss 160(1), 163, Sch 10, para 35(b), Sch 12. Date in force: this repeal came into force on 25 May 2007 being the date on which the initial period ended (following the appointment of the First Minister): see the Government of Wales Act 2006, ss 46, 161(4), (5).

322 Orders as to costs of parties where no local inquiry held

(1) This section applies to proceedings under this Act where the Secretary of State is required, before reaching a decision, to give any person an opportunity of appearing before and being heard by a person appointed by him.

[*(1A) This section also applies to proceedings under this Act to which section 319A applies.*]

[(1AA) This section also applies to proceedings under this Act to which section 319B applies.]

[(1B) Section 250(4) of the Local Government Act 1972 applies to costs incurred by the Secretary of State, or a person appointed by the Secretary of State, in relation to proceedings in England to which this section applies which do not give rise to a local inquiry as it applies to costs incurred in relation to a local inquiry.

(1C) In its application for that purpose, section 250(4) of that Act has effect as if—

(a) after 'the costs incurred by him in relation to the inquiry' there were inserted ', or such portion of those costs as he may direct,', and

(b) after 'the amount of the costs so incurred' there were inserted 'or, where he directs a portion of them to be paid, the amount of that portion'.

(1D) Section 42 of the Housing and Planning Act 1986 (recovery of Minister's costs) applies to costs incurred in relation to proceedings in England to which this section applies which do not give rise to a local inquiry as it applies to costs incurred in relation to an inquiry.]

(2) The Secretary of State has the same power to make orders under section 250(5) of the Local Government Act 1972 (orders with respect to the costs of the parties) in relation to proceedings to which this section applies which do not give rise to a local inquiry as he has in relation to a local inquiry.

Town and Country Planning Act 1990

Amendment

This section is temporarily omitted by the Planning (Consequential Provisions) Act 1990, s 6, Sch 4, paras 1, 6, until such day as may be appointed by order made by the Secretary of State under that Schedule: the Planning (Consequential Provisions) Act 1990 (Appointed Day No 1 and Transitional Provisions) Order 1991, SI 1991/2698, appoints 2 January 1992 only for the purposes of the awards of costs in relation to proceedings which give rise to a hearing and the Planning (Consequential Provisions) Act 1990 (Appointed Day No 2 and Transitional Provision (England) Order 2009, SI 2009/849, appoints 6 April 2009 only for the purposes of proceedings which do not give rise to an inquiry or hearing.

Sub-s (1A): inserted by the Planning Act 2008, s 196(4), Sch 10, paras 1, 10. Date in force (for certain purposes): 6 April 2009: see SI 2009/400, art 3(j); for savings see art 6(2) thereof. Date in force (for remaining purposes): to be appointed: see the Planning Act 2008, s 241(8).

Sub-s (1AA): inserted, in relation to Wales, by SI 2014/2773, art 3, Sch 1, paras 1, 9. Date in force: 11 November 2014: see SI 2014/2773, art 1(2).

Sub-ss (1B)–(1D): inserted by the Growth and Infrastructure Act 2013, s 2(2). Date in force: 1 October 2013: see SI 2013/2143, art 2(1)(b).

[322A Orders as to costs: supplementary]

[(1) This section applies where—
  (a) for the purposes of any proceedings under this Act—
    (i) the Secretary of State is required, before a decision is reached, to give any person an opportunity, or ask any person whether he wishes, to appear before and be heard by a person appointed by him; and
    (ii) arrangements are made for a local inquiry or hearing to be held;
  (b) the inquiry or hearing does not take place; and
  (c) if it had taken place, the Secretary of State or a person appointed by him would have had power to make an order under section 250(5) of the Local Government Act 1972 requiring any party to pay any costs of any other party.

[(1A) This section also applies where—
  (a) arrangements are made for a local inquiry or a hearing to be held pursuant to a determination under section 319A;
  (b) the inquiry or hearing does not take place; and
  (c) if it had taken place, the Secretary of State or a person appointed by the Secretary of State would have had power to make an order under section 250(5) of the Local Government Act 1972 requiring any party to pay any costs of any other party.]

[(1B) This section also applies where—
  (a) arrangements are made for a local inquiry or a hearing to be held pursuant to a determination of the Welsh Ministers under section 319B;
  (b) the inquiry or hearing does not take place; and
  (c) if it had taken place, the Welsh Ministers or a person appointed by the Welsh Ministers would have had power to make an order under section 250(5) of the Local Government Act 1972 requiring any party to pay any costs of any other party.]

(2) Where this section applies the power to make such an order may be exercised, in relation to costs incurred for the purposes of the inquiry or hearing, as if it had taken place.

Part XV Miscellaneous and General Provisions

[(3) Where this section applies in the case of an inquiry or hearing which was to take place in England but did not, section 250(4) of that Act applies to costs incurred by the Secretary of State or a person appointed by the Secretary of State as if—

    (a) in the case of an inquiry, the inquiry had taken place;

    (b) in the case of a hearing, the hearing were an inquiry which had taken place.

(4) In its application for that purpose, section 250(4) of that Act has effect as if—

    (a) after 'the costs incurred by him in relation to the inquiry' there were inserted ', or such portion of those costs as he may direct,', and

    (b) after 'the amount of the costs so incurred' there were inserted 'or, where he directs a portion of them to be paid, the amount of that portion'.

(5) Section 42 of the Housing and Planning Act 1986 (recovery of Minister's costs) applies to costs incurred in relation to a hearing of the kind referred to in subsection (1) or (1A) which was to take place in England but did not as it applies to costs incurred in relation to an inquiry which was to take place but did not.]]

Amendment

Inserted by the Planning and Compensation Act 1991, s 30(1).

Sub-s (1A): inserted by the Planning Act 2008, s 196(4), Sch 10, paras 1, 11. Date in force (for certain purposes): 6 April 2009: see SI 2009/400, art 3(j); for savings see art 6(2) thereof. Date in force (for remaining purposes): to be appointed: see the Planning Act 2008, s 241(8).

Sub-s (1B): inserted, in relation to Wales, by SI 2014/2773, art 3, Sch 1, paras 1, 10. Date in force: 11 November 2014: see SI 2014/2773, art 1(2).

Sub-ss (3)–(5): inserted by the Growth and Infrastructure Act 2013, s 2(3). Date in force: 1 October 2013: see SI 2013/2143, art 2(1)(b).

[322B Local inquiries in London: special provision as to costs in certain cases]

[(1) This section applies where—

    (a) the local planning authority for a London borough refuse an application for planning permission,

    (b) that refusal is in compliance with a direction made by the Mayor of London in accordance with provision made in a development order by virtue of section 74(1B)(a), and

    (c) an appeal against the refusal is made to the Secretary of State under section 78.

(2) If the Secretary of State causes a local inquiry to be held under section 320(1) to determine the appeal, in its application to the inquiry section 250 of the 1972 Act shall be treated as if—

    (a) for subsection (4) there were substituted the subsection set out at subsection (5) below, and

    (b) for subsection (5) there were substituted the subsection set out at subsection (6) below.

(3) If the appeal does not give rise to a local inquiry under section 320, in the application of section 322(2) in relation to the appeal the reference to section 250(5) of the 1972 Act shall be treated as if it were a reference to that provision as modified by subsection (2)(b) above.

Town and Country Planning Act 1990

(4) If arrangements are made for a local inquiry in relation to the appeal and the inquiry does not take place, in the application of section 322A in relation to the appeal the reference to section 250(5) of the 1972 Act shall be treated as if it were a reference to that provision as modified by subsection (2)(b) above.

(5) The subsection referred to in subsection (2)(a) above is as follows—

'( ) Where this subsection applies to an inquiry, the costs incurred by the Secretary of State in relation to the inquiry[, or such portion of those costs as he may direct,] shall be paid—

(a) by the Mayor of London, if he is not a party to the inquiry and if the Secretary of State decides that the Mayor acted unreasonably in making the direction in accordance with which the local planning authority refused the planning permission, or

(b) if the Mayor is a party or if the Secretary of State does not so decide, by such local authority or party to the inquiry as he may direct;

and the Secretary of State may cause the amount of the costs so incurred [or, where he directs a portion of them to be paid, the amount of that portion] to be certified, and any amount so certified and directed to be paid by the Mayor or by any authority or person shall be recoverable from the Mayor or from that authority or person by the Secretary of State summarily as a civil debt.'

(6) The subsection referred to in subsection (2)(b) above is as follows—

'( ) Where this subsection applies to an inquiry, or to costs incurred for the purposes of an inquiry, the Secretary of State may make orders as to the costs of the parties to the inquiry and as to the parties by whom the costs are to be paid; and—

(a) the parties by whom the costs are ordered to be paid may include the Mayor of London if he is not a party to the inquiry and if the Secretary of State decides that the Mayor acted unreasonably in making the direction in accordance with which the local planning authority refused the planning permission;

(b) every such order may be made a rule of the High Court on the application of any party named in the order.'

(7) In this section 'the 1972 Act' means the Local Government Act 1972.]

Amendment

Inserted by the Greater London Authority Act 1999, s 345. Date in force: 3 July 2000: see SI 2000/801, art 2(2)(c), Schedule, Pt 3.

Sub-s (5): words ', or such portion of those costs as he may direct,' in square brackets inserted by the Growth and Infrastructure Act 2013, s 2(4)(a). Date in force: 1 October 2013: see SI 2013/2143, art 2(1)(b).

Sub-s (5): words 'or, where he directs a portion of them to be paid, the amount of that portion' in square brackets inserted by the Growth and Infrastructure Act 2013, s 2(4)(b). Date in force: 1 October 2013: see SI 2013/2143, art 2(1)(b).

323 Procedure on certain appeals and applications

(1) The Secretary of State may by regulations prescribe the procedure to be followed in connection with proceedings under this Act where he is required,

Part XV Miscellaneous and General Provisions

before reaching a decision, to give any person an opportunity of appearing before and being heard by a person appointed by him and which are to be disposed of without an inquiry or hearing to which rules under [section 9 of the Tribunals and Inquiries Act 1992] apply.

[(1A) The Secretary of State may by regulations prescribe the procedure to be followed in connection with proceedings under this Act which, pursuant to a determination under section 319A, are to be considered on the basis of representations in writing.]

[(1B) The Welsh Ministers may by regulations prescribe the procedure to be followed in connection with proceedings under this Act which, pursuant to a determination under section 319B, are to be considered on the basis of representations in writing.]

(2) *The regulations may* [Regulations under this section may] in particular make provision as to the procedure to be followed—

 (a) where steps have been taken with a view to the holding of *such an inquiry or hearing* [an inquiry or hearing to which rules under section 9 of the Tribunals and Inquiries Act 1992 would apply] which does not take place, or

 (b) where steps have been taken with a view to the determination of any matter by a person appointed by the Secretary of State and the proceedings are the subject of a direction that the matter shall instead be determined by the Secretary of State, or

 (c) where steps have been taken in pursuance of such a direction and a further direction is made revoking that direction,

 and may provide that such steps shall be treated as compliance, in whole or in part, with the requirements of the regulations.

(3) *The regulations may* [Regulations under this section may] also—

 (a) provide for a time limit within which any part to the proceedings must submit representations in writing and any supporting documents;

 (b) prescribe the time limit (which may be different for different classes of proceedings) or enable the Secretary of State to give directions setting the time limit in a particular case or class of case;

 (c) empower the Secretary of State to proceed to a decision taking into account only such written representations and supporting documents as were submitted within the time limit; and

 (d) empower the Secretary of State, after giving the parties written notice of his intention to do so, to proceed to a decision notwithstanding that no written representations were made within the time limit, if it appears to him that he has sufficient material before him to enable him to reach a decision on the merits of the case.

[(4) Regulations made by the Secretary of State under this section may include provision as to the circumstances in which, in proceedings in England such as are mentioned in subsection (1) or (1A)—

 (a) directions may be given under section 250(4) of the Local Government Act 1972 as applied by a prescribed provision of this Act;

 (b) orders for costs may be made under section 250(5) of that Act as so applied.]

Town and Country Planning (Use Classes) Order 1987

Amendment

Sub-s (1): words in square brackets substituted by the Tribunals and Inquiries Act 1992, s 18(1), Sch 3, para 26.

Sub-s (1A): inserted by the Planning Act 2008, s 196(4), Sch 10, paras 1, 12(1), (2). Date in force (for certain purposes): 6 April 2009: see SI 2009/400, art 3(j); for savings see art 6(2) thereof. Date in force (for remaining purposes): to be appointed: see the Planning Act 2008, s 241(8).

Sub-s (1B): inserted, in relation to Wales, by SI 2014/2773, art 3, Sch 1, paras 1, 11(1), (2). Date in force: 11 November 2014: see SI 2014/2773, art 1(2).

Sub-s (2): words 'The regulations may' in italics repealed and subsequent words in square brackets substituted by the Planning Act 2008, s 196(4), Sch 10, paras 1, 12(1), (3) and by SI 2014/2773, Sch 1, paras 1, 11(1), (3). Date in force (in relation to England for certain purposes): 6 April 2009: see SI 2009/400, art 3(j); for savings see art 6(2) thereof. Date in force (in relation to Wales): 11 November 2014: see SI 2014/2773, art 1(2). Date in force (in relation to England for remaining purposes): to be appointed: see the Planning Act 2008, s 241(8).

Sub-s (2): in para (a) words 'such an inquiry or hearing' in italics repealed and subsequent words in square brackets substituted by the Planning Act 2008, s 196(4), Sch 10, paras 1, 12(1), (4). Date in force (for certain purposes): 6 April 2009: see SI 2009/400, art 3(j); for savings see art 6(2) thereof. Date in force (for remaining purposes): to be appointed: see the Planning Act 2008, s 241(8).

Sub-s (3): words 'The regulations may' in italics repealed and subsequent words in square brackets substituted by the Planning Act 2008, s 196(4), Sch 10, paras 1, 12(1), (3) and by SI 2014/2773, art 3, Sch 1, paras 1, 11(1), (3). Date in force (in relation to England for certain purposes): 6 April 2009: see SI 2009/400, art 3(j); for savings see art 6(2) thereof. Date in force (in relatioin to Wales): 11 November 2014: see SI 2014/2773, art 1(2). Date in force (in relation to England for remaining purposes): to be appointed: see the Planning Act 2008, s 241(8).

Sub-s (4): inserted by the Growth and Infrastructure Act 2013, s 2(5). Date in force: 1 October 2013: see SI 2013/2143, art 2(1)(b).

(SI 1987/764)

Town and Country Planning (Use Classes) Order 1987

1 Citation and commencement

This Order may be cited as the Town and Country Planning (Use Classes) Order 1987 and shall come into force on 1st June 1987.

2 Interpretation

In this Order, unless the context otherwise requires:—

Town and Country Planning (Use Classes) Order 1987

'care' means personal care for people in need of such care by reason of old age, disablement, past or present dependence on alcohol or drugs or past or present mental disorder, and in class C2 also includes the personal care of children and medical care and treatment;

'day centre' means premises which are visited during the day for social or recreational purposes or for the purposes of rehabilitation or occupational training, at which care is also provided;

...

'industrial process' means a process for or incidental to any of the following purposes:—

(a) the making of any article or part of any article (including a ship or vessel, or a film, video or sound recording);

(b) the altering, repairing, maintaining, ornamenting, finishing, cleaning, washing, packing, canning, adapting for sale, breaking up or demolition of any article; or

(c) the getting, dressing or treatment of minerals;

in the course of any trade or business other than agriculture, and other than a use carried out in or adjacent to a mine or quarry;

'Schedule' means the Schedule to this Order;

'site' means the whole area of land within a single unit of occupation.

Amendment

Definitions omitted revoked by SI 1992/657, art 2(1).

3 Use Classes

(1) Subject to the provisions of this Order, where a building or other land is used for a purpose of any class specified in the Schedule, the use of that building or that other land for any other purpose of the same class shall not be taken to involve development of the land.

(2) References in paragraph (1) to a building include references to land occupied with the building and used for the same purposes.

(3) A use which is included in and ordinarily incidental to any use in a class specified in the Schedule is not excluded from the use to which it is incidental merely because it is specified in the Schedule as a separate use.

(4) Where land on a single site or on adjacent sites used as parts of a single undertaking is used for purposes consisting of or including purposes falling [within classes B1 and B2] in the Schedule, those classes may be treated as a single class in considering the use of that land for the purposes of this Order, so long as the area used for a purpose falling [within class B2] is not substantially increased as a result.

(5) ...

(6) No class specified in the Schedule includes use—

(a) as a theatre,

(b) as an amusement arcade or centre, or a funfair,

Town and Country Planning (Use Classes) Order 1987

[(c) as a launderette,]
(d) for the sale of fuel for motor vehicles,
(e) for the sale or display for sale of motor vehicles,
(f) for a taxi business or business for the hire of motor vehicles,
(g) as a scrapyard, or a yard for the storage or distribution of minerals or the breaking of motor vehicles,
[(h) for any work registrable under the Alkali, etc. Works Regulation Act 1906],
[(i) as a hostel]
[(j) as a waste disposal installation for the incineration, chemical treatment (as defined in Annex I to Directive 2008/98/EC under heading D9) or landfill of hazardous waste as defined (in relation to England) in regulation 6 of the Hazardous Waste (England and Wales) Regulations 2005 or (in relation to Wales) in regulation 6 of the Hazardous Waste (Wales) Regulations 2005,]
[(k) as a retail warehouse club being a retail club where goods are sold, or displayed for sale, only to persons who are members of that club;
(l) as a night-club],
[(m) as a casino],
[(n) as a betting office,
(o) as a pay day loan shop].

[(6A) For the purpose of paragraph (6)—

'high-cost short-term credit' has the meaning given in the edition of the Financial Conduct Authority's Handbook which came into effect on 1st April 2014 (following an amendment by the Authority in the Consumer Credit (Consequential and Supplementary Amendments) Instrument 2014); and

'pay day loan shop' means premises—
(a) from which high-cost short-term credit is provided principally to visiting members of the public and includes premises from which such credit is provided in addition to other financial or professional services, and
(b) which, but for provision made in this article, would fall within Class A2 (financial and professional services) of the Schedule to this Order.]

[(7) Where a building or other land is situated in Wales, class B8 (storage or distribution) does not include use of that building or land for the storage of, or as a distribution centre for, radioactive material or radioactive waste.

(8) *For the purpose of paragraph (7), 'radioactive material' and 'radioactive waste' have the meanings assigned to those terms in the Radioactive Substances Act 1993.*]

[(8) For the purpose of paragraph (7), 'radioactive material' and 'radioactive waste' have the same meaning as in the Environmental Permitting (England and Wales) Regulations 2010.]

Amendment
Para (4): words in square brackets substituted by SI 1995/297, art 2(1).

Para (5): revoked by SI 1992/657, art 2(2).

Para (6): sub-para (c) substituted by SI 1991/1567, art 2(1).

Para (6): sub-para (h) inserted by SI 1992/610, art 2(1)(b).

Para (6): sub-para (i) inserted by SI 1994/724, art 2(1).

Para (6): sub-para (j) substituted by SI 2011/988, reg 48(3), Sch 4, Pt 2, para 8. Date in force: 29 March 2011: see SI 2011/988, reg 1(2).

Para (6): sub-paras (k), (l) inserted, in relation to England, by SI 2005/84, art 2(1). Date in force: 21 April 2005: see SI 2005/84, art 1(1).

Para (6): sub-para (m) inserted, in relation to England, by SI 2006/220, art 2(1), (2). Date in force: 6 April 2006: see SI 2006/220, art 1(1).

Para (6): sub-paras (n), (o) inserted, in relation to England, by SI 2015/597, art 2(1), (2). Date in force: 15 April 2015: see SI 2015/597, art 1(1); for transitional provisions see reg 3.

Para (6A): inserted, in relation to England, by SI 2015/597, art 2(1), (3). Date in force: 15 April 2015: see SI 2015/597, art 1(1); for transitional provisions see reg 3.

Paras (7), (8): inserted, in relation to Wales, by SI 2002/1875, art 2. Date in force: 12 August 2002: see SI 2002/1875, art 1(1).

Para (8): substituted, in relation to England and Wales, by SI 2010/675, reg 107, Sch 26, Pt 2, para 3. Date in force: 6 April 2010 (immediately after the coming into force of the Environmental Permitting (England and Wales) (Amendment) (No 2) Regulations 2009, SI 2009/3381): see SI 2010/675, reg 1(1)(b).

4 Change of use of part of building or land

In the case of a building for a purpose within class C3 (dwellinghouses) in the Schedule, the use as a separate dwellinghouse of any part of the building or of any land occupied with and used for the same purposes as the building is not, by virtue of this Order, to be taken as not amounting to development.

5 Revocation

...

Amendment

This article revokes SI 1972/1385 and SI 1983/1614.

SCHEDULE

Article 3, 4

PART A

Class A1. Shops

Use for all or any of the following purposes—

(a) for the retail sale of goods other than hot food,

(b) as a post office,

(c) for the sale of tickets or as a travel agency,

(d) for the sale of sandwiches or other cold food for consumption off the premises,

(e) for hairdressing,

Town and Country Planning (Use Classes) Order 1987

(f) for the direction of funerals,
(g) for the display of goods for sale,
(h) for the hiring out of domestic or personal goods or articles,
[(i) for the washing or cleaning of clothes or fabrics on the premises,
(j) for the reception of goods to be washed, cleaned or repaired,]
[(k) as an internet café; where the primary purpose of the premises is to provide facilities for enabling members of the public to access the internet,]

where the sale, display or service is to visiting members of the public.

Class A2. Financial and professional services

Use for the provision of—
(a) financial services, or
(b) professional services (other than health or medical services), or
(c) any other services *(including use as a betting office)* which it is appropriate to provide in a shopping area,

where the services are provided principally to visiting members of the public.

Class A3. Food and drink

Use for the sale of food and drink for consumption on the premises or of hot food for consumption off the premises.

[Class A3. Restaurants and cafes

Use for the sale of food and drink for consumption on the premises.

Class A4. Drinking establishments

Use as a public house, wine-bar or other drinking establishment

Class A5. Hot food takeaways

Use for the sale of hot food for consumption off the premises.]

Amendment

Class A1: paras (i), (j) substituted by SI 1991/1567, art 2(2).

Class A1: para (k) inserted, in relation to England, by SI 2005/84, art 2(2)(a). Date in force: 21 April 2005: see SI 2005/84, art 1(1).

Class A2: in para (c) words '(including use as a betting office)' in italics revoked, in relation to England, by SI 2015/597, art 2(1), (4). Date in force: 15 April 2015: see SI 2015/597, art 1(1); for transitional provisions see reg 3.

Classes A3–A5: substituted, for Class A3 as originally enacted, in relation to England, by SI 2005/84, art 2(2)(b). Date in force: 21 April 2005: see SI 2005/84, art 1(1).

PART B

Class B1. Business

Use for all or any of the following purposes—

Town and Country Planning (Use Classes) Order 1987

(a) as an office other than a use within class A2 (financial and professional services),
(b) for research and development of products or processes, or
(c) for any industrial process,

being a use which can be carried out in any residential area without detriment to the amenity of that area by reason of noise, vibration, smell, fumes, smoke, soot, ash, dust or grit.

Class B2. General industrial

Use for the carrying on of an industrial process other than one falling within Class B1 above ... .

Class B3. Special Industrial Group A

...

Class B4–Class B7.

...

Class B8. Storage or distribution.

Use for storage or as a distribution centre.

Amendment

In entry relating to Class B2 words omitted revoked by SI 1995/297, art 2(2)(a).
Entry relating to Class B3 revoked by SI 1992/610, art 2(b).
Entries relating to Classes B4 to B7 revoked by SI 1995/297, art 2(2)(b).

PART C

[Class C1. Hotels

Use as a hotel or as a boarding or guest house where, in each case, no significant element of care is provided.]

Class C2. Residential institutions

Use for the provision of residential accommodation and care to people in need of care (other than a use within Class C3 (dwelling houses)).

Use as a hospital or nursing home.

Use as a residential school, college or training centre.

[*Class C2A. Secure residential institutions*

Use for the provision of secure residential accommodation, including use as a prison, young offenders institution, detention centre, secure training centre, custody centre, short-term holding centre, secure hospital, secure local authority accommodation or use as military barracks.]

[Class C2A. Secure residential institutions

Use for the provision of secure residential accommodation, including use as a prison, young offenders institution, detention centre, secure training centre, custody centre,

Town and Country Planning (Use Classes) Order 1987

short-term holding centre, secure hospital, secure local authority accommodation or use as military barracks.]

Class C3. Dwellinghouses

Use as a dwellinghouse (whether or not as a sole or main residence)—

(a) *by a single person or by people living together as a family, or*

(b) *by not more than 6 residents living together as a single household (including a household where care is provided for residents).*

[Class C3. Dwellinghouses

Use as a dwellinghouse (whether or not as a sole or main residence) by—

(a) a single person or by people to be regarded as forming a single household;

(b) not more than six residents living together as a single household where care is provided for residents; or

(c) not more than six residents living together as a single household where no care is provided to residents (other than a use within Class C4).

Interpretation of Class C3

For the purposes of Class C3(a) 'single household' shall be construed in accordance with section 258 of the Housing Act 2004.]

[Class C4. Houses in multiple occupation

Use of a dwellinghouse by not more than six residents as a 'house in multiple occupation'.

Interpretation of Class C4

For the purposes of Class C4 a 'house in multiple occupation' does not include a converted block of flats to which section 257 of the Housing Act 2004 applies but otherwise has the same meaning as in section 254 of the Housing Act 2004.]

Amendment

Class C1: substituted by SI 1994/724, art 2(2).

Class C2A: inserted in relation to England by SI 2006/1282, art 5(1), (2) and in relation to Wales by SI 2006/1386, art 2(1), (2). Date in force (in relation to England): 7 June 2006: see SI 2006/1282, art 1. Date in force (in relation to Wales): 7 June 2006: see SI 2006/1386, art 1(1).

Class C2A: substituted, in relation to England, by SI 2010/653, art 2(1), (2). Date in force: 6 April 2010: see SI 2010/653, art 1(1).

Class C3: substituted, in relation to England, by SI 2010/653, art 2(1), (3). Date in force: 6 April 2010: see SI 2010/653, art 1(1).

Class C4: inserted, in relation to England, by SI 2010/653, art 2(1), (4). Date in force: 6 April 2010: see SI 2010/653, art 1(1).

PART D

Class D1. Non-residential institutions

Any use not including a residential use—

(a) for the provision of any medical or health services except the use of premises attached to the residence of the consultant or practitioner,
(b) as a creche, day nursery or day centre,
(c) for the provision of education,
(d) for the display of works of art (otherwise than for sale or hire),
(e) as a museum,
(f) as a public library or public reading room,
(g) as a public hall or exhibition hall,
(h) for, or in connection with, public worship or religious instruction,
[(i) as a law court].

Class D2. Assembly and leisure

Use as—
(a) a cinema,
(b) a concert hall,
(c) a bingo hall *or casino*,
(d) a dance hall,
(e) a swimming bath, skating rink, gymnasium or area for other indoor or outdoor sports or recreations, not involving motorised vehicles or firearms.

Amendment

Class D1: para (i) inserted in relation to England by SI 2006/1282, art 5(1), (3) and in relation to Wales by SI 2006/1386, art 2(1), (3). Date in force (in relation to England): 7 June 2006: see SI 2006/1282, art 1. Date in force (in relation to Wales): 7 June 2006: see SI 2006/1386, art 1(1).

Class D2: in para (c) words 'or casino' in italics revoked, in relation to England, by SI 2006/220, art 2(1), (3). Date in force: 6 April 2006: see SI 2006/220, art 1(1).

(SI 2000/1624)

Town and Country Planning (Inquiries Procedure) (England) Rules 2000

1 Citation, commencement, and extent

(1) These Rules may be cited as the Town and Country Planning (Inquiries Procedure) (England) Rules 2000.

(2) These Rules shall come into force on 1st August 2000.

Town and Country Planning (Inquiries Procedure) (England) Rules 2000

(3) These Rules extend to England only.

Amendment

Revoked, in relation to the inquiry procedure for major infrastructure projects in England, by virtue of SI 2002/1223, r 26(1).

Date in force: 7 June 2002 (except in relation to any application or appeal which has not been determined on that date): see SI 2002/1223, rr 1(2), 26(1).

2 Interpretation

[(1)] *In these Rules—*

'applicant' *in the case of an appeal, means the appellant;*

'assessor' *means a person appointed by the Secretary of State to sit with an inspector at an inquiry or re-opened inquiry to advise the inspector on such matters arising as the Secretary of State may specify;*

'the Commission' *means the Historic Buildings and Monuments Commission for England;*

...

'development order' *has the meaning given in section 59 of the Planning Act;*

'document' *includes a photograph, map or plan;*

[*'electronic communication' has the meaning given in section 15(1) of the Electronic Communications Act 2000;*]

'inquiry' *means a local inquiry in relation to which these Rules apply;*

'inspector' *means a person appointed by the Secretary of State to hold an inquiry or a re-opened inquiry;*

'land' *means the land or building to which an inquiry relates;*

'the Listed Buildings Act' *means the Planning (Listed Buildings and Conservation Areas) Act 1990;*

'listed building consent' *has the meaning given in section 8(7) of the Listed Buildings Act;*

'local planning authority' *means in relation to—*

  (i) *a referred application, the body who would otherwise have dealt with the application;*

  (ii) *an appeal, the body who were responsible for dealing with the application occasioning the appeal;*

'outline statement' *means a written statement of the principal submissions which a person proposes to put forward at an inquiry;*

'the Planning Act' *means the Town and Country Planning Act 1990;*

'pre-inquiry meeting' *means a meeting held before an inquiry to consider what may be done with a view to securing that the inquiry is conducted efficiently and expeditiously, and where two or more such meetings are held references to the conclusion of a pre-inquiry meeting are references to the conclusion of the final meeting;*

'questionnaire' *means a document in the form supplied by the Secretary of State to local planning authorities for the purpose of proceedings under these Rules* [, *and for this purpose a form is taken to be supplied where the Secretary of State has published it on a website and has notified the local planning authority of—*

Town and Country Planning (Inquiries Procedure) (England) Rules 2000

    (i) publication of the form on the website,

    (ii) the address of the website, and

    (iii) the place on the website where the form may be accessed, and how it may be accessed];

'referred application' means an application of any description mentioned in rule 3(1) which is referred to the Secretary of State for determination;

...

'the 1992 Rules' means the Town and Country Planning (Inquiries Procedure) Rules 1992;

['starting date' means the date of the notice given by the Secretary of State under rule 3A;]

'statement of case' means, and is comprised of, a written statement which contains full particulars of the case which a person proposes to put forward at an inquiry and a list of any documents which that person intends to refer to or put in evidence;

'statement of common ground' means a written statement prepared jointly by the local planning authority and the applicant, which contains agreed factual information about the proposal, which is the subject of the application or appeal;

'statutory party' means—

    (a) a person mentioned in paragraph (1)(b)(i) of article 19 of the Town and Country Planning (General Development Procedure) Order 1995 whose representations the Secretary of State is required by paragraph (3) of that article to take into account in determining the referred application or appeal to which an inquiry relates; and, in the case of an appeal, such a person whose representations the local planning authority were required by paragraph (1) of that article to take into account in determining the application occasioning the appeal; and

    (b) a person whose representations the Secretary of State is required by paragraphs (3)(b) and (5) of regulation 6 of the Planning (Listed Buildings and Conservation Areas) Regulations 1990 to take into account in determining the referred application or appeal to which an inquiry relates; and, in the case of an appeal, a person whose representations the local planning authority were required by paragraph (3)(b) of that regulation to take into account in determining the application occasioning the appeal.

[(2) In these Rules, and in relation to the use of electronic communications for any purpose of these Rules which is capable of being carried out electronically—

    (a) the expression 'address' includes any number or address used for the purposes of such communications, except that where these Rules impose an obligation on any person to provide a name and address to any other person, the obligation shall not be fulfilled unless the person on whom it is imposed provides a postal address;

    (b) references to statements, notices, or other documents, or to copies of such documents, include references to such documents or copies of them in electronic form.

Town and Country Planning (Inquiries Procedure) (England) Rules 2000

(3) Paragraphs (4) to (8) apply where an electronic communication is used by a person for the purpose of fulfilling any requirement in these Rules to give or send any statement, notice or other document to any other person ('the recipient').

(4) The requirement shall be taken to be fulfilled where the notice or other document transmitted by means of the electronic communication is—

(a) capable of being accessed by the recipient,

(b) legible in all material respects, and

(c) sufficiently permanent to be used for subsequent reference.

(5) In paragraph (4), 'legible in all material respects' means that the information contained in the statement, notice or document is available to the recipient to no lesser extent than it would be if sent or given by means of a document in printed form.

(6) Where the electronic communication is received by the recipient outside the recipient's business hours, it shall be taken to have been received on the next working day; and for this purpose 'working day' means a day which is not a Saturday, Sunday, Bank Holiday or other public holiday.

(7) A requirement in these Rules that any document should be in writing is fulfilled where that document meets the criteria in paragraph (4), and 'written' and cognate expressions are to be construed accordingly.

(8) A requirement in these Rules to send more than one copy of a statement or other document may be complied with by sending one copy only of the statement or other document in question.]

Amendment

Para (1): numbered as such by SI 2003/956, art 12(1), Sch 2, para 1. Date in force: 31 March 2003: see SI 2003/956, art 1(1).

Revoked, in relation to the inquiry procedure for major infrastructure projects in England, by virtue of SI 2002/1223, r 26(1). Date in force: 7 June 2002 (except in relation to any application or appeal which has not been determined on that date): see SI 2002/1223, rr 1(2), 26(1).

Para (1): definition 'conservation area consent' (omitted) revoked by SI 2013/2146, art 3, Schedule, para 3(a). Date in force: 1 October 2013: see SI 2013/2146, art 1; for savings see art 4 thereof and for transitional provisions see SI 2013/2148, art 5(4)(a).

Para (1): definition 'electronic communication' inserted by SI 2003/956, art 12(1), Sch 2, para 1(a). Date in force: 31 March 2003: see SI 2003/956, art 1(1).

Para (1): in definition 'questionnaire' words from ', and for this purpose' to 'may be accessed' in square brackets inserted by SI 2003/956, art 12(1), Sch 2, para 1(b). Date in force: 31 March 2003: see SI 2003/956, art 1(1).

Para (1): definition 'relevant notice' (omitted) revoked by SI 2009/455, r 4(1), (2)(a). Date in force: 6 April 2009 (in relation to appeals and applications made on or after that date): see SI 2009/455, r 1(1), (2)(a).

Para (1): definition 'starting date' substituted by SI 2009/455, r 4(1), (2)(b). Date in force: 6 April 2009 (in relation to appeals and applications made on or after that date): see SI 2009/455, r 1(1), (2)(a).

Paras (2)–(8): inserted by SI 2003/956, art 12(1), Sch 2, para 2. Date in force: 31 March 2003: see SI 2003/956, art 1(1).

Town and Country Planning (Inquiries Procedure) (England) Rules 2000

3 Application of Rules

(1)   These Rules apply in relation to any local inquiry caused by the Secretary of State to be held in England before he determines—

(a)   *an application for planning permission referred to him under section 77, or an appeal to him under section 78 [(including an appeal under section 78 as applied by regulations made under section 220)], of the Planning Act;*

(b)   *an application for listed building consent referred to him under section 12, or for variation or discharge of conditions referred to him under that section as applied by section 19, or an appeal to him under section 20, of the Listed Buildings Act;*

(c)   ...

....

(2)   Where these Rules apply in relation to an appeal which at some time fell to be disposed of in accordance with the Town and Country Planning Appeals (Determination by Inspectors) (Inquiries Procedure) (England) Rules 2000 or Rules superseded by those Rules any step taken or thing done under those Rules which could have been done under any corresponding provision of these Rules shall have effect as if it had been taken or done under that corresponding provision.

Amendment

Revoked, in relation to the inquiry procedure for major infrastructure projects in England, by virtue of SI 2002/1223, r 26(1). Date in force: 7 June 2002 (except in relation to any application or appeal which has not been determined on that date): see SI 2002/1223, rr 1(2), 26(1).

Para (1): in sub-para (a) words from '(including an appeal' to 'under section 220)' in square brackets inserted by SI 2015/316, r 2(1), (2)(a). Date in force: 6 April 2015: see SI 2015/316, r 1(1).

Para (1): sub-para (c) revoked by SI 2013/2146, art 3, Schedule, para 3(b). Date in force: 1 October 2013: see SI 2013/2146, art 1; for savings see art 4 thereof and for transitional provisions see SI 2013/2148, art 5(4)(a).

Para (1): words omitted revoked by SI 2015/316, r 2(1), (2)(b). Date in force: 6 April 2015: see SI 2015/316, r 1(1).

[3A Notice from the Secretary of State]

[(1)   In the case of an appeal under section 78 of the Planning Act [(including an appeal under section 78 of the Planning Act as applied by regulations made under section 220 of that Act),] as soon as practicable after a determination has been made under section 319A of the Planning Act that the appeal is to proceed at an inquiry, the Secretary of State shall send a notice to this effect to the appellant and the local planning authority.

(2)   In the case of any other appeal or application to which these Rules apply, the Secretary of State shall as soon as practicable after receipt of all the documents required to enable the appeal or application to proceed, send a notice to the applicant and the local planning authority, informing them that an inquiry is to be held.]

Amendment

Inserted by SI 2009/455, r 4(1), (3). Date in force: 6 April 2009 (in relation to appeals and applications made on or after that date): see SI 2009/455, r 1(1), (2)(a).

Para (1): words from '(including an appeal' to 'of that Act),' in square brackets inserted by SI 2015/316, r 3. Date in force: 6 April 2015: see SI 2015/316, r 1(1).

4 Preliminary information to be supplied by local planning authority

(1) The local planning authority shall, on receipt of the [notice under rule 3A], forthwith inform the Secretary of State and the applicant in writing of the name and address of any statutory party who has made representations to them; and the Secretary of State shall, as soon as practicable thereafter, inform the applicant and the local planning authority in writing of the name and address of any statutory party who has made representations to him.

(2) This paragraph applies where—

(a) the Secretary of State has given to the local planning authority a direction restricting the grant of planning permission for which application was made; or

(b) in a case relating to listed building consent, the Commission has given a direction to the local planning authority pursuant to section 14(2) of the Listed Buildings Act as to how the application is to be determined; or

(c) the Secretary of State or any other Minister of the Crown or any government department, or any body falling within rule 11(1)(c), has expressed in writing to the local planning authority the view that the application should not be granted either wholly or in part, or should be granted only subject to conditions; or

(d) any person consulted in pursuance of a development order has made representations to the local planning authority about the application.

(3) Where paragraph (2) applies, the local planning authority shall forthwith after the starting date inform the person concerned of the inquiry and, unless they have already done so, that person shall thereupon give the local planning authority a written statement of the reasons for making the direction, expressing the view or making the representations, as the case may be.

(4) Subject to paragraph (5), the local planning authority shall ensure that within 2 weeks of the starting date—

(a) the Secretary of State and the applicant have received a completed questionnaire and a copy of each of the documents referred to in it;

(b) any—

(i) statutory party; and

(ii) other person who made representations to the local planning authority about the application occasioning the appeal,

has been notified [in writing] that an appeal has been made and of the address to which and of the period within which they may make representations to the Secretary of State.

(5) The requirements of the previous paragraph do not apply in respect of referred applications.

Amendment

Revoked, in relation to the inquiry procedure for major infrastructure projects in England, by virtue of SI 2002/1223, r 26(1). Date in force: 7 June 2002 (except in relation to any application or appeal which has not been determined on that date): see SI 2002/1223, rr 1(2), 26(1).

Town and Country Planning (Inquiries Procedure) (England) Rules 2000

Para (1): words 'notice under rule 3A' in square brackets substituted by SI 2009/455, r 4(1), (4)(a). Date in force: 6 April 2009 (in relation to appeals and applications made on or after that date): see SI 2009/455, r 1(1), (2)(a).

Para (4): in sub-para (b) words 'in writing' in square brackets inserted by SI 2009/455, r 4(1), (4)(b). Date in force: 6 April 2009 (in relation to appeals and applications made on or after that date): see SI 2009/455, r 1(1), (2)(a).

5 Procedure where Secretary of State causes pre-inquiry meeting to be held

(1)   The Secretary of State shall hold a pre-inquiry meeting—

(a)   if he expects an inquiry to last for 8 days or more, unless he considers it is unnecessary;

(b)   in respect of shorter inquiries, if it appears to him necessary.

(2)   Where the Secretary of State decides to hold a pre-inquiry meeting the following provisions shall apply—

(a)   the Secretary of State shall send with the relevant notice—

(i)   notice of his intention to hold a pre-inquiry meeting;

(ii)   a statement of the matters about which he particularly wishes to be informed for the purposes of his consideration of the application or appeal in question and where another Minister of the Crown or a government department has expressed in writing to the Secretary of State a view which is mentioned in rule 4(2)(c), the Secretary of State shall set this out in his statement;

(b)   the Secretary of State shall send a copy of the statement described in the previous paragraph to the Minister or government department concerned;

(c)   the local planning authority shall publish in a newspaper circulating in the locality in which the land is situated a notice of the Secretary of State's intention to hold a pre-inquiry meeting and of the statement sent in accordance with paragraph (2)(a)(ii) above; and

(d)   the applicant and the local planning authority shall ensure that within 8 weeks of the starting date 2 copies of their outline statement have been received by the Secretary of State.

(3)   The Secretary of State shall, as soon as practicable after receipt, send a copy of the local planning authority's outline statement to the applicant and a copy of the applicant's outline statement to the local planning authority.

(4)   Where rule 4(2) applies, the local planning authority shall—

(a)   include in their outline statement—

(i)   the terms of any direction given together with a statement of the reasons for it; and

(ii)   any view expressed or representation made on which they intend to rely in their submissions at the inquiry; and

(b)   within the period mentioned in paragraph (2)(d) send a copy of their outline statement to the person concerned.

(5)   The Secretary of State may in writing require any other person who has notified him of an intention or a wish to appear at the inquiry to send an outline statement to him, the applicant and the local planning authority and the person

shall ensure that they are received by the Secretary of State, the applicant and the local planning authority within 4 weeks of the date of the Secretary of State's written requirement.

(6) The pre-inquiry meeting (or, where there is more than one, the first pre-inquiry meeting) shall be held within 16 weeks of the starting date.

(7) The Secretary of State shall give not less than 3 weeks written notice of the pre-inquiry meeting to—

   (a) the applicant;

   (b) the local planning authority;

   (c) any person known at the date of the notice to be entitled to appear at the inquiry; and

   (d) any other person whose presence at the pre-inquiry meeting appears to him to be desirable,

and he may require the local planning authority to take, in relation to notification of the pre-inquiry meeting, one or more of the steps which he may under rule 10(6) require them to take in relation to notification of the inquiry.

(8) The inspector—

   (a) shall preside at the pre-inquiry meeting;

   (b) shall determine the matters to be discussed and the procedure to be followed;

   (c) may require any person present at the pre-inquiry meeting who, in his opinion, is behaving in a disruptive manner to leave; and

   (d) may refuse to permit that person to return or to attend any further pre-inquiry meeting, or may permit him to return or attend only on such conditions as he may specify.

(9) Where a pre-inquiry meeting has been held pursuant to paragraph (1), the inspector may hold a further pre-inquiry meeting and he shall arrange for such notice to be given of a further pre-inquiry meeting as appears to him necessary; and paragraph (8) shall apply to such a pre-inquiry meeting.

(10) If the Secretary of State requests any further information from the applicant or the local planning authority at the pre-inquiry meeting, they shall ensure that 2 copies of it have been received by him and a copy has been received by any statutory party within 4 weeks of the conclusion of the pre-inquiry meeting and the Secretary of State shall, as soon as practicable after receipt, send a copy of the further information received from the applicant to the local planning authority and a copy of the further information received from the local planning authority to the applicant.

Amendment

Revoked, in relation to the inquiry procedure for major infrastructure projects in England, by virtue of SI 2002/1223, r 26(1). Date in force: 7 June 2002 (except in relation to any application or appeal which has not been determined on that date): see SI 2002/1223, rr 1(2), 26(1).

6 Receipt of statements of case etc

(1) The local planning authority shall ensure that within—

Town and Country Planning (Inquiries Procedure) (England) Rules 2000

    (a) 6 weeks of the starting date, or

    (b) where a pre-inquiry meeting is held pursuant to rule 5, 4 weeks of the conclusion of that pre-inquiry meeting,

2 copies of their statement of case have been received by the Secretary of State and a copy of their statement of case has been received by any statutory party.

(2) The local planning authority shall—

    (a) include in their statement of case—

        [(i) details of the time and place where the opportunity to inspect and take copies described in paragraph (13) below shall be afforded (including, in any case in which the local planning authority rely on paragraph (13A), the details mentioned in that paragraph);] and

        (ii) where rule 4(2) applies, the matters mentioned in rule 5(4)(a)(ii), unless they have already included these in an outline statement; and

    (b) where rule 4(2) applies, within the period specified in paragraph (1) send a copy of their statement of case to the person concerned.

(3) The applicant shall ensure that within—

    (a) in the case of an appeal or a referred application where no pre-inquiry meeting is held pursuant to rule 5, 6 weeks of the starting date, or

    (b) in any case where a pre-inquiry meeting is held pursuant to rule 5, 4 weeks of the conclusion of that pre-inquiry meeting,

2 copies of their statement of case have been received by the Secretary of State and a copy of their statement of case has been received by any statutory party.

(4) The Secretary of State shall, as soon as practicable after receipt, send a copy of the local planning authority's statement of case to the applicant and a copy of the applicant's statement of case to the local planning authority.

(5) The applicant and the local planning authority may in writing each require the other to send them a copy of any document, or of the relevant part of any document, referred to in the list of documents comprised in the party's statement of case; and any such document, or relevant part, shall be sent, as soon as practicable, to the party who required it.

(6) The Secretary of State may in writing require any other person, who has notified him of an intention or wish to appear at an inquiry, to send [within 4 weeks of being so required]—

    (a) 3 copies of their statement of case to him …; and

    (b) a copy of their statement of case to any statutory party,

and the Secretary of State shall, as soon as practicable after receipt, send a copy of each such statement of case to the local planning authority and to the applicant.

(7) The Secretary of State shall as soon as practicable—

    (a) send to a person from whom he requires a statement of case in accordance with paragraph (6) a copy of the statements of case of the applicant and the local planning authority; and

    (b) inform that person of the name and address of every person to whom his statement of case is required to be sent.

Town and Country Planning (Inquiries Procedure) (England) Rules 2000

(8) The Secretary of State or the inspector may in writing require any person, who has sent to him a statement of case in accordance with this rule, to provide such further information about the matters contained in the statement of case as he may specify and may specify the time within which the information shall be received by him.

(9) A local planning authority or applicant required to provide further information, shall ensure that—

(a) 2 copies of that information ... have been received by the Secretary of State, or as the case may be the inspector, within the specified time; and

(b) a copy has been received by any statutory party within the specified time,

and the Secretary of State, or as the case may be the inspector, shall, as soon as practicable after receipt, send a copy of the further information received from the local planning authority to the applicant and a copy of the further information received from the applicant to the local planning authority.

(10) Any other person required to provide further information shall ensure that—

(a) 3 copies of that information ... have been received by the Secretary of State, or as the case may be the inspector, within the specified time; and

(b) a copy has been received by any statutory party within the specified time,

and the Secretary of State, or as the case may be the inspector, shall, as soon as practicable after receipt, send a copy of the further information to the local planning authority and the applicant.

(11) Any person other than the applicant who sends a statement of case to the Secretary of State shall send with it a copy of—

(a) any document; or

(b) the relevant part of any document,

referred to in the list comprised in that statement, unless a copy of the document or part of the document in question is already available for inspection pursuant to paragraph (13).

(12) Unless he has already done so, the Secretary of State shall within 12 weeks of the starting date send a written statement of the matters referred to in rule 5(2)(a)(ii) to—

(a) the applicant;

(b) the local planning authority;

(c) any statutory party; and

(d) any person from whom he has required a statement of case.

(13) The local planning authority shall afford to any person who so requests a reasonable opportunity to inspect and, where practicable, take copies of—

(a) any statement of case, ... information or other document a copy of which has been sent to the local planning authority in accordance with this rule; and

(b) the local planning authority's completed questionnaire and statement of case together with a copy of any document, or of the relevant part of any document, referred to in the list comprised in that statement, and ... information or other documents sent by the local planning authority pursuant to this rule.

Town and Country Planning (Inquiries Procedure) (England) Rules 2000

[*(13A) For the purposes of the previous paragraph an opportunity is to be taken to have been afforded to a person where the person is notified of—*

(a) *publication on a website of the documents mentioned in that paragraph;*

(b) *the address of the website;*

(c) *the place on the website where the documents may be accessed, and how they may be accessed.*]

(14) ...

(15) ...

(16) The Secretary of State shall, as soon as practicable after receipt, send to the inspector any statement of case, document or further information ... sent to him in accordance with this rule and received by him within the relevant period, if any, specified in this rule.

Amendment

Revoked, in relation to the inquiry procedure for major infrastructure projects in England, by virtue of SI 2002/1223, r 26(1). Date in force: 7 June 2002 (except in relation to any application or appeal which has not been determined on that date): see SI 2002/1223, rr 1(2), 26(1).

Para (2): sub-para (a)(i) substituted by SI 2003/956, art 12(1), Sch 2, para 3(a). Date in force: 31 March 2003: see SI 2003/956, art 1(1).

Para (6): words 'within 4 weeks of being so required' in square brackets inserted by SI 2009/455, r 4(1), (5)(a)(i). Date in force: 6 April 2009 (in relation to appeals and applications made on or after that date): see SI 2009/455, r 1(1), (2)(a).

Para (6): in sub-para (a) words omitted revoked by SI 2009/455, r 4(1), (5)(a)(ii). Date in force: 6 April 2009 (in relation to appeals and applications made on or after that date): see SI 2009/455, r 1(1), (2)(a).

Para (9): in sub-para (a) words omitted revoked by SI 2009/455, r 4(1), (5)(b). Date in force: 6 April 2009 (in relation to appeals and applications made on or after that date): see SI 2009/455, r 1(1), (2)(a).

Para (10): in sub-para (a) words omitted revoked by SI 2009/455, r 4(1), (5)(c). Date in force: 6 April 2009 (in relation to appeals and applications made on or after that date): see SI 2009/455, r 1(1), (2)(a).

Para (13): in sub-para (a) words omitted revoked by SI 2009/455, r 4(1), (5)(d)(i). Date in force: 6 April 2009 (in relation to appeals and applications made on or after that date): see SI 2009/455, r 1(1), (2)(a).

Para (13): in sub-para (b) words omitted revoked by SI 2009/455, r 4(1), (5)(d)(ii). Date in force: 6 April 2009 (in relation to appeals and applications made on or after that date): see SI 2009/455, r 1(1), (2)(a).

Para 13A: inserted by SI 2003/956, art 12(1), Sch 2, para 3(b). Date in force: 31 March 2003: see SI 2003/956, art 1(1).

Paras (14), (15): revoked by SI 2009/455, r 4(1), (5)(e). Date in force: 6 April 2009 (in relation to appeals and applications made on or after that date): see SI 2009/455, r 1(1), (2)(a).

Para (16): words omitted revoked by SI 2009/455, r 4(1), (5)(f). Date in force: 6 April 2009 (in relation to appeals and applications made on or after that date): see SI 2009/455, r 1(1), (2)(a).

7 Further power of inspector to hold pre-inquiry meetings

(1) Where no pre-inquiry meeting is held pursuant to rule 5, an inspector may hold one if he thinks it necessary.

Town and Country Planning (Inquiries Procedure) (England) Rules 2000

(2) An inspector shall give not less than 2 weeks written notice of a pre-inquiry meeting he proposes to hold under paragraph (1) to—

   (a) the applicant;

   (b) the local planning authority;

   (c) any person known at the date of the notice to be entitled to appear at the inquiry; and

   (d) any other person whose presence at the pre-inquiry meeting appears to him to be desirable.

(3) Rule 5(8) shall apply to a pre-inquiry meeting held under this rule.

Amendment

Revoked, in relation to the inquiry procedure for major infrastructure projects in England, by virtue of SI 2002/1223, r 26(1). Date in force: 7 June 2002 (except in relation to any application or appeal which has not been determined on that date): see SI 2002/1223, rr 1(2), 26(1).

8 Inquiry timetable

(1) The inspector shall arrange a timetable for the proceedings at, or at part of, an inquiry where—

   (a) a pre-inquiry meeting is held pursuant to rule 5; or

   (b) it appears to the Secretary of State likely that an inquiry will last for 8 days or more.

(2) The inspector may arrange a timetable for the proceedings at, or at part of, any other inquiry.

(3) The inspector may, at any time, vary the timetable arranged under the preceding paragraphs.

(4) The inspector may specify in a timetable arranged pursuant to this rule a date by which any proof of evidence and summary sent in accordance with rule 13(1) shall be received by the Secretary of State.

Amendment

Revoked, in relation to the inquiry procedure for major infrastructure projects in England, by virtue of SI 2002/1223, r 26(1). Date in force: 7 June 2002 (except in relation to any application or appeal which has not been determined on that date): see SI 2002/1223, rr 1(2), 26(1).

9 Notification of appointment of assessor

Where the Secretary of State appoints an assessor, he shall notify [in writing] every person entitled to appear at the inquiry of the name of the assessor and of the matters on which he is to advise the inspector.

Amendment

Revoked, in relation to the inquiry procedure for major infrastructure projects in England, by virtue of SI 2002/1223, r 26(1). Date in force: 7 June 2002 (except in relation to any application or appeal which has not been determined on that date): see SI 2002/1223, rr 1(2), 26(1).

Words 'in writing' in square brackets inserted by SI 2009/455, r 4(1), (6). Date in force: 6 April 2009 (in relation to appeals and applications made on or after that date): see SI 2009/455, r 1(1), (2)(a).

Town and Country Planning (Inquiries Procedure) (England) Rules 2000

10 Date and notification of inquiry

(1) The date fixed by the Secretary of State for the holding of an inquiry shall be, unless he considers such a date impracticable, not later than—

    (a) Subject to paragraph (b), 22 weeks after the starting date; or

    (b) in a case where a pre-inquiry meeting is held pursuant to rule 5, 8 weeks after the conclusion of that meeting.

(2) Where the Secretary of State considers it impracticable to fix a date in accordance with paragraph (1), the date fixed shall be the earliest date after the end of the relevant period mentioned in that paragraph which he considers to be practicable.

(3) Unless the Secretary of State agrees a lesser period of notice with the applicant and the local planning authority, he shall give not less than 4 weeks written notice of the date, time and place fixed by him for the holding of an inquiry to every person entitled to appear at the inquiry.

[(3A) A written notice shall be taken to have been given by the Secretary of State for the purposes of paragraph (3) where he and any person entitled to appear at the inquiry have agreed that notice of the matters mentioned in that paragraph may instead be accessed by that person via a website, and—

    (a) the notice is a notice to which that agreement applies;

    (b) the Secretary of State has published that notice on the website;

    (c) not less than 4 weeks before the date fixed by the Secretary of State for the holding of the inquiry, the person is notified of—

        (i) the publication of the notice on a website,

        (ii) the address of the website, and

        (iii) the place on the website where the notice may be accessed, and how it may be accessed.]

(4) The Secretary of State may vary the date fixed for the holding of an inquiry, whether or not the date as varied is within the relevant period mentioned in paragraph (1); and [paragraphs (3) and (3A)] shall apply to a variation of a date as it applied to the date originally fixed.

(5) The Secretary of State may vary the time or place for the holding of an inquiry and shall give such notice of any variation as appears to him to be reasonable.

(6) The Secretary of State may in writing require the local planning authority to take one or more of the following steps—

    (a) not less than 2 weeks before the date fixed for the holding of an inquiry, to publish a notice of the inquiry in one or more newspapers circulating in the locality in which the land is situated;

    (b) to send a notice of the inquiry to such persons or classes of persons as he may specify, within such period as he may specify; or

    (c) to post a notice of the inquiry in a conspicuous place near to the land, within such period as he may specify.

(7) Where the land is under the control of the applicant he shall—

    (a) if so required in writing by the Secretary of State, affix a notice of the inquiry firmly to the land or to some object on or near the land, in such manner as to be readily visible to and legible by members of the public; and

Town and Country Planning (Inquiries Procedure) (England) Rules 2000

(b) not remove the notice, or cause or permit it to be removed, for such period before the inquiry as the Secretary of State may specify.

(8) Every notice of inquiry published, sent or posted pursuant to paragraph (6), or affixed pursuant to paragraph (7), shall contain—

(a) a clear statement of the date, time and place of the inquiry and of the powers enabling the Secretary of State to determine the application or appeal in question;

(b) a written description of the land sufficient to identify approximately its location;

(c) a brief description of the subject matter of the application or appeal; and

(d) details of where and when copies of the local planning authority's completed questionnaire and any documents sent by and copied to the authority pursuant to rule 6 may be inspected.

Amendment

Revoked, in relation to the inquiry procedure for major infrastructure projects in England, by virtue of SI 2002/1223, r 26(1). Date in force: 7 June 2002 (except in relation to any application or appeal which has not been determined on that date): see SI 2002/1223, rr 1(2), 26(1).

Para (3A): inserted by SI 2003/956, art 12(1), Sch 2, para 4(a). Date in force: 31 March 2003: see SI 2003/956, art 1(1).

Para (4): words 'paragraphs (3) and (3A)' in square brackets substituted by SI 2003/956, Sch 2, para 4(b). Date in force: 31 March 2003: see SI 2003/956, art 1(1).

11 Appearances at inquiry

(1) The persons entitled to appear at an inquiry are—

(a) the applicant;

(b) the local planning authority;

(c) any of the following bodies if the land is situated in their area and they are not the local planning authority—

(i) a county or district council;

(ii) an enterprise zone authority designated under Schedule 32 to the Local Government, Planning and Land Act 1980;

(iii) the Broads Authority, within the meaning of the Norfolk and Suffolk Broads Act 1988;

(iv) a housing action trust specified in an order made under section 67(1) of the Housing Act 1988;

(d) where the land is in an area previously designated as a new town, [the Homes and Communities Agency];

(e) any statutory party;

(f) the council of the parish in which the land is situated, if that council made representations to the local planning authority in respect of the application in pursuance of a provision of a development order;

(g) where the application was required to be notified to the Commission under section 14 of the Listed Buildings Act, the Commission;

(h) any other person who has sent a statement of case in accordance with rule 6(6) or who has sent an outline statement in accordance with rule 5(5).

Town and Country Planning (Inquiries Procedure) (England) Rules 2000

(2)   Nothing in paragraph (1) shall prevent the inspector from permitting any other person to appear at an inquiry, and such permission shall not be unreasonably withheld.

(3)   Any person entitled or permitted to appear may do so on his own behalf or be represented by any other person.

Amendment

Revoked, in relation to the inquiry procedure for major infrastructure projects in England, by virtue of SI 2002/1223, r 26(1). Date in force: 7 June 2002 (except in relation to any application or appeal which has not been determined on that date): see SI 2002/1223, rr 1(2), 26(1).

Para (1): in sub-para (d) words 'the Homes and Communities Agency' in square brackets substituted by SI 2008/2831, art 6, Sch 4, para 1. Date in force: 1 December 2008 (being the date on which the Housing and Regeneration Act 2008, s 5 came into force): see SI 2008/2831, art 1(2) and SI 2008/3068, arts 1(2), 2(1)(b); for transitional provisions and savings see SI 2008/2831, art 6, Sch 4, paras 5, 6 and SI 2008/3068, arts 9, 10.

12 Representatives of government departments and other authorities at inquiry

(1)   Where—

(a)   the Secretary of State or the Commission has given a direction described in rule 4(2)(a) or (b); or

(b)   the Secretary of State or any other Minister of the Crown or any government department, or any body falling within rule 11(1)(c), has expressed a view described in rule 4(2)(c) and the local planning authority have included the terms of the expression of view in a statement sent in accordance with rule 5(2) or 6(1); or

(c)   another Minister of the Crown or any government department has expressed a view described in rule 4(2)(c) and the Secretary of State has included its terms in a statement sent in accordance with rule 5(2) or 6(12),

the applicant, the local planning authority or a person entitled to appear may, not later than 4 weeks before the date of an inquiry, apply in writing to the Secretary of State for a representative of the Secretary of State or of the other Minister, department or body concerned to be made available at the inquiry.

(2)   Where an application is made in accordance with paragraph (1), the Secretary of State shall make a representative available to attend the inquiry or, as the case may be, send the application to the other Minister, department or body concerned, who shall make a representative available to attend the inquiry.

(3)   Any person attending an inquiry as a representative in pursuance of this rule shall state the reasons for the direction or expressed view and shall give evidence and be subject to cross-examination to the same extent as any other witness.

(4)   Nothing in paragraph (3) shall require a representative of a Minister or a government department to answer any question which in the opinion of the inspector is directed to the merits of government policy.

Amendment

Revoked, in relation to the inquiry procedure for major infrastructure projects in England, by virtue of SI 2002/1223, r 26(1). Date in force: 7 June 2002 (except in relation to any application or appeal which has not been determined on that date): see SI 2002/1223, rr 1(2), 26(1).

Town and Country Planning (Inquiries Procedure) (England) Rules 2000

13 Proofs of evidence

(1) Any person entitled to appear at an inquiry, who proposes to give, or to call another person to give evidence at the inquiry by reading a proof of evidence, shall—

    (a) send 2 copies, in the case of the local planning authority and the applicant, or 3 copies in the case of any other person, of the proof of evidence together with any written summary, to the Secretary of State; and

    (b) simultaneously send copies of these to any statutory party,

and the Secretary of State shall, as soon as practicable after receipt, send a copy of each proof of evidence together with any summary to the local planning authority and the applicant.

(2) No written summary shall be required where the proof of evidence proposed to be read contains no more than 1500 words.

(3) The proof of evidence and any summary shall be received by the Secretary of State no later than—

    (a) 4 weeks before the date fixed for the holding of the inquiry, or

    (b) where a timetable has been arranged pursuant to rule 8 which specifies a date by which the proof of evidence and any summary shall be received by the Secretary of State, that date.

(4) The Secretary of State shall send to the inspector, as soon as practicable after receipt, any proof of evidence together with any summary sent to him in accordance with this rule and received by him within the relevant period, if any specified in this rule.

(5) Where a written summary is provided in accordance with paragraph (1), only that summary shall be read at the inquiry, unless the inspector permits or requires otherwise.

(6) Any person, required by this rule to send copies of a proof of evidence to the Secretary of State, shall send with them the same number of copies of the whole, or the relevant part, of any document referred to in the proof of evidence, unless a copy of the document or part of the document in question is already available for inspection pursuant to rule 6(13).

(7) The local planning authority shall afford to any person who so requests a reasonable opportunity to inspect and, where practicable, take copies of any document sent to or by them in accordance with this rule.

[(8) For the purposes of the previous paragraph an opportunity shall be taken to have been afforded to a person where the person is notified of—

    (a) publication of the relevant document on a website,

    (b) the address of the website,

    (c) the place on the website where the document may be accessed, and how it may be accessed.]

Amendment

Revoked, in relation to the inquiry procedure for major infrastructure projects in England, by virtue of SI 2002/1223, r 26(1). Date in force: 7 June 2002 (except in relation to any application or appeal which has not been determined on that date): see SI 2002/1223, rr 1(2), 26(1).

Town and Country Planning (Inquiries Procedure) (England) Rules 2000

Para (8): inserted by SI 2003/956, art 12(1), Sch 2, para 5. Date in force: 31 March 2003: see SI 2003/956, art 1(1).

14 Statement of common ground

(1) The local planning authority and the applicant shall—

(a) *together prepare an agreed statement of common ground; and*

(b) *ensure that the Secretary of State receives it and that any statutory party receives a copy of it [within 6 weeks of the starting date].*

(2) *The local planning authority shall afford to any person who so requests, a reasonable opportunity to inspect, and where practicable, take copies of the statement of common ground sent to the Secretary of State.*

[(3) For the purposes of the previous paragraph an opportunity shall be taken to have been afforded to a person where the person is notified of—

(a) publication of the statement of common ground on a website,

(b) the address of the website,

(c) the place on the website where the document may be accessed, and how it may be accessed.]

Amendment

Revoked, in relation to the inquiry procedure for major infrastructure projects in England, by virtue of SI 2002/1223, r 26(1). Date in force: 7 June 2002 (except in relation to any application or appeal which has not been determined on that date): see SI 2002/1223, rr 1(2), 26(1).

Para (1): in sub-para (b) words 'within 6 weeks of the starting date' in square brackets substituted by SI 2009/455, r 4(1), (7). Date in force: 6 April 2009 (in relation to appeals and applications made on or after that date): see SI 2009/455, r 1(1), (2)(a).

Para (3): inserted by SI 2003/956, art 12(1), Sch 2, para 6. Date in force: 31 March 2003: see SI 2003/956, art 1(1).

15 Procedure at inquiry

(1) *Except as otherwise provided in these Rules, the inspector shall determine the procedure at an inquiry.*

(2) *At the start of the inquiry the inspector shall identify what are, in his opinion, the main issues to be considered at the inquiry and any matters on which he requires further explanation from the persons entitled or permitted to appear.*

(3) *Nothing in paragraph (2) shall preclude any person entitled or permitted to appear from referring to issues which they consider relevant to the consideration of the application or appeal but which were not issues identified by the inspector pursuant to that paragraph.*

(4) *Unless in any particular case the inspector otherwise determines, the local planning authority shall begin and the applicant shall have the right of final reply; and the other persons entitled or permitted to appear shall be heard in such order as the inspector may determine.*

(5) *A person entitled to appear at an inquiry shall be entitled to call evidence and the applicant, the local planning authority and any statutory party shall be entitled to cross-examine persons giving evidence, but, subject to the foregoing and paragraphs (6) and [(9)], the calling of evidence and the cross-examination of persons giving evidence shall otherwise be at the discretion of the inspector.*

Town and Country Planning (Inquiries Procedure) (England) Rules 2000

(6) The inspector may refuse to permit the—
   (a) giving or production of evidence;
   (b) cross-examination of persons giving evidence; or
   (c) presentation of any other matter,

which he considers to be irrelevant or repetitious; but where he refuses to permit the giving of oral evidence, the person wishing to give the evidence may submit to him any evidence or other matter in writing before the close of the inquiry.

(7) Where a person gives evidence at an inquiry by reading a summary of his proof of evidence in accordance with rule 13(5)—
   (a) the proof of evidence referred to in rule 13(1) shall be treated as tendered in evidence, unless the person required to provide the summary notifies the inspector that he now wishes to rely on the contents of that summary alone; and
   (b) the person whose evidence the proof of evidence contains shall then be subject to cross-examination on it to the same extent as if it were evidence he had given orally.

(8) The inspector may direct that facilities shall be afforded to any person appearing at an inquiry to take or obtain copies of documentary evidence open to public inspection.

(9) The inspector may—
   (a) require any person appearing or present at an inquiry who, in his opinion, is behaving in a disruptive manner to leave; and
   (b) refuse to permit that person to return; or
   (c) permit him to return only on such conditions as he may specify,

but any such person may submit to him any evidence or other matter in writing before the close of the inquiry.

(10) The inspector may allow any person to alter or add to a statement of case received by the Secretary of State or him under rule 6 so far as may be necessary for the purposes of the inquiry; but he shall (if necessary by adjourning the inquiry) give every other person entitled to appear who is appearing at the inquiry an adequate opportunity of considering any fresh matter or document.

(11) The inspector may proceed with an inquiry in the absence of any person entitled to appear at it.

(12) The inspector may take into account any written representation or evidence or any other document received by him from any person before an inquiry opens or during the inquiry provided that he discloses it at the inquiry.

(13) The inspector may from time to time adjourn an inquiry and, if the date, time and place of the adjourned inquiry are announced at the inquiry before the adjournment, no further notice shall be required.

(14) In respect of any inquiry that the Secretary of State expects to last for 8 or more days, any person, who appears at the inquiry and makes closing submissions, shall by the close of the inquiry provide the inspector with a copy of their closing submission in writing.

Town and Country Planning (Inquiries Procedure) (England) Rules 2000

Amendment
Revoked, in relation to the inquiry procedure for major infrastructure projects in England, by virtue of SI 2002/1223, r 26(1). Date in force: 7 June 2002 (except in relation to any application or appeal which has not been determined on that date): see SI 2002/1223, rr 1(2), 26(1).

Para (5): reference to '(9)' in square brackets substituted by SI 2009/455, r 4(1), (8). Date in force: 6 April 2009 (in relation to appeals and applications made on or after that date): see SI 2009/455, r 1(1), (2)(a).

16 Site inspections

(1) The inspector may make an unaccompanied inspection of the land before or during an inquiry without giving notice of his intention to the persons entitled to appear at the inquiry.

(2) During an inquiry or after its close, the inspector—

   (a) may inspect the land in the company of the applicant, the local planning authority and any statutory party; and

   (b) shall make such an inspection if so requested by the applicant or the local planning authority before or during an inquiry.

(3) In all cases where the inspector intends to make an accompanied site inspection he shall announce during the inquiry the date and time at which he proposes to make it.

(4) The inspector shall not be bound to defer an inspection of the kind referred to in paragraph (2) where any person mentioned in that paragraph is not present at the time appointed.

Amendment
Revoked, in relation to the inquiry procedure for major infrastructure projects in England, by virtue of SI 2002/1223, r 26(1). Date in force: 7 June 2002 (except in relation to any application or appeal which has not been determined on that date): see SI 2002/1223, rr 1(2), 26(1).

17 Procedure after inquiry

(1) After the close of an inquiry, the inspector shall make a report in writing to the Secretary of State which shall include his conclusions and his recommendations or his reasons for not making any recommendations.

(2) Where an assessor has been appointed, he may, after the close of the inquiry, make a report in writing to the inspector in respect of the matters on which he was appointed to advise.

(3) Where an assessor makes a report in accordance with paragraph (2), the inspector shall append it to his own report and shall state in his own report how far he agrees or disagrees with the assessor's report and, where he disagrees with the assessor, his reasons for that disagreement.

(4) When making his decision the Secretary of State may disregard any written representations, evidence or any other document received after the close of the inquiry.

(5) If, after the close of an inquiry, the Secretary of State—

   (a) differs from the inspector on any matter of fact mentioned in, or appearing to him to be material to, a conclusion reached by the inspector; or

Town and Country Planning (Inquiries Procedure) (England) Rules 2000

> (b) *takes into consideration any new evidence or new matter of fact (not being a matter of government policy),*
>
> and is for that reason disposed to disagree with a recommendation made by the inspector, he shall not come to a decision which is at variance with that recommendation without first notifying [in writing] the persons entitled to appear at the inquiry who appeared at it of his disagreement and the reasons for it; and affording them an opportunity of making written representations to him or (if the Secretary of State has taken into consideration any new evidence or new matter of fact, not being a matter of government policy) of asking for the re-opening of the inquiry.

(6) *Those persons making written representations or requesting the inquiry to be re-opened under paragraph (5), shall ensure that such representations or requests are received by the Secretary of State within 3 weeks of the date of the Secretary of State's notification under that paragraph.*

(7) *The Secretary of State may, as he thinks fit, cause an inquiry to be re-opened, and he shall do so if asked by the applicant or the local planning authority in the circumstances mentioned in paragraph (5) and within the period mentioned in paragraph (6); and where an inquiry is re-opened (whether by the same or a different inspector)—*

> (a) *the Secretary of State shall send to the persons entitled to appear at the inquiry who appeared at it a written statement of the matters with respect to which further evidence is invited; and*
>
> (b) *paragraphs (3) to (8) of rule 10 shall apply as if the references to an inquiry were references to a re-opened inquiry.*

Amendment

Revoked, in relation to the inquiry procedure for major infrastructure projects in England, by virtue of SI 2002/1223, r 26(1). Date in force: 7 June 2002 (except in relation to any application or appeal which has not been determined on that date): see SI 2002/1223, rr 1(2), 26(1).

Para (5): words 'in writing' in square brackets inserted by SI 2009/455, r 4(1), (9). Date in force: 6 April 2009 (in relation to appeals and applications made on or after that date): see SI 2009/455, r 1(1), (2)(a).

18 Notification of decision

(1) *The Secretary of State shall, as soon as practicable, notify his decision on an application or appeal, and his reasons for it in writing to—*

> (a) *all persons entitled to appear at the inquiry who did appear, and*
>
> (b) *any other person who, having appeared at the inquiry, has asked to be notified of the decision.*

[(1A) *Notification in writing of a decision and reasons shall be taken to have been given to a person for the purposes of this rule where—*

> (a) *the Secretary of State and the person have agreed that decisions and reasons required under this rule to be given in writing may instead be accessed by that person on a website;*
>
> (b) *the decision and reasons are a decision and reasons to which that agreement applies;*
>
> (c) *the Secretary of State has published the decision and reasons on a website;*

Town and Country Planning (Inquiries Procedure) (England) Rules 2000

(d) *the person is notified, in a manner for the time being agreed between him and the Secretary of State, of—*
  (i) *the publication of the decision and reasons on a website;*
  (ii) *the address of the website;*
  (iii) *the place on the website where the decision and reasons may be accessed, and how they may be accessed.*]

(2) *Where a copy of the inspector's report is not sent with the notification of the decision, the notification shall be accompanied by a statement of his conclusion and of any recommendations made by him, and if a person entitled to be notified of the decision has not received a copy of that report, he shall be supplied with a copy of it on written application to the Secretary of State.*

(3) *In this rule 'report' includes any assessor's report appended to the inspector's report but does not include any other documents so appended; but any person who has received a copy of the report may apply to the Secretary of State in writing, within 6 weeks of the date of the Secretary of State's decision, for an opportunity of inspecting any such documents and the Secretary of State shall afford him that opportunity.*

[(3A) *For the purposes of the previous paragraph an opportunity shall be taken to have been afforded to a person where that person is notified of—*
  (a) *publication of the relevant documents on a website;*
  (b) *the address of the website;*
  (c) *the place on the website where the documents may be accessed, and how they may be accessed.*]

(4) *Any person applying to the Secretary of State under paragraph (2) shall ensure that his application is received by the Secretary of State within 4 weeks of the Secretary of State's determination.*

Amendment

Revoked, in relation to the inquiry procedure for major infrastructure projects in England, by virtue of SI 2002/1223, r 26(1). Date in force: 7 June 2002 (except in relation to any application or appeal which has not been determined on that date): see SI 2002/1223, rr 1(2), 26(1).

Para (1A): inserted by SI 2003/956, art 12(1), Sch 2, para 7(a). Date in force: 31 March 2003: see SI 2003/956, art 1(1).

Para (3A): inserted by SI 2003/956, art 12(1), Sch 2, para 7(b). Date in force: 31 March 2003: see SI 2003/956, art 1(1).

19 Procedure following quashing of decision

(1) *Where a decision of the Secretary of State on an application or appeal in respect of which an inquiry has been held is quashed in proceedings before any court, the Secretary of State—*
  (a) *shall send to the persons entitled to appear at the inquiry who appeared at it a written statement of the matters with respect to which further representations are invited for the purposes of his further consideration of the application or appeal;*
  (b) *shall afford to those persons the opportunity of making written representations to him in respect of those matters or of asking for the re-opening of the inquiry; and*

Town and Country Planning (Inquiries Procedure) (England) Rules 2000

(c) may, as he thinks fit, cause the inquiry to be re-opened (whether by the same or a different inspector) and if he does so paragraphs (3) to (8) of the rule 10 shall apply as if the references to an inquiry were references to a re-opened inquiry.

(2) Those persons making representations or asking for the inquiry to be re-opened under paragraph (1)(b) shall ensure that such representations or requests are received by the Secretary of State within 3 weeks of the date of the written statement sent under paragraph (1)(a).

Amendment

Revoked, in relation to the inquiry procedure for major infrastructure projects in England, by virtue of SI 2002/1223, r 26(1). Date in force: 7 June 2002 (except in relation to any application or appeal which has not been determined on that date): see SI 2002/1223, rr 1(2), 26(1).

20 Allowing further time

The Secretary of State may at any time in any particular case allow further time for the taking of any step which is required or enabled to be taken by virtue of these Rules, and references in these Rules to a day by which, or a period within which, any step is required or enabled to be taken shall be construed accordingly.

Amendment

Revoked, in relation to the inquiry procedure for major infrastructure projects in England, by virtue of SI 2002/1223, r 26(1). Date in force: 7 June 2002 (except in relation to any application or appeal which has not been determined on that date): see SI 2002/1223, rr 1(2), 26(1).

21 Additional copies

(1) The Secretary of State may at any time before the close of an inquiry request from any person entitled to appear additional copies of the following—

(a) an outline statement sent in accordance with rule 5;

(b) a statement of case … sent in accordance with rule 6;

(c) a proof of evidence sent in accordance with rule 13; or

(d) any other document or information sent to the Secretary of State before or during an inquiry,

and may specify the time within which such copies should be received by him.

(2) Any person so requested shall ensure that the copies are received by the Secretary of State within the period specified.

Amendment

Revoked, in relation to the inquiry procedure for major infrastructure projects in England, by virtue of SI 2002/1223, r 26(1). Date in force: 7 June 2002 (except in relation to any application or appeal which has not been determined on that date): see SI 2002/1223, rr 1(2), 26(1).

Para (1): in sub-para (b) words omitted revoked by SI 2009/455, r 4(1), (10). Date in force: 6 April 2009 (in relation to appeals and applications made on or after that date): see SI 2009/455, r 1(1), (2)(a).

[22 Sending of notices etc]

[Notices or documents required or authorised to be sent or supplied under these Rules may be sent or supplied—

Town and Country Planning (Inquiries Procedure) (England) Rules 2000

(a) by post; or

(b) by using electronic communications to send or supply the notice or document (as the case may be) to a person at such address as may for the time being be specified by the person for that purpose.]

Amendment

Substituted by SI 2003/956, art 12(1), Sch 2, para 8. Date in force: 31 March 2003: see SI 2003/956, art 1(1).

[22A Withdrawal of consent to use of electronic communications]

[Where a person is no longer willing to accept the use of electronic communications for any purpose of these Rules which is capable of being effected electronically, he shall give notice in writing—

(a) withdrawing any address notified to the Secretary of State or to a local planning authority for that purpose, or

(b) revoking any agreement entered into with the Secretary of State or with a local planning authority for that purpose,

and such withdrawal or revocation shall be final and shall take effect on a date specified by the person in the notice but not less than seven days after the date on which the notice is given.]

Amendment

Inserted by SI 2003/956, art 12(1), Sch 2, para 9. Date in force: 31 March 2003: see SI 2003/956, art 1(1).

23 Mayor of London

(1) In this rule 'the Mayor' means the Mayor of London.

(2) Where an inquiry is held into an application, or an appeal arising from such an application, in respect of which the Mayor has directed the local planning authority to refuse the application these Rules shall apply subject to the following modifications—

[(a) in rule 3A—

(i) in paragraph (1), after 'the appellant' insert ', the Mayor';

(ii) in paragraph (2), after 'the applicant' insert ', the Mayor';]

(b) in rule 4—

(i) in paragraph (1) after 'inform the Secretary of State' and after 'inform the applicant' insert ', the Mayor';

(ii) in paragraph (2) after sub-paragraph (d) insert—

'or

(e) the Mayor has given to the local planning authority a direction to refuse the application for planning permission.';

(iii) in paragraph (4)(a) after the 'Secretary of State' insert ', the Mayor';

(c) in rule 5—

(i) in paragraph (2)(d) after 'the applicant' insert ', the Mayor';

(ii) for paragraph (3) substitute—

'The Secretary of State shall as soon as practicable after receipt send—

    (a) copies of the outline statements of the applicant and the Mayor to the local planning authority;

    (b) copies of the outline statements of the applicant and the local planning authority to the Mayor; and

    (c) copies of the outline statements of the local planning authority and the Mayor to the applicant.';

(iii) in paragraph (5) after both references to 'the applicant' insert ', the Mayor';

(iv) in paragraph (10) after the first reference to 'from the applicant' insert 'the Mayor', for '2' substitute '3' and for 'send a copy of the further information received from the applicant to the local planning authority and a copy of the further information received from the local planning authority to the applicant' substitute—

'send—

    (a) copies of the further information received from the applicant and the Mayor to the local planning authority;

    (b) copies of the further information received from the applicant and the local planning authority to the Mayor; and

    (c) copies of the further information received from the local planning authority and the Mayor to the applicant.';

(d) in rule 6—

(i) in paragraph (1) after 'The local planning authority' insert 'and the Mayor' and for '2' substitute '3';

(ii) in paragraph (3) for '2' substitute '3';

(iii) for paragraph (4) substitute—

'The Secretary of State shall as soon as practicable after receipt send—

    (a) copies of the statements of case of the applicant and the Mayor to the local planning authority;

    (b) copies of the statements of case of the applicant and the local planning authority to the Mayor; and

    (c) copies of the statements of case of the local planning authority and the Mayor to the applicant.';

(iv) in paragraph (5) for 'The applicant and the local planning authority may in writing each require the other' substitute—

'Any party required to provide a statement of case pursuant to paragraph (1) or (3) may in writing require any other party so required';

(v) in paragraph (6) for '3' substitute '4' and after 'the local planning authority' insert ', to the Mayor';

(vi) in paragraph (7)(a) after 'the applicant' insert ', the Mayor';

Town and Country Planning (Inquiries Procedure) (England) Rules 2000

> (vii) *in paragraph (9) after 'A local planning authority' insert ', the Mayor', in sub-paragraph (a) for '2' substitute '3' and for 'send a copy of the further information received from the local planning authority to the applicant and copy of the further information received from the applicant to the local planning authority' substitute—*
>
> *'send—*
> *(a) copies of the further information received from the applicant and the Mayor to the local planning authority;*
> *(b) copies of the further information received from the applicant and the local planning authority to the Mayor; and*
> *(c) copies of the further information received from the local planning authority and the Mayor to the applicant.';*
>
> (viii) *in paragraph (10) for '3' substitute '4' and after 'the local planning authority' insert ', the Mayor';*
>
> (ix) *in paragraph (12) at the end of sub-paragraph (c) delete 'and' and after paragraph (d) add—*
>
> *'and*
> *(e) the Mayor.';*
>
> (x) ...
>
> (xi) ....
>
> (e) *in rule 7(2)—*
> (i) *at the end of sub-paragraph (c) delete 'and',*
> (ii) *after sub-paragraph (d) add—*
>
> *'and*
> *(e) the Mayor.';*
>
> (f) *in rule 10(3) after 'the applicant' insert ', the Mayor';*
>
> (g) *in rule 11(1) after sub-paragraph (h) insert—*
>
> *'(i) the Mayor in relation to an inquiry arising from an application in respect of which he has given to the local planning authority a direction to refuse the application.';*
>
> (h) *in rule 12—*
> (i) *after paragraph(1)(c) insert—*
>
> *'or*
> *(d) the Mayor has given to the local planning authority a direction to refuse the application for planning permission,'; and*
>
> (ii) *after 'body concerned' insert 'or of the Mayor';*
>
> (i) *in rule 13—*
> (i) *in paragraph (1)(a) after 'the local planning authority' insert ', the Mayor', for '2' substitute '3' and for '3' substitute '4'; and*
> (ii) *in paragraph (1) after 'summary to the local planning authority' insert ', the Mayor';*

Town and Country Planning (Inquiries Procedure) (England) Rules 2000

    (j)   in rule 14(1) after 'The local planning authority' insert ', the Mayor';

    (k)   in rule 15(5) after 'the local planning authority' insert ', the Mayor';

    (l)   in rule 17(7) after 'the applicant' insert ', the Mayor'.

(3)   Where an inquiry is held into an application or an appeal arising from such an application, in respect of which the local planning authority was required to notify the Mayor but which is not an application or an appeal falling within paragraph (2) these Rules shall apply as if the Mayor were a statutory party.

Amendment

Revoked, in relation to the inquiry procedure for major infrastructure projects in England, by virtue of SI 2002/1223, r 26(1). Date in force: 7 June 2002 (except in relation to any application or appeal which has not been determined on that date): see SI 2002/1223, rr 1(2), 26(1).

Para (2): sub-para (a) substituted by SI 2009/455, r 4(1), (11)(a). Date in force: 6 April 2009 (in relation to appeals and applications made on or after that date): see SI 2009/455, r 1(1), (2)(a).

Para (2): sub-para (d)(x), (xi) revoked by SI 2009/455, r 4(1), (11)(b). Date in force: 6 April 2009 (in relation to appeals and applications made on or after that date): see SI 2009/455, r 1(1), (2)(a).

[23A Modifications where national security direction given and for urgent Crown development or works]

[(1)   The modifications set out in Part 1 of the Schedule shall have effect where a direction is given by the Secretary of State under—

    (a)   section 321(3) of the Planning Act (planning inquiries to be held in public subject to certain exceptions); or

    (b)   paragraph 6(6) of Schedule 3 to the Listed Buildings Act (determination of certain appeals by person appointed by the Secretary of State).

(2)   The modifications set out in Part 2 of the Schedule shall have effect where either section 293A of the Planning Act (urgent Crown development) or section 82B of the Listed Buildings Act (urgent works relating to Crown land), or both, apply.]

Amendment

Inserted by SI 2006/1282, art 24(1), (2). Date in force: 7 June 2006: see SI 2006/1282, art 1.

[23B Modifications for most appeals]

[(1)   Subject to paragraph (2) these Rules shall apply subject to the modifications set out in this rule in relation to an appeal made under—

    (a)   section 78 of the Planning Act; [or]

    (b)   section 20 of the Listed Buildings Act…

    (c)   ….

(2)   These modifications shall not apply—

    (a)   where a direction is given by the Secretary of State under section 321(3) of the Planning Act or paragraph 6(6) of Schedule 3 to the Listed Buildings Act (matters related to national security);

    (b)   where section 293A of the Planning Act or section 82B of the Listed Buildings Act (urgent Crown development) applies;

    (c)   in relation to type A or type B appeals within the meaning in article 33(7) of the Town and Country Planning (Development Management Procedure) (England) Order 2010 (appeals); …

Town and Country Planning (Inquiries Procedure) (England) Rules 2000

- (d) in relation to any appeal transferred out of Part 1 of the Town and Country Planning (Appeals) (Written Representations Procedure) (England) Regulations 2009 under regulation 9 of those Regulations[; or
- (e) in relation to any appeal made under section 78 of the Planning Act as applied by regulations made under section 220 of that Act].

(3) In rule 2 (interpretation)—
- (a) after the definition of 'document' insert—
  ''draft statement of common ground' means the draft statement of common ground (if any) submitted in accordance with article 33 of the 2010 Order or regulation 8 of the Listed Buildings Regulations';
- (b) after the definition of 'electronic communication' insert—
  ''full statement of case'—
  - (a) means, in relation to the applicant, the full statement of case submitted with their notice of appeal under article 33 of the 2010 Order or regulation 8 of the Listed Buildings Regulations; and
  - (b) in relation to everyone else means, and is comprised of, a written statement which contains full particulars of the case which a person proposes to put forward and copies of any documents which that person intends to refer to or put in evidence;';
- (c) after the definition of 'the Listed Buildings Act' insert—
  ''the Listed Buildings Regulations' means the Planning (Listed Buildings and Conservation Areas) Regulations 1990;';
- (d) after the definition of 'local planning authority' insert—
  ''the 2010 Order' means the Town and Country Planning (Development Management Procedure) (England) (Order) 2010';
- (e) for the definition of 'outline statement' substitute—
  ''outline statement' means—
  - (a) in relation to the applicant, the full statement of case submitted with their notice of appeal under article 33 of the 2010 Order or regulation 8 of the Listed Buildings Regulations; and
  - (b) in relation to everyone else, a written statement of the principal submissions which a person proposes to put forward at an inquiry.'; and
- (f) omit the definition of 'statement of case'.

(4) In rule 5 (procedure where Secretary of State causes pre-inquiry meeting to be held)—
- (a) in paragraph (2)(d) omit 'the applicant and'; and
- (b) in paragraph (3) omit the words from 'and a copy of the applicant's' to the end.

(5) In rule 6 (receipt of statements of case etc)—
- (a) in the title insert 'full' before 'statements of case';
- (b) substitute 'full statement of case' for 'statement of case' wherever it appears;
- (c) for paragraph (3) substitute—

  '(3) As soon as practicable after receiving the information in rule 4(1) (preliminary information to be supplied by local planning authority) the applicant shall ensure that a copy of their full statement of case has been received by any statutory party.

(3A) In any case where a pre-inquiry meeting is held pursuant to rule 5, the applicant may modify their full statement of case following that meeting.

(3B) Where paragraph 3A applies, and the applicant wishes to make modifications, they shall ensure that a copy of their modified full statement of case has been received by the Secretary of State, the local planning authority and any statutory party within 4 weeks of the conclusion of that pre-inquiry meeting.';

(d) in paragraph (4) omit the words from 'and a copy of the applicant's' to the end;

(e) omit paragraph (5);

(f) in paragraph (8)—
  (i) substitute 'either of them' for the first 'him'; and
  (ii) insert ', article 33 of the 2010 Order, or regulation 8 of the Listed Buildings Regulations' after 'in accordance with this rule';

(g) omit paragraph (11);

(h) in paragraph (13)—
  (i) in sub-paragraph (a) insert ', article 33 of the 2010 Order, or regulation 8 of the Listed Buildings Regulations' after 'in accordance with this rule'; and
  (ii) in sub-paragraph (b) omit from 'together with a copy' to 'comprised in that statement'; and

(i) in paragraph (16) insert ', article 33 of the 2010 Order, or regulation 8 of the Listed Buildings Regulations,' after 'in accordance with this rule', and omit 'in this Rule'.

(6) In rule 10(8)(d) insert ', article 33 of the 2010 Order, or regulation 8 of the Listed Buildings Regulations,' after 'pursuant to rule 6'.

(7) In rule 11(1)(h) (appearances at inquiry) substitute 'full statement of case' for 'statement of case'.

(8) In rule 15(10) (procedure at inquiry)—
  (a) substitute 'full statement of case' for 'statement of case' and
  (b) insert ', article 33 of the 2010 Order, or regulation 8 of the Listed Buildings Regulations,' after 'under rule 6'.

(9) In rule 21(1)(b) (additional copies)—
  (a) substitute 'full statement of case' for 'statement of case'; and
  (b) insert ', article 33 of the 2010 Order, or regulation 8 of the Listed Buildings Regulations' after 'with rule 6'.

(10) In rule 23(2)(c) (Mayor of London: modifications to rule 5)—
  (a) for paragraph (i) substitute—
    '(i) in paragraph (2)(d) after 'the local planning authority' insert 'and the Mayor';'

Town and Country Planning (Inquiries Procedure) (England) Rules 2000

    (b) in paragraph (ii) in the substituted paragraph (3)—

        (i) in sub-paragraph (a) substitute 'statement' for 'statements' and omit 'the applicant and'; and

        (ii) in sub-paragraph (b) substitute 'statement' for 'statements' and omit 'the applicant and'.

(11) In rule 23(2)(d) (Mayor of London: modifications to rule 6)—

    (a) substitute 'full statement of case' for 'statement of case' wherever it appears;

    (b) for paragraph (ii) substitute—

        '(ii) in paragraph (3) insert 'and the Mayor, and that the Mayor has received a copy of their draft statement of common ground' after 'any statutory party';

        (iia) in paragraph (3B) insert ', the Mayor' after 'local planning authority';'

    (c) in paragraph (iii) in the substituted paragraph (4)—

        (i) in sub-paragraph (a) substitute 'statement' for 'statements' and omit 'the applicant and';

        (ii) in sub-paragraph (b) substitute 'statement' for 'statements' and omit 'the applicant and'; and

    (d) omit paragraph (iv).]

Amendment

Inserted by SI 2013/2137, r 3(1), (2). Date in force: 1 October 2013: see SI 2013/2137, r 1; for transitional provisions see r 7 thereof.

Para (1): in sub-para (a) word 'or' in square brackets inserted by SI 2015/316, r 4(a). Date in force: 6 April 2015: see SI 2015/316, r 1(1).

Para (1): in sub-para (c) and word omitted immediately preceding it revoked by SI 2015/316, r 4(b), (c). Date in force: 6 April 2015: see SI 2015/316, r 1(1).

Para (2): in sub-para (c) word omitted revoked by SI 2015/316, r 4(d)(i). Date in force: 6 April 2015: see SI 2015/316, r 1(1).

Para (2): sub-para (e) and word '; or' immediately preceding it inserted by SI 2015/316, r 4(d)(ii), (iii). Date in force: 6 April 2015: see SI 2015/316, r 1(1).

24 Revocation, savings and transitional provisions

(1) Subject to paragraph (2) the Town and Country Planning (Inquiries Procedure) Rules 1992 are hereby revoked in relation to England except rule 21 of those Rules so far as it makes provision for the continued application of the Town and Country Planning (Inquiries Procedure) Rules 1974.

(2) Subject to paragraph (3) any application or appeal to which the 1992 Rules applied which has not been determined on the date when these Rules come into force shall be continued under the 1992 Rules.

(3) Where a decision of the Secretary of State on an application or appeal to which the 1992 Rules applied is subsequently quashed in proceedings before any court, the decision shall be re-determined in accordance with these Rules.

Amendment

Revoked, in relation to the inquiry procedure for major infrastructure projects in England, by virtue of SI 2002/1223, r 26(1). Date in force: 7 June 2002 (except in relation to any application or appeal which has not been determined on that date): see SI 2002/1223, rr 1(2), 26(1).

[SCHEDULE]

[Rule 23A]

[PART 1 MODIFICATIONS WHERE NATIONAL SECURITY DIRECTION GIVEN]

[Interpretation

1

In rule 2(1)—

    (a) after the definition of 'applicant' insert—

        "'appointed representative' means a person appointed under—

            (a) section 321(5) or (6) of the Planning Act; or

            (b) paragraph 6A(1) or (2) of Schedule 3 to the Listed Buildings Act;';

    (b) after the definition of 'assessor' insert—

        "'closed evidence' means evidence which is subject to a security direction;';

    (c) after the definition of 'the 1992 Rules' insert—

        "'security direction' means a direction given by the Secretary of State under—

            (a) section 321(3) of the Planning Act (matters related to national security); or

            (b) paragraph 6(6) of Schedule 3 to the Listed Buildings Act (matters related to national security);'; and

    (d) in the definition of 'statement of common ground' after 'local planning authority' insert ', or appointed representative, as the case may be,'.

Procedure where Secretary of State causes a pre-inquiry meeting to be held

2

In rule 5—

    (a) for paragraph (3) substitute—

        '(3) The Secretary of State shall, as soon as practicable after receipt, send a copy of the local planning authority's outline statement to the applicant, a copy of the applicant's outline statement to the appointed representative and a copy of the applicant's open outline statement to the local planning authority.

        (3A) In this rule 'open outline statement' means such part (if any) of an outline statement as does not include or refer to closed evidence.';

    (b) in paragraph (5) after 'statement to him,' insert 'and the open outline statement to'; and

    (c) after paragraph (5) insert—

        '(5A) The Secretary of State shall, as soon as practicable after receipt, send to the appointed representative any outline statement received in accordance with paragraph (5).'.

Town and Country Planning (Inquiries Procedure) (England) Rules 2000

Receipt of statement of case etc

3

In rule 6—
- (a) in paragraph (3) for 'copy of their statement of case' substitute 'copy of their open statement';
- (b) in paragraph (4) for 'statement of case to the local planning authority' substitute 'open statement to the local planning authority';
- (c) in paragraph (6)—
    - (i) in sub-paragraph (b) for 'statement of case' substitute 'open statement';
    - (ii) for 'send a copy of each such statement of case' substitute 'send a copy of any open statement received by him in accordance with sub-paragraph (a)';
- (d) in paragraph (7)—
    - (i) in sub-paragraph (a) for 'statements of case of the applicant and the local planning authority' substitute 'open statement of the applicant and the statement of case of the local planning authority';
    - (ii) in sub-paragraph (b) for 'statement of case' substitute 'open statement';
- (e) in paragraph (16) after 'inspector' insert 'and appointed representative'; and
- (f) after paragraph (16) insert—

    '(17) For the purposes of this rule 'open statement' means such part (if any) of a statement of case as does not include or refer to closed evidence.'.

Appearances at inquiry

4

In rule 11(1) after sub-paragraph (a) insert—

'(aa)   the appointed representative;'.

Proofs of evidence

5

In rule 13—
- (a) in paragraph (1) for 'Any person' substitute 'Subject to paragraph (1A), any person'; and
- (b) after paragraph (1) insert—

    '(1A) Paragraph (1B) applies where the proof of evidence includes or refers to closed evidence.

    (1B) Where this paragraph applies, any person entitled to appear at an inquiry, who proposes to give, or to call another person to give evidence at the inquiry by reading a proof of evidence, shall—
    - (a) send to the Secretary of State 2 copies, in the case of the local planning authority and the applicant, or 3 copies in the case of any other person, of—
        - (i) the proof of evidence including closed evidence together with any written summary of it;

(ii) the proof of evidence excluding closed evidence ('the open proof') together with any written summary of it; and

(b) simultaneously send copies of the open proof and any written summary of it to any statutory party,

and the Secretary of State shall, as soon as practicable after receipt, send a copy of each open proof together with any written summary of it to the local planning authority and the applicant.';

(c) in paragraph (4) after 'inspector' insert 'and appointed representative'; and

(d) in paragraph (5) after 'paragraph (1)' insert 'or (1B)'.

Statement of common ground

6

In rule 14—

(a) in paragraph (1)(a) after 'ground' insert 'insofar as it does not relate to closed evidence'; and

(b) after paragraph (3) insert—

'(4) Where the application or appeal is made by or on behalf of the Crown, the appointed representative and the applicant shall—

(a) together prepare an agreed statement of common ground insofar as it relates to closed evidence; and

(b) ensure that the Secretary of State receives it not less than 4 weeks before the date fixed for the holding of the inquiry.'.

Site inspections

7

In rule 16—

(a) in paragraph (1) for 'The inspector' substitute 'Subject to paragraph (1A), the inspector';

(b) after paragraph (1) insert—

'(1A) Paragraph (1) does not apply where a site inspection will involve inspection of closed evidence.';

(c) in paragraph (2) for 'During' substitute 'Subject to paragraph (2A), during';

(d) after paragraph (2) insert—

'(2A) Where an accompanied site inspection will involve the inspection of closed evidence, paragraph (2) does not apply and the inspector—

(a) may inspect the land in the company of the applicant and the appointed representative, where one has been appointed; and

(b) shall make such an inspection if so requested by the applicant or the appointed representative before or during an inquiry.'; and

(e) in paragraph (4) after 'paragraph (2)' insert 'or (2A)'.

Town and Country Planning (Inquiries Procedure) (England) Rules 2000

Procedure after inquiry

8

In rule 17—
- (a) after paragraph (3) insert—

    '(3A) Where closed evidence was considered at the inquiry—
    - (a) the inspector and assessor, where one has been appointed, shall set out in a separate part ('the closed part') of their reports any description of that evidence together with any conclusions or recommendations in relation to that evidence; and
    - (b) where an assessor has been appointed, the inspector shall append the closed part of the assessor's report to the closed part of his own report and shall state in the closed part of his own report how far he agrees or disagrees with the closed part of the assessor's report and, where he disagrees with the assessor, his reasons for that disagreement.';

- (b) at the beginning of paragraph (5) insert 'Subject to paragraph (5A)'; and
- (c) after paragraph (5) insert—

    '(5A) Where the Secretary of State differs from the inspector on any matter of fact mentioned in, or appearing to him to be material to, a conclusion reached by the inspector in relation to a matter in respect of which closed evidence has been given, the notification referred to in paragraph (5) shall include the reasons for the Secretary of State's disagreement unless—
    - (a) the notification is addressed to a person who is neither the appointed representative nor any person specified, or of a description specified, in the security direction; and
    - (b) inclusion of the reasons would disclose any part of the closed evidence.'.

Notification of decision

9

In rule 18—
- (a) in paragraph (1) for 'the Secretary of State' substitute 'Subject to paragraph (1B), the Secretary of State';
- (b) after paragraph (1A) insert—

    '(1B) Where the Secretary of State's reasons for a decision relate to matters in respect of which closed evidence has been given, nothing in paragraph (1) requires the Secretary of State to notify those reasons to any person other than—
    - (a) the appointed representative; or
    - (b) a person specified, or of any description specified, in the security direction.';

- (c) in paragraph (2) for 'Where a copy' substitute 'Subject to paragraph (2A), where a copy'; and

(d) after paragraph (2) insert—

'(2A) Nothing in paragraph (2) requires the disclosure of the closed part of the inspector's report referred to in rule 17(2A) to a person other than—
  (a) the appointed representative; or
  (b) a person specified, or of any description specified, in the security direction.'.

Procedure following quashing of decision

10

In rule 19—
(a) at the beginning of sub-paragraph (a) of paragraph (1) insert 'subject to paragraph (1A)'; and
(b) after paragraph (1) insert—

'(1A) Where the matters referred to in paragraph (1)(a) will involve consideration of closed evidence, the Secretary of State shall only send the written statement to—
  (a) the appointed representative; and
  (b) a person specified, or of any description specified, in the security direction.'.

Closed evidence not to be disclosed

11

After rule 22A insert—

'22B Closed evidence not to be disclosed

Nothing in these Rules shall be taken to require or permit closed evidence to be disclosed to a person other than—
  (a) the Secretary of State;
  (b) the appointed representative; or
  (c) a person specified, or of any description specified, in the security direction.']

Amendment
Inserted by SI 2006/1282, art 24(1), (3), Sch 2. Date in force: 7 June 2006: see SI 2006/1282, art 1.

[PART 2 MODIFICATIONS FOR URGENT CROWN DEVELOPMENT OR URGENT WORKS AFFECTING CROWN LAND]

[Interpretation

1

In rule 2(1) in paragraph (a) of the definition of 'statutory party' after 'in determining the' insert 'application,'.

Town and Country Planning (Inquiries Procedure) (England) Rules 2000

Application of Rules

2

In rule 3—
- (a) after paragraph (1)(a) insert—
  '(aa) an application for planning permission made to the Secretary of State under section 293A of the Planning Act (urgent Crown development);'; and
- (b) after paragraph (1)(b) insert—
  '(bb) an application for listed building consent made to the Secretary of State under section 82B of the Listed Buildings Act (urgent works relating to Crown land);'.

Preliminary information to be supplied

3

For rule 4 substitute—

'4 Preliminary information to be supplied by the Secretary of State

(1) The Secretary of State shall, as soon as practicable after the date of the relevant notice inform the applicant and the local planning authority in writing of the name and address of any statutory party who has made representations to him.

(2) This paragraph applies where—
   (a) any Minister of the Crown (other than the Secretary of State), any government department, or any body falling within rule 11(1)(c), has expressed in writing to the Secretary of State the view that the application should not be granted either wholly or in part, or should be granted subject only to conditions; or
   (b) any person consulted in pursuance of a development order has made representations to the Secretary of State about the application.

(3) Where paragraph (2) applies, the Secretary of State shall forthwith after the date of the relevant notice inform the person concerned of the inquiry and, unless they have already done so, that person shall thereupon give the Secretary of State a written statement of the reasons for expressing the view or making the representations, as the case may be.'.

Procedure where Secretary of State causes pre-inquiry meeting to be held

4

In rule 5—
- (a) in paragraph (2)(d) for '8' substitute '6';
- (b) in paragraph (5) for '4' substitute '3';
- (c) in paragraph (6) for '16' substitute '10';
- (d) in paragraph (7) for '3' substitute '2'; and
- (e) in paragraph (10) for '4' substitute '3'.

Town and Country Planning (Inquiries Procedure) (England) Rules 2000

Receipt of statements of case etc

5

In rule 6—
- (a) in paragraph (1)(a) for '6' substitute '4';
- (b) in paragraph (1)(b) for '4' substitute '3';
- (c) in paragraph (3)(a) for '6' substitute '4';
- (d) in paragraph (3)(b) for '4' substitute '3';
- (e) in paragraph (6)(a) for '4' substitute '3';
- (f) in paragraph (12) for '12' substitute '8';
- (g) in paragraph (14) for '9' substitute '6'; and
- (h) in paragraph (15) for '4' substitute '3'.

Date and notification of inquiry

6

In rule 10—
- (a) in paragraph (1)(a) for '22' substitute '14';
- (b) in paragraph (1)(b) for '8' substitute '5'; and
- (c) in paragraph (6)—
    - (i) omit 'in writing require the local planning authority to';
    - (ii) in sub-paragraph (a) omit 'to';
    - (iii) in sub-paragraphs (b) and (c) omit the first 'to' in each place.

Proofs of evidence

7

In rule 13(3)(a) for '4' substitute '3'.]

Amendment

Inserted by SI 2006/1282, art 24(1), (3), Sch 2. Date in force: 7 June 2006: see SI 2006/1282, art 1.

814

Town and Country Planning Appeals (Determination by Inspectors) Rules 2000

(SI 2000/1625)

Town and Country Planning Appeals (Determination by Inspectors) (Inquiries Procedure) (England) Rules 2000

1 Citation, commencement and extent

(1) These Rules may be cited as the Town and Country Planning Appeals (Determination by Inspectors) (Inquiries Procedure) (England) Rules 2000.

(2) These Rules shall come into force on 1st August 2000.

(3) These Rules extend to England only.

2 Interpretation

[(1)] In these Rules, unless the context otherwise requires—

'assessor' means a person appointed by the Secretary of State to sit with an inspector at an inquiry or re-opened inquiry to advise the inspector on such matters arising as the Secretary of State may specify;

'the Commission' means the Historic Buildings and Monuments Commission for England;

...

'development order' has the meaning given in section 59 of the Planning Act;

'document' includes a photograph, map or plan;

['draft statement of common ground' means the draft statement of common ground (if any) submitted in accordance with article 33 of the 2010 Order or regulation 8 of the Listed Buildings Regulations;]

['electronic communication' has the meaning given in section 15(1) of the Electronic Communications Act 2000;]

['full statement of case'—

(a) means, in relation to the applicant, the full statement of case submitted with their notice of appeal under article 33 of the 2010 Order or regulation 8 of the Listed Buildings Regulations; and

(b) in relation to everyone else means, and is comprised of, a written statement which contains full particulars of the case which a person proposes to put forward and copies of any documents which that person intends to refer to or put in evidence;]

'inquiry' means a local inquiry in relation to which these Rules apply;

'inspector' means a person appointed by the Secretary of State under Schedule 6 to the Planning Act or, as the case may be, Schedule 3 to the Listed Buildings Act to determine an appeal;

'land' means the land or building to which an inquiry relates;

'the Listed Buildings Act' means the Planning (Listed Buildings and Conservation Areas) Act 1990;

['the Listed Buildings Regulations' means the Planning (Listed Buildings and Conservation Areas) Regulations 1990;]

'listed building consent' has the meaning given in section 8(7) of the Listed Buildings Act;

'local planning authority' means the body who were responsible for dealing with the application occasioning the appeal;

['the 2010 Order' means the Town and Country Planning (Development Management Procedure) (England) (Order) 2010;]

'the Planning Act' means the Town and Country Planning Act 1990;

'pre-inquiry meeting' means a meeting held before an inquiry to consider what may be done with a view to securing that the inquiry is conducted efficiently and expeditiously, and where two or more such meetings are held references to the conclusion of a pre-inquiry meeting are references to the conclusion of the final meeting;

'questionnaire' means a document in the form supplied by the Secretary of State to local planning authorities for the purpose of proceedings under these Rules[, and for this purpose a form is taken to be supplied where the Secretary of State has published it on a website and has notified the local planning authority, in a manner for the time being agreed between the Secretary of State and the authority for that purpose, of—

(i) publication of the form on the website,

(ii) the address of the website, and

(iii) the place on the website where the form may be accessed, and how it may be accessed];

...

'the 1992 Rules' means the Town and Country Planning Appeals (Determination by Inspectors) (Inquiries Procedure) Rules 1992;

['starting date' means the date of the notice given by the Secretary of State under rule 3A;]

...

'statement of common ground' means a written statement prepared jointly by the local planning authority and the appellant and which contains agreed factual information about the proposal which is the subject of the appeal;

'statutory party' means—

(a) a person mentioned in paragraph (1)(b)(i) of article 19 of the Town and Country Planning (General Development Procedure) Order 1995 whose representations the inspector is required by paragraph (3) of that article to take into account in determining the appeal to which an inquiry relates, and such a person whose representations the local planning authority were required by paragraph (1) of that article to take into account in determining the application occasioning the appeal; and

Town and Country Planning Appeals (Determination by Inspectors) Rules 2000

   (b) a person whose representations the inspector is required by paragraphs (3)(b) and (5) of regulation 6 of the Planning (Listed Buildings and Conservation Areas) Regulations 1990 to take into account in determining the appeal to which an inquiry relates, and a person whose representations the local planning authority were required by paragraph (3)(b) of that regulation to take into account in determining the application occasioning the appeal.

[(2) In these Rules, and in relation to the use of electronic communications for any purpose of these Rules which is capable of being carried out electronically—

  (a) the expression 'address' includes any number or address used for the purposes of such communications, except that where these Rules impose an obligation on any person to provide a name and address to any other person, the obligation shall not be fulfilled unless the person on whom it is imposed provides a postal address;

  (b) references to statements, notices or other documents, or to copies of such documents, include references to such documents or copies of them in electronic form.

(3) Paragraphs (4) to (8) apply where an electronic communication is used by a person for the purpose of fulfilling any requirement in these Rules to give or send any statement, notice or other document to any other person ('the recipient').

(4) The requirement shall be taken to be fulfilled where the document transmitted by means of the electronic communication is—

  (a) capable of being accessed by the recipient,

  (b) legible in all material respects, and

  (c) sufficiently permanent to be used for subsequent reference.

(5) In paragraph (4), 'legible in all material respects' means that the information contained in the document is available to the recipient to no lesser extent than it would be if sent or given by means of a document in printed form.

(6) Where the electronic communication is received by the recipient outside the recipient's business hours, it shall be taken to have been received on the next working day; and for this purpose, 'working day' means a day which is not a Saturday, Sunday, Bank Holiday or other public holiday.

(7) A requirement in these Rules that any document should be in writing is fulfilled where that document meets the criteria in paragraph (4), and 'written' and cognate expressions are to be construed accordingly.

(8) A requirement in these Rules to send more than one copy of a statement or other document may be complied with by sending one copy only of the statement or other document in question.]

Amendment

 Para (1): numbered as such by SI 2003/956, art 12(2), Sch 3, para 1. Date in force: 31 March 2003: see SI 2003/956, art 1(1).

 Para (1): definition 'conservation area consent' (omitted) revoked by SI 2013/2146, art 3, Schedule, para 4(a). Date in force: 1 October 2013: see SI 2013/2146, art 1; for savings see art 4 thereof and for transitional provisions see SI 2013/2148, art 5(4)(a).

Town and Country Planning Appeals (Determination by Inspectors) Rules 2000

Para (1): definition 'draft statement of common ground' inserted by SI 2013/2137, r 4(1), (2)(a). Date in force: 1 October 2013: see SI 2013/2137, r 1; for transitional provisions and savings see rr 6, 7 thereof.

Para (1): definition 'electronic communication' inserted by SI 2003/956, art 12(2), Sch 3, para 1(a). Date in force: 31 March 2003: see SI 2003/956, art 1(1).

Para (1): definition 'full statement of case' inserted by SI 2013/2137, r 4(1), (2)(b). Date in force: 1 October 2013: see SI 2013/2137, r 1; for transitional provisions and savings see rr 6, 7 thereof.

Para (1): definition 'the Listed Buildings Regulations' inserted by SI 2013/2137, r 4(1), (2)(c). Date in force: 1 October 2013: see SI 2013/2137, r 1; for transitional provisions and savings see rr 6, 7 thereof.

Para (1): definition 'the 2010 Order' inserted by SI 2013/2137, r 4(1), (2)(d). Date in force: 1 October 2013: see SI 2013/2137, r 1; for transitional provisions and savings see rr 6, 7 thereof.

Para (1): in definition 'questionnaire' words from ', and for this' to 'may be accessed' in square brackets inserted by SI 2003/956, art 12(2), Sch 3, para 1(b). Date in force: 31 March 2003: see SI 2003/956, art 1(1).

Para (1): definition 'relevant notice' (omitted) revoked by SI 2009/455, r 3(1), (2)(a). Date in force: 6 April 2009 (in relation to appeals and applications made on or after that date): see SI 2009/455, r 1(1), (2)(a).

Para (1): definition 'starting date' substituted by SI 2009/455, r 3(1), (2)(b). Date in force: 6 April 2009 (in relation to appeals and applications made on or after that date): see SI 2009/455, r 1(1), (2)(a).

Para (1): definition 'statement of case' (omitted) revoked by SI 2013/2137, r 4(1), (2)(e). Date in force: 1 October 2013: see SI 2013/2137, r 1; for transitional provisions and savings see rr 6, 7 thereof.

Paras (2)–(8): inserted by SI 2003/956, art 12(2), Sch 3, para 2. Date in force: 31 March 2003: see SI 2003/956, art 1(1).

3 Application of Rules

(1) These Rules apply in relation to any local inquiry held in England by an inspector before he determines—

   (a) an appeal to the Secretary of State in relation to an application for planning permission under section 78 of the Planning Act;

   (b) an appeal to the Secretary of State in relation to listed building consent under section 20 of the Listed Buildings Act...,

   ....

[(1A) These Rules apply in relation to any local inquiry held in England by an inspector before he determines an appeal under section 78 of the Planning Act (as applied by regulations made under section 220 of that Act) subject to the modifications in rule 24A.]

(2) Where these Rules apply in relation to an appeal which at some time fell to be disposed of in accordance with the Town and Country Planning (Inquiries Procedure) (England) Rules 2000 or Rules superseded by those Rules, any step taken or thing done under those Rules which could have been done under any corresponding provision of these Rules shall have effect as if it had been taken or done under that corresponding provision.

Amendment

Para (1): in sub-para (b) words omitted revoked by SI 2013/2146, art 3, Schedule, para 4(b). Date in force: 1 October 2013: see SI 2013/2146, art 1; for savings see art 4 thereof and for transitional provisions see SI 2013/2148, art 5(4)(a).

Town and Country Planning Appeals (Determination by Inspectors) Rules 2000

Para (1): words omitted revoked by SI 2015/316, r 5(1), (2)(a). Date in force: 6 April 2015: see SI 2015/316, r 1(1).

Para (1A): inserted by SI 2015/316, r 5(1), (2)(b). Date in force: 6 April 2015: see SI 2015/316, r 1(1).

[3A Notice from the Secretary of State]

[(1) In the case of an appeal under section 78 of the Planning Act [(including an appeal under section 78 of the Planning Act as applied by regulations made under section 220 of that Act),] as soon as practicable after a determination has been made under section 319A of the Planning Act that the appeal is to proceed at an inquiry, the Secretary of State shall send a notice to this effect to the appellant and the local planning authority.

(2) In the case of any other appeal to which these Rules apply, the Secretary of State shall as soon as practicable after receipt of all the documents required to enable the appeal to proceed, send a notice to the appellant and the local planning authority, informing them that an inquiry is to be held.]

Amendment
Inserted by SI 2009/455, r 3(1), (3). Date in force: 6 April 2009 (in relation to appeals and applications made on or after that date): see SI 2009/455, r 1(1), (2)(a).

Para (1): words from '(including an appeal' to 'of that Act),' in square brackets inserted by SI 2015/316, r 5(1), (3). Date in force: 6 April 2015: see SI 2015/316, r 1(1).

4 Preliminary information to be supplied by local planning authority

(1) The local planning authority shall, on receipt of the [notice under rule 3A], forthwith inform the Secretary of State and the appellant in writing of the name and address of any statutory party who has made representations to them; and the Secretary of State shall, as soon as practicable thereafter, inform the appellant and the local planning authority in writing of the name and address of any statutory party who has made representations to him.

(2) This paragraph applies where—

   (a) the Secretary of State has given to the local planning authority a direction restricting the grant of planning permission for which application was made; or

   (b) in a case relating to listed building consent, the Commission has given a direction to the local planning authority pursuant to section 14(2) of the Listed Buildings Act as to how the application is to be determined; or

   (c) the Secretary of State or any other Minister of the Crown or any government department, or any body falling within rule 11(1)(c), has expressed in writing to the local planning authority the view that the application should not be granted either wholly or in part, or should be granted only subject to conditions; or

   (d) any person consulted in pursuance of a development order has made representations to the local planning authority about the application.

(3) Where paragraph (2) applies, the local planning authority shall forthwith after the starting date inform the person concerned of the inquiry and, unless they have already done so, that person shall thereupon give the local planning authority a written statement of the reasons for making the direction, expressing the view or making the representations, as the case may be.

Town and Country Planning Appeals (Determination by Inspectors) Rules 2000

(4) The local planning authority shall ensure that within [1 week] of the starting date—

(a) the Secretary of State and the appellant have received a completed questionnaire and a copy of each of the documents referred to in it; and

(b) any—

(i) statutory party; and

(ii) other person who made representations to the local planning authority about the application occasioning the appeal,

have been notified [in writing] that an appeal has been made and of the address to which and of the period within which they may make representations to the Secretary of State.

Amendment

Para (1): words 'notice under rule 3A' in square brackets substituted by SI 2009/455, r 3(1), (4)(a). Date in force: 6 April 2009 (in relation to appeals and applications made on or after that date): see SI 2009/455, r 1(1), (2)(a).

Para (4): words '1 week' in square brackets substituted by SI 2013/2137, r 4(1), (3). Date in force: 1 October 2013: see SI 2013/2137, r 1; for transitional provisions and savings see rr 6, 7 thereof.

Para (4): words 'in writing' in square brackets inserted by SI 2009/455, r 3(1), (4)(b). Date in force: 6 April 2009 (in relation to appeals and applications made on or after that date): see SI 2009/455, r 1(1), (2)(a).

5 Notification of name of inspector

(1) Subject to paragraph (2), the Secretary of State shall notify [in writing] the name of the inspector to every person entitled to appear at the inquiry.

(2) Where the Secretary of State appoints another inspector instead of the person previously appointed and it is not practicable to notify the new appointment before the inquiry is held, the inspector holding the inquiry shall, at its commencement, announce his name and the fact of his appointment.

Amendment

Para (1): words 'in writing' in square brackets inserted by SI 2009/455, r 3(1), (5). Date in force: 6 April 2009 (in relation to appeals and applications made on or after that date): see SI 2009/455, r 1(1), (2)(a).

6 Receipt of [full] statements of case etc

(1) The local planning authority shall ensure that, within [5 weeks] of the starting date, 2 copies of their [full statement of case] have been received by the Secretary of State; and a copy of their [full statement of case] has been received by any statutory party.

(2) The local planning authority shall—

(a) include in their [full statement of case]—

[(i) details of the time and place where the opportunity to inspect and take copies described in paragraph 13 below shall be afforded (including, in any case in which the local planning authority rely on paragraph 13A, the details mentioned in that paragraph);] and

(ii) where rule 4(2) applies, the terms of any direction given together with a statement of the reasons therefor together with any view expressed or representation made on which they intend to rely in their submissions at the inquiry; and

(b) where rule 4(2) applies, within the period mentioned in paragraph (1) send a copy of their [full statement of case] to the person concerned.

[(3) As soon as practicable after receiving the information in rule 4(1) (preliminary information to be supplied by local planning authority), the appellant shall ensure that a copy of their full statement of case has been received by any statutory party.]

(4) The Secretary of State shall, as soon as practicable after receipt, send a copy of the local planning authority's [full statement of case] to the appellant ....

(5) ...

(6) The Secretary of State may in writing require any other person who has notified him of an intention or a wish to appear at an inquiry, to send [within 4 weeks of being so required]—

(a) 3 copies of their [full statement of case] to him ...; and

(b) a copy of their [full statement of case] to any statutory party;

and the Secretary of State shall, as soon as practicable after receipt, send a copy of each such [full statement of case] to the local planning authority and the appellant.

(7) The Secretary of State shall, as soon as practicable—

(a) send to any person from whom he requires a [full statement of case] in accordance with paragraph (6) a copy of the statements of case of the appellant and the local planning authority; and

(b) inform that person of the name and address of every person to whom his [full statement of case] is required to be sent.

(8) The Secretary of State may in writing require any person who has sent a [full statement of case] in accordance with these Rules[, article 33 of the 2010 Order, or regulation 8 of the Listed Buildings Regulations,] to provide such further information about the matters contained in the [full statement of case] as he may specify and may specify the time within which the information shall be received by him.

(9) A local planning authority or appellant required to provide further information shall ensure that—

(a) 2 copies of that information ... have been received by the Secretary of State within the specified time; and

(b) a copy has been received by any statutory party within the specified time,

and the Secretary of State shall, as soon as practicable after receipt, send a copy of the further information received from the local planning authority to the appellant and a copy of the further information received from the appellant to the local planning authority.

(10) Any other person required to provide further information shall ensure that—

(a) 3 copies of that information ... have been received by the Secretary of State within the specified time; and

(b) a copy has been received by any statutory party within the specified time, and the Secretary of State shall, as soon as practicable after receipt, send a copy of the further information to the local planning authority and the appellant.

(11) ...

(12) The Secretary of State shall, as soon as practicable after receipt, send to the inspector any [full statement of case], document, further information ... sent to him in accordance with this rule[, article 33 of the 2010 Order, or regulation 8 of the Listed Buildings Regulations,] and received by him within the relevant period, if any, specified ....

(13) The local planning authority shall afford to any person who so requests a reasonable opportunity to inspect and, where practicable, take copies of—

(a) any [full statement of case], ... information or other document a copy of which has been sent to the local planning authority in accordance with this rule[, article 33 of the 2010 Order, or regulation 8 of the Listed Buildings Regulations]; and

(b) the local planning authority's completed questionnaire, and [full statement of case] ..., and ... information or other documents sent by the local planning authority pursuant to this rule.

[(13A) For the purposes of the previous paragraph an opportunity shall be taken to have been afforded to a person where the person is notified of—

(a) publication on a website of the documents mentioned in that paragraph;

(b) the address of the website;

(c) the place on the website where the documents may be accessed, and how they may be accessed.]

(14) ...

(15) ...

Amendment

Provision heading: word 'full' in square brackets inserted by SI 2013/2137, r 4(1), (4)(a). Date in force: 1 October 2013: see SI 2013/2137, r 1; for transitional provisions and savings see rr 6, 7 thereof.

Para (1): words '5 weeks' in square brackets substituted by SI 2013/2137, r 4(1), (4)(c). Date in force: 1 October 2013: see SI 2013/2137, r 1; for transitional provisions and savings see rr 6, 7 thereof.

Para (1): words 'full statement of case' in square brackets in both places they occur substituted by SI 2013/2137, r 4(1), (4)(b). Date in force: 1 October 2013: see SI 2013/2137, r 1; for transitional provisions and savings see rr 6, 7 thereof.

Para (2): in sub-paras (a), (b) words 'full statement of case' in square brackets substituted by SI 2013/2137, r 4(1), (4)(b). Date in force: 1 October 2013: see SI 2013/2137, r 1; for transitional provisions and savings see rr 6, 7 thereof.

Para (2): sub-para (a)(i) substituted by SI 2003/956, art 12(2), Sch 3, para 3(a). Date in force: 31 March 2003: see SI 2003/956, art 1(1).

Para (3): substituted by SI 2013/2137, r 4(1), (4)(d). Date in force: 1 October 2013: see SI 2013/2137, r 1; for transitional provisions and savings see rr 6, 7 thereof.

Para (4): words 'full statement of case' in square brackets substituted by SI 2013/2137, r 4(1), (4)(b). Date in force: 1 October 2013: see SI 2013/2137, r 1; for transitional provisions and savings see rr 6, 7 thereof.

Para (4): words omitted revoked by SI 2013/2137, r 4(1), (4)(e). Date in force: 1 October 2013: see SI 2013/2137, r 1; for transitional provisions and savings see rr 6, 7 thereof.

Town and Country Planning Appeals (Determination by Inspectors) Rules 2000

Para (5): revoked by SI 2013/2137, r 4(1), (4)(f). Date in force: 1 October 2013: see SI 2013/2137, r 1; for transitional provisions and savings see rr 6, 7 thereof.

Para (6): words 'within 4 weeks of being so required' in square brackets inserted by SI 2009/455, r 3(1), (6)(a)(i). Date in force: 6 April 2009 (in relation to appeals and applications made on or after that date): see SI 2009/455, r 1(1), (2)(a).

Para (6): words 'full statement of case' in square brackets in each place they occur substituted by SI 2013/2137, r 4(1), (4)(b). Date in force: 1 October 2013: see SI 2013/2137, r 1; for transitional provisions and savings see rr 6, 7 thereof.

Para (6): in sub-para (a) words omitted revoked by SI 2009/455, r 3(1), (6)(a)(ii). Date in force: 6 April 2009 (in relation to appeals and applications made on or after that date): see SI 2009/455, r 1(1), (2)(a).

Para (7): in sub-paras (a), (b) words 'full statement of case' in square brackets substituted by SI 2013/2137, r 4(1), (4)(b). Date in force: 1 October 2013: see SI 2013/2137, r 1; for transitional provisions and savings see rr 6, 7 thereof.

Para (8): words 'full statement of case' in square brackets in both places they occur substituted by SI 2013/2137, r 4(1), (4)(b). Date in force: 1 October 2013: see SI 2013/2137, r 1; for transitional provisions and savings see rr 6, 7 thereof.

Para (8): words ', article 33 of the 2010 Order, or regulation 8 of the Listed Buildings Regulations,' in square brackets inserted by SI 2013/2137, r 4(1), (4)(g). Date in force: 1 October 2013: see SI 2013/2137, r 1; for transitional provisions and savings see rr 6, 7 thereof.

Para (9): in sub-para (a) words omitted revoked by SI 2009/455, r 3(1), (6)(b). Date in force: 6 April 2009 (in relation to appeals and applications made on or after that date): see SI 2009/455, r 1(1), (2)(a).

Para (10): in sub-para (a) words omitted revoked by SI 2009/455, r 3(1), (6)(c). Date in force: 6 April 2009 (in relation to appeals and applications made on or after that date): see SI 2009/455, r 1(1), (2)(a).

Para (11): revoked by SI 2013/2137, r 4(1), (4)(h). Date in force: 1 October 2013: see SI 2013/2137, r 1; for transitional provisions and savings see rr 6, 7 thereof.

Para (12): words 'full statement of case' in square brackets substituted by SI 2013/2137, r 4(1), (4)(b). Date in force: 1 October 2013: see SI 2013/2137, r 1; for transitional provisions and savings see rr 6, 7 thereof.

Para (12): first words omitted revoked by SI 2009/455, r 3(1), (6)(d). Date in force: 6 April 2009 (in relation to appeals and applications made on or after that date): see SI 2009/455, r 1(1), (2)(a).

Para (12): words ', article 33 of the 2010 Order, or regulation 8 of the Listed Buildings Regulations,' in square brackets inserted by SI 2013/2137, r 4(1), (4)(i). Date in force: 1 October 2013: see SI 2013/2137, r 1; for transitional provisions and savings see rr 6, 7 thereof.

Para (12): final words omitted revoked by SI 2013/2137, r 4(1), (4)(i). Date in force: 1 October 2013: see SI 2013/2137, r 1; for transitional provisions and savings see rr 6, 7 thereof.

Para (13): in sub-paras (a), (b) words 'full statement of case' in square brackets substituted by SI 2013/2137, r 4(1), (4)(b). Date in force: 1 October 2013: see SI 2013/2137, r 1; for transitional provisions and savings see rr 6, 7 thereof.

Para (13): in sub-para (a) words omitted revoked by SI 2009/455, r 3(1), (6)(e)(i). Date in force: 6 April 2009 (in relation to appeals and applications made on or after that date): see SI 2009/455, r 1(1), (2)(a).

Para (13): in sub-para (a) words ', article 33 of the 2010 Order, or regulation 8 of the Listed Buildings Regulations' in square brackets inserted by SI 2013/2137, r 4(1), (4)(j)(i). Date in force: 1 October 2013: see SI 2013/2137, r 1; for transitional provisions and savings see rr 6, 7 thereof.

Town and Country Planning Appeals (Determination by Inspectors) Rules 2000

Para (13): in sub-para (b) first words omitted revoked by SI 2013/2137, r 4(1), (4)(j)(ii). Date in force: 1 October 2013: see SI 2013/2137, r 1; for transitional provisions and savings see rr 6, 7 thereof.

Para (13): in sub-para (b) second words omitted revoked by SI 2009/455, r 3(1), (6)(e)(ii). Date in force: 6 April 2009 (in relation to appeals and applications made on or after that date): see SI 2009/455, r 1(1), (2)(a).

Para (13A): inserted by SI 2003/956, art 12(2), Sch 3, para 3(b). Date in force: 31 March 2003: see SI 2003/956, art 1(1).

Paras (14), (15): revoked by SI 2009/455, r 3(1), (6)(f). Date in force: 6 April 2009 (in relation to appeals and applications made on or after that date): see SI 2009/455, r 1(1), (2)(a).

7 Statement of matters and pre-inquiry meetings

(1) An inspector may, within [12 weeks] of the starting date, send to the appellant, the local planning authority and any statutory party a written statement of the matters about which he particularly wishes to be informed for the purposes of his consideration of the appeal.

(2) An inspector shall hold a pre-inquiry meeting—

  (a) if he expects an inquiry to last for 8 days or more, unless he considers it is unnecessary; or

  (b) in respect of shorter inquiries, if it appears to him necessary.

(3) An inspector shall give not less than 2 weeks written notice of a pre-inquiry meeting to—

  (a) the appellant;

  (b) the local planning authority;

  (c) any statutory party;

  (d) any other person known to be entitled to appear at the inquiry; and

  (e) any other person whose presence at the meeting appears to him to be desirable.

(4) The inspector—

  (a) shall preside at the pre-inquiry meeting;

  (b) shall determine the matters to be discussed and the procedure to be followed;

  (c) may require any person present at the pre-inquiry meeting who, in his opinion, is behaving in a disruptive manner to leave; and

  (d) may refuse to permit that person to return or to attend any further pre-inquiry meeting, or may permit him to return or attend only on such conditions as he may specify.

(5) If the inspector requests any further information from the appellant or the local planning authority at the pre-inquiry meeting, they shall ensure that 2 copies of it have been received by him and a copy has been received by any statutory party within 4 weeks of the conclusion of the pre-inquiry meeting and the inspector shall, as soon as practicable after receipt, send a copy of the further information received from the local planning authority to the appellant and a copy of the further information received from the appellant to the local planning authority.

Amendment

Para (1): words '12 weeks' in square brackets substituted by SI 2015/316, r 5(1), (5). Date in force: 6 April 2015: see SI 2015/316, r 1(1).

8 Inquiry timetable

(1) In respect of all inquiries that appear to the Secretary of State likely to last for 8 days or more, the inspector shall prepare a timetable for the proceedings.

(2) In respect of shorter inquiries, the inspector may at any time prepare a timetable for the proceedings at, or at part of, an inquiry.

(3) The inspector may, at any time, vary the timetable arranged under the preceding paragraphs.

(4) The inspector may specify in a timetable arranged pursuant to this rule a date by which any proof of evidence and summary sent in accordance with rule 14(1) shall be received by him.

9 Notification of appointment of assessor

Where the Secretary of State appoints an assessor, he shall notify [in writing] every person entitled to appear at the inquiry of the name of the assessor and of the matters on which he is to advise the inspector.

Amendment
Words 'in writing' in square brackets inserted by SI 2009/455, r 3(1), (7). Date in force: 6 April 2009 (in relation to appeals and applications made on or after that date): see SI 2009/455, r 1(1), (2)(a).

10 Date and notification of inquiry

(1) The date fixed by the Secretary of State for the holding of an inquiry shall be—

   (a) not later than [20 weeks] after the starting date unless he considers such a date impracticable; or

   (b) the earliest date after that period which he considers to be practicable.

(2) Unless the Secretary of State agrees a lesser period of notice with the appellant and the local planning authority, he shall give not less than 4 weeks written notice of the date, time and place fixed by him for the holding of an inquiry to every person entitled to appear at the inquiry.

[(2A) A written notice shall be taken to have been given by the Secretary of State for the purposes of paragraph (2) where he and any person entitled to appear at the inquiry have agreed that notice of the matters mentioned in that paragraph may instead be accessed by that person on a website, and—

   (a) the notice is a notice to which that agreement applies;

   (b) the Secretary of State has published that notice on a website;

   (c) not less than 4 weeks before the date fixed by the Secretary of State for the holding of the inquiry, the person is notified of—

      (i) the publication of the notice on a website,

      (ii) the address of the website, and

      (iii) the place on the website where the notice may be accessed, and how it may be accessed.]

(3) The Secretary of State may vary the date fixed for the holding of an inquiry, whether or not the date as varied is within the period of [20 weeks] mentioned in paragraph (1); and [paragraphs (2) to (2A)] shall apply to the variation of a date as it applied to the date originally fixed.

Town and Country Planning Appeals (Determination by Inspectors) Rules 2000

(4) The Secretary of State may vary the time or place for the holding of an inquiry and shall give such notice of any such variation as appears to him to be reasonable.

(5) The Secretary of State may in writing require the local planning authority to take one or more of the following steps—
   (a) not less than 2 weeks before the date fixed for the holding of an inquiry, to publish a notice of the inquiry in one or more newspapers circulating in the locality in which the land is situated;
   (b) to send a notice of the inquiry to such persons or classes of persons as he may specify, within such period as he may specify; or
   (c) to post a notice of the inquiry in a conspicuous place near to the land, within such period as he may specify.

(6) Where the land is under the control of the appellant he shall—
   (a) if so required in writing by the Secretary of State, affix a notice of the inquiry firmly to the land or to some object on or near the land, in such manner as to be readily visible to and legible by members of the public; and
   (b) not remove the notice, or cause or permit it to be removed, for such period before the inquiry as the Secretary of State may specify.

(7) Every notice of inquiry published, sent or posted pursuant to paragraph (5), or affixed pursuant to paragraph (6), shall contain—
   (a) a clear statement of the date, time and place of the inquiry and of the powers enabling the inspector to determine the appeal in question;
   (b) a written description of the land sufficient to identify approximately its location;
   (c) a brief description of the subject matter of the appeal; and
   (d) details of where and when copies of the local planning authority's completed questionnaire and any documents sent by and copied to the authority pursuant to rule 6[, article 33 of the 2010 Order, or regulation 8 of the Listed Buildings Regulations,] may be inspected.

Amendment

Para (1): in sub-para (a) words '20 weeks' in square brackets substituted by SI 2015/316, r 5(1), (6)(a). Date in force: 6 April 2015: see SI 2015/316, r 1(1).

Para (2A): inserted by SI 2003/956, art 12(2), Sch 3, para 4(a). Date in force: 31 March 2003: see SI 2003/956, art 1(1).

Para (3): words '20 weeks' in square brackets substituted by SI 2015/316, r 5(1), (6)(b). Date in force: 6 April 2015: see SI 2015/316, r 1(1).

Para (3): words 'paragraphs (2) to (2A)' in square brackets substituted by SI 2003/956, art 12(2), Sch 3, para 4(b). Date in force: 31 March 2003: see SI 2003/956, art 1(1).

Para (7): in sub-para (d) words from ', article 33 of' to 'Listed Buildings Regulations,' in square brackets inserted by SI 2013/2137, r 4(1), (6)(c). Date in force: 1 October 2013: see SI 2013/2137, r 1; for transitional provisions and savings see rr 6, 7 thereof.

11 Appearances at inquiry

(1) The persons entitled to appear at an inquiry are—
   (a) the appellant;
   (b) the local planning authority;

(c) any of the following bodies if the land is situated in their area and they are not the local planning authority—
   - (i) a county or district council;
   - (ii) an enterprise zone authority designated under Schedule 32 to the Local Government, Planning and Land Act 1980;
   - (iii) the Broads Authority, within the meaning of the Norfolk and Suffolk Broads Act 1988;
   - (iv) a housing action trust specified in an order made under section 67(1) of the Housing Act 1988;
   (d) where the land is in an area previously designated as a new town, [the Homes and Communities Agency];
   (e) any statutory party;
   (f) the council of the parish in which the land is situated, if that council made representations to the local planning authority in respect of the application in pursuance of a provision of a development order;
   (g) where the application was required to be notified to the Commission under section 14 of the Listed Buildings Act, the Commission;
   (h) any other person who has sent a [full statement of case] in accordance with rule 6(6).

(2) Nothing in paragraph (1) shall prevent the inspector from permitting any other person to appear at an inquiry, and such permission shall not be unreasonably withheld.

(3) Any person entitled or permitted to appear may do so on his own behalf or be represented by any other person.

Amendment
Para (1): in sub-para (d) words 'the Homes and Communities Agency' in square brackets substituted by SI 2008/2831, art 6, Sch 4, para 1. Date in force: 1 December 2008 (being the date on which the Housing and Regeneration Act 2008, s 5 came into force): see SI 2008/2831, art 1(2) and SI 2008/3068, arts 1(2), 2(1)(b); for transitional provisions and savings see SI 2008/2831, art 6, Sch 4, paras 5, 6 and SI 2008/3068, arts 9, 10.
Para (1): in sub-para (h) words 'full statement of case' in square brackets substituted by SI 2013/2137, r 4(1), (7). Date in force: 1 October 2013: see SI 2013/2137, r 1; for transitional provisions and savings see rr 6, 7 thereof.

12 Representatives of government departments and other authorities at inquiry

(1) Where—
   (a) the Secretary of State or the Commission has given a direction described in rule 4(2)(a) or (b); or
   (b) the Secretary of State or any other Minister of the Crown or any government department, or any body falling within rule 11(1)(c), has expressed a view described in rule 4(2)(c) and the local planning authority have included its terms in a statement served in accordance with rule 6(1),

the appellant, the local planning authority or a person entitled to appear may, not later than 4 weeks before the date of an inquiry, apply in writing to the Secretary of State for a representative of the Secretary of State or of the other Minister, department or body concerned to be made available at the inquiry.

Town and Country Planning Appeals (Determination by Inspectors) Rules 2000

(2) Where an application is made in accordance with paragraph (1), the Secretary of State shall make a representative available to attend the inquiry or, as the case may be, send the application to the other Minister, department or body concerned, who shall make a representative available to attend the inquiry.

(3) Any person attending an inquiry as a representative in pursuance of this rule shall state the reasons for the direction or expressed view and shall give evidence and be subject to cross-examination to the same extent as any other witness.

(4) Nothing in paragraph (3) shall require a representative of a Minister or a government department to answer any question which in the opinion of the inspector is directed to the merits of government policy.

13 Inspector may act in place of Secretary of State

An inspector may in place of the Secretary of State take such steps as the Secretary of State is required or enabled to take under or by virtue of rule 6(6) to (10), ... rule 10, rule 12(1), rule 12(2), rule 21 and rule 22; and where an inspector requires further information or copies pursuant to rules 6(8) or 22, that information or copies shall be sent to him.

Amendment
Words omitted revoked by SI 2009/455, r 3(1), (8). Date in force: 6 April 2009 (in relation to appeals and applications made on or after that date): see SI 2009/455, r 1(1), (2)(a).

14 Proofs of evidence

(1) Any person entitled to appear at an inquiry who proposes to give, or to call another person to give, evidence at the inquiry by reading a proof of evidence shall simultaneously send—
   (a) 2 copies of the proof of evidence, in the case of the local planning authority and the appellant, and 3 copies in the case of any other person, to the Secretary of State together with any written summary; and
   (b) one copy of these to any statutory party;

and the Secretary of State shall, as soon as practicable after receipt, send a copy of each proof of evidence together with any summary to the local planning authority and the appellant.

(2) No written summary shall be required where the proof of evidence proposed to be read contains no more than 1500 words.

(3) The proof of evidence and any summary shall be received by the Secretary of State no later than—
   (a) 4 weeks before the date fixed for the holding of the inquiry, or
   (b) where a timetable has been arranged pursuant to rule 8, which specifies a date by which the proof of evidence and any summary shall be received by the Secretary of State, that date.

(4) The Secretary of State shall send to the inspector, as soon as practicable after receipt, any proof of evidence together with any summary sent to him in accordance with this rule and received by him within the relevant period, if any, specified in this rule.

(5) Where a written summary is provided in accordance with paragraph (1), only that summary shall be read at the inquiry, unless the inspector permits or requires otherwise.

(6) Any person required by this rule to send copies of a proof of evidence to the inspector shall send with them the same number of copies of the whole, or the relevant part, of any document referred to in the proof of evidence, unless a copy of the document or part of the document in question is already available for inspection pursuant to rule 6(13).

(7) The local planning authority shall afford to any person who so requests a reasonable opportunity to inspect and, where practicable, take copies of any document sent to or by them in accordance with this rule.

[(8) For the purposes of the previous paragraph an opportunity shall be taken to have been afforded to a person where the person is notified, in a manner for the time being agreed between him and the local planning authority for that purpose, of—

(a) publication of the relevant document on a website,

(b) the address of the website,

(c) the place on the website where the document may be accessed, and how it may be accessed.]

Amendment

Para (8): inserted by SI 2003/956, art 12(2), Sch 3, para 5. Date in force: 31 March 2003: see SI 2003/956, art 1(1).

15 Statement of common ground

(1) The local planning authority and the appellant shall—

(a) together prepare an agreed statement of common ground; and

(b) ensure that the Secretary of State and any statutory party receives a copy of it, [within [6 weeks] of the starting date].

(2) The local planning authority shall afford to any person, who so requests, a reasonable opportunity to inspect and, where practicable, take copies of the statement of common ground sent to the Secretary of State.

[(3) For the purposes of the previous paragraph an opportunity shall be taken to have been afforded to a person where the person is notified, in a manner for the time being agreed between him and the local planning authority for that purpose, of—

(a) publication of the statement of common ground on a website,

(b) the address of the website,

(c) the place on the website where the document may be accessed, and how it may be accessed.]

Amendment

Para (1): in sub-para (b) words from 'within' to 'the starting date' in square brackets substituted by SI 2009/455, r 3(1), (9). Date in force: 6 April 2009 (in relation to appeals and applications made on or after that date): see SI 2009/455, r 1(1), (2)(a).

Para (1): in sub-para (b) words '6 weeks' in square brackets substituted by SI 2015/316, r 5(1), (7). Date in force: 6 April 2015: see SI 2015/316, r 1(1).

Para (3): inserted by SI 2003/956, art 12(2), Sch 3, para 6. Date in force: 31 March 2003: see SI 2003/956, art 1(1).

16 Procedure at inquiry

(1) Except as otherwise provided in these Rules, the inspector shall determine the procedure at an inquiry.

Town and Country Planning Appeals (Determination by Inspectors) Rules 2000

(2) At the start of the inquiry the inspector shall identify what are, in his opinion, the main issues to be considered at the inquiry and any matters on which he requires further explanation from the persons entitled or permitted to appear.

(3) Nothing in paragraph (2) shall preclude any person entitled or permitted to appear from referring to issues which they consider relevant to the consideration of the appeal but which were not issues identified by the inspector pursuant to that paragraph.

(4) Unless in any particular case the inspector otherwise determines, the local planning authority shall begin and the appellant shall have the right of final reply; and the other persons entitled or permitted to appear shall be heard in such order as the inspector may determine.

(5) A person entitled to appear at an inquiry shall be entitled to call evidence and the appellant, the local planning authority and any statutory party shall be entitled to cross-examine persons giving evidence, but, subject to the foregoing and paragraphs (6) and [(9)], the calling of evidence and the cross-examination of persons giving evidence shall otherwise be at the discretion of the inspector.

(6) The inspector may refuse to permit the—

   (a) giving or production of evidence;

   (b) cross-examination of persons giving evidence; or

   (c) presentation of any other matter,

   which he considers to be irrelevant or repetitious; but where he refuses to permit the giving of oral evidence, the person wishing to give the evidence may submit to him any evidence or other matter in writing before the close of the inquiry.

(7) Where a person gives evidence at an inquiry by reading a summary of his proof of evidence in accordance with rule 14(5)—

   (a) the proof of evidence referred to in rule 14(1) shall be treated as tendered in evidence, unless the person required to provide the summary notifies the inspector that he now wishes to rely on the contents of the summary alone; and

   (b) the person whose evidence the proof of evidence contains shall then be subject to cross-examination on it to the same extent as if it were evidence he had given orally.

(8) The inspector may direct that facilities shall be afforded to any person appearing at an inquiry to take or obtain copies of documentary evidence open to public inspection.

(9) The inspector may—

   (a) require any person appearing or present at an inquiry who, in his opinion, is behaving in a disruptive manner to leave; and

   (b) refuse to permit that person to return; or

   (c) permit him to return only on such conditions as he may specify,

   but any such person may submit to him any evidence or other matter in writing before the close of the inquiry.

(10) The inspector may allow any person to alter or add to a [full statement of case] received by the Secretary of State or him under rule 6[, article 33 of the

2010 Order, or regulation 8 of the Listed Buildings Regulations,] so far as may be necessary for the purposes of the inquiry; but he shall (if necessary by adjourning the inquiry) give every other person entitled to appear who is appearing at the inquiry an adequate opportunity of considering any fresh matter or document.

(11) The inspector may proceed with an inquiry in the absence of any person entitled to appear at it.

(12) The inspector may take into account any written representation or evidence or any other document received by him from any person before an inquiry opens or during the inquiry provided that he discloses it at the inquiry.

(13) The inspector may from time to time adjourn an inquiry and, if the date, time and place of the adjourned inquiry are announced before the adjournment, no further notice shall be required.

(14) In respect of any inquiry that the Secretary of State expects to last for 8 or more days, any person, who appears at the inquiry and makes closing submissions, shall by the close of the inquiry provide the inspector with a copy of their closing submissions in writing.

Amendment

Para (5): reference to '(9)' in square brackets substituted by SI 2009/455, r 3(1), (10). Date in force: 6 April 2009 (in relation to appeals and applications made on or after that date): see SI 2009/455, r 1(1), (2)(a).

Para (10): words 'full statement of case' in square brackets substituted by SI 2013/2137, r 4(1), (9)(a). Date in force: 1 October 2013: see SI 2013/2137, r 1; for transitional provisions and savings see rr 6, 7 thereof.

Para (10): words from ', article 33 of' to 'Listed Buildings Regulations,' in square brackets inserted by SI 2013/2137, r 4(1), (9)(b). Date in force: 1 October 2013: see SI 2013/2137, r 1; for transitional provisions and savings see rr 6, 7 thereof.

17 Site inspections

(1) The inspector may make an unaccompanied inspection of the land before or during an inquiry without giving notice of his intention to the persons entitled to appear at the inquiry.

(2) During an inquiry or after its close, the inspector—
  (a) may inspect the land in the company of the appellant, the local planning authority and any statutory party; and
  (b) shall make such an inspection if so requested by the appellant or the local planning authority before or during an inquiry.

(3) In all cases where the inspector intends to make an accompanied inspection he shall announce during the inquiry the date and time at which he proposes to make it.

(4) The inspector shall not be bound to defer an inspection of the kind referred to in paragraph (2) where any person mentioned in that paragraph is not present at the time appointed.

18 Procedure after inquiry

(1) Where an assessor has been appointed, he may, after the close of the inquiry make a report in writing to the inspector in respect of the matters on which he

was appointed to advise, and where he does so the inspector shall state in his notification of his decision pursuant to rule 19 that such a report was made.

(2) When making his decision the inspector may disregard any written representations or evidence or any other document received after the close of the inquiry.

(3) If, after the close of an inquiry, an inspector proposes to take into consideration any new evidence or any new matter of fact (not being a matter of government policy) which was not raised at the inquiry and which he considers to be material to his decision, he shall not come to a decision without first—

   (a) notifying [in writing] the persons entitled to appear at the inquiry who appeared at it of the matter in question; and

   (b) affording them an opportunity of making written representations to him or of asking for the re-opening of the inquiry,

and they shall ensure that such written representations or request to re-open the inquiry are received by the Secretary of State within 3 weeks of the date of the notification.

(4) An inspector may, as he thinks fit, cause an inquiry to be re-opened, and he shall do so if asked by the appellant or the local planning authority in the circumstances and within the period mentioned in paragraph (3); and where an inquiry is re-opened—

   (a) the inspector shall send to the persons entitled to appear at the inquiry who appeared at it a written statement of the matters with respect to which further evidence is invited; and

   (b) paragraphs (2) to (7) of rule 10 shall apply as if the references to an inquiry were references to a re-opened inquiry.

Amendment

Para (3): in sub-para (a) words 'in writing' in square brackets inserted by SI 2009/455, r 3(1), (11). Date in force: 6 April 2009 (in relation to appeals and applications made on or after that date): see SI 2009/455, r 1(1), (2)(a).

19 Notification of decision

(1) The inspector shall, as soon as practicable, notify his decision on an appeal, and his reasons for it, in writing to—

   (a) all persons entitled to appear at the inquiry who did appear, and

   (b) any other person who, having appeared at the inquiry, has asked to be notified of the decision.

[(1A) Notification in writing of a decision and reasons shall be taken to have been given to a person for the purposes of this rule where—

   (a) the Secretary of State and the person have agreed that decisions and reasons required under this rule to be given in writing may instead be accessed by that person via a website;

   (b) the decision and reasons are a decision and reasons to which that agreement applies;

   (c) the Secretary of State has published the decision and reasons on a website;

   (d) the person is notified, in a manner for the time being agreed between him and the Secretary of State, of—

Town and Country Planning Appeals (Determination by Inspectors) Rules 2000

- (i) the publication of the decision and reasons on a website;
- (ii) the address of the website;
- (iii) the place on the website where the decision and reasons may be accessed, and how they may be accessed.]

(2) Any person entitled to be notified of the inspector's decision under paragraph (1) may apply to the Secretary of State in writing for an opportunity to inspect any documents listed in the notification and any report made by an assessor and the Secretary of State shall afford him that opportunity.

[(2A) For the purposes of the previous paragraph an opportunity shall be taken to have been afforded to a person where that person is notified of—

- (a) publication of the relevant documents on a website;
- (b) the address of the website;
- (c) the place on the website where the documents may be accessed, and how they may be accessed.]

(3) Any application made pursuant to paragraph (2) shall be received by the Secretary of State within 6 weeks of the date of the decision.

Amendment

Para (1A): inserted by SI 2003/956, art 12(2), Sch 3, para 7(a). Date in force: 31 March 2003: see SI 2003/956, art 1(1).

Para (2A): inserted by SI 2003/956, art 12(2), Sch 3, para 7(b). Date in force: 31 March 2003: see SI 2003/956, art 1(1).

20 Procedure following quashing of decision

(1) Where a decision of an inspector on an appeal in respect of which an inquiry has been held is quashed in proceedings before any court, the Secretary of State—

- (a) shall send to the persons entitled to appear at the inquiry who appeared at it a written statement of the matters with respect to which further representations are invited for the purposes of his further consideration of the appeal; and
- (b) shall afford to those persons the opportunity of making written representations to him in respect of those matters or of asking for the re-opening of the inquiry; and
- (c) may, as he thinks fit, cause the inquiry to be re-opened (whether by the same or a different inspector), and if he does so paragraphs (2) to (7) of rule 10 shall apply as if the references to an inquiry were references to a re-opened inquiry.

(2) Those persons making representations or asking for the inquiry to be re-opened under paragraph (1)(b) shall ensure that such representations or requests are received by the Secretary of State within 3 weeks of the date of the written statement sent under paragraph (1)(a).

21 Allowing further time

The Secretary of State may at any time in any particular case allow further time for the taking of any step which is required or enabled to be taken by virtue of these Rules, and references in these Rules to a day by which, or a period within which, any step is required or enabled to be taken shall be construed accordingly.

22 Additional copies

(1) The Secretary of State may at any time before the close of an inquiry request from any person entitled to appear additional copies of the following—

    (a) a [full statement of case] sent in accordance with rule 6[, article 33 of the 2010 Order, or regulation 8 of the Listed Buildings Regulations];

    (b) a proof of evidence sent in accordance with rule 14; or

    (c) any other document or information sent to the Secretary of State before or during an inquiry,

and may specify the time within which such copies should be received by him.

(2) Any person so requested shall ensure that the copies are received by the Secretary of State within the period specified.

Amendment

Para (1): in sub-para (a) words 'full statement of case' in square brackets substituted by SI 2013/2137, r 4(1), (10)(a). Date in force: 1 October 2013: see SI 2013/2137, r 1; for transitional provisions and savings see rr 6, 7 thereof.

Para (1): in sub-para (a) words ', article 33 of the 2010 Order, or regulation 8 of the Listed Buildings Regulations' in square brackets inserted by SI 2013/2137, r 4(1), (10)(b). Date in force: 1 October 2013: see SI 2013/2137, r 1; for transitional provisions and savings see rr 6, 7 thereof.

[23 Sending of notices etc]

[Notices or documents required or authorised to be sent or supplied under these Rules may be sent or supplied—

    (a) by post; or

    (b) by using electronic communications to send or supply the notice or document (as the case may be) to a person at such address as may for the time being be specified by the person for that purpose.]

Amendment

Substituted by SI 2003/956, art 12(2), Sch 3, para 8. Date in force: 31 March 2003: see SI 2003/956, art 1(1).

[23A Withdrawal of consent to use of electronic communications]

[Where a person is no longer willing to accept the use of electronic communications for any purpose which, under these Rules, is capable of being carried out using such communications, he shall give notice in writing—

    (a) withdrawing any address notified to the Secretary of State or (as the case may be) to a local planning authority for that purpose, or

    (b) revoking any agreement entered into with the Secretary of State or (as the case may be) with a local planning authority for that purpose,

and such withdrawal or revocation shall be final and shall take effect on a date specified by the person in the notice but not less than seven days after the date on which the notice is given.]

Amendment

Inserted by SI 2003/956, art 12(2), Sch 3, para 9. Date in force: 31 March 2003: see SI 2003/956, art 1(1).

Town and Country Planning Appeals (Determination by Inspectors) Rules 2000

24 Mayor of London

(1) In this rule 'the Mayor' means the Mayor of London.

(2) Where an inquiry is held into an appeal arising from an application in respect of which the Mayor has directed the local planning authority to refuse the application these Rules shall apply subject to the following modifications—

[(a) in rule 3A—

(i) in paragraph (1), after 'the appellant' insert ', the Mayor';

(ii) in paragraph (2), after 'the appellant' insert ', the Mayor';]

(b) in rule 4—

(i) in paragraph (1) after 'inform the Secretary of State' and after 'inform the appellant' insert ', the Mayor';

(ii) in paragraph (2) after sub-paragraph (d) insert

'or

(e) the Mayor has given to the local planning authority a direction to refuse the application for planning permission.';

(iii) in paragraph (4)(a) after the 'Secretary of State' insert ', the Mayor';

(c) in rule 6—

(i) in paragraph (1) after 'The local planning authority' insert 'and the Mayor' and for '2' substitute '3';

[(ii) in paragraph (3) for '2' substitute '3';]

(iii) for paragraph (4) substitute—

'The Secretary of State shall, as soon as practicable after receipt, send—

(a) copies of the [statements] of case of [the appellant and] ... the Mayor to the local planning authority;

(b) copies of the [statements] of case of [the appellant and] ... the local planning authority to the Mayor; and

(c) copies of the statements of case of the local planning authority and the Mayor to the appellant.';

[(iiia) in paragraph (5) for 'The appellant and the local planning authority may in writing each require the other' substitute 'Any party required to provide a statement of case pursuant to paragraph (1) or (3) may in writing require any other party so required';]

(iv) ...

(v) in paragraph (6) for '3' substitute '4' and after 'the local planning authority' insert ', the Mayor';

(vi) in paragraph (7)(a) after 'the appellant' insert ', the Mayor';

(vii) in paragraph (9) after 'local planning authority' insert ', the Mayor', in sub-paragraph (a) for '2' substitute '3' and for 'send a copy of the further information received from the local planning authority to the appellant and a copy of the further information received from the appellant to the local planning authority' substitute—

'send—
(a) copies of the further information received from the appellant and the local planning authority to the Mayor;
(b) copies of the further information received from the appellant and the local planning authority to the Mayor; and
(c) copies of the further information received from the local planning authority and the Mayor to the appellant.';

(viii) in paragraph (10) for '3' substitute '4' and after 'the local planning authority' insert ', the Mayor';

(ix) ...

(x) ...

(d) in rule 7—
  (i) in paragraph (1) after 'the local planning authority' insert ', the Mayor'; and
  (ii) in paragraph (5) after 'from the appellant' insert ', the Mayor', for '2' substitute '3' and delete all the words after 'receipt,' and substitute—

  'send—
  (a) copies of the further information received from the appellant and the Mayor to the local planning authority;
  (b) copies of the further information received from the appellant and the local planning authority to the Mayor; and
  (c) copies of the further information received from the local planning authority and the Mayor to the appellant';

(e) in rule 10(2) after 'the appellant' insert ', the Mayor';

(f) in rule 11 after paragraph (1)(h) insert—
  '(i) the Mayor in relation to an inquiry arising from an application in respect of which he has given to the local planning authority a direction to refuse the application for planning permission.';

(g) in rule 12—
  (i) after paragraph (1)(b) insert—

  'or
  (c) the Mayor has given to the local planning authority a direction to refuse the application for planning permission,'; and

  (ii) after 'body concerned' insert 'or of the mayor';

(h) in rule 14—
  (i) in paragraph (1)(a) after 'the local planning authority' insert ', the Mayor', for '2' substitute '3' and for '3' substitute '4'; and
  (ii) in paragraph (1) for 'summary to the local planning authority and the appellant' substitute 'summary to the local planning authority, the Mayor and the appellant';

(i) in rule 15(1) after 'The local planning authority' insert ', the Mayor';

(j) in rule 16(5) after 'the local planning authority' insert ', the Mayor'; and

Town and Country Planning Appeals (Determination by Inspectors) Rules 2000

    (k) in rule 18(4) after 'by the appellant' insert ', the Mayor'.

(3) Where an inquiry is held into an appeal arising from an application which the local planning authority was required to notify to the Mayor but which is not an appeal falling within paragraph (1), these Rules shall apply as if the Mayor were a statutory party.

Amendment

Para (2): sub-para (a) substituted by SI 2009/455, r 3(1), (12)(a). Date in force: 6 April 2009 (in relation to appeals and applications made on or after that date): see SI 2009/455, r 1(1), (2)(a).

Para (2): sub-para (c)(ii) further substituted by SI 2015/316, r 5(1), (8)(a). Date in force: 6 April 2015: see SI 2015/316, r 1(1).

Para (2): in sub-para (c)(iii), in r 6(4)(a) (as set out) word 'statements' in square brackets substituted by SI 2015/316, r 5(1), (8)(b)(i). Date in force: 6 April 2015: see SI 2015/316, r 1(1).

Para (2): in sub-para (c)(iii), in r 6(4)(a) (as set out) words 'the appellant and' in square brackets inserted by SI 2015/316, r 5(1), (8)(b)(i). Date in force: 6 April 2015: see SI 2015/316, r 1(1).

Para (2): in sub-para (c)(iii), in r 6(4)(a) (as set out) words omitted revoked by SI 2013/2137, r 4(1), (11)(c)(i). Date in force: 1 October 2013: see SI 2013/2137, r 1; for transitional provisions and savings see rr 6, 7 thereof.

Para (2): in sub-para (c)(iii), in r 6(4)(b) (as set out) word 'statements' in square brackets substituted by SI 2015/316, r 5(1), (8)(b)(ii). Date in force: 6 April 2015: see SI 2015/316, r 1(1).

Para (2): in sub-para (c)(iii), in r 6(4)(b) (as set out) words 'the appellant and' in square brackets inserted by SI 2015/316, r 5(1), (8)(b)(ii). Date in force: 6 April 2015: see SI 2015/316, r 1(1).

Para (2): in sub-para (c)(iii), in r 6(4)(b) (as set out) words omitted revoked by SI 2013/2137, r 4(1), (11)(c)(ii). Date in force: 1 October 2013: see SI 2013/2137, r 1; for transitional provisions and savings see rr 6, 7 thereof.

Para (2): sub-para (c)(iiia) inserted by SI 2015/316, r 5(1), (8)(c). Date in force: 6 April 2015: see SI 2015/316, r 1(1).

Para (2): sub-para (c)(iv) revoked by SI 2013/2137, r 4(1), (11)(d). Date in force: 1 October 2013: see SI 2013/2137, r 1; for transitional provisions and savings see rr 6, 7 thereof.

Para (2): sub-para (c)(ix), (x) revoked by SI 2009/455, r 3(1), (12)(b). Date in force: 6 April 2009 (in relation to appeals and applications made on or after that date): see SI 2009/455, r 1(1), (2)(a).

[24A Advertisement appeals]

[(1) Where an inquiry is held into an appeal under section 78 of the Planning Act, as applied by regulations made under section 220 of that Act, these Rules shall apply, subject to the modifications in this rule.

(2) In rule 2 (interpretation), after the definition of 'starting date', insert—

    "'statement of case' means, and is comprised of, a written statement which contains full particulars of the case which a person proposes to put forward at an inquiry and a list of any documents which that person intends to refer to or put in evidence;'.

(3) In rule 4(4) (preliminary information to be supplied by local planning authority) for '1 week' substitute '2 weeks'.

(4) In rule 6 (receipt of full statements of case etc)—

Town and Country Planning Appeals (Determination by Inspectors) Rules 2000

    (a) in the heading, omit the word 'full';
    (b) for 'full statement of case' substitute 'statement of case' wherever it appears;
    (c) in paragraph (1) for '5 weeks' substitute '6 weeks';
    (d) for paragraph (3) substitute—

        '(3) The appellant shall ensure that, within 6 weeks of the starting date, 2 copies of their statement of case have been received by the Secretary of State and a copy has been received by any statutory party.';

    (e) in paragraph (4) after 'to the appellant' insert 'and a copy of the appellant's statement of case to the local planning authority';
    (f) after paragraph (4) insert—

        '(5) The appellant and the local planning authority may in writing each require the other to send them a copy of any document, or of the relevant part of any document, referred to in the list of documents comprised in their statement of case; and any such document or relevant part, shall be sent, as soon as practicable, to the party who required it.';

    (g) after paragraph (10), insert—

        '(11) Any person other than the appellant who sends a statement of case to the Secretary of State shall send with it a copy of—

            (a) any document; or
            (b) the relevant part of any document,

        referred to in the list comprised in that statement, unless a copy of the document or part of the document in question is already available for inspection pursuant to paragraph (13).';

    (h) in paragraph (12) after 'specified' insert 'in this rule'; and
    (i) in paragraph (13)(b) after 'statement of case' insert 'together with a copy of any document, or of the relevant part of any document referred to in the list comprised in that statement'.]

Amendment
Inserted by SI 2015/316, r 5(1), (4). Date in force: 6 April 2015: see SI 2015/316, r 1(1).

25 Revocation, savings and transitional provisions

(1) Subject to paragraph (2), the Town and Country Planning Appeals (Determination by Inspectors) (Inquiries Procedure) Rules 1992 are hereby revoked in relation to England.

(2) Subject to paragraph (3) any appeal to which the 1992 Rules applied which has not been determined on the date when these Rules come into force, shall be continued under the 1992 Rules.

(3) Where a decision of an inspector on an appeal to which the 1992 Rules applied is subsequently quashed in proceedings before any court, the decision shall be re-determined in accordance with the Town and Country Planning (Inquiries Procedure) (England) Rules 2000.

(SI 2000/1626)

Town and Country Planning (Hearings Procedure) (England) Rules 2000

1 Citation, commencement and extent

(1) These Rules may be cited as the Town and Country Planning (Hearings Procedure) (England) Rules 2000.

(2) These Rules shall come into force on 1st August 2000.

(3) These Rules extend to England only.

2 Interpretation

[(1)] In these Rules—

'document' includes a photograph, map or plan;

['draft statement of common ground' means the draft statement of common ground (if any) submitted in accordance with article 33 of the 2010 Order or regulation 8 of the Listed Buildings Regulations;]

['electronic communication' has the meaning given in section 15(1) of the Electronic Communications Act 2000;]

['full statement of case'—

(a) means, in relation to the appellant, the full statement of case submitted with their notice of appeal under article 33 of the 2010 Order or regulation 8 of the Listed Buildings Regulations; and

(b) in relation to everyone else means, and is comprised of, a written statement which contains full particulars of the case which a person proposes to put forward and copies of any documents which that person intends to refer to or put in evidence;]

'hearing' means a hearing in relation to which these Rules apply;

...

'inquiry' means a local inquiry in relation to which the Town and Country Planning (Inquiries Procedure) (England) Rules 2000 or the Town and Country Planning Appeals (Determination by Inspectors) (Inquiries Procedure) (England) Rules 2000 apply;

'inspector' means—

(a) in relation to a transferred appeal, a person appointed by the Secretary of State to determine an appeal;

(b) in relation to a non-transferred appeal, a person appointed by the Secretary of State to hold a hearing or a re-opened hearing;

'land' means the land or building to which a hearing relates;

'the Listed Buildings Act' means the Planning (Listed Buildings and Conservation Areas) Act 1990;

['the Listed Buildings Regulations' means the Planning (Listed Buildings and Conservation Areas) Regulations 1990;]

'local planning authority' means the body who were responsible for dealing with the application occasioning the appeal;

'non-transferred appeal' means an appeal which falls to be determined by the Secretary of State, including an appeal which falls to be so determined by virtue of a direction under paragraph 3(1) of Schedule 6 to the Planning Act or paragraph 3(1) of Schedule 3 to the Listed Buildings Act;

['the 2010 Order' means the Town and Country Planning (Development Management Procedure) (England) (Order) 2010;]

'the Planning Act' means the Town and Country Planning Act 1990;

'questionnaire' means a document in the form supplied by the Secretary of State to local planning authorities for the purpose of proceedings under these Rules[, and for this purpose a form is taken to be supplied where the Secretary of State has published it on a website and has notified the local planning authority of—

(i) publication of the form on the website,

(ii) the address of the website, and

(iii) the place on the website where the form may be accessed, and how it may be accessed];

...

['starting date' means the date of the notice given by the Secretary of State under rule 3A;]

['statement of common ground' means a written statement prepared jointly by the local planning authority and the appellant, which contains agreed factual information about the proposal which is the subject of the appeal;]

'statutory party' means—

(a) a person mentioned in paragraph (1)(b)(i) of article 19 of the Town and Country Planning (General Development Procedure) Order 1995 whose representations the Secretary of State is required by paragraph (3) of that article to take into account in determining the appeal to which a hearing relates; and such a person whose representations the local planning authority were required by paragraph (1) of that article to take into account in determining the application occasioning the appeal; and

(b) a person whose representations the Secretary of State is required by paragraphs (3)(b) and (5) of regulation 6 of the Planning (Listed Buildings and Conservation Areas) Regulations 1990 to take into account in determining the appeal to which a hearing relates; and a person whose representations the local planning authority were required by paragraph (3)(b) of that regulation to take into account in determining the application occasioning the appeal; and

'transferred appeal' means an appeal which falls to be determined by a person appointed by the Secretary of State under Schedule 6 to the Planning Act or Schedule 3 to the Listed Buildings Act.

Town and Country Planning (Hearings Procedure) (England) Rules 2000

[(2) In these Rules, and in relation to the use of electronic communications for any purpose of these Rules which is capable of being effected electronically—

(a) the expression 'address' includes any number or address used for the purposes of such communications, except that where these Rules impose an obligation on any person to provide a name and address to any other person, the obligation shall not be fulfilled unless the person on whom it is imposed provides a postal address;

(b) references to statements, notices, or other documents, or to copies of such documents, include references to such documents or copies of them in electronic form.

(3) Paragraphs (4) to (8) apply where an electronic communication is used by a person for the purpose of fulfilling any requirement in these Rules to give or send any statement, notice or other document to any other person ('the recipient').

(4) The requirement shall be taken to be fulfilled where the document transmitted by means of the electronic communication is—

(a) capable of being accessed by the recipient,

(b) legible in all material respects, and

(c) sufficiently permanent to be used for subsequent reference.

(5) In paragraph (4), 'legible in all material respects' means that the information contained in the statement, notice or document is available to the recipient to no lesser extent than it would be if sent or given by means of a document in printed form.

(6) Where the electronic communication is received by the recipient outside the recipient's business hours, it shall be taken to have been received on the next working day; and for this purpose 'working day' means a day which is not a Saturday, Sunday, Bank Holiday or other public holiday.

(7) A requirement in these Rules that any document should be in writing is fulfilled where that document meets the criteria in paragraph (4), and 'written' and cognate expressions are to be construed accordingly.

(8) A requirement in these Rules to send more than one copy of a statement or other document may be complied with by sending one copy only of the statement or other document in question.]

Amendment

Para (1): numbered as such by SI 2003/956, art 12(3), Sch 4, para 1. Date in force: 31 March 2003: see SI 2003/956, art 1(1).

Para (1): definition 'draft statement of common ground' inserted by SI 2013/2137, r 5(1), (2)(a). Date in force: 1 October 2013: see SI 2013/2137, r 1; for transitional provisions and savings see rr 6, 7 thereof.

Para (1): definition 'electronic communication' inserted by SI 2003/956, art 12(3), Sch 4, para 1(a). Date in force: 31 March 2003: see SI 2003/956, art 1(1).

Para (1): definition 'full statement of case' inserted by SI 2013/2137, r 5(1), (2)(b). Date in force: 1 October 2013: see SI 2013/2137, r 1; for transitional provisions and savings see rr 6, 7 thereof.

Para (1): definition 'hearing statement' (omitted) revoked by SI 2013/2137, r 5(1), (2)(c). Date in force: 1 October 2013: see SI 2013/2137, r 1; for transitional provisions and savings see rr 6, 7 thereof.

Town and Country Planning (Hearings Procedure) (England) Rules 2000

Para (1): definition 'the Listed Buildings Regulations' inserted by SI 2013/2137, r 5(1), (2)(d). Date in force: 1 October 2013: see SI 2013/2137, r 1; for transitional provisions and savings see rr 6, 7 thereof.

Para (1): definition 'the 2010 Order' inserted by SI 2013/2137, r 5(1), (2)(e). Date in force: 1 October 2013: see SI 2013/2137, r 1; for transitional provisions and savings see rr 6, 7 thereof.

Para (1): in definition 'questionnaire' words from ', and for this' to 'may be accessed' in square brackets inserted by SI 2003/956, art 12(3), Sch 4, para 1(b). Date in force: 31 March 2003: see SI 2003/956, art 1(1).

Para (1): definition 'the relevant notice' (omitted) revoked by SI 2009/455, r 2(1), (2)(a). Date in force: 6 April 2009 (in relation to appeals and applications made on or after that date): see SI 2009/455, r 1(1), (2)(a).

Para (1): definition 'starting date' substituted by SI 2009/455, r 2(1), (2)(b). Date in force: 6 April 2009 (in relation to appeals and applications made on or after that date): see SI 2009/455, r 1(1), (2)(a).

Para (1): definition 'statement of common ground' inserted by SI 2013/2137, r 5(1), (2)(f). Date in force: 1 October 2013: see SI 2013/2137, r 1; for transitional provisions and savings see rr 6, 7 thereof.

Paras (2)–(8): inserted by SI 2003/956, art 12(3), Sch 4, para 2. Date in force: 31 March 2003: see SI 2003/956, art 1(1).

3 Application of Rules

(1) These Rules apply in relation to any hearing held in England for the purposes of a non-transferred or a transferred appeal made on or after 1st August 2000 under—

    (a) section 78 of the Planning Act;

    (b) section 20 of the Listed Buildings Act…

    (c) …

….

[(1A) These Rules apply in relation to any hearing held in England for the purposes of a non-transferred or a transferred appeal under section 78 of the Planning Act (as applied by regulations made under section 220 of that Act) subject to the modifications in rule 20A.]

(2) Where these Rules apply in relation to an appeal which at some time fell to be disposed of in accordance with the Town and Country Planning (Inquiries Procedure) (England) Rules 2000 or the Town and Country Planning Appeals (Determination by Inspectors) (Inquiries Procedure) (England) Rules 2000, any step taken or thing done under those Rules which could have been done under any corresponding provision of these Rules shall have effect as if it had been taken or done under that corresponding provision.

Amendment

Para (1): in sub-para (b) semi-colon omitted revoked by SI 2015/316, r 6(1), (2)(a). Date in force: 6 April 2015: see SI 2015/316, r 1(1).

Para (1): sub-para (c) revoked by SI 2013/2146, art 3, Schedule, para 5. Date in force: 1 October 2013: see SI 2013/2146, art 1; for savings see art 4 thereof and for transitional provisions see SI 2013/2148, art 5(4)(a).

Para (1): words omitted revoked by SI 2015/316, r 6(1), (2)(a). Date in force: 6 April 2015: see SI 2015/316, r 1(1).

Para (1A): inserted by SI 2015/316, r 6(1), (2)(b). Date in force: 6 April 2015: see SI 2015/316, r 1(1).

Town and Country Planning (Hearings Procedure) (England) Rules 2000

[3A Notice from the Secretary of State]

[(1) In the case of an appeal under section 78 of the Planning Act [(including an appeal under section 78 of the Planning Act as applied by regulations made under section 220 of that Act)] as soon as practicable after a determination has been made under section 319A of the Planning Act that the appeal is to proceed at a hearing, the Secretary of State shall send a notice to this effect to the appellant and the local planning authority.

(2) In the case of any other appeal to which these Rules apply, the Secretary of State shall, as soon as practicable after receipt of all the documents required to enable the appeal to proceed, send a notice to the appellant and the local planning authority, informing them that a hearing is to be held.]

Amendment

Inserted by SI 2009/455, r 2(1), (3). Date in force: 6 April 2009 (in relation to appeals and applications made on or after that date): see SI 2009/455, r 1(1), (2)(a).

Para (1): words from '(including an appeal' to 'of that Act)' in square brackets inserted by SI 2015/316, r 6(1), (3). Date in force: 6 April 2015: see SI 2015/316, r 1(1).

4 Preliminary information to be supplied by local planning authority

(1) The local planning authority shall, on receipt of the [notice under rule 3A], forthwith inform the Secretary of State and the appellant in writing of the name and address of any statutory party who has made representations to them; and the Secretary of State shall, as soon as practicable thereafter, inform the appellant and the local planning authority in writing of the name and address of any statutory party who has made representations to him.

(2) The local planning authority shall ensure that within [1 week] of the starting date—
   (a) the Secretary of State and the appellant have received a completed questionnaire and a copy of each of the documents referred to in it;
   (b) any—
      (i) statutory party; and
      (ii) other person who made representations to the local planning authority about the application occasioning the appeal,
      has been notified [in writing] that an appeal has been made and of the address to which and of the period within which they may make representations to the Secretary of State.

Amendment

Para (1): words 'notice under rule 3A' in square brackets substituted by SI 2009/455, r 2(1), (4)(a). Date in force: 6 April 2009 (in relation to appeals and applications made on or after that date): see SI 2009/455, r 1(1), (2)(a).

Para (2): words '1 week' in square brackets substituted by SI 2013/2137, r 5(1), (3). Date in force: 1 October 2013: see SI 2013/2137, r 1; for transitional provisions and savings see rr 6, 7 thereof.

Para (2): in sub-para (b) words 'in writing' in square brackets inserted by SI 2009/455, r 2(1), (4)(b). Date in force: 6 April 2009 (in respect of appeals and applications made on or after that date): see SI 2009/455, r 1(1), (2)(a).

5 Notification of name of inspector

(1) This rule applies where a hearing is to be held for the purposes of a transferred appeal.

(2) Subject to paragraph (3), the Secretary of State shall notify [in writing] the name of the inspector to every person entitled to appear at the hearing.

(3) Where the Secretary of State appoints another inspector instead of the person previously appointed and it is not practicable to notify the new appointment before the hearing is held, the inspector holding the hearing shall, at its commencement, announce his name and the fact of his appointment.

Amendment
Para (2): words 'in writing' in square brackets inserted by SI 2009/455, r 2(1), (5). Date in force: 6 April 2009 (in relation to appeals and applications made on or after that date): see SI 2009/455, r 1(1), (2)(a).

6 Receipt of [full statements of case] etc

[(1) As soon as practicable after receiving the information in rule 4(1) (preliminary information to be supplied by local planning authority), the appellant shall ensure that a copy of their full statement of case has been received by any statutory party.

(1A) The local planning authority shall ensure that, within 5 weeks of the starting date, 2 copies of their full statement of case have been received by the Secretary of State, and that a copy has been received by any statutory party.]

(2) The Secretary of State may in writing require the appellant and the local planning authority to provide such further information about the matters contained in their [full statement of case] as he may specify; such information shall be provided in writing and the appellant or the local planning authority, as the case may be, shall ensure that 2 copies are received by the Secretary of State and a copy is received by any statutory party within such period as the Secretary of State may reasonably require.

(3) Any statutory party, and any person who made representations to the local planning authority about the application occasioning the appeal or who was notified about the application occasioning the appeal, shall ensure that the Secretary of State has received 3 copies of any written comments they wish to make concerning the appeal within [5 weeks] of the starting date.

(4) ...

(5) The Secretary of State shall send, as soon as practicable after receipt, a copy of any—

    (a) [full statement of case] received by him pursuant to [paragraph (1A)], [and] further information provided pursuant to paragraph (2) ... from, in each case, the appellant or the local planning authority to the other of those two parties; and

    (b) written comments made by persons pursuant to paragraph (3), to the local planning authority and the appellant.

(6) The local planning authority shall afford to any person who so requests a reasonable opportunity to inspect, and where practicable, take copies of—

(a) the local planning authority's completed questionnaire, [full statement of case] and any document copied to the authority under paragraph (5) [, article 33 of the 2010 Order, or regulation 8 of the Listed Buildings Regulations]; and

(b) further information provided by the authority under paragraph (2) ...,

and shall specify in their [full statement of case] the time and place where such opportunity shall be afforded.

[(6A) For the purposes of the previous paragraph an opportunity shall be taken to have been afforded to a person where the person is notified of—

(a) publication on a website of any document mentioned in sub-paragraph (a) or (b) of the previous paragraph;

(b) the address of the website;

(c) the place on the website where the document may be accessed, and how it may be accessed.]

(7) The Secretary of State shall send to the inspector, as soon as practicable after receipt, any [full statement of case], document, part of any document or written comments received by the Secretary of State within the relevant period specified for receiving such documents pursuant to [paragraphs (1A) to (3), article 33 of the 2010 Order, or regulation 8 of the Listed Buildings Regulations].

(8) In the case of a non-transferred appeal, the Secretary of State, and in the case of a transferred appeal, the inspector, may in determining the appeal disregard any comments made pursuant to [paragraph (3)] which are received after the relevant period specified for receipt.

Amendment

Provision heading: words 'full statements of case' in square brackets substituted by SI 2013/2137, r 5(1), (4)(a). Date in force: 1 October 2013: see SI 2013/2137, r 1; for transitional provisions and savings see rr 6, 7 thereof.

Paras (1), (1A): substituted, for para (1) as originally enacted, by SI 2013/2137, r 5(1), (4)(c). Date in force: 1 October 2013: see SI 2013/2137, r 1; for transitional provisions and savings see rr 6, 7 thereof.

Para (2): words 'full statement of case' in square brackets substituted by SI 2013/2137, r 5(1), (4)(b). Date in force: 1 October 2013: see SI 2013/2137, r 1; for transitional provisions and savings see rr 6, 7 thereof.

Para (3): words '5 weeks' in square brackets substituted by SI 2013/2137, r 5(1), (4)(d). Date in force: 1 October 2013: see SI 2013/2137, r 1; for transitional provisions and savings see rr 6, 7 thereof.

Para (4): revoked by SI 2009/455, r 2(1), (6)(a). Date in force: 6 April 2009 (in relation to appeals and applications made on or after that date): see SI 2009/455, r 1(1), (2)(a).

Para (5): in sub-para (a) words 'full statement of case' in square brackets substituted by SI 2013/2137, r 5(1), (4)(b). Date in force: 1 October 2013: see SI 2013/2137, r 1; for transitional provisions and savings see rr 6, 7 thereof.

Para (5): in sub-para (a) words 'paragraph (1A)' in square brackets substituted by SI 2013/2137, r 5(1), (4)(e). Date in force: 1 October 2013: see SI 2013/2137, r 1; for transitional provisions and savings see rr 6, 7 thereof.

Para (5): in sub-para (a) word 'and' in square brackets inserted by SI 2009/455, r 2(1), (6)(b)(i). Date in force: 6 April 2009 (in relation to appeals and applications made on or after that date): see SI 2009/455, r 1(1), (2)(a).

Para (5): in sub-para (a) words omitted revoked by SI 2009/455, r 2(1), (6)(b)(ii). Date in force: 6 April 2009 (in relation to appeals and applications made on or after that date): see SI 2009/455, r 1(1), (2)(a).

Para (6): words 'full statement of case' in square brackets in both places they occur substituted by SI 2013/2137, r 5(1), (4)(b). Date in force: 1 October 2013: see SI 2013/2137, r 1; for transitional provisions and savings see rr 6, 7 thereof.

Para (6): in sub-para (a) words ', article 33 of the 2010 Order, or regulation 8 of the Listed Buildings Regulations' in square brackets inserted by SI 2013/2137, r 5(1), (4)(f). Date in force: 1 October 2013: see SI 2013/2137, r 1; for transitional provisions and savings see rr 6, 7 thereof.

Para (6): in sub-para (b) words omitted revoked by SI 2009/455, r 2(1), (6)(c). Date in force: 6 April 2009 (in relation to appeals and applications made on or after that date): see SI 2009/455, r 1(1), (2)(a).

Para (6A): inserted by SI 2003/956, art 12(3), Sch 4, para 3. Date in force: 31 March 2003: see SI 2003/956, art 1(1).

Para (7): words 'full statement of case' in square brackets substituted by SI 2013/2137, r 5(1), (4)(b). Date in force: 1 October 2013: see SI 2013/2137, r 1; for transitional provisions and savings see rr 6, 7 thereof.

Para (7): words 'paragraphs (1A) to (3), article 33 of the 2010 Order, or regulation 8 of the Listed Buildings Regulations' in square brackets substituted by SI 2013/2137, r 5(1), (4)(g). Date in force: 1 October 2013: see SI 2013/2137, r 1; for transitional provisions and savings see rr 6, 7 thereof.

Para (8): words 'paragraph (3)' in square brackets substituted by SI 2009/455, r 2(1), (6)(e). Date in force: 6 April 2009 (in relation to appeals and applications made on or after that date): see SI 2009/455, r 1(1), (2)(a).

[6A …]

[…]

Amendment

Inserted by SI 2013/2137, r 5(1), (5). Date in force: 1 October 2013: see SI 2013/2137, r 1; for transitional provisions and savings see rr 6, 7 thereof.

Revoked by virtue of SI 2015/316, r 6(1), (6). Date in force: 6 April 2015: see SI 2015/316, r 1(1).

7 Date and notification of hearing

(1) The date fixed by the Secretary of State for the holding of a hearing shall be—

    (a) not later than [12 weeks] after the starting date, unless he considers such a date impracticable; or

    (b) the earliest date after that period which he considers to be practicable.

(2) Unless the Secretary of State agrees a lesser period of notice with the appellant and the local planning authority, he shall give not less than 4 weeks written notice of the date, time and place fixed by him for the holding of a hearing to every person entitled to appear at the hearing.

[(2A) A written notice shall be taken to have been given by the Secretary of State for the purposes of paragraph (2) where he and any person entitled to appear at the hearing have agreed that notice of the matters mentioned in that paragraph may instead be accessed by that person via a website, and—

    (a) the notice is a notice to which that agreement applies;

(b) the Secretary of State has published the notice on a website;

(c) not less than 4 weeks before the date fixed by the Secretary of State for the holding of the inquiry, the person is notified of—

(i) the publication of the notice on a website,

(ii) the address of the website, and

(iii) the place on the website where the notice may be accessed, and how it may be accessed.]

(3) The Secretary of State may vary the date fixed for the holding of a hearing, whether or not the date as varied is within the period of [12 weeks] mentioned in paragraph (1); and [paragraphs (2) and (2A)] shall apply to a variation of a date as it applied to the date originally fixed.

(4) The Secretary of State may vary the time or place for the holding of a hearing and shall give such notice of any variation as appears to him to be reasonable.

(5) The Secretary of State may in writing require the local planning authority to take one or both of the following steps—

(a) not less than 2 weeks before the date fixed for the holding of a hearing, to publish a notice of the hearing in one or more newspapers circulating in the locality in which the land is situated;

(b) to send a notice of the hearing to such persons or classes of persons as he may specify, within such period as he may specify.

(6) Every notice of hearing published or sent pursuant to paragraph (5) shall contain—

(a) a clear statement of the date, time and place of the hearing and of the powers enabling the Secretary of State or inspector to determine the appeal in question;

(b) a written description of the land sufficient to identify approximately its location;

(c) a brief description of the subject matter of the appeal; and

(d) details of where and when copies of the local planning authority's completed questionnaire and documents sent by and copied to the authority pursuant to rule 6[, article 33 of the 2010 Order, or regulation 8 of the Listed Buildings Regulations,] may be inspected.

Amendment

Para (1): in sub-para (a) words '12 weeks' in square brackets substituted by virtue of SI 2015/316, r 6(1), (7)(a). Date in force: 6 April 2015: see SI 2015/316, r 1(1).

Para (2A): inserted by SI 2003/956, art 12(3), Sch 4, para 4(a). Date in force: 31 March 2003: see SI 2003/956, art 1(1).

Para (3): words '12 weeks' in square brackets substituted by virtue of SI 2015/316, r 6(1), (7)(b). Date in force: 6 April 2015: see SI 2015/316, r 1(1).

Para (3): words 'paragraphs (2) and (2A)' in square brackets substituted by SI 2003/956, art 12(3), Sch 4, para 4(b). Date in force: 31 March 2003: see SI 2003/956, art 1(1).

Para (6): in sub-para (d) words from ', article 33 of' to 'Listed Buildings Regulations,' in square brackets inserted by SI 2013/2137, r 5(1), (6)(c). Date in force: 1 October 2013: see SI 2013/2137, r 1; for transitional provisions and savings see rr 6, 7 thereof.

Town and Country Planning (Hearings Procedure) (England) Rules 2000

8 Method of procedure

(1) [Subject to paragraphs (3) and (4), if] either the appellant or the local planning authority at any time before or during the hearing is of the opinion that the hearings procedure is inappropriate in determining the appeal and that the appeal should not proceed in this way then they may inform the Secretary of State [in writing], before the hearing, or the inspector, during the hearing, of their opinion and the reasons for it, and—

   (a) the Secretary of State, before the hearing, shall, after consulting the other party who may inform the Secretary of State of his opinion [in writing] pursuant to this paragraph, decide whether an inquiry should be arranged instead; or

   (b) the inspector, during the hearing, shall, after consulting the other party who may inform the inspector of his opinion pursuant to this paragraph, decide whether the hearing should be closed and an inquiry held instead.

(2) [Except in the case of an appeal under section 78 of the Planning Act [(including an appeal under section 78 of the Planning Act as applied by regulations made under section 220 of that Act)], if] at any time during a hearing it appears to the inspector that the hearings procedure is inappropriate, he may, after consulting the appellant and the local planning authority, decide to close the proceedings and arrange for an inquiry to be held instead.

[(3) In the case of an appeal under section 78 of the Planning Act [(including an appeal under section 78 of the Planning Act as applied by regulations made under section 220 of that Act)], if either the appellant or the local planning authority at any time before or during a hearing is of the opinion that the hearings procedure is inappropriate to determine the appeal and that the appeal should not proceed in this way then they may inform the Secretary of State in writing, before the hearing, or the inspector, during the hearing and the reasons for it.

(4) Where paragraph (3) applies, Secretary of State shall consult the other party, who may inform the Secretary of State of their opinion in writing pursuant to this paragraph, before exercising the power in section 319A(4) of the Planning Act.]

Amendment

Para (1): words 'Subject to paragraphs (3) and (4), if' in square brackets substituted by SI 2009/455, r 2(1), (7)(a). Date in force: 6 April 2009 (in relation to appeals and applications made on or after that date): see SI 2009/455, r 1(1), (2)(a).

Para (1): words 'in writing' in square brackets inserted by SI 2009/455, r 2(1), (7)(b). Date in force: 6 April 2009 (in relation to appeals and applications made on or after that date): see SI 2009/455, r 1(1), (2)(a).

Para (1): in para (a) words 'in writing' in square brackets inserted by SI 2009/455, r 2(1), (7)(c). Date in force: 6 April 2009 (in relation to appeals and applications made on or after that date): see SI 2009/455, r 1(1), (2)(a).

Para (2): words in square brackets beginning with the words 'Except in the' substituted by SI 2009/455, r 2(1), (8). Date in force: 6 April 2009 (in relation to appeals and applications made on or after that date): see SI 2009/455, r 1(1), (2)(a).

Para (2): words from '(including an appeal' to 'of that Act)' in square brackets inserted by SI 2015/316, r 6(1), (4)(a). Date in force: 6 April 2015: see SI 2015/316, r 1(1).

Paras (3), (4): inserted by SI 2009/455, r 2(1), (9). Date in force: 6 April 2009 (in relation to appeals and applications made on or after that date): see SI 2009/455, r 1(1), (2)(a).

Para (3): words from '(including an appeal' to 'of that Act)' in square brackets inserted by SI 2015/316, r 6(1), (4)(b). Date in force: 6 April 2015: see SI 2015/316, r 1(1).

9 Appearances at hearing

(1) The persons entitled to appear at the hearing are—
   (a) the appellant;
   (b) the local planning authority; and
   (c) any statutory party.

(2) Nothing in paragraph (1) shall prevent the inspector from permitting any other person to appear at a hearing, and such permission shall not be unreasonably withheld.

(3) Any person entitled or permitted to appear may do so on his own behalf or be represented by any other person.

10 Inspector may act in place of Secretary of State in respect of transferred appeals

(1) This rule applies where a hearing is to be held or has been held in respect of a transferred appeal.

(2) An inspector may in place of the Secretary of State take such steps as the Secretary of State is required or enabled to take under or by virtue of rules 6(2), 6(5), 7 and 18; and where an inspector requires further information or copies pursuant to rules 6(2) or 18(2) that information or copies shall be sent to him.

11 Procedure at hearing

(1) Except as otherwise provided in these Rules, the inspector shall determine the procedure at a hearing.

(2) A hearing shall take the form of a discussion led by the inspector and cross-examination shall not be permitted unless the inspector considers that cross-examination is required to ensure a thorough examination of the main issues.

(3) Where the inspector considers that cross-examination is required under paragraph (2) he shall consider, after consulting the appellant and the local planning authority, whether the hearing should be closed and an inquiry held instead.

(4) At the start of the hearing the inspector shall identify what are, in his opinion, the main issues to be considered at the hearing and any matters on which he requires further explanation from any person entitled or permitted to appear.

(5) Nothing in paragraph (4) shall preclude any person entitled or permitted to appear from referring to issues which they consider relevant to the consideration of the appeal but which were not issues identified by the inspector pursuant to that paragraph.

(6) A person entitled to appear at a hearing shall be entitled to call evidence but, subject to the foregoing and paragraphs (7) and (8), the calling of evidence shall otherwise be at the inspector's discretion.

(7) The inspector may refuse to permit the—
   (a) giving or production of evidence; or
   (b) presentation of any other matter,

which he considers to be irrelevant or repetitious; but where he refuses to permit the giving of oral evidence, the person wishing to give the evidence may submit to him any evidence or other matter in writing before the close of the hearing.

(8) The inspector may—
 (a) require any person appearing or present at a hearing who, in his opinion, is behaving in a disruptive manner to leave; and
 (b) refuse to permit that person to return; or
 (c) permit him to return only on such conditions as he may specify,

 but any such person may submit to him any evidence or other matter in writing before the close of the hearing.

(9) The inspector may allow any person to alter or add to a [hearing statement] received under rule 6[, article 33 of the 2010 Order, or regulation 8 of the Listed Buildings Regulations,] so far as may be necessary for the purposes of the hearing; but he shall (if necessary by adjourning the hearing) give every other person entitled to appear who is appearing at the hearing an adequate opportunity of considering any fresh matter or document.

(10) The inspector may proceed with a hearing in the absence of any person entitled to appear at it.

(11) The inspector may take into account any written representation or evidence or any other document received by him from any person before a hearing opens or during the hearing provided that he discloses it at the hearing.

(12) The inspector may from time to time adjourn a hearing and, if the date, time and place of the adjourned hearing are announced at the hearing before the adjournment, no further notice shall be required.

Amendment

Para (9): words 'hearing statement' in square brackets substituted by SI 2015/316, r 6(1), (8). Date in force: 6 April 2015: see SI 2015/316, r 1(1).

Para (9): words from ', article 33 of' to 'Listed Buildings Regulations,' in square brackets inserted by SI 2013/2137, r 5(1), (7)(b). Date in force: 1 October 2013: see SI 2013/2137, r 1; for transitional provisions and savings see rr 6, 7 thereof.

12 Site inspections

(1) Where it appears to the inspector that one or more matters would be more satisfactorily resolved by adjourning the hearing to the appeal site he may adjourn the hearing to that site and conclude the hearing there provided he is satisfied that—
 (a) the hearing would proceed satisfactorily and that no party would be placed at a disadvantage;
 (b) all parties present at the hearing would have the opportunity to attend the adjourned hearing; and
 (c) the local planning authority, the appellant or any statutory party has not raised reasonable objections to it being continued at the appeal site.

(2) Unless the hearing is to be adjourned to the appeal site pursuant to paragraph (1), the inspector—
 (a) may inspect the land during the hearing or after its close; and
 (b) shall inspect the land if requested to do so by the appellant or the local planning authority before or during the hearing.

(3) Where the inspector intends to make an inspection under paragraph (2), he shall ask the appellant and the local planning authority whether they wish to be present.

Town and Country Planning (Hearings Procedure) (England) Rules 2000

(4) Where the appellant or the local planning authority have indicated that they wish to be present the inspector shall announce the date and time at which he proposes to make the inspection during the hearing and shall make the inspection in the company of—

    (a) the appellant and the local planning authority; and

    (b) at the inspector's discretion, any other person entitled or permitted to appear at the hearing who is appearing or did appear at it.

(5) The inspector shall not be bound to defer an inspection of the kind referred to in paragraph (2) where any person mentioned in paragraph (4) is not present at the time appointed.

13 Procedure after hearing—non-transferred appeals

(1) This rule applies where a hearing has been held for the purposes of a non-transferred appeal.

(2) After the close of the hearing, the inspector shall make a report in writing to the Secretary of State which shall include his conclusions and his recommendations or his reasons for not making any recommendations.

(3) When making his determination the Secretary of State may disregard any written representations, evidence or other document received after the hearing has closed.

(4) If, after the close of the hearing, the Secretary of State—

    (a) differs from the inspector on any matter of fact mentioned in, or appearing to him to be material to, a conclusion reached by the inspector, or

    (b) takes into consideration any new evidence or new matter of fact (not being a matter of government policy),

and is for that reason disposed to disagree with a recommendation made by the inspector, he shall not come to a decision which is at variance with that recommendation without first notifying [in writing] the persons entitled to appear at the hearing who appeared at it of his disagreement and the reasons for it; and affording them an opportunity of making written representations to him or (if the Secretary of State has taken into consideration any new evidence or new matter of fact, not being a matter of government policy) of asking for the re-opening of the hearing.

(5) Those making written representations or requesting the hearing to be re-opened pursuant to paragraph (4), shall ensure that such representations or request are received by the Secretary of State within 3 weeks of the date of the Secretary of State's notification under that paragraph.

(6) The Secretary of State may, as he thinks fit, cause a hearing to be re-opened, and he shall do so if asked by the appellant or the local planning authority in the circumstances mentioned in paragraph (4) and within the period mentioned in paragraph (5); and where a hearing is re-opened (whether by the same or a different inspector)—

    (a) the Secretary of State shall send to the persons entitled to appear at the hearing who appeared at it a written statement of the matters with respect to which further evidence is invited; and

    (b) paragraphs (2) to (6) of rule 7 shall apply as if the references to a hearing were references to a re-opened hearing.

Town and Country Planning (Hearings Procedure) (England) Rules 2000

Amendment
Para (4): words 'in writing' in square brackets inserted by SI 2009/455, r 2(1), (10). Date in force: 6 April 2009 (in relation to appeals and applications made on or after that date): see SI 2009/455, r 1(1), (2)(a).

14 Procedure after hearing—transferred appeals

(1) This rule applies where a hearing has been held for the purposes of a transferred appeal.

(2) When making his decision the inspector may disregard any written representations, or evidence or any other document received after the hearing has closed.

(3) If, after the close of the hearing, an inspector proposes to take into consideration any new evidence or any new matter of fact (not being a matter of government policy) which was not raised at the hearing and which he considers to be material to his decision, he shall not come to a decision without first—

    (a) notifying [in writing] persons entitled to appear at the hearing who appeared at it of the matter in question; and

    (b) affording them an opportunity of making written representations to him or of asking for the re-opening of the hearing,

and they shall ensure that such written representations or request to re-open the hearing are received by the Secretary of State within 3 weeks of the date of the notification.

(4) An inspector may, as he thinks fit, cause a hearing to be re-opened and he shall do so if asked by the appellant or the local planning authority in the circumstances and within the period mentioned in paragraph (3); and where a hearing is re-opened—

    (a) the inspector shall send to the persons entitled to appear at the hearing who appeared at it a written statement of the matters with respect to which further evidence is invited; and

    (b) paragraphs (2) to (6) of rule 7 shall apply as if the references to a hearing were references to a re-opened hearing.

Amendment
Para (3): in sub-para (a) words 'in writing' in square brackets inserted by SI 2009/455, r 2(1), (11). Date in force: 6 April 2009 (in relation to appeals and applications made on or after that date): see SI 2009/455, r 1(1), (2)(a).

15 Notification of decision—non-transferred appeals

(1) This rule applies where a hearing has been held for the purposes of a non-transferred appeal.

(2) The Secretary of State shall notify his decision on an appeal, and his reasons for it, in writing to—

    (a) all persons entitled to appear at the hearing who did appear; and

    (b) any other person who, having appeared at the hearing, has asked to be notified of the decision.

[(2A) Notification in writing of a decision and reasons shall also be taken to have been given to a person for the purposes of this rule where—

(a) the Secretary of State and the person have agreed that decisions and reasons required under this rule to be given in writing may instead be accessed by that person on a website;
(b) the decision and reasons are a decision and reasons to which that agreement applies;
(c) the Secretary of State has published the decision and reasons on a website;
(d) the person is notified of—
   (i) the publication of the decision and reasons on a website;
   (ii) the address of the website;
   (iii) the place on the website where the decision and reasons may be accessed, and how they may be accessed.]

(3) Where a copy of the inspector's report is not sent with the notification of the decision, the notification shall be accompanied by a statement of his conclusions and of any recommendations made by him; and if a person entitled to be notified of the decision has not received a copy of that report, he shall be supplied with a copy of it on written application to the Secretary of State.

(4) In this rule 'report' does not include any documents appended to the inspector's report; but any person who has received a copy of the report may apply to the Secretary of State in writing for an opportunity of inspecting any such documents and the Secretary of State shall afford him that opportunity.

[(4A) For the purposes of the previous paragraph an opportunity shall be taken to have been afforded to a person where that person is notified of—
(a) publication of the relevant documents on a website;
(b) the address of the website;
(c) the place on the website where the documents may be accessed, and how they may be accessed.]

(5) A person applying to the Secretary of State under—
(a) paragraph (3) shall ensure that his application is received by the Secretary of State within 4 weeks;
(b) paragraph (4) shall ensure that his application is received by the Secretary of State within 6 weeks,

of the date of the Secretary of State's decision.

Amendment

Para (2A): inserted by SI 2003/956, art 12(3), Sch 4, para 5(a). Date in force: 31 March 2003: see SI 2003/956, art 1(1).

Para (4A): inserted by SI 2003/956, art 12(3), Sch 4, para 5(b). Date in force: 31 March 2003: see SI 2003/956, art 1(1).

16 Notification of decision—transferred appeals

(1) This rule applies where a hearing has been held for the purposes of a transferred appeal.

(2) An inspector shall notify his decision on an appeal, and his reason for it, in writing to—
(a) all persons entitled to appear at the hearing who did appear; and

(b) any other person who, having appeared at the hearing, has asked to be notified of the decision.

(3) Any person entitled to be notified of the inspector's decision under paragraph (2) may apply to the Secretary of State in writing, for an opportunity of inspecting any documents listed in the notification and the Secretary of State shall afford him that opportunity.

(4) Any person making an application under paragraph (3) shall ensure that it is received by the Secretary of State within 6 weeks of the date of the inspector's decision.

[(4A) For the purposes of the previous paragraph an opportunity shall be taken to have been afforded to a person where that person is notified of—

(a) publication of the relevant documents on a website;
(b) the address of the website;
(c) the place on the website where the documents may be accessed, and how they may be accessed.]

Amendment

Para (4A): inserted by SI 2003/956, art 12(3), Sch 4, para 6. Date in force: 31 March 2003: see SI 2003/956, art 1(1).

17 Procedure following quashing of decision

(1) Where a decision of the Secretary of State or an inspector on an appeal in respect of which a hearing has been held is quashed in proceedings before any court, the Secretary of State—

(a) shall send to the persons entitled to appear at the hearing who appeared at it a written statement of the matters with respect to which further representations are invited for the purposes of his further consideration of the appeal;
(b) shall afford to those persons the opportunity of making written representations to him in respect of those matters or of asking for the re-opening of the hearing; and
(c) may, as he thinks fit, cause the hearing to be re-opened or an inquiry held instead (whether by the same or a different inspector) and if he re-opens the hearing paragraphs (2) to (6) of rule 7 shall apply as if the references to a hearing were to a re-opened hearing.

(2) Those persons making representations or asking for the hearing to be re-opened under paragraph (1)(b) shall ensure that such representations or request are received by the Secretary of State within 3 weeks of the date of the written statement sent under paragraph (1)(a).

18 Further time and additional copies

(1) The Secretary of State may at any time in any particular case allow further time for the taking of any step which is required or enabled to be taken by virtue of these Rules, and references in these Rules to a day by which, or a period within which, any step is required or enabled to be taken shall be construed accordingly.

(2) The Secretary of State may at any time before the close of a hearing request from any person entitled to appear additional copies of the following—

Town and Country Planning (Hearings Procedure) (England) Rules 2000

(a) a [hearing statement] or comments sent in accordance with rule 6[, article 33 of the 2010 Order, or regulation 8 of the Listed Buildings Regulations]; or

(b) any other document or information sent to the Secretary of State before or during a hearing,

and may specify the time within which such copies should be received by him and any person so requested shall ensure that the copies are received within the period specified.

Amendment

Para (2): in sub-para (a) words 'hearing statement' in square brackets substituted by SI 2015/316, r 6(1), (9). Date in force: 6 April 2015: see SI 2015/316, r 1(1).

Para (2): in sub-para (a) words from ', article 33 of' to 'Listed Buildings Regulations' in square brackets inserted by SI 2013/2137, r 5(1), (8)(b). Date in force: 1 October 2013: see SI 2013/2137, r 1; for transitional provisions and savings see rr 6, 7 thereof.

[19 Sending of notices etc]

[Notices or documents required or authorised to be sent or supplied under these Rules may be sent or supplied—

(a) by post; or

(b) by using electronic communications to send or supply the notice or document (as the case may be) to a person at such address as may for the time being be specified by the person for that purpose.]

Amendment

Substituted by SI 2003/956, art 12(3), Sch 4, para 7. Date in force: 31 March 2003: see SI 2003/956, art 1(1).

[19A Withdrawal of consent to use of electronic communications]

[Where a person is no longer willing to accept the use of electronic communications for any purpose under these Rules which is capable of being effected electronically, the person shall give notice in writing—

(a) withdrawing any address notified to the Secretary of State or to a local planning authority for that purpose, or

(b) revoking any agreement entered into with the Secretary of State or with a local planning authority for that purpose,

and such withdrawal or revocation shall be final and shall take effect on a date specified by the person in the notice but not less than seven days after the date on which the notice is given.]

Amendment

Inserted by SI 2003/956, art 12(3), Sch 4, para 8. Date in force: 31 March 2003: see SI 2003/956, art 1(1).

20 Mayor of London

(1) In this rule 'the Mayor' means the Mayor of London.

(2) Where a hearing is held into an appeal arising from an application in respect of which the Mayor has directed the local planning authority to refuse the application these Rules shall apply subject to the following modifications—

[(a) in rule 3A—
  (i) in paragraph (1), after 'the appellant' insert ', the Mayor';
  (ii) in paragraph (2), after 'the appellant' insert ', the Mayor';]
(b) in rule 4—
  (i) in paragraph (1), after 'inform the Secretary of State' and after 'inform the appellant' insert ', the Mayor';
  (ii) in paragraph (2)(a) after 'the Secretary of State' insert ', the Mayor';
  (iii) in paragraph (2)(b)(i), after 'statutory party' insert 'and the Mayor';
(c) in rule 6—
  [(i) in paragraph (1), after 'The appellant' insert ', the Mayor' and for '2' substitute '3';]
  (ii) in paragraph (2), after both references to 'the appellant' insert ', the Mayor' and for '2' substitute '3';
  (iii) in paragraph (3), for '3' substitute '4';
  (iv) …
  (v) in paragraph (5)(a), after 'the appellant' insert ', the Mayor' and for 'of those two parties' substitute 'parties required to provide such documents';
  (vi) in paragraph (5)(b), after 'the local planning authority' insert ', the Mayor'.
[(ca) …]
(d) in rule 7(2) after 'the appellant' insert ', the Mayor';
(e) in rule 8—
  (i) in paragraph (1), for 'If either the appellant' substitute 'If the appellant, the Mayor', for each reference to 'party' substitute 'parties' and for each reference to 'his opinion' substitute 'their opinions';
  (ii) in paragraph (2), after 'the appellant' insert ', the Mayor';
  [(iii) in paragraph (3), for 'If either the appellant' substitute 'If the appellant, the Mayor';
  (iv) in paragraph (4), for 'party' substitute 'parties'];
(f) in rule 9(1)—
  (i) at the end of sub-paragraph (b) delete 'and';
  (ii) after sub-paragraph (c) add—

  'and

  (d) the Mayor.';

(g) in rules 13(6) and 14(4), after 'the appellant' insert ', the Mayor'.

(3) Where a hearing is held into an appeal arising from an application which a local planning authority was required to notify to the Mayor but which is not an appeal falling within paragraph (2), these Rules shall apply as if the Mayor were a statutory party.

Amendment
Para (2): sub-para (a) substituted by SI 2009/455, r 2(1), (12)(a). Date in force: 6 April 2009 (in relation to appeals and applications made on or after that date): see SI 2009/455, r 1(1), (2)(a).

Town and Country Planning (Hearings Procedure) (England) Rules 2000

Para (2): sub-para (c)(i) substituted, for sub-para (c)(i), (ia) as originally enacted by SI 2015/316, r 6(1), (10). Date in force: 6 April 2015: see SI 2015/316, r 1(1).

Para (2): sub-para (c)(iv) revoked by SI 2009/455, r 2(1), (12)(b). Date in force: 6 April 2009 (in relation to appeals and applications made on or after that date): see SI 2009/455, r 1(1), (2)(a).

Para (2): sub-para (ca) inserted by SI 2013/2137, r 5(1), (10). Date in force: 1 October 2013: see SI 2013/2137, r 1; for transitional provisions and savings see rr 6, 7 thereof.

Para (2): sub-para (ca) revoked by SI 2015/316, r 6(1), (11). Date in force: 6 April 2015: see SI 2015/316, r 1(1).

Para (2): sub-para (e)(iii), (iv) inserted by SI 2009/455, r 2(1), (12)(c). Date in force: 6 April 2009 (in relation to appeals and applications made on or after that date): see SI 2009/455, r 1(1), (2)(a).

[20A Advertisement appeals]

[(1) Where a hearing is held into an appeal under section 78 of the Planning Act as applied by regulations made under section 220 of that Act, these Rules apply subject to the modifications in this rule.

(2) In rule 2 (interpretation), after the definition of 'hearing', insert—

"'hearing statement' means, and is comprised of, a written statement which contains full particulars of the case which a person proposes to put forward at a hearing and a list of any documents which that person intends to refer to or put in evidence;'.

(3) In rule 4(2) (preliminary information to be supplied by local planning authority) for '1 week' substitute '2 weeks'.

(4) In rule 6 (receipt of hearing statements etc)—

(a) in the heading, for 'full statement of case' substitute 'hearing statements';

(b) for 'full statement of case' substitute 'hearing statement' wherever it appears;

(c) for paragraphs (1) and (1A) substitute—

'(1) The appellant and the local planning authority shall ensure that, within 6 weeks of the starting date, 2 copies of their hearing statement have been received by the Secretary of State and a copy has been received by any statutory party.';

(d) in paragraph (3) for '5 weeks' substitute '6 weeks';

(e) in paragraph (5)(a) for 'paragraph (1A)' substitute 'paragraph (1)'; and

(f) in paragraph (7) for 'paragraphs (1A) to (3)' substitute 'paragraphs (1) to (3)'.]

Amendment

Inserted by SI 2015/316, r 6(1), (5). Date in force: 6 April 2015: see SI 2015/316, r 1(1).

(SI 2009/452)

Town and Country Planning (Appeals) (Written Representations Procedure) (England) Regulations 2009

1 Citation and commencement

These Regulations may be cited as the Town and Country Planning (Appeals) (Written Representations Procedure) (England) Regulations 2009 and shall come into force on 6th April 2009.

2 Interpretation

(1)   In these Regulations—

'the Act' means the Town and Country Planning Act 1990;

['advertisement application' means an application for express consent to display an advertisement made under Part 3 of the Town and Country Planning (Control of Advertisements) (England) Regulations 2007; and

'advertisement consent appeal' means an appeal under section 78(1) of the Act (as applied by regulations made under section 220 of the Act) in relation to an advertisement application, except an appeal against the grant of any consent which is granted subject to conditions];

'appellant' means a person giving notice of appeal to the Secretary of State;

'document' includes a photograph, map or plan;

'dwellinghouse' does not include a building containing one or more flats, or a flat contained within such a building;

'electronic communication' has the meaning given in section 15(1) of the Electronic Communications Act 2000;

['full statement of case'—

(a)   means, in relation to the appellant, the full statement of case (if any) submitted by the appellant with their notice of appeal under article 33 of the Town and Country Planning (Development Management Procedure) (England) Order 2010 (appeals); and

(b)   in relation to everyone else, means and is comprised of, a written statement which contains full particulars of the case which a person proposes to put forward and copies of any documents which that person intends to refer to or put in evidence;]

'householder appeal' means an appeal under section 78(1) of the Act in relation to a householder application, except an appeal against the grant of any planning permission, consent, agreement or approval which is granted subject to conditions;

'householder application' means—
  (a) an application for planning permission for development of an existing dwellinghouse, or development within the curtilage of such a dwellinghouse for any purpose incidental to the enjoyment of the dwellinghouse, or
  (b) an application for any consent, agreement or approval required by or under a planning permission, development order or local development order in relation to such development,
  but does not include—
  (i) an application for change of use,
  (ii) an application to change the number of dwellings in a building;

'local planning authority' means the body who were responsible for dealing with the application occasioning the appeal;

['minor commercial appeal' means an appeal under section 78(1) of the Act in relation to a minor commercial application, except an appeal against the grant of any planning permission, consent, agreement or approval which is granted subject to conditions;

'minor commercial application' means—
  (a) an application for planning permission for development of an existing building or part of a building currently in use for any of the purposes set out in the Schedule to these Regulations, or
  (b) an application for any consent, agreement or approval required by or under a planning permission, development order or local development order in relation to such development,
  where such an application does not include a change of use, a change to the number of units in a building, or development that is not wholly at ground floor level or that would increase the gross internal area of a building;]

'notice of appeal' means a notice of appeal under section 78 of the Act;

'questionnaire' means a document in the form supplied by the Secretary of State to local planning authorities for the purpose of proceedings under these Regulations, and for this purpose a form is taken to be supplied where the Secretary of State has published it on a website and has notified the local planning authority of—
  (a) publication of the form on the website,
  (b) the address of the website, and
  (c) the place on the website where the form may be accessed, and how it may be accessed;

'starting date' means the date of the notice under regulation 4 or 11, as the case may be;

'working day' means a day which is not a Saturday, Sunday, Bank Holiday or other public holiday; and

'written representations' includes supporting documents.

(2) In these Regulations, and in relation to the use of electronic communications for any purpose of these Regulations which is capable of being effected electronically—
  (a) the expression 'address' includes any number or address used for the purposes of such communications, except that where these Regulations

impose an obligation on any person to provide a name and address to any other person, the obligation shall not be fulfilled unless the person on whom it is imposed provides a postal address;

(b) references to notices, representations or other documents, or to copies of such documents, include references to such documents or copies of them in electronic form.

(3) Paragraphs (4) to (7) apply where an electronic communication is used by a person for the purpose of fulfilling any requirement in these Regulations to give or send any statement, notice or other document to any other person ('the recipient').

(4) The requirement shall be taken to be fulfilled where the notice or other document transmitted by means of the electronic communication is—

(a) capable of being accessed by the recipient,

(b) legible in all material respects, and

(c) sufficiently permanent to be used for subsequent reference.

(5) In paragraph (4), 'legible in all material respects' means that the information contained in the notice or other document is available to the recipient to no lesser extent than it would be if sent or given by means of a document in printed form.

(6) Where the electronic communication is received by the recipient outside the recipient's business hours, it shall be taken to have been received on the next working day.

(7) A requirement in these Regulations that any document should be in writing is fulfilled where that document meets the criteria in paragraph (4), and 'written' and cognate expressions are to be construed accordingly.

Amendment

Para (1): definitions 'advertisement application' and 'advertisement consent appeal' inserted by SI 2013/2114, reg 2(1), (2)(a). Date in force: 1 October 2013: see SI 2013/2114, reg 1(1); for savings see reg 4(1) thereof.

Para (1): definition 'full statement of case' inserted by SI 2013/2114, reg 2(1), (2)(b). Date in force: 1 October 2013: see SI 2013/2114, reg 1(1); for savings see reg 4(1) thereof.

Para (1): definitions 'minor commercial appeal' and 'minor commercial application' inserted by SI 2013/2114, reg 2(1), (2)(c). Date in force: 1 October 2013: see SI 2013/2114, reg 1(1); for savings see reg 4(1) thereof.

3 Application

(1) These Regulations apply in relation to England only.

(2) Part 1 of these Regulations only applies where—

[(a) either—

(i) a householder appeal is made in relation to an application which was made on or after 6th April 2009; or

(ii) an advertisement consent or minor commercial appeal is made in relation to an application which was made on or after 1st October 2013; and]

(b) the Secretary of State has determined under section 319A (determination of procedure of certain proceedings) of the Act that it is a matter which is to be determined on the basis of representations in writing.

Part 1 Procedure for Householder Appeals

(3) Part 2 of these Regulations only applies where—

[(a) an appeal which is not a householder, advertisement consent or minor commercial appeal is made—

(i) under section 78 of the Act in relation to an application which was made on or after 6th April 2009; or

(ii) under section 78 of the Act, as applied by regulations made under section 220 of the Act, in relation to an application determined, or a discontinuance notice served, on or after 1st October 2013; and]

(b) the Secretary of State has determined under section 319A of the Act that it is a matter which is to be determined on the basis of representations in writing.

[(3A) For the purposes of paragraph (3)(a)(ii) an application is deemed to be determined if—

(a) a determination has not been made; and

(b) the period after which an appeal can be made has expired.]

(4) Where the Secretary of State varies a determination under section 319A(4) so that an appeal proceeding at a local inquiry or at a hearing is to continue on the basis of representations in writing, in accordance with Part 1 or Part 2 of these Regulations, as the case may be, these Regulations apply in relation to the proceedings to such extent as the Secretary of State may specify having regard to any steps already taken in relation to those proceedings.

(5) Where the Secretary of State varies a determination under section 319A(4) so that an appeal proceeding on the basis of representations in writing is to continue at a local inquiry or at a hearing, these Regulations shall cease to apply.

Amendment

Para (2): sub-para (a) substituted by SI 2013/2114, reg 2(1), (3)(a). Date in force: 1 October 2013: see SI 2013/2114, reg 1(1); for savings see reg 4(1) thereof.

Para (3): sub-para (a) substituted by SI 2013/2114, reg 2(1), (3)(b). Date in force: 1 October 2013: see SI 2013/2114, reg 1(1); for transitional provision and savings savings see regs 4(1), 5(1)–(3) thereof.

Para (3A): inserted by SI 2013/2114, reg 2(1), (3)(c). Date in force: 1 October 2013: see SI 2013/2114, reg 1(1); for savings see reg 4(1) thereof.

PART 1 PROCEDURE FOR HOUSEHOLDER[, ADVERTISEMENT CONSENT AND MINOR COMMERCIAL] APPEALS

Amendment

Part heading: words ', Advertisement Consent and Minor Commercial' in square brackets inserted by SI 2013/2114, reg 2(1), (4). Date in force: 1 October 2013: see SI 2013/2114, reg 1(1); for savings see reg 4 thereof.

4 Notification of receipt of appeal

The Secretary of State shall, as soon as practicable after a determination has been made under section 319A of the Act, advise the appellant and the local planning authority in writing—

(a) of the reference number allocated to the appeal;

(b) that the appeal will follow the procedures set out in Part 1 of these Regulations; and

(c) of the address to which written communications to the Secretary of State about the appeal are to be sent.

5 Questionnaire

The local planning authority shall, within 5 working days of the starting date, send to the Secretary of State and copy to the appellant—

    (a) a completed questionnaire; and

    (b) a copy of each of the documents referred to in it.

6 Notice to interested persons

(1) The local planning authority shall give written notice of the appeal within 5 working days of the starting date to—

    (a) any person notified or consulted in accordance with the Act or a development order about the application which has given rise to the appeal; and

    (b) any other person who made representations to the local planning authority about that application.

(2) A notice under paragraph (1) shall—

    (a) state the name of the appellant and the address of the site to which the appeal relates;

    (b) describe the application;

    (c) state the starting date;

    (d) set out the matters notified to the appellant and the local planning authority under regulation 4(a) and (b); and

    (e) state that any representations made to the local planning authority in relation to the application, before it was determined, will be sent to the Secretary of State and the appellant by the local planning authority and will be considered by the Secretary of State when determining the appeal unless they are withdrawn in writing within 4 weeks of the starting date.

7 Representations

(1) The notice of appeal and the documents accompanying it shall comprise the appellant's representations in relation to the appeal.

(2) The completed questionnaire and documents sent with it shall comprise the local planning authority's representations in relation to the appeal.

(3) The Secretary of State shall, as soon as practicable after receipt, send a copy of the representations made by the local planning authority to the appellant and shall send a copy of the representations made by the appellant to the local planning authority.

8 Further information

(1) The Secretary of State may in writing require the appellant, local planning authority and other interested persons, to provide such further information relevant to the appeal as may be specified.

(2) Such information must be provided in writing within such period as the Secretary of State may specify.

(3) The Secretary of State may disregard any further information unless that information has been requested pursuant to paragraph (1).

9 Transfer of appeal from Part 1

(1) At any time before an appeal is determined, the Secretary of State may determine that the procedures set out in this Part are no longer suitable for that appeal.

(2) Where such a determination is made the Secretary of State shall notify the appellant and the local planning authority in writing that—

(a) the appeal is to be transferred from the procedures set out in Part 1 of these Regulations; and

(b) the appeal will proceed in accordance with Part 2 of these Regulations to such extent as the Secretary of State may specify having regard to any steps already taken in relation to those proceedings.

10 Decision on householder[, advertisement consent and minor commercial appeals] under Part 1

(1) The Secretary of State may, after giving the appellant and the local planning authority written notice of the intention to do so, proceed to a decision on an appeal taking into account only those representations which have been sent within the relevant time limits, where it appears that there is sufficient material to enable a decision to be reached.

(2) In paragraph (1) 'relevant time limits' means the time limits prescribed by these Regulations, or where the Secretary of State has exercised the power under regulation 17, any later time limit.

Amendment

Provision heading: words ', advertisement consent and minor commercial appeals' in square brackets substituted by SI 2013/2114, reg 2(1), (5). Date in force: 1 October 2013: see SI 2013/2114, reg 1(1); for savings see reg 4 thereof.

PART 2 PROCEDURES FOR OTHER APPEALS

11 Notification of receipt of appeal

The Secretary of State shall, as soon as practicable after a determination has been made under section 319A of the Act, advise the appellant and the local planning authority in writing—

(a) of the reference number allocated to the appeal;

(b) that the appeal will follow the procedures set out in Part 2 of these Regulations; and

(c) of the address to which written communications to the Secretary of State about the appeal are to be sent.

12 Questionnaire

The local planning authority shall, within [1 week] of the starting date, send to the Secretary of State and copy to the appellant—

(a) a completed questionnaire; and

Town and Country Planning (Appeals) Regulations 2009

    (b) a copy of each of the documents referred to in it.

Amendment

Words '1 week' in square brackets substituted by SI 2013/2114, reg 2(1), (6). Date in force: 1 October 2013: see SI 2013/2114, reg 1(1); for savings see reg 4 thereof.

13 Notice to interested persons

(1) The local planning authority shall give written notice of the appeal within [1 week] of the starting date to—

    (a) any person notified or consulted in accordance with the Act or a development order about the application which has given rise to the appeal; and

    (b) any other person who made representations to the local planning authority about that application.

(2) A notice under paragraph (1) shall—

    (a) state the name of the appellant and the address of the site to which the appeal relates;

    (b) describe the application;

    (c) state the starting date;

    (d) set out the matters notified to the appellant and the local planning authority under regulation 11;

    (e) state that any representations made to the local planning authority in relation to the application, before it was determined, will be sent to the Secretary of State and the appellant by the local planning authority and will be considered by the Secretary of State when determining the appeal unless they are withdrawn, in writing, within [5 weeks] of the starting date; and

    (f) state that further written representations may be sent to the Secretary of State within 6 weeks of the starting date.

Amendment

Para (1): words '1 week' in square brackets substituted by SI 2013/2114, reg 2(1), (7)(a). Date in force: 1 October 2013: see SI 2013/2114, reg 1(1); for savings see reg 4 thereof.

Para (2): in sub-para (e) words '5 weeks' in square brackets substituted by SI 2013/2114, reg 2(1), (7)(b). Date in force: 1 October 2013: see SI 2013/2114, reg 1(1); for savings see reg 4 thereof.

14 Representations

(1) The notice of appeal and the documents accompanying it shall comprise the appellant's representations in relation to the appeal.

(2) The local planning authority may elect to treat the questionnaire and the documents sent with it as their representations in relation to the appeal; and, where this is done, they shall notify the Secretary of State and the appellant accordingly when sending the questionnaire or sending the copy in accordance with regulation 12.

(3) Where the local planning authority do not elect as described in paragraph (2), they shall send 2 copies of their [full statement of case] to the Secretary of State within [5 weeks] of the starting date.

(4) …

(5) The Secretary of State shall, as soon as practicable after receipt, send a copy of any representations made by the local planning authority to the appellant ….

Part 2 Procedures for Other Appeals

[(6) The appellant shall send 2 copies of any comments they have on the local planning authority's representations to the Secretary of State within 7 weeks of the starting date; and the Secretary of State shall, as soon as practicable after receipt, send a copy of those further comments to the local planning authority.]

(7) The Secretary of State may disregard further information from the appellant ... which was not sent within [7 weeks] of the starting date unless that further information has been requested by the Secretary of State.

[(7A) Subject to regulation 15(2)(b) (third party representations) the Secretary of State may disregard further information from the local planning authority which was not sent within 5 weeks of the starting date unless that further information has been requested by the Secretary of State.]

(8) Where a party to which this regulation applies elects to use electronic communications for submitting, sending, copying or sending a copy of any representations, questionnaire or other documents, references to '2 copies of' in paragraphs (3)... and (6) shall be omitted.

Amendment

Para (3): words 'full statement of case' in square brackets substituted by SI 2013/2114, reg 2(1), (8)(a). Date in force: 1 October 2013: see SI 2013/2114, reg 1(1); for savings see reg 4 thereof.

Para (3): words '5 weeks' in square brackets substituted by SI 2013/2114, reg 2(1), (8)(a). Date in force: 1 October 2013: see SI 2013/2114, reg 1(1); for savings see reg 4 thereof.

Para (4): revoked by SI 2013/2114, reg 2(1), (8)(b). Date in force: 1 October 2013: see SI 2013/2114, reg 1(1); for savings see reg 4 thereof.

Para (5): words omitted revoked by SI 2013/2114, reg 2(1), (8)(c). Date in force: 1 October 2013: see SI 2013/2114, reg 1(1); for savings see reg 4 thereof.

Para (6): substituted by SI 2013/2114, reg 2(1), (8)(d). Date in force: 1 October 2013: see SI 2013/2114, reg 1(1); for savings see reg 4 thereof.

Para (7): words omitted revoked by SI 2013/2114, reg 2(1), (8)(e). Date in force: 1 October 2013: see SI 2013/2114, reg 1(1); for savings see reg 4 thereof.

Para (7): words '7 weeks' in square brackets substituted by SI 2013/2114, reg 2(1), (8)(e). Date in force: 1 October 2013: see SI 2013/2114, reg 1(1); for savings see reg 4 thereof.

Para (7A): inserted by SI 2013/2114, reg 2(1), (8)(f). Date in force: 1 October 2013: see SI 2013/2114, reg 1(1); for savings see reg 4 thereof.

Para (8): reference omitted revoked by SI 2013/2114, reg 2(1), (8)(g). Date in force: 1 October 2013: see SI 2013/2114, reg 1(1); for savings see reg 4 thereof

15 Third party representations

(1) If a person notified under regulation 13(1) wishes to send representations to the Secretary of State, they shall do so, in writing, within [5 weeks] of the starting date.

(2) The Secretary of State shall—

  (a) send to the appellant and the local planning authority, as soon as practicable after receipt, a copy each of all of such representations; and

  (b) specify a period [ending within 7 weeks of the starting date] within which any comments on these representations must be sent to the Secretary of State.

Amendment

Para (1): words '5 weeks' in square brackets substituted by SI 2013/2114, reg 2(1), (9)(a). Date in force: 1 October 2013: see SI 2013/2114, reg 1(1); for savings see reg 4 thereof.

Para (2): in sub-para (b) words 'ending within 7 weeks of the starting date' in square brackets substituted by SI 2013/2114, reg 2(1), (9)(b). Date in force: 1 October 2013: see SI 2013/2114, reg 1(1); for savings see reg 4 thereof.

16 Decision on appeal

(1) The Secretary of State may proceed to a decision on an appeal taking into account only such written representations as have been sent within the relevant time limits.

(2) The Secretary of State may, after giving the appellant and the local planning authority written notice of the intention to do so, proceed to a decision on an appeal even though no written representations have been made within the relevant time limits by the local planning authority or any other third parties, if it appears that there is sufficient material to enable a decision on the merits of the case to be reached.

(3) In this regulation 'relevant time limits' means the time limits prescribed by these Regulations, or where the Secretary of State has exercised the power under regulation 17, any later time limit.

PART 3 MISCELLANEOUS

17 Allowing further time

The Secretary of State may in a particular case give directions setting later time limits than those prescribed by these Regulations.

18 Mayor of London

(1) In this regulation 'the Mayor' means the Mayor of London.

(2) Where an appeal arises from an application in respect of which the Mayor has directed the local planning authority to refuse the application and where the Secretary of State has determined under section 319A of the Act that it is a matter which is to be determined on the basis of representations in writing these Regulations shall apply subject to the following modifications—

(a) in regulations 4 and 11, after 'advise the appellant' insert ', the Mayor';

(b) in regulations 5 and 12, after 'and copy to the appellant' insert 'and the Mayor';

(c) in regulation 8, after 'local planning authority' insert ', the Mayor';

(d) in regulation 9(2), after 'the appellant' insert ', the Mayor';

(e) in regulations 10(1), after 'the appellant' insert ', the Mayor';

(f) in regulation 14—

(i) for '2 copies' substitute '3 copies' where ever it occurs;

[(ia) after paragraph (1) insert—

'(1A) Where the documents referred to in paragraph (1) include a full statement of case, the appellant shall send that full statement of case to the Mayor as soon as practicable after the starting date.']

Part 3 Miscellaneous

      (ii)   in paragraph (2), after 'Secretary of State' insert ', the Mayor';
      (iii)   after paragraph (4) insert—

           '(4A) If the Mayor wishes to make any representations in relation to the appeal, the Mayor shall [do so in the form of a full statement of case and] submit 3 copies of [that full statement of case] to the Secretary of State within [5 weeks] of the starting date.'

     [(iv) at the end of paragraph (5) insert 'and the Mayor, and shall send a copy of any representations made to the Secretary of State by the Mayor to the appellant and to the local planning authority';
      (v)   in paragraph (6), after 'the local planning authority's' insert 'or the Mayor's', and after 'local planning authority' insert 'and the Mayor';
      (vi)   after paragraph (6) insert—

           '(6A) The local planning authority and the Mayor shall send 3 copies of any comments they have on each other's representations to the Secretary of State within 7 weeks of the starting date; and the Secretary of State shall, as soon as practicable after receipt, send a copy of those further comments to the other party and the appellant.';

      (vii) for paragraphs (7) and (7A) substitute—

          '(7)   The Secretary of State may disregard further information from the appellant, the Mayor and the local planning authority which was not sent within 7 weeks of the starting date unless that further information has been requested by the Secretary of State.';

      (viii) in paragraph (8) substitute '(3), (4A), (6) and (6A)' for '(3) and (6)'.]
  (g) in regulation 15, in paragraph (2)(a), after 'the appellant' insert ', the Mayor';
  (h) in regulation 16, in paragraph (2), after 'the appellant' insert ', the Mayor'.

Amendment

Para (2): sub-para (f)(ia) inserted by SI 2013/2114, reg 2(1), (10)(a). Date in force: 1 October 2013: see SI 2013/2114, reg 1(1); for savings see reg 4 thereof.

Para (2): in sub-para (f)(iii) in para (4A) (as set out) words 'do so in the form of a full statement of case and' in square brackets inserted by SI 2013/2114, reg 2(1), (10)(b)(i). Date in force: 1 October 2013: see SI 2013/2114, reg 1(1); for savings see reg 4 thereof.

Para (2): in sub-para (f)(iii) in para (4A) (as set out) words 'that full statement of case' in square brackets substituted by SI 2013/2114, reg 2(1), (10)(b)(ii). Date in force: 1 October 2013: see SI 2013/2114, reg 1(1); for savings see reg 4 thereof.

Para (2): in sub-para (f)(iii) in para (4A) (as set out) words '5 weeks' in square brackets substituted by SI 2013/2114, reg 2(1), (10)(b)(iii). Date in force: 1 October 2013: see SI 2013/2114, reg 1(1); for savings see reg 4 thereof.

Para (2): sub-para (f)(iv)–(viii) substituted, for sub-para (f)(iv)–(vii) as originally enacted, by SI 2013/2114, reg 2(1), (10)(c). Date in force: 1 October 2013: see SI 2013/2114, reg 1(1); for savings see reg 4 thereof.

19 Withdrawal of consent to use of electronic communications

Where a person is no longer willing to accept the use of electronic communications for any purpose of these Regulations which is capable of being effected electronically, the person shall give notice in writing—

(a) withdrawing any address notified to the Secretary of State or to a local planning authority for that purpose, or

(b) revoking any agreement entered into with the Secretary of State or with a local planning authority for that purpose,

and such withdrawal or revocation shall be final and shall take effect on a date specified by the person in the notice but not less than 1 week after the date on which the notice is given.

20 Revocation transitional and saving provision

(1) Subject to paragraphs (2), the Town and Country Planning (Appeals) (Written Representations Procedure) (England) Regulations 2000 ('the 2000 Regulations') are revoked.

(2) Subject to paragraph (3), where an appeal in relation to an application made before the 6th April 2009 is to be considered on the basis of representations in writing, the appeal shall be continued under the 2000 Regulations.

(3) Where a decision of the Secretary of State on an appeal to which the 2000 Regulations applied is subsequently quashed in proceedings before any court, the decision shall be redetermined in accordance with Part 2 of these Regulations.

[SCHEDULE
MINOR COMMERCIAL DEVELOPMENT USES]

Amendment

Inserted by SI 2013/2114, reg 2(1), (11). Date in force: 1 October 2013: see SI 2013/2114, reg 1(1); for savings see reg 4 thereof.

[Regulation 2(1)]

[Shops

1

Use for all or any of the following purposes—

(a) for the retail sale of goods other than hot food,

(b) as a post office,

(c) for the sale of tickets or as a travel agency,

(d) for the sale of sandwiches or other cold food for consumption off the premises,

(e) for hairdressing,

(f) for the direction of funerals,

(g) for the display of goods for sale,

(h) for the hiring out of domestic or personal goods or articles,

(i) for the washing or cleaning of clothes or fabrics on the premises,

(j) for the reception of goods to be washed, cleaned or repaired,

(k) as an internet café, where the primary purpose of the premises is to provide facilities for enabling members of the public to access the internet,

where the sale, display or service is to visiting members of the public.

Financial and professional services

2

Use for the provision of—

(a) financial services,

(b) professional services (other than health or medical services), or

(c) any other services (including use as a betting office) which it is appropriate to provide in a shopping area,

where the services are provided principally to visiting members of the public.

Restaurants and cafes

3

Use for the sale of food and drink for consumption on the premises.

Drinking establishments

4

Use as a public house, wine-bar or other drinking establishment.

Hot food takeaways

5

Use for the sale of hot food for consumption off the premises.]

Amendment

Inserted by SI 2013/2114, reg 2(1), (11). Date in force: 1 October 2013: see SI 2013/2114, reg 1(1); for savings see reg 4 thereof.

(SI 2015/595)

Town and Country Planning (Development Management Procedure) (England) Order 2015

PART 1 PRELIMINARY

1 Citation, commencement and application

(1) This Order may be cited as the Town and Country Planning (Development Management Procedure) (England) Order 2015 and comes into force on 15th April 2015.

Town and Country Planning (Development Management Procedure) Order 2015

(2) This Order applies in relation to England only.

(3) This Order applies to all land in England, but where the land is the subject of a special development order, whether made before or after the commencement of this Order, this Order applies to that land only to such extent and subject to such modifications as may be specified in the special development order.

(4) Nothing in this Order applies to any permission which is deemed to be granted under section 222 of the 1990 Act (planning permission not needed for advertisements complying with regulations).

2 Interpretation

(1) In this Order, unless the context otherwise requires—

'the 1990 Act' means the Town and Country Planning Act 1990;

'the 2004 Act' means the Planning and Compulsory Purchase Act 2004;

'the 2011 Regulations' mean the Town and Country Planning (Environmental Impact Assessment Regulations 2011;

'access', in relation to reserved matters, means the accessibility to and within the site, for vehicles, cycles and pedestrians in terms of the positioning and treatment of access and circulation routes and how these fit into the surrounding access network; where 'site' means the site or part of the site in respect of which outline planning permission is granted or, as the case may be, in respect of which an application for such a permission has been made;

'appearance' means the aspects of a building or place within the development which determines the visual impression the building or place makes, including the external built form of the development, its architecture, materials, decoration, lighting, colour and texture;

'contaminated land' has the same meaning as in Part 2A of the Environmental Protection Act 1990;

'dwellinghouse' does not include a building containing one or more flats, or a flat contained within such a building;

'EIA application', 'EIA development', 'environmental information' and 'environmental statement' have the same meanings respectively as in regulation 2(1) of the 2011 Regulations (interpretation);

'electronic communication' has the same meaning as in section 15(1) of the Electronic Communications Act 2000 (general interpretation);

'flat' means a separate and self-contained set of premises constructed or adapted for use for the purpose of a dwelling and forming part of a building from some other part of which it is divided horizontally;

'flood' has the same meaning as in section 1 of the Flood and Water Management Act 2010;

'floor space' means the total floor space in a building or buildings;

'householder application' means—

(a) an application for planning permission for development for an existing dwellinghouse, or development within the curtilage of such a dwellinghouse for any purpose incidental to the enjoyment of the dwellinghouse, or

Part 1 Preliminary

    (b) an application for any consent, agreement or approval required by or under a planning permission, development order or local development order in relation to such development,

but does not include an application for change of use or an application to change the number of dwellings in a building;

'infrastructure manager' means any person who in relation to relevant railway land—

    (a) is responsible for developing or maintaining the land; or

    (b) manages or uses the land, or permits the land to be used for the operation of a railway;

'landscaping', in relation to a site or any part of a site for which outline planning permission has been granted or, as the case may be, in respect of which an application for such permission has been made, means the treatment of land (other than buildings) for the purpose of enhancing or protecting the amenities of the site and the area in which it is situated and includes—

    (a) screening by fences, walls or other means;

    (b) the planting of trees, hedges, shrubs or grass;

    (c) the formation of banks, terraces or other earthworks;

    (d) the laying out or provision of gardens, courts, squares, water features, sculpture or public art; and

    (e) the provision of other amenity features;

'layout' means the way in which buildings, routes and open spaces within the development are provided, situated and orientated in relation to each other and to buildings and spaces outside the development;

'listed building' has the same meaning as in section 1 of the Planning (Listed Buildings and Conservation Areas) Act 1990 (listing of buildings of special architectural or historic interest);

'major development' means development involving any one or more of the following—

    (a) the winning and working of minerals or the use of land for mineral-working deposits;

    (b) waste development;

    (c) the provision of dwellinghouses where—

        (i) the number of dwellinghouses to be provided is 10 or more; or

        (ii) the development is to be carried out on a site having an area of 0.5 hectares or more and it is not known whether the development falls within sub-paragraph (c)(i);

    (d) the provision of a building or buildings where the floor space to be created by the development is 1,000 square metres or more; or

    (e) development carried out on a site having an area of 1 hectare or more;

'mining operations' means the winning and working of minerals in, on or under land, whether by surface or underground working;

'minor commercial application' means—

    (a) an application for planning permission for development of an existing building or part of a building currently in use for any of the purposes falling within Part A of the Schedule to the Town and Country Planning (Use Classes) Order 1987, or

(b) an application for any consent, agreement or approval required by or under a planning permission, development order or local development order in relation to such development,

where such an application does not include a change of use, a change to the number of units in a building, or development that is not wholly at ground floor level or that would increase the gross internal area of a building,

'outline planning permission' means a planning permission for the erection of a building, which is granted subject to a condition requiring the subsequent approval of the local planning authority with respect to one or more reserved matters;

'the Permitted Development Order' means Town and Country Planning (General Permitted Development) Order 2015;

'planning obligation' means an obligation entered into by agreement or otherwise by any person interested in land pursuant to section 106 of the 1990 Act (planning obligations);

'proposed highway' has the same meaning as in section 329 of the Highways Act 1980 (further provision as to interpretation);

'qualifying European site' means—

(a) a European offshore marine site within the meaning of regulation 15 of the Offshore Marine Conservation (Natural Habitats, &c) Regulations 2007; or

(b) a European site within the meaning of regulation 8 of the Conservation of Habitats and Species Regulations 2010;

'relevant railway land' means land—

(a) forming part of any operational railway; or

(b) which is authorised to be used for the purposes of an operational railway under—

  (i) a planning permission granted or deemed to be granted,

  (ii) a development consent granted by an order made under the Planning Act 2008, or

  (iii) an Act of Parliament,

including viaducts, tunnels, retaining walls, sidings, shafts, bridges, or other structures used in connection with an operational railway and excluding car parks, offices, shops, hotels or any other land which, by its nature or situation, is comparable with land in general rather than land which is used for the purpose of an operational railway;

'reserved matters' in relation to an outline planning permission, or an application for such permission, means any of the following matters in respect of which details have not been given in the application—

(a) access;

(b) appearance;

(c) landscaping;

(d) layout; and

(e) scale;

Part 1 Preliminary

'scale' except in the term 'identified scale', means the height, width and length of each building proposed within the development in relation to its surroundings;

'section 278 agreement' means an agreement entered into pursuant to section 278 of the Highways Act 1980 (agreements as to execution of works);

'by site display' means by the posting of the notice by firm fixture to some object, sited and displayed in such a way as to be easily visible and legible by members of the public;

'site of special scientific interest' has the same meaning as in Part 2 of the Countryside and Wildlife Act 1981;

'special road' means a highway or proposed highway which is a special road in accordance with section 16 of the Highways Act 1980 (general provision as to special roads);

'strategic highways company' means a company for the time being appointed under Part 1 of the Infrastructure Act 2015

'trunk road' means a highway or proposed highway which is a trunk road by virtue of sections 10(1) (general provision as to trunk roads) or 19 (certain special roads and other highways to become trunk roads) of the Highways Act 1980 or any other enactment or any instrument made under any enactment; and

'waste development' means any operational development designed to be used wholly or mainly for the purpose of, or material change of use to, treating, storing, processing or disposing of refuse or waste materials.

(2) In this Order and in relation to the use of electronic communications or electronic storage for any purpose of this Order which is capable of being carried out electronically—

(a) the expression 'address' includes any number or address used for the purpose of such communications or storage, except that where this Order imposes any obligation on any person to provide a name and address to any other person, the obligation is not fulfilled unless the person on whom it is imposed provides a postal address; and

(b) references to documents, maps, plans, drawings, certificates or other documents, or to copies of such things, include references to such documents or copies of them in electronic form.

(3) Paragraphs (4) to (7) apply where an electronic communication is used by a person for the following purposes—

(a) fulfilling any requirement in this Order to give or send any application, notice or other document to any other person; or

(b) lodging an application, certificate or other document referred to in article 34(4) or (5) with an authority mentioned in that article,

and in those paragraphs, 'the recipient' means the person mentioned in sub-paragraph (a) of this paragraph, or the authority mentioned in sub-paragraph (b), as the case may be.

(4) The requirement is fulfilled, or (as the case may be) the application or other document is taken to have been lodged, if the document transmitted by the electronic communications is—

Town and Country Planning (Development Management Procedure) Order 2015

    (a) capable of being accessed by the recipient;
    (b) legible in all material respects; and
    (c) sufficiently permanent to be used for subsequent reference.

(5) In paragraph (4), 'legible in all material respects' means that the information contained in the notice or document is available to the recipient to no lesser extent than it would be if sent or given by means of a document in printed form.

(6) Where the electronic communication is received by the recipient outside the recipient's business hours, it is taken to have been received on the next working day; and for this purpose—
    (a) 'working day' means a day which is not a Saturday, Sunday, bank holiday or other public holiday; and
    (b) 'bank holiday' has the same meaning as in paragraph 1 of Schedule 1 to the Banking and Financial Dealings Act 1971;

(7) A requirement in this Order that any application, notice or other document should be in writing is fulfilled where the document meets the criteria in paragraph (4), and 'written' and related expressions are to be construed accordingly.

PART 2 PRE-APPLICATION CONSULTATION

3 Consultation before applying for planning permission

(1) Subject to paragraph (2), for the purposes of section 61W of the 1990 Act (requirement to carry out pre-application consultation) a person must carry out consultation on a proposed application for planning permission for any development involving an installation for the harnessing of wind power for energy production where—
    (a) the development involves the installation of more than 2 turbines; or
    (b) the hub height of any turbine exceeds 15 metres.

(2) Paragraph (1) does not apply to—
    (a) applications made pursuant to section 73 of the 1990 Act (determination of applications to develop land without compliance with conditions previously attached); or
    (b) applications of the description contained in article 20(1)(b) or (c) (consultations before the grant of a replacement planning permission subject to a new time limit).

4 Particulars of pre-application consultation

Where consultation is required by virtue of article 3(1), an application for planning permission must be accompanied by particulars of—
    (a) how the applicant complied with section 61W(1) of the 1990 Act;
    (b) any responses to the consultation that were received by the applicant; and
    (c) the account taken of those responses by the applicant.

PART 3 APPLICATIONS

5 Applications for outline planning permission

(1) Where an application is made to the local planning authority for outline planning permission, the authority may grant permission subject to a condition specifying reserved matters for the authority's subsequent approval.

(2) Where the authority who are to determine an application for outline planning permission are of the opinion that, in the circumstances of the case, the application ought not to be considered separately from all or any of the reserved matters, the authority must within the period of 1 month beginning with the date of receipt of the application notify the applicant that they are unable to determine it unless further details are submitted, specifying the further details they require.

(3) Where access is a reserved matter, the application for outline planning permission must state the area or areas where access points to the development proposed will be situated.

6 Applications for approval of reserved matters

An application for approval of reserved matters—
    (a) must be made in writing to the local planning authority and give sufficient information to enable the authority to identify the outline planning permission in respect of which it is made;
    (b) must include such particulars, and be accompanied by such plans and drawings, as are necessary to deal with the matters reserved in the outline planning permission; and
    (c) except where the authority indicate that a lesser number is required, or where the application is made using electronic communications, must be accompanied by 3 copies of the application and of the plans and drawings submitted with it.

7 General requirements: applications for planning permission including outline planning permission

(1) Subject to paragraphs (3) to (5), an application for planning permission must—
    (a) be made in writing to the local planning authority on a form published by the Secretary of State (or a form to substantially the same effect);
    (b) include the particulars specified or referred to in the form;
    (c) except where the application is made pursuant to section 73 (determination of applications to develop land without conditions previously attached) or section 73A(2)(c) (planning permission for development already carried out) of the 1990 Act or is an application of a kind referred to in article 20(1)(b) or (c), be accompanied, whether electronically or otherwise, by—
        (i) a plan which identifies the land to which the application relates;
        (ii) any other plans, drawings and information necessary to describe the development which is the subject of the application;
        (iii) except where the application is made by electronic communications or the local planning authority indicate that a lesser number is required, 3 copies of the form; and

Town and Country Planning (Development Management Procedure) Order 2015

(iv) except where they are submitted by electronic communications or the local planning authority indicate that a lesser number is required, 3 copies of any plans, drawings and information accompanying the application.

(2) Any plans or drawings required to be provided by paragraph (1)(c)(i) or (ii) must be drawn to an identified scale and, in the case of plans, must show the direction of North.

(3) Except where article 5(3) applies, an application for outline planning permission does not need to give details of any reserved matters.

(4) Subject to paragraph (5), an application for planning permission for development consisting of mining operations or the use of land for mineral-working deposits must—

(a) be made on a form provided by the local planning authority (or on a form to substantially the same effect);

(b) include the particulars specified or referred to in the form; and

(c) comply with the requirements of paragraph (1)(c).

(5) In the case of an application for planning permission for development consisting of mining operations for the winning and working of oil or natural gas by underground operations (including exploratory drilling)—

(a) where the application is made pursuant to section 73 or 73A(2)(c) of the 1990 Act or is an application of a kind referred to in article 20(1)(b) or (c), the application must be made in accordance with paragraph (4);

(b) in any other case, the application must be made in accordance with paragraph (1).

(6) Where an application is made using electronic communications to transmit a form to the local planning authority, the applicant is taken to have agreed—

(a) to the use of such communications by the local planning authority for the purposes of the application;

(b) that the applicant's address for those purposes is the address incorporated into, or otherwise logically associated with, the application; and

(c) that the applicant's deemed agreement under this paragraph subsists until the applicant gives notice in writing of the withdrawal of consent to the use of electronic communications under article 46.

8 Applications in respect of Crown land

An application for planning permission in respect of Crown land must be accompanied by—

(a) a statement that the application is made in respect of Crown land; and

(b) where the application is made by a person authorised in writing by the appropriate authority, a copy of that authorisation.

9 Design and access statements

(1) Paragraph (2) applies to an application for planning permission which is for—

(a) development which is major development; or

Part 3 Applications

    (b) where any part of the development is in a designated area, development consisting of—
        (i) the provision of one or more dwellinghouses; or
        (ii) the provision of a building or buildings where the floor space created by the development is 100 square metres or more.

(2) An application for planning permission to which this paragraph applies must, except where paragraph (4) applies, be accompanied by a statement ('a design and access statement') about—
    (a) the design principles and concepts that have been applied to the development; and
    (b) how issues relating to access to the development have been dealt with.

(3) A design and access statement must—
    (a) explain the design principles and concepts that have been applied to the development;
    (b) demonstrate the steps taken to appraise the context of the development and how the design of the development takes that context into account;
    (c) explain the policy adopted as to access, and how policies relating to access in relevant local development documents have been taken into account;
    (d) state what, if any, consultation has been undertaken on issues relating to access to the development and what account has been taken of the outcome of any such consultation; and
    (e) explain how any specific issues which might affect access to the development have been addressed.

(4) Paragraph (2) does not apply to an application for planning permission which is—
    (a) for permission to develop land without compliance with conditions previously attached, made pursuant to section 73 of the 1990 Act;
    (b) of the description contained in article 20(1)(b) or (c);
    (c) for engineering or mining operations;
    (d) for a material change in use of the land or buildings; or
    (e) for development which is waste development.

(5) In paragraph (1)—
    'designated area' means—
        (a) a conservation area; or
        (b) a property appearing on the World Heritage List kept under article 11(2) of the 1972 UNESCO Convention Concerning the Protection of the World Cultural and National Heritage (a World Heritage Site).

10 Applications for non-material changes to planning permission

(1) This article applies in relation to an application made under section 96A(4) of the 1990 Act (power to make non-material changes to planning permission).

(2) An application must be made in writing to the local planning authority on a form published by the Secretary of State (or a form substantially to the same effect).

Town and Country Planning (Development Management Procedure) Order 2015

(3) At the same time as making that application the applicant must give notice to any person (other than the applicant) who is an owner of the land to which the application relates or a tenant of an agricultural holding any part of which is comprised in the land to which the application relates, stating—

(a) what the application is for and where the person can view a copy of it; and

(b) that any representations about the application must be made to the local planning authority within 14 days of the date when the notice is given.

(4) Where notice is given under paragraph (3), the local planning authority must, in determining the application, take into account any representations made within 14 days beginning with the date when the notice was given.

(5) Where a local planning authority receive an application made in accordance with paragraph (2) they must give the applicant notice in writing of their decision on the application within 28 days of receipt of the application or such longer period as may be agreed in writing between the applicant and the authority.

11 General provisions relating to applications

(1) An application made under article 5, 6 or 7, must be made—

(a) where the application relates to land which is in a National Park, to the National Park authority;

(b) where the application relates to land in Greater London or a metropolitan county, which is not land in a National Park, to the local planning authority;

(c) where the application relates to land which is not in a National Park, Greater London or a metropolitan county, and the application relates to a county matter—

(i) to the county planning authority; or

(ii) where there is no county planning authority in relation to the land, to the district planning authority;

(d) in any other case—

(i) to the district planning authority; or

(ii) where there is no district planning authority in relation to the land, to the county planning authority.

(2) When the local planning authority with whom the application has to be lodged receive—

(a) in the case of an application made under article 5, 6 or 7, an application which complies with the requirements of article 5, 6 or 7, as the case may be;

(b) the certificate required by article 14;

(c) in a case to which article 9 applies, the design and access statement;

(d) in a case where pre-application consultation is required in accordance with article 3, the particulars in article 4;

(e) subject to paragraph (3), the particulars or evidence required by the authority under section 62(3) of the 1990 Act (applications for planning permission); and

(f) the fee required to be paid in respect of the application,

Part 3 Applications

the authority must, as soon as is reasonably practicable, send to the applicant an acknowledgement of the application in the terms (or substantially in the terms) set out in Schedule 1.

(3) Paragraph (2)(e) only applies if—
   (a) before the application is made the local planning authority publish or republish, for the purposes of article 34(4) and (5), a list of requirements on their website;
   (b) the particulars or evidence that the authority require to be included in the application fall within that list;
   (c) the particulars or evidence the authority require to be included in the application—
      (i) are reasonable having regard, in particular, to the nature and scale of the proposed development; and
      (ii) are about a matter which it is reasonable to think will be a material consideration in the determination of the application; and
   (d) the list mentioned in sub-paragraph (a) was published (or republished) during the 2 year period immediately before the date on which the application is made.

(4) Where an application is made to a county planning authority, in accordance with paragraph (1), that authority must, as soon as reasonably practicable, send a copy of the application and of any accompanying plans, drawings and information to the district planning authority, if any.

(5) Where, after sending an acknowledgement as required by paragraph (2), the local planning authority consider that the application is invalid, they must as soon as reasonably practicable notify the applicant that the application is invalid.

(6) In this article—
   (a) 'county matter' has the same meaning as in paragraph 1(1) of Schedule 1 to the 1990 Act (local planning authorities: distribution of functions); and
   (b) an application is invalid if it is not a valid application within the meaning of article 34(4) or it is not a non-validated application within the meaning of article 34(5).

12 Validation dispute

(1) Where—
   (a) a local planning authority require particulars or evidence to be included in an application; and
   (b) the applicant considers any particulars or evidence required do not meet the requirements set out in article 34(6)(c),
   the applicant may send a notice to the authority.

(2) The notice must—
   (i) specify which particulars or evidence the applicant considers do not meet the requirements set out in article 34(6)(c);
   (ii) set out the reasons the applicant relies upon in holding that view; and
   (iii) request the authority to waive the requirement to include those particulars or evidence in the application.

(3) Following receipt of the notice mentioned in paragraph (1) and not later than the date specified in paragraph (3), the local planning authority must notify the applicant either that—

    (i) the authority no longer require the applicant to provide the particulars or evidence ('a validation notice'); or

    (ii) the authority continues to require the applicant to provide the particulars or evidence ('non-validation notice').

(4) The date specified in this paragraph is—

    (a) the date the period specified or referred to in article 34(2) ('the determination period') ends; or

    (b) where the notice mentioned in paragraph (1) is received—

        (i) during the 7 working days immediately preceding the end of the determination period; or

        (ii) on the final day of, or after the end of, the determination period,

    the date which is 7 working days after the date the notice is received by the local planning authority.

(5) In this article 'working day' has the same meaning as in article 2(6).

13 Notice of applications for planning permission

(1) Except where paragraph (2) applies, an applicant for planning permission must give requisite notice of the application to any person (other than the applicant) who on the prescribed date is an owner of the land to which the application relates, or a tenant—

    (a) by serving the notice on every such person whose name and address is known to the applicant; and

    (b) where the applicant has taken reasonable steps to ascertain the names and addresses of every such person, but has been unable to do so, by publication of the notice after the prescribed date in a newspaper circulating in the locality in which the land to which the application relates is situated.

(2) Subject to paragraph (3), in the case of an application for planning permission for development consisting of the winning and working of minerals by underground operations, the applicant must give requisite notice of the application to any person (other than the applicant) who on the prescribed date is an owner of any of the land to which the application relates, or a tenant—

    (a) by serving the notice on every such person whom the applicant knows to be such a person and whose name and address is known to the applicant;

    (b) by publication of the notice after the prescribed date in a newspaper circulating in the locality in which the land to which the application relates is situated; and

    (c) by site display in at least one place in every parish within which there is situated any part of the land to which the application relates, leaving the notice in position for not less than 7 days in the period of 21 days immediately preceding the making of the application to the local planning authority.

(3) In the case of an application for planning permission for development consisting of the winning and working of oil or natural gas (including exploratory drilling)—

Part 3 Applications

    (a) the applicant is not required to serve a notice under paragraph (2)(a) in relation to any land which is to be used solely for underground operations;

    (b) where any part of the land to which the application relates is in an unparished area, the applicant must give notice under paragraph (2)(c) in relation to that part of the land as if for 'parish' there were substituted 'ward'; and

    (c) where sub-paragraph (b) applies, references in this article to notices required by paragraph (2)(c) include notices required by paragraph (2)(c) as modified by sub-paragraph (b).

(4) The notice required by paragraph (2)(c) must (in addition to any other matters required to be contained in it) specify a place within the area of the local planning authority to whom the application is made where a copy of the application for planning permission, and of all plans and other documents submitted with it, will be open to inspection by the public at all reasonable hours during such period as may be specified in the notice.

(5) Where a local planning authority maintain a website for the purpose of advertisement of applications for planning permission, the notice required by paragraph (2)(c) must (in addition to any other matters required to be contained in it) state the address of the website where a copy of the application, and of all plans and other documents submitted with it, will be published.

(6) Where the notice is, without any fault or intention of the applicant, removed, obscured or defaced before the period of 7 days referred to in paragraph (2)(c) has elapsed, the applicant is to be treated as having complied with the requirements of that paragraph if the applicant has taken reasonable steps for protection of the notice and, if need be, its replacement.

(7) The date prescribed for the purposes of section 65(2) of the 1990 Act (notice etc of applications for planning permission) and the 'prescribed date' for the purposes of this article, is the day 21 days before the date of the application.

(8) The applications prescribed for the purposes of paragraph (c) of the definition of 'owner' in section 65(8) of the 1990 Act are minerals applications and the minerals prescribed for the purposes of that paragraph are any minerals other than oil, gas, coal, gold or silver.

(9) In this article—

    'minerals applications' mean applications for planning permission for development consisting of the winning and working of minerals;

    'requisite notice' means notice in the appropriate form set out in Schedule 2 or in a form substantially to the same effect, but does not include notice served using electronic communications; and

    'tenant' means the tenant of an agricultural holding any part of which is comprised in the land to which an application relates.

14 Certificates in relation to notice of applications for planning permission

(1) Where an application for planning permission is made, the applicant must certify, in a form published by the Secretary of State or in a form substantially to the same effect, that the relevant requirements of article 13 have been satisfied.

(2) If an applicant has cause to rely on article 13(6), the certificate must state the relevant circumstances.

Town and Country Planning (Development Management Procedure) Order 2015

15 Publicity for applications for planning permission

(1) An application for planning permission must be publicised by the local planning authority to which the application is made in the manner prescribed by this article.

(2) In the case of an application for planning permission for development which—

(a) is an EIA application accompanied by an environmental statement,

(b) does not accord with the provisions of the development plan in force in the area in which the land to which the application relates is situated, or

(c) would affect a right of way to which Part 3 of the Wildlife and Countryside Act 1981 (public rights of way) applies,

the application must be publicised in the manner specified in paragraph (3).

(3) An application falling within paragraph (2) ('a paragraph (2) application') must be publicised in accordance with the requirements in paragraph (7) and by giving requisite notice—

(a) by site display in at least one place on or near the land to which the application relates for not less than 21 days; and

(b) by publication of the notice in a newspaper circulating in the locality in which the land to which the application relates is situated.

(4) In the case of an application for planning permission which is not a paragraph (2) application, if the development proposed is major development the application must be publicised in accordance with the requirements in paragraph (7) and by giving requisite notice—

(a) (i) by site display in at least one place on or near the land to which the application relates for not less than 21 days; or

(ii) by serving the notice on any adjoining owner or occupier; and

(b) by publication of the notice in a newspaper circulating in the locality in which the land to which the application relates is situated.

(5) In a case to which neither paragraph (2) nor paragraph (4) applies, the application must be publicised in accordance with the requirements in paragraph (7) and by giving requisite notice—

(a) by site display in at least one place on or near the land to which the application relates for not less than 21 days; or

(b) by serving the notice on any adjoining owner or occupier.

(6) Where the notice is, without any fault or intention of the local planning authority, removed, obscured or defaced before the period of 21 days referred to in paragraph (3)(a), (4)(a)(i) or (5)(a) has elapsed, the authority is to be treated as having complied with the requirements of the relevant paragraph if they have taken reasonable steps for protection of the notice and, if need be, its replacement.

(7) The following information must be published on a website maintained by the local planning authority—

(a) the address or location of the proposed development;

(b) a description of the proposed development;

(c) the date by which any representations about the application must be made, which must not be before the last day of the period of 14 days beginning with the date on which the information is published;

Part 3 Applications

(d) where and when the application may be inspected;

(e) how representations may be made about the application; and

(f) that, in the case of a householder or minor commercial application, in the event of an appeal that proceeds by way of the expedited procedure, any representations made about the application will be passed to the Secretary of State and there will be no opportunity to make further representations.

(8) Subject to paragraph (9), if the local planning authority have failed to satisfy the requirements of this article in respect of an application for planning permission at the time the application is referred to the Secretary of State under section 77 (reference of applications to Secretary of State) of the 1990 Act, or any appeal to the Secretary of State is made under section 78 of the 1990 Act, this article continues to apply as if such referral or appeal to the Secretary of State had not been made.

(9) Where paragraph (8) applies, the local planning authority must inform the Secretary of State as soon as they have satisfied the relevant requirements in this article.

(10) In this article—

'adjoining owner or occupier' means any owner or occupier of any land adjoining the land to which the application relates; and

'requisite notice' means notice in the appropriate form set out in Schedule 3 or in a form substantially to the same effect.

(11) Paragraphs (1) to (6) apply to applications made to the Secretary of State under section 293A of the 1990 Act (urgent Crown development: application) as if the references to a local planning authority were references to the Secretary of State.

16 Publicity for applications for planning permission within 10 metres of relevant railway land

(1) This article applies where the development to which the application relates is situated within 10 metres of relevant railway land.

(2) The local planning authority must, except where paragraph (3) applies, publicise an application for planning permission by serving requisite notice on any infrastructure manager of relevant railway land.

(3) Where an infrastructure manager has instructed the local planning authority in writing that they do not require notification in relation to a particular description of development, type of building operation or in relation to specified sites or geographical areas ('the instruction'), the local planning authority is not required to notify that infrastructure manager.

(4) The infrastructure manager may withdraw the instruction at any time by notifying the local planning authority in writing.

(5) In paragraph (2) 'requisite notice' means a notice in the appropriate form as set out in Schedule 3 or in a form substantially to the same effect.

17 Notice of reference of applications to the Secretary of State

On referring any application to the Secretary of State under section 77 (reference of applications to Secretary of State) of the 1990 Act pursuant to a direction made under that section, a local planning authority must serve on the applicant a notice—

Town and Country Planning (Development Management Procedure) Order 2015

    (a) setting out the terms of the direction and any reasons given by the Secretary of State for issuing it; and

    (b) stating that the application has been referred to the Secretary of State.

PART 4 CONSULTATION

18 Consultations before the grant of permission

(1) Before granting planning permission for development which, in their opinion, falls within a category set out in the Table in Schedule 4, a local planning authority must consult the authority or person mentioned in relation to that category, except where—

    (a) the local planning authority are the authority so mentioned;

    (b) the local planning authority are required to consult the authority so mentioned under paragraph 7 of Schedule 1 to the 1990 Act (local planning authorities: distribution of functions) or article 24;

    (c) the authority or person so mentioned has advised the local planning authority that they do not wish to be consulted;

    (d) the development is subject to any standing advice published by the authority or person so mentioned in relation to the category of development; or

    (e) the development is not EIA development and is the subject of an application in relation to which article 20 applies.

(2) The exception in paragraph (1)(c) does not apply where, in the opinion of the local planning authority, development falls within paragraph (zb) of the Table in Schedule 4.

(3) The exception in paragraph (1)(d) does not apply where—

    (a) the development is EIA development; or

    (b) the standing advice was published more than 2 years before the date of the application for planning permission for the development and the guidance has not been amended or confirmed as being current by the authority or person within that period.

(4) The Secretary of State may give directions to a local planning authority requiring that authority to consult any person or body named in the directions, in any case or class of case specified in the directions.

(5) Where, by or under this article or article 20, a local planning authority are required to consult any person or body ('consultee') before granting planning permission—

    (a) they must, unless an applicant has served a copy of an application for planning permission on the consultee, give notice of the application to the consultee; and

    (b) subject to paragraph (6), they must not determine the application until at least 21 days after the date on which notice is given under sub-paragraph (a) or, if earlier, 21 days after the date of service of a copy of the application on the consultee by the applicant.

(6) Paragraph (5)(b) does not apply if before the end of the period referred to in that sub-paragraph—

Part 4 Consultation

(a) the local planning authority have received representations concerning the application from all consultees; or

(b) all consultees give notice that they do not intend to make representations.

(7) The local planning authority must, in determining the application, take into account any representations received from any consultee.

19 Consultations before the grant of planning permission: urgent Crown development

(1) This article applies in relation to applications made to the Secretary of State under section 293A of the 1990 Act (urgent Crown development: application).

(2) Before granting planning permission for development which, in the opinion of the Secretary of State, falls within a category set out in the Table in Schedule 4, the Secretary of State must consult the authority or person mentioned in relation to that category, except where—

(a) the Secretary of State is required to consult the authority so mentioned under section 293A(9)(a) of the 1990 Act;

(b) the authority or person so mentioned has advised the Secretary of State that they do not wish to be consulted; or

(c) the development is subject to any standing advice published by the authority or person so mentioned to the Secretary of State in relation to the category of development.

(3) The exception in paragraph (2)(b) does not apply where, in the opinion of the Secretary of State, development falls within paragraph (zb) of the Table in Schedule 4.

(4) The exception in paragraph (2)(c) does not apply where—

(a) the development is EIA development; or

(b) the standing advice was issued more than 2 years before the date of the application for planning permission for the development and the guidance has not been amended or confirmed as being current by the authority or person within that period.

(5) Where, by or under this article, the Secretary of State is required to consult any person or body ('consultee') before granting planning permission—

(a) the Secretary of State must, unless an applicant has served a copy of an application for planning permission on the consultee, give notice of the application to the consultee; and

(b) subject to paragraph (6), the Secretary of State must not determine the application until at least 21 days after the date on which notice is given under sub-paragraph (a) or, if earlier, 21 days after the date of service of a copy of the application on the consultee by the applicant.

(6) Paragraph (5)(b) does not apply if before the end of the period referred to in that sub-paragraph—

(a) the Secretary of State has received representations concerning the application from the consultee; or

(b) all consultees give notice that they do not intend to make representations.

(7) The Secretary of State must, in determining the application, take into account any representations received from any consultee.

20 Consultations before the grant of planning permission pursuant to section 73 or the grant of a replacement planning permission subject to a new time limit

(1) Paragraph (2) applies in relation to an application—

    (a) made pursuant to section 73 of the 1990 Act (determination of applications to develop land without conditions previously attached);

    (b) for planning permission where the development that is the subject of the application—

        (i) has not yet begun; and

        (ii) was granted planning permission on or before 1st October 2010 subject to a time limit imposed by or under section 91 (general condition limiting duration of planning permission) or 92 (outline planning permission) of the 1990 Act which has not expired; or

    (c) for outline planning permission where the development that is the subject of the application—

        (i) has begun in accordance with the terms of, and any reserved matters approved under, an outline planning permission which is required or expressly permitted to be implemented in phases, other than a permission granted on an application made under sub-paragraph (b); and

        (ii) was granted that outline planning permission on or before 1st October 2010 subject to a time limit imposed by or under section 91 or 92 of the 1990 Act which has not expired.

(2) Before granting planning permission on an application in relation to which this paragraph applies, the local planning authority must consult such authorities or persons falling within a category set out in the Table in Schedule 4 as the local planning authority consider appropriate.

21 Consultation with county planning authority

The period prescribed for the purposes of paragraph 7(7)(c) of Schedule 1 to the 1990 Act (local planning authorities: distribution of functions) is 21 days.

22 Duty to respond to consultation

(1) The requirements to consult which are prescribed for the purposes of section 54(2)(b) of the 2004 Act (duty to respond to consultation) are those contained in—

    (a) articles 18 and 19 and Schedule 4, except as provided for in paragraph (2);

    (b) article 20;

    (c) article 24;

    (d) paragraphs W(5) and (6) of Part 3 of Schedule 2 to the Permitted Development Order (change of use);

    (e) paragraph E.3(5) and (6) of Part 4 of Schedule 2 to the Permitted Development Order (filming);

Part 4 Consultation

    (f) paragraph A.3(5)(a) of Part 16 of Schedule 2 to the Permitted Development Order (development by electronic communications code operators);

    (g) section 71(3) of the 1990 Act (consultations in connection with determinations under section 70);

    (h) paragraph 4(2) of Schedule 1 to the 1990 Act;

    (i) paragraph 7 of Schedule 1 to the 1990 Act; and

    (j) paragraph 3(b) of Schedule 4 to the Planning (Listed Buildings and Conservation Areas) Act 1990 (further provisions as to exercise of functions by different authorities).

(2) A requirement to consult under paragraph (zb)(iii) of Schedule 4 is not a prescribed requirement for the purposes of section 54(2)(b) of the 2004 Act.

(3) The period prescribed for the purposes of section 54(4)(a) of the 2004 Act is the period of 21 days beginning with the day on which—

    (a) the document on which the views of consultees are sought, or

    (b) where there is more than one such document and they are sent on different days, the last of those documents,

is received by the consultee, or such other period as may be agreed in writing between the consultee and the consultor.

(4) The information to be provided to the consultee for the purposes of the consultation, pursuant to section 54(5)(b) of the 2004 Act, is such information as will enable that person to provide a substantive response.

(5) For the purposes of this article and article 23 and pursuant to section 54(5)(c) of the 2004 Act, a substantive response is one which—

    (a) states that the consultee has no comment to make;

    (b) states that, on the basis of the information available, the consultee is content with the development proposed;

    (c) refers the consultor to current standing advice by the consultee on the subject of the consultation; or

    (d) provides advice to the consultor.

23 Duty to respond to consultation: annual reports

(1) Each consultee who is, by virtue of section 54 of the 2004 Act and article 22, under a duty to respond to consultation, must give to the Secretary of State, not later than 1st July in each year, a report as to that consultee's compliance with section 54(4) of the 2004 Act.

(2) The report must relate to the period of 12 months commencing on 1st April in the preceding year ('the report year').

(3) The report must contain, in respect of any report year—

    (a) a statement as to the number of occasions on which the consultee was consulted by a person other than a local planning authority;

    (b) a statement as to the number of occasions on which a substantive response was given to a person other than a local planning authority within the period referred to in section 54(4) of the 2004 Act;

    (c) a statement as to the number of occasions on which the consultee was consulted by a local planning authority;

(d) a statement as to the number of occasions on which a substantive response was given to a local planning authority within the period referred to in section 54(4) of the 2004 Act; and

(e) in relation to occasions on which the consultee has given a substantive response outside the period referred to in section 54(4) of the 2004 Act, a summary of the reasons why the consultee failed to comply with the duty to respond within that period.

24 Recommendations by district planning authority before determination of county matters application

(1) Subject to paragraph (2), a county planning authority must, before determining—

(a) an application for planning permission under Part 3 of the 1990 Act (control over development),

(b) an application for a certificate of lawful use or development under section 191 or 192 of the 1990 Act (certificates of lawfulness of existing or proposed use or development), or

(c) an application for approval of reserved matters,

give the district planning authority, if any, for the area in which the relevant land lies a period of at least 21 days, from the date of receipt of the application by the district authority, within which to make recommendations about the manner in which the application must be determined; and must take any such recommendations into account.

(2) Paragraph (1) does not prevent a county planning authority determining an application if before the end of the period referred to in that paragraph—

(a) the county planning authority have received recommendations concerning the application from the district planning authority; or

(b) the district planning authority give notice to the county planning authority that they do not intend to make recommendations.

(3) A county planning authority must—

(a) on determining an application of a kind mentioned in paragraph (1), as soon as reasonably practicable notify the district planning authority, if any, of the terms of their decision; or

(b) if any such application is referred to the Secretary of State, inform the district planning authority, if any, of the date when it was so referred and, when notified to them, of the terms of the decision.

25 Representations by parish council before determination of application

(1) Where the council of a parish are given information in relation to an application pursuant to paragraph 8(1) of Schedule 1 to the 1990 Act (local planning authorities: distribution of functions), they must, as soon as practicable, notify the local planning authority who are determining the application whether they propose to make any representations about the manner in which the application should be determined, and must make any representations to that authority within 21 days of the notification to them of the application.

(2) A local planning authority must not determine any application in respect of which a parish are required to be given information before—

Part 5 Applications Made Under a Planning Condition

(a) the council of the parish inform them that they do not propose to make any representations;
(b) representations are made by that council; or
(c) the period of 21 days mentioned in paragraph (1) has elapsed,

whichever occurs first; and in determining the application the authority must take into account any representations received from the council of the parish.

(3) The appropriate authority must notify the council of the parish of—
   (a) the terms of the decision on any such application; or
   (b) where the application is referred to the Secretary of State—
      (i) the date when it was so referred; and
      (ii) when notified to the appropriate authority, the terms of the Secretary of State's decision.

(4) For the purposes of paragraph (3), the 'appropriate authority' is—
   (a) where the parish is situated in a National Park, the National Park authority;
   (b) where the parish is situated in Greater London or a metropolitan county, and is not situated in a National Park, the local planning authority;
   (c) where the parish is situated in a district which has no district council and is not situated in a National Park, the county planning authority;
   (d) in any other case, the district planning authority.

26 Notification of mineral applications

(1) Where notice has been given for the purposes of this article to a mineral planning authority as respects land which is in their area and it is specified in the notice—
   (a) by the Coal Authority that the land contains coal,
   (b) by the Secretary of State for Energy and Climate Change that the land contains gas or oil, or
   (c) by the Crown Estate Commissioners that the land contains silver or gold,

the mineral planning authority must not determine any application for planning permission to win and work any mineral on that land without first notifying the body or person who gave the notice that an application has been made.

(2) In paragraph (1)(a), 'coal' means coal other than that—
   (a) won or worked during the course of operations which are carried on exclusively for the purpose of exploring for coal; or
   (b) which it is necessary to dig or carry away in the course of activities carried on for purposes which do not include the getting of coal or any product of coal.

PART 5 APPLICATIONS MADE UNDER A PLANNING CONDITION

27 Applications made under a planning condition

(1) Subject to paragraph (3), an application for any consent, agreement or approval required by a condition or limitation attached to a grant of planning permission must—

Town and Country Planning (Development Management Procedure) Order 2015

      (a) be made in writing to the local planning authority and must give sufficient information to enable the authority to identify the planning permission in respect of which it is made; and

      (b) include such particulars, and be accompanied by such plans and drawings, as are necessary to deal with the application.

(2) The authority must give notice to the applicant of their decision on the application within a period of 8 weeks beginning with the day immediately following that on which the application is received by the authority, or such longer period as may be agreed by the applicant and the authority in writing.

(3) Paragraphs (1) and (2) do not apply to an application for approval—

      (a) of reserved matters; or

      (b) under Schedule 2 to the Permitted Development Order.

28 Deemed discharge

(1) Subject to article 30, a planning condition to which section 74A(2) of the 1990 Act applies is deemed to be discharged with effect from the date provided for paragraph (2) where—

      (a) the applicant has applied to the local planning authority under article 27; and

      (b) the applicant has given notice, in relation to that condition, in accordance with article 29; and

      (c) the period for the authority to give notice to the applicant of their decision on the application has elapsed without the authority giving notice to the applicant of their decision.

(2) Deemed discharge takes effect on the date specified in the notice given under article 29 or on such later date as may be agreed by the applicant and the authority in writing, unless the authority has given notice to the applicant of their decision on the application under article 27 before that date.

29 Deemed discharge notice

(1) In order for a planning condition to be deemed discharged under article 28, the applicant must give a notice ('the deemed discharge notice') to the local planning authority.

(2) A deemed discharge notice may not be given unless—

      (a) at least 6 weeks have elapsed beginning with the day immediately following that on which the application under article 27 is received by the local planning authority; or

      (b) such shorter period as may be agreed in writing between the applicant and the local planning authority for serving a deemed discharge notice has elapsed.

(3) The deemed discharge notice must—

      (a) provide details of the application submitted under article 27 and identify the planning condition to which it relates;

      (b) where the period referred to in article 27 has elapsed, confirm that no appeal has been made under section 78 of the 1990 Act; and

      (c) specify the date on which deemed discharge is to take effect.

Part 6 Determination

(4) The date specified under paragraph (3)(c) must be no earlier than—

(a) the date the period referred to in article 27 elapses, or

(b) 14 days after the day immediately following that on which the deemed discharge notice is received by the local planning authority,

whichever is later.

30 Exemptions

Deemed discharge under article 28 does not apply to a condition attached to the grant of planning permission where—

(a) the condition falls within the exemptions listed in Schedule 6; or

(b) in relation to that condition, the applicant for planning permission and the local planning authority have agreed in writing that the provisions of section 74A of the 1990 Act (deemed discharge of planning conditions) do not apply.

PART 6 DETERMINATION

31 Directions by the Secretary of State

(1) The Secretary of State may give directions restricting the grant of permission by a local planning authority, either indefinitely or during such a period as may be specified in the directions, in respect of any development or in respect of development of any class so specified.

(2) The Secretary of State may give directions that development, which is both of a description set out in column 1 of the table to Schedule 2 to the 2011 Regulations (descriptions of development and applicable thresholds and criteria for the purposes of the definition of 'Schedule 2 development') and of a class described in the direction, is EIA development for the purposes of those Regulations.

(3) A local planning authority must deal with applications for planning permission for development to which a direction given under paragraph (1) or (2) applies, in such manner as to give effect to the direction.

32 Development not in accordance with the development plan

A local planning authority may in such cases and subject to such conditions as may be prescribed by directions given by the Secretary of State under this Order, grant permission for development which does not accord with the provisions of the development plan in force in the area in which the land to which the application relates is situated.

33 Representations to be taken into account

(1) A local planning authority must, in determining an application for planning permission, take into account any representations made where any notice of, or information about, the application has been—

(a) given by site display under article 13 or 15, within 21 days beginning with the date when the notice was first displayed by site display;

(b) served on—

Town and Country Planning (Development Management Procedure) Order 2015

(i) an owner of the land or a tenant of an agricultural holding under article 13;

(ii) an adjoining owner or occupier under article 15; or

(iii) an infrastructure manager under article 16,

within 21 days beginning with the date when the notice was served on that person, provided that the representations are made by any person who they are satisfied is such an owner, tenant, occupier or infrastructure manager; or

(c) published in a newspaper under article 13 or 15 or on a website under article 15, within the period of 14 days beginning with the date on which the notice or information was published,

and the representations and periods in this article are representations and periods prescribed for the purposes of section 71(2)(a) of the 1990 Act (consultations in connection with determinations under section 70).

(2) A local planning authority must give notice of their decision to every person who has made representations which they were required to take into account in accordance with paragraph (1)(b)(i), and such notice is the notice prescribed for the purposes of section 71(2)(b) of the 1990 Act.

(3) Paragraphs (1) and (2) apply to applications referred to the Secretary of State under section 77 (reference of applications to Secretary of State) of the 1990 Act and to applications made to the Secretary of State under section 293A(2) of the 1990 Act (applications for urgent Crown development) and paragraphs (1)(b) and (2) apply to appeals to the Secretary of State made under section 78 of the 1990 Act (right to appeal against planning decisions and failure to take such decisions), as if the references to—

(a) a local planning authority were to the Secretary of State; and

(b) determining an application for planning permission were to determining such application or appeal, as the case may be.

34 Time periods for decisions

(1) Subject to paragraph (9), where a valid application or a non-validated application has been received by a local planning authority, the authority must within the period specified or referred to in paragraph (2) or (3) give the applicant notice of their decision or determination or notice that the application has been referred to the Secretary of State.

(2) The period specified or referred to in this paragraph is—

(a) in relation to an application for major development, 13 weeks beginning with the day immediately following that on which the application is received by the local planning authority;

(b) in relation to an application for development which is not major development, 8 weeks beginning with the day immediately following that on which the application is received by the local planning authority; or

(c) in relation to any development, unless the applicant has already given notice of appeal to the Secretary of State, such extended period as may be agreed in writing between the applicant and the local planning authority.

(3) In relation to a non-validated application, where the notice mentioned in article 12(1) is received—

Part 6 Determination

    (a) during the 7 working days immediately before the end of the period specified or referred to in paragraph (2) ('the initial determination period'); or

    (b) on the final day of, or after the end of, the initial determination period,

the period specified or referred to in this paragraph is 7 working days beginning with the date the notice mentioned in article 12(1) is received by the local planning authority.

(4) In this article 'valid application' means an application which consists of—

    (a) an application which complies with the requirements of article 5, 6 or 7, as the case may be,

    (b) in a case to which article 9 applies, the design and access statement,

    (c) the certificate required by article 14,

    (d) in a case where pre-application consultation is required in accordance with article 3, the particulars specified in article 4,

    (e) subject to paragraph (6), the particulars or evidence required by the authority under section 62(3) of the 1990 Act (applications for planning permission), and

    (f) any fee required to be paid in respect of the application and, for this purpose, lodging a cheque for the amount of a fee is to be taken as payment,

and a valid application is taken to have been received when the application, and such of the documents, particulars or evidence referred to above as are required to be included in, or to accompany, the application have been lodged with the appropriate authority mentioned in article 11(1) and the fee required to be paid has been paid.

(5) In this article 'non-validated application' means an application which consists of—

    (a) an application which complies with the requirements of article 5, 6 or 7, as the case may be;

    (b) in a case to which article 9 applies, the design and access statement;

    (c) the certificate required by article 14;

    (d) in a case where pre-application consultation is required in accordance with article 3, the particulars referred to in article 4;

    (e) subject to paragraph (6), the particulars or evidence required by the authority under section 62(3) of the 1990 Act (applications for planning permission) except the particulars or evidence specified by the applicant in a notice sent to the local planning authority under article 12(1); and

    (f) any fee required to be paid in respect of the application and, for this purpose, lodging a cheque for the amount of a fee is to be taken as payment,

and a non-validated application is taken to have been received when the application, and such of the documents, particulars or evidence (except the particulars or evidence specified by the applicant in a notice sent to the authority under article 12(1)) referred to above as required to be included in, or, to accompany, the application have been lodged with the appropriate authority mentioned in article 11(1), and the fee required to be paid has been paid.

(6) Paragraphs (4)(e) and (5)(e) only apply if—

(a) before the application is made the local planning authority publish or republish, for the purposes of paragraphs (4) and (5), a list of requirements on their website; and

(b) the particulars or evidence that the authority require to be included in the application fall within that list;

(c) the particulars or evidence the authority require to be included in the application—

(i) are reasonable having regard, in particular, to the nature and scale of the proposed development; and

(ii) are about a matter which it is reasonable to think will be a material consideration in the determination of the application; and

(d) the list mentioned in sub-paragraph (a) was published (or republished) during the 2 year period immediately before the date on which the application is made.

(7) Where a fee due in respect of an application has been paid by a cheque which is subsequently dishonoured—

(a) sub-paragraph (a) or (b) of paragraph (2), as the case may be, has effect as if, for 'the application is received by the local planning authority', there were substituted 'the local planning authority are satisfied that they have received the full amount of the fee'; and

(b) sub-paragraph (c) of that paragraph has effect as if, at the end, there were added 'once the authority are satisfied that they have received the full amount of the fee'.

(8) A local planning authority must provide such information about applications made under article 5, 6 or 7 (including information as to the manner in which any such application has been dealt with) as the Secretary of State may by direction require; and any such direction may include provision as to the persons to be informed and the manner in which the information is to be provided.

(9) A local planning authority must not determine an application for planning permission where any notice of, or information about, the application has been—

(a) given by site display under article 13 or 15, before the end of the period of 21 days beginning with the date when the notice was first displayed by site display;

(b) served on—

(i) an owner of the land or a tenant of an agricultural holding under article 13;

(ii) an adjoining owner or occupier under article 15; or

(iii) an infrastructure manager under article 16,

before the end of the period of 21 days beginning with the date when the notice was served on that person; or

(c) published in a newspaper under article 13 or 15 or on a website under article 15, within the period of 14 days beginning with the date on which the notice or information was published,

and the periods in this paragraph are periods prescribed for the purposes of section 71(1) of the 1990 Act (consultations in connection with determinations under section 70).

Part 6 Determination

35 Written notice of decision or determination relating to a planning application

(1) When the local planning authority give notice of a decision or determination on an application for planning permission or for approval of reserved matters—

  (a) where planning permission is granted subject to conditions, the notice must state clearly and precisely their full reasons—

    (i) for each condition imposed; and

    (ii) in the case of each pre-commencement condition, for the condition being a pre-commencement condition;

  (b) where planning permission is refused, the notice must state clearly and precisely their full reasons for the refusal, specifying all policies and proposals in the development plan which are relevant to the decision;

  (c) where—

    (i) the Secretary of State has given a direction restricting the grant of planning permission for the development for which application is made; or

    (ii) the Secretary of State or a government department has expressed the view that the permission should not be granted (either wholly or in part) or should be granted subject to conditions,

  the notice must give details of the direction or of the view expressed.

(2) Where paragraph (1)(a) or (b) applies, the notice must also include a statement explaining, whether, and if so how, in dealing with the application, the local planning authority have worked with the applicant in a positive and proactive manner based on seeking solutions to problems arising in relation to dealing with a planning application.

(3) Where paragraph (1)(a), (b) or (c) applies, the notice must be accompanied by a notification in the terms (or substantially in the terms) set out in Schedule 5.

(4) Where—

  (a) an applicant for planning permission has submitted an environmental statement; and

  (b) the local planning authority have decided (having taken environmental information into consideration) to grant permission (whether unconditionally or subject to conditions),

  the notice given to the applicant in accordance with article 34(1) must include a statement that environmental information has been taken into consideration by the authority.

(5) In paragraph (1)(a)(ii) 'pre-commencement condition' means a condition imposed on the grant of a planning permission which must be complied with—

  (a) before any building or other operation comprised in the development is begun; or

  (b) where the development consists of a material change in the use of any buildings or other land, before the change of use is begun.

PART 7 APPEALS

36 Notice of appeal

Articles 13 and 14 apply to any appeal to the Secretary of State under section 78 of the 1990 Act (right to appeal against planning decisions and failure to take such decisions) as those articles apply to applications for planning permission.

37 Appeals

(1) An applicant who wishes to appeal to the Secretary of State under section 78 of the 1990 Act must give notice of appeal to the Secretary of State by—

    (a) serving on the Secretary of State within—

        (i) the time limit specified in paragraph (2); or

        (ii) such longer period as the Secretary of State may, at any time, allow,

a completed appeal form, obtained from the Secretary of State, together with such of the documents specified in paragraph (3) as are relevant to the appeal; and

    (b) serving on the local planning authority a copy of the completed appeal form mentioned in sub-paragraph (a), as soon as reasonably practicable, together with a copy of the documents mentioned in paragraph (3)(b) (viii) to (x) (where those paragraphs apply), and any relevant documents mentioned in paragraph (3)(a)(ii) or paragraph (3)(b)(v), as the case may be.

(2) The time limit mentioned in paragraph (1) is—

    (a) in the case of a householder or minor commercial appeal, other than a type A or a type B appeal, 12 weeks from the date of the notice of the decision or determination giving rise to the appeal;

    (b) in the case of a type A appeal, 28 days from—

        (i) the date of the notice of the decision or determination giving rise to the appeal; or

        (ii) the expiry of the specified period;

    (c) in the case of a type B appeal, 28 days from the date on which the enforcement notice is served;

    (d) in all other cases, 6 months from—

        (i) the date of the notice of the decision or determination giving rise to the appeal;

        (ii) in a case in which the authority have served a notice on the applicant in accordance with article 5(2) that they require further information, and the applicant has not provided the information, the date of service of that notice; or

        (iii) in any other case, the expiry of the specified period.

(3) The documents mentioned in paragraph (1) are—

    (a) in the case of a householder or minor commercial appeal—

        (i) a copy of the application which was sent to the local planning authority which has occasioned the appeal;

        (ii) any other plans, documents or drawings relating to the application which were not sent to the authority, except any plans, documents or

Part 7 Appeals

drawings relating to amendments to the application proposed after the authority have made their determination; and

(iii) the notice of the decision or determination;

(b) in all other cases—

(i) a copy of the application which was sent to the local planning authority which has occasioned the appeal;

(ii) all plans, drawings and documents sent to the authority in connection with the application;

(iii) all correspondence with the authority relating to the application;

(iv) any certificate provided to the authority under article 14;

(v) any other plans, documents or drawings relating to the application which were not sent to the authority, except any plans, documents or drawings relating to amendments to the application proposed after the authority have made their determination;

(vi) the notice of the decision or determination, if any;

(vii) if the appeal relates to an application for approval of certain matters in accordance with a condition on a planning permission, the application for that permission, the plans submitted with that application and the planning permission granted;

(viii) subject to paragraph (4), the applicant's full statement of case (if they wish to make additional representations);

(ix) subject to paragraph (4), a statement of which procedure (written representations, a hearing or an inquiry) the applicant considers should be used to determine the appeal; and

(x) subject to paragraph (4), a draft statement of common ground if the applicant considers that the appeal should be determined through a hearing or an inquiry.

(4) The relevant documents required in paragraph (3)(b)(viii) to (x) are not required to accompany the notice under paragraph (1)—

(a) where a direction is given by the Secretary of State under section 321(3) of the 1990 Act (matters related to national security);

(b) where section 293A of the 1990 Act (urgent Crown development) applies; or

(c) in relation to type A or type B appeals.

(5) The Secretary of State may refuse to accept a notice of appeal from an applicant if the completed appeal form required under paragraph (1)(a) and the documents required under paragraph (3) are not served on the Secretary of State within the time limit specified in paragraph (2).

(6) The Secretary of State may provide, or arrange for the provision of, a website for use for such purposes as the Secretary of State thinks fit which—

(a) relate to appeals under section 78 of the 1990 Act and this article; and

(b) are capable of being carried out electronically.

Town and Country Planning (Development Management Procedure) Order 2015

(7) Where a person gives notice of appeal to the Secretary of State using electronic communications, the person is taken to have agreed—

   (a) to the use of such communications for all purposes relating to the appeal which are capable of being carried out electronically;

   (b) that the person's address for the purpose of such communications is the address incorporated into, or otherwise logically associated with, the person's notice of appeal; and

   (c) that the person's deemed agreement under this paragraph subsists until notice is given in accordance with article 46 that the person wishes to revoke the agreement.

(8) In this article—

   'draft statement of common ground' means a written statement containing factual information about the proposal which is the subject of the appeal that the applicant reasonably considers will not be disputed by the local planning authority;

   'full statement of case' means, and is comprised of, a written statement which contains full particulars of the case which a person proposes to put forward and copies of any documents which that person intends to refer to or put in evidence;

   'householder appeal' means an appeal under section 78(1) of the 1990 Act in respect of a householder application, except an appeal against the grant of any planning permission, consent, agreement or approval which is granted subject to conditions;

   'minor commercial appeal' means an appeal under section 78(1) of the 1990 Act in relation to a minor commercial application, except an appeal against the grant of any planning permission, consent, agreement or approval which is granted subject to conditions;

   'specified period' means the period specified in article 27 or article 34, as the case may be;

   'type A appeal' means an appeal under section 78(1) or 78(2) of the 1990 Act in respect of an application relating to land and development which are the same or substantially the same as the land and development in respect of which an enforcement notice—

   (a) has been served no earlier than 2 years before the application is made;

   (b) has been served before—

      (i) the date of the notice of the decision or determination giving rise to the appeal; or

      (ii) the expiry of the specified period; and

   (c) is not withdrawn before the expiry of the period of 28 days from the date specified in sub-paragraph (b); and

   'type B appeal' means an appeal under section 78(1) or 78(2) of the 1990 Act in respect of an application relating to land and development which are the same or substantially the same as the land and development in respect of which an enforcement notice—

   (a) is served on or after—

      (i) the date of the notice of the decision or determination giving rise to the appeal, or

(ii) the expiry of the specified period;

(b) is served earlier than 28 days before the expiry of the time limit specified—

(i) in the case of a householder or minor commercial appeal, in paragraph (2)(a); or

(ii) in any other case, in paragraph (2)(d); and

(c) is not withdrawn before the expiry of the period of 28 days from the date on which the enforcement notice is served.

PART 8 MISCELLANEOUS

38 Local development orders

(1) Where a local planning authority propose to make a local development order they must first prepare—

(a) a draft of the order; and

(b) a statement of their reasons for making the order.

(2) The statement of reasons must contain—

(a) a description of the development which the order would permit; and

(b) a plan or statement identifying the land to which the order would relate.

(3) Where a local planning authority have prepared a draft local development order, they must consult, in accordance with paragraph (5), such of the following persons whose interests the authority consider would be affected by the order if made—

(a) if the local planning authority is a London borough council, the Mayor of London;

(b) a local planning authority, county council or parish council any part of whose area is in or adjoins the area of the local planning authority;

(c) Natural England;

(d) the Environment Agency;

(e) the Historic England;

(f) where the Secretary of State is the highway authority for any highway in the area of the local planning authority, the Secretary of State for Transport;

(g) a strategic highways company any part of whose area is in or adjoins the area of the local planning authority;

(h) any person—

(i) to whom the electronic communications code applies by virtue of a direction given under section 106(3)(a) of the Communications Act 2003 (application of the electronic communications code); and

(ii) who owns or controls electronic communications apparatus situated in any part of the area of the local planning authority;

(i) any of the following persons who exercise functions in any part of the area of the local planning authority—

(i) a clinical commissioning group;

(ii) the National Health Service Commissioning Board;

(iii) a person to whom a licence has been granted under section 6(1)(b) and (c) of the Electricity Act 1989 (licences authorising supply, etc);

(iv) a person to whom a licence has been granted under section 7(2) of the Gas Act 1986 (licensing of gas transporters);

(v) a sewerage undertaker;

(vi) a water undertaker;

(j) voluntary bodies some or all of whose activities benefit any part of the local planning authority's area;

(k) bodies which represent the interests of persons who share a protected characteristic in the local planning authority's area;

(l) bodies which represent the interests of persons carrying on business in the local planning authority's area.

(4) The local planning authority must also consult any person with whom they would have been required to consult on an application for planning permission for the development proposed to be permitted by the order.

(5) In consulting in accordance with paragraphs (3) and (4) the local planning authority must—

(a) send a copy of the draft order and the statement of reasons to the consultees;

(b) specify a consultation period of not less than 28 days; and

(c) take account of all representations received by them during the period specified.

(6) A local planning authority must, during any consultation under paragraphs (3) and (4)—

(a) make a copy of the draft local development order, the environmental statement and statement of reasons available for inspection—

(i) at their principal office during normal working hours; and

(ii) at such other places within their area as they consider appropriate;

(b) publish on their website—

(i) the draft local development order, the environmental statement and the statement of reasons;

(ii) a statement that those documents are available for inspection and the places where and times when they can be inspected; and

(iii) the date by which representations on the draft local development order must be received, which must be not less than 28 days after the date of first publication on the website; and

(c) give notice by local advertisement of—

(i) the draft local development order, the environmental statement and the statement of reasons;

(ii) the availability of those documents for inspection, and the places where and times when they can be inspected; and

(iii) the date by which representations on the draft local development order must be received, which must be not less than 28 days from the date on which the notice was first published.

Part 8 Miscellaneous

(7) Where the draft local development order would grant planning permission for development specified in the order, the local planning authority must also give notice of their proposal to make the order—

   (a) by site display in at least one place on or near to the site to which the order relates a notice in the appropriate form set out in Schedule 7 or in a form substantially to the same effect, and, subject to paragraph (8), leaving the notice in position for a period of not less than 28 days beginning with the date on which it is first displayed by site display; and

   (b) by serving a copy of that notice on every person whom the authority knows to be the owner or tenant of any part of the site whose name and address is known to the authority,

   and specifying in the notice a date by which representations on the draft local development order must be received, which must be not less than 28 days from the date on which the notice was displayed by site display or served, as the case may be.

(8) Where the notice referred to in paragraph (7)(a) is, without any fault or intention of the authority, removed, obscured or defaced before the period referred to in that paragraph has elapsed, the authority is treated as having complied with the requirements of that paragraph if they have taken reasonable steps for the protection of the notice, and, if necessary, its replacement.

(9) Paragraph (10) applies where any notice of the proposal has been—

   (a) published on the authority's website or by local advertisement in accordance with paragraph (6);

   (b) given by site display under paragraph (7)(a); or

   (c) served on an owner of the land or a tenant under paragraph (7)(b).

(10) A local planning authority must, in considering what modifications should be made to the draft local development order or whether such an order should be adopted, take into account any representations made in relation to that order and received by the authority by the date specified on the website or in the notices, in accordance with paragraph (6) or (7) as the case may be, as the date by which representations should be made (or, if the dates on the website or in the notices differ from each other, the latest of such dates).

(11) A local planning authority must send a copy of—

   (a) the local development order,

   (b) the statement of reasons relating to the making of that order, and

   (c) any environmental statement relating to that order prepared in accordance with regulation 29(4)(a) of the 2011 Regulations, to the Secretary of State as soon as reasonably practicable, and no later than 28 days, after the local planning authority has adopted the order.

(12) A local development order must not be made so as to grant planning permission—

   (a) for development affecting a listed building, or

   (b) for development which is Schedule 1 development within the meaning of regulation 2(1) of the 2011 Regulations (interpretation).

(13) Where a local planning authority revoke a local development order the authority must—

(a) publish on their website a statement that the local development order has been revoked;

(b) give notice of the revocation by local advertisement; and

(c) give written notice of the revocation to every person whom the local planning authority consulted under paragraphs (3) or (4) before making the order.

(14) In this article, a requirement to give notice by local advertisement is a requirement to publish the notice in as many newspapers as will secure that the press coverage (taken as a whole) extends to the whole of the area to which the local development order relates.

39 Certificate of lawful use or development

(1) An application for a certificate under section 191(1) or 192(1) of the 1990 Act (certificates of lawfulness of existing or proposed use or development) must be made on a form published by the Secretary of State (or on a form substantially to the same effect) and must, in addition to specifying the land and describing the use, operations or other matter in question in accordance with those sections, include the particulars specified or referred to in the form.

(2) An application to which paragraph (1) applies must be accompanied by—

(a) a plan identifying the land to which the application relates drawn to an identified scale and showing the direction of North;

(b) such evidence verifying the information included in the application as the applicant can provide; and

(c) a statement setting out the applicant's interest in the land, the name and address of any other person known to the applicant to have an interest in the land and whether any such other person has been notified of the application.

(3) Where an application for a certificate under section 192(1) of the 1990 Act is made in respect of Crown land, it must, in addition to the documents required by paragraph (2), be accompanied by—

(a) a statement that the application is made in respect of Crown land; and

(b) where the application is made by a person authorised in writing by the appropriate authority, a copy of that authorisation.

(4) Where such an application specifies two or more uses, operations or other matters, the plan which accompanies the application must indicate to which part of the land each such use, operation or matter relates.

(5) Where an application is made using electronic communications to transmit a form to the local planning authority, the applicant is taken to have agreed—

(a) to the use of such communications by the local planning authority for the purposes of the application;

(b) that the applicant's address for those purposes is the address incorporated into, or otherwise logically associated with, the application; and

(c) that the applicant's deemed agreement under this paragraph subsists until notice is given in writing of the withdrawal of the applicant's consent to the use of electronic communications under article 46.

(6) Articles 11(1) and 34(8) apply to an application for a certificate to which paragraph (1) applies as they apply to an application for planning permission.

Part 8 Miscellaneous

(7) When the local planning authority receive an application which complies with the requirements of paragraphs (1) to (4) and any fee required to be paid with respect to the application, they must, as soon as reasonably practicable, send to the applicant an acknowledgement of the application in the terms (or substantially in the terms) set out in Schedule 1.

(8) Where, after sending an acknowledgement as required by paragraph (7), the local planning authority consider that the application is invalid they must, as soon as reasonably practicable, notify the applicant that the application is invalid.

(9) The local planning authority may by notice in writing require the applicant to provide such further information as may be specified to enable them to deal with the application.

(10) Where a valid application has been received, the local planning authority must give the applicant written notice of their decision within—

    (a) the period of 8 weeks beginning with the day immediately following that on which the application is received; or

    (b) unless the applicant has already given notice of appeal to the Secretary of State, within such extended period as may be agreed in writing between the applicant and the authority.

(11) Where a fee due in respect of an application has been paid by a cheque which is subsequently dishonoured—

    (a) sub-paragraph (a) of paragraph (10) has effect as if, for 'the application is received', there were substituted 'the authority are satisfied that they have received the full amount of the fee'; and

    (b) sub-paragraph (b) of that paragraph has effect as if, at the end, there were added 'once the authority are satisfied that they have received the full amount of the fee'.

(12) In this article, 'valid application' means an application which—

    (a) complies with the requirements of paragraphs (1) to (4); and

    (b) is accompanied by the appropriate fee,

and a valid application is taken to have been received when the application and all of the documents, particulars or evidence referred to in paragraphs (1) to (4) have been lodged with the appropriate authority mentioned in article 11(1) and the fee has been paid.

(13) Where an application is refused, in whole or in part (including a case in which the authority modify the description of the use, operations or other matter in the application or substitute an alternative description for that description), the notice of decision must state clearly and precisely the authority's full reasons for their decision and include a statement to the effect that if the applicant is aggrieved by the decision the applicant may appeal to the Secretary of State under section 195 of the 1990 Act (appeals against refusal or failure to give decision on application).

(14) A certificate under section 191 or 192 of the 1990 Act must be in the form set out in Schedule 8 or in a form substantially to the same effect.

(15) Where a local planning authority propose to revoke a certificate issued under section 191 or 192 of the 1990 Act in accordance with section 193(7) of the

1990 Act (certificates under sections 191 and 192: supplementary provisions), they must, before they revoke the certificate, give notice of that proposal to—

(a) the owner of the land affected;

(b) the occupier of the land affected;

(c) any other person who will in their opinion be affected by the revocation; and

(d) in the case of a certificate issued by the Secretary of State under section 195 of the 1990 Act, the Secretary of State.

(16) A notice issued under paragraph (15) must invite the person on whom the notice is served to make representations on the proposal to the authority within 14 days of service of the notice and the authority must not revoke the certificate until all such periods allowed for making representations have expired.

(17) An authority must give written notice of any revocation under section 193(7) of the 1990 Act to every person on whom notice of the proposed revocation was served under paragraph (15).

PART 9 MONITORING

40 Register of applications

(1) In this article and in articles 41 and 42, 'the local planning register authority' means—

(a) in relation to land in a National Park, the National Park authority (and references to the area of the local planning register authority are, in this case, to the National Park);

(b) in relation to land in Greater London or a metropolitan county, which is not land in a National Park, the local planning authority (and references to the area of the local planning register authority are, in this case, to the area of the local planning authority other than any part of their area within a National Park);

(c) in relation to any other land—

(i) the district planning authority; or

(ii) where there is no district planning authority in relation to the land, the county planning authority,

(and references to the area of the local planning register authority are, in this case, to the area of the district planning authority or the area of the county planning authority, as the case may be, other than any part of their area within a National Park).

(2) Each local planning register authority must keep, in two parts, a register ('the register') of every application for planning permission relating to their area.

(3) Part 1 of the register must contain in respect of each such application and any application for approval of reserved matters made in respect of an outline planning permission granted on such an application, made or sent to the local planning register authority and not finally disposed of—

(a) a copy (which may be photographic or in electronic form) of the application together with any accompanying plans and drawings;

(b) a copy (which may be photographic or in electronic form) of any planning obligation or section 278 agreement proposed or entered into in connection with the application;

(c) a copy (which may be photographic or in electronic form) of any other planning obligation or section 278 agreement entered into in respect of the land the subject of the application which the applicant considers relevant; and

(d) particulars of any modification to any planning obligation or section 278 agreement included in Part 1 of the register in accordance with sub-paragraphs (b) and (c).

(4) Part 2 of the register must contain, in respect of every application for planning permission relating to the local planning register authority's area—

(a) a copy (which may be photographic or in electronic form) of the application and of plans and drawings submitted in relation thereto and of any accompanying design and access statement provided in accordance with article 9;

(b) particulars of any direction given under the 1990 Act or this Order in respect of the application;

(c) the decision, if any, of the local planning authority in respect of the application, including details of any conditions subject to which permission was granted, the date of such decision and the name of the local planning authority;

(d) the reference number, the date and effect of any decision of the Secretary of State in respect of the application, whether on appeal, on an application under section 293A(2) of the 1990 Act (urgent Crown development: application) or on a reference under section 77 of the 1990 Act (reference of applications to Secretary of State);

(e) the date of any subsequent approval (whether approval of reserved matters or any other approval required) given in relation to the application;

(f) a copy (which may be photographic or in electronic form) of any planning obligation or section 278 agreement entered into in connection with any decision of the local planning authority or the Secretary of State in respect of the application;

(g) a copy (which may be photographic or in electronic form) of any other planning obligation or section 278 agreement taken into account by the local planning authority or the Secretary of State when making the decision; and

(h) particulars of any modification to or discharge of any planning obligation or section 278 agreement included in Part 2 of the register in accordance with sub-paragraphs (f) or (g) or paragraph (6).

(5) The register must also contain the following information in respect of every application made under article 10 relating to their area—

(a) a copy (which may be photographic or in electronic form) of the application together with any accompanying plans and drawings; and

(b) the decision, if any, of the local planning authority in respect of the application, the date of such decision and the name of the local planning authority.

(6) Where, on any appeal to the Secretary of State under section 174 of the 1990 Act (appeal against enforcement notice), the appellant is deemed to have made

Town and Country Planning (Development Management Procedure) Order 2015

an application for planning permission and the Secretary of State has granted permission, the local planning register authority must, on receipt of notification of the Secretary of State's decision, enter into Part 2 of the register particulars of the development concerned, the land on which it was carried out, and the date and effect of the Secretary of State's decision together with a copy (which may be photographic or in electronic form) of—

(a) any planning obligation or section 278 agreement entered into in connection with the decision; and

(b) any other planning obligation or section 278 agreement taken into account by the Secretary of State when making the decision.

(7) The register must also contain the following information in respect of every application for a certificate under section 191 or 192 of the 1990 Act (certificates of lawfulness of existing or proposed use or development) relating to the authority's area—

(a) the name and address of the applicant;

(b) the date of the application;

(c) the address or location of the land to which the application relates;

(d) the description of the use, operations or other matter included in the application;

(e) the decision, if any, of the local planning authority in respect of the application and the date of such decision; and

(f) the reference number, date and effect of any decision of the Secretary of State on an appeal in respect of the application.

(8) The register must contain the following information about simplified planning zone schemes in the area of the authority—

(a) brief particulars of any action taken by the authority or the Secretary of State in accordance with section 83 of, or Schedule 7 to, the 1990 Act (making of simplified planning zone schemes etc) to establish or approve any simplified planning zone scheme, including the date of adoption or approval, the date on which the scheme or alteration becomes operative and the date on which it ceases to be operative;

(b) a copy of any simplified planning zone scheme, or alteration to an existing scheme, including any diagrams, illustrations, descriptive matter or any other prescribed material which has been made available for inspection under Schedule 7 to the 1990 Act; and

(c) an index map showing the boundary of any operative or proposed simplified planning zone schemes, including alterations to existing schemes where appropriate, together with a reference to the entries in the register under sub-paragraphs (a) and (b).

(9) To enable any person to trace any entry in the register, every register must include an index together with a separate index of applications for development involving mining operations or the creation of mineral working deposits.

(10) Subject to paragraph (11), every entry in the register must be made within 14 days of the receipt of an application, or of the giving or making of the relevant direction, decision or approval as the case may be.

Part 9 Monitoring

(11) A copy of any application made under section 293A(2) of the 1990 Act (urgent Crown development: application) and of any plans and drawings submitted in relation to it must be placed on the register within 14 days of the date on which the local planning authority is consulted on the application by the Secretary of State.

(12) The register must either be kept at the principal office of the local planning register authority or that part of the register which relates to land in part of that authority's area must be kept at a place situated in or convenient to that part.

(13) For the purposes of paragraph (3), an application is not treated as finally disposed of unless and until—

   (a) it has been decided by the authority (or the appropriate period specified or referred to in article 34(2) or (3) has expired without their giving a decision) and the time limit specified in article 37(2) has expired without any appeal having been made to the Secretary of State;

   (b) if it has been referred to the Secretary of State under section 77 of the 1990 Act or an appeal has been made to the Secretary of State under section 78 of the 1990 Act (right to appeal against planning decisions and failure to take such decisions), the Secretary of State has issued a decision and the period of 6 weeks specified in section 288 of the 1990 Act (proceedings for questioning the validity of other orders, decisions and directions) has expired without any application having been made to the High Court under that section;

   (c) an application has been made to the High Court under section 288 of the 1990 Act and the matter has been finally determined, either by final dismissal of the application by a court or by the quashing of the Secretary of State's decision and the issue of a fresh decision (without a further application under the said section 288); or

   (d) it has been withdrawn before being decided by the authority or the Secretary of State, as the case may be, or an appeal has been withdrawn before the Secretary of State has issued a decision.

(14) Where the register kept by a local planning register authority under this article is kept using electronic storage, the authority may make the register available for inspection by the public on a website maintained by the authority for that purpose.

41 Register of local development orders

(1) The register kept by each local planning register authority under article 40 must also include as Part 3 a Part relating to local development orders.

(2) Part 3 of the register must consist of 2 sections—

   (a) the first section of Part 3 must contain copies of draft local development orders which have been prepared but not adopted by the authority; and

   (b) the second section of Part 3 must contain—

      (i) copies of local development orders which have been adopted by the authority;

      (ii) particulars of the revocation of any local development order made by the authority, including the date on which the revocation took effect; and

(iii) particulars of the revision of any local development order, including the date on which the revision took effect.

(3) A copy of each draft local development order must be placed on the register when the draft is sent for consultation in accordance with article 38(3).

(4) A copy of each local development order must be placed on the register within 14 days of the date of its adoption.

(5) A requirement under this article to place a copy of a draft order or order on the register includes a requirement to do the same with the statement of reasons for making that order.

42 Register of neighbourhood development orders

(1) The register kept by each local planning register authority under article 40 must also include as Part 4 a Part with two sections relating to neighbourhood development orders.

(2) The first section of Part 4 must contain copies of draft neighbourhood development orders which have been submitted to the authority by a qualifying body and not finally disposed of and such of the following as have been submitted with each such order—

(a) a copy of any plan or statement identifying the land to which the proposal relates;

(b) copies of any other accompanying plans or drawings;

(c) copies of any planning obligation or section 278 agreement entered into, or proposed to be entered into, in connection with any planning permission proposed to be granted by the draft neighbourhood development order; and

(d) in the case of a draft community right to build order, details of any enfranchisement rights which the qualifying body proposes are not exercisable, and the properties, or types of properties, in relation to which those rights are not exercisable.

(3) For the purposes of paragraph (2), a draft neighbourhood development order is not finally disposed of unless and until—

(a) the proposal for the order has been withdrawn before the authority have made a decision under paragraph 12 of Schedule 4B (consideration by authority of recommendations made by examiner etc) or paragraph 10 of Schedule 4C (examination of proposals for community right to build orders etc) to the 1990 Act;

(b) the authority have refused the proposal for the order in accordance with paragraph 6(4) of Schedule 4B to the 1990 Act (consideration of proposals by authority);

(c) the order has not been made following a referendum because a majority of persons voting have not voted in favour of it, or as a result of a decision made under section 61E(5) or (8) of the 1990 Act (neighbourhood development orders); or

(d) the order has been made (with or without modifications).

(4) The second section of Part 4 must contain copies of neighbourhood development orders which have been made by the authority and with respect to each such order—

(a) a copy of any accompanying plan or statement identifying the land to which the order relates;

(b) copies of any other accompanying plans or drawings;

(c) if the order is revoked, particulars of the revocation, including the date on which the revocation took effect;

(d) the date on which any subsequent approval is given which the order specifies is required;

(e) a copy of any planning obligation or section 278 agreement entered into in connection with any planning permission granted by the order; and

(f) in the case of a community right to build order, details of any enfranchisement rights which are not exercisable and the properties, or types of properties, in relation to which those rights are not exercisable.

(5) A reference in this article to a copy includes a reference to a copy in photographic or electronic form.

43 Register of enforcement and stop notices and other enforcement action

(1) A register under section 188 of the 1990 Act (register of enforcement and stop notices and other enforcement action) ('the enforcement register') must contain the following information with respect to every planning enforcement order made in relation to land in the area of the authority maintaining the register—

(a) the address of the land to which the order relates or a plan by reference to which its situation can be ascertained;

(b) the name of the applying authority;

(c) the name of the court that made the order;

(d) the date on which the court's decision to make the order was given;

(e) the day which marks the beginning of the enforcement year for the order;

(f) the day which marks the end of that year;

(g) information on any postponement of the day which marks the beginning of the enforcement year for the order by reason of section 171BA(4) of the 1990 Act (time limits in cases involving concealment) and the date of the final determination or withdrawal of any application;

(h) the apparent breach of planning control identified in the order; and

(i) in relation to any enforcement notice issued or breach of condition notice served in respect of that breach, details of where in the register the information specified in paragraphs (2) and (3) in relation to that notice is to be found.

(2) The enforcement register must also contain the following information with respect to every enforcement notice issued in relation to land in the area of the authority maintaining the register—

(a) the address of the land to which the notice relates or a plan by reference to which its situation can be ascertained;

(b) the name of the issuing authority;

(c) the date of issue of the notice;

(d) the date of service of copies of the notice;

Town and Country Planning (Development Management Procedure) Order 2015

  (e) a statement or summary of the breach of planning control alleged and the requirements of the notice, including the period within which any required steps are to be taken;

  (f) the date specified in the notice as the date on which it is to take effect;

  (g) information on any postponement of the date specified as the date on which the notice will take effect by reason of section 175(4) of the 1990 Act (appeals: supplementary provisions) and the date of the final determination or withdrawal of any appeal;

  (h) the date of service and, if applicable, of withdrawal of any stop notice referring to the enforcement notice, together with a statement or summary of the activity prohibited by any such stop notice; and

  (i) the date, if any, on which the local planning authority are satisfied that steps required by the notice for a purpose mentioned in section 173(4)(b) of the 1990 Act (contents and effect of notice: remedying any injury to amenity) have been taken.

(3) The enforcement register must also contain the following information with respect to every breach of condition notice served in relation to land in the area of the authority maintaining the register—

  (a) the address of the land to which the notice relates or a plan by reference to which its situation can be ascertained;

  (b) the name of the serving authority;

  (c) the date of service of the notice;

  (d) details of the relevant planning permission sufficient to enable it to be identified; and

  (e) a statement or summary of the condition which has not been complied with and the requirements of the notice, including the period allowed for compliance.

(4) All entries relating to a planning enforcement order, enforcement notice, stop notice or breach of condition notice must be removed as soon as reasonably practicable from the enforcement register if—

  (a) in the case of a planning enforcement order, the order—

    (i) is rescinded; or

    (ii) the enforcement year for the order expires without enforcement action having been taken during that year;

  (b) in the case of an enforcement notice or stop notice, the relevant enforcement notice is quashed by the Secretary of State or is withdrawn; and

  (c) in the case of a breach of condition notice, the notice is quashed by a court or is withdrawn.

(5) Every enforcement register must include an index for enabling a person to trace any entry in the register by reference to the address of the land to which the notice relates.

(6) Paragraph (7) applies where a magistrates' court make a planning enforcement order on the application of a county planning authority or a county planning authority issue an enforcement notice or serve a stop notice or a breach of condition notice.

(7) The county planning authority must—

(a) supply the information specified in paragraph (1), (2) or (3), as the case may be, in relation to the order or notice to the district planning authority (if any) in whose area the land to which the order or notice relates is situated; and

(b) inform that authority if the order is rescinded or expires without enforcement action having been taken during the enforcement year for that order or the relevant enforcement notice or breach of condition notice is withdrawn or quashed.

(8) The information prescribed in paragraphs (1), (2) and (3) must be entered in the enforcement register as soon as practicable and in any event within 14 days of the occurrence to which it relates, and information must be supplied under paragraph (7) so that entries may be made within that period of 14 days.

(9) The enforcement register must either be kept at the principal office of the authority maintaining the enforcement register or that part of that register which relates to land in part of that authority's area must be kept at a place situated in or convenient to that part.

PART 10 GENERAL

44 Development to include certain internal operations

(1) The amount specified under section 55(2A) of the 1990 Act (meaning of 'development' and 'new development') is 200 square metres.

(2) The circumstances in which section 55(2) of the 1990 Act does not apply to operations mentioned in paragraph (a) of that subsection which have the effect of increasing the floor space of the building by more than 200 square metres are that the building is used for the retail sale of goods other than hot food.

(3) In paragraph (2), the reference to a building used for the retail sale of goods includes a building used as a retail warehouse club, being a retail club where goods are sold, or displayed for sale, only to members who are members of that club.

45 Directions

Any power conferred by this Order to give a direction includes power to cancel or vary the direction by a subsequent direction.

46 Withdrawal of consent to use of electronic communications

Where a person is no longer willing to accept the use of electronic communications for any purpose of this Order which is capable of being carried out electronically, that person must give notice in writing—

(a) withdrawing any address notified to the Secretary of State or to a local planning authority for that purpose; or

(b) revoking any agreement entered into or deemed to have been entered into with the Secretary of State or with a local planning authority for that purpose,

and such withdrawal or revocation takes effect on the date specified by the person in the notice but not less than 7 days after the date on which the notice is given.

Town and Country Planning (Development Management Procedure) Order 2015

47 Revocations, transitional provisions and savings

(1) The statutory instruments specified in the first column of the table in Schedule 9 are revoked, in so far as they apply to England, to the extent specified in the corresponding row of the third column of the table.

(2) In respect of an application for planning permission made before 15th April 2015, the following articles of this Order do not apply—

(i) article 15 (publicity for applications for planning permission)

(ii) article 16 (publicity for applications for planning permission within 10 metres of relevant railway land);

(iii) Schedule 3 (publicity for planning permission);

(iv) article 35 (written notice of determination relating to a planning application); and

(v) Schedule 4 (consultations before the grant of planning permission).

(3) In respect of an application for planning permission made before 15th April 2015, the following articles of the Town and Country Planning (Development Management Procedure) (England) Order 2010 ('the 2010 Order') apply as they applied immediately prior to 15th April 2015—

(i) article 13 (publicity for applications for planning permission);

(ii) article 31 (written notice of determination relating to a planning application);

(iii) Schedule 5 (consultations before the grant of planning permission); and

(iv) Schedule 6 (notification where planning permission refused or granted subject to conditions).

(4) In respect of an application for planning permission made before 15th April 2015, the following provisions of this Order should be read as if—

(i) the reference in article 35 of this Order to article 34 were a reference to article 29 in the 2010 Order;

(ii) the reference to article 15 in Schedule 3 of this Order were a reference to article 13 in the 2010 Order;

(iii) the references to articles 18, 19 and 20 in Schedule 4 of this Order were references to articles 16, 17 and 18 of the 2010 Order; and

(iv) the reference to article 35 in Schedule 5 of this Order were a reference to article 31 in the 2010 Order.

(5) In respect of an application for consent, agreement, or approval required by a condition or limitation attached to a grant of planning permission, where the application for the grant of planning permission was made before 15th April 2015—

(a) Part 5 of this Order does not apply; and

(b) article 30 of the 2010 Order applies as that article applied immediately prior to 15th April 2015.

(6) Paragraph (7) applies in respect of an application made before 1st June 2015 for development falling within paragraph (zc) of Schedule 5 to the 2010 Order.

(7) Where this paragraph applies—

(a) Schedule 4 of this Order should be read as if paragraph (zb) of the Schedule were a reference to paragraph (zc) of Schedule 5 to the 2010 Order;

(b) paragraph 1(k) (interpretation of table) of Schedule 4 to this Order should be read as if it were a reference to paragraph 1(l) of (interpretation of table) in Schedule 5 to the 2010 Order; and

(c) the references in article 18(2) and 19(3) of this Order to paragraph (zb) of Schedule 4 to this Order should be read as if they are references to paragraph (zc) of Schedule 5 of the 2010 Order.

SCHEDULE 1
Letter to be Sent to Applicant on Receipt of Application

Article 11 and 39

Letter to be sent to applicant on receipt of application
Letter to be sent by a local planning authority when they receive an application for planning permission or for a certificate of lawful use or development

Thank you for your application dated ....

which I received on ....

I am still examining your application form and the accompanying plans and documents to see whether they comply with the law.*

If I find that your application is invalid because it does not comply with the statutory requirements then I will write to you again as soon as I can

If, by *(insert date at end of period of, in the case of applications for major development, 13 weeks, or in all other cases, 8 weeks, beginning with the day immediately following the date when the application was received)*...you have not been given a decision in writing and:

- you have not been told that your application is invalid; or

- * you have not been told that your fee cheque has been dishonoured; or

- you have not agreed in writing to extend the period m which the decision may be given.

then you can appeal to the Secretary of State under section 78/section 195* of the Town and Country Planning Act 1990. This does not apply if your application has already been referred to the Secretary of State. You must use a form which you can get online from www.gov.uk/govemment/organisations/planning-inspectorate or from the Planning Inspectorate at Temple Quay House, 2 The Square, Temple Quay, Bristol BS1 6PN. If you appeal:

- within 12 weeks [*in the case o f a householder or minor commercial appeal other than type A Appeal or type B Appeal] from* ....
.............., or

- if an enforcement notice relating to the same or substantially the same land and development as in your application has been served before *[insert the relevant date]* (but no earlier than 2 years before your application) and has not been withdrawn, you should appeal within 28 days from *[insert the relevant date]*, or

- if an enforcement notice relating to the same or substantially the same land and development as in your application is served on or after *[insert the relevant date]* but no later than *[insert date that is 28 days before expiry of 6 months from the relevant date]* and has not been withdrawn, you should appeal within 28 days from the date on which the enforcement notice is served, or

Town and Country Planning (Development Management Procedure) Order 2015

- you should appeal within 6 months from *[insert date at end of period of, in the case of applications for major development, 13 weeks, or in all other cases, 8 weeks, beginning with the day immediately following the date when the application was received ('the relevant date')]* ....

*delete where inappropriate

SCHEDULE 2
NOTICES UNDER ARTICLES 13 AND 36

Article 13 and 36

TOWN AND COUNTRY PLANNING (DEVELOPMENT MANAGEMENT PROCEDURE) (ENGLAND) ORDER 2015

NOTICE UNDER ARTICLE 13 OF APPLICATION FOR PLANNING PERMISSION

(to be published in a newspaper and, where relevant, on a website or to be served on an owner* or a tenant**)

Proposed development at (a)..

I give notice that (b) ....

is applying to the [(c) ....Council] [Secretary of State]+

for planning permission to (d)..

Any owner* of the land or tenant** who wishes to make representations about this application

should write to the [Council][Secretary of State]+ at (e) ....

by (f) ....

* 'owner' means a person having a freehold interest or a leasehold interest the unexpired term of which is not less than 7 years, or, in the case of development consisting of the winning or working of minerals, a person entitled to an interest in a mineral in the land (other than oil, gas, coal, gold or silver).

** 'tenant' means a tenant of an agricultural holding any part of which is comprised in the land.

Signed..

+On behalf of ....

Date ....

Statement of owners' rights

The grant of planning permission does not affect owners' rights to retain or dispose of their property, unless there is some provision to the contrary in an agreement or in a lease.

Statement of agricultural tenants' rights

The grant of planning permission for non-agricultural development may affect agricultural tenants' security of tenure.

+ delete where inappropriate

Insert:

(a) address or location of the proposed development

(b) applicant's name

(c) name of the Council

(d) description of the proposed development

(e) address of the Council or the Secretary of State as appropriate

(f) date giving a period of 21 days beginning with the date of service, or 14 days beginning with the date of publication, of the notice (as the case may be)

TOWN AND COUNTRY PLANNING (DEVELOPMENT MANAGEMENT PROCEDURE) (ENGLAND) ORDER 2015

NOTICE UNDER ARTICLE 13 OF APPLICATION FOR PLANNING PERMISSION FOR HOUSEHOLDER DEVELOPMENT

(to be published in a newspaper and, where relevant, on a website or to be served on an owner * or a tenant** in the case of an application for planning permission for householder development***)

Proposed householder development*** at (a)...

I give notice that (b) ....

is applying to the (c) ....

Council for planning permission to (d) ....

Any owner* of the land or tenant** who wishes to make representations about this application should write to the Council at (e)..

by (f) ....

In the event that an appeal is made against a decision of the Council to refuse to grant planning permission for the proposed development, and that appeal then proceeds by way of the expedited procedure under the written representations procedure+, any representations made by the owner* or tenant** to the Council about this application will be passed to the Secretary of State and there will be no opportunity to make further representations. Any owner or tenant wishing to make representations should do so by the date given above.

* 'owner' means a person having a freehold interest or a leasehold interest the unexpired term of which is not less than 7 years.

** 'tenant' means a tenant of an agricultural holding any part of which is comprised in the land.

*** 'householder development' means development of an existing dwellinghouse, or development within the curtilage of such a dwellinghouse for any purpose incidental to the enjoyment of the dwellinghouse. It does not include a change of use or a change to the number of dwellings in a building.

+ The expedited procedures in relation to written representations are set out in Part 1 of the Town and Country Planning (Appeals) (Written Representations Procedure) (England) Regulations 2009 (S.I. 2009/452).

Signed...

On behalf of (delete if not applicable)...

Date ....

Town and Country Planning (Development Management Procedure) Order 2015

Statement of owners, rights

The grant of planning permission does not affect owners' rights to retain or dispose of their property, unless there is some provision to the contrary in an agreement or in a lease.

Statement of agricultural tenants' rights

The grant of planning permission for non-agricultural development may affect agricultural tenants' security of tenure.

Insert:

(a) address or location of the proposed development

(b) applicant's name

(c) name of the Council

(d) description of the proposed development

(e) address of the Council

(f) date giving a period of 21 days beginning with the date of service, or 14 days beginning with the date of publication, of the notice (as the case may be)

TOWN AND COUNTRY PLANNING (DEVELOPMENT MANAGEMENT PROCEDURE) (ENGLAND) ORDER 2015

NOTICE UNDER ARTICLE 13 OF APPLICATION FOR PLANNING PERMISSION FOR MINOR COMMERCIAL DEVELOPMENT

(to be published in a newspaper and, where relevant, on a website or to be served on an owner* or a tenant** in the case of an application for planning permission or consent for minor commercial development***)

Proposed minor commercial development*** at (a)..

I give notice that (b)..

is applying to the (c) ....

Council for planning permission to (d)...

Any owner* of the land or tenant** who wishes to make representations about this application

should write to the Council at (e)...

by (f)...

In the event that an appeal is made against a decision of the Council to refuse to grant planning permission for the proposed development, and that appeal then proceeds by way of the expedited procedure under the written representations procedure+, any representations made by the owner* or tenant** to the Council about this application will be passed to the Secretary of State and there will be no opportunity to make further representations. Any owner or tenant wishing to make representations should do so by the date given above.

* 'owner' means a person having a freehold interest or a leasehold interest the unexpired term of which is not less than 7 years.

** "tenant' means a tenant of an agricultural holding any part of which is comprised in the land.

*** 'minor commercial development' means development of an existing building, or part of a building, in use for certain commercial purposes. It does not include a change of use, development not wholly at ground floor level, an increase in floor space or a change to the number of units in a building.

Part 10 General

+The expedited procedures in relation to written representations are set out in Part 1 of the Town and Country Planning (Appeals) (Written Representations Procedure) (England) Regulations 2009 (S.I. 2009/452).

Signed..

On behalf of (delete if not applicable) ....

Date ....

Statement of owners' rights

The grant of planning permission does not affect owners' rights to retain or dispose of their property, unless there is some provision to the contrary in an agreement or in a lease.

Statement of agricultural tenants' rights

The grant of planning permission for non-agricultural development may affect agricultural tenants' security of tenure.

Insert:

(a) address or location of the proposed development

(b) applicant's name

(c) name of the Council

(d) description of the proposed development

(e) address of the Council

(f) date giving a period of 21 days beginning with the date of service, or 14 days beginning with the date of publication, of the notice (as the case may be)

TOWN AND COUNTRY PLANNING (DEVELOPMENT MANAGEMENT PROCEDURE) (ENGLAND) ORDER 2015

NOTICE UNDER ARTICLE 13 OF APPLICATION FOR PLANNING PERMISSION FOR THE WINNING AND WORKING OF MINERALS BY UNDERGROUND OPERATIONS

(to be posted in the case of an application for planning permission for development consisting of the winning and working of minerals by underground operations (in addition to the service or publication of any other requisite notices in this Schedule))

Proposed development at (a) ....

I give notice that (b) ....

is applying to the [(c) ....Council] [Secretary of State]+

for planning permission to (d) ....

Members of the public may inspect copies of:

- the application
- the plans
- and other documents submitted with it

at (e) ....

during all reasonable hours until (f)..

Town and Country Planning (Development Management Procedure) Order 2015

Anyone who wishes to make representations about this application should write to the [Council][Secretary of State]+ at (g) ....
by (f) ....

Signed..
+On behalf of ....
Date ....

+delete where inappropriate

Insert:

(a) address or location of the proposed development

(b) applicant's name

(c) name of the Council

(d) description of the proposed development

(e) address at which the application may be inspected (the applicant is responsible for making the application available for inspection within the area of the local planning authority)

(f) date giving a period of 21 days beginning with the date when the notice is posted

(g) address of the Council or the Secretary of State as appropriate

TOWN AND COUNTRY PLANNING (DEVELOPMENT MANAGEMENT PROCEDURE) (ENGLAND) ORDER 2015

NOTICE UNDER ARTICLES 13 AND 36 OF APPEAL

(to be published in a newspaper and, where relevant, on a website or to be served on an owner* or a tenant**)

Proposed development at (a) ....

I give notice that (b) ....

having applied to the (c) ....Council to (d)

....is appealing to the Secretary of State

against the decision of the Council +

on the failure of the Council to give notice of a decision +

Any owner* of the land or tenant** who wishes to make representations about this appeal should write to the Secretary of State at Temple Quay House, 2 The Square, Temple Quay, Bristol BS1 6PN or using the website at

by (e)...

* 'owner' means a person having a freehold interest or a leasehold interest the unexpired term of which is not less than 7 years, or. in the case of development consisting of the winning or working of minerals, a person entitled to an interest in a mineral in the land (other than oil, gas, coal, gold or silver).

*** 'tenant' means a tenant of an agricultural holding any part of which is comprised in the land.

Signed..

+On behalf of ....

Date ....

Statement of owners' rights

The grant of planning permission does not affect owners' rights to retain or dispose of their property, unless there is some provision to the contrary in an agreement or in a lease.

Statement of agricultural tenants' rights

The grant of planning permission for non-agricultural development may affect agricultural tenants' security of tenure.

+ delete where inappropriate

Insert:

(a) address or location of the proposed development

(b) applicant's name

(c) name of the Council

(d) description of the proposed development

(e) date giving a period of 21 days beginning with the date of service, or 14 days beginning with the date of publication, of the notice (as the case may be)

TOWN AND COUNTRY PLANNING (DEVELOPMENT MANAGEMENT PROCEDURE) (ENGLAND) ORDER 2015

NOTICE UNDER ARTICLES 13 AND 36 OF APPEAL

*(to be published in a newspaper and, where relevant, on a website or to be served on an owner * or a tenant** in the case of an appeal against the refusal to grant planning permission for householder development***)*

Proposed householder development*** at (a) ....

I give notice that (b)...

having applied to the (c) ....Council to (d)

....is appealing to the Secretary of State against the refusal of the Council to grant planning permission for the proposed development.

In the event that the appeal is dealt with by the expedited procedure under the written representations procedure+. any representations made by the owner* of the land or tenant** to the Council about the application will be passed to the Secretary of State and there will be no opportunity to make further representations in relation to the appeal.

* 'owner' means a person having a freehold interest or a leasehold interest the unexpired term of which is not less than 7 years.

** 'tenant' means a tenant of an agricultural holding any part of which is comprised in the land.

Town and Country Planning (Development Management Procedure) Order 2015

*** 'householder development' means development of an existing dwellinghouse, or development within the curtilage of such a dwellinghouse for any purpose incidental to the enjoyment of the dwellinghouse. It does not include a change of use or a change to the number of dwellings in a building.

+ The expedited procedures in relation to written representations are set out in Part 1 of the Town and Country Planning (Appeals) (Written Representations Procedure) (England) Regulations 2009 (S.I. 2009/452).

Signed..

On behalf of (delete ii not applicable)...............................

Date ....

Statement of owners' rights

The grant of planning permission does not affect owners' rights to retain or dispose of their property, unless there is some provision to the contrary in an agreement or in a lease.

Statement of agricultural tenants' rights

The grant of planning permission for non-agricultural development may affect agricultural tenants5 security of tenure.

Insert:

(a) address or location of the proposed development

(b) applicant's name

(c) name of the Council

(d) description of the proposed development

TOWN AND COUNTRY PLANNING (DEVELOPMENT MANAGEMENT PROCEDURE) (ENGLAND) ORDER 2015

NOTICE UNDER ARTICLES 13 AND 36 OF APPEAL

(to be posted in the case of an application for planning permission for development consisting of the winning an d working of minerals by underground operations (in addition to the service or publication of arty other requisite notices in this Schedule))

Proposed development at (a)...

I give notice that (b)...

having applied to the (c)..Council to (d)

.... is appealing to the Secretary of State

against the decision of the Council +

on the failure of the Council to give notice of a decision +

Members of the public may inspect copies of
- the application
- the plans
- and other documents submitted with it

at (e)..
during all reasonable hours until (f)...

Anyone who wishes to make representations about this appeal should write to the Secretary of State at Temple Quay House, 2 The Square, Temple Quay, Bristol BS1 6PN or online at www.gov.uk/government/organisations/planning-inspectorate
by (f) ....

Signed...
+On behalf of ....
Date ....

+ delete where inappropriate
Insert:

(a) address or location of the proposed development

(b) applicant's name

(c) name of the Council

(d) description of the proposed development

(e) address of the Council

(f) date giving a period of 21 days beginning with the date when the notice is posted

Town and Country Planning (Development Management Procedure) (England) Order 2015

NOTICE UNDER ARTICLES 13 AND 36 OF APPEAL

(to be published in a newspaper and, where relevant, on a website or to be served on an owner* or a tenant** in the case of an appeal against the refusal to grant planning permission for minor commercial development***)

Proposed minor commercial development*** at (a)...

I give notice that (b)...

having applied to the (c)...Council to (d)

.... is appealing to the Secretary of State against the refusal of the Council to grant planning permission for the proposed development.

In the event that the appeal is dealt with by the expedited procedure under the written representations procedure+, any representations made by the owner* of the land or tenant** to the Council about the application will be passed to the Secretary of State and there will be no opportunity to make further representations in relation to the appeal.

* 'owner' means a person having a freehold interest or a leasehold interest the unexpired term of which is not less than 7 years.

** 'tenant' means a tenant of an agricultural holding any part of which is comprised in the land.

*** 'minor commercial development' means development of an existing building, or part of a building, in use for certain commercial purposes. It does not include a change of use, development not wholly at ground floor level, an increase in floor space or a change to the number of units in a building.

Town and Country Planning (Development Management Procedure) Order 2015

+The expedited procedures in relation to mitten representations are set out in Part 1 of the Town and Country Planning (Appeals) (Written Representations Procedure) (England) Regulations 2009 (S.I. 2009/452).

Signed..

On behalf of (delete if not applicable)...............................

Date ....

Statement of owners' rights

The grant of planning permission does not affect owners' rights to retain or dispose of their property, unless there is some provision to the contrary in an agreement or in a lease.

Statement of agricultural tenants' rights

The grant of planning permission for non-agricultural development may affect agricultural tenants' security of tenure.
Insert:

(a) address or location of the proposed development

(b) applicant's name

(c) name of the Council

(d) description of the proposed development

SCHEDULE 3
PUBLICITY FOR APPLICATIONS FOR PLANNING PERMISSION

Articles 15 or 16

TOWN AND COUNTRY PLANNING (DEVELOPMENT MANAGEMENT PROCEDURE) (ENGLAND) ORDER 2015

NOTICE UNDER ARTICLE 15(4) OR (5) OR ARTICLE 16 OF APPLICATION FOR PLANNING PERMISSION

(to be published in a newspaper, displayed by site display on or near the site, or served on owners and/or occupiers of adjoining land, or infrastructure managers)

Proposed development at (a)..

I give notice that (b)..

is applying to the (c)..Council

for planning permission to (d) ....

The proposed development does not accord with the provisions of the development plan in force in the area in which the land to which the application relates is situated.*

The proposed development to which the application relates is situated within 10 metres of relevant railway land*

Members of the public may inspect copies of

- the application
- the plans
- and other documents submitted with it

at(e).. during all reasonable hours
until(f)... Anyone who wishes to make representations about this application should write to the Council at (g)...
by (f)...

In the event that an appeal is made against a decision of the Council to refuse to grant planning permission for the proposed development, and that appeal then proceeds by way of the expedited procedure under the written representations procedure+, any representations made by the owner* or tenant** to the Council about this application will be passed to the Secretary of State and there will be no opportunity to make further representations. Any owner or tenant wishing to make representations should do so by the date given above.

Signed..(Council's authorised officer)

On behalf of..Council

Date ....

*delete where inappropriate
Insert:

(a) address or location of the proposed development

(b) applicant's name

(c) name of the Council

(d) description of the proposed development

(e) address at which the application may be inspected

(f) date giving a period of 21 days, beginning with the date when the notice is first displayed where visible or accessible on or near the site or served on an owner and/or occupier of adjoining land, or a period of 14 days, beginning with the date when the notice is published in a newspaper (as the case may be)

(g) address of the Council

TOWN AND COUNTRY PLANNING (DEVELOPMENT MANAGEMENT PROCEDURE) (ENGLAND) ORDER 2015

NOTICE UNDER ARTICLE 15(3) OR ARTICLE 16 OF APPLICATION FOR PLANNING PERMISSION ACCOMPANIED BY AN ENVIRONMENTAL STATEMENT

(to be published in a newspaper and displayed by site display on or near the site)

Proposed development at (a) ....

I give notice that (b) ....

is applying to the (c) ....

Council for planning permission to (d) ....

and that the application is accompanied by an environmental statement.

The proposed development does not accord with the provisions of the development plan in force in the area in which the land to which the application relates is situated.*

The proposed development to which the application relates is situated within 10 metres of relevant railway land*

Members of the public may inspect copies of

- the application

Town and Country Planning (Development Management Procedure) Order 2015

- the plans
- the environmental statement
- and other documents submitted with the application

at (e) .... during all reasonable hours
until (f) ....
Members of the public may obtain copies of the environmental statement from (g)
....
at a charge of (h) ....
Anyone who wishes to make representations about this application should write to the

Council at (i)..

by (f) ....

Signed……........................(Council's authorised officer)
On behalf of ....Council
Date ....

* delete where inappropriate

Insert:

(a) address or location of the proposed development

(b) applicant's name

(c) name of the Council

(d) description of the proposed development

(e) address at which the application may be inspected

(f) date giving a period of 21 days, beginning with the date when the notice is first displayed where visible or accessible on or near the site, or a period of 14 days, beginning with the date when the notice is published in a newspaper (as the case may be)

(g) address from where copies of the environmental statement may be obtained (whether or not the same as (e))

(h) amount of charge, if any

(i) address of the Council

SCHEDULE 4
CONSULTATIONS BEFORE THE GRANT OF PERMISSION

Articles 18, 19 and 20

Table

Para	Description of Development	Consultee
(a)	Development likely to affect land in a National Park	The National Park authority concerned
(b)	Development likely to affect land in Greater London or in a metropolitan county other than land in a National Park	The local planning authority concerned
(c)	Development likely to affect land in a non-metropolitan county other than land in a National Park	The district planning authority concerned or, where there is no district planning authority in relation to the land, the county planning authority concerned
(d)	Development, in relation to which an application for planning permission has been made to the Secretary of State under section 293A of the 1990 Act (urgent Crown development: application)(a), where that development is likely to affect land in the area of a parish council	The parish council
(e)	Development within an area which has been notified to the local planning authority by the Health and Safety Executive for the purpose of this provision because of the presence within the vicinity of toxic, highly reactive, explosive or inflammable substances (otherwise than on a relevant nuclear site) and which involves the provision of— (i) residential accommodation; (ii) more than 250 square metres of retail floor space; (iii) more than 500 square metres of office floor space; or (iv) more than 750 square metres of floor space to be used for an industrial process, or which is otherwise likely to result in a material increase in the number of persons working within or visiting the notified area	The Health and Safety Executive
(f)	Development within an area which has been notified to the local planning authority by the Office for Nuclear Regulation for the purpose of this provision because of the presence within the vicinity of toxic, highly reactive, explosive or inflammable substances on a relevant nuclear site and which involves the provision of— (i) residential accommodation;	The Office for Nuclear Regulation

Para	Description of Development	Consultee
	(ii) more than 250 square metres of retail floor space; or	
	(iii) more than 500 square metres of office floor space; or	
	(iv) more than 750 square metres of floor space to be used for an industrial process.	
	or which is otherwise likely to result in a material increase in the number of persons working within or visiting the notified area.	

(a) 1990 c. 8. Section 293A was inserted by section 82(1) of the 2004 Act.

(g)	Development other than minor development, likely to result in an adverse impact on the safety of, or queuing, on a trunk road	The highway authority for the trunk road
(h)	Development likely to prejudice the improvement or construction of a trunk road	The highway authority for the trunk road
(i)	Development which consists of or includes the construction, formation or laying out of access to or from a trunk road	The highway authority for the trunk road
(j)	Development which is likely to result in a material increase in the volume or a material change in the character of traffic using a level crossing over a railway	The operator of the network which includes or consists of the railway in question, and the Secretary of State for Transport
(k)	Development likely to result in a material increase in the volume or a material change in the character of traffic entering or leaving a classified road or proposed highway	The local highway authority concerned
(l)	Development likely to prejudice the improvement or construction of a classified road or proposed highway	The local highway authority concerned
(m)	Development involving—	
	(i) the formation, laying out or alteration of any means of access to a highway (other than a trunk road); or	The local highway authority concerned
	(ii) the construction of a highway or private means of access to premises affording access to a road in relation to which a toll order is in force	The local highway authority concerned, and in the case of a road subject to a concession, the concessionaire
(n)	Development which consists of or includes the laying out or construction of a new street	The local highway authority
(o)	Development which involves the provision of a building or pipeline in an area of coal working notified by the Coal Authority to the local planning authority	The Coal Authority

Part 10 General

Para	Description of Development	Consultee
(p)	Development involving or including mining operations	The Environment Agency
(q)	Development of land involving the demolition, in whole or in part, or the material alteration of a Listed building which is classified as Grade I or Grade II*	Historic England(a)
(r)	Development likely to affect the site of a scheduled monument	Historic England

(a) *See* section 32 of the National Heritage Act 1983 (c. 47). This body is also known as the Historic Buildings and Monuments Commission for England.

Para	Description of Development	Consultee
(s)	Development likely to affect any battlefield, garden or park of special historic interest which is registered in accordance with section 8C of the Historic Buildings and Ancient Monuments Act 1953 (register of gardens)(a)	(a) Historic England in relation to any battlefield, and any garden or park which is classified as Grade I or Grade II*; and (b) the Garden History Society in relation to all registered gardens or parks
(t)	Development involving the carrying out of works or operations in the bed of, or within 20 metres of the top of a bank of, a main river which has been notified to the local planning authority by the Environment Agency as a main river for the purposes of this provision	The Environment Agency
(u)	Development for the purpose of refining or storing mineral oils and their derivatives	The Environment Agency
(v)	Development relating to the use of land as a cemetery	The Environment Agency
(w)	Development in or likely to affect a site of special scientific interest	Natural England
(x)	Development involving any land on which there is a theatre	The Theatres Trust
(y)	Development which is not for agricultural purposes and is not in accordance with the provisions of a development plan and involves— (i) the loss of not less than 20 hectares of grades 1, 2 or 3a agricultural land(b) which is for the time being used (or was last used) for agricultural purposes; or (ii) the loss of less than 20 hectares of grades 1, 2 or 3a agricultural land which is for the time being used (or was last used) for agricultural purposes, in circumstances in which the development is likely to lead to a further loss of agricultural land amounting cumulatively to 20 hectares or more	Natural England

Town and Country Planning (Development Management Procedure) Order 2015

Para	Description of Development	Consultee
(z)	Development which—	Sport England(c)
	(i) is likely to prejudice the use, or lead to the loss of use' of land being used as a playing Held; or	
	(ii) is on land which has been—	
	(aa) used as a playing field at any time in the 5 years before the making of the relevant application and which remains undeveloped; or	

(a) 1953 c. 49; section 8C was inserted by paragraph 10 of Schedule 4 to the National Heritage Act 1983 (c. 47).

(b) *See* Natural England publication for the agricultural land classification system. TIN049 edition 2 - Agricultural Land Classification: protecting the best and most versatile agricultural land available from http://publications.naturalengland.org.uk.publication/35012?category=9001.

(c) Sport England is also known as the English Sports Council.

	(bb) allocated for use as a playing field in a development plan or in proposals for such a plan or its alteration or replacement; or	
	(iii) involves the replacement of the grass surface of a playing pitch on a playing field with an artificial, man-made or composite surface	
(za)	Development likely to affect—	The Canal & River Trust
	(i) any inland waterway (whether natural or artificial) or reservoir owned or managed by the Canal & River Trust; or	
	(ii) any canal feeder channel, watercourse, let off or culvert,	
	which is within an area which has been notified for the purposes of this provision to the local planning authority by the Canal & River Trust	
(zb)	Development falling within any of the following descriptions—	(a) The COMAH competent authority;
	(i) development involving the siting of new establishments;	(b) where it appears to the local planning authority that an area of particular natural sensitivity or interest may be affected, Natural England; and

Part 10 General

Para	Description of Development	Consultee
(ii)	development consisting of modifications to existing establishments covered by Article 11 of Directive 2012/18EU of the European Parliament and of the Council on the control of major-accident hazards involving dangerous substances(a); or	(c) in the case of development falling within paragraph (iii), any person who according to—
(iii)	new developments including transport routes, locations of public use and residential areas in the vicinity of establishments, where the siting or development may be the source of or increase the risk or consequences of a major accident.	(i) the register held by the hazardous substances authority under regulation 20 of the Planning (Hazardous) Substances) Regulations 2015(b), or
		(ii) a notice submitted under regulation 32(1)(b) of those Regulations where the local authority has been notified under regulation 32(3) of those Regulations. is the person in control of the land on which any establishment is located.

(a) O.JL 197,24.7.2012:

(b) S I. 2015/627.

(zc)	Development, other than minor development, which is to be carried out on land—	The Environment Agency
	(i) in an area within Flood Zone 2 or Flood Zone 3; or	
	(ii) in an area within Flood Zone 1 which has critical drainage problems and which has been notified for the purpose of this provision to the local planning authority by the Environment Agency	
(zd)	Major development which does not use the services of a sewerage undertaker for the disposal of sewage	The Environment Agency
(ze)	Major development with surface water drainage	The Lead local flood authority
(zf)	Development involving the boring for or getting of oil and natural gas from shale	Any water or sewerage undertaker in whose area of appointment the development is proposed and, in the case where the development is likely to affect water resources in the area of appointment of another water or sewerage undertaker, that undertaker

Para Description of Development	Consultee

Interpretation of Table

1. In the above Table—
    (a) in paragraph (e)(iv), 'industrial process' means a process for or incidental to any of the following purposes—
        (i) the making of any article or part of any article (including a ship or vessel, or a film, video or sound recording);
        (ii) the altering, repairing, maintaining, ornamenting, finishing, cleaning, washing, packing, canning, adapting for sale, breaking up or demolition of any article; or
        (iii) the getting, dressing or treatment of minerals in the course of any trade or business other than agriculture, and other than a process carried out on land used as a mine or adjacent to and occupied together with a mine (and in this paragraph, 'mine' means any site on which mining operations are carried out);
    (b) in paragraph (g). 'minor development' means—
        (i) development of an existing dwellinghouse, or development within the curtilage of such a dwellinghouse, for any purpose incidental to the enjoyment of the dwellinghouse as such;
        (ii) the extension of an existing building used for non-domestic purposes where the floor space created by the development does not exceed 250 square metres; and
        (iii) the alteration of an existing building where the alteration does not increase the size of the building.
    (c) in paragraph (j). 'network' and 'operator' have the same meaning as in Part 1 of the Railways Act 1993 (the provision of railway services)(a);

(a) 1993 c. 43; *see* section 83.

    (d) in paragraphs (k) and (l) 'classified road' means a highway or proposed highway which—
        (i) is a classified road or a principal road by virtue of section 12(1) of the Highways Act 1980 (general provision as to principal and classified roads) (a); or
        (ii) is classified for the purposes of any enactment by the Secretary of State by virtue of section 12(3) of that Act;
    (e) in paragraph (m), 'concessionaire', 'road subject to a concession' and 'toll order' have the same meaning as in Part 1 of the New Roads and Street Works Act 1991 (new roads in England and Wales)(b);
    (f) in paragraph (n), 'street' has the same meaning as in section 48(1) of the New Roads and Street Works Act 1991 (streets, street works and undertakers), and 'new street' includes a continuation of an existing street;
    (g) in paragraph (r), 'scheduled monument' has the same meaning as in section 1(11) of the Ancient Monuments and Archaeological Areas Act 1979 (schedule of monuments)(c);
    (h) in paragraph (t), 'main river' has the same meaning as in section 113 of the Water Resources Act 1991 (interpretation of Part 4 ☒ flood defence)(d);

Part 10 General

Para	Description of Development	Consultee

(i) in paragraph (x), 'theatre' has the same meaning as in section 5 of the Theatres Trust Act 1976 (interpretation)(e);

(j) in paragraph (z)—

  (i) 'playing field' means the whole of a site which encompasses at least one playing pitch;

  (ii) 'playing pitch' means a delineated area which, together with any run-off area, is of 0.2 hectares or more, and which is used for association football, American football, rugby, cricket, hockey, lacrosse, rounders, baseball, softball, Australian football, Gaelic football, shinty, hurling, polo or cycle polo;

(k) in paragraph (zb)—

  (i) expressions appearing both in that paragraph and in Directive 2012/18/EU have the same meaning as in that Directive;

  (ii) 'COMAH competent authority' has the meaning in regulation 2(1) of the Planning (Hazardous Substances) Regulations 2015; and

(l) in paragraph (zc)—

'Flood Zone 1' means land which has a less than a 1 in 1000 annual probability of river or sea flooding(f);

'Flood Zone 2' means land which has—

  (i) between a 1 in 100 and 1 in 1000 annual probability of river flooding; or

  (ii) between a 1 in 200 and 1 in 1000 annual probability of sea flooding;

'Flood Zone 3' means land which has—

  (i) a 1 in 100 or greater annual probability or river flooding; or

  (ii) a 1 in 200 or greater annual probability of sea flooding; and 'minor development' has the same meaning as in paragraph (g).

(a) 1980 c. 66.

(b) 1991 c.22.

(c) 1979 c. 46.

(d) 1991 c. 57.

(e) 1976 c. 27.

(f) Maps showing the various Flood Zones are available from the Environment Agency at http://www.environment-agency.gov.uk.

Town and Country Planning (Development Management Procedure) Order 2015

SCHEDULE 5
NOTIFICATION WHERE PLANNING PERMISSION REFUSED OR GRANTED SUBJECT TO CONDITIONS

Article 35

TOWN AND COUNTRY PLANNING ACT 1990

NOTIFICATION TO BE SENT TO AN APPLICANT WHEN A LOCAL PL ANNING AUTHORITY REFUSE PL ANNING PERMISSION O R GRANT IT SUBJECT TO CONDITIONS *(TO BE ENDORSED ON NOTICES OF DECISION) (PAGE 1 OF 2)**

Appeals to the Secretary of State

- If you are aggrieved by the decision of your local planning authority to refuse permission for the proposed development or to grant it subject to conditions, then you can appeal to the Secretary of State under section 78 of the Town and Country Planning Act 1990.

- As this is a decision on a planning application relating to the same or substantially the same land and development as is already the subject of an enforcement notice [reference], if you want to appeal against your local planning authority's decision on your application, then you must do so within 28 days of the date of this notice.*

- If an enforcement notice is served relating to the same or substantially the same land and development as in your application and if you want to appeal against your local planning authority's decision on your application, then you must do so within: 28 days of the date of service of the enforcement notice, or within 6 months [12 weeks in the case of a householder appeal] of the date of tins notice, whichever period expires earlier.*

- As this is a decision to refuse planning permission for a householder application, if you want to appeal against your local planning authority's decision then you must do so within 12 weeks of the date of this notice.*

- If you want to appeal against your local planning authority's decision then you must do so within 6 months of the date of this notice.*

- Appeals must be made using a form which you can get from the Secretary of State at Temple Quay House, 2 The Square, Temple Quay, Bristol BS1 6PN or online at www.gov.uk/govemment/organisations/planning-inspectorate.

- The Secretary of State can allow a longer period for giving notice of an appeal, but will not normally be prepared to use this power unless there are special circumstances which excuse the delay in giving notice of appeal.

- The Secretary of State need not consider an appeal if it seems to the Secretary of State that the local planning authority could not have granted planning permission for the proposed development or could not have granted it without the conditions they imposed, having regard to the statutory requirements, to the provisions of any development order and to any directions given under a development order.

* delete where inappropriate

Part 10 General

TOWN AND COUNTRY PLANNING ACT 1990

NOTIFICATION TO BE SENT TO AN APPLICANT WHEN A LOCAL PLANNING AUTHORITY REFUSE PLANNING PERMISSION OR GRANT IT SUBJECT TO CONDITIONS *(TO BE ENDORSED ON NOTICES OF DECISION) (PAGE 2 OF 2)**

- In practice, the Secretary of State does not refuse to consider appeals solely because the local planning authority based their decision on a direction given by the Secretary of State.

Purchase Notices

- If either the local planning authority or the Secretary of State refuses permission to develop land or grants it subject to conditions, the owner may claim that the owner can neither put the land to a reasonably beneficial use in its existing state nor render the land capable of a reasonably beneficial use by the carrying out of any development which has been or would be permitted.

- In these circumstances, the owner may serve a purchase notice on the Council (that is, where the land is situated in a National Park, the National Park authority for that Park, or in any other case the district council (or county council which is exercising the functions of a district council in relation to an area for which there is no district council). London borough council or Common Council of the City of London in whose area the land is situated). This notice will require the Council to purchase the owner's interest in the land in accordance with the provisions of Chapter I of Part 6 of the Town and Country Planning Act 1990.

* delete where inappropriate

SCHEDULE 6
DEEMED DISCHARGE: EXEMPTIONS

Articles 28, 29 and 30

1. For the purposes of article 30, the following planning conditions are exempt under section 74A(6) of the 1990 Act (deemed discharge of planning conditions)(a).

Environment

2.—(1) A condition attached to the grant of planning permission where the development permitted—

(a) is EIA development;

(b) would have been EIA development apart from that condition;

(c) is likely to have a significant effect on a qualifying European site and is not directly connected with or necessary to the management of that site; or

(d) would have been likely to have a significant effect on a qualifying European site apart from that condition and is not directly connected with or necessary to the management of that site.

(2) In sub-paragraph (1)—

(a) reference to development which is. or would have been, likely to have significant effect on a qualifying European site includes development which is, or would have been, likely to that effect in combination with other plans or projects;

(b) reference to the development which would have been of a particular kind apart from a condition imposed on the grant of planning permission for the development include development which would have been of that kind apart from—

    (i) that condition; and

    (ii) any other condition attached to the grant of planning permission for the development.

Flooding

3. A condition attached to the grant of planning permission, intended to manage the risk of flood.

Sites of special scientific interest

4.—(1) A condition attached to the grant of planning permission for the development of land which is or forms part of a site of special scientific interest—

    (a) which is likely to have a significant effect on such a site; or

    (b) which would have been likely to have a significant effect on such a site apart from that condition.

(2) In sub-paragraph (1)—

    (a) the reference to development of land which is. or would have been, likely to have a significant effect on a site of special scientific interest includes development which is, or would have been, likely to have that effect in combination with other plans or projects.

    (b) the reference to development which would have been likely to have a significant effect on a site of special scientific interest apart from a condition includes a development which would have been likely to have that effect apart from—

(a) Section 74A was inserted by section 29 of the Infrastructure Act 2015 (c. 7).

    (i) that condition; and

    (ii) any other condition attached to the grant of planning permission for the development.

Contaminated land

5. A condition attached to the grant of planning permission which relates to the—

    (a) assessment of whether the land to which the planning permission relates is contaminated land; or

    (b) remediation of contaminated land (whether or not the remediation is to the land to which the planning permission relates).

Archaeology

6. A condition attached to the grant of planning permission which relates to investigation of the archaeological potential of the land to which the planning permission relates.

Highways

7. A condition attached to the grant of planning permission which—

    (a) relates to access between the development and the highway; or

    (b) requires a section 278 agreement to be entered into.

Approval of reserved matters

8. A condition attached to the grant of an outline planning permission in relation to the approval of any reserved matter.

Part 10 General

Planning obligations

9. A condition attached to the grant of planning permission that requires a planning obligation to be entered into.

Development orders

10. A condition attached to the grant of planning permission under a—

(a) development order pursuant to section 59 of the 1990 Act(a); or

(b) special development order pursuant to section 264 of the 1990 Act(b);

(c) local development order pursuant to section 61A of the 1990 Act(c); or

(d) neighbourhood development order pursuant to section 61E(d) of the 1990 Act.

(a) Section 59 was amended by section 1(2) of: and paragraphs 1 and 4 of Schedule 1 to, the Growth and Infrastructure Act 2013 (c. 27).

(b) Section 264 was amended by section 40(2)00 of the 2004 Act. There are amendments to section 264 not relevant to this Order.

(c) Section 61A was inserted by section 40(1) of the 2004 Act.

(d) Section 61E was inserted by section 116 of, and Schedule 9 to: the Localism Act 2011(c. 20).

Simplified planning zones or enterprise zones

11. A condition attached to the grant of planning permission in relation to land in—

(a) a simplified planning zone(a) where the development permitted is specified, or of a class specified, in the simplified planning zone scheme; or

(b) an enterprise zone(b) where the development permitted is specified, or of a class specified, in the enterprise zone scheme.

Crown development or government authorisation

12. A condition attached to the grant of planning permission under—

(a) section 90 of the 1990 Act (government authorisation)(c);

(b) section 293A of the 1990 Act (urgent Crown development)(d).

(a) *See* section 84.

(b) *See* section 88 which was amended in ways not relevant to this Order.

(c) Section 90 was amended by section 78 of, and paragraph 32(4) of Schedule 10, to the Environment Act 1995

(d) Section 293A was inserted by section 82(1) of the Planning and Compulsory Purchase Act 2004 (c. 5).

SCHEDULE 7
NOTICES UNDER ARTICLE 38

TOWN AND COUNTRY PLANNING (DEVELOPMENT MANAGEMENT PROCEDURE) (ENGLAND) ORDER 2015

NOTICE UNDER ARTICLE 38 OF PROPOSAL FOR LOCAL DEVELOPMENT ORDER GRANTING PLANNING PERMISSION

(to be displayed by site display on or near the site to which the order relates and to be served on an owner* or a tenant**)

Proposed development at (a) ....

I give notice that the (b) ....Council proposes to make a local development order granting planning permission to (c)...

....

A copy of the draft order and a statement of the Council's reasons for making the order are available for inspection at..

(d) and are published on the Council's website at ....(e)

Anyone who wishes to make representations about this proposed local development order should write to the Council at (f) ....

....

by (g) ....

* 'owner' means a person having a freehold interest or a leasehold interest the unexpired term of which is not less than 7 years, or. in the case of development consisting of the winning or working of minerals, a person entitled to an interest in a mineral in the land (other than oil. gas. coal, gold or silver).

** 'tenant' means a tenant of an agricultural holding any part of which is comprised in the land.

Signed..(Council's authorised officer)
On behalf of .... Council
Date ....

Statement of owners' rights

The grant of planning permission does not affect owners' rights to retain or dispose of their property, unless there is some provision to the contrary in an agreement or in a lease.

Statement of agricultural tenants' rights

The grant of planning permission for non-agricultural development may affect agricultural tenants' security of tenure.

Insert:

(a) address or location of the proposed development

(b) name of the Council

(c) description of the proposed development
(d) places where and times when the documents are available for inspection

(e) website address where the documents are published

(f) address of the Council

(g) date giving a period of not less than 28 days beginning with the [date the notice is first displayed where visible or accessible on or near the site, or the date of service of the notice (as the case may be)

SCHEDULE 8
CERTIFICATE OF LAWFUL USE OR DEVELOPMENT

Article 39

TOWN AND COUNTRY PLANNING ACT 1990: SECTIONS 191 AND 192 TOWN AND COUNTRY PLANNING (DEVELOPMENT MANAGEMENT PROCEDURE) (ENGLAND) ORDER 2015: ARTICLE 39

CERTIFICATE OF LAWFUL USE OR DEVELOPMENT

The (a) .... Council hereby certify that on (b) .... the use/operations/matter* described in the First Schedule to this certificate in respect of the land specified in the Second Schedule to this certificate and edged/hatched/coloured* (c)....................... on the plan attached to this certificate, was/were/would have been/would be* lawful within the meaning of section 191/192* of the Town and Country Planning Act 1990 for the following reason(s):

....
....

Signed..(Council's authorised officer)

On behalf of (a)...Council

Date..

First Schedule

(d)

Second Schedule

(e)

Notes

1   This certificate is issued solely for the purpose of section 191/192* of the Town and Country Planning Act 1990.

2   It certifies that the use/operations/matter* specified in the First Schedule taking place on the land described in the Second Schedule was/were/would have been/would be* lawful, on the specified date and, therefore, was not/were not/would not have been* liable to enforcement action under Part 7 of the 1990 Act on that date.

3   This certificate applies only to the extent of the use/operations/matter* described in the First Schedule and to the land specified in the Second Schedule and identified on the attached plan. Any use/operations/matter* which is/are* materially different from that/those* described or which relate/s* to other land may render the owner or occupier liable to enforcement action.

*4 The effect of the certificate is also qualified by the proviso in section 192(4) of the 1990 Act. which states that the lawfulness of a described use or operation is only conclusively presumed where there has been no material change, before the use is instituted or the operations are begun, in any of the matters relevant to determining such lawfulness.

*delete where inappropriate

Insert:

(a) name of Council

(b) date of application to the Council

(c) colour used on the plan

(d) full description of use, operations or other matter, if necessary, by reference to details in the application or submitted plans, including a reference to the use class, if any, specified in an order under section 55(2)(f) of the 1990 Act, within which the use referred to in this certificate falls

(e) address or location of the site

SCHEDULE 9
REVOCATIONS IN RELATION TO ENGLAND

Article 47

Title of Instrument	Reference	Extent of revocation
The Town and Country Planning (Development Management Procedure) (England) Order 2010	S.I. 2010/2184	The whole of the Order
The Town and Country Planning (Environmental Impact Assessment) Regulations 2011	S.I. 2011/1824	Paragraphs 17 to 20 of Schedule 6 to the Order
The Town and Country Planning (Development Management Procedure) (England) (Amendment) Order 2012	S.I. 2012/636	The whole of the Order
The Town and Country Planning (Development Management Procedure) (England) (Amendment No. 2) Order 2012	S.I. 2012/2274	The whole of the Order
The Town and Country Planning (Development Management Procedure) (England) (Amendment No. 3) Order 2012	S.I. 2012/3109	The whole of the Order
The National Treatment Agency (Abolition) and the Health and Social Care Act 2012 (Consequential, Transitional and Saving Provisions) Order 2013	S.I. 2013/235	Paragraph 155 of Part 1 of Schedule 2 to the Order

Town and Country Planning (General Permitted Development) Order 2015

Title of Instrument	Reference	Extent of revocation
The Town and Country Planning (Development Management Procedure) (England) (Amendment) Order 2013	S.I. 2013/1238	The whole of the Order
The Town and Country Planning (Development Management Procedure) (England) (Amendment No. 2) Order 2013	S.I. 2013/2136	The whole of the Order
The Growth and Infrastructure Act 2013 (Local Development Orders) (Consequential Provisions) (England) Order 2013	S.I. 2013/2879	Articles 2 and 4 of the Order
The Town and Country Planning (Development Management Procedure and Section 62A Applications) (England) (Amendment) Order 2013	S.I. 2013/2932	Article 2
The Town and Country Planning (Development Management Procedure and Section 62A Applications) (England) (Amendment No 2) Order 2013	S.I. 2013/3194	Article 2
The Energy Act 2013 (Office for Nuclear Regulation) (Consequential Amendments, Transitional Provisions and Savings) Order 2014	S.I. 2014/469	Paragraph 201 of Part 5 of Schedule 3 to the Order
The Town and Country Planning (General Permitted Development) (Amendment and Consequential Provision) (England) Order 2014	S.I. 2014/564	Article 8
The Town and Country Planning (Development Management Procedure and Section 62 A Applications) (England) (Amendment) Order	S.I. 2014/1532	Article 2
The Infrastructure Act 2015 (Strategic Highways Companies) (Consequential, Transitional and Savings Provisions) Regulations 2015	S.I. 2015/377	Paragraphs 47 to 51 of the Schedule to the Regulations

(SI 2015/596)

Town and Country Planning (General Permitted Development) (England) Order 2015

1 Citation, commencement and application

(1) This Order may be cited as the Town and Country Planning (General Permitted Development) (England) Order 2015 and comes into force on 15th April 2015.

Town and Country Planning (General Permitted Development) Order 2015

(2) This Order applies to all land in England, but where land is the subject of a special development order, whether made before or after the commencement of this Order, this Order applies to that land only to such extent and subject to such modifications as may be specified in the special development order.

(3) Nothing in this Order applies to any permission which is deemed to be granted under section 222 of the Act (planning permission not needed for advertisements complying with regulations).

2 Interpretation

(1) In this Order—

'the 1960 Act' means the Caravan Sites and Control of Development Act 1960;

'the Act' means the Town and Country Planning Act 1990;

'adjoining owner or occupier' means any owner or occupier of any premises or land adjoining the site;

'aerodrome' means an aerodrome as defined in article 255 of the Air Navigation Order 2009 (interpretation) which is—

(a) licensed under that Order,

(b) a Government aerodrome,

(c) one at which the manufacture, repair or maintenance of aircraft is carried out by a person carrying on business as a manufacturer or repairer of aircraft,

(d) one used by aircraft engaged in the public transport of passengers or cargo or in aerial work, or

(e) one identified to the Civil Aviation Authority before 1st March 1986 for inclusion in the UK Aerodrome Index,

and, for the purposes of this definition, the terms 'aerial work', 'Government aerodrome' and 'public transport' have the meanings given in article 255 of that Order;

'aqueduct' does not include an underground conduit;

'area of outstanding natural beauty' means an area designated as such by an order made by Natural England under section 82 of the Countryside and Rights of Way Act 2000 (designation of areas) as confirmed by the Secretary of State;

'building'—

(a) includes any structure or erection and, except in Class F of Part 2, Class B of Part 11, Classes A to I of Part 14, Classes A, B and C of Part 16 and Class T of Part 19, of Schedule 2, includes any part of a building; and

(b) does not include plant or machinery and, in Schedule 2, except in Class F of Part 2 and Class C of Part 11, does not include any gate, fence, wall or other means of enclosure;

'caravan' has the same meaning as for the purposes of Part 1 of the 1960 Act (caravan sites);

'caravan site' means land on which a caravan is stationed for the purpose of human habitation and land which is used in conjunction with land on which a caravan is so stationed;

'classified road' means a highway or proposed highway which—

(a) is a classified road or a principal road by virtue of section 12(1) of the Highways Act 1980 (general provision as to principal and classified roads); or

(b) is classified by the Secretary of State for the purposes of any enactment by virtue of section 12(3) of that Act;

'cubic content' means the cubic content of a structure or building measured externally;

'dwellinghouse', except in Part 3 of Schedule 2 to this Order (changes of use), does not include a building containing one or more flats, or a flat contained within such a building;

'electronic communication' has the meaning given in section 15(1) of the Electronic Communications Act 2000;

'erection', in relation to buildings, includes extension, alteration, or re-erection;

'existing', in relation to any building or any plant or machinery or any use, means (except in the definition of 'original') existing immediately before the carrying out, in relation to that building, plant, machinery or use, of development described in this Order;

'flat', except in the expression 'flat roof', means a separate and self-contained set of premises constructed or adapted for use for the purpose of a dwelling and forming part of a building from some other part of which it is divided horizontally;

'Flood Zone 1', 'Flood Zone 2' and 'Flood Zone 3' have the meaning given in Schedule 4 to the Procedure Order;

'floor space' means the total floor space in a building or buildings;

'industrial process' means a process for or incidental to any of the following purposes—

(a) the making of any article or part of any article (including a ship or vessel, or a film, video or sound recording);

(b) the altering, repairing, maintaining, ornamenting, finishing, cleaning, washing, packing, canning, adapting for sale, breaking up or demolition of any article; or

(c) the getting, dressing or treatment of minerals in the course of any trade or business other than agriculture, and other than a process carried out on land used as a mine or adjacent to and occupied together with a mine;

'land drainage' has the same meaning as in section 116 of the Land Drainage Act 1976 (interpretation);

'listed building' has the same meaning as in section 1 of the Planning (Listed Buildings and Conservation Areas) Act 1990 (listing of buildings of special architectural or historic interest);

'local advertisement' means publication of the notice in at least one newspaper circulating in the locality in which—

(a) in the case of a direction, the area or, as the case may be, the whole or relevant part of the conservation area to which the direction relates is situated; and

(b) in any other case, the land to which the proposed development relates is situated;

'machinery' includes any structure or erection in the nature of machinery;

'microwave' means that part of the radio spectrum above 1,000 MHz;

'microwave antenna' means a satellite antenna or a terrestrial microwave antenna;

'military explosives storage area' means an area, including an aerodrome, depot or port, within which the storage of military explosives has been licensed by the Secretary of State for Defence, and identified on a safeguarding map provided to the local planning authority for the purposes of a direction made by the Secretary of State in exercise of powers conferred by article 33(1) of the Procedure Order (or any previous powers to the like effect);

'mine' means any site on which mining operations are carried out;

'mining operations' means the winning and working of minerals in, on or under land, whether by surface or underground working;

'network' and 'operator', for the purposes of Part 3 and 4 of Schedule 2, have the same meaning as in Part 1 of the Railways Act 1993 (the provision of railway services);

'notifiable pipe-line' means a major accident hazard pipeline (as described in regulation 18 of the Pipelines Safety Regulations 1996) but does not include a pipeline the construction of which has been authorised under section 1 of the Pipe-lines Act 1962;

'operational Crown building' means a building which is operational Crown land;

'operational Crown land' means—

(a) Crown land which is used for operational purposes; and

(b) Crown land which is held for those purposes,

but does not include—

(i) land which, in respect of its nature and situation, is comparable rather with land in general than with land which is used, or held, for operational purposes;

(ii) Crown land—

(aa) belonging to Her Majesty in right of the Crown and forming part of the Crown Estate;

(bb) in which there is an interest belonging to Her Majesty in right of Her private estates;

(cc) in which there is an interest belonging to Her Majesty in right of the Duchy of Lancaster; or

(dd) belonging to the Duchy of Cornwall;

'operational purposes' means the purposes of carrying on the functions of the Crown or of either House of Parliament;

'original' means—

(a) in relation to a building, other than a building which is Crown land, existing on 1st July 1948, as existing on that date;

(b) in relation to a building, other than a building which is Crown land, built on or after 1st July 1948, as so built;

(c) in relation to a building which is Crown land on 7th June 2006, as existing on that date; and

(d) in relation to a building built on or after 7th June 2006 which is Crown land on the date of its completion, as so built;

'plant' includes any structure or erection in the nature of plant;

'private way' means a highway not maintainable at the public expense and any other way other than a highway;

'Procedure Order' means the Town and Country Planning (Development Management Procedure) (England) Order 2015;

'proposed highway' has the same meaning as in section 329 of the Highways Act 1980 (further provision as to interpretation);

'public service vehicle' means—

(a) a public service vehicle within the meaning of section 1 of the Public Passenger Vehicles Act 1981 (definition of public service vehicles), or

(b) a tramcar or trolley vehicle within the meaning of section 192(1) of the Road Traffic Act 1988 (general interpretation);

'safety hazard area' means an area notified to the local planning authority—

(a) by the Health and Safety Executive for the purposes of paragraph (e) of the Table in Schedule 4 to the Procedure Order (or any previous powers to the like effect); or

(b) by the Office for Nuclear Regulation for the purposes of paragraph (f) of that Table;

'satellite antenna' means apparatus designed for transmitting microwave radio energy to satellites or receiving it from them, and includes any mountings or brackets attached to such apparatus;

'scheduled monument' has the same meaning as in section 1(11) of the Ancient Monuments and Archaeological Areas Act 1979 (schedule of monuments);

'site display' means the posting of the notice by firmly attaching it to some object, sited and displayed in such a way as to be easily visible and legible by members of the public;

'site of archaeological interest' means land which—

(a) is included in the schedule of monuments compiled by the Secretary of State under section 1 of the Ancient Monuments and Archaeological Areas Act 1979 (schedule of monuments);

(b) is within an area of land which is designated as an area of archaeological importance under section 33 of that Act (designation of areas of archaeological importance), or

(c) is within a site registered in any record adopted by resolution by a county council and known as the County Sites and Monuments Record;

'site of special scientific interest' means land to which section 28(1) of the Wildlife and Countryside Act 1981 (sites of special scientific interest, notification of additional land and enlargement of SSSI) applies;

'statutory undertaker' includes, in addition to any person mentioned in section 262(1) of the Act (meaning of statutory undertakers)—

Town and Country Planning (General Permitted Development) Order 2015

    (a) a universal service provider (within the meaning of Part 3 of the Postal Services Act 2011) in connection with the provision of a universal postal service (within the meaning of that Part);
    (b) the Civil Aviation Authority;
    (c) a person who holds a licence under Chapter 1 of Part 1 of the Transport Act 2000 (air traffic services);
    (d) the Environment Agency;
    (e) any water undertaker;
    (f) any gas transporter; and
    (g) any licence holder under section 6 of the Electricity Act 1989;

'terrestrial microwave antenna' means apparatus designed for transmitting or receiving terrestrial microwave radio energy between two fixed points;

'trunk road' means a highway or proposed highway which is a trunk road by virtue of section 10(1) or 19 of the Highways Act 1980 (general provision as to trunk roads, and certain special roads and other highways to become trunk roads) or any other enactment or any instrument made under any enactment;

'the Use Classes Order' means the Town and Country Planning (Use Classes) Order 1987; and

'World Heritage Site' means a property appearing on the World Heritage List kept under article 11(2) of the UNESCO Convention for the Protection of the World Cultural and Natural Heritage adopted at Paris on 16th November 1972.

(2) Unless the context otherwise requires, any reference in this Order to the height of a building or of plant or machinery is to be construed as a reference to its height when measured from ground level; and for the purposes of this paragraph 'ground level' means the level of the surface of the ground immediately adjacent to the building or plant or machinery in question or, where the level of the surface of the ground on which it is situated or is to be situated is not uniform, the level of the highest part of the surface of the ground adjacent to it.

(3) The land referred to elsewhere in this Order as article 2(3) land is the land described in Part 1 of Schedule 1 to this Order (National Parks, areas of outstanding natural beauty and conservation areas etc).

(4) The land referred to elsewhere in this Order as article 2(4) land is the land described in Part 2 of Schedule 1 to this Order (National Parks and adjoining land and the Broads).

(5) The land referred to elsewhere in this Order as article 2(5) land is the land described in Part 3 of Schedule 1 to this Order (exempt commercial areas).

(6) Paragraphs (7) to (11) apply where an electronic communication is used by a person for the purpose of fulfilling any requirement in this Order or in any Schedule to this Order to give or send any statement, notice or other document to any other person ('the recipient').

(7) The requirement referred to in paragraph (6) is taken to be fulfilled where the notice or other document transmitted by means of the electronic communication is—
    (a) capable of being accessed by the recipient,

(b) legible in all material respects, and

(c) sufficiently permanent to be used for subsequent reference.

(8) In paragraph (7), 'legible in all material respects' means that the information contained in the notice or document is available to the recipient to no lesser extent than it would be if sent or given by means of a document in printed form.

(9) Where the electronic communication is received by the recipient outside the recipient's business hours, it is taken to have been received on the next working day; and for this purpose 'working day' means a day which is not a Saturday, Sunday, Christmas Day, Good Friday or a day which is a bank holiday in England under the Banking and Financial Dealings Act 1971.

(10) A requirement in this Order or in any Schedule to this Order that any document should be in writing is fulfilled where that document meets the criteria in paragraph (7), and 'written' and related expressions are to be construed accordingly.

(11) References in this Order or in any Schedule to this Order to plans, drawings, notices or other documents, or to copies of such documents, include references to such documents or copies of them in electronic form.

(12) For the purposes of this Order, development carried out by or on behalf of any person in whom control of accommodation in any part of the Palace of Westminster or its precincts is vested is treated (so far as it would not otherwise be treated) as development by or on behalf of the Crown.

3 Permitted development

(1) Subject to the provisions of this Order and regulations 73 to 76 of the Conservation of Habitats and Species Regulations 2010 (general development orders), planning permission is hereby granted for the classes of development described as permitted development in Schedule 2.

(2) Any permission granted by paragraph (1) is subject to any relevant exception, limitation or condition specified in Schedule 2.

(3) References in this Order to permission granted by Schedule 2 or by any Part, Class or paragraph of that Schedule are references to the permission granted by this article in relation to development described in that Schedule or that provision of that Schedule.

(4) Nothing in this Order permits development contrary to any condition imposed by any planning permission granted or deemed to be granted under Part 3 of the Act otherwise than by this Order.

(5) The permission granted by Schedule 2 does not apply if—

(a) in the case of permission granted in connection with an existing building, the building operations involved in the construction of that building are unlawful;

(b) in the case of permission granted in connection with an existing use, that use is unlawful.

(6) The permission granted by Schedule 2 does not, except in relation to development permitted by Classes A, B, D and E of Part 9 and Class A of Part 18 of that Schedule, authorise any development which requires or involves the formation, laying out or material widening of a means of access to an existing

Town and Country Planning (General Permitted Development) Order 2015

highway which is a trunk road or classified road, or creates an obstruction to the view of persons using any highway used by vehicular traffic, so as to be likely to cause danger to such persons.

(7) Any development falling within Class A of Part 18 of Schedule 2 authorised by an Act or order subject to the grant of any consent or approval is not to be treated for the purposes of this Order as authorised unless and until that consent or approval is obtained, except where the Act was passed or the order made after 1st July 1948 and it contains provision to the contrary.

(8) Schedule 2 does not grant permission for the laying or construction of a notifiable pipe-line, except in the case of the laying or construction of a notifiable pipe-line by a gas transporter in accordance with Class A of Part 15 of that Schedule.

(9) Except as provided in Classes B and C of Part 11, Schedule 2 does not permit any development which requires or involves the demolition of a building, but in this paragraph 'building' does not include part of a building.

(10) Subject to paragraph (12), Schedule 1 development or Schedule 2 development within the meaning of the Town and Country Planning (Environmental Impact Assessment) Regulations 2011 ('the EIA Regulations') is not permitted by this Order unless—

 (a) the local planning authority has adopted a screening opinion under regulation 5 of those Regulations that the development is not EIA development;

 (b) the Secretary of State has made a screening direction under regulation 4(7) or 6(4) of those Regulations that the development is not EIA development; or

 (c) the Secretary of State has given a direction under regulation 4(4) of those Regulations that the development is exempted from the application of those Regulations.

(11) Where—

 (a) the local planning authority has adopted a screening opinion under regulation 5 of the EIA Regulations that development is EIA development and the Secretary of State has in relation to that development neither made a screening direction to the contrary under regulation 4(8) or 6(4) of those Regulations nor directed under regulation 4(4) of those Regulations that the development is exempted from the application of those Regulations; or

 (b) the Secretary of State has directed that development is EIA development,

that development is treated, for the purposes of paragraph (10), as development which is not permitted by this Order.

(12) Paragraph (10) does not apply to—

 (a) development which consists of the carrying out by a drainage body, within the meaning of the Land Drainage Act 1991, of improvement works within the meaning of the Environmental Impact Assessment (Land Drainage Improvement Works) Regulations 1999;

 (b) development for which permission is granted by Class E of Part 6, Class K of Part 7, Class B of Part 12, Class A(a) of Part 15, Class D, E or I of Part 17 or Class A of Part 18 of Schedule 2;

 (c) development for which permission is granted by Class F, H or K of Part 17 of Schedule 2 where the land in, on or under which the development is to be carried out is—

Town and Country Planning (General Permitted Development) Order 2015

      (i) in the case of Class F of Part 17, on the same authorised site,

      (ii) in the case of Class H of Part 17, on the same premises or, as the case may be, the same ancillary mining land,

      (iii) in the case of Class K of Part 17, on the same land or, as the case may be, on land adjoining that land,

    as that in, on or under which development of any description permitted by the same Class has been carried out before 14th March 1999;

  (d) the completion of any development begun before 14th March 1999;

  (e) development for which permission is granted by Class B of Part 9 of Schedule 2.

(13) Where a person uses electronic communications for making any application required to be made under any of Part of Schedule 2, that person is taken to have agreed—

  (a) to the use of electronic communications for all purposes relating to that person's application which are capable of being effected using such communications;

  (b) that the address for the purpose of such communications is the address incorporated into, or otherwise logically associated with, that person's application; and

  (c) that the deemed agreement under this paragraph subsists until that person gives notice in writing revoking the agreement (and such revocation is final and takes effect on a date specified by the person but not less than 7 days after the date on which the notice is given).

4 Directions restricting permitted development

(1) If the Secretary of State or the local planning authority is satisfied that it is expedient that development described in any Part, Class or paragraph in Schedule 2, other than Class K or M of Part 17, should not be carried out unless permission is granted for it on an application, the Secretary of State or (as the case may be) the local planning authority, may make a direction under this paragraph that the permission granted by article 3 does not apply to—

  (a) all or any development of the Part, Class or paragraph in question in an area specified in the direction; or

  (b) any particular development, falling within that Part, Class or paragraph, which is specified in the direction,

and the direction must specify that it is made under this paragraph.

(2) A direction under paragraph (1) does not affect the carrying out of—

  (a) development permitted by any Class in Schedule 2 which is expressed to be subject to prior approval where, in relation to that development, the prior approval date occurs before the date on which the direction comes into force and the development is completed within a period of 3 years starting with the prior approval date;

  (b) development permitted by Class B of Part 9 of Schedule 2;

  (c) development mentioned in Class A of Part 16 of Schedule 2, unless the direction specifically so provides;

Town and Country Planning (General Permitted Development) Order 2015

(d) development permitted by Class A of Part 18 of Schedule 2 authorised by an Act passed after 1st July 1948 or by an order requiring the approval of both Houses of Parliament approved after that date;

(e) development permitted by Class Q, R, S or T of Part 19 of Schedule 2;

(f) development permitted under Schedule 2 in an emergency.

(3) A direction made or having effect as if made under this article does not, unless the direction so provides, affect the carrying out by a statutory undertaker of the following descriptions of development—

(a) the maintenance of bridges, buildings and railway stations;

(b) the alteration and maintenance of railway track, and the provision and maintenance of track equipment, including signal boxes, signalling apparatus and other appliances and works required in connection with the movement of traffic by rail;

(c) the maintenance of docks, harbours, quays, wharves, canals and towing paths;

(d) the provision and maintenance of mechanical apparatus or appliances (including signalling equipment) required for the purposes of shipping or in connection with the embarking, disembarking, loading, discharging or transport of passengers, livestock or goods at a dock, quay, harbour, bank, wharf or basin;

(e) any development required in connection with the improvement, maintenance or repair of watercourses or drainage works;

(f) the maintenance of buildings, runways, taxiways or aprons at an aerodrome; or

(g) the provision, alteration and maintenance of equipment, apparatus and works at an aerodrome, required in connection with the movement of traffic by air (other than buildings, the construction, erection, reconstruction or alteration of which is permitted by Class F of Part 8 of Schedule 2).

(4) The procedures which must be followed in making, modifying or cancelling any direction made under article 4(1) are set out in Schedule 3.

(5) In this article and in Schedule 3—

'local planning authority' means the local planning authority whose function it would be to determine an application for planning permission for the development to which the direction relates or is proposed to relate; and

'prior approval date' means the date on which—

(a) prior approval is given;

(b) a determination that such approval is not required is given, or

(c) any period for giving such a determination has expired without the applicant being notified whether prior approval is required, given or refused.

5 Directions restricting certain minerals permitted development

(1) If, on receipt of a notification from any person proposing to carry out development within Class K or M of Part 17 of Schedule 2, a mineral planning authority are satisfied as mentioned in paragraph (2), they may, within a period of 21 days beginning with the receipt of the notification, direct that the

permission granted by article 3 does not apply to the development, or to such part of the development as is specified in the direction.

(2) The mineral planning authority may make a direction under this article if they are satisfied that it is expedient that the development, or any part of it, should not be carried out unless permission for it is granted on an application because—

(a) the land on which the development is to be carried out is within—
  (i) a National Park;
  (ii) an area of outstanding natural beauty;
  (iii) a site of archaeological interest, and the operation to be carried out is not one described in the Schedule to the Areas of Archaeological Importance (Notification of Operations) (Exemption) Order 1984 (exempt operations);
  (iv) a site of special scientific interest; or
  (v) the Broads;
(b) the development, either taken by itself or taken in conjunction with other development which is already being carried out in the area or in respect of which notification has been given under the provisions of Class K or M of Part 17 of Schedule 2 would cause serious detriment to the amenity of the area in which it is to be carried out or would adversely affect the setting of a Grade I listed building;
(c) the development would constitute a serious nuisance to the inhabitants of a nearby residential building, hospital or school; or
(d) the development would endanger aircraft using a nearby aerodrome.

(3) A direction made under this article must contain a statement as to the day on which (if it is not disallowed under paragraph (5)) it comes into force, which must be 29 days from the date on which notice of it is sent to the Secretary of State in accordance with paragraph (4).

(4) As soon as is reasonably practicable a copy of a direction under this article must be sent by the mineral planning authority to the Secretary of State and to the person who gave notice of the proposal to carry out development.

(5) The Secretary of State may, at any time within a period of 28 days beginning with the date on which the direction is made, disallow the direction; and immediately upon receipt of notice in writing from the Secretary of State disallowing the direction, the mineral planning authority must give notice in writing, to the person who gave notice of the proposal, stating that the person is authorised to proceed with the development.

6 Directions: general

Any power conferred by this Order to give a direction includes power to cancel or vary the direction by a subsequent direction.

7 Prior approval applications: time periods for decision

Where, in relation to development permitted by any Class in Schedule 2 which is expressed to be subject to prior approval, an application has been made to a local planning authority for such approval or a determination as to whether such approval is required, the decision in relation to the application must be made by the authority—

(a) within the period specified in the relevant provision of Schedule 2,
(b) where no period is specified, within a period of 8 weeks beginning with the day immediately following that on which the application is received by the authority, or
(c) within such longer period as may be agreed by the applicant and the authority in writing.

8 Revocations and saving

(1) Subject to paragraph (2), the statutory instruments specified in Schedule 4 are revoked insofar as they apply to England.

(2) For the purposes only of development specified in article 6(2) of the Amending Order, the Town and Country Planning (General Permitted Development) Order 1995, in the form in which it existed immediately before the coming into force of the Amending Order, continues to apply in relation to that development.

(3) The saving provision in paragraph (2) ceases to have effect at the end of the 3 year period beginning with the day on which this Order comes into force.

(4) In this article, 'the Amending Order' means the Town and Country Planning (General Permitted Development) (Amendment) (England) Order 2015.

SCHEDULE 1

Article 2(3) to (5)

PART 1 ARTICLE 2(3) LAND

1

Land within—
(a) an area designated as a conservation area under section 69 of the Planning (Listed Buildings and Conservation Areas) Act 1990 (designation of conservation areas);
(b) an area of outstanding natural beauty;
(c) an area specified by the Secretary of State for the purposes of section 41(3) of the Wildlife and Countryside Act 1981 (enhancement and protection of the natural beauty and amenity of the countryside);
(d) the Broads;
(e) a National Park; and
(f) a World Heritage Site.

PART 2 ARTICLE 2(4) LAND

2

(1) Land within the following areas—
(a) a National Park;
(b) the Broads; or

Town and Country Planning (General Permitted Development) Order 2015

    (c) land outside the boundaries of a National Park which is within the parishes listed in sub-paragraph (2).

(2) The parishes are—

    (a) in the district of Allerdale—

Blindcrake, Bothel and Threapland, Bridekirk, Brigham, Broughton, Broughton Moor, Camerton, Crosscanonby, Dean, Dearham, Gilcrux, Great Clifton, Greysouthen, Little Clifton, Loweswater, Oughterside and Allerby, Papcastle, Plumbland, Seaton, Winscales;

    (b) in the borough of Copeland—

Arlecdon and Frizington, Cleator Moor, Distington, Drigg and Carleton, Egremont, Gosforth, Haile, Irton with Santon, Lamplugh, Lowca, Lowside Quarter, Millom, Millom Without, Moresby, Parton, Ponsonby, St Bees, St Bridget's Beckermet, St John's Beckermet, Seascale, Weddicar;

    (c) in the district of Eden—

Ainstable, Asby, Bandleyside, Bolton, Brough, Brough Sowerby, Brougham, Castle Sowerby, Catterlen, Clifton, Cliburn, Crackenthorpe, Crosby Garrett, Crosby Ravensworth, Culgaith, Dacre, Dufton, Glassonby, Great Salkeld, Great Strickland, Greystoke, Hartley, Hesket, Hillbeck, Hunsonby, Hutton, Kaber, Kings Meaburn, Kirkby Stephen, Kirby Thore, Kirkoswald, Langwathby, Lazonby, Little Strickland, Long Marton, Lowther, Mallerstang, Milburn, Morland, Mungrisdale, Murton, Musgrave, Nateby, Newbiggin, Newby, Orton, Ousby, Ravenstonedale, Shap, Skelton, Sleagill, Sockbridge and Tirril, Soulby, Stainmore, Tebay, Temple Sowerby, Thrimby, Waitby, Warcop, Wharton, Winton, Yanwath and Eamont Bridge;

    (d) in the borough of High Peak—

Chapel-en-le-Frith, Charlesworth, Chinley Buxworth and Brownside, Chisworth, Green Fairfield, Hartington Upper Quarter, Hayfield, King Sterndale, Tintwistle, Wormhill;

    (e) in the district of South Lakeland—

Aldingham, Angerton, Arnside, Barbon, Beetham, Blawith and Subberthwaite, Broughton West, Burton, Casterton, Docker, Egton-with-Newland, Fawcett Forest, Firbank, Grayrigg, Helsington, Heversham, Hincaster, Holme, Hutton Roof, Killington, Kirkby Ireleth, Kirkby Lonsdale, Lambrigg, Levens, Lower Allithwaite, Lower Holker, Lowick, Lupton, Mansergh, Mansriggs, Middleton, Milnthorpe, Natland, New Hutton, Old Hutton and Holmescales, Osmotherley, Pennington, Preston Patrick, Preston Richard, Scalthwaiterigg, Sedgwick, Skelsmergh, Stainton, Strickland Ketel, Strickland Roger, Urswick, Whinfell, Whitwell and Selside;

    (f) in the district of West Derbyshire—

Aldwark, Birchover, Stanton.

PART 3 ARTICLE 2(5) LAND

3

Land within the areas named in column 1 of the table in this Part is designated by reference to the area bounded externally by the outer edge of the boundary line shown on the corresponding map specified in column 3 of the table.

Town and Country Planning (General Permitted Development) Order 2015

Table

Column 1—name of area	Column 2—local planning authority for the area	Column 3—map number (colour / style of boundary line)
Central Activities Zone and Tech City, London	Common Council of the City of London	1.1 (red line)
	London Borough Council of Islington	1.2 (red line)
	London Borough Council of Hackney	1.3 to 1.7 (blue line)
	London Borough Council of Tower Hamlets	1.8 and 1.9 (red line and black borough boundary line, green line and black borough boundary line and pink line)
	London Borough Council of Southwark	1.10 (red line)
	London Borough Council of Lambeth	1.11 (red line)
	London Borough Council of Wandsworth	1.12 (blue line and black-dashed borough boundary line)
	Westminster City Council	1.13 (red line)
	Royal Borough Council of Kensington and Chelsea	1.14 (red line)
	London Borough Council of Camden	1.15 (red line)
The whole of the Royal Borough of Kensington and Chelsea (so far as not already designated under the entry for Central Activities Zone and Tech City)	Royal Borough Council of Kensington and Chelsea	1.14 (red line)
Areas in the Isle of Dogs (so far as not already designated under the entry for Central Activities Zone and Tech City)	London Borough Council of Tower Hamlets	1.8 and 1.9 (blue line)
3 areas known as the Royal Docks Enterprise Zone	London Borough Council of Newham	1.16 (red line)
2 areas known as Milton Park Enterprise Zone	Vale of the White Horse Borough Council	1.17 (red line)
Harwell Oxford Enterprise Zone	Vale of the White Horse Borough Council	1.18 (red line)
2 areas known as Manchester City Centre Core	Manchester City Council	1.19 (red line)
13 areas within the Gunnels Wood Employment Area	Stevenage Borough Council	1.20 (red line)
8 areas in and around De Beauvoir	London Borough of Hackney	1.21 (blue line)

Town and Country Planning (General Permitted Development) Order 2015

Column 1—name of area	Column 2—local planning authority for the area	Column 3—map number (colour / style of boundary line)
6 areas in and around Mare Street	London Borough of Hackney	1.22 (blue line)
BT Building, London Road	Sevenoaks District Council	1.23 (black line)
An area in London Road	Sevenoaks District Council	1.24 (black line)
Crown Inn, Westerham	Sevenoaks District Council	1.25 (black line)
Trading Centre, Westerham		
Ashford Commercial Quarter	Ashford Borough Council	1.26 (red line)
Petersfield Parish	East Hampshire District Council	1.27 (red line)
Alton Parish	East Hampshire District Council	1.28 (red line)
An area in Whitehall and Bordon	East Hampshire District Council	1.29 (red line)
Horndean Parish	East Hampshire District Council	1.30 (red line)
Liss Parish	East Hampshire District Council	1.31 (red line)
Bramshott and Liphook Ward and Parish	East Hampshire District Council	1.32 (red line)
Ropley Parish	East Hampshire District Council	1.33 (red line)
Bentley Parish	East Hampshire District Council	1.34 (red line)
Grayshott Ward and Parish	East Hampshire District Council	1.35 (red line)
Four Marks and Medstead Ward	East Hampshire District Council	1.36 (red line)

4

In this Part reference to a map is to one of the maps numbered 1.1 to 1.36 and entitled 'Maps of areas exempt from office to residential change of use permitted development right 2013', of which copies, signed by a member of the Senior Civil Service in the Department for Communities and Local Government, are available for inspection at the Planning Directorate, Department for Communities and Local Government, 2 Marsham Street, London, SW1P 4DF.

SCHEDULE 2
PERMITTED DEVELOPMENT RIGHTS

Article 3

PART 1 DEVELOPMENT WITHIN THE CURTILAGE OF A DWELLINGHOUSE

Class A—enlargement, improvement or other alteration of a dwellinghouse

Permitted Development

A   *The enlargement, improvement or other alteration of a dwellinghouse.*

Development not permitted

A.1

Development is not permitted by Class A if—

(a) permission to use the dwellinghouse as a dwellinghouse has been granted only by virtue of Class M, N, P or Q of Part 3 of this Schedule (changes of use);

(b) as a result of the works, the total area of ground covered by buildings within the curtilage of the dwellinghouse (other than the original dwellinghouse) would exceed 50% of the total area of the curtilage (excluding the ground area of the original dwellinghouse);

(c) the height of the part of the dwellinghouse enlarged, improved or altered would exceed the height of the highest part of the roof of the existing dwellinghouse;

(d) the height of the eaves of the part of the dwellinghouse enlarged, improved or altered would exceed the height of the eaves of the existing dwellinghouse;

(e) the enlarged part of the dwellinghouse would extend beyond a wall which—

   (i) forms the principal elevation of the original dwellinghouse; or

   (ii) fronts a highway and forms a side elevation of the original dwellinghouse;

(f) subject to paragraph (g), the enlarged part of the dwellinghouse would have a single storey and—

   (i) extend beyond the rear wall of the original dwellinghouse by more than 4 metres in the case of a detached dwellinghouse, or 3 metres in the case of any other dwellinghouse, or

   (ii) exceed 4 metres in height;

(g) until 30th May 2019, for a dwellinghouse not on article 2(3) land nor on a site of special scientific interest, the enlarged part of the dwellinghouse would have a single storey and—

   (i) extend beyond the rear wall of the original dwellinghouse by more than 8 metres in the case of a detached dwellinghouse, or 6 metres in the case of any other dwellinghouse, or

   (ii) exceed 4 metres in height;

(h) the enlarged part of the dwellinghouse would have more than a single storey and—

(i) extend beyond the rear wall of the original dwellinghouse by more than 3 metres, or
(ii) be within 7 metres of any boundary of the curtilage of the dwellinghouse opposite the rear wall of the dwellinghouse;
(i) the enlarged part of the dwellinghouse would be within 2 metres of the boundary of the curtilage of the dwellinghouse, and the height of the eaves of the enlarged part would exceed 3 metres;
(j) the enlarged part of the dwellinghouse would extend beyond a wall forming a side elevation of the original dwellinghouse, and would—
(i) exceed 4 metres in height,
(ii) have more than a single storey, or
(iii) have a width greater than half the width of the original dwellinghouse; or
(k) it would consist of or include—
(i) the construction or provision of a verandah, balcony or raised platform,
(ii) the installation, alteration or replacement of a microwave antenna,
(iii) the installation, alteration or replacement of a chimney, flue or soil and vent pipe, or
(iv) an alteration to any part of the roof of the dwellinghouse.

A.2

In the case of a dwellinghouse on article 2(3) land, development is not permitted by Class A if—
(a) it would consist of or include the cladding of any part of the exterior of the dwellinghouse with stone, artificial stone, pebble dash, render, timber, plastic or tiles;
(b) the enlarged part of the dwellinghouse would extend beyond a wall forming a side elevation of the original dwellinghouse; or
(c) the enlarged part of the dwellinghouse would have more than a single storey and extend beyond the rear wall of the original dwellinghouse.

Conditions

A.3

Development is permitted by Class A subject to the following conditions—
(a) the materials used in any exterior work (other than materials used in the construction of a conservatory) must be of a similar appearance to those used in the construction of the exterior of the existing dwellinghouse;
(b) any upper-floor window located in a wall or roof slope forming a side elevation of the dwellinghouse must be—
(i) obscure-glazed, and
(ii) non-opening unless the parts of the window which can be opened are more than 1.7 metres above the floor of the room in which the window is installed; and
(c) where the enlarged part of the dwellinghouse has more than a single storey, the roof pitch of the enlarged part must, so far as practicable, be the same as the roof pitch of the original dwellinghouse.

Town and Country Planning (General Permitted Development) Order 2015

A.4

(1) The following conditions apply to development permitted by Class A which exceeds the limits in paragraph A.1(f) but is allowed by paragraph A.1(g).

(2) Before beginning the development the developer must provide the following information to the local planning authority—

(a) a written description of the proposed development including—

(i) how far the enlarged part of the dwellinghouse extends beyond the rear wall of the original dwellinghouse;

(ii) the maximum height of the enlarged part of the dwellinghouse; and

(iii) the height of the eaves of the enlarged part of the dwellinghouse;

(b) a plan indicating the site and showing the proposed development;

(c) the addresses of any adjoining premises;

(d) the developer's contact address; and

(e) the developer's email address if the developer is content to receive communications electronically.

(3) The local planning authority may refuse an application where, in the opinion of the authority—

(a) the proposed development does not comply with, or

(b) the developer has provided insufficient information to enable the authority to establish whether the proposed development complies with,

the conditions, limitations or restrictions applicable to development permitted by Class A which exceeds the limits in paragraph A.1(f) but is allowed by paragraph A.1(g).

(4) Sub-paragraphs (5) to (7) and (9) do not apply where a local planning authority refuses an application under sub-paragraph (3) and for the purposes of section 78 (appeals) of the Act such a refusal is to be treated as a refusal of an application for approval.

(5) The local planning authority must notify each adjoining owner or occupier about the proposed development by serving on them a notice which—

(a) describes the proposed development, in cluding—

(i) how far the enlarged part of the dwellinghouse extends beyond the rear wall of the original dwellinghouse;

(ii) the maximum height of the enlarged part of the dwellinghouse; and

(iii) the height of the eaves of the enlarged part of the dwellinghouse;

(b) provides the address of the proposed development;

(c) specifies the date when the information referred to in sub-paragraph (2) was received by the local planning authority and the date when the period referred to in sub-paragraph (10)(c) would expire; and

(d) specifies the date (being not less than 21 days from the date of the notice) by which representations are to be received by the local planning authority.

(6) The local planning authority must send a copy of the notice referred to in sub-paragraph (5) to the developer.

(7) Where any owner or occupier of any adjoining premises objects to the proposed development, the prior approval of the local planning authority is required as

to the impact of the proposed development on the amenity of any adjoining premises.

(8) The local planning authority may require the developer to submit such further information regarding the proposed development as the authority may reasonably require in order to determine the application.

(9) The local planning authority must, when considering the impact referred to in sub-paragraph (7)—

  (a) take into account any representations made as a result of the notice given under sub-paragraph (5); and

  (b) consider the amenity of all adjoining premises, not just adjoining premises which are the subject of representations.

(10) The development must not begin before the occurrence of one of the following—

  (a) the receipt by the developer from the local planning authority of a written notice that their prior approval is not required;

  (b) the receipt by the developer from the local planning authority of a written notice giving their prior approval; or

  (c) the expiry of 42 days following the date on which the information referred to in sub-paragraph (2) was received by the local planning authority without the local planning authority notifying the developer as to whether prior approval is given or refused.

(11) The development must be carried out—

  (a) where prior approval is required, in accordance with the details approved by the local planning authority;

  (b) where prior approval is not required, or where sub-paragraph (10)(c) applies, in accordance with the information provided under sub-paragraph (2),

unless the local planning authority and the developer agree otherwise in writing.

(12) The local planning authority may grant prior approval unconditionally or subject to conditions reasonably related to the impact of the proposed development on the amenity of any adjoining premises.

(13) The development must be completed on or before 30th May 2019.

(14) The developer must notify the local planning authority of the completion of the development as soon as reasonably practicable after completion.

(15) The notification referred to in sub-paragraph (14) must be in writing and must include—

  (a) the name of the developer;

  (b) the address or location of the development, and

  (c) the date of completion.

Town and Country Planning (General Permitted Development) Order 2015

Class B—additions etc to the roof of a dwellinghouse

Permitted development

B *The enlargement of a dwellinghouse consisting of an addition or alteration to its roof.*

Development not permitted

B.1

Development is not permitted by Class B if—

- (a) permission to use the dwellinghouse as a dwellinghouse has been granted only by virtue of Class M, N, P or Q of Part 3 of this Schedule (changes of use);
- (b) any part of the dwellinghouse would, as a result of the works, exceed the height of the highest part of the existing roof;
- (c) any part of the dwellinghouse would, as a result of the works, extend beyond the plane of any existing roof slope which forms the principal elevation of the dwellinghouse and fronts a highway;
- (d) the cubic content of the resulting roof space would exceed the cubic content of the original roof space by more than—
    - (i) 40 cubic metres in the case of a terrace house, or
    - (ii) 50 cubic metres in any other case;
- (e) it would consist of or include—
    - (i) the construction or provision of a verandah, balcony or raised platform, or
    - (ii) the installation, alteration or replacement of a chimney, flue or soil and vent pipe; or
- (f) the dwellinghouse is on article 2(3) land.

Conditions

B.2

Development is permitted by Class B subject to the following conditions—

- (a) the materials used in any exterior work must be of a similar appearance to those used in the construction of the exterior of the existing dwellinghouse;
- (b) the enlargement must be constructed so that—
    - (i) other than in the case of a hip-to-gable enlargement or an enlargement which joins the original roof to the roof of a rear or side extension—
        - (aa) the eaves of the original roof are maintained or reinstated; and
        - (bb) the edge of the enlargement closest to the eaves of the original roof is, so far as practicable, not less than 0.2 metres from the eaves, measured along the roof slope from the outside edge of the eaves; and
    - (ii) other than in the case of an enlargement which joins the original roof to the roof of a rear or side extension, no part of the enlargement extends beyond the outside face of any external wall of the original dwellinghouse; and

Town and Country Planning (General Permitted Development) Order 2015

    (c) any window inserted on a wall or roof slope forming a side elevation of the dwellinghouse must be—
        (i) obscure-glazed, and
        (ii) non-opening unless the parts of the window which can be opened are more than 1.7 metres above the floor of the room in which the window is installed.

Interpretation of Class B

B.3

For the purposes of Class B, 'resulting roof space' means the roof space as enlarged, taking into account any enlargement to the original roof space, whether permitted by this Class or not.

B.4

For the purposes of paragraph B.2(b)(ii), roof tiles, guttering, fascias, barge boards and other minor roof details overhanging the external wall of the original dwellinghouse are not to be considered part of the enlargement.

Class C—other alterations to the roof of a dwellinghouse

Permitted development

C   *Any other alteration to the roof of a dwellinghouse.*

Development not permitted

C 1

Development is not permitted by Class C if—
    (a) permission to use the dwellinghouse as a dwellinghouse has been granted only by virtue of Class M, N, P or Q of Part 3 of this Schedule (changes of use);
    (b) the alteration would protrude more than 0.15 metres beyond the plane of the slope of the original roof when measured from the perpendicular with the external surface of the original roof;
    (c) it would result in the highest part of the alteration being higher than the highest part of the original roof; or
    (d) it would consist of or include—
        (i) the installation, alteration or replacement of a chimney, flue or soil and vent pipe, or
        (ii) the installation, alteration or replacement of solar photovoltaics or solar thermal equipment.

Conditions

C 2

Development is permitted by Class C subject to the condition that any window located on a roof slope forming a side elevation of the dwellinghouse must be—
    (a) obscure-glazed; and

Town and Country Planning (General Permitted Development) Order 2015

(b) non-opening unless the parts of the window which can be opened are more than 1.7 metres above the floor of the room in which the window is installed.

Class D—porches

Permitted development

D   *The erection or construction of a porch outside any external door of a dwellinghouse.*

Development not permitted

D.1

Development is not permitted by Class D if—

(a) permission to use the dwellinghouse as a dwellinghouse has been granted only by virtue of Class M, N, P or Q of Part 3 of this Schedule (changes of use);

(b) the ground area (measured externally) of the structure would exceed 3 square metres;

(c) any part of the structure would be more than 3 metres above ground level; or

(d) any part of the structure would be within 2 metres of any boundary of the curtilage of the dwellinghouse with a highway.

Class E—buildings etc incidental to the enjoyment of a dwellinghouse

Permitted development

E   *The provision within the curtilage of the dwellinghouse of—*

(a) any building or enclosure, swimming or other pool required for a purpose incidental to the enjoyment of the dwellinghouse as such, or the maintenance, improvement or other alteration of such a building or enclosure; or

(b) a container used for domestic heating purposes for the storage of oil or liquid petroleum gas.

Development not permitted

E.1

Development is not permitted by Class E if—

(a) permission to use the dwellinghouse as a dwellinghouse has been granted only by virtue of Class M, N, P or Q of Part 3 of this Schedule (changes of use);

(b) the total area of ground covered by buildings, enclosures and containers within the curtilage (other than the original dwellinghouse) would exceed 50% of the total area of the curtilage (excluding the ground area of the original dwellinghouse);

(c) any part of the building, enclosure, pool or container would be situated on land forward of a wall forming the principal elevation of the original dwellinghouse;

(d) the building would have more than a single storey;
(e) the height of the building, enclosure or container would exceed—
   (i) 4 metres in the case of a building with a dual-pitched roof,
   (ii) 2.5 metres in the case of a building, enclosure or container within 2 metres of the boundary of the curtilage of the dwellinghouse, or
   (iii) 3 metres in any other case;
(f) the height of the eaves of the building would exceed 2.5 metres;
(g) the building, enclosure, pool or container would be situated within the curtilage of a listed building;
(h) it would include the construction or provision of a verandah, balcony or raised platform;
(i) it relates to a dwelling or a microwave antenna; or
(j) the capacity of the container would exceed 3,500 litres.

E.2

In the case of any land within the curtilage of the dwellinghouse which is within—
(a) an area of outstanding natural beauty;
(b) the Broads;
(c) a National Park; or
(d) a World Heritage Site,

development is not permitted by Class E if the total area of ground covered by buildings, enclosures, pools and containers situated more than 20 metres from any wall of the dwellinghouse would exceed 10 square metres.

E.3

In the case of any land within the curtilage of the dwellinghouse which is article 2(3) land, development is not permitted by Class E if any part of the building, enclosure, pool or container would be situated on land between a wall forming a side elevation of the dwellinghouse and the boundary of the curtilage of the dwellinghouse.

Interpretation of Class E

E.4

For the purposes of Class E, 'purpose incidental to the enjoyment of the dwellinghouse as such' includes the keeping of poultry, bees, pet animals, birds or other livestock for the domestic needs or personal enjoyment of the occupants of the dwellinghouse.

Class F—hard surfaces incidental to the enjoyment of a dwellinghouse

Permitted development

F   *Development consisting of—*
   (a) *he provision within the curtilage of a dwellinghouse of a hard surface for any purpose incidental to the enjoyment of the dwellinghouse as such; or*
   (b) *the replacement in whole or in part of such a surface.*

Town and Country Planning (General Permitted Development) Order 2015

Development not permitted

F.1

Development is not permitted by Class F if permission to use the dwellinghouse as a dwellinghouse has been granted only by virtue of Class M, N, P or Q of Part 3 of this Schedule (changes of use).

Conditions

F.2

Development is permitted by Class F subject to the condition that where—
   (a) the hard surface would be situated on land between a wall forming the principal elevation of the dwellinghouse and a highway, and
   (b) the area of ground covered by the hard surface, or the area of hard surface replaced, would exceed 5 square metres,

either the hard surface is made of porous materials, or provision is made to direct run-off water from the hard surface to a permeable or porous area or surface within the curtilage of the dwellinghouse.

Class G—chimneys, flues etc on a dwellinghouse

Permitted development

G   *The installation, alteration or replacement of a chimney, flue or soil and vent pipe on a dwellinghouse.*

Development not permitted

G.1

Development is not permitted by Class G if—
   (a) permission to use the dwellinghouse as a dwellinghouse has been granted only by virtue of Class M, N, P or Q of Part 3 of this Schedule (changes of use);
   (b) the height of the chimney, flue or soil and vent pipe would exceed the highest part of the roof by 1 metre or more; or
   (c) in the case of a dwellinghouse on article 2(3) land, the chimney, flue or soil and vent pipe would be installed on a wall or roof slope which—
      (i) fronts a highway, and
      (ii) forms either the principal elevation or a side elevation of the dwellinghouse.

Class H—microwave antenna on a dwellinghouse

Permitted development

H   *The installation, alteration or replacement of a microwave antenna on a dwellinghouse or within the curtilage of a dwellinghouse.*

Development not permitted

H.1

Development is not permitted by Class H if—

(a) permission to use the dwellinghouse as a dwellinghouse has been granted only by virtue of Class M, N, P or Q of Part 3 of this Schedule (changes of use);
(b) it would result in the presence on the dwellinghouse or within its curtilage of—
   (i) more than 2 antennas;
   (ii) a single antenna exceeding 1 metre in length;
   (iii) 2 antennas which do not meet the relevant size criteria;
   (iv) an antenna installed on a chimney, where the length of the antenna would exceed 0.6 metres;
   (v) an antenna installed on a chimney, where the antenna would protrude above the chimney; or
   (vi) an antenna with a cubic capacity in excess of 35 litres;
(c) in the case of an antenna to be installed on a roof without a chimney, the highest part of the antenna would be higher than the highest part of the roof;
(d) in the case of an antenna to be installed on a roof with a chimney, the highest part of the antenna would be higher than the highest part of the chimney, or 0.6 metres measured from the highest part of the ridge tiles of the roof, whichever is the lower; or
(e) in the case of article 2(3) land, it would consist of the installation of an antenna—
   (i) on a chimney, wall or roof slope which faces onto, and is visible from, a highway;
   (ii) in the Broads, on a chimney, wall or roof slope which faces onto, and is visible from, a waterway; or
   (iii) on a building which exceeds 15 metres in height.

Conditions

H.2

Development is permitted by Class H subject to the following conditions—
(a) an antenna installed on a building must, so far as practicable, be sited so as to minimise its effect on the external appearance of the building; and
(b) an antenna no longer needed for reception or transmission purposes is removed as soon as reasonably practicable.

Interpretation of Class H

H.3

For the purposes of Class H—
(a) the relevant size criteria for the purposes of paragraph H.1(b)(iii) are that—
   (i) only 1 of the antennas may exceed 0.6 metres in length; and
   (ii) any antenna which exceeds 0.6 metres in length must not exceed 1 metre in length;

(b) the length of the antenna is to be measured in any linear direction, and excludes any projecting feed element, reinforcing rim, mounting or brackets.

Interpretation of Part 1

I

For the purposes of Part 1—

'highway' includes an unadopted street or a private way;

'raised' in relation to a platform means a platform with a height greater than 0.3 metres; and

'terrace house' means a dwellinghouse situated in a row of 3 or more dwellinghouses used or designed for use as single dwellings, where—
- (a) it shares a party wall with, or has a main wall adjoining the main wall of, the dwellinghouse on either side; or
- (b) if it is at the end of a row, it shares a party wall with or has a main wall adjoining the main wall of a dwellinghouse which fulfils the requirements of paragraph (a); and

'unadopted street' means a street not being a highway maintainable at the public expense within the meaning of the Highways Act 1980.

PART 2 MINOR OPERATIONS

Class A—gates, fences, walls etc

Permitted development

A *The erection, construction, maintenance, improvement or alteration of a gate, fence, wall or other means of enclosure.*

Development not permitted

A.1

Development is not permitted by Class A if—
- (a) the height of any gate, fence, wall or means of enclosure erected or constructed adjacent to a highway used by vehicular traffic would, after the carrying out of the development, exceed—
  - (i) for a school, 2 metres above ground level, provided that any part of the gate, fence, wall or means of enclosure which is more than 1 metre above ground level does not create an obstruction to the view of persons using the highway as to be likely to cause danger to such persons;
  - (ii) in any other case, 1 metre above ground level;
- (b) the height of any other gate, fence, wall or means of enclosure erected or constructed would exceed 2 metres above ground level;
- (c) the height of any gate, fence, wall or other means of enclosure maintained, improved or altered would, as a result of the development, exceed its former height or the height referred to in paragraph (a) or (b) as the height appropriate to it if erected or constructed, whichever is the greater; or
- (d) it would involve development within the curtilage of, or to a gate, fence, wall or other means of enclosure surrounding, a listed building.

Interpretation of Class A

A.2

For the purposes of Class A, 'school' includes—
- (a) premises which have changed use under Class S or T of Part 3 of this Schedule (changes of use) to become a state-funded school or registered nursery as defined in paragraph X of Part 3; and
- (b) a building permitted by Class C of Part 4 of this Schedule (temporary buildings and uses) to be used temporarily as a school, from the date the local planning authority is notified as provided in paragraph C 2(b) of Part 4.

Class B—means of access to a highway

Permitted development

B   *The formation, laying out and construction of a means of access to a highway which is not a trunk road or a classified road, where that access is required in connection with development permitted by any Class in this Schedule (other than by Class A of this Part).*

Class C—exterior painting

Permitted development

C   *The painting of the exterior of any building or work.*

Development not permitted

C 1

Development is not permitted by Class C if the painting is for the purpose of advertisement, announcement or direction.

Interpretation of Class C

C 2

In Class C, 'painting' includes any application of colour.

Class D—electrical outlet for recharging vehicles

Permitted development

D   *The installation, alteration or replacement, within an area lawfully used for off-street parking, of an electrical outlet mounted on a wall for recharging electric vehicles.*

Development not permitted

D.1

Development is not permitted by Class D if the outlet and its casing would—
- (a) exceed 0.2 cubic metres;
- (b) face onto and be within 2 metres of a highway;
- (c) be within a site designated as a scheduled monument; or
- (d) be within the curtilage of a listed building.

Town and Country Planning (General Permitted Development) Order 2015

Conditions

D.2

Development is permitted by Class D subject to the conditions that when no longer needed as a charging point for electric vehicles—

    (a) the development is removed as soon as reasonably practicable; and

    (b) the wall on which the development was mounted or into which the development was set is, as soon as reasonably practicable, and so far as reasonably practicable, reinstated to its condition before that development was carried out.

Class E—electrical upstand for recharging vehicles

Permitted development

E   *The installation, alteration or replacement, within an area lawfully used for off-street parking, of an upstand with an electrical outlet mounted on it for recharging electric vehicles.*

Development not permitted

E.1

Development is not permitted by Class E if the upstand and the outlet would—

    (a) exceed 1.6 metres in height from the level of the surface used for the parking of vehicles;

    (b) be within 2 metres of a highway;

    (c) be within a site designated as a scheduled monument;

    (d) be within the curtilage of a listed building; or

    (e) result in more than 1 upstand being provided for each parking space.

Conditions

E.2

Development is permitted by Class E subject to the conditions that when the development is no longer needed as a charging point for electric vehicles—

    (a) the development is removed as soon as reasonably practicable; and

    (b) the land on which the development was mounted or into which the development was set is, as soon as reasonably practicable, and so far as reasonably practicable, reinstated to its condition before that development was carried out.

Class F—closed circuit television cameras

Permitted development

F   *The installation, alteration or replacement on a building of a closed circuit television camera to be used for security purposes.*

Development not permitted

F.1

Development is not permitted by Class F if—

(a) the building on which the camera would be installed, altered or replaced is a listed building or a scheduled monument;
(b) the dimensions of the camera including its housing exceed 0.75 metres by 0.25 metres by 0.25 metres;
(c) any part of the camera would, when installed, altered or replaced, be less than 2.5 metres above ground level;
(d) any part of the camera would, when installed, altered or replaced, protrude from the surface of the building by more than 1 metre when measured from the surface of the building;
(e) any part of the camera would, when installed, altered or replaced, be in contact with the surface of the building at a point which is more than 1 metre from any other point of contact;
(f) any part of the camera would be less than 10 metres from any part of another camera installed on a building;
(g) the development would result in the presence of more than 4 cameras on the same side of the building; or
(h) the development would result in the presence of more than 16 cameras on the building.

Conditions

F.2

Development is permitted by Class F subject to the following conditions—
(a) the camera is, so far as practicable, sited so as to minimise its effect on the external appearance of the building on which it is situated; and
(b) the camera is removed as soon as reasonably practicable after it is no longer required for security purposes.

Interpretation of Class F

F.3

For the purposes of Class F—

'camera', except in paragraph F.1(b), includes its housing, pan and tilt mechanism, infra-red illuminator, receiver, mountings and brackets; and

'ground level' means the level of the surface of the ground immediately adjacent to the building or, where the level of the surface of the ground is not uniform, the level of the highest part of the surface of the ground adjacent to it.

PART 3 CHANGES OF USE

Class A—restaurants, cafes, takeaways or pubs to retail

Permitted development

A *Development consisting of a change of use of a building from a use falling within Class A3 (restaurants and cafes), A4 (drinking establishments) or A5 (hot food takeaways) of the Schedule to the Use Classes Order, to a use falling within Class A1 (shops) or Class A2 (financial and professional services) of that Schedule.*

Town and Country Planning (General Permitted Development) Order 2015

Development not permitted

A.1

Development is not permitted by Class A during the specified period if the building is a specified building.

Conditions

A.2

In the case of a building which is not a community asset, which is used for a purpose falling within Class A4 (drinking establishments) of the Schedule to the Use Classes Order, development is permitted by Class A subject to the following conditions.

(2) Before beginning the development the developer must send a written request to the local planning authority as to whether the building has been nominated, which must include—

(a) the address of the building;

(b) the developer's contact address; and

(c) the developer's email address if the developer is content to receive communications electronically.

(3) If the building is nominated, whether at the date of request under paragraph A.2(2) or on a later date, the local planning authority must notify the developer as soon as is reasonably practicable after it is aware of the nomination, and on notification development is not permitted for the specified period.

(4) The development must not begin before the expiry of a period of 56 days following the date of request under paragraph A.2(2) and must be completed within a period of 1 year of the date of that request.

Interpretation of Class A

A.3

For the purposes of Class A—

'community asset' means a building which has been entered onto a list of assets of community value, including any building which has been subsequently excluded from that list under regulation 2(b) of the Assets of Community Value (England) Regulations 2012;

'list of assets of community value' means a list of land of community value maintained by a local authority under section 87(1) of the Localism Act 2011;

'nomination' means a nomination made under section 89(2) of the Localism Act 2011 for a building to be included in a list of assets of community value and 'nominated' is to be interpreted accordingly;

'specified building' means a building used for a purpose falling within Class A4 (drinking establishments) of the Schedule to the Use Classes Order—

(a) which is a community asset; or

(b) in relation to which the local planning authority has notified the developer of a nomination under paragraph A.2(3); and

'specified period' means—
(a) in relation to a building which is subject to a nomination of which the local planning authority have notified the developer under paragraph A.2(3), the period from the date of that notification to the date on which the building is entered onto—
  (i) a list of assets of community value; or
  (ii) a list of land nominated by unsuccessful community nominations under section 93 of the Localism Act 2011;
(b) in relation to a building which is a community asset—
  (i) 5 years beginning with the date on which the building was entered onto the list of assets of community value; or
  (ii) where the building was removed from that list—
    (aa) under regulation 2(c) of the Assets of Community Value (England) Regulations 2012 following a successful appeal against listing or because the local authority no longer consider the land to be land of community value; or
    (bb) under section 92(4)(a) of the Localism Act 2011 following the local authority's decision on a review that the land concerned should not have been included in the local authority's list of assets of community value,
  the period from the date on which the building was entered onto the list of assets of community value to the date on which it was removed from that list.

Class B—takeaways or pubs to restaurants and cafes

Permitted development

B *Development consisting of a change of use of a building from a use falling within Class A4 (drinking establishments) or Class A5 (hot food takeaways) of the Schedule to the Use Classes Order, to a use falling within Class A3 (restaurants and cafes) of that Schedule.*

Development not permitted

B.1

Development is not permitted by Class B during the specified period if the building is a specified building.

Conditions

B.2

In the case of a building which is not a community asset, which is used for a purpose falling within Class A4 (drinking establishments) of the Schedule to the Use Classes Order, development is permitted by Class B subject to the conditions set out in paragraphs A.2(2) to (4).

Town and Country Planning (General Permitted Development) Order 2015

Interpretation of Class B

B.3

For the purposes of Class B, 'community asset', 'specified building' and 'specified period' have the meaning given in paragraph A.3.

Class C—retail, betting office or pay day loan shop or casino to restaurant or cafe

Permitted development

C   Development consisting of—
(a) a change of use of a building from a use—
  (i) *falling within Class A1 (shops) or Class A2 (financial and professional services) of the Schedule to the Use Classes Order,*
  (ii) *as a betting office or pay day loan shop, or*
  (iii) *as a casino,*
  to a use falling within Class A3 (restaurants and cafes) of the Schedule to the Use Classes Order, and
(b) *building or other operations for the provision of facilities for—*
  (i) *ventilation and extraction (including the provision of an external flue), and*
  (ii) *the storage of rubbish,*
  reasonably necessary to use the building for a use falling within Class A3 (restaurants and cafes) of that Schedule.

Development not permitted

C 1

Development is not permitted by Class C if—
(a) the cumulative floor space of the existing building changing use under Class C exceeds 150 square metres;
(b) the development (together with any previous development under Class C) would result in more than 150 square metres of floor space in the building having changed use under Class C;
(c) the land or the site on which the building is located is or forms part of—
  (i) a site of special scientific interest;
  (ii) a safety hazard area; or
  (iii) a military explosives storage area;
(d) the site is, or contains, a scheduled monument; or
(e) the land or building is a listed building or is within the curtilage of a listed building.

Conditions

C 2

(1) Where the development proposed is development under Class C(a) together with development under Class C(b), development is permitted subject to the

condition that before beginning the development, the developer must apply to the local planning authority for a determination as to whether the prior approval of the authority will be required as to—

(a) noise impacts of the development,

(b) odour impacts of the development,

(c) impacts of storage and handling of waste in relation to the development,

(d) impacts of the hours of opening of the development,

(e) transport and highways impacts of the development,

(f) whether it is undesirable for the building to change to a use falling within Class A3 (restaurants and cafes) of the Schedule to the Use Classes Order because of the impact of the change of use—

- (i) on adequate provision of services of the sort that may be provided by a building falling within Class A1 (shops) or, as the case may be, Class A2 (financial and professional services) of that Schedule, but only where there is a reasonable prospect of the building being used to provide such services, or

- (ii) where the building is located in a key shopping area, on the sustainability of that shopping area, and

(g) the siting, design or external appearance of the facilities to be provided under Class C(b),

and the provisions of paragraph W (prior approval) of this Part apply in relation to that application.

(2) Where the development proposed is development under Class C(a) only, development is permitted subject to the condition that before beginning the development, the developer must apply to the local planning authority for a determination as to whether the prior approval of the authority will be required as to the items referred to in sub-paragraphs (1)(a) to (f) and the provisions of paragraph W (prior approval) of this Part apply in relation to that application.

(3) Development under Class C is permitted subject to the condition that development under Class C(a), and under Class C(b), if any, must begin within a period of 3 years starting with the prior approval date.

Class D—shops to financial and professional

Permitted development

D   *Development consisting of a change of use of a building within its curtilage from a use falling within Class A1 (shops) of the Schedule to the Use Classes Order, to use falling within Class A2 (financial and professional services) of that Schedule.*

Class E—financial and professional or betting office or pay day loan shop to shops

Permitted development

E   *Development consisting of a change of use of a building with a display window at ground floor level from—*

   (a) a use falling within Class A2 (financial and professional services) of the Schedule to the Use Classes Order, or

(b) *a use as a betting office or a pay day loan shop,*

to a use falling within Class A1 (shops) of the Schedule to the Use Classes Order.

Class F—betting offices or pay day loan shops to financial and professional

Permitted development

F *Development consisting of a change of use of a building from a use as a betting office or a pay day loan shop to a use falling within Class A2 (financial and professional services) of the Schedule to the Use Classes Order.*

Class G—retail or betting office or pay day loan shop to mixed use

Permitted development

G *Development consisting of a change of use of a building—*
   (a) from a use for any purpose within Class A1 (shops) of the Schedule to the Use Classes Order, to a mixed use for any purpose within Class A1 (shops) of that Schedule and as up to 2 flats;
   (b) from a use for any purpose within Class A1 (shops) of the Schedule to the Use Classes Order, to a mixed use for any purpose within Class A2 (financial and professional services) of that Schedule and as up to 2 flats;
   (c) from a use—
      (i) for any purpose within Class A2 (financial and professional services) of the Schedule to the Use Classes Order, or
      (ii) as a betting office or a pay day loan shop,
      to a mixed use for any purpose within Class A2 (financial and professional services) of that Schedule and as up to 2 flats;
   (d) where that building has a display window at ground floor level, from a use—
      (i) for any purpose within Class A2 (financial and professional services) of the Schedule to the Use Classes Order, or
      (ii) as a betting office or a pay day loan shop,
      to a mixed use for any purpose within Class A1 (shops) of the Schedule to the Use Classes Order and as up to 2 flats;
   (e) from a use as a betting office or a pay day loan shop to a mixed use as a betting office or a pay day loan shop and as up to 2 flats.

Conditions

G.1

Development permitted by Class G is subject to the following conditions—
   (a) some or all of the parts of the building used as a betting office or pay day loan shop or for any purposes within Class A1 or Class A2, as the case may be, of the Schedule to the Use Classes Order is situated on a floor below the lowest part of the building used as a flat;

(b) where the development consists of a change of use of any building with a display window at ground floor level, the ground floor must not be used in whole or in part as a flat;

(c) a flat must not be used otherwise than as a dwelling (whether or not as a sole or main residence)—

(i) by a single person or by people living together as a family, or

(ii) by not more than 6 residents living together as a single household (including a household where care is provided for residents).

Interpretation of Class G

G.2

For the purposes of Class G, 'care' means personal care for people in need of such care by reason of old age, disablement, past or present dependence on alcohol or drugs or past or present mental disorder.

Class H—mixed use to retail

Permitted development

H *Development consisting of a change of use of a building—*

(a) *from a mixed use for any purpose within Class A1 (shops) of the Schedule to the Use Classes Order and as up to 2 flats, to a use for any purpose within Class A1 (shops) of that Schedule;*

(b) *from a mixed use for any purpose within Class A1 (shops) of the Schedule to the Use Classes Order and as up to 2 flats, to a use for any purpose within Class A2 (financial and professional services) of that Schedule;*

(c) *from a mixed use—*

(i) *for any purpose within Class A2 (financial and professional services) of the Schedule to the Use Classes Order and as up to 2 flats,*

(ii) *as a betting office or pay day loan shop and as up to 2 flats,*

to a use for any purpose within Class A2 (financial and professional services) of that Schedule;

(d) *where that building has a display window at ground floor level, from a mixed use for any purpose—*

(i) *within Class A2 (financial and professional services) of the Schedule to the Use Classes Order and as up to 2 flats, or*

(ii) *as a betting office or pay day loan shop and as up to 2 flats,*

to a use for any purpose within Class A1 (shops) of the Schedule to the Use Classes Order;

(e) *from a mixed use as a betting office or pay day loan shop and as up to 2 flats to a use as a betting office or pay day loan shop.*

Development not permitted

H.1

Development is not permitted by Class H unless each part of the building used as a flat was, immediately prior to being so used, used for any purpose within Class A1

Town and Country Planning (General Permitted Development) Order 2015

(shops) or Class A2 (financial and professional services) of the Schedule to the Use Classes Order or, as the case may be, used as a betting office or pay day loan shop.

Class I—industrial and general business conversions

Permitted development

I Development consisting of a change of use of a building—
   (a) *from any use falling within Class B2 (general industrial) or B8 (storage or distribution) of the Schedule to the Use Classes Order, to a use for any purpose falling within Class B1 (business) of that Schedule;*
   (b) *from any use falling within Class B1 (business) or B2 (general industrial) of the Schedule to the Use Classes Order, to a use for any purpose falling within Class B8 (storage or distribution) of that Schedule.*

Development not permitted

I.1

Development is not permitted by Class I, where the change is to or from a use falling within Class B8 of that Schedule, if the change of use relates to more than 500 square metres of floor space in the building.

Class J—retail or betting office or pay day loan shop to assembly and leisure

Permitted development

J Development consisting of a change of use of a building from a use—
   (a) *falling within Class A1 (shops) or Class A2 (financial and professional services) of the Schedule to the Use Classes Order, or*
   (b) *as a betting office or pay day loan shop,*

   to a use falling within Class D2 (assembly and leisure) of that Schedule.

Development not permitted

J.1

Development is not permitted by Class J if—
   (a) the building was not used solely for a use falling within Class J(a) or (b)—
       (i) on 5th December 2013, or
       (ii) in the case of a building which was in use before that date but was not in use on that date, on the date it was last in use, or
       (iii) in the case of a building which is brought into use after 5th December 2013, for a period of at least 5 years before the date development under Class J begins;
   (b) the cumulative floor space of the existing building changing use under Class J exceeds 200 square metres;
   (c) the development (together with any previous development under Class J) would result in more than 200 square metres of floor space in the building having changed use under Class J;
   (d) the building is on article 2(3) land;

Town and Country Planning (General Permitted Development) Order 2015

(e) the land or the site on which the building is located is or forms part of—
  (i) a site of special scientific interest;
  (ii) a safety hazard area; or
  (iii) a military explosives storage area;
(f) the land or building is, or contains, a scheduled monument; or
(g) the land or building is a listed building or is within the curtilage of a listed building.

Conditions

J.2

(1) Class J is permitted subject the condition that before beginning the development, the developer must apply to the local planning authority for a determination as to whether the prior approval of the authority will be required as to—
  (a) noise impacts of the development,
  (b) impacts of the hours of opening of the development,
  (c) transport and highways impacts of the development, and
  (d) whether it is undesirable for the building to change to a use falling within Class D2 (assembly and leisure) of the Schedule to the Use Classes Order because of the impact of the change of use—
    (i) on adequate provision of services of the sort that may be provided by a building falling within Class A1 (shops) or, as the case may be, Class A2 (financial and professional services) of that Schedule, but only where there is a reasonable prospect of the building being used to provide such services, or
    (ii) where the building is located in a key shopping area, on the sustainability of that shopping area, and

and the provisions of paragraph W (prior approval) of this Part apply in relation to that application.

(2) Subject to sub-paragraph (3), development under Class J must begin within a period of 3 years starting with the prior approval date.

(3) Where, in relation to a particular development under Class J, planning permission is granted on an application in respect of associated operational development before the end of the period referred to in sub-paragraph (2), then development under Class J must begin within the period of 3 years starting with the date that planning permission is granted.

(4) For the purposes of sub-paragraph (3), 'associated operational development' means building or other operations in relation to the same building or land which are reasonably necessary to use the building or land for the use proposed under Class J.

Class K—casinos to assembly and leisure

Permitted Development

K *Development consisting of a change of use of a building from a use as a casino to a use falling within Class D2 (assembly and leisure) of the Schedule to the Use Classes Order.*

Town and Country Planning (General Permitted Development) Order 2015

Class L—small HMOs to dwellinghouses and vice versa

Permitted development

L Development consisting of a change of use of a building—
   (a) from a use falling within Class C4 (houses in multiple occupation) of the Schedule to the Use Classes Order, to a use falling within Class C3 (dwellinghouses) of that Schedule;
   (b) from a use falling within Class C3 (dwellinghouses) of the Schedule to the Use Classes Order, to a use falling within Class C4 (houses in multiple occupation) of that Schedule.

Development not permitted

L 1

Development is not permitted by Class L if it would result in the use—
   (a) as two or more separate dwellinghouses falling within Class C3 (dwellinghouses) of the Schedule to the Use Classes Order of any building previously used as a single dwellinghouse falling within Class C4 (houses in multiple occupation) of that Schedule; or
   (b) as two or more separate dwellinghouses falling within Class C4 (houses in multiple occupation) of that Schedule of any building previously used as a single dwellinghouse falling within Class C3 (dwellinghouses) of that Schedule.

Class M—retail or betting office or pay day loan shop to dwellinghouses

Permitted development

M Development consisting of—
   (a) a change of use of a building from—
       (i) a use falling within Class A1 (shops) or Class A2 (financial and professional services) of the Schedule to the Use Classes Order;
       (ii) a use as a betting office or pay day loan shop, or
       (iii) a mixed use combining use as a dwellinghouse with—
           (aa) a use as a betting office or pay day loan shop, or
           (bb) a use falling within either Class A1 (shops) or Class A2 (financial and professional services) of that Schedule (whether that use was granted permission under Class G of this Part or otherwise),
       to a use falling within Class C3 (dwellinghouses) of that Schedule, and
   (b) building operations reasonably necessary to convert the building referred to in paragraph (a) to a use falling within Class C3 (dwellinghouses) of that Schedule.

Development not permitted

M.1

Development is not permitted by Class M if—
   (a) the building was not used for one of the uses referred to in Class M(a)—

(i) on 20th March 2013, or

(ii) in the case of a building which was in use before that date but was not in use on that date, when it was last in use;

(b) permission to use the building for a use falling within Class A1 (shops) or Class A2 (financial and professional services) of the Schedule to the Use Classes Order has been granted only by this Part;

(c) the cumulative floor space of the existing building changing use under Class M exceeds 150 square metres;

(d) the development (together with any previous development under Class M) would result in more than 150 square metres of floor space in the building having changed use under Class M;

(e) the development would result in the external dimensions of the building extending beyond the external dimensions of the existing building at any given point;

(f) the development consists of demolition (other than partial demolition which is reasonably necessary to convert the building to a use falling within Class C3 (dwellinghouses) of the Schedule to the Use Classes Order); or

(g) the building is—

(i) on article 2(3) land;

(ii) in a site of special scientific interest;

(iii) in a safety hazard area;

(iv) in a military explosives storage area;

(v) a listed building; or

(vi) a scheduled monument.

Conditions

M.2

(1) Where the development proposed is development under Class M(a) together with development under Class M(b), development is permitted subject to the condition that before beginning the development, the developer must apply to the local planning authority for a determination as to whether the prior approval of the authority will be required as to—

(a) transport and highways impacts of the development,

(b) contamination risks in relation to the building,

(c) flooding risks in relation to the building,

(d) whether it is undesirable for the building to change to a use falling within Class C3 (dwellinghouses) of the Schedule to the Use Classes Order because of the impact of the change of use—

(i) on adequate provision of services of the sort that may be provided by a building falling within Class A1 (shops) or, as the case may be, Class A2 (financial and professional services) of that Schedule, but only where there is a reasonable prospect of the building being used to provide such services, or

(ii) where the building is located in a key shopping area, on the sustainability of that shopping area, and

Town and Country Planning (General Permitted Development) Order 2015

(e) the design or external appearance of the building,

and the provisions of paragraph W (prior approval) of this Part apply in relation to that application.

(2) Where the development proposed is development under Class M(a) only, development is permitted subject to the condition that before beginning the development, the developer must apply to the local planning authority for a determination as to whether the prior approval of the authority will be required as to the items referred to in sub-paragraphs (1)(a) to (d) and the provisions of paragraph W (prior approval) of this Part apply in relation to that application.

(3) Development under Class M is permitted subject to the condition that—
   (a) development under Class M(a), and under Class M(b), if any, must be completed within a period of 3 years starting with the prior approval date; and
   (b) a building which has changed use under Class M is to be used as a dwellinghouse within the meaning of Class C3 of the Schedule to the Use Classes Order and for no other purpose, except to the extent that the other purpose is ancillary to the primary use as such a dwellinghouse.

Class N—specified sui generis uses to dwellinghouses

Permitted development

N   *Development consisting of—*
   (a) a change of use of a building and any land within its curtilage from a use as—
      (i) an amusement arcade or centre, or
      (ii) a casino,
      to a use falling within Class C3 (dwellinghouses) of the Schedule to the Use Classes Order; and
   (b) building operations reasonably necessary to convert the building referred to in paragraph (a) to a use falling within Class C3 (dwellinghouses) of that Schedule.

Development not permitted

N.1

Development is not permitted by Class N if—
   (a) the building was not used solely for one of the uses specified in Class N(a)—
      (i) on 19th March 2014, or
      (ii) in the case of a building which was in use before that date but was not in use on that date, when it was last in use;
   (b) the cumulative floor space of the existing building changing use under Class N exceeds 150 square metres;
   (c) the development (together with any previous development under Class N) would result in more than 150 square metres of floor space in the building having changed use under Class N;

(d) the development under Class N(b) would consist of building operations other than—
  (i) the installation or replacement of—
    (aa) windows, doors, roofs, or exterior walls, or
    (bb) water, drainage, electricity, gas or other services,
    to the extent reasonably necessary for the building to function as a dwellinghouse; and
  (ii) partial demolition to the extent reasonably necessary to carry out building operations allowed by paragraph (d)(i);
(e) the building is within—
  (i) an area of outstanding natural beauty;
  (ii) an area specified by the Secretary of State for the purposes of section 41(3) of the Wildlife and Countryside Act 1981;
  (iii) the Broads;
  (iv) a National Park; or
  (v) a World Heritage Site;
(f) the site is, or forms part of—
  (i) a site of special scientific interest;
  (ii) a safety hazard area;
  (iii) a military explosives storage area;
(g) the building is a listed building or is within the curtilage of a listed building; or
(h) the site is, or contains, a scheduled monument.

Conditions

N.2

(1) Where the development proposed is development under Class N(a) together with development under Class N(b), development is permitted subject to the condition that before beginning the development, the developer must apply to the local planning authority for a determination as to whether the prior approval of the authority will be required as to—
  (a) transport and highways impacts of the development,
  (b) contamination risks in relation to the building,
  (c) flooding risks in relation to the building, and
  (d) the design or external appearance of the building,
  and the provisions of paragraph W (prior approval) of this Part apply in relation to that application.

(2) Where the development proposed is development under Class N(a) only, development is permitted subject to the condition that before beginning the development, the developer must apply to the local planning authority for a determination as to whether the prior approval of the authority will be required as to the items referred to in sub-paragraphs (1)(a) to (c) and the provisions of paragraph W (prior approval) of this Part apply in relation to that application.

Town and Country Planning (General Permitted Development) Order 2015

(3) Development under Class N is permitted subject to the condition that development under Class N(a), and under Class N(b), if any, must be completed within a period of 3 years starting with the prior approval date.

Class O—offices to dwellinghouses

Permitted development

O   *Development consisting of a change of use of a building and any land within its curtilage from a use falling within Class B1(a) (offices) of the Schedule to the Use Classes Order, to a use falling within Class C3 (dwellinghouses) of that Schedule.*

Development not permitted

O.1

Development is not permitted by Class O if—

(a) the building is on article 2(5) land;

(b) the building was not used for a use falling within Class B1(a) (offices) of the Schedule to the Use Classes Order—

    (i) on 29th May 2013, or

    (ii) in the case of a building which was in use before that date but was not in use on that date, when it was last in use;

(c) the use of the building falling within Class C3 (dwellinghouses) of that Schedule was begun after 30th May 2016;

(d) the site is, or forms part of, a safety hazard area;

(e) the site is, or forms part of, a military explosives storage area;

(f) the building is a listed building or is within the curtilage of a listed building; or

(g) the site is, or contains, a scheduled monument.

Conditions

O.2

Development under Class O is permitted subject to the condition that before beginning the development, the developer must apply to the local planning authority for a determination as to whether the prior approval of the authority will be required as to—

(a) transport and highways impacts of the development;

(b) contamination risks on the site; and

(c) flooding risks on the site,

and the provisions of paragraph W (prior approval) apply in relation to that application.

Class P—storage or distribution centre to dwellinghouses

Permitted development

P   *Development consisting of a change of use of a building and any land within its curtilage from a use falling within Class B8 (storage or distribution centre) of the Schedule to the Use Classes Order to a use falling within Class C3 (dwellinghouses) of that Schedule.*

Development not permitted

P1

Development is not permitted by Class P if—

 (a) the building was not used solely for a storage or distribution centre use on 19th March 2014 or in the case of a building which was in use before that date but was not in use on that date, when it was last in use;

 (b) the building was not used solely for a storage or distribution centre use for a period of at least 4 years before the date development under Class P begins;

 (c) the use of the building falling within Class C3 (dwellinghouses) of that Schedule was begun after 15th April 2018;

 (d) the gross floor space of the existing building exceeds 500 square metres;

 (e) the site is occupied under an agricultural tenancy, unless the express consent of both the landlord and the tenant has been obtained;

 (f) less than 1 year before the date the development begins—

  (i) an agricultural tenancy over the site has been terminated, and

  (ii) the termination was for the purpose of carrying out development under this Class,

 unless both the landlord and the tenant have agreed in writing that the site is no longer required for agricultural purposes;

 (g) the building is within—

  (i) an area of outstanding natural beauty;

  (ii) an area specified by the Secretary of State for the purposes of section 41(3) of the Wildlife and Countryside Act 1981;

  (iii) the Broads; or

  (iv) a National Park;

  (v) a World Heritage Site;

 (h) the site is, or forms part of—

  (i) a site of special scientific interest;

  (ii) a safety hazard area;

  (iii) a military explosives storage area;

 (i) the building is a listed building or is within the curtilage of a listed building; or

 (j) the site is, or contains, a scheduled monument.

Conditions

P2

Development is permitted by Class P subject to the condition that before beginning the development, the developer must—

 (a) submit a statement, which must accompany the application referred to in paragraph (b), to the local planning authority setting out the evidence the developer relies upon to demonstrate that the building was used solely for a storage or distribution centre use on the date referred to in paragraph P1(a) and for the period referred to in paragraph P1(b);

Town and Country Planning (General Permitted Development) Order 2015

(b) apply to the local planning authority for a determination as to whether the prior approval of the authority will be required as to—

(i) impacts of air quality on the intended occupiers of the development;

(ii) transport and highways impacts of the development,

(iii) contamination risks in relation to the building,

(iv) flooding risks in relation to the building,

(v) noise impacts of the development, and

(vi) where the authority considers the building to which the development relates is located in an area that is important for providing storage or distribution services or industrial services or a mix of those services, whether the introduction of, or an increase in, a residential use of premises in the area would have an adverse impact on the sustainability of the provision of those services,

and the provisions of paragraph W (prior approval) of this Part apply in relation to that application.

Interpretation of Class P

P3

For the purposes of Class P—

'curtilage' (except in paragraph P1(i)) means—

(a) the piece of land, whether enclosed or unenclosed, immediately beside or around the building in storage or distribution centre use, closely associated with and serving the purposes of that building, or

(b) an area of land immediately beside or around the building in storage or distribution centre use no larger than the land area occupied by the building,

whichever is the lesser;

'general industrial use' means a use falling within Class B2 (general industrial) of the Schedule to the Use Classes Order;

'industrial services' means services provided from premises with a light industrial use or general industrial use;

'light industrial use' means a use falling within Class B1(c) (light industrial) of the Schedule to the Use Classes Order;

'storage or distribution centre use' means a use falling within Class B8 (storage or distribution) of the Schedule to the Use Classes Order; and

'storage or distribution services' means services provided from premises with a storage or distribution centre use.

Class Q—agricultural buildings to dwellinghouses

Permitted development

Q *Development consisting of—*

(a) a change of use of a building and any land within its curtilage from a use as an agricultural building to a use falling within Class C3 (dwellinghouses) of the Schedule to the Use Classes Order; and

Town and Country Planning (General Permitted Development) Order 2015

    (b) building operations reasonably necessary to convert the building referred to in paragraph (a) to a use falling within Class C3 (dwellinghouses) of that Schedule.

Development not permitted

Q.1

Development is not permitted by Class Q if—

    (a) the site was not used solely for an agricultural use as part of an established agricultural unit—

        (i) on 20th March 2013, or

        (ii) in the case of a building which was in use before that date but was not in use on that date, when it was last in use, or

        (iii) in the case of a site which was brought into use after 20th March 2013, for a period of at least 10 years before the date development under Class Q begins;

    (b) the cumulative floor space of the existing building or buildings changing use under Class Q within an established agricultural unit exceeds 450 square metres;

    (c) the cumulative number of separate dwellinghouses developed under Class Q within an established agricultural unit exceeds 3;

    (d) the site is occupied under an agricultural tenancy, unless the express consent of both the landlord and the tenant has been obtained;

    (e) less than 1 year before the date development begins—

        (i) an agricultural tenancy over the site has been terminated, and

        (ii) the termination was for the purpose of carrying out development under Class Q,

    unless both the landlord and the tenant have agreed in writing that the site is no longer required for agricultural use;

    (f) development under Class A(a) or Class B(a) of Part 6 of this Schedule (agricultural buildings and operations) has been carried out on the established agricultural unit—

        (i) since 20th March 2013; or

        (ii) where development under Class Q begins after 20th March 2023, during the period which is 10 years before the date development under Class Q begins;

    (g) the development would result in the external dimensions of the building extending beyond the external dimensions of the existing building at any given point;

    (h) the development under Class Q (together with any previous development under Class Q) would result in a building or buildings having more than 450 square metres of floor space having a use falling within Class C3 (dwellinghouses) of the Schedule to the Use Classes Order;

    (i) the development under Class Q(b) would consist of building operations other than—

        (i) the installation or replacement of—

(aa) windows, doors, roofs, or exterior walls, or

(bb) water, drainage, electricity, gas or other services,

to the extent reasonably necessary for the building to function as a dwellinghouse; and

(ii) partial demolition to the extent reasonably necessary to carry out building operations allowed by paragraph Q.1(i)(i);

(j) the site is on article 2(3) land;

(k) the site is, or forms part of—

(i) a site of special scientific interest;

(ii) a safety hazard area;

(iii) a military explosives storage area;

(l) the site is, or contains, a scheduled monument; or

(m) the building is a listed building.

Conditions

Q.2

(1) Where the development proposed is development under Class Q(a) together with development under Class Q(b), development is permitted subject to the condition that before beginning the development, the developer must apply to the local planning authority for a determination as to whether the prior approval of the authority will be required as to—

(a) transport and highways impacts of the development,

(b) noise impacts of the development,

(c) contamination risks on the site,

(d) flooding risks on the site,

(e) whether the location or siting of the building makes it otherwise impractical or undesirable for the building to change from agricultural use to a use falling within Class C3 (dwellinghouses) of the Schedule to the Use Classes Order, and

(f) the design or external appearance of the building,

and the provisions of paragraph W (prior approval) of this Part apply in relation to that application.

(2) Where the development proposed is development under Class Q(a) only, development is permitted subject to the condition that before beginning the development, the developer must apply to the local planning authority for a determination as to whether the prior approval of the authority will be required as to the items referred to in sub-paragraphs (1)(a) to (e) and the provisions of paragraph W (prior approval) of this Part apply in relation to that application.

(3) Development under Class Q is permitted subject to the condition that development under Class Q(a), and under Class Q(b), if any, must be completed within a period of 3 years starting with the prior approval date.

Class R—agricultural buildings to a flexible commercial use

Permitted development

R Development consisting of a change of use of a building and any land within its curtilage from a use as an agricultural building to a flexible use falling within Class A1 (shops), Class A2 (financial and professional services), Class A3 (restaurants and cafes), Class B1 (business), Class B8 (storage or distribution), Class C1 (hotels) or Class D2 (assembly and leisure) of the Schedule to the Use Classes Order.

Development not permitted

R.1

Development is not permitted by Class R if—
- (a) the building was not used solely for an agricultural use as part of an established agricultural unit—
    - (i) on 3rd July 2012;
    - (ii) in the case of a building which was in use before that date but was not in use on that date, when it was last in use, or
    - (iii) in the case of a building which was brought into use after 3rd July 2012, for a period of at least 10 years before the date development under Class R begins;
- (b) the cumulative floor space of buildings which have changed use under Class R within an established agricultural unit exceeds 500 square metres;
- (c) the site is, or forms part of, a military explosives storage area;
- (d) the site is, or forms part of, a safety hazard area; or
- (e) the building is a listed building or a scheduled monument.

Conditions

R.2

Development is permitted by Class R subject to the following conditions—
- (a) a site which has changed use under Class R may, subject to paragraph R.3, subsequently change use to another use falling within one of the use classes comprising the flexible use;
- (b) for the purposes of the Use Classes Order and this Order, after a site has changed use under Class R the site is to be treated as having a sui generis use;
- (c) after a site has changed use under Class R, the planning permissions granted by Class G of Part 7 of this Schedule apply to the building, subject to the following modifications—
    - (i) 'curtilage' has the meaning given in paragraph X (interpretation) of this Part;
    - (ii) any reference to 'office building' is to be read as a reference to the building which has changed use under Class R.

R.3

(1) Before changing the use of the site under Class R, and before any subsequent change of use to another use falling within one of the use classes comprising the flexible use, the developer must—

Town and Country Planning (General Permitted Development) Order 2015

    (a) where the cumulative floor space of the building or buildings which have changed use under Class R within an established agricultural unit does not exceed 150 square metres, provide the following information to the local planning authority—

        (i) the date the site will begin to be used for any of the flexible uses;

        (ii) the nature of the use or uses; and

        (iii) a plan indicating the site and which buildings have changed use;

    (b) where the cumulative floor space of the building or buildings which have changed use under Class R within an established agricultural unit exceeds 150 square metres, apply to the local planning authority for a determination as to whether the prior approval of the authority will be required as to—

        (i) transport and highways impacts of the development;

        (ii) noise impacts of the development;

        (iii) contamination risks on the site; and

        (iv) flooding risks on the site,

and the provisions of paragraph W (prior approval) apply in relation to that application.

(2) Subject to sub-paragraph (3), development under Class R of the type described in paragraph R.3(1)(b) must begin within a period of 3 years starting with the prior approval date.

(3) Where, in relation to a particular development under Class R of the type described in paragraph R.3(1)(b), planning permission is granted on an application in respect of associated operational development before the end of the period referred to in sub-paragraph (2), then development under Class R must begin within the period of 3 years starting with the date that planning permission is granted.

(4) For the purposes of sub-paragraph (3), 'associated operational development' means building or other operations in relation to the same building or land which are reasonably necessary to use the building or land for the use proposed under Class R.

Interpretation of Class R

R.4

For the purposes of Class R, 'flexible use' means use of any building or land for a use falling within the list of uses set out in Class R and change of use (in accordance with Class R) between any use in that list.

Class S—agricultural buildings to state-funded school or registered nursery

Permitted development

S   *Development consisting of a change of use of a building and any land within its curtilage from a use as an agricultural building to use as a state-funded school or a registered nursery.*

Town and Country Planning (General Permitted Development) Order 2015

Development not permitted

S.1

Development is not permitted by Class S if—

(a) the building was not used solely for an agricultural use as part of an established agricultural unit—
   (i) on 20th March 2013, or
   (ii) in the case of a building which was in use before that date but was not in use on that date, when it was last in use, or
   (iii) in the case of a building which was brought into use after 20th March 2013, for a period of at least 10 years before the date development under Class S begins;

(b) the cumulative area of—
   (i) floor space within the existing building or buildings, and
   (ii) land within the curtilage of that building or those buildings,
   changing use under Class S within an established agricultural unit exceeds 500 square metres;

(c) the site is occupied under an agricultural tenancy, unless the express consent of both the landlord and the tenant has been obtained;

(d) less than 1 year before the date development begins—
   (i) an agricultural tenancy over the site has been terminated, and
   (ii) the termination was for the purpose of carrying out development under Class S,
   unless both the landlord and the tenant have agreed in writing that the site is no longer required for agricultural use;

(e) development under Class A(a) or Class B(a) of Part 6 of this Schedule (agricultural buildings and operations) has been carried out on the established agricultural unit—
   (i) since 20th March 2013; or
   (ii) where development under Class Q begins after 20th March 2023, during the period which is 10 years before the date development under Class Q begins;

(f) the site is, or forms part of—
   (i) a site of special scientific interest;
   (ii) a safety hazard area; or
   (iii) a military explosives storage area;

(g) the site is, or contains, a scheduled monument; or

(h) the building is a listed building.

Conditions

S.2

(1) Development is permitted by Class S subject to the following conditions—

(a) the site is to be used as a state-funded school or, as the case may be, as a registered nursery and for no other purpose, including any other purpose falling within Class D1 (non-residential institutions) of the Schedule to the Use Classes Order, except to the extent that the other purpose is ancillary to the primary use of the site as a state-funded school or, as the case may be, as a registered nursery; and

(b) before changing the use of the site under Class S the developer must apply to the local planning authority for a determination as to whether the prior approval of the authority will be required as to—

(i) transport and highways impacts of the development,

(ii) noise impacts of the development,

(iii) contamination risks on the site,

(iv) flooding risks on the site, and

(v) whether the location or siting of the building makes it otherwise impractical or undesirable for the building to change to use as a state-funded school or, as the case may be, a registered nursery,

and the provisions of paragraph W (prior approval) of this Part apply in relation to that application.

(2) Subject to sub-paragraph (3), development under Class S must begin within a period of 3 years starting with the prior approval date.

(3) Where, in relation to a particular development under Class S, planning permission is granted on an application in respect of associated operational development before the end of the period referred to in sub-paragraph (2), then development under Class S must begin within the period of 3 years starting with the date that planning permission is granted.

(4) For the purposes of sub-paragraph (3), 'associated operational development' means building or other operations in relation to the same building or land which are reasonably necessary to use the building or land for the use proposed under Class S.

Class T—business, hotels etc to state-funded schools or registered nursery

Permitted development

T *Development consisting of a change of use of a building and any land within its curtilage from a use falling within Class B1 (business), Class C1 (hotels), Class C2 (residential institutions), Class C2A (secure residential institutions) or Class D2 (assembly and leisure) of the Schedule to the Use Classes Order, to use as a state-funded school or a registered nursery.*

Development not permitted

T.1

Development is not permitted by Class T if—

(a) permission to use the site for a use falling within Class D2 (assembly and leisure) of the Schedule to the Use Classes Order has been granted only by virtue of Class J of this Part;

(b) the site is, or forms part of, a military explosives storage area;

(c) the site is, or forms part of, a safety hazard area; or

(d) the building is a listed building or a scheduled monument.

Conditions

T.2

(1) Development is permitted by Class T subject to the following conditions—

   (a) the site is to be used as a state-funded school or, as the case may be, as a registered nursery and for no other purpose, including any other purpose falling within Class D1 (non-residential institutions) of the Schedule to the Use Classes Order, except to the extent that the other purpose is ancillary to the primary use of the site as a state-funded school or, as the case may be, as a registered nursery;

   (b) before beginning the development, the developer must apply to the local planning authority for a determination as to whether the prior approval of the local planning authority will be required as to—

   (i) transport and highways impacts of the development;

   (ii) noise impacts of the development; and

   (iii) contamination risks on the site,

   and the provisions of paragraph W (prior approval) of this Part apply in relation to that application.

(2) Subject to sub-paragraph (3), development under Class T must begin within a period of 3 years starting with the prior approval date.

(3) Where, in relation to a particular development under Class T, planning permission is granted on an application in respect of associated operational development before the end of the period referred to in sub-paragraph (2), then development under Class T must begin within the period of 3 years starting with the date that planning permission is granted.

(4) For the purposes of sub-paragraph (3), 'associated operational development' means building or other operations in relation to the same building or land which are reasonably necessary to use the building or land for the use proposed under Class T.

Class U—return to previous use from converted state-funded school or registered nursery

Permitted development

U   *Development consisting of a change of use of land from a use permitted by Class T to the previous lawful use of the land.*

Class V—changes of use permitted under a permission granted on an application

Permitted development

V   *Development consisting of a change of use of a building or other land from a use permitted by planning permission granted on an application, to another use which that permission would have specifically authorised when it was granted.*

Development not permitted

V.1

Development is not permitted by Class V if—

(a) the application for planning permission referred to was made before 5th December 1988;

(b) it would be carried out more than 10 years after the grant of planning permission;

(c) the development would consist of a change of use of a building to use as betting office or pay day loan shop; or

(d) it would result in the breach of any condition, limitation or specification contained in that planning permission in relation to the use in question.

Procedure for applications for prior approval under Part 3

W

(1) The following provisions apply where under this Part a developer is required to make an application to a local planning authority for a determination as to whether the prior approval of the authority will be required.

(2) The application must be accompanied by—

(a) a written description of the proposed development, which, in relation to development proposed under Class C, M, N or Q of this Part, must include any building or other operations;

(b) a plan indicating the site and showing the proposed development;

(c) the developer's contact address;

(d) the developer's email address if the developer is content to receive communications electronically; and

(e) where sub-paragraph (6) requires the Environment Agency to be consulted, a site-specific flood risk assessment,

together with any fee required to be paid.

(3) The local planning authority may refuse an application where, in the opinion of the authority—

(a) the proposed development does not comply with, or

(b) the developer has provided insufficient information to enable the authority to establish whether the proposed development complies with,

any conditions, limitations or restrictions specified in this Part as being applicable to the development in question.

(4) Sub-paragraphs (5) to (8) and (10) do not apply where a local planning authority refuses an application under sub-paragraph (3) and for the purposes of section 78 (appeals) of the Act such a refusal is to be treated as a refusal of an application for approval.

(5) Where the application relates to prior approval as to transport and highways impacts of the development, on receipt of the application, where in the opinion of the local planning authority the development is likely to result in a material increase or a material change in the character of traffic in the vicinity of the site, the local planning authority must consult—

(a) where the increase or change relates to traffic entering or leaving a trunk road, the highway authority for the trunk road;

(b) the local highway authority, where the increase or change relates to traffic entering or leaving a classified road or proposed highway, except where the local planning authority is the local highway authority; and

(c) the operator of the network which includes or consists of the railway in question, and the Secretary of State for Transport, where the increase or change relates to traffic using a level crossing over a railway.

(6) Where the application relates to prior approval as to the flooding risks on the site, on receipt of the application, the local planning authority must consult the Environment Agency where the development is—

(a) in an area within Flood Zone 2 or Flood Zone 3; or

(b) in an area within Flood Zone 1 which has critical drainage problems and which has been notified to the local planning authority by the Environment Agency for the purpose of paragraph (zc)(ii) in the Table in Schedule 4 to the Procedure Order.

(7) The local planning authority must notify the consultees referred to in sub-paragraphs (5) and (6) specifying the date by which they must respond (being not less than 21 days from the date the notice is given).

(8) The local planning authority must give notice of the proposed development—

(a) by site display in at least one place on or near the land to which the application relates for not less than 21 days of a notice which—

   (i) describes the proposed development;

   (ii) provides the address of the proposed development;

   (iii) specifies the date by which representations are to be received by the local planning authority; or

(b) by serving a notice in that form on any adjoining owner or occupier.

(9) The local planning authority may require the developer to submit such information as the authority may reasonably require in order to determine the application, which may include—

(a) assessments of impacts or risks;

(b) statements setting out how impacts or risks are to be mitigated; or

(c) details of proposed building or other operations.

(10) The local planning authority must, when determining an application—

(a) take into account any representations made to them as a result of any consultation under sub-paragraphs (5) or (6) and any notice given under sub-paragraph (8);

(b) have regard to the National Planning Policy Framework issued by the Department for Communities and Local Government in March 2012, so far as relevant to the subject matter of the prior approval, as if the application were a planning application; and

(c) in relation to the contamination risks on the site—

   (i) determine whether, as a result of the proposed change of use, taking into account any proposed mitigation, the site will be contaminated land as described in Part 2A of the Environmental Protection Act 1990, and in doing so have regard to the Contaminated Land Statutory Guidance issued by the Secretary of State for the Environment, Food and Rural Affairs in April 2012, and

(ii) if they determine that the site will be contaminated land, refuse to give prior approval.

(11) The development must not begin before the occurrence of one of the following—
   (a) the receipt by the applicant from the local planning authority of a written notice of their determination that such prior approval is not required;
   (b) the receipt by the applicant from the local planning authority of a written notice giving their prior approval; or
   (c) the expiry of 56 days following the date on which the application under sub-paragraph (2) was received by the local planning authority without the authority notifying the applicant as to whether prior approval is given or refused.

(12) The development must be carried out—
   (a) where prior approval is required, in accordance with the details approved by the local planning authority;
   (b) where prior approval is not required, or where sub-paragraph (11)(c) applies, in accordance with the details provided in the application referred to in sub-paragraph (1),

   unless the local planning authority and the developer agree otherwise in writing.

(13) The local planning authority may grant prior approval unconditionally or subject to conditions reasonably related to the subject matter of the prior approval.

Interpretation of Part 3

X

For the purposes of Part 3—

'agricultural building' means a building (excluding a dwellinghouse) used for agriculture and which is so used for the purposes of a trade or business; and 'agricultural use' refers to such uses;

'agricultural tenancy' means a tenancy under—
   (a) the Agricultural Holdings Act 1986; or
   (b) the Agricultural Tenancies Act 1995;

'curtilage' means, for the purposes of Class Q, R or S only—
   (a) the piece of land, whether enclosed or unenclosed, immediately beside or around the agricultural building, closely associated with and serving the purposes of the agricultural building, or
   (b) an area of land immediately beside or around the agricultural building no larger than the land area occupied by the agricultural building,
   whichever is the lesser;

'established agricultural unit' means agricultural land occupied as a unit for the purposes of agriculture—
   (a) for the purposes of Class R, on or before 3rd July 2012 or for 10 years before the date the development begins; or
   (b) for the purposes of Class Q or S, on or before 20th March 2013 or for 10 years before the date the development begins;

'pay day loan shop' has the meaning given in the Use Classes Order;

'prior approval date' means the date on which—
  (a) prior approval is given; or
  (b) a determination that such approval is not required is given or the period for giving such a determination set out in paragraph W(11)(c) of this Part has expired without the applicant being notified whether prior approval is required, given or refused;

'registered nursery' means non-domestic premises in respect of which a person is registered under Part 3 of the Childcare Act 2006 to provide early years provision;

'site' means the building and any land within its curtilage;

'state-funded school' means a school funded wholly or mainly from public funds, including—
  (a) an Academy school, an alternative provision Academy or a 16 to 19 Academy established under the Academies Act 2010;
  (b) a school maintained by a local authority, as defined in section 142(1) of the School Standards and Framework Act 1998; and

'sui generis use' means a use for which no class is specified in the Schedule to the Use Classes Order.

PART 4 TEMPORARY BUILDINGS AND USES

Class A—temporary buildings and structures

Permitted development

A *The provision on land of buildings, moveable structures, works, plant or machinery required temporarily in connection with and for the duration of operations being or to be carried out on, in, under or over that land or on land adjoining that land.*

Development not permitted

A.1

Development is not permitted by Class A if—
  (a) the operations referred to are mining operations, or
  (b) planning permission is required for those operations but is not granted or deemed to be granted.

Conditions

A.2

Development is permitted by Class A subject to the conditions that, when the operations have been carried out—
  (a) any building, structure, works, plant or machinery permitted by Class A is removed, and
  (b) any adjoining land on which development permitted by Class A has been carried out is, as soon as reasonably practicable, reinstated to its condition before that development was carried out.

Town and Country Planning (General Permitted Development) Order 2015

Class B—temporary use of land

Permitted development

B   The use of any land for any purpose for not more than 28 days in total in any calendar year, of which not more than 14 days in total may be for the purposes of—

    (a) the holding of a market;

    (b) motor car and motorcycle racing including trials of speed, and practising for these activities,

and the provision on the land of any moveable structure for the purposes of the permitted use.

Development not permitted

B.1

Development is not permitted by Class B if—

    (a) it would consist of development of a kind described in Class E of this Part (temporary use of land for film-making);

    (b) the land in question is a building or is within the curtilage of a building;

    (c) the use of the land is for a caravan site;

    (d) the land is, or is within, a site of special scientific interest and the use of the land is for—

        (i) motor car and motorcycle racing including trials of speed or other motor sports, and practising for these activities;

        (ii) clay pigeon shooting; or

        (iii) any war game, or

    (e) the use of the land is for the display of an advertisement.

Class C—use as a state-funded school for a single academic year

Permitted development

C   *The use of a building and any land within its curtilage as a state-funded school for a single academic year.*

Development not permitted

C 1

Development is not permitted by Class C if—

    (a) the existing use of the site is not a class of use specified in the Schedule to the Use Classes Order;

    (b) the site is, or forms part of, a military explosives storage area;

    (c) the site is, or forms part of, a safety hazard area;

    (d) the building is a listed building or a scheduled monument; or

    (e) the building is a specified building and the development is undertaken during the specified period, regardless of whether any approval or notification has been given in accordance with paragraphs C 2(a) or (b).

Town and Country Planning (General Permitted Development) Order 2015

Conditions

C 2

Development is permitted by Class C subject to the following conditions—

(a) the site must be approved for use as a state-funded school by the relevant Minister;

(b) the relevant Minister must notify the local planning authority of the approval and of the proposed opening date of the school;

(c) the site is to be used as a state-funded school and for no other purpose, including any other purpose falling within Class D1 (non-residential institutions) of the Schedule to the Use Classes Order, except to the extent that the other purpose is ancillary to the primary use of the site as a state-funded school;

(d) the permission is granted for one academic year and it may be used only once in relation to a particular site;

(e) the site reverts to its previous lawful use at the end of the academic year; and

(f) in the case of a building which is not a community asset, which is used for a purpose falling within Class A4 (drinking establishments) of the Schedule to the Use Classes Order—

(i) before beginning the development the developer must send a written request to the local planning authority as to whether the building has been nominated, which must include;

(aa) the address of the building;

(bb) the developer's contact address; and

(cc) the developer's email address if the developer is content to receive communications electronically;

(ii) if the building is nominated, whether at the date of request under paragraph (f)(i) or on a later date, the local planning authority must notify the developer as soon as is reasonably practicable after it is aware of the nomination, and on notification development is not permitted for the specified period;

(iii) the development must not begin before the expiry of a period of 56 days following the date of request under paragraph (f)(i) and must be completed within a period of 1 year of the date of that request.

Interpretation of Class C

C 3

For the purposes of Class C—

'academic year' means any period beginning with 1st August and ending with the next 31st July;

'community asset' means a building which has been entered onto a list of assets of community value, including any building which has been subsequently excluded from that list under regulation 2(b) of the Assets of Community Value (England) Regulations 2012;

Town and Country Planning (General Permitted Development) Order 2015

'list of assets of community value' means a list of land of community value maintained by a local authority under section 87(1) of the Localism Act 2011;

'nomination' means a nomination made under section 89(2) of the Localism Act 2011 for a building to be included in a list of assets of community value and 'nominated' is to be interpreted accordingly;

'relevant Minister' means the Secretary of State with policy responsibility for schools;

'state-funded school' means a school funded wholly or mainly from public funds, including—

(a) an Academy school, an alternative provision Academy or a 16 to 19 Academy established under the Academies Act 2010;

(b) a school maintained by a local authority, as defined in section 142(1) of the School Standards and Framework Act 1998;

'specified building' means a building used for a purpose falling within Class A4 (drinking establishments) of the Schedule to the Use Classes Order—

(a) which is a community asset; or

(b) in relation to which the local planning authority has notified the developer of a nomination under paragraph C 2(f)(ii); and

'specified period' means—

(a) in relation to a building which is subject to a nomination of which the local planning authority have notified the developer under paragraph C 2(f)(ii), the period from the date of that notification to the date on which the building is entered onto—

(i) a list of assets of community value; or

(ii) a list of land nominated by unsuccessful community nominations under section 93 of the Localism Act 2011;

(b) in relation to a building which is a community asset—

(i) 5 years beginning with the date on which the building was entered onto the list of assets of community value; or

(ii) where the building was removed from that list—

(aa) under regulation 2(c) of the Assets of Community Value (England) Regulations 2012 following a successful appeal against listing or because the local authority no longer consider the land to be land of community value; or

(bb) under section 92(4)(a) of the Localism Act 2011 following the local authority's decision on a review that the land concerned should not have been included in the local authority's list of assets of community value,

the period from the date on which the building was entered onto the list of assets of community value to the date on which it was removed from that list.

Class D—shops, financial, cafes, takeaways, pubs etc to temporary flexible use

Permitted development

D *Development consisting of a change of use of a building and any land within its curtilage—*

Town and Country Planning (General Permitted Development) Order 2015

(a) from—
  (i) a use falling within Class A1 (shops), Class A2 (financial and professional services), Class A3 (restaurants and cafes), Class A4 (drinking establishments), Class A5 (hot food takeaways), Class B1 (business), Class D1 (non-residential institutions) and Class D2 (assembly and leisure) of the Schedule to the Use Classes Order, or
  (ii) a use as a betting office or pay day loan shop,
(b) to a flexible use falling within Class A1 (shops), Class A2 (financial and professional services), Class A3 (restaurants and cafes) or Class B1 (business) of that Schedule,

for a single continuous period of up to 2 years beginning on the date the building and any land within its curtilage begins to be used for the flexible use or on the date given in the notice under paragraph D.2(a), whichever is the earlier.

Development not permitted

D.1

Development is not permitted by Class D if—
  (a) the change of use relates to more than 150 square metres of floor space in the building;
  (b) the site has at any time in the past relied upon the permission granted by Class D;
  (c) the site is, or forms part of, a military explosives storage area;
  (d) the site is, or forms part of, a safety hazard area;
  (e) the building is a listed building or a scheduled monument; or
  (f) the building is a specified building and the development is undertaken during the specified period, regardless of whether any notification has been given in accordance with paragraph D.2(a).

Conditions

D.2

Development is permitted by Class D subject to the following conditions—
  (a) the developer must notify the local planning authority of the date the site will begin to be used for one of the flexible uses, and what that use will be, before the use begins;
  (b) at any given time during the 2 year period referred to in Class D the site is used for a purpose or purposes falling within just one of the use classes comprising the flexible use;
  (c) the site may at any time during the 2 year period change use to a use falling within one of the other use classes comprising the flexible use, subject to further notification as provided in paragraph (a);
  (d) for the purposes of the Use Classes Order and this Order, during the period of flexible use the site retains the use class it had before changing to any of the flexible uses under Class D;
  (e) the site reverts to its previous lawful use at the end of the period of flexible use;

Town and Country Planning (General Permitted Development) Order 2015

(f) in the case of a building which is not a community asset, which is used for a purpose falling within Class A4 (drinking establishments) of the Schedule to the Use Classes Order, the conditions set out in paragraphs C 2(f)(i) to (iii) apply.

Interpretation of Class D

D.3

For the purposes of Class D—

'community asset', 'specified building' and 'specified period' have the meaning given in paragraph C 3; and

'flexible use' means use of any building or land for a use falling within the list of uses set out in Class D(b) and change of use (in accordance with Class D) between any use in that list.

Class E—temporary use of buildings or land for film-making purposes

Permitted development

E   Development consisting of—

(a) the temporary use of any land or buildings for a period not exceeding 9 months in any 27 month period for the purpose of commercial film-making; and

(b) the provision on such land, during the filming period, of any temporary structures, works, plant or machinery required in connection with that use.

Development not permitted

E.1

Development is not permitted by Class E if—

(a) the land in question, or the land on which the building in question is situated, is more than 1.5 hectares;

(b) the use of the land is for overnight accommodation;

(c) the height of any temporary structure, works, plant or machinery provided under Class E(b) exceeds 15 metres, or 5 metres where any part of the structure, works, plant or machinery is within 10 metres of the curtilage of the land;

(d) the land or building is on article 2(3) land;

(e) the land or the site on which the building is located is or forms part of—

(i) a site of special scientific interest;

(ii) a safety hazard area; or

(iii) a military explosives storage area;

(f) the land or building is, or contains, a scheduled monument; or

(g) the land or building is a listed building or is within the curtilage of a listed building.

Conditions

E.2

(1) Class E development is permitted subject to the condition that—

(a) any structure, works, plant or machinery provided under the permission must, as soon as practicable after the end of each filming period, be removed from the land; and

(b) the land on which any development permitted by Class E has been carried out must, as soon as reasonably practicable after the end of the filming period, be reinstated to its condition before that development was carried out.

(2) Class E development is permitted subject to the condition that before the start of each new filming period the developer must apply to the local planning authority for a determination as to whether the prior approval of the authority will be required as to—

(a) the schedule of dates which make up the filming period in question and the hours of operation,

(b) transport and highways impacts of the development,

(c) noise impacts of the development,

(d) light impacts of the development, in particular the effect on any occupier of neighbouring land of any artificial lighting to be used, and

(e) flooding risks on the site,

and the provisions of paragraph E.3 apply in relation to that application.

Procedure for applications for prior approval under Class E

E.3

(1) The following provisions apply where under Class E a developer is required to make an application to a local planning authority for a determination as to whether the prior approval of the authority will be required.

(2) The application must be accompanied by—

(a) a written description of the proposed development;

(b) a plan indicating the site and showing the proposed development;

(c) the developer's contact address;

(d) the developer's email address if the developer is content to receive communications electronically; and

(e) a site-specific flood risk assessment,

together with any fee required to be paid.

(3) The local planning authority may refuse an application where, in the opinion of the authority—

(a) the proposed development does not comply with, or

(b) the developer has provided insufficient information to enable the authority to establish whether the proposed development complies with,

any conditions, limitations or restrictions specified in Class E as being applicable to the development in question.

(4) Sub-paragraphs (5) to (8) and (10) do not apply where a local planning authority refuses an application under sub-paragraph (3) and for the purposes of section 78 (appeals) of the Act such a refusal is to be treated as a refusal of an application for approval.

Town and Country Planning (General Permitted Development) Order 2015

(5) On receipt of the application, where in the opinion of the local planning authority the development is likely to result in a material increase or a material change in the character of traffic in the vicinity of the site, the local planning authority must consult—

(a) where the increase or change relates to traffic entering or leaving a trunk road, the highway authority for the trunk road;

(b) the local highway authority, where the increase or change relates to traffic entering or leaving a classified road or proposed highway, except where the local planning authority is the local highway authority; and

(c) the operator of the network which includes or consists of the railway in question, and the Secretary of State for Transport, where the increase or change relates to traffic using a level crossing over a railway.

(6) On receipt of the application, the local planning authority must consult the Environment Agency where the development is—

(a) in an area within Flood Zone 2 or Flood Zone 3; or

(b) in an area within Flood Zone 1 which has critical drainage problems and which has been notified to the local planning authority by the Environment Agency for the purpose of paragraph (zc)(ii) in the Table in Schedule 4 to the Procedure Order.

(7) The local planning authority must notify the consultees referred to in sub-paragraphs (5) and (6) specifying the date by which they must respond (being not less than 21 days from the date the notice is given).

(8) The local planning authority must give notice of the proposed development—

(a) by site display in at least one place on or near the land to which the application relates for not less than 21 days of a notice which—

(i) describes the proposed development;

(ii) provides the address of the proposed development;

(iii) specifies the date by which representations are to be received by the local planning authority; or

(b) by serving a notice in that form on any adjoining owner or occupier.

(9) The local planning authority may require the developer to submit such information as the authority may reasonably require in order to determine the application, which may include—

(a) assessments of impacts or risks; or

(b) statements setting out how impacts or risks are to be mitigated.

(10) The local planning authority must, when determining an application—

(a) take into account any representations made to them as a result of any consultation under sub-paragraphs (5) or (6) and any notice given under sub-paragraph (8); and

(b) have regard to the National Planning Policy Framework issued by the Department for Communities and Local Government in March 2012, so far as relevant to the subject matter of the prior approval, as if the application were a planning application.

(11) The development must not begin before the occurrence of one of the following—

(a) the receipt by the applicant from the local planning authority of a written notice of their determination that such prior approval is not required;

(b) the receipt by the applicant from the local planning authority of a written notice giving their prior approval; or

(c) the expiry of 56 days following the date on which the application under sub-paragraph (2) was received by the local planning authority without the authority notifying the applicant as to whether prior approval is given or refused.

(12) The development must be carried out—

(a) where prior approval is required, in accordance with the details approved by the local planning authority;

(b) where prior approval is not required, or where sub-paragraph (11)(c) applies, in accordance with the details provided in the application referred to in sub-paragraph (2),

unless the local planning authority and the developer agree otherwise in writing.

(13) The local planning authority may grant prior approval unconditionally or subject to conditions reasonably related to the subject matter of the prior approval.

Interpretation of Class E

E.4

For the purposes of Class E—

'broadcast or transmission' means—

(a) broadcast of the film or television programme by—

(i) a television programme provider, or

(ii) any other person for commercial gain,

(b) transmission of it, including over the internet, by—

(i) a television programme provider, or

(ii) any other person for commercial gain, or

(c) theatrical release of it at the commercial cinema;

'commercial film-making' means filming for broadcast or transmission but does not include the filming of persons paying to visit the site to participate in any leisure activity on that site including—

(a) motor car and motorcycle racing including trials of speed or other motor sports, and practising for those activities, or

(b) clay pigeon shooting or any war game;

'filming period' means a period, not exceeding 9 months in total, during which the land or building is used for commercial film-making (including activities preparatory to, or otherwise related to, that film-making) under Class E; and

'television programme provider' has the meaning given in section 99(2) of the Broadcasting Act 1996.

Interpretation of Part 4

F

For the purposes of Part 4—

Town and Country Planning (General Permitted Development) Order 2015

'site' means the building and any land within its curtilage; and

'war game' means an enacted, mock or imaginary battle conducted with weapons which are designed not to injure (including smoke bombs, or guns or grenades which fire or spray paint or are otherwise used to mark other participants), but excludes military activities or training exercises organised by or with the authority of the Secretary of State for Defence.

PART 5 CARAVAN SITES AND RECREATIONAL CAMPSITES

Class A—use of land as caravan site

Permitted development

A   *The use of land, other than a building, as a caravan site in the circumstances referred to in paragraph A.2.*

Condition

A.1

Development is permitted by Class A subject to the condition that the use is discontinued when the circumstances specified in paragraph A.2 cease to exist, and all caravans on the site are removed as soon as reasonably practicable.

Interpretation of Class A

A.2

The circumstances mentioned in Class A are those specified in paragraphs 2 to 10 of Schedule 1 to the 1960 Act (cases where a caravan site licence is not required), but in relation to those mentioned in paragraph 10 do not include use for winter quarters.

Class B—development on caravan site required by conditions

Permitted development

B   *Development required by the conditions of a site licence for the time being in force under the 1960 Act.*

Class C—use of land by members of certain recreational organisations

Permitted development

C   *The use of land by members of a recreational organisation for the purposes of recreation or instruction, and the erection or placing of tents on the land for the purposes of the use.*

Development not permitted

C 1

Development is not permitted by Class C if the land is a building or is within the curtilage of a dwellinghouse.

Town and Country Planning (General Permitted Development) Order 2015

Interpretation of Class C

C 2

For the purposes of Class C, 'recreational organisation' means an organisation holding a certificate of exemption under section 269 of the Public Health Act 1936 (power of local authority to control use of moveable dwellings).

PART 6 AGRICULTURAL AND FORESTRY

Class A—agricultural development on units of 5 hectares or more

Permitted development

A   The carrying out on agricultural land comprised in an agricultural unit of 5 hectares or more in area of—
- (a) *works for the erection, extension or alteration of a building; or*
- (b) *any excavation or engineering operations,*

which are reasonably necessary for the purposes of agriculture within that unit.

Development not permitted

A.1

Development is not permitted by Class A if—
- (a) the development would be carried out on a separate parcel of land forming part of the unit which is less than 1 hectare in area;
- (b) it would consist of the erection or extension of any agricultural building on an established agricultural unit (as defined in paragraph X of Part 3 of this Schedule) where development under Class Q or S of Part 3 (changes of use) of this Schedule has been carried out within a period of 10 years ending with the date on which development under Class A(a) begins;
- (c) it would consist of, or include, the erection, extension or alteration of a dwelling;
- (d) it would involve the provision of a building, structure or works not designed for agricultural purposes;
- (e) the ground area which would be covered by—
    - (i) any works or structure (other than a fence) for accommodating livestock or any plant or machinery arising from engineering operations; or
    - (ii) any building erected or extended or altered by virtue of Class A,

    would exceed 465 square metres, calculated as described in paragraph D.1(2)(a) of this Part;
- (f) the height of any part of any building, structure or works within 3 kilometres of the perimeter of an aerodrome would exceed 3 metres;
- (g) the height of any part of any building, structure or works not within 3 kilometres of the perimeter of an aerodrome would exceed 12 metres;
- (h) any part of the development would be within 25 metres of a metalled part of a trunk road or classified road;

Town and Country Planning (General Permitted Development) Order 2015

    (i) it would consist of, or include, the erection or construction of, or the carrying out of any works to, a building, structure or an excavation used or to be used for the accommodation of livestock or for the storage of slurry or sewage sludge where the building, structure or excavation is, or would be, within 400 metres of the curtilage of a protected building;

    (j) it would involve excavations or engineering operations on or over article 2(4) land which are connected with fish farming; or

    (k) any building for storing fuel for or waste from a biomass boiler or an anaerobic digestion system—

        (i) would be used for storing waste not produced by that boiler or system or for storing fuel not produced on land within the unit; or

        (ii) is or would be within 400 metres of the curtilage of a protected building.

Conditions

A.2

(1) Development is permitted by Class A subject to the following conditions—

    (a) where development is carried out within 400 metres of the curtilage of a protected building, any building, structure, excavation or works resulting from the development are not used for the accommodation of livestock except in the circumstances described in paragraph D.1(3) of this Part or for the storage of slurry or sewage sludge, for housing a biomass boiler or an anaerobic digestion system, for storage of fuel or waste from that boiler or system, or for housing a hydro-turbine;

    (b) where the development involves—

        (i) the extraction of any mineral from the land (including removal from any disused railway embankment); or

        (ii) the removal of any mineral from a mineral-working deposit,

    the mineral is not moved off the unit;

    (c) waste materials are not brought on to the land from elsewhere for deposit except for use in works described in Class A(a) or in the provision of a hard surface and any materials so brought are incorporated forthwith into the building or works in question.

(2) Subject to sub-paragraph (3), development consisting of—

    (a) the erection, extension or alteration of a building;

    (b) the formation or alteration of a private way;

    (c) the carrying out of excavations or the deposit of waste material (where the relevant area, as defined in paragraph D.1(4) of this Part, exceeds 0.5 hectares); or

    (d) the placing or assembly of a tank in any waters,

    is permitted by Class A subject to the following conditions—

        (i) the developer must, before beginning the development, apply to the local planning authority for a determination as to whether the prior approval of the authority will be required as to the siting, design and external appearance of the building, the siting and means of construction of the private way, the siting of the excavation or deposit or the siting and appearance of the tank, as the case may be;

(ii) the application must be accompanied by a written description of the proposed development and of the materials to be used and a plan indicating the site together with any fee required to be paid;

(iii) the development must not begin before the occurrence of one of the following—

(aa) the receipt by the applicant from the local planning authority of a written notice of their determination that such prior approval is not required;

(bb) where the local planning authority give the applicant notice within 28 days following the date of receiving the applicant's application of their determination that such prior approval is required, the giving of such approval; or

(cc) the expiry of 28 days following the date on which the application under sub-paragraph (2)(ii) was received by the local planning authority without the local planning authority making any determination as to whether such approval is required or notifying the applicant of their determination;

(aa) the receipt by the applicant from the local planning authority of a written notice of their determination that such prior approval is not required;

(bb) where the local planning authority give the applicant notice within 28 days following the date of receiving the applicant's application of their determination that such prior approval is required, the giving of such approval; or

(cc) the expiry of 28 days following the date on which the application under sub-paragraph (2)(ii) was received by the local planning authority without the local planning authority making any determination as to whether such approval is required or notifying the applicant of their determination;

(iv) where the local planning authority give the applicant notice that such prior approval is required, the applicant must—

(aa) display a site notice by site display on or near the land on which the proposed development is to be carried out, leaving the notice in position for not less than 21 days in the period of 28 days from the date on which the local planning authority gave the notice to the applicant; and

(bb) where the site notice is, without any fault or intention of the applicant, removed, obscured or defaced before the period of 21 days referred to in sub-paragraph (iv)(aa) has elapsed, the applicant is treated as having complied with the requirements of that sub-paragraph if the applicant has taken reasonable steps for protection of the notice and, if need be, its replacement;

(aa) display a site notice by site display on or near the land on which the proposed development is to be carried out, leaving the notice in position for not less than 21 days in the period of 28 days from the date on which the local planning authority gave the notice to the applicant; and

(bb) where the site notice is, without any fault or intention of the applicant, removed, obscured or defaced before the period of

Town and Country Planning (General Permitted Development) Order 2015

        21 days referred to in sub-paragraph (iv)(aa) has elapsed, the applicant is treated as having complied with the requirements of that sub-paragraph if the applicant has taken reasonable steps for protection of the notice and, if need be, its replacement;

    (v) the development must, except to the extent that the local planning authority otherwise agree in writing, be carried out—

        (aa) where prior approval is required, in accordance with the details approved;

        (bb) where prior approval is not required, in accordance with the details submitted with the application; and

        (aa) where prior approval is required, in accordance with the details approved;

        (bb) where prior approval is not required, in accordance with the details submitted with the application; and

    (vi) the development must be carried out—

        (aa) where approval has been given by the local planning authority, within a period of 5 years from the date on which approval was given;

        (bb) in any other case, within a period of 5 years from the date on which the local planning authority were given the information referred to in paragraph (d)(ii).

        (aa) where approval has been given by the local planning authority, within a period of 5 years from the date on which approval was given;

        (bb) in any other case, within a period of 5 years from the date on which the local planning authority were given the information referred to in paragraph (d)(ii).

(3) The conditions in sub-paragraph (2) do not apply to the extension or alteration of a building if the building is not on article 2(4) land except in the case of a significant extension or a significant alteration.

(4) Development consisting of the significant extension or the significant alteration of a building may only be carried out once by virtue of Class A(a).

(5) Where development consists of works for the erection, significant extension or significant alteration of a building and—

    (a) the use of the building or extension for the purposes of agriculture within the unit permanently ceases within 10 years from the date on which the development was substantially completed; and

    (b) planning permission has not been granted on an application, or has not been deemed to be granted under Part 3 of the Act, for development for purposes other than agriculture, within 3 years from the date on which the use of the building or extension for the purposes of agriculture within the unit permanently ceased,

then, unless the local planning authority have otherwise agreed in writing, the building or, in the case of development consisting of an extension, the extension, must be removed from the land and the land must, so far as is practicable, be restored to its condition before the development took place, or to such condition as may have been agreed in writing between the local planning authority and the developer.

(6) Where an appeal has been made, under the Act, in relation to an application for development described in sub-paragraph (5)(b), within the period described in that paragraph, that period is extended until the appeal is finally determined or withdrawn.

(7) Where development is permitted by Class A(a), within 7 days of the date on which the development is substantially completed, the developer must notify the local planning authority in writing of that fact.

Class B—agricultural development on units of less than 5 hectares

Permitted development

B *The carrying out on agricultural land comprised in an agricultural unit, of not less than 0.4 but less than 5 hectares in area, of development consisting of—*
- *(a) the extension or alteration of an agricultural building;*
- *(b) the installation of additional or replacement plant or machinery;*
- *(c) the provision, rearrangement or replacement of a sewer, main, pipe, cable or other apparatus;*
- *(d) the provision, rearrangement or replacement of a private way;*
- *(e) the provision of a hard surface;*
- *(f) the deposit of waste; or*
- *(g) the carrying out of any of the following operations in connection with fish farming, namely, repairing ponds and raceways; the installation of grading machinery, aeration equipment or flow meters and any associated channel; the dredging of ponds; and the replacement of tanks and nets,*

where the development is reasonably necessary for the purposes of agriculture within the unit.

Development not permitted

B.1

Development is not permitted by Class B if—
- (a) the development would be carried out on a separate parcel of land forming part of the unit which is less than 0.4 hectares in area;
- (b) the external appearance of the premises would be materially affected;
- (c) any part of the development would be within 25 metres of a metalled part of a trunk road or classified road;
- (d) it would consist of, or involve, the carrying out of any works to a building or structure used or to be used for the accommodation of livestock or the storage of slurry or sewage sludge where the building or structure is within 400 metres of the curtilage of a protected building;
- (e) it would relate to fish farming and would involve the placing or assembly of a tank on land or in any waters or the construction of a pond in which fish may be kept or an increase (otherwise than by the removal of silt) in the size of any tank or pond in which fish may be kept; or
- (f) any building for storing fuel for or waste from a biomass boiler or an anaerobic digestion system would be used for storing waste not produced

by that boiler or system or for storing fuel not produced on land within the unit.

B.2

Development is not permitted by Class B(a) if—

(a) the height of any building would be increased;

(b) the cubic content of the original building would be increased by more than 10%;

(c) any part of any new building would be more than 30 metres from the original building;

(d) it would consist of the extension or provision of any agricultural building on an established agricultural unit (as defined in paragraph X of Part 3 (changes of use) of this Schedule) where development under Class Q or S of Part 3 (changes of use) of this Schedule has been carried out within a period of 10 years ending with the date on which development under Class B(a) begins;

(e) the development would involve the extension, alteration or provision of a dwelling;

(f) any part of the development would be carried out within 5 metres of any boundary of the unit; or

(g) the ground area of any building extended by virtue of Class B(a) would exceed 465 square metres.

B.3

Development is not permitted by Class B(b) if—

(a) the height of any additional plant or machinery within 3 kilometres of the perimeter of an aerodrome would exceed 3 metres;

(b) the height of any additional plant or machinery not within 3 kilometres of the perimeter of an aerodrome would exceed 12 metres;

(c) the height of any replacement plant or machinery would exceed that of the plant or machinery being replaced; or

(d) the area to be covered by the development would exceed 465 square metres calculated as described in paragraph D.1(2)(a) of this Part.

B.4

Development is not permitted by Class B(e) if the area to be covered by the development would exceed 465 square metres calculated as described in paragraph D.1(2)(a) of this Part.

Conditions

B.5

(1) Development permitted by Class B and carried out within 400 metres of the curtilage of a protected building is subject to the condition that any building which is extended or altered, or any works resulting from the development, is not used for the accommodation of livestock except in the circumstances described in paragraph D.1(3) of this Part or for the storage of slurry or sewage sludge, for housing a biomass boiler or an anaerobic digestion system, for storage of fuel or waste from that boiler or system, or for housing a hydro-turbine.

(2) Development consisting of the extension or alteration of a building situated on article 2(4) land or the provision, rearrangement or replacement of a private way on such land is permitted subject to—
   (a) the condition that the developer must, before beginning the development, apply to the local planning authority for a determination as to whether the prior approval of the authority will be required as to the siting, design and external appearance of the building as extended or altered or the siting and means of construction of the private way; and
   (b) the conditions set out in paragraphs A.2(2)(ii) to (vi) of this Part.

(3) Development is permitted by Class B(f) subject to the following conditions—
   (a) that waste materials are not brought on to the land from elsewhere for deposit unless they are for use in works described in Class B(a), (d) or (e) and are incorporated forthwith into the building or works in question; and
   (b) that the height of the surface of the land will not be materially increased by the deposit.

(4) Development is permitted by Class B(a) subject to the following conditions—
   (a) where development consists of works for the significant extension or significant alteration of a building and—
      (i) the use of the building or extension for the purposes of agriculture within the unit permanently ceases within 10 years from the date on which the development was substantially completed; and
      (ii) planning permission has not been granted on an application, or has not been deemed to be granted under Part 3 of the Act, for development for purposes other than agriculture, within 3 years from the date on which the use of the building or extension for the purposes of agriculture within the unit permanently ceased,

then, unless the local planning authority have otherwise agreed in writing, the extension, in the case of development consisting of an extension, must be removed from the land and the land must, so far as is practicable, be restored to its condition before the development took place, or to such condition as may have been agreed in writing between the local planning authority and the developer;
   (b) where an appeal has been made, under the Act, in relation to an application for development described in paragraph (a)(ii), within the period described in that paragraph, that period is extended until the appeal is finally determined or withdrawn.

(5) Where development is permitted by Class B(a), within 7 days of the date on which the development is substantially completed, the developer must notify the local planning authority in writing of that fact.

Class C—mineral working for agricultural purposes

Permitted development

C   *The winning and working on land held or occupied with land used for the purposes of agriculture of any minerals reasonably necessary for agricultural purposes within the agricultural unit of which it forms part.*

Town and Country Planning (General Permitted Development) Order 2015

Development not permitted

C 1

Development is not permitted by Class C if any excavation would be made within 25 metres of a metalled part of a trunk road or classified road.

Condition

C 2

Development is permitted by Class C subject to the condition that no mineral extracted during the course of the operation is moved to any place outside the land from which it was extracted, except to land which is held or occupied with that land and is used for the purposes of agriculture.

Interpretation of Classes A to C

D.1

(1) For the purposes of Classes A, B and C—

'agricultural land' means land which, before development permitted by this Part is carried out, is land in use for agriculture and which is so used for the purposes of a trade or business, and excludes any dwellinghouse or garden;

'agricultural unit' means agricultural land which is occupied as a unit for the purposes of agriculture, including—

(a) any dwelling or other building on that land occupied for the purpose of farming the land by the person who occupies the unit, or

(b) any dwelling on that land occupied by a farmworker;

'building' does not include anything resulting from engineering operations;

'fish farming' means the breeding, rearing or keeping of fish or shellfish (which includes any kind of crustacean and mollusc);

'livestock' includes fish or shellfish which are farmed;

'protected building' means any permanent building which is normally occupied by people or would be so occupied, if it were in use for purposes for which it is designed; but does not include—

(a) a building within the agricultural unit; or

(b) a dwelling or other building on another agricultural unit which is used for or in connection with agriculture;

'significant extension' or 'significant alteration' means any extension or alteration, as the case may be, of the building where the cubic content of the original building would be exceeded by more than 10% or the height of the building as extended or altered would exceed the height of the original building;

'site notice' means a notice containing—

(a) the name of the applicant,

(b) the address or location of the proposed development,

(c) a description of the proposed development and of the materials to be used,

Town and Country Planning (General Permitted Development) Order 2015

>> (d) a statement that the prior approval of the authority will be required as to the siting, design and external appearance of the building or, as the case may be, the siting and means of construction of the private way,
>> (e) the name and address of the local planning authority,
>>
>> and which is signed and dated by or on behalf of the applicant;
>
> 'slurry' means animal faeces and urine (whether or not water has been added for handling); and
>
> 'tank' includes any cage and any other structure for use in fish farming.

(2) For the purposes of Classes A, B and C—

> (a) an area 'calculated as described in paragraph D.1(2)(a)' comprises the ground area which would be covered by the proposed development, together with the ground area of any building (other than a dwelling), or any structure, works, plant, machinery, ponds or tanks within the same unit which are being provided or have been provided within the preceding 2 years and any part of which would be within 90 metres of the proposed development;
> (b) a reference to 400 metres in paragraphs A.1(i) and (k), A.2(1)(a), B.1(d) and B.5(1) of this Part is a reference to distance measured along the ground.

(3) The circumstances referred to in paragraphs A.2(1)(a) and B.5(1) of this Part are—

> (a) that no other suitable building or structure, 400 metres or more from the curtilage of a protected building, is available to accommodate the livestock; and
> (b) (i) that the need to accommodate the livestock arises from quarantine requirements, or an emergency due to another building or structure in which the livestock could otherwise be accommodated being unavailable because it has been damaged or destroyed by fire, flood or storm; or
>> (ii) in the case of animals normally kept out of doors, they require temporary accommodation in a building or other structure because they are sick or giving birth or newly born, or to provide shelter against extreme weather conditions.

(4) For the purposes of paragraph A.2(2)(c) of this Part, the relevant area is the area of the proposed excavation or the area on which it is proposed to deposit waste together with the aggregate of the areas of all other excavations within the unit which have not been filled and of all other parts of the unit on or under which waste has been deposited and has not been removed.

(5) For the purposes of Class B—

> (a) the erection of any additional building within the curtilage of another building is to be treated as the extension of that building and the additional building is not to be treated as an original building;
> (b) where 2 or more original buildings are within the same curtilage and are used for the same undertaking they are to be treated as a single original building in making any measurement in connection with the extension or alteration of either of them.

(6) In Class C, 'the purposes of agriculture' includes fertilising land used for the purposes of agriculture and the maintenance, improvement or alteration of any

buildings, structures or works occupied or used for such purposes on land so used.

(7) In Class A(a), 'reasonably necessary for the purposes of agriculture' includes, in relation to the erection, extension or alteration of a building, for housing a biomass boiler or an anaerobic digestion system; for storage of fuel for or waste from that boiler or system; or for housing a hydro-turbine.

(8) In Class B(a), 'reasonably necessary for the purposes of agriculture' includes, in relation to the extension or alteration of an agricultural building, for housing a biomass boiler or an anaerobic digestion system; for storage of fuel for or waste from that boiler or system; or for housing a hydro-turbine.

Class E—forestry developments

Permitted development

E *The carrying out on land used for the purposes of forestry, including afforestation, of development reasonably necessary for those purposes consisting of—*

    (a) works for the erection, extension or alteration of a building;

    (b) the formation, alteration or maintenance of private ways;

    (c) operations on that land, or on land held or occupied with that land, to obtain the materials required for the formation, alteration or maintenance of such ways;

    (d) other operations (not including engineering or mining operations).

Development not permitted

E.1

Development is not permitted by Class E if—

    (a) it would consist of or include the provision or alteration of a dwelling;

    (b) the height of any building or works within 3 kilometres of the perimeter of an aerodrome would exceed 3 metres in height;

    (c) any part of the development would be within 25 metres of the metalled portion of a trunk road or classified road; or

    (d) any building for storing fuel for, or waste from, a biomass boiler or an anaerobic digestion system would be used for storing waste not produced by that boiler or system or for storing fuel not produced on land which is occupied together with that building for the purposes of forestry.

Conditions

E.2

(1) Subject to sub-paragraph (3), development consisting of the erection of a building or the extension or alteration of a building or the formation or alteration of a private way is permitted by Class E subject to the following conditions—

    (a) the developer must, before beginning the development, apply to the local planning authority for a determination as to whether the prior approval

Town and Country Planning (General Permitted Development) Order 2015

of the authority will be required as to the siting, design and external appearance of the building or, as the case may be, the siting and means of construction of the private way;

(b) the application must be accompanied by a written description of the proposed development, the materials to be used and a plan indicating the site together with any fee required to be paid;

(c) the development must not begin before the occurrence of one of the following—

　(i) the receipt by the applicant from the local planning authority of a written notice of their determination that such prior approval is not required;

　(ii) where the local planning authority give the applicant notice within 28 days following the date of receiving the applicant's application of their determination that such prior approval is required, the giving of such approval;

　(iii) the expiry of 28 days following the date on which the application under sub-paragraph (1)(b) was received by the local planning authority without the local planning authority making any determination as to whether such approval is required or notifying the applicant of their determination;

(d) where the local planning authority give the applicant notice that such prior approval is required, the applicant must—

　(i) display a site notice by site display on or near the land on which the proposed development is to be carried out, leaving the notice in position for not less than 21 days in the period of 28 days from the date on which the local planning authority gave the notice to the applicant;

　(ii) where the site notice is, without any fault or intention of the applicant, removed, obscured or defaced before the period of 21 days referred to in paragraph (d)(i) has elapsed, the applicant is treated as having complied with the requirements of that sub-paragraph if the applicant has taken reasonable steps for protection of the notice and, if need be, its replacement;

(e) the development must, except to the extent that the local planning authority otherwise agree in writing, be carried out—

　(i) where prior approval is required, in accordance with the details approved;

　(ii) where prior approval is not required, in accordance with the details submitted with the application; and

(f) the development must be carried out—

　(i) where approval has been given by the local planning authority, within a period of 5 years from the date on which approval was given,

　(ii) in any other case, within a period of 5 years from the date on which the local planning authority were given the information referred to in paragraph (b).

(2) In the case of development consisting of the significant extension or the significant alteration of the building such development may be carried out only once.

(3) Sub-paragraph (1) does not preclude the extension or alteration of a building if the building is not on article 2(4) land except in the case of a significant extension or a significant alteration.

Interpretation of Class E

E.3

(1) For the purposes of Class E—

'significant extension' or 'significant alteration' means any extension or alteration, as the case may be, of the building where the cubic content of the original building would be exceeded by more than 10% or the height of the building as extended or altered would exceed the height of the original building; and

'site notice' means a notice containing—

(a) the name of the applicant,

(b) the address or location of the proposed development,

(c) a description of the proposed development and of the materials to be used,

(d) a statement that the prior approval of the authority will be required as to the siting, design and external appearance of the building or, as the case may be, the siting and means of construction of the private way,

(e) the name and address of the local planning authority,

and which is signed and dated by or on behalf of the applicant.

(2) For the purposes of Class E, development that is reasonably necessary for the purposes of forestry includes works for the erection, extension or alteration of a building for housing a biomass boiler or an anaerobic digestion system; for storage of fuel for or waste from that boiler or system; or for housing a hydro-turbine.

PART 7 NON-DOMESTIC EXTENSIONS, ALTERATIONS ETC

Class A—extensions etc of shops or financial or professional premises

Permitted development

A *The extension or alteration of a shop or financial or professional services establishment.*

Development not permitted

A.1

Development is not permitted by Class A if—

(a) the gross floor space of the original building would be exceeded by more than—

(i) in respect of an original building or a development on—

(aa) article 2(3) land, or

(bb) a site of special scientific interest,

25% or 50 square metres (whichever is the lesser);

(ii) in any other case, 50% or 100 square metres (whichever is the lesser);
(b) the height of the building as extended would exceed 4 metres;
(c) any part of the development (other than an alteration)—
  (i) is on land which—
    (aa) adjoins other premises which are used for a purpose falling within any of the classes in Part C (residential premises or institutions) of the Schedule to the Use Classes Order,
    (bb) is article 2(3) land, or
    (cc) is a site of special scientific interest, and
  (ii) is within 2 metres of any boundary of the curtilage of the premises;
(d) the development would be within the curtilage of a listed building;
(e) any alteration would be on article 2(3) land;
(f) the development would consist of or include the construction or provision of a verandah, balcony or raised platform;
(g) any part of the development would extend beyond an existing shop front;
(h) the development would involve the insertion or creation of a new shop front or the alteration or replacement of an existing shop front; or
(i) the development would involve the installation or replacement of a security grill or shutter on a shop front.

Conditions

A.2

Development is permitted by Class A subject to the following conditions—
(a) any alteration is at ground floor level only;
(b) any extension is, in the case of article 2(3) land, constructed using materials which have a similar external appearance to those used for the building being extended; and
(c) any extension or alteration is only to be used as part of, or for a purpose incidental to, the use of the shop or financial or professional services establishment.

Interpretation of Class A

A.3

For the purposes of Class A—

'raised platform' means a platform with a height greater than 0.3 metres; and

'shop or financial or professional services establishment' means a building, or part of a building, used for any purpose within Classes A1 or A2 of the Schedule to the Use Classes Order and includes buildings with other uses in other parts as long as the other uses are not within the parts being altered or extended,

and where 2 or more original buildings are within the same curtilage and are used for the same undertaking, they are to be treated as a single original building in making any measurement.

Town and Country Planning (General Permitted Development) Order 2015

Class B—construction of shop trolley stores

Permitted development

B   *The erection or construction of a trolley store within the curtilage of a shop.*

Development not permitted

B.1

Development is not permitted by Class B if—
- (a) the gross floor space of the building or enclosure erected would exceed 20 square metres;
- (b) any part of the building or enclosure erected would be—
  - (i) within 20 metres of any boundary of the curtilage of; or
  - (ii) above or below,

  any building used for any purpose within Part C (residential premises or institutions) of the Schedule to the Use Classes Order or as a hostel;
- (c) the height of the building or enclosure would exceed 2.5 metres;
- (d) the development would be within the curtilage of a listed building; or
- (e) the development would be between a shop front and a highway where the distance between the shop front and the boundary of the curtilage of the premises is less than 5 metres.

Condition

B.2

Development is permitted by Class B subject to the condition that the building or enclosure is only used for the storage of shopping trolleys.

Interpretation of Class B

B.3

For the purposes of Class B—
- 'shop' means a building used for any purpose within Class A1 (shops) of the Schedule to the Use Classes Order; and
- 'trolley store' means a building or enclosure designed to be used for the storage of shopping trolleys.

Class C—click and collect facilities

Permitted development

C   *Development consisting of the erection or construction of a collection facility within the curtilage of a shop.*

Development not permitted

C 1

Development is not permitted by Class C if—

(a) the development would result in more than 1 collection facility within the curtilage of a shop;

(b) the gross floor space of the building or structure would exceed 20 square metres;

(c) the height of the building or structure would exceed 4 metres;

(d) any part of the development would be within 2 metres of any boundary of the curtilage;

(e) any part of the development would be between a shop front and a highway where the distance between the shop front and the boundary of the curtilage of the premises is less than 5 metres; or

(f) any part of the development would be—

(i) on article 2(3) land;

(ii) in a site of special scientific interest; or

(iii) within the curtilage of a listed building or a scheduled monument.

Conditions

C 2

(1) Development is permitted by Class C subject to the condition that the developer must, before beginning the development, apply to the local planning authority for a determination as to whether the prior approval of the authority will be required as to the siting, design and external appearance of the development and the following sub-paragraphs apply in relation to that application.

(2) The application must be accompanied by—

(a) a written description of the proposed development, which must include details of any building operations proposed;

(b) a plan indicating the site and showing the proposed development;

(c) the developer's contact address; and

(d) the developer's email address if the developer is content to receive communications electronically,

together with any fee required to be paid.

(3) The local planning authority may refuse an application where, in the opinion of the authority—

(a) the proposed development does not comply with, or

(b) the developer has provided insufficient information to enable the authority to establish whether the proposed development complies with,

any conditions, limitations or restrictions specified in Class C as being applicable to the development in question.

(4) Sub-paragraphs (5) and (7) do not apply where a local planning authority refuses an application under sub-paragraph (3) and for the purposes of section 78 (appeals) of the Act such a refusal is to be treated as a refusal of an application for approval.

(5) The local planning authority must give notice of the proposed development—

(a) by site display in at least one place on or near the land to which the application relates for not less than 21 days of a notice which—

(i) describes the proposed development;

(ii) provides the address of the proposed development;

(iii) specifies the date by which representations are to be received by the local planning authority; or

(b) by serving a notice in that form on any adjoining owner or occupier.

(6) The local planning authority may require the developer to submit such information as the authority may reasonably require in order to determine the application.

(7) The local planning authority must, when determining an application—

(a) take into account any representations made to them as a result of any notice given under sub-paragraph (5);

(b) have regard to the National Planning Policy Framework issued by the Department for Communities and Local Government in March 2012, so far as relevant to the subject matter of the prior approval, as if the application were a planning application.

(8) The development must not begin before the occurrence of one of the following—

(a) the receipt by the applicant from the local planning authority of a written notice of their determination that such prior approval is not required;

(b) the receipt by the applicant from the local planning authority of a written notice giving their prior approval; or

(c) the expiry of 56 days following the date on which the application under sub-paragraph (2) was received by the local planning authority without the authority notifying the applicant as to whether prior approval is given or refused.

(9) The development must be carried out—

(a) where prior approval is required, in accordance with the details approved by the local planning authority;

(b) where prior approval is not required, or where sub-paragraph (8)(c) applies, in accordance with the details provided in the application referred to in sub-paragraph (2),

unless the local planning authority and the developer agree otherwise in writing.

(10) The local planning authority may grant prior approval unconditionally or subject to conditions reasonably related to the subject matter of the prior approval.

Interpretation of Class C

C 3

For the purposes of Class C—

'collection facility' means a building or structure designed to be used by visiting members of the public for the collection of any goods and for the storage of goods awaiting such collection; and

'shop' means a building used for any purpose within Class A1 (shops) of the Schedule to the Use Classes Order.

Town and Country Planning (General Permitted Development) Order 2015

Class D—modification of shop loading bays

Permitted development

D   *Development consisting of modification of a loading bay of a shop.*

Development not permitted

D.1

Development is not permitted by Class D if—
- (a) the size of the original loading bay, when measured in any dimension, would be increased by more than 20%; or
- (b) any part of the development would be—
  - (i) on article 2(3) land;
  - (ii) in a site of special scientific interest; or
  - (iii) within the curtilage of a listed building or a scheduled monument.

Conditions

D.2

Development is permitted by Class D subject to the condition that the materials used must be of a similar appearance to those used in the construction of the exterior of the shop.

Interpretation of Class D

D.3

For the purposes of Class D—
'goods vehicle' has the meaning given in section 192 of the Road Traffic Act 1988;
'loading bay' means any facility, including vehicle ramps, for the loading or unloading of goods vehicles; and
'shop' means a building used for any purpose within Class A1 (shops) of the Schedule to the Use Classes Order.

Class E—hard surfaces for shops, catering or financial or professional premises

Permitted development

E   *Development consisting of—*
- *(a) the provision of a hard surface within the curtilage of a shop or catering, financial or professional services establishment; or*
- *(b) the replacement in whole or in part of such a surface.*

Development not permitted

E.1

Development is not permitted by Class E if—
- (a) the cumulative area of ground covered by a hard surface within the curtilage of the premises (other than hard surfaces already existing on 6th April 2010) would exceed 50 square metres; or

Town and Country Planning (General Permitted Development) Order 2015

(b) the development would be within the curtilage of a listed building.

Conditions

E.2

Development is permitted by Class E subject to the following conditions—
- (a) where there is a risk of groundwater contamination, the hard surface is not made of porous materials; and
- (b) in all other cases, either—
  - (i) the hard surface is made of porous materials, or
  - (ii) provision is made to direct run-off water from the hard surface to a permeable or porous area or surface within the curtilage of the undertaking.

Interpretation of Class E

E.3

For the purposes of Class E, 'shop or catering, financial or professional services establishment' means a building used for any purpose within Classes A1 to A5 of the Schedule to the Use Classes Order.

Class F—extensions etc of office buildings

Permitted development

F   *The extension or alteration of an office building.*

Development not permitted

F.1

Development is not permitted by Class F if—
- (a) the gross floor space of the original building would be exceeded by more than—
  - (i) in respect of an original building or a development on—
    - (aa) article 2(3) land, or
    - (bb) on a site of special scientific interest,
    25% or 50 square metres (whichever is the lesser);
  - (ii) in any other case, 50% or 100 square metres (whichever is the lesser);
- (b) the height of the building as extended would exceed—
  - (i) if within 10 metres of a boundary of the curtilage of the premises, 5 metres; or
  - (ii) in all other cases, the height of the building being extended;
- (c) any part of the development, other than an alteration, would be within 5 metres of any boundary of the curtilage of the premises;
- (d) any alteration would be on article 2(3) land; or
- (e) the development would be within the curtilage of a listed building.

Conditions

F.2

Development is permitted by Class F subject to the following conditions—
    (a) any office building as extended or altered is only used as part of, or for a purpose incidental to, the use of that office building;
    (b) any extension is, in the case of article 2(3) land, constructed using materials which have a similar external appearance to those used for the building being extended; and
    (c) any alteration is at ground floor level only.

Interpretation of Class F

F.3

For the purposes of Class F, where 2 or more original buildings are within the same curtilage and are used for the same undertaking, they are to be treated as a single original building in making any measurement.

Class G—hard surfaces for office buildings

Permitted development

G Development consisting of—
    (a) the provision of a hard surface within the curtilage of an office building to be used for the purpose of the office concerned; or
    (b) the replacement in whole or in part of such a surface.

Development not permitted

G.1

Development is not permitted by Class G if—
    (a) the cumulative area of ground covered by a hard surface within the curtilage (excluding hard surfaces already existing on 6th April 2010) would exceed 50 square metres; or
    (b) the development would be within the curtilage of a listed building.

Conditions

G.2

Development is permitted by Class G subject to the following conditions—
    (a) where there is a risk of groundwater contamination, the hard surface is not made of porous materials; and
    (b) in all other cases, either—
        (i) the hard surface is made of porous materials, or
        (ii) provision is made to direct run-off water from the hard surface to a permeable or porous area or surface within the curtilage of the office building.

Town and Country Planning (General Permitted Development) Order 2015

Class H—extensions etc of industrial and warehouse

Permitted development

H *The erection, extension or alteration of an industrial building or a warehouse.*

Development not permitted

H.1

Development is not permitted by Class H if—
- (a) the gross floor space of any new building erected would exceed—
  - (i) for a building on article 2(3) land or on a site of special scientific interest, 100 square metres;
  - (ii) in any other case, would exceed 200 square metres;
- (b) the gross floor space of the original building would be exceeded by more than—
  - (i) in respect of an original building or a development on article 2(3) land, 10% or 500 square metres (whichever is lesser);
  - (ii) in respect of an original building or a development on a site of special scientific interest, 25% or 1,000 square metres (whichever is the lesser);
  - (iii) in any other case, 50% or 1,000 square metres (whichever is the lesser);
- (c) the height of any part of the new building erected would exceed—
  - (i) if within 10 metres of a boundary of the curtilage of the premises, 5 metres;
  - (ii) in all other cases, the height of the highest building within the curtilage of the premises or 15 metres, whichever is lower;
- (d) the height of the building as extended or altered would exceed—
  - (i) if within 10 metres of a boundary of the curtilage of the premises, 5 metres;
  - (ii) in all other cases, the height of the building being extended or altered;
- (e) any part of the development would be within 5 metres of any boundary of the curtilage of the premises;
- (f) the development would lead to a reduction in the space available for the parking or turning of vehicles; or
- (g) the development would be within the curtilage of a listed building.

Conditions

H.2

Development is permitted by Class H subject to the following conditions—
- (a) the development is within the curtilage of an existing industrial building or warehouse;
- (b) any building as erected, extended or altered is only to be used—
  - (i) in the case of an industrial building, for the carrying out of an industrial process for the purposes of the undertaking, for research and

development of products or processes, or the provision of employee facilities ancillary to the undertaking;

(ii) in the case of a warehouse, for storage or distribution for the purposes of the undertaking or the provision of employee facilities ancillary to the undertaking;

(c) no building as erected, extended or altered is used to provide employee facilities—

(i) between 7.00pm and 6.30am, for employees other than those present at the premises of the undertaking for the purpose of their employment; or

(ii) at all, if a quantity of a dangerous substance is present at the premises of the undertaking in a quantity equal to or exceeding the quantity listed in the entry for that substance in Parts 2 or 3 of Schedule 1 to the Control of Major Accident Hazards Regulations 1999;

(d) any new building erected is, in the case of article 2(3) land, constructed using materials which have a similar external appearance to those used for the existing industrial building or warehouse; and

(e) any extension or alteration is, in the case of article 2(3) land, constructed using materials which have a similar external appearance to those used for the building being extended or altered.

Interpretation of Class H

H.3

For the purposes of Class H, where 2 or more original buildings are within the same curtilage and are used for the same undertaking, they are to be treated as a single original building in making any measurement.

H.4

For the purposes of Class H—

'dangerous substance' has the meaning given in regulation 2 of the Control of Major Accident Hazards Regulations 1999;

'employee facilities' means social, care or recreational facilities provided for employees of the undertaking, including crèche facilities provided for the children of such employees; and

'original building' does not include any building erected at any time under Class H.

Class I—developments relating to an industrial process

Permitted development

I *Development carried out on industrial land for the purposes of an industrial process consisting of—*

(a) *the installation of additional or replacement plant or machinery;*

(b) *the provision, rearrangement or replacement of a sewer, main, pipe, cable or other apparatus, or*

(c) *the provision, rearrangement or replacement of a private way, private railway, siding or conveyor.*

Town and Country Planning (General Permitted Development) Order 2015

Development not permitted

I.1

Development described in Class I(a) is not permitted if—

    (a) it would materially affect the external appearance of the premises of the undertaking concerned; or

    (b) any plant or machinery would exceed a height of 15 metres above ground level or the height of anything replaced, whichever is the greater.

Interpretation of Class I

I.2

For the purposes of Class I, 'industrial land' means land used for the carrying out of an industrial process, including land used for the purposes of an industrial undertaking as a dock, harbour or quay but does not include land in or adjacent to and occupied together with a mine.

Class J—hard surfaces for industrial and warehouse premises

Permitted development

J   *Development consisting of—*

    (a) the provision of a hard surface within the curtilage of an industrial building or warehouse to be used for the purpose of the undertaking concerned; or

    (b) the replacement in whole or in part of such a surface.

Development not permitted

J.1

Development is not permitted by Class J if the development would be within the curtilage of a listed building.

Conditions

J.2

Development is permitted by Class J subject to the following conditions—

    (a) where there is a risk of groundwater contamination the hard surface must not be made of porous materials; and

    (b) in all other cases, either—

        (i) the hard surface is made of porous materials, or

        (ii) provision is made to direct run-off water from the hard surface to a permeable or porous area or surface within the curtilage of the industrial building or warehouse.

Class K—waste deposits from an industrial process

Permitted development

K   *The deposit of waste material resulting from an industrial process on any land comprised in a site which was used for that purpose on 1st July 1948* *whether or not the superficial area or the height of the deposit is extended as a result.*

Development not permitted

K.1

Development is not permitted by Class K if—

(a) the waste material is or includes material resulting from the winning and working of minerals; or

(b) the use on 1st July 1948 was for the deposit of material resulting from the winning and working of minerals.

Class L—development at waste management facilities

Permitted development

L   *Development carried out on land used for the purposes of a waste management facility consisting of—*

    (a) the extension or alteration of a building; and

    (b) the installation of replacement plant or machinery.

Development not permitted

L 1

Development described in Class L is not permitted if—

(a) the gross floor space occupied by the replacement plant or machinery would exceed by more than 15% the gross floor space of the plant or machinery it replaced;

(b) the development under Class L (together with any previous development under Class L) would result in the area occupied by buildings, plant or machinery on the site exceeding the original area occupied by buildings, plant or machinery by more than—

    (i) 50%; or

    (ii) 100 square metres,

   whichever is the lesser;

(c) the height of any building as extended or altered would exceed—

    (i) if within 10 metres of a boundary of the curtilage of the site, 5 metres; or

    (ii) in all other cases, the height of the building being extended or altered or 15 metres, whichever is the lower;

(d) the height of any replacement plant or machinery would exceed—

    (i) if within 10 metres of a boundary of the curtilage of the site, 5 metres; or

    (ii) in all other cases, 15 metres;

(e) any part of the development would be within 5 metres of any boundary of the curtilage of the site;

(f) the development would lead to a reduction in the space available for the parking or turning of vehicles;

Town and Country Planning (General Permitted Development) Order 2015

(g) the development would be—
  (i) on article 2(3) land; or
  (ii) in a site of special scientific interest;
(h) the building is a listed building or is within the curtilage of a listed building; or
(i) the site is, or contains, a scheduled monument.

Conditions

L 2

Development is permitted by Class L subject to the condition that any building as extended or altered is only used as part of, or for a purpose incidental to, the use of the site as a waste management facility.

Interpretation

L 3

For the purposes of Class L—

'waste management facility' means premises and associated land used for the purposes of any waste operation for which an environmental permit is required under Part 2 of the Environmental Permitting (England and Wales) Regulations 2010 or which is an exempt facility under those Regulations; and

'waste operation' has the meaning given in the Environmental Permitting (England and Wales) Regulations 2010.

Class M—extensions etc for schools, colleges, universities and hospitals

Permitted development

M   The erection, extension or alteration of a school, college, university or hospital building.

Development not permitted

M.1

Development is not permitted by Class M—
(a) if the cumulative gross floor space of any buildings erected, extended or altered would exceed—
  (i) 25% of the gross floor space of the original school, college, university or hospital buildings; or
  (ii) 100 square metres,
  whichever is the lesser;
(b) if any part of the development would be within 5 metres of a boundary of the curtilage of the premises;
(c) if, as a result of the development, any land used as a playing field at any time in the 5 years before the development commenced and remaining in this use could no longer be so used;

Town and Country Planning (General Permitted Development) Order 2015

    (d) if the height of any new building erected would exceed 5 metres;
    (e) if the height of the building as extended or altered would exceed—
        (i) if within 10 metres of a boundary of the curtilage of the premises, 5 metres; or
        (ii) in all other cases, the height of the building being extended or altered;
    (f) if the development would be within the curtilage of a listed building; or
    (g) unless—
        (i) in the case of school, college or university buildings, the predominant use of the existing buildings on the premises is for the provision of education;
        (ii) in the case of hospital buildings, the predominant use of the existing buildings on the premises is for the provision of any medical or health services.

Conditions

M.2

Development is permitted by Class M subject to the following conditions—
    (a) the development is within the curtilage of an existing school, college, university or hospital;
    (b) the development is only used as part of, or for a purpose incidental to, the use of that school, college, university or hospital;
    (c) any new building erected is, in the case of article 2(3) land, constructed using materials which have a similar external appearance to those used for the original school, college, university or hospital buildings; and
    (d) any extension or alteration is, in the case of article 2(3) land, constructed using materials which have a similar external appearance to those used for the building being extended or altered.

Interpretation of Class M

M.3

For the purposes of Class M—
    'original school, college, university or hospital building' means any original building which is a school, college, university or hospital building, as the case may be, other than any building erected at any time under Class M; and
    'school' does not include a building which changed use by virtue of Class S of Part 3 of this Schedule (changes of use),
where 2 or more original buildings are within the same curtilage and are used for the same institution, they are to be treated as a single original building in making any measurement.

Class N—hard surfaces for schools, colleges, universities or hospitals

Permitted development

N   *Development consisting of—*

Town and Country Planning (General Permitted Development) Order 2015

(a) the provision of a hard surface within the curtilage of any school, college, university or hospital to be used for the purposes of that school, college, university or hospital; or

(b) the replacement in whole or in part of such a surface.

Development not permitted

N.1

Development is not permitted by Class N if—

(a) the cumulative area of ground covered by a hard surface within the curtilage of the site (other than hard surfaces already existing on 6th April 2010) would exceed 50 square metres;

(b) as a result of the development, any land used as a playing field at any time in the 5 years before the development commenced and remaining in this use could no longer be so used; or

(c) the development would be within the curtilage of a listed building.

Conditions

N.2

Development is permitted by Class N subject to the following conditions—

(a) where there is a risk of groundwater contamination, the hard surface is not made of porous materials; and

(b) in all other cases, either—

(i) the hard surface is made of porous materials, or

(ii) provision is made to direct run-off water from the hard surface to a permeable or porous area or surface within the curtilage of the institution.

Interpretation of Part 7

O

For the purposes of Part 7—

'industrial building' means a building used for the carrying out of an industrial process and includes a building used for the carrying out of such a process on land used as a dock, harbour or quay for the purposes of an industrial undertaking and land used for research and development of products or processes, but does not include a building on land in or adjacent to and occupied together with a mine;

'office building' means a building used for any purpose within Class B1(a) of the Schedule to the Use Classes Order (offices);

'registered nursery' and 'state-funded school' have the meanings given in paragraph X of Part 3 of this Schedule (changes of use);

'school'—

(a) includes a building permitted by Class C of Part 4 (temporary buildings and uses) to be used temporarily as a school, from the date the local planning authority is notified as provided in paragraph C 2(b) of Part 4;

(b) except in Class M (extensions etc for schools), includes premises which have changed use under Class S of Part 3 of this Schedule (changes of use) to become a state-funded school or registered nursery; and

(c) includes premises which have changed use under Class T of Part 3 of this Schedule (changes of use) to become a state-funded school or registered nursery; and

'warehouse' means a building used for any purpose within Class B8 (storage or distribution) of the Schedule to the Use Classes Order but does not include a building on land in or adjacent to and occupied together with a mine.

PART 8 TRANSPORT RELATED DEVELOPMENT

Class A—railway or light railway undertakings

Permitted development

A **Development by railway undertakers on their operational land, required in connection with the movement of traffic by rail.**

Development not permitted

A.1

Development is not permitted by Class A if it consists of or includes—
- (a) the construction of a railway;
- (b) the construction or erection of a hotel, railway station or bridge; or
- (c) the construction or erection otherwise than wholly within a railway station of—
  - (i) an office, residential or educational building, or a building used for an industrial process, or
  - (ii) a car park, shop, restaurant, garage, petrol filling station or other building or structure provided under transport legislation.

Interpretation of Class A

A.2

For the purposes of Class A, references to the construction or erection of any building or structure include references to the reconstruction or alteration of a building or structure where its design or external appearance would be materially affected.

Class B—dock, pier, harbour, water transport, canal or inland navigation undertakings

Permitted development

B **Development on operational land by statutory undertakers or their lessees in respect of dock, pier, harbour, water transport, or canal or inland navigation undertakings, required—**

(a) for the purposes of shipping, or

Town and Country Planning (General Permitted Development) Order 2015

(b) in connection with the embarking, disembarking, loading, discharging or transport of passengers, livestock or goods at a dock, pier or harbour, or with the movement of traffic by canal or inland navigation or by any railway forming part of the undertaking.

Development not permitted

B.1

Development is not permitted by Class B if it consists of or includes—
- (a) the construction or erection of a hotel, or of a bridge or other building not required in connection with the handling of traffic; or
- (b) the construction or erection otherwise than wholly within the limits of a dock, pier or harbour of—
    - (i) an educational building, or
    - (ii) a car park, shop, restaurant, garage, petrol filling station or other building provided under transport legislation.

Interpretation of Class B

B.2

For the purposes of Class B—
- (a) references to the construction or erection of any building or structure include references to the reconstruction or alteration of a building or structure where its design or external appearance would be materially affected, and
- (b) the reference to operational land includes land designated by an order made under section 14 or 16 of the Harbours Act 1964 (orders for securing harbour efficiency etc, and orders conferring powers for improvement, construction etc, of harbours), and which has come into force, whether or not the order was subject to the provisions of the Statutory Orders (Special Procedure) Act 1945.

Class C—works to inland waterways

Permitted development

C   *The improvement, maintenance or repair of an inland waterway (other than a commercial waterway or cruising waterway) to which section 104 of the Transport Act 1968 (classification of waterways)applies, and the repair or maintenance of a culvert, weir, lock, aqueduct, sluice, reservoir, let-off valve or other work used in connection with the control and operation of such a waterway.*

Class D—dredging by transport undertakings

Permitted development

D   *The use of any land by statutory undertakers in respect of dock, pier, harbour, water transport, canal or inland navigation undertakings for the spreading of any dredged material.*

Town and Country Planning (General Permitted Development) Order 2015

Class E—development for the aid of shipping

Permitted development

E   *Development required for the purposes of the functions of a general or local lighthouse authority under the Merchant Shipping Act 1995 and any other statutory provision made with respect to a local lighthouse authority, or in the exercise by a local lighthouse authority of rights, powers or duties acquired by usage prior to the 1995 Act.*

Development not permitted

E.1

Development is not permitted by Class E if it consists of or includes the erection of offices, or the reconstruction or alteration of offices where their design or external appearance would be materially affected.

Class F—development at an airport

Permitted development

F   *The carrying out on operational land by a relevant airport operator or its agent of development (including the erection or alteration of an operational building) in connection with the provision of services and facilities at a relevant airport.*

Development not permitted

F.1

Development is not permitted by Class F if it would consist of or include—

(a) the construction or extension of a runway;

(b) the construction of a passenger terminal the floor space of which would exceed 500 square metres;

(c) the extension or alteration of a passenger terminal, where the floor space of the building as existing at 5th December 1988 or, if built after that date, of the building as built, would be exceeded by more than 15%;

(d) the erection of a building other than an operational building; or

(e) the alteration or reconstruction of a building other than an operational building, where its design or external appearance would be materially affected.

Condition

F.2

Development is permitted by Class F subject to the condition that the relevant airport operator consults the local planning authority before carrying out any development, unless that development falls within the description in paragraph F.4.

Interpretation of Class F

F.3

For the purposes of paragraph F.1, floor space is calculated by external measurement and without taking account of the floor space in any pier or satellite.

Town and Country Planning (General Permitted Development) Order 2015

F.4

Development falls within this paragraph if—

(a) it is urgently required for the efficient running of the airport, and

(b) it consists of the carrying out of works, or the erection or construction of a structure or of an ancillary building, or the placing on land of equipment, and the works, structure, building, or equipment do not exceed 4 metres in height or 200 cubic metres in capacity.

Class G—air traffic services development at an airport

Permitted development

G *The carrying out on operational land within the perimeter of a relevant airport by a relevant airport operator or its agent of development in connection with the provision of air traffic services.*

Class H—air traffic services development near an airport

Permitted development

H *The carrying out on operational land outside but within 8 kilometres of the perimeter of a relevant airport by a relevant airport operator or its agent of development in connection with the provision of air traffic services.*

Development not permitted

H.1

Development is not permitted by Class H if—

(a) any building erected would be used for a purpose other than housing equipment used in connection with the provision of air traffic services;

(b) any building erected would exceed a height of 4 metres; or

(c) it would consist of the installation or erection of any radar or radio mast, antenna or other apparatus which would exceed 15 metres in height, or, where an existing mast, antenna or apparatus is replaced, the height of that mast, antenna or apparatus, if greater.

Class I—development by an air traffic services licence holder within an airport

Permitted development

I *The carrying out by an air traffic services licence holder or its agents within the perimeter of an airport of development in connection with the provision of air traffic services.*

Class J—development by an air traffic services licence holder on operational land

Permitted development

J *The carrying out on operational land of an air traffic services licence holder by that licence holder or its agents of development in connection with the provision of air traffic services.*

Development not permitted

J.1

Development is not permitted by Class J if—

(a) any building erected would be used for a purpose other than housing equipment used in connection with the provision of air traffic services;

(b) any building erected would exceed a height of 4 metres; or

(c) it would consist of the installation or erection of any radar or radio mast, antenna or other apparatus which would exceed 15 metres in height, or, where an existing mast, antenna or apparatus is replaced, the height of that mast, antenna or apparatus, if greater.

Class K—development by an air traffic services licence holder in an emergency

Permitted development

K   *The use of land by or on behalf of an air traffic services licence holder in an emergency to station moveable apparatus replacing unserviceable apparatus.*

Condition

K.1

Development is permitted by Class K subject to the condition that on or before the expiry of a period of 6 months beginning with the date on which the use began, the use ceases, and any apparatus is removed, and the land is restored to its condition before the development took place, or to any other condition as may be agreed in writing between the local planning authority and the developer.

Class L—development by an air traffic services licence holder involving moveable structures

Permitted development

L   *The use of land by or on behalf of an air traffic services licence holder to provide services and facilities in connection with the provision of air traffic services and the erection or placing of moveable structures on the land for the purposes of that use.*

Condition

L 1

Development is permitted by Class L subject to the condition that, on or before the expiry of the period of 6 months beginning with the date on which the use began, the use ceases, and any structure is removed, and the land is restored to its condition before the development took place, or to any other condition as may be agreed in writing between the local planning authority and the developer.

Class M—development by the Civil Aviation Authority for surveys etc

Permitted development

M   *The use of land by or on behalf of the Civil Aviation Authority for the stationing and operation of apparatus in connection with the carrying out of surveys or investigations.*

Town and Country Planning (General Permitted Development) Order 2015

Condition

M.1

Development is permitted by Class M subject to the condition that on or before the expiry of the period of 6 months beginning with the date on which the use began, the use ceases, and any apparatus is removed, and the land is restored to its condition before the development took place, or to any other condition as may be agreed in writing between the local planning authority and the developer.

Class N—use of airport buildings managed by relevant airport operators

Permitted development

N   *The use of buildings within the perimeter of an airport managed by a relevant airport operator for purposes connected with air transport services or other flying activities at that airport.*

Interpretation of Part 8

O

For the purposes of Part 8—

> 'air traffic services' has the same meaning as in section 98 of the Transport Act 2000 (air traffic services);
>
> 'air traffic services licence holder' means a person who holds a licence under Chapter 1 of Part 1 of the Transport Act 2000;
>
> 'air transport services' has the same meaning as in section 82 of the Airports Act 1986;
>
> 'operational building' means a building, other than a hotel, required in connection with the movement or maintenance of aircraft, or with the embarking, disembarking, loading, discharge or transport of passengers, livestock or goods at a relevant airport;
>
> 'relevant airport' means an airport to which Part 5 of the Airports Act 1986 (status of certain airport operators as statutory undertakers etc) applies;
>
> 'relevant airport operator' means a relevant airport operator within the meaning of section 57A of the Airports Act 1986 (scope of Part 5); and
>
> 'transport legislation' means section 14(1)(d) of the Transport Act 1962 (supplemental provisions relating to the Boards' powers) or section 10(1)(x) of the Transport Act 1968 (general powers of Passenger Transport Executive).

PART 9 DEVELOPMENT RELATING TO ROADS

Class A—development by highways authorities

Permitted development

A   *The carrying out by a highway authority—*

> *(a) on land within the boundaries of a road, of any works required for the maintenance or improvement of the road, where such works involve development by virtue of section 55(2)(b) of the Act; or*

Town and Country Planning (General Permitted Development) Order 2015

(b) on land outside but adjoining the boundary of an existing highway of works required for or incidental to the maintenance or improvement of the highway.

Class B—development by the Secretary of State or a strategic highways company under the Highways Act 1980

Permitted development

B   *The carrying out by the Secretary of State or a strategic highways company of works in exercise of the functions of the Secretary of State or the company under the Highways Act 1980, or works in connection with, or incidental to, the exercise of those functions.*

Interpretation of Class B

B.1

For the purposes of Class B, 'strategic highways company' means a company for the time being appointed under Part 1 of the Infrastructure Act 2015.

Class C—tramway or road transport undertakings

Permitted development

C   *Development required for the purposes of the carrying on of any tramway or road transport undertaking consisting of—*

(a) *the installation of posts, overhead wires, underground cables, feeder pillars or transformer boxes in, on, over or adjacent to a highway for the purpose of supplying current to public service vehicles;*

(b) *the installation of tramway tracks, and conduits, drains and pipes in connection with such tracks for the working of tramways;*

(c) *the installation of telephone cables and apparatus, huts, stop posts and signs required in connection with the operation of public service vehicles;*

(d) *the erection or construction and the maintenance, improvement or other alteration of passenger shelters and barriers for the control of people waiting to enter public service vehicles;*

(e) *any other development on operational land of the undertaking.*

Development not permitted

C.1

Development is not permitted by Class C if it would consist of—

(a) in the case of any Class C(a) development, the installation of a structure exceeding 17 cubic metres in capacity;

(b) in the case of any Class C(e) development—

   (i) the erection of a building or the reconstruction or alteration of a building where its design or external appearance would be materially affected;

   (ii) the installation or erection by way of addition or replacement of any plant or machinery which would exceed 15 metres in height or the

Town and Country Planning (General Permitted Development) Order 2015

> height of any plant or machinery it replaces, whichever is the greater; or
>
> (iii) development, not wholly within a bus or tramway station, in pursuance of powers contained in transport legislation.

Interpretation of Class C

C 2

For the purposes of Class C, 'transport legislation' means section 14(1)(d) of the Transport Act 1962 (supplemental provisions relating to the Boards' powers) or section 10(1)(x) of the Transport Act 1968 (general powers of Passenger Transport Executive).

Class D—toll road facilities

Permitted development

D *Development consisting of—*
   (a) *the setting up and the maintenance, improvement or other alteration of facilities for the collection of tolls;*
   (b) *the provision of a hard surface to be used for the parking of vehicles in connection with the use of such facilities.*

Development not permitted

D.1

Development is not permitted by Class D if—
   (a) it is not located within 100 metres (measured along the ground) of the boundary of a toll road;
   (b) the height of any building or structure would exceed—
      (i) 7.5 metres excluding any rooftop structure; or
      (ii) 10 metres including any rooftop structure; or
   (c) the aggregate area of the floor space at or above ground level of any building or group of buildings within a toll collection area, excluding the floor space of any toll collection booth, would exceed 1,500 square metres.

Conditions

D.2

In the case of any article 2(3) land, development is permitted by Class D subject to the following conditions—
   (a) the developer must, before beginning the development, apply to the local planning authority for a determination as to whether the prior approval of the authority will be required as to the siting, design and external appearance of the facilities for the collection of tolls;
   (b) the application must be accompanied by a written description, together with plans and elevations, of the proposed development and any fee required to be paid;
   (c) the development must not begin before the occurrence of one of the following—

(i) the receipt by the applicant from the local planning authority of a written notice of their determination that such prior approval is not required;

(ii) where the local planning authority give the applicant notice within 28 days following the date of receiving the application of their determination that such prior approval is required, the giving of such approval; or

(iii) the expiry of 28 days following the date on which the application was received by the local planning authority without the local planning authority making any determination as to whether such approval is required or notifying the applicant of their determination;

(d) the development must, except to the extent that the local planning authority otherwise agree in writing, be carried out—

(i) where prior approval is required, in accordance with the details approved;

(ii) where prior approval is not required, or where paragraph (c)(iii) applies, in accordance with the details submitted with the application; and

(e) the development must be carried out—

(i) where approval has been given by the local planning authority, within a period of 5 years from the date on which the approval was given;

(ii) in any other case, within a period of 5 years from the date on which the local planning authority were given the information referred to in paragraph (b).

Interpretation of Class D

D.3

For the purposes of Class D—

'facilities for the collection of tolls' means such buildings, structures, or other facilities as are reasonably required for the purpose of or in connection with the collection of tolls in pursuance of a toll order;

'ground level' means the level of the surface of the ground immediately adjacent to the building or group of buildings in question or, where the level of the surface of the ground on which it is situated or is to be situated is not uniform, the level of the highest part of the surface of the ground adjacent to it;

'rooftop structure' means any apparatus or structure which is reasonably required to be located on and attached to the roof, being an apparatus or structure which is—

(a) so located for the provision of heating, ventilation, air conditioning, water, gas or electricity;

(b) lift machinery; or

(c) reasonably required for safety purposes;

'toll' means a toll which may be charged pursuant to a toll order;

'toll collection area' means an area of land where tolls are collected in pursuance of a toll order, and includes any facilities for the collection of tolls;

Town and Country Planning (General Permitted Development) Order 2015

'toll collection booth' means any building or structure designed or adapted for the purpose of collecting tolls in pursuance of a toll order;

'toll order' has the same meaning as in Part 1 of the New Roads and Street Works Act 1991 (new roads in England and Wales); and

'toll road' means a road which is the subject of a toll order.

Class E—repairs to unadopted streets and private ways

Permitted development

E   *The carrying out on land within the boundaries of an unadopted street or private way of works required for the maintenance or improvement of the street or way.*

Interpretation of Class E

E.1

For the purposes of Class E, 'unadopted street' means a street not being a highway maintainable at the public expense within the meaning of the Highways Act 1980.

PART 10 REPAIRS TO SERVICES

Class A

Permitted development

A   *The carrying out of any works for the purposes of inspecting, repairing or renewing any sewer, main, pipe, cable or other apparatus, including breaking open any land for that purpose.*

PART 11 HERITAGE AND DEMOLITION

Class A—development by Historic England

Permitted development

A   *Development by or on behalf of Historic England, consisting of—*
   (a) the maintenance, repair or restoration of any building or monument;
   (b) the erection of screens, fences or covers designed or intended to protect or safeguard any building or monument; or
   (c) the carrying out of works to stabilise ground conditions by any cliff, watercourse or the coastline;
   where such works are required for the purposes of securing the preservation of any building or monument.

Development not permitted

A.1

Development is not permitted by Class A(a) if the works involve the extension of the building or monument.

Condition

A.2

Except for development also falling within Class A(a), Class A(b) development is permitted subject to the condition that any structure erected in accordance with that permission is removed at the expiry of a period of 6 months (or such longer period as the local planning authority may agree in writing) from the date on which work to erect the structure was begun.

Interpretation of Class A

A.3

For the purposes of Class A, 'building or monument' means any building or monument in the guardianship of Historic England or owned, controlled or managed by it.

Class B—demolition of buildings

Permitted development

B *Any building operation consisting of the demolition of a building.*

Development not permitted

B.1

Development is not permitted by Class B if—

    (a) the building has been rendered unsafe or otherwise uninhabitable by the action or inaction of any person having an interest in the land on which the building stands and it is practicable to secure safety or health by works of repair or works for affording temporary support;

    (b) the demolition is 'relevant demolition' for the purposes of section 196D of the Act (demolition of an unlisted etc building in a conservation area); or

    (c) the building is a specified building and the development is undertaken during the specified period, regardless of whether, in relation to the development, a prior approval event has occurred.

Conditions

B.2

Development is permitted by Class B subject to the following conditions—

    (a) where demolition is urgently necessary in the interests of safety or health and the measures immediately necessary in such interests are the demolition of the building the developer must, as soon as reasonably practicable, give the local planning authority a written justification of the demolition;

    (b) where the demolition does not fall within paragraph (a) and is not excluded demolition—

        (i) the developer must, before beginning the development—

            (aa) in all cases, apply to the local planning authority for a determination as to whether the prior approval of the authority

Town and Country Planning (General Permitted Development) Order 2015

will be required as to the method of demolition and any proposed restoration of the site; and

(bb) in cases where the building is not a community asset and is used for a purpose falling within Class A4 (drinking establishments) of the Schedule to the Use Classes Order, send a written request to the local planning authority as to whether the building has been nominated;

(ii) an application described in paragraph (b)(i)(aa) must be accompanied by a written description of the proposed development, a statement that a notice has been posted in accordance with paragraph (b)(iv) and any fee required to be paid;

(iii) a request described in paragraph (b)(i)(bb) must include the address of the building, the developer's contact address and, if the developer is content to receive communications electronically, the developer's email address;

(iv) subject to paragraph (b)(v), the applicant must display a site notice by site display on or near the land on which the building to be demolished is sited and must leave the notice in place for not less than 21 days in the period of 28 days beginning with the date on which the application was submitted to the local planning authority;

(v) where the site notice is, without any fault or intention of the applicant, removed, obscured or defaced before the period of 21 days referred to in paragraph (b)(iv) has elapsed, the applicant is treated as having complied with the requirements of that paragraph if the applicant has taken reasonable steps for protection of the notice and, if need be, its replacement;

(vi) where the building is used for a purpose falling within Class A4 (drinking establishments) of the Schedule to the Use Classes Order and the building is nominated, whether at the date of request under paragraph (b)(i)(bb) or on a later date, the local planning authority must notify the developer as soon as is reasonably practicable after it is aware of the nomination, and on notification development is not permitted for the specified period;

(vii) subject to paragraph (b)(x), the development must not begin before the occurrence of one of the following—

(aa) the receipt by the applicant from the local planning authority of a written notice of their determination that such prior approval is not required;

(bb) where the local planning authority give the applicant notice within 28 days following the date of receiving the application of their determination that such prior approval is required, the giving of such approval; or

(cc) the expiry of 28 days following the date on which the application was received by the local planning authority without the local planning authority making any determination as to whether such approval is required or notifying the applicant of their determination;

(viii) the development must, except to the extent that the local planning authority otherwise agree in writing, be carried out—

(aa) where prior approval is required, in accordance with the details approved;

(bb) where prior approval is not required, in accordance with the details submitted with the application;

(ix) subject to paragraph (b)(x), the development must be carried out—

(aa) where approval has been given by the local planning authority, within a period of 5 years from the date on which approval was given;

(bb) in any other case, within a period of 5 years from the date on which the local planning authority were given the information referred to in paragraph (b)(ii); and

(x) where the building is used for a purpose falling within Class A4 (drinking establishments) of the Schedule to the Use Classes Order, in addition to the requirements of paragraph (b)(vii) and (ix), the development must not begin before the expiry of a period of 56 days following the date of request under paragraph (b)(i)(bb) and must be completed within a period of 1 year of the date of that request.

Interpretation of Class B

B.3

For the purposes of Class B—

'community asset' means a building which has been entered onto a list of assets of community value including any building which has been subsequently excluded from that list under regulation 2(b) of the Assets of Community Value (England) Regulations 2012;

'excluded demolition' means demolition—

(a) on land which is the subject of a planning permission, for the redevelopment of the land, granted on an application or deemed to be granted under Part 3 of the Act (control over development),

(b) permitted to be carried out by a consent under Part 1 of the Ancient Monuments and Archaeological Areas Act 1979 (scheduled monument consent),

(c) permitted to be carried out by a consent under Part 1 of the Planning (Listed Buildings and Conservation Areas) Act 1990 (listed building consent),

(d) required or permitted to be carried out by or under any other enactment, or

(e) required to be carried out by virtue of a relevant obligation;

'list of assets of community value' means a list of land of community value maintained by a local authority under section 87(1) of the Localism Act 2011;

'nomination' means a nomination made under section 89(2) of the Localism Act 2011 for a building to be included in a list of assets of community value and 'nominated' is to be interpreted accordingly;

'prior approval event' means, in relation to a particular development—

(a) the giving of prior approval by the local planning authority in relation to the matters in paragraph B.2(b)(i)(aa);

(b) a determination that such approval is not required to be given, or

(c) the expiry of the period for giving such a determination without the applicant being notified whether prior approval is required, given or refused;

'relevant obligation' means—

(a) an obligation arising under an agreement made under section 106 of the Act, as originally enacted (agreements regulating development or use of land);

(b) a planning obligation entered into under section 106 of the Act, as substituted by section 12 of the Planning and Compensation Act 1991 (planning obligations), or under section 299A of the Act (Crown planning obligations);

(c) an obligation arising under, or under an agreement made under, any provision corresponding to section 106 of the Act, as originally enacted or as substituted by the Planning and Compensation Act 1991, or to section 299A of the Act;

'site notice' means a notice containing—

(a) the name of the applicant,

(b) a description, including the address, of the building or buildings which it is proposed to be demolished,

(c) a statement that the applicant has applied to the local planning authority for a determination as to whether the prior approval of the authority will be required as to the method of demolition and any proposed restoration of the site,

(d) the date on which the applicant proposes to carry out the demolition, and

(e) the name and address of the local planning authority,

and which is signed and dated by or on behalf of the applicant;

'specified building' means a building used for a purpose falling within Class A4 (drinking establishments) of the Schedule to the Use Classes Order—

(a) which is a community asset; or

(b) in relation to which the local planning authority has notified the developer of a nomination under paragraph B.2(b)(vi); and

'specified period' means—

(a) in relation to a building which is subject to a nomination of which the local planning authority have notified the developer under paragraph B.2(b)(vi), the period from the date of that notification to the date on which the building is entered onto—

(i) a list of assets of community value; or

(ii) a list of land nominated by unsuccessful community nominations under section 93 of the Localism Act 2011;

(b) in relation to a building which is a community asset—

(i) 5 years beginning with the date on which the building was entered onto the list of assets of community value; or

(ii) where the building was removed from that list—

(aa) under regulation 2(c) of the Assets of Community Value (England) Regulations 2012 following a successful appeal against listing or because the local authority no longer consider the land to be land of community value; or

(bb) under section 92(4)(a) of the Localism Act 2011 following the local authority's decision on a review that the land concerned should not have been included in the local authority's list of assets of community value,

the period from the date on which the building was entered onto the list of assets of community value to the date on which it was removed from that list.

Class C—demolition of gates, fences, walls etc

Permitted development

C *Any building operation consisting of the demolition of the whole or any part of any gate, fence, wall or other means of enclosure.*

Development not permitted

C 1

Development is not permitted by Class C if the demolition is 'relevant demolition' for the purposes of section 196D of the Act (demolition of an unlisted etc building in a conservation area).

PART 12 DEVELOPMENT BY LOCAL AUTHORITIES

Class A

Permitted development

A *The erection or construction and the maintenance, improvement or other alteration by a local authority or by an urban development corporation of—*

(a) any small ancillary building, works or equipment on land belonging to or maintained by them required for the purposes of any function exercised by them on that land otherwise than as statutory undertakers;

(b) lamp standards, information kiosks, passenger shelters, public shelters and seats, telephone boxes, fire alarms, public drinking fountains, horse troughs, refuse bins or baskets, barriers for the control of people waiting to enter public service vehicles, electric vehicle charging points and any associated infrastructure, and similar structures or works required in connection with the operation of any public service administered by them.

Interpretation of Class A

A.1

For the purposes of Class A, 'urban development corporation' has the same meaning as in Part 16 of the Local Government, Planning and Land Act 1980 (urban development).

A.2

The reference in Class A to any small ancillary building, works or equipment is a reference to any ancillary building, works or equipment not exceeding 4 metres in height or 200 cubic metres in capacity.

Town and Country Planning (General Permitted Development) Order 2015

Class B

Permitted development

B *The deposit by a local authority of waste material on any land comprised in a site which was used for that purpose on 1st July 1948 whether or not the superficial area or the height of the deposit is extended as a result.*

Development not permitted

B.1

Development is not permitted by Class B if the waste material is or includes material resulting from the winning and working of minerals.

Interpretation of Part 12

C

For the purposes of Part 12, 'local authority' includes a parish council.

PART 13 WATER AND SEWERAGE

Class A—Water or hydraulic power undertakings

Permitted development

A *Development for the purposes of their undertaking by statutory undertakers for the supply of water or hydraulic power consisting of—*
   (a) development not above ground level required in connection with the supply of water or for conserving, redistributing or augmenting water resources, or for the conveyance of water treatment sludge;
   (b) development in, on or under any watercourse and required in connection with the improvement or maintenance of that watercourse;
   (c) the provision of a building, plant, machinery or apparatus in, on, over or under land for the purpose of survey or investigation;
   (d) the maintenance, improvement or repair of works for measuring the flow in any watercourse or channel;
   (e) the installation in a water distribution system of a booster station, valve house, meter or switch-gear house;
   (f) any works authorised by or required in connection with an order made under section 73 of the Water Resources Act 1991 (power to make ordinary and emergency drought orders);
   (g) any other development in, on, over or under operational land other than the provision of a building but including the extension or alteration of a building.

Development not permitted

A.1

Development is not permitted by Class A if—

Town and Country Planning (General Permitted Development) Order 2015

(a) in the case of any Class A(a) development, it would include the construction of a reservoir;

(b) in the case of any Class A(e) development involving the installation of a station or house exceeding 29 cubic metres in capacity, that installation is carried out at or above ground level or under a highway used by vehicular traffic;

(c) in the case of any Class A(g) development, it would consist of or include the extension or alteration of a building so that—

   (i) its design or external appearance would be materially affected;

   (ii) the height of the original building would be exceeded, or the cubic content of the original building would be exceeded by more than 25%, or

   (iii) the floor space of the original building would be exceeded by more than 1,000 square metres; or

(d) in the case of any Class A(g) development, it would consist of the installation or erection of any plant or machinery exceeding 15 metres in height or the height of anything it replaces, whichever is the greater.

Condition

A.2

Development is permitted by Class A(c) subject to the condition that, on completion of the survey or investigation, or at the expiration of 6 months from the commencement of the development, whichever is the sooner, all such operations cease and all such buildings, plant, machinery and apparatus are removed and the land restored as soon as reasonably practicable to its former condition (or to any other condition which may be agreed with the local planning authority).

Class B—development by or on behalf of sewerage undertakers

Permitted development

B   *Development by or on behalf of a sewerage undertaker consisting of—*

   (a) development not above ground level required in connection with the provision, improvement, maintenance or repair of a sewer, outfall pipe, sludge main or associated apparatus;

   (b) the provision of a building, plant, machinery or apparatus in, on, over or under land for the purpose of survey or investigation;

   (c) the maintenance, improvement or repair of works for measuring the flow in any watercourse or channel;

   (d) the installation in a sewerage system of a pumping station, valve house, control panel house or switch-gear house;

   (e) any works authorised by or required in connection with an order made under section 73 of the Water Resources Act 1991 (power to make ordinary and emergency drought orders);

   (f) any other development in, on, over or under their operational land, other than the provision of a building but including the extension or alteration of a building.

Town and Country Planning (General Permitted Development) Order 2015

Development not permitted

B.1

Development is not permitted by Class B if—

(a) in the case of any Class B(d) development involving the installation of a station or house exceeding 29 cubic metres in capacity, that installation is carried out at or above ground level or under a highway used by vehicular traffic;

(b) in the case of Class B(f) development, it would consist of or include the extension or alteration of a building so that—

(i) its design or external appearance would be materially affected;

(ii) the height of the original building would be exceeded, or the cubic content of the original building would be exceeded, by more than 25%; or

(iii) the floor space of the original building would be exceeded by more than 1,000 square metres; or

(c) in the case of Class B(f) development, it would consist of the installation or erection of any plant or machinery exceeding 15 metres in height or the height of anything it replaces, whichever is the greater.

Condition

B.2

Development is permitted by Class B(b) subject to the condition that, on completion of the survey or investigation, or at the expiration of 6 months from the commencement of the development concerned, whichever is the sooner, all such operations cease and all such buildings, plant, machinery and apparatus are removed and the land restored as soon as reasonably practicable to its former condition (or to any other condition which may be agreed with the local planning authority).

Interpretation of Class B

B.3

For the purposes of Class B—

'associated apparatus', in relation to any sewer, main or pipe, means pumps, machinery or apparatus associated with the relevant sewer, main or pipe; and

'sludge main' means a pipe or system of pipes (together with any pumps or other machinery or apparatus associated with it) for the conveyance of the residue of water or sewage treated in a water or sewage treatment works as the case may be, including final effluent or the products of the dewatering or incineration of such residue, or partly for any of those purposes and partly for the conveyance of trade effluent or its residue.

Class C—development by drainage bodies

Permitted development

C   *Development by a drainage body in, on or under any watercourse or land drainage works required in connection with the improvement, maintenance or repair of that watercourse or those works.*

Town and Country Planning (General Permitted Development) Order 2015

Interpretation of Class C

C 1

For the purposes of Class C, 'drainage body' has the same meaning as in section 72(1) of the Land Drainage Act 1991 (interpretation) other than the Environment Agency.

Class D—development by the Environment Agency

Permitted development

D   Development by the Environment Agency for the purposes of its functions, consisting of—
   (a) development not above ground level required in connection with conserving, redistributing or augmenting water resources;
   (b) development in, on or under any watercourse or land drainage works and required in connection with the improvement, maintenance or repair of that watercourse or those works;
   (c) the provision of a building, plant, machinery or apparatus in, on, over or under land for the purpose of survey or investigation;
   (d) the maintenance, improvement or repair of works for measuring the flow in any watercourse or channel;
   (e) any works authorised by or required in connection with an order made under section 73 of the Water Resources Act 1991 (power to make ordinary and emergency drought orders);
   (f) any other development in, on, over or under their operational land, other than the provision of a building but including the extension or alteration of a building.

Development not permitted

D.1

Development is not permitted by Class D if—
   (a) in the case of any Class D(a) development, it would include the construction of a reservoir;
   (b) in the case of any Class D(f) development, it would consist of or include the extension or alteration of a building so that—
      (i) its design or external appearance would be materially affected,
      (ii) the height of the original building would be exceeded, or the cubic content of the original building would be exceeded by more than 25%, or
      (iii) the floor space of the original building would be exceeded by more than 1,000 square metres; or
   (c) in the case of any Class D(f) development, it would consist of the installation or erection of any plant or machinery exceeding 15 metres in height or the height of anything it replaces, whichever is the greater.

Condition

D.2

Development is permitted by Class D(c) subject to the condition that, on completion of the survey or investigation, or at the expiration of 6 months from the commencement of the development concerned, whichever is the sooner, all such operations cease and all such buildings, plant, machinery and apparatus are removed and the land restored as soon as reasonably practicable to its former condition (or to any other condition which may be agreed with the local planning authority).

PART 14 RENEWABLE ENERGY

Class A—installation or alteration etc of solar equipment on domestic premises

Permitted development

A The installation, alteration or replacement of microgeneration solar PV or solar thermal equipment on—
  (a) a dwellinghouse or a block of flats; or
  (b) a building situated within the curtilage of a dwellinghouse or a block of flats.

Development not permitted

A.1

Development is not permitted by Class A if—
  (a) the solar PV or solar thermal equipment would protrude more than 0.2 metres beyond the plane of the wall or the roof slope when measured from the perpendicular with the external surface of the wall or roof slope;
  (b) it would result in the highest part of the solar PV or solar thermal equipment being higher than the highest part of the roof (excluding any chimney);
  (c) in the case of land within a conservation area or which is a World Heritage Site, the solar PV or solar thermal equipment would be installed on a wall which fronts a highway;
  (d) the solar PV or solar thermal equipment would be installed on a site designated as a scheduled monument; or
  (e) the solar PV or solar thermal equipment would be installed on a building within the curtilage of the dwellinghouse or block of flats if the dwellinghouse or block of flats is a listed building.

Conditions

A.2

Development is permitted by Class A subject to the following conditions—
  (a) solar PV or solar thermal equipment is, so far as practicable, sited so as to minimise its effect on the external appearance of the building;
  (b) solar PV or solar thermal equipment is, so far as practicable, sited so as to minimise its effect on the amenity of the area; and
  (c) solar PV or solar thermal equipment is removed as soon as reasonably practicable when no longer needed.

Class B—installation or alteration etc of stand-alone solar equipment on domestic premises

Permitted development

B The installation, alteration or replacement of stand-alone solar for microgeneration within the curtilage of a dwellinghouse or a block of flats.

Town and Country Planning (General Permitted Development) Order 2015

Development not permitted

B.1

Development is not permitted by Class B if—
- (a) in the case of the installation of stand-alone solar, the development would result in the presence within the curtilage of more than 1 stand-alone solar;
- (b) any part of the stand-alone solar—
  - (i) would exceed 4 metres in height;
  - (ii) would, in the case of land within a conservation area or which is a World Heritage Site, be installed so that it is nearer to any highway which bounds the curtilage than the part of the dwellinghouse or block of flats which is nearest to that highway;
  - (iii) would be installed within 5 metres of the boundary of the curtilage;
  - (iv) would be installed within the curtilage of a listed building; or
  - (v) would be installed on a site designated as a scheduled monument; or
- (c) the surface area of the solar panels forming part of the stand-alone solar would exceed 9 square metres or any dimension of its array (including any housing) would exceed 3 metres.

Conditions

B.2

Development is permitted by Class B subject to the following conditions—
- (a) stand-alone solar is, so far as practicable, sited so as to minimise its effect on the amenity of the area; and
- (b) stand-alone solar is removed as soon as reasonably practicable when no longer needed.

Class C—installation or alteration etc of ground source heat pumps on domestic premises

Permitted development

C   *The installation, alteration or replacement of a microgeneration ground source heat pump within the curtilage of a dwellinghouse or a block of flats.*

Class D—installation or alteration etc of water source heat pumps on domestic premises

Permitted development

D   *The installation, alteration or replacement of a microgeneration water source heat pump within the curtilage of a dwellinghouse or a block of flats.*

Class E—installation or alteration etc of flue for biomass heating system on domestic premises

Permitted development

E   *The installation, alteration or replacement of a flue, forming part of a micro-generation biomass heating system, on a dwellinghouse or a block of flats.*

Town and Country Planning (General Permitted Development) Order 2015

Development not permitted

E.1

Development is not permitted by Class E if—

    (a) the height of the flue would exceed the highest part of the roof by 1 metre or more; or

    (b) in the case of land within a conservation area or which is a World Heritage Site, the flue would be installed on a wall or roof slope which fronts a highway.

Class F—installation or alteration etc of flue for combined heat and power on domestic premises

Permitted development

F   *The installation, alteration or replacement of a flue, forming part of a microgeneration combined heat and power system, on a dwellinghouse or a block of flats.*

Development not permitted

F.1

Development is not permitted by Class F if—

    (a) the height of the flue would exceed the highest part of the roof by 1 metre or more; or

    (b) in the case of land within a conservation area or which is a World Heritage Site, the flue would be installed on a wall or roof slope which fronts a highway.

Class G—installation or alteration etc of air source heat pumps on domestic premises

Permitted Development

G   *The installation, alteration or replacement of a microgeneration air source heat pump—*

    (a) on a dwellinghouse or a block of flats; or

    (b) within the curtilage of a dwellinghouse or a block of flats, including on a building within that curtilage.

Development not permitted

G.1

Development is not permitted by Class G unless the air source heat pump complies with the MCS Planning Standards or equivalent standards.

G.2

Development is not permitted by Class G if—

    (a) in the case of the installation of an air source heat pump, the development would result in the presence of more than 1 air source heat pump on the same building or within the curtilage of the building or block of flats;

(b) in the case of the installation of an air source heat pump, a wind turbine is installed on the same building or within the curtilage of the dwellinghouse or block of flats;

(c) in the case of the installation of an air source heat pump, a stand-alone wind turbine is installed within the curtilage of the dwellinghouse or block of flats;

(d) the volume of the air source heat pump's outdoor compressor unit (including any housing) would exceed 0.6 cubic metres;

(e) any part of the air source heat pump would be installed within 1 metre of the boundary of the curtilage of the dwellinghouse or block of flats;

(f) the air source heat pump would be installed on a pitched roof;

(g) the air source heat pump would be installed on a flat roof where it would be within 1 metre of the external edge of that roof;

(h) the air source heat pump would be installed on a site designated as a scheduled monument;

(i) the air source heat pump would be installed on a building or on land within the curtilage of the dwellinghouse or the block of flats if the dwellinghouse or the block of flats is a listed building;

(j) in the case of land within a conservation area or which is a World Heritage Site the air source heat pump—

  (i) would be installed on a wall or a roof which fronts a highway; or

  (ii) would be installed so that it is nearer to any highway which bounds the curtilage than the part of the dwellinghouse or block of flats which is nearest to that highway; or

(k) in the case of land, other than land within a conservation area or which is a World Heritage Site, the air source heat pump would be installed on a wall of a dwellinghouse or block of flats if—

  (i) that wall fronts a highway; and

  (ii) the air source heat pump would be installed on any part of that wall which is above the level of the ground floor storey.

Conditions

G.3

Development is permitted by Class G subject to the following conditions—

(a) the air source heat pump is used solely for heating purposes;

(b) the air source heat pump is, so far as practicable, sited so as to minimise its effect on the external appearance of the building;

(c) the air source heat pump is, so far as practicable, sited so as to minimise its effect on the amenity of the area; and

(d) the air source heat pump is removed as soon as reasonably practicable when no longer needed.

Town and Country Planning (General Permitted Development) Order 2015

Class H—*installation or alteration etc of wind turbine on domestic premises*

Permitted Development

H   *The installation, alteration or replacement of a microgeneration wind turbine on—*
   (a) a detached dwellinghouse; or
   (b) a detached building situated within the curtilage of a dwellinghouse or a block of flats.

Development not permitted

H.1

Development is not permitted by Class H unless the wind turbine complies with the MCS Planning Standards or equivalent standards.

H.2

Development is not permitted by Class H if—
   (a) in the case of the installation of a wind turbine the development would result in the presence of more than 1 wind turbine on the same building or within the curtilage;
   (b) in the case of the installation of a wind turbine, a stand-alone wind turbine is installed within the curtilage of the dwellinghouse or the block of flats;
   (c) in the case of the installation of a wind turbine, an air source heat pump is installed on the same building or within its curtilage;
   (d) the highest part of the wind turbine (including blades) would either—
      (i) protrude more than 3 metres above the highest part of the roof (excluding the chimney); or
      (ii) exceed more than 15 metres in height,
      whichever is the lesser;
   (e) the distance between ground level and the lowest part of any blade of the wind turbine would be less than 5 metres;
   (f) any part of the wind turbine (including blades) would be positioned so that it would be within 5 metres of any boundary of the curtilage of the dwellinghouse or the block of flats;
   (g) the swept area of any blade of the wind turbine would exceed 3.8 square metres;
   (h) the wind turbine would be installed on safeguarded land;
   (i) the wind turbine would be installed on a site designated as a scheduled monument;
   (j) the wind turbine would be installed within the curtilage of a building which is a listed building;
   (k) in the case of land within a conservation area, the wind turbine would be installed on a wall or roof slope of—
      (i) the detached dwellinghouse; or
      (ii) a building within the curtilage of the dwellinghouse or block of flats, which fronts a highway; or

Town and Country Planning (General Permitted Development) Order 2015

(l) the wind turbine would be installed on article 2(3) land other than land within a conservation area.

Conditions

H.3

Development is permitted by Class H subject to the following conditions—
  (a) the blades of the wind turbine is made of non-reflective materials;
  (b) the wind turbine is, so far as practicable, sited so as to minimise its effect on the external appearance of the building;
  (c) the wind turbine is, so far as practicable, sited so as to minimise its effect on the amenity of the area; and
  (d) the wind turbine is removed as soon as reasonably practicable when no longer needed.

Class I—installation or alteration etc of stand-alone wind turbine on domestic premises

Permitted Development

I ***The installation, alteration or replacement of a stand-alone wind turbine for microgeneration within the curtilage of a dwellinghouse or a block of flats.***

Development not permitted

I.1

Development is not permitted by Class I unless the stand-alone wind turbine complies with the MCS Planning Standards or equivalent standards.

I.2

Development is not permitted by Class I if—
  (a) in the case of the installation of a stand-alone wind turbine, the development would result in the presence of more than 1 stand-alone wind turbine within the curtilage of the dwellinghouse or block of flats;
  (b) in the case of the installation of a stand-alone wind turbine, a wind turbine is installed on the dwellinghouse or on a building within the curtilage of the dwellinghouse or the block of flats;
  (c) in the case of the installation of a stand-alone wind turbine, an air source heat pump is installed on the dwellinghouse or block of flats or within the curtilage of the dwellinghouse or block of flats;
  (d) the highest part of the stand-alone wind turbine would exceed 11.1 metres in height;
  (e) the distance between ground level and the lowest part of any blade of the stand-alone wind turbine would be less than 5 metres;
  (f) any part of the stand-alone wind turbine (including blades) would be located in a position which is less than a distance equivalent to the overall height (including blades) of the stand-alone wind turbine plus 10% of its height when measured from any point along the boundary of the curtilage;

(g) the swept area of any blade of the stand-alone wind turbine exceeds 3.8 square metres;

(h) the stand-alone wind turbine would be installed on safeguarded land;

(i) the stand-alone wind turbine would be installed on a site designated as a scheduled monument;

(j) the stand-alone wind turbine would be installed within the curtilage of a building which is a listed building;

(k) in the case of land within a conservation area, the stand-alone wind turbine would be installed so that it is nearer to any highway which bounds the curtilage than the part of the dwellinghouse or block of flats which is nearest to that highway; or

(l) the stand-alone wind turbine would be installed on article 2(3) land other than land within a conservation area.

Conditions

I.3

Development is permitted by Class I subject to the following conditions—

(a) the blades of the stand-alone wind turbine is made of non-reflective materials;

(b) the stand-alone wind turbine is, so far as practicable, sited so as to minimise its effect on the amenity of the area; and

(c) the stand-alone wind turbine is removed as soon as reasonably practicable when no longer needed.

Class J—installation or alteration etc of solar equipment on non-domestic premises

Permitted development

J *The installation, alteration or replacement of—*

(a) microgeneration solar thermal equipment on a building;

(b) microgeneration solar PV equipment on a building; or

(c) other solar PV equipment on the roof of a building,

other than a dwellinghouse or a block of flats.

Development not permitted

J.1

Development is not permitted by Class J if—

(a) the solar PV equipment or solar thermal equipment would be installed on a pitched roof and would protrude more than 0.2 metres beyond the plane of the roof slope when measured from the perpendicular with the external surface of the roof slope;

(b) the solar PV equipment or solar thermal equipment would be installed on a flat roof, where the highest part of the solar PV equipment would be higher than 1 metre above the highest part of the roof (excluding any chimney);

(c) the solar PV equipment or solar thermal equipment would be installed within 1 metre of the external edge of that roof;

- (d) in the case of a building on article 2(3) land, the solar PV equipment or solar thermal equipment would be installed on a roof slope which fronts a highway;
- (e) the solar PV equipment or solar thermal equipment would be installed on a site designated as a scheduled monument; or
- (f) the solar PV equipment or solar thermal equipment would be installed on a listed building or on a building within the curtilage of a listed building.

J.2

Development is not permitted by Class J(a) or (b) if—
- (a) the solar PV equipment or solar thermal equipment would be installed on a wall and would protrude more than 0.2 metres beyond the plane of the wall when measured from the perpendicular with the external surface of the wall;
- (b) the solar PV equipment or solar thermal equipment would be installed on a wall and within 1 metre of a junction of that wall with another wall or with the roof of the building; or
- (c) in the case of a building on article 2(3) land, the solar PV equipment or solar thermal equipment would be installed on a wall which fronts a highway.

J.3

Development is not permitted by Class J(c) if the capacity of the solar PV equipment installed (together with any solar PV equipment installed under Class J(b)) to generate electricity exceeds 1 megawatt.

Conditions

J.4

(1) Class J development is permitted subject to the following conditions—
- (a) the solar PV equipment or solar thermal equipment must, so far as practicable, be sited so as to minimise its effect on the external appearance of the building and the amenity of the area; and
- (b) the solar PV equipment or solar thermal equipment is removed as soon as reasonably practicable when no longer needed.

(2) Class J(c) development is permitted subject to the condition that before beginning the development the developer must apply to the local planning authority for a determination as to whether the prior approval of the authority will be required as to the design or external appearance of the development, in particular the impact of glare on occupiers of neighbouring land, and the following sub-paragraphs apply in relation to that application.

(3) The application must be accompanied by—
- (a) a written description of the proposed development;
- (b) a plan indicating the site and showing the proposed development;
- (c) the developer's contact address; and
- (d) the developer's email address if the developer is content to receive communications electronically;

together with any fee required to be paid.

Town and Country Planning (General Permitted Development) Order 2015

(4) The local planning authority may refuse an application where, in the opinion of the authority—

(a) the proposed development does not comply with, or

(b) the developer has provided insufficient information to enable the authority to establish whether the proposed development complies with,

any conditions, limitations or restrictions specified in Class J applicable to the development in question.

(5) Sub-paragraphs (6) and (8) do not apply where a local planning authority refuses an application under sub-paragraph (4) and for the purposes of section 78 (appeals) of the Act such a refusal is to be treated as a refusal of an application for approval.

(6) The local planning authority must give notice of the proposed development—

(a) by site display in at least one place on or near the land to which the application relates for not less than 21 days of a notice which—

(i) describes the proposed development;

(ii) provides the address of the proposed development;

(iii) specifies the date by which representations are to be received by the local planning authority; or

(b) by serving a notice in that form on any adjoining owner or occupier.

(7) The local planning authority may require the developer to submit such information as the authority may reasonably require in order to determine the application.

(8) The local planning authority must, when determining an application—

(a) take into account any representations made to them as a result of any notice given under sub-paragraph (6); and

(b) have regard to the National Planning Policy Framework issued by the Department for Communities and Local Government in March 2012, so far as relevant to the subject matter of the prior approval, as if the application were a planning application.

(9) The development must not begin before the occurrence of one of the following—

(a) the receipt by the applicant from the local planning authority of a written notice of their determination that such prior approval is not required;

(b) the receipt by the applicant from the local planning authority of a written notice giving their prior approval; or

(c) the expiry of 56 days following the date on which the application under sub-paragraph (3) was received by the local planning authority without the authority notifying the applicant as to whether prior approval is given or refused.

(10) The development must be carried out—

(a) where prior approval is required, in accordance with the details approved by the local planning authority;

(b) where prior approval is not required, or where sub-paragraph (9)(c) applies, in accordance with the details provided in the application referred to in sub-paragraph (3), unless the local planning authority and the developer agree otherwise in writing.

(11) The local planning authority may grant prior approval unconditionally or subject to conditions reasonably related to the subject matter of the prior approval.

Class K—installation or alteration etc of stand-alone solar equipment on non-domestic premises

Permitted development

K   The installation, alteration or replacement of stand-alone solar for microgeneration within the curtilage of a building other than a dwellinghouse or a block of flats.

Development not permitted

K.1

Development is not permitted by Class K if—
   (a) in the case of the installation of stand-alone solar, the development would result in the presence within the curtilage of more than 1 stand-alone solar;
   (b) any part of the stand-alone solar—
      (i) would exceed 4 metres in height;
      (ii) would, if installed on any article 2(3) land, be installed so that it is nearer to any highway which bounds the curtilage than the part of the building which is nearest to that highway;
      (iii) would be installed within 5 metres of the boundary of the curtilage;
      (iv) would be installed within the curtilage of a listed building; or
      (v) would be installed on a site designated as a scheduled monument; or
   (c) the surface area of the solar panels forming part of the stand-alone solar would exceed 9 square metres or any dimension of its array (including any housing) would exceed 3 metres.

Conditions

K.2

Development is permitted by Class K subject to the following conditions—
   (a) the stand-alone solar must, so far as practicable, be sited so as to minimise its effect on the amenity of the area; and
   (b) the stand-alone solar is removed as soon as reasonably practicable when no longer needed.

Class L—installation or alteration etc of ground source heat pump on non-domestic premises

Permitted development

L   The installation, alteration or replacement of a microgeneration ground source heat pump within the curtilage of a building other than a dwellinghouse or a block of flats.

Town and Country Planning (General Permitted Development) Order 2015

Conditions

L 1

Development is permitted by Class L subject to the following conditions—
- (a) the total area of excavation must not exceed 0.5 hectares;
- (b) the development must not result in the presence within the curtilage of more than 1 ground source heat pump; and
- (c) a pump is removed as soon as reasonably practicable when no longer needed and the land is, as far as reasonably practicable, restored to its condition before the development took place, or to such condition as may have been agreed in writing between the local planning authority and the developer.

Class M—installation or alteration etc of water source heat pump on non-domestic premises

Permitted development

M   *The installation, alteration or replacement of a microgeneration water source heat pump within the curtilage of a building other than a dwellinghouse or a block of flats.*

Conditions

M.1

Development is permitted by Class M subject to the condition that the total surface area covered by the water source heat pump (including any pipes) must not exceed 0.5 hectares.

Class N—installation etc of flue for biomass heating system on non-domestic premises

Permitted development

N   *The installation, alteration or replacement of a flue, forming part of a microgeneration biomass heating system, on a building other than—*
- *(a) a dwellinghouse or a block of flats; or*
- *(b) a building situated within the curtilage of a dwellinghouse or a block of flats.*

Development not permitted

N.1

Development is not permitted by Class N if—
- (a) the capacity of the system that the flue would serve exceeds 45 kilowatts thermal;
- (b) the height of the flue would exceed either—
    - (i) the highest part of the roof by 1 metre or more, or
    - (ii) the height of an existing flue which is being replaced, whichever is the highest;

Town and Country Planning (General Permitted Development) Order 2015

(c) the installation of the flue would result in the installation on the same building of more than 1 flue forming part of either a biomass heating system or a combined heat and power system;

(d) the flue would be installed on a listed building, within the curtilage of a listed building or on a site designated as a scheduled monument; or

(e) in the case of a building on article 2(3) land, the flue would be installed on a wall or roof slope which fronts a highway.

Class O—installation etc of flue for combined heat and power on non-domestic premises

Permitted development

O   *The installation, alteration or replacement of a flue, forming part of a microgeneration combined heat and power system, on a building other than—*

(a) *a dwellinghouse or a block of flats; or*

(b) *a building situated within the curtilage of a dwellinghouse or a block of flats.*

Development not permitted

O.1

Development is not permitted by Class O if—

(a) the capacity of the system that the flue would serve exceeds 45 kilowatts thermal;

(b) the height of the flue would exceed either—

(i) the highest part of the roof by 1 metre or more, or

(ii) the height of an existing flue which is being replaced,

whichever is the highest;

(c) the installation of the flue would result in the installation on the same building of more than 1 flue forming part of either a biomass heating system or a combined heat and power system;

(d) the flue would be installed on a listed building, within the curtilage of a listed building, or on a site designated as a scheduled monument; or

(e) in the case of a building on article 2(3) land, the flue would be installed on a wall or roof slope which fronts a highway.

Interpretation of Part 14

P

For the purposes of Part 14—

'aerodrome'—

(a) means any area of land or water designed, equipped, set apart, or commonly used for affording facilities for the landing and departure of aircraft; and

(b) includes any area or space, whether on the ground, on the roof of a building or elsewhere, which is designed, equipped or set apart for

Town and Country Planning (General Permitted Development) Order 2015

affording facilities for the landing and departure of aircraft capable of descending or climbing vertically; but

(c) does not include any area the use of which for affording facilities for the landing and departure of aircraft has been abandoned and has not been resumed;

'air traffic services licence holder' means a person who holds a licence under Chapter 1 of Part 1 of the Transport Act 2000;

'block of flats' means a building which consists wholly of flats;

'detached dwellinghouse' or 'detached building' means a dwellinghouse or building, as the case may be, which does not share a party wall with a neighbouring building;

'MCS Planning Standards' means the standards specified in the Microgeneration Certification Scheme for air source heat pumps (being MCS 007) and for small and micro wind turbines (being MCS 006);

'microgeneration' has the same meaning as in section 82(6) of the Energy Act 2004;

'safeguarded land' means land which—

(a) is necessary to be safeguarded for aviation or defence purposes; and

(b) has been notified as such, in writing, to the Secretary of State by an aerodrome operator, an air traffic services licence holder or the Secretary of State for Defence for the purposes of this Part;

'solar PV' means solar photovoltaics;

'stand-alone solar' means solar PV or solar thermal equipment which is not installed on a building;

'stand-alone wind turbine' means a wind turbine which is not fixed to a building; and

'water source heat pump' means a heat pump where the collecting medium is water.

PART 15 POWER RELATED DEVELOPMENT

Class A—gas transporters

Permitted development

A *Development by a gas transporter required for the purposes of its undertaking consisting of—*

(a) the laying underground of mains, pipes or other apparatus;

(b) the installation in a gas distribution system of apparatus for measuring, recording, controlling or varying the pressure, flow or volume of gas, and structures for housing such apparatus;

(c) the construction in any storage area or protective area specified in an order made under section 4 of the Gas Act 1965 (storage authorisation orders), of boreholes, and the erection or construction in any such area of any plant or machinery required in connection with the construction of such boreholes;

(d) the placing and storage on land of pipes and other apparatus to be included in a main or pipe which is being or is about to be laid or

constructed in pursuance of planning permission granted or deemed to be granted under Part 3 of the Act (control over development);

(e) the erection on operational land of the gas transporter of a building solely for the protection of plant or machinery;

(f) any other development carried out in, on, over or under the operational land of the gas transporter.

Development not permitted

A.1

Development is not permitted by Class A if—

(a) in the case of any Class A(b) development involving the installation of a structure for housing apparatus exceeding 29 cubic metres in capacity, that installation would be carried out at or above ground level, or under a highway used by vehicular traffic;

(b) in the case of any Class A(c) development—

   (i) the borehole is shown in an order approved by the Secretary of State for the purpose of section 4(6) of the Gas Act 1965; or

   (ii) any plant or machinery would exceed 6 metres in height;

(c) in the case of any Class A(e) development, the building would exceed 15 metres in height; or

(d) in the case of any Class A(f) development—

   (i) it would consist of or include the erection of a building, or the reconstruction or alteration of a building where its design or external appearance would be materially affected;

   (ii) it would involve the installation of plant or machinery exceeding 15 metres in height, or capable without the carrying out of additional works of being extended to a height exceeding 15 metres; or

   (iii) it would consist of or include the replacement of any plant or machinery, by plant or machinery exceeding 15 metres in height or exceeding the height of the plant or machinery replaced, whichever is the greater.

Conditions

A.2

Development is permitted by Class A subject to the following conditions—

(a) in the case of any Class A(a) development, not less than 8 weeks before the beginning of operations to lay a notifiable pipe-line, the gas transporter must give notice in writing to the local planning authority of its intention to carry out that development, identifying the land under which the pipe-line is to be laid;

(b) in the case of any Class A(d) development, on completion of the laying or construction of the main or pipe, or at the expiry of a period of 9 months from the beginning of the development, whichever is the sooner, any pipes or other apparatus still stored on the land are removed and the land restored as soon as reasonably practicable to its condition before the development took place (or to any other condition which may be agreed with the local planning authority); and

(c) in the case of any Class A(e) development, approval of the details of the design and external appearance of the building must be obtained, before the development is begun, from—

(i) in Greater London or a metropolitan county, the local planning authority,

(ii) in a National Park, outside a metropolitan county, the county planning authority,

(iii) in any other case, the district planning authority.

Class B—electricity undertakings

Permitted development

B   *Development by statutory undertakers for the generation, transmission, distribution or supply of electricity for the purposes of their undertaking consisting of—*

(a) the installation or replacement in, on, over or under land of an electric line and the construction of shafts and tunnels and the installation or replacement of feeder or service pillars or transforming or switching stations or chambers reasonably necessary in connection with an electric line;

(b) the installation or replacement of any electronic communications line which connects any part of an electric line to any electrical plant or building, and the installation or replacement of any support for any such line;

(c) the sinking of boreholes to ascertain the nature of the subsoil and the installation of any plant or machinery reasonably necessary in connection with such boreholes;

(d) the extension or alteration of buildings on operational land;

(e) the erection on operational land of the undertaking or a building solely for the protection of plant or machinery;

(f) any other development carried out in, on, over or under the operational land of the undertaking.

Development not permitted

B.1

Development is not permitted by Class B if—

(a) in the case of any Class B(a) development—

(i) it would consist of or include the installation or replacement of an electric line to which section 37(1) of the Electricity Act 1989 (consent required for overhead lines) applies; or

(ii) it would consist of or include the installation or replacement at or above ground level or under a highway used by vehicular traffic, of a chamber for housing apparatus and the chamber would exceed 29 cubic metres in capacity;

(b) in the case of any Class B(b) development—

(i) the development would take place in a National Park, an area of outstanding natural beauty, or a site of special scientific interest;

Town and Country Planning (General Permitted Development) Order 2015

    (ii) the height of any support would exceed 15 metres; or

    (iii) the electronic communications line would exceed 1,000 metres in length;

(c) in the case of any Class B(d) development—

    (i) the height of the original building would be exceeded;

    (ii) the cubic content of the original building would be exceeded by more than 25% or, in the case of any building on article 2(3) land, by more than 10%, or

    (iii) the floor space of the original building would be exceeded by more than 1,000 square metres or, in the case of any building on article 2(3) land, by more than 500 square metres;

(d) in the case of any Class B(e) development, the building would exceed 15 metres in height, or

(e) in the case of any Class B(f) development, it would consist of or include—

    (i) the erection of a building, or the reconstruction or alteration of a building where its design or external appearance would be materially affected, or

    (ii) the installation or erection by way of addition or replacement of any plant or machinery exceeding 15 metres in height or the height of any plant or machinery replaced, whichever is the greater.

Conditions

B.2

Development is permitted by Class B subject to the following conditions—

(a) in the case of any Class B(a) development consisting of or including the replacement of an existing electric line, compliance with any conditions contained in a planning permission relating to the height, design or position of the existing electric line which are capable of being applied to the replacement line;

(b) in the case of any Class B(a) development consisting of or including the installation of a temporary electric line providing a diversion for an existing electric line, on the ending of the diversion or at the end of a period of 6 months from the completion of the installation (whichever is the sooner) the temporary electric line is removed and the land on which any operations have been carried out to install that line is restored as soon as reasonably practicable to its condition before the installation took place;

(c) in the case of any Class B(c) development, on the completion of that development, or at the end of a period of 6 months from the beginning of that development (whichever is the sooner) any plant or machinery installed is removed and the land is restored as soon as reasonably practicable to its condition before the development took place; and

(d) in the case of any Class B(e) development, approval of details of the design and external appearance of the buildings must be obtained, before development is begun, from—

    (i) in Greater London or a metropolitan county, the local planning authority,

    (ii) in a National Park, outside a metropolitan county, the county planning authority,

    (iii) in any other case, the district planning authority.

Town and Country Planning (General Permitted Development) Order 2015

Interpretation of Class B

B.3

For the purposes of Class B(a), 'electric line' has the meaning given by section 64(1) of the Electricity Act 1989 (interpretation etc of Part 1).

B.4

For the purposes of Class B(b)—

'electrical plant' has the meaning given by section 64(1) to that Act; and

'electronic communications line' means a line which forms part of an electronic communications apparatus, (and both line and electronic communications apparatus have the meaning given in paragraph 1 of Schedule 2 to the Telecommunications Act 1984 (the electronic communications code)).

B.5

For the purposes of Class B(d), (e) and (f), the land of the holder of a licence under section 6(1) of the Electricity Act 1989 (licensing of supply etc) is treated as operational land if it would be operational land within section 263 of the Act (meaning of 'operational land') if such licence holders were statutory undertakers for the purpose of that section.

PART 16 COMMUNICATIONS

Class A—electronic communications code operators

Permitted development

A   *Development by or on behalf of an electronic communications code operator for the purpose of the operator's electronic communications network in, on, over or under land controlled by that operator or in accordance with the electronic communications code, consisting of—*

       (a) the installation, alteration or replacement of any electronic communications apparatus,

       (b) the use of land in an emergency for a period not exceeding 6 months to station and operate moveable electronic communications apparatus required for the replacement of unserviceable electronic communications apparatus, including the provision of moveable structures on the land for the purposes of that use, or

       (c) development ancillary to radio equipment housing.

Development not permitted

Development not permitted: ground-based apparatus

A.1

(1)   Development is not permitted by Class A(a) if—

       (a) in the case of the installation of apparatus (other than on a building or other structure) the apparatus, excluding any antenna, would exceed a height of 15 metres above ground level;

(b) in the case of the alteration or replacement of apparatus already installed (other than on a building or other structure), the apparatus, excluding any antenna, would when altered or replaced exceed the height of the existing apparatus or a height of 15 metres above ground level, whichever is the greater; or

(c) in the case of the alteration or replacement of an existing mast (other than on a building or other structure, on article 2(3) land or on any land which is, or is within, a site of special scientific interest)—

    (i) the mast, excluding any antenna, would when altered or replaced—

        (aa) exceed a height of 20 metres above ground level;

        (bb) at any given height exceed the width of the existing mast at the same height by more than one third; or

    (ii) where antenna support structures are altered or replaced, the combined width of the mast and any antenna support structures would exceed the combined width of the existing mast and any antenna support structures by more than one third.

Development not permitted: building-based apparatus

(2) Development is not permitted by Class A(a) if—

(a) in the case of the installation, alteration or replacement of apparatus on a building or other structure, the height of the apparatus (taken by itself) would exceed—

    (i) 15 metres, where it is installed, or is to be installed, on a building or other structure which is 30 metres or more in height; or

    (ii) 10 metres in any other case;

(b) in the case of the installation, alteration or replacement of apparatus on a building or other structure, the highest part of the apparatus when installed, altered or replaced would exceed the height of the highest part of the building or structure by more than—

    (i) 10 metres, in the case of a building or structure which is 30 metres or more in height;

    (ii) 8 metres, in the case of a building or structure which is more than 15 metres but less than 30 metres in height; or

    (iii) 6 metres in any other case;

(c) in the case of the installation, alteration or replacement of an antenna on a building or structure (other than a mast) which is less than 15 metres in height; on a mast located on such a building or structure; or, where the antenna is to be located below a height of 15 metres above ground level, on a building or structure (other than a mast) which is 15 metres or more in height—

    (i) the antenna is to be located on a wall or roof slope facing a highway which is within 20 metres of the building or structure on which the antenna is to be located;

    (ii) in the case of dish antennas, the size of any dish would exceed 0.9 metres or the aggregate size of all of the dishes on the building, structure or mast would exceed 4.5 metres, when measured in any dimension;

(iii) in the case of antennas other than dish antennas, the development (other than the installation, alteration or replacement of 1 small antenna or a maximum of 2 small cell antennas) would result in the presence on the building or structure of—

(aa) more than 3 antenna systems; or

(bb) any antenna system operated by more than 3 electronic communications code operators; or

(iv) the building or structure is a listed building or a scheduled monument; or

(d) in the case of the installation, alteration or replacement of an antenna on a building or structure (other than a mast) which is 15 metres or more in height, or on a mast located on such a building or structure, where the antenna is located at a height of 15 metres or above, measured from ground level—

(i) in the case of dish antennas, the size of any dish would exceed 1.3 metres or the aggregate size of all of the dishes on the building, structure or mast would exceed 10 metres, when measured in any dimension;

(ii) in the case of antennas other than dish antennas, the development (other than the installation, alteration or replacement of a maximum of 2 small antennas or 2 small cell antennas) would result in the presence on the building or structure of—

(aa) more than 5 antenna systems; or

(bb) any antenna system operated by more than 3 electronic communications code operators; or

(iii) the building or structure is a listed building or a scheduled monument.

Development ot permitted: apparatus on masts

(3) Development is not permitted by Class A(a) if, in the case of the installation, alteration or replacement of apparatus (other than an antenna) on a mast, the height of the mast would, when the apparatus was installed, altered or replaced, exceed any relevant height limit specified in respect of apparatus in paragraphs A.1(1)(a), (b) and (c), and A.1(2)(a) and (b), and for the purposes of applying the limit specified in paragraph A.1(2)(a), the words '(taken by itself)' in that paragraph are omitted.

Development not permitted: ground or base area

(4) Development is not permitted by Class A(a) if, in the case of the installation, alteration or replacement of any apparatus other than—

(a) a mast;

(b) an antenna;

(c) a public call box;

(d) any apparatus which does not project above the level of the surface of the ground; or

(e) radio equipment housing,

the ground or base area of the structure would exceed 1.5 square metres.

Town and Country Planning (General Permitted Development) Order 2015

Development not permitted: antennas installed, replaced or altered on article 2(3) land or SSSIs

(5) Development is not permitted by Class A(a) if—
  (a) in the case of development on any article 2(3) land or any land which is, or is within, a site of special scientific interest, it would consist of—
    (i) the installation or alteration of an antenna or of any apparatus which includes or is intended for the support of such an antenna; or
    (ii) the replacement of such an antenna or such apparatus by an antenna or apparatus which differs from that which is being replaced,
  unless the development is carried out in an emergency or is allowed by paragraphs A.1(5)(b), (9)(a), (9)(b) or (10)(b); or
  (b) in the case of the installation of an additional antenna on existing electronic communications apparatus on a building or structure (including a mast) on article 2(3) land—
    (i) in the case of dish antennas, the size of any additional dishes would exceed 0.6 metres, and the number of additional dishes on the building or structure would exceed 3; or
    (ii) in the case of antennas other than dish antennas, any additional antennas would exceed 3 metres in height, and the number of additional antennas on the building or structure would exceed 3.

Development not permitted: driver information systems

(6) Development is not permitted by Class A(a) if it would consist of the installation, alteration or replacement of system apparatus within the meaning of section 8(6) of the Road Traffic (Driver Licensing and Information Systems) Act 1989 (definitions of driver information systems etc).

Development not permitted: apparatus near a highway

(7) Development is not permitted by Class A(a) if, in the case of the installation of a mast, on a building or structure which is less than 15 metres in height, such a mast would be within 20 metres of a highway.

Development not permitted: radio equipment housing

(8) Development is not permitted by Class A(a) if, in the case of the installation, alteration or replacement of radio equipment housing—
  (a) the development is not ancillary to the use of any other electronic communications apparatus;
  (b) the cumulative volume of such development would exceed 90 cubic metres or, if located on the roof of a building, the cumulative volume of such development would exceed 30 cubic metres; or
  (c) on any article 2(3) land, or on any land which is, or is within, a site of special scientific interest, any single development would exceed 2.5 cubic metres, unless the development is carried out in an emergency.

Development not permitted: antennas installed, replaced or altered on a dwellinghouse

(9) Development is not permitted by Class A(a) if—

Town and Country Planning (General Permitted Development) Order 2015

    (a) in the case of the installation, alteration or replacement on a dwellinghouse or within the curtilage of a dwellinghouse of any electronic communications apparatus, that apparatus—

        (i) is not a small antenna;

        (ii) being a small antenna, would result in the presence on that dwellinghouse or within the curtilage of that dwellinghouse of more than 1 such antenna; or

        (iii) being a small antenna, is to be located on a roof or on a chimney so that the highest part of the antenna would exceed in height the highest part of that roof or chimney respectively; or

    (b) in the case of the installation, alteration or replacement on article 2(3) land of a small antenna on a dwellinghouse or within the curtilage of a dwellinghouse, the antenna is to be located—

        (i) on a chimney;

        (ii) on a building which exceeds 15 metres in height;

        (iii) on a wall or roof slope which fronts a highway; or

        (iv) in the Broads, on a wall or roof slope which fronts a waterway.

Development not permitted: antennas installed, replaced or altered not on a dwellinghouse

(10) Development is not permitted by Class A(a) if—

    (a) in the case of the installation, alteration or replacement of a small antenna on a building which is not a dwellinghouse or within the curtilage of a dwellinghouse—

        (i) the building is on article 2(3) land;

        (ii) the building is less than 15 metres in height, and the development would result in the presence on that building of more than 1 such antenna; or

        (iii) the building is 15 metres or more in height, and the development would result in the presence on that building of more than 2 such antennas; or

    (b) in the case of the installation, alteration or replacement of a small cell antenna on a building or structure which is not a dwellinghouse or within the curtilage of a dwellinghouse—

        (i) the building or structure is on any land which is, or is within, a site of special scientific interest; or

        (ii) the development would result in the presence on the building or structure of more than 2 such antennas.

Conditions

A.2

(1) Class A(a) and Class A(c) development is permitted subject to the condition that any antenna or supporting apparatus, radio equipment housing or development ancillary to radio equipment housing constructed, installed, altered or replaced on a building in accordance with that permission is, so far as is practicable, sited so as to minimise its effect on the external appearance of the building.

(2) Class A(a) and Class A(c) development is permitted subject to the condition that any apparatus or structure provided in accordance with that permission is removed from the land, building or structure on which it is situated—
  (a) if such development was carried out in an emergency on any article 2(3) land or on any land which is, or is within, a site of special scientific interest, at the expiry of the relevant period, or
  (b) in any other case, as soon as reasonably practicable after it is no longer required for electronic communications purposes,

  and such land, building or structure is restored to its condition before the development took place, or to any other condition as may be agreed in writing between the local planning authority and the developer.

(3) Class A(b) development is permitted subject to the condition that any apparatus or structure provided in accordance with that permission must, at the expiry of the relevant period, be removed from the land and the land restored to its condition before the development took place.

(4) Subject to sub-paragraph (5), Class A development—
  (a) on article 2(3) land or land which is, or is within, a site of special scientific interest, or
  (b) on any other land and consisting of the construction, installation, alteration or replacement of—
    (i) a mast;
    (ii) an antenna on a building or structure (other than a mast) where the antenna (including any supporting structure) would exceed the height of the building or structure at the point where it is installed or to be installed by 6 metres or more;
    (iii) a public call box;
    (iv) radio equipment housing, where the volume of any single development is in excess of 2.5 cubic metres,

  is permitted subject, except in case of emergency (in which case only paragraph A.3(11) applies), to the conditions set out in paragraph A.3.

(5) The conditions set out in paragraph A.3 (prior approval) do not apply in relation to Class A development on any article 2(3) land which consists of the construction, installation, alteration or replacement of a telegraph pole, cabinet or line, in connection with the provision of fixed-line broadband, provided that the development is completed on or before 30th May 2018.

A.3

(1) The developer must give notice of the proposed development to any person (other than the developer) who is an owner of the land to which the development relates, or a tenant, before making the application required by sub-paragraph (3)—
  (a) by serving a developer's notice on every such person whose name and address is known to the developer; and
  (b) where the developer has taken reasonable steps to ascertain the names and addresses of every such person, but has been unable to do so, by local advertisement.

Town and Country Planning (General Permitted Development) Order 2015

(2) Where the proposed development consists of the installation of a mast within 3 kilometres of the perimeter of an aerodrome, the developer must notify the Civil Aviation Authority, the Secretary of State for Defence or the aerodrome operator, as appropriate, before making the application required by sub-paragraph (3).

(3) Before beginning the development, the developer must apply to the local planning authority for a determination as to whether the prior approval of the authority will be required as to the siting and appearance of the development.

(4) The application must be accompanied—
   (a) by a written description of the proposed development and a plan indicating its proposed location together with any fee required to be paid;
   (b) by the developer's contact address, and the developer's email address if the developer is content to receive communications electronically;
   (c) where sub-paragraph (1) applies, by evidence that the requirements of sub-paragraph (1) have been satisfied; and
   (d) where sub-paragraph (2) applies, by evidence that the Civil Aviation Authority, the Secretary of State for Defence or the aerodrome operator, as the case may be, has been notified of the proposal.

(5) Subject to sub-paragraph (7)(c) and (d), upon receipt of the application under sub-paragraph (4) the local planning authority must—
   (a) for development which, in their opinion, falls within a category set out in the Table in Schedule 4 to the Procedure Order (consultations before the grant of permission), consult the authority or person mentioned in relation to that category, except where—
      (i) the local planning authority are the authority so mentioned; or
      (ii) the authority or person so mentioned has advised the local planning authority that they do not wish to be consulted,
   and must give the consultees at least 14 days within which to comment;
   (b) in the case of development which does not accord with the provisions of the development plan in force in the area in which the land to which the application relates is situated or which would affect a right of way to which Part 3 of the Wildlife and Countryside Act 1981 (public rights of way) applies, must give notice of the proposed development, in the appropriate form set out in Schedule 2 to the Procedure Order (notice of applications for planning permission)—
      (i) by site display in at least one place on or near the land to which the application relates for not less than 21 days, and
      (ii) by local advertisement;
   (c) in the case of development which does not fall within paragraph (b) but which involves development carried out on a site having an area of 1 hectare or more, must give notice of the proposed development, in the appropriate form set out in Schedule 2 to the Procedure Order—
      (i) by—
         (aa) site display in at least one place on or near the land to which the application relates for not less than 21 days, or
         (bb) serving notice on any adjoining owner or occupier, and
      (ii) by local advertisement;

Town and Country Planning (General Permitted Development) Order 2015

  (d) in the case of development which does not fall within paragraph (b) or (c), must give notice of the proposed development, in the appropriate form set out in Schedule 2 to the Procedure Order—

    (i) by site display in at least one place on or near the land to which the application relates for not less than 21 days, or

    (ii) by serving the notice on any adjoining owner or occupier.

(6) The local planning authority must take into account any representations made to them as a result of consultations or notices given under paragraph A.3, when determining the application made under sub-paragraph (3).

(7) The development must not begin before the occurrence of one of the following—

  (a) the receipt by the applicant from the local planning authority of a written notice of their determination that such prior approval is not required;

  (b) where the local planning authority gives the applicant written notice that such prior approval is required, the giving of that approval to the applicant, in writing, within a period of 56 days beginning with the date on which they received the applicant's application;

  (c) where the local planning authority gives the applicant written notice that such prior approval is required, the expiry of a period of 56 days beginning with the date on which the local planning authority received the application under sub-paragraph (4) without the local planning authority notifying the applicant, in writing, that such approval is given or refused; or

  (d) the expiry of a period of 56 days beginning with the date on which the local planning authority received the application without the local planning authority notifying the applicant, in writing, of their determination as to whether such prior approval is required.

(8) The development must, except to the extent that the local planning authority otherwise agree in writing, be carried out—

  (a) where prior approval has been given as mentioned in sub-paragraph (7)(b) in accordance with the details approved;

  (b) in any other case, in accordance with the details submitted with the application.

(9) The agreement in writing referred to in sub-paragraph (8) requires no special form of writing, and in particular there is no requirement on the developer to submit a new application for prior approval in the case of minor amendments to the details submitted with the application for prior approval.

(10) The development must begin—

  (a) where prior approval has been given as mentioned in sub-paragraph (7)(b), not later than the expiration of 5 years beginning with the date on which the approval was given;

  (b) in any other case, not later than the expiration of 5 years beginning with the date on which the local planning authority were given the information referred to in sub-paragraph (4).

(11) In a case of emergency, development is permitted by Class A subject to the condition that the operator must give written notice to the local planning authority of such development as soon as possible after the emergency begins.

Town and Country Planning (General Permitted Development) Order 2015

Interpretation of Class A
A.4

For the purposes of Class A—

'aerodrome operator' means the person for the time being having the management of an aerodrome or, in relation to a particular aerodrome, the management of that aerodrome;

'antenna system' means a set of antennas installed on a building or structure and operated in accordance with the electronic communications code;

'developer's notice' means a notice signed and dated by or on behalf of the developer and containing—

(a) the name of the developer;

(b) the address or location of the proposed development;

(c) a description of the proposed development (including its siting and appearance and the height of any mast);

(d) a statement that the developer will apply to the local planning authority for a determination as to whether the prior approval of the authority will be required as to the siting and appearance of the development;

(e) the name and address of the local planning authority to whom the application will be made;

(f) a statement that the application is available for public inspection at the offices of the local planning authority during usual office hours;

(g) a statement that any person who wishes to make representations about the siting and appearance of the proposed development may do so in writing to the local planning authority;

(h) the date by which any such representations should be received by the local planning authority, being a date not less than 14 days from the date of the notice; and

(i) the address to which such representations should be made;

'development ancillary to radio equipment housing' means the construction, installation, alteration or replacement of structures, equipment or means of access which are ancillary to and reasonably required for the purposes of the radio equipment housing, and except on any land which is, or is within, a site of special scientific interest includes—

(a) security equipment;

(b) perimeter walls and fences; and

(c) handrails, steps and ramps;

'electronic communications apparatus', 'electronic communications code' and 'electronic communications service' have the same meaning as in the Communications Act 2003;

'existing electronic communications apparatus' means electronic communications apparatus which is already sending or receiving electronic communications;

'existing mast' means a mast with attached electronic communications apparatus which existed and was sending or receiving electronic communications at 3rd May 2013;

'fixed-line broadband' means a service or connection (commonly referred to as being 'always on'), via a fixed-line network, providing a bandwidth greater than narrowband;

'land controlled by the operator' means land occupied by the operator in right of a freehold interest or a leasehold interest under a lease granted for a term of not less than 10 years;

'mast' means a radio mast or a radio tower;

'narrowband' means a service or connection providing data speeds up to 128 k bit/s;

'owner' means any person who is the estate owner in respect of the fee simple, or who is entitled to a tenancy granted or extended for a term of years certain of which not less than 7 years remain unexpired;

'relevant period' means a period which expires—

(a) 6 months from the commencement of the construction, installation, alteration or replacement of any apparatus or structure permitted by Class A(a) or Class A(c) or from the commencement of the use permitted by Class A(b), as the case may be, or

(b) when the need for such apparatus, structure or use ceases,

whichever occurs first;

'site display' means the posting of the notice by firmly attaching it to some object, sited and displayed in such a way as to be easily visible and legible by members of the public;

'small antenna' means an antenna which—

(a) is for use in connection with a telephone system operating on a point to fixed multi-point basis;

(b) does not exceed 0.5 metres in any linear measurement; and

(c) does not, in two-dimensional profile, have an area exceeding 1,591 square centimetres,

and any calculation for the purposes of paragraph (b) and (c) excludes any feed element, reinforcing rim mountings and brackets;

'small cell antenna' means an antenna which—

(a) operates on a point to multi-point or area basis in connection with an electronic communications service;

(b) may be variously referred to as a femtocell, picocell, metrocell or microcell antenna;

(c) does not, in any two-dimensional measurement, have a surface area exceeding 5,000 square centimetres; and

(d) does not have a volume exceeding 50,000 cubic centimetres,

and any calculation for the purposes of paragraph (c) and (d) includes any power supply unit or casing, but excludes any mounting, fixing, bracket or other support structure; and

'tenant' means the tenant of an agricultural holding any part of which is comprised in the land to which the application relates.

Town and Country Planning (General Permitted Development) Order 2015

A.5

Where Class A permits the installation, alteration or replacement of any electronic communications apparatus, the permission extends to any—

(a) casing or covering;
(b) mounting, fixing, bracket or other support structure;
(c) perimeter walls or fences;
(d) handrails, steps or ramps; or
(e) security equipment,

reasonably required for the purposes of the electronic communications apparatus.

A.6

Nothing in paragraph A.5 extends the permission in Class A to include the installation, alteration or replacement of anything mentioned in paragraph A.5(a) to (e) on any land which is, or is within, a site of special scientific interest if the inclusion of such an item would not have been permitted by Class A, as read without reference to paragraph A.5.

Class B—other telecommunications development

Permitted development

B   *The installation, alteration or replacement on any building or other structure of a height of 15 metres or more of a microwave antenna and any structure intended for the support of a microwave antenna.*

Development not permitted

B.1

Development is not permitted by Class B if—

(a) the building is a dwellinghouse or the building or structure is within the curtilage of a dwellinghouse;
(b) it would consist of development of a kind described in Class A of this Part;
(c) it would consist of the installation, alteration or replacement of system apparatus within the meaning of section 8(6) of the Road Traffic (Driver Licensing and Information Systems) Act 1989 (definitions of driver information systems etc);
(d) it would result in the presence on the building or structure of more than 4 antennas;
(e) in the case of an antenna installed on a chimney, the length of the antenna would exceed 0.6 metres;
(f) in all other cases, the length of the antenna would exceed 1.3 metres;
(g) it would consist of the installation of an antenna with a cubic capacity in excess of 35 litres;
(h) the highest part of the antenna or its supporting structure would be more than 3 metres higher than the highest part of the building or structure on which it is installed or is to be installed; or
(i) in the case of article 2(3) land, it would consist of the installation of an antenna—

(i) on a chimney, wall or roof slope which faces onto, and is visible from, a highway;

(ii) in the Broads, on a chimney, wall or roof slope which faces onto, and is visible from, a waterway.

Conditions

B.2

Development is permitted by Class B subject to the following conditions—

(a) the antenna is, so far as is practicable, sited so as to minimise its effect on the external appearance of the building or structure on which it is installed; and

(b) an antenna no longer needed for reception or transmission purposes is removed from the building or structure as soon as reasonably practicable.

Class C—other telecommunications development: microwave antenna

Permitted development

C   *The installation, alteration or replacement on any building or other structure of a height of less than 15 metres of a microwave antenna.*

Development not permitted

C 1

Development is not permitted by Class C if—

(a) the building is a dwellinghouse or other structure within the curtilage of a dwellinghouse;

(b) it would consist of development of a kind described in Class A of this Part;

(c) it would consist of the installation, alteration or replacement of system apparatus within the meaning of section 8(6) of the Road Traffic (Driver Licensing and Information Systems) Act 1989 (definitions of driver information systems etc);

(d) it would result in the presence on the building or structure of—

(i) more than 2 antennas;

(ii) a single antenna exceeding 1 metre in length;

(iii) 2 antennas which do not meet the relevant size criteria;

(iv) an antenna installed on a chimney, where the length of the antenna would exceed 0.6 metres;

(v) an antenna installed on a chimney, where the antenna would protrude over the chimney;

(vi) an antenna with a cubic capacity in excess of 35 litres;

(e) in the case of an antenna to be installed on a roof without a chimney, the highest part of the antenna would be higher than the highest part of the roof;

(f) in the case of an antenna to be installed on a roof with a chimney, the highest part of the antenna would be higher than the highest part of the chimney stack, or 0.6 metres measured from the highest part of the ridge tiles of the roof, whichever is the lowest; or

Town and Country Planning (General Permitted Development) Order 2015

(g) in the case of article 2(3) land, it would consist of the installation of an antenna—
   (i) on a chimney, wall or roof slope which faces onto, and is visible from, a highway;
   (ii) in the Broads, on a chimney, wall or roof slope which faces onto, and is visible from, a waterway.

Condition

C 2

Development is permitted by Class C subject to the following conditions—
   (a) the antenna is, so far as practicable, sited so as to minimise its effect on the external appearance of the building or structure on which it is installed; and
   (b) an antenna no longer needed for reception or transmission purposes is removed from the building or structure as soon as reasonably practicable.

Interpretation of Class C

C 3

The relevant size criteria for the purposes of paragraph C 1(d)(iii) are that:
   (a) only 1 of the antennas may exceed 0.6 metres in length; and
   (b) any antenna which exceeds 0.6 metres in length must not exceed 1 metre in length.

Class D—driver information systems

Permitted development

D   The installation, alteration or replacement of system apparatus by or on behalf of a driver information system operator.

Development not permitted

D.1

Development is not permitted by Class D if—
   (a) in the case of the installation, alteration or replacement of system apparatus other than on a building or other structure—
      (i) the ground or base area of the system apparatus would exceed 1.5 square metres; or
      (ii) the system apparatus would exceed a height of 15 metres above ground level; or
   (b) in the case of the installation, alteration or replacement of system apparatus on a building or other structure—
      (i) the highest part of the apparatus when installed, altered, or replaced would exceed in height the highest part of the building or structure by more than 3 metres; or
      (ii) the development would result in the presence on the building or structure of more than 2 microwave antennas.

Conditions

D.2

Development is permitted by Class D subject to the following conditions—

(a) any system apparatus is, so far as practicable, sited so as to minimise its effect on the external appearance of any building or other structure on which it is installed; and

(b) any system apparatus which is no longer needed for a driver information system is removed as soon as reasonably practicable.

Interpretation of Class D

D.3

For the purposes of Class D—

'driver information system operator' means a person granted an operator's licence under section 10 of the Road Traffic (Driver Licensing and Information Systems) Act 1989 (operators' licences); and

'system apparatus' has the meaning assigned to that term by section 8(6) of that Act (definitions of driver information systems etc).

Class E—universal postal service providers

Permitted development

E *Development required for the purposes of a universal service provider (within the meaning of Part 3 of the Postal Services Act 2011) in connection with the provision of a universal postal service (within the meaning of that Part) consisting of—*

(a) the installation of posting boxes or self-service machines,

(b) any other development carried out in, on, over or under the operational land of the undertaking.

Development not permitted

E.1

Development is not permitted by Class E if—

(a) it would consist of or include the erection of a building, or the reconstruction or alteration of a building where its design or external appearance would be materially affected, or

(b) it would consist of or include the installation or erection by way of addition or replacement of any plant or machinery which would exceed 15 metres in height or the height of any existing plant or machinery, whichever is the greater.

Interpretation of Part 16

F.1

For the purposes of Part 16, the length of an antenna is to be measured in any linear direction and excludes any projecting feed element, reinforcing rim, mounting or brackets.

Town and Country Planning (General Permitted Development) Order 2015

PART 17 MINING AND MINERAL EXPLORATION

Class A—extensions, alterations etc ancillary to mining operations

Permitted development

A   *The carrying out of operations for the erection, extension, installation, rearrangement, replacement, repair or other alteration of any—*
- *(a) plant or machinery,*
- *(b) buildings,*
- *(c) private ways or private railways or sidings, or*
- *(d) sewers, mains, pipes, cables or other similar apparatus,*

on land used as a mine.

Development not permitted

A.1

Development is not permitted by Class A—
- (a) in relation to land at an underground mine—
  - (i) on land which is not an approved site; or
  - (ii) on land to which the description in paragraph N.2(1)(b) of this Part applies, unless a plan of that land was deposited with the mineral planning authority before 5th June 1989;
- (b) if the principal purpose of the development would be any purpose other than—
  - (i) purposes in connection with the winning and working of minerals at that mine or of minerals brought to the surface at that mine; or
  - (ii) the treatment, storage or removal from the mine of such minerals or waste materials derived from them;
- (c) if the external appearance of the mine would be materially affected;
- (d) if the height of any building, plant or machinery which is not in an excavation would exceed—
  - (i) 15 metres above ground level; or
  - (ii) the height of the building, plant or machinery, if any, which is being rearranged, replaced or repaired or otherwise altered,

  whichever is the greater;
- (e) if the height of any building, plant or machinery in an excavation would exceed—
  - (i) 15 metres above the excavated ground level; or
  - (ii) 15 metres above the lowest point of the unexcavated ground immediately adjacent to the excavation; or
  - (iii) the height of the building, plant or machinery, if any, which is being rearranged, replaced or repaired or otherwise altered,

  whichever is the greatest;
- (f) if any building erected (other than a replacement building) would have a floor space exceeding 1,000 square metres; or

Town and Country Planning (General Permitted Development) Order 2015

    (g) if the cubic content of any replaced, extended or altered building would exceed by more than 25% the cubic content of the building replaced, extended or altered or the floor space would exceed by more than 1,000 square metres the floor space of that building.

Condition

A.2

Development is permitted by Class A subject to the condition that before the end of the period of 24 months from the date when the mining operations have permanently ceased, or any longer period which the mineral planning authority agree in writing—

    (a) all buildings, plant and machinery permitted by Class A are removed from the land unless the mineral planning authority have otherwise agreed in writing; and

    (b) the land is restored, so far as is practicable, to its condition before the development took place, or restored to such condition as may have been agreed in writing between the mineral planning authority and the developer.

Class B—other developments ancillary to mining operations

Permitted development

B   The carrying out, on land used as a mine or on ancillary mining land of operations for the erection, installation, extension, rearrangement, replacement, repair or other alteration of any—

    (a) plant or machinery,

    (b) buildings, or

    (c) structures or erections.

Development not permitted

B.1

Development is not permitted by Class B—

    (a) in relation to land at an underground mine—

        (i) on land which is not an approved site; or

        (ii) on land to which the description in paragraph N.2(1)(b) of this Part applies, unless a plan of that land was deposited with the mineral planning authority before 5th June 1989; or

    (b) if the principal purpose of the development would be any purpose other than—

        (i) purposes in connection with the operation of the mine;

        (ii) the treatment, preparation for sale, consumption or utilization of minerals won or brought to the surface at that mine; or

        (iii) the storage or removal from the mine of such minerals, their products or waste materials derived from them.

Town and Country Planning (General Permitted Development) Order 2015

Condition

B.2

(1) Subject to sub-paragraph (2), development is permitted by Class B subject to the prior approval of the mineral planning authority of detailed proposals for the siting, design and external appearance of the building, plant or machinery proposed to be erected, installed, extended or altered.

(2) The prior approval referred to in sub-paragraph (1) may not be refused or granted subject to conditions unless the authority are satisfied that it is expedient to do so because—

 (a) the proposed development would injure the amenity of the neighbourhood and modifications can reasonably be made or conditions reasonably imposed in order to avoid or reduce that injury; or

 (b) the proposed development ought to be, and could reasonably be, sited elsewhere.

B.3

Development is permitted by Class B subject to the condition that before the end of the period of 24 months from the date when the mining operations have permanently ceased, or any longer period which the mineral planning authority agree in writing—

 (a) all buildings, plant, machinery, structures and erections permitted by Class B is removed from the land unless the mineral planning authority have otherwise agreed in writing; and

 (b) the land is restored, so far as is practicable, to its condition before the development took place or restored to such condition as may have been agreed in writing between the mineral planning authority and the developer.

Class C—developments for maintenance or safety

Permitted development

C   The carrying out of development required for the maintenance or safety of a mine or a disused mine or for the purposes of ensuring the safety of the surface of the land at or adjacent to a mine or a disused mine.

Development not permitted

C 1

Development is not permitted by Class C if it is carried out by the Coal Authority or any licensed operator within the meaning of section 65 of the Coal Industry Act 1994 (interpretation).

Conditions

C 2

(1) Subject to sub-paragraphs (2) and (3), development is permitted by Class C subject to the prior approval of the mineral planning authority of detailed proposals for the siting, design and external appearance of the building, plant or machinery proposed to be erected, installed, extended or altered.

Town and Country Planning (General Permitted Development) Order 2015

(2) The prior approval referred to in sub-paragraph (1) is not required if—
   (a) the external appearance of the mine or disused mine at or adjacent to which the development is to be carried out would not be materially affected;
   (b) no building, plant, machinery, structure or erection—
      (i) would exceed a height of 15 metres above ground level, or
      (ii) where any building, plant, machinery, structure or erection is rearranged, replaced or repaired, would exceed a height of 15 metres above ground level or the height of what was rearranged, replaced or repaired, whichever is the greater, and
   (c) the development consists of the extension, alteration or replacement of an existing building, within the limits set out in sub-paragraph (4).
(3) The prior approval referred to in sub-paragraph (1) may not be refused or granted subject to conditions unless the authority are satisfied that it is expedient to do so because—
   (a) the proposed development would injure the amenity of the neighbourhood and modifications could reasonably be made or conditions reasonably imposed in order to avoid or reduce that injury; or
   (b) the proposed development ought to be, and could reasonably be, sited elsewhere.
(4) The limits referred to in paragraph C 2(2)(c) are—
   (a) that the cubic content of the building as extended, altered or replaced does not exceed that of the existing building by more than 25%; and
   (b) that the floor space of the building as extended, altered or replaced does not exceed that of the existing building by more than 1,000 square metres.

Class D—coal mining development by the Coal Authority and licensed operators

Permitted development

D *Development by a licensee of the Coal Authority, in a mine started before 1st July 1948, consisting of—*
   (a) the winning and working underground of coal or coal-related minerals in a designated seam area; or
   (b) the carrying out of development underground which is required in order to gain access to and work coal or coal-related minerals in a designated seam area.

Conditions

D.1

Development is permitted by Class D subject to the following conditions—
   (a) subject to paragraph (b)—
      (i) except in a case where there is an approved restoration scheme or mining operations have permanently ceased, the developer must, before 31st December 1995 or before any later date which the mineral planning authority may agree in writing, apply to the mineral planning authority for approval of a restoration scheme;
      (ii) where there is an approved restoration scheme, reinstatement, restoration and aftercare is carried out in accordance with that scheme;

(iii) if an approved restoration scheme does not specify the periods within which reinstatement, restoration or aftercare should be carried out, it is subject to conditions that—

 (aa) reinstatement or restoration, if any, is to be carried out before the end of the period of 24 months from either the date when the mining operations have permanently ceased or the date when any application for approval of a restoration scheme under paragraph (a)(i) has been finally determined, whichever is later, and

 (bb) aftercare, if any, in respect of any part of a site, is to be carried out throughout the period of 5 years from either the date when any reinstatement or restoration in respect of that part is completed or the date when any application for approval of a restoration scheme under paragraph (a)(i) has been finally determined, whichever is later;

(iv) where there is no approved restoration scheme—

 (aa) all buildings, plant, machinery, structures and erections used at any time for or in connection with any previous coal-mining operations at that mine are removed from any land which is an authorised site unless the mineral planning authority have otherwise agreed in writing; and

 (bb) that land is, so far as practicable, restored to its condition before any previous coal-mining operations at that mine took place or to such condition as may have been agreed in writing between the mineral planning authority and the developer,

before the end of the period specified in paragraph (a)(v);

(v) the period referred to in paragraph (a)(iv) is—

 (aa) the period of 24 months from the date when the mining operations have permanently ceased or, if an application for approval of a restoration scheme has been made under paragraph (a)(i) before that date, 24 months from the date when that application has been finally determined, whichever is later, or

 (bb) any longer period which the mineral planning authority have agreed in writing;

(vi) for the purposes of paragraph (a), an application for approval of a restoration scheme has been finally determined when the following conditions have been met—

 (aa) any proceedings on the application, including any proceeding on or in consequence of an application under section 288 of the Act (proceedings for questioning the validity of certain orders, decisions and directions), have been determined, and

 (bb) any time for appealing under section 78 (right to appeal against planning decisions and failure to take such decisions), or applying or further applying under section 288, of the Act (where there is a right to do so) has expired; and

(b) paragraph (a) does not apply to land in respect of which there is an extant planning permission which—

 (i) has been granted on an application under Part 3 of the Act; and

 (ii) has been implemented.

Town and Country Planning (General Permitted Development) Order 2015

Interpretation of Class D

D.2

For the purposes of Class D—

'approved restoration scheme' means a restoration scheme which is approved when an application made under paragraph D.1(a)(i) is finally determined, as approved (with or without conditions), or as subsequently varied with the written approval of the mineral planning authority (with or without conditions);

'coal-related minerals' means minerals other than coal which are, or may be, won and worked by coal-mining operations;

'designated seam area' means land identified, in accordance with paragraph (a) of the definition of 'seam plan', in a seam plan which was deposited with the mineral planning authority before 30th September 1993;

'a licensee of the Coal Authority' means any person who is for the time being authorised by a licence under Part 2 of the Coal Industry Act 1994 to carry on coal-mining operations to which section 25 of that Act (coal-mining operations to be licensed) applies;

'previous coal-mining operations' has the same meaning as in section 54(3) of the Coal Industry Act 1994 (obligations to restore land affected by coal-mining operations) and references in Class D to the use of anything in connection with any such operations include references to its use for or in connection with activities carried on in association with, or for purposes connected with, the carrying on of those operations;

'restoration scheme' means a scheme which makes provision for the reinstatement, restoration or aftercare (or a combination of these) of any land which is an authorised site and has been used at any time for or in connection with any previous coal-mining operations at that mine; and

'seam plan' means a plan on a scale of not less than 1 to 25,000 showing—

(a) land comprising the maximum extent of the coal seam or seams that could have been worked from shafts or drifts existing at a mine at 13th November 1992, without further development on an authorised site other than development permitted by Class B of Part 20 of Schedule 2 to the Town and Country Planning General Development Order 1988, as originally enacted;

(b) any active access used in connection with the land referred to in paragraph (a) of this definition;

(c) the National Grid lines and reference numbers shown on Ordnance Survey maps;

(d) a typical stratigraphic column showing the approximate depths of the coal seam referred to in paragraph (a) of this definition.

Class E—coal mining development by a licensee of the British Coal Corporation

Permitted development

E   *Development by a licensee of the British Coal Corporation, in a mine started before 1st July 1948, consisting of—*

(a) the winning and working underground of coal or coal-related minerals in a designated seam area; or

(b) the carrying out of development underground which is required in order to gain access to and work coal or coal-related minerals in a designated seam area.

Interpretation of Class E

E.1

For the purposes of Class E—

'coal-related minerals' means minerals other than coal which can only be economically worked in association with the working of coal or which can only be economically brought to the surface by the use of a mine of coal;

'designated seam area' has the same meaning as in paragraph D.2 of this Part; and

'a licensee of the British Coal Corporation' means any person who is for the time being authorised by virtue of section 25(3) of the Coal Industry Act 1994 (coal-mining operations to be licensed) to carry on coal-mining operations to which section 25 of that Act applies.

Class F—coal-mining development on an authorised site

Permitted development

F Any development required for the purposes of a mine which is carried out on an authorised site at that mine by a licensed operator in connection with coal-mining operations.

Development not permitted

F.1

Development is not permitted by Class F if—

(a) the external appearance of the mine would be materially affected;

(b) any building, plant or machinery, structure or erection or any deposit of minerals or waste—

(i) would exceed a height of 15 metres above ground level, or

(ii) where a building, plant or machinery would be rearranged, replaced or repaired, the resulting development would exceed a height of 15 metres above ground level or the height of what was rearranged, replaced or repaired, whichever is the greater;

(c) any building erected (other than a replacement building) would have a floor space exceeding 1,000 square metres;

(d) the cubic content of any replaced, extended or altered building would exceed by more than 25% the cubic content of the building replaced, extended or altered or the floor space would exceed by more than 1,000 square metres, the floor space of that building;

(e) it would be for the purpose of creating a new surface access to underground workings or of improving an existing access (which is not an active access) to underground workings; or

Town and Country Planning (General Permitted Development) Order 2015

(f) it would be carried out on land to which the description in paragraph N.2(2)(b) of this Part applies, and a plan of that land had not been deposited with the mineral planning authority before 5th June 1989.

Conditions

F.2

Development is permitted by Class F subject to the condition that before the end of the period of 24 months from the date when the mining operations have permanently ceased, or any longer period which the mineral planning authority agree in writing—

(a) all buildings, plant, machinery, structures and erections and deposits of minerals or waste permitted by Class F are removed from the land unless the mineral planning authority have otherwise agreed in writing; and

(b) the land is, so far as is practicable, restored to its condition before the development took place or to such condition as may have been agreed in writing between the mineral planning authority and the developer.

F.3

(1) Subject to sub-paragraphs (2) and (3), development is permitted by Class F subject to the prior approval of the mineral planning authority of detailed proposals for the siting, design and external appearance of any building, plant or machinery proposed to be erected, installed, extended or altered.

(2) The prior approval referred to in sub-paragraph (1) is not required for any building, plant or machinery which does not exceed the limits set out in paragraph F.1(b), (c) or (d).

(3) The prior approval referred to in sub-paragraph (1) may not be refused or granted subject to conditions unless the authority are satisfied that it is expedient to do so because—

(a) the proposed development would injure the amenity of the neighbourhood and modifications could reasonably be made or conditions reasonably imposed in order to avoid or reduce that injury; or

(b) the proposed development ought to be, and could reasonably be, sited elsewhere.

Class G—coal-mining development by the Coal Authority etc for maintenance or safety

Permitted development

G   *The carrying out by the Coal Authority or a licensed operator of development required for the maintenance or safety of a mine or a disused mine or for the purposes of ensuring the safety of the surface of the land at or adjacent to a mine or a disused mine.*

Conditions

G.1

(1) Subject to sub-paragraphs (2) and (3), development is permitted by Class G subject to the prior approval of the mineral planning authority of detailed proposals for the siting, design and external appearance of the building, plant or machinery proposed to be erected, installed, extended or altered.

Town and Country Planning (General Permitted Development) Order 2015

(2) The prior approval referred to in sub-paragraph (1) is not required if—
  (a) the external appearance of the mine or disused mine at or adjacent to which the development is to be carried out would not be materially affected;
  (b) no building, plant or machinery, structure or erection—
    (i) would exceed a height of 15 metres above ground level; or
    (ii) where any building, plant, machinery, structure or erection is rearranged, replaced or repaired, would exceed a height of 15 metres above ground level or the height of what was rearranged, replaced or repaired, whichever is the greater, and
  (c) the development consists of the extension, alteration or replacement of an existing building, within the limits set out in sub-paragraph (4).

(3) The prior approval referred to in sub-paragraph (1) may not be refused or granted subject to conditions unless the authority are satisfied that it is expedient to do so because—
  (a) the proposed development would injure the amenity of the neighbourhood and modifications could reasonably be made or conditions reasonably imposed in order to avoid or reduce that injury; or
  (b) the proposed development ought to be, and could reasonably be, sited elsewhere.

(4) The limits referred to in paragraph G.1(2)(c) are—
  (a) that the cubic content of the building as extended, altered or replaced does not exceed that of the existing building by more than 25%; and
  (b) that the floor space of the building as extended, altered or replaced does not exceed that of the existing building by more than 1,000 square metres.

Class H—waste tipping at a mine

Permitted development

H **The deposit, on premises used as a mine or on ancillary mining land already used for the purpose, of waste derived from the winning and working of minerals at that mine or from minerals brought to the surface at that mine, or from the treatment or the preparation for sale, consumption or utilization of minerals from the mine.**

Development not permitted

H.1

Development is not permitted by Class H if—
  (a) in the case of waste deposited in an excavation, waste would be deposited at a height above the level of the land adjoining the excavation, unless that is provided for in a waste management scheme or a relevant scheme; or
  (b) in any other case, the superficial area or height of the deposit (measured as at 21st October 1988) would be increased by more than 10%, unless such an increase is provided for in a waste management scheme or in a relevant scheme.

Conditions

H.2

Development is permitted by Class H subject to the following conditions—

    (a) except in a case where a relevant scheme or a waste management scheme has already been approved by the mineral planning authority, the developer must, if the mineral planning authority so require, within 3 months or such longer period as the authority may specify, submit a waste management scheme for that authority's approval; and

    (b) where a waste management scheme or a relevant scheme has been approved, the depositing of waste and all other activities in relation to that deposit is carried out in accordance with the scheme as approved.

Interpretation of Class H

H.3

For the purposes of Class H—

    'ancillary mining land' means land adjacent to and occupied together with a mine at which the winning and working of minerals is carried out in pursuance of planning permission granted or deemed to be granted under Part 3 of the Act (control over development); and

    'waste management scheme' means a scheme required by the mineral planning authority to be submitted for their approval in accordance with the condition in paragraph H.2(a) which makes provision for—

        (a) the manner in which the depositing of waste (other than waste deposited on a site for use for filling any mineral excavation in the mine or on ancillary mining land in order to comply with the terms of any planning permission granted on an application or deemed to be granted under Part 3 of the Act) is to be carried out after the date of the approval of that scheme;

        (b) where appropriate, the stripping and storage of the subsoil and topsoil;

        (c) the restoration and aftercare of the site.

Class I—waste tipping from a mine on sites used since 1948

Permitted development

I   *The deposit on land comprised in a site used for the deposit of waste materials or refuse on 1st July 1948 of waste resulting from coal-mining operations.*

Development not permitted

I.1

Development is not permitted by Class I unless it is in accordance with a relevant scheme approved by the mineral planning authority before 5th December 1988.

Interpretation of Class J

I.2

For the purposes of Class I, 'coal-mining operations' has the same meaning as in section 65 of the Coal Industry Act 1994 (interpretation).

Town and Country Planning (General Permitted Development) Order 2015

Class J—temporary use of land etc for mineral exploration

Permitted development

J Development on any land during a period not exceeding 28 consecutive days consisting of—
- (a) the drilling of boreholes;
- (b) the carrying out of seismic surveys; or
- (c) the making of other excavations,

for the purpose of mineral exploration, and the provision or assembly on that land or adjoining land of any structure required in connection with any of those operations.

Development not permitted

J.1

Development is not permitted by Class J if—
- (a) it consists of the drilling of boreholes for petroleum exploration;
- (b) any operation would be carried out within 50 metres of any part of an occupied residential building or a building occupied as a hospital or school;
- (c) any operation would be carried out within a National Park, an area of outstanding natural beauty, a site of archaeological interest or a site of special scientific interest;
- (d) any explosive charge of more than 1 kilogram would be used;
- (e) any excavation referred to in Class J(c) would exceed 10 metres in depth or 12 square metres in surface area;
- (f) in the case described in Class J(c) more than 10 excavations would, as a result, be made within any area of 1 hectare within the land during any period of 24 months; or
- (g) any structure assembled or provided would exceed 12 metres in height, or, where the structure would be within 3 kilometres of the perimeter of an aerodrome, 3 metres in height.

Conditions

J.2

Development is permitted by Class J subject to the following conditions—
- (a) no operations are carried out between 6.00pm and 7.00am;
- (b) no trees on the land are removed, felled, lopped or topped and no other thing is done on the land likely to harm or damage any trees, unless the mineral planning authority have so agreed in writing;
- (c) before any excavation (other than a borehole) is made, any topsoil and any subsoil is separately removed from the land to be excavated and stored separately from other excavated material and from each other;
- (d) within a period of 28 days from the cessation of operations unless the mineral planning authority have agreed otherwise in writing—
    - (i) any structure permitted by Class J and any waste material arising from other development so permitted is removed from the land;

Town and Country Planning (General Permitted Development) Order 2015

  (ii) any borehole is adequately sealed;
  (iii) any other excavation is filled with material from the site;
  (iv) the surface of the land on which any operations have been carried out is levelled and any topsoil replaced as the uppermost layer, and
  (v) the land is, so far as is practicable, restored to its condition before the development took place, including the carrying out of any necessary seeding and replanting.

Class K—use of land etc for mineral exploration

Permitted development

K *Development on any land consisting of—*
 (a) the drilling of boreholes;
 (b) the carrying out of seismic surveys; or
 (c) the making of other excavations,

for the purposes of mineral exploration, and the provision or assembly on that land or on adjoining land of any structure required in connection with any of those operations.

Development not permitted

K.1

Development is not permitted by Class K if—
 (a) it consists of the drilling of boreholes for petroleum exploration;
 (b) the developer has not previously notified the mineral planning authority in writing of its intention to carry out the development (specifying the nature and location of the development);
 (c) the relevant period has not elapsed;
 (d) any explosive charge of more than 2 kilograms would be used;
 (e) any excavation referred to in Class K(c) would exceed 10 metres in depth or 12 square metres in surface area; or
 (f) any structure assembled or provided would exceed 12 metres in height.

Conditions

K.2

Development is permitted by Class K subject to the following conditions—
 (a) the development is carried out in accordance with the details in the notification referred to in paragraph K.1(b), unless the mineral planning authority have otherwise agreed in writing;
 (b) no trees on the land are removed, felled, lopped or topped and no other thing is done on the land likely to harm or damage any trees, unless specified in detail in the notification referred to in paragraph K.1(b) or the mineral planning authority have otherwise agreed in writing;
 (c) before any excavation other than a borehole is made, any topsoil and any subsoil is separately removed from the land to be excavated and stored separately from other excavated material and from each other;

Town and Country Planning (General Permitted Development) Order 2015

(d) within a period of 28 days from operations ceasing, unless the mineral planning authority have agreed otherwise in writing—
  (i) any structure permitted by Class K and any waste material arising from other development so permitted is removed from the land;
  (ii) any borehole is adequately sealed;
  (iii) any other excavation is filled with material from the site;
  (iv) the surface of the land is levelled and any topsoil replaced as the uppermost layer, and
  (v) the land is, so far as is practicable, restored to its condition before the development took place, including the carrying out of any necessary seeding and replanting, and
(e) the development ceases no later than a date 6 months after the elapse of the relevant period, unless the mineral planning authority have otherwise agreed in writing.

Interpretation of Class K

K.3

For the purposes of Class K, 'relevant period' means the period elapsing—
(a) where a direction is not issued under article 5, 28 days after the notification referred to in paragraph K.1(b) or, if earlier, on the date on which the mineral planning authority notify the developer in writing that they will not issue such a direction, or
(b) where a direction is issued under article 5, 28 days from the date on which notice of that decision is sent to the Secretary of State, or, if earlier, the date on which the mineral planning authority notify the developer that the Secretary of State has disallowed the direction.

Class L—removal of material from a stockpile

Permitted development

L *The removal of material of any description from a stocpile.*

Class M—removal of material from mineral-working deposits

Permitted development

M *The removal of material of any description from a mineral-working deposit other than a stockpile.*

Development not permitted

M.1

Development is not permitted by Class M if—
(a) the developer has not previously notified the mineral planning authority in writing of its intention to carry out the development and supplied them with the appropriate details;
(b) the deposit covers a ground area exceeding 2 hectares, unless the deposit contains no mineral or other material which was deposited on the land more than 5 years before the development; or

Town and Country Planning (General Permitted Development) Order 2015

(c) the deposit derives from the carrying out of any operations permitted under Class A, B or C of Part 6 (agricultural development) of this Schedule or any Class in a previous development order which it replaces.

Conditions

M.2

Development is permitted by Class M subject to the following conditions—

(a) it is carried out in accordance with the details given in the notice sent to the mineral planning authority referred to in paragraph M.1(a), unless that authority have agreed otherwise in writing;

(b) if the mineral planning authority so require, the developer must within a period of 3 months from the date of the requirement (or such other longer period as that authority may provide) submit to them for approval a scheme providing for the restoration and aftercare of the site;

(c) where such a scheme is required, the site is restored and aftercare is carried out in accordance with the provisions of the approved scheme; and

(d) development is not be commenced until the relevant period has elapsed.

Interpretation of Class M

M.3

For the purposes of Class M—

'appropriate details' means—

(a) the nature of the development;

(b) the exact location of the mineral-working deposit from which the material would be removed;

(c) the proposed means of vehicular access to the site at which the development is to be carried out, and

(d) the earliest date at which any mineral presently contained in the deposit was deposited on the land; and

'relevant period' means the period elapsing—

(a) where a direction is not issued under article 5, 28 days after the notification referred to in paragraph M.1(a) or, if earlier, on the date on which the mineral planning authority notify the developer in writing that they will not issue such a direction; or

(b) where a direction is issued under article 5, 28 days from the date on which notice of that direction is sent to the Secretary of State, or, if earlier, the date on which the mineral planning authority notify the developer that the Secretary of State has disallowed the direction.

Interpretation of Part 17

N.1

For the purposes of Part 17—

'active access' means a surface access to underground workings which is in normal and regular use for the transportation of coal, materials, spoil or persons;

Town and Country Planning (General Permitted Development) Order 2015

'ancillary mining land' means land adjacent to and occupied together with a mine at which the winning and working of minerals is carried out in pursuance of planning permission granted or deemed to be granted under Part 3 of the Act (control over development);

'coal-mining operations' has the same meaning as in section 65 of the Coal Industry Act 1994 (interpretation) and references to any development or use in connection with coal-mining operations include references to development or use for or in connection with activities carried on in association with, or for purposes connected with, the carrying on of those operations;

'licensed operator' has the same meaning as in section 65 of the Coal Industry Act 1994;

'mineral exploration' means ascertaining the presence, extent or quality of any deposit of a mineral with a view to exploiting that mineral;

'minerals' does not include any coal other than coal won or worked during the course of operations which are carried on exclusively for the purpose of exploring for coal or confined to the digging or carrying away of coal that it is necessary to dig or carry away in the course of activities carried on for purposes which do not include the getting of coal or any product of coal;

'normal and regular use' means use other than intermittent visits to inspect and maintain the fabric of the mine or any plant or machinery;

'relevant scheme' means a scheme, other than a waste management scheme, requiring approval by the mineral planning authority in accordance with a condition or limitation on any planning permission granted or deemed to be granted under Part 3 of the Act (control over development), for making provision for the manner in which the deposit of waste is to be carried out and for the carrying out of other activities in relation to that deposit;

'stockpile' means a mineral-working deposit consisting primarily of minerals which have been deposited for the purposes of their processing or sale;

'structure' includes a building, plant or machinery; and

'underground mine' is a mine at which minerals are worked principally by underground methods.

N.2

(1) An area of land is an approved site for the purposes of Class A and B of this Part if—

(a) it is identified in a grant of planning permission or any instrument by virtue of which planning permission is deemed to be granted, as land which may be used for development described in this Part; or

(b) in any other case, it is land immediately adjoining an active access to an underground mine which, on 5th December 1988, was in use for the purposes of that mine, in connection with the purposes described in paragraph A.1(b)(i) or (ii) or paragraph B.1(b)(i) to (iii) of this Part.

(2) Subject to sub-paragraph (3), land is an authorised site for the purposes of Class D and F of this Part if—

(a) it is identified in a grant of planning permission or any instrument by virtue of which planning permission is deemed to be granted as land which may be used for development described in this Part; or

(b) in any other case, it is land immediately adjoining an active access which, on 5th December 1988, was in use for the purposes of that mine in connection with coal-mining operations.

(3) For the purposes of sub-paragraph (2), land is not to be regarded as in use in connection with coal-mining operations if—
 (a) it is used for the permanent deposit of waste derived from the winning and working of minerals; or
 (b) there is on, over or under it a railway, conveyor, aerial ropeway, roadway, overhead power line or pipe-line which is not itself surrounded by other land used for those purposes.

PART 18 MISCELLANEOUS DEVELOPMENT

Class A—development under local or private Acts or Order

Permitted development

A Development authorised by—
 (a) a local or private Act of Parliament,
 (b) an order approved by both Houses of Parliament, or
 (c) an order under section 14 or 16 of the Harbours Act 1964 (orders for securing harbour efficiency etc, and orders conferring powers for improvement, construction etc of harbours),

which designates specifically the nature of the development authorised and the land upon which it may be carried out.

Conditions

A.1

Development is not permitted by Class A if it consists of or includes—
 (a) the erection, construction, alteration or extension of any building, bridge, aqueduct, pier or dam; or
 (b) the formation, laying out or alteration of a means of access to any highway used by vehicular traffic,

unless the prior approval of the appropriate authority to the detailed plans and specifications is first obtained.

A.2

The prior approval referred to in paragraph A.1 is not to be refused by the appropriate authority nor are conditions to be imposed unless they are satisfied that—
 (a) the development (other than the provision of or works carried out to a dam) ought to be and could reasonably be carried out elsewhere on the land; or
 (b) the design or external appearance of any building, bridge, aqueduct, pier or dam would injure the amenity of the neighbourhood and is reasonably capable of modification to avoid such injury.

Interpretation of Class A

A.3

For the purposes of Class A, 'appropriate authority' means—

(a) in Greater London or a metropolitan county, the local planning authority;

(b) in a National Park, outside a metropolitan county, the county planning authority; and

(c) in any other case, the district planning authority.

Class B—development at amusement parks

Permitted development

B *Development on land used as an amusement park consisting of—*

(a) the erection of booths or stalls or the installation of plant or machinery to be used for or in connection with the entertainment of the public within the amusement park; or

(b) the extension, alteration or replacement of any existing booths or stalls, plant or machinery so used.

Development not permitted

B.1

Development is not permitted by Class B if—

(a) the plant or machinery would—

(i) if the land or pier is within 3 kilometres of the perimeter of an aerodrome, exceed a height of 25 metres or the height of the highest existing structure (whichever is the lesser), or

(ii) in any other case, exceed a height of 25 metres;

(b) in the case of an extension to an existing building or structure, that building or structure would as a result exceed 5 metres above ground level or the height of the roof of the existing building or structure, whichever is the greater; or

(c) in any other case, the height of the building or structure erected, extended, altered or replaced would exceed 5 metres above ground level.

Interpretation of Class B

B.2

For the purposes of Class B—

'amusement park' means an enclosed area of open land, or any part of a seaside pier, which is principally used (other than by way of a temporary use) as a funfair or otherwise for the purposes of providing public entertainment by means of mechanical amusements and side-shows; but, where part only of an enclosed area is commonly so used as a funfair or for such public entertainment, only the part so used is to be regarded as an amusement park; and

'booths or stalls' includes buildings or structures similar to booths or stalls.

PART 19 DEVELOPMENT BY THE CROWN OR FOR NATIONAL SECURITY PURPOSES

Class A—general development by the Crown

Permitted development

A The erection or construction and the maintenance, improvement or other alteration by or on behalf of the Crown of—
   (a) any small ancillary building, works or equipment on Crown land required for operational purposes;
   (b) lamp standards, information kiosks, passenger shelters, shelters and seats, telephone boxes, fire alarms, drinking fountains, refuse bins or baskets, barriers for the control of people and vehicles, and similar structures or works required in connection with the operational purposes of the Crown.

Interpretation of Class A

A.1

The reference in Class A to any small ancillary building, works or equipment is a reference to any ancillary building, works or equipment not exceeding 4 metres in height or 200 cubic metres in capacity.

Class B—extension or alteration of an operational Crown building

Permitted development

B The extension or alteration by or on behalf of the Crown of an operational Crown building.

Development not permitted

B.1

Development is not permitted by Class B if—
   (a) the building as extended or altered is to be used for purposes other than those of—
      (i) the Crown; or
      (ii) the provision of employee facilities;
   (b) the height of the building as extended or altered would exceed the height of the original building;
   (c) the cubic content of the original building would be exceeded by more than—
      (i) 10%, in respect of development on any article 2(3) land; or
      (ii) 25%, in any other case;
   (d) the floor space of the original building would be exceeded by more than—
      (i) 500 square metres in respect of development on any article 2(3) land; or
      (ii) 1,000 square metres in any other case;

Town and Country Planning (General Permitted Development) Order 2015

    (e) the external appearance of the original building would be materially affected;

    (f) any part of the building as extended or altered would be within 5 metres of any boundary of the curtilage of the original building; or

    (g) the development would lead to a reduction in the space available for the parking or turning of vehicles.

Interpretation of Class B

B.2

For the purposes of Class B—

    (a) the erection of any additional building within the curtilage of another building (whether by virtue of Class B or otherwise) and used in connection with it is to be treated as the extension of that building, and the additional building is not to be treated as an original building;

    (b) where 2 or more original buildings are within the same curtilage and are used for the same operational purposes, they are to be treated as a single original building in making any measurement; and

    (c) 'employee facilities' means social, care or recreational facilities provided for employees or servants of the Crown, including crèche facilities provided for the children of such employees or servants.

Class C—developments on operational Crown land

Permitted development

C   *Development carried out by or on behalf of the Crown on operational Crown land for operational purposes consisting of—*

    (a) the installation of additional or replacement plant or machinery;

    (b) the provision, rearrangement or replacement of a sewer, main, pipe, cable or other apparatus; or

    (c) the provision, rearrangement or replacement of a private way, private railway, siding or conveyor.

Development not permitted

C.1

Development described in Class C(a) is not permitted if—

    (a) it would materially affect the external appearance of the premises; or

    (b) any plant or machinery would exceed a height of 15 metres above ground level or the height of anything replaced, whichever is the greater.

Interpretation of Class C

C.2

In Class C, 'Crown land' does not include land in or adjacent to and occupied together with a mine.

Town and Country Planning (General Permitted Development) Order 2015

Class D—hard surfaces for operational Crown buildings

Permitted development

D   The provision by or on behalf of the Crown of a hard surface within the curtilage of an operational Crown building.

Class E—development on operational Crown land relating to an airbase

Permitted development

E   The carrying out on operational Crown land, by or on behalf of the Crown, of development (including the erection or alteration of an operational building) in connection with the provision of services and facilities at an airbase.

Development not permitted

E.1

Development is not permitted by Class E if it would consist of or include—

(a) the construction or extension of a runway;

(b) the construction of a passenger terminal the floor space of which would exceed 500 square metres;

(c) the extension or alteration of a passenger terminal, where the floor space of the building as existing at 7th June 2006 or, if built after that date, of the building as built, would be exceeded by more than 15%;

(d) the erection of a building other than an operational building; or

(e) the alteration or reconstruction of a building other than an operational building, where its design or external appearance would be materially affected.

Condition

E.2

Development is permitted by Class E subject to the condition that the relevant airbase operator consults the local planning authority before carrying out any development, unless that development falls within the description in paragraph E.4.

Interpretation of Class E

E.3

For the purposes of paragraph E.1, floor space is calculated by external measurement and without taking account of the floor space in any pier or satellite.

E.4

Development falls within this paragraph if—

(a) it is urgently required for the efficient running of the airbase; and

(b) it consists of the carrying out of works, or the erection or construction of a structure or of an ancillary building, or the placing on land of equipment, and the works, structure, building, or equipment do not exceed 4 metres in height or 200 cubic metres in capacity.

Town and Country Planning (General Permitted Development) Order 2015

E.5

For the purposes of Class E, 'operational building' means an operational Crown building, other than a hotel, required in connection with the movement or maintenance of aircraft, or with the embarking, disembarking, loading, discharge or transport of passengers, military or civilian personnel, goods, military equipment, munitions and other items.

Class F—development on operational land within an airbase

Permitted development

F *The carrying out on operational land within the perimeter of an airbase, by or on behalf of the Crown, of development in connection with the provision of air traffic services.*

Class G—development on operational land outside an airbase

Permitted development

G *The carrying out on operational land outside but within 8 kilometres of the perimeter of an airbase, by or on behalf of the Crown, of development in connection with the provision of air traffic services.*

Development not permitted

G.1

Development is not permitted by Class G if—
  (a) any building erected would be used for a purpose other than housing equipment used in connection with the provision of air traffic services;
  (b) any building erected would exceed a height of 4 metres; or
  (c) it would consist of the installation or erection of any radar or radio mast, antenna or other apparatus which would exceed 15 metres in height, or, where an existing mast, antenna or apparatus is replaced, the height of that mast, antenna or apparatus, if greater.

Class H—development on operational land by the Crown connected with air traffic services

Permitted development

H *The carrying out on operational land, by or on behalf of the Crown, of development in connection with the provision of air traffic services.*

Development not permitted

H.1

Development is not permitted by Class H if—
  (a) any building erected would be used for a purpose other than housing equipment used in connection with the provision of air traffic services;
  (b) any building erected would exceed a height of 4 metres; or
  (c) it would consist of the installation or erection of any radar or radio mast, antenna or other apparatus which would exceed 15 metres in height, or,

Town and Country Planning (General Permitted Development) Order 2015

where an existing mast, antenna or apparatus is replaced, the height of that mast, antenna or apparatus, if greater.

Class I—emergency use of land by the Crown connected with air traffic services

Permitted development

I   *The use of land by or on behalf of the Crown in an emergency to station moveable apparatus replacing unserviceable apparatus in connection with the provision of air traffic services.*

Condition

I.1

Development is permitted by Class I subject to the condition that on or before the expiry of a period of 6 months beginning with the date on which the use began, the use ceases, and any apparatus is removed, and the land is restored to its condition before the development took place, or to such other state as may be agreed in writing between the local planning authority and the developer.

Class J—use of land etc by the Crown connected with air traffic services

Permitted development

J   *The use of land by or on behalf of the Crown to provide services and facilities in connection with the provision of air traffic services and the erection or placing of moveable structures on the land for the purposes of that use.*

Condition

J.1

Development is permitted by Class J subject to the condition that, on or before the expiry of the period of 6 months beginning with the date on which the use began, the use ceases, any structure is removed, and the land is restored to its condition before the development took place, or to such other state as may be agreed in writing between the local planning authority and the developer.

Class K—use of land by the Crown in relation to surveys etc

Permitted development

K   *The use of land by or on behalf of the Crown for the stationing and operation of apparatus in connection with the carrying out of surveys or investigations.*

Condition

K.1

Development is permitted by Class K subject to the condition that on or before the expiry of the period of 6 months beginning with the date on which the use began, the use ceases, any apparatus is removed, and the land is restored to its condition before the development took place, or to such other state as may be agreed in writing between the local planning authority and the developer.

Town and Country Planning (General Permitted Development) Order 2015

Class L—use of buildings by the Crown on an airbase connected to air transport services etc

Permitted development

L   *The use of buildings by or on behalf of the Crown within the perimeter of an airbase for purposes connected with air transport services or other flying activities at that airbase.*

Interpretation of Class L

L 1

For the purposes of Class L, 'air transport services' has the same meaning as in section 82 of the Airports Act 1986.

Class M—development by the Crown on operational Crown land connected to rail

Permitted development

M   *Development by or on behalf of the Crown on operational Crown land, required in connection with the movement of traffic by rail.*

Development not permitted

M.1

Development is not permitted by Class M if it consists of or includes—
  (a) the construction of a railway;
  (b) the construction or erection of a hotel, railway station or bridge; or
  (c) the construction or erection otherwise than wholly within a railway station of an office, residential or educational building, car park, shop, restaurant, garage, petrol filling station or a building used for an industrial process.

Interpretation of Class M

M.2

For the purposes of Class M, references to the construction or erection of any building or structure include references to the reconstruction or alteration of a building or structure where its design or external appearance would be materially affected.

Class N—development by the Crown on operational Crown land connected to shipping etc

Permitted development

N   *Development by or on behalf of the Crown or its lessees on operational Crown land where the development is required—*
  (a) for the purposes of shipping; or
  (b) at a dock, pier, pontoon or harbour in connection with the embarking, disembarking, loading, discharging or transport of military or civilian personnel, military equipment, munitions, or other items.

Town and Country Planning (General Permitted Development) Order 2015

Development not permitted

N.1

Development is not permitted by Class N if it consists of or includes the construction or erection of a bridge or other building not required in connection with the handling of traffic.

Interpretation of Class N

N.2

For the purposes of Class N, references to the construction or erection of any building or structure include references to the reconstruction or alteration of a building or structure where its design or external appearance would be materially affected.

Class O—use of land by the Crown for spreading of dredged material

Permitted development

O *The use of any land by or on behalf of the Crown for the spreading of any dredged material resulting from a dock, pier, harbour, water transport, canal or inland navigation undertaking.*

Class P—development by the Crown on operational Crown land etc relating to aids to shipping

Permitted development

P *Development by or on behalf of the Crown on operational Crown land, or for operational purposes, consisting of—*
   (a) the use of the land as a lighthouse, with all requisite works, roads and appurtenances;
   (b) the extension of, alteration, or removal of a lighthouse; or
   (c) the erection, placing, alteration or removal of a buoy or beacon.

Development not permitted

P1

Development is not permitted by Class P if it consists of or includes the erection of offices, or the reconstruction or alteration of offices where their design or external appearance would be materially affected.

Interpretation of Class P

P2

For the purposes of Class P—
   'buoy or beacon' includes all other marks and signs of the sea; and
   'lighthouse' includes any floating and other light exhibited for the guidance of ships, and also any sirens and any other description of fog signals.

Town and Country Planning (General Permitted Development) Order 2015

Class Q—development by the Crown relating to an emergency

Permitted development

Q   *Development by or on behalf of the Crown on Crown land for the purposes of—*
- (a) preventing an emergency;
- (b) reducing, controlling or mitigating the effects of an emergency; or
- (c) taking other action in connection with an emergency.

Conditions

Q.1

Development is permitted by Class Q subject to the following conditions—
- (a) the developer must, as soon as practicable after commencing development, notify the local planning authority of that development; and
- (b) on or before the expiry of the period of 6 months beginning with the date on which the development began—
  - (i) any use of that land for a purpose of Class Q ceases and any buildings, plant, machinery, structures and erections permitted by Class Q is removed; and
  - (ii) the land is restored to its condition before the development took place, or to such other state as may be agreed in writing between the local planning authority and the developer.

Interpretation of Class Q

Q.2

(1) For the purposes of Class Q, 'emergency' means an event or situation which threatens serious damage to—
- (a) human welfare in a place in the United Kingdom;
- (b) the environment of a place in the United Kingdom; or
- (c) the security of the United Kingdom.

(2) For the purposes of sub-paragraph (1)(a), an event or situation threatens damage to human welfare only if it involves, causes or may cause—
- (a) loss of human life;
- (b) human illness or injury;
- (c) homelessness;
- (d) damage to property;
- (e) disruption of a supply of money, food, water, energy or fuel;
- (f) disruption of a system of communication;
- (g) disruption of facilities for transport; or
- (h) disruption of services relating to health.

(3) For the purposes of sub-paragraph (1)(b), an event or situation threatens damage to the environment only if it involves, causes or may cause—
- (a) contamination of land, water or air with biological, chemical or radioactive matter; or
- (b) disruption or destruction of plant life or animal life.

Town and Country Planning (General Permitted Development) Order 2015

Class R—erection etc of gates, fences etc by the Crown for national security purposes

Permitted development

R   *The erection, construction, maintenance, improvement or alteration of a gate, fence, wall or other means of enclosure by or on behalf of the Crown on Crown land for national security purposes.*

Development not permitted

R.1

Development is not permitted by Class R if the height of any gate, fence, wall or other means of enclosure erected or constructed would exceed 4.5 metres above ground level.

Class S—closed circuit television cameras for national security purposes

Permitted development

S   *The installation, alteration or replacement by or on behalf of the Crown on Crown land of a closed circuit television camera and associated lighting for national security purposes.*

Development not permitted

S.1

Development is not permitted by Class S if—

(a) the dimensions of the camera including its housing exceed 0.75 metres by 0.25 metres by 0.25 metres; or

(b) the uniform level of lighting provided exceeds 10 lux measured at ground level.

Conditions

S.2

Development is permitted by Class S subject to the following conditions—

(a) the camera is, so far as practicable, sited so as to minimise its effect on the external appearance of any building to which it is fixed; and

(b) the camera is removed as soon as reasonably practicable after it is no longer required for national security purposes.

Interpretation of Class S

S.3

For the purposes of Class S—

'camera', except in paragraph S.1(a), includes its housing, pan and tilt mechanism, infra-red illuminator, receiver, mountings and brackets; and

'ground level' means the level of the surface of the ground immediately adjacent to the building to which the camera is attached or, where the level of the surface of the ground is not uniform, the level of the lowest part of the surface of the ground adjacent to it.

Town and Country Planning (General Permitted Development) Order 2015

Class T—electronic communication apparatus etc for national security purposes

Permitted development

T   Development by or on behalf of the Crown for national security purposes in, on, over or under Crown land, consisting of—
- (a) the installation, alteration or replacement of any electronic communications apparatus;
- (b) the use of land in an emergency for a period not exceeding 6 months to station and operate moveable electronic communications apparatus required for the replacement of unserviceable electronic communications apparatus, including the provision of moveable structures on the land for the purposes of that use; or
- (c) development ancillary to radio equipment housing.

Development not permitted

T.1

Development is not permitted by Class T(a) if—
- (a) in the case of the installation of apparatus (other than on a building) the apparatus, excluding any antenna, would exceed a height of 15 metres above ground level;
- (b) in the case of the alteration or replacement of apparatus already installed (other than on a building), the apparatus, excluding any antenna, would, when altered or replaced, exceed the height of the existing apparatus or a height of 15 metres above ground level, whichever is the greater;
- (c) in the case of the installation, alteration or replacement of apparatus on a building, the height of the apparatus (taken by itself) would exceed the height of the existing apparatus or—
    - (i) 15 metres, where it is installed, or is to be installed, on a building which is 30 metres or more in height; or
    - (ii) 10 metres in any other case,

  whichever is the greater;
- (d) in the case of the installation, alteration or replacement of apparatus on a building, the highest part of the apparatus when installed, altered or replaced would exceed the height of the highest part of the building by more than the height of the existing apparatus or—
    - (i) 10 metres, where it is installed, or is to be installed, on a building which is 30 metres or more in height;
    - (ii) 8 metres, in the case of a building which is more than 15 metres but less than 30 metres in height; or
    - (iii) 6 metres in any other case,

  whichever is the greater;
- (e) in the case of the installation, alteration or replacement of apparatus (other than an antenna) on a mast, the height of the mast and the apparatus supported by it would, when the apparatus was installed, altered or replaced, exceed any relevant height limit specified in respect of apparatus in paragraphs (a), (b), (c) and (d), and for the purposes of applying the limit specified in paragraph (c), the words '(taken by itself)' in that paragraph are disregarded;

Town and Country Planning (General Permitted Development) Order 2015

(f) in the case of the installation, alteration or replacement of any apparatus other than—
  (i) a mast;
  (ii) an antenna;
  (iii) any apparatus which does not project above the level of the surface of the ground; or
  (iv) radio equipment housing,
  the ground or base area of the structure would exceed the ground or base area of the existing structure or 1.5 square metres, whichever is the greater;

(g) in the case of the installation, alteration or replacement of an antenna on a building (other than a mast) which is less than 15 metres in height; on a mast located on such a building; or, where the antenna is to be located below a height of 15 metres above ground level, on a building (other than a mast) which is 15 metres or more in height—
  (i) the antenna is to be located on a wall or roof slope facing a highway which is within 20 metres of the building on which the antenna is to be located, unless it is essential for operational purposes that the antenna is located in that position; or
  (ii) in the case of dish antennas, the size of any dish would exceed the size of the existing dish when measured in any dimension or 1.3 metres when measured in any dimension, whichever is the greater;

(h) in the case of the installation, alteration or replacement of a dish antenna on a building (other than a mast) which is 15 metres or more in height, or on a mast located on such a building, where the antenna is located at a height of 15 metres or above, measured from ground level the size of any dish would exceed the size of the existing dish when measured in any dimension or 1.3 metres when measured in any dimension, whichever is the greater;

(i) in the case of the installation of a mast, on a building which is less than 15 metres in height, such a mast would be within 20 metres of a highway, unless it is essential for operational purposes that the mast is installed in that position; or

(j) in the case of the installation, alteration or replacement of radio equipment housing—
  (i) the development is not ancillary to the use of any other electronic communications apparatus; or
  (ii) the development would exceed 90 cubic metres or, if located on the roof of a building, the development would exceed 30 cubic metres.

T.2

Development consisting of the installation of apparatus is not permitted by Class T(a) on article 2(3) land unless—

(a) the land on which the apparatus is to be installed is, or forms part of, a site on which there is existing electronic communication apparatus;
(b) the existing apparatus was installed on the site on or before the relevant day; and
(c) the site was Crown land on the relevant day.

Town and Country Planning (General Permitted Development) Order 2015

T.3

(1) Subject to sub-paragraph (2), development is not permitted by Class T(a) if it will result in the installation of more than 1 item of apparatus ('the original apparatus') on a site in addition to any item of apparatus already on that site on the relevant day.

(2) In addition to the original apparatus which may be installed on a site by virtue of Class T(a), for every 4 items of apparatus which existed on that site on the relevant day, 1 additional item of small apparatus may be installed.

(3) In sub-paragraph (2), 'small apparatus' means—

　(a) a dish antenna, other than on a building, not exceeding 5 metres in diameter and 7 metres in height;

　(b) an antenna, other than a dish antenna and other than on a building, not exceeding 7 metres in height;

　(c) a hard standing or other base for any apparatus described in paragraphs (a) and (b), not exceeding 7 metres in diameter;

　(d) a dish antenna on a building, not exceeding 1.3 metres in diameter and 3 metres in height;

　(e) an antenna, other than a dish antenna, on a building, not exceeding 3 metres in height;

　(f) a mast on a building, not exceeding 3 metres in height;

　(g) equipment housing not exceeding 3 metres in height and of which the area, when measured at ground level, does not exceed 9 square metres.

Conditions

T.4

(1) Class T(a) and Class T(c) development is permitted subject to the condition that any antenna or supporting apparatus, radio equipment housing or development ancillary to radio equipment housing constructed, installed, altered or replaced on a building in accordance with that permission is, so far as is practicable, sited so as to minimise its effect on the external appearance of the building.

(2) Class T(a) development consisting of the installation of any additional apparatus on article 2(3) land is permitted subject to the condition that the apparatus is installed as close as is reasonably practicable to any existing apparatus.

(3) Class T(b) development is permitted subject to the condition that any apparatus or structure provided in accordance with that permission is, at the expiry of the relevant period, removed from the land and the land restored to its condition before the development took place.

(4) Class T development—

　(a) on article 2(3) land or land which is, or is within, a site of special scientific interest; or

　(b) on any other land and consisting of the construction, installation, alteration or replacement of a mast; or of an antenna on a building or structure (other than a mast) where the antenna (including any supporting structure) would exceed the height of the building or structure at the point where it is installed or to be installed by 4 metres or more; or of radio equipment

Town and Country Planning (General Permitted Development) Order 2015

housing with a volume in excess of 2.5 cubic metres; or of development ancillary to radio equipment housing,

is permitted subject, except in case of emergency, to the conditions set out in T.5.

T.5

(1) The developer must, before commencing development, give notice of the proposed development to any person (other than the developer) who is an owner or tenant of the land to which the development relates—

    (a) by serving the appropriate notice on every such person whose name and address is known to the developer; and

    (b) where the developer has taken reasonable steps to ascertain the names and addresses of every such person, but has been unable to do so, by local advertisement.

(2) Where the proposed development consists of the installation of a mast within 3 kilometres of the perimeter of an aerodrome, the developer must, before commencing development, notify the Civil Aviation Authority, the Secretary of State for Defence or the aerodrome operator, as appropriate.

Interpretation of Class T

T.6

For the purposes of Class T—

'aerodrome operator' means the person who is for the time being responsible for the management of the aerodrome;

'appropriate notice' means a notice signed and dated by or on behalf of the developer and containing—

    (a) the name of the developer;

    (b) the address or location of the proposed development;

    (c) a description of the proposed development (including its siting and appearance and the height of any mast);

'development ancillary to radio equipment housing' means the construction, installation, alteration or replacement of structures, equipment or means of access which are ancillary to and reasonably required for the purposes of the radio equipment housing;

'mast' means a radio mast or a radio tower;

'owner' means any person who is the estate owner in respect of the fee simple, or who is entitled to a tenancy granted or extended for a term of years certain of which not less than 7 years remain unexpired;

'relevant day' means—

    (a) 7th June 2006; or

    (b) where apparatus is installed pursuant to planning permission granted on or after 7th June 2006, the date when that apparatus is finally installed pursuant to that permission,

whichever is later;

'relevant period' means a period which expires—

    (a) 6 months from the commencement of the construction, installation, alteration or replacement of any apparatus or structure permitted by Class T(a) or Class T(c) or from the commencement of the use permitted by Class T(b), as the case may be; or

(b) when the need for such apparatus, structure or use ceases,

whichever occurs first; and

'tenant' means the tenant of an agricultural holding any part of which is comprised in the land to which the proposed development relates.

Interpretation of Part 19

U

For the purposes of Part 19—

'airbase' means the aggregate of the land, buildings and works comprised in a Government aerodrome within the meaning of article 255 of the Air Navigation Order 2009; and

'air traffic services' has the same meaning as in section 98 of the Transport Act 2000 (air traffic services).

SCHEDULE 3
PROCEDURES FOR ARTICLE 4 DIRECTIONS

Article 4

Procedure for article 4(1) directions without immediate effect

1

(1) Subject to paragraph 2, notice of any direction made under article 4(1) of this Order must, as soon as practicable after the direction has been made, be given by the local planning authority—

  (a) by local advertisement;
  (b) by site display at no fewer than 2 locations within the area to which the direction relates, or, if the direction is made under article 4(1)(b), on the site of the particular development to which the direction relates, for a period of not less than 6 weeks; and
  (c) subject to sub-paragraph (2), by serving the notice on the owner and occupier of every part of the land within the area or site to which the direction relates.

(2) In a case where this paragraph applies, the local planning authority need not serve notice on an owner or occupier in accordance with sub-paragraph (1)(c), if they consider that—

  (a) individual service on that owner or occupier is impracticable because it is difficult to identify or locate that person or
  (b) the number of owners or occupiers within the area to which the direction relates makes individual service impracticable.

(3) Sub-paragraph (2) does not apply where the owner or occupier is a statutory undertaker or the Crown.

(4) The notice referred to in sub-paragraph (1) must—

(a) include a description of the development and the area to which the direction relates, or the site to which it relates, as the case may be, and a statement of the effect of the direction;

(b) specify that the direction is made under article 4(1) of this Order;

(c) name a place where a copy of the direction, and a copy of a map defining the area to which it relates, or the site to which it relates, as the case may be, may be seen at all reasonable hours;

(d) specify a period of at least 21 days, stating the date on which that period begins, within which any representations concerning the direction may be made to the local planning authority; and

(e) specify the date on which it is proposed that the direction will come into force, which must be at least 28 days but no longer than 2 years after the date referred to in paragraph (d).

(5) Where a notice given by site display is, without any fault or intention of the local planning authority, removed, obscured or defaced before the period referred to in sub-paragraph (4)(d) has elapsed, the authority is treated as having complied with the requirements of that paragraph if they have taken reasonable steps for the protection of the notice, including, if need be, its replacement.

(6) The local planning authority must send a copy of the direction and the notice under sub-paragraph (1), including a copy of a map defining the area to which it relates, or the site to which it relates, as the case may be, to the Secretary of State on the same day that notice of the direction is first published or displayed in accordance with sub-paragraph (1).

(7) The direction comes into force in respect of any part of the land within the area to which it relates on the date specified in accordance with sub-paragraph (4)(e) but does not come into force unless confirmed by the local planning authority in accordance with sub-paragraphs (9) and (10).

(8) On making a direction under article 4(1)—

(a) a county planning authority must give notice of it to any district planning authority in whose district the area or part of the area to which the direction relates is situated; and

(b) except in metropolitan districts, a district planning authority must give notice of it to the county planning authority, if any.

(9) In deciding whether to confirm a direction made under article 4(1), the local planning authority must take into account any representations received during the period specified in accordance with sub-paragraph (4)(d).

(10) The local planning authority must not confirm a direction until after the expiration of—

(a) a period of at least 28 days following the latest date on which any notice relating to the direction was served or published; or

(b) such longer period as may be specified by the Secretary of State following the notification by the local planning authority to the Secretary of State of the direction.

(11) The local planning authority must, as soon as practicable after a direction has been confirmed—

Town and Country Planning (General Permitted Development) Order 2015

(a) give notice of such confirmation and the date on which the direction will come into force; and

(b) send a copy of the direction as confirmed to the Secretary of State.

(12) Notice under sub-paragraph (11)(a) must be given in the manner described in sub-paragraphs (1) and (4)(a) to (c); and sub-paragraphs (2) and (3) apply for this purpose as they apply for the purpose of sub-paragraph (1)(c).

(13) A local planning authority may, by making a subsequent direction, cancel any direction made by them under article 4(1); and the Secretary of State may, subject to paragraphs 2(3) and (4), make a direction cancelling or modifying any direction under article 4(1) made by a local planning authority at any time before or after its confirmation.

(14) Sub-paragraphs (1) to (12) apply in relation to any direction made under sub-paragraph (13) by a local planning authority unless the direction it is cancelling is a direction to which paragraph 2 applied.

(15) Paragraphs 2(2) to (10) apply in relation to any direction made by a local planning authority under sub-paragraph (13) cancelling a direction to which paragraph 2 applied.

(16) The Secretary of State must notify the local planning authority as soon as practicable after making a direction under sub-paragraph (13).

(17) Sub-paragraphs (1) to (3) and (4)(a) to (c) apply to any direction made under sub-paragraph (13) by the Secretary of State.

(18) A direction made under sub-paragraph (13) by the Secretary of State comes into force in respect of any part of the land within the area to which it relates—

(a) on the date on which the notice is served in accordance with sub-paragraph (1)(c) on the occupier of that part of the land or, if there is no occupier, on the owner; or

(b) if sub-paragraph (2) applies, on the date on which the notice is first published or displayed in accordance with sub-paragraph (1).

Procedure for article 4(1) directions with immediate effect

2

(1) This paragraph applies where—

(a) a direction relating only to development permitted by any of Parts 1 to 4, or Class B or C of Part 11, of Schedule 2 has been made by the local planning authority under article 4(1) and the authority consider that the development to which the direction relates would be prejudicial to the proper planning of their area or constitute a threat to the amenities of their area; or

(b) a direction within the whole or part of any conservation area has been made by the local planning authority under article 4(1) which the authority consider should have immediate effect and the development to which the direction relates is described in paragraphs (a) to (j) of sub-paragraph (3).

(2) Subject to sub-paragraphs (3), (4) and (9), paragraphs 1(1) to (3), (4)(a) to (d), (5), and (8) to (10) apply in relation to a direction to which this paragraph applies; and the planning authority must notify the Secretary of State of the direction on the same day that notice is given under paragraph 1(1).

(3) The Secretary of State may not make a direction under paragraph 1(13) within the whole or part of any conservation area where the development to which the direction relates is described in—

  (a) Class A of Part 1 of Schedule 2, consisting of the enlargement, improvement or other alteration of a dwellinghouse, where any part of the enlargement, improvement or alteration would front a relevant location;

  (b) Class C of Part 1 of that Schedule, where the alteration would be to a roof slope which fronts a relevant location;

  (c) Class D of Part 1 of that Schedule, where the external door in question fronts a relevant location;

  (d) Class E of Part 1 of that Schedule, where the building or enclosure, swimming or other pool to be provided would front a relevant location, or where the part of the building or enclosure maintained, improved or altered would front a relevant location;

  (e) Class F of Part 1 of that Schedule, where the hard surface would front a relevant location;

  (f) Class G of Part 1 of that Schedule, consisting of the installation, alteration or replacement of a chimney on a dwellinghouse;

  (g) Class H of Part 1 of that Schedule, where the part of the building or other structure on which the antenna is to be installed, altered or replaced fronts a relevant location;

  (h) Class A of Part 2 of that Schedule, where the gate, fence, wall or other means of enclosure would be within the curtilage of a dwellinghouse and would front a relevant location;

  (i) Class C of Part 2 of the Schedule, consisting of the painting of the exterior of any part of—

    (i) a dwellinghouse; or

    (ii) any building or enclosure within the curtilage of a dwellinghouse,

    which fronts a relevant location;

  (j) Class C of Part 11 of that Schedule, where the gate, fence, wall or other means of enclosure is within the curtilage of a dwellinghouse and fronts a relevant location.

(4) The Secretary of State may not modify a direction to which this paragraph applies or a direction which relates to—

  (a) a listed building;

  (b) a building which is notified to the authority by the Secretary of State as a building of architectural or historic interest; or

  (c) development within the curtilage of a listed building,

  and does not relate to land of any other description.

(5) The direction comes into force in respect of any part of the land within the area to which it relates—

  (a) on the date on which the notice is served in accordance with paragraph 1(1)(c) on the occupier of that part of the land or, if there is no occupier, on the owner; or

  (b) if paragraph 1(2) applies, on the date on which the notice is first published or displayed in accordance with paragraph 1(1).

(6) A direction to which this paragraph applies expires at the end of the period of 6 months beginning with the date on which it comes into force unless confirmed by the local planning authority in accordance with paragraphs 1(9) and (10) before the end of the 6 month period.

(7) The local planning authority must, as soon as practicable after a direction has been confirmed—

   (a) give notice of their confirmation; and

   (b) send a copy of the direction as confirmed to the Secretary of State.

(8) Notice under sub-paragraph (7)(a) must be given in the manner described in paragraphs 1(1) and (4)(a) to (c); and paragraphs 1(2) and (3) apply for this purpose as they apply for the purpose of paragraph 1(1)(c).

(9) Sub-paragraph (7)(b) does not apply in relation to a direction to which sub-paragraph (3) applies or to a direction which relates to—

   (a) a listed building;

   (b) a building which is notified to the authority by the Secretary of State as a building of architectural or historic interest; or

   (c) development within the curtilage of a listed building,

   and does not relate to land of any other description.

(10) In this paragraph, 'relevant location' means a highway, waterway or open space.

SCHEDULE 4
STATUTORY INSTRUMENTS REVOKED IN SO FAR AS THEY APPLY TO ENGLAND

Article 8

1

The Town and Country Planning (General Permitted Development) Order 1995.

2

The Town and Country Planning (General Permitted Development) (Amendment) Order 1996.

3

The Town and Country Planning (General Permitted Development) (Amendment) Order 1997.

4

The Town and Country Planning (General Permitted Development) (Amendment) Order 1998.

5

The Town and Country Planning (General Permitted Development) (Amendment) Order 1999.

6

The Town and Country Planning (General Permitted Development) (Amendment) (England) Order 2001.

7

The Town and Country Planning (General Permitted Development) (Amendment) (England) Order 2005;

8

The Town and Country Planning (General Permitted Development) (England) (Amendment) (No 2) Order 2005.

9

The Town and Country Planning (General Permitted Development) (Amendment) (England) Order 2006.

10

The Town and Country Planning (General Permitted Development) (Amendment) (England) Order 2007.

11

The Town and Country Planning (General Permitted Development) (Amendment) (England) Order 2008.

12

The Town and Country Planning (General Permitted Development) (Amendment) (No 2) (England) Order 2008.

13

The Town and Country Planning (General Permitted Development) (Amendment) (England) Order 2010.

14

The Town and Country Planning (General Permitted Development) (Amendment) (No2) (England) Order 2010.

15

The Town and Country Planning (General Permitted Development) (Amendment) (England) Order 2011.

16

The Town and Country Planning (General Permitted Development) (Amendment) (England) Order 2012.

17

The Town and Country Planning (General Permitted Development) (Amendment) (No 2) (England) Order 2012.

Town and Country Planning (General Permitted Development) Order 2015

18

The Town and Country Planning (General Permitted Development) (Amendment) (England) Order 2013.

19

The Town and Country Planning (General Permitted Development) (Amendment) (No 2) (England) Order 2013.

20

The Town and Country Planning (General Permitted Development) (Amendment) (England) (No 3) Order 2013.

21

The Town and Country Planning (General Permitted Development) (Amendment) (England) (No 4) Order 2013.

22

The Town and Country Planning (General Permitted Development) (Amendment and Consequential Provisions) (England) Order 2014.

23

The Town and Country Planning (General Permitted Development) (Amendment) (England) Order 2015.

Index

[*All references are to para numbers*]

A
Amusement park
  permitted development, 5.176
Appeal
  advertisement appeal, simplified regime—
    application of, 20.4
    Minister's discretion to depart from, 20.4
    scope for bringing, 20.5
    written representations, 20.12
  alternatives to, 19.39, 19.43
  amendment of schemes on, 19.44–19.46
  costs *see* **Costs** (planning appeals and call-ins, in)
  decision to appeal—
    factors to consider—
      non-determination, in case of, 19.42
      refusal, in case of, 19.40
    other options, 19.39, 19.43
  determining—
    generally, 19.12, 24.1
    mode of—
      England, in, 19.51, 19.52
      generally, 19.48–19.50
      hearing, 19.52
      inquiry, 19.52
      ministerial discretion as to, 19.48
      options available, 19.48–19.50
      statutory reform, 19.50
      Wales, in, 19.53
      written representations, 19.52
    see also **Decision**
  dual jurisdiction, 19.36–19.38
  evidence, restriction on Ministers introducing, 19.15
  factors to consider—
    non-determination, in case of, 19.42
    refusal, in case of, 19.40
  fairness in raising points, 19.15
  form, submission of, 19.24, 19.26, 19.30
  further application as alternative to, 19.43
  grant of permission subject to conditions, following, 19.41
  hearing *see* **Hearing**

Appeal – *contd*
  householder or minor commercial appeal—
    accompanying documents, 19.25, 19.26, 20.18–20.20
    householder application: meaning—
      England, in, 20.6, 20.7
      Wales, in, 20.13
    minor commercial application: meaning—
      England, in, 20.8
      Wales, in, 20.15
    simplified procedure—
      accompanying documents, 20.18–20.20
      amendments requiring consultation, 20.32
      application of, 20.4
      assumptions behind, 20.30
      caution, appellant's need to exercise, 20.31
      commencement of appeal, 20.18
      further representations and issues, 20.30–20.32
      importance of representations, 20.21
      information about appeal, right to, 20.24, 20.25
      introduction, 20.1
      Minister's discretion to depart from, 20.4
      nature of, 20.1
      notice of procedure, Secretary of State giving, 20.22
      Planning Inspectorate standard form letter, sue of, 20.24
      popularity of, 20.1
      publicity of original planning application, relevance, 20.11
      questionnaire, LPA sending, 20.23
      scope for bringing, 20.5
      site visits, 20.26–20.29
      statutory authority for, 20.2
      time limit for bringing, 20.17, 20.20
      use classes, application of, 20.9, 20.10
      written representations case—
        England, in, 20.6–20.12
        stages and regulations in, 20.3
        Wales, in, 20.13–20.16

Index

Appeal – *contd*
  matters to have regard to, 19.13, 19.14
  Mayor of London, from decision of *see under* **Mayor of London**
  methods of determining, 19.3
  non-determination for timing etc, inability to appeal for, 19.22
  notice of—
    accompanying documents—
      appeal form, along with, 19.30
      environmental statement etc, 19.31
      householder or minor commercial appeal, 19.25, 19.26
      not required, where, 19.29
      other cases, 19.27
      Wales, in, 19.31–19.34
    agricultural tenants, for, 19.35
    generally, 19.24
    owners, for, 19.35
    reform of process, effect, 19.23
    statutory authority for, 19.24
    Wales, in, 19.32–19.34
  planning application, effect on, 19.9
  range of appeals available, 19.1, 19.6
  recovery of *see under* **Planning application** (calling in)
  reform of procedures, 19.23
  refusal of planning application, against—
    excluded, where, 19.2
    factors to consider, 19.40
    generally, 6.91–6.93, 19.1–19.3, 19.39, 19.40
    jurisdiction to hear, 1.68
    other options, 19.39
    procedural guidance on, 1.70
    procedures for determining, 1.67
    right of, 1.66
    start of time for submission, 14.4
    time limit for bringing, 1.66
    written decision as to, 1.69
    see also right of *below*
  requirements, 19.27
  right of—
    application determined before appeal submitted, 19.9
    expiry, 19.8
    judicial review giving rise to, 19.22
    non-applicant, not available to, 19.11, 19.22
    not arising, where, 19.8
    person able to exercise, 19.10
    range of appeals, 19.6
    statutory authority, 19.4, 19.5
    time when arising, 19.7
  role of, 19.12–19.15
  statement of case, 19.28

Appeal – *contd*
  time limits—
    development order, as prescribed in, 19.16
    EIA required, where, 19.16
    England, in, 19.16
    exceptions, 19.16
    generally, 19.16
    householder application: meaning, 19.17
    late submission, 19.21
    minor commercial application: meaning, 19.18
    non-determination appeals, 19.22, 19.42
    non-EIA major development, in case of, 19.16
    Wales, in, 19.19, 19.20
  Wales—
    determining application after being appealed in, 19.36–19.38
    dual jurisdiction, introduction, 19.37
    mode of determination, 19.53
    notice of appeal, 19.32–19.34
    time limits, 19.19, 19.20
  withdrawal, 19.47
  written representations *see* **Written representations**

B
Broads Authority
  planning authority, as, 1.12
Building
  meaning, 5.91
Building operations
  meaning, 1.14

C
Change of use
  advertisements, display of, 2.48
  agriculture and forestry, 2.39–2.42
  carrying on use, 2.34–2.36
  cessation of use where more than one, 2.28
  character of use, broad nature of, 2.24
  curtilage of building, to, 2.38
  description of use, change in, 2.25
  examples of material change of use, 2.45–2.48
  exceptions to material change, 2.37–2.44
  horses, keeping or breeding of, 2.41
  identity of user, whether material, 2.26
  inactivity, survival despite, 2.35
  judicial approach to, 2.27
  landfilling of hazardous waste, 2.47
  material change: meaning, 2.24
  mixed uses, in case of, 2.44

Change of use – *contd*
  planning unit, determining, 2.32, 2.33
  primary use, uses incidental or ancillary to, 2.29–2.31, 2.44
  refuse or waste, deposit of, 2.46
  sale of produce, 2.40
  short-term lettings in London, 2.49–2.52
  start of use, identifying, 2.36
  time for, 2.24
  use classes *see* **Use classes**
Community Infrastructure Levy
  meaning, 27.4
  annual amendments, 27.3
  appeals—
    challenging appeal decision, 27.42
    charitable relief, by person claiming, 27.39
    eligible persons, 27.38
    generally, 27.37
    interested person, by, 27.40
    liability for development, by person assuming, 27.39
    owner of material interest, by, 27.39
    procedure, 27.42
    self-build housing exemption, by person claiming, 27.41
    to whom made, 27.41
    written representation procedure, determined under, 27.42
  charging schedule, need to adopt, 27.4
  different rates for different reasons, 27.5
  draft charging schedule, 27.6
  exclusions from liability—
    development not subject for timing reasons, 27.30, 27.31
    retained and replacement floorspace, exclusion of, 27.26–27.29
    see also exemptions and reliefs *below*
  exemptions and reliefs—
    charities, 27.15
    exceptional circumstances relief, 27.24, 27.25
    generally, 27.11
    minor development, 27.12
    residential annexes or extensions, 27.13, 27.14
    self-build housing, 27.20–27.23
    social housing, 27.16–27.19
    unacceptable impact on economic viability, 27.24, 27.25
  generally, 27.1–27.3
  historical background to, 27.1, 27.2
  introduction, 27.3
  liability to pay—
    apportionment, 27.36
    assumption of, 27.36

Community Infrastructure Levy – *contd*
  liability to pay – *contd*
    development categories subject to, 27.9, 27.10
    development not subject for timing reasons, 27.30, 27.31
    elements giving rise to, 27.7
    exemptions and reliefs *see* exemptions and reliefs *above*
    nature of development, 27.8
    retained and replacement floorspace, exclusion of, 27.26–27.29
    see also rates applied *below*
  matters to be taken into account in setting rate, 27.4
  payment, 27.43–27.45
  persons able to levy, 27.4
  planning obligation, effect on, 12.40–12.46
  publication of charging schedule, need for, 27.6
  purpose, 27.4
  rates, setting, 27.4
  rates applied—
    apportionment, 27.36
    assumption of liability, 27.36
    calculation of chargeable amount, 27.35
    development under general consent, 27.34
    development where planning application granted, 27.33
    source of, 27.32
Completion notice
  completion condition, 4.20
  confirmation by Ministers, 4.24
  further period specified within, 4.23
  generally, 4.19
  hearing as to, 4.24
  refusal to confirm, 4.24
  right to give, 4.21, 4.23
  service—
    development carried out before, 4.24
    persons on whom served, 4.23
    right to be heard following, 4.24
    right to serve, 4.23
  time for taking effect, 4.23
  unopposed, 4.23
  use of, circumstances for, 4.22
  withdrawal, 4.24
Conditions *see under* **Planning permission**
Contractual agreement
  disposal of land by, 12.105
  enforcement, 12.105
  local authority's power to enter into, 12.105

1117

Index

Costs
High Court appeals and applications *see under* **High Court**
parties with power to award, 25.26
planning appeals and call-ins, in—
  application—
    close of inquiry or hearing, following, 24.43
    comment, opportunity for, 24.44
    documentation relevant to, introduction of, 24.48
    form for making, 24.48
    late, 24.42
    making, procedure for, 24.45–24.48
    oral, 24.47
    time for making, 24.40–24.44
    types, 24.45
    withdrawal of appeal, following, 24.43
  challenge to decision *see* **High Court** (challenge to costs decision in planning appeal)
  essential elements of, 24.30
  generally, 24.28–24.30
  interested parties, 24.49–24.52
  parties meeting own, 24.28
  power to award, 24.28
  reasons for award of, 24.28
  statutory authority for, 24.29
  unreasonable behaviour—
    examples, 24.31
    generally, 24.31
    Planning Practice Guidance, 24.34
    procedural, 24.28, 24.32, 24.36, 24.37
    substantive, 24.28, 24.32, 24.33, 24.34, 24.25
    wasted expenditure, 24.38, 24.39

County council
consultation with district, 6.134

Crown
permitted development *see under* **Development rights**
urgent development—
  appropriate authority applying, 18.30
  called in, treated as if, 18.33
  challenge to ministerial decision, 18.33
  fee, 18.31
  generally, 18.29–18.33
  inquiry in case of, 23.149
  public inspection, right of, 18.32
  publicity and consultation requirements, 18.30, 18.31, 18.32
  removal of exemption from planning control, 18.29

Crown land
planning application, and, 6.61–6.63

Custom housebuilding
Housing and Planning Bill, 9.108
legislation, 9.108, 9.111
meeting demand for, 9.111
registers, 9.111

D

Decision
call-in or recovered appeal decisions *see* ministerial decision-making *below*
costs *see* **Costs**
effect, 24.53
Environmental Impact Assessment, subject to, 24.25–24.27
errors in, correction of—
  advisability of reading decisions carefully, 24.61
  apology as alternative to, 24.61
  correctable error—
    meaning, 24.55
    applicable decisions, 24.54
    consent needed, in Wales, 24.58
    correction notice, 24.59, 24.60
    decisions outside regime, 24.56
    effect, 24.54
    legislative intention, 24.57
    minor but unnecessary changes, slip rule used for, 24.58
    need for, 24.54
  generally, 24.53, 24.54
  legal challenge, heading off, 24.61
  statutory authority, 24.53, 24.54
final nature of, 24.53
generally, 24.1
inspector's decision-making—
  new matters following close of inquiry or hearing, 24.16, 24.17
  reasons *see* reasons *below*
  reopening of inquiry, 24.15
  split decisions, 24.18
  writing up decision, process for, 24.15
ministerial decision-making—
  briefing report from civil servants, 24.10
  decision letter, 24.13
  inquiry—
    assessor's report, 24.7
    inspector's report following, 24.5, 24.6, 24.8, 24.9
    procedural rules following, 24.4
  inspector reporting to Ministers, 24.2
  'minded to' letter, 24.14
  Minister differing from inspector, 24.11, 24.12
  reasons *see* reasons *below*
  report from inspector, 24.3
  Secretary of State, by, 24.2

1118

Decision – *contd*
ministerial decision-making – *contd*
Secretary of State, jointly with Minister, 24.2
statutory undertakers as alternative to, 24.2
reasons—
adequacy of, 24.21
case-law, 24.21–24.23
disagreement with expert witnesses, where, 24.24
generally, 24.19
to whom sent, 24.20
written, need for, 24.19
withdrawal of issued decision, prohibition on, 24.62–24.67
Demolition
development, following, 4.4
heritage, and, 5.145, 5.146
planning control, 2.22
Development
meaning, 1.3, 1.14, 2.2
change of use *see* **Change of use**
Crown *see under* **Crown**
generally, 2.1–2.4
operational *see* **Operational development**
planning permission for *see* **Planning permission**
principles applicable to, 2.4
statutory powers to remove right of *see* **Completion notice; Discontinuation order**
types of, 2.3
Development consent order
generally, 1.71
statutory authority for, 1.71
Development order
construction, 5.88
dealing with permission under, 5.2
general order, 5.3
grant of—
flexible nature of methods involved, 5.6
generally, 5.3
legislation, general nature of, 5.6
permitted rights *see under* **Development rights**
special development order, 5.3
Development plan
approach to, 9.17–9.26
councils' duty to prepare strategy, 1.23
county councils' duties, 1.24
England, in, 1.28, 9.15
importance of, 9.14
local plans, 1.27
Localism Act, effect, 1.25
London's Spatial Development Strategy, 1.23

Development plan – *contd*
neighbourhood plan, 1.26
preparation, 1.21
recent history of system, 1.22–1.26
Regional Spatial Strategy, 1.23
Wales, in, 1.28, 9.16
Development rights
permitted—
agriculture and forestry, 5.133–5.139
amusement parks, 5.176
application for, where necessary, 1.30
art 4 directions, making of—
conditional authority to make, 5.70
conservation area direction, 5.77
constitutional authority to check, need to check, 5.71
consultation procedures, 5.72, 5.78
effective date of non-immediate direction, 5.74
England, in, 5.66–5.80
expiry of immediate effect direction, 5.79
generally, 5.65
immediate effect, having, 5.76
modification or cancellation, 5.75
National Planning Policy Framework guidance, 5.80
statutory consultation, 5.72
Wales, in, 5.81–5.84
art 5 directions, 5.85
avian flu, in case of, 5.190
caravan site, use of land for, 5.130, 5.131
change of use—
consultation process, 5.116
documents to accompany application, 5.114
flexible planning permissions, 5.119
mixed use, in case of, 5.118
prior approval process, 5.113–5.117
recent legal developments, 5.111
refusal of application for, 5.115
restrictions and conditions, complex nature of, 5.112
statutory authority, 5.110
temporary buildings and structures *see* temporary buildings and structures *below*
changes to—
art 4 direction, effect, 5.60–5.62
designation of land, affecting, 5.63
GPDO, changes to, 5.56–5.59
reasons for, 5.54
retrospective effect, prohibition on, 5.55
underlying circumstances on the ground, affecting, 5.64

Index

Development rights – *contd*
  permitted – *contd*
    communications—
      driver information systems operator, 5.162
      electronic *see* electronic communications code operators *below*
      generally, 5.155
      National Planning Policy Framework guidance, 5.164
      universal postal service operator, 5.163
    conditions withdrawing, 5.15–5.19
    consents, no effect on, 1.31
    Crown, and—
      avian flu, 5.190
      Class A rights, 5.178, 5.190
      Class B rights, 5.179
      Class C rights, 5.180
      Class D rights, 5.181
      Class E rights, 5.182
      Class K, 5.184
      Class M, 5.185
      Class N, 5.186
      Class O, 5.187
      Class P, 5.187
      Class Q, 5.188
      Classes F-J rights, 5.183
      Classes R, S and T, 5.189
      emergency powers, 5.188
      generally, 5.177
      national security purposes, 5.189
    development order *see* **Development order**
    electricity suppliers, 5.154
    electronic communications code operators—
      Class A rights, 5.156
      Class B rights, 5.161
      Class C rights, 5.161
      Class D rights, 5.162
      limitations, 5.158
      siting and design prior approval process, 5.159, 5.160
      statutory authorisation, 5.157
    emergency powers, 5.188
    England, in, 5.4
    Environmental Impact Assessment and, 5.23–5.25
    environmental restrictions, 1.31
    gas transporters, 5.153
    general principles, 5.8–5.11
    generally, 1.29–1.31, 5.1–5.7, 5.99
    GPDO, grant under, 5.8–5.11
    habitats, and, 5.26–5.31
    heritage and demolition, 5.145, 5.146

Development rights – *contd*
  permitted – *contd*
    highway used by vehicular traffic, and, 5.109
    household rights, 5.100–5.107
    interpretation—
      building: meaning, 5.90–5.96
      dwellinghouse: meaning, 5.94
      generally, 5.88, 5.89
      highway: meaning, 5.95
      machinery: meaning, 5.92, 5.93
      plant: meaning, 5.92, 5.93
      statutory undertaker, 5.96
    lawful development, need for, 5.20–5.22
    local authorities, development by, 5.147, 5.148
    mining and mineral exploration—
      Class A rights, 5.166
      Class B rights, 5.167
      Class C rights, 5.168
      Class L, 5.172
      Class M, 5.173
      Classes D-G, 5.169
      Classes H and I, 5.170
      Classes J and K, 5.171
      coal mining, 5.169
      directions restricting, 5.85
      generally, 5.165
      mineral waste tipping, 5.170
      removal other than from stockpile, 5.173
      stockpile, removal of material from, 5.172
    minor operations, 5.108, 5.109
    miscellaneous development, 5.174–5.176
    national security purposes, 5.189
    non-domestic extensions, alterations etc, 5.140
    particular acts limited to particular rights, 5.32–5.34
    power-related development, 5.153, 5.154
    prior approval of details—
      appeals, 5.47
      applicable rights, 5.35
      application forms, 5.40
      conditions attached to, 5.50–5.52
      determination, effect of, 5.48, 5.49
      elements involved, 5.39
      extensions to dwellinghouses, 5.42
      extent of details, 5.37
      failure to give notice of decision, 5.43–5.47
      fees, 5.40
      generally, 5.35–5.42

1120

Development rights – *contd*
  permitted – *contd*
    prior approval of details – *contd*
      modification to approval, 5.47
      planning obligations and, 5.53
      post-2014 rights, 5.36
      publicity requirements and practices, 5.41
      time for receipt of application, 5.45
      time period, starting date, 5.46
      validity of application, 5.45
    rationale behind, 1.29
    recreational campsites, 5.129, 5.132
    renewable energy, 5.151, 5.152
    restricted categories of land, 5.97, 5.98
    restrictions etc subject to, 5.7, 5.12–5.14
    roads, relating to, 5.143
    Secretary of State's power to authorise, 5.2
    services, repairs to, 5.144
    temporary buildings and structures—
      building and land within curtilage, change of use of, 5.127
      commercial film-making, use of land for, 5.28
      generally, 5.121–5.123
      state-funded school, change to, 5.126
      statutory authority, 5.120
      temporary uses, 5.124, 5.125
    test for excluding, 3.12
    transport-related development, 5.141, 5.142
    types, 5.87
    Wales, in, 5.4
    water and sewerage, 5.149, 5.150
    Welsh Ministers' power to authorise, 5.2
    withdrawal—
      conditions resulting in, 5.15–5.19
      revocation of order, following, 5.57

Discontinuance order
  challenge to confirmed order, 4.37
  compensation, whether recoverable, 4.36
  confirmation, need for, 4.37
  disadvantages, 4.40
  entry powers etc, 4.39
  grant of planning permission under, 4.35
  offence in connection with, 4.38
  power to make—
    local planning authority, by, 4.33
    Secretary of State, by, 4.38
    Welsh Ministers, by, 4.38
  rare use of, 4.40
  right to require discontinuance, 4.33
  statutory authority, 4.34
  withdrawal, 4.37

Dwellinghouse
  meaning, 5.94

E

Enterprise zone
  generally, 26.60
  means of granting permission, 26.60
  nature of planning permission, 26.60
  scheme, power to make, 26.60
  scope of permission granted by, 26.60

Environmental Impact Assessment
  arising, where, 7.1
  categories of project—
    generally 1.40, 7.3
    infrastructure projects, 7.15, 7.16
    matter of law, as, 7.16
    projects outside sensitive areas, 7.19
    Sch 1, under, 7.11, 7.16, 7.20
    Sch 2, under, 7.12, 7.14–7.19, 7.21
    sensitive area, in, 7.13
    urban development projects, 7.15, 7.16
    waste disposal installation, 7.17
  decision—
    case-law, 7.38–7.42
    error of law, example of, 7.43
    errors affecting, 7.44
    insufficient information to make, 7.43
    mitigation measures, taking, 7.38
    planning register, kept on or with, 7.52, 7.53
    publicity, 7.78
    reasons, 7.45–7.51
    selection criteria, 7.36
  direction, adopting—
    selection criteria, 7.36
    see also decision *above*
  Directive, prescribed in, 1.39, 7.2
  EIA application: meaning, 7.9
  environmental statement, need for *see* **Environmental statement**
  generally, 7.1–7.5
  introduction, 7.2
  legislation in UK, 7.4
  mitigation measures, 7.38
  need for, 7.6, 7.37
  permissions subject to, 7.8
  permitted development rights, and, 5.23–5.25
  regulations as to, 1.41
  screening—
    changes to scheme post-screening, 7.54
    decision *see* decision *above*
    generally, 7.22
    insufficient information for, 7.43
    need for, 7.22

Index

Environmental Impact Assessment – *contd*
screening – *contd*
 opinion—
  meaning, 7.23
  application below threshold screening decisions, 7.33–7.35
  decision *see* decision *above*
  development assessed in, 7.25
  further information, request for, 7.26, 7.28
  Minister's direction as to, 7.27
  new road, whether within relevant threshold or criteria, 7.32
  positive, production of, 7.28
  request to adopt, 7.24
  Sch 1 or Sch 2 development, 7.31, 7.32
  Secretary of State requested to make, 7.28
  selection criteria, need to consider, 7.36
  time for adopting, 7.27, 7.30
 planning application, on receipt of, 7.29–7.32
significant effects likely, where, 7.37, 7.42
stages in process, 1.42, 7.5
subsequent applications, for, 7.7, 7.10, 7.76, 7.77

Environmental statement
meaning, 7.62
additional information, submission of, 7.70–7.72
availability to public concerned, 7.68
consultation following submission, 7.61, 7.68, 7.69
contents, 7.64–7.66
generally, 7,66
information—
 duty to supply, 7.61
 environmental, consideration of, 7.73–7.75
limited nature of, 7.66
minimum information in, 7.63
preparation, 7.55, 7.61
publicity, 7.68, 7.69
purpose, 7.55
requirements, 7.65, 7.66
scoping decision, effect, 7.60
scoping opinion—
 binding on LPA or Minister, whether, 7.60
 effect, 7.60
 failure to adopt within timescale, 7.59
 request for—
  adoption following, 7.58
  consultation following, 7.57
  documents to accompany, 7.56

Environmental statement – *contd*
scoping opinion – *contd*
 request for – *contd*
  generally, 7.56
  right to make, 7.56
  screening opinion, submitted with request for, 7.56
  timescale for adoption following, 7.58
 scoping direction—
  effect, 7.60
  request for, 7.59
 structure, 7.67
 submission, service of notice and, 7.61

F
Fish farming
planning control, 2.23

G
Greater London
agreements and undertakings in, enforcement etc, 12.108
Green Belt
meaning, 9.68
characteristics, 9.68
development in—
 appropriateness generally, 9.71–9.73
 cemeteries, 9.74, 9.75, 9.76, 9.77
 inappropriateness generally, 9.71–9.73
 mobile homes, 9.79
 oil and gas exploration, 9.78
 outdoor sport, 9.74, 9.75, 9.77
 questions, relevant, 9.70
 recreation, 9.74, 9.75, 9.77
 very special circumstances, in, 9.80–9.85
policy, 9.68
purposes, 9.69

H
Habitats
permitted development rights, and, 5.26–5.31
Hearing
meaning, 22.1
accommodation at, 22.26
adjournment to site, 22.36, 22.37
appearances at, 22.22
conduct at, 22.33
cross-examination, limits on, 22.1, 22.30
date—
 notice of, 22.24, 22.25
 time limit for setting, 22.23
detailed legal submissions at, 22.1
determination, potential to change mode of, 22.19–22.21

1122

Index

Hearing – *contd*
discussion at, nature of, 22.29
evidence—
  late, 22.34
  no formal calling of, 22.31
  time for production of, 22.2
five-week statement *see* statement of case *below*
informal nature of venue, 22.26
information, Minister's right to further, 22.14
late evidence, 22.17
legislation, relevant, 22.3
mode of determination, decision on, 22.6
natural justice, adherence to rules of, 22.29
nature of, 22.1
notice of, 22.7
opening matters at, 22.28
procedure at, 22.28–22.33
questionnaire, completion and submission, 22.9
questions at, 22.29
representation at, 22.31, 22.32
rigour of, 22.27
rules, relevant, 22.4
site visit—
  closure of hearing, following, 22.38, 22.39
  inspector's presence, 22.39
  request for, 22.39
  rules as to, 22.39
stages in, 22.4
start of discussion at, 22.29
starting date, 22.7
statement of case—
  availability, 22.13
  circulation, 22.13
  comments on, 22.11
  copies, submission, 22.11
  duplication of documents unnecessary, 22.10
  inspection, 22.13
  none-week comments, 22.16
  response to submission, 22.10
  time limit for submission—
    England, in, 22.10, 22.17
    Wales, in, 22.12
statement of common ground, 22.18
statutory parties—
  meaning, 22.8
  provision of details to appellant, 22.8
  statement of case provided to, 22.8
submission of appeal, 22.5
tactics and preparation, 22.35
third party appearance at, 22.32

Hearing – *contd*
third-party representations—
  availability, 22.13
  circulation, 22.13
  inspection, 22.13
  time limit to make, 22.12
timetable, start of, 22.7
venue, 22.26
virtues of format, 22.1
Heritage
demolition, and, 5.145, 5.146
High Court
administrative reform, 25.1
application under s 288—
  acknowledgment of service, 25.61, 25.62
  commencement *see* commencement of s 287 or 288 proceedings *below*
  cross-examination, 25.79, 25.80
  evidence *see* evidence *below*
  former s 288 procedure, 25.68–25.70
  generally, 25.31
  grounds of challenge, 25.32–25.34
  interim orders, 25.81
  person aggrieved—
    meaning, 25.35
    EIA carried out, where, 25.37
    refused, where, 25.39
  protocol, not subject to, 25.54
  service, 25.58, 25.59
  standing to bring—
    EIA carried out, where, 25.36, 25.37
    generally, 25.35
    person aggrieved *see* person aggrieved *supra*
    third party pressure groups, 25.38
  summary grounds of resistance, 25.61, 25.62
authorities, agreed bundle of, 25.82, 25.83
challenge to costs decision in planning appeal—
  costs decision only being challenged, 25.29
  decision made after 26 October 2015, 25.27
  judicial concerns, 25.29
  merits, effect of wider context of case, 25.28
  public law grounds, on, 25.26
  substantive appeal decision also challenged, 25.28
challenge to planning decision—
  alternative remedies, 25.24, 25.25
  bodies other than LPAs, of, 25.23
  costs decisions, 25.17
  decisions not open to challenge, 25.15, 25.16

1123

Index

High Court – *contd*
  challenge to planning decision – *contd*
    decisions open to challenge—
      method of challenging, 25.14
      simplified planning zone schemes, 25.14
      statutory list of, 25.13
    generally, 1.81, 25.11
    historical background, 25.2
    judicial review—
      challenge to decision, as alternative to, 25.19
      decisions of public bodies, 25.11
      exceptional case where allowed, 25.25
      non-planning application provisions, 25.18
      reasons adopted in appeal decision, as to, 25.21
      reasons for not bringing proceedings, 25.24
    lawfulness of eventual decision, challenging, 25.19
    mechanisms available, 25.12
    potential problems facing disgruntled victor, 25.22
    procedures *see* procedures *below*
    public law grounds *see* public law grounds of review *below*
    reasons adopted in appeal decision, against, 25.21
    statutory authority, 25.3
    steps in application process, 25.20
    types of proceedings, 1.81
  commencement of s 287 or 288 proceedings—
    acknowledgment of service, 25.61, 25.62
    authority for, 25.41
    consideration of permission application, 25.63–25.66
    details accompanying claim form, 25.43, 25.44, 25.56
    generally, 25.57
    information to be given, 25.42
    Part 8 claim form, 25.41
    parties, 25.41
    permission to proceed required, 25.60
    post-permission procedure, 25.67
    service, 25.58, 25.59
    summary grounds of resistance, 25.61, 25.62
    time for, 25.45–25.51
    with notice nature of process, 25.60
  costs—
    additional, payment of, 25,97
    apportionment, 25.94

High Court – *contd*
  costs – *contd*
    discretionary nature of, 25.94
    general rule, 25.94
    more than one set of, restriction on paying, 25.95–25.97
    protection for parties—
      Aarthus Convention claims in judicial review, 25.99–25.101
      Environmental Impact assessment cases, in, 25.103, 25.104
      generally, 25.98, 25.102
      Industrial Emissions Directive cases, in, 25.103, 25.104
    winner usually recovering, 25.94
  Court of Appeal, appeal to, 25.105–25.107
  cross-examination, 25.79, 25.80
  disclosure—
    application made without notice, where, 25.77
    documentation refused prior to commencement, where, 25.78
    duty to make full and frank, 25.76, 25.77
    internal notes and e-mails, 25.75
    no automatic duty of, 25.75
    onerous, where, 25.77
    request in context of proceedings, 25.78
    specific, application for, 25.78
  evidence—
    disclosure *see* disclosure *above*
    exhibiting documents, dealt with by, 25.73
    generally, 25.71–25.73
    nature of, 25.71, 25.72
    not in the decision-making process, where, 25.72
    reasoning process, about, 25.74
  hearing—
    agreed bundle of authorities, 25.82, 25.83
    judge at, 25.84
    procedure at, 25.84
    skeleton argument, provision of, 25.82
    statement of factual matters, agreement as to, 25.82
    trial bundle, filing of, 25.82
  judicial review proceedings—
    cross-examination, 25.79, 25.80
    evidence *see* evidence *above*
    former s 288 procedure, 25.68–25.70
    interim orders, 25.81
    pre-action processes *see* pre-action processes *below*

1124

Index

High Court – *contd*
  judicial review proceedings – *contd*
    s 288, and—
      acknowledgment of service, 25.61, 25.62
      commencement, 25.57
      consideration of permission application, 25.63–25.66
      documentation filed with proceedings, 25.56
      former s 288 procedure, 25.68–25.70
      generally, 25.55
      permission to proceed required, 25.60
      post-permission procedure, 25.67
      service of proceedings, 25.58, 25.59
      summary grounds of resistance, 25.61
      with notice nature of process, 25.60
    standing in, 25.40
  Planning Court *see* **Planning Court**
  pre-action processes—
    matters to be included in pre-action letters, 25.53
    protocol, subject to, 25.52
    reduced period for bringing proceedings, 25.54
  procedures—
    application under s 288 *see* application under s 288 *above*
    generally, 25.30
    pre-action processes *see* pre-action processes *above*
    statutory authority, 25.30
  public law grounds of review—
    generally, 25.4
    illegality error going to jurisdiction, 25.5
    irrationality, 25.6, 25.7
    natural justice, 25.8–25.10
    perversity, 25.7
    procedural impropriety, 25.8–25.10
    unreasonableness, 25.6, 25.7
    Wednesbury unreasonableness, 25.7
  quashing, effect of—
    declaration as to planning status of land, 25.115
    generally, 25.108
    redetermination of appeal or call-in following—
      bespoke timetable, working up, 25.112
      compensation arrangements, 25.113
      consultation with claimant, 25.111
      costs, whether recoverable, 25.112, 25.113
      error by inspector, where, 25.113
      generally, 25.109–25.113

High Court – *contd*
  quashing, effect of – *contd*
    redetermination of appeal or call-in following – *contd*
      initial procedure, 25.110
      representations, request for, 25.111
      redetermination of planning application, 25.114
    remedies—
      generally, 25.85–25.90
      judicial review decisions in—
        approach to exercise of discretion, 25.88, 25.89
        flexible nature of court's powers, 25.85
        orders available, 25.85
        severance of unlawful part of decision, 25.91–25.93
      new material, whether needing to be produced, 25.90
    quashing—
      effect *see* quashing, effect of *above*
      generally, 25.85–25.88, 25.91
      s 288 applications, in—
        approach to exercise of discretion to quash, 25.88
        quashing decision, 25.85–25.88, 25.91
        relevant requirements, where failure to comply with, 25.87
        starting point, 25.86
        severance of unlawful part of decision, 25.91–25.93
    skeleton argument, contents of, 25.82
    statement of factual matters, agreement as to, 25.82
    trial bundle, filing of, 25.82
Highway
  meaning, 5.95
Historic England
  guidance from, as material consideration, 9.40

I

Inquiry
  meaning, 23.1
  adjournment, 23.107
  advocate—
    conduct of case, constraints on, 23.61
    role of, 23.58, 23.60
  assessors, 23.62
  closure of, 23.106
  commencement of process—
    English inspector cases, 23.7
    English Ministerial cases, 23.6
    generally, 23.4
    rules applicable to, 23.5
    Welsh inspector cases, 23.9
    Welsh Ministerial cases, 23.8

Index

Inquiry – *contd*
  conduct, 23.108–23.112
  Crown development, urgent, 23.149
  date—
    judicial review, amenable to, 23.49
    notification of, 23.50–23.57
    rules, as set out in, 23.3
    setting, 23.48
    variation, 23.48, 23.51
  decisions *see* **Decision**
  evidence—
    exceptions to public nature of, 23.82
    inspector's role during giving of, 23.135, 23.136
    material not produced by parties, reference to—
      breach of natural justice test, 23.140, 23.141
      case law, 23.137
      consultation, lack of, 23.139
      decisions by inspectors or Ministers, 23.137
      generally, 23.137–23.141
      national security cases, 23.142–23.148
      not having effect on decision, 23.138
    national security case, in case of, 23.142–23.148
    offence of destroying, 23.81
    proof of *see* proof of evidence *below*
    public nature of, 23.82
    statement of, in Wales—
      duty to prepare, 23.64
      see also proof of evidence *below*
    summons to attend or produce documents, 23.80, 23.81
    witness *see* witness *below*
    see also under procedure *below*
  failure to attend, offence, 23.81
  fairness of proceedings—
    general principles, 23.129–23.134
    inspector's role during giving of evidence, 23.135, 23.136
  guidance, 23.2
  inspector—
    communication with, outside formal hearing, 23.113–23.116
    conduct in general, 23.120
    conflict of interests, need to avoid, 23.117–23.119
    powers and duties, 24.1
    previous decisions, examination of, 23.57
    professional background, knowledge of, 23.57
    role during giving of evidence, 23.135, 23.136

Inquiry – *contd*
  inspector's pre-inquiry meeting—
    meaning, 23.28
    agenda, inspector circulating, 23.31
    conduct of, 23.32
    generally, 23.28–23.35
    inspector presiding over, 23.31
    long inquiry, for, 23.28
    note of, inspector circulating, 23.34
    notice, 23.30
    persons entitled to appear at *see* persons entitled to appear at *below*
    procedural points, raising, 23.33
    programming matters, 23.32
    purpose, 23.28
    rules, need to adhere to, 23.35
    timescales, relaxation of, 23.35
    venue arrangements, 23.32
  local nature of, 23.83
  material not produced by parties, reference to *see under* evidence *above*
  Mayor of London, status of, 23.23
  national security cases, evidence in case of, 23.142–23.148
  nature of, 23.1
  persons entitled to appear at—
    England, in, 23.39
    government departments, 23.44–23.47
    inspector's discretionary powers, 23.43
    locally based public authorities, 23.41
    Mayor of London, 23.41
    neighbourhood fora, 23.42
    notification of date to, 23.57
    Wales, in, 23.40
  pre-inquiry meeting—
    inspector presiding over, 23.18, 23.31
    inspector's right to call *see* inspector's pre-inquiry meeting *above*
    major inquiry, usefulness in, 23.14
    Minister's power to call, 23.13, 23.29
    notice of, 23.15, 23.18
    outline statement of case, provision of, 23.16, 23.17, 23.30
    persons entitled to appear at *see* persons entitled to appear at *above*
    rules, need to adhere to, 23.35
    time for holding, 23.18
    timescales, relaxation of, 23.35
  procedure at—
    addressing of parties, 23.110
    adjournment, 23.107
    appellant's opening speech, 23.90
    closing submissions, 23.104, 23.105
    closure of inquiry, 23.106
    conditions to be imposed, discussion as to, 23.103

Inquiry – *contd*
  procedure at – *contd*
    evidence—
      giving of, 23.93
      objectors', timing of, 23.100
      refusal to allow, 23.98
      third party cross-examination, 23.102
      witnesses *see* witnesses *infra*
      written representations, disclosure of, 23.100
    formal nature of, 23.108
    inspector's opening statement, 23.89
    order of speeches, 23.92
    preliminary matters, 23.87–23.89
    qualified privilege of statements, 23.112
    seating of parties, 23.109
    skeleton arguments etc, 23.91
    summary, reading out, 23.94
    unruly behaviour etc, dealing with, 23.111
    witnesses—
      appellant calling, 23.101
      calling of, 23.93, 23.99, 23.101
      cross-examination, 23.96, 23.97, 23.101, 23.102
      examination on oath, 23.95
      inspector questioning, 23.99
      re-examination, 23.98
  proof of evidence—
    meaning, 23.63
    appendices, 23.71
    approach to dealing with, 23.65
    calling a witness by reading, 23.72
    contents, 23.66
    copies, where necessary, 23.72, 23.73
    cross-reference to other documents, 23.71
    ease of use and understanding, 23.71
    expert evidence in, 23.69
    limited length, 23.67
    numbering of pages and paragraphs, 23.71
    statement of truth in, 23.70
    submission, time for, 23.63
    summary, where advisable, 23.68
    supplementary proofs, 23.74
    'taken as read', 23.65
    third parties not obliged to serve, 23.75
  purpose, 23.1
  recording of, 23.121, 23.122
  rules as to holding of, 23.3
  site visit—
    accompanied, 23.106, 23.124, 23.125, 23.126
    entry onto site necessary, 23.127
    generally, 23.123–23.128

Inquiry – *contd*
  site visit – *contd*
    insufficient nature of, 23.128
    need for, 23.123
    pre-inquiry, 23.123
    private property, 23.125
    unaccompanied, 23.123, 23.128
    viewing site insufficient, 23.127
  stages in, 23.3
  statement of case in—
    appellant's, 23.20, 23.21
    copies, to whom sent, 23.26
    England, in, 23.20
    further information, Minister's right to demand, 23.27
    local planning authority's, 23.22
    outline statement, provision of, 23.16, 23.17
    referenced documents, Wales, in, 23.19
  statement of common ground in, 23.76–23.79
  statement of evidence *see* proof of evidence *below*
  statement of matters, 23.36
  statutory authority, 23.2
  summons to attend or produce documents, 23.80, 23.81
  third parties' r 6 status, 23.24, 23.25
  timetabling—
    bespoke programme, arranging, 23.10
    conduct of inquiry, as to, 23.10
    evidence, as to, 23.10
    extension of time, 23.10
    generally, 23.10
    initial publicity, 23.11, 23.12
    Minister's power to vary, 23.48
    pre-inquiry meeting *see* pre-inquiry meeting *above*
    statement of case *see* statement of case *above*
    submission of proofs, for, 23.10
    timetable, preparation etc, 23.37, 23.38
  venue—
    essential requirement, 23.85
    generally, 23.83–23.86
    local nature of, 23.83
    Minister's power to vary, 23.48, 23.51
    practical requirements to be met, 23.85
    responsibility for finding, 23.84
    site, proximity to, 23.84
    suitability of room, 23.85
    time within which available, 23.86
  witness—
    cross-examination, 23.59
    local residents, 23.59
    role of, 23.58

Index

Inquiry – *contd*
  witness – *contd*
    types of evidence given, 23.58
    view on merits of scheme, giving, 23.59
    see also under procedure *above*

L

Local authority
  contractual agreement, power to enter into, 12.105
  permitted development by, 5.147, 5.148
  restrictive covenants, enforcement of, 12.107

Local development order
  additional to other permissions, 26.8
  amendment, 26.21
  calling in—
    Secretary of State's power, repeal of, 26.18
    Welsh Ministers, by, 26.17
  conditional or unconditional, 26.8
  conservation matters, restrictions in case of, 26.9
  direction restricting development in, effect of revocation etc, 26.21
  direction-making power in, 26.8
  EIA, subject to, 26.9
  generally, 26.7
  listed building, 26.9
  making of, 26.7
  National Planning Policy Framework guidance, 26.19
  process for making—
    calling in *see* calling in *above*
    consultation—
      duty of, 26.13
      England, in, 26.11
      persons with right to, 26.13
      Wales, in, 26.12
    draft preparation by LPA, 26.10
    publicity, 26.14
    representations, consideration of, 26.16
    Secretary of State, submission to by LPA, 26.18
    site notice, 26.15
    statement of reasons, 26.10
  register, 26.23
  revision, 26.22
  revocation, 26.20, 26.21
  Wales, in—
    calling in, 26.17
    restrictions, 26.9
    Welsh Government Circular guidance, 26.19

Local planning authority
  application to, 1.32
  application to develop own land, 6.18
  criteria for designating, 18.9
  designation—
    England, in, 18.9, 18.10
    Wales, in, 18.18
  generally, 6.16
  planning application followed by disposal of land, 6.18
  published policies giving rise to legitimate expectation, 6.151
  relevant, 6.16
  revocation of designation, 18.10
  single-tier council, 6.16
  two areas, planning permission required in, 6.19
  two-tier authority areas, 6.17, 6.18
  underperforming, where, 1.32
  wrong authority taking decision, 6.20

London
  generally, 10.1–10.4
  Greater London Authority, establishment, 10.2, 10.4
  Mayor *see* **Mayor of London**
  planning control—
    difficulties, 10.1
    historical background, 10.2
    legislation, 10.4
    Mayor's role *see* **Mayor of London**

M

Machinery
  meaning, 5.92, 5.93

Material considerations
  meaning, 9.3
  appeal, risks arising on, 9.210
  areas of outstanding natural beauty—
    development in, 9.118, 9.119
    policies, 9.120–9.9.123
  biodiversity, 9.146
  Broads, development in—
    generally, 9.115–9.117
    policies, 9.120–9.9.123
  daylight and sunlight, 9.55
  debate over, extensive nature of, 9.8
  examples, 9.4
  fumes and smells, 9.55
  generally, 9.1, 9.2
  Green Belt development *see under* **Green Belt**
  guidance from specialist bodies, 9.40
  health implications, 9.86
  historic development, 9.87–9.99
  Historic England, guidance from, 9.40
  housing—
    affordable housing, 9.104–9.107

Index

Material considerations – *contd*
  housing – *contd*
    five-year housing supply, need for, 9.101–9.103
    policy, 9.100–9.103
    technical standards, effect, 9.209
  human rights implications, 9.149–9.152
  immaterial considerations, and, 9.3
  landscape impacts, 9.112
  light pollution, 9.56
  local finance considerations, 9.5
  minerals policy, 9.124
  National Parks, development in—
    generally, 9.113, 9.114
    policies, 9.120–9.9.123
  nature conservation—
    European sites and species, 9.126–9.131
    generally, 9.125
    Habitats Directive, 9.126–9.130
    protected species, sanctions etc to protect, 9.131
    sites protection, 9.132–9.139
    species protection in planning, 9.140–9.144
  need to have regard to, 9.3
  noise, 9.55
  overbearing and overshadowing, 9.55
  overlooking, 9.56
  personal circumstances and impacts, relevance, 9.148
  planning decision, aspects of—
    appeal, risks on, 9.210
    effect of other regulatory regimes on decision, 9.207, 9.208
    fallback position, 9.191, 9.192
    generally, 9.190
    previous decisions—
      generally, 9.193–9.199
      judicial approach to, 9.194–9.196
      material consideration, as, 9.193
      other sites, decisions on, 9.197–9.199
      unlawfulness of, 9.200
  planning uses—
    effect of application on existing permission, 9.206
    existing or proposed uses and users, protection of, 9.201–9.204
    existing unlawful development, 9.205
    housing technical standards, 9.209
  policy—
    interpretation, 9.41–9.44
    national policy *see under* **Planning policy**
  public sector equality duty, 9.153–9.155
  sites of special scientific interest, 9.145

Material considerations – *contd*
  statutory duties to have regard to various matters, 9.13
  structural—
    alternatives, 9.161–9.168
    draft policy, 9.181
    emerging local policy, advice on weight to be given to, 9.182
    financial considerations—
      generally, 9.169–9.171
      local, 9.172–9.175
    interference with other legal rights, 9.176, 9.177
    precedent, 9.178–9.180
    prematurity, 9.183–9.189
  substantive—
    amenity effects on occupants of proposed development, 9.59
    coal mining operations, 9.62
    economical development, 9.65, 9.66
    external costs, 9.67
    extremely sensitive neighbours and users, 9.60, 9.61
    generally, 9.45, 9.46
    Green Belt land *see* **Green Belt** (development in)
    major accident hazards, safety and control of, 9.63, 9.64
    neighbouring land and amenity, effects on, 9.53–9.58
    services, impact on, 9.67
    sustainable development, 9.47–9.52
  test of, 9.7
  time for addressing, 9.11, 9.12
  trees, 9.147
  visual impacts, 9.112
  waste—
    facilities for dealing with, provision of, 9.156
    Landfill Directive, 9.159
    regulations, 9.158
    Waste Framework Directive, 9.157
  Welsh language, use of, 9.160
  wide potential range of, 9.6
  wind turbines, effect of, 9.58
  work environments, impact on, 9.57
Mayor of London
  appeal from decision of—
    costs, 10.35
    generally, 10.34, 10.35
    Secretary of State, to, 10.4
  consultation with—
    protected vistas, as to, 10.36–10.38
    safeguarded wharves, as to, 10.36, 10.37
  directions to consult on applications, 10.36–10.38

Index

Mayor of London – *contd*
  legislation, 10.4
  local planning authority, power to
    become, 10.25–10.32
  London Plan, responsibility for, 1.23
  matters to have regard to, 10.19
  Mayoral development order *see* **Mayoral development order**
  Ministers' right to call in planning applications, 10.4
  planning authority, as, 1.11, 1.12
  planning obligation, agreement to, 12.30
  potential strategic importance, applications of—
    consultation—
      initial, 10.14
      pre-application, 10.13
      prior to decision being issued, 10.15–10.17
    directions to refuse permission, 10.18–10.24
    legislation, 10.8
    refused or taken over, 10.9–10.11
    statement of reasons on refusal, 10.22
    time for exercise of powers, 10.12
    types of development, 10.9, 10.10
  powers—
    directed refusals, 10.6, 10.18–10.24
    generally, 10.5–10.7
    involvement generally, 10.39
    Mayoral development order, to grant, 10.40
    potential strategic importance, applications of *see* potential strategic importance, applications *above*
    private nature of process, criticism of, 10.21, 10.32
    statutory authority, 10.7
    time for exercise of, 10.12
  protected vistas, right of consultation, 10.36, 10.38
  referral to, 1.65
  refusal of application—
    directed refusals, 10.6, 10.18–10.24
    local planning authority subsequently refusing, 10.23
    matters to have regard to, 10.19
    own view, Mayor required to form, 10.24
    potential strategic importance, applications, 10.9–10.11
  reserved matters, determination of, 10.33
  right to comment on applications, 10.39
  s 106BA application, determining, 12.85
  safeguarded wharves, right of consultation, 10.36, 10.37

Mayor of London – *contd*
  Secretary of State—
    appeal to, 10.4
    power to call in application, 10.24, 10.32
    site visits, 10.32
    strategic developments, need to form own view, 10.24
  two-fold nature of powers, 10.3
Mayoral development order
  appeals, 26.50
  condition in, developer objecting to, 26.51
  content, 26.50
  legislative amendments, 26.48
  power to grant, 10.40, 26.40
  revocation or revision, 26.52, 26.53
  scope of, 26.47
  Secretary of State's role, 26.49
  sites for development, 26.47
  statutory authority, 26.46
Mining operations
  examples, 2.11, 2.13
  minerals: meaning, 2.12
  mineral-working deposit: meaning, 2.12
Minister *see also* **Secretary of State; Welsh Ministers**
  calling in, powers as to *see under* **Planning application**
  conduct of planning matters, 17.66, 17.67
  planning application—
    made directly to—
      generally, 17.5, 18.1, 18.2
      mechanisms for, 18.2
    see also under **Secretary of State** (right to apply to)
    role in *see under* Planning application
  Planning Inquiry Commission, power to appoint, 17.68–17.72
  urgent Crown development *see under* **Crown**

N
National park authority
  consultation by, 6.134
  planning authority, as, 1.12
National security
  permitted development for purposes of, 5.189
Natural England
  advice from, reasons for rejecting, 8.120
Neighbourhood development plan
  initiation, 1.26
Neighbourhood planning
  community right to build order—
    conditions or limitations, subject to, 26.29
    exclusions under, 26.28

1130

Index

Neighbourhood planning – *contd*
  community right to build order – *contd*
    permission granted under, 26.28
    policy on, 26.44
    register of, 26.45
    see also neighbourhood development order *below*
  essence of, 26.24
  introduction, 26.24
  neighbourhood areas, designation, 26.25
  neighbourhood development order—
    basic conditions, need to meet, 26.38
    Cockermouth Order 2014, 26.43
    community right to build order, as, 26.29
    conditions or limitations, subject to, 26.29
    conservation provisions, 26.33
    consultation and publicity provisions, 26.30, 26.31, 26.35, 26.36
    EIA provisions, 26.33
    examination—
      examiner, appointment of, 26.36
      hearing, 26.39
      LPA making different decision, 26.40
      matters for consideration, 26.37–26.39
      reasoned report, provision of, 26.40
      written representations, 26.39
    exclusions under, 26.28
    finalisation and submission of proposals, 26.32
    guidance, 26.44
    LPA's power to decline order proposal, 26.34
    permission granted under, 26.28
    policy on, 26.44
    promotion of, 26.30
    publicity, 26.35
    referendum—
      business area, in, 26.41
      holding of, 26.41
      order following vote in favour, 26.42
      register of, 26.45
    scope, 26.28
  neighbourhood development plan, 26.27
  neighbourhood forum, 26.26
  parish council's role, 26.26

O
Operational development
  building operations, 2.6–2.9
  demolition, 2.22
  engineering operations, 2.10

Operational development – *contd*
  exclusions from—
    demolition, 2.23
    external appearance affected, where, 2.18
    fish farming, 2.23
    generally, 2.15–2.21
    highway works, 2.20
    internal works, 2.16, 2.17, 2.19
    mezzanine floors, installation of, 2.19
    sewers, pipes etc, works as to, 2.21
    statutory authority, 2.15
  fish farming, 2.23
  floor space, increasing, 2.19
  generally, 2.5, 2.14
  highway works, exception for, 2.20
  mining operations, 2.11–2.13

P
Planning
  appeal *see* **Appeal**
  consent regimes, 1.74–1.76
  legislation, 1.13
  local level, at, 1.11
  ministerial conduct of planning matters, 17.66, 17.67
  political nature of process, 17.2, 17.61
Planning application
  accompanying documents—
    drawings, 6.59, 6.60
    generally, 6.58
  acknowledgment of valid application, 6.86
  amendment to, 6.149, 6.150
  appeal against refusal *see under* **Appeal**
  area planning committee—
    access to reports etc *see under* documents *below*
    bias—
      appearance rather than fact, 8.69
      case-law, consideration of, 8.70–8.74
      disqualified member, role of, 8.86–8.89
      generally, 8.61
      Localism Act 2011, effect, 8.75–8.77
      non-committee members, role of, 8.83–8.85
      one person tainting committee, 8.78
      personal interest, arising from, 8.69
      persons subject to rules on, 8.81–8.82
      predetermination, 8.66, 8.67, 8.79, 8.80
      principles, 8.62–8.64
      test involved, 8.68
    decision-making process *see* decision-making process *below*

1131

Index

Planning application – *contd*
  area planning committee – *contd*
    generally, 8.12–8.15
    issues arising, 8.13
    majority vote, decision by, 8.109
    meetings—
      advice etc at, 8.58
      bias *see* bias *supra*
      commencement, 8.56
      format for considering application, 8.57
      generally, 8.56–8.59
      indefensible prospective decision, 8.58
      multiple applications, dealing with, 8.56
      officers present at, 8.58
      procedure at, 8.58
      public nature of, 8.59
      recording, 8.111–8.114
      resolutions, 8.60
      unlawful prospective decision, 8.58
    membership, 8.12
    pecuniary interest, councillor having, 8.84
    reports, 8.18–8.23
    representations to, power to make—
      approaching councillors not on committee, 8.51
      brevity of submission, 8.47
      caution in dealings, 8.50
      copying letter to planning department, 8.49
      methods, 8.43
      oral, 8.52–8.55
      points to avoid, 8.46
      report published, after, 8.45
      time for making, 8.44
      writing to councillors direct, 8.48
  calling in—
    appeals *see* recovery of appeals *infra*
    case-law on challenges to, 17.43–17.45
    challenge to decision whether or not to call in, 17.42–17.45
    contents of request for, 17.39
    costs *see* **Costs** (planning appeals and call-ins, in)
    Crown development, urgent, 18.33
    decisions *see* **Decision**
    developer seeking, 17.41
    direction, exercise of power by—
      generally, 17.33
      local planning authority, direction given to, 17.53
      notification, 17.54, 17.55
      parish council requesting notification, 17.55

Planning application – *contd*
  calling in – *contd*
    direction, exercise of power by – *contd*
      right to be heard, 17.56
      to whom sent, 17.53
    effects of, 17.41
    generally, 17.52–17.57
    major infrastructure projects in England, s 76A and, 17.46–17.50
    Ministers' powers—
      arising, how, 17.37
      Caborn principles, guidance from, 17.36
      decisions, power to take, 17.52
      direction, exercise by, 17.33
      informal nature of direction, 17.35
      limit on power, 17.35
      policy, 17.36–17.41
      practice directions, 17.34
      relevant planning issues, 17.36
      where exercised, 17.32
    persons resisting, response by, 17.41
    process—
      direction, exercise of power by *see* direction, exercise of power by *supra*
      s 62A application direct to Secretary of State, 17.57
    recovery of appeals—
      decisions *see* **Decision**
      generally, 17.63
      ministerial statement as to, 17.59
      planning inspectors, ministers differing from, 17.63
      Planning Practice Guidance, 17.59
      procedure, 17.64, 17.65
      relevant proposals etc, 17.59, 17.60
      Secretary of State's power to recover jurisdiction, 17.61
      to whom appeals made, 17.58
      transfer to inspectors, 17.58
      used, where, 17.62
    request for, 17.39
    revocation of decision to call in, 17.51
    Secretary of State's policy on, 1.64
    Secretary of State's powers—
      decisions, power to take, 17.52
      generally, 17.30, 17.31
      see also Ministers' powers *supra*
    time for, 17.40
    Welsh Ministers' powers, 17.30
  changes to scheme post-screening, 7.54
  consultation—
    amendment to application, effect, 6.149, 6.150
    change in material considerations, failure to consult after, 6.130

Index

Planning application – *contd*
  consultation – *contd*
    conditions on permission, effect of imposition, 6.149
    consultee's right to bring proceedings, 6.129
    county councils with districts, by, 6.133
    county planning authorities, with, 6.131, 6.132
    detailed list of requirements, 6.127, 6.128
    duty to consult, 6.25
    failure to consult, effect, 6.130
    generally, 6.125
    guidance, duties set out in, 6.128
    legislation, 6.125
    local planning authority's duty, 1.37
    National park authorities, by, 6.134
    period for, with statutory bodies, 6.137, 6.138
    renewals, on, 6.135
    responses—
      making, 6.139–6.147
      taking into account, 6.148
    s 73 applications, on, 6.135, 6.136
    time for, 6.129
  Crown land, 6.61–6.63
  decision notice—
    appeal notice to accompany, 14.18
    contents—
      conditions and notes, 14.9, 14.10
      date of decision, 14.8
      generally, 14.7
    drawings identified in, 14.13
    England, positive working statement in, 14.14, 14.15
    Environment Agency's rights, 14.19
    environmental information considered, 14.17
    errors in—
      judicial approach to, 14.20, 14.21
      potential remedies, 14.22–14.24
      prohibition on withdrawal etc, 14.20
    events between resolution and, 14.5, 14.6
    generally, 1.50, 14.1
    Health and Safety Executive's rights, 14.1
    judicial review proceedings, 14.20
    Natural England's rights, 14.19
    planning register, kept in, 14.19
    publicity, 14.19
    quashing, 14.20
    refusal, in case of, 14.11, 14.12
    revocation, 14.20
    second, inability to issue, 14.20, 14.21

Planning application – *contd*
  decision notice – *contd*
    Wales—
      community councils' right to be notified, 14.19
      duty to give notice of commencement of development in, 14.16
      revision in, 16.43
  decision-making process—
    area planning committee, by *see* area planning committee *above*
    bias *see under* area planning committee *above*
    conflict of interest within same authority, 8.8
    decision notice *see* decision notice *above*
    delegation—
      common arrangements, 8.11
      compliance with scheme of, 8.16, 8.17
      constitutional nature of powers, 8.10
      powers of, 8.9
      restriction on, 8.9, 8.11
    historical background, 8.2
    immaterial considerations, 9.3
    Local Government Act 1972, powers under, 8.5
    Local Government Act 2000, effect, 8.3
    material considerations *see* **Material considerations**
    Natural England, reasons for rejecting advice from, 8.120
    non-executive nature of function, 8.3, 8.4
    officers, by, restriction on powers, 8.9, 8.11
    reasons for decision—
      adoption of officer recommendation, where, 8.103
      clarity etc, need for, 8.102
      departing from officers' analysis, 8.104
      duty to give, 8.90
      English duty to give, 8.91
      former English duty, 8.94–8.100
      generally, 8.92
      given where not obliged to, 8.102
      meeting, proposed at, 8.107
      members disagreeing with officer recommendation, 8.105
      motion proposed at meeting, where, 8.106
      need for, 8.101–8.110
      officer decisions, 8.115–8.118
      practices to be discouraged, 8.108
      predetermination, need to avoid, 8.106
      Wales, duty in, 8.93

Index

Planning application – *contd*
  decision-making process – *contd*
    refusal, reasons for, 8.119
    two or more authorities jointly, by, 8.7
    voting—
      errors in course of, 8.110
      majority, 8.109
      procedure, 8.109
      second or casting vote, 8.109
  design and access statement—
    curtailed need for, 6.70
    England, in, 6.74
    need for, 1.34, 6.70, 6.73
    not required, where, 6.72, 6.73
    purpose, 6.70
    relevant applications, 6.71
    Wales, in, 6.76–6.78
  determination—
    access to documents *see under*
      documents *below*
    agenda and reports, publication, 1.44
    appeal against non-determination, 19.42
    by whom, 1.43
    decision notice *see* decision notice *above*
    decision-making process *see* decision-making process *above*
    generally, 8.1, 14.1
    issue of planning permission *see under* **Planning permission**
    matters for consideration—
      England, in, 1.45
      judicial approach to, 1.47–1.49
      Wales, in, 1.46
      see also **Material considerations**
    permission or refusal, 1.50
    persons determining, 8.1
  documents—
    access to—
      confidential papers, removal of, 8.39
      Data Protection Act 1998, 8.31, 8.32
      Environmental Information Regulations 2004, under, 8.26–8.29
      Freedom of Information Act 2000, 8.30
      generally, 8.24, 8.25
      legitimate expectation of publication, 8.38
      Local Government Act 1972, reports etc under, 8.33–8.37
      public interest test, 8.40
      unredacted financial reports, 8.41
      viability reports and sensitive information, 8.39–8.42

Planning application – *contd*
  documents – *contd*
    accompanying application—
      drawings of plans, 6.59, 6.60
      effect of failure to submit, 6.87–6.90
    England, in, 1.34
    Environmental Impact Assessment case law, and, 6.14, 6.15
    environmental statement, 6.79
  fee—
    changes to, for different applicants, 6.66–6.69
    consolidation of existing mineral permissions, 6.68
    different categories, development within, 6.65
    disabled access etc, 6.66
    generally, 1.34
    gross floorspace: meaning, 6.65
    list of, 6.64
    parish or community council application, 6.68
    reserved matters applications, 6.69
    site area: meaning, 6.65
    statutory authority for, 6.64
  form for, 6.57
  formal nature of, 1.33
  generally, 1.32–1.34, 6.1, 6.2, 6.57, 6.58
  immaterial considerations, 9.3
  legislation, 6.2
  legitimate expectation—
    examples, 6.117
    procedural rules, and requirements in, 6.111
    statement of community involvement, and, 6.112–6.116, 6.151
  local lists, 6.80–6.85
  local planning authorities *see* **Local planning authority**
  material considerations *see* **Material considerations**
  matters deferred for later approval, 6.4, 6.5
  Ministers' role—
    appeal, recovering jurisdiction over, 17.6
    application direct to *see under* **Minister**
    calling in *see under* calling in *above*
    directions to prevent determination of application—
      art 31 directions, 17.11, 17.12
      England, in, 17.9, 17.11
      generally, 17.8–17.12
      persuading Minister to lift, 17.14
      persuading Minister to make, 17.13
      Wales, in, 17.10

Planning application – *contd*
  Ministers' role – *contd*
    duties to refer application to Minister—
      consultation with Secretary of State, 17.17, 17.18
      England, in, 17.16–17.19
      extraction of aggregates, 17.20
      flood risk area development, 17.16, 17.20
      generally, 17.15
      Green Belt development, 17.16
      health and safety advice, effect, 17.28
      Lee Valley Regional Park Authority, rights of, 17.29
      minerals development, 17.20
      playing field development, 17.16
      safeguarded aerodromes, 17.23, 17.24
      safeguarded meteorological sites, 17.25
      safeguarded military explosives storage areas, 17.23, 17.24
      safeguarded technical sites, 17.23, 17.24
      significant residential development, 17.20
      time limit for granting permission, 17.19, 17.21
      transport routes, safeguarding direction to protect, 17.26, 17.27
      Wales, in, 17.20–17.22
      waste development, 17.20
      Welsh Ministers' right to documents, 17.22
      World Heritage Site, 17.16
    generally, 17.4
    interventionary powers, 17.4–17.7
    planning permission without application, power to grant, 17.7
    underperforming council areas, in, 17.5
    see also **Secretary of State** (planning application)
  notice of—
    failure to give, 6.87–6.90, 6.129
    generally, 1.35, 1.36
    inaccurate certificate of notice, offence, 6.56
    owner, to, 6.50
    persons to whom given, 6.49
    significance, 6.51
    statutory authority, 6.49
    tenant, to, 6.50
    underground mining, in case of, 6.52–6.55

Planning application – *contd*
  outline—
    meaning, 6.5
    factory outlet cases, 6.13
  persons able to make, 6.48
  planning register *see* **Planning register**
  plans to accompany, 6.59, 6.60
  press releases, 1.36
  publicity—
    categories, 6.119
    conservation areas, as to, 6.124
    listed buildings, as to, 6.124
    manner of, 6.120–6.123
    statutory authority, 6.118
  referral—
    Mayor of London, to, 1.65
    Secretary of State, to, 1.60–1.64
    Welsh Ministers, to, 1.60–1.63
  refusal to determine —
    appeal against *see under* **Appeal**
    conditions justifying, 6.103
    discretionary power, 6.109, 6.110
    overlapping application, in case of, 6.104–6.106
    power to refuse, 6.101, 6.102
    pre-existing enforcement notice, and, 6.107, 6.108
    procedural rules, requirements in, 6.111
    similar applications, in case of, 6.104–6.106
    statement of community involvement and legitimate expectations, 6.111–6.116
  reserved matters—
    meaning, 6.6
    access in relation to, 6.7
    alteration to, 6.150
    appeal on application, 16.42
    appearance: meaning, 6.8
    approval—
      application for, 16.18–16.20
      conditions on, 16.16, 16.17
      EIA, and *see* EIA and subsequent applications *infra*
      fee for application, 16.21
      publicity and consultation, 16.22
    consultation, 16.22
    EIA and subsequent applications—
      generally, 16.23–16.26
      multiple applications and approvals, 16.27–16.29
    generally, 16.1, 16.2
    landscaping, hard and soft, 6.9
    layout: meaning, 6.10
    merits, approach to considering, 16.8
    number of dwellings determined later, 16.7

Index

Planning application – *contd*
  reserved matters – *contd*
    omission of approved elements, 16.12–16.15
    planning authority bound by decision, 16.4
    precise details in permission, 16.6
    publicity, 16.22
    relevant considerations, 16.10, 16.11
    scale: meaning, 6.11
    scope of details under, 16.3–16.11
    unlawful refusal, 16.9
  Secretary of State's role—
    calling in *see* calling in *above*
    generally, 17.1–17.3
    power to restrict grant of planning permission etc, 17.8
    right to apply to *see under* **Secretary of State** (right to apply to)
  stages in—
    acceptable development, determining, 6.28
    common applications, 6.23
    consent requirements, tailoring aspirations to, 6.26
    Environmental Impact Assessment, 6.31
    generally, 6.21
    harm to public interest, consideration of, 6.26
    legislation, relevant, 6.21
    list of, 6.21
    local authority policies, 6.41
    objective, decision as to, 6.22
    new buildings, scheme for, 6.29
    planning performance agreement, 6.38
    planning policies, need to consider, 6.26
    pre-application advice, 6.32–6.37
    pre-application consultation—
      generally, 6.39, 6.40
      local authority policies, and, 6.41
      non-statutory, 6.46, 6.47
      statutory, 6.42–6.45
    professional input, question of, 6.30
    regulatory constraints, need to consider, 6.27
    scale of development, effect, 6.24, 6.25
    working up the scheme, 6.22–6.31
  statement of community involvement—
    legitimate expectation, giving rise to, 6.151
    status, 6.113
    statutory authority, 1.38, 6.112
  statutory publicity, 1.36
  to whom made, 1.32

Planning application – *contd*
  types—
    generally, 6.3–6.15
    hybrid, 6.4
    prospective, 6.4
    reserved matters *see* reserved matters *above*
    retrospective, 6.4
  validity—
    acknowledgment of valid application, 6.86
    appeal, right of, 6.91
    determining, 6.91–6.95
  Wales, in—
    generally, 1.34
    Ministers' power to restrict grant of planning permission etc, 17.8
Planning authority
  generally, 1.11, 1.12
  local level, at, 1.11, 1.12
  Mayor of London as, 1.11, 1.12
  Wales, in, 1.11
Planning conditions *see under* **Planning permission**
Planning control
  breach of—
    meaning, 1.77
    measures available, 1.78
    s 215 notice on condition of land, 1.80
    time limits, 1.79
  consent regimes, 1.74–1.76
  High Court challenges, 1.81
Planning Court
  historical background, 25.116
  issue of claims in, 25.117
  judges, 25.129–25.131
  jurisdiction—
    claim: meaning, 25.119, 25.124
    environmental law, 25.122
    generally, 25.119–25.124
    Practice Direction, 25.124
    topics, wide range of, 25.121
    transfer of cases to, 25.123
    types of claim, 25.120
  Lead Judge in charge of, 25.118
  Planning Court claim: meaning, 25.119
  Planning Fast Track, as evolution of, 25.117
  Planning Liaison Judge, 25.118
  significant cases, 25.125, 25.126
  specialist list, as, 25.117
  timetabling—
    interests of justice, subject to objective of, 25.128
    significant cases, 25.126
    to deal with cases justly, 25.127

Index

Planning Inquiry Commission
appointment, 17.68
constitution, 17.70
grounds for establishing, 17.69
membership, 17.70
multiple applications or appeals, dealing with, 17.70
non-use of, 17.72
report to Minister, 17.71
research, right to commission or carry out, 17.71
right to be heard before, 17.71

Planning obligation
meaning, 1.56, 12.1
breach—
    effect, 29.44
    example, 29.44
    nature of, 29.44
    not discharged by, 12.97
commencement of development defined in, 29.45
Community Infrastructure Levy, effect, 12.41–12.47
consultation, 12.30, 12.31
content, tests to be satisfied, 1.59
contractual interpretation—
    judicial application, 12.55, 12.56
    summary of principles, 12.54
    use of material outside obligation, 12.57
counterparty basis, entry in to on, 12.28
deed, in—
    execution, 12.20, 12.23, 12.25, 12.26
    generally, 12.3
    need for, 12.20
    person making, 12.3
    several obligations in, 12.4
discharge *see* modification or discharge *below*
enforcement, 1.57, 12.58
execution—
    before issue of planning decision, 12.29
    company, by, 12.26
    deed, as, 12.20, 12.23, 12.25, 12.26
    individual, by, 12.25
interpretation *see* contractual interpretation *above*
formal requirements—
    consultation, 12.30, 12.31
    counterparty basis, 12.28
    deed, need for *see* deed, in *above*
    development consent obligation, in case of, 12.22
    execution *see* execution *above*
    generally, 12.19
    nature of obligation, identifying, 12.21–12.29
    publicity, 12.32

Planning obligation – *contd*
formal requirements – *contd*
    statement of obligation, 12.21
    statutory requirements, compliance with, 12.24
    transfer of land, providing for, 12.27
generally, 12.1, 12.2
land, interest in—
    generally, 12.14–12.18
    identification of land, 12.16
    identification of person entering into obligation, 12.17
    interested in land: meaning, 12.15
    interests bound by, extent of, 12.18
    need for, 12.14
land transfer, as to, 12.7
lawful, whether—
    generally, 1.58, 12.8, 12.9
    planning permission, relationship with—
        generally, 12.33, 12.34
        reg 122, tests in, 12.35–12.40
        reg 123, restrictions in, 12.41–12.47
        relevant infrastructure: meaning, 12.42
limits of, 12.5–12.9
made, where, 1.59
Mayor of London's agreement to, 12.30
model, 12.49
modification or discharge—
    affordable housing, for purposes of *see* s 106B application *infra*
    agreement, by, 12.60, 12.61
    applications for, 12.62, 12.63
    appropriate authority, 12.59
    early modification, avoiding need for, 12.96
    generally, 1.57, 12.59
    methods, 12.59
    s 106BC appeals, 12.91–12.95
    s 106A application—
        amendment, restriction on, 12.75
        appeal against decision, 12.77
        contents, 12.68
        determination of, 12.71–12.78
        different modification agreed, 12.75
        formal nature of, 12.68
        generally, 12.64–12.78
        map to accompany, 12.68
        notice, 12.69, 12.70
        person making, 12.65
        procedure for making, 12.68
        publicity, 12.69, 12.70
        representations, right to make, 12.78
        time for notice of decision, 12.76
        time limits, 12.66, 12.67
        useful purpose, nature of, 12.72–12.74

1137

Index

Planning obligation – *contd*
modification or discharge – *contd*
  s 106BA application—
    appeal against decision, 12.90–12.95
    background to introduction of, 12.79
    determination, 12.85, 12.86
    different modification, power to make, 12.87
    discretion, exercise of, 12.89
    generally, 12.80–12.89
    Mayor of London determining, 12.85
    procedure, 12.84
    public involvement, 12.84
    reasons for decision, 12.89
    requirement, nature of, 12.80
    second or subsequent application, approach on, 12.88
    test to be applied, 12.82, 12.83
    varied approaches, 12.81
negotiating parties, 12.30
payments—
  Localism Act 2011, general power in, 12.104
  use of planning conditions to require, 12.103
Planning Inspectorate—
  copies not originals to be sent to, 12.51
  guidance deadlines, 12.50
  regulatory tests met, need to prove, 12.53
  title, need to demonstrate to inspector, 12.52
planning register, in, 12.32
pre-1991 Act planning agreements—
  amendment, 12.100
  enforcement, 12.101
  generally, 12.98 12.102
  modification or discharge, 12.102
  preservation of, 12.98
  running with land, 12.101
  statutory authority, 12.99
publicity, 12.32
requirements, 12.3, 12.5
signatures to, 1.57
statutory authority for, 1.56, 12.2, 12.3
submission—
  heads of terms in appeal, and, 12.50–12.53
  heads of terms in application, and, 12.48, 12.49
  planning appeal, in, 12.50–12.53
  planning application, in, 12.48, 12.49
title, need to demonstrate, 12.52
transfer of land, providing for, 12.27
unilateral imposition of land or obligations, 12.10–12.13

Planning permission
abandonment of lawful use, 4.12–4.14
amendment, non-material—
  appeal, right of, 15.21
  case law on statutory rights, 15.13
  challenge to decision, 15.21, 15.22
  effect, 15.7
  generally, 15.1, 15.2
  implicit ability to make, 15.3–15.6
  judicial review, 15.22
  local planning authority's power to make, 15.8
  material nature of change, determining, 15.10, 15.11
  mechanisms for allowing, 15.2
  persons able to apply for, 15.12
  procedure for making—
    consultation, 15.17
    decision, 15.18–15.20
    different change, authority making, 15.20
    fee, 15.14
    form for, 15.14
    generally, 15.14–15.17
    notification, 15.15, 15.16
    planning authority's approach, 15.19, 15.20
    planning register, application etc to be kept on, 15.17
    publication of application, as good practice 15.17
    representations, 15.16
    writing, application in, 15.14
    Wales, site notice etc in, 15.17
  reasons for making, 15.1
  scope of power to make, 15.9
  statutory rights, 15.7–15.13
  third party's right of appeal against decision, 15.22
  use of, 15.23, 15.24
appeal, start of time period for submitting, 14.4
building operations: meaning, 1.14
completion notice *see* **Completion notice**
conditions—
  agreement as to, advisability of, 11.51
  agreements, requiring, 11.35–11.38
  appeal, on, 11.52
  appeal against, 19.41
  approval of details under, application for—
    accompanying documents, 16.30
    agriculture, aftercare condition specifying use for, 16.36
    appeals, 16.42
    clarity, need for, 16.30
    contents, 16.30

Index

Planning permission – *contd*
  conditions – *contd*
    approval of details under, application for – *contd*
      development plan, regard to, 16.35
      fees, 16.31, 16.32
      forestry, aftercare condition specifying use for, 16.36
      generally, 16.30–16.37
      material considerations, regard to, 16.34
      mineral planning authority's role, 16.36, 16.37
      planning register, date of approval on, 16.33
      writing, need for, 16.30
    breach of condition notice, failure to comply with, 11.17–11.19
    call-in, on, 11.52
    completion within certain period, as to, 4.20
    consultation, effect of imposition on, 6.149
    consultees proposing, 11.51
    deemed discharge of details under, 16.38–16.41
    deferment of certain matters to later submission and approval, 16.1
    determining, 11.51, 11.52
    discussion as to, 11.51
    effect, 6.149
    existing lawful uses, affecting, 11.26
    fairness, when granting lesser permission, 11.50
    generally, 11.1
    geographical extent—
      application site, 11.13, 11.14
      generally, 11.12
      land outside site or applicant's control *see* land outside site or applicant's control *infra*
      other land under applicant's control, 11.15
    highway agreements, 11.39
    implementation in accordance with—
      breach of legitimate expectation, 29.26
      care, need to interpret conditions with, 29.35
      case-law, 29.18–29.34
      compulsory purchase order, operation of, 29.27
      conditions precedent, whether, 29.30
      demolition, whether possible without further consent, 29.25
      different outcomes for different conditions, 29.31

Planning permission – *contd*
  conditions – *contd*
    implementation in accordance with – *contd*
      drainage details, failure to submit, 29.28
      exceptions to general principle, 29.19, 29.20
      general principle, 29.18
      generally, 29.18–29.35
      Hart Aggregates approach, implications of, 29.33
      importance of breach, effect, 29.30
      informal representations not giving rise to estoppel, 29.21
      matters not going to heart of permission, 29.32
      'no development' conditions and *Whitley* principle, 29.29
      partial reserved matters, whether development proceeding under, 29.35
      public law concepts, application of, 29.24
      safeguards for third parties and public generally, 29.22, 29.23, 29.26
      reserved matters approved for only part of development, 29.21
      transport and works order and deemed permission, 29.25
      vehicle movement conditions, failure to comply with, 29.34
      whether development commencing prior to expiry of permission, 29.21
    imposition of, 11.51
    interpretation of, 28.20–28.23
    land outside site or applicant's control—
      failure to comply with breach of condition notice, 11.17–11.19
      scope of conditions, 11.17–11.19
    legal tests for—
      fairly and reasonably relating to development, 11.9, 11.10
      generally, 1.54
      judicial analysis, 11.6
      Newbury tests, 1.54, 11.7
      planning purpose, need to serve, 11.8
      statutory authority, 11.6
      unreasonable, prohibition on being, 11.11
    lesser permission, grant of, 11.50
    matters not otherwise subject to control, affecting, 11.24

Index

Planning permission – *contd*
  conditions – *contd*
    mineral extraction—
      aftercare standards, 11.48
      amenity sues, suitability of, 11.48
      duration, as to, 11.46
      generally, 11.45–11.48
      restoration, 11.47
    negative, 1.53, 11.20–11.23
    objecting to, options available, 19.41
    partial approval, 11.50
    payments, requiring the making of, 11.32, 12.103
    permitted development rights, removal of, 11.25
    policy tests for—
      National Planning Policy Framework, in, 11.30
      Wales, in, 11.31
    positive, 1.53, 11.20–11.23
    power to impose—
      judicial analysis, 11.5
      statutory authority, 11.3–11.5
    relevant situations, 1.52
    reserved matters *see under* **Planning permission**
    restriction on imposition, 1.58
    site of special scientific interest, protection for, 11.49
    statutory authority for, 1.51
    substance of permission, whether affecting—
      generally, 11.27
      later approval of details, providing for, 11.28
      later variations to approved details, providing for, 11.29
      limits on, 11.27
    time for implementing permission—
      extension of time if consent challenged, 11.43, 11.44
      full permission, 11.41
      generally, 11.40, 29.5
      outline permission, 11.42
    transfer of land, requiring, 11.33, 11.34
    use class order rights, removal of, 11.25
  conflicting permissions, carrying out of, 29.47–29.51
  decision notice *see under* **Planning application**
  deemed—
    meaning, 26.61
    authorisation by government department, 26.62
    circumstances for grant of, 26.61
    electricity generation, in case of, 26.63–26.65

Planning permission – *contd*
  deemed – *contd*
    power to grant, 26.3, 26.61
    Town and Country Planning Act 1990—
      application of, 26.67
      not a determination under, 26.67
    transport and works order, on making of, 26.66
  delay in issue, 1.50
  development—
    meaning, 1.14
    demolition following, effect, 4.4
    in part, partial demolition, 4.5
    repeated, authorisation for, 4.7
    statutory powers to remove right *see* **Completion notice; Discontinuation order**
    to be carried out once only, 4.4
  discontinuation order *see* **Discontinuation order**
  effect—
    ambiguity in permission, of, 28.11, 28.13
    benefit to land unless specified otherwise, 28.6, 28.7
    careful consideration required, 28.5
    development implicit in permission, 28.2
    extrinsic evidence, need to consider, 28.14
    generally, 28.2–28.5
    issue arising as to, 28.1
    not stated on face of permission, 28.3
    Town and Country Planning Act 1990 s 75, application of, 28.3–28.5
    use of new building in, 28.4
    see also interpretation *below*
  enterprise zone, in *see* **Enterprise zone**
  exceptions—
    enforcement notice, effect of issue, 4.9
    existing use, in case of, 4.10
    generally, 1.15, 4.8
    resumption of various sues, in case of, 4.10
    unnecessary, where, 4.11
  grant of—
    decision notice *see under* **Planning application**
    deemed permission *see* deemed *above*
    development consent order, 26.3
    enterprise zone *see* **Enterprise zone**
    generally, 1.50, 4.3, 26.1, 26.3
    Housing and Planning Bill 2015, under *see* Housing and Planning Bill 2015, under *below*

Index

Planning permission – *contd*
grant of – *contd*
local development order *see* **Local development order**
mayoral development order *see* **Mayoral development order**
mechanisms available for, 26.1
neighbourhood planning *see* **Neighbourhood planning**
orders, by, 1.72
simplified planning zone *see* **Simplified planning zone**
special development order, 26.4–26.6
time of, 14.3
zoning, 1.73, 26.2
see also issue *below*
Housing and Planning Bill 2015, under—
generally, 26.68, 26.69
planning permission in principle—
application, grant on, 26.77, 26.78
development order, grant by, 26.70–26.76
introduction of, 26.68
routes to, 26.69
technical details consent, followed by, 26.69, 26.79–26.82
implementation—
meaning, 29.1
conflicting permissions, carrying out of, 29.47–29.51
development begun: meaning, 29.4
initiated: meaning, 29.4
Pilkington approach—
case law as to, 29.52–29.54
pragmatic nature of, 29.56
second permission with different conditions or obligation, 29.55
prospective *see* prospective *below*
retrospective, 29.3, 29.46
time for commencing development: meaning, 29.4
types of permission, 29.2
interpretation—
broad principles, use of, 28.17, 28.18
building, as to, 28.4
conditions, of, 28.20–28.23
construction as a whole, 28.12
designed: meaning, 28.4
drawing and details in application, importance of, 28.9
extrinsic evidence, need to consider, 28.14
framework of relevant law, taking place within, 28.16
full permission, 28.9
generally, 28.8–28.19
implied conditions, 28.21

Planning permission – *contd*
interpretation – *contd*
intention disclosed by application documents, 28.4
issue arising as to, 28.1
matter of law, as, 28.8
meaning of words, approach to, 28.15
narrow range of documentation, within, 28.15
outline permission, 28.8, 28.10
perverse, sanctioning of, 28.19
public document, permission as, 28.11
summary of principles, 28.8
see also effect *below*
issue—
decision notice *see under* **Planning application**
events between resolution and decision notice, 14.5, 14.6
generally, 14.3, 14.4
matters between decision to grant and, 14.2
time periods for giving of notice, 14.4
see also grant of *above*
lawful use—
abandonment, 4.12–4.14
interventions ending, 4.15–4.18
need for—
change of use, effect, 4.6
completion notice *see* **Completion notice**
discontinuation order *see* **Discontinuation order**
exceptions *see* exceptions *above*
generally, 1.14–1.17, 4.1–4.7
lawful use *see* lawful use *above*
legislation as to, 4.2
once-only development, 4.4
partial construction, rebuilding following, 4.5
repeated development, 4.7
revocation etc *see* revocation or modification *below*
neighbourhood planning *see* **Neighbourhood planning**
outline, 6.12
prospective—
meaning, 29.2
implementation—
conditions, in accordance with *see under* conditions *above*
elements to, 29.6
material operations, 29.7–29.10
minerals cases, in, 29.9
no need for intention to implement, 29.36–29.42

1141

Index

Planning permission – *contd*
  prospective – *contd*
    implementation – *contd*
      non-material operations,
        commencement of works being,
        29.10
      planning obligations, 29.44, 29.45
      time of, 29.3, 29.5
      Wales, duty to give and display
        notice of commencement in,
        29.43
      works not in exact accord with
        permission, 29.11–29.17
  replacement—
    determination of application, 13.32
    fallback position, effect, 13.32
    fees, 13.38
    generally, 13.1, 13.2
    matters to be taken into account, 13.32
    procedures, 13.34, 13.35
    purpose of procedure, 13.31
    time limits, 13.30
    Wales, renewal application in, 13.33,
      13.38
  retrospective—
    meaning, 29.2, 29.46
    conservation area, demolition within,
      13.23
    fees, 13.38
    generally, 13.1, 13.2
    implementation, time of, 29.3, 29.46
    interpretation issues, 13.28
    issues, scope of, 13.24
    minor material amendments, 13.27
    partially completed development,
      13.25
    procedures, 13.36, 13.37
    s 73 or s 73A, deciding between, 13.29
    scope of power, 13.21, 13.22
    statutory authority, 13.20
    submission of further details, 13.26
  revocation or modification—
    compensation for, 4.31
    confirmation from Minister, 4.28
    development to be dealt with, 4.27
    failure to comply with order for, 4.32
    matters for consideration, 4.26
    Secretary of State's power, 4.30
    statutory authority, 4.25, 4.26
    unopposed order, talking effect as, 4.29
    Welsh Ministers' power, 4.30
  s 73 variations—
    meaning, 13.1, 13.4
    breadth of s 73 consideration, 13.6–
      13.8
    conditions, permissible, 13.7, 13.8
    constraints on scope, 13.5

Planning permission – *contd*
  s 73 variations – *contd*
    extant permission, need for, 13.9,
      13.10
    fees, 13.38
    fundamental alteration, example pf,
      13.5
    generally, 13.1, 13.2
    material considerations, 13.6–13.8
    modifying effect of conditions, 13.5
    permissible conditions, 13.5
    procedures, 13.34, 13.35
    reserved matters, 13.16–13.19
    scope of permissible changes, 13.5
    statutory authority, 13.3
    time limits, extension, 13.11–13.15
  types—
    renewals in Wales, 13.33
    replacement *see* replacement *above*
    retrospective *see* retrospective *above*
    variations *see* s 73 variations *above*
  variations *see* s 73 variations *above*
  Wales, renewal application in, 13.33,
    13.38
  zoning, 1.72, 1.73
Planning policy
  development plan *see* **Development plan**
  England, in, 1.18
  generally, 1.18–1.28
  guides, 1.20
  gypsies and travellers, as to, 9.31
  local policy—
    England, categories of documents in,
      9.28
    generally, 9.27
    Wales, in, 9.28
  material consideration, as—
    interpretation, 9.41–9.44
    national policy *see* national *below*
  national—
    England, in—
      cancelled guidance, 9.37
      energy, as to, 9.35
      generally, 9.36
      gypsies and travellers, as to, 9.31
      National Planning Policy
        Framework, 9.29–9.32
      national policy statements, 9.34,
        9.35
      Planning Practice Guidance, 9.33
      transport, as to, 9.35
      waste, as to, 9.30, 9.35
      water, as to, 9.35
    Wales, in, 9.38, 9.39
  nature of, 1.18
  Wales, in, 1.19
  waste, as to, 9.30

Planning register
 contents, 6.97
 decision notice, copy of, 14.19
 final disposal of application, 6.98
 generally, 6.96–6.100
 inspection, 6.96
 need to keep, 6.97
 Part 1, 6.97, 6.98, 6.99
 Part 2, 6.97, 6.100
 planning obligation in, 12.32
 s 278 agreement in, 12.32
 screening decisions kept on or with, 7.52, 7.53

Planning system
 development *see* **Development** 1.13
 environmental dimension, 1.7, 1.9
 European dimension, 1.7
 framework, parliamentary discussion as to, 1.8
 purpose—
  generally, 1.2–1.10
  National Planning Policy Framework, as set out in, 1.10
  parliamentary discussion as to, 1.8

Plant
 meaning, 5.92, 5.93

R

Regional Strategies
 revocation, 1.25

Renewable energy
 permitted development rights, and, 5.151, 5.152

Restrictive covenant
 enforcement, 12.106, 12.107
 inclusion on disposal of land, 12.106

S

Secretary of State *see also* **Minister; Welsh Ministers**
 development order, power to authorise, 5.2
 discontinuance order, power to make, 4.38
 planning application—
  determining, methods of, 18.16
  fees, 18.14
  hearing procedure, flexibility of, 18.16
  listed building consent, connected, 18.13
  parish council involvement, 18.15
  Planning Inspector determining, 18.16
  refusal to determine, 18.14
  right to apply to—
   criteria for designating local planning authorities, 18.9
   designating local planning authorities, 18.9, 18.10

Secretary of State – *contd*
 planning application – *contd*
  right to apply to – *contd*
   discretionary areas, 18.4
   generally, 18.3–18.10
   major development: meaning, 18.8
   political angle to power, 18.5
   process, 18.11–18.16
   risks involved, 18.4
   stages involved, list of, 18.12
   statutory authority, 18.2, 18.3
   statutory regime, 18.6, 18.7
   timescale, 18.3
  role in determining—
   calling in *see under* **Planning application**
   generally, 17.1–17.3
   power to restrict grant of planning permission etc, 17.8
   stages involved, list of, 18.12

Self-build
 Housing and Planning Bill, 9.108, 9.111
 legislation, 9.108, 9.111
 meeting demand for, 9.111
 registers, 9.111

Sewerage
 permitted development rights, and, 5.149, 5.150

Simplified planning zone
 alteration, 26.55
 consultation, 26.57
 contents, 26.55
 direction from Minister, 26.56
 generally, 26.54
 introduction, 26.54
 legislation, 26.54
 making of, 26.55
 matters specified by, 26.55
 nature of permission granted by, 26.55
 notification to Minister, 26.56
 objections following local inquiry, 26.58
 persons able to request making of, 26.56
 planning permission granted by, 26.55
 promotion, 26.56
 representations as to making of, 26.56
 restrictions on permission granted by, 26.59

Starter home
 meaning, 9.109
 generally, 9.109
 Housing and Planning Bill, 9.108
 planning obligation as to, 9.110
 planning permission for, 9.110
 promotion of supply of, 9.110

Statutory undertaker
 meaning, 5.96

Index

U
Use *see* **Use of land**
Use classes
  meaning, 3.1
  basis of, 3.2–3.4
  business and industrial uses—
    business, 3.24
    class B3 Special Industrial Group A, 3.30
    class B4 Special Industrial Group B, 3.31
    class B5 Special Industrial Group C, 3.32
    class B6 Special Industrial Group D, 3.33
    class B7 Special Industrial Group E, 3.34
    general industrial, 3.24
    generally, 3.24
    industrial process—
      meaning, 3.26
      sui generis categories pertinent to, 3.27
    mixed use site, 3.28
    office: meaning, 3.25
    storage or distribution, 3.24, 3.29
  categorisation—
    business and industrial uses *see* business and industrial uses *above*
    community use *see* community use *below*
    generally, 3.17
    residential uses *see* residential uses *below*
    shopping area uses *see* class A *below*
  class A—
    financial and professional services, 3.20, 3.21
    food and drink, 3.22, 3.23
    generally, 3.18
    shops, 3.19
  class B *see* business and industrial uses *above*
  class C *see* residential uses *below*
  class D *see* community use *below*
  community use—
    assembly and leisure, 3.50
    non-residential institutions, 3.50
    sports stadium used for concerts, 3.51
  generally, 3.1
  legislation, 3.2, 3.3, 3.52
  pay day loan shop, 3.7
  removal by planning condition, 3.10–3.16
  residential uses—
    dwellinghouse—
      dual use of premises, 3.49
      examples, 3.44
      generally, 3.42, 3.43
      holiday accommodation, 3.45, 3.46
      house in multiple occupation, 3.43
      purpose of C4 class, 3.48
      small community care home, 3.47

Use classes – *contd*
  residential uses – *contd*
    hostel, 3.36–3.38
    hotel, 3.35
    residential institution—
      care: meaning, 3.40
      generally, 3.39
      secure, 3.41
  Use Classes Order, effect, 3.5
  uses outside—
    generally, 3.6–3.8
    removal by planning condition, 3.10–3.16
    subdivision of land or buildings in same use class, 3.9
    sui generis, reasons for, 3.8
Use of land
  abandonment of lawful use, 4.12–4.14
  carrying on, 2.34–2.36
  change *see* **Change of use**
  classes *see* **Use classes**
  inactivity, survival despite, 2.35
  lawful use—
    abandonment, 4.12–4.14
    interventions ending, 4.15–4.18
  mixed uses, 2.44
  primary use, incidental or ancillary to, 2.29–2.31, 2.44
  start of, identifying, 2.36

W
Wales
  appeals in *see under* **Appeals**
  decision notice in planning application *see under* **Planning application** (decision notice)
  local development order in *see under* **Local development order**
  nationally significant development in, applications for—
    generally, 18.21–18.25
    s 62D procedure, 18.26–18.28
    secondary consents, 18.24, 18.25
  Welsh Ministers, right to apply to *see under* **Welsh Ministers**
  written representations procedure in *see under* **Wales**
Water
  permitted development rights, and, 5.149, 5.150
Welsh Ministers
  mode of determination, right to decide, 19.53
  right to apply to—
    community council, notification to, 18.20
    connected application made on same day, 18.19

Welsh Ministers – *contd*
  right to apply to – *contd*
    designation of local planning authority, 18.18
    grounds for making, 18.17
    nationally significant development, 18.22
    planning or reserved matters application, 18.17
    procedure, 18.20
    s 62D application procedure, 18.26–18.28
    secondary consents, 18.24, 18.25
    statutory authority, 18.17
Written representations
  England, procedure in—
    2013 amendments, prior to—
      fairness *see* fairness *infra*
      generally, 21.19
      main submissions, time for making, 21.24
      time limits, 21.19, 21.23, 21.24
    2013 amendments, under—
      absence of representations, determination in, 21.18
      commencement of process, 21.4
      explanation etc provided by LPA, 21.11
      five-week representations by LPA, 21.12, 21.13
      further information, Secretary of State requesting, 21.17
      generally, 21.4, 21.5
      inspectors' limited time to deal with, 21.4
      late representations, disregarding, 21.18
      new material, attempt to introduce, 21.13
      Planning Inspectorate's right to be informed of changes etc, 21.17
      questionnaire from LPA, 21.9–21.11
      report setting out officer analysis, 21.10
      responses to five-week representations, 21.16–21.18
      starting date, 21.6
      statement of case, submission, 21.4, 21.5
      third parties, notice to, 21.7, 21.8
      third party representations, 21.14, 21.15
      time limits, enforcement, 21.18

Written representations – *contd*
  England, procedure in – *contd*
    fairness—
      generally, 21.25–21.32
      late submission of evidence, 21.30
      natural justice principles, application of, 21.25–21.27
      new issues occurring to inspector, 21.32
      new point raised, effect on time limit for comments, 21.29
      pre-2013 case-law, 21.28–21.31
      time limit for restriction on comments, 21.28
  generally, 19.52, 21.1
  householder or minor commercial appeal—
    England, in, 20.6–20.12
    stages and regulations in, 20.3
    Wales, in, 20.13–20.16
  site visit—
    accompanied, remission of decision due to, 21.35
    forms of, 21.33
    unaccompanied, 21.34
  stages in case, 21.3
  statutory authorisation, 21.2
  Wales, procedure in—
    2015 regulations, effect, 21.19
    22 June 2015, applications made before, 21.22
    fairness—
      generally, 21.25–21.32
      late submission of evidence, 21.30
      natural justice principles, application of, 21.25–21.27
      new issues occurring to inspector, 21.32
      new point raised, effect on time limit for comments, 21.29
      pre-2013 case-law, 21.28–21.31
      time limit for restriction on comments, 21.28
    generally, 21.19–21.14
    main submissions, time for making, 21.24
    reasoned decision, sending of, 21.21
    third parties, effect of failure to notify, 21.20
    time limits, 21.19, 21.20, 21.22, 21.24